THE
CONCORD
DESK ENCYCLOPEDIA

VOLUME

3

O-Z

15th letter and fourth vowel of the English ALPHABET. It began as the Semitic 'ayin (eye), and the Greek Omicron, and became the 14th letter of the Roman alphabet. It also represents the number zero, and the element oxygen.

OAHU, third-largest island (608sq mi) of Hawaii, containing Honolulu (the state capital), the naval base at Pearl Harbor and 80% of Hawaii's population. A fertile valley growing pineapples and sugarcane, it is flanked by coastal mountain ranges. Pop 761,964.

OAKLEY, Annie (1860–1926), US entertainer, born Phoebe Anne Oakley Mozee. Known as "Little Sure Shot" (she was only 5ft tall), she was a sharpshooter star of BUFFALO BILL's Wild West Show, together with her husband Frank Butler.

OAK RIDGE, city in E Tenn., 17mi W of Knoxville. The site was chosen in 1942 as the WWII headquarters of the atomic energy program (the MANHATTAN PROJECT) because of its isolation and easy access to necessary resources. It is still a major research center, and houses the American Museum of Atomic Energy. Pop 27,662.

OAS. See ORGANIZATION OF AMERICAN STATES.

OATES, Joyce Carol (1938–), prolific US novelist, short story writer, poet, playwright and critic whose work often deals with insanity, violence and other nightmarish aspects of society. Among her many books are the novels *A Garden of Earthly Delights* (1967), *Them* (1969, National Book Award 1970); and *Bellefleur* (1980), *The Seduction and Other Stories* (1975), the poems *The Fabulous Beasts* (1975) and the play *Psychiatric Service* (1976).

OATES, Titus (1649–1705), English conspirator who in 1678 claimed to have discovered a Roman Catholic plot against Charles II—known as the POPISH PLOT. No such plot existed, but his story set off a wave of persecution in which some 35 persons were executed. Exposed and imprisoned in 1685, he was freed and pensioned (1689) after the GLORIOUS REVOLUTION.

OBADIAH (or Abdias), Book of, shortest book of the Old Testament, fourth book of the MINOR PROPHETS. Probably written in the 6th century BC, its 21 verses foretell the triumph of Israel over its rival EDOM. Nothing is known of Obadiah himself.

OBERAMMERGAU, village in the Bavarian Alps of West Germany, famous for its Passion Play. Every 10 years inhabitants of the village reenact the suffering, death and resurrection of Christ, in fulfillment of a vow made by the villagers in 1633 during a plague. Pop 4,603.

OBERTH, Hermann (1894–), pioneering German astrophysicist who established many of the basic principles of space-flight in his *Means of Space Travel* (1929), and *The Rocket into Interplanetary Space* (1934). He worked with Werner von BRAUN's V-2 team during WWII, and on space research for the US Army 1955–58.

OBESITY, the condition of a subject's having excessive weight for his height, build and age. It is common in Western society, overfeeding in infancy being a possible cause. Excess ADIPOSE TISSUE is found in subcutaneous tissue and the ABDOMEN. Obesity predisposes to or is associated with numerous DISEASES including ARTERIOSCLEROSIS and high blood pressure; here premature DEATH is usual. Strict diet is essential for cure.

OBOE, soprano WIND INSTRUMENT consisting of a double-reed mouthpiece at the end of a conically-bored tube. It is controlled by keys and finger holes. It was developed in 17th-century France, where it was called the *hautbois* (high wood), whence oboe. An orchestral instrument, it has also had important solo music written for it by composers from Purcell onwards.

OBREGÓN, Álvaro (1880–1928), President of Mexico from 1920 to 1924. A planter, he joined CARRANZA in overthrowing President HUERTA in 1913. He subsequently served in Carranza's government, but led the revolt against him in 1920. As president, Obregón promoted important economic and educational reforms. Four years after leaving office he was elected to another term, but was assassinated by a religious fanatic before taking office.

OBSCENITY. See PORNOGRAPHY.

OBSTETRICS, the care of women during PREGNANCY, delivery and the puerperium, a branch of MEDICINE and SURGERY usually linked with GYNECOLOGY. Antenatal care and the avoidance or control of risk factors for both mother and baby—ANEMIA, TOXEMIA. high blood pressure, DIABETES, VENEREAL DISEASE, frequent MISCARRIAGE, etc.—have greatly contributed to the reduction of maternal and fetal deaths. The monitoring and control of labor and BIRTH, with early recognition of complications; induction of labor and the prevention of post-partum HEMORRHAGE with OXYTOCIN; safe forceps delivery and CESARIAN SECTION, and improved ANESTHETICS are important factors in obstetric safety. ASEPSIS has made PUERPERAL FEVER a rarity.

O'CASEY, Sean (1880–1964), Irish playwright whose sardonic dramas depict the effects of poverty and war on the Irish. His early plays, such as *Juno and the Paycock* (1924), are the most highly regarded. His later works were written in self-imposed exile due to hostility both from theater managements and from Irish nationalists who objected to his unglamorous portrayal of the independence movement.

OCCAM'S RAZOR. See OCKHAM, WILLIAM OF.

OCCUPATIONAL THERAPY, the ancillary speciality of MEDICINE concerned with practical measures to circumvent or overcome disability due to DISEASE. It includes the design or modification of everyday items such as cutlery, dressing aids, bath and lavatory aids, and wheelchairs. Assessment and education in domestic skills and industrial retraining are also important. Diversional activities are arranged for long-stay patients.

OCEAN CURRENTS, large-scale permanent or semipermanent movements of water at or beneath the surface of the OCEANS. Currents may be divided into those caused by winds and those caused by differences in DENSITY of seawater. In the former case, FRICTION between the prevailing wind and the water surface causes horizontal motion, and this motion is both modified by and in part transferred to deeper layers by further friction. Density variations may result from temperature differences, differing salinities, etc. The direction of flow of all currents is affected by the CORIOLIS EFFECT. Best known, perhaps, are the GULF STREAM and HUMBOLDT CURRENT.

OCEANIA, vast section of the Pacific Ocean, stretching roughly from Hawaii to New Zealand and from New Guinea to Easter Island, divided into three broad cultural areas: MELANESIA in the SW, MICRONESIA in the NW and POLYNESIA in the E. The area has islands ranging from large masses of ancient rock to minute coral atolls—many of volcanic origin—and the vegetation varies from lush jungle to scanty palm trees. The Pacific Islands were probably peopled from SE Asia, though HEYERDAHL has shown the possibility of influences from South America. The native

islanders live mainly by fishing an farming; their basic diet is vegetable, bu some pigs and poultry are kept. Firs European contact was made by MAGELLA in 1519, but the earliest comprehensiv exploration of the area was that of Captai James COOK in the 18th century. Many c the islands were colonized, first by Britai and France and later by the US and Japar They brought trade and missionaries, bu also new diseases which wiped ou thousands. The influence of Wester culture upon the fragile island societies wa generally destructive. Many of the island are now independent.

OCEANIC LANGUAGES include som 200 aboriginal languages of Australia about 500 Papuan languages (spoke mostly in New Guinea), and more than 50(MALAYO-POLYNESIAN LANGUAGES.

OCEANS. The oceans cover some 71% o the earth's surface and comprise about 97% of the water of the planet (se HYDROSPHERE). They provide man wit food, chemicals, minerals and transporta tion; and, by acting as a reservoir of sola heat energy, they ameliorate the effects o seasonal and diurnal temperature extreme for much of the world. With th atmosphere, they largely determine th world's CLIMATE (see also HYDROLOGIC CYCLE).

Oceanography is the study of all aspects of and phenomena associated with, the ocean and seas. Most modern maps of the sea floo are compiled by use of ECHO SOUNDERS (see also SONAR), the vessel's position at sea being accurately determined by RADAR or otherwise. Water sampling, in order tc determine, for example, salinity and oxyger content, is also important. Sea-floor sampling, to determine the composition of the sea floor, is carried out by use of dredges, grabs, etc. (see DREDGING), and especially by use of hollow DRILLS which bring up cores of rock. OCEAN CURRENTS can be studied by use of buoys, drift bottles, etc. and often simply by accurate determinations of the different positions of a ship allowed to drift. Further information about the sea bottom can be obtained by direct observation (see BATHYSCAPHE; BATHY SPHERE) or by study of the deflections of seismic waves (see EARTHQUAKE).

Oceanographers generally regard the world's oceans as a single, large ocean. Geographically, however, it is useful to divide this into smaller units: the Atlantic, Pacific, Indian, Arctic and Antarctic (or Southern) Oceans (though the Arctic is often considered as part of the Atlantic, the Antarctic as parts of the Atlantic, Pacific

nd Indian). Of these, the Pacific is by far
ie largest and, on average, the deepest.
lowever, the Atlantic has by far the longest
astline: its many bays and inlets, ideal for
atural harbors, have profoundly affected
/ civilization's history.

cean trenches are long, narrow depressions
f V-shaped cross-section running, typical-
·, roughly parallel to continental coastal
OUNTAIN ranges or volcanic island arcs
see VOLCANISM). **Midocean ridges** are
ibmarine mountain belts: the first to be
iscovered was that running roughly N-S in
ie Atlantic. They are important sites of
arthquakes and volcanic activity (see
LATE TECTONICS; SEA-FLOOR SPREADING).

(See also ABYSSAL PLAINS; FISHERIES;
YDROGRAPHY; HYDROLOGY; ICEBERG;
IARINE BIOLOGY; OCEAN WAVES; OOZES;
UBMARINE CANYON; TIDES; TSUNAMI.)

CELOT, *Panthera pardalis*, a South
American cat related to the MARGAY. A
mall leopard-like cat, it has a beautifully
narked coat. Ocelots feed on small birds
nd mammals, and are capable of bringing
own prey the size of deer fawns.

CHOA, Severo (1905–), Spanish-
orn US biochemist who shared with
ORNBERG the 1959 Nobel Prize for
hysiology or Medicine for his first
ynthesis of a NUCLEIC ACID (or RNA).

CHS, Adolph Simon (1858–1935), US
ewspaper publisher largely responsible for
:reating the prestige of the *New York
Times*. Born in Cincinnati, Ohio, he
iecame the paper's manager in 1896,
adopting the slogan "All the news that's fit
o print."

CKHAM (or Occam), William of
c1285–1349), English scholar who for-
nulated the principle now known as
)ccam's Razor: "Entities must not
nnecessarily be multiplied." This princi-
ole, interpreted roughly as "the simplest
heory that fits the facts corresponds most
:losely to reality," has many applications
hroughout science.

'CONNELL, Daniel (1775–1847), Irish
statesman, called "the Liberator," who led
:he fight for Catholic emancipation. He
'ounded the Catholic Association (1823)
ind after his election (1828) to Parliament
refused to take his seat until public opinion
precipitated the CATHOLIC EMANCIPATION
ACT. He contested the 1801 act uniting
Ireland with Britain.

O'CONNOR, Flannery (May Flannery
O'Connor; 1925–1964), US fiction writer
noted for her brilliant style and her
grotesque vision of life in the South. Her
novels include *Wise Blood* (1952).

O'CONNOR, Frank (1903–1966), Irish
short-story writer whose works are admired
for their oral quality and portrayals of Irish
life. His many collections include *Guests of
the Nation* (1931), *Bones of Contention and
Other Stories* (1936) and *A Set of
Variations* (1969). O'Connor also published poetry, criticism and translations of
old Irish literature from the Gaelic.

O'CONNOR, Sandra Day (1930–),
first woman to serve on the US Supreme
Court. A lawyer, she was assistant attorney
general of Arizona and a state senator. She
then served as a trial judge and on the state
court of appeals. In 1981 President Reagan
nominated her to the Supreme Court and
she was confirmed unanimously by the
Senate.

OCTAVE, in music, the interval between
two pitches of which one has twice the
frequency of the other. In the diatonic scale
these are the first and the eighth tones.
Because of its unique consonance, the
octave gives an aural impression of a single
tone duplicated.

OCTOBER, the tenth month of the year. It
contains 31 days. Its name comes from the
Latin *octo* (eight), since it was the eighth
month in the Roman calendar.

OCTOBRISTS, Russian political party
formed in 1905 by Alexander Ivanovich
Guchkov (1862–1935). It was so called
because its members (mainly moderates of
the upper middle class) supported the new
constitution established by the October
Manifesto of that year, promising a wider
franchise and a parliament with legislative
power.

OCTOPUS, a cephalopod MOLLUSK whose
most striking feature is the possession of
eight tentacle-like "arms" which surround
the mouth. Behind the beaked head is a
sac-like body containing the viscera.
Octopods can alter body form and outline,
and also change color, and thus have
excellent protective camouflage. In addition, a black pigment, SEPIA, can be ejected
into the water from a special sac, forming a
smoke screen which foils predators.

ODD FELLOWS, Independent Order of, a
secret benevolent fraternity. Probably
founded in 18th-century England, it was
first established in the US (Baltimore) in
1819. It has a world membership of over one
million.

ODE, a stately lyric poem usually
expressing praise. It is often addressed to
the person, object or concept (such as "Joy"
or "Autumn") being celebrated. It
originated in the ancient Greek choral
songs. PINDAR used a tripartite structure in
his odes: strophe, antistrophe (both in the
same meter) and epode (in a different

meter). HORACE'S odes were in stanzaic form. Poets of the 19th century, such as KEATS and SHELLEY, wrote odes with irregular structures.

ODER-NEISSE LINE, since 1945, the border between East Germany and Poland, formed by the ODER river and its tributary the Neisse.

ODESSA, city and port in the Ukrainian SSR, USSR, on the Black Sea. It is a major transportation, industrial, commercial and cultural center. It was the scene of an abortive workers' revolt in 1905. Pop 1,057,000.

ODETS, Clifford (1906–1963), US playwright and screenwriter famous for his social-protest dramas about ordinary people caught in the Depression. He was a leading figure in the GROUP THEATER. His works include *Awake and Sing!* (1935), *Waiting for Lefty* (1935) and *Golden Boy* (1937).

ODETTA (Odetta Holmes; 1930–   ), US folksinger who gained national prominence during the folk music revival of the late 1950s and remained popular through the 1980s. Her powerful, dusky, contralto voice and emotional intensity sustained a repertoire that included spirituals, blues and ballads.

ODIN, in Germanic mythology, the chief of the gods, also known as Wotan or Woden (whose name gave us Wednesday). He was the god of war, poetry, wisdom, learning and magic. He had a single all-seeing eye. He made the world from the body of the giant Ymir, man from an ash tree and woman from an elm.

ODOACER (c435–493), Germanic chief who overthrew the last of the West Roman emperors in 476 and was proclaimed king of Italy. The East Roman Emperor Zeno sent THEODORIC THE GREAT to depose him. After a long war, Odoacer was treacherously killed by Theodoric.

ODYSSEUS, or Ulysses, legendary hero of ancient Greece, son and successor of King Laertes of Ithaca and husband of PENELOPE. He was the crafty counselor of the TROJAN WAR (described in Homer's ILIAD). After 10 years' adventures (subject of Homer's ODYSSEY) he returned home disguised as a beggar and, with his son TELEMACHUS, killed the suitors beleaguering his wife.

ODYSSEY, famous ancient Greek epic poem ascribed to HOMER, one of the masterpieces of world literature. Its 24 books relate the adventures of ODYSSEUS and his Greek friends after the TROJAN WAR. Rescued from the land of the Lotus-Eaters, they encountered the one-eyed cyclops POLYPHEMUS, the cannibal Laestrygonians and the sorceress CIRCE. They resisted the SIRENS and the perils of SCYLLA AND CHARYBDIS but Odysseus alone survived shipwreck at Trinacria. For seven years he lingered with the nymph CALYPSO before he finally reached his home, Ithaca, to be reunited after twenty years with his wife PENELOPE.

OEDIPUS, in Greek legend, King of Thebes who was fated to kill his father King Laius and marry his mother Jocasta. Laius, warned by an oracle that he would be killed by his son, abandoned him to die. Oedipus survived and was adopted by the King of Corinth. As a young man he learned his fate from the oracle and fled Corinth, home of his supposed parents. On the road he killed Laius, an apparent stranger. Reaching Thebes, he solved the riddle of the SPHINX and was rewarded with the hand of the widowed Jocasta. He later discovered the truth and blinded himself. His story and that of his daughter ANTIGONE inspired tragedies by SOPHOCLES.

OEDIPUS COMPLEX, COMPLEX typical of INFANTILE SEXUALITY, comprising mainly UNCONSCIOUS desires to exclude the parent of the same SEX and possess the parent of the opposite sex. In boys, mother FIXATION and consequent rivalry with the father may lead to a CASTRATION COMPLEX.

OERSTED, Hans Christian (1777–1851), Danish physicist whose discovery that a magnetized needle can be deflected by an electric current passing through a wire (1820) gave birth to the science of ELECTROMAGNETISM.

O'FAOLAIN, Sean (1900–   ), Irish short-story writer, novelist and biographer whose works often give an unflattering, yet sympathetic view of everyday Irish life. Among his many works are *Midsummer Night Madness and Other Stories* (1932), the novel *A Nest of Simple Folk* (1933), *The Great O'Neill: A Biography of Hugh O'Neill* (1942) and his autobiography *Vive Moi!* (1964).

OFF-BROADWAY THEATER refers to theater performed in NYC outside the Times Square Theater district, usually in houses that can seat fewer than 300 persons. Although some activity of the kind had been taking place for decades, the modern development of Off-Broadway is considered to have begun with a 1948 production of SARTRE'S *The Respectful Prostitute*, and, in 1949, five theater groups formed the Off-Broadway League of Theatres, eventually winning the cooperation of Actors' Equity. Modern Off-Broadway was influenced by Eva Le Gallienne's Civic Repertory Theater (1928) and by two Greenwich Village theaters of the early

00s, the Theater Guild, famous for oductions of Eugene O'Neill's plays, and e Provincetown Players. Like those early eaters, modern Off-Broadway seeks to velop actors, directors and writers in an mosphere removed from commercial essures, although general audience terest to some degree has pushed this aim, ading to development of "Off-f-Broadway" theaters for the production the most experimental work. Early ff-Broadway theaters included the down-wn Circle-in-the-Square, founded by Jose ıINTERO and Theodore Mann, and the ıoenix Theater. Numerous important ays have originated in Off-Broadway oductions, including BECKETT's *Endgame* 958) and SHEPARD's *Curse of the Starving lass* (1977).

FFENBACH, Jacques (1819–1880), ˘ench composer. He wrote over 100 ıerettas including the immensely popular ˘*pheus in the Underworld* (1858), ˙ntaining the famous can-can, and *La ılle Hélène* (1864). His masterpiece is ˙nsidered to be the more serious *Tales of ˙offman*, first produced in 1881.

FFICE EQUIPMENT, Electronic. See ˙ORD PROCESSING.

FFICE OF STRATEGIC SERVICES, US ˙overnment agency formed in 1942 to ˙ollect and analyze strategic information ˙ıring WWII. It was dissolved in 1945.

FFSET LITHOGRAPHY. See PRINTING.

'FLAHERTY, Liam (1897–   ), Irish ˙ovelist known for his realistic stories of ˙rdinary people in trouble, such as *The ˙lack Soul* (1924), *The Informer* (1925) ˙nd *The Assassins* (1928).

GILVY, David MacKenzie (1911–   ), ˙ritish-born US businessman who was a ˙ɔ-founder of the New York advertising ˙rm of Hewitt, Ogilvy, Benson and Mather ˙ater Ogilvy & Mather) in 1948. He ˙reated "long copy" ads, perfected ˙ıass-marketing techniques and helped to ˙ıild the ad agency into one of the world's ˙ırgest.

GLETHORPE, James Edward ˙696–1785), English philanthropist, ˙eneral and member of parliament who ˙btained (1732) a charter to found the ˙olony of Georgia. He settled the colony as a ˙efuge for jailed debtors and was governor ˙ntil he returned to England in 1743.

'HAIR, Madalyn Murray (1919–   ), ˙JS atheist who initiated the law suit against ˙he Baltimore public schools (1960) which ˙ed to the US Supreme Court decision ˙ɔanning prayer in the public schools (1963). ˙ɔhe founded the American Atheist Center ˙1965) and wrote several books on atheism.

O'HARA, John Henry (1905–1970), US fiction writer known principally for his vigorous accounts of urban and suburban life in America. His novels include *Appointment in Samarra* (1934), *Butterfield 8* (1935) and *A Rage to Live* (1949).

O. HENRY. See HENRY, O.

O'HIGGINS, family famous in South American history. **Ambrosio O'Higgins** (c1720–1801), born in Ireland and educated in Spain, went to South America and rose to be governor of Chile (1789) and viceroy of Peru (1796). **Bernardo O'Higgins** (1778–1842), his natural son, liberated Chile from Spanish rule and became its dictator (1817). His reforms aroused such opposition that he was exiled to Peru in 1823.

Name of state: Ohio
Capital: Columbus
Statehood: March 1, 1803 (17th state)
Familiar name: Buckeye State
Area: 41,222sq mi
Population: 10,797,419
Elevation: Highest—1,550ft, Campbell Hill in Logan County. Lowest—433ft, Ohio River in Hamilton County
Motto: With God, All Things Are Possible
State flower: Scarlet carnation
State bird: Cardinal
State tree: Buckeye
State song: "Beautiful Ohio"

OHIO, N central state of the US. It is bounded N by Mich. and Lake Erie, E by Pa. and W.Va., S by W.Va. and Ky., and W by Ind. The Ohio R forms the Ky. and W.Va. borders.

Land. Ohio has four land regions: the highland area of the Appalachian Plateau in the E; the narrow strip of Great Lakes Plains bordering Lake Erie; the Till Plains in the SW, the easternmost section of the great fertile Midwestern Corn Belt; and a small wedge of the Blue Grass region extending from Ky. into S Ohio. Excellent ports on Lake Erie have made the state a major transportation hub of the Midwest. Ohio's climate is humid continental with an average annual precipitation of 37in.

People. About 80% of Ohio's citizens live in urban areas. The state's largest cities are Cleveland, Columbus, Cincinnati and Toledo.

Economy. Ohio is one of the country's major industrial states. Widely varied manufactures include non-electrical machinery, primary metals, transportation equipment and fabricated metal products. Ohio leads the nation in the production of tires, machine tools, playing cards, business machines, glassware and other products. Rubber, coal, and iron ore are important resources. New deposits of oil and gas were discovered in SE Ohio in the 1960s. Major agricultural products are livestock, cereal crops, fruit and dairy foods. Tourism is also important.

History. The Iroquois were the dominant Indian group in the area when La Salle investigated the Ohio valley in 1669. His voyage formed the basis for French claims to the entire Ohio valley, but English fur traders also frequented the region and Va. and other seaboard colonies had been granted parts of the Ohio country in their royal charters. Anglo-French rivalry culminated in the last of the FRENCH AND INDIAN WARS, as a result of which England was awarded the territory. After the Revolution the region was included by Congress (1787) in the NORTHWEST TERRITORY. The first permanent settlement was Marietta, founded in 1788. Ohio itself became a territory in 1799 and was the 17th state to enter the Union (1803). Rapid expansion in the 19th century was aided (1825) by the opening of the ERIE CANAL. In the period leading up to the Civil War, Ohio had an active UNDERGROUND RAILROAD. Ohio has contributed seven presidents to the nation. The state's cultural and educational facilities are outstanding, but the state has been plagued in recent years with many of the environmental, economic, and social problems common to other highly industrialized states. Strip mining of coal has scarred much of its landscape and pollution of Lake Erie poses a serious threat to the many cities that rely on it for water supplies. A long slump in the state's economy has been aggravated by the decline in the nation's auto industry, in which many Ohio firms are involved, and unemployment has been high—8.8% in 1980. Its cities, particularly Cleveland, have suffered eroding tax bases, as middle- and upper-income people crowd into the suburbs, while poorer people crowd in, many coming from rural areas, where farms, in Ohio as in other states, are becoming at once larger and more mechanized. The state itself has

been edging toward fiscal crisis, whic probably can be averted only by th unhappy combination of higher taxes an reduced services. In many ways the typica American state, Ohio's economy is likely t improve only as the national economy itsel grows stronger.

OHIO RIVER, the main eastern tributar of the Mississippi River, which it joins a Cairo, Ill. It is formed at Pittsburgh, Pa., b the junction of the Allegheny an Monongahela rivers and flows generall southwest for about 980mi. Together wit its main tributaries, it drains over 203,000s mi and is navigable throughout.

OHIRA, Masayoshi (1910–1980), Japan ese prime minister (1978–80). First electe to parliament as a member of the Libera Democratic Party in 1952, he hel numerous ministerial posts before becomin party leader and prime minister in 1978 Unable to hold together warring factions o his party, he was campaigning when he die ten days before new parliamentar elections.

OHM'S LAW, the statement due to G. S OHM in 1827 that the electric POTENTIA difference across a conductor is proportion al to the current flowing through it, th constant of proportionality being known a the RESISTANCE of the conductor. It holds well for most materials and objects including solutions, provided that the passage of the current does not heat the conductor, but ELECTRON TUBES and SEMICONDUCTOR devices show a much more complicated behavior.

O'HORGAN, Tom (1926–   ), US composer and stage director given to flamboyant scenic effects and crowd scenes His Broadway productions include *Hai* (1968) and *Lenny* (1971).

OIL, any substance that is insoluble ir water, soluble in ETHER and greasy to the touch. There are three main groups: minera oils (see PETROLEUM); fixed vegetable and animal oils (see FATS; LIPIDS), and volatile vegetable oils (see ESSENTIAL OILS). Oils are classified as fixed or volatile according to the ease with which they vaporize when heated. Mineral oils include GASOLINE and many other fuel oils, heating oils and lubricants. Fixed vegetable oils are usually divided into three subgroups depending on the physical change that occurs when they absorb oxygen: oils such as linseed and tung which form a hard film, are known as "drying oils"; "semidrying oils," such as cottonseed or soybean oil, thicken consider- ably but do not harden; "nondrying oils," such as castor and olive oil, thicken only slightly. Fixed animal oils include the "marine oils," such as cod-liver and whale oil. Fixed animal and vegetable fats such as butterfat and palm oil are often also classified as oils. Examples of volatile vegetable oils, which usually have a very distinct odor and flavor, include such oils as bitter almond, peppermint and TURPENTINE. When dissolved in alcohol, they are called "essences."

OIL PAINTS, in art, ground pigments combined with oil (usually linseed), a stabilizer, a plasticizer and often a drier to ensure uniformity of drying time. In applying such paints, the artist may add more oil or a thinner, usually turpentine. Oil paints were developed during the 1400s and 1500s in response to the needs of the radically innovative Renaissance painters. Because they are so predictable, versatile, and durable, these pigments gradually displaced other media. They remain the most popular painter's colors today.

OIL SHALE, a fine-grained, dark-colored sedimentary rock from which oil suitable for refining can be extracted. The rock contains an organic substance called kerogen, which may be distilled to yield OIL (see also DISTILLATION). Important deposits occur in Wyo., Col. and adjacent states. (See also SEDIMENTARY ROCKS: SHALE.)

OISTRAKH, David Feodorovich (1908–1974), Russian violinist. His brilliant technique and strong emotional interpretation (especially of the romantic composers) brought him worldwide acclaim. PROKOFIEV and SHOSTAKOVICH wrote works for him. His son, **Igor** (1931–   ), is also a violinist and conductor of world renown.

OJIBWA INDIANS (or Chippewa), one of the largest ALGONQUIN-speaking tribes of North America. They lived as small bands of hunter-gatherers, mainly in woodland areas around Lakes Superior and Huron, and to the west. They fought frequently with the SIOUX. but had little contact with early white settlers. LONGFELLOW's *The Song of Hiawatha* was based on a study of Ojibwa mythology. Today some 60,000 Ojibwas live on US and Canadian reservations.

O'KEEFFE, Georgia (1887–   ), US painter, noted for her delicate, abstract designs incorporating symbolic motifs drawn from observations of nature. She is also known for large symbolic flower paintings such as *Black Iris* (1926). Her paintings were first exhibited in 1916 by Alfred STIEGLITZ, whom she married in 1924.

OKEFENOKEE SWAMP, swamp and wildlife refuge in SE Ga. and NE Fla. Covering over 650sq mi, it is drained by the St. Marys and Suwannee rivers and has densely forested areas, grassy bog savannas, hummock islands, sand bars and large swamp areas of dark water overgrown by heavy brush and trees. The abundant wildlife includes alligators, deer, bears, raccoons and many species of birds and fish.

OKINAWA, largest (454sq mi) and most important of the Ryukyu Islands in the W Pacific, about 500mi SW of Japan. The island is part of Japan's Okinawa prefecture and Naha is its capital city. The island is mountainous and jungle-covered in the S, and hilly in the N. It is fertile—sugarcane, sweet potatoes and rice are grown, and there are good fisheries. Captured by the US during WWII, Okinawa was formally returned to Japan in 1972.

Name of state: Oklahoma
Capital: Oklahoma City
Statehood: Nov. 16, 1907 (46th state)
Familiar name: Sooner State
Area: 69,919sq mi
Population: 3,025,266
Elevation: Highest—4,973ft., Black Mesa in Cimarron County. Lowest—287ft, Little River in McCurtain County
Motto: Labor Omnia Vincit (Labor Conquers All Things)
State flower: Mistletoe
State bird: Scissortailed flycatcher
State tree: Redbud
State song: "Oklahoma!"

OKLAHOMA, state, S central US, bounded to the E by Mo. and Ark., to the S by Tex., to the W by Tex. and N.M. and to the N by Col. and Kans. The state is shaped somewhat like a saucepan, with a 34mi wide "panhandle" extending W 167mi.

Land. The state's 69,919sq mi show a wide variation of terrain. Plains in the W give way to rolling hills in the central region and mountain ranges in the E; scrubby sagebrush country contrasts with rich forestlands. The highest point in the state, Black Mesa (4,973ft), is in the far NW corner of the state. Over 65% of Okla. is in the Arkansas R basin and the rest is in the Red R drainage area. Numerous lakes, most of them man-made, provide sources of irrigation and hydroelectric power. All of the larger rivers drain into the Mississippi R. Rainfall is light in the W and heavy in the E. Extremes of temperature occur: the midsummer average is about 83°F, but the overall state average is about 40°F. Timber is a major natural resource with forest and good stands of varied hard- and softwood trees. Wildlife is abundant.

People. The population is more than 85% white, and 5% American Indian. About 55% are urban dwellers, and many live in one of the state's three major cities: Oklahoma City, Tulsa and Lawton.

Economy. Originally a farming state, Oklahoma now depends chiefly upon mineral production and manufacturing. It ranks third among the oil- and natural gas-producing states and also has large reserves of coal, zinc, lead, granite, salt, gravel, gypsum and helium. Manufactures are based mainly on local agricultural and mineral production, but also include non-electrical machinery, transportation equipment, aircraft and fabricated metal, stone, glass and clay products. A large proportion of agricultural income is based on livestock. Major crops are wheat, cotton, corn, beans, peanuts, oats, hay and barley.

History. Oklahoma was acquired by the US as part of the LOUISIANA PURCHASE, and in 1834 the land was designated INDIAN TERRITORY and became a Federal dumping ground for many Indian tribes. Homesteading runs and "land lotteries" (1889–1910) brought a rush of settlers. The first major oilfield was opened in 1901; and on Nov. 16, 1907, after a constitution had been ratified by popular vote, Okla. was admitted to the Union. The state was hard hit by the great drought of the 1930s, which turned many farms to dust and forced the farmers to migrate, but its economy expanded and diversified during WWII, providing the basis for relatively slow but solid growth in the postwar period. Oklahoma's population rose 18.2% in the 1970s but unemployment, at 4.3% in 1980, remained low. Unlike many other US states, Oklahoma maintains its particular Indian and pioneering heritage amidst a flourishing modern economy.

OKLAHOMA CITY, the capital city of Okla., centrally located on the North Canadian R. It is a major processing and trading center for livestock and farm products and for petroleum and natural gas. It was founded on Apr. 22, 1889, the same day that the first portion of INDIAN TERRITORY was officially opened to pioneer settlement. Pop 403,213.

OLAV V (1903–   ), King of Norway from 1957. He was active in the fight for his country's liberation from the Germans in WWII and in 1944 took command of the Norwegian forces.

OLD BELIEVERS, seceders from the Russian ORTHODOX CHURCH who would not accept the liturgical reforms of Patriarch NIKON; they were excommunicated as schismatics 1667 and persecuted until the late 19th century. The major group depended on seceding priests until they could set up a hierarchy (1846); many small, extravagant lay sects also sprang up.

OLD CATHOLICS, group of churches which have seceded from the ROMAN CATHOLIC CHURCH. The Jansenist Church of Utrecht separated in 1724, followed after 1870 by churches in Germany, Austria and Switzerland, led by von DÖLLINGER, which would not accept the dogmas of papal infallibility and jurisdiction defined by the First VATICAN COUNCIL. Several smaller Slavic churches later separated. Virtually high Anglican in doctrine and practice, Old Catholics have been in full communion with the Church of England since 1932.

OLD CHURCH SLAVONIC, a language of the Slavic subfamily of the Indo-European family of languages, devised in the 9th century by the Greek scholars and saints CYRIL and METHODIUS; presumed to be the first written Slavic language. Its descendant, Church Slavonic, was used as a literary language (from 1100 AD to c1700 AD) and is still the most widely used liturgical language in the Eastern Orthodox churches. (See also SLAVONIC LANGUAGES.)

OLDENBURG, Claes (1929–   ), Swedish-born US artist best known for "soft" sculptures that satirize America. His hamburgers, ice cream cones, telephones and bathroom fixtures are usually larger than life.

OLD FAITHFUL, name given to an intermittent hot spring, or geyser, a tourist attraction at YELLOWSTONE NATIONAL PARK, Wyo., which at intervals of 66min, varying at times from 33 to 148min, erupts for about 5min up to heights of 150ft.

OLDFIELD, Barney (Berner Eli Oldfield; 1877–1946), pioneer US auto-racing driver. Victorious in Henry FORD's racing team driving the Ford-Cooper "999," he became the first mile-a-minute motorist (1903 at Indianapolis) and in 1910 set a world speed record of 131.724 mph.

OLDS, Ransom Eli (1864–1950), pioneer US automobile engineer and manufacturer. He produced the Oldsmobile and Reo cars, and is generally considered the founder of the US automobile industry. His first powered vehicle was a steam-driven three-wheeler (1886). He established the Olds Motor Vehicle Company in 1899, marketed a 3hp Oldsmobile in 1901—the first commercially successful American car—and established the Reo Motor Car Company in 1904.

OLD TESTAMENT, or the Hebrew Bible, the first part of the Christian Bible (for list of books see BIBLE), describing God's covenant with Israel. The Jewish CANON was fixed by the 1st century AD and is followed by the Protestant churches; the Greek SEPTUAGINT version, containing also the APOCRYPHA, was followed by the VULGATE and hence by the Roman Catholic Church. The standard MASORETIC TEXT of the Hebrew Old Testament is now largely confirmed for most books by the DEAD SEA SCROLLS (almost 1000 years earlier). The Old Testament is traditionally divided into three parts: the Law (see PENTATEUCH), the Prophets—the Former Prophets being the earlier historical books, the Latter being the three Major Prophets and the MINOR PROPHETS—and the Writings, including the later historical books, Daniel and the poetic and "wisdom" books. Christianity regards the Old Testament as an inspired record of God's dealings with His people in preparation for the coming of Christ, containing in embryo much New Testament teaching.

OLDUVAI GORGE, a 300ft-deep canyon in N Tanzania, gouged through lake sediment, volcanic ash and other material deposited over the past few million years. In Bed I, the lowest of five layers into which the walls are divided, the anthropologists Louis and Mary LEAKEY found early fossil remains of PREHISTORIC MAN.

OLIGARCHY, a form of government rule, or control of a state or some other organization by a small elite group. The term often carries an implication that rule by an oligarchy is essentially interested. (See also GOVERNMENT.)

OLIGOCENE, the third epoch of the TERTIARY, extending from about 40 to 25 million years ago. (See also GEOLOGY.)

OLIGOPOLY, a market situation such as in the US steel and car industries where identical or very similar products are produced by a few firms. (See also MONOPOLY.)

OLIPHANT, Patrick (1935–), US editorial cartoonist who revolutionized the art with his horizontal, "gag-cartoon" format and his reduction of the use of labels. He received a Pulitzer Prize in 1967.

OLIVER, Joseph "King" (1885–1938), American jazz musician. A leader of the New Orleans style of jazz, his band, the Creole Jazz Band, played blues pieces and tunes based on rags and marches. Oliver himself was a cornetist.

OLIVES, Mount of, ridge of hills E of Jerusalem. On the W slope is the Garden of GETHSEMANE where Jesus went with his disciples after the Last Supper. It is also the site of Christ's Ascension.

OLIVETTI, Adriano (1901–1960), Italian industrialist who inherited a small typewriter factory and transformed it into one of the world's largest manufacturing companies, with 25,000 employees and with plants in six countries. He was president of the company from 1938 until his death.

OLIVIER, Laurence Kerr, Baron Olivier of Brighton (1907–), English actor, producer and director. Immensely versatile and brilliant in classical as well as modern roles, such as John OSBORNE's *The Entertainer*, he made and acted in such films as *Henry V* (1944) and *Hamlet* (1948), which won an Academy Award. In 1962 he was appointed director of Britain's National Theatre.

OLMEC INDIANS, a people of the SE coastal lowlands of ancient Mexico. Their culture, earliest of the major Mexican cultures, flourished from between 1000 BC and 500 BC until c1100 AD. They were skilled in artistic work with stone and produced huge sculptured basalt heads, beautiful jewelry, fine jade, white ware and mosaics. They knew how to record time and had a hieroglyphic form of writing. Their culture may have influenced the ZAPOTECS and TOLTECS.

OLMSTED (or OLMSTEAD), Frederick Law (1822–1903), American landscape architect and writer. With Calvert Vaux he planned Central Park, New York, and himself designed other parks in Philadelphia, Brooklyn, Montreal and Chicago. In the 1850s he was well known for his perceptive travel books on the South.

OLNEY, Richard (1835–1917), US attorney general (1893–95) and secretary of state (1895–97) under President Cleveland. He is remembered for calling out troops to deal with workers involved in the PULLMAN STRIKE in 1894. He announced the controversial "Olney Corollary" to the Monroe Doctrine in 1895, declaring bluntly United States willingness to interfere in the internal affairs of South America.

OLYMPIC GAMES, the oldest international sporting contest traditionally for amateurs, held every four years. The games probably developed from the ancient Greek athletic contests in honor of a god or dead hero. Events such as boxing, wrestling, long jump, discus, javelin, distance running and chariot racing were added to the original sole event, a 210yd race, held in 776 BC at Olympia in honor of ZEUS. The games at Olympia lasted seven days. They lost popularity, largely through the growth of cheating, and were abolished by Emperor Theodosius I in 394 AD. In 1896 the first modern Olympic Games were held in Athens, organized by Pierre de COUBERTIN. Since then the games have been held in different cities, once every four years except 1916, 1940 and 1944. In 1924 the Winter Olympics were started at Chamonix, France. The 1972 games in Munich were marred by the terrorist massacre of 11 Israelis. In 1976, 21 African countries withdrew, protesting New Zealand's rugby tour of South Africa. In 1980, 62 of the more than 125 nations invited boycotted the Summer Games in Moscow, protesting the Russian invasion of Afghanistan. Occasionally, the Olympic games can generate considerable national pride, as they did in the US in 1980 when, at the Winter Games at Lake Placid, N.Y., the underdog US ice hockey team defeated the favored Soviet team and ultimately won the gold medal.

OLYMPIO, Silvanus (1902–1963), African politician, first president of Togo 1961–63. He was prime minister from 1958 until independence from France was granted in 1960. His authoritarian regime brought about his assassination.

OLYMPUS, Mount, highest mountain in Greece, rises 9,570ft at the E end of the 25mi range along the Thessaly-Macedonia border. The summit is snowcapped for most of the year. The Ancient Greeks believed it to be the home of Zeus and most other gods (the Olympians).

OM, Sanskrit sacred syllable (see MANTRA) signifying the primordial sound and divine energy; in HINDUISM it often represents the Trimurti, and in Buddhism the Absolute. It is commonly chanted repetitively to purify and concentrate the mind for meditation. LAMAISM often uses the mantra *om mani padme hum* (ah! the jewel is indeed in the lotus!).

OMAN (formerly Muscat and Oman), an independent sultanate along the SE Arabian peninsula on the Arabian Sea. A peninsula separated from the rest of Oman by the United Arab Emirates juts into the strategic Strait of Hormuz. Much of Oman is barren, with little rainfall and temperatures reaching 130°F. Dates are grown on the Batinah coastal plain, NW of Muscat (the capital) and the Dhofar Province is noted for sugarcane and cattle. Grains and fruits are grown around Jebel Akhdar. Oil was discovered in 1964, and over 100 million barrels are produced yearly. Closely associated with Britain since 1798, Oman has a population that is mostly Arab, but includes blacks, Indians and Pakistanis. In 1970 the reformist Sultan Qabus bin Said ousted his father and has become a prominent moderate in Middle Eastern affairs. A 1976 ceasefire largely ended guerrilla warfare in the S but the situation remains tense.

Official name: The Sultanate of Oman
Capital: Muscat
Area: 120,000sq mi
Population: 850,000
Languages: Arabic, English
Religions: Muslim
Monetary unit(s): 1 rial Omani = 1,000 baiza

OMAN, Gulf of, arm of the Arabian Sea between Oman and Iran. It is 350mi long and joins with the Persian Gulf through the Hormuz Strait.

OMAR KHAYYAM, 11th-century Persian poet, astronomer and mathematician. His epic poem *Rubaiyat*, dealing with nature and love, is known in the West through its translation by Edward FITZGERALD.

ONASSIS, Aristotle Socrates (1906–1975), Turkish-born Greek shipowner and financier. In the 1920s he was a tobacco merchant in Buenos Aires. In 1925 he acquired Argentinian and Greek nationality. Buying his first ships in the early 1930s, he came to own many super-tankers and became one of the world's richest men. In 1968 he married Jacqueline KENNEDY.

ONEIDA COMMUNITY, a religious commune founded by J. H. NOYES in 1848 near Oneida, N.Y. The group shared both possessions and partners and thought of themselves as a "family" of God. They set up successful businesses in silver and steel products. The flourishing community was made a joint stock company in 1881 and social experiments were ended.

O'NEILL, Eugene (Gladstone) (1888–1953), arguably the US's greatest playwright, winner of the 1936 Nobel Prize for Literature. Son of a popular actor, after

-ying the sea, journalism and gold rospecting he started to write plays during convalescence from tuberculosis and was nitially involved in early off-Broadway fforts to introduce European seriousness nto American theater. Whether expres- ionistic (*The Emperor Jones*, 1920), aturalistic (*Anna Christie*, 1921), ymbolist (*The Hairy Ape*, 1922) or pdated Greek tragedy (*Mourning ecomes Electra*, 1931), his large body of ork was ambitious in scope and elentlessly tragic (except for the comedy *4h, Wilderness!*, 1935), and culminated in nasterpieces such as *The Iceman Cometh* 1946) and *Long Day's Journey Into Night* 1955).

O'NEILL, Margaret "Peggy" 1796–1879), the daughter of a tavern keeper and wife of John EATON. President *ACKSON*'s secretary of war. The wives of other cabinet ministers snubbed her socially, provoking a cabinet crisis in which VAN BUREN replaced CALHOUN as vice-president.

O'NEILL, Thomas P. ("Tip"), Jr. 1912–), US legislator. Elected to the US House (1952), he became majority whip 1972) and then (1977) Speaker. An 'old-fashioned" liberal, he was an early opponent of the Vietnam War and a critic of budget cuts for domestic programs by Presidents Carter and Reagan.

ONO, Yoko (1933–), Japanese-born avant-garde artist, musician and film- maker, who married (1969) and collaborat- ed with BEATLES member John Lennon (1940–1980).

ONSAGER, Lars (1903–1975), Norwegian-born US chemist awarded the 1968 Nobel Prize for Chemistry for his fundamental work on irreversible chemical and thermodynamic processes.

Name of province: Ontario
Joined Confederation: July 1, 1867
Capital: Toronto
Area: 412,582sq mi
Population: 8,570,000

ONTARIO, the richest and most populous province of Canada.

Land. In the N part of Ontario lies the Hudson Bay Lowland, a poorly drained area covered by low forests, tundra and swamps, stretching 100mi to 200mi inland from the coast of Hudson Bay and James Bay. S of this is the CANADIAN SHIELD. covering half of Ontario's surface. Nickel, iron, platinum, copper, gold and uranium are among the valuable ores mined there. The Great Lakes Lowland, lying along Lakes Huron, Erie and Ontario, is the site of rich farmland as well as most of the province's industry. There are many rivers and 250,000 lakes in Ontario, and Ontario has vast resources of hydroelectric power.

People. Between 1970 and 1980 Ontario's population grew by 10%; the fastest growth rates were in the metropolitan areas. Nearly 90% of Ontarians live in the 10% of the province that lies S of the French River and Lake Nipissing, and 80% of the people live in towns. About three-fifths of the people are of British origin and the second largest ethnic group are the French Canadians in eastern and northern Ontario. Since WWII over a million European immigrants, including British, Italians, Dutch, Germans and Poles have settled in Ontario.

Economy. Ontario is responsible for about half Canada's manufactured goods, a third of its agricultural wealth and a fourth of its mineral production. Metropolitan Toronto is the most important industrial center. There is car manufacturing in Oakville, Oshawa and Windsor, iron and steelmaking in Hamilton, nickel processing in Port Colborne and a petrochemical industry in Sarnia. The SW area of the Great Lakes Lowland is the main field crop region, where hay, tobacco, soybeans, oats, tomatoes and corn are grown. Because of mechanization and specialization, farms have become very productive. Corn is the leading crop. Rich orchards and vineyards lie in the Niagara fruit belt. Beef and dairy cattle are reared in the NE of the Great Lakes Lowland. The number of beef cattle has doubled since 1965. About two-thirds of farm income is derived from livestock. Ontario provides about 20% of Canada's commercial lumber. The most important wood product is newsprint.

In the 1960s deposits of zinc and copper were found near Porcupine Lake. The Sudbury basin provides more than a third of the world's nickel, 40% of Canada's copper and a large amount of platinum. The Pickering station, opened in 1971, is the world's largest commercial nuclear power facility.

History. In the early 17th century Ontario was explored by Étienne BRULÉ and Samuel de CHAMPLAIN. By 1671 the English Hudson Bay Company had set up a trading post at Moose Factory, and N Ontario became the scene of Anglo-French rivalry until 1763, at the end of the French and Indian Wars, when French North America was ceded to Britain. In the 1780s many American Loyalists settled in S Ontario. In 1791 Ontario broke from Quebec and became the colony of Upper Canada. After the rebellion of 1837–38, led by W. L. MACKENZIE, there were political reforms and in 1840 came reunion with Quebec. The Dominion of CANADA was established in 1867 with Ontario, Quebec, New Brunswick and Nova Scotia as original members. At the end of the 1800s many Ontarians left for richer agricultural lands westward and in the US. The coming of industry and the accessibility of rich mines and lumbering areas in the N led to rapidly increasing prosperity which was accelerated by the opening of the SAINT LAWRENCE SEAWAY in 1959.

ONTARIO, Lake, the smallest (about 7,600sq mi) and farthest E of the five GREAT LAKES. The lake, bisected by the US-Canadian border, is about 193mi long and up to 53mi wide, with a maximum sounded depth of 802ft. A major link in the GREAT LAKES-SAINT LAWRENCE SEAWAY system, its cargo traffic includes coal, grain, lumber and iron ore. Principal ports are Toronto, Hamilton and Kingston (Ontario), and Oswego and Rochester (N.Y.).

OOSTENDE, town, fishing port and resort in NW Belgium. It dates from the 9th century, and now has shipbuilding industries. Pop 56,954.

ONTOGENY AND PHYLOGENY, terms respectively descriptive of the developmental (particularly embryonic) history of an individual organism and of the evolutionary history of its race. E. H. HAECKEL's "biogenetic law" proposed that "ontogeny recapitulates (repeats) phylogeny."

ONTOLOGY. a branch of philosophy, sometimes viewed as a subdivision of METAPHYSICS, which inquires about the nature of being or the senses in which something is said "to be." The ontological argument for the existence of God argues from the idea of God to his necessary existence.

OPAL, cryptocrystalline variety of porous hydrated SILICA. deposited from aqueous solution in all kinds of rocks, and also formed by replacement of other minerals. Opals are variously colored; the best GEM varieties are translucent, with milky or pearly opalescence and iridescence due to light scattering and interference from internal cracks and cavities. Common opal is used as an abrasive, filler and insulator.

OP ART, abstract art style in which patterns and color values are composed to produce an illusion of movement on the picture-surface. The best-known artists in the style, which developed in the 1960s, are Victor Vasarely and Bridget Riley.

OPEC. See ORGANIZATION OF PETROLEUM EXPORTING COUNTRIES.

OPEN DOOR POLICY, policy of equal commercial rights for all nations involved in

an area, usually referring to its enunciati in 1899 and during the BOXER REBELLION US Secretary of State John Hay in notes the main powers concerned with China. roots lay in the Nanking Treaty after t OPIUM WAR. It was confirmed 1921–22 (s WASHINGTON, TREATIES OF), and ended wi the clash with Japan's "New Order" in t 1930s and with WWII.

OPEN SHOP. See RIGHT-TO-WORK LAW.

OPERA, staged dramatic form in which t text is wholly or partly sung to instrumental or orchestral accompanime It originated in 17th-century Italy, in attempt to recreate Greek drama; this w combined with the popular semi-music mystery plays and religious dramas in *dramma per musica* (drama throu music), and spread through Europe. Mu early opera was a mere excuse for spectacl but works by MONTEVERDI, CAVALLI, LULL PURCELL and others greatly advanced the a and are again popular today. Dramat standards had declined by the early 18 century (despite fine works by HANDEL being caught up in stilted convention. GLUC sought to avoid this by unifying plot, mus and staging into a dramatic whole, whi MOZART introduced greater depth of feelir into the music and realism of character c stage. The form was still further enriche by the Romantics, BEETHOVEN and WEBER Germany and BERLIOZ and BIZET in Franc The great Italians BELLINI, DONIZETTI an ROSSINI developed the more stylized BE CANTO form to which VERDI, in his late operas, gave greater depth and naturalism a trend carried further in the seminal worl and theories of Richard WAGNER. He sough to add a philosophical basis to Gluck synthesis by creating *Gesamtkunstwerk* the total work of art and in his later wor made extensive use of leitmotifs, sho musical statements representing a cha acter, things or idea. Much of the music i *Der Ring des Nibelungen* consists c leitmotifs woven together, then develope and varied. Wagner influenced many late composers such as Richard STRAUSS an DEBUSSY. The recent Italian *verism* (naturalistic) school produced smalle scale, often sensational works: PUCCIN mastered both this and a more epic fantastic style. Among the greates 20th-century opera composers ar JANAČEK, BERG and BRITTEN. (See als individual composers, especially BOITO GOUNOD; MASCAGNI; MEYERBEER MUSSORGSKY; TCHAIKOVSKY.)

OPERA BUFFA (Italian: comic opera) light operatic form, generally consisting o musical numbers linked by *recitativo secco* lightly-accompanied RECITATIVE more spoken than sung.

OPERA COMIQUE, French light opera of the 18th century, with spoken dialogue rather than recitative linking musical numbers. After c1800 the term was extended to cover any opera using spoken dialogue.

OPERETTA, light opera with elements of romance and satire, such as the works of Johann STRAUSS, Franz LEHAR, Jacques OFFENBACH and in England W. S. GILBERT and Sir Arthur SULLIVAN. Operetta was one of the ancestors of 20th-century MUSICAL COMEDY.

OPHTHALMOLOGY, the branch of MEDICINE and SURGERY concerned with diseases of VISION and the EYE. In infancy, congenital BLINDNESS and STRABISMUS, and in adults, glaucoma, uveitis, CATARACT, retinal detachment and vascular diseases are common, as are ocular manifestations of systemic diseases—hypertension and DIABETES. Disorders of eye movement, lids and TEAR production; color vision; infection, and injury are also seen. Surgery to the lens, CORNEA (including corneal grafting), eye muscles and lids may be used, and cryosurgery (freezing) or coagulation employed in retinal disease.

OPHTHALMOSCOPE, instrument for examining the RETINA and structures of the inner EYE. A powerful light and lens system, combined with the CORNEA and lens of the eye allows the retina and eye blood vessels to be seen at high magnification. It is a valuable aid to diagnosis in OPHTHALMOLOGY and internal MEDICINE.

OPINION POLL. See POLL, PUBLIC OPINION.

OPIUM, NARCOTIC extract from the immature fruits of the opium poppy, *Papaver somniferum,* which is native to Greece and Asia Minor. The milky juice is refined to a powder which has a sharp, bitter taste. Drugs, some drugs of abuse (see DRUG ADDICTION), obtained from opium include the narcotic ANALGESICS, HEROIN, MORPHINE and CODEINE. (Synthetic analogues of these include methadone and pethidine.) Older opium preparations, now rarely used, include LAUDANUM and PAREGORIC. The extraction of opium outside the pharmaceutical industry is strictly controlled in the West.

OPIUM WAR (1839–42), fought in China by the British, the first in a series aimed at opening ports and gaining tariff concessions. The pretext was the burning of 20,000 chests of opium by the Chinese. China had banned the opium trade in 1799, but with the aid of corrupt Chinese officials British merchants still made enormous profits from it. British troops occupied Hong Kong in 1841, and the fall of Chinkiang in 1842 threatened Peking itself. The Treaty of Nanking ceded Hong Kong to Britain and granted British merchants full rights of residence in the ports of Amoy, Canton, Foochow, Ningpo and Shanghai; Britain was to receive over $50 million war indemnity. The US gained trade facilities by the 1844 Treaty of Wanghai. Further hostilities, in which French joined British troops (1856), led to more concessions, notably in the Treaties of Tientsin (1858) to which Britain, France, Russia and the US were parties and which legalized the opium trade, and in 1860, when Kowloon was ceded to Britain and part of Manchuria to Russia.

OPOSSUMS, primitive arboreal MARSUPIALS of the Americas. The name has also been applied to Australian forms but these are now usually distinguished as POSSUMS. Opossums are carnivorous and usually have a prehensile tail. The pouch is developed only in some species, but all have an uneven number of teats, as many as 17 in the Virginian opossum. (The teats of all Australian marsupials are paired.) In size, opossums vary from mouse-like to forms about the size of a domestic cat. Family: Didelphidae.

OPPENHEIMER, Julius Robert (1904–1967), US physicist whose influence as an educator is still felt today and who headed the MANHATTAN PROJECT, which developed the ATOMIC BOMB. His main aim was the peaceful use of nuclear power (he fought against the construction of the HYDROGEN BOMB but was overruled by Truman in 1949); but, because of his left-wing friendships, was unable to pursue his researches in this direction after being labeled a security risk (1954). He also worked out much of the theory of BLACK HOLES.

OPTICAL FIBER, a fine strand of transparent material, usually high-purity glass coated with protective material, that is able to guide light through it by repeated internal reflection from its surface. The technology of these fibers and their applications is called **fiber optics.** A bundle of parallel fibers can transmit an image no matter how the bundle is bent, each fiber carrying a dot of light from one end to the corresponding point at the other end. Fiber optics is used in this way in medical instruments to explore the gastrointestinal tract. Optical fibers are coming into use as a substitute for telephone cables, the voice information being converted into pulses of

LASER light. Communications are expected to be the major application of fiber optics in the future.

OPTICS, the science of light and vision. Physical optics deal with the nature of LIGHT (see also COLOR; DIFFRACTION; INTERFERENCE; POLARIZED LIGHT; SPECTROSCOPY). Geometrical optics consider the behavior of light in optical instruments (see ABERRATION, OPTICAL; CAMERA; DISPERSION LENS, OPTICAL; MICROSCOPE; MIRROR; PRISM; REFLECTION; REFRACTION; SPECTRUM; TELESCOPE). Physiological optics are concerned with vision (see EYE).

ORANGE, House of, an important dynasty in the Netherlands since the 16th century. The line has included WILLIAM III of England and, since 1815, the monarchs of the Netherlands, including the present Queen Beatrix.

ORANGE FREE STATE, province of South Africa, covering 49,866sq mi of inland plateau between the Orange and Vaal rivers. Agriculture is based on livestock, cereals and fruit; gold, diamonds and coal are mined. The capital is Bloemfontein. (See also BOER WAR; SOUTH AFRICA.) Pop 1,649,306.

ORANGEMEN, or Loyal Orange Institution, a Protestant (chiefly Ulster) society, which since the first (1795) Lodge has identified with the Protestant ascendancy in Ireland and, more recently, union with Britain. The name is from William of Orange (see also BOYNE, BATTLE OF; WILLIAM III).

ORANGUTAN, *Pongo pygmaeus,* a large, red, anthropoid ape of Sumatra and Borneo. Animals of thick rain forests, they are truly arboreal apes—walking quadrupedally along branches, or bipedally, with the arms holding on above. Occasionally the orangutan brachiates for short distances. They can move along the ground, but rarely descend from the trees. Orangutans are vegetarians, feeding mainly on leaves, buds and fruit.

ORATORIANS, Roman Catholic congregation founded c1575 in Rome by St. Philip NERI. Members, organized in autonomous congregations, are secular priests who take no vows. NEWMAN founded oratories in Birmingham –(1848) and London (1849). A separate society was founded in 1611 in Paris by Pierre de Bérulle.

ORATORIO, a musical composition for vocal soloists, chorus and orchestra, usually with a religious subject. The form evolved c1600 from medieval sacred drama. Early oratorio composers include SCARLATTI, J. S. BACH and HANDEL, whose *Messiah* is probably the most famous oratorio. Amon later oratorio composers are BEETHOVEN MENDELSSOHN and ELGAR. (See als PASSION.)

ORBIT, the path followed by one celestia body revolving under the influence o gravity (see GRAVITATION) about another. I the SOLAR SYSTEM, the planets orbit the sun and the moons the planets, in elliptica paths, although Triton's orbit of NEPTUNE i as far as can be determined perfectl circular. The point in the planetary asteroidal or cometary orbit closest to th sun is called its *perihelion;* the farthes point is termed *aphelion.* In the case of a moon or artificial satellite orbiting a plane or other moon, the corresponding terms are *perigee* and *apogee.* (See also APSIDES, LINE OF: KEPLER'S LAWS.) Celestial objects o similar masses may orbit each other particularly DOUBLE STARS.

ORCAGNA, (or ARCAGNOLD) (c1308–1368), painter, sculptor and architect of Florence, Italy, leading artist in the Byzantine Gothic style. His work includes the Strozzi chapel altarpiece in S. Maria Novella and the Or San Michele tabernacle, Florence.

ORCHESTRA, the name given to most instrumental groups of more than a few players. The modern orchestra dates from the birth of OPERA c1600. The first great operatic composer, MONTEVERDI, wrote for orchestra, and for some time opera and orchestral music were closely linked. As the VIOLIN family replaced VIOLS, composers like VIVALDI, J. S. BACH and HANDEL began to write purely orchestral music. The SYMPHONY was developed around the same time (1700) from the operatic overture. In the 18th century HAYDN organized the orchestra into four groups: string, woodwind, brass and percussion—a basic pattern that has not altered. With the great 18th- and 19th-century composers, the orchestra came to dominate the musical scene. New and more numerous instruments were introduced, permanent orchestras established, and the art of conducting developed. The 20th century has seen a movement to return to smaller ensembles.

ORCHIDS, plants of the very large family Orchidaceae (15,000–30,000 species) which produce colorful and elaborate flowers. Some species are native to cold and temperate regions, but most occur in tropical, damp climates. Some grow as EPIPHYTES on forest trees. Orchid flowers are specially adapted to insect POLLINATION, some requiring a particular SPECIES of insect. Orchids produce minute seeds that are devoid of stored food and thus require the aid of fungi to supply the nourishment needed for germination (see MYCORRHIZA). Orchids are of little economic importance except as curious ornamental plants; cultivation has developed into an extensive hobby throughout the world. As house plants they should be grown in sunny windows at average house temperatures; they do well in fluorescent-light gardens. The soil should be drenched and then not watered again until almost dry. Propagation is by planting divisions.

ORDER. See TAXONOMY.

ORDINAL NUMBER, one that describes the order of an element in a SET. For example, in the phrase "my second and third candies," 2 and 3 are ordinal numbers. (See also CARDINAL NUMBER.)

ORDINATION, in the Christian Church, the ceremonial appointment to one of the orders of MINISTRY. The ordination of BISHOPS is usually called consecration. Regarded by the Roman Catholic Church as a SACRAMENT, ordination is performed in episcopal churches by a bishop (see also APOSTOLIC SUCCESSION), and in presbyterian churches by the presbytery. The rite includes prayer and the laying on of hands, traditionally in a eucharistic context.

ORDOVICIAN, the second period of the PALEOZOIC, which lasted from about 500 to 440 million years ago and immediately followed the CAMBRIAN. (See GEOLOGY.)

ORE, aggregate of minerals and rocks from which it is commercially worthwhile to extract minerals (usually metals). An ore has three parts: the country rock in which the deposit is found; the gangue, the unwanted ROCKS and minerals of the deposit; and the desired MINERAL itself. MINING techniques depend greatly on the form and position of the deposit (see PLACER MINING; STRIP MINING).

Name of state: Oregon
Capital: Salem
Statehood: Feb. 14, 1859 (33rd state)
Familiar name: Beaver State
Area: 96,981sq mi
Population: 2,632,663
Elevation: Highest—11,245ft, Mount Hood. Lowest—sea level, Pacific Ocean
Motto: The Union
State flower: Oregon grape
State bird: Western meadowlark
State tree: Douglas fir
State song: "Oregon, My Oregon"

OREGON, a US state of the Pacific Northwest, bounded to the N by Wash., across the Columbia R., E by Ida., S by Nev. and Cal., and W by the Pacific Ocean. It is known to its millions of visitors for its lofty mountains, deep gorges and fine coastline.

Land. Oregon is divided in two by the Cascade Range of mountains which stretch north-south across the entire state. Between the Coastal Range and the Cascades lies Willamette Valley, which contains the state's most fertile land and most of its population and industries. This area has a mild and moist marine climate. Most of the land E of the Cascades is part of the Columbia Plateau, occupying two-thirds of Oregon. This area is drier and experiences a greater range of temperatures. Half of Oregon is forested.

People. Two-thirds of Oregon's population live in or around Portland, Eugene and Salem in the Willamette Valley. Oregon's original constitution of 1859 is still in effect, with the amendments of 1902 providing for the initiative and referendum. These two measures, together with direct primaries and procedures for the recall of elected officials, became known as the "Oregon system" and were adopted by many states before WWI.

Economy. The most important manufactures are wood-processing and food-processing (especially fish canning). Other leading industries are machinery, transportation equipment, and metal processing, in which cheap hydroelectric power is used. Wheat, grown in E Oregon, is the most important crop. Livestock and turkey farming are also of importance. Commercial deposits of natural gas were tapped in 1979 in NW Oregon, and there is a large geothermal potential. Tourism is also of increasing importance to the state's economy.

History. The first American to visit the area (1792) was Captain Robert GRAY. The LEWIS AND CLARK EXPEDITION of 1805–06 to the mouth of the Columbia R reinforced American claims to the region. Although pioneers settled in Oregon from the 1840s (see OREGON TRAIL), development was slow until the coming of the railroad in the 1880s. The first two decades of this century saw the rapid development of the lumbering industry, and the post-WWII period has seen new developments in the metallurgical and electrochemical industries. The state has been growing quickly, with population increasing 25.9% during the 1970's, but the local economy has kept pace, with unemployment, at 6.9% in 1980, being less than the national average. Oregon's cities have not suffered the same deterioration as older cities in the East, freeing the state to give more emphasis now to conserving its natural resources.

OREGON TRAIL, famous pioneer wagon route of 19th-century America between Independence, Mo., on the Missouri, and the Columbia R region of the Pacific Northwest. The 2,000mi trail was most popular in the 1840s, before the beginning of the Californian GOLD RUSH. In that decade at least 10,000 pioneers made the arduous trek from NE Kansas, along the R Platte in Nebraska, to Fort Laramie, Wyoming. From there they crossed the Rockies at South Pass and passed through Snake River country to Fort Vancouver. The journey was recounted in Francis Parkman's classic, *The Oregon Trail* (1849).

ORESTES, in Greek mythology, son of AGAMEMNON and CLYTEMNESTRA. After Clytemnestra had killed Agamemnon, Orestes avenged his father by killing his mother and her lover, with the aid of his sister ELECTRA. Pursued by the FURIES, he stole the image of Artemis from Tauris to atone for his murders, helped this time by his sister IPHIGENIA.

ORFF, Carl (1895–   ), German composer and music teacher. His works are marked by short melodic motifs and strong rhythms from a large and varied percussion section.

ORGAN, a musical instrument in which air is blown into pipes of different shape and size to produce a range of notes. Organ pipes are of two kinds: flue pipes which work like a flute or recorder, and reed pipes which operate on the same principle as a clarinet or oboe. Although organs go back to ancient times, the main developments in organ building took place between the 14th and the 18th centuries. Composers like SWEELINCK and BUXTEHUDE paved the way for J. S. BACH, the greatest of all composers for the organ. Bach and HANDEL wrote for the baroque organ, a relatively small instrument. In the 19th century many great organs were built, precursors of the huge electric-powered organs built in the 1920s and 1930s in cinemas and theaters. The modern Hammond organ produces its sound electronically. Small electronic organs are now frequently used by pop groups. (See also HARMONIUM.)

ORGAN, in biology, a functionally adapted part of an organism. Organs, such as the vermiform APPENDIX in man, which persist in a species although no longer of any use to it, are termed *vestigial organs.*

ORGANIC CHEMISTRY, major branch of CHEMISTRY comprising the study of CARBON compounds containing hydrogen (simple carbon compounds such as carbon dioxide being usually deemed inorganic). This apparently specialized field is in fact wide and varied, because of carbon's almost unique ability to form linked chains of atoms to any length and complexity; far more organic compounds are known than inorganic. Organic compounds form the basic stuff of living tissue (see also BIOCHEMISTRY), and until the mid-19th century, when organic syntheses were achieved, a "vital force" was thought necessary to make them. The 19th-century development of quantitative ANALYSIS by J. LIEBIG and J. B. A. DUMAS, and of structural theory by S. CANNIZZARO and F. A. KEKULÉ, laid the basis for modern organic chemistry. Organic compunds are classified as aliphatic, alicyclic, aromatic and heterocyclic compounds (see HYDROCARBONS), according to the structure of the skeleton of the molecule, and are further subdivided in terms of the FUNCTIONAL GROUPS present.

ORGANIZATION FOR ECONOMIC COOPERATION AND DEVELOPMENT (OECD), a consultative organization set up in 1961 to coordinate economic policies and encourage economic growth and world trade. The founder-states were 18 W European countries, the US and Canada. Japan, Finland, New Zealand and Australia are also members.

ORGANIZATION OF AFRICAN UNITY (OAU), an association of the independent African states (excluding South Africa) which aims to promote unity and eradicate colonialism in Africa. Founded in 1963, the OAU has a permanent secretariat in Addis Ababa, Ethiopia, and has had great influence at the United Nations.

ORGANIZATION OF AMERICAN STATES (OAS), an association of 28 republics of the Americas which aims to settle disputes peacefully, to create a collective security system, and to coordinate the work of other intra-American bodies. The OAS was founded in Bogotá, Colombia, in 1948 and has a permanent secretariat, the Pan American Union. Its activities have included support for the US blockade of Cuba in 1962, and mediation between Britain and Guatemala in 1972.

ORGANIZATION OF PETROLEUM EXPORTING COUNTRIES (OPEC), an association founded in 1960 by Iran, Iraq, Kuwait, Libya, Saudi Arabia and Venezuela. OPEC's membership expanded to include Qatar, Indonesia, United Arab Emirates, Algeria, Nigeria, Ecuador and Gabon and its power increased dramatically in the 1970s, when many countries in the world became increasingly dependent on its oil to run their economies. OPEC was accused of shamelessly raising the price of oil by acting as an international cartel; its members agreed on a unified price for crude oil of $34 per barrel in Oct. 1981. But the world oil surplus of the early 1980s worked to decrease OPEC's power.

ORIGAMI, the Japanese art of paper folding. In Japan it is divided into two categories—the making of *no shi*, decorations attached to gifts, and the making of plant, animal and human figures. Origami has become popular in the West since WWII.

ORIGINAL SIN, in Christian theology, the state of sinfulness in which all mankind is born, and which is the root cause of all actual SINS. According to St. PAUL, when Adam disobeyed God (the Fall), the whole human race fell in solidarity with him and inherited his sin and guilt, losing supernatural GRACE and communion with God, and our FREE WILL was made spiritually inoperative. In Catholic theology, original sin is washed away in BAPTISM.

ORINOCO RIVER, great river of Venezuela, N South America, about 1,700mi long. It rises in the Parima highlands of SE Venezuela and eventually flows into the Atlantic Ocean through a 7,000sq mi delta. It is mostly navigable.

ORKNEY ISLANDS, group of about 70 islands north of Scotland, of which they are part. Their total area is 376sq mi but fewer than half are inhabited. The climate is mild and the soil fertile. Farming is the chief activity (grains, sheep, cattle, poultry), with some fishing.

ORLANDO, Vittorio Emanuele (1860–1952), Italian statesman, prime minister 1917–19. He led the Italian delegation at the VERSAILLES Peace Conference of 1919–20. Orlando retired from politics with the advent of fascism, but returned after the fall of Mussolini.

ORLÉANS, family name of two branches of the French royal line. The House of Valois-Orléans was founded by Louis, Duke of Orléans (1372–1407), whose grandson ascended the throne (1498) as LOUIS XII. The House of Bourbon-Orléans was founded by Philippe, Duke of Orléans (1640–1701), a brother of king LOUIS XIV. His son, Philippe (1674–1723), was regent of France 1715–23. LOUIS PHILIPPE was the sole member of the House to become king.

ORMANDY, Eugene (1899–), Hungarian-born US conductor, a famous interpreter of Romantic works. Trained as a violinist, he became permanent conductor of the Philadelphia Orchestra in 1938.

ORNITHOLOGY, the scientific study of BIRDS. The observation of birds in their natural environment has a long history and is now so popular as to be the most widespread of zoological hobbies.

OROZCO, José Clemente (1883–1949), major Mexican painter, who exploited the fresco technique in his large-scale murals, which express strong social convictions. His most famous works include the fresco *Prometheus* (1930) and a mural *Epic Culture in the New World* (1932–34).

ORPHEUS, in Greek mythology, famous musician of Thrace. Son of the Muse CALLIOPE, he could tame wild beasts with his lyre-playing. After the death of his wife Eurydice, Orpheus sought her in HADES. He was allowed to lead her back to earth providing he did not look back, but he could not resist the temptation, and Eurydice vanished forever. He is said to have been killed by the women followers of DIONYSUS in Thrace. He was regarded as the founder of the Orphic MYSTERY cult.

ORR, Bobby (1948–), US ice hockey player. Perhaps the best defenseman in hockey history, he revolutionized the game with his attacking style of play. He set an NHL record with 102 assists in 1971 and twice led the league in scoring while winning eight consecutive Norris Trophies as top defensive player, 1968–75.

ORTEGA Y GASSET, José (1883–1955), Spanish philosopher, whose best-known work, *The Revolt of the Masses* (1929), attributes Western decadence to the revolt of "mass man" against an intellectual elite. His philosophy attempts to reconcile reason with individual lives and needs.

ORTHODONTICS. See DENTISTRY.

ORTHODOX CHURCHES, the family of Christian churches that developed out of the EASTERN CHURCH, remaining orthodox when the NESTORIANS and MONOPHYSITE CHURCHES separated. They finally broke with Rome in the GREAT SCHISM of 1054. Each church is independent, but all are in full communion and acknowledge the honorary primacy of the ecumenical patriarch of Constantinople; some are patriarchates, others are governed by SYNODS. The ancient patriarchates of Constantinople, Alexandria, Antioch and Jerusalem are dwarfed by the more recent churches of Russia, Serbia, Romania, Bulgaria, Georgia, Greece, Cyprus and others. There are now more than 123 million Orthodox worldwide, including 3 million in the US. Orthodoxy accepts the first seven ECUMENICAL COUNCILS, but often prefers not to define dogma very closely; it is characterized by MONASTICISM, veneration of ICONS and the importance of the laity. It rejects papal claims, the IMMACULATE CONCEPTION and PURGATORY, and does not require clerical celibacy.

ORTHOPEDICS, speciality within SURGERY, dealing with BONE and soft-tissue disease, damage and deformity. Its name derives from 17th-century treatments designed to produce "straight children." Until the advent of anesthetics, ASEPSIS and X-RAYS, its methods were restricted to AMPUTATION and manipulation for dislocation, etc. Treatment of congenital deformity; FRACTURES and TUMORS of bone; OSTEOMYELITIS; ARTHRITIS, and JOINT dislocation are common in modern orthopedics. Methods range from the use of splints, PHYSIOTHERAPY and manipulation, to surgical correction of deformity, fixing of fractures and refashioning or replacement of joints. Suture or transposition of TENDONS, MUSCLES or nerves are performed.

ORWELL, George (1903–1950), pen name of the English novelist Eric Arthur Blair, famous principally for *Animal Farm* (1945), a savage satire on communist revolution, and *Nineteen Eighty-Four* (1949), depicting a dehumanizing totalitarian society. Orwell was also a critic and essayist. Other works include the semi-autobiographical *The Road to Wigan Pier* (1937), and *Homage to Catalonia* (1938), an account of his experiences in the SPANISH CIVIL WAR.

ORY, Edward "Kid" (1886–1973), US jazz trombonist and band leader. A jazz pioneer, he led one of the most famous New Orleans jazz bands (1910–19) which, at various times, included King OLIVER, Sidney BECHET and Louis ARMSTRONG.

OSAGE INDIANS, Plains Indian tribe of the Siouan language group who lived in what is now W Mo. and Ark. in the late 17th century. In 1872 they were moved to a reservation in Okla., and became one of the richest communities in the world when oil was discovered on their reservation in the 19th century.

OSAKA, third largest city in Japan, a major port on the S coast of Honshu Island. It is the center of the populous industrial area called the Kinki, and is one of Japan's most important commercial and industrial centers with a great diversity of manufactures. It is also a major educational and cultural center. An ancient city, it developed as Japan's leading trading center after the 16th century. Pop 2,682,200.

OSBORN, Fairfield (1887–1969), US naturalist and conservationist. As the flamboyant president of the New York Zoological Society (1940–68) he attracted millions of visitors to the Bronx Zoo and Coney Island Aquarium. His popular environmental books included *Our Plundered Planet* (1948) and *The Limits of the Earth* (1953).

OSBORNE, John (1929–   ), British dramatist whose *Look Back in Anger* (1956) made him the first ANGRY YOUNG MAN of the 1950s and established a new and vigorous realism in the theater. Later plays include *The Entertainer* (1957), *Luther* (1961) and *Inadmissible Evidence* (1964).

OSCARS. See ACADEMY AWARDS.

OSCEOLA (c1804–1838), Indian leader in the Second Seminole War against the US (1835–42), who used guerrilla tactics to resist a US plan to transport the Seminole Indians from Fla. to Okla. He was taken prisoner in 1837 and died in prison.

OSCILLATOR, a device converting direct to alternating current (see ELECTRICITY), used, for example, in generating RADIO waves. Most types are based on an electronic AMPLIFIER, a small portion of the output being returned via a FEEDBACK circuit to the input, so as to make the oscillation self-sustaining. The feedback signal must have the same PHASE as the input: by varying the components of the feedback circuit, the frequency for which this occurs can be varied, so that the oscillator is easily "tuned." "Crystal" oscillators incorporate a piezoelectric crystal (see PIEZOELECTRICITY) in the tuning circuit for stability; in "heterodyne" oscillators, the output is the beat frequency between two higher frequencies.

OSCILLOSCOPE, a device using a CATHODE RAY TUBE to produce line GRAPHS of rapidly varying electrical signals. Since nearly every physical effect can be converted into an electrical signal, the oscilloscope is very widely used. Typically, the signal controls the vertical deflection of the beam while the horizontal deflection increases steadily, producing a graph of the signal as a function of time. For periodic (repeating) signals, synchronization of the horizontal scan with the signal is achieved by allowing the attainment by the signal of some preset value to "trigger" a new scan after one is finished. Most models allow two signals to be displayed as functions of each other; dual-beam instruments can display two as a function of time. Oscilloscopes usually operate from DC to high requencies, and will display signals as low s a few millivolts.

OSLER, Sir William (1849–1919), Canadian-born physician and educator best known for his work on platelets (see BLOOD) and for the informality of his educational techniques.

OSLO, capital, largest city and chief seaport of Norway. Founded c1050, it was rebuilt after the great fire of 1624. Between 1625 and 1925 it was known as Christiania or Kristiania. Today it is Norway's chief commercial, industrial and cultural center. Oslo has many fine museums, castles and parks. The Viking Ship Museum and the Vigeland Sculpture Park are especially noteworthy. Pop 454,900.

OSMOSIS, the diffusion of a solvent through a semipermeable membrane that separates two solutions of different concentration, the movement being from the more dilute to the more concentrated solution, owing to the thermodynamic tendency to equalize the concentrations. The liquid flow may be opposed by applying pressure to the more concentrated solution: the pressure required to reduce the flow to zero from a pure solvent to a given solution is known as the *osmotic pressure of the solution*. Osmosis was studied by Thomas Graham, who coined the term (1858); in 1886 Van't Hoff showed that, for dilute solutions (obeying Henry's Law), the osmotic pressure varies with temperature and concentration as if the solute were a GAS occupying the volume of the solution. This enables MOLECULAR WEIGHTS to be calculated from osmotic pressure measurements, and degrees of ionic DISSOCIATION to be estimated. Osmosis is important in DIALYSIS and in water transport in living tissue.

OSPREY, *Pandion haliaetus*, a large fish-eating bird of prey, found throughout the world, except in South America. Also known as the **fish hawk**, the osprey occupies both marine and freshwater areas, cruising above the water and plunging to take the fish in its talons. The future of the osprey is in some doubt in both Europe and North America, where it has suffered from increased use of persistent pesticides.

OSSIAN, legendary Gaelic bard who wrote of Finn Mac Cumhaill's heroic acts in S Ireland in about the 3rd century AD. James MACPHERSON's forgeries popularized the figure of Ossian in ROMANTICISM.

OSTEND MANIFESTO, agreement drawn up in Oostende (Ostend), Belgium in 1854 by three proslavery US diplomats, James BUCHANAN, John Y. MASON and Pierre SOULÉ. The manifesto implied that if Spain refused to sell Cuba the US would forcibly

seize the island. The diplomats, who probably hoped to make Cuba a Union slave state, were denounced by all the political parties.

OSTEOMYELITIS, BACTERIAL infection of BONE, usually caused by STAPHYLOCOCCUS, STREPTOCOCCUS and SALMONELLA carried to the bone by the BLOOD, or gaining access through open FRACTURES. It commonly affects children, causing FEVER and local pain. If untreated or partially treated, it may become chronic with bone destruction and a discharging SINUS. ANTIBIOTICS and surgical drainage are frequently necessary.

OSTEOPATHY, system of treatment based on theory that DISEASE arises from the mechanical and structural disorder of the body skeleton. Prevention and treatment are practiced by manipulation, often of the spine. While it may have a role in treatment of chronic musculo-skeletal pain, its methods may be hazardous, especially to the SPINAL CORD. Furthermore, serious disease may be overlooked. Osteopathy is best regarded as an adjunct to, rather than a replacement for, orthodox medicine.

OSTRICH, *Struthio camelus*, the largest living bird, at one time found throughout Africa and SW Asia, but now common in the wild only in E Africa. They are flightless birds, well adapted to a terrestrial life. They have long powerful legs, with two toes on each foot, an adaptation for running over dry grassland parallel to the reduction of digits in the horse's hoof (see HORSE). Ostriches are polygamous, living in groups of a single male and his harem.

OSTROGOTHS (East Goths), branch of the GOTHS, a Germanic people who originally occupied the lands to the N of the Black Sea. The accession of their king THEODORIC THE GREAT in 471 heralded an alliance with Zeno, Emperor of the East Roman Empire. On Zeno's orders, Theodoric invaded Italy in 488 and reduced it to Ostrogothic rule in 493, ruling from Ravenna. The Byzantine general BELISARIUS destroyed Ostrogothic rule in the 530s; a subsequent Ostrogothic revolt was swiftly crushed in 552.

OSTWALD, Friedrich Wilhelm (1853–1932), Latvian-born German physical chemist regarded as a father of physical chemistry, and awarded the 1909 Nobel Prize for Chemistry for his work on CATALYSIS. He also developed the Ostwald process for manufacturing NITRIC ACID.

OSWALD, Lee Harvey, the alleged assassin of President John F. KENNEDY in Dallas, Texas on Nov. 22, 1963, and of a local police officer. A former marine, he had lived in the USSR 1959–62. He was himself shot dead by Dallas nightclub owner Jack RUBY while being transferred from the city to the county jail on Nov. 24. The WARREN REPORT declared Oswald the sole assassin.

OTIS, Elisha Graves (1811–1861), US inventor of the safety ELEVATOR (1852), first installed for passenger use in 1856, New York City.

OTTAWA, capital city of Canada, situated at the junction of Ottawa and Rideau Rivers, in SE Ontario. Ottawa is principally a government center; a major tourist attraction is the group of Parliament buildings, built in Victorian Gothic style. The city was built as a logging community, Bytown, in 1827, during the construction of the Rideau canal which divides the city. It became Ottawa (an anglicization of the local Outawouais Indians) in 1854, and capital in 1867. Pop 304,465.

OTTAWA INDIANS, large North American tribe of the Algonquian family originally inhabiting, with the OJIBWA and POTAWATAMI INDIANS, the region N of the Great Lakes. The Ottawa later moved to Manitoulin Island. They were active traders and negotiated with the French.

OTTERS, aquatic or semiaquatic carnivores of the weasel family, subfamily Lutrinae. There are five freshwater genera and one marine genus. The body is lithe and muscular, built for vigorous swimming, and covered with thick fur. The paws are generally webbed. The nostrils and eyes may be shut when swimming underwater. The prey consists of small fish, eels, crayfish and frogs. The sea otter's diet is more specialized: sea otters have powerful rounded molars adapted for crushing sea urchins, abalones and mussels. A tool-using animal, it floats on its back, breaking open the urchin- or mussel-shell on a stone anvil balanced on its chest. Unlike most other wild animals, otters remain playful as adults.

OTTO, Nikolaus August (1832–1891), German engineer who built the first four-stroke INTERNAL-COMBUSTION ENGINE (1876), which rapidly replaced the STEAM ENGINE in many applications and facilitated the development of the automobile.

OTTOMAN EMPIRE, vast empire of the Ottoman Turks which at its height, during the reign of Sultan SULEIMAN I stretched from the far shore of the Black Sea and the Persian Gulf in the E to Budapest in the N and Algiers in the W. The Ottoman Turks, led by OSMAN I, entered Asia Minor in the late 1200s and, expanding rapidly, made Bursa their capital in 1326. They crossed to the Balkan Peninsula (1345) and in 1453 CONSTANTINOPLE fell to MOHAMMED II. The empire continued to expand in the 16th century under Selim I, the Terrible, 1512–20 and reached its zenith under Suleiman I. However, Suleiman I failed to capture Vienna (1529) and was driven back at Malta (1565). Directly after his death, the Ottoman fleet was annihilated at the naval battle of LEPANTO (1571). During the 1700s and 1800s the decaying empire fought against Russia and Greece won its independence. The reformist Young Turk movement led the empire into WWI on the German side, with disastrous results. Finally, the nationalists, led by ATATURK, deposed and exiled the last Sultan, Mohammed VI, and proclaimed the Turkish republic in 1922.

OUIDA, pen name of Maria Louise de la Ramée (1839–1908), melodramatic English novelist. Among her works are *Under Two Flags* (1867), *A Dog of Flanders* (1872), and *Moths* (1880).

OUTCAULT, Richard Felton (1863–1928), US cartoonist who created the comic urchin "Yellow Kid" for the *New York World* 1896–97. His other famous strip was "Buster Brown," which was published in the *New York Herald* from 1902.

OUTER MONGOLIA. See MONGOLIAN PEOPLE'S REPUBLIC.

OVARY, the female reproductive organ. In plants it contains the ovules (see FLOWER); in humans, the FOLLICLES in which the eggs (*ova*) develop (see ESTROGEN; FERTILIZATION; GAMETE; PROGESTERONE; REPRODUCTION).

OVERLAND TRAIL, name of westward migration routes in the US, in particular for the S alternative route to the OREGON TRAIL, and for the route to the Cal. goldfields. This latter trail went from Fort Bridger to Sutter's Fort, Cal., and duplicated in part the Mormon Trail.

OVER-THE-COUNTER STOCKS, those securities which are not traded on any of the nine US stock exchanges. The market in over-the-counter stocks has been regulated by the SECURITIES AND EXCHANGE COMMISSION since 1964.

OVERTURE, orchestral piece played at the beginning of most operas, oratorios or plays with incidental music. Operatic overtures developed in the 17th century; GLUCK was one of the first composers to link the tunes of the overture with those of the subsequent opera. Self-contained works for the concert hall are also called overtures.

OVERWEIGHT. See DIETING; OBESITY.

OVETT, Steve (1955–   ), British runner. In the space of 10 days in 1981, Ovett and countryman Sebastian COE traded the world mile record three times. Ovett won the gold medal in the 800-meter n at the 1980 Olympics.

VID (Publius Ovidius Naso; 43 BC–18
), Latin poet. Popular in his time, he was
led by the emperor Augustus to the Black
a in 8 AD and died there; his *Sorrows* and
ters from Pontus are pleas for his return.
was a master of erotic poetry, as in his
nores and *Art of Love*, but his
etamorphoses, a collection of myths
ked by their common theme of change, is
nerally considered to be his finest work.

JULATION. See MENSTRUATION.

VEN, two industrialists and social
ormers. **Robert Owen** (1771–1858), was
socialist and pioneer of the cooperative
vement. He introduced better conditions
his cotton mills in Scotland and was
tive in the trade union movement in
tain. In the US Owen set up short-lived
llages of cooperation," such as that at
w HARMONY, Ind. **Robert Dale Owen**
301–1877), his son campaigned in the US
birth control, women's property rights,
te public schools and slave emancipation.
was a member of Congress from Ind.
43–47.

VEN, Steve (1898–1964), pro football
ach. He led the New York Giants from
1930s into the "modern" football era of
1950s. He coached only six losing teams
23 seasons and won two NFL titles.

VEN, Wilfred (1893–1918), British poet
o wrote movingly of the savagery and
man sacrifice in WWI; he was deeply
luenced by Siegfried SASSOON. Owen was
led in action a week before the end of
WI. Nine of his poems form the text of
TTEN's *War Requiem* (1962), a powerful
ti-war statement.

VENS, Jesse (1913–1980), famous US
gro athlete. In 1935–36 he broke three
rld records at college track meets. By
nning the 100- and 200-meter dash, the
0-meter relay and the broad jump at the
36 Berlin Olympics, he shattered Hitler's
empt to demonstrate "Aryan
periority."

VINGS, Nathaniel Alexander
903–   ), US architect. As develop-
nt supervisor of the 1933 Chicago
position, he worked with Louis Skidmore
design many inexpensive pavillions. The
ir co-founded an architectural firm
936; known as Skidmore, Owings and
errill after 1939) that became one of the
ost prestigious in America.

VLS, soft-plumaged, nocturnal BIRDS OF
EY. Owls have large eyes, directed
rward, and all have pronounced facial
sks. Some species develop ear tufts and
ost have extremely sensitive hearing.
any species hunt primarily on auditory

cues. The eyes are also extremely powerful:
some 35–100 times more sensitive than our
own. All owls are soft-feathered and their
flight is completely silent. There are two
main families, the Tytonidae, or Barn owls,
with heart-shaped facial disks, and the
Strigidae, which contain the orders
Buboninae, to which the majority of species
belong, and the Striginae.

OX, term zoologically applied to many
members of the BOVIDAE; also, in common
usage, a castrated bull used for draft
purposes or for its meat.

OXFORD MOVEMENT, 19th-century
religious movement aiming to revitalize the
Church of England by reintroducing
traditional Catholic practices and doctrines.
It started in 1833 in Oxford; its leaders,
John Keble, J. H. NEWMAN and, later,
Edward PUSEY, wrote a series of *Tracts for
the Times* to publish their opinions. They
became known as the "Tractarians."
Despite violent controversy over the
Romeward tendency of some—culminating
in Newman's conversion to Roman
Catholicism (1845)—and over ritualism
(from 1850), the movement has had great
influence in the Anglican Church.

OXFORD UNIVERSITY, English university in Oxford comprising nearly 50
affiliated but autonomous colleges and
halls, a great center of learning since its
foundation in the 12th century. The oldest
mens' college is University (1249) and the
oldest womens' college Lady Margaret Hall
(1879). The major university library is the
famous BODLEIAN.

OXUS. See AMU DARYA.

OXYGEN (O), gaseous nonmetal in Group
VIA of the PERIODIC TABLE, comprising 21%
by volume of the ATMOSPHERE and about
50% by weight of the earth's crust. It was
first prepared by SCHEELE and PRIESTLEY,
and named *oxygene* by LAVOISIER. Gaseous
oxygen is colorless, odorless and tasteless;
liquid oxygen is pale blue. Oxygen has two
allotropes (see ALLOTROPY): OZONE (O_3),
which is metastable; and normal oxygen
(O_2), which shows paramagnetism (see
MAGNETISM) because its diatomic molecule
has two electrons with unpaired SPINS.
Oxygen is prepared in the laboratory by
heating mercuric oxide or potassium
chlorate (with manganese dioxide catalyst).
It is produced industrially by fractional
distillation of liquid air. Oxygen is very
reactive, yielding OXIDES with almost all
other elements, and in some cases
PEROXIDES. Almost all life depends on
chemical reactions with oxygen to produce
energy. Animals receive oxygen from the
air, as do fish from the water (see

RESPIRATION): it is circulated through the body in the bloodstream. The amount of oxygen in the air, however, remains constant because of PHOTOSYNTHESIS in plants and the decomposition of the sun's ultraviolet rays of water vapor in the upper atmosphere.

Oxygen is used in vast quantities in metallurgy: smelting and refining, especially of iron and steel. Oxygen and ACETYLENE are used in oxyacetylene torches for cutting and WELDING metals. Liquid oxygen is used in rocket fuels. Oxygen has many medical applications and is used in mixtures breathed by divers and high-altitude fliers. It is also widely used in chemical synthesis. AW 16.0, mp—218°C, bp—183°C.

OYSTERS, bivalve MOLLUSKS of shallow coastal waters. The edible oysters, as distinct from the Pearl oysters (see PEARL), belong to the family Ostreidae. While other bivalves are able to move by means of a muscular "foot," oysters have lost this foot and the animal lives cemented to the left valve of the shell to some hard substrate. Like all bivalves, oysters feed by removing suspended organic particles from a feeding current of water drawn into the shell. Food particles are trapped on highly filamentous gill plates. Oysters are extensively fished and cultivated all over the world.

OZARK PLATEAU, mountainous tableland in the S central US, covering about 50,000 sq mi from SW Mo. across NW Ark. into E Okla. Farming and lead and zinc mining are the chief economic activities; the forest scenery, numerous reservoirs and limestone caves attract tourism.

OZAWA, Seiji (1935–   ), Japanese conductor, best known for his fiery interpretations of Romantic and modern French composers. He became director of the San Francisco Symphony Orchestra in 1970 and of the Boston Symphony Orchestra and the Berkshire Music Festival in 1973.

OZONE (O_3), triatomic allotrope of OXYGEN (see ALLOTROPY); blue gas with a pungent odor. It is a very powerful oxidizing agent, and yields ozonides with OLEFINS. It decomposes rapidly above 100°C. The upper ATMOSPHERE contains a layer of ozone, formed when ULTRAVIOLET RADIATION acts on oxygen; this layer protects the earth from the sun's ultraviolet rays. Ozone is made by subjecting oxygen to a high-voltage electric discharge. It is used for killing germs, bleaching, removing unpleasant odors from foods, sterilizing water and in the production of azelaic acid. mp—193°C, bp—112°C.

16th letter of the English alphabet. It i descended from the Semitic *Pe*, the word fo mouth. It then became the Greek *pi*, an was incorporated into Latin and English.

PABST, Georg Wilhelm (1885–1967) distinguished German film director note for his imaginative treatment of realism i *The Joyless Street* (1925), *Pandora's Bo* (1928), and *West Front 1918* (1930).

PACIFIC ISLANDS, Trust Territory o the, UN trust territory administered by th US 1946–81. It included 2,141 islands (onl 96 inhabited) scattered over three million s mi of the Pacific Ocean within the are known as MICRONESIA. The formerl German Islands were mandated to Japan i 1922 and after US occupation in WWII t the US. Among constituent territories, th MARIANAS gained separate status as th NORTHERN MARIANAS and in 1978 became US commonwealth; the Marshall Island became (1979) self-governing; the island of Truk, Yap, Ponape, and Kosrae becam (1978) the Federated States of Micronesia and Palau self-governing (1981) as th Republic of BELAU.

PACIFIC OCEAN, world's largest an deepest ocean. Named by the 16th-centur navigator MAGELLAN, it extends from th Arctic to the Antarctic Ocean and from th coasts of the Americas to those of Asia. It area of 70 million sq mi is one third of th earth's total surface. The equator divide the ocean into the North Pacific and th South Pacific. The average depth of th Pacific is about 14,000ft and the deepes point is 36,198ft in the Challenger Deep Mariana Trench, SW of Guam. Plateaux ridges, trenches (some over 6mi deep), se mountains and GUYOTS make for man variations in depth. Japan, the Philippine New Zealand and the thousands of OCEANI islands lie on the connected series of ridge running from the Bering Straits to th South China Sea, and SE. Despite its nam the ocean is not a calm area. In the tropica and subtropical zones over 130 cyclone occur per year. Many bring much-neede rain, but the winds of at least 150mph, th torrential rain and tempestuous seas of the HURRICANES in the NE, E and S, and the 400mph tidal wave, the TSUNAMI, are highly destructive. The first European to sight the Pacific was BALBOA in 1513 and the first to cross it was Magellan, 1520–21. It was explored by DRAKE, TASMAN, BOUGAINVILLE, BERING, Captain COOK and VANCOUVER. The ocean was the site of the WAR OF THE PACIFIC in WWII.

PACIFISM, belief that violence is never justified, and hence that peaceful means should always be employed to settle disputes. A pacifist may not only refuse to use force himself, but also to abet its use, as by refusing to help produce weapons of war. Pacifists who refuse to serve in the armed forces are called CONSCIENTIOUS OBJECTORS. Supporters of nuclear DISARMAMENT or opponents of a specific war are not necessarily pacifist. Among the most successful pacifist statesmen was Mahatma GANDHI. (See also NEUTRALITY.)

PADDLE TENNIS, form of tennis, with similar rules, first introduced in New York City playgrounds in the early 1920s. It is now played on a smaller court than is lawn tennis, and players use a wooden bat, or paddle, and a slow-bouncing sponge rubber ball. Shots may be played on the carom off the wire screens that surround the court.

PADEREWSKI, Ignace Jan (1860–1941), Polish statesman, composer and celebrated concert pianist. He was the first prime minister of the Polish republic (1919) and in 1940–41 led the Polish government in exile.

PADUA, historic city in N Italy, a famous RENAISSANCE center and noted for its architecture. Its art treasures include works by GIOTTO, DONATELLO, MANTEGNA and TITIAN. GALILEO taught at its university. It is now an industrial, agricultural and commercial center. Pop 242,800.

PAGANINI, Niccolo (1782–1840), Italian violinist, one of the great virtuosos. By his use of adventurous techniques, such as diverse tuning of strings and the exploitation of harmonics, he extended the compass of the instrument. His best-known compositions are his 24 *Caprices.*

PAGNOL, Marcel (1895–1974), French playwright, screen writer, director, producer, and critic. He wrote the screenplays of *Marius* (1930) and *Topaze* (1932), both adapted from his own plays. *Marius* was the first in his Provençal trilogy, which also included *Fanny* and *César.*

PAIGE, "Satchel" (Leroy Robert Paige: 1906–   ), outstanding US baseball pitcher. Barred as a Negro from the major leagues until 1948, he played with the Cleveland Indians through 1951, and with the St. Louis Browns from 1951 until his retirement in 1953.

PAIN, the detection by the nervous system of harmful stimuli. The function of pain is to warn the individual of imminent danger: even the most minor tissue damage will cause pain, so that avoiding action can be taken at a very early stage. The level at which pain can only just be felt is the *pain threshold.* This threshold level varies slightly among individuals, and can be raised by, for example, HYPNOSIS, ANESTHETICS, ANALGESICS and the drinking of alcohol. In some psychological illnesses, especially the NEUROSES, it is lowered. The receptors of pain are unencapsulated nerve endings (see NERVOUS SYSTEM), distributed variably about the body. Deep pain, from the internal organs, may be felt as surface pain or in a different part of the body. This phenomenon, *referred pain,* is probably due to the closeness of the nerve tracts entering the SPINAL CORD. In psychoanalysis, "pain" refers to the distress felt when tension caused through frustration of INSTINCT goes unrelieved.

PAINE, Thomas (1737–1809), English-born writer and radical, a leading figure of the American Revolution. He emigrated to America in 1774; his highly influential pamphlet, *Common Sense,* 1776, urged the American colonies to declare independence. His patriotic pamphlets, *The Crisis* (1776–83), inspired the CONTINENTAL ARMY. He returned to England and wrote *The Rights of Man,* 1791–92, a defense of the FRENCH REVOLUTION and republicanism. Forced to flee to France, he was elected to the National Convention. His controversially deistic *The Age of Man* (1794–95) alienated his US support; he returned there in 1802, and died in obscurity.

PAINTING, the depiction in terms of line and color of a subject, rendered representationally or abstractly, on a two-dimensional surface. (For art preceding that of the RENAISSANCE see ALTAMIRA; LASCAUX CAVE; Ancient EGYPT; Ancient GREECE; ETRUSCANS; ROMAN ART; BYZANTINE ART; ROMANESQUE ART; GOTHIC ART. See also CHINESE ART; JAPANESE ART; ISLAMIC ART.)

Italian painting, 1300–1600. Giotto's FRESCO works broke away from Byzantine art by his realistic depiction of people and their emotions. His monumental, sculptural style was generally followed in 14th-century Florence. In Siena, the decorative linear style of DUCCIO and Simone MARTINI prevailed. The Florentine discovery of linear perspective was first employed by MASACCIO, and the tradition was continued by Fra ANGELICO, PIERO DELLA FRANCESCA and BOTTICELLI. Western painting reached an apogee in the High Renaissance works of LEONARDO DA VINCI, RAPHAEL and MICHELANGELO. MANNERISM, developed by GIULIO ROMANO and ANDREA DEL SARTO, influenced the arresting style of EL GRECO. From the mid-15th century a distinct Venetian school emerged, notable particularly for its use of color. The most influential Venetian artists were Titian, Tintoretto and Veronese.

Painting outside Italy, 1400–1600. Flemish art was finely detailed, as in the work of Jan Van Eyck who, with his brother Hubert, is credited with innovating oil painting. A more emotional style was developed by Van der Weyden, while Bosch and Pieter Bruegel developed grotesque fantasy pictures. In the late-15th century, German art became influential with Durer's woodcuts and engravings, Grunewald's Isenheim altar and Hans Holbein's portraits.

Painting, 1600–1850. The prominent artists of the BAROQUE period were the Italian painter Caravaggio; the brilliant and imaginative Flemish painter Rubens; the Spaniard Velazquez; two classical French painters, Poussin and Claude; and Rembrandt. Dutch painters like Steen and Vermeer specialized in GENRE scenes. The ROCOCO style was characterized by elegant, sensuous, often frivolous works by painters like Watteau and Boucher. English portraiture was developed by Reynolds and Gainsborough, influencing the first important American artists, Copley and Benjamin West. The Spanish Rococo painter, Goya, adapted his style to depict the savagery of the Napoleonic wars. The first half of the 19th century in France was dominated by the CLASSICISM of Ingres and the ROMANTICISM of Delacroix.

Painting since 1850. Courbet promoted the rendering of large-scale pictures of ordinary life and Manet influenced IMPRESSIONISM. Monet and Renoir pioneered painting out of doors and experimented with the effects of light. The POST-IMPRESSIONISTS Gauguin and Van Gogh, through their novel use of paint and simplified forms, greatly influenced EXPRESSIONISM and FAUVISM. Cézanne's work was crucial to the development of CUBISM, which was largely invented by Picasso and Braque. Kandinsky and Malevich developed forms of ABSTRACT ART. SURREALISM used imagery taken from dreams, as in the works of Dali and Ernst. In the 1960s POP ART was developed by Jasper Johns, Robert Rauschenberg and Andy

Warhol. Later in the decade, OP ART followed. A resurgence of interest in various aspects of REALISM occurred in the 1970s and 1980s.

PAIUTE INDIANS, several North American Indian tribes of the SHOSHONE INDIANS. They can be divided into the North Paiute of N Cal. and Nev. and the South Paiute (or Digger Indians) of Ariz. and S Nev. The Paiute GHOST DANCE religion, which began in 1870, led by WOVOKA, led to violent uprisings. Today about 4,000 Paiute live on reservations.

Official name: Islamic Republic of Pakistan
Capital: Islamabad
Area: 310,403sq mi
Population: 76,770,000
Languages: Urdu, Sindhi, Punjabi, Pushtu, English
Religion: Muslim
Monetary unit(s): 1 Pakistani Rupee=100 paisa

PAKISTAN (Urdu: land of the Pure), formerly West Pakistan, republic in the NW Indian subcontinent.

Land. Pakistan, located on the Arabian Sea, between Afghanistan to the NW and India to the SE, with Jammu and KASHMIR to the NE, comprises four provinces: Punjab, Sind, Baluchistan and the North-West Frontier Province. High mountains dominate the N, and dry high plateaus and mountain ranges the W. The S includes part of the THAR DESERT and borders on the barren RANN OF KUTCH. Most of Pakistan consists of the huge INDUS alluvial plain, which receives the five rivers of the Punjab. One of the largest irrigated regions of the world, it has high agricultural productivity. The climate has extremes of temperature, ranging from below freezing to 120°F. Annual rainfall averages less than 10 in.
People. Most of the population are relatively light-skinned Punjabis. Other groups include the tall, fairer and often blue-eyed Pathans, possibly of Semitic origin, and the Baluchi, an Aryan people; there are many tribal and linguistic differences. Islam is the state religion. The literacy rate is about 16%. The majority of

the population live in small villages. The largest cities are Karachi, Lahore, Lyallpur, Hyderabad and Rawalpindi.

Economy. Pakistan is among the world's poorest countries. It has few natural resources, and is dependent on its agriculture. Wheat is the main subsistence crop but fruit and livestock are important in the N. The diverse mineral resources are still to be developed but low-grade coal and iron ore, chromite, gypsum and limestone are being mined. Deposits of natural gas and oil are potentially large. Pakistan exports wool and cotton textiles (some from cottage industries), and leather goods.

History. Demands for a Muslim state independent of Hindu India grew strong in the early 1900s. In 1906 the MUSLIM LEAGUE was founded and led from 1916 by Mohammed Ali JINNAH. He became first governor-general of the independent dominion of Pakistan, formed in 1947; Liaquat ALI KHAN was the prime minister. The country consisted of two parts, East and West Pakistan, separated by 1000mi of Indian territory. The new states of India and Pakistan fought bitterly, particularly over Kashmir. In the 1950s tension grew between Bengali East Pakistan and Punjabi West Pakistan which dominated the civil service and army. Pakistan was a republic from 1956, and General AYUB KHAN seized power in 1958. He introduced a new political system, "Basic Democracy," and land reforms. Political riots in 1969 and government policies led to the secession of East Pakistan as BANGLADESH in 1971. In the ensuing civil war West Pakistan was quickly defeated with the aid of Indian troops. The secession halved Pakistan's population and meant the loss of the valuable jute crop. Pakistan formally recognized Bangladesh in 1974. During the 1970s there was increasing separatist violence in the W provinces. In 1977 Zulfigar Ali Bhutto was reelected prime minister; the opposition declared the vote a fraud, and in the ensuing disorders Bhutto was deposed and a martial-law regime was set up under Gen. Mohammad Zia ul-Haq. Bhutto was tried for treason (among other charges) and executed in 1979. General Zia postponed promised elections (1979) indefinitely.

PALEOBOTANY. See PALEONTOLOGY.

PALEOCENE, the first epoch of the TERTIARY period, which extended between about 65 and 55 million years ago. (See also GEOLOGY.)

PALEOMAGNETISM, the study of past changes in the EARTH's magnetic field by examination of rocks containing certain iron-bearing minerals (e.g., HEMATITE, MAGNETITE). Reversals of the field and movements of the magnetic poles can be charted and information on CONTINENTAL DRIFT may be obtained. (See also SEA-FLOOR SPREADING; PLATE TECTONICS.)

PALEONTOLOGY, or **paleobiology**, the study of fossils or evidences of ancient life. The two principal branches are *paleobotany* and *paleozoology*, dealing with plants and animals respectively. An important subdivision of paleobotany is PALYNOLOGY, the study of pollen and spores. Paleozoology is divisible into *vertebrate paleontology* and *invertebrate paleontology*. The term *micropaleontology* refers to the study of microscopic fossils or microfossils, which include both plant and animal representatives. Paleontologic studies are essential to STRATIGRAPHY, and provide important evidence for EVOLUTION and CONTINENTAL DRIFT theories. (See also FOSSILS; PALEOCLIMATOLOGY; RADIOCARBON DATING.)

PALEOZOIC, the earliest era of the PHANEROZOIC EON, comprising two sub-eras: the Lower Paleozoic, 570–400 million years ago, containing the CAMBRIAN, ORDOVICIAN and SILURIAN periods; and the Upper Paleozoic, 400–225 million years ago, containing the DEVONIAN, MISSISSIPPIAN, PENNSYLVANIAN and PERMIAN periods. (See GEOLOGY.)

PALERMO, capital of Sicily, its largest city and chief seaport, on the NW coast. Shipbuilding, textiles and chemicals are leading industries. Palermo was founded by Phoenicians in the 8th–6th centuries BC. Its notable medieval architecture has Byzantine, Norman and Muslim features. The SICILIAN VESPERS and other uprisings took place there. Pop 687,600.

PALESTINE, the biblical Holy Land, named for the PHILISTINES and also called CANAAN. Its boundaries, often imprecise, have varied widely. Palestine now usually refers to the region bounded W by the Mediterranean, E by the Jordan R and Dead Sea, N by Mt Hermon on the Syria-Lebanon border and S by the Sinai Peninsula. It thus lies almost entirely within modern Israel, though extending into Jordan. There were Paleolithic and Mesolithic cultures in Palestine, and Neolithic JERICHO emerged by 7000 BC. SEMITES arrived c3000 BC and built a Bronze-Age civilization (3000–1500 BC). Soon after 2000 BC, Hebrew tribes under Abraham came from Mesopotamia (see JEWS). In 1479 BC Egyptians invaded, enslaving many Hebrews (or Israelites) in Egypt. Their descendants returned under MOSES c1200 BC. Successful wars against

Canaanites and Philistines helped unite Hebrew tribes in one kingdom (c1020 BC), ruled by Saul, then David, then Solomon. After Solomon died the kingdom split into (N) Israel and (S) Judah (later JUDAEA), hence the term "Jew." Both kingdoms worshiped the One God, Yahweh (JEHOVAH), and Judaism developed under religious leaders called prophets. In 721 BC Assyrians overran Israel and in 587 BC Babylonians conquered Judah, deporting many Jews who returned only after Babylonia fell to Persia's CYRUS THE GREAT in 539 BC. Palestine was later controlled by Alexander the Great (332–323 BC), the Ptolemies of Egypt (323–198 BC) and the Seleucids of Syria (198–168 BC). Then JUDAS MACCABEUS began a national revolt which established the Jewish HASMONEAN dynasty (143–37 BC) in Judaea. Roman rule (63 BC–395 AD) saw the birth of Christianity, but also repression climaxed by the Roman destruction of Jerusalem (70 AD) followed by massive Jewish emigration. Control passed to the Byzantines (395–611 and 628–633 AD), Persians (611–628), and Arabs, whose conquest in the 630s began 1,300 years of Muslim rule, disturbed by the CRUSADES. In 1918 the OTTOMAN EMPIRE collapsed and British rule followed. Jewish immigration which had begun in the 1850s, increased rapidly after the British government's BALFOUR DECLARATION (1917) promising the Jews a national home in Palestine. Britain had also promised (1915–16) the Arabs an independent state in SE Asia. The British claim that Palestine was excluded from this promise has never been accepted by the Arabs. The appalling fate of the Jews in Europe after the rise of NAZISM brought widespread support for the creation of a Jewish state. In 1948 Jews, but not Arabs, accepted a UN recommendation to split Palestine into Jewish and Arab states. Jews proclaimed the state of Israel, and at the same time nearby Arab nations invaded the area, the first major step in an Arab-Israeli conflict which has continued into the 1980s. (See also ISRAEL; JORDAN; ARAB-ISRAELI WARS; PALESTINE LIBERATION ORGANIZATION.)

PALESTINE LIBERATION ORGANIZATION (PLO), coordinating body of Palestinian refugee groups, aiming to establish a Palestinian state on land regained from Israel and recognized by many Arabs as the PALESTINE government. Led by Yassir ARAFAT, it committed many acts of terrorism, though official PLO policy became more moderate in the face of worldwide criticism. First using Jordan as a base of operations until forced out in 1970, the PLO later found a haven in Lebanon, from which it engaged Israel in sporadic conflict.

PALESTRINA, Giovanni Pierluigi da (c1525–1594), Italian RENAISSANCE composer of unaccompanied choral church music. He wrote over 100 masses and is perhaps best known for his *Missa Papae Marcelli*. He was organist and choirmaster in several Roman churches.

PALLADIO, Andrea (1508–1580), Italian architect, born Andrea di Pietro. He created the immensely influential Palladian style. His designs for villas, palaces and churches stressed harmonic proportions and classical symmetry. Palladio's *The Four Books of Architecture* (1570) helped to spread his style through Europe, notably (via Inigo JONES) to England.

PALM, any of over 3,000 species of trees and shrubs of the family Palmae, mainly native to tropical and subtropical regions. Palms are characterized by having an unbranched stem bearing at the tip a bunch of feather-like (pinnate) or fan-like (palmate) leaves. Flowers are greenish, borne in spikes, and the fruits are either dry or fleshy. Palm products are of great economic importance, both locally and in world trade. The COCONUT PALM and DATE PALM produce staple crops; wax is obtained from the CARNAUBA palm; the OIL PALM yields oils used in food, soap, toiletries and industrial processes (see also SAGO). Several palms make good house plants. Indoors, they grow well at average house temperatures and should be placed in a moderately sunny position. The soil should be kept wet to moist, though palms do not tolerate standing water. The foliage should be misted often. They can be propagated from seeds or by planting divisions.

PALMER, Alexander Mitchell (1872–1936), US attorney general (1919–21) notorious for the "Palmer Raids"—mass arrests of supposed subversives, many of whom were deported as aliens. A congressman 1909–15, he was US alien property custodian in WWI.

PALMER, Arnold (1929–   ), US golfer, the first to win the US Masters Tournament four times (1958, 1960, 1962, and 1964). He won the US Open in 1960 and the British Open in 1961 and 1962 and was one of the most popular of golf champions, the hero of a host of fans dubbed "Arnold's Army."

PALMER, Daniel David (1845–1913), Canadian-born US founder of CHIROPRACTIC (1895).

PALMERSTON, Henry John Temple, 3rd Viscount (1784–1865), British statesman remembered for his successful and often aggressive foreign policy. As foreign secretary 1830–34, 1835–41 and 1846–51, he was instrumental in securing Belgian independence (1830–31), in upholding the OTTOMAN EMPIRE (1839–41), and in maintaining peace in Europe during the REVOLUTIONS OF 1848. As prime minister 1855–58 and 1859–65, he led Britain to victory in the CRIMEAN WAR and kept out of the American Civil War, despite the TRENT AFFAIR.

PALM SUNDAY, the Sunday before EASTER and the first day of HOLY WEEK, commemorating Christ's triumphal entry into Jerusalem riding on an ass, when palm leaves were spread in his path. Palm leaves are blessed and carried in procession.

PAMIRS, mountainous region of central Asia. It forms a hub from which radiate the Hindu Kush, Karakorum, Kunlun and Tien Shan ranges. Most of it lies in the Tadzhik SSR, but parts are in Afghanistan, China and Kashmir. The highest peaks are Communism Peak (24,590ft) and Lenin Peak (23,508ft), both in the USSR.

PAMPAS, grassy plains of SE South America. They stretch about 300,000sq mi over Argentina and into Uruguay. The humid E Pampa bears some crops. The dry W Pampa supports livestock.

Official name: Republic of Panama
Capital: Panama
Area: 29,201sq mi
Population: 1,881,400
Language: Spanish
Religion: Roman Catholic
Monetary unit(s): 1 Balboa=100 centésimos

PANAMA, central American republic occupying the Isthmus of Panama (see PANAMA, ISTHMUS OF), and cut in half by the PANAMA CANAL.

Land. Panama is traversed by mountain ranges, flanked by well-watered valleys and plains. The climate is hot and rainy. Much of E Panama is dense tropical forest; the Pacific coast has savanna and forest.

People. The population is more than 70% mestizos, about 14% pure Negro and 12% European (mainly Spanish). There are about 60,000 Amerindians, mainly in E Panama and on the San Blas Islands off the Caribbean coast. Nearly one third of Panamanians live in Panama City or Colón, the largest centers. The literacy rate is about 80%.

Economy. The canal provides 25% of the gross national product but the economy is basically agricultural. The farms, mostly under 25 acres, produce rice, corn, beans, bananas, cacao and coffee. Only half of all arable land is farmed, and Panama imports most of its food. Industry is chiefly consumer oriented. Major exports by value are bananas, shrimps, coffee, sugar, fishmeal and petroleum products. Food, industrial raw materials and manufactured goods largely account for Panama's huge trading deficit. The chief ports are Cristóbal and Balboa. In 1973 Panama had the world's 8th largest merchant fleet by tonnage, foreign shipowners registering in Panama to profit from low fees and easy labor laws. Panama is also a center of international banking.

History. First sighted by Europeans in 1501, claimed by Spain and colonized under BALBOA and DÁVILA. Panama became a springboard for Spanish conquests in the Americas and a route for transshipping Peruvian gold to Spain. Panama lost importance in the 18th century after buccaneer attacks forced treasure ships from Peru to sail around South America. In 1821 Panama broke free from Spain and became part of Colombia. In 1903, Panama gained independence with US support. The completion (1914) of the PANAMA CANAL brought some prosperity, but discontent with US control over the canal led to riots in 1959, 1962 and 1964. Gen. Omar Torrijos Herrera came to power after a military coup in 1968; following 1978 elections Gen. Torrijos resigned and political parties were again allowed. In 1977, US and Panama signed two treaties about gradual takeover by Panama of the canal, to be completed in 1999.

PANAMA CANAL, ship canal which crosses the Isthmus of PANAMA to link the Atlantic and Pacific oceans. It runs 40mi SE from Colón on the Caribbean to Balboa on the Pacific. Ships are lifted to 85ft above sea level and lowered again by means of the Gatún Pedro Miguel and Miraflores locks. Minimum depth is 41ft. Minimum width is 100ft. A French company led by de LESSEPS bought a Colombian canal-building concession, but after eight years' work in Panama (1881–89), labor problems and disease bankrupted the firm. A second French company bought the franchise in 1894, largely to keep it alive. The US negotiated the HAY-PAUNCEFOTE TREATY with Britain (1901) and aimed to build a canal through Nicaragua. The French offered the US the rights to the Panamanian project, but Colombia refused the US terms (see HAY-HERRAN TREATY, 1903). In 1903, a US warship and US troops helped Panama successfully revolt against Colombia and the ensuing HAY-BUNAU-VARILLA TREATY gave the US rights in perpetuity to a 10mi-wide strip across the isthmus. The US completed the canal in 1914, due mainly to the work of the engineer G. W. GOETHALS and the government health officer Dr. W. C. GORGAS. After WWII there was US-Panamanian friction over canal sovereignty. In 1977 US and Panamanian representatives signed a new treaty handing control to Panama. Construction of a second canal, large enough to accommodate super-tankers, is being discussed.

PANAMA CANAL TREATIES, two treaties that determine the status of the Panama Canal. On Apr. 18, 1978, almost 75 years after signing of the HAY-BUNAU-VARILLA TREATY of 1903 that gave the US full sovereignty over the 10-mile strip of land used for building the Panama Canal, the US Senate ratified by a vote of 68–32—one more than the two-thirds majority needed—a new treaty under which the canal will be returned to Panama on Dec. 31, 1999. An accompanying treaty, approved the previous month by the Senate, also by a 68–32 margin, guaranteed the neutrality of the canal after the year 2000 and assured that the canal would be open to passage by ships of all countries. The US and Panama had signed the treaty in 1977 and Panama had approved it that year in a plebiscite.

PANAMA CANAL ZONE, formerly a strip of land extending 5mi on either side of the PANAMA CANAL. It was controlled by the US and the governor, normally a US army officer, was a presidential appointee. Panama took control over the territory in October 1979, after US and Panama signed and ratified two treaties about gradual takeover of the canal by Panama.

PAN-AMERICAN HIGHWAY, highway system linking Latin American countries with each other and with the Interstate Highway system of the US. By the mid 1970s engineers in Panama and Colombia were closing the last big gap in the system. The highway was conceived at the Fifth International Conference of American States (1923).

PAN AMERICANISM, movement aimed at creating closer cultural, economic political and social ties among the republics of the Western Hemisphere. It dates from 1826, when BOLÍVAR called a conference of Latin American states which agreed on a treaty of union and assistance. Further conferences followed. US involvement dates from the First International Conference of American States (1889–90) which founded the International Union of American Republics, reorganized in 1910 as the Pan American Union. Later landmarks in cooperation included the founding of the PAN-AMERICAN HIGHWAY, the PAN-AMERICAN GAMES and the ORGANIZATION OF AMERICAN STATES. The ALLIANCE FOR PROGRESS, initiated by President Kennedy in 1961, improved US relations with Latin America, but Pan Americanism is still an ideal rather than a reality.

PANCHEN LAMA, second-highest lama in Tibetan BUDDHISM (preceded only by the DALAI LAMA), revered as a reincarnation of Amitabha, the Buddha of Light. After the Dalai Lama fled to India, the Panchen Lama nominally ruled TIBET 1959–64.

PANCREAS, organ consisting partly of exocrine GLAND tissue, secreting into the DUODENUM, and partly of ENDOCRINE GLAND tissue (the *islets of Langerhans*), whose principal HORMONES include INSULIN and GLUCAGON. The pancreas lies on the back wall of the upper ABDOMEN, much of it within the duodenal loop. Powerful digestive-system ENZYMES (pepsin, trypsin, lipase, amylase) are secreted into the gut; this secretion is in part controlled by intestinal hormones (SECRETIN) and in part by nerve REFLEXES. Insulin and glucagon have important roles in glucose and fat METABOLISM (see DIABETES); other pancreatic hormones affect GASTROINTESTINAL-TRACT secretion and activity. Acute INFLAMMATION of pancreas due to VIRUS disease, ALCOHOLISM or duct obstruction by gall-stones, may lead to severe abdominal pain with SHOCK and prostration caused by the release of digestive enzymes into the abdomen. Chronic pancreatitis leads to functional impairment and malabsorption. CANCER of the pancreas may cause JAUNDICE by obstructing the BILE duct.

PANDAS, two species of raccoon-like mammals of uncertain relation found in montane bamboo forests of Yunnan and Szechwan. Both have an unusual sixth digit, a modified wristbone which has evolved to thumb-like size and flexibility in the Giant panda, *Ailuropoda melanoleuca*, remaining vestigial in the Lesser or Red panda, *Ailurus fulgens*. Though they have evolved from carnivores, both pandas are vegetarians, their diet largely comprising bamboo shoots. The Giant panda has been adopted as the emblem of the World Wildlife Fund.

PANDIT, Vijaya Läkshmi (1900–   ), Indian diplomat and political leader, sister of NEHRU. She was active in the struggle for India's independence and helped implement India's postwar policy of nonalignment. She was ambassador to the US 1949–51 and the first woman president of the UN General Assembly 1953–54.

PANKHURST, Emmeline (1858–1928), English suffragist. In 1903 she and her daughters **Christabel Pankhurst** (1880–1958) and **Sylvia Pankhurst** (1882–1960) founded the Woman's Social and Political Union, which soon became militant. She was constantly in prison and on hunger strike 1908–14. She died a month before women gained full voting equality with men. (See WOMEN'S RIGHTS.)

PAN-SLAVISM, movement for the cultural and political solidarity of the SLAVS. It began in the 1830s. Pan-Slav Congresses were held in Prague (1848) and Moscow (1867). Pan-Slavism was a factor in the events leading to the Russo-Turkish War (1877–78), the Balkan Wars (1912, 1913) and WWI. Both pre- and post-communist Russia attempted to use Pan-Slavism as a cloak for Russian expansionism.

PANTHEISM, religious or philosophical viewpoint in which God and the universe are identified, stressing God's IMMANENCE and denying his TRANSCENDENCE. Religious pantheists see finite beings as merely part of God; others deify the universe, nature being the supreme principle. Pantheism is found in HINDUISM, STOICISM, IDEALISM and notably in SPINOZA's thought; Christian MYSTICISM may tend to it.

PANTHEON, historically, a temple dedicated to the worship of all the gods. In modern times it refers to a structure where a nation's heroes are buried or honored. The most famous pantheon is an ancient circular temple (now a church) in Rome, built c120 AD and having a 142ft-diameter dome.

PANTOMIME, originally a drama performed entirely in MIME. Popular in Roman times, it was developed by the COMMEDIA DELL' ARTE and further adapted to become the traditional British Christmas pantomime (or "panto"), with its dialogue, song, spectacle and comedy loosely based on a well-known fairy story.

PAPACY, the office and institution of the pope. As bishop of Rome in succession to St. PETER, the first bishop of Rome, the pope claims to be Christ's representative, with supremacy over all other bishops. This claim is accepted only by Roman Catholics.

The title pope, meaning father, was originally applied to all bishops. The authority of the pope at Rome was established in the West during the first five centuries AD but the refusal of the Eastern churches to accept it resulted (1054) in the first GREAT SCHISM. The papacy had strengthened its secular power in the West after LEO III crowned Charlemagne Holy Roman Emperor in 800. By 1200 the pope had more feudal vassals than any other power and CANON LAW was enforceable throughout Christian Europe. But growing secular forces weakened papal political authority by the late Middle Ages, and the second Great Schism (1378–1417) gravely divided the papacy. Renaissance popes worked to strengthen the PAPAL STATES and created a culturally brilliant papal court, but Church corruption led to demands for reform which culminated in the Protestant REFORMATION. The papacy reacted by founding the JESUITS (1540), reinforcing the INQUISITION (1542), and calling the reformist Council of TRENT. In the 17th and 18th centuries, the power of the papacy was weakened from within by disputes over JANSENISM and from without by increasing secularism and skepticism. In the 19th century the papacy recovered influence as a bulwark of tradition against revolution, and asserted its renewed confidence in such pronouncements as the doctrine of papal infallibility (1870), which held that the pope was infallible in matters of faith and morals when speaking as the vicar of Christ. The Papal States were lost in 1870 but the LATERAN TREATY of 1929 established VATICAN CITY as an independent papal domain. In recent times popes such as JOHN XXIII and JOHN PAUL II have opposed totalitarian rule, encouraged social justice and backed initiatives to renew the Church while maintaining its historic doctrines. (See also ROMAN CATHOLIC CHURCH; VATICAN COUNCILS.)

PAPADOPOULOS, George (1919–   ), Greek army officer, prime minister (1967–73) and president (June–Nov. 1973) of Greece under the military junta. In 1974, under civilian rule, he and others were tried and found guilty of crimes against the state. His death sentence was commuted to life imprisonment.

PAPAL STATES, lands held by the popes as temporal rulers, 754–1870. The states date from PEPIN THE SHORT's donation of conquered Lombard lands to the papacy. Later gifts and conquests meant that by the early 1200s the states stretched from coast to coast across central Italy. VICTOR EMMANUEL II annexed the papal states, including, eventually, Rome itself (1870) during the RISORGIMENTO. The papacy refused to accept its loss of lands until the LATERAN TREATY (1929) created an independent VATICAN CITY.

PAPEN, Franz von (1879–1969), German statesman. Lacking support as chancellor (June–Nov. 1932), he resigned and helped engineer the appointment of Hitler, supporting the Nazis as a bulwark against communism. He was Hitler's vicechancellor 1933–34, and as German minister to Vienna (1934–38), he paved the way for German annexation of Austria.

PAPER, felted or matted sheets of CELLULOSE fibers, formed on a wire screen from a water suspension, and used for writing and printing. Rags and cloth—still used for special high-grade papers—were the raw materials used until generally replaced by wood pulp processes developed in the mid-19th century. Logs are now pulped by three methods. Mechanical pulping normally uses a revolving grindstone. In full chemical pulping, wood chips are cooked under pressure in a solution that dissolves all but the cellulose: the kraft process uses alkaline sodium sulfide solution; the sulfite process uses various bisulfites with excess sulfur dioxide. Semichemical pulping employs mild chemical softening followed by mechanical grinding. The pulp is bleached, washed and refined—i.e., the fibers are crushed, frayed and cut by mechanical beaters. This increases their surface area and bonding power. At this stage various substances are added: fillers (mainly clay and chalk) to make the paper more opaque, sizes (rosin and alum) for resistance, and dyes and pigments as necessary. A dilute aqueous slurry of the pulp is fed to the paper machine, flowing onto a moving belt or cylindrical drum of fine wire mesh, most of the water being drained off by gravity and suction. The newly-formed continuous sheet is pressed between rollers, dried by evaporation, and subjected to CALENDERING. Some paper is coated to give a special surface.

PAPIER-MACHE, molding material of pulped paper mixed with flour paste, glue or resin. It is usually molded while wet but in some industrial processes is pressuremolded. The technique of making papier-mâché decorative objects began in the Orient, and reached Europe in the 18th century.

PAPP, Joseph (1921–   ), US stage producer and director who made free Shakespeare in Central Park a New York City tradition. His Public Theatre, dedicated to new American playwrights,

presented *That Championship Season* (1973) and *A Chorus Line* (1975), both of which won Tony Awards and Pulitzer Prizes.

PAP SMEAR TEST, or Papanicolaou test, CANCER screening test in which cells scraped from the cervix of the WOMB are examined for abnormality under the microscope using the method of G. N. PAPANICOLAOU.

Official name: Papua New Guinea
Capital: Port Moresby
Area: 178,704
Population: 3,078,600 .
Language: local languages; pidgin and standard English
Religions: Christian; tribal religions, animism
Monetary unit(s): 1 Kina = 100 toea

PAPUA NEW GUINEA, independent nation (since 1975), located just N of Australia. The E half of NEW GUINEA Island, just N of Australia, comprises five-sixths of its territory which also includes the islands of BOUGAINVILLE, Buka and the Bismarck Archipelago to the NE and smaller islands to the SE.

Land and People. It is a mountainous, densely forested region with high temperature and rainfall and a rich variety of plant and animal life. The isolating nature of the environment has resulted in a great variety of racial groups and languages: Melanesian in the E and islands, Papuan and sporadic pygmy Negrito groups on the mainland. Most practice animism or tribal religions. In the interior some Stone Age cultures survive.

Economy. Plantation farming replaces traditional subsistence agriculture in some areas. Exports include timber and coconut products, rubber, cocoa, tea, and coffee. Rich mineral deposits, largely undeveloped, include gold, copper and petroleum. Forestry, with exports mainly to Japan, is important.

History. The N mainland and islands were part of German New Guinea 1884–1914. Seized by Australia in 1914, they later became the Trust Territory of New Guinea. The S area was British New Guinea

1884–1905, then, as the Territory of Papua, under Australian rule. The two areas were merged administratively in 1949 as the Australian-administered Territory of Papua and New Guinea. It was renamed Papua New Guinea in 1971, became self-governing in 1973, and independent in 1975. A border treaty with Indonesia (1979) ended efforts by Papuan nationalists in neighboring IRIAN JAYA to unite with Papua New Guinea.

PAPYRUS, or paper reed, *Cyperus papyrus*, a stout, reed-like SEDGE, used in ancient civilizations as a writing material. It was also used for making sails, baskets and clothing, and the pith prepared as food. Family: Cyperaceae.

PARACELSUS, Philippus Aureolus (1493–1541), Swiss alchemist and physician who channeled the arts of ALCHEMY toward the preparation of medical remedies. Born Theophrastus Bombast von Hohenheim, he adopted the name Paracelsus, boasting that he was superior to the renowned 1st-century Roman medical writer Celsus.

PARACHUTE, collapsible umbrella-like structure used to retard movement through the air. It was invented in the late-18th century, being used for descent from balloons, and made successively from canvas, silk and nylon. When opened—either manually by pulling a ripcord or by a line attached to the aircraft—the canopy fills with air, trapping a large air mass which, because of the parachute's movement, is at a higher pressure than that outside, producing a large retarding force. The canopy consists of numerous strong panels sewn together. Parachutes are used for safe descent of paratroops and others, for dropping airplanes or missiles, and returning space capsules. Sport parachuting, or SKYDIVING, has become popular.

Official name: Republic of Paraguay
Capital: Asunción
Area: 157,042sq mi
Population: 2,888,000
Languages: Spanish, Guarani
Religion: Roman Catholic

Monetary unit(s): 1 Guaraní = 100 céntimos
PARAGUAY, landlocked republic of South America, bordered by Brazil, Argentina and Bolivia. The Paraguay R flows N-S and divides the country into two distinct regions.
Land. The sparsely populated W region known as the Chaco Boreal (part of the GRAN CHACO) is flat, scrubby country, increasingly arid to the W. The smaller but far richer E region is where most of the people live; it is itself divided into two regions by a clifflike ridge running N from the Alton Paraná R near Encarnación. The sparsely populated and densely forested Paraná Plateau lies to the E. To the W, rolling country, rarely above 2,000ft, falls away to more populous low-lying terrain. The climate is mild and constant, with abundant rains especially in the E.
People and Economy. The majority of the people are mestizo, with Guaraní Indian stock predominating over Spanish influence. More than 50% of the working population is employed on the land, and over a third of the gross national product comes from agriculture. Products of ranch, farm (cotton, tobacco, coffee) and forest (timber, tannin, oils) are the chief exports. Industry, which developed rapidly in the late 1970s, is represented mainly by agricultural product processing. No commercially valuable minerals have been found, though oil deposits exist in the Chaco. Although over half the country is forested, even this resource is mainly unexploited.
History. The country was originally inhabited by Guaranís, settled Indian farmers. Spanish exploration and settlement began in the early 16th century and by the 1550s the region had become Spain's power base in SE South America. Jesuit influence 1609–1767 contributed significantly to the merging of Guaraní and Spanish cultures. During 1776–1811, Paraguay was part of the Spanish viceroyalty of La Plata. It gained independence in 1811 after a relatively peaceful revolt. Its third ruler, Francisco Solano López led the disastrous War of the Triple Alliance against Brazil, Uruguay and Argentina (1865–70). Paraguay was laid waste and more than half the population died. Clashes with Bolivia over a border dispute led to the CHACO WAR (1932–35). Paraguay gained territory but was ruined economically. President Morínigo's comparatively stable and constructive rule (1940–48) ended in civil war. The incumbent president, Gen. Alfredo STROESSNER, seized power in 1954.

The regime was often accused of human rights violations.

PARAKEETS, small or medium-sized PARROTS with long tails. They do not form a natural group, the name being given to species of many different genera. Most parakeets are brightly-colored, gregarious birds, feeding on fruits, buds and flowers in semiarid regions throughout the tropics.

PARALYSIS, temporary or permanent loss of MUSCLE power or control. It may consist of inability to move a limb or part of a limb or individual muscles, paralysis of the muscles of breathing, swallowing and VOICE production being especially serious. Paralysis may be due to disease of the BRAIN (e.g., STROKE; TUMOR); SPINAL CORD (POLIOMYELITIS); nerve roots (SLIPPED DISK); peripheral NERVOUS SYSTEM (NEURITIS); neuromuscular junction (MYASTHENIA GRAVIS), or muscle (MUSCULAR DYSTROPHY). Disturbance of blood POTASSIUM levels can also lead to paralysis.

PARAMETER, a VARIABLE whose value determines a distinct set (see SET THEORY) of cases in a mathematical statement. Parametric equations are those expressed in terms of parameters. For example,

$$f(x) = ax^2 + b$$

is the general equation (see ANALYTIC GEOMETRY) of a set of points corresponding to a parabola (see CONIC SECTIONS), expressed in terms of the parameters a and b. Substitutions of specific values of these define a particular set. In STATISTICS, the parameters of a distribution are those elements of it which can be used to loosely define it. They may be location parameters, such as the MEAN, MEDIAN AND MODE, or parameters of dispersion, such as the STANDARD DEVIATION.

PARANÁ RIVER, or **Alto Paranná** R, formed by the confluence of the Rio Grande and the Paranaíba R in S central Brazil. An important commercial artery, it flows 1,827mi S and SW to join the Paraguay R. One of the world's largest hydroelectric plants is under construction at Itaipó.

PARANOIA, a PSYCHOSIS characterized by delusions of persecution (hence the popular term, **persecution mania**) and grandeur, often accompanied by HALLUCINATIONS. The delusions may form a self-consistent system which replaces reality. (See also MENTAL ILLNESS; SCHIZOPHRENIA.)

PARAPLEGIA, PARALYSIS involving the lower part of the body, particularly the legs. Injury to the SPINAL CORD is often the cause.

PARAPSYCHOLOGY, or **Psychic Research,** a field of study concerned with scientific evaluation of two distinct types of phenomena: those collectively termed ESP, and those concerned with life after death, reincarnation, etc., particularly including claims to communication with souls of the dead (spiritism or, incorrectly, spiritualism). Tests of the former have generally been inconclusive, of the latter almost exclusively negative. But in both cases many "believers" hold that such phenomena, being beyond the bounds of science, cannot be subjected to laboratory evaluation. In spiritism, the prime site of the alleged communication is the séance, in which one individual (the medium) goes into a trance before communicating with the souls of the dead, often through a spirit guide (a spirit associated particularly with the medium). The astonishing disparity among different accounts of the spirit world has led to the whole field being treated with skepticism.

PARASITE, an organism that is for some part of its life-history physiologically dependent on another, the host, from which it obtains nutrition and which may form its total environment. Nearly all the major groups of animals and plants from viruses to vertebrates and BACTERIA and angiosperms, have some parasitic members. The most important parasites, besides the viruses which are a wholly parasitic group, occur in the bacteria, Protozoa, Flatworms and Roundworms. Study of the parasitic worms, the platyhelminths, nematodes and acanthocephalans, is termed helminthology. Bloodsucking arthropods, such as mosquitoes, Tsetse flies and ticks, are also important because they transmit PARASITIC DISEASES and serve as vectors or transport-hosts for other parasites.

PARCHMENT, the skin of sheep, ewes or lambs, cleaned, polished, stretched and dried to make a material which can be written on, and also used to make drums and for bookbinding. Invented in the 2nd century BC as a substitute for PAPYRUS, it was widely used for manuscripts until superseded by paper in the 15th century, except for legal documents. Vellum is fine-quality parchment made from lamb, kid or calf skin. Both terms are now applied to high-quality paper. Vegetable parchment is paper immersed briefly in sulfuric acid and so made strong and parchment-like.

PARENT-TEACHER ASSOCIATION (PTA), National, voluntary US alliance which aims to further education and productive school-community relations with about 6.5 million members. The PTA grew from the National Congress of Mothers, founded 1897 by Alice McLellan Birney and Phoebe Apperson Hearst. The name was changed in 1924.

PARETO, Vilfredo (1848–1923), Italian economist and sociologist. He followed Walras in applying mathematics to economic theory. (See ECONOMICS.) His theories on elites, developed in *Mind and Society* (1916), influenced Mussolini's fascists.

PARIS, capital and largest city of France. It is in the middle of the fertile ILE DE FRANCE region. The Seine R winds through Paris, spanned by 30 bridges, and flows 110mi NW to the English Channel. World-famous for its beauty, social and cultural life, Paris is an important port and France's chief manufacturing center. In the city itself, tourism, dressmaking and luxury trades predominate. Heavier industry (chiefly autos) is based further out in the metropolitan area. On the Left Bank of the Seine lies the SORBONNE in the Latin Quarter, associated with students and artists. Over 2 million tourists a year come to enjoy the EIFFEL TOWER, LOUVRE museum, NOTRE DAME cathedral, MONTMARTRE, the cafés, gardens and nightlife.

The Parisii Gauls inhabited the Île de la Cité when the Romans set up a colony at this important crossroads in 52 BC. In the early 6th century King Clovis I of the Franks made Paris his capital, a status confirmed when Hugh Capet became King of France in 987 (see CAPETIANS). Growth increased in Philip II's reign (1180–1223) and was maintained even when Louis XIV moved the court to Versailles (1682). The rebuilding of Paris after the FRENCH REVOLUTION (1789) included Georges Haussman's great tree-lined boulevards. The work was interrupted 1870–71 by the FRANCO-PRUSSIAN WAR and by the PARIS COMMUNE. Though occupied by the Germans during WWII, Paris was little damaged; it was liberated in Aug. 1944. Postwar expansion was particularly striking beyond the western edge of the city. Pop 2,317,200; met pop. 8,549,900.

PARIS, Treaties of, name given to several treaties concluded at Paris. The **Treaty of Paris, 1763,** ended the SEVEN YEARS WAR including the FRENCH AND INDIAN WARS in America. France lost her military rights in E India (and thus any chance of ousting the British) and her American possessions. Britain gained Florida and parts of Louisiana, and Spain regained Cuba and the Philippines. Freed from the French threat, American colonists stepped up the struggle for independence, which was finally confirmed by the **Treaty of Paris, 1783,** ending the REVOLUTIONARY WAR. US boundaries were agreed as Canada in the N,

the Mississippi in the W and Florida (regained by Spain) in the S, and the US won fishing rights off Newfoundland. The **Treaty of Paris, 1814,** attempted to end the NAPOLEONIC WARS after Napoleon's first abdication. France under the restored Bourbon monarchy was allowed to retain her 1792 boundaries and most of her colonies. The **Treaty of Paris, 1815,** signed after Napoleon's final defeat at WATERLOO, dealt with France more harshly. French boundaries were reduced to those of 1790 and France had to pay reparations and support an army of occupation for up to five years. The **Treaty of Paris, 1856,** ending the CRIMEAN WAR, was signed by Russia, Britain, France, Turkey and Sardinia. Designed largely to protect Turkey from Russia, it guaranteed Turkish independence, declared the Black Sea neutral, opened Danube navigation to all nations, and established MOLDAVIA and WALACHIA (later Romania) as independent states under Turkish suzerainty. The **Treaty of Paris, 1898,** ended the SPANISH-AMERICAN WAR and effectively ended the Spanish empire. Cuba became independent, and the US gained Puerto Rico, Guam and the Philippines. After WWI the treaties of NEUILLY, SAINT-GERMAIN, SÈVRES, TRIANON and VERSAILLES were concluded at the Paris Peace Conference. Treaties were also signed at Paris after WWII.

PARIS, UNIVERSITY OF, France's greatest, and the world's most venerable, institution of higher learning. Growing out of the medieval cathedral schools of Notre Dame, it has granted Master's degrees since 1170. The SORBONNE (founded 1253) became its single most famous college. Reconstituted during the Napoleonic era as a modern university, it was reorganized again in 1970 into 13 autonomous units.

PARIS COMMUNE, insurrection of radical Parisians against the pro-royalist National Assembly, March–May 1871, following the humiliation of the FRANCO-PRUSSIAN WAR. The Communards drove the Assembly out of Paris, and elected their own Commune government, while similar movements broke out elsewhere. The Assembly sent in 130,000 troops who crushed the movement in a week of bloody street fighting, killing some 20,000 people.

PARK CHUNG HEE, (1917–1979), president of South Korea 1963–1979. He served with the Japanese in WWII, became a general in the Korean army and led the 1961 military coup. Becoming progressively more dictatorial, in 1972 he assumed almost unlimited power. He was a strong ally of the

US. He was assassinated by the director of the Korean Central Intelligence Agency.

PARKER, Charlie (Charles Christopher Parker, 1920–1955), US jazz musician, known as "Bird" or "Yardbird." An alto saxophonist and composer, he was one of the most innovative improvisers in jazz history.

PARKER, Dorothy (1893–1967), American writer, critic and wit. She wrote short stories, satirical verse and newspaper columns, and was a celebrated conversationalist. Her tone is poignant, ironical and often cruelly witty and cynical.

PARKINSON'S DISEASE, a common disorder in the elderly, causing a characteristic mask-like facial appearance, shuffling gait, slowness to move, muscular rigidity and tremor at rest; mental ability is preserved except in those cases following ENCEPHALITIS lethargica. It is a disorder of the basal ganglia of the BRAIN and may be substantially helped by DRUGS (e.g., L-Dopa) that affect impulse transmission in these sites.

PARKMAN, Francis (1823–1893), great US historian of the Frontier and of the Anglo-French struggle for North America. His chief work is the seven volumes collectively called *France and England in North America* (1865–92). Other works include his *History of the Conspiracy of Pontiac* (1851) and *The Oregon Trail* (1849), an enormously popular account of a journey made in 1846. He later became an expert horticulturalist.

PARKS, Gordon (1912–   ), US photographer. After his photo-essay on Harlem gangs came to the attention of *Life* magazine, Parks was hired as a staff photographer (1948–68). He is also a poet and composer who directed the movie version of his novel *The Learning Tree* (1963) and the "Shaft" films.

PARLEMENT, French high court of justice in Paris which operated from the Middle Ages until 1789. It had some political influence through its power of questioning the king's edicts. Membership became a hereditary privilege. There were also 12 provincial parlements. As bastions of reaction, they were swept away in the French Revolution.

PARLIAMENT, body of elected representatives responsible for a country's legislation and finance. The term parliamentary government is used to describe a system (distinct from the presidential system) in which the government's chief ministers, including the PRIME MINISTER, are elected members of parliament. This system operates in Britain, most Commonwealth countries and Scandinavia.

In a parliamentary system the head of state (a monarch or president) exists outside parliament and exercises only limited powers; real power rests with the prime minister, who leads the majority party or a coalition of parties. He rules with the help of a CABINET chosen from other elected members. The government in power has the right to dissolve parliament and call a new election before its term of office ends, but is obliged to resign if it fails to command a majority vote of members. All these features differ from presidential government as practiced in the US. The chief model for modern parliamentary government is the British Parliament, which began to take on its present form in the Middle Ages. (See also HOUSE OF COMMONS; HOUSE OF LORDS; LEGISLATURE; PRESIDENCY.)

PARMENIDES (flourished c475 BC), Greek philosopher of Elea in southern Italy; foremost of the ELEATICS. His philosophy, anchored on the proposition "What *is*," denied the reality of multiplicity and change. His uncompromising attempt to deduce the properties of the Real—a single eternal solid, all-embracing yet undifferentiated— marks the beginning of the Western tradition of philosophical reasoning. (See also PRE-SOCRATICS.)

PARNASSIANS, group of 19th-century French poets led by LECONTE DE LISLE. Influenced by GAUTIER's "art for art's sake" theories, they emphasized technical skill, restraint and objectivity.

PARNASSUS, mountain in central Greece, N of DELPHI and the Gulf of Corinth. It was once sacred to Dionysus and Apollo and celebrated as a home of the MUSES. It is 8,061 ft high.

PARNELL, Charles Stewart (1846–1891), Irish nationalist, leader of the Irish HOME RULE movement from within the British parliament from 1877. He obstructed parliamentary business and demanded Irish land reform, and his supporters' agitation persuaded GLADSTONE to adopt a home rule policy. His political career ended in 1890 when he was named corespondent in a divorce case.

PARRINGTON, Vernon Louis (1871–1929), US literary historian who stressed the influence of social and economic affairs upon American writers. His *Main Currents in American Thought* (1927–30) won a Pulitzer prize.

PARRISH, Maxfield (1870–1966), US painter and illustrator with an elegant, richly decorative style. He is noted for murals, posters and book and magazine illustrations.

PARROTS, a family, Psittacidae, of about

20 species of birds distributed throughout the tropics. Most are brightly-colored birds with heavy, hooked bills, of which both mandibles articulate with the skull. Most are arboreal and diurnal, feeding on fruits, berries and leaves. There are four subfamilies: the Strigopinae (with only the KAKAPO of New Zealand), the Cacatuinae (the COCKATOOS) and the Lorinae (the LORIES and lorikeets, pygmy parrots and fig parrots). The fourth subfamily, the Psittacinae, contains some 200 species of "true" parrots, including the 130 species of American parrots.

PARSEES, or Parsis, religious group centered in Bombay and NW India who practice ZOROASTRIANISM. Their ancestors came from Persia in the 8th century to escape Muslim persecution. They now number about 120,000. The Parsees, many of whom are traders, are among the wealthiest and best educated groups in India. They worship at fire temples and expose their dead.

PARSONS, Talcott (1902–   ), US sociologist, who taught at Harvard 1927–74. An inveterate theorizer, he advocated a "structural-functional" analysis of the units that make up a stable social system. Works include *The Structure of Social Action* (1937), *The Social System* (1951) and *Politics and Social Structure* (1969).

PARTCH, Harry (1901–1974), US composer who devised a special notation for his unique microtonal music, which was based on an octave divided into 43 intervals instead of the traditional 12. His works received scant public attention as they could only be performed on bizarre instruments of his own devising.

PARTHENON, the most famous Greek temple, on the ACROPOLIS at Athens. Sacred to the city's patron goddess, Athena Parthenos, it was built of marble 447–432 BC by ICTINUS and CALLICRATES, with PHIDIAS supervising the sculptures. It featured a roof on Doric columns, an inner room, and fine sculptures and friezes including the ELGIN MARBLES. The Parthenon remained well preserved until 1687 when a Venetian bombardment exploded a Turkish powder magazine inside it. It is now threatened by industrial pollution. (See also GREEK ART AND ARCHITECTURE.)

PARTISANS, term usually used to describe the resistance movements in German-occupied territories in WWII. The original partisans were the communist supporters (*partizani*) of TITO in Yugoslavia. (See also GUERRILLA WARFARE; MAQUIS.)

PARTNERSHIP, business arrangement between two or more people combining labor, funds or property with a view to sharing profits. In law, partners are assumed to exercise joint control and can be held responsible for the liabilities of the partnership. The arrangement is common in professions such as law and accountancy and in small-scale service businesses. In limited partnerships a partner's liability is limited to his investment in the partnership.

PARTON, Dolly (1946–   ), US country singer whose buxom figure, backwoods innocence and flamboyant costumes and coiffures made her a pop superstar in the late 1970s. She appeared in the film *Nine to Five* (1981).

PARTRIDGES, several genera of game birds distributed through Europe, Asia and Africa. Best known is the Gray or Common partridge, *Perdix perdix*, of Europe, with a chestnut horseshoe on the breast.

PASCAL, Blaise (1623–1662), French mathematician, physicist and religious philosopher. Though not the first to study what is now called PASCAL'S TRIANGLE, he was first to use it in PROBABILITY studies, the mathematical treatment of which he and FERMAT evolved together, though in different ways. His studies of the CYCLOID inspired others to formulate the CALCULUS. His experiments (performed by his brother-in-law) observing the heights of the column of a BAROMETER at different altitudes on the mountain Puy-de-Dôme (1646) confirmed that the atmospheric air had weight. He also pioneered HYDRODYNAMICS and HYDROSTATICS, in doing so discovering PASCAL'S LAW, the basis of HYDRAULICS. His religious thought, which emphasizes "the reasons of the heart" over those of dry logic and intellect, is expressed in his *Provincial Letters* (1656–57) and his posthumously published *Pensées* (1670 onward).

PASCAL'S LAW, in HYDROSTATICS, states that the pressure in an enclosed body of fluid arising from forces applied to its boundaries is transmitted equally in all directions with unchanged intensity. This pressure acts at right angles to the surface of the fluid container.

PASSENGER PIGEON, *Ectopistes migratorius,* extinct member of the PIGEON family Columbidae, extremely common until the 19th century over most of North America. They were highly gregarious and social birds migrating in huge flocks. They fed on invertebrates, fruits and grain, often doing extensive damage to crops. Hunted by man both as a pest and for food, they finally became extinct in 1914.

PASSION PLAY, dramatic presentation of

Christ's suffering and death. It was one of the popular medieval MYSTERY PLAYS, performed by amateurs at religious festivals. The most famous passion play still performed is that at OBERAMMERGAU, staged every ten years since 1634.

PASSOVER, ancient major Jewish festival held for eight days from 14th *Nisan* (March/April). It celebrates the Israelites' escape from Egyptian slavery, when each family slew a paschal lamb and sprinkled its blood on the doorposts, and the destroying angel passed over (see also PLAGUES OF EGYPT). At the *Seder* feast, on the evening of the first two days, special dishes symbolize the Israelites' hardships and the story of the Exodus is read from the HAGGADAH. During Passover unleavened bread (matzoth) is eaten, and no LEAVEN may be used, a reminder of the hasty departure. (See also LAST SUPPER.)

PASTEL, drawing medium resembling a stick of colored chalk, and the pictures formed with it. The color is applied in broad areas and may be rubbed with the finger to form different tones. Usually it covers an entire surface, resembling painting rather than drawing. Masters of the art include J. B. S. CHARDIN and DEGAS.

PASTERNAK, Boris Leonidovich (1890–1960), Russian writer, best known for his only novel *Doctor Zhivago* (1958). He won the 1958 Nobel Prize for Literature but official pressure forced him to decline it. He was also a gifted translator of Shakespeare and Goethe, and the author of poems, short stories and an autobiography.

PASTEUR, Louis (1822–1895), French microbiologist and chemist. In his early pioneering studies in STEREOCHEMISTRY he discovered optical ISOMERISM. His attentions then centered around FERMENTATION, in which he demonstrated the role of microorganisms. He developed PASTEURIZATION as a way of stopping wine and beer from souring, and experimentally disproved the theory of SPONTANEOUS GENERATION. His "germ theory" of DISEASE proposed that diseases are spread by living germs (i.e., BACTERIA); and his consequent popularization of the STERILIZATION of medical equipment saved many lives. While studying ANTHRAX in cattle and sheep he developed a form of VACCINATION rather different from that of JENNER: he found inoculation with dead anthrax germs gave future IMMUNITY from the disease. Treating RABIES similarly, he concluded that it was caused by a germ too small to be seen—i.e., a VIRUS. The Pasteur Institute was founded in 1888 to lead the fight against rabies.

PASTEURIZATION, a process for partially sterilizing MILK originally invented by L. PASTEUR for improving the storage qualities of wine and beer. Originally the milk was held at 63°C for 30min in a vat. But today the usual method is a continuous process whereby the milk is held at 72°–85°C for 16s. Disease-producing BACTERIA, particularly those causing TUBERCULOSIS, are thus destroyed with a minimum effect on the flavor of the product. Since the process also destroys a majority of the harmless bacteria which sour milk, its keeping properties are also improved.

PASTORAL LITERATURE idealizes simple shepherd life, free from the corruption of the city. Typical forms are the verse elegy, prose romance and drama. Originating with THEOCRITUS in the 3rd century BC, the form was used by VERGIL, and later in England, after a Renaissance revival, by SHAKESPEARE (in *As You Like It*), Sir Philip SIDNEY (in *Arcadia*) and MILTON (in *Comus*).

PATAGONIA, that part of South America S of the Rio Negro or, more usually, the dry tableland in this region between the Andes and Atlantic, including Tierra del Fuego. Both areas lie mainly in Argentina, partly in Chile. Sheep-raising is the main activity of the few inhabitants, and there are oil, iron ore and coal deposits.

PATENT, a grant of certain specified rights by the government of a particular country, usually to a person whose claim to be the true and first inventor of a new invention (or the discoverer of a new process) is upheld. Criteria of the "novelty" of an invention are defined in law. The term derives from "letters patent"—the "open letters" by which a sovereign traditionally confers a special privilege or right on a subject. An inventor (or his assignee) who files an application for and is granted a patent is exclusively entitled to make, use or sell his invention for a limited period—17 years from the granting date, in the US and Canada. By granting the inventor a temporary monopoly, patent law aims to stimulate inventive activity and the rapid exploitation of new inventions for the public benefit.

PATHÉ, Charles (1873–1957), French photographer and originator of the Pathé news, which he introduced as a regular feature c1909 in a Paris theater.

PATHET LAO, pro-communist nationalist movement long active in N and E Laos, more recently dominating the government and comprising Lao People's Party and a broader Lao Patriotic Front. Its chairman, Prince Souphanouvong, became president of the new Lao People's Democratic epublic.

ATHOLOGY, study of the ANATOMY of SEASE. Morbid anatomy, the dissection of odies after DEATH with a view to scovering the cause of disease and the ature of its manifestaions, is complement-d and extended by HISTOLOGY. In addition AUTOPSY, BIOPSIES and surgical specimens e examined; these provide information at may guide treatment. It has been said at pathology is to MEDICINE what anatomy to PHYSIOLOGY.

ATON, Alan Stewart (1903–   ), South frican writer. His novel *Cry the Beloved ountry* (1948), drawing on his experience s principal of a reform school for Africans, escribes APARTHEID. In 1953 he became resident of the Liberal Party, banned in 968.

ATRIARCH, Old Testament title of the ead of a family or tribe, especially the sraelite fathers, Abraham, Isaac, Jacob nd Jacob's sons (see TWELVE TRIBES OF RAEL). The title was adopted by the early hristian bishops of Rome, Alexandria and ntioch, and now extends to certain other ees, especially of the ORTHODOX CHURCHES. implies jurisdiction over other bishops.

ATRICK, Saint, 5th-century missionary ishop, patron saint of Ireland. Controversy rrounds his identity, dates and works. In ie popular and official version he was born Britain c385, was captured by pagan ish and was a slave six years. After aining in Gaul he returned c432 to convert eland, with spectacular success in Ulster nd at Tara. He founded his see at Armagh. uthor of the autobiographical *Con-ssions*, he died c461. His feast day, an rish festival the world over, is 17 March.

ATROONS, holders of huge estates in the utch colony of NEW NETHERLAND (now I.Y.). From 1629 patroonships, with tax xemptions, monopolies and feudal rights, ere granted by the Dutch West India Company to sponsors of 50 or more settlers. he VAN RENSSELAER patroon excepted, the ystem did not encourage colonization, but estiges remained until the ANTI-RENT WAR f 1839–46.

ATTERSON, Floyd (1935–   ), US oxer. He won an Olympic gold medal in 952 and at 21 knocked out Archie Moore o become boxing's youngest world eavyweight champion. Also the first to egain the title (from Ingemar Johansson in 960), he lost it to Sonny Liston in 1962.

ATTON, George Smith, Jr (1885–1945), US general. His ruthlessness and tactical rilliance as a tank commander won him the ickname "Old Blood and Guts." Born of a nilitary family, he graduated from West

Point in 1909 and commanded a tank brigade in WWI. In WWII he was highly successful in N Africa and led the Third Army's rapid drive through France to SW Germany. He was killed in an automobile accident in Dec., 1945.

PAUL, name of six popes. **Paul III** (1468–1549), pope from 1534, encouraged the first major reforms of the COUNTER-REFORMATION, recognized the Jesuit order, and convened the Council of TRENT (1545). **Paul IV** (1476–1559), reigned from 1555, increased the powers of the Roman Inquisition, enforced segregation of the Jews in Rome and introduced strict censorship. His fanatical reformism proved self-defeating by creating widespread hostility. **Paul V** (1552–1621), pope from 1605, came into conflict with the Venetian Republic over papal jurisdiction, and, as a member of the Borgia family, was notorious for nepotism. **Paul VI** (1897–1978), elected in 1963, continued the modernizing reforms of his predecessor, JOHN XXIII, confirmed the Roman Catholic Church's ban on contraception, and became the first pope to travel widely.

PAUL, Saint (d. c65 AD), APOSTLE to the Gentiles, major figure in the early Christian Church. His life is recorded in the ACTS OF THE APOSTLES. Son of a Roman citizen, he was a zealous Jew, active in the persecution of the Christians until a vision of Christ on the road to Damascus made him a fervent convert to the new faith. He went on extensive missionary journeys to Cyprus, Asia Minor and Greece. Returning to Jerusalem, he was violently attacked by the Jews and imprisoned for two years. An appeal to the Emperor brought a transfer (c60 AD) to Rome, where, according to tradition, he was executed after two years' house arrest. His epistles, some of which are preserved in the NEW TESTAMENT, have had an incalculable influence on Christian belief and practice.

PAUL I (Pavel Petrovich; 1754–1801), emperor of Russia from 1796. His despotism at home and erratic policies abroad caused widespread discontent. He was assassinated by army officers anxious to secure the succession of his son Alexander.

PAULI, Wolfgang (1900–1958), Austrian-born physicist awarded the 1945 Nobel Prize for Physics for his discovery of the Pauli EXCLUSION PRINCIPLE, that no two fermions (see SUBATOMIC PARTICLES) in a system may have the same four quantum numbers. In terms of the ATOM, this means that at most two electrons may occupy the same ORBITAL (the two having opposite SPIN).

PAUL I (1901–1964), king of Greece from 1947, on the death of his brother George II. During his reign Greece was the recipient of US economic aid, and generally followed anti-communist policies. He was succeeded by his son Constantine (r. 1964-73).

PAULING, Linus Carl (1901–   ), US chemist and pacifist awarded the 1954 Nobel Prize for Chemistry for his work on the chemical BOND and the 1962 Nobel Peace Prize for his support of unilateral nuclear disarmament.

PAULIST FATHERS, officially the Society of Missionary Priests of St. Paul the Apostle, an evangelical order of Roman Catholic priests in the US, founded by Isaac HECKER (1858).

PAVAROTTI, Luciano (1935–   ), Italian tenor. A leading singer since his debut as Rodolfo in LA BOHÈME in 1961, he has been called the best Italian BEL CANTO tenor of his day. He became a Metropolitan Opera star after his debut there in 1968.

PAVESE, Cesare (1908–1950), Italian post-WWII novelist and, with Elio Vittorini, a major translator of American writing into Italian.

PAVLOV, Ivan Petrovich (1849–1936), Russian physiologist best known for his work on the conditioned REFLEX. Regularly, over long periods, he rang a bell just before feeding dogs, and found that eventually they salivated on hearing the bell, even when there was no food forthcoming. He also studied the physiology of the DIGESTIVE SYSTEM, and for this received the 1904 Nobel Prize for Physiology or Medicine.

PAVLOVA, Anna Matveyevna (1882–1931), Russian ballerina, considered the greatest of her time. She formed her own company and was famed for her roles in *Giselle* and *The Dying Swan* choreographed for her by Michel FOKINE.

PAWNBROKING, the business activity of lending on the security of personal possessions, which are left with the pawnbroker in return for a sum of money (usually well below the value of the article). The borrower receives a ticket with which he can redeem his property within a certain time, after which it may be sold.

PEABODY, Elizabeth Palmer (1804–1894), US educator, author and publisher who started the first US kindergarten and introduced FROEBEL's methods of education to the US. She wrote widely on educational theory, published early works of Nathaniel HAWTHORNE, and was an exponent of TRANSCENDENTALISM.

PEABODY, George (1795–1869), US financier and philanthropist. From 1837 he lived in London, where he set up an immensely prosperous investment banking house. His donations made possible such foundations as the Peabody Institute of Baltimore and the George Peabody College in Nashville, Tenn., as well as museums at Harvard and Yale.

PEACE CORPS, agency of the US government established by President John F. KENNEDY in 1961. The aim of the Peace Corps is to help raise living standards in developing countries, and to promote international friendship and understanding. Peace Corps projects, ranging from farm assistance to nursing instruction, are established at the request of the host country. Its 6,000 volunteers normally serve for two years.

PEACE PIPE, or *calumet* (French: reed), a tobacco pipe, long-stemmed and elaborately decorated, smoked by most North American Indian peoples on ceremonial occasions such as the signing of peace treaties. The peace pipe was a symbol of its owner's power and honor, and as such was held sacred.

PEACE RIVER, in W Canada, the main branch of the Mackenzie R. Formed by the junction of the Finlay and Parsnip rivers in central British Columbia, it flows 1,065mi E into Alberta to join the Slave R near Lake Athabaska.

PEACOCKS, properly **Peafowl,** large exotic ground birds of two genera, *Pavo* and *Afropavo*, well known as ornamental birds. The male, the peacock, has a train of up to 150 tail feathers, which can be erected in display to form a showy fan.

PEALE, an important family of early US painters. The prolific and versatile **Charles Willson Peale** (1741–1827) is best known for his portraits of Washington and other leading figures of the revolutionary period. He studied with Benjamin WEST in London and in 1784 founded a museum in Philadelphia, later moved to Independence Hall, which housed a portrait gallery together with natural history and technology exhibits. His younger brother **James Peale** (1749–1831) was best known for his portrait miniatures. Charles' many sons included **Raphaelle Peale** (1774-1825), a pioneer of US still-life painting, and **Rembrandt Peale** (1778-1860), a portraitist and founder of the Peale Museum, Baltimore. His most famous work is a portrait of Thomas Jefferson (1805).

PEALE, Norman Vincent (1898–   ), US Protestant minister and author of best-selling books on the power of self-confidence and a positive outlook, such as *A Guide to Confident Living* (1948) and *The Power of Positive Thinking* (1952).

PEARL HARBOR, natural land-locked harbor on the island of Oahu in Hawaii, US. Of great strategic importance, it is best known as the scene of the Japanese bombing of the US Pacific fleet on Dec. 7, 1941. Most of the fleet was in the harbor when Japanese carrier-based planes attacked without warning. Along with many smaller ships, eight battleships were damaged—three destroyed and another capsized; on the ground at Wheeler Field 188 planes were destroyed. The raid caused over 2,200 casualties with negligible losses to the Japanese. The attack brought the US into WWII.

PEARLS, white spherical gems produced by bivalve mollusks, particularly by Pearl oysters, *Pinctada*. In response to an irritation by foreign matter within the shell, the mantle secretes calcium carbonate in the form of NACRE (MOTHER OF PEARL) around the irritant body. Over several years, this encrustation forms the pearl. Cultured pearls may be obtained by "seeding" the oyster with an artificial irritant such as a small bead. Pearls are variable and may be black or pink as well as the usual white. Another bivalve group producing marketable pearls is the freshwater Pearl mussel, *Margaritifera margaritifera*.

PEARLY NAUTILUS, a shelled member of the cephalopod mollusks, with six species in the genus *Nautilus*, found in the southwestern Indo-Pacific. The shell is coiled and chambered. The growing animal lives always in the last chamber, the empty ones being gas-filled for flotation.

PEARSON, Drew (1897-1969), pen name of Andrew Russell Pearson, US journalist who wrote the syndicated column *The Washington Merry-go-round* (begun 1932), which specialized in exposés of national politics and political figures.

PEARSON, Karl (1857-1936), British mathematician best known for his pioneering work on STATISTICS (e.g., devising the CHI-SQUARED TEST) and for his *The Grammar of Science* (1892), an important contribution to the philosophy of mathematics. He was also an early worker in the field of EUGENICS.

PEARSON, Lester Bowles (1897-1972), Canadian diplomat, prime minister (1963-68) and winner of the 1957 Nobel Peace Prize for his mediation in the Suez crisis (1956). In 1928 he joined the Department of External Affairs, becoming first secretary, and in 1945 he was appointed ambassador to the US. As secretary of state (1948-57) he made notable contributions to the UN and NATO. In 1958 he became the Liberal leader. After resigning as prime minister he headed the WORLD BANK commission which produced the Pearson Report on developing countries.

PEARY, Robert Edwin (1856-1920), US Arctic explorer who discovered the North Pole. He entered the US Navy in 1881, and first journeyed to the interior of Greenland in 1886. On leaves of absence from the navy, he led a series of exploratory expeditions to Greenland which culminated in his reaching the North Pole on April 6, 1909. Peary's books, including *The North Pole* (1910) and *Secrets of Polar Travel* (1917), give an account of his journeys and an impression of his extraordinary stamina and courage.

PEASANTS' WAR, popular revolt (1524-26), which began in SW Germany and spread to many parts of Germany and Austria. The social turmoil created by the REFORMATION and the decay of FEUDALISM seem to have been at the root of the discontent. The movement collapsed when LUTHER denounced the uprising and supported its ruthless suppression.

PEAT, partly decayed plant material found in layers, usually in marshy areas. It is composed mainly of the peat mosses SPHAGNUM and Hypnum, but also of sedges, trees, etc. Under the right geological conditions, peat forms COAL. It is used as a MULCH and burned for domestic heating.

PECCARIES, pig-like mammals of the southwestern US and northern South America, inhabiting bushy thickets or forests. There are two species within the family Tayassuidae, the Collared peccary (*Pecari tajacu*) and White-lipped peccary (*Tayassu pecari*). Both are long-legged, with thick bristly hair and an erectile mane along the back.

PECK, Gregory (1916–   ), US film actor, a leading man in such popular movies as *Spellbound* (1944), *Duel in the Sun* (1946), *Gentleman's Agreement* (1947) and *Moby Dick* (1956). He won an Academy Award for his performance in *To*

Kill a Mockingbird (1963).

PECK ORDER, the term given to a DOMINANCE HIERARCHY in BIRDS. The top bird can peck all others; the second can peck all but the top bird, and so on down to the bottom bird who is pecked by all but can peck none. Frenzied pecking soon decides the rank of any new bird introduced to the group.

PEDIATRICS, branch of MEDICINE concerned with care of children. This starts with newborn, especially premature, babies for whom intensive care is required to protect the baby from and adapt it to the environment outside the WOMB. An important aspect is the recognition and treatment of congenital DISEASES in which structural or functional defects occur due to inherited disease (e.g., MONGOLISM) or disease acquired during development of EMBRYO or FETUS (e.g., SPINA BIFIDA). Otherwise, INFECTIOUS DISEASE, failure to grow or develop normally, MENTAL RETARDATION, DIABETES, ASTHMA and EPILEPSY form the bulk of pediatric practice.

PEEL, Sir Robert (1788–1850), British statesman. As home secretary in the 1820s, Peel set up the British police force and sponsored the CATHOLIC EMANCIPATION ACT (1829). Though he opposed the REFORM BILL (1832), he became more progressive, and after a brief term (1834–35) as prime minister, he organized the new Conservative Party out of the old Tory Party, aided by young politicians such as DISRAELI and GLADSTONE. His second term in office (1841–46) saw the introduction of an income tax, banking controls and Irish land reforms, and the further removal of discriminatory laws against Roman Catholics. The repeal of the CORN LAWS (1846) led to an era of FREE TRADE but caused a party split which led to his resignation.

PEGLER, James Westbrook (1894–1969), US journalist who won a Pulitzer Prize (1941) for his reporting. His column featured exposés, especially of labor racketeering, and was syndicated nationally 1944–62.

PÉGUY, Charles Pierre (1873–1914), French poet and essayist known for his spiritual ideals. As editor of *Cahiers de la quinzaine*, he defended Dreyfus. An ardent Catholic and nationalist, Péguy wished France to become a Catholic, socialist state.

PEI, Ieoh Ming (1917–   ), Chinese-born US architect of public buildings and urban complexes, e.g., the Mile High Center in Denver, Place Ville Marie in Montreal, the John Hancock Tower in Boston and the National Gallery's East Wing in Washington, DC. Most are noted for their simplicity and environmental harmony.

PEIRCE, Charles Sanders (1839–1914), US philosopher, best known as a pioneer of PRAGMATISM. He is also known for his work on the logic of relations, theory of signs, and other contributions in logic and the philosophy of science. Although he was a rigorous thinker who dealt with all main branches of philosophy, he wrote no comprehensive work but published numerous articles in philosophical journals.

PEKING, (also Beijing), capital of the People's Republic of China, lying within Hopeh Province, but administratively independent. It is the political, commercial, cultural and communications center of the country, and embraces a massive industrial complex. The city's rectangular layout was the work of KUBLAI KHAN in the 13th century, and its splendors were described by Marco POLO. It became the permanent capital of China in 1421. Its occupation by French and British troops from 1860 was a contributing cause of the BOXER REBELLION (1900). In 1928 Peking (renamed Peiping) was superseded by Nanking (Nanjing), but regained its capital status and its name with the communist victory in 1949. Peking has two historic districts: the Inner City, enclosing the Imperial City and the Forbidden City; and the Outer City. Pop 8,490,000.

PEKINGESE, lap-dog, bred for centuries only in the Chinese court, now a popular pet. It stands only 6–9in high, is longhaired and has a flat skull.

PELAGIANISM, Christian heresy based on the teachings of the British theologian **Pelagius** (c353–c425); an ascetic movement chiefly of aristocratic laity. Pelagius held that men are not naturally sinful, and have FREE WILL to take the first steps to salvation by their own efforts. This challenged the basic Christian doctrines relating to GRACE, ORIGINAL SIN and Christ's ATONEMENT. Pelagianism was opposed by St. AUGUSTINE and condemned by the Council of Ephesus in 431. A middle position, **Semi-Pelagianism,** was dominant in Gaul until condemned by the Council of Orange (529).

PELÉ (Edson Arantes do Nascimento; 1940–   ), Brazilian soccer player. Often rated as the best player of all time, he led the Brazilian national team to an unprecedented three World Cup titles (1958, 1962, 1970), then gave the North American Soccer League instant credibility by joining the N.Y. Cosmos (1975–77). He scored 1,281 goals during his career.

PELÉE, Mount, active volcano on MARTINIQUE, in the French West Indies;

4,583ft high. Its eruption in 1902 destroyed the town of St. Pierre and killed some 40,000 people.

PELICANS, large aquatic birds of the genus *Pelecanus*. The long bills are provided with an expansible pouch attached to the lower mandible, used, not for storage, but simply as a catching apparatus, a scoop-net. They are social birds, breeding in large colonies. Most species also fish in groups, swimming together, herding the fish in horseshoe formation. All are fine fliers.

PELLAGRA, VITAMIN deficiency DISEASE (due to lack of niacin), often found in maize- or millet-dependent populations. A DERMATITIS, initially resembling sunburn, but followed by thickening, scaling and pigmentation, is characteristic; internal EPITHELIUM is affected (sore tongue, DIARRHEA). Confusion, DELIRIUM, hallucination and ultimately dementia may ensue. Niacin replacement is essential and food enrichment is an important preventitive measure.

PELOPONNESIAN WAR, (431–404 BC), war between the rival Greek city-states of ATHENS and SPARTA which ended Athenian dominance and marked the beginning of the end of Greek civilization. The war was fought in two phases. The first (431–421) was inconclusive because Athenian sea power was matched by Spartan land power, and a stalemate was acknowledged by the Peace of NICIAS. Nicias had been the third Athenian leader in the war following PERICLES and CLEON, and his leadership was now challenged by ALCIBIADES, who initiated the second and decisive phase of the conflict (418–404). In an attack on Syracuse in 413, the Athenians suffered a major defeat. The Spartans, with Persian aid, built up a powerful fleet under the leadership of LYSANDER who blockaded Athens and forced her final surrender. (See also GREECE, ANCIENT.)

PELOPONNESUS, peninsula forming the S part of the Greek mainland, linked with the N by Isthmus of Corinth. It is mostly mountainous but its fertile lowlands provide wheat, tobacco, and fruit crops. Its largest city and port is Patras. In ancient times it was the center of the MYCENAEAN CIVILIZATION and, later, was dominated by SPARTA in the SE.

PEN, acronym of the International Association of Poets, Playwrights, Editors, Essayists and Novelists. Founded in 1922, the association aims to promote international intercourse and cooperation between men of letters.

PENANCE, a SACRAMENT of the Roman Catholic Church. A priest, after receiving the CONFESSION of a penitent, may (as the agent of God) grant ABSOLUTION, imposing a penance and requiring restitution for harm done to others. The penance— now usually prayers, though formerly a rigorous ascetic discipline—represents the temporal punishment for sin. (See also INDULGENCE.)

PENDERECKI, Krzysztof (1933–   ), Polish composer. His innovative works used such unorthodox sounds as sawing and typing, scraping instruments and hissing singers, and include *Threnody for the Victims of Hiroshima* (1960) and *St. Luke's Passion* (1965).

PENDERGAST, Thomas Joseph (1872–1945), US politician. He was the Democratic political boss of Kansas City and Mo. during the 1920s and 30s. Pendergast was convicted and imprisoned for evading income tax (1939).

PENDLETON ACT, US Federal law (1883) by which Federal employment was given on the basis of merit rather than political affiliation, thus establishing the modern CIVIL SERVICE. Sponsored by Senator Pendleton of Ohio after public disquiet at corruption, the law provided for selection by open competitive examination.

PENDULUM, a rigid body mounted on a fixed horizontal axis that is free to rotate under the influence of gravity. Many types of pendulum exist (e.g., Kater's and the FOUCAULT PENDULUM), the most common consisting of a large weight (the bob) supported at the end of a light string or bar. An idealized simple pendulum, with a string of negligible weight and length, l, the weight of its bob concentrated at a point and a small swing amplitude, executes SIMPLE HARMONIC MOTION. The time, T, for a complete swing (to and fro) is given by $T = 2\pi \sqrt{l/g}$ depending only on the string length and the local value of the gravitational ACCELERATION, g. Actual physical or compound pendulums approximate this behavior if they have a small angle of swing. They are used for measuring absolute values of g or its variation with geographical position, and as control elements in CLOCKS.

PENGUINS, the most highly-specialized of all aquatic birds, with 17 species in the order Sphenisciformes, restricted to the S hemisphere. Completely flightless, the wings are reduced to flippers for "flying" through the water. Ungainly on land, penguins only leave the water to breed. The nest is usually a skimpy affair; Emperor and King penguins brood their single eggs on their feet covered by a flap of skin. Most species nest in colonies. Penguins are long-lived birds: the Yellow-eyed penguin may live for 20 years or more.

PENICILLIN, substance produced by a class of FUNGI which interferes with cell wall production by BACTERIA and which was one of the first, and remains among the most useful, ANTIBIOTICS. The property was noted by A. FLEMING in 1928 and production of penicillin for medical use was started by E. B. CHAIN and H. W. FLOREY in 1940. Since then numerous penicillin derivatives have been manufactured, extending the range of activity, overcoming resistance in some organisms and allowing some to be taken by mouth. STAPHYLOCOCCUS, STREPTOCOCCUS and the bacteria causing the VENEREAL DISEASES of gonorrhea and syphilis are among the bacteria sensitive to natural penicillin, while bacilli negative to GRAM'S STAIN, which cause urinary-tract infection, SEPTICEMIA, etc., are destroyed by semisynthetic penicillins.

PENINSULAR WAR (1808–1814), part of the NAPOLEONIC WARS, in which the French, fighting against the British, Portuguese and Spanish, were driven out of the Iberian Peninsula. Anxious to increase his security in Europe, NAPOLEON sent General JUNOT to occupy Portugal (1807), and in 1808 dispatched Murat to occupy Spain, although she was an ally. The Spanish and the Portuguese soon rebelled, and, with the aid of the British under Arthur Wellesley (later Duke of WELLINGTON), the French were driven out of Portugal (1809). In the long struggle that followed, the British—aided by Portuguese and Spanish guerrillas—gradually gained the upper hand, despite many reverses. By 1813 the French forces in Spain had been defeated, and Wellesley invaded S France. The war ended on Napoleon's abdication.

PENIS, male reproductive organ for introducing sperm and semen into the female vagina and womb; its urethra also carries URINE from the BLADDER. The penis is made of connective tissue and specialized blood vessels which become engorged with BLOOD in sexual arousal and which cause the penis to become stiff and erect; this facilitates the intromission of semen in sexual intercourse. A protective fold, the foreskin, covers the tip and is often removed for ethnic or medical reasons in circumcision.

PENKOVSKIY, Oleg (1919–1963), Soviet chief of military intelligence who passed secret information to the British and Americans during the early 1960s. Caught and tried by Soviet authorities in 1963, he was sentenced to death and executed. His memoirs, *The Penkovskiy Papers* (1965), divulged a wealth of information about Soviet strategy and intentions.

PENN, William (1644–1718), English QUAKER, advocate of religious tolerance, and founder of PENNSYLVANIA. He wrote numerous tracts on Quaker beliefs and was several times imprisoned for his nonconformity. In 1675 he became involved in American colonization as a trustee for one of the proprietors of W N.J. (then West Jersey). In 1681, he and 11 others bought the rights to E N.J. (then East Jersey), and he received a vast province on the W bank of the Delaware R in settlement of a debt owed by Charles II to Penn's father. Thousands of European Quakers emigrated there in search of religious and political freedom. In 1682 Penn visited the colony and witnessed the fulfillment of his plans for the city of Philadelphia. He returned in 1699 to revise the constitution.

PENNAMITE WARS (1769–71, 1775–84), two major conflicts amid a series of clashes between Conn. and Pa. over their long-standing rivalry for the Wyoming Valley. Both wars ended with the Conn. settlers in possession of the valley, and the controversy ended only in 1799 when Conn. yielded to the claims of Pa., by then legally recognized. A compromise was reached, and the New England culture of the Conn. settlers became a major influence on the state.

PENNELL, Joseph (1857–1926), US etcher and writer, noted for his prolific and original book illustrations. He spent much of his life in London, but returned to the US in WWI. He wrote a biography (1908) of WHISTLER, by whom he was influenced.

PENNSYLVANIA, Middle Atlantic state of the US, one of the original 13 colonies. It is bounded on the N by Lake Erie and N.Y., E by N.Y. and N.J., S by Del., Md. and W. Va., and W by W. Va. and Ohio.

Land. The state embraces the vast ranges of the APPALACHIAN and ALLEGHENY Mts; its only lowlands are the coastal plains SE and NW. The main rivers are the Delaware and the Susquehanna in the E and the Allegheny and Monongahela in the W. The state is still richly forested, and many of its spectacularly beautiful inland regions retain an air of wilderness. Pa. has a moist climate with pronounced seasonal variations.

People. Pennsylvania is the fourth-largest state in population. About 10% are black and nearly two thirds of the people are urban, the largest cities being PHILADELPHIA and PITTSBURGH. Religious freedom in colonial times attracted diverse groups of immigrants including QUAKERS and the PENNSYLVANIA DUTCH.

onomy. Manufacturing dominates the
ate's diversified economy. The pig-iron
d steel industry, centered in Pittsburgh,
oduces one-fifth of the national total.
her major manufactures include elec-
cal and other machinery, processed food,
etal products and clothing. Tourism,
riculture (mainly livestock) and coal
ning are also of major importance. The
tstanding communications and distribu-
n facilities of Pennsylvania include the
o great ports of Philadelphia and Erie.
story. When Henry Hudson entered
elaware Bay in 1609, the region was
habited by ALGONQUIAN and IROQUOIS
dians. The first permanent settlement
as made by the Swedes in 1643. Swedish
le gave way to control by the Dutch in
55, and in 1664 the region was captured
the English. It was granted (1681) to
illiam PENN. Under Penn's guidance, the
lony became a tolerant, peaceful and
osperous community, initially on good
rms with the Indians. The peace was
oken by the FRENCH AND INDIAN WARS
754–63) and again by the REVOLUTIONARY
AR. in which the location and resources of
. were vital. The Declaration of
dependence was signed in Philadelphia,
e nation's capital from 1790 to 1800 and
r long its foremost city. Pennsylvanian
uakers had been outspoken opponents of
avery, and the state entered the Civil War
the Union side. It was the scene of the
ucial Battle of GETTYSBURG (1863).
For nearly a century, from the end of the
vil War to the end of WWII, the state's

ame of state: Pennsylvania
apital: Harrisburg
tatehood: Dec 12, 1787 (2nd state)
amiliar name: Keystone State
rea: 45,333sq mi
opulation: 11,866,728
levation: Highest—3,213ft. Mount Davis.
owest—sea level, Delaware River
lotto: Virtue, Liberty and Independence
tate flower: Mountain laurel
tate bird: Ruffled grouse
tate tree: Hemlock
tate song: None

steady growth in prosperity was interrupted
only by severe floods in 1889 and the Great
Depression of the 1930s. After WWII,
however, Pennsylvania's economy was
buffeted from various directions: out-
of-state (and out-of-country) competitors
took business away from the old, relatively
inefficient plants of the local iron and steel
industry; textile mills moved south in search
of cheaper labor; the railroads entered a
seemingly irreversible decline, and unemployment became chronic in coal-mining
regions as users switched to other fuels.

Pittsburgh was substantially renovated in
the 1950s and its air quality dramatically
improved, changing one of the dirtiest cities
into one of the cleanest; but Pennsylvania's
other major cities, particularly Philadelphia, are in need of renewal. Despite its
present dificulties, including a 7.9%
unemployment rate in 1980, Pennsylvania's
economic base is still so large and so strong
that it remains by any measure-one of the
wealthiest and most powerful states in the
US.

PENNSYLVANIA DUTCH (from German *Deutsch*, meaning German), descendants of German-speaking immigrants who
came to Pa. during the 17th and 18th
centuries in search of religious freedom.
They were mainly Lutheran and Reformed
Protestants, but included such Pietist sects
as the AMISH. DUNKERS, MENNONITES and
MORAVIANS. who still retain their original
culture.

PENNSYLVANIAN, the penultimate period of the PALEOZOIC, stretching between
about 315 and 280 million years ago. (See
CARBONIFEROUS; GEOLOGY.)

PENOBSCOT RIVER, longest river in Me.
(350mi from the head of its longest branch).
Rising near the Canadian border it flows E
and S to Penobscot Bay on the Atlantic. The
Penobscot valley saw a number of battles
between the English and French from 1673
to 1759, and between the English and
Americans during the Revolution and the
War of 1812.

PENOLOGY. See PRISONS; PUNISHMENT.

PENSION, regular payment made to
people after they retire from employment
because of age or disability, received from
the government under SOCIAL SECURITY
programs, or from private employers, or
both. In the US, almost all large
corporations provide pension plans for their
employees, based on salary and length of
service, and financed either by the company
alone or jointly by company and employee
(contributory plans). The most common
forms are the trust fund, administered by a
bank or trust company; the group annuity in

which an insurance company collects payments from the corporation to build up the retirement fund; and profit-sharing plans, in which pension funds are accumulated annually as a percentage of company profits.

PENTAGON, The, five-sided building in Arlington, Va., which houses the US Department of Defense, built in 1941–43. The largest office building in the world, it consists of five concentric pentagons covering a total area of 34 acres.

PENTAGON PAPERS, a 2.5-million-word, top-secret history of American involvement in Indochina from 1945 to 1968, compiled by order of Secretary of Defense Robert S. McNamara, and leaked by Daniel Ellsberg, a former government researcher, to the *New York Times*, which began publishing articles about the history on June 13, 1971. The Justice Department obtained a court order on June 15 barring further articles, but the US Supreme Court on June 30 allowed publication to proceed under protection of the First Amendment. The government brought Ellsberg to trial but the judge threw the case out of court on May 11, 1973, after learning of illegal FBI taps of 15 of Ellsberg's telephone conversations and of the White House attempt to gather derogatory information on Ellsberg by having a team of burglars (the plumbers, of Watergate fame) break into the offices of his psychiatrist.

PENTATEUCH (Greek: five books), the first five books of the OLD TESTAMENT: GENESIS, EXODUS, LEVITICUS, NUMBERS and DEUTERONOMY. They were traditionally assigned to MOSES, but are now regarded as a compilation of four or more documents (J, E, P and D) dating from the 9th to the 5th centuries BC and distinguished by style and theological bias. (See also TORAH.)

PENTATHLON. See TRACK AND FIELD.

PENTECOST (Greek: 50th), distinct Jewish and Christian festivals. The Jewish Pentecost, called SHAVUOT, celebrated on the 50th day after PASSOVER, is a harvest feast. The Christian Pentecost (Whitsunday)—the 50th day inclusively after, Easter commemorates the descent of the HOLY SPIRIT upon the Apostles, marking the birth of the Christian Church.

PENTECOSTAL CHURCHES, Protestant churches, fundamentalist (see FUNDAMENTALISM) and revivalist, that emphasize holiness and spiritual power as initiated by an experience ("baptism in the Spirit") in which the recipient "speaks in tongues" (see GLOSSOLALIA). They base their distinctive doctrines and practice of CHARISMATA on New Testament teaching

and accounts of the bestowal of the H Spirit. Pentecostalism began c1906 a spread rapidly; it is now influential in ma major denominations. The largest Pentec tal churches in the US are the Assemblies God and the United Pentecos Church.

PENTOTHAL SODIUM, or thiopentone BARBITURATE drug injected into a vein produce brief general ANESTHESIA, also us in PSYCHIATRY as a relaxant to remo inhibitions (a so-called "truth drug").

PENZIAS, Arno (1933–   ), Germa born US physicist who shared the 19 Nobel Prize in Physics for discoveri cosmic MICROWAVE radiation emanati from outside of the GALAXY while doi communications research for the B Telephone Laboratories. The discove provided evidence for the "big bang" theo of the origins of the universe.

PEONAGE, form of coercive servitude which a laborer (peon) worked off l debts—often inescapable and lifelong— his creditor-master. In Spanish Americ where it was most prevalent, and in t Southern states of the US (in a modifi form), peonage did not end until the 20 century.

PEP, Willie (1922–   ), US feathe weight boxer. He won the world title in 19 and 1949. He won 229 of 241 fights, 65 knockouts. From 1940–43 he won consecutive bouts and from 1943–48 scor 73 wins and one draw.

PEPSIN, an ENZYME which breaks dov PROTEINS in the DIGESTIVE SYSTEM.

PEPYS, Samuel (1633–1703), Engli diarist. Although he was a successf reforming naval administrator and pre ident of the Royal Society (1684–85), it his talent in recording contemporary affai and his own private life for which he famed today. His diary, written in ciph 1660–69, was not decoded and publishe until 1825.

PEQUOT INDIANS, North America Indians of the ALGONQUIAN language grou who lived in S New England. Their murd of a colonial trader by whom they had be mistreated led to the **Pequot War** (1637 the first major white massacre of Indians North America, in which almost the enti tribe was slaughtered or enslaved. T Pequot were resettled (1655) on Connecticut reservation.

PERCEPTION, the recognition or ide tification of something. External percepti relies on the SENSES, internal perceptio which is introverted, relying on t CONSCIOUSNESS. Some psychologists ho that perception need not be CONSCIOUS;

articular, subliminal perception involves reaction of the UNCONSCIOUS to external timuli and its subsequent influencing of the conscious (see GESTALT; SUGGESTION).

PERCHES, a family of spiny-finned fishes with protrusible upper jaw and sharp-edged scales. The true perches are all freshwater and belong to the family Percidae, but the name perch is often used for other perch-like fishes within the order Perciformes. True perches include both the European and the American perch, both predatory fishes.

PERCUSSION INSTRUMENTS, musical instruments from which sound is produced by striking. These are divided into two main classes: **idiophones**, such as BELLS, CASTANETS, CYMBALS and GONGS, whose wood or metal substance vibrates to produce sound, and **membranophones**, chiefly DRUMS and TAMBOURINES, in which sound is produced by vibrating a stretched skin. Although the PIANO, CELESTA, TRIANGLE, XYLOPHONE and GLOCKENSPIEL can be classed as percussion, the term commonly denotes those instruments used chiefly for rhythmic effect. (See also TIMPANI.)

PEREGRINE, *Falco peregrinus*, one of the largest and most widespread of the FALCONS. They are found in mountainous areas or on sea cliffs, feeding on birds up to the size of a duck, caught in the air. Numbers are declining all over Europe and North America with the increased use of pesticides.

PERELMAN, Sidney Joseph (1904–1979), US humorous writer noted for his collaboration as screen writer on several MARX BROTHERS films, and for many articles which appeared in the *New Yorker*. He won an Academy Award in 1956.

PERENNIAL, any plant that continues to grow for more than two years. Trees and shrubs are examples of the perennials that have woody stems that thicken with age. The herbaceous perennials such as the PEONY and DAFFODIL have stems that die down each winter and regrow in the spring from underground perennating organs, such as TUBERS and BULBS. (See ANNUAL; BIENNIAL.)

PÉREZ JIMÉNEZ, Marcos (1914–   ), president of Venezuela 1952–58. One of a three-man junta from 1948, he seized sole power in 1952. Inadequate reforms and corrupt rule led to his overthrow and flight. Extradited from the US and imprisoned 1963–68, he was, upon his release, exiled to Madrid.

PERFECT NUMBER, a NATURAL NUMBER equal to the SUM of its FACTORS. Two such numbers are 6 (divisible by 1, 2, 3, and 1+2+3=6) and 28 (1, 2, 7, 4, 14). Only 23 perfect numbers are known.

PERFUME, a blend of substances made from plant oils and synthetic materials which produce a pleasant odor. Perfumes were used in ancient times as INCENSE in religious rites, in medicines and later for adornment. Today they are utilized in cosmetics, toilet waters, soaps and detergents, and polishes. A main source of perfumes are ESSENTIAL OILS extracted from different parts of plants, e.g., the flowers of the ROSE, the leaves of LAVENDER, CINNAMON from bark and PINE from wood. They are extracted by steam distillation; by using volatile solvents; by coating petals with fat, or by pressing. Animal products, such as AMBERGRIS from the sperm whale, are used as fixatives to preserve fragrance. The development of synthetic perfumes began in the 19th century. There are now a number of synthetic chemicals with flowerlike fragrance, for example citronellol for rose and benzyl acetate for JASMINE.

PERGOLESI, Giovanni Battista (1710–1736), Italian opera composer famed for his comic intermezzo *The Maid as Mistress* (1733). He also composed serious opera and religious music, such as the *Mass in F* (1734) and *Stabat Mater* (1736).

PERI, Jacopo (1561–1633), Italian composer whose *Dafne* (1597) may have been the first opera. Only his opera *Euridice* (1600) and the sensitive madrigals of *Le varie musiche* (1609) survive.

PERICLES (c495–429 BC), Athenian general and statesman. A strong critic of the conservative AREOPAGUS council, he obtained (461) the OSTRACISM of Cimon and became supreme leader of the Athenian democracy. The years 462–454 BC saw the furthering of that democracy, with salaried state offices and supremacy of the assembly. Pericles' expansionist foreign policy led to a defeat of Persia (449), truce with Sparta (445), and the transformation of the DELIAN LEAGUE into an Athenian empire. The peace of 445–431 saw the height of Athenian culture under his rule. The PARTHENON and PROPYLAEA were both built at Pericles' request. One of the instigators of the PELOPONNESIAN WAR, he was deposed but reelected in 429; his death in a plague soon after may have lost Athens the war.

PERIODIC TABLE, a table of the ELEMENTS in order of atomic number (see ATOM), arranged in rows and columns to illustrate periodic similarities and trends in physical and chemical properties. Such classification of the elements began in the early 19th century, when Johann Wolfgang

Döbereiner (1780–1849) discovered certain "triads" of similar elements (e.g. calcium, strontium, barium) whose atomic weights were in arithmetic progression. By the 1860s many more elements were known, and their atomic weights determined, and it was noted by John Alexander Reina Newlands (1837–1898) that similar elements recur at intervals of eight—his "law of octaves"—in a sequence in order of atomic weight. In 1869 MENDELEYEV published the first fairly complete periodic table, based on his discovery that the properties of the elements vary periodically with atomic weight. There were gaps in the table corresponding to elements then unknown, whose properties Mendeleyev predicted with remarkable accuracy. Modern understanding of atomic structure has shown that the numbers and arrangement of the electrons in the atom are responsible for the periodicity of properties; hence the atomic number, rather than the atomic weight, is the basis of ordering. Each row, or period, of the table corresponds to the filling of an electron "shell"; hence the numbers of elements in the periods are 2, 8, 8, 18, 18, 32, 32. (There are n^2 ORBITALS in the nth shell.) The elements are arranged in vertical columns or groups containing those of similar atomic structure and properties, with regular gradation of properties down each group. The longer groups, with members in the first three (short) periods, are known as the Main Groups, usually numbered IA to VIIA, and 0 for the NOBLE GASES. The remaining groups, the TRANSITION ELEMENTS, are numbered IIIB to VIII (a triple group), IB and IIB. The characteristic VALENCE of each group is equal to its number N, or to $(8-N)$ for some nonmetals. Two series of 14 elements each, the LANTHANIDES and ACTINIDES, form a transition block in which the inner f ORBITALS are being filled; their members have similar properties, and they are usually counted in Group IIIB. (See also TRANSURANIUM ELEMENTS.)

PERIPATETIC SCHOOL, in philosophy, the name given to the school of philosophy founded by ARISTOTLE and THEOPHRASTUS. The term derives from the covered arcade (*peripatos*) at the Lyceum where Aristotle taught in Athens.

PERISCOPE, optical instrument that permits an observer to view his surroundings along a displaced axis, and hence from a concealed, protected or submerged position. The simplest periscope, used in tanks, has two parallel reflecting surfaces (prisms or mirrors). An auxiliary telescopic gunsight may be added. Submarine periscopes have a series of lenses within the tube to widen the field of view, crosswires and a range-finder, and can rotate and retract.

PERISTALSIS, the coordinated movements of hollow visceral organs, especially the GASTROINTESTINAL TRACT, which cause forward propulsion and mixing of the contents. It is effected by autonomic NERVOUS SYSTEM plexuses acting on visceral MUSCLE layers.

PERITONITIS, INFLAMMATION of PERITONEUM, usually caused by BACTERIAL INFECTION or chemical irritation of peritoneum when internal organs become diseased (as with APPENDICITIS) or when GASTROINTESTINAL TRACT contents escape (as with a perforated peptic ULCER). Characteristic pain, sometimes with SHOCK FEVER, and temporary cessation of bowel activity (ileus), are common. Urgent treatment of the cause is required, often with SURGERY; ANTIBIOTICS may also be needed.

PERKINS, Frances (1882–1965), US secretary of labor 1933–45, first US woman cabinet member. From 1910 she was active in N.Y. state factory and labor affairs. Appointed labor secretary by President F. D. ROOSEVELT, she administered NEW DEAL programs.

PERLMAN, Itzhak (1945–   ), Israeli-born violinist who was recognized as one of the leading violinists of his generation. A favorite of concert audiences, he performed throughout the world, appeared frequently on TV and made several notable recordings.

PERMAFROST, permanently frozen ground, typical of the treeless plains of Siberia (see TUNDRA), though common throughout polar regions.

PERMIAN, the last period of the PALEOZOIC, stretching between about 280 and 225 million years ago. (See also GEOLOGY.)

PERMUTATIONS AND COMBINATIONS, respectively, the different orders that can be given to the elements of a SET; and the different selections of elements that may be taken from the set, every selection being of the same size, no element being a member of more than one selection, and order within each selection being immaterial. For a set of n elements there are $n(n-1)(n-2)$ ... 2.1 ($=n!$—see FACTORIAL) permutations, taking the elements singly; and, taking the elements in *ordered* subsets each containing k elements, there are $n(n-1)(n-2)$ ... $(n-(k-1))(=\frac{n!}{(n-k)!})$ permutations. For the same set, taking k

elements in each *unordered* subset, there are $\frac{n!}{k!(n-k)!}$ combinations.

PERÓN, Isabel (María Estela Martínez de Perón 1931–), president of Argentina 1974–76. Personal secretary to Juan PERÓN from 1956, she married him in 1961, She was elected vice-president in 1973 and became president on her husband's death. Deposed by a military junta in 1976, she was held under house arrest until 1979.

PERÓN, Juan Domingo (1895–1974), president of Argentina 1946–55, 1973–74. As head of an army clique, he helped overthrow Castillo in 1943. He won union loyalty as secretary of labor. Elected president (after police intervention), he began with his first wife Eva (1919–1952) a program of industrialization and social reform. Church and army opposition to corruption and repression forced him into exile. Peronist influence survived, however; he returned in 1973, and was reelected president. He served until his death and was succeeded by his third wife, Isabel.

PERPENDICULAR STYLE, name given to the period of English Gothic architecture from the 14th to the middle 16th century. It is characterized by the vertical tracery on windows and wall panels and by fan vaults. King's College chapel, Cambridge, is a famous example of the style.

PERPETUAL MOTION, an age-old goal of inventors: a machine which would work forever without external interference, or at least with 100% efficiency. No such machine has worked or can work, though many are plausible on paper. Perpetual motion machines of the *first kind* are those whose efficiency exceeds 100%—they do work without energy being supplied. They are disallowed by the First Law of THERMODYNAMICS. Those of the *second kind* are machines that take heat from a reservoir (such as the ocean) and convert it wholly into work. Although energy is conserved, they are disallowed by the Second Law of Thermodynamics. Those of the *third kind* are machines that do no work, but merely continue in motion forever. They are approachable but not actually achievable, because some energy is always dissipated as heat by friction, etc. An example, however, of what is in a sense perpetual motion of the third kind is electric current flowing in a superconducting ring (see SUPERCON-DUCTIVITY), which continues undiminished indefinitely.

PERRAULT, name of two eminent French brothers. **Charles Perrault** (1628–1703), poet, fairy-tale writer and man of letters, is best known for his *Contes de ma mère l'Oye* (*Tales of Mother Goose*; 1697) which include "Little Red Riding Hood," "Cinderella" and "Puss in Boots." **Claude Perrault** (1613–1688), architect, scientist and physician, is remembered for his buildings, notably the colonnade of the Louvre (1667–70), the Paris Observatory (1667–72) and for his translation of the works of VITRUVIUS (1673).

PERRY, two US brothers who became distinguished naval officers. **Matthew Calbraith Perry** (1794–1858) was instrumental in opening Japan to the US and world trade. He commanded the first US steam warship, the *Fulton II* (1838) and led US naval forces suppressing the slave trade; he fought in the MEXICAN WAR. In 1853 Perry took four vessels into Tokyo Bay and remained there until a Japanese envoy agreed to receive President FILLMORE'S request for a diplomatic and trade treaty. He returned in Feb. 1854 to conclude the treaty, which was a turning point in US-Japan relations. **Oliver Hazard Perry** (1785–1819), became a hero of the WAR OF 1812. After assembling a fleet of nine ships at Erie, Pa., he defeated six British warships on Sep. 10, 1813 off Put-in-Bay, Ohio, in the battle of Lake ERIE. He announced his victory in the famous message "We have met the enemy and they are ours."

PERSE, St.-John (1887–1975), pen name of Alexis Saint-Léger Léger, French poet and diplomat. He was secretary general of the French foreign office (1933–40). His poetry includes *Anabase* (1924), translated by T. S. ELIOT, and *Amers* (1957). In 1960 he was awarded the Nobel Prize for Literature.

PERSHING, John Joseph (1860–1948), US general. After distinguished service in the Indian Wars (1886, 1890–91), the Spanish-American War (1898) and in the Philippines (1899–1903), he was promoted to brigadier general (1906). He led a punitive expedition to Mexico against VILLA (1916) and a year later became commander of the AMERICAN EXPEDITIONARY FORCE in Europe. Pershing insisted on independent authority over US forces. In 1919 he became general of the armies, and was chief of staff from 1921 until 1924.

PERSIA, Ancient, the high plateau of Iran, home of several great civilizations. In the 2nd millenium BC the literate civilization of ELAM developed in the SW of the plateau, with its capital at SUSA. Its W neighbors, BABYLONIA and ASSYRIA. had trading and political interests in the state and attempted takeovers. The civilization was ended in 639 BC by the invasion of Ashurbanipal of Assyria. Assyrian downfall followed in 612 after the sacking of NINEVEH by the

Babylonians and the MEDES, an Aryan kingdom S of the Caspian Sea. The area of Parsumash to the S of the Medes was ruled by the ACHAEMENIANS. CYRUS THE GREAT expanded the Achaemenid empire and at his death (529) he controlled the Middle East from the Mediterranean to the Indus R. Under DARIUS I (522–486) PERSEPOLIS succeeded PASAGARDAE as capital; a road system linked the great empire, a canal linked the Nile and Red Sea. Flourishing trade, commerce and public works continued under XERXES I (586–465). Xerxes' murder by his son was followed by intrigues and rebellions that weakened the Achaemenians. In c330 the empire was conquered by ALEXANDER THE GREAT and at his death most of it became part of the brief empire of the SELEUCIDS, who were conquered by the Parthians from SW of the Caspian. The empire of PARTHIA (3rd century BC–3rd century AD) had its capital at CTESIPHON and halted the nomads in the NE and the Romans in the W, defeating CRASSUS in 53 BC and later Mark Anthony. In 224 AD, a successful revolt by Ardashir, ruler of the Fars (the S Persian homeland), established the vigorous SASSANIAN empire. Arts, architecture and religion (ZOROASTRIANISM) revived, the wars with Rome continued, and in 260 AD Shapur, the son of Ardashir, captured the Emperor Valerian. Later, after constant struggles with the Byzantines, the Sassanian empire was overwhelmed by the Arabs in 651.

PERSIAN, the language of Iran, where 12 million of its 15 million speakers live (the others are in Afghanistan). It is an INDO-EUROPEAN LANGUAGE. Modern Persian emerged after the Arab conquest in the 7th century. It has many borrowed Arabic words and a modified Arabic alphabet.

PERSIAN CAT, long-haired type of cat, first introduced into Europe from Turkey and Persia at the end of the 16th century; in the US the official name for the group of long-haired breeds with cobby bodies, short legs and round heads which may be a variety of colors in tabby, self-color, particolor or smoke. Breeders have developed cats with flowing and luxuriant silky coats which require daily grooming, for they cannot be kept in condition by the cat itself.

PERSIAN GULF, or **Arabian Gulf**, an arm of the Arabian Sea between Iran and Arabia. About 550mi long and 120mi wide, the gulf is entered from the Gulf of Oman by the Straits of Hormuz. The bordering regions of Iran, Kuwait, Saudi Arabia, Bahrain, Qatar and the United Arab Emirates contain more than half the world's oil and natural gas resources.

PERSIAN WARS (500–449 BC), wars between Greek states and the Persian empire. Athenian support of the revolt of Greek states within the empire precipitated Persian offensives in Greece. However, by 449 BC Greek strength had secured Europe from further Persian invasions. (See GREECE, ANCIENT.)

PERSPIRATION, or **sweat**, watery fluid secreted by the SKIN as a means of reducing body temperature. Sweating is common in hot climates, after EXERCISE and in the resolution of FEVER, where the secretion and subsequent evaporation of sweat allow the skin and thus the body to be cooled. Humid atmospheres and high secretion rates delay the evaporation, leaving perspiration on the surface. Excessive fluid loss in sweat, and of salt in the abnormal sweat of CYSTIC FIBROSIS, may lead to SUNSTROKE. Most sweating is regulated by the HYPOTHALAMUS and autonomic NERVOUS SYSTEM. But there is also a separate system of sweat glands, especially on the palms, which secretes at times of stress. *Hyperidrosis* is a condition of abnormally profuse sweating.

PERTUSSIS. See WHOOPING COUGH.

Official name: Republic of Peru
Capital: Lima
Area: 496,093sq mi
Population: 16,820,000
Languages: Spanish, Quechua, Aymara
Religion: Roman Catholic
Monetary unit(s): 1 Sol = 100 centavos
PERU, third-largest nation in South America. It has a mountainous backbone and a 1,400mi coastline bordering the Pacific.

Land. Peru is divided into three geographical regions. The coastal zone, averaging 40mi in width, contains a third of the population and most of the large cities. It is mainly arid, but fertile where irrigated by rivers flowing down from the mountains. The mountainous region (the *Sierra*) of the Andes consists of parallel ranges, some with peaks over 20,000ft. Although conditions are harsh, over half the population live in the Sierra. The *Montaña*, consisting of the lower slopes of the E Andes and the E plains, forms part of the tropical forest of the Amazon basin. Rainfall is very low (less than 2in per year) in the coastal zone, moderate in the Sierra and heavy (100in or more) in the E. An earthquake in 1970 was the hemisphere's worst natural disaster, with about 50,000 dead.

People. Peru's population is composed of about 50% Amerindians, 40% *mestizos* (mixed white and Indian) and 10% whites. Spanish and Quechua are both official languages. There is a great division between the poor, less-educated Indians and *mestizos*, and the wealthier, predominantly white Spanish-speakers. About 30% of the population are illiterate.

Economy. Subsistence agriculture provides the means of livelihood for less than half of the population. Cotton, sugarcane and coffee are the main export crops. Peru is the world's leading fishing country, the main catch being *anchovetas*, which are processed into fishmeal, the country's chief export. Copper, iron, silver, phosphates and other minerals are mined and exported, and manufacturing industry is developing. The high mountains make communications difficult, and transportation problems hinder economic growth.

History. The ancient INCA Empire in Peru was destroyed by the Spanish conquistador PIZARRO (1532). Spanish rule, based at Lima, lasted until the revolutions led by BOLIVAR and SAN MARTÍN (1820–24). After independence power continued to be concentrated in the hands of a small number of wealthy landowners. This century has been characterized by unstable governments and military coups. In 1968 General Juan Velasco Alvarado instituted a program of social reform, suspended the constitution and seized US-owned companies. Alvarado was overthrown in a military coup in 1975 led by Francisco Morales Bermudez. The country returned to constitutional rule in 1980 and Fernando Belaúnd Terry (who had been president 1963–68) was reelected president.

PERUGIA, historic city in Umbria, central Italy. Once an Etruscan city, the walled, hilltop town is renowned for its architecture, paintings and archaeological museum. Its 13th-century municipal palace was decorated with paintings by Perugino, who lived in the city, assisted by his young pupil, Raphael.

PERUGINO (Pietro Vannucci, c1446–1523), Italian Renaissance painter, teacher of RAPHAEL. His frescoes in the Vatican SISTINE CHAPEL, including the *Christ Giving the Keys to St. Peter* (1481), established his fame. He worked much in Florence, and later in his native Umbria.

PERUZZI, Baldassare (1481–1536), Italian High Renaissance architect and painter. In Rome he built the Villa Farnesina, which he decorated with illusionist paintings (1508–11), and the Mannerist Palazzo Massimo (1532–36).

PESCADORES, group of about 64 small islands, about 50sq mi of land area, belonging to Taiwan, in the Formosa strait. The chief occupations are fishing and farming.

PESTALOZZI, Johann Heinrich (1746–1827), famous Swiss educator. At his school at Yverdon he stressed the importance of the individual, and based his methods on the child's direct experience, rather than mechanical learning. His teacher-training methods also became renowned. *How Gertrude Teaches Her Children* (1801) was his most influential work.

PESTICIDE, any substance used to kill plants or animals responsible for economic damage to crops, either growing or under storage, or ornamental plants, or which prejudice the well-being of man and domestic or conserved wild animals. Pesticides are subdivided into INSECTICIDES (which kill insects); miticides (which kill mites); herbicides (which kill plants—see WEEDKILLER); FUNGICIDES (which kill fungi), and rodenticides (which kill rats and mice). Substances used in the treatment of infectious BACTERIAL DISEASES are not generally regarded as pesticides. The efficient control of pests is of enormous economic importance for man, particularly as farming becomes more intensive. A major question with all pesticides is the possibility of unfortunate environmental side effects (see ECOLOGY; POLLUTION).

PÉTAIN, Henri Philippe (1856–1951), French WWI hero who became chief of state in the collaborationist VICHY regime (1940). Famous for his defense of Verdun (1916), he was made chief-of-staff (1917), and subsequently held important military offices. In 1934 he served briefly as war minister. Recalled from his post as ambassador to Spain in June 1940, he became premier and negotiated an armistice with the Nazis. As head of the Vichy government, he aided the Nazis, and in 1945 was tried for treason and sentenced to life imprisonment.

PETER, name of three tsars of Russia. **Peter I, the Great** (1672–1725) became joint tsar in 1682 and sole tsar in 1696. As a young man he traveled in W Europe (1697–98), learning techniques of war and industry and recruiting experts to bring back to Russia. His war against Turkey was intended to gain access to the Mediterranean, and the long conflict with Sweden (1700–21) led to Russian domination of the Baltic Sea. He established his new capital of St. Petersburg on the Baltic, as a symbol of his policy of westernization. Domestically, he introduced sweeping military, administrative and other reforms. A man of enormous size, strength and demonic energy, Peter was also savage in the exercise of power, and although he modernized, reformed and strengthened Russia, it was at great cost. **Peter II** (1715–1730) ruled from 1727. **Peter III** (1728–1762) ruled in 1762.

PETER, Epistles of, two New Testament letters, traditionally attributed to St. PETER. The first is written to encourage persecuted Christians in Asia Minor; the second closely parallels the Epistle of JUDE and refers to the Second Coming. The authorship is doubtful, particularly of the second, which some scholars date c150 AD and which was admitted late to the CANON.

PETER, PAUL AND MARY, US folksinging group. The trio of Peter Yarrow (1938–   ), Mary Travers (1937–   ) and Paul Stookey (1937–   ) was formed in 1962 and soon became a major force in the folk music boom of the early 1960s.

PETER, Saint (Simon Peter; d. c64 AD), leader of the 12 APOSTLES, and regarded by Roman Catholics as the first pope. A Galilean fisherman when Jesus called him to be a disciple, he was a dominating but impulsive figure, and denied Jesus after his arrest. He played a leading role in the early Church, especially in Jerusalem, as related in Acts. By tradition, he died a martyr at Rome.

PETER I (1844–1921), king of Serbia. A Serbian prince, he spent years in exile, and joined the anti-Turkish Herzegovinian revolt in 1875. He became an honorary senator of Montenegro in 1883, and was elected king of Serbia in 1903.

PETER II (1923–1970), king of Yugoslavia. On the death of his father ALEXANDER I his cousin governed as regent (1934–41). Peter fled to London after the Nazi invasion (1941), and set up an exile government. In 1945 Yugoslavia became a republic, and Peter a pretender.

PETER LOMBARD. See LOMBARD, PETER.

PETERLOO MASSACRE, name applied to the meeting held Aug. 16, 1819, in St. Peter's Fields, Manchester, England. When 60,000 radicals demonstrated peacefully to demand a reform of Parliament, the local magistrates, fearing a riot, ordered the militia to stop the meeting. Their cavalry support charged the crowd, killing 11 and wounding over 400.

PETERSON, Oscar (1925–   ), Canadian-born virtuoso jazz pianist who became an instant jazz celebrity with his first recordings, such as *Oscar's Blues* (1947). He has recorded both with his own eminent trio and with many of the most highly regarded contemporary jazz musicians.

PETERSON, Roger Tory (1908–   ), US naturalist. Considered to be the foremost ornithologist of his time in the US, Peterson was associated with the National Audubon Society (from 1934). Among his many books was the best-selling *Guide to the Birds* (1934), *A Field Guide to Western Birds* (1941) and *Penguins* (1979).

PETER THE HERMIT (c1050–1115), French monk who preached the First CRUSADE (1095). He led an army into Asia Minor which was annihilated, and later played an undistinguished part at Antioch and Jerusalem.

PETIPA, Marius (1819–1910), French dancer and choreographer who created the modern classical ballet. An outstanding dancer and mime, he joined the Russian ballet at St. Petersburg in 1847, becoming chief choreographer in 1869. There he created over 60 full-length ballets, including *The Nutcracker*, *Swan Lake* and *The Sleeping Beauty*.

PETIT, Roland (1924–   ), French dancer and choreographer. A founder (1945) and premier danseur of Les Ballets des Champs-Élysées, in 1948 he formed Les Ballets de Paris. He choreographed *Carmen* (1949), *La Croqueuse de Diamants* (1950) and many other ballets for stage and film.

PETITION OF RIGHT, document presented to CHARLES I of England by Parliament (1628) in protest against his arbitrary fiscal methods. It asserted four principles: no taxation without parliamentary consent; no imprisonment of subjects without due legal cause; no billeting of soldiers in private houses without payment; no declaring of MARTIAL LAW in peacetime. Accepted but later disregarded by the king, it represents a landmark in English constitutional history.

PETRARCH (Francesco Petrarca; 1304–1374), Italian poet and early HUMANIST. Supported by influential patrons, he spent his life in study, travel and writing. He wrote poetry, epistles and other prose works in Latin, but also much in vernacular Italian, of which he is one of the earliest masters. He himself rated his Latin works highest, but his great fame now rests on the Italian *Canzoniere*, mostly sonnets inspired by his love for the enigmatic Laura, who ied of plague in 1348.

PETRELS, seabirds of the tubenosed-bird order, Procellariiformes, particularly the typical petrels and shearwaters of the family Procellariidae. All have webbed feet and hooked bills, with nostrils opening through horny tubes on the upper mandible. They are marine birds which swim and fly expertly, feeding far from the shore on fish, squids and offal. Normally they go ashore only to breed.

PETRIFIED FOREST NATIONAL PARK, a park of 147sq mi in E Ariz. The fossil remains of a TRIASSIC forest are exposed on the surface, creating the largest display of petrified wood in the world.

PETROCHEMICALS, chemicals made from PETROLEUM and NATURAL GAS, i.e., all organic chemicals, plus the inorganic substances carbon black, sulfur, ammonia and hydrogen peroxide. Many petrochemicals are still made also from other raw materials, but the petrochemical industry has grown rapidly since about 1920. Polymers, detergents, solvents and nitrogen fertilizers are major products.

PETROLEUM, naturally-occurring mixture of HYDROCARBONS, usually liquid "crude oil," but sometimes taken to include NATURAL GAS. Petroleum is believed to be formed from organic debris, chiefly of plankton and simple plants, which has been rapidly buried in fine-grained sediment under marine conditions unfavorable to oxidation. After some biodegradation, increasing temperature and pressure cause CRACKING, and oil is produced. As the source rock is compacted, oil and water are forced out, and slowly migrate to porous reservoir rocks, chiefly sandstone or limestone. Finally, secondary migration occurs within the reservoir as the oil coagulates to form a pool, generally capped by impervious strata, and often associated with natural gas. Some oil seeps to the earth's surface: this was used by the early Mesopotamian civilizations. The first oil well was drilled in W Pa. in 1859. The industry thus begun has grown so fast that it now supplies about half the world's energy, as well as the raw materials for PETROCHEMICALS. Modern technology has made possible oil-well drilling to a depth of 5km, and deep-sea wells in 150m of water. Rotary drilling is used, with pressurized mud to carry the rock to the surface and to prevent escape of oil. When the well is completed, the oil rises to the surface, usually under its own pressure, though pumping may be required. The chief world oil-producing regions are the Persian Gulf, the US (mainly Tex., La., Okla. and Cal.), the USSR, N and W Africa, and Venezuela. After removing salt and water, the petroleum is refined by fractional DISTILLATION producing the fractions GASOLINE, KEROSENE, diesel oil, fuel oil, lubricating oil, and ASPHALT. Undesirable compounds may be removed by solvent extraction, treatment with sulfuric acid, etc., and less valuable components converted into more valuable ones by cracking, reforming, alkylation and polymerization. The chemical composition of crude petroleum is chiefly alkanes, saturated alicyclic compounds, and aromatic compounds, (see HYDROCARBONS) with some sulfur compounds, oxygen compounds (carboxylic acids and phenols), nitrogen and salt. (See also OIL SHALE.)

PETROLEUM INDUSTRY, US, comprises firms engaged in producing, transporting, refining and selling oil and natural gas. Edwin L. Drake drilled the first oil well at Titusville, Pa., in 1859 and began a boom in oil production as new fields were developed and the base for huge fortunes was established. John D. ROCKEFELLER expanded part-ownership of an oil refinery into an empire, the Standard Oil Co.—some 40 firms organized into a trust—that by the 1880s controlled almost the entire oil refining capacity of the US. The Supreme Court dissolved the trust in 1911. Many former trust firms merged into organizations that have become the giant oil corporations of today. With development of the gasoline engine, oil—until then used mainly for kerosene—became the world's most important product and, beginning in the 1950s, the prime raw material in chemical and fertilizer production. Although the US possessed major oil resources, to meet worldwide demand oil firms leased and developed oil fields throughout the world, but gradually ceded majority control to foreign governments as the fields were nationalized after WWII. With the formation of OPEC in 1960, US companies also lost control over oil pricing, although they still maintain hegemony in transport and refining. Oil is the largest single industry in the US. Six oil companies are listed among the ten largest US industrial corporations: Exxon, Mobile, Texaco, Standard Oil of Ohio, Gulf, and Atlantic Richfield.

PETROLOGY, branch of geology concerned with the history, composition, occurrence, properties and classification of rocks. (See GEOLOGY; ROCKS.)

PETRONIUS ARBITER, Gaius (d. 66 AD), Roman satirist. He became NERO'S "Arbiter of Taste," but fell from favor and committed suicide. *Trimalchio's Dinner* is the best-known fragment of his *Satyricon*, a sensual, amoral and often obscene romance.

PETTY, Richard (1937–   ), US stock car racer. The greatest money-winner that auto-racing has produced, he earned over $3 million from more than 200 victories on the NASCAR circuit and is a seven-time Winston Cup Grand National champion.

PEVSNER, Antoine (1886–1962), Russian-born sculptor who studied in Paris 1911–13 and settled there from 1922. In 1920 he launched CONSTRUCTIVISM with his brother NAUM GABO in Moscow. Light and space play important roles in his sculptures.

PEWTER, class of ALLOYS consisting chiefly of TIN, now hardened with copper and antimony, and usually containing lead. Roman pewter was high in lead and darkened with age. Pewter has been used for bowls, drinking vessels and candlesticks.

PEYOTE, *Lophophora williamsii* and related cactus species, native to Texas and Mexico. The cut, dried tops are chewed by Indians to release the hallucinogenic drug MESCALINE. This habit was first described in 1560. Family: Cactaceae.

PHALANX, ancient Greek infantry formation, consisting of rows of eight men, each heavily armed with an overlapping shield and long pike. PHILIP II of Macedon developed a phalanx 16 men deep, which his son ALEXANDER THE GREAT used in defeating the Persians. Only after defeat by Rome in 168 BC did the phalanx become outmoded.

PHANEROZOIC, the eon of visible life, the period of time represented by rock strata in which skeletonized FOSSILS appear, running from about 570 million years ago through to the present and containing the PALEOZOIC, MESOZOIC and CENOZOIC eras. (See also CRYPTOZOIC; GEOLOGY; PRECAMBRIAN.)

PHARISEES, an ancient Jewish sect devoted to strict observance of the Holy Law and strongly opposed to pagan practices absorbed by Judaism, and to the SADDUCEES. Their moral fervor and initially progressive nature made them an important political force. Tradition has made them synonymous with hypocrisy and self-righteousness, but Jesus only attacked the debasement of their ideals.

PHARMACOLOGY, the study of DRUGS, their chemistry, mode of action, routes of absorption, excretion METABOLISM, interaction, toxicity and side-effects. New drugs, based on older drugs, traditional remedies, chance observations etc., are tested for safety and efficacy, and manufactured by the pharmaceutical industry. The dispensing of drugs is PHARMACY. Drug prescription is the cornerstone of the medical treatment of DISEASE.

PHARAOH, Hebrew form of the title of the kings of ancient Egypt. The term (actually *per-'o*: great house) described his palace and, by association, the king. The Egyptians believed the pharoah to be the personification of the gods HORUS and, later, AMON.

PHAROS, a peninsula near Alexandria, Egypt, whose lighthouse was one of the SEVEN WONDERS OF THE WORLD. The tower of white marble was completed about 280 BC. From pictures it seems to have been about 400ft high with a ramp leading to the top, where a beacon was kept burning day and night. It stood for some 1,600 years, until demolished by an earthquake in 1302.

PHEASANTS, game birds of the 16 genera of subfamily Phasianinae. They originated in Asia, but are now found all over the world. They are ground birds which scratch the earth for seeds and insects. When they fly they rise almost vertically on short broad wings. Males are usually brightly-colored, and many species are kept as ornamentals.

PHELPS, William Lyon (1865–1943), US literary critic and teacher of modern drama and fiction during his 41 years at Yale. He was a very popular lecturer and columnist.

PHENOMENOLOGY, a school of philosophy based largely on a method of approach developed by Edmund HUSSERL. Unlike the NATURALIST, who describes objects without reference to the subjectivity of the observer, the phenomenologist attempts to describe the "invariant essences" of objects as objects "intended" by consciousness. As a first step toward achieving this, he performs the "phenomenological reduction," which involves as far as possible a suspension of all preconceptions about experience. Phenomenology has become a leading tendency in 20th-century philosophy.

PHENOTYPE, the appearance of, and characteristics actually present in an organism, as contrasted with its GENOTYPE (its genetic make-up). Heterozygotes and homozygotes with a dominant GENE have the same phenotype but differing genotypes. Organisms may also have an identical genotype but differing phenotype due to environmental influences.

PHENYLKETONURIA (PKU), inherited DISEASE in which phenylalanine METABOLISM is disordered due to lack of an ENZYME. It rapidly causes MENTAL RETARDATION, as well as irritability and vomiting, unless DIETARY FOODS low in phenylalanine are given soon after birth and indefinitely. Screening of the newborn by urine tests (with confirmation by blood tests) facilitates prompt treatment.

PHI BETA KAPPA, the most prestigious

honor society for college and university
dents in the liberal arts and sciences.
embers are generally elected in their third
fourth year on the basis of academic
hievements. The oldest Greek letter
ciety in the US, the fraternity was
unded at William and Mary College, Va.
1776.

IDIAS (c500–c432 BC), perhaps the
eatest Greek sculptor, whose work
owed the human form idealized and with
eat nobility. As none of his works survive,
s reputation rests on contemporary
counts, on Roman copies and on the
RTHENON statues made under his
rection. Under Pericles he had artistic
ntrol over the ACROPOLIS.

HILADELPHIA, historic city in SE Pa.,
e fourth largest in the US. It is a key
ipping port with important metal,
achinery, clothing, petroleum, chemical
d food industries. It has long been a
nter for publishing, education and the
ts, and was one of the first planned cities.
s founder, William PENN, created his
lony in 1682 as a "holy experiment" in
hich all sects could find freedom.
hiladelphia (Greek: brotherly love)
tracted immigrants and brought com-
erce that made it the largest and
ealthiest of US cities. In the Old City,
ar the Delaware R, is the INDEPENDENCE
ATIONAL PARK, whose buildings include
DEPENDENCE HALL, where both the Declar-
ion of Independence and the Constitution
ere adopted. The city was US capital
790–1800; subsequent corruption in
overnment and growth of slums ac-
mpanied a decline. In the 1950s massive
rban renewal projects were initiated.
oday the city has the world's largest
eshwater port, linked with the Atlantic by
e Delaware R. Philadelphia is part of an
rban complex stretching from Boston to
Vashington D.C. Pop 1,688,210.

HILEMON, Epistle to, New Testament
tter written c61 AD by St. PAUL to
hilemon, a Colossian Christian, asking
im to forgive his runaway slave Onesimus,
ho had become a Christian and who
eturned with the letter.

HILIP, Saint, one of the 12 APOSTLES. Born
Bethsaida, he was according to legend
artyred at Hierapolis in Phrygia.

HILIP, six kings of France. Philip I
1052–1108), reigned from 1059. He
nlarged his small territories and prevented
nion of England and Normandy. His
ractice of simony and his disputed second
narriage led him into conflict with the
apacy. **Philip II** (Philip Augustus;
165–1223), reigned from 1179, estab-

lished France as a European power. He
joined the CRUSADES, only to quarrel with
RICHARD the Lion Heart and seize his
French territories. By 1204 he had added
Normandy, Maine, Anjou, Tourraine and
Brittany to his domain, in which he set up
new towns and a system of royal bailiffs.
Philip III (the Bold; 1245–85), reigned from
1270, secured Auvergne, Poitou and
Toulouse for France. **Philip IV** (the Fair;
1268–1314), reigned from 1285, added
Navarre and Champagne to the kingdom,
but attempts to overrun Flanders led to his
defeat at Courtrai in 1302. He seized Pope
BONIFACE VIII in a quarrel about taxation of
clergy, obtained the election of CLEMENT V, a
puppet pope residing at Avignon (see
BABYLONIAN CAPTIVITY), and seized the land
of the crusading order of the KNIGHTS
TEMPLAR. **Philip V** (1294–1322), reigned
from 1317, invoked the SALIC LAW of male
succession and carried out reforms to
strengthen royal power. The succession in
1328 of **Philip VI** (1293–1350) through the
Salic Law was disputed and led to the
HUNDRED YEARS' WAR against England.

PHILIP II (382–336 BC), king of
Macedonia from c359 and father of
ALEXANDER THE GREAT. His powerfully
reorganized army (see PHALANX) conquered
N Greece, acquiring the gold mines of
Thrace and advancing S as far as
Thermopylae, the key to central Greece. He
defeated Athens and Thebes at Chaeronea
(338) and became ruler of all Greece. His
reign marked the end of the independent
and warring city-states.

PHILIP, five kings of Spain. Philip I
(1478–1506) was archduke of Austria,
duke of Burgundy and inheritor of the
Netherlands. He became first Hapsburg
king of Castile in 1506, ruling jointly with
his wife Joanna. **Philip II** (1527–1598),
crowned in 1556, united the Iberian
peninsula and ruled an empire which
included Milan, Naples, Sicily, the
Netherlands and vast tracts of the New
World. Though son of the Holy Roman
Emperor CHARLES V, he never became
emperor. A fanatical Catholic, he married
MARY I of England, supported the
Inquisition and tried in vain to crush the
Protestant Netherlands. He was recognized
king (Philip I) of Portugal in 1580, but lost
naval supremacy to England after the
ARMADA (1588). His son **Philip III**
(1578–1621), crowned in 1598, made peace
with England and the Netherlands but was
frustrated in Italy by the THIRTY YEARS'
WAR. **Philip IV** (1605–1655), crowned in
1621, son of Philip III and last Hapsburg
king of Spain, was the patron of VELÁZQUEZ.

He attempted unsuccessfully to dominate Europe by fighting France, Germany and Holland in the THIRTY YEARS' WAR, but lost Portugal in the process (1640). **Philip V** (1683–1746), crowned in 1700, founder of the BOURBON line, restored influence but his accession in 1700 led to the war of the SPANISH SUCCESSION. By the Treaty of UTRECHT (1713) his title was recognized, though he ceded possessions in Italy and the Netherlands to Austria.

PHILIP, Prince, Duke of Edinburgh (1921–   ), consort of Queen ELIZABETH II of England. The son of Prince Andrew of Greece and Princess Alice of Battenburg, he renounced his Greek title, became a British subject and married the then Princess Elizabeth in 1947; he was created prince in 1957.

PHILIP NERI, Saint (Filippo Neri; 1515–1595), a leading figure of the COUNTER-REFORMATION, and founder of the secular order of the Congregation of the Oratory which was devoted to care of the poor and sick. He was canonized in 1622.

PHILIPPIANS, Epistle to the, NEW TESTAMENT letter written by St. PAUL from prison in Rome (c62 AD) to the Christians at PHILIPPI. whom he himself had converted. He encourages them affectionately, and quotes an early hymn on Christ's humility.

Official name: Republic of the Philippines
Capital: Quezon City
Area: 115,830sq mi
Population: 39,769,000
Languages: Tagalog; English; Spanish
Religions: Roman Catholic; Muslim; Protestant
Monetary unit(s): 1 Philippine peso=100 centavos

PHILIPPINES, republic in the SW Pacific Ocean, between the equator and the Tropic of Cancer, comprising more than 7,000 islands.

Land. The islands range in size from tiny rocks to LUZON (41,845sq mi), the largest. The other principal islands include Mindanao, Samar, Negros, Panay, Mindoro and Leyte. Only 730 of the islands are inhabited, and 11 of these account for most

of the total land area and most of the population. All the larger islands are volcanic and mountainous. The climate is the lowlands is humid, with temperature averaging 80°F.

People. The population is predominantly of Malay origin, but includes groups of Chinese, Indonesians, MOROS, Negritos (descendants of the earliest inhabitants) and people of mixed blood. Filipino, based on Tagalog, was adopted as the national language in 1946; numerous native languages are also spoken. The majority of the population is Roman Catholic.

Economy. About 55% of Filipinos work on the land. The leading crops are rice, coconut, corn and sugar. Abaca (manilla hemp) and lumber are important exports. The islands are rich in mineral resources, the most important of which are lead, nickel, zinc, copper and cobalt. Manila, the largest city is the main industrial center. Manufactures include wood products, processed foods, textiles, aluminum and tobacco.

History. The islands were first visited by Europeans on MAGELLAN's expedition (1521), and were later named in honor of the future Philip II of Spain. By the 1570s Spanish rule there was secure and lasted until the end of the SPANISH-AMERICAN WAR (1898), when the Philippines were ceded to the US. A revolutionary nationalist movement, under the leadership of Emilio AGUINALDO, helped the US defeat Spain. The issue of independence loomed large in US politics until the establishment (1935) of the internally self-governing Commonwealth of the Philippines, with Manuel QUEZON as president. Occupied by the Japanese during WWII, the country was made an independent republic in 1946, with Manuel ROXAS and later Ramon MAGSAYSAY as presidents. Communist revolutionary movements have been active since 1949. The powers of the presidency were greatly increased (1973) with the introduction of martial law under President Marcos and his family. Martial law was nominally ended in 1981.

PHILISTINES, a non-Semitic people who lived in PALESTINE from the 12th century BC. They were hostile to the Israelites and for a time held considerable power. The term "philistine" may nowadays denote an uncultured person.

PHILLIPS CURVE, in economics, describes the mathematical relationship between the rate of price change and the percentage of unemployment, and between unemployment and inflation. The curve was developed by Prof. A.W. Phillips of the

London School of Economics.

PHILO JUDEAS (c20 BC–c50 AD), Alexandrine Jewish philosopher whose attempt to fuse Greek philosophical thought with Jewish Biblical religion had a profound influence on both Christian and Jewish theology.

PHILOLOGY, the study of literature and the language employed in it. The term is used also for those branches of LINGUISTICS concerned with the evolution of languages, especially those dealing with the interrelationships between different languages (comparative philology).

PHILOSOPHES, 18th-century French school of thinkers, scientists and men of letters who believed that the methodology of science should be applied to contemporary social, economic and political problems. Inspired by DESCARTES and the school of SCEPTICISM, they included MONTESQUIEU, VOLTAIRE, DIDEROT and ROUSSEAU.

PHILOSOPHY (from *philosophia*, lover of wisdom), term applied to any body of doctrine or opinion as to the nature and ultimate significance of human experience considered as a whole. It is perhaps more properly applied to the critical evaluation of all claims to knowledge—including its own *and* anything that is presupposed about its own nature and task. In this latter respect, it is widely argued, philosophy differs fundamentally from all other disciplines. What philosophy "is" (what methods the philosopher should employ, what criteria he should appeal to, and what goals he should set himself) is as perennial a question for the philosopher as any other. Traditionally, philosophers have concerned themselves with four main topic areas: LOGIC, the study of the formal structure of valid arguments; METAPHYSICS, usually identified with ontology—the study of the nature of "Being" or ultimate reality; EPISTEMOLOGY, or theory of knowledge, sometimes treated as a branch of metaphysics; and axiology, or theory of value—including AESTHETICS, the philosophy of taste (especially as applied to the arts), ETHICS, or moral philosophy, and political philosophy (see POLITICAL SCIENCE). In modern times, as traditional philosophy has yielded up the subject matters of the natural sciences, of other descriptive studies such as PSYCHOLOGY and SOCIOLOGY, and of such formal studies as logic and mathematics, all once numbered among its legitimate concerns, philosophers have become increasingly conscious of their critical role. Most now tend to interest themselves in special philosophies, e.g., philosophy *of* logic, philosophy *of* science (see SCIENTIFIC METHOD) and philosophy *of* religion. The first attempts to answer distinctively philosophical questions were made from about 600 BC by certain Greek philosophers known collectively as the PRESOCRATICS; their intellectual heirs were SOCRATES, PLATO and ARISTOTLE, the three towering figures in ancient philosophy. Later ancient philosophies include EPICUREANISM, STOICISM and NEOPLATONISM. Foremost among medieval philosophers were St. AUGUSTINE and St. Thomas AQUINAS. (See also SCHOLASTICISM; THOMISM; NOMINALISM; REALISM.) Modern philosophy begins with René DESCARTES and a parallel development of RATIONALISM and EMPIRICISM culminating in the philosophy of Immanuel KANT. The IDEALISM of G. F. W. HEGEL and the POSITIVISM of Auguste COMTE were major forces in 19th-century philosophy. The DIALECTICAL MATERIALISM of Karl MARX had its roots in both. (See also MATERIALISM.) The philosophical orientations of most 20th-century philosophers are developments of MARXISM, KANTIANISM, LOGICAL POSITIVISM, PRAGMATISM, PHENOMENOLOGY or EXISTENTIALISM.

PHLEBITIS, INFLAMMATION of the VEINS, usually causing THROMBOSIS (thrombophlebitis) and obstruction to BLOOD flow. It is common in the superficial veins of the legs, especially VARICOSE VEINS, and visceral veins close to inflamed organs or ABSCESSES. Phlebitis may complicate intravenous INJECTIONS of DRUGS or indwelling cannulae for intravenous fluids. Pain, swelling and ERYTHEMA over the vein are typical with it becoming a thick tender cord. Occasionally, phlebitis indicates systemic DISEASE (e.g., CANCER).

PHLOGISTON, the elementary principle postulated by G. H. STAHL to be lost from substances when they burn. The phlogiston concept provided 18th-century CHEMISTRY with its unifying principle. The phlogiston theory of COMBUSTION found general acceptance until displaced by its inverse—LAVOISIER's oxygen theory.

PHNOM-PENH, capital and river port of Kampuchea (formerly Cambodia), on the Tônlé Sap R where it joins the Mekong. It is the country's administrative, commercial, communications and cultural center. Founded in the 14th century, it was first made Khmer capital in the 1430s, Phnom Penh was the focus of a massive civil war campaign 1970–75. Pop 200,000.

PHOBIA, a NEUROSIS characterized by exaggerated ANXIETY on confrontation with a specific object or situation; or the anxiety itself. Phobia is sometimes linked with OBSESSIONAL NEUROSIS, sometimes with HYSTERIA; in each case the object of phobia is usually merely symbolic. Classic phobias are AGORAPHOBIA and CLAUSTROPHOBIA.

PHOENICIA, ancient territory corresponding roughly to the coastal region of modern Lebanon, inhabited by the Phoenicians (originally called Canaanites) from c3000 BC. It included the city-states of SIDON and TYRE. Being on the trade route between Asia Minor, Mesopotamia and Egypt, Phoenicia became an important center of commerce. By 1200 BC, with the decline of Egyptian dominance, Phoenicians led the Mediterranean world in trading and seafaring. They colonized many Mediterranean areas which later became independent states, such as CARTHAGE and UTICA. From the 9th century BC Phoenicia was intermittently dominated by ASSYRIA, and in 538 came under Persian rule. By the time ALEXANDER THE GREAT conquered Tyre (332) Phoenician civilization had largely been eclipsed. The Greeks were the inheritors of their outstanding cultural legacy—most notably their alphabetic script, from which the modern Western alphabet is descended.

PHOENIX, largest city and capital of Ariz., seat of Maricopa Co. on the Salt R. It is a major center for agricultural marketing, electronics research and production, and manufactures such as aluminum products, aircraft, chemicals and textiles. Pop 764,911.

PHONETICS, the systematic examination of the sounds made in speech, concerned not only with the classification of these sounds but also with physical and physiological aspects of their production and transmission, and with their reception and interpretation by the listener. **Phonology,** the study of phonetic patterns in languages, is of importance in comparative LINGUISTICS. **Phonemics** is the study of PHONEMES.

PHOSGENE, or **carbonyl chloride** ($COCl_2$), colorless, reactive gas, hydrolyzed by water, made by catalytic combination of CARBON monoxide and CHLORINE, and used to make RESINS and DYES. Highly toxic, it was a poison gas in WWI.

PHOSPHATES, derivatives of phosphoric acid (see PHOSPHORUS): either phosphate ESTERS, or salts containing the various phosphate ions. Like SILICATES, these are numerous and complex, the simplest being orthophosphate, PO_4^{3-}. Of many phosphate minerals, the most important is APATITE. This is treated with sulfuric acid or phosphoric acid to give calcium dihydrogenphosphate ($Ca[H_2PO_4]_2$), known as **superphosphate**—the major phosphate FERTILIZER. The alkaline trisodium phosphate (TSP) (Na_3PO_4) is used as a cleansing agent and water softener. Phosphates are used in making GLASS, SOAPS and DETERGENTS.

PHOSPHOR, a substance exhibiting LUMINESCENCE, i.e., emitting LIGHT (or other ELECTROMAGNETIC RADIATION) on nonthermal stimulation. Important phosphors include those used in TELEVISION picture tubes (where stimulation is by ELECTRONS) and those coated on the inside wall of fluorescent lamp tubes to convert ULTRAVIOLET RADIATION into visible light.

PHOSPHORUS (P), reactive nonmetal in Group VA of the PERIODIC TABLE, occurring naturally as APATITE. This is heated with silica and coke, and elementary phosphorus is produced. Phosphorus has three main allotropes (see ALLOTROPY): white phosphorus, a yellow waxy solid composed of P_4 molecules, spontaneously flammable in air, soluble in carbon disulfide, and very toxic; red phosphorus, a dark-red powder, formed by heating white phosphorus, less reactive, and insoluble in carbon disulfide; and black phosphorus, a flaky solid, resembling GRAPHITE, consisting of corrugated layers of atoms. Phosphorus burns in air to give the trioxide and the pentoxide, and also reacts with the halogens, sulfur and some metals. It is used in making matches, ammunition, pesticides, steels, phosphor bronze, phosphoric acid and phosphate fertilizers. Phosphorus is of great biological importance. AW 31.0 mp (wh) 44°C, bp (wh) 280°C, sg (wh) 1.82, (red) 2.20, (bl) 2.69. Phosphorus forms phosphorus (trivalent) and phosphoric (pentavalent) compounds. **Phosphine** (PH_3), is a colorless, flammable gas, highly toxic, and with an odor of garlic. It is a weak BASE, resembling AMMONIA, and forms phosphonium salts (PH_4^+). **Phosphoric acid** (H_3PO_4), is a colorless crystalline solid, forming a syrupy aqueous solution. It is used to flavor food, in dyeing, to clean metals, and to make PHOSPHATES. **Phosphorus Pentoxide** (P_4O_{10}), is a white powder made by burning phosphorus in excess air. It is very deliquescent (forming phosphoric acid), and is used as a dehydrating agent.

PHOTOCHEMISTRY, branch of PHYSICAL CHEMISTRY dealing with chemical reactions that produce LIGHT (see CHEMILUMINESCENCE; COMBUSTION), or that are initiated by light (visible or ultraviolet). Important examples include PHOTOSYNTHESIS, PHOTOGRAPHY and bleaching by sunlight. One PHOTON of light of suitable wavelength may be absorbed by a molecule, raising it to an electronically excited state. Re-emission may occur by fluorescence or phosphorescence (see

LUMINESCENCE), the energy may be transferred to another molecule, or a reaction may occur, commonly DISSOCIATION to form FREE RADICALS. The *quantum yield,* or efficiency, of the reaction is the number of molecules of reactant used (or product formed) per photon absorbed; this may be very large for chain reactions. (See also FLASH PHOTOLYSIS; LASER; RADIATION CHEMISTRY.)

PHOTOELECTRIC CELL, a device with electrical properties which vary according to the LIGHT falling on it. There are three types: PHOTOVOLTAIC CELLS; PHOTOCONDUCTIVE DETECTORS and phototubes (see PHOTOELECTRIC EFFECT).

PHOTOELECTRIC EFFECT, properly **photoemissive effect,** the emission of ELECTRONS from a surface when struck by ELECTROMAGNETIC RADIATION such as LIGHT. In 1905 EINSTEIN laid one of the twin foundations of QUANTUM THEORY by explaining photoemission in terms of the action of individual PHOTONS. The effect is used in phototubes (ELECTRON TUBES having a photoemissive cathode), often employed as "electric eye" switches. Special types are used in image intensifiers and in the Image Orthicon TELEVISION camera. The Einstein photoelectric law is: $E_k = hv - \omega$
where E_k is the maximum kinetic energy of emitted electrons, h is Planck's constant, v is the frequency of the radiation and ω is the surface work function for photoemission.

PHOTOGRAPHY, the use of light-sensitive materials to produce permanent visible images (photographs). The most familiar photographic processes depend on the light-sensitivity of the SILVER halides. A photographic emulsion is a preparation of tiny crystals of these salts suspended in a thin layer of gelatin coated on a glass, film or paper support. On brief exposure to light in a CAMERA or other apparatus, a latent image in activated silver salt is formed wherever light has fallen on the emulsion. This image is made visible in development, when the activated silver halide crystals (but not the unexposed ones) are reduced to metallic silver (black) using a weak organic reducing agent (the developer). The silver image is then made permanent by fixing, in the course of which it becomes possible to examine the image in the light for the first time. Fixing agents (fixers) work by dissolving out the silver halide crystals which were not activated on exposure. The image made in this way is densest in silver where the original subject was brightest and lightest where the original was darkest; it is thus a "negative" image. To produce a positive image, the negative (which is usually made on a film or glass support) is itself made the original in the above process, the result being a positive "print" usually on a paper carrier. An alternative method of producing a positive image is to bleach away the developed image on the original film or plate before fixing, and reexpose the unactivated halide in diffuse light. This forms a second latent image which on development produces a positive image of the original subject (reversal processing).

The history of photography from the earliest work of NIÉPCE, DAGUERRE and Fox TALBOT to the present has seen successive refinements in materials, techniques and equipment. Photography became a popular hobby after EASTMAN first marketed roll film in 1889. The silver halides are sensitive to light only from the blue end of the SPECTRUM so that in the earliest photographs other colors appear dark. The color-sensitivity of emulsions was improved from the 1870s onward as small quantities of sensitizing dyes were incorporated. "Orthochromatic" plates became available after 1884 and "panchromatic" from 1906.

New sensitizing dyes also opened up the way to infrared and color photography. Modern "tripack" color films have three layers of emulsion, one each sensitive to blue, green and red light from the subject. Positive color transparencies are made using a reversal processing method in which the superposed, positive, silver images are replaced with yellow, magenta and cyan dyes respectively.

Motion-picture photography dates from 1890, when EDISON built a device to expose Eastman's roll film, and rapidly became an important art form (SEE MOTION PICTURES). Not all modern photographic methods employ the silver-halide process; XEROGRAPHY and the BLUEPRINT and OZALID processes work differently. FALSE-COLOR PHOTOGRAPHY and the diffusion process used in the Polaroid Land camera are both developments of the silver-halide process.

The photographers themselves have achieved a great diversity of pictorial results. The great portraitists, from Nadar and Julia Margaret Cameron to Richard AVEDON, have demonstrated an ability to breach the surface and capture the souls of their subjects. Documentary work, much of which has earned recognition as art, has ranged from the 19th-century western views of William Henry JACKSON and Timothy O'Sullivan to the scenes of war captured by witnesses from Matthew BRADY to Gene Smith and Robert CAPA. Those who helped establish photography as art included Alfred STIEGLITZ, Edward STEICHEN and

Paul STRAND. The natural world has been idealized in the fine prints of Edward WESTON, Ansel ADAMS and Eliot Porter. André Kertesz, Henri CARTIER-BRESSON and Robert Frank discovered art in the everyday movements of common men and women. Photography seems certain to remain the most expensive and experimental of the arts. (See also articles about many of the photographers mentioned above.)

PHOTOMETRY, the science of the measurement of LIGHT, particularly as it affects illumination engineering. Because the brightness experienced when light strikes the human EYE depends not only on the POWER conveyed by the radiation but also on the wavelength of the light (the visual sensation for a given power reaching a maximum at 555nm), a special arbitrary set of units is used in photometric calculations. In SI UNITS, the photometric base quantity is luminous intensity which measures the intensity of light radiated from a small source. The base unit of luminous intensity is the CANDELA (cd). The luminous flux (the photometric equivalent of the power radiating) from a point source is measured in lumens where 1 lumen (lm) is the flux radiating from a 1 cd source through a solid angle of steradian. The illuminance falling on a surface (formerly known as its illumination) is measured in luxes where 1 lux (lx) is the level of illuminance occurring when a luminous flux of 1 lm falls on each m² of the surface. Up to the 1970s considerable confusion reigned among scientists regarding the concepts and terminology best to be used in photometry and many alternative units—APOSTILBS, BLONDELS, FOOT-CANDLES and LAMBERTS—are still commonly encountered. (See also LUMINANCE.)

PHOTON, the quantum of electromagnetic energy (see QUANTUM THEORY), often thought of as the particle associated with LIGHT or other ELECTROMAGNETIC RADIATION. Its ENERGY is given by hv where h is the PLANCK CONSTANT and v the frequency of the radiation.

PHOTOSYNTHESIS, the process by which green plants convert the ENERGY of sunlight into chemical energy which is then stored as CARBOHYDRATE. Overall, the process may be written as:

$$6CO_2 + 6H_2O \xrightarrow{light} C_6H_{12}O_6 + 6O_2$$

Although in detail photosynthesis is a complex sequence of reactions, two principal stages can be identified. In the "light reaction," CHLOROPHYLL (the key chemical in the whole process) is activated by absorbing a quantum of LIGHT, initiating a sequence of reactions in which the energy-rich compounds ATP (adenosine triphosphate—see NUCLEOTIDES) and TPNH (the reduced form of triphosphopyridine nucleotide—TPN) are made, water being decomposed to give free oxygen in the process. In the second stage, the "dark reaction," the ATP and TPNH provide the energy for the assimilation of carbon dioxide gas, yielding a variety of SUGARS from which other sugars and carbohydrates, including STARCH, can be built up.

PHOTOVOLTAIC CELL, a device for converting LIGHT radiation into ELECTRICITY, used in LIGHT METERS and for providing spacecraft power supplies. The photovoltage is usually developed in a layer of SEMICONDUCTOR (e.g., SELENIUM) sandwiched between a transparent electrode and one providing support. (See also SOLAR CELL.)

PHRENOLOGY, study of the shape and detailed contours of the SKULL as indicators of personality, intelligence and individual characteristics. The method, developed by F. J. GALL and promoted in the UK and US by George Combe (1788–1858), had many 19th-century followers and may have contributed to the more enlightened treatment of offenders and the mentally ill. Today it has little scientific backing.

PHRYGIA, ancient region and sometime kingdom (8th–6th centuries BC) in present-day central Turkey. Its early kings included MIDAS and Gordius. Excavation shows the Phrygians to have been highly cultured. The Phrygian worship of CYBELE was taken over by the Greeks. (See also GORDIAN KNOT.)

PHYFE, Duncan (c1768–1854), US cabinetmaker, designer of the most distinctive US neoclassical furniture. He came to the US from Scotland in 1784, and based his work on European styles such as the SHERATON and the EMPIRE STYLE.

PHYLOGENY. See ONTOGENY AND PHYLOGENY.

PHYLUM. See TAXONOMY.

PHYSICAL CHEMISTRY, major branch of CHEMISTRY, in which the theories and methods of PHYSICS are applied to chemical systems. Physical chemistry underlies all the other branches of chemistry and includes theoretical chemistry. Its main divisions are the study of molecular structure; COLLOIDS; CRYSTALS; ELECTROCHEMISTRY; chemical EQUILIBRIUM; GAS laws; chemical kinetics; MOLECULAR WEIGHT determination; PHOTOCHEMISTRY; SOLUTION; SPECTROSCOPY, and chemical THERMODYNAMICS.

PHYSICAL THERAPY. See PHYSIOTHERAPY.

PHYSICS, originally, the knowledge of natural things (=natural science); now, the science dealing with the interaction of MATTER and ENERGY (but usually taken to exclude CHEMISTRY). Until the "scientific revolution" of the Renaissance, physics was a branch of PHILOSOPHY dealing with the natures of things. The physics of the heavens, for instance, was quite separate from (and often conflicted with) the descriptions of mathematical and positional ASTRONOMY. But from the time of GALILEO, and particularly through the efforts of HUYGENS and NEWTON, physics became identified with the mathematical description of nature; occult qualities were banished from physical science. Firm on its Newtonian foundation, classical physics gathered more and more phenomena under its wing until, by the late 19th century, comparatively few phenomena seemed to defy explanation. But the interpretation of these effects (notably BLACKBODY RADIATION and the PHOTOELECTRIC EFFECT) in terms of new concepts due to PLANCK and EINSTEIN involved the thoroughgoing reformulation of the fundamental principles of physical science (see QUANTUM THEORY; RELATIVITY). Physics today is divided into many specialisms, themselves subdivided many-fold. The principal of these are ACOUSTICS; ELECTRICITY and MAGNETISM; MECHANICS; NUCLEAR PHYSICS; OPTICS; QUANTUM MECHANICS; RELATIVITY, and THERMODYNAMICS.

PHYSIOCRATS, 18th-century French school of economists founded by François QUESNAY, who held that agriculture, rather than industry or commerce, was the basis of a nation's prosperity, and that land alone should be subject to tax. Their belief in a natural economic law, which merely required non-interference to be successful, is reflected in their famous formula *laissez faire* (let it be). The physiocrats influenced Adam SMITH.

PHYSIOLOGY, the study of function in living organisms. Based on knowledge of ANATOMY, physiology seeks to demonstrate the manner in which organs perform their tasks, and in which the body is organized and maintained in a state of HOMEOSTASIS. Normal responses to various stresses on the whole or on parts of an organism are studied. Important branches of physiology deal with RESPIRATION, BLOOD CIRCULATION, the NERVOUS SYSTEM, the DIGESTIVE SYSTEM, the KIDNEYS, the fluid and electrolyte balance, the ENDOCRINE GLANDS and METABOLISM. Methods of study include experimentation on anesthetized animals and on human volunteers. Knowledge and understanding of physiology is basic to MEDICINE and provides the physician with a perspective in which to view the body's disordered function in DISEASE.

PHYSIOTHERAPY, system of physical treatment for disease or disability. Active and passive muscle movement; electrical stimulation; balancing exercises; HEAT, ULTRAVIOLET or shortwave RADIATION, and manual vibration of the CHEST wall with postural drainage, are some of the techniques used. Rehabilitation after FRACTURE, SURGERY, STROKE or other neurological disease, and the treatment of LUNG infections (PNEUMONIA, BRONCHITIS), are among the aims.

PI (Greek π), the ratio between the circumference of a CIRCLE and its diameter. π is an IRRATIONAL NUMBER whose value to five decimal places is 3.14159. Approximate values of π have been known to several ancient civilizations, such as Babylonia, where the accepted value was 3.0.

PIAF, Edith (1915–1963), French singer of cabaret and music-hall. Born Edith Giovanna Gassion, she began singing for a living at 15 and won international fame with such songs as *Milord* and *Je ne regrette rien*.

PIAGET, Jean (1896–1980), Swiss psychologist whose theories of the mental development of children, though now often criticized, have been of paramount importance. His many books include *The Psychology of the Child* (1969), and *Biology and Knowledge* (1971).

PIANO, keyboard instrument in which depression of the keys causes the strings to be struck with hammers. These hammers rebound immediately after striking, so that the strings go on sounding their notes until the keys are released, when the strings' vibrations are stopped with dampers. Bartolommeo Cristofori made the first piano in 1709, and by 1800 it had overtaken the HARPSICHORD and the CLAVICHORD in popularity. Today the two basic types of piano are the upright piano with vertical strings, and the grand piano with horizontal strings, which has a range of seven octaves. Composers noted for their writing for the piano include C.P.E. BACH, MOZART, BEETHOVEN, CHOPIN, LISZT, and RACHMANINOV. (See also KEYBOARD INSTRUMENTS.)

PICARESQUE NOVEL, early type of the novel in which the episodic adventures of a roguish, antiheroical character are narrated in the first person. Of 16th-century Spanish origin, the picaresque novel was popular until the mid-1700s, and included notable

English examples such as Defoe's *Moll Flanders* (1722).

PICASSO, Pablo Ruiz y (1881–1973), Spanish-born French painter, sculptor, graphic artist and ceramist, considered by many the greatest artist of the 20th century. An extraordinarily precocious painter, after his melancholy "blue period" and his lyrical "rose period" (1901–06) he was influenced by African and Primitive art, as shown in *Les Demoiselles d'Avignon*, 1907. Together he and BRAQUE created CUBISM, 1907–14. His friends at this time included APOLLINAIRE, DIAGHILEV (for whom he made stage designs), and Gertrude STEIN. In 1921 he painted both the cubist *Three Musicians* and the classical *Three Women at the Fountain*. In the 1930s he adopted the style of SURREALISM, using it to horrify in the large anti-war canvas *Guernica*, 1937 (see GUERNICA). His later work employed cubist and surrealist forms and could be beautiful, tender or grotesque. His output was enormous and near the end of his life he produced a brilliant series of etchings.

PICCARD, Auguste Antoine (1884–1962) and **Jean Felix** (1884–1963), Swiss scientists who were twin brothers. Auguste, a physicist, set a world ballooning altitude record (1931), and an ocean-depth record (1953) in the BATHYSCAPHE that he designed. Jean, a chemist, measured cosmic radiation during a 57,000-foot balloon ascent (1934).

PICCOLO. See FLUTE.

PICKETT, George Edward (1825–1875), Confederate general in the US CIVIL WAR who led the disastrous assault (July 3, 1863) on Cemetery Ridge in the Battle of GETTYSBURG. Of the 15,000 Confederate troops who charged the Union line some 6,000 were killed. Pickett later suffered a second major defeat at the Battle of FIVE FORKS (April 1, 1865).

PICKETT, Wilson (1941–), US singer known for his raucous singing style and orange-trimmed purple jackets with ruffled lilac shirts. He recorded such hits as "You're So Fine" (1959) and "Sugar, Sugar" (1970).

PICKFORD, Mary (1893–1979), U movie actress, born Gladys Smith. Her rol in such films as *Daddy Long Legs*, under t direction of D. W. GRIFFITH, won her t title of "America's sweetheart." In 1919 s and her husband, Douglas FAIRBANK helped found United Artists.

PICKLE, food that has been preserved VINEGAR or BRINE to prevent the develo ment of putrefying BACTERIA. Spices a usually added for flavor. Cucumber onions, beets, tomatoes and cauliflowers a used to make popular pickles. Pigs' feet ar corned beef are also sometimes pickle (See FOOD PRESERVATION.)

PICO DELLA MIRANDOLA, Cou Giovanni (1463–1494), Italian Renaissan philosopher and humanist who attempted reconcile Christianity with NEOPLATONIS He was a member of Lorenzo de MEDIC Platonic Academy in Florence. Short before his death he became a follower SAVONAROLA. (See also HUMANISM.)

PICTS, ancient inhabitants of Scotlan whose forebears probably came from th European continent c1000 BC. By the 8 century their kingdom extended from Fi to Caithness. In 843 they united with th kingdom of the SCOTS, and were assimilate into the Scottish nation.

PIDGIN, a language of simplified gramma and vocabulary, most often based on western European language. Pidgi originate as a means of communication (e. for trading purposes) between peoples wit different mother tongues. Varieties pidgin English were developed in China an elsewhere. (See also LINGUA FRANCA.)

PIERCE, Franklin (1804–1869), fou teenth president of the US (1853–57). Th youngest president the nation had th known, Pierce was the inexperience compromise candidate of a badly divide Democratic Party, and he was unable t cope with the sectional strife that heralde the Civil War. Born in New Hampshir Pierce trained and practiced as a lawye before entering politics. After rapi advancement he spent two terms (1833–37 as a Democratic member of the House o Representatives, and then became member of the Senate. In 1842 he retire from national politics, but 10 years later, a a time when he was virtually unknown, h won the Democratic nomination after th four leading candidates had brought th Baltimore convention to deadlock. In th 1852 election Pierce easily defeate Winfield Scott, last national candidate o the declining Whig Party. As presiden Pierce proved to be fatally pliable an vacillating. His initial concentration o fulfilling the electoral promise of an expansionist foreign policy led to such conspicuous failures as his attempt to procure Hawaii and Alaska for the US, and to annex Cuba from Spain (see OSTEND MANIFESTO). On the domestic scene, apart from the acquisition of the GADSDEN PURCHASE from Mexico, Pierce's administration proved equally inept. Pierce had pledged loyalty to the COMPROMISE OF 1850, but in 1854, yielding to pressure, he passed the KANSAS-NEBRASKA ACT. This repealed the MISSOURI COMPROMISE which had prohibited slavery in the Kansas region. The dormant slavery controversy was reopened and the Northern part of the Democratic Party split to form the new "Republicans." A wild rush of slavery and anti-slavery supporters poured into Kansas, leading to a local civil war. Pierce's mishandling of the crisis wrecked his administration and his chances of renomination. He left office a discredited figure, retired from public life and died in virtual obscurity.

PIERCE, John Robinson (1910–   ), US engineer. A pioneer in MICROWAVE and RADAR technology, he was the first to write of the possibility of space-satellite radio communication (1955). He persuaded the US government to develop the first COMMUNICATIONS SATELLITE (Echo I, 1960), thus initiating the revolution in international communications.

PIERO DELLA FRANCESCA (c1420–1492), Italian painter, one of the greatest RENAISSANCE artists. His concern for the harmonious relationship of figures to their setting was expressed through simple, elegant forms, clear colors and tones, atmospheric light and perspective as is found in his FRESCO, *Legend of the True Cross*, 1452–59 in AREZZO.

PIERO DI COSIMO (1462–1521), Italian RENAISSANCE painter in Florence, remembered for curious poetic pictures like *Death of Procris; Venus, Cupid and Mars* and *Battle of the Centaurs and Lapiths*, which is based on OVID.

PIERPONT MORGAN LIBRARY, library in New York City created from the private collections of American financier J.P. MORGAN (1837–1913) and established as a public institution by his son in 1924. Its choice holdings include more than 65,000 first and rare editions and rich collections of illuminated manuscripts, authors' manuscripts and prints and drawings, of which those by William BLAKE are especially notable.

PIERRE, capital of S.D. and seat of Hughes Co., on the Missouri R. It is the trade and shipping center of a large agricultural region. Pop 11,973.

PIETA, subject in art representing the Virgin Mary supporting the body of the dead Christ after the Deposition. It originated in N Europe in the 14th century and was popular in the Italian RENAISSANCE and carved three times by MICHELANGELO.

PIETISM, 17th-century evangelical revivalist movement in the German LUTHERAN CHURCH. It attacked the prevalent dead orthodoxy and stressed individual piety and devotion, but tended to MYSTICISM and anti-intellectualism. It influenced the Moravians, Methodists, and American Lutherans.

PIETRO DA CORTONA (1596–1669), Italian BAROQUE painter whose facade for *Santa Maria della Pace*, Rome, 1656–57, made him a leading architect of the period. Another masterpiece was the ceiling painting, *Divine Providence*, 1633–39, an allegory for the BARBERINIS' fortunes.

PIG. See HOG.

PIGEONS, a family, Columbidae, of some 255 species of birds, with worldwide distribution. They are a diverse group, but the typical pigeon is a pastel gray, pink or brown bird with contrasting patches of brighter colors. The body is compact, the neck short and the head and bill fairly small. Most species are gregarious and many are seen in very large flocks. The food may be stored in a distensible crop.

PIGMENTS, Natural, chemical substances imparting colors to animals and plants. In animals the most important examples include MELANIN (black), RHODOPSIN (purple) and the respiratory pigments, HEMOGLOBIN (red) and HEMOCYANIN (blue). (See also MIMICRY; PROTECTIVE COLORATION.) In plants, the CHLOROPHYLLS (green) are important as the key chemicals in PHOTOSYNTHESIS. Other plant pigments include the carotenes and xanthophylls (red-yellow), the anthocyanins (red-blue) and the anthoxanthins (yellow-orange). In nature, whiteness results from the absence of pigment (see ALBINO) and is comparatively uncommon.

PIKE, freshwater fishes of the N hemisphere. They are mottled fish with a long head and snout and large jaws. The fins are set well back on the body—a characteristic of predatory fishes that lie in wait for prey and make a sudden dash to catch it. The genus *Esox* includes the European or Northern pike, the MUSKELLUNGE, and the PICKERELS.

PIKES PEAK, mountain, 14,110ft, in E central Col., part of the Rocky Mts., near Colorado Springs, one of the most famous in the US. Its solitary position and commanding vistas make it a popular tourist attraction.

PILATE, Pontius, Roman procurator of Judea (26–36 AD) who ordered the crucifixion of Christ, afterwards washing his hands to disclaim responsibility. Hated by the Jews, he was recalled to Rome after his behavior had provoked a riot which had to be put down by troops.

PILGRIM FATHERS, 102 English emigrants on the MAYFLOWER, including 35 PURITAN separatists formerly settled in the Netherlands, who became the first English settlers in New England (1620). Their settlement was named PLYMOUTH COLONY. (See also ALDEN, JOHN; BRADFORD, WILLIAM; BREWSTER, WILLIAM; CARVER, JOHN; STANDISH, MILES.)

PILGRIMS, those who journey to a holy place for penance or to seek divine help. Pilgrimages today include those by Roman Catholics to ROME, LOURDES and FÁTIMA; by Hindus to VARANASI; by Muslims to MECCA, Shi'ites to KARBALA and by Buddhists to KANDY.

PILLARS OF HERCULES, the rocky summits on each side of the Strait of Gibraltar, in Greek myth set up by HERCULES, and held to mark the W limits of the seas he had made safe for sailing.

PILSUDSKI, Józef (1867–1935), Polish general and statesman. Imprisoned several times for his nationalism, he led a private army against Russia in WWI and directed the RUSSO-POLISH WAR. From 1918 to 1922 he was president of the new Polish republic. After a coup d'etat in 1926 he became virtual dictator.

PILTDOWN MAN, *Eoanthropus dawsoni.* In 1908–15 were found under Piltdown Common, Sussex, UK, a skull with ape-like jaw but large, human cranium and teeth worn down in a way unlike those of any extant ape, surrounded by FOSSIL animals that indicated an early PLEISTOCENE date. Piltdown Man was held by many as an ancestor of *Homo sapiens* until 1953, when the fraud was exposed: the skull was human but relatively recent; the even more recent jaw that of an orangutan; the teeth had been filed down by hand; and the fossil animals were not of British origin. The remains had been artificially stained to increase confusion.

PINBALL, an electrified mechanical game in which a player tries to direct a small metal ball to high-score areas on a glass-covered, slanted board. A series of flippers and bumpers help the player to keep the ball in play. Pinball machines made their first appearance in the 1930s and pinball "parlors," frequented mainly by young people, have been common in the US and Europe since the mid-1940s.

PINCHOT, Gifford (1865–1946), US conservationist who was largely responsible for making CONSERVATION a public issue. He headed the Division of Forestry (US Dept. of Agriculture; 1898–1910) and influenced President Theodore Roosevelt to transfer millions of acres of forest land to public reserves. He was a founder of the PROGRESSIVE PARTY (1912) and served as governor of Pennsylvania (1923–27; 1931–35).

PINCKNEY'S TREATY, or Treaty of San Lorenzo el Real. After years of US–Spanish dispute, in 1795 Thomas PINCKNEY negotiated a treaty which established trade arrangements, set the US boundary at the 31st parallel, and gave the Americans the right to navigate the entire Mississippi R and of tax-free deposit at the port of New Orleans.

PINDAR (c518–c438 BC), Theban noble and greatest of Greek lyric poets, perfector of the choral *epinician* ODE celebrating a victory in the national games. His odes combine lofty praise of athlete, patron and gods with extended mythical metaphor. From them was developed the Pindaric ode, consisting of a strophe, antistrophe and epode, chiefly used in 17th- and 18th-century English poetry.

PING-PONG. See TABLE TENNIS.

PINKERTON, Allan (1819–1884), Scottish-born founder of America's most famous pioneer detective agency. He organized a Civil War espionage network which became the Federal Secret Service. "Pinkerton Men" became famous; they were used to break the HOMESTEAD STRIKE in 1890 and were responsible for destroying the MOLLY MAGUIRES.

PINKEYE, common name for CONJUNCTIVITIS.

PINOCHET UGARTE, Augusto (1915–), president of Chile (1974–). A right-wing general, he led the bloody coup that overthrew the Marxist president, Salvador Allende, in 1973. His authoritarian regime was affirmed by a plebiscite in 1980.

PINOCHLE, card game played mainly in the US, probably brought by German immigrants. It is played with a 48-card pack, containing two of each suit of ace, king, queen, jack, 10 and 9. Varieties include two-hand, partnership and, most popular, auction pinochle, which is a bidding game, like BRIDGE. Points are scored for card combinations declared by the winner of a trick.

PINTER, Harold (1930–), English

dramatist and director. His "comedies of menace" have ambiguous and deceptively casual dialogue, cat-and-mouse situations and a fine balance of humor and tension; notable are *The Caretaker* (1960), *The Homecoming* (1965) and *No Man's Land* (1974). He has written several successful screenplays.

PINTURICCHIO (Bernardino di Betto c1454–1513), Italian (Umbrian) RENAISSANCE painter. A pupil of PERUGINO, he helped paint the SISTINE CHAPEL. His most important frescoes are in the Vatican and in the Siena cathedral library.

PINYIN, the official system of the People's Republic of China for transliterating Chinese into the Roman alphabet. In the 1970s the new spellings began to replace those of the earlier Wade-Giles system in English-speaking countries. Pinyin spellings include "Beijing" for the conventional "Peking" and "Mao Zedong" instead of "Mao Tse-tung."

PIONEER PROBES, US space probe series started in 1958. Pioneers 1–3 studied the VAN ALLEN RADIATION BELTS. Pioneers 5–8 were launched into solar orbit to study interplanetary space and the sun itself. Pioneers 10 and 11 were Jupiter "fly-by" probes.

PIRACY, armed robbery on the high seas; the plundering of shipping by freebooters. It has existed since earliest times, though efficient navies and communications have virtually ended it today. Piracy was rife in the Mediterranean in ancient times. POMPEY suppressed it, but later the ruthless CORSAIRS, based in Algiers and TRIPOLI, were much feared PRIVATEERS (licensed by government). Piracy also flourished in northern seas and the HANSEATIC LEAGUE was formed partly to protect its member cities. New World shipping gave piracy a fresh impetus and BUCCANEERS seized much of the West Indies for England. Chinese pirates operated until WWII. (See also HIJACKING; SKYJACKING; BARBARY WARS; BLACKBEARD; DRAKE, SIR FRANCIS; KIDD, WILLIAM; LAFITTE, JEAN; MORGAN, SIR HENRY.)

PIRAEUS, chief port and third largest city of Greece, 6mi SW of Athens, whose ancient history it shares. It handles over half the country's seaborne trade. Its industries include shipbuilding, engineering and textiles. Pop 187,458.

PIRANDELLO, Luigi (1867–1936), Italian dramatist and author of novels and short stories. A most influential writer, he won the Nobel Prize for Literature in 1934. He is noted for his grimly humorous treatment of psychological themes and of the reality of art compared with "real" life, as in his best-known play *Six Characters in Search of an Author* (1921).

PIRANESI, Giovanni Battista (1720–1778), Italian etcher, draftsman and architect, known for his prints of old and contemporary Roman buildings, *Views of Rome* (begun 1748), and for a series of fantastic *Imaginary Prisons* (c1745). They are notable for their grandeur and lighting contrasts.

PIRANHAS, or **Caribes**, small, but extremely ferocious, shoaling freshwater fish from South America. The jaws are short but powerful, armed with sharp cutting teeth. They quickly strip the flesh from other fish and mammals and have even been known to attack humans on river crossings. Family: Characidae.

PISA, historic city of NW central Italy, on the Arno R in Tuscany. GALILEO was born at Pisa, which is famous for its marble campanile (see LEANING TOWER OF PISA) and rich in architecture and art. Pop 103,800.

PISANELLO (Antonio Pisano; c1395–c1455), Italian Renaissance painter and medalist, best known for his portrait medals, frescoes (including *St. George and the Princess*) in Verona, and a complete set of drawings now in the Louvre, Paris.

PISANO, two sculptors, father and son, of Pisa, Italy: Nicolo Pisano (c1220–1284?), who revived the art of sculpture in Italy; and Giovanni Pisano (c1250–after 1314). They combined classical and Gothic forms in works which include richly decorated pulpits at Pisa, Siena and Pistoia, a fountain at Perugia and the facade of Siena cathedral.

PISCES (the Fishes), a large, faint constellation on the ECLIPTIC, the 12th sign of the ZODIAC. The vernal EQUINOX now lies in Pisces.

PISSARRO, Camille (1830–1903), leading French Impressionist painter. Born in the West Indies, he came to Paris in 1855. Influenced by the BARBIZON SCHOOL at first, he was with CÉZANNE, MONET and RENOIR a founder of IMPRESSIONISM. His works, most notably landscapes and street scenes, are famous for their freshness, vividness and luminous color.

PISTOL, small FIREARM that can be conveniently held and operated in one hand. It developed in parallel with the shoulder weapon from the 14th century, first becoming practical in the early 16th century with the invention of the wheel-lock firing mechanism, soon superseded by the FLINTLOCK. Modern rapid-fire pistols are usually either REVOLVERS or automatics. Automatic pistols, such as the Colt .45

Automatic, contain a magazine of cartridges in the butt and are automatically reloaded and cocked by the energy of recoil when a round is fired (see AMMUNITION).

PISTON, Walter (1894–1976), US neoclassical composer, professor of music at Harvard from 1944 to 1961. His austere but dynamic music incorporates complex rhythm and harmonics in traditional forms. His *7th Symphony* (1961) won a Pulitzer Prize.

PITCAIRN ISLAND, small British colony (2sq mi) in the Pacific midway between New Zealand and Panama, famous as the uninhabited island settled by BOUNTY mutineers and Tahitian women (1790), from whom the present 90-odd English-speaking islanders are descended.

PITCH, Musical, refers to the FREQUENCY of the vibrations constituting a SOUND. The frequency associated with a given pitch name (e.g., Middle C) has varied considerably over the years. The present international standard sets Concert A at 440Hz.

PITCHBLENDE, or **Uraninite,** brown, black or greenish radioactive mineral, the most important source of URANIUM, RADIUM and POLONIUM. The composition varies between UO_2 and $UO_{2.6}$; thorium, radium, polonium, lead and helium are also present. Principal deposits are in Zaire, Bohemia, at Great Bear Lake, Canada, and in the Mountain States.

PITCHER, Molly (1754–1832), popular heroine of the American Revolution. Born Mary Ludwig, she earned her nickname by carrying water for the Continental soldiers during the battle of MONMOUTH. According to legends, she manned her husband's gun when he collapsed.

PITMAN, Sir Isaac (1813–1897), English school teacher who invented a famous SHORTHAND based on phonetic principles, still one of the most widely used systems of stenography in English.

PITT, the name of two British statesmen. **William Pitt, Earl of Chatham** (1708–1778), known as "Pitt the Elder," was an outstanding war minister and empire builder during the SEVEN YEARS' WAR. He was also famous for his defense of the rights of the American colonists. By 1761 he had completely transformed Britain's position in Europe and throughout the world. He strengthened the British navy, and extended British control in Canada and India. **William Pitt** (1759–1806), second son of the Earl of Chatham, known as "Pitt the Younger." At 24 he became Britain's youngest prime minister, at the invitation of GEORGE III, and he dominated British politics

until his death. In his 1783–1801 ministry he strengthened national finances but war with France and agitation at home forced him to shelve parliamentary reform measures. His 1804–06 ministry was marked by defeats on land but victory at sea in the NAPOLEONIC WARS.

PITTSBURGH, steel-producing city in SW Penn., seat of Allegheny Co., and the state's second largest city. It occupies over 55sq mi around its business center, the "Golden Triangle" where the Allegheny and Monongahela rivers meet to form the Ohio. Its economic wealth is based on steel mills, coke from Allegheny coal, pig iron, glass and a variety of manufactured products. It has an impressive transport system and is the biggest inland river port in the US. Pittsburgh is rich in cultural institutions, with universities, a symphony orchestra, opera company, and many other amenities. A subway system is planned for completion in the 1980s. Pop 423,938.

PITUITARY GLAND, major ENDOCRINE GLAND situated just below the BRAIN, under the control of the adjacent HYPOTHALAMUS and in its turn controlling other endocrine glands. The posterior pituitary is a direct extension of certain cells in the hypothalamus and secretes VASOPRESSIN and OXYTOCIN into the BLOOD stream. The anterior pituitary develops separately and consists of several cell types which secrete different HORMONES, including growth hormone, FOLLICLE STIMULATING HORMONE, LUTEINIZING HORMONE, PROLACTIN, thyrotrophic hormone (which stimulates thyroid gland) and adrenocorticotrophic hormone (ACTH). Growth hormone is concerned with skeletal growth and development as well as regulation of blood sugar (anti-INSULIN activity). The anterior pituitary hormones are controlled by releasing hormones secreted by the hypothalamus into local blood vessels; the higher centers of the brain and environmental influences act by this route. FEEDBACK from the organs controlled occurs at both the hypothalamic and pituitary levels. Pituitary TUMORS or loss of blood supply may cause loss of function, while some tumors may be functional and produce syndromes such as GIGANTISM or acromegaly (due to growth hormone imbalance). Pituitary tumors may also affect VISION by compressing the nearby optic nerves. Sophisticated tests of pituitary function are now available.

PIUS, name of twelve popes. **Saint Pius V** (1504–1572) succeeded in 1566. With some severity he restored a degree of discipline and morality to the papacy in the face of the Protestant challenge, and organized the

Spanish-Venetian expedition which defeated the Turks at LEPANTO in 1571. **Pius VI** (1717–1799), elected in 1775, drained the Pontine marshes and completed St. Peter's. The French Revolution led to the occupation of the papal territories and Pius' death in captivity. **Pius VII** (1740–1823) succeeded him in 1800. Under an 1801 CONCORDAT French troops were withdrawn, but the PAPAL STATES were later annexed by Napoleon, whom Pius had consecrated emperor in 1804. **Pius IX** (1792–1878) began the longest papal reign in 1846 with liberal reforms, but became an extreme reactionary in both politics and dogma after the REVOLUTIONS OF 1848. The Immaculate Conception became an article of dogma (1854), and papal infallibility was proclaimed in 1870 by the first VATICAN COUNCIL (see ULTRAMONTANISM). In 1871 the new kingdom of Italy passed The Law of Guaranties defining relations between the state and the papacy, but Pius refused to accept the position. **Saint Pius X** (1835–1914), elected in 1903, condemned modernism in the Church. **Pius XI** (1857–1939), elected in 1922, concluded the LATERAN TREATY (1929) with the Italian state and issued encyclicals condemning communism, fascism and racism. **Pius XII** (1876–1958), who reigned from 1939, was an active diplomat in a difficult period and undertook a considerable amount of humanitarian work during WWII although he was criticized for refusing to condemn Nazi policy toward the Jews. His encyclical *Mediator Dei* led to changes in the Mass.

PIZARRO, Francisco (c1474–1541), Spanish conquistador who destroyed the INCA empire in the course of his conquest of PERU. He was with BALBOA when he discovered the Pacific (1513). In 1524 and 1526–27 Pizarro attempted to conquer Peru with Diego de ALMAGRO and Fernando de Luque. In 1531, with royal assent, he began a new campaign and found Peru in an unsettled state under the Inca emperor ATAHUALPA. At Cajamarca in the Andes Pizarro's small band, at first pretending friendship, kidnapped Atahualpa and massacred his unarmed followers; he forced the emperor to pay a massive ransom, then executed him. A vicious and greedy man, Pizarro cheated Almagro and eventually had him killed; he was himself assassinated by Almagro's followers.

PLACENTAL MAMMALS, Eutheria, or True mammals, those mammals, distinct from MARSUPIALS and MONOTREMES, in which the FETUS is nourished in the womb attached to a highly organized PLACENTA until a comparatively late state in its development. By contrast, marsupials give birth to far less well developed young, further development occurring while the young is attached to the mother's teat. Other differences are in the structure of the reproductive system and in the BRAIN. Placental mammals have larger brains and possess a *corpus callosum*: threads of tissue connecting the two halves of the brain.

PLAGUE, a highly infectious disease due to a bacterium carried by rodent fleas. It causes greatly enlarged LYMPH nodes (buboes, hence bubonic plague), SEPTICEMIA with FEVER, prostration and COMA; plague PNEUMONIA is particularly severe. If untreated, DEATH is common and EPIDEMICS occur in areas of overcrowding and poverty. It still occurs on a small rural scale in the Far East; massive epidemics such as the **Black Death,** which perhaps halved the population of Europe in the mid-14th century, are rare. Rat and flea control, disinfection and ANTIBIOTICS are the mainstay of current prevention and treatment.

PLAINSONG, or plainchant, one of the earliest forms of music in Christian Europe, still used in the Roman Catholic Church. It is a sung version of the LITURGY in which an unaccompanied line of melody, at its simplest all on one note (psalmodic intonation), follows the rhythm of the words. The "Ambrosian chant" developed in Milan under St. AMBROSE (c340–397). Today's Gregorian chant was developed in Rome and codified in the time of Pope GREGORY I (c540–604), adapting Greek modes. (See MODE; NOTATION; POLYPHONY.)

PLANCK, Max Karl Ernst Ludwig (1858–1947), German physicist whose QUANTUM THEORY, with the Theory of RELATIVITY, ushered physics into the modern era. Initially influenced by CLAUSIUS, he made fundamental researches in THERMODYNAMICS before turning to investigate BLACKBODY RADIATION. To describe the electromagnetic radiation emitted from a BLACKBODY he evolved the **Planck Radiation Formula,** which implied that ENERGY, like MATTER, is not infinitely subdivisible—that it can exist only as quanta (see PLANCK CONSTANT). Planck himself was unconvinced of this, even after EINSTEIN had applied the theory to the PHOTOELECTRIC EFFECT and BOHR in his model of the ATOM; but for his achievement he received the 1918 Nobel Prize.

PLANCK CONSTANT, h ($= 6.6256 \times 10^{-34}$Js), a quantity fundamental to quantum physics, named for Max PLANCK, who in 1900 solved a long-standing problem in radiation physics with the hypothesis that the energy of a system vibrating with frequency *v* had to be a whole-number multiple of *hv*. The Planck constant also governs the accuracy with which different properties can be measured simultaneously (see UNCERTAINTY PRINCIPLE) and the wavelength of the wave associated with a particle (see QUANTUM MECHANICS).

PLANETARIUM, an instrument designed to represent the relative positions and motions of celestial objects. Originally a mechanical model of the SOLAR SYSTEM (see ORRERY), the planetarium of today is an intricate optical device that projects disks and points of light representing sun, moon, planets and stars on to the interior of a fixed hemispherical dome. The various cyclic motions of these bodies as seen from a given latitude on earth can be simulated. Of great assistance to students of ASTRONOMY and celestial NAVIGATION, planetariums also attract large public audiences. The first modern planetarium, built in 1923 by the firm of Carl ZEISS, is still in use at the Deutsches Museum, Munich, West Germany.

PLANKTON, microscopic animals and plants that live in the sea. They drift under the influence of OCEAN CURRENTS and are vitally important links in the marine food chain (see ECOLOGY). A major part of plankton comprises minute plants (phytoplankton), which are mainly ALGAE, but include DINOFLAGELLATES and DIATOMS. Phytoplankton may be so numerous as to color the water and cause it to have a "bloom." They are eaten by animals (zooplankton), which comprise the eggs, larvae and adults of a vast array of animal types, from Protozoa to JELLYFISH. Zooplankton is an important food for large animals such as WHALES and countless fishes such as HERRING. Phytoplankton is confined to the upper layers of the sea where light can reach, but zooplankton has been found at great depths. (See also OCEANS.)

PLANNED PARENTHOOD—WORLD POPULATION (PPWP), the chief organization in the US for promoting FAMILY PLANNING, the use of BIRTH CONTROL methods and the availability of devices for CONTRACEPTION. Founded in 1914 by Margaret SANGER, its affiliates operate some 400 clinics in over 150 US cities. PPWP is funded by donations.

PLANT, a living organism belonging to the PLANT KINGDOM. Green plants are unique in being able to synthesize their own organic molecules from carbon dioxide and water using light energy by the process known as PHOTOSYNTHESIS. Mineral nutrients are absorbed from the environment. Plants are the primary source of food for all other living organisms (see ECOLOGY). The possession of CHLOROPHYLL, the green photosynthetic pigment, is probably the most important distinction between plants and animals, but there are several other differences. Plants are stationary, have no nervous system and the cell wall contains large amounts of CELLULOSE. But there are exceptions. Some plants, such as ALGAE and BACTERIA, can move about, and others, including FUNGI, bacteria and some PARASITES do not contain chlorophyll and cannot synthesize their own organic molecules, but absorb them from their environment. Some INSECTIVOROUS PLANTS obtain their food by trapping insects.

Although the more primitive plants vary considerably in their overall structure, the higher plants (GYMNOSPERMS and ANGIOSPERMS) are much the same in their basic anatomy and morphology. In a typical angiosperm, four main regions can be recognized: ROOT, STEM, LEAF and FLOWER. Each region has one or more basic functions.

When examined under the microscope, a piece of plant tissue can be seen to consist of thousands of tiny CELLS, generally packed tightly together. The cells are not all alike and each one is adapted to do a certain job. All are derived, however, from a basic pattern. This basic plant cell tends to be rectangular and it has a tough wall of cellulose which gives it its shape, but the living boundary of the cell is the delicate cell membrane just inside the wall. Inside the membrane is the PROTOPLASM, which contains the nucleus, the CHLOROPLASTS and many other microscopic structures. In the center of the protoplasm there is a large sap-filled vacuole, which maintains the cell's shape and plays an important part in the working of the whole plant.

Both sexual and asexual REPRODUCTION are widespread throughout the plant kingdom. Many plants are capable of both forms and in some cases the life cycle of the plant may involve the two different forms. (See ALTERNATION OF GENERATIONS.) (See also BOTANY; FERTILIZATION; FRUIT; GERMINATION; GROWTH; OSMOSIS; PLANT DISEASES; POLLINATION; TRANSPIRATION.)

PLANTAGENETS, name given to the branch of the ANGEVIN dynasty descended from GEOFFREY PLANTAGENET which ruled England 1154–1485. From HENRY II until the deposition of RICHARD II in 1399 the succession was direct. Thereafter the crown passed to other branches of the family until the defeat of the Yorkist Plantagenet RICHARD III at the hands of Henry Tudor

(HENRY VII), who had remote Plantagenet connections.

PLANT DISEASES cause serious losses to crop production; they may kill plants completely, but more often they simply reduce the yield. Most plant diseases are caused by microorganisms which infect the tissues, the most important being FUNGI, including MILDEW, RUSTS and SMUTS. Control methods are based on FUNGICIDES. VIRUSES are the next most damaging group of plant pathogens. Most of them are carried by aphids and other sap-sucking insects and control is largely a matter of controlling these insect carriers. BACTERIA are less important, their main role being in secondary infection, causing the tissues to rot. Deficiency diseases are caused by a lack of available minerals in the soil. Insect pests, such as the BOLL WEEVIL on cotton, can also cause serious crop damage.

PLANT KINGDOM, the second great group of living organisms. The plant and ANIMAL KINGDOMS together embrace all living things except VIRUSES, and only overlap in the most primitive organisms. The plant kingdom is extremely diverse (over 400,000 species are now known), and they are found in almost every conceivable habitat. They range in size from microscopic BACTERIA to 100m (330ft) SEQUOIAS. The plant kingdom can be arranged into an orderly hierarchical pattern of classification (see TAXONOMY) containing divisions, classes, orders, families, genera and species. Indeed, several systems have been evolved to do this. In the classical Eichler system there are four divisions: the THALLOPHYTA, including bacteria, SLIME MOULDS, ALGAE and FUNGI; the BRYOPHYTA, including LIVERWORTS, HORNWORTS and MOSSES; the PTERIDOPHYTA, including FERNS, CLUB MOSSES and HORSETAILS; and the SPERMATOPHYTA, including GYMNOSPERMS and ANGIOSPERMS, the latter being divided into DICOTYLEDONS and MONOCOTYLEDONS. However, this system has been replaced recently by a more natural arrangement of 11 divisions: Schizophyta, bacteria and blue-green algae; Euglenophyta, euglenoids; Chlorophyta, green algae; Xanthophyta, yellow-green algae; Chrysophyta, golden algae and DIATOMS; Phaeophyta, brown algae; Rhodophyta, red algae; Pyrrophyta, dino-flagellates and cryptomonads; Mycota, slime molds and fungi; Bryophyta, liverworts and mosses; and Tracheophyta, the vascular plants, including horsetails, ferns, gymnosperms and angiosperms. Under this system some authorities break the plant kingdom into three kingdoms: the Monera, including the division Schizophyta; the Metaphyta, including the Bryophyta and Tracheophyta; and the Protista, which includes all the other divisions.

PLASMA, almost completely ionized GAS, containing equal numbers of free ELECTRONS and positive IONS. Plasmas such as those forming stellar atmospheres (see STAR) or regions in an electron discharge tube are highly conducting but electrically neutral and many phenomena occur in them that are not seen in ordinary gases. The TEMPERATURE of a plasma is theoretically high enough to support a controlled nuclear FUSION reaction. Because of this, plasmas are being widely studied particularly in MAGNETOHYDRODYNAMICS research. Plasmas are formed by heating low-pressure gases until the ATOMS have sufficient energy to ionize each other. Unless the plasma can be successfully contained by electric or magnetic fields, rapid cooling and recombination occurs; indeed the high temperatures needed for thermonuclear reactions cannot as yet be maintained in the laboratory for sufficiently long.

PLASMA, the part of the BLOOD remaining when all CELLS have been removed, and which includes CLOTTING factors. It may be used in resuscitation from SHOCK.

PLASTICS, materials that can be molded (at least in production) into desired shapes. A few natural plastics are known, e.g., BITUMEN, RESINS and RUBBER, but almost all are man-made, mainly from PETROCHEMICALS, and are available with a vast range of useful properties: hardness, elasticity, transparency, toughness, low density, insulating ability, inertness and corrosion resistance, etc. They are invariably high POLYMERS with carbon skeletons, each molecule being made up of thousands or even millions of atoms. Plastics fall into two classes: thermoplastic and thermosetting. **Thermoplastics** soften or melt reversibly on heating; they include celluloid and other cellulose plastics, LUCITE, NYLON, POLYETHYLENE, STYRENE polymers, VINYL polymers, polyformaldehyde and polycarbonates. **Thermosetting** plastics, although moldable when produced as simple polymers, are converted by heat and pressure, and sometimes by an admixed hardener, to a cross-linked, infusible form. These include bakelite and other phenol resins, EPOXY RESINS, polyesters, SILICONES, urea-formaldehyde and melamine-formaldehyde resins, and some polyureth-anes. Most plastics are mixed with stabilizers, fillers, dyes or pigments and plasticizers if needed. There are several fabrication processes: making films by calendering (squeezing between rollers), casting or extrusion, and making objects by compression molding, injection molding (melting and forcing into a cooled mold) and casting. (See also LAMINATES; SYNTHETIC FIBERS.)

PLASTIC SURGERY, the branch of SURGERY devoted to reconstruction or repair of deformity, surgical defect or the results of injury. Using bone, cartilage, tendon, and skin from other parts of the body, or artificial substitutes, function and appearance may in many cases be restored. In skin grafting, the most common procedure, a piece of skin is cut, usually from the thigh, and stitched to the damaged area. Bone and cartilage (usually from the ribs or hips), or sometimes plastic, are used in cosmetic remodeling and facial reconstruction after injury. Congenital defects such as HARELIP and CLEFT PALATE can be treated in infancy. "Face lifting," the cosmetic removal of excess fat and tightening of the skin, is a delicate and often unsuccessful operation, carrying the added risk of infection.

PLATA, Riò de la. See RÍO DE LA PLATA.

PLATELET. See BLOOD.

PLATE TECTONICS, revolutionary unifying theory of modern GEOLOGY, developed in the 1960s when new information concerning the topography of the ocean floor and paleomagnetic studies become available. The theory is now broadly supported by additional evidence from many branches of geology. Plate tectonics explains the earth's dynamics in terms of a series of moving rigid slab-like plates of the LITHOSPHERE that are driven slowly by convection currents in the ASTHENOSPHERE. Plate boundaries, outlined by their seismicity and volcanic activity, are of three types: divergent (constructive) boundaries, usually located along major oceanic ridges where the plates are slowly spreading apart, allowing molten rock (MAGMA) to rise to the surface and solidify to form new oceanic crust; convergent (destructive) boundaries, located at deep oceanic trenches, where the leading edge of one plate plunges beneath the other in a SUBDUCTION ZONE and remelts in the upper MANTLE, often rising in a molten state through the upper plate to form an arc of volcanic islands fringing the trench; and transform fault (passive) boundaries where plates slip past each other along fracture zones. The theory provides for the mechanism (and for the necessity) of CONTINENTAL DRIFT, as continents are carried as integral parts of the conveyor-like plates. It also explains the origin of ocean basins through the location of divergent boundaries under continental land masses;

the origin of major continental mountain chains through orogenic folding and faulting of sediments trapped in zones of convergence; and it suggests answers for many questions relating to the migration, extinction and EVOLUTION of life through paleogeographic reconstruction of ancient continental locations and paleoclimates. Plate tectonics also has implications in the search for the earth's mineral resources by suggesting likely places for the localization of oil, gas and metallic ores. (See also SEA-FLOOR SPREADING, SUBDUCTION ZONE; BENIOFF ZONE; OROGENIES; PALEO-MAGNETISM.)

PLATH, Sylvia (1932–1963), US poet whose taut, melodic, highly imagistic works explore the nature of womanhood and her fixation with death. *Ariel* (1965), which appeared after her suicide, won her international acclaim as a major US "confessional" poet. Her other works include *The Bell Jar* (1963), a semi-autobiographical novel about a young woman's emotional breakdown, and her *Complete Poems* (1981) edited by Ted HUGHES.

PLATO, Greek philosopher (c427–347 BC). A pupil of SOCRATES, c385 BC he founded the ACADEMY, where ARISTOTLE studied. His early dialogues present a portrait of Socrates as critical arguer, but in the great middle dialogues he develops his own doctrines such as the Theory of Forms (*Republic*), the immortality of the soul (*Phaedo*), knowledge as recollection of the Forms by the soul (*Meno*), virtue as knowledge (*Protagoras*), and attacks hedonism and the idea that "might is right" (*Gorgias*). The *Symposium* and *Phaedrus* sublimate love into a beatific vision of the Forms of the Good and the Beautiful. The late dialogues (*Sophist, Theaetetus, Politicus, Philebus, Parmenides*) deal with problems of epistemology, ontology, and logic; the *Timaeus* contains cosmological speculation. In the *Republic* Plato posits abstract Forms as the supreme reality. The highest function of the human soul is to achieve the vision of the Form of the Good. Drawing an analogy between the soul and the state, he presents his famous ideal state ruled by philosophers, who correspond to the rational part of the soul. In the late *Laws* Plato develops in detail his ideas of the state. His idealist philosophy, his insistence on order and harmony, his moral fervor and asceticism and his literary genius have made Plato a dominant figure in Western thought.

PLATYPUS, or **Duck-billed platypus,** *Ornithorhynchus anatinus,* an amphibious

MONOTREME (egg-laying mammal) found in Australia and Tasmania. They have webbed feet and thick fur (equipping them for an aquatic life); a short, thick tail, and a flat, toothless, bill-like mouth used for taking insects and crustaceans off the surface of the water. Like ECHIDNAS, the other monotreme group, they retain many reptilian characteristics. There is no scrotum; the TESTES are internal. The mammary glands are diffuse and lack distinct teats. Moreover, in the platypus, the right ovary and oviduct are nonfunctional.

PLAUTUS, Titus Maccius (c254–184 BC), Roman writer of comedies, 21 of which have survived. He based them on Greek New Comedy, especially MENANDER, but adapted them to Roman tastes and situations, and added his own brand of lively, bawdy humor. Popular in his time, he influenced SHAKESPEARE and MOLIÈRE among others.

PLAY, a distinctive type of behavior of both adult and juvenile animals, of unknown function and involving the incomplete, ritualized expression of normal adult behavior patterns. Movements are extravagant and exaggerated. Play occurs particularly in carnivores, primates and certain birds.

PLAYER, Gary (1935–), South African golfer, a touring pro from the 1950s. He won all the major championships (US and British Opens, Masters and PGA), the first non-US golfer to achieve this.

PLAYER PIANO, a PIANO with a mechanism for playing automatically, first patented as the Pianola in 1897. A roll of paper is perforated with holes so placed that as it moves, air pumped through them strikes the hammers. The player piano was originally operated by foot pedals, but later became fully automatic with an electric motor. The popularity of the instrument declined with the widespread distribution of the radio and phonograph, but the performance of a number of famous composers and pianists are preserved on rolls made for player pianos.

PLAYING CARDS, pieces of card with numerical and pictorial sequences marked on them, used in games of skill and chance. Probably originating in the Orient, they were known in Europe by the 14th century. Developed from the TAROT deck, the modern pack has 52 cards in four *suits* (Clubs, Diamonds, Hearts, Spades). In most card games players attempt to make winning combinations of cards following a particular set of rules. (See BLACKJACK; BRIDGE; CANASTA; PINOCHLE; POKER; RUMMY; WHIST.)

PLEA BARGAINING involves an agreement between the accused and the prosecutor under which the accused agrees to plead guilty to a lesser offense in order to receive a lighter sentence from the judge. Plea bargaining has been accepted by judges, prosecutors and lawyers as necessary though undesirable. Necessary, to save time and speed up the work of dangerously overcrowded courts; it also gives guilty parties less time in prison than they would get if they went to trial and were convicted. Undesirable, because it denies the accused a fair trial and does not require the prosecutor to prove the accused's guilt beyond a reasonable doubt.

PLEASURE PRINCIPLE, a concept of FREUD, the avoidance of PAIN or unpleasantness, the sole influence on the mind before the EGO has developed. In later stages, it is modified by the **reality principle**, which recognizes physical and social constraints.

PLEBISCITE, in Roman history, a law enacted by the plebeian *comitia*, or assembly of tribes. In modern times a plebiscite is a direct vote of the whole body of citizens on some specific issue (for instance, acceptance of a new constitution).

PLÉIADE, seven French poets of the 16th century, the chief being RONSARD and DU BELLAY. Named for an ancient Alexandrian school, they aimed to develop French as a literary language, while imitating classical and Italian forms.

PLEIADES, a GALACTIC CLUSTER in the constellation TAURUS. Seven of the stars can be seen by the naked eye, and these are named after the seven daughters of ATLAS. The Pleiades are about 153pc from the sun and are surrounded by a bright NEBULA.

PLEISTOCENE, the earlier epoch of the QUATERNARY Period, also known as "The Great Ice Age," stretching from between about 2–3 million through 10,000 years ago. (See also GEOLOGY; HOLOCENE.)

PLESSY v. FERGUSON, important US Supreme Court ruling on segregation in 1896, which held that the provision of "separate but equal" accomodations for blacks on railroad trains did not violate the "equal protection of the laws" clause of the 14th Amendment. This decision was reversed in 1954 when the Supreme Court unanimously ruled against segregation in the case of BROWN V. BOARD OF EDUCATION.

PLEURISY, INFLAMMATION of the pleura, the two thin connective tissue layers covering the outer LUNG surface and the inner CHEST wall. It causes a characteristic chest pain, which may be localized and is made worse by deep breathing and coughing. It may be caused by infection (e.g., PNEUMONIA, TUBERCULOSIS) or TUMORS and inflammatory disease.

PLIMSOLL MARK, a line on the side of a seagoing ship indicating the safe loading limit. Samuel Plimsoll (1824–1898) first secured its compulsory marking on British ships in 1876.

PLINY, name of two Roman authors. **Pliny the Elder** (c23-79 AD) is known for his *Natural History*, a vast compendium of ancient sciences, which though of little scientific merit was popular throughout antiquity and the Middle Ages. He died attempting to help the citizens of POMPEII in the eruption of Vesuvius. **Pliny the Younger** (c61-113 AD), a nephew of Pliny the Elder, was a lawyer, statesman and administrator, primarily known for his elegant *Letters*, which throw much light on the political, economic and social life of the Roman Empire.

PLIOCENE, the final period of the TERTIARY, immediately preceding the QUATERNARY, lasting from about 10 to 4 million years ago. (See also GEOLOGY.)

PLISETSKAYA, Maya (1925–   ), Soviet dancer. A leading performer with the Bolshoi Ballet from 1943, she became famous for her Odette-Odile in *Swan Lake*. She choreographed and created the title role in *Anna Karenina* (1972).

PLOTINUS (205–270 AD), Greco-Roman philosopher, founder of NEOPLATONISM. Probably born in Egypt, he became a teacher in Rome; his work, the *Enneads*, was edited by his pupil PORPHYRY. His complex philosophical cosmology involves a hierarchy of degrees of being, the highest being the ineffable One or Good which controls the rest, down to the lowest (the physical world), by a process of *emanations*. The human soul reaches its highest state in the mystical contemplation of the One.

PLOVERS, small or medium-sized wading birds of the family Charadriidae. The family contains the LAPWINGS and the true plovers. Fairly leggy birds, most plovers have an olive or brown back, with lighter underparts. Typically, they have a dark band across the belly and a white band on a black head. Plovers feed on insects or crustacea in mud and sand.

PLUNKET, Saint Oliver (1629–1681), Irish churchman, primate of all Ireland from 1669. Falsely accused by Titus OATES of planning a foreign invasion of Ireland, he became the last Roman Catholic martyr in England.

PLUTARCH (c46–c120 AD), Greek philosopher and biographer. A native of BOEOTIA, he visited Rome and lectured there, and was for 30 years a priest at DELPHI. His *Parallel Lives* of famous Greeks and Romans, grouped in pairs for comparison,

exemplifies the private virtues or vices of great men and has had great influence on European literature, notably on SHAKESPEARE. His *Moralia* is a vast collection of philosophical essays.

PLUTO, the ninth planet of the SOLAR SYSTEM, orbiting the sun at a mean distance of 39.53AU in 248.4 years. Pluto was discovered in 1930 following observations of perturbations in NEPTUNE's orbit. Because of its great distance from us, little is known of Pluto's composition, atmosphere, mass (probably less than 0.1 that of the earth), or diameter (probably 5,000–6,000km). Its orbit is very eccentric: indeed, it is occasionally closer to the sun than is Neptune and may be an escaped satellite of that planet. In 1978 Pluto was discovered to have a satellite, named Charon, large enough to make the two bodies a double planet system, like the earth and its moon. At the same time, the total mass of Pluto and Charon was found to be about 0.002 times the mass of the earth.

PLUTONISM, the geological theory, often associated with the followers of J. HUTTON, that the rocks of the earth were originally molten in origin. In the early 19th century, plutonism rivalled NEPTUNISM for acceptance as the fundamental geological principle.

PLUTONIUM (Pu), the most important TRANSURANIUM ELEMENT, used as fuel for NUCLEAR REACTORS and for the ATOMIC BOMB. It is one of the ACTINIDES and chemically resembles URANIUM. Pu^{239} is produced in BREEDER REACTORS by neutron irradiation of uranium (U^{238}); like U^{235}, it undergoes nuclear FISSION, and was used for the Nagasaki bomb in WWII. mp 640°C, bp 3235°C, sg 19.84 (α; 25°C).

PLYMOUTH, historic town in SE Mass., seat of Plymouth Co., where the PILGRIM FATHERS landed from the MAYFLOWER in 1620, and established PLYMOUTH COLONY. Its tourist features include PLYMOUTH ROCK and a reconstruction of the original settlement. Pop 35,913.

PLYMOUTH COLONY, first English settlement in what is now New England, and the second permanent English settlement in America, founded by the PILGRIM FATHERS in Dec., 1620. In 1691 it was merged with Massachusetts Bay Colony to form Massachusetts. The colony was founded by a group of Puritan Separatists from the Church of England, who were blown off their course to Virginia and agreed in the famous MAYFLOWER COMPACT to form a government where they landed. The settlers included John CARVER and William BRADFORD, the first two governors. Half the colony died during a bitter first winter, but the survivors were helped by the friendly Indian chief MASSASOIT, and by 1624 it was thriving.

PLYMOUTH COMPANY, speculative joint-stock company founded in 1606 by a group of English "merchant adventurers." Its purpose was to colonize the coast of North America and thus increase English wealth and trade. It had exclusive rights to the region between 45°N and 41°N. After the failure of its first and only colony on the Kennebec R in Me. (1607–08), it was reorganized in 1620 as the COUNCIL FOR NEW ENGLAND.

PLYMOUTH ROCK, a granite boulder on the shore at Plymouth, Mass., on which, according to tradition, the PILGRIM FATHERS first set foot in America in 1620. There is no documentary evidence confirming the legend.

PNEUMOCONIOSIS, restrictive disease of the LUNGS caused by deposition of dusts in the lung substance, inhaled during years of exposure, often in extractive industries. SILICOSIS, anthracosis and asbestosis are the principal kinds, although aluminum, iron, tin and cotton fiber also cause pneumoconiosis. Characteristic X-RAY changes are seen in the lungs.

PNEUMONIA, INFLAMMATION and consolidation of LUNG tissue. It is usually caused by bacteria (pneumococcus, STAPHYLOCOCCUS, GRAM'S STAIN negative bacilli), but rarely results from pure VIRUS infection (INFLUENZA, MEASLES); other varieties occur if food, secretions or chemicals are aspirated or inhaled. The inflammatory response causes lung tissue to be filled with exudate and PUS, which may center on the bronchi (**bronchopneumonia**) or be restricted to a single lobe (**lobar pneumonia**). Cough with yellow or green sputum (sometimes containing BLOOD); FEVER; malaise, and breathlessness are common. The involvement of the pleural surfaces causes PLEURISY. ANTIBIOTICS and PHYSIOTHERAPY are essential in treatment.

PNEUMOTHORAX, presence of air in the pleural space between the LUNG and the CHEST wall. This may result from trauma, rupture of lung bullae in EMPHYSEMA or in ASTHMA, TUBERCULOSIS, PNEUMOCONIOSIS, CANCER etc., or, in tall thin athletic males, it may occur without obvious cause. Drainage of the air through a tube inserted in the chest wall allows lung re-expansion.

PÔRTO ALEGRE, city in SE Brazil. It is a major port with industries mostly connected with processing food and farm products from the interior, and also an important commercial center. Pop 885,564.

PO, the longest river in Italy. Rising in the Cottain Alps near the French border, it winds E for 405mi through N Italy to the Adriatic Sea S of Venice. The Po drains almost all N Italy, and helps to make the plain of Lombardy Italy's richest agricultural region.

POCAHONTAS (c1595–1617), daughter of the North American Indian chief POWHATAN, who befriended the settlers at Jamestown, Virginia. According to Captain John SMITH, leader of the colony, Pocahontas saved his life when he had been captured by her father and was about to be executed. In 1614 she was christened, married John ROLFE and went to England, where she died of smallpox.

POCONO MOUNTAINS, mountain range in NE Pa., c2,000ft high, part of the Appalachian system and a popular resort area.

PODGORNY, Nikolai Viktorovich (1903–   ), Russian political leader. After rising through the Communist Party ranks in the Ukraine, he was named to the party secretariat of the Soviet Union (1963). After Khrushchev's fall he became (1965) chairman of the Presidium of the Supreme Soviet, or head of state, holding the post until 1977.

PODHORETZ, Norman (1930–   ), US editor of the influential Jewish monthly *Commentary* (from 1960). He rejected the radicalism of the 1960s and emerged in the late 1970s as a leader of neoconservativism, advocating a strong anti-Soviet foreign policy. His books include his memoirs, *Making It* (1968) and *Breaking Ranks* (1979), and a political analysis, *The Present Danger* (1980).

PODIATRY, or chiropody, care of the FEET, concerned with the nails, CORNS AND CALLUSES, bunions and toe deformities. Care of the SKIN of the feet is especially important in the elderly and in diabetics.

POE, Edgar Allan (1809–1849), US short-story writer, poet and critic, famous for his tales of mystery and the macabre, such as *The Murders in the Rue Morgue* (1841) and *The Purloined Letter* (1844), prototypes of the detective story, and *The Fall of the House of Usher* (1839). His poems, including "The Raven" (1845) and "Annabel Lee" (1849), are musical and striking in imagery. Poe discussed beauty and form in art in *The Philosophy of Composition* (1846), which influenced BAUDELAIRE and the French Symbolists.

POET LAUREATE, royal appointment held by a British poet. Traditionally he writes poems for state occasions, but the title is now largely honorific. DRYDEN first had the title in 1668, but the custom started when Ben JONSON received a royal pension in 1616.

POETRY, meaningful arrangement of words into an imaginative or emotional discourse, always with a strong rhythmic pattern. The language, seeking to evoke image and idea, uses IMAGERY and METAPHOR. RHYME or alliteration may also be important elements. The length of poems may vary from brief LYRIC POETRY to long narrative poems such as COLERIDGE's *Ancient Mariner* or EPIC poetry with the length and scope of a novel, such as BYRON's *Don Juan*. The poet may choose BLANK VERSE, FREE VERSE or any simple or complex rhyme scheme as his medium. Traditional forms also exist; BALLADS are often rhymed in QUATRAINS. The poet has a number of devices available that would be obtrusive or pretentious in prose, such as alliteration or onomatopoeia. The kind of forms and devices used most often or most successfully in poetry depends on the language of the poet. Since the sense of poetry is so intimately tied to its sound it is extremely difficult to translate. The heightening of thought as well as of language, however, and the intensifying and concentration of emotion and observation have meant that the great poets of each country and time have become in some measure accessible to the world as a whole. In most cultures poetry, linked by its rhythmic elements to music and dance, develops before prose literature; the poetic form aids oral transmission. Eventually it is written down; a "higher" form then develops, poetry destined largely for the printed page, although a vital oral tradition may accompany it. Even such written poetry, however, must remain to some extent "musical"; this and its great association with the THEATER still remind one of poetry's origins. (See also articles on individual poets.)

POGROM, term (from the Russian for devastation or riot) for the officially condoned mob attacks on Jewish communities in Russia between 1881 and 1921. More generally, it is used to describe any massacre of a defenseless minority, particularly JEWS, such as those organized by the NAZIS. The pogroms were a major factor in the large-scale emigration of European Jews to the US.

POINCARÉ, Jules Henri (1854–1912), French mathematician, cosmologist and scientific philosopher, best known for his many contributions to pure and applied MATHEMATICS and celestial mechanics.

POINCARÉ, Raymond Nicholas Landry (1860–1934), French statesman, three times premier (1912, 1922–24, 1926–29) and president 1913–20. A strongly nationalist conservative, he ordered the French occupation of the RUHR (1923). His financial policies succeeded in stabilizing the currency (1928).

POINTER, sporting or gun dog bred in England. Standing 23–26in high at the shoulder, Pointers have a smooth coat, usually white with black or reddish-brown markings, and a long muzzle. Scenting out their quarry, they stiffen and point towards it.

POINT FOUR PROGRAM, technical assistance plan for underdeveloped nations proposed by President Harry TRUMAN in his Inaugural Address of Jan., 1949, so named because it was the fourth point in the speech. Launched in 1950 and later merged with other aid programs, it provided technical, educational and health assistance, and aimed to encourage private investment and increase US influence.

POINTILLISM, painting technique, in which tiny paint dots of color are juxtaposed on the canvas to build up the form. The dots of color are additively mixed by the eye of the observer. This method was developed by the impressionist painters, SEURAT and SIGNAC, to achieve more luminosity and greater control of tone.

POISONING, the taking, via ingestion or other routes, of substances which are liable to produce illness or DEATH. Poisoning may be accidental, homicidal, suicidal or as a suicidal gesture. DRUGS and medications are often involved, either taken by children in ignorance of their nature from accessible places, or by adults in suicide or attempted suicide. Easily available drugs such as ASPIRIN, paracetamol and mild SEDATIVES are often taken, though in serious suicidal attempts, BARBITURATES and ANTIDEPRESSANTS are more common. Chemicals, such as disinfectants and weedkillers, cosmetics and paints are frequently swallowed as drinks by children, while poisonous berries may appear attractive. Poisoning by domestic gas or carbon monoxide has been used for suicide and homicide. Heavy metals (see LEAD POISONING, MERCURY POISONING, ARSENIC), INSECTICIDES and CYANIDES are common industrial poisons as well as being a risk in the community. Poisons may act by damaging body structures (e.g., weedkillers); preventing OXYGEN uptake by HEMOGLOBIN (carbon monoxide); acting on the NERVOUS SYSTEM (heavy metals); interfering with essential ENZYMES (cyanides, insecticides); with HEART action (antidepressants), or with the control of RESPIRATION (barbiturates). In some cases, antidotes are available which, if used early, can minimize poisoning, but in most cases, life is supported until the poison is eliminated.

POISON IVY, POISON OAK, and POISON SUMAC, vines or shrubs of the genus *Rhus* native to North America. They contain a poisonous agent, urushiol, that causes itching or blisters, by contact or indirectly through contaminated clothes. Immediate washing with an alkaline soap may prevent the irritation. Family: Anacardiaceae.

POITIER, Sidney (1927–   ), US film actor who was the first black leading man in Hollywood movies. He won an Academy Award for his performance in *Lilies of the Field* (1963) and starred in such other hits as *The Defiant Ones* (1958), *In the Heat of the Night* (1967) and *Guess Who's Coming to Dinner* (1967).

POITIERS, Battle of, famous English victory in the HUNDRED YEARS' WAR, fought in 1356, near Poitiers in W central France. The English, led by EDWARD THE BLACK PRINCE, were outnumbered four to one by their French opponents, but won a brilliant victory over JOHN II and PHILIP THE BOLD.

POKER, a card game whose earliest forms date back to c1520 in Europe, developing into such bet-and-bluff games as *brag* in England, *pochen* ("bluff") in Germany and *poque* in France. *Poque* was taken by the French to America c1800, where it was developed and reexported to Europe as poker, c1870. It is now one of the world's top three card games. There are many variations, but basically five or seven cards are dealt and each player tries to make up a winning combination, on which he bets and bluffs in a contest of skill and nerves against the unknown combinations of his opponents.

Official name: Polish People's Republic
Capital: Warsaw
Area: 120,633sq mi
Population: 35,580,000
Language: Polish
Religion: Roman Catholic
Monetary unit(s): 1 zloty = 100 groszy

POLAND, people's republic in central Europe on the Baltic Sea, lying between East Germany and the USSR and N of Czechoslovakia.

Land. Poland is very flat with about 90% of the land under 1,000ft, though in the S are the peaks of the Silesian and Carpathian Mountains, forming a natural barrier between Poland and Czechoslovakia. The main rivers, the Vistula (which flows through Warsaw and Kráków), the Oder, Neisse, Bug and Warta, are important for transportation to the large Baltic ports. The principal cities are Warsaw, Lodz, Kraków, Wroclaw, Poznan and Gdánsk (Danzig). The climate is moderate in summer with temperatures averaging about 60°F. Winters are generally cold (32°F–24°F). About 50% of Poland comprises arable land and 25% forests.

People. Most of the population are of Polish descent. After WWI Poland had sizeable minorities of Ukrainians, Jews and Belorussians, comprising over 30% of its people. By the mid-1960s there were only small minority groups, and an estimated 10 million Poles lived abroad.

Economy. Poland was an agricultural country until WWII; since then it has been rapidly industrialized. State agricultural collectivization was resisted by the peasants and there are now very few state farms. The chief products are wheat, rye, barley, oats, potatoes and sugar beet. Industry is largely state-owned. Poland is a big producer of coal, zinc, steel, petroleum and sulfur. Manufactures include machinery, textiles, cement and chemicals. There is a sizeable shipbuilding industry at Gdánsk. The principal exports are coal, textiles, metal products and processed meat.

History. Poland's recorded history dates back to the 10th century, when the local Slavic tribes first united. Later Germans settled in Poland, particularly on the Baltic coast. After Swedish invasions in the 17th century, Poland was divided between Austria, Prussia and Russia in 1772. This lasted until 1918. In 1919 the Treaty of VERSAILLES established a new Poland, formed the POLISH CORRIDOR and made GDÁNSK a free city. In 1939 Germany invaded Poland, occupying the E region. The USSR occupied the W. The population was decimated by massacre, starvation and imprisonment in concentration camps like AUSCHWITZ. The Germans were expelled in 1945 and a provisional government was set up under Soviet auspices. The communists dominated the 1947 elections, and the

Russian ROKOSSOVSKY was made minister of defence (1949). The 1952 constitution was modeled on Russian lines. After STALIN's death, opposition to Soviet control led to widespread rioting in 1956, and GOMULKA became leader of the anti-Soviet revolt. He freed Cardinal WYSZYNSKI, and for several years there was considerable freedom in Poland. But by the early 1960s Gomulka was following Russian policies. In 1970 Edward GIEREK replaced Gomulka, and instituted many reforms and controled inflation. In 1972 Germany and Poland ratified the Oder-Neisse line as Poland's W boundary. In the late 1970s a new wave of unrest swept the country, stimulated by higher food prices. Polish workers formed the independent trade union *Solidarnośc* (Solidarity) in 1980 and demanded a greater measure of workers' control in industry. Gierek fell from power in the same year. Unrest continued into early 1982.

POLANSKI, Roman (1933–   ), Paris-born Polish film director noted especially for macabre tales such as *Repulsion* (1965) and *Rosemary's Baby* (1968). His other films include *Knife in the Water* (in Polish, 1961), *Chinatown* (1974) and *Tess of the D'Urbervilles* (1980).

POLAR BEAR, *Thalarctos maritimus*, the most carnivorous of the BEARS. Essentially an aquatic and polar animal, rarely found south of 70°N, it can swim strongly and is also agile on land. It hunts seals, whale calves, fishes, and, on land, arctic foxes and even lemmings. A large bear, up to 750kg (1,650lb), it is well adapted to withstand cold conditions.

POLARIS (Alpha Ursae Minoris), a CEPHEID VARIABLE star in the LITTLE DIPPER. Because of its close proximity to the N celestial pole (see CELESTIAL SPHERE), Polaris is also known as the Polestar or North Star, and has been used in navigation for centuries: owing to precession, (motion of the earth's axis), Polaris is moving away from the N celestial pole.

POLARIS MISSILE, two-stage, solid-propellant guided MISSILE. It is 31ft long, has a 2,875mi range and attains 7,800mph. Developed from 1957, it is designed to be armed with a nuclear warhead and to be fired underwater from nuclear-powered submarines. All single-warhead Polaris missiles have now been phased out due to the emergence of the multiple independently targetable reentry vehicle (MIRV). (See also ROCKET.)

POLARIZED LIGHT, LIGHT in which the orientation of the wave vibrations displays a definite pattern. In ordinary unpolarized light the wave vibrations (which occur at right-angles to the direction in which the radiation is propagated) are distributed randomly about the axis of propagation. In *plane-polarized light* (produced in reflection from a DIELECTRIC such as glass or by transmission through a NICOL PRISM or polarizing filter), the vibrations all occur in a single plane. Polaroid filters work by subtracting the components of light orientated in a particular plane; two filters in sequence with their transmission planes crossed transmit no light. In *elliptically polarized light* (produced when plane-polarized light is reflected from a polished metallic surface) and *circularly polarized light* (produced on transmission through certain CRYSTALS exhibiting double refraction), the electric vector of the radiation at any point describes an ellipse or a circle. Much of the light around us—that of the blue sky, or reflected from lakes, walls and highways—is partially polarized. Polarizing sunglasses reduce glare by eliminating the light polarized by reflection from horizontal surfaces. Polariscopes employing two polarizing filters have proved to be valuable tools in organic chemistry.

POLAROID LAND CAMERA, See CAMERA.

POLAR REGIONS. See ANTARCTICA; ARCTIC REGIONS.

POLDERS, name given in the Netherlands to areas of agricultural land reclaimed by constructing dikes and canals and draining swamps, lakes or shallows. Much of the land around IJSSELMEER consists of polders below sea level.

POLE. See NORTH POLE; SOUTH POLE.

POLECATS, members of the WEASEL family, best known for the pungent odor secreted by their anal glands. With thick, yellowish underfur and black or black-tipped guard hairs, they are lithe and loose-limbed, giving an amazing impression of fluidity. A domestic strain used for flushing rabbits from burrows is the FERRET.

POLESTAR. See POLARIS.

POLICE, civil body charged with maintaining public order and protecting persons and property from unlawful acts. While most civilizations have had some kind of law enforcement agency, most modern forces are descended from the Metropolitan Police established in London by Sir Robert PEEL in 1829; in the US, Boston introduced a similar force in 1838, and New York City soon afterwards. Today in the US the police are organized into around 40,000 separate forces, consisting of local, district, county and state police and the sheriffs and deputies of around 35,000 towns and villages. There are also federal police agencies such as the FBI, the Bureau of Narcotics and Dangerous Drugs, the Border Patrol and the Internal Revenue Service, each responsible to its own civil governing authority. Uniformed police are largely responsible for maintaining public order, regulating traffic, highways and crowds, patrolling the streets and arresting lawbreakers in the course of these duties. In many countries they are also responsible for helping strangers, tracing runaway children and many other duties not involving crime. With the increasing complexity and sophistication of crime, however, most forces have introduced "plainclothes" branches, some specially to deal with homicide, robbery and burglary, vice, and crime involving fraud, narcotics, computer fraud, art thefts, and forgery. There are also specialized services such as forensic science laboratories, information and statistics services. Police powers are in most countries strictly circumscribed by law and constitution. In the US and Great Britain they are obliged to inform an arrested person of his rights.

POLICE POWER, in US law, the inherent power of the state to regulate personal and property rights in the public interest. Although not provided for in the Constitution, the courts have held that it does not violate the 14th Amendment.

POLIOMYELITIS, or **infantile paralysis,** VIRAL DISEASE causing muscle PARALYSIS as a result of direct damage to motor nerve cells in the SPINAL CORD. The virus usually enters by the mouth or GASTROINTESTINAL TRACT and causes a mild feverish illness, after which PARESIS or paralysis begins, often affecting mainly those muscles that have been most used in preceding days. Treatment is with bed rest and avoidance or treatment of complications: contracture; bed sores; venous THROMBOSIS; secondary infection; MYOCARDITIS; respiratory failure, and swallowing difficulties. Current polio vaccine is a live attenuated strain taken by mouth and which colonizes the gut and induces IMMUNITY. Poliomyelitis VACCINATION, developed by Dr. Jonas Salk in the mid-1950s, has been one of the most successful developments in preventive medicine.

POLISH, one of the W group of the Slavic languages. It is the official and literary language of Poland where it is spoken by more than 30 million people. In the US it is the language of over three million. Modern literary Polish, dating from the 16th century, was originally based on dialects in the vicinity of Poznań.

POLISH CORRIDOR, strip of Polish land about 25mi–65mi wide and 90mi long. Formerly German, it was granted to Poland in 1919 to give her access to the Baltic Sea. The predominantly German port of Danzig (now GDAŃSK) adjoining the Corridor was declared a free city. The separation of East Prussia from the rest of Germany by the Corridor precipitated the German invasion of Poland (1939).

POLITBURO, in the USSR, permanent secretariat of top political officials, first formed in 1917, which dominates the Central Committee of the Soviet Communist of top political officials, first formed in 1917, which the Communist Party and to a large extent of the USSR. It has about 11 full and nine alternative members.

POLITIAN. See POLIZIANO, ANGELO.

POLITICAL ECONOMY, a social science, equivalent to modern ECONOMICS, concerned with how a state raises, increases and uses its revenues. The study evolved with the 17th-century rise of MERCANTILISM and was developed by Adam SMITH, David RICARDO and John Stuart MILL, whose *Principles of Political Economy* (1848) is a classic statement. The term had fallen out of use by the 20th century.

POLITICAL PARTY, body or organization which puts forward candidates for public office and contends for power in elections. Parties pose alternative programs and candidates and provide a means by which voters can make their desires and opinions felt. Party connections and party loyalty help to coordinate the separate branches and levels of government necessary in the US system. Primarily, however, political parties institutionalize conflict and the struggle for power. The alternation of parties in office is a peaceful means of replacing those in power, thus ensuring change without revolution.

In some countries a **two-party system** exists while in others there is a multiplicity of parties. The US and many English-speaking powers are dominated by two major parties, and a third party may poll a significant number of votes overall without having a single representative elected. By contrast, in European legislatures, representatives are generally chosen under the system of **proportional representation** which allows the election of candidates from a number of parties in exact proportion to their popular strength. Often in such cases no one party may have a simple overall majority and a coalition will be necessary. Communist states and many newly independent states have a **single-party system,** and the political party is in effect part of the state apparatus. (See also DEMOCRATIC PARTY; REPUBLICAN PARTY; TORY; WHIG.)

POLITICAL SCIENCE, the study of government and political institutions and processes. It was initiated by PLATO's *Republic* and ARISTOTLE's *Politics*, and well-known political theories have included those of MACHIAVELLI, BODIN, HOBBES, LOCKE, MONTESQUIEU, BENTHAM, Jean Jacques ROUSSEAU and MARX. Traditionally, the study had been primarily concerned with the nature of the state, of SOVEREIGNTY and of government. Today greater emphasis is placed on the human associations, the behavior of interest groups and the decision-making processes. The basis of the study is human power over other humans. This leads to a study of social organization. Pertinent areas of inquiry concern the institutions that dispose of power, the systems through which they operate and the motives of those who run them. These questions are closely connected with the question of the morality of power and general theories of man and society. Past theories cannot provide for the complexity of modern society and a standard view today is to regard society as a set of interacting interdependent systems.

In the US almost all advanced students of political science concentrate on some aspect of one of the following areas: political theory, philosophy and methodology; public administration; international organization; politics and law; foreign governments; government and policies of the US; constitutional and administrative law in the US; and US state and local government.

POLIZIANO, Angelo, or **Politian** (1454–1494), Italian poet, scholar and humanist. Perhaps the greatest RENAISSANCE classical scholar, he also wrote the first Italian play, *Orfeo* (1480), and the famous lyrical love poem *Stanze per la Giostra* (1475–78).

POLK, James Knox (1795–1849), eleventh President of the US, 1845–49, elected on a Democratic platform pledged to expand the existing territories of the nation according to the doctrine of MANIFEST DESTINY.

In 1825 Polk was elected to the US House of Representatives and during Andrew JACKSON's presidency he became the administration's leading spokesman in the House. After Jackson's reelection (1832) Polk became chairman of the Ways and Means Committee in 1833. He was speaker of the House 1835–39, and governor of Tennessee 1839–41. Chosen as a compromise candidate by the Democrats, Polk defeated Henry CLAY and was inaugurated as president on May 4, 1845, having campaigned on five main objectives, each of which he managed to achieve. The first, the annexation of Texas, was in fact achieved before Polk took up office, for the outgoing President, John TYLER, had already accepted the Democratic victory as a mandate and sanctioned the admission of Texas as a slave state of the Union (March, 1845). The second objective was to extend the boundary in Oregon Territory to a latitude of 54°40′. In the event, he compromised with Great Britain in the Oregon Treaty (1846) which established the boundary between the US and British America at the 49th parallel. The third objective, to acquire California from Mexico, involved the US in the MEXICAN WAR, 1846–48. By the Treaty of GUADALUPE HIDALGO (1848) Mexico ceded all her claims to the territory of California and New Mexico and recognized the border at the Rio Grande. The fourth objective, a promise to the South to lower the tariff, was enacted by the Walker Tariff (1846). Polk's final objective, to reestablish an INDEPENDENT TREASURY SYSTEM, was achieved by the Independent Treasury Act (1846) which survived with some modifications until 1913. Broken in health by overwork, he chose not to run for reelection and died shortly afterwards, having achieved impressive successes in fulfilling his aims.

POLKA, dance with a basic 2/4 rhythm originating as a folk dance in Bohemia. It became fashionable in the 19th century and has been especially popular as a dance and musical form in the US, especially among Polish-Americans.

POLL, Public Opinion, technique for measuring the range of opinions held by the general public or by specifically limited groups of people. It developed during the 1920s. Opinion polls rely on certain statistical laws which show that small carefully chosen samples of any group can accurately represent the range of opinions of the whole group or population. The population in question, known as the "universe," may be a general one (all voters in the US) or a limited one (all car workers in Detroit). Accuracy depends on the care with which the sample is constructed and on the size of the sample. Since 1944 all polls have adopted the method of random selection pioneered by the US Census Bureau in which each member of the "universe" has an equal chance of being questioned. Pioneers in US public-opinion polling included George Gallup, Louis Harris and Elmo Roper.

POLLAIUOLO, Antonio (c1431–1498),

Florentine goldsmith and painter. Often collaborating with his brother **Piero**, his works include the *Martyrdom of St Sebastian* (1475), many portraits of women in profile and the tomb of Pope Innocent VIII in St. Peter's, Rome. His pictures are noted for their landscapes and his figures for anatomical detail.

POLLINATION, in plants, the transfer of the male GAMETES (*pollen*) from the anthers of a FLOWER to the stigma of the same or another flower, where subsequent growth of the pollen leads to the fertilization of the female gametes (or EGGS) contained in the ovules and the production of SEEDS and FRUIT. Wind-pollinated plants, such as grasses, produce inconspicuous flowers with large feathery stamens and stigmas and usually large quantities of pollen. Insect-pollinated flowers have large conspicuous and colorful flowers, produce NECTAR and have small stigmas. (See PLANT: REPRODUCTION.)

POLLOCK (Paul Jackson (1912–1956), US painter, leader of ABSTRACT EXPRESSIONISM. Influenced by SURREALISM, he developed "action painting"—dripping paint on canvas placed flat on the floor, and forming marks in it with sticks, trowels, knives. His pictures, like *Number 32* (1950) and *Blue Poles* (1953) comprise intricate networks of lines.

POLL TAX, a tax levied equally on each individual in a community. In the US a special poll tax was levied on voters in elections, which effectively disenfranchised the blacks and poor whites. This was banned for federal elections by the 24th amendment to the Constitution (1964), and the ban was extended to local elections in 1966.

POLLUTION, the contamination of one substance by another so that the former is unfit for an intended use; or, more broadly, the addition to any natural environmental resource on which life or the quality of life depends or any substance or form of energy at a rate resulting in abnormal concentrations of what is then termed the "pollutant." Air (see AIR POLLUTION), water and soil are the natural resources chiefly affected. Some forms of pollution, such as urban sewage and garbage or inshore petroleum spillage, pose an immediate and obvious environmental threat; other forms, such as those involving potentially toxic substances found in industrial wastes and agricultural PESTICIDES, present a more insidious hazard: they may enter biological food chains and, by affecting the metabolism of organisms, create an ecological imbalance (see ECOLOGY). Populations of organisms thriving abnormally at the expense of other populations may themselves be regarded as pollutants. Forms of energy pollution include: NOISE, e.g., factory, airport and traffic noise; THERMAL POLLUTION, e.g., the excessive heating of lakes and rivers by industrial effluents; light pollution, e.g., the glare of city lights when it interferes with astronomical observations, and radiation from radioactive wastes (see RADIOACTIVITY: FALL-OUT). The need to control environmental pollution in all its aspects is now widely recognized. (See also RECYCLING.)

POLO, game played on horseback with a ball and mallets. It is played between two teams of four on a field 300yds long and 200yds wide, with a goal at each end. The object is to score points by striking the 4½ inch diameter ball into the goal with the mallet. The game originated in Persia and spread through Turkey, Tibet and India, China and Japan. It was revived in 19th-century India and learned by British army officers, and introduced into England in 1869 and the US in 1876.

POLO, Marco (c1254–1324), Venetian explorer famous for his overland journey to China, 1271–95. Reaching China in 1275 he served as an envoy to the ruler KUBLAI KHAN. He was appointed governor of Yangchow for three years and assisted in the capture of the city of Sainfu. He returned home to Venice (1295) laden with a treasure in precious stones. He commanded a galley against the Genoese at the battle of Curzola (1298) and was captured. In prison, he wrote an important account of his travels which later inspired explorers such as Christopher COLUMBUS to search for a sea passage to the East.

POLONAISE, slow Polish dance in ¾ time, probably developed from the *promenade*. Polonaises were written by MOZART. BEETHOVEN, CHOPIN and many others.

POLYCLITUS THE ELDER, 5th-century BC Greek sculptor, renowned for his bronze statues of athletes, of which numerous marble copies survive. His most famous works were a colossal statue of Hera, now lost, and the *Doryphoros* (Spear Bearer), which became the models for ideal proportion. *Polyclitus the Younger* was known primarily as an architect but also produced figures of athletes.

POLYETHYLENE, white, translucent RESIN, a POLYMER of ETHYLENE made catalytically at high pressure. Tough, elastic and inert, it is used to make plastic film, molded items, and SYNTHETIC FIBERS.

POLYGAMY, marriage in which husbands may have several wives at one time (*polygyny*), or wives several husbands (*polyandry*). It is still practised in parts of

Asia and Africa; both the Muslim and Hindu religions permit polygyny. It was once also a custom of US MORMONS; always illegal.

POLYGRAPH. See LIE DETECTOR.

POLYMER, substance composed of very large MOLECULES (macromolecules) built up by repeated linking of small molecules (monomers). Many natural polymers exist, including PROTEINS, NUCLEIC ACIDS, polysaccharides (see CARBOHYDRATES), RESINS, RUBBER, and many minerals (e.g., quartz). The ability to make synthetic polymers to order lies at the heart of modern technology (see PLASTICS; SYNTHETIC FIBERS). Polymerization, which requires that each monomer has two or more FUNCTIONAL GROUPS capable of linkage, takes place by two processes: CONDENSATION with elimination of small molecules, or simple addition. CATALYSIS is usually required, or the use of an initiator to start a chain reaction of FREE RADICALS. If more than one kind of monomer is used, the result is a copolymer with the units arranged at random in the chain. Under special conditions it is possible to form stereoregular polymers, with the groups regularly oriented in space; these have useful properties. Linear polymers may form crystals in which the chains are folded sinuously, or they may form an amorphous tangle. Stretching may orient and extend the chains, giving increased tensile strength useful in synthetic fibers. Some crosslinking between the chains produces elasticity; a high degree of cross-linking yields a hard, infusible product (a thermosetting PLASTIC).

POLYMORPHISM, in zoology the existence of more than two forms or types of individual within the same species of animal. An example is seen in some social insects such as ants and bees in which many different types of worker are structurally adapted for different tasks within the colony.

POLYNESIA, archipelagos and islands in the central Pacific, part of Oceania. They include the Hawaiian, Cook, Phoenix, Ellice, and Easter islands, Samoa, French Polynesia, Tonga, and ethnologically if not geographically New Zealand. They are either of volcanic origin, or are atolls built up by coral reefs.

POLYP, benign TUMOR of EPITHELIUM extending above the surface, usually on a stalk. Polyps may cause NASAL obstruction and some (as in the GASTROINTESTINAL TRACT) may have a tendency to become a CANCER.

POLYPHONY (from Greek: many sounds), music made up of several independent but harmonically linked melodic lines. The name is usually applied to the sacred choral music of the late Renaissance, particularly that of PALESTRINA, LASSUS and William BYRD.

POLYTHEISM, belief in many gods, as opposed to MONOTHEISM or DUALISM; characteristic of most religions, notably HINDUISM and Greek and Roman religion. It may arise from the personification of forces worshiped at a more primitive level in ANIMISM. One god may dominate the others (e.g. ZEUS); sometimes a supreme Being is recognized, transcending the gods. (See also MYTHOLOGY.)

POLYWATER, or **"anomalous water,"** a liquid formerly supposed to be a polymeric form of WATER. First reported in 1962, it is made by condensing water in very fine glass or silica capillary tubes, and has unusual properties (mp $-40°C$, bp c500°C, sg 1.4). It is now thought to contain substances dissolved from the glass.

POMERANIAN, small dog with a pointed face and small pointed ears, related to sled-dogs. Varied in color, it stands 6–7in high.

POMPADOUR, Jeanne Antoinette Poisson, Marquise de (1721–1764), famous mistress of King LOUIS XV of France from 1745. She was a patroness of the arts and had much influence on the political and artistic life of France.

POMPEII, ancient Roman city in S Italy, buried by an eruption of Mt VESUVIUS in 79 AD. It was rediscovered in 1748. Excavations have revealed a town preserved much as it was on the day of its destruction, even to several bodies. The site has yielded invaluable information of Roman urban life and beautiful examples of Roman art.

POMPEY (Gnaeus Pompeius Magnus; 106 BC–48 BC) known as the Great, Roman general and statesman. He crushed the rebellion in Spain (76 BC), defeated SPARTACUS (72 BC), and King MITHRIDATES (63 BC). In 61 BC he entered the First TRIUMVIRATE, becoming the colleague and later rival of Julius CAESAR. In the civil war following the latter's return from Gaul, Pompey was defeated at PHARSALUS in 48 BC and fled to Egypt, where he was assassinated.

POMPIDOU, Georges Jean Raymond (1911–1974), French statesman, president of France 1969–74. He joined the DE GAULLE government in 1944 and again in 1958. In 1961 he prepared the truce negotiation with the FLN, the Algerian nationalist organization. He was prime minister 1962–68, and succeeded de Gaulle as president in 1969. He died in office, of cancer.

PONCE DE LEON, Juan (c1460–1521), Spanish discoverer of Florida. He sailed with Christopher COLUMBUS in 1493, and in 1508 he conquered Puerto Rico and became its governor. Leading an expedition, possibly to find the mythical Fountain of Youth, he discovered and named Florida in 1513, but when he attempted to colonize it in 1521 he was driven off and mortally wounded by Indians.

PONCHIELLI, Amilcare (1834–1886), Italian opera composer. His best-known works are *I Promessi Sposi* (1856) and *La Gioconda* (1876), with its famous ballet, *Dance of the Hours*.

PONIES, small, sturdy HORSES, usually less than 15 hands (1.5m), hardy and able to live on small amounts of poor food. Races of pony include the Exmoor, Dartmoor, Welsh, Shetland, Iceland and Mongolian. All derive from a Celtic stock of prehistoric British and Scandinavian work horses.

PONSELLE, Rosa (1897–1981), US soprano, born Rosa Ponzillo. She sang in vaudeville before her sensational Metropolitan Opera debut in 1918 opposite Enrico CARUSO in Verdi's *La Forza del destino*. Until retiring in 1936 she was one of the company's leading dramatic sopranos.

PONTIAC (c1720–1769), chief of the Ottawa Indians. He opposed the English during the FRENCH AND INDIAN WARS, and was one of the leaders of an unsuccessful war against them, called **Pontiac's Rebellion** (1763–65), in which Pa., Va. and Md. were seriously threatened. He signed a peace treaty in 1766.

PONTIFEX, high priest of ancient Rome, one of the 16 members of the Pontifical College presiding over the state religion. The highest religious authority was the *pontifex maximus* (supreme pontiff); this title was adopted by the emperors and later the popes.

PONY EXPRESS, famous relay mail service between St. Joseph, Mo., and Sacramento, Cal., from April 1860 to October 1861. It used horses, not ponies, with riders chosen for their small size. The route covered 1,966mi, with stations at 10–15mi intervals. The goal of 10-day delivery was often met, and only one delivery was ever lost. It was superseded by the transcontinental telegraph.

PONZI, Charles (1872–1943), Italian-born US financial swindler. During WWI he established the Securities Exchange Co. and promised investors a 50% interest payment on loans to his company for purported foreign financial dealings. In 1920 it was revealed that no such foreign

exchanges had taken place and that the company's dividends had been paid from funds supplied by investors. After being imprisoned, he was deported to Italy upon his release in 1934.

POODLE, thick-coated breed of dog originally bred in 16th-century Germany. There are three varieties, of differing height: the *toy* poodle is 10in or below, the *miniature* is between 10–15in, and the *standard* poodle is over 15in high.

POOL, See BILLIARDS.

POOR CLARES, Franciscan closed order of nuns, founded by St. CLARE and St. FRANCIS OF ASSISI in 1212. They are a mainly ascetic and contemplative order.

POOR LAWS, laws developed in England from the 16th century enforcing parish assistance to the aged, sick and poor. It was revised in 1834 to provide minimal relief for the able-bodied poor, and after WWI was replaced by a system of public welfare services under the social legislature.

POP ART, modern art movement dating from the mid-1950s, based on images of advertising, commercial illustration and mass-produced objects. Developed in England and the US, it included artists like Richard Hamilton, David HOCKNEY, Andy WARHOL and Robert RAUSCHENBERG.

POPE, Alexander (1688–1744), the greatest English poet and satirist of the AUGUSTAN AGE. Only 4ft 6in tall, he was partly crippled by tuberculosis. He first set out his literary ideals in his *Essay on Criticism* (1711), written in rhymed (heroic) couplets. His best-known works are the mock epic *The Rape of the Lock* (1712), his translations of the *Iliad* (1720) and the *Odyssey* (1726), *The Dunciad* (1728 and 1743), a satirical attack on literary critics, and his essays on moral philosophy, *An Essay on Man* (1733–34) and *Moral Essays* (1731–35).

POPE, John (1822–1892), US Union general. Born in Louisville, Ky., he commanded the newly-organized army of Va. in 1862. He was defeated at the second battle of BULL RUN, and was deprived of the command.

POPE, John Russell (1874–1937), US architect who designed, in neoclassical style, the Jefferson Memorial and the National Gallery in Washington, D.C., both completed after his death.

POP MUSIC, the popular music of the latter half of the 20th century. Much of its vitality derives from the interaction of its diverse styles, all largely affected by commercial pressures. Most have their roots in American FOLK MUSIC, especially in the BLUES and its descendant, rhythm'n'blues.

This latter led in the 1950s to rock'n'roll, a form based on electronic amplification and a simple, dominant beat. In the 1960s, British performers such as the BEATLES and the ROLLING STONES experimented lyrically and musically with pop and traditional forms; while the US underwent a "folk revival" led by Bob DYLAN who, like Joe HILL and Woody GUTHRIE before him, adapted folk styles in pursuit of contemporary relevance, at first chiefly through quasipolitical protest. With increased lyrical sophistication came folk-rock; and its fusion with the "British" style, by now adopted and adapted in the US, was responsible for much of the pop of the late 1960s and early 1970s. Indian (and later, African) music and JAZZ influenced form and instrumentation; technological advance stimulated closer ties with "serious" music; and a reaction from such complexities resulted in the resurgence of the unsophistication of rock'n'roll. (See also ROCK MUSIC.)

POPPER, Sir Karl Raimund (1902–   ), Austrian-born British philosopher, best known for his theory of falsification in the philosophy of science. Popper contends that scientific theories are never more than provisionally adopted and remain acceptable only as long as scientists are devising new experiments to test (falsify) them. His attacks on the doctrine of historicism are in *The Open Society and Its Enemies* (1945) and *The Poverty of Historicism* (1957).

POPULAR FRONT, coalition of left-wing and center parties formed in the 1930s to present a united front against FASCISM. Reflecting a change in Soviet policy, the idea was proclaimed at the 1935 meeting of the Communist International, and communists cooperated with socialist and liberal parties in forming anti-fascist governments. A Popular Front government led by BLUM ruled France 1936–37; the Spanish Popular Front, elected in 1936, was eventually overthrown by FRANCO.

POPULATION, the inhabitants of a designated territory. For the world as a whole, population doubled between 1930 and 1975, from 2 to 4 billion, with a possible 6 billion forecast for the year 2000. The sharpest increases have been in developing nations least able to provide food, education and jobs for all. Averting world famine depends on the few countries able to export food. Many nations now have population-control programs, but the control of infectious diseases and increases in the food supply because of modern growing techniques have combined to encourage population growth. In some societies, however, fertility rates have declined somewhat, and an increase in abortions, approaching the number of live births in a few countries, has helped defuse the population bomb, though not without great controversy. In the US, a "baby boom" occurred after WWII, but after 1957 the birth rate declined and by the 1980s gave indications of approaching ZERO POPULATION GROWTH!

POPULISM, generally, a "grass roots" political movement which is basically agrarian, but which incorporates a farmer-labor coalition. Specifically, it refers to the doctrines of the US People's Party. This grew from the post-Civil War farm depression which created agrarian reform movements such as the GRANGE and the FARMERS' ALLIANCE. In 1891–92 delegates from the Farmers' Alliance and labor organizations set up the People's Party, which fielded J. B. WEAVER as presidential candidate in 1892 on a platform including an eight-hour day, government ownership of railroads, graduated income tax, government postal savings banks, direct election of Senators, increase of the money supply and FREE SILVER. Weaver gained over 1,000,000 votes, and the party gained support rapidly. In the 1896 presidential elections, however, the Democratic candidate, W. J. BRYAN, captured most of the populist vote by campaigning on the issue of free silver, and thereafter the People's Party declined. It failed because its money-supply and free silver theories did not present a sound economic analysis, and because it did not gain urban support.

The term populism is also sometimes applied to be any policies aimed at appealing to the "little man," such as those advocated by Huey LONG and George WALLACE.

PORCUPINES, large spiny vegetarian rodents of two quite distinct families: one, Erithizontidae, confined to the Americas, the other, Hystricidae, to the tropics of the Old World. Old World forms include about a dozen species in Africa and S Asia. They are among the largest of rodents and the entire body is covered with spines. The American porcupines have an equal armory of spines, but when relaxed, these are concealed in a thick underfur.

PORGIES, a family, Sparidae, of food fishes found in many parts of the world. Perchlike fishes, they have large scales and a spiny dorsal fin. In addition they have strong teeth, some species showing a differentiation between front and side teeth.

PORK BARREL, term for a US

congressional appropriation for local improvements or public works, often unnecessary, supported by politicians for the patronage benefits accruing as a local spin-off; in other words, corruption. (See also LOG-ROLLING.)

PORNOGRAPHY AND OBSCENITY LAWS, in the US are held to exist for the protection of public morality. Pornography may be defined as material designed by its explicitness to appeal exclusively to a prurient interest in sex. The often explicit contents of genuine works of art and literature and medical texts are thus not pornographic, although in certain circumstances may be deemed obscene. Obscenity, like pornography, is not well defined in law, but may be said to be anything tending to corrupt public morals, generally in a sexual sense. Obscenity laws vary widely from country to country, and in the US from state to state, as does the degree of toleration extended by police and public. US Supreme Court decisions such as *US v Roth* (1957) tended to relax legal strictures, against obscenity by taking as their standard of acceptability that of the "average reasonable adult" and laying down that a work must be judged as a whole. This made the law vaguer and hence hard to administer, with the result that a great deal of "hardcore" pornography became freely available. Supreme Court decisions since then tended to reverse the trend without, however, clarifying the definition.

PORPHYRIA, metabolic disease due to disordered HEMOGLOBIN synthesis. It runs in families and may cause episodic abdominal pain, skin changes, NEURITIS and mental changes. Certain DRUGS can precipitate acute attacks. Porphyria may have been the cause of the "madness" of George III of England.

PORPHYRY, an IGNEOUS ROCK having many large crystals (phenocrysts) set in a very fine-grained matrix, occurring in DIKES and SILLS. More generally, rocks are said to have porphyritic texture if they contain some phenocrysts in a finer-grained matrix (e.g., porphyritic granite).

PORPOISES, small toothed whales, family Phocaenidae. Distinguished from DOLPHINS in being smaller, rather tubby and having a rounded head with no projecting beak-like mouth, they feed mainly on shoaling fishes. Unfortunately the name is now also loosely applied in the US to the various species of dolphin kept in captivity.

PORT, a sweet wine, usually red, fortified with brandy. It comes from grapes grown in the Douro valley, Portugal, and is shipped from Oporto, whence its name.

PORT ARTHUR, now *Lüshin* and *Lüda*, two ports at the S end of the Liaotung peninsula, China first developed under Russian (1898) and Japanese (1905) control. Port Arthur is a strategically important naval base, and Dairen a major commercial port and industrial city. Pop Port Arthur 200,000; Dairen 1,500,000.

PORTER, Cole (1893–1964), US popular song composer. After WWI, he achieved great success as a sophisticated writer of songs and musical comedies, providing both the words and music. His prolific output included *Anything Goes* (1934), *Kiss Me, Kate* (1948), *Can-Can* (1953), the film score for *High Society* (1956) and many classic songs.

PORTER, Katherine Anne (1890–1980), US short-story writer and novelist who won the 1966 Pulitzer Prize for her *Collected Short Stories* (1965). Her first collection of stories was *Flowering Judas* (1930), followed by *Pale Horse, Pale Rider* (1939). *Ship of Fools* (1962) is her only novel.

PORTER, William Sidney. See HENRY, O.

PORTINARI, Candido (1903–1962), Brazilian painter. His early canvases utilized warm earth tones to depict agricultural scenes in his native land. His later work became increasingly abstract. Two of his murals, *War* and *Peace*, decorate the UN General Assembly Building in NYC.

PORTLAND CEMENT, widely-used CEMENT made by calcining a mixture of lime and clays, reputedly named for the resemblance of the set cement mortar to limestone from the Isle of Portland, England.

PORTSMOUTH, Treaty of, the treaty which ended the 1904–05 Russo-Japanese War. After mediation by President Roosevelt, it was signed Sept. 5, 1905, at Portsmouth Navy Yard, N.H. Russia conceded Japanese supremacy in Korea, and Manchuria was restored to China.

PORTUGAL, republic of the W Iberian Peninsula, between Spain and the Atlantic, and including the Azores and Madeira.

Land. The N half of Portugal consists of mountains and high plateaus, cut by deep valleys. The S is characterized by lower, rolling countryside and plains. Two large rivers, the Tagus and Douro, cut the country from E to W. The climate is mild and humid in winter and warm and dry in summer.

Economy. Portugal is one of Europe's poorer countries. Agriculture still plays an important part in the economy, with most of the population living in villages and small towns. Most farms are very small and poor, although there are some large estates in the

S. Grain, livestock, wine, olives, citrus fruits and almonds are the principal products. There are large forests in the mountainous areas, and Portugal is the world's biggest producer of cork. Fishing is important, the chief catches being sardines and tuna. Industries include food-processing, textiles, metals, mining and hydroelectricity. The principal cities are Lisbon, Oporto, Coimbra and Setúbal. Chief exports are cork, wine, sardines and fruit.

History. Portugal became an independent kingdom in 1143, under Alfonso I. In 1385, John I founded the Aviz dynasty. His reign started a period of colonial expansion, leading to an empire that by the second half of the sixteenth century included much of South America, Africa and S and SE Asia. In 1580 King Philip II of Spain seized Portugal, and Spanish kings ruled until the successful revolt of 1640 which established the ruling house of Braganza. Portugal had already lost much of her power, especially in the Far East, and in the ensuing period of increasing absolutism never recovered it. During the NAPOLEONIC WARS she was invaded by the French and Spanish (see PENINSULAR WAR). By 1825 Brazil became an independent empire, and a period of conflict and unrest led to the Portuguese republic being declared in 1910. In 1926 there was a military coup, after which Dr SALAZAR became virtual dictator until he was succeeded by Marcello CAETANO in 1968. In 1974 a military coup brought about a new government under General SPÍNOLA which restored freedom of political expression, and promised popular elections and independence for Portugal's overseas territories. In the struggle between leftist and rightist forces that followed, he was replaced in Sept. 1974 by General Costa Gomes. Continuing strife led to his

Official name: Republic of Portugal
Capital: Lisbon
Area: 35,510sq mi
Population: 9,930,000
Language: Portuguese
Religion: Roman Catholic
Monetary unit(s): 1 Escudo = 100 centavos

resignation (1976) and the election of General Eanes for a five-year term. Of Portugal's overseas territories, GUINEA-BISSAU became independent in 1974, followed by ANGOLA, the CAPE VERDE ISLANDS, MOZAMBIQUE and SÃO TOME and PRÍNCIPE in 1975; in 1976 Portuguese TIMOR became part of Indonesia and MACAO gained greater autonomy.

PORTUGUESE, official language of Portugal and Brazil. It is one of the ROMANCE LANGUAGES and developed from the Latin spoken in Roman Iberia. Brazilian Portuguese has absorbed words and phrases from the languages of the Indian and African slave populations.

PORTUGUESE MAN-O'-WAR, *Physalia physalis,* a colorful jellyfish of the Siphonophora. A colonial Cnidarian, it consists of an assemblage of four kinds of POLYPS: the most obvious of which is a gas-filled bladder 300mm (1ft) long, which carries a high crest and is colored blue or purple. Below this float are supported other polyps including the long stinging tentacles used for catching prey. The sting can be painful to humans.

POSITIVISM, philosophical theory of knowledge associated with the 19th-century French philosopher Auguste COMTE. It holds that the observable, or "positive," data of sense experience constitute the sole basis for assertions about matters of fact; only the truths of logic and mathematics are additionally admitted. The speculative claims of theology and metaphysics, regarded as the primitive antecedents of "positive" or scientific thought, are discounted. (See also LOGICAL POSITIVISM.)

POSITRON, the antiparticle corresponding to the ELECTRON. (See ANTIMATTER.)

POSSUMS, Australian marsupial mammals, members of the Phalangeridae (see PHALANGERS). The term is also used, wrongly, for the OPOSSUMS of the New World.

POST, Emily (1873–1960), US writer who became an accepted authority on correct social behavior through her book *Etiquette* (1922). She broadcast regularly and her daily column was syndicated to over 200 newspapers.

POST, Wiley (1899–1935), US aviator, who made a record-breaking world flight in 1931 and repeated the performance solo in 1933. He and his passenger, humorist Will ROGERS, died in a plane crash.

POSTAL SERVICE, the collection, transmission and delivery of mail. Postal systems grew out of the military and administrative needs of the early empires. Communications were maintained by networks of runners or mounted couriers in Egypt by 2000 BC, in China by 1000 BC, and in the Persian Empire by CYRUS THE GREAT; in Europe the Roman Empire had a network whose efficiency was not matched again until the 19th century.

Modern postal services originated in the late Middle Ages. There was an international network in the Hapsburg empire in the 15th century, and CHARLES I of England and LOUIS XIV of France set up regular postal services in the 17th century. As the amount of traffic increased private enterprise gave way to government monopoly, and modern postal systems are all government controlled. First stagecoaches, then railways and steamships, and finally airplanes have dramatically reduced delivery times, and a milestone in the organization of the post was the "penny post" (1840) in England, with prepaid adhesive stamps and a single rate (see HILL, ROWLAND). International standardization of procedures was achieved in 1875 (see UNIVERSAL POSTAL UNION). The international postal system now handles enormous numbers of items every day, but is faced with great financial and administrative problems. In recent years the vast volume of mail has been handled at steadily rising costs. (See also POST OFFICE, US.)

POSTER, printed placard, posted up to advertise an event, product or service, or for propaganda purposes. The invention of LITHOGRAPHY made it possible to produce brightly-colored posters cheaply and quickly. Famous artists who designed posters include Jules Chéret, TOULOUSE-LAUTREC and Aubrey BEARDSLEY.

POSTIMPRESSIONISM, term coined to describe the work of certain painters (c1880–90) whose styles, though dissimilar, flowed from IMPRESSIONISM. CÉZANNE, GAUGUIN, SEURAT, and VAN GOGH are considered the principal Postimpressionists.

POST OFFICE, US, formerly a US government department, since 1970 an independent agency. It administers the POSTAL SERVICE of the US, under the direction of the postmaster-general, formerly a cabinet member, but now appointed by a corporate board of governors. By far the largest in the world, the US Post Office employs 700,000 people and operates 33,000 post offices, handling around 100,000,000,000 items of mail every year. Rural free delivery has operated since 1896.

POTASSIUM (K), a soft, silvery-white, highly reactive ALKALI METAL. It is the seventh most abundant element, and is extensively found as SYLVITE, carnallite and other mixed salts; it is isolated by ELECTROLYSIS of fused potassium hydroxide.

Potassium is chemically very like sodium, but even more reactive. It has one natural radioactive isotope, K^{40}, which has a half-life of 1.28 billion yr. K^{40} decays into Ar^{40}, an isotope of argon; the relative amounts of each are used to date ancient rocks. Potassium salts are essential to plant life (hence their use as fertilizers), and are important in animals for the transmission of impulses through the nervous system. AW 39.1, mp 64°C, bp 774°C, sg 0.862 (20°C).

Potassium carbonate (K_2CO_3), or **Potash,** is a hygroscopic colorless crystalline solid, made from potassium hydroxide and carbon dioxide, an ALKALI used for making glass.

Potassium chloride (KCl), is a colorless crystalline solid, found as sylvite. Used in fertilizers and as the raw material for other potassium compounds.

Potassium nitrate (KNO_3), or **Saltpeter,** is a colorless crystalline solid, soluble in water, which decomposes to give off oxygen when heated to 400°C. It is made from sodium nitrate and potassium chloride by fractional crystallization, and is used in GUNPOWDER, matches, fireworks, some rocket fuels, and as a fertilizer.

POTATO, *Solanum tuberosum,* herbaceous plant with an edible, fleshy tuberous underground stem, originating in the South American Andes. The tubers became a popular European foodstuff in the 18th century, the Irish in particular becoming dependent on the crop. Family: Solanaceae.

POTATO FAMINE, in 19th-century Ireland, famine caused by potato blight. The 1845 and 1846 potato crops failed, and in the subsequent famine nearly a million people died and over a million emigrated, particularly to the US. Ireland's population fell from about 8,500,000 in 1845 to 6,550,000 in 1851.

POTAWATOMI INDIANS, a North American Indian tribe of the ALGONQUIAN language family. In the 18th century they lived around the S of Lake Michigan. They allied with the French colonists and joined chief PONTIAC in his rebellion (1763). They later supported the British in the Revolutionary War and in the War of 1812. Coming under pressure from settlers, they moved W, and in 1846 most of them were forced into a reservation in Kan. The Potawatomi in Kansas have preserved much of the aboriginal culture. Other groups live in Mich., Okla. and Wis.

POTEMKIN, Prince Grigori Aleksandrovich (1739–1791), Russian soldier, statesman and favorite of Catherine the Great. For the last 20 years of his life, he was the most powerful man in Russia. He enlarged the Russian army and navy, and annexed the Crimea in 1782.

POTLATCH, in many tribal cultures, especially among the Indians of the American NW coast, an elaborate ceremonial feast at which the host distributes or destroys wealth to gain status or office in his tribe. Wealthier guests are expected to match or exceed this in turn. Although banned for a while in Canada the potlatch is still an important tribal institution.

POTOMAC RIVER, US river flowing through Washington, D.C. Formed by the confluence of the 110mi long N Branch and the 140mi long S Branch, it flows 287mi into Chesapeake Bay. Navigation for large ships is prevented above Washington D.C., by the Great Falls. The river is noted for its scenic attraction.

POTSDAM CONFERENCE (July–Aug. 1945), a "summit" meeting at Potsdam, Germany, between STALIN. TRUMAN and, in succession, CHURCHILL and Clement ATTLEE. They agreed that a four-power Allied Control Council would rule defeated Germany, disarming it and fostering democratic government; Poland would gain part of E Germany; the German economy would be decentralized; Germans in Hungary, Poland and Czechoslovakia would be repatriated. The conference also discussed reparations payments and issued an ultimatum to Japan. The agreements were almost all breached as the COLD WAR hardened. (See also YALTA CONFERENCE.)

POTTER, Beatrix (1866–1943), British author of children's books. Her works, illustrated by herself, include *Peter Rabbit* (1902), *The Tailor of Gloucester* (1903), *Benjamin Bunny* (1904), *Mrs Tiggy-Winkle* (1905), *Jemima Puddle-Duck* (1908) and *Pigling Bland* (1913). Her books have become children's classics and remain widely popular.

POTTERY AND PORCELAIN, CERAMIC articles, especially vessels, made of CLAY (generally KAOLIN) and hardened by firing. The simplest and oldest type of pottery, **earthenware** (nonvitreous), is soft, porous and opaque, usually glazed and used for common tableware. TERRA COTTA is a primitive unglazed kind. Earthenware is fired to about 1000°C. **Stoneware**, the first vitreous ware (of low porosity), was developed in China from the 5th to the 7th centuries AD. Fired to about 1200°C, it is a hard, strong, nonabsorbent ware, opaque and cream to brown in color. From stoneware evolved **porcelain** during the Sung dynasty (960–1279). This is a hard, nonporous vitreous ware, white and

translucent. Made from flint, kaolin and feldspar, it is fired to about 1350°C.

In the manufacture of pottery the clay is made plastic by blending with water. The article is then shaped: traditionally by hand, but building up layers of strips (coiled pottery), by "throwing" on the potter's wheel or by molding; industrially by high-pressure molding or by a rotating template. The clay is fired in a kiln, slowly at first, then at higher temperatures to oxidize and consolidate it. The **glaze** (if desired) is then applied by spraying or dipping, and the article refired. Glazes are mixtures of fusible minerals and pigments, similar to those used for ENAMEL, powdered and mixed with water.

Among the most celebrated potters were the ancient Greeks (see GREEK ART) and the Chinese. Chinese porcelain had a profound influence on the ceramic arts of both Islam and W Europe. From the 9th century the Muslims used tin glaze to imitate Chinese ware, and this was in turn imitated in the European FAÏENCE and MAJOLICA wares. Porcelain was developed as a luxury ware in Europe in the 18th century, the greatest centers being Dresden (see DRESDEN CHINA) and SÈVRES. In England the great ceramics manufacturers were Josiah SPODE (see also BONE CHINA) and Josiah WEDGWOOD. (See also DELFT.)

POULENC, Francis (1899–1963), French composer, member of the post-WWI group of composers called *Les Six*. His music is light in texture, although serious. His best-known works include *Mouvements perpetuels* for piano (1918), the ballet *Les Biches* (1924) and the operas *Les Mamelles de Tirésias* and *Dialogue des Carmélites* (1957). He was also a notable songwriter.

POUND, Ezra Loomis (1885–1972), major 20th-century US poet, critic and translator. A gifted linguist, he went to Europe in 1908, and soon won recognition. His most important works are *Homage to Sextus Propertius* (1918), *Hugh Selwyn Mauberley* (1920) and the epic *Cantos* (1925–60). He championed the IMAGIST and VORTICIST movements, and influenced T. S. ELIOT, Robert FROST and W. B. YEATS, among others. He supported MUSSOLINI, and after broadcasting pro-fascist propaganda during WWII he was indicted for treason by the Americans, found unfit to plead, and confined to a mental institution until 1958.

POUND (lb), the name of various units of weight (see WEIGHTS AND MEASURES). The pound avoirdupois is defined as being exactly 0.453,592,37kg. The "metric pound" commonly used in continental Europe is 500g.

POUSSIN, Nicolas (1594–1665), the greatest 17th-century French BAROQUE painter. He worked mostly in Rome, and based his style on RAPHAEL and antiquities. His classical and religious subjects, such as *Shepherds of Arcadia* (c1629), *The Rape of the Sabine Women* (c1635) and *The Seven Sacraments* (1644–48) are rich in color, austere in handling, dramatic, and evocative in mood. He influenced Jacques DAVID, CÉZANNE and PICASSO.

POVERTY, a shortage of the income or resources considered necessary for a minimum standard of living in a particular society. Because of the differences between societies, it is impossible to define precisely; an American may be considered poor if he does not possess an automobile, while the poor in Africa, Asia or South America may be actually starving to death. The vast gap between rich and poor, and especially between rich and poor countries, is a major fact of the modern world. In the underdeveloped countries, whose populations are increasing fast, many people suffer from MALNUTRITION, and are poor by any standards. Despite aid from the rich and technologically advanced nations, the gap is increasing.

In 1978, 24.5 million people, or 11.4% of the total population, were living below the poverty level in the US, where the poverty threshold for a nonfarm family of four was defined as $6,662, or one-third the median income for four-member families. Blacks constituted 31.1% of the poor, Hispanics 10.6%, though these minorities represented only 11.6% and 5.6%, respectively, of the total population. Other groups disproportionately represented among the poor were Indians, families headed by women, and the elderly.

Poverty may be regarded as almost inevitable in certain circumstances. In many nations too few jobs, especially remunerative ones, exist, creating a pattern of large-scale UNEMPLOYMENT or underemployment. Lack of opportunities to gain either education or skills reinforces such a pattern. In other nations where more opportunities exist, the path from poverty may be closed because of discrimination based on race, religion or sex. The effects of poverty on individuals may include poor health, lower energy and productivity, drug addiction, a penchant for crime, greater abuse from authorities and a shorter life.

A nation wealthy enough to do so may aid its poor in several ways. It may seek to avoid the onset of poverty by providing SOCIAL SECURITY, medical aid for the aged (see also MEDICARE), comprehensive health insurance, survivor's benefits, unemployment compensation, and workmen's compensation. For those who are already poor, FOOD STAMPS, public housing or support for fatherless families may be provided. Still other programs seek to help the poor by improving their nutrition, education and health or by training them for jobs (See also COMPREHENSIVE EMPLOYMENT AND TRAINING ACT; JOB CORPS; WAR ON POVERTY).

A summit conference at Cancún, Mexico, in 1981, attended by more than 20 heads of government, represented an ambitious attempt to deal with poverty on a worldwide basis, with special attention to how rich nations could assist the poor ones.

POWELL, Adam Clayton Jr. (1908–1972), US politician. A clergyman, he was New York's first black councillor (1941). He founded *The People's Voice* (1942) and, as the flamboyant "Voice of Harlem," was a Democratic Representative 1945–70. Excluded from Congress for alleged misuse of funds (1967), he was reelected twice, but defeated in 1970.

POWELL, Anthony (Dymoke) (1905–), English novelist, best known for his contemporary comedy of manners *A Dance to the Music of Time*, a series of novels which started with *A Question of Upbringing* (1951).

POWELL, Enoch (1912–), British political leader who entered Parliament in 1950 as a Conservative and served as minister of health 1960–63. He aroused much controversy for his opposition to British entry into the Common Market and for demagogic speeches calling for a halt to non-white immigration into the UK.

POWELL, John Wesley (1834–1902), US geologist and ethnologist best known for his geological and topographical surveys, and for his anthropological studies of the AMERINDS.

POWELL, Lewis Franklin, Jr. (1907–), associate justice of the US Supreme Court (1971–). A lawyer and former president of the American Bar Association, he was appointed to the court by President Nixon.

POWELL, Mel (1923–), US composer. He played jazz piano and arranged for Benny GOODMAN before studying with Paul Hindemith. As a Yale faculty member, he established an electronic music studio. *Haiku Settings* (1961) is a characteristic work.

POWER, the rate at which WORK is performed, or ENERGY dissipated. Power is thus measured in units of work (energy) per unit time, the SI UNIT being the watt (=joule/second) and other units including the horsepower (=745.70W) and the cheval-vapeur (=735.5W). Frequently in engineering (and particularly in transportation) contexts, what matters is the power that a given machine can deliver or utilize—the rate at which it can handle energy—and not the absolute energies involved. A high-power machine is one which can convert or deliver energy quickly. While mechanical power may be derived as a product of a FORCE and a VELOCITY (linear or angular), the electrical power utilized in a circuit is a product of the potential drop and the current flowing in it (volts × amperes = watts). Where the electrical supply is alternating, the root-mean-square (rms) value of the voltage must be used.

POWER OF ATTORNEY, in US law, a legal document authorizing a person to act on behalf of the signatory, usually in business and financial matters. To be officially recorded, it must usually be certified by a notary public. A general power allows the agent to act for the signatory in all circumstances, while a special power covers only items listed.

POWERS, Francis Gary (1929–1977), US military officer who piloted a U-2 spy plane and was shot down over the Soviet Union in 1960; the incident precipitated an international crisis. Sentenced to 10 years in a Soviet prison, he was released 1962 in exchange for a convicted Russian spy, Rudolph Abel.

POWHATAN (c1550–1618), personal name Wahunsonacock, chief of the POWHATAN INDIANS and head of the Powhatan Confederacy of tribes which he enlarged until it covered most of the Virginia tidewater region and part of Maryland. He befriended the JAMESTOWN settlers under their leader John SMITH (1608). Later hostilities were settled when his daughter POCAHONTAS married John ROLFE (1614).

POWYS, John Cowper (1872–1963), English writer. His work included novels such as Wolf Solent (1929) and A Glastonbury Romance (1932), his Autobiography (1934), poems, essays and lectures.

PRAETORIAN GUARD, the elite household troops of the Roman emperors, consisting of 9 (later 10) cohorts of 1,000 foot soldiers with higher rank and pay than ordinary troops. Instituted by Augustus in 2 BC, they assumed enough power to overthrow emperors. Constantine disbanded them in 312.

PRAETORIUS, Michael (German name Schultheiss; 1571–1621), prolific German composer of choral church music and

dances, and author of Syntagma musicum (1614–20), a historically important treatise on theory and instruments.

PRAGMATIC SANCTION, an edict by a ruler pronouncing on an important matter of state, such as the succession. The most famous was issued by the Holy Roman Emperor Charles VI in 1713 (published 1718), declaring that his eldest daughter MARIA THERESA should inherit the throne in the absence of a male heir. This resulted in the War of the AUSTRIAN SUCCESSION.

PRAGMATISM, a philosophical theory of knowledge whose criterion of truth is relative to events and not, as in traditional philosophy, absolute and independent of human experience. A theory is pragmatically true if it "works"—if it has an intended or predicted effect. All human undertakings are viewed as attempts to solve problems in the world of action; if theories are not trial solutions capable of being tested, they are pointless. The philosophy of pragmatism was developed in reaction to late 19th-century IDEALISM mainly by the US philosophers C. S. PEIRCE, William JAMES and John DEWEY. (See also INSTRUMENTALISM.)

PRAGUE (Praha), capital of Czechoslovakia, on the Vltava R. One of Europe's great historic cities, it became prominent under Emperor Charles IV, who founded the university, the first in central Europe (1348). The Hapsburgs ruled Prague for nearly 300 years, until Czechoslovakia's independence after WWI. Prague was invaded by the Nazis in 1939 and by Warsaw Pact countries in 1968. The city has great cultural, commercial and industrial importance and is the center of the country's engineering industry. Pop 1,193,300.

PRAGUE SCHOOL, or **Linguistic Circle of Prague,** an association of linguists founded by Vilélm Mathesius in 1926, which included the Russian émigrés Nikolay S. Trubetskoy and Roman JAKOBSON. The Prague School sought to relate structuralist concepts to an understanding of the vital role played in language formation by the functions language performs. These scholars were also noted for work in phonology and stylistics.

PRAIRIE DOGS, GROUND SQUIRRELS of the genus Cynomys. Social animals of the open plains of North America, they live in large colonies in burrows. They are short-tailed marmot-like creatures; active by day, feeding, grooming or sunbathing near their burrows. They frequently raise themselves on their hindlegs to watch for danger. A sharp whistle, given as warning, sends the colony dashing into the burrows.

PRAIRIE PROVINCES, the popular name for the Canadian provinces of Manitoba, Saskatchewan and Alberta.

PRAIRIES, the rolling GRASSLANDS that once covered much of interior North America. There are three types: tallgrass, midgrass (or mixed-grass) and shortgrass, which is found in the driest areas. Typical prairie animals are the coyote, badger, prairie dog and jackrabbit, and the now largely vanished bison and wolf. (See also STEPPES.)

PRAIRIE SCHOONER, the "ship of the plains," the typical canvas covered wagon used in migration to the West. It developed about 1820 from the CONESTOGA WAGON but was lighter and often drawn by oxen.

PRAWNS, zoologically, shrimp-like crustaceans of the suborder Natantia, specifically those groups which possess a pointed rostrum projecting between the eyes. In common language, the term is often used interchangeably with SHRIMP, and applied to any large shrimp.

PRAXITELES (active about 370–330 BC), greatest Greek sculptor of his time. Of his major works, which introduced a new delicacy, grace and sinuosity of line, only a marble statue of Hermes carrying the infant Dionysus survives. There are Roman copies of his *Aphrodite of Cnidus* and *Apollo Sauroctonus*. (See GREEK ART AND ARCHITECTURE.)

PRAYER, in all religions, communication with the sacred; the major element in most private and public worship, often associated with SACRIFICE. It includes adoration, praise, thanksgiving, confession of sin and intercession for others as well as asking for one's own material and spiritual needs. Prayer ranges from the ardent spiritual experience of the mystic (see MYSTICISM) to traditional formal LITURGY. In Islam a set prayer is recited five times daily towards Mecca. In Christianity prayer is made through Jesus Christ and on his authority; it is based on God's power and PROVIDENCE. (See also LORD'S PRAYER.) Praying to the SAINTS is practiced in the Roman Catholic and Orthodox Churches.

PRAYING MANTIS. See MANTISES.

PRECAMBRIAN, the whole of geological time from the formation of the planet earth to the start of the PHANEROZOIC (the eon characterized by the appearance of abundant FOSSILS in rock strata), and thus lasting from about 4,550 to 570 million years ago. It is essentially equivalent to the Cryptozoic eon. (See also GEOLOGY.)

PRECESSION, the gyration of the rotational axis of a spinning body, such as a GYROSCOPE, describing a right circular CONE whose vertex lies at the center of the spinning body. Precession is caused by the action of a TORQUE on the body. **Precession of the equinoxes** occurs because the earth is not spherical, but bulges at the EQUATOR, which is at an angle of 23.5° to the ECLIPTIC. Because of the gravitational attraction of the sun, the earth is subject to a torque which attempts to pull the equatorial bulge into the same plane as the ecliptic, therefore causing the planet's poles, and hence the intersections of the equator and ecliptic (the equinoxes), to precess in a period of about 26,000 years. The moon (see NUTATION) and planets similarly affect the direction of the earth's rotational axis.

PRE-COLUMBIAN ART, art of what is now Latin America prior to COLUMBUS' discovery of the Americas in 1492. The two main cultural areas were the central Andes (S Colombia, Ecuador, Peru, Bolivia, NW Argentina and N Chile) and Meso-America (Mexico and Central America). In both areas artistic development took place after c3000 BC. Monochrome-decorated pottery, female figurines and elaborately designed textiles have been discovered in Ecuador and Peru dating from 3000–2500 BC. The great Andean classical period noted for textiles, ceramics, gold and silver work, jewelry and stone masonry took place in 1000 BC–800 AD prior to the INCA kingdom. The great city buildings at CUZCO, MACHU PICCHU and TIAHUANACO are striking achievements. The Meso-Americans excelled in the graphic and plastic arts. From about 1000 AD the illuminated codex writings of the MAYAS, MIXTECS and AZTECS recorded mythological stories. Their temples, as at CHICHEN-ITZA, were decorated with elaborately carved stone sculptures and reliefs, with wall frescoes inside. The OLMECS made small jade carvings and colossal stone heads. In Colombia the CHIBCHA INDIANS were skilled in ceramics, textiles and jewelry.

PREDESTINATION, in theology, the belief that through God's decree certain persons (the elect) are destined to be saved. Premised on God's omniscience and omnipotence and buttressed by the doctrines of God's PROVIDENCE and GRACE, predestination was taught especially by St. Paul and was elaborated by St. AUGUSTINE in opposition to PELAGIANISM. CALVINISM taught additionally the predestination of the nonelect to damnation, unlike Catholicism denying individual FREE WILL and regarding saving grace as irresistible and wholly gratuitious. JANSENISM was a similar Roman movement. Islam likewise teaches absolute predestination. (See also ARMINIANS.)

PREGNANCY, in humans the nine-month period from the fertilization and IMPLANTATION of an EGG, the development of EMBRYO and FETUS through the BIRTH of a child. Interruption of MENSTRUATION and change in the structure and shape of the BREASTS are early signs; morning sickness, which may be mild or incapacitating is a common symptom. Later an increase in abdominal size is seen and other abdominal organs are pushed up by the enlarging WOMB. LIGAMENTS and JOINTS become more flexible in preparation for delivery. MULTIPLE PREGNANCY, hydatidiform mole, spontaneous ABORTION, antepartum HEMORRHAGE, toxemia and premature labor are common disorders of pregnancy. The time following birth is known as the puerperium.

PREHISTORIC AND PRIMITIVE ART, the earliest forms of art. Prehistoric art is the art of the STONE AGE. The first known works of art date from c15,000 BC when man was carving statuettes of "mother-goddesses," like the *Venus of Willendorf*, in ivory, bone and out of walls, as at ALTIMIRA and the LASCAUX CAVES. Such depiction possibly had a magical function, helping hunters to capture their prey. In the NW European Mesolithic period (c8000–3000 BC) Scandinavian and Spanish cave painters depicted inter-tribal wars, harvest scenes and hunts. Complex rock paintings in the central Sahara regions of Africa, at Tassili-n-Ajjer, date from the Neolithic period (8000–3000 BC).

Primitive art is that of primitive societies in general. Primitive art in this sense should not be confused with that of unschooled artist of W Europe and the US referred to as PRIMITIVES. Such primitive societies are usually hunting or agricultural groups. However unsophisticated their artistic materials and workmanship, their art tends to be functional, related to religion, magic and rituals. Ancestor worship and the power of dead spirits, and thus spirit masks, are very important, especially in SE Asia. Ornamental skulls—heads were thought to be the home of the spirit—are common in New Zealand and New Guinea, and the motif of the squatting figure found in South America, Indochina and Indonesia suggests contact between their primitive peoples at some time. Some of the finest primitive art works are the magnificent 14th-century bronze-cast heads produced by the African IFE and BENIN tribes. (See PRIMITIVE MAN.)

PREHISTORIC MAN. Homo sapiens sapiens, or modern man, appeared on the earth relatively recently. Though the planet's age is estimated at 4.5 billion years, man in his present form may have existed for only some 100,000 years. By comparison, one-celled life began about 3.2 billion years ago, while mammals have flourished for about 200 million years.

Study of early man is hampered by the difficulty of distinguishing between what was to become *Homo sapiens* and the ancestors of our modern apes. The actual point of separation of the two strains is so long ago, probably before either bore any resemblance to their modern descendants, that it is unlikely ever to be discovered. The earliest known form of man may have been **Ramapithecus**, though there is still debate as to whether he should be classed as of the Hominidae (family of man), of the Pongidae (anthropoid-ape family) or of a third lineage that left no descendants. Only small fragments of Ramapithecus fossil skeletons exist, the earliest of these dating from some 15 million years ago, the latest from some 8 million years ago. The first certain ancestor of modern man is **Australopithecus afarensis,** discovered in 1978. This species flourished in Ethiopia and Tanzania from 3.8 to 2.5 million years ago. Adult individuals walked erect at a height of about 4ft and had a brain of about 400cc. They inhabited grasslands and ate a wide variety of food including some meat. *A. afarensis* is one of several species of the genus *Australopithecus*. Another, *A. africanus*, was slightly taller and lighter boned. Still another, *A. robustus*, was, as its name implies, a taller and more robust species. These two species seem to have established family relationships and relied on meat diets, but both are believed to have been evolutionary dead ends.

The genus **Homo,** or true human being, dates back two million years in the form of *H. habilia*, who used primitive tools and had a brain capacity of 500 to 750cc. *H. habilia* hunted in groups. *H. erectus* appeared about 1.5 million years ago and had a brain size of 800cc—about half that of modern man—which gradually increased to 1,300cc over a period of one million years. *H. erectus* spread from Africa into Europe and Asia, and originated the use of fire and the ax. The species gradually evolved into *H. sapiens* and into our own subspecies, *H. sapiens sapiens*. During this gradual change, beginning 400,000 years ago, our ancestors cooked meat, wore clothes, made wooden tools and built huts. Facial features continued to flatten into close resemblance to our own. A variant, **Neanderthal man,** who flourished from about 75,000 to 35,000 years ago, may have become extinct or may have been in man's direct line of descent. Not the brute often depicted, the Neanderthal in fact developed a sense of the spiritual.

There is some evidence that *H. sapiens sapiens* may have appeared in southern Africa 115,000 years ago; but he is not known in Europe until 30,000 years ago. There, he is often designated as **Cro-Magnon man** for the site in France where his remains were first discovered. Cro-Magnon man closely resembled modern man; he used a variety of tools and domesticated animals about 18,000 years ago and plants about 12,000 years ago. The lovely cave paintings of France and Spain, 15–20,000 years old, represent another major stride in the development of modern man.

PRELUDE, an instrumental, usually keyboard, introduction to a musical work. It was employed by J. S. BACH to introduce FUGUES and SUITES. In later piano music it is often a self-contained composition, as in the *Preludes* of CHOPIN, SCRIABIN or DEBUSSY.

PREMINGER, Otto Ludwig (1906–   ), Austrian-born film director, who came to the US in 1936. Noted for his mastery of dramatic suspense, he directed *Laura* (1944), *The Man with the Golden Arm* (1955), *Anatomy of a Murder* (1959), *Exodus* (1960) and *The Cardinal* (1963).

PRENDERGAST, Maurice Brazil (1859–1924), US painter influenced by POSTIMPRESSIONISM, a member of the EIGHT. His work includes *Umbrellas in the Rain* (1899) and *Central Park* (1901).

PREPPY, adjective designating a certain living style associated with the exclusive prep (preparatory) schools of the Northeast. Although the word has pejorative connotations, the style itself, especially as it relates to fashions in dress, has been quite popular and influential. The term preppy was given increased currency with the publication in 1980 of the mock guide, *The Preppy Handbook.*

PRE-RAPHAELITES, influential group of English artists who formed a "brotherhood" in 1848 in reaction against the prevailing academic style. An allegorical subject, bright colors and minute naturalistic detail are typical of their work, as in *Christ in the Carpenter Shop* (1850) by MILLAIS or *The Scapegoat* (1854) by H. HUNT. A third founder member was D. G. ROSSETTI, while BURNE-JONES and William MORRIS were later followers. Critic John RUSKIN was an advocate of the Pre-Raphaelites.

PRESBYOPIA, a defect of VISION coming on with advancing age in which the LENS of the EYE hardens, causing loss of the ability to accommodate (focus) nearby and often distant objects. The condition is corrected by supplying two pairs of GLASSES (one for close work, the other for distant vision), though these may be combined in bifocal lenses.

PRESBYTER (from Greek *presbyteros*, elder), office of MINISTRY in the early Church. There were several presbyters in each congregation, ordained as leaders and teachers. At first identical with the "overseers" (or "bishops"), presbyters became by the 2nd century a distinct order of PRIESTS. (See also BISHOP; ELDER.)

PRESBYTERIANISM, form of church government by ELDERS. Midway between episcopacy and congregationalism, it was espoused at the Reformation by the REFORMED CHURCHES, who viewed it as a rediscovery of the apostolic practice of government by PRESBYTERS. There is a hierarchy of church courts: the *kirk-session*, the minister and elders elected by the local congregation; the *presbytery*, representative ministers and elders from a given area; the SYNOD, members chosen from several presbyteries; and the *general assembly*, the supreme body, consisting of ministers and elders from all the presbyteries. (Various names are used for these courts.) Presbyterian doctrine is biblical CALVINISM, usually with the WESTMINSTER CONFESSION as a subordinate standard. Worship is simple and dignified.

PRESCOTT, Samuel (1751–c1777), American patriot who in a famous ride with Paul REVERE escaped to warn his home town CONCORD, Mass., of the British advance (1775). Later captured, he died in prison.

PRESCOTT, William (1726–1795), American Revolutionary colonel. He commanded the militia in the Battle of BUNKER HILL (1775) and took part in the battles of LONG ISLAND (1776) and SARATOGA (1777).

PRESCOTT, William Hickling (1796–1859), US historian. Despite the handicap of near blindness he became an authority on Spain and the Spanish conquest of America. His *History of the Reign of Ferdinand and Isabella the Catholic* (1837), *History of the Conquest of Mexico* (1843) and *History of the Conquest of Peru* (1847) became classics, admired for their narrative skill as well as their historical rigor.

PRESIDENCY, in many countries the office of head of state and often of chief executive; also of the head of many business, educational and other organizations. The US president is both head of state and chief executive. The Founding Fathers intended the presidency to act as a point of unity for the separate states and provide a commander in chief for joint defense. The office has been molded by events and by the elected presidents themselves and has steadily grown in power. President and vice-president are the only elected US federal executives. A candidate for president must be over 35 years of age and be a "natural-born" US citizen who has resided in the US for at least 14 years. By a majority vote the ELECTORAL COLLEGE chooses a president for a four-year term. With the adoption of the 22nd Amendment, a president may serve not more than two terms.

The Constitution empowers the president to appoint, with the advice and consent of the Senate, cabinet secretaries, Supreme Court justices, ambassadors and other high officials. The president similarly appoints heads of boards, agencies and commissions set up by Congress. He has powers under the Constitution and statutes to issue EXECUTIVE ORDERS in times of emergency; the TAFT-HARTLEY ACT gives powers to intervene in labor-management disputes. As commander in chief, the president represents the supremacy of civil authority over the military. He plays a customary role of great importance in foreign policy, owing to his ability to use speed, flexibility and secrecy in negotiations. This role is enhanced by his sole authority in determining the use of nuclear weapons. Although the president cannot declare war, he can create a condition of war by sending troops into combat, as did Kennedy, Johnson and Nixon in Laos, Cambodia and Vietnam. Under the Constitution, the LEGISLATURE, like the JUDICIARY, is independent of the authority of the president, who is responsible for the execution of laws. But the president's ability to VETO legislation and to initiate it through his party carry great weight in the lawmaking process.

The Executive Office of the President provides the agencies, bureaus and councils vital to the execution of presidential duties. The White House Office Staff includes the president's secretaries, military aides, advisors and his personal physician.

The office's great power of political leadership depends ultimately on the political skills of the president. His control of patronage, his leadership of one of the major political parties and his ability to exert pressure on the legislative and judicial branches of government by appealing directly to the people are powerful weapons for the maintenance of presidential power.

(See also CHECKS AND BALANCES; SEPARATION OF POWERS; CONGRESS OF THE UNITED STATES; UNITED STATES CONSTITUTION; WATERGATE.)

PRESIDIUM, in the USSR, the supreme state authority between sessions of the SUPREME SOVIET, responsible for legislation. The Supreme Soviet elects its chairman, who is titular head of state, 15 vice-chairmen (one from each union republic), 20 members and secretary. At different times the POLITBURO has also been termed Presidium.

PRESLEY, Elvis (1935–1977), the first major rock'n'roll star and a present-day cult hero. From 1956 until the mid 1960s, Presley's belted-out versions of rhythm-and-blues songs (*Hound Dog*) and ballads (*Love Me Tender*) were instant hits, as were his 33 films. His Memphis home is today a shrine for his many fans.

PRE-SOCRATIC PHILOSOPHY, term applied to the thought of the early Greek philosophers (c600–400 BC) whose work came before the influence of SOCRATES. Their works survive mostly in obscure fragments, but their fame and importance lie in their being the first to attempt rational explanations of the universe. They are grouped into the IONIAN school in Asia Minor (THALES, ANAXIMANDER, ANAXIMENES, XENOPHANES, HERACLITUS, ANAXAGORAS, and the ATOMISTS, LEUCIPPUS and DEMOCRITUS) the Pythagoreans (see PYTHAGORAS); and the ELEATICS (PARMENIDES, ZENO and EMPEDOCLES).

PRESSBURG, Treaty of (1805), between Napoleon and Holy Roman Emperor Francis II after Austria's defeat at AUSTERLITZ. Among other concessions, Austria lost her Italian possessions and recognized Napoleon as King of Italy. (See NAPOLEONIC WARS.)

PRESSURE, the FORCE per unit area acting on a surface. The SI UNIT of pressure is the PASCAL ($Pa = newton/(metre)^2$) but several other pressure units, including the atmosphere (101.325kPa), the bar (100kPa) and the millimetre of mercury (mmHg = 133.322Pa), are in common use. In the universe, the pressure varies from roughly zero in interstellar space to an atmospheric pressure of roughly 100kPa at the surface of the earth and much higher pressures within massive bodies and in STARS. According to the KINETIC THEORY of matter, the pressure in a closed container of GAS arises from the bombardment of the container walls by gas molecules: it is proportional to the temperature and inversely proportional to the volume of the gas.

PRESSURE COOKER, small AUTOCLAVE

used for domestic cooking. Water boils inside the vessel at a pressure greater than atmospheric (commonly 2atm), at which pressure its BOILING POINT is considerably higher than 100°C, so that the food cooks much more rapidly than if boiled normally. The pressure, regulated by a weighted or spring-loaded valve, is due to the steam produced by the boiling water.

PRESTER JOHN, legendary Christian priest-king. A purported letter from "Presbyter John," probably of Western authorship, reached the papal court in 1165. It described a great Christian utopia in the "three Indies," identified in later legend as Ethiopia.

PRETORIA, administrative capital of South Africa and capital of the Transvaal. Named for PRETORIUS, it has fine government buildings, art galleries and museums. Its industries include iron, steel, chemicals, glassware, engineering and paint. Pop 543,950.

PRETORIUS, Andries Wilhelmus Jacobus (1799–1835), commandant of the BOERS and GREAT TREK leader. His defeat of the ZULUS at Blood R (1838) led to the founding of Natal. He led the 1848 trek into the Transvaal.

PRÉVERT, Jacques (1900–   ), French writer. His popular poems, sometimes satirical, sometimes melancholy, include *Paroles* (1946). Among his screenplays is that for Carné's *Les Enfants du paradis* (1944).

PREVIN, André (1929–   ), German-US pianist, conductor and arranger. Originally an adapter of stage musicals for the screen, he won Academy Awards for his work on the films *Kiss Me Kate* (1953) and *Gigi* (1958). He later took up symphony conducting, becoming director of the Houston Symphony (1964), the London Symphony (1968) and the Pittsburgh Symphony (1976). Also a jazz pianist, he made several successful recordings with small groups.

PRÉVOST D'EXILES, Antoine François (Abbé Prévost) (1697–1763), French writer, priest and adventurer. *Manon Lescaut* (1731), a love story, is the masterpiece among his many novels.

PRIBILOF ISLANDS, a group of four small islands of volcanic origin in the Bering Sea. They lie about 300mi SW of Alaska and were acquired by the US in 1867. The two largest are St. Paul and St. George. Every spring, about 80% of the world's fur seals visit the islands to breed. Since 1911 the seal herds have been protected and the US regulates the harvesting of seals.

PRICE, the amount of money (or goods in a barter system) for which a commodity or service is exchanged. In theory, prices are set in a FREE ENTERPRISE SYSTEM by SUPPLY AND DEMAND, while in a planned economy (see SOCIALISM) the state decides prices centrally. (See also MONEY; WAGE AND PRICE CONTROL.)

PRICE, Leontyne (1927–   ), US soprano. Her first success was as Bess in Gershwin's *Porgy and Bess*. Following opera debuts on television (1955) and with the San Francisco Opera (1957) she won international fame in VERDI and PUCCINI operas.

PRICE CONTROL. See WAGE AND PRICE CONTROL.

PRIDE, Charley (1938–   ), US singer who was the first major black recording star in the country music field. He won the Country Music Association's Performer of the Year Award in 1971.

PRIEST, in most religions, a cultic officer who mediates the sacred to the people; a spiritual leader, expert in ritual and generally the offerer of SACRIFICE. In the Old Testament an initial patriarchal priesthood was later restricted to the descendants of AARON, assisted by LEVITES (see also HIGH PRIEST). In the Christian Church PRESBYTERS came to be called priests—an order of the threefold MINISTRY—with powers to grant ABSOLUTION and to offer the sacrifice of the MASS. At the Reformation the priesthood of Christ and through him that of all believers, was emphasized. (See also ORDINATION.)

PRIESTLEY, Joseph (1733–1804), British theologian and chemist. Encouraged and supported by Benjamin FRANKLIN, he wrote *The History and Present State of Electricity* (1767). His most important discovery was OXYGEN (1774; named later by LAVOISIER), whose properties he investigated. However, he never abandoned the PHLOGISTON theory of COMBUSTION. He later discovered many other gases—AMMONIA, CARBON monoxide, hydrogen sulfide—and found that green plants require sunlight and give off oxygen. He coined the name RUBBER. His association in the 1780s with the LUNAR SOCIETY brought him into contact with scientists such as James WATT and Erasmus DARWIN. His theological writings and activity were important in leading the English Presbyterians into Unitarianism; indeed he is regarded as a principal architect of the Unitarian Church. Hostile opinion over this and his support of the French Revolution led to his emigration to the US (1794).

PRIESTLY, J. B. (John Boynton Priestly; 1894–   ), English man of letters. His writings include many plays but he is best known for such popular novels as *The Good Companions* (1929) and *Angel Pavement* (1930) and for his major critical work *Literature and Western Man* (1960).

PRIGOGINE, Ilya (1917–   ), Russian-born Belgian chemist who was awarded the 1977 Nobel Prize in Chemistry for his contributions to nonequilibrium THERMODYNAMICS, the study of how heat is created and dissipated by the action of molecules in "open" or nonconfined systems. His work made thermodynamic principles applicable to such fields as SOCIOLOGY, CITY PLANNING and ECOLOGY.

PRIMAL SCREAM THERAPY, a type of intensive, short-term psychotherapy created by psychologist Arthur JANOV. The patient is led to relive infant experiences which, according to Janov's theory, have caused a lifelong neurotic reaction; this recreates primal pain and the patient is encouraged to respond with a "primal scream," a profound reaction in which the pain and tension of the neurosis are released. Janov explained his theory in *The Primal Scream* (1970).

PRIMARY ELECTION, in the US, an election in which party members elect candidates to run in a subsequent general election. Primary elections are used throughout the US for choosing candidates for Congress, state offices and local government posts. In some states the candidates are proposed by petition; in others they simply file for the office. An election determines which candidate is the party's choice. Most states operate "closed" primaries in which only registered party members may vote. Presidential primaries are but a prelude to the party's national convention, held every four years. Although some states choose delegates to the national convention by the caucus system, most have adopted the presidential primary in one form or another; voters indicate their preference for president directly or by voting for delegate-candidates who are pledged to a particular presidential candidate.

PRIMATES, the order of MAMMALS containing MAN, the ANTHROPOID APES, MONKEYS, TARSIERS, POTTOS, BUSHBABIES and LEMURS. Compared with most mammal groups, primates are peculiarly un-specialized; the brain, however, is proportionately larger and more developed. The stages in the evolution of primates are mostly represented in extant forms. From tarsier-like forms evolved the lemurs and lorises; from the EOCENE Omomyidae arose the Anthropoidea; the Catarrhini, Platyrrhini and Hominoidea.

PRIME MINISTER, or premier, head of the executive in a parliamentary system. The prime minister appoints and directs his own CABINET, which is the source of all major legislation. He also has the power to make and dismiss ministers and to call an election before the full term of a government. The office developed in England at the time of Robert WALPOLE. Most parliamentary democracies distinguish between the head of state (a monarch or president) and the prime minister, who is head of the government. (See also PARLIAMENT.)

PRIME NUMBER, a NATURAL NUMBER which cannot be expressed as the PRODUCT of other natural numbers, e.g. 1, 2, 3, 5, 7, 11, 13, 17 and 19.

PRIME RATE, in the US, the rate of INTEREST on short-term loans charged to the major corporations by commercial banks. It largely determines the other interest rates charged by commercial banks.

PRIMITIVE ART. See PREHISTORIC AND PRIMITIVE ART.

PRIMITIVE MAN, term for societies whose culture has reached a level little, if any, higher than the STONE AGE. Although technologically limited and economically unsophisticated, primitive societies may have extremely complex social structures with extensive rules governing behavior such as MARRIAGE, kinship and religion (see TABOOS). Most contemporary primitive societies are Neolithic; that is, they practice agriculture, make pots, weave textiles and work stone to make tools. A few, however, are Paleolithic, such as the AUSTRALIAN ABORIGINES, the Tasady of Mindanao in the Philippines, and the recently extinguished TASMANIANS. PREHISTORIC MAN probably first formed primitive societies about 250,000 years ago.

PRIMITIVES, in art history, a term describing several groups of painters: the pre-1500 Netherlandish or Flemish school, including VAN EYCK; all Italian painters between GIOTTO and RAPHAEL; and more recent naive, untrained artists such as Henri ROUSSEAU, and the Americans Edward HICKS and Grandma MOSES.

PRIMO DE RIVERA, Miguel (1870–1930), Spanish general and politician. Supported by King Alfonso XIII, he overthrew the government in 1923 and became dictator. Popular discontent, economic failure and loss of army support forced him to resign in 1930. His son, José Antonio Primo de Rivera, founded the FALANGE and was executed by loyalists in 1936.

PRIMOGENITURE, law by which the

eldest son inherits family lands. It originated in medieval Europe for the support of the son who gave military service to his king. Never widely established in the US, primogeniture is still customary in England.

PRIMROSE, William (1904–   ), Scottish violist, US resident since 1937. He cofounded the Festival Quartet in 1956. Several composers, including Bartók, have written works especially for him.

PRINCE, Harold (1928–   ), US theatrical producer. He collaborated with Robert Griffith to produce *Pajama Game* (1954) and *West Side Story* (1957) and himself produced *Fiddler on the Roof* (1964), *Evita* (1980) and *Cabaret* (1966), which he also directed.

PRINCE EDWARD ISLAND, Canadian maritime province. It is Canada's smallest province, both in area and in population, but it is the most densely populated.

Land. The island lies in the Gulf of St. Lawrence and is separated from the mainland by the Northumberland Strait. Its length is about 145mi and greatest width 35mi. There are many tidal inlets, known as "rivers," and no point is more than 10mi from the sea. The surface is gently rolling with small hills in the center and SE; the highest point is 450ft above sea level. The climate is milder than on the mainland and often humid. Annual precipitation averages 40in and heavy snowfalls are common in winter.

People. The population had remained at about 110,000 for many decades; emigration to the mainland had held down the growth rate. But in the last 15 years, the trend has been a rising population. Some 80% of the population descends from British and 15% from original inhabitants of ACADIA. There are several hundred MICMAC INDIANS living on reservations.

Economy. Prince Edward Island's economy is based on farming, fishing, tourism and light industry. Now self-sufficient in grain production, it will soon become an exporter of grain, while tobacco, strawberry and blueberry crops are already valuable exports. Hog production is profitable, and the potato crop, always the most important to the economy, is now relying more on processing industries. Nearly half the crop is processed, mainly into frozen french fries. The processing of lumber is important to the island, as is lobster fishing and the more recent oyster cultivation, or aquaculture, operated by the government. Manufacturing of agricultural and fisheries products is becoming more important.

History. Jacques CARTIER was the first European known to have explored the island and in 1603 CHAMPLAIN claimed it for France. Settled by the French in 1719, it became part of the British colony of Nova Scotia in 1763 and was named Prince Edward Island in 1799 for the future father of Queen Victoria. In 1851 the island won control of its own affairs and it hosted the Confederation Conference of 1864 which led to the foundation of the Dominion of Canada. Prince Edward Island joined the Dominion in 1873 and gained financial support for its depressed economy. It has remained basically rural but after WWII the central government mounted large construction and aid programs for the islanders.

Name of province: Prince Edward Island
Capital: Charlottetown
Area: 2,184sq mi
Population: 124,000

PRINCETON UNIVERSITY, private university in Princeton, N.J. Chartered as the College of New Jersey in 1746, it was renamed in 1896. One of the leading universities in the US, it includes world-famous graduate schools of engineering, architecture and scientific research. It has admitted women since 1969.

PRINCIP, Gavrilo (1895–1918), Serbian nationalist who assassinated Archduke Francis Ferdinand of Austria-Hungary on June 28, 1914 at SARAJEVO. The incident precipitated WWI.

PRINTING, the reproduction of words and pictures in ink on paper or other suitable media. Despite the advent of INFORMATION RETRIEVAL systems, the dissemination and storage of knowledge are still based primarily on the printed word. Modern printing begins with the work of Johann GUTENBERG, who probably invented movable type and type metal in the 15th century. Individual characters could be used several times. The process was little changed for 400 years until the invention of machines that could cast type as it was required (see LINOTYPE; MONOTYPE). Letterpress and lithography are today the two most used printing techniques. **Letterpress** uses raised type that is a mirror image of the printed impression. The type is inked and the paper pressed to it. A number of typeset pages (usually 8, 12, 16, 24 or 32) are tightly locked in a metal form such that, when a sheet of paper has been printed on both sides, it may be folded and trimmed to give a *signature* of up to 64 pages. The arrangement of the pages of type is the *imposition*. Most newspapers use **rotary letterpress:** the forms are not flat but curved backward, so that two may be clamped around a cylinder. Paper is fed between this cylinder and another, the impression cylinder. This technique is especially swift when the paper is fed in as a continuous sheet (a *web*). **Lithography** depends on the mutual repulsion of water and oil or grease. In the fine arts, a design is drawn with a grease crayon on the surface of a flat, porous stone, which is then wetted. The water is repelled by the greasy areas; but ink is repelled by the damp and adheres to the greasy regions. Modern mechanized processes use the same principle. Commonest is **photo-offset**, where the copy to be printed is photographed and the image transferred to a plate such that the part to be printed is oleophilic (oil-loving), the rest hydrophilic (water-loving). The plate is clamped around a cylinder and inked. The impression is made on an intermediate "blanket cylinder," which prints onto the paper. **Gravure** is another major printing technique. The plate is covered with a pattern of recessed cells in which the ink is held, greater depth of cell increasing printed intensity. Gravure is good for color and the plates long-lasting, but high initial plate-making costs render it suitable only for long runs. Little-used for books, it is much used in packaging as it also prints well on media other than paper. **Illustrations**, in letterpress, are reproduced using line or HALFTONE blocks (see also ETCHING). In photo-offset black and white illustrations are printed much as is text; and gravure is inherently suitable for printing tones. For COLOR, the illustration is photographed for each of the colors magenta, cyan, yellow and black, and separate plates or blocks made: the four images are superimposed in printing to give a full-color effect. (See also INK; PAPER; PHOTOGRAPHY.)

PRISONER OF WAR, in wartime, combatant who has been captured by or has surrendered to an enemy state. The Hague Convention of 1907 and the GENEVA CONVENTIONS of 1929 and 1949 established rules in international law for the protection of such prisoners, notably that they should not be maltreated nor required to give any information other than their name, rank, and serial number, and that they should be repatriated upon the cessation of hostilities.

PRISONS, institutions for confining people accused and/or convicted of breaking a law. There are three types of prisons in the US. Jails and lockups are run by city and county governments mainly for those awaiting trial, but also for some convicts serving short sentences. State prisons are operated by the individual states and contain the majority of those convicted of serious crimes. Federal prisons house those convicted of offenses relating to the drug and liquor laws, income tax or immigration laws, misuse of the mails, threats to national security and crimes carried out across state borders.

By the early 1800s, most of the Western world had adopted imprisonment (rather than CORPORAL PUNISHMENT, CAPITAL PUNISHMENT, or exile to PENAL COLONIES) as the chief method of dealing with criminals. The purpose of prisons is threefold: (1) to punish the wrongdoer; (2) to protect society; and (3) to act as a deterrent. Whether more than the first of these functions is fulfilled by modern prison facilities is often debated. Opportunities to learn a useful trade, the provision of psychiatric care, and the relatively normal living and working conditions afforded by open, or minimum-security, facilities or work-release programs and conjugal visits—along with the parole system developed in the 19th century, which gives convicts a chance to readapt to society toward the end of their sentences—are obviously conducive to rehabilitation. Of these, however, only parole is a realistic possibility for the majority of inmates. Prisoners are more likely to do unskilled work, which is underpaid in prison and will again draw low wages on the outside; to experience hostility or mistreatment at the hands of guards; and to live in an environment characterized by serious overcrowding, racial tension, lack of differentiation between violent and non-violent, hardened or novice criminals, and routine violence including widespread sexual abuse. Such conditions led to serious riots at the Attica (N.Y.) State Correctional Facility in 1971, where 42 died, and the New Mexico State Penitentiary in 1980, where 33 died, as well as to violent incidents at many other prisons. Poor conditions have caused the courts to close a number of facilities. Nevertheless, in 1981 the Supreme Court ruled that two prisoners may be kept in a cell built for one if as a whole prison conditions are humane. At present, US federal and state prisons hold about 350,000 inmates, or 0.1% of the total US population.

PRITCHETT,   V(ictor)   S(awdon) (1900–   ), English novelist, short-story writer and literary critic. Based on his travels, many of his works are about Spain, such as *Marching Spain* (nonfiction, 1928), *The Spanish Temper* (nonfiction, 1954), and *Clare Drummer* (novel, 1929). *A Cab at the Door* (1968) and *Midnight Oil* (1971) are autobiographical.

PRIVACY, customary right of a citizen to

An Atlas of Human Anatomy

The study of anatomy is as old as that of medicine itself, but it is only within the last few centuries that physicians have begun to understand the inner workings of the human body in all their marvelous complexity. With this knowledge, gained largely by painstaking dissection of dead bodies, comes the ability to heal the living.

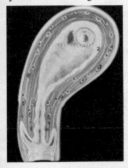

The beginning of life. At left: *Human embryo in the womb, or uterus, during the first month of pregnancy: (1) muscle, (2) the mucous membrane, or endometrium, of the womb, (3) the embryo. In this stage of development, called implantation, the fertilized egg has begun dividing into cells and attached itself to the mucous membrane. The interface between embryo and membrane will develop into the placenta around the fetus.* Below: *The first and last stages of the birth process.* At left: *The baby's head is just above the cervix, the opening of the womb.* At right: *The baby's upper body turns so that it can pass down the birth canal, while the doctor supports the head.*

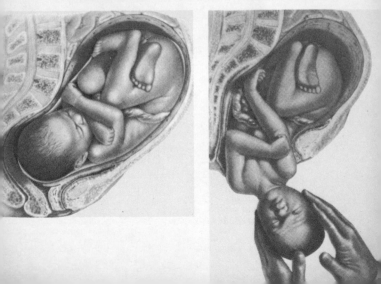

1. Skull
2. Spinal column
3. Clavicle
4. Sternum
5. Pelvis
6. Arm:
   (a) humerus
   (b) ulna
   (c) radius

7. Legs:
   (a) neck of femur
   (b) femur
   (c) tibia
   (d) patella
   (e) fibula
   (f) talus

8. Hand:
   (a) carpus
   (b) hand bones
   (metacarpels)
   (c) fingers

9. Foot:
   (a) tarsals
   (b) calcaneum
   (c) metatarsals
   (d) toes

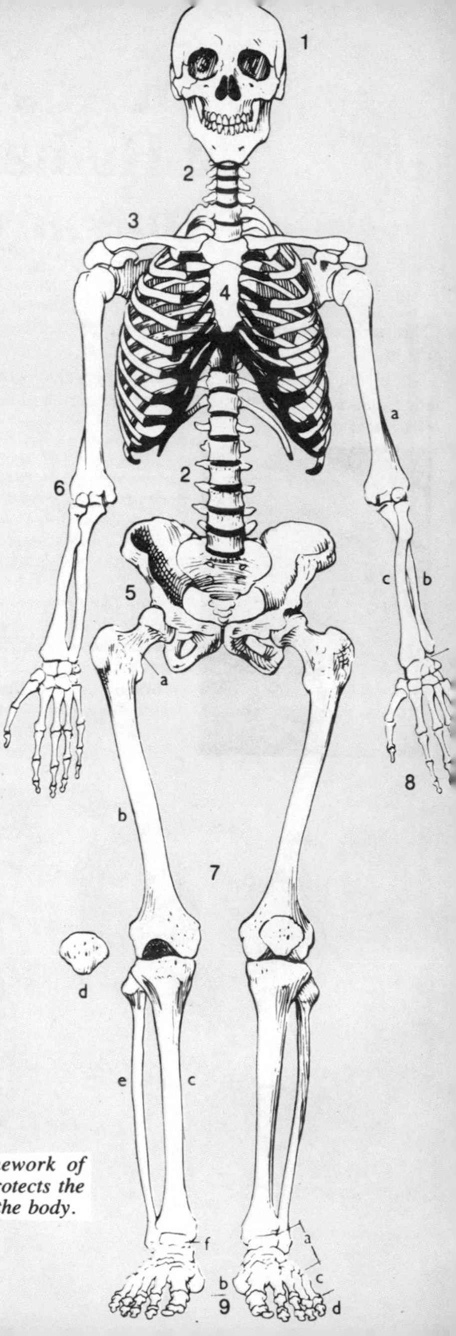

The skeleton is the framework of bones that supports and protects the soft tissues and organs of the body.

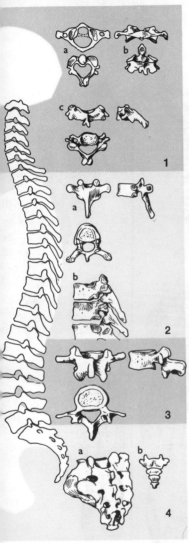

1. Vertebrae of the neck—
   (a) top and (b) back views of
   atlas and axis, and
   (c) other neck vertebrae

2. Thoracic vertebrae—
   (a) *left:* from behind;
   right: side view;
   below: from above

3. Lumbar vertebrae

4. Sacral vertebrae—(a) as fused
   into one in humans, and (b) the
   tail vertebrae or coccyx,
   consisting of 3 or 4 fused
   vertebrae.

*The backbone or spinal column,
composed of bones called vertebrae,
is the central pillar of the human
skeleton.*

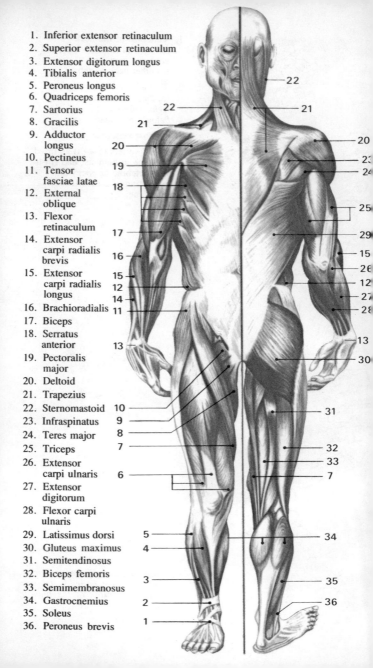

1. Inferior extensor retinaculum
2. Superior extensor retinaculum
3. Extensor digitorum longus
4. Tibialis anterior
5. Peroneus longus
6. Quadriceps femoris
7. Sartorius
8. Gracilis
9. Adductor longus
10. Pectineus
11. Tensor fasciae latae
12. External oblique
13. Flexor retinaculum
14. Extensor carpi radialis brevis
15. Extensor carpi radialis longus
16. Brachioradialis
17. Biceps
18. Serratus anterior
19. Pectoralis major
20. Deltoid
21. Trapezius
22. Sternomastoid
23. Infraspinatus
24. Teres major
25. Triceps
26. Extensor carpi ulnaris
27. Extensor digitorum
28. Flexor carpi ulnaris
29. Latissimus dorsi
30. Gluteus maximus
31. Semitendinosus
32. Biceps femoris
33. Semimembranosus
34. Gastrocnemius
35. Soleus
36. Peroneus brevis

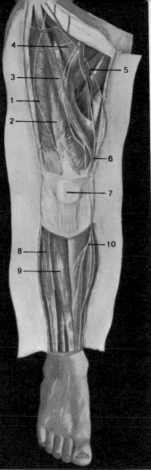

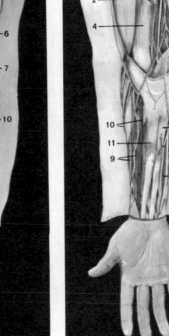

Frontal view of dissected leg
(1) vastus lateralis, (2) rectus
femoris, (3) sartorius,
(4) iliopsoas, (5) pectineus,
(6) nerves (yellow), artery (red)
and veins (blue) of the femur,
(7) patella, (8) extensor digitorum
longus, (9) tibialis anterior,
(10) superficial lower leg artery
and nerve.

Muscles and nerves of the arm
(1) deltoid, (2) biceps,
(3) coracobrachialis,
(4) brachialis, (5) brachial artery,
(6) median nerve, (7) ulnar nerve,
(8) pronator teres, (9) branches of
radial nerve, (10) radial artery and
vein, (11) flexor carpi radialis,
(12) palmaris longus, (13) ulnar
artery

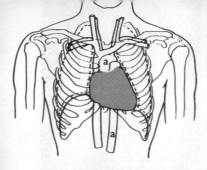

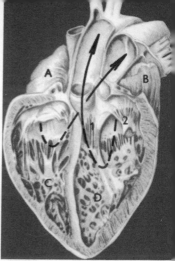

Above: *Located between the lungs and supported by the diaphragm, the heart pumps blood from the left ventricle through the aorta (a).* Right: *(A) right atrium, (B) left atrium, (C) right ventricle, (D) left ventricle.*

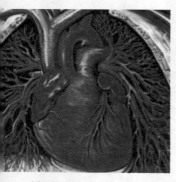

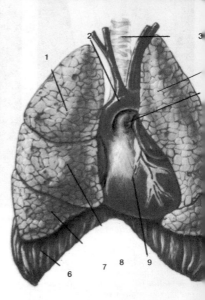

Above: *Coronary arteries (red) branch out from the aorta (top) to supply the heart itself with blood.* Right: *The lungs — (1) right superior lobe, (2) aorta, (3) trachea, (4) left superior lobe, (5) pulmonary artery, (6) diaphragm, (7) right inferior lobe, (8) middle lobe, (9) heart*

SECTION THROUGH NORMAL HEART

Blood carrying carbon dioxide (blue arrows) is pumped to lungs, oxygenated, and returned to heart (red arrows).

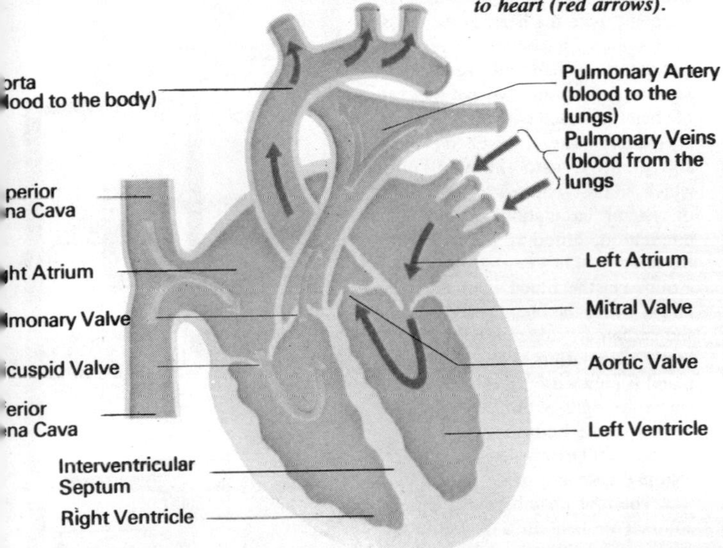

Aorta (blood to the body)

Superior Vena Cava

Right Atrium

Pulmonary Valve

Tricuspid Valve

Inferior Vena Cava

Interventricular Septum

Right Ventricle

Pulmonary Artery (blood to the lungs)

Pulmonary Veins (blood from the lungs)

Left Atrium

Mitral Valve

Aortic Valve

Left Ventricle

LOCATIONS OF SOME CONGENITAL DEFECTS

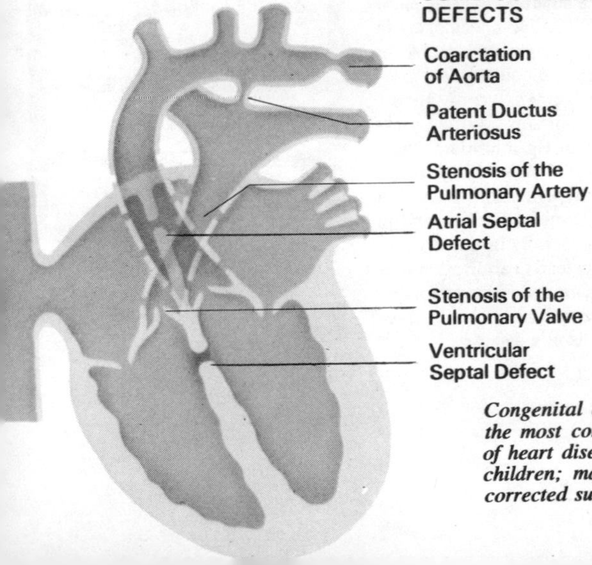

Coarctation of Aorta

Patent Ductus Arteriosus

Stenosis of the Pulmonary Artery

Atrial Septal Defect

Stenosis of the Pulmonary Valve

Ventricular Septal Defect

Congenital defects are the most common form of heart disease among children; many can be corrected surgically.

The human circulatory system has two distinct parts: pulmonary circulation and systemic circulation. The two parts can be thought of as a figure eight, with the heart at the crossover point. The heart powers both circulatory systems but keeps them separate by having two parallel sets of chambers, each with an atrium and a ventricle. The atria receive blood and pump it into the ventricles which, in turn, pump it into the lungs or systemic circulation. In pulmonary circulation, blood is pumped from the heart's right ventricle to the left atrium via the blood vessels of the lungs, where the blood is oxygenated and carbon dioxide removed. In systemic circulation, the oxygenated blood is pumped from the left ventricle to the right atrium via the blood vessels of the body tissues where—in the capillaries—it is deoxygenated and carbon dioxide is taken up.

The four chambers of the heart contract or beat in a wavelike sequence. The "heart beat," which is a complete cycle of these contractions, originates with an electrical discharge from a small region (the sinoatrial node or cardiac pacemaker) in the wall of the right atrium. As it leaves the heart, blood is under considerable pressure—about 120mmHg maximum (systolic pressure) and 80mmHg minimum (diastolic pressure). Sustained high blood pressure, or hypertension, occurs in kidney and hormone diseases and in old age, but generally its cause is unknown. It may lead to arteriosclerosis and heart, brain, and kidney damage. Low pressure occurs in shock, trauma, and Addison's disease.

BLOOD CIRCULATION

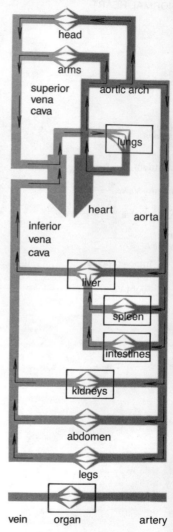

The digestive system. Food passes from mouth (a) through esophagus (b) to stomach (c) where it mixes with gastric juice. Absorption continues in duodenum (d) where bile from gall bladder (e) and salts from liver (f) are introduced. Food then passes to cecum (g) to which appendix (h) is attached, and enters colon (i) where most of the water is absorbed. The residue is eliminated through the rectum.

Most digestive processes for converting food into a form that is absorbable and usable by the body takes place in the gastrointestinal tract.

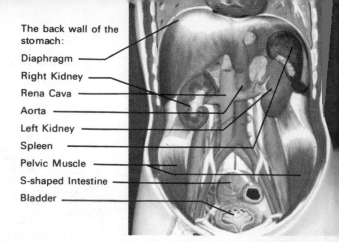

The back wall of the stomach:

Diaphragm ——

Right Kidney ——

Rena Cava ——

Aorta ——

Left Kidney ——

Spleen ——

Pelvic Muscle ——

S-shaped Intestine ——

Bladder ——

The abdomen in humans and other vertebrates is the part of the body between the chest and the pelvis. In human beings, it contains most of the gastrointestinal tract (from the stomach to the colon) together with the liver, gall bladder, and spleen in a potential cavity lined by a transparent membrane called the

Section through abdomen showing the bladder and urethra in the female (left) and male (right). Urine trickles constantly from the kidneys into the *bladder, which slowly swells, causing the desire to urinate through the urethra.*

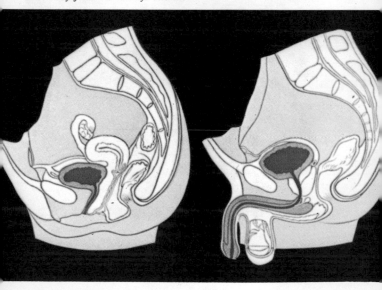

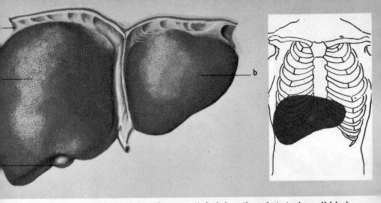

The liver, seen from the front, lies just below the diaphragm (a) atop the abdominal cavity. On the liver's lower surface, between the left and right lobes (b and c), is the gall bladder, which acts as a reservoir for bile.

peritoneum. This cavity also contains fluid, allowing the organs to move over each other. Behind this space lie the kidneys, adrenal glands, and pancreas, along with the abdominal aorta and inferior vena cava. The entire abdomen is protected by a muscular wall attached to the spine, ribs, and pelvic bones, and it is separated from the chest by the diaphragm.

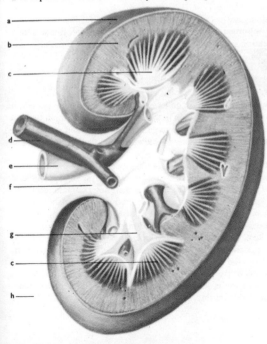

Kidney section: Under protective capsule (a) is renal cortex (b). Rounded projections called pyramids (c) empty into renal calyxes (g) of renal pelvis (f), where urine from collecting tubules is gathered. Urine drains off to bladder through ureter (h), which lies close to renal artery (d) and renal vein (e).

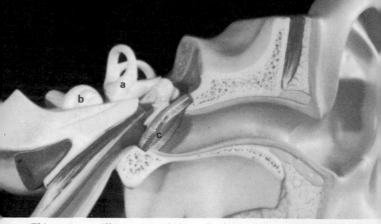

This cutaway illustration of the human ear shows

(a) the semicircular, fluid-bearing canals, essential to the sense of balance;

(b) the cochlea, containing the cochlear fluid, which activates the hearing receptor cells; and

(c) the tympanic membrane or eardrum, which conveys sonar vibrations.

All the bodily systems are necessary to the support of life, but the nervous system is the most important among them, for it governs and coordinates their operations. The beating of the heart, the secretion of glands, breathing, and digestion, for example, are all triggered, monitored, and adjusted by nervous impulses. Moreover, the nervous system is also the physical basis of all mental activities and properties: consciousness, sensation, thought, speech, memory, emotion, character, and skill.

The nervous system has a certain gross similarity to a telephone system: It works electrically, it carries information in the form of electrical impulses, and all the nervous pathways of the body converge upon the brain and spinal cord, which together form a "central exchange" and constitute the Central Nervous System.

As we see in these pictures of the ear, some aspects of the system depend upon relatively simple mechanical devices; however, the system as a whole is highly complex and sophisticated. At birth the human body contains some 10 billion nerve cells (neurons)—a number which gradually diminishes, for as nerve cells die they are not replaced, although existing ones may grow in size.

A nerve cell consists of a body (soma) and long, threadlike processes, the axon and the dendrites. The dendrites carry an impulse toward the cell body; the axon carries it oppositely. The ends of an axon lie very close to the dendrites of other neurons, the distance between being called the synapse.

At the outer limits of the sensory pathways are sensory receptors, which translate stimulation of various sorts into electrical energy which is then transmitted by nerve cells to the brain.

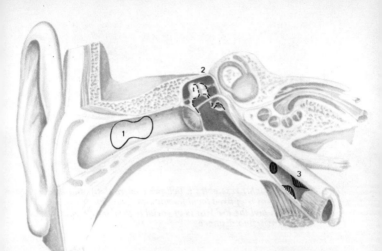

Loss or distortion of perception can be caused by a disturbance at any point in the neurophysiological system. Thus, causes of deafness include

(1) obstruction of the external auditory canal;

(2) degeneration of the auditory ossicles;

(3) plugging of the eustachian tube;

(4) inflammation of the inner ear extending to the petrous bone;

(5) infection of the auditory nerve;

(6) middle-ear inflammation. (In the illustrations, the external ear is shown in blue, the middle ear in red, and the inner ear in green.)

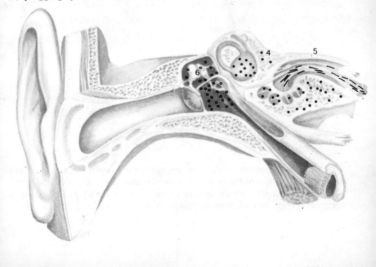

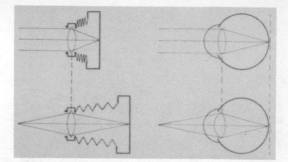

The eye (right) resembles a bellows camera (left). But the camera lens is of fixed focal length with a variable lens-film distance, and the eye lens is of variable focal length with a fixed lens-retina distance.

A cross section of the eye:
(1) optical axis, (2) visual axis,
(3) cornea, (4) anterior chamber
(aqueous fluid), (5) iris,
(6) posterior chamber, (7) ciliary
body, (8) lens capsule,
(9) vitreous humor, (10) optic
nerve, (11) fovea, (12) retina

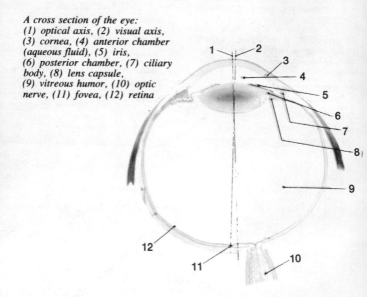

Touch receptors convert mechanical energy; heat receptors convert thermal energy; the receptors of the inner ear convert sound energy; the rods and cones of the retina convert light energy; and taste buds and olfactory cells convert chemical energy. Not all these receptors are on the surface of the body: there

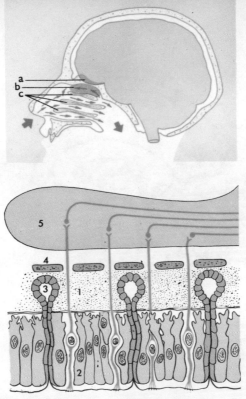

Top: *olfactory system of the head, with bone in yellow and nervous tissue in violet.*
(a) brain's olfactory bulb,
(b) olfactory epithelium, and
(c) nasal turbinals.

Bottom: *(1) sensory cells with long processes in the olfactory epithelium,*
(2) supporting cells, (3) secretory cells, (4) openings in the bone for the olfactory nerve threads,
(5) the olfactory bulb of the brain.

are touch receptors at all bone joints, in most muscles, and in the gut (we know, e.g., when we are "stuffed" from overeating). Also, as we see in the illustrations of the olfactory system of the head, there are olfactory receptor cells in the epithelium (membrane) which lies at the end of the nasal turbinals; the air which enters through these passages comes into contact with the receptors, and the information is passed through openings in the cribriform plate, the bone protecting the brain, to the olfactory bulb of the brain. Curiously, there are no receptors in the brain itself, so that if a metal probe were to be pressed solely into the brain, it would not be felt.

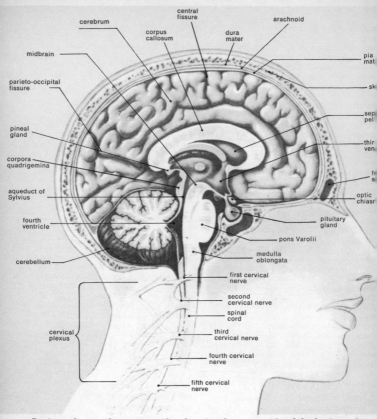

cerebrum

central fissure

corpus callosum

dura mater

arachnoid

pia mat

midbrain

parieto-occipital fissure

sk

pineal gland

sep pel

corpora quadrigemina

thir ven

aqueduct of Sylvius

f s

optic chiasr

fourth ventricle

pituitary gland

cerebellum

pons Varolii

medulla oblongata

first cervical nerve

second cervical nerve

spinal cord

cervical plexus

third cervical nerve

fourth cervical nerve

fifth cervical nerve

Brain: the cerebrum (convoluted) governs sensation, motor action, thought, and speech; the corpus callosum has millions of tiny fibers go-ing from one side of the brain to the other; the cerebellum governs motor feedback.

In the past few decades, much progress has been made in matching up precise points in the brain with the parts of the body to which they are neurally connected. Also, although it has long been known that the right half of the brain controls the left side of the body and vice versa, in recent years we have reached a far more elaborate understanding of the roles of the brain's hemispheres, and some of the basic concepts have entered the popular culture, with common references to people who are highly verbal and logical as "left-brained" and those who are intuitive, artistic, and sensitive to spatial relations as "right-brained." Nevertheless, we have still taken only the first steps toward a complete study of the workings of the brain.

maintain his private life without "undue" interference or publicity. In many countries, the right of privacy is written into the constitution. The concept represents a balance of interests between the individual and the state. In general, privacy may only be interfered with by constitutionally-approved means such as powers given to the police or other government bodies. In the US, a major threat to privacy arises from government and commercial organizations having acquired and computerized large bodies of information about individuals.

PRIVATEER, armed vessel which was privately owned, but commissioned by a government to prey upon enemy ships in wartime. Privateers thus often supplemented a nation's navy. The practice of privateering was outlawed (1856) by the Declaration of Paris, but the US refused to sign it, and privateers operated during the American Civil War. The practice has since been abandoned by all nations.

PRIVY COUNCIL, in British history, an advisory council to the monarch, by whom its members were chosen. Powerful in the 15th and 16th centuries, it declined thereafter with the ascendancy of Parliament.

PROBABILITY, the statistical ratio between the number n of particular outcomes and the number N of possible outcomes: n/N; where all of N are equally likely. For example, when throwing a die there is one way in which a six can turn up and five ways in which a "not six" can turn up. Thus $n=1$ and $N=5+1=6$, and the ratio $n:N=1/6$. If two dice are thrown there are 6×6 (=36) possible pairs of numbers that can turn up: the chance of throwing two sixes is $1/36$. This does not mean that if a six has just been thrown there is only a $1/36$ chance of throwing another: the two events are independent; the probability of their occurring *together* is $1/36$.

Probability theory is intimately linked with STATISTICS. More advanced probability theory has contributed vital understandings in many fields of physics, as in STATISTICAL MECHANICS, behavior of particles in a COLLOID (see BROWNIAN MOTION) or molecules in a GAS.

PROBATE, the legal process of proving that a WILL is valid. Before a will can take effect, it must be shown that it is genuine, that it was the deceased's last will, that he signed it voluntarily and that he was of sound mind. Probate requires all possible heirs of the testator's property to be notified before a special hearing is held in a probate court, where objections can be lodged.

PROBATION, an alternative to prison, whereby convicted offenders are placed under the supervision of a probation officer, on condition that they maintain good behavior. The aim is to encourage reform, particularly for the young, when a spell in prison might simply reinforce criminal tendencies. (See also PAROLE; PUNISHMENT.)

PROCESS PHILOSOPHY, a radical alternative to positivistic philosophies (see POSITIVISM), in which the physicists' "spatial" notion of TIME is rejected and interest centers in the developmental process. First propounded by Henri BERGSON, process philosophy influenced William JAMES, George SANTAYANA and Alfred North WHITEHEAD.

PROCLAMATION OF 1763, proclamation made by the British at the end of the FRENCH AND INDIAN WARS, establishing territorial rights for North American Indians. It aimed both to appease the Indians and to prevent land disputes, but it angered (and was in many respects disregarded by) the colonialists.

PRODUCER PRICE INDEX, three separate indexes issued monthly by the US Department of Labor, reflecting the monthly price changes in three categories of goods: crude goods (raw materials such as corn and coal); intermediate goods (corn meal and machine parts); and finished products (packaged foods, freezers). The indexes are based on a monthly collection of some 10,000 prices supplied by major producers.

PROGESTERONE, female SEX HORMONE produced by the corpus luteum under the influence of LUTEINIZING HORMONE. It prepares the WOMB lining for IMPLANTATION and other body organs for the changes of PREGNANCY. It is used in some oral CONTRACEPTIVES to suppress ovulation or implantation.

PROGRAMMED LEARNING, teaching method whereby matter to be learned is arranged in a coherent sequence of small clear steps (programmed) and presented in such a way that the student is able to instruct, test and, if necessary, correct himself at each step. The learning program is usually embodied in a book or booklet or adapted for use in conjunction with a TEACHING MACHINE. It enables the student to learn at his own pace, with a minimum of wasted effort. There are two basic kinds of programs. The "linear program," based on the work of the Harvard psychologist B. F. SKINNER, obliges the student to compare his own response at each step with the correct response. The "intrinsic (or branching) program," originally developed for instructing US Air Force technicians, offers a limited choice of responses at each step. The correct response is immediately reinforced; an incorrect response obliges the student to follow a corrective subprogram leading back to the point at which the error occurred.

PROGRAM MUSIC, music with extra-musical meaning. It may describe an event, as in Byrd's *The Battell*, or a place, as in Vaughan Williams' *London Symphony*, or it may express specific feelings, as in Beethoven's *Pastoral Symphony*.

PROGRESSIVE CONSERVATIVE PAR-TY, one of Canada's two major political parties. It is generally more conservative on most issues than Canada's Liberal Party. Called the Conservative Party from its formation in 1854, it was the nation's dominant political party for nearly a century. After changing its name in 1942, the Progressive Conservatives have won only two national elections and have governed Canada only twice, in 1957–63 under John G. Diefenbaker and for only six months in 1979 under Joe Clark. His Progressive Conservative-Social Credit coalition was forced to resign after losing a vote of confidence in the House of Commons on Clark's austerity budget. The party's seating in the House was reduced from 136 to 101 members as the result of the elections on Feb 18, 1980.

PROGRESSIVE EDUCATION, an educational reform movement which grew from the idea that schooling should cater to the emotional as well as the intellectual development of the child, and that the basis of learning should be the child's natural and individual curiosity, rather than an enforced discipline. In the US the movement, led by John DEWEY, was most active c1890–1950. (See also EDUCATION.)

PROGRESSIVE PARTY, the name of three American political organizations which fought in 20th century presidential campaigns. Each was largely characterized by programs of social and economic reform. The Progressive Party of 1912 (better known by its nickname, the Bull Moose Party) chose ex-President Theodore Roosevelt as its nominee. It seceded from the Republican Party after the nomination of TAFT, but was reunited with it during the campaign of 1916.

The Progressive Party of 1924 was formed by farm and labor leaders dissatisfied with the conservatism of the Republican administration. Its position, like that of the Bull Moose Party, was that there should be government control of trusts, and it upheld the right of government intervention in private wealth. Its presiden-tial nominee was Robert LA FOLLETTE. The Progressive Party of 1948 nominated former Democratic Vice-President H. A. WALLACE for the presidency. The party sought better relations with the USSR and an end to the Cold War. It had support from many left-wing groups but was labeled a "Communist front" organization. It polled little more than a million votes out of 48 million.

PROHIBITION, restriction or prevention of the manufacture and sale of alcoholic drinks. It refers in particular to the period from 1919 to 1933 when (by means of the 18th Amendment to the Constitution) there was a Federal prohibition law in the US. In spite of the intensive economic and group pressures which had brought it about, it soon became apparent that the law was too unpopular and too expensive to enforce. A now-notorious time of gangsterism followed, with a vast illegal liquor business (the activities involved were known as bootlegging) in the control of men such as Al CAPONE. Prohibition was repealed (1933) by the 21st Amendment. A few states in the US maintained local prohibition laws as late as 1966. (See also VOLSTEAD ACT, NATION, CARRY; WOMEN'S CHRISTIAN TEMPERANCE UNION.)

PROJECTION, in PSYCHOLOGY and PSYCHIATRY, the attribution to others of characteristics which the individual denies in himself. In PSYCHOANALYSIS, the term describes the interpretation of situations or the actions of others in such a way as to justify one's self-opinion or beliefs, as in PARANOIA and paranoid SCHIZOPHRENIA.

PROJECTION TEST, test whereby an individual's personality may be gauged by his completion of unfinished sentences, his interpretation of "pictures" from inkblots, etc.

PROKOFIEV, Sergei (1891–1953), Russian composer. A student at the St. Petersburg Conservatory with RIMSKY-KORSAKOV. Prokofiev created a fierce, dynamic, unemotive style which later became somewhat softer and more eclectic. His works include the popular Classical Symphony, the operas *The Love for Three Oranges* (1921) and *War and Peace* (1943); *Peter and the Wolf* (1936), for narrator and orchestra; *Romeo and Juliet* (1936), a ballet; six symphonies; concertos for piano, violin and cello; film scores and chamber music.

PROLETARIAT, name given to industrial employees as a social and economic class. In Marxist theory, the proletariat is exploited by and inimical to the bourgeois class of employers and property owners.

PROMETHEUS, a demi-god of Greek mythology, one of the TITANS and a brother of ATLAS. He was sometimes said to have created humankind out of earth and water. In a widespread legend, Prometheus stole fire from the gods for the benefit of mankind. ZEUS punished Prometheus by having him bound to a rock, where his liver was devoured by an eagle.

PRONGHORN, *Antilocapra americana,* the only horned animal that sheds its horn sheath, and the only one with branched HORNS as distinct from ANTLERS. They live in groups in arid grasslands and semi-desert of western North America, feeding on forbs and browse plants. Conservation efforts have restored numbers from an estimated 30,000 in 1924 to a present 400,000.

PROPAGANDA, selected information, true or false, which is promoted with the aim of persuading people to adopt a particular belief, attitude or course of action. During the 20th century all the major political ideologies have employed propaganda and made use of modern media to reach a mass audience. It has an important role in modern warfare and by WWII separate bureaus and ministries were established to promote morale and subvert the enemy. The Nazi Ministry of Propaganda, headed by GOEBBELS, was one of the most effective. In the West there has been an increase in professional propagandists such as people in public relations and ADVERTISING.

PROPERTY, social concept and legal term indicating the ownership of, or the right to enjoy, something of value; it may also be an interest in something owned by another. Under some systems such as FEUDALISM or COMMUNISM, ownership of some or all kinds of property is vested not in the individual but in the state or its head. The US Constitution establishes the individual's right to property. COMMON LAW distinguishes between *real property,* land and generally non-transportable goods such as houses and trees, and *personal property,* all other kinds; financial rights such as copyrights or patent holdings are personal. The law treats the two kinds differently in such areas as tax, debt, inheritance and other significant obligations and relationships. (See also DEED; ESTATE; MORTGAGE.)

PROPHETS, in the Old Testament, men who by special REVELATION proclaimed the word of God by oracles and symbolic actions; originally seers and ecstatics. Often a scourge of the establishment, they were religious and social reformers who called for righteousness and faithfulness to God, and pronounced judgment on the ungodly. (See also ESCHATOLOGY; MINOR PROPHETS; OLD TESTAMENT.) In the early Church prophecy was a recognized CHARISMA, but soon died out except in Montanism (see MONTANUS). It was revived among ANABAPTISTS, QUAKERS, MORMONS and PENTECOSTALS. In Islam Mohammed is the last and greatest prophet. Oracular prophets are found in many religions. (See also ORACLE; SHAMANISM.)

PROPORTIONAL REPRESENTATION. See ELECTION.

PROPOSITION 13, a 1978 ballot initiative in Cal., created and publicized by businessman Howard A. Jarvis. It called most notably for a two-thirds reduction of the state property tax and the requirement of a two-thirds vote in the legislature to impose new taxes. The passage of Proposition 13 by a wide margin marked the beginning of the taxpayer revolt that culminated in the elections of President Ronald Reagan and of a Republican-majority Senate in 1980. The immediate impact of Proposition 13 on California was minor because the state had a multibillion-dollar budget surplus at the time. But three years later, many municipalities and the state itself, having used up the budget surplus, were suffering a financial crisis.

PROPRIETARY COLONIES, in US colonial history, English colonies granted by royal charter to an individual or small group, mostly in the period 1660–90. Large tracts of land in N.Y., N.J., Pa., N.C. and S.C. were allocated in this way. The proprietors had almost despotic power in theory, but in practice had to yield rights to the colonists, and the system was ended after the REVOLUTIONARY WAR.

PROSPECTING, the hunt for MINERALS economically worth exploiting. The simplest technique is direct observation of local surface features characteristically associated with specific mineral deposits. This is often done by prospectors on the ground, but increasingly aerial photography is employed (see PHOTOGRAMMETRY; REMOTE SENSING). Other techniques include examining the seismic waves caused by explosions—these supply information about the structures through which they have passed; testing local magnetic fields to detect magnetic metals or the metallic gangues associated with nonmagnetic minerals; and especially for metallic sulfides, testing electric CONDUCTIVITY.

PROSTATE GLAND, male reproductive GLAND which surrounds the urethra at the base of the BLADDER and which secretes semen. This carries sperm made in the TESTES to the PENIS. Benign enlargement of prostate in old age is very common and may cause retention of the urine. CANCER of the prostate is also common in the elderly but responds to HORMONE treatment. Both conditions benefit from surgical removal.

PROSTHETICS, mechanical or electrical devices inserted into or onto the body to replace or supplement the function of defective or diseased organs. Artificial limbs designed for persons with AMPUTATIONS were among the first prosthetics; but metal or plastic JOINT replacements or BONE fixations for subjects with severe ARTHRITIS, FRACTURE or deformity are now also available. Replacement TEETH for those lost by CARIES or trauma are included in prosthodontics (see also DENTISTRY). The valves of the HEART may fail as a result of rheumatic or congenital heart disease or bacterial endocarditis, and may need replacement with mechanical valves (usually of ball-and-wire or flap types) sutured in place of the diseased valves under cardiorespiratory bypass. If the natural pacemaker of the heart fails, an electrical substitute can be implanted to stimulate the heart muscle at a set rate.

PROSTITUTION, the exchange of sexual favors for money or gifts, usually by women. Male prostitutes, while less common, make themselves available to other men or even, rarely, to women. An alarming aspect is the exploitation by adults of young children, often runaways, for prostitution.

Though universally deplored through the ages, prostitutes do have a social scale. At the bottom are the streetwalkers, who openly solicit in selected areas of major cities, above them are the bar girls, who frequent nightclubs or bars and encourage men to spend money, while other women work out of "massage parlors," or thinly disguised brothels. At the top of the pyramid are call girls, who serve a wealthier clientele from their homes.

Women usually rely on the help of a pimp who, in return for a part of the prostitute's earnings, may provide a home, bail money, clothing and a steady sexual partnership. Money is the principal attraction for prostitutes, who often need large sums to support a drug habit. The greatest danger, far more so than harassment by police, is venereal disease.

Not without reason, prostitution is known as the world's oldest profession, and its survival as a service in constant demand suggests that attempts to eliminate it may always be futile. Persons favoring decriminalizing prostitution argue that it is a "victimless" crime (though, in fact, many customers are robbed, just as many prostitutes are exploited) and that police and the courts have more serious crimes to contend with. In the US, Nevada law permits any county to allow prostitution. Many other countries do not consider prostitution a criminal offense.

PROTAGORAS (c490–421 BC), most famous of the Greek SOPHISTS, remembered for the maxim "man is the measure of all things." A respected figure in Athens, where he spent most of his life, he taught RHETORIC and the proper conduct of life ("virtue"), and was appointed lawmaker to the Athenian colony of Thurii in 444 BC. Little is known of his teaching, but he is thought to have been a relativist concerning knowledge and a sceptic about the gods, although he upheld conventional morality.

PROTECTIONISM, in INTERNATIONAL TRADE, a policy by which a country seeks to protect its own industries by controlling the import and export of goods. It generally takes the form of restrictive TARIFFS or QUOTAS on imported goods. The US has had a long tradition of protectionism, and still has a number of restrictive import quotas, in spite of the general world trend towards freer trade (see GENERAL AGREEMENT ON TARIFFS AND TRADE).

PROTECTIVE COLORATION. Many animals have adapted their coloration as a means of defense against predators. Except where selection favors bright coloration for breeding or territorial display, most higher animals are colored in such a way that they blend in with their backgrounds—by pure coloration, by disruption of outline with bold lines or patches, or by a combination of the two. The most highly developed camouflage is found in ground-nesting birds, for example, NIGHTJARS, or insects, such as WALKING STICKS or LEAF INSECTS. Associated with this coloration must be special behavior patterns enabling the animal to seek out the correct background for its camouflage and to "freeze" against it. Certain animals can change the body texture and coloration to match different backgrounds: OCTOPUSES, CHAMELEONS, and some FLATFISHES. An alternative strategy adopted by some animals, particularly insects, is the use of shock-coloration. When approached by a predator these insects flick open dowdy wings to expose bright colors, often in the form of staring "eyes," to scare the predator.

PROTECTORATE, a country which is nominally independent, but surrenders part of its SOVEREIGNTY, such as control over foreign policy, in return for protection by a stronger state. The degree of control and dependency may vary. Many states in the European colonial empires were governed as protectorates.

PROTECTORATE, The, period of English history from 1653 to 1659 when the country was ruled by a Lord Protector, a Council of State, and Parliament. It was in effect, a dictatorship. Oliver CROMWELL was the first Lord Protector, succeeded in 1658 by his son Richard, who, unable to control army and Parliament, resigned in 1659, paving the way for the RESTORATION.

PROTEIN, a high-molecular-weight compound which yields AMINO ACIDS on HYDROLYSIS. Although hundreds of different amino acids are possible, only 20 are found in appreciable quantities in proteins, and these are all α-amino acids. Proteins are found throughout all living organisms. Muscle, the major structural material in animals, is mainly protein; the 20% of blood which is not water is mainly protein. ENZYMES may contain other components, but basically they too are protein. Approximately 700 different proteins are known. Of these 200–300 have been studied and over 150 obtained in crystalline form. Some proteins, such as those found in the hides of cattle which can be converted to LEATHER, are very stable, while others are so delicate that even exposure to air will destroy their capability as enzymes. The most important and strongest bond in a protein is the PEPTIDE bond joining the amino acids in a chain. Other bonds hold the different chains together: HYDROGEN BONDING, together with strong disulfide bonds and secondary peptide links are important here. The three dimensional structure of proteins helps to determine their properties; X-RAY studies have shown that the amino acid chain is sometimes coiled in a spiral or helix. Although proteins are very large molecules (with molecular weights ranging from 12,000 to over 1 million), many of them are partly ionized and hence are soluble in water. Such differences in size, solubility and electrical charge are exploited in methods of separating and purifying proteins. The separation of proteins in an electrical field (ELECTROPHORESIS) is widely applied to human serum in the diagnosis of certain diseases.

PROTESTANT EPISCOPAL CHURCH. See EPISCOPAL CHURCH, PROTESTANT.

PROTESTANT ETHIC, set of attitudes thought to be embodied in Calvinistic PROTESTANTISM, especially the value placed on hard work, "for the greater glory of God." The term was introduced by M. WEBER in *The Protestant Ethic and the Spirit of Capitalism* (1904–05), which argued that the Protestant ethic was responsible for the rise of capitalism.

PROTESTANTISM, the principles of the REFORMATION. The name derives from the *Protestatio* of the minority reforming delegates at the Diet of SPEYER (1529). Protestantism is characterized by subordinating TRADITION to the Bible as the basis for doctrine and practice, and stresses JUSTIFICATION BY FAITH, biblical preaching and a high personal morality (see also EVANGELICALISM). In reaction to Roman Catholicism it rejected papal claims, the MASS and the worship of the SAINTS. The main original branches were LUTHERANISM, CALVINISM, ANGLICANISM and Zwinglianism (see ZWINGLI, HULDREICH), with small ANABAPTIST sects on the left wing. Exercise of the right of private judgment in interpreting Scripture led to much fragmentation, a trend reversed in recent decades by the ECUMENICAL MOVEMENT. Protestant churches of later genesis include the CONGREGATIONAL CHURCHES, BAPTISTS, QUAKERS, METHODISTS, the MORAVIAN CHURCH, the SALVATION ARMY and the PENTECOSTAL CHURCHES. Initial rapid expansion (see REFORMATION), followed by consolidation and scholastic doctrinal orthodoxy (17th century), was succeeded by a period of liberalism influenced by romantic subjectivism (see SCHLEIERMACHER) and the ENLIGHTENMENT. From this sprang MODERNISM, opposed in different ways by FUNDAMENTALISM and NEOORTHODOXY. In some churches desire for détent with Rome has led to repudiation of the term "protestant."

PROTON, stable elementary particle found in the nucleus of all ATOMS. It has a positive charge, equal in magnitude to that of the ELECTRON, and rest mass of 1.67252×10^{-27} kg (slightly less than the NEUTRON mass but 1,836.1 times the electron mass). As the HYDROGEN ion, the proton is chemically important, particularly in aqueous solutions (see ACID), and is widely used in physics as a projectile for bombarding atoms and nuclei.

PROTOPLASM, the substance including and contained within the plasma membrane of animal CELLS but in plants forming only the cell's contents. It is usually differentiated into the nucleus and the cytoplasm. The latter is usually a transparent viscous fluid containing a number of specialized structures; it is the medium in which the main chemical reactions of the cell take place. The nucleus contains the cell's genetic material.

PROTOZOA, animals consisting of a single CELL, with all life functions carried on within that cell, distinct from the METAZOA, multicelled organisms in which cells are differentiated in function and are united into groups in ORGANS or TISSUES. Nearly 50,000 species of Protozoans have been described. They occur all over the world in every possible kind of habitat. They are divided into four classes: the Mastigophora, or flagellated Protozoa; the Sarcodina, which move using PSEUDOPODIA; the Sporozoa, nonmotile and parasitic, and the Ciliata, ciliated forms.

PROUDHON, Pierre Joseph (1809–1865), French social thinker, and a founder of modern ANARCHISM. From a poor family, he gained an education through scholarships, and also became a printer. He first gained notoriety with his book *What is Property?* (1840), to which his famous answer was "Property is theft." However, he was not a socialist, but believed in a society in which property would be distributed among free individuals who cooperated spontaneously outside a framework of state authority—a philosophy he called *mutualism.* In 1847 he clashed with MARX, and started a struggle between libertarian and authoritarian views on socialism which continued long after his death. Proudhon spent his life propagating his ideas, writing much of his work in prison (1849–1852) and in exile (1858–1862). His influence can be traced in SYNDICALISM, and in French radicalism.

PROUST, Joseph Louis (1754–1826), French chemist who established the law of definite proportions, or Proust's Law (see COMPOSITION, CHEMICAL).

PROUST, Marcel (1871–1922), French novelist whose seven-part work *Remembrance of Things Past* is one of the greatest novels of the 20th century. It was written during the period 1907–19, after Proust, who suffered continually from asthma, had retired from Parisian high society and become virtually a recluse. A semi-autobiographical exploration of time, memory and consciousness, with an underlying theme of the transcendency of art over the futility of man's best efforts, it broke new ground in the art of the novel, and was enormously influential.

PROVENÇAL, or *langue d'oc,* a ROMANCE LANGUAGE developed from the Latin spoken in S France, principally Provence. During the Middle Ages, Provençal produced a notable literature which reached its highest point with the courtly love poetry of the TROUBADOURS.

PROVENCE, region and former province of France, embracing the lower Rhone R (including the CAMARGUE) and the French Riviera. The chief cities are Nice, Marseilles, Toulon, Avignon, Arles and Aix-en-Provence (the historic capital). It is a

sunny and picturesque region, famous for historical associations and its fruit, vineyards and olives. It was the first transalpine Roman province (hence the name), and later it became an independent kingdom (879–933), finally passing to the French kings in 1486.

PROVERBS, Book of, book of the OLD TESTAMENT; an example of the "wisdom literature" popular in post-exilic Judaism. Its eight sections, attributed in their headings to various authors including SOLOMON, consist of numerous pithy proverbs, mostly unconnected moral maxims, probably dating between the 9th and 2nd centuries BC.

PROVIDENCE, state capital of R.I., at the head of Providence Bay. It is a busy port, and industries include textiles, jewelry, machinery and metal products. It is also an important educational center, and the home of the Rhode Island School of Design and BROWN University. Founded by Roger WILLIAMS in 1636, it is one of the oldest cities in the US. Pop 156,804.

PROVIDENCE, in THEISM, the government by God of the universe. By His almighty power, He infallibly determines and regulates all events—in general providence by means of natural laws: in specific providence by MIRACLES or other direct actions. CALVINISM stresses the providential government of free human actions. (See also CREATION.)

PRUSSIA, militaristic state of N central Europe that dominated Germany until the rise of NAZISM. At the height of its strength it stretched from W of the Rhine to Poland and Russia. The Baltic territory later known as East Prussia was Germanized by the TEUTONIC KNIGHTS in the 1200s and later became the duchy of Prussia. In 1618 it came under the rule of the Electors of nearby Brandenburg, the Hohenzollerns, and FREDERICK I declared himself king of Prussia in 1701. Under his successors, particularly FREDERICK THE GREAT, the Prussian state expanded to become the strongest military power in N Europe. It received a setback in the NAPOLEONIC WARS, but recovered. In 1862 BISMARCK became premier, and as a result of a planned series of wars and skilful diplomacy conducted under his direction, King WILLIAM I of Prussia was declared Emperor of Germany in 1871. Prussia was the largest and most powerful of the states of the united Germany, and continued so until 1934, when by a decree of HITLER the separate German states ceased to exist as political entities. After WWII former Prussian territory was divided between East

Germany, Poland and the USSR.

PSALMS, Book of, collection of 150 songs in the OLD TESTAMENT, used as the HYMN book of Judaism since the return from exile, and prominent in Christian LITURGY. Metrical psalms are sung in the REFORMED CHURCHES. Many psalms are traditionally ascribed to DAVID; modern scholars date them between the 10th and 2nd centuries BC. Their fine poetry embodies a rich variety of religious experience, both national and individual. (See also BAY PSALM BOOK.)

PSALTERY, musical instrument related to the dulcimer and consisting of strings stretched over a flat soundbox, and plucked. Of Near Eastern origin, it enjoyed great popularity in the West in the 13th–15th centuries. No medieval examples are extant.

PSEUDEPIGRAPHA (Greek: writings falsely ascribed), uncanonical books excluded from the APOCRYPHA and generally pseudonymous. Such Jewish works, written largely from c150 BC to c100 AD, include the *Book of Enoch*, *Assumption of Moses* and *Apocalypse of Baruch*. Christian pseudepigrapha, also called New Testament apocrypha, include numerous Gospels, Acts of most of the apostles, and spurious epistles; they are mostly fanciful and heretical.

PSITTACOSIS, or Parrot fever, LUNG disease with FEVER, cough and breathlessness caused by a bedsonia, an organism intermediate between BACTERIA and VIRUSES. It is carried by parrots, pigeons, domestic fowl and related birds. TETRACYCLINES provide effective treatment, but any infected birds must be destroyed.

PSORIASIS, common SKIN condition characterized by patches of red, thickened and scaling skin. It often affects the elbows, knees and scalp but may be found anywhere. Several forms are recognized and the manifestations may vary in each individual with time. Coal tar preparations are valuable in treatment but STEROID creams and cytotoxic CHEMOTHERAPY may be needed. There is also an associated ARTHRITIS.

PSYCHE, Greek word meaning soul. In the 5th century BC the soul was personified as a beautiful woman, with whom the god of love, Eros (CUPID), fell in love and tormented.

PSYCHE, in psychology, the mind.

PSYCHEDELIC DRUGS. See HALLUCINOGENIC DRUGS.

PSYCHIATRY, the branch of medicine concerned with the study and treatment of MENTAL ILLNESS. It has two major branches:

one is PSYCHOTHERAPY, the application of psychological techniques to the treatment of mental illnesses where a physiological origin is either unknown or does not exist (see also PSYCHOANALYSIS); the other, medical therapy, where attack is made either on the organic source of the disease or, at least, on its physical or behavioral symptoms. (Psychotherapy and medical therapy are often used in tandem.) As a rule of thumb, the former deals with NEUROSES, the latter with PSYCHOSES. (See also PSYCHOLOGY.) DRUGS are perhaps the most widely used tools of psychiatry. Many emotional and other disturbances can be simply treated by the use of mild SEDATIVES or TRANQUILIZERS. (See also PSYCHOPHARMACOLOGY.) Another somatic therapy is electro shock (electroconvulsive therapy—ECT). In electroshock treatment, an electric current is passed through the brain, producing convulsions and, often unconsciousness: it is used in cases of severe depression. Both techniques are unpredictable in result. LOBOTOMY, a surgical operation which severs certain of the neural pathways, is now rarely used.

PSYCHICAL RESEARCH. See PARAPSYCHOLOGY.

PSYCHOANALYSIS, a system of psychology having as its base the theories of Sigmund FREUD; also, the psychotherapeutic technique based on that system. The distinct forms of psychoanalysis developed by JUNG and ADLER are respectively more correctly termed analytical psychology and individual psychology. Freud's initial interest was in the origins of the NEUROSES. On developing the technique of FREE ASSOCIATION to replace that of HYPNOSIS in his therapy, he observed that certain patients could in some cases associate freely only with difficulty. He decided that this was due to the memories of certain experiences being held back from the CONSCIOUS mind (see REPRESSION) and noted that the most sensitive areas were in connection with sexual experiences. He thus developed the concept of the UNCONSCIOUS (later to be called the ID), and suggested (for a while) that ANXIETY was the result of repression of the LIBIDO. He also defined "resistance" by the conscious to acceptance of ideas and impulses from the unconscious, and TRANSFERENCE, the idea that relationships with people or objects in the past affect the individual's relationships with people or objects in the present. (Other important psychoanalytic ideas include CENSORSHIP; DEFENSE MECHANISM; EGO; INHIBITION; PLEASURE PRINCIPLE; SUPEREGO. See also DREAMS; GROUP INSTINCT;

METAPSYCHOLOGY; PROJECTION; SEX.)

PSYCHOHISTORY, history written with special attention to psychodynamic factors. The term gained currency in the 1960s with reference to the historical writing of psychoanalyst Erik H. Erikson, especially his biographies of Luther and Gandhi. The psychohistorical approach has been criticized for substituting speculation for research, but its value depends largely on how carefully and intelligently it is done. A recent work in this genre is Doris Kearns' biography of Lyndon B. Johnson.

PSYCHOLINGUISTICS. See LINGUISTICS.

PSYCHOLOGICAL TESTS, measures, or sets of tasks, devised to elicit information about the psychological characteristics of individuals. Such characteristics may relate to the INTELLIGENCE, vocation, personality or aptitudes of the individual. Tests must be both consistent and accurate to be of value. (See also GRAPHOLOGY; IQ; PROJECTION TEST; PSYCHOLOGY; STANFORD-BINET TEST.)

PSYCHOLOGICAL WARFARE, the use of psychological pressure to undermine an enemy's will to resist. It usually consists of printed or broadcast PROPAGANDA aimed at civilians or armed forces, and is often preceded or accompanied by supporting economic or military measures.

PSYCHOLOGY, originally the branch of philosophy dealing with the mind, then the science of mind, and now, considered in its more general context, the science of behavior, whether human or animal, and of human thought processes. (See also ANIMAL BEHAVIOR.) Clearly, psychology is closely connected with, on the one side, MEDICINE and PSYCHIATRY and, on the other, SOCIOLOGY. There are a number of closely interrelated branches of human psychology. **Experimental psychology** embraces all psychological investigations undertaken by the psychologist. His experiments may center on the individual or GROUP, in which latter case STATISTICS will play a large part in the research. **Social psychologists** use statistical and other methods to investigate the effect of the group on the behavior of the individual. In **applied psychology**, the discoveries and theories of psychology are put to practical use as in INDUSTRIAL PSYCHOLOGY. **Comparative psychology** deals with the different behavioral organizations of animals (including man). **Physiological psychology** attempts to understand the NEUROLOGY and PHYSIOLOGY of behavior. **Clinical psychologists** diagnose and treat mental disorders, principally using psychological tests, psychotherapy and behavior therapy. They also do research on psychological factors affecting mental illness. (See also Alfred BINET; Francis GALTON; William JAMES; Wilhelm WUNDT; and BEHAVIORISM; GESTALT PSYCHOLOGY; IDEA; INTELLIGENCE; PARAPSYCHOLOGY; PSYCHOLOGICAL TESTS; PSYCHOPHARMACOLOGY.)

PSYCHOPATH, a mentally disturbed individual who is unconcerned about others to the point of being completely antisocial. Such individuals are lacking in conscience and are often manipulative and exploitative.

PSYCHOPHARMACOLOGY, the study of the effects of DRUGS on the mind, and particularly the development of drugs for treating MENTAL ILLNESS.

PSYCHOSIS, in contrast with NEUROSIS, any MENTAL ILLNESS, whether of neurological (see NEUROLOGY) or purely psychological origins, which renders the individual incapable of distinguishing reality from unreality or fantasy. If the loss of mental capacity is progressive, the illness is termed a deteriorative psychosis.

PSYCHOSOMATIC ILLNESS, any illness in which some mental activity, usually ANXIETY or the INHIBITION of the EMOTIONS (see also REPRESSION), causes or substantially contributes to physiological malfunction. There is debate as to which disorders are psychosomatic, but among the most likely candidates are gastric ULCERS, ulcerative COLITIS and certain types of ASTHMA.

PSYCHOTHERAPY, the application of the theories and discoveries of PSYCHOLOGY to the treatment of MENTAL ILLNESS. Psychotherapy does not involve physical techniques, such as the use of drugs or surgery (see PSYCHIATRY).

PTA. See PARENTS AND TEACHERS ASSOCIATION.

PTERODACTYLS, a name which has come to be used for all Pterosaurs or flying reptiles, though originally reserved for a single genus. Pterosaurs were a large and diverse group of reptiles adapted for different kinds of flight. The wings consisted of a naked membrane supported by the fourth finger only. Pterosaurs were almost certainly warm-blooded and had a thick fur. *Pteranodon* was the most specialized, with a wing-span of 9m (29.5ft), adapted for soaring and gliding over sea cliffs.

PTOLEMY, name used by all 15 Egyptian kings of the Macedonian dynasty (323–30 BC). **Ptolemy I Soter** (c367–283 BC) was one of Alexander the Great's generals. He secured Egypt for himself after Alexander's death and defended it in a series of wars against the other DIADOCHI. He founded the library of Alexandria, which became a center of HELLENISTIC CULTURE. **Ptolemy II Philadelphus** (308–246 BC) succeeded in 285. Under him Alexandria reached its height; he completed the PHAROS and appointed CALLIMACHUS librarian. **Ptolemy III Euergetes** (c280–221 BC), succeeded in 246. He extended the empire to include most of Asia Minor, the E Mediterranean and Aegean Islands. After 221 the Ptolemaic empire entered a long period of decline, gradually losing its overseas possessions. **Ptolemy XV Caesarion** ("son of Caesar"; 47–30 BC) ruled from 44 BC jointly with his mother CLEOPATRA VII. On their defeat at the battle of Actium (31 BC), Egypt became a Roman province.

PTOLEMY, or **Claudius Ptolemaeus** 2nd century AD), Alexandrian astronomer, mathematician and geographer. Most important in his book on ASTRONOMY, now called *Almagest* ("the greatest"), a synthesis of Greek astronomical knowledge, especially that of HIPPARCHUS: his geocentric cosmology dominated Western scientific thought until the Copernican Revolution of the 16th century (see COPERNICUS, N.). His *Geography* confirmed Columbus' belief in the westward route to Asia. In his *Optics* he attempts to solve the astronomical problem of atmospheric refraction.

PTOMAINE POISONING, old name for FOOD POISONING.

PUBERTY, the time during the GROWTH of a person at which sexual development occurs, commonly associated with a growth spurt. Female puberty involves several stages—the acquisition of BREAST buds; of sexual hair, and the onset of MENSTRUATION— which may each begin at different times. Male puberty involves sexual-hair development; VOICE change, and growth of the TESTES and PENIS. Precocious puberty is the abnormally early development of pubertal features (before 9 years in females). The average age of puberty has fallen in recent years.

PUBLIC BROADCASTING SYSTEM (PBS). See BROADCASTING NETWORKS, US.

PUBLIC DEFENDER, in US law, an official paid to defend in court those unable to pay a lawyer. The defender is employed and compensated by the state, county or city.

PUBLIC DOMAIN, in US law, ownership of a property or resource by the people. In 1978 public domain or public land made up 34% of US land. Processes, plans and creative works not protected by PATENT or COPYRIGHT are said to be in the public domain.

PUBLIC HEALTH, the practice and organization of preventative MEDICINE

within a community. Many threats to health are beyond individual control. DISEASE, EPIDEMICS, POLLUTION of the air and purity of WATER can only be effectively regulated by laws and health authorities. Among the strictest controls are those on SEWAGE and WASTE DISPOSAL. Most advanced countries have pure food laws controlling food purity, freshness and additives. In the US, these controls are the responsibility of the FOOD AND DRUG ADMINISTRATION. The work of individual countries in the public health field is coordinated by the WORLD HEALTH ORGANIZATION. Some countries have complete public health services which provide free or low-cost medical treatment of all kinds. (See also HEALTH, AND HUMAN SERVICES; WELFARE; MEDICARE; JENNER, EDWARD; PASTEUR, LOUIS.)

PUBLIC HEALTH SERVICE (PHS), the chief US health agency, set up in 1870. In 1953, it became a division of the new Department of Health, Education, and Welfare, now the Department of HEALTH AND HUMAN SERVICES.

PUBLIC OPINION POLL. See POLL, PUBLIC OPINION.

PUBLIC RELATIONS (PR), general term for fostering goodwill for a person, corporation, institution, or product without actually paying for advertisements. Practitioners of PR supply information to the media in the hope that the media will not bother to make any changes in what they want to have said. PR people suggest improvements in behavior, grooming, packaging, etc., to a client or employer. The term "public realtions" is thought to have been used first by Ivy L. LEE, who styled himself an "advisor" on "public relations" as early as 1919.

PUCCI, Emilio (1914–   ), Italian fashion designer who became internationally famous for the casual elegance of his print dresses and accessories.

PUCCINI, Giacomo (1858–1924), Italian opera composer. His first international success, *Manon Lescaut* (1893), was followed by *La Bohème* (1896), *Tosca* (1900), *Madame Butterfly* (1904) and *Turandot* (uncompleted at Puccini's death). A lyric style and strong orchestration are characteristic of his operas, which have great dramatic and emotional power. Puccini's works are among the most popular in the operatic repertoire.

PUBLIC WORKS ADMINISTRATION (PWA), or Federal Emergency Administration of Public Works, a NEW DEAL agency set up in 1933 to stimulate employment and purchasing power. Under H. L. ICKES it made loans and grants, mainly to government bodies, for projects which included the GRAND COULEE and BONNEVILLE dams. The PWA was phased out from 1939.

PUEBLO INCIDENT, the seizure of the US Navy spy ship *Pueblo* on Jan. 23, 1968, by North Koreans and the subsequent imprisonment of the 83-man crew; the ship was taken within or near Korea's 12mi limit. The loss of the ship (with its invaluable electronic equipment) and the long (10-month), embarrassing negotiations to obtain the release of those captured provoked bitterness in a nation already frustrated by the Vietnam War. There were some official calls for the court martial of the captain, Commander Lloyd M. Bucher, who signed a confession, although it was known that his men had been tortured and he said that he had feared they would be killed; no such action was taken.

PUEBLO INDIANS, several American Indian tribes living in SW US (Ariz. and N.M.) in permanent villages (*pueblos*). They have the oldest and most developed pre-Columbian civilization N of Mexico. The various tribes, which include the HOPI and ZUNI, are descended from the BASKET MAKERS and CLIFF DWELLERS. Pueblo Indians are noted for their handiworks; their social system and religious practices remain largely intact today. (See also INDIANS, NORTH AMERICAN.)

PUERPERAL FEVER, disease occurring in puerperal women, usually a few days after the BIRTH of the child and caused by infection of the WOMB, often with STREPTOCOCCUS. It causes FEVER, abdominal pain and discharge of PUS from the womb. The introduction of ASEPSIS in OBSTETRICS by I. P. SEMMELWEISS greatly reduced its incidence. Today, ANTIBIOTICS are required if it develops.

Name of territory Commonwealth of Puerto Rico
Capital: San Juan
Became a Commonwealth: July 25, 1952
Area: 3,435sq mi
Population: 3,187,566
Elevation: Highest—4,389, Cerro de Punta. Lowest—sea level.
Motto: Joannes est Nomien (John is His Name)
Commonwealth song: "La Borinqueña"

PUERTO RICO, West Indian island, farthest E of the Greater Antilles. It is a self-governing commonwealth freely associated with the US.

Land and Climate. Roughly rectangular in shape, Puerto Rico extends 133mi E–W and 41mi N–S. The Cordillera Central, which rises to 4,398ft, gives way to foothills, valleys and a fertile coastal plain 1–12mi wide. The mild tropical climate, drier in the S, varies little apart from occasional storms July–Nov.

People. Puerto Ricans are US citizens but pay no federal taxes and may not vote in national elections. The Spanish element is predominant in the people's African and Spanish origins. The island is densely populated; two-thirds of the population is in San Juan, Ponce and Mayagüez. Unemployment has led many Puerto Ricans to migrate, mainly to New York.

Economy. Formerly a single-crop economy based on sugar, Puerto Rico now depends largely on manufacturing. From the 1940s "Operation Bootstrap" attracted investment. Today metals, chemicals, oil-refining, textiles and sugar products are the principal exports. The US is the main trading partner. Most of the remaining third of goods produced comprises sugarcane, coffee, tobacco and foods.

History. The island was discovered by Columbus in 1493. In 1508, Juan PONCE DE LEON founded a colony. The native ARAWAK INDIANS died out under Spanish rule and, from c1510, Negro slaves were imported to work on sugar plantations. Puerto Rico remained under Spanish rule until 1898 when, as a result of the SPANISH-AMERICAN WAR, the island was ceded to the US. In 1917, Puerto Ricans received US citizenship and the right to elect both houses of their legislature, but nationalism, active since the late 1800s, continued. In 1952, the island became a free commonwealth with its own constitution, a status approved in a 1967 plebiscite.

With Operation Bootstrap, started in 1950, Puerto Rico has experienced vigorous economic development. Continuing into the 1980s it enjoys one of the highest standards of living in the Caribbean region, although unemployment, at least 19%, remained extremely high by US standards. The island's relationship to the US is a perennial political issue, with a minority calling for complete independence and the mainstream parties favoring statehood or maintenance of Commonwealth status; the latter group, led by Romero Barceló of the New Progressive Party, narrowly prevailed in the 1980 elections.

PUFENDORF, Samuel, Baron von (1632–1694), German jurist, philosopher and historian. In his great Latin work *On the Law of Nature and of Nations* (1672) he stressed NATURAL LAW as opposed to positive (man-made) law in international relations.

PUFFINS, stubby sea birds of the AUK family, Alcidae. Black or black-and-white birds, they are characterized by their large and laterally compressed bills, which, at the beginning of the breeding season, become still further enlarged and brightly patterned. Puffins live in colonies on sea cliffs, nesting in burrows.

PUG, small dog of Chinese origin with a short, deeply wrinkled face, and tail curled tightly over its back. The body is sturdy, 11in high and weighs 14-18lb. Its short smooth coat is usually fawn, but can be black.

PUGET SOUND, irregular inlet of the Pacific in NW Wash. It extends S about 100mi to Olympia and is navigable by large ships (US navy yard at Bremerton). Seattle and Tacoma lie on its shores and the state's fish and lumber industries are centered in the area. It was first explored by George VANCOUVER in 1792.

PUGWASH CONFERENCES, series of international conferences on nuclear disarmament, so-called because the first, in 1957, was held in Pugwash, Nova Scotia. Attended by scientists from many nations (40 countries were represented in 1981), the conferences have provided forums in which American and Soviet scientists can meet for informal, theoretically unofficial exchanges.

PULASKI, Casimir, Count (1748-1779), Polish soldier, hero of the anti-Russian revolt of 1768 who, exiled from Poland, fought in the American Revolutionary War. He fought at the Battles of BRANDYWINE and GERMANTOWN. In 1778, he formed his own cavalry unit, the Pulaski Legion. He was mortally wounded at the siege of Savannah.

PULITZER, Joseph (1847-1911), Hungarian-born US publisher who created the PULITZER PRIZES. In 1883, he bought the New York *World* and raised the circulation tenfold in seven years by aggressive reporting (the term YELLOW JOURNALISM was coined to describe its style). In the 1890s Pulitzer was involved in a circulation war with William Randolph HEARST's New York *Journal*. He consistently ran liberal crusades. He also endowed the school of journalism at Columbia U.

PULITZER PRIZES, awards for achievement in US journalism and letters, given every May since 1917 through a foundation created by the estate of Joseph PULITZER and administered by Columbia U. There are eight cash awards for journalism, five for literature and four travelling scholarships. An award for music was added in 1943.

PULLEY, grooved wheel mounted on a block and with a cord or belt passing over it. A pulley is a simple MACHINE applying the equilibrium of TORQUES to obtain a mechanical advantage. Thus, the block and tackle is a combination of ropes and pulleys used for hoisting heavy weights. A belt and pulley combination can transmit motion from one part of a machine to another. Variable speed can be obtained from a single-speed driving shaft by the use of stepped or cone-shaped pulleys with diameters that give the correct speed ratios and belt tensions. To help prevent excessive belt wear and slipping, the rim surface of a pulley is adapted to the material of the belt used.

PULLMAN, George Mortimer (1831-1897), US industrialist and inventor of the first modern railroad sleeping car—the "Pullman." In 1880, he built a model company town—Pullman, Ill. (now part of Chicago), later site of the PULLMAN STRIKE.

PULLMAN STRIKE, May-July 1894, famous boycott of rolling stock of the Pullman Palace Car Co., Pullman, Ill. by E. V. DEBS' American Railway Union to protest the company's wage cuts and victimization of union representatives. After the owners obtained a federal injunction the strike was broken by federal troops, and the US labor movement suffered a major setback.

PULQUE, or pulke, intoxicating Mexican national drink made from freshly fermented sap of several species of MAGUEY (AGAVE) plants. The alcoholic content is about 6%.

PULSAR, short for pulsating radio star, a celestial radio source emitting brief extremely regular pulses of ELECTROMAGNETIC RADIATION (with one exception, entirely radio-frequency). Each pulse lasts a few hundredths of a second and the period between pulses is of the order of one second or less; the pulse frequency varies from pulsar to pulsar. The first pulsar was discovered in 1967 by HEWISH and S. J. Bell. The fastest pulsar yet observed has a period of 0.033s, emitting pulses of the same frequency in the X-ray and visible regions of the spectrum. It is likely that there are some 10,000 pulsars in the MILKY WAY, though less than 100 have as yet been discovered. It is believed that pulsars are the neutron STAR remnants of SUPERNOVAE. rapidly spinning and radiating through loss of rotational energy.

PULSE, the palpable impulse conducted in the ARTERIES representing the transmitted beat of the HEART. A normal pulse rate is between 68 and 80, but athletes may have slower pulses. FEVER, heart disease, ANOXIA and ANXIETY increase the rate. The pulse character may suggest specific conditions, loss of pulse possibly indicating arterial block or cessation of the heart.

PUMA, *Felis concolor,* the **Cougar** or **Mountain lion,** the most widespread of the big CATS of the Americas, occupying an amazing variety of habitats. Powerful cats, resembling a slender and sinuous lioness with a small head, they lead solitary lives preying on various species of deer. The lifespan of a puma in the wild is about 18 years. A puma can cover up to 6m (20ft) in a bound, and will regularly travel up to 80km (50mi) when hunting.

PUMICE, porous, frothy volcanic glass, usually silica-rich; formed by the sudden release of vapors as LAVA cools under low pressures. It is used as an ABRASIVE, an AGGREGATE and a railroad ballast.

PUMP, device for taking in and forcing out a fluid, thus giving it kinetic or potential ENERGY. The HEART is a pump for circulating blood around the body. Pumps are commonly used domestically and industrially to transport fluids, to raise liquids, to compress gases or to evacuate sealed containers. Their chief use is to force fluids along pipelines (see PIPES AND PIPELINES). The earliest pumps were waterwheels, endless chains of buckets, and the ARCHIMEDES screw. Piston pumps, known in classical times, were developed in the 16th and 17th centuries, the suction types (working by atmospheric pressure) being usual, though unable to raise water more than about 10.4m (34ft). The STEAM ENGINE was developed to power pumps for pumping out mines. Piston pumps—the simplest of which is the SYRINGE—are reciprocating **volume-displacement pumps,** as are diaphragm pumps, with a pulsating diaphragm instead of the piston. One-way inlet and outlet valves are fitted in the cylinder. Rotary volume-displacement pumps have rotating gear wheels or wheels with lobes or vanes. **Kinetic pumps,** or FANS, work by imparting momentum to the fluid by means of rotating curved vanes in a housing: centrifugal pumps expel the fluid radially outward, and propeller pumps axially forward. **Air compressors** use the TURBINE principle (see also JET PROPULSION). **Air pumps** use compressed air to raise liquids from the bottom of wells, displacing one fluid by another. If the fluid must not come into direct contact with the pump, as in a nuclear reactor, **electromagnetic pumps** are used: an electric current and a magnetic field at right angles induce the conducting fluid to flow at right angles to both (see MOTOR, ELECTRIC); or the principle of the linear INDUCTION MOTOR may be used. To achieve a very high vacuum, the **diffusion pump** is used, in which atoms of condensing mercury vapor entrain the remaining gas molecules.

PUNCH AND JUDY, leading characters in a children's handpuppet show of the same name. Punch is descended from Pulcinella (Punchinello) of the COMMEDIA DELL'ARTE. He is a hooknosed, hunchbacked, wifebeating rogue who usually ends on the gallows or in a crocodile's mouth. He is accompanied by his shrewish wife Judy (originally called Joan) and their dog, Toby. The Devil, Baby, Hangman, Policeman and Doctor may also appear. (See also PUPPET.)

PUNIC WARS, three wars between ancient Rome and CARTHAGE, each marking a crucial phase in the expansion of Roman empire in the western Mediterranean, the third culminating in the total destruction of Carthage itself. (The Carthaginians, PHOENICIAN by descent, were known to the Romans as *Poeni*; hence *Punic*.) The **First Punic War** (264–241 BC) turned on a struggle for the strategically important island of Sicily. The Carthaginians had some success on land, notably under Xanthippus and HAMILCAR BARCA, but were defeated at sea, the decisive battle being fought off the Aegadian Isles in 241. Rome's naval supremacy was thenceforth unchallenged. The **Second Punic War** (218–201 BC), provoked by Roman moves to check Carthaginian expansion in Spain, began with HANNIBAL's daring invasion of Italy via an overland route which obliged him to cross the Alps in winter. Despite several remarkable victories, including the virtual annihilation of a strong Roman army at CANNAE (216), his plan to isolate Rome from her Italian allies was ultimately frustrated. Roman counterattacks in Spain and then in Africa—at ZAMA (202), under SCIPIO Africanus—forced a Carthaginian surrender on terms which included the forfeiture of her Spanish empire and war fleet. Roman misgivings at the subsequent revival of Carthage as a mercantile power led to the **Third Punic War** (149–146 BC). After a two-year siege of Carthage, SCIPIO Aemilianus took the city and razed it to the ground. Carthaginian territory became the Roman province of "Africa."

PUNISHMENT, imposition of pain or suffering, deprivation or discomfort, on a person who has infringed the law, rule or custom of the community. The ancient individual exaction of "an eye for an eye" in retaliation or revenge has given way to socially imposed retribution. Supernatural or religious authority may be adduced, though this has yielded to arguments based on the wellbeing of a community. Today revenge is seen by most people as only one aspect of punishment. Another important aspect is to function as a deterrent, and in the 19th and 20th centuries, the work of reformers such as John HOWARD and Elizabeth FRY led to reform and rehabilitation being considered important factors. (See CRIMINAL LAW; CAPITAL PUNISHMENT; CORPORAL PUNISHMENT; PRISONS.)

PUNJAB (Sanskrit: five rivers), large wheat-growing region in the NW of the Indian subcontinent, on the upper Indus R plain. Formerly the British Indian province of Punjab, it was divided in 1947 into what became known as **Punjab (Pakistan)** and **Punjab (India)**. In 1966 Punjab (India) was divided into two further provinces, **Punjab** and **Haryāna**.

PUPA, an immature stage in the development of those insects which have a LARVA completely different in structure from the adult, and in which "complete" METAMORPHOSIS occurs. The pupa is a resting stage in which the larval structure is reorganized to form the adult: all but the nervous system changes. Feeding and locomotion are meanwhile suspended.

PUPPET, figure of a person or animal manipulated in dramatic presentations. There are hand, or glove, and finger puppets; jointed *marionettes* string controlled from above; and rod puppets, often used in shadow plays. Puppetry, with which VENTRILOQUISM is associated, is an ancient, flexible entertainment, popular in many countries. (See also PUNCH AND JUDY; MUPPETS.)

PURCELL, Henry (c1659–1695), English composer, the foremost of his time. A master of melody and counterpoint, he wrote in every form and style of the period: odes and anthems for royal occasions, many choral and instrumental works, and music for plays and masques, including his opera *Dido and Aeneas* (1689).

PURE FOOD AND DRUG LAWS. See CONSUMER PROTECTION; FOOD AND DRUG ADMINISTRATION.

PURGATORY, in Roman Catholicism, the place where Christians after death undergo purifying punishment and expiate unforgiven venial sins before admission to HEAVEN. INDULGENCES, MASSES and prayers for the dead are held to lighten their suffering.

PURIM, the Feast of Lots, Jewish festival of the 14th day of Adar (Feb.–March), a joyful celebration of the deliverance from massacre of Persian Jews, through intervention by ESTHER and Mordecai. The story is told in the Book of Esther.

PURITANS, English reforming Protestants who aimed for a simpler form of worship expressly warranted by Scripture, devout personal and family life, and the abolition of clerical hierarchy. They stressed self-discipline, work as a vocation and the christianizing of all spheres of life. Most were strict Calvinists. The term "puritan" was first used in the 1560s of those dissatisfied with the compromise of the Elizabethan settlement of the CHURCH OF ENGLAND; under James I, after the unsuccessful HAMPTON COURT CONFERENCE, some separated from the Church of England. Archbishop LAUD set about systematic repression of puritanism, causing some to emigrate to America (see PILGRIM FATHERS). The English CIVIL WAR—known also as the Puritan Revolution—led to the establishment of PRESBYTERIANISM, but under Oliver CROMWELL puritan dominance was weakened by internal strife. Most puritans were forced to leave the Church after the Restoration (1660), becoming NONCONFORMISTS. Many New England settlers were puritan, and their influence on America was marked, especially their concern for education and church democracy. (See also COVENANTERS; HALF-WAY COVENANT.)

PURKINJE, Johannes Evangelista (1787–1869), Bohemian-born Czech physiologist and pioneer of HISTOLOGY, best known for his observations of nerve cells (see NERVOUS SYSTEM) and discovery of the Purkinje Effect, that at different overall light intensities the eye is more sensitive to different colors (see VISION).

PUS, off-white or yellow liquid consisting of inflammatory exudate, the debris of white BLOOD cells and BACTERIA resulting from localized INFLAMMATION, especially ABSCESSES. Pus contained in cavities is relatively inaccessible to ANTIBIOTICS and may require drainage by SURGERY. Pus suggests but does not prove the presence of bacterial infection.

PUSEY, Edward Bouverie (1800–1882), English clergyman, professor of Hebrew at Oxford University (1828) and a leader of the OXFORD MOVEMENT. He preached the REAL PRESENCE, helped found the first Anglican sisterhood (1845) and established private confession as an Anglican practice.

PUSHKIN, Alexander (1799–1837), poet, widely recognized as the founder of modern Russian literature. A sympathizer of the DECEMBRIST REVOLT, he spent his adult life in exile or under police surveillance. His poetic range included the political, humorous, erotic, lyrical, epic, and verse tales or novels like *Ruslan and Ludmila* (1820), *The Prisoner of the Caucasus* (1822) and his masterpiece *Eugene Onegin* (1833). Other works are the great drama *Boris Godunov* (1831) and such prose works as *The Queen of Spades* (1834) and *The Captain's Daughter* (1836).

PUTREFACTION, the natural decomposition of dead organic matter, in particular the anaerobic decomposition of its PROTEIN by BACTERIA and FUNGI. This process produces foul-smelling substances such as AMMONIA, hydrogen SULFIDE and organic SULFUR compounds. The amino-acid nitrogen of the protein is recycled by incorporation in the bacteria and fungi.

P'U YI, Henry (also known as Hsüan-t'ung; 1906–1967), last Chinese Emperor of the CH'ING (Manchu) dynasty (1908–12) and Japan's puppet emperor of MANCHUKUO (MANCHURIA), 1934–45. He died in Peking.

PYGMALION, in Greek mythology, king of Cyprus who fell in love with and married a statue brought to life by Aphrodite. The story inspired G. B. SHAW's *Pygmalion*. In Virgil's *Aeneid* Pygmalion is the king of Tyre and brother of DIDO.

PYGMY, term used to denote those peoples whose adult males are on average less than 1.5m tall. Some Kalahari Desert Bushmen are of pygmy size, but the most notable pygmys are the Mbuti, or Bambuti, of the Ituri Forest, Zaire, who, through their different blood type, skin color and other characteristics, are regarded as distinct from the surrounding peoples and were probably the original inhabitants of the region. A Stone Age people, they are nomadic hunters, living in groups of 50 to 100. Asian pygmies are generally termed Negritos. Peoples rather larger than pygmies are described as pygmoid.

PYLE, Ernie (Ernest Taylor Pyle; 1900–1945), US journalist and war correspondent. He accompanied US troops to all the major fronts in Europe and N Africa, and his popular news column won a Pulitzer Prize in 1944. He was killed by Japanese machine-gun fire during the Okinawa campaign.

PYLE, Howard (1853–1911), US writer and illustrator of children's books such as *The Merry Adventures of Robin Hood* (1883) and *The Story of King Arthur and His Knights* (1903).

PYM, John (c1584–1643), English statesman. A PURITAN, he led parliamentary opposition to CHARLES I and organized the impeachment of the Duke of BUCKINGHAM (1626). Dominating the SHORT and LONG PARLIAMENTS, he narrowly escaped arrest by the king in 1642, and arranged an alliance with the COVENANTERS (1643).

PYNCHON, Thomas (1937–), US novelist whose works, influenced by James JOYCE and Vladimir NABOKOV, are noted for their ingenious wordplay and complexity. His novels include *V* (1963), *The Crying of Lot 49* (1966) and *Gravity's Rainbow* (1973), a National Book Award winner.

P'YONGYANG, capital and largest city of North Korea. It lies on the Taedong R in an important coal-mining area and is a major industrial center producing iron, steel, machinery and textiles. An ancient settlement, it was the capital of the Choson kingdom in the 3rd century BC. The city was severely damaged during the Korean War. Pop 1,500,000.

PYORRHEA, or flow of PUS, usually used to refer to the pus related to poor oral hygiene and exuding from the margins of the gums and TEETH; it causes loosening of the teeth and HALITOSIS.

PYRENEES, mountain range between France and Spain, stretching 270mi from the Bay of Biscay to the Mediterranean and rising to Pico de Aneto (11,168ft) in the central section. The average height is about 3,500ft and the maximum width about 50mi. There are extensive forests and pasture land. Mineral deposits include iron, zinc, bauxite and talc, and there are sports and health resorts and a growing tourist industry.

PYRITE, or iron pyrites (FeS_2, iron (II) disulfide), a hard, yellow, common SULFIDE known as fool's gold from its resemblance to gold. Of worldwide occurence, it is an ore of SULFUR. It crystallizes in the isometric system, usually as cubes. It alters to GOETHITE and LIMONITE.

PYROMETER, a temperature measuring device used for high temperatures. Platinum resistance thermometers and pyrometers operating on the principle of the THERMOCOUPLE have the disadvantage that they must be in contact with the hot body, but optical and radiation pyrometers can be used at a distance. Optical pyrometers estimate temperature from the light intensity in a narrow band of the visible spectrum by optical comparison of a glowing filament with an image of the hot body. Radiation pyrometers focus the body's heat radiation on a responsive thermal element such as a thermocouple.

PYRRHO OF ELIS (c360–c270 BC), Greek philosopher, the founder of SKEPTICISM. He taught that, as nothing can be known with certainty, suspension of judgment and imperturbability of mind are the true wisdom and source of happiness.

PYRRHUS (c319–272 BC), king of Epirus, NW Greece. King at 12, he served with DEMETRIUS I of Macedonia in Asia Minor, was helped by PTOLEMY I of Egypt to regain his throne, and later won and lost Macedonia. His costly defeat of the Romans at Asculum (279), during an Italian campaign, gave rise to the term "Pyrrhic victory." Further campaigns in Macedonia and Sparta failed. He was killed in Argos.

PYTHAGORAS (c570–c500 BC), Greek philosopher who founded the Pythagorean school. Attributed to the school are: the proof of PYTHAGORAS' THEOREM; the suggestion that the earth travels around the sun, the sun in turn around a central fire; observation of the ratios between the lengths of vibrating strings that sound in mutual harmony, and ascription of such ratios to the distances of the planets, which sounded the "harmony of the spheres," and the proposition that all phenomena may be reduced to numerical relations. The Pythagoreans were also noted for their concept of the soul, the life of moderation, and their interest in medicine. They exerted great influence on Plato and ancient philosophizing generally.

PYTHAGORAS' THEOREM, or **Pythagorean Theorem,** the statement that, for any right-angled TRIANGLE, the SQUARE of the HYPOTENUSE is equal to the sum of the squares of the other two sides. The earliest known formal statement of the theorem is in the *Elements* of EUCLID, but it seems that the basis of it was known long before this time and, indeed, long before the time of PYTHAGORAS himself. (See also EUCLIDEAN GEOMETRY.)

PYTHIAN GAMES, one of four great festivals of ancient Greece, held at Delphi to celebrate Apollo's slaying of the PYTHON. Staged every eighth year, then after the Delphic AMPHICTYONY took control c582 BC every four years, they included dramatic, poetic, musical, athletic and equestrian contests and continued until at least 424 AD.

PYTHONS, the Old World equivalent of the New World BOAS, like them SNAKES bearing small spurs as the vestiges of hindlimbs. These two groups are clearly the closest relatives of the ancestral snake type. Like boas, pythons are nonvenomous constrictors. They are found from Africa to Australia in a wide variety of habitats. All have bold color patterns in browns and yellows. The largest species, the Reticulate python of Asia, reaches 10m (33ft). Pythons feed on small mammals, birds, reptiles and frogs; the larger African species also take small antelope.

17th letter of the alphabet, traceable to the Semitic letter *koph* and the archaic Greek letter *koppa*. Q is used to designate a hypothetical source of the SYNOPTIC GOSPELS.

QADDAFI (or Gaddafi) Muammar al- (1942–   ), Libyan leader. One of a group of army officers who deposed King Idris in 1969, he became chairman of the ruling Revolutionary Command Council and commander-in-chief of the armed forces. One of the world's most intemperate heads of state, he was vehemently anti-Israel and supported several insurgent and terrorist groups around the world. The vast oil resources in Libya increased his influence.

Official name: State of Qatar
Capital: Doha
Area: 4,247sq mi
Population: 250,000
Language: Arabic; English for commercial use
Religion: Muslim
Monetary unit(s): 1 Qatar riyal=100 dirhams

QATAR, oil-rich state on a peninsula in the Persian Gulf bordering Saudi Arabia on the west. Mainly desert, it is dominated by the oil industry, centered in the Dukhan oilfield in W Qatar, one of the richest in the Middle East. A British protectorate from 1916, the country became independent in 1971, and with the wealth from its oil revenues is undergoing rapid economic development.

QATTARA DEPRESSION, barren low-lying area in NW Egypt, 130mi W of Cairo. Its area is about 7,000sq mi and at one point it is 436ft below sea level.

Q FEVER, or query fever, INFECTIOUS DISEASE due to *Coxiella*, an organism intermediate between BACTERIA and VIRUSES, causing FEVER, HEADACHE and often dry cough and chest pain. It is transmitted by ticks from various farm animals and is common among farm workers and veterinarians. Its course is benign but TETRACYCLINES may be used in treatment.

QUADRAPHONIC SOUND. See HIGH FIDELITY.

QUADRUPLE ALLIANCE, an alliance of four countries. Historically, the most famous are: (1) An alliance between England, France, Austria and the Netherlands formed in 1718 to prevent Spain from changing the terms of the Peace of UTRECHT. Spain later joined the alliance. (2) An alliance between Britain, Austria, Russia and Prussia, signed in 1814 and renewed in 1815. Its purpose was to defeat Napoleon and after his defeat and first abdication to ensure that France abided by the terms of the 1815 Treaty of PARIS.

QUAI D'ORSAY, a quay in Paris on the left bank of the Seine. It is the location of the French Foreign Office, and the ministry and its policies are often referred to by that name.

QUAILS, two distinct groups of game birds: Old World and New World quails. Small, rounded ground birds of open country, they feed on insects, grain and shoots. They rarely fly even when disturbed. The tiny painted quail was carried by Chinese mandarins to warm the hands. Family: Phasianidae.

QUAKERS, or the Society of Friends, a church known for its pacifism, humanitarianism and emphasis on inner quiet. Founded in 17th-century England by George FOX, it was persecuted for its rejection of organized churches and of any dogmatic creed, and many Quakers emigrated to America, where in spite of early persecution they were prominent among the colonizers. In 1681 William PENN established his "Holy Experiment" in Pennsylvania, and from that point the church's main growth took place in America.

The early Quakers adopted a distinctive, simple style of dress and speech, and simplicity of manner is still a characteristic Quaker trait. They have no formal creed and no clergy, and put their trust in the "Inward Light" of God's guidance. Their meetings for worship, held in "Meeting Houses," follow a traditional pattern of beginning in silence, with no set service and no single speaker.

The Quakers have exercised a moral influence disproportionate to their numbers through actually practicing what they believe, particularly pacifism. In the US they were prominent abolitionists and have been among the pioneers of social reform. They today number about 126,000 in the US.

QUANT, Mary (1934–), British fashion designer whose mini and mod designs expressed the spirit of the 1960s Beatles' generation. Her fabrics were also unconventional; she showed denim for evening wear and lace for daytime.

QUANTITY THEORY OF MONEY, theory relating changes in the level of prices to changes in the amount of MONEY in circulation; i.e., distinguishing between money, whose value may alter with price fluctuations, and true wealth. In the 19th century it was used to support FREE TRADE against protectionism. After the work of KEYNES in the 1930s it lost favor, but it regained popularity in the 1960s, when control of the money supply was seen as important in the fight against inflation. See CHICAGO SCHOOL; MONETARISM.

QUANTRILL, William Clarke (1837–1865), Confederate guerrilla leader in the American CIVIL WAR. A criminal before the war, Quantrill was made a Confederate captain in 1862. On Aug. 21, 1863, with a force of 450 men he attacked the town of Lawrence, Kan., and slaughtered 150 civilians. He was killed while on a raid in Kentucky.

QUANTUM MECHANICS, fundamental theory of small-scale physical phenomena (such as the motions of ELECTRONS within ATOMS), developed during the 20th century when it became clear that the existing laws of classical mechanics and electromagnetic theory were not successfully applicable to such systems. Because quantum mechanics treats physical events that we cannot directly perceive, it has many concepts unknown in everyday experience. DE BROGLIE struck out from the old QUANTUM THEORY when he suggested that particles have a wavelike nature, with a wavelength h/p (h being the Planck constant and p the particle momentum). This wavelike nature is significant only for particles on the molecular scale or smaller. These ideas were developed by SCHRÖDINGER and others into the branch of quantum mechanics known as WAVE MECHANICS. HEISENBERG worked along parallel lines with a theory incorporating only observable quantities such as ENERGY, using matrix algebra techniques. The UNCERTAINTY PRINCIPLE is fundamental to quantum mechanics, as is Pauli's EXCLUSION PRINCIPLE. DIRAC incorporated relativistic ideas into quantum mechanics.

QUANTUM THEORY, theory developed at the beginning of the 20th century to account for certain phenomena that could not be explained by classical PHYSICS. PLANCK described the previously unexplained distribution of radiation from a BLACK BODY by assuming that ELECTROMAGNETIC RADIATION exists in discrete bundles known as quanta, each with an ENERGY $E=hv$ (v being the radiation frequency and h a universal constant—the PLANCK CONSTANT). EINSTEIN also used the idea of quanta to explain the PHOTOELECTRIC EFFECT, establishing that electromagnetic radiation has a dual nature, behaving both as a WAVE MOTION and as a stream of particle-like quanta. Measurements of other physical quantities, such as the frequencies of lines in atomic spectra and the energy losses of electrons on colliding with atoms, showed that these quantities could not have a continuous range of values, discrete values only being possible. With RUTHERFORD's discovery in 1911 that ATOMS consist of a small positively charged nucleus surrounded by ELECTRONS, attempts were made to understand this atomic structure in the light of quantum ideas, since classically the electrons would radiate energy continuously and collapse into the nucleus. BOHR postulated that an atom only exists in certain stationary (i.e., nonradiating) states with definite energies and that quanta of radiation are emitted or absorbed in transitions between these states; he successfully calculated the stationary states of hydrogen. Some further progress was made along these lines by Bohr and others, but it became clear that the quantum theory was fundamentally weak in being unable to calculate intensities of spectral lines. The new QUANTUM MECHANICS was developed c1925 to take its place.

QUARK. See SUBATOMIC PARTICLES.

QUARTERMASTER CORPS, the section of the US Army responsible for providing food, clothing, accommodation and equipment for the troops. Its functions were taken over in 1962 by the newly set up Army Materiel Command.

QUARTZ, rhombohedral form of SILICA, usually forming hexagonal prisms, colorless when pure ("rock crystal"). A common mineral, it is the chief constituent of SAND, SANDSTONE, QUARTZITE and FLINT, an essential constituent of high-silica igneous rocks such as GRANITE, rhyolite and

pegmatite, and also occurs as the GEMS: CHALCEDONY; AGATE; JASPER, and ONYX. Quartz is piezoelectric (see PIEZOELECTRICITY) and is used to make oscillators for clocks, radio and radar; and also to make windows for optical instruments. Crude quartz is used to make glass, glazes and abrasives, and as a flux.

QUASAR, or quasi-stellar object, a telescopically star-like celestial object whose SPECTRUM shows an abnormally large RED SHIFT. Quasars may be extremely distant objects—perhaps the inexplicably bright cores of galaxies near the limits of the known universe—receding from us at high velocities. The spectra of quasars, however, do not seem to be affected by the interpolation of intergalactic gas. Quasars also show variability in light and radio emission (although the first quasars were discovered by RADIO ASTRONOMY, not all are radio sources). These phenomena might indicate that quasars instead are comparatively small objects less than 0 3pc across, and that they are comparatively close to us (larger—and more distant—objects being unlikely to vary in this way). There are about 200 quasars in each square degree of the sky.

QUASIMODO, Salvatore (1901–1968), Italian poet and translator of poetry awarded the 1959 Nobel Prize for Literature. During and after WWII he turned (originally because of his opposition to Fascism) from a complex, introverted hermetic style to social protest and examination of the plight of the individual, as in *Day after Day* (1947).

QUATERNARY, the period of the CENOZOIC whose beginning is marked by the advent of man. It has lasted about 4 million years up to and including the present. (See also TERTIARY; GEOLOGY.)

Name of province: Quebec—Québec
Joined Confederation: July 1, 1867
Capital: Quebec
Area: 594,860sq mi
Population: 6,303,000

QUEBEC, the largest province in Canada, stretching from Hudson Bay to S of the St. Lawrence R.
Land. Over 90% of the province lies within the CANADIAN SHIELD, a great rocky plateau, much of it an uninhabited wilderness of forests, lakes and streams. South of the Shield are the agricultural St. Lawrence Lowlands containing most of the cities of Quebec. The third major region is the Appalachian Uplands in the SE. The St. Lawrence R, running through Quebec, has played a key role in its development. The province has severe winters and warm

humid summers.

People. Quebec's population is concentrated in the S. About 85% are urban dwellers. French-Canadians, most of them descendants of 17th- and 18th-century settlers, constitute 80% of the population; over 80% speak French, and there are separate radio and TV stations and newspapers. French was made the official language of education, business and government by the French Language Charter of 1977. Roman Catholicism dominates the religious life of the province.

Economy. Quebec has vast resources of raw materials and almost limitless hydroelectric power that are still being developed. Industries include paper, aluminum processing, foodstuffs, textiles, chemicals and metal products. Montreal and Quebec City are the leading manufacturing centers with ships, automobiles, aircraft, and railway rolling stock the principal manufactures. The chief mineral products are iron ore, asbestos and copper. Dairying is the most important branch of agriculture, and Quebec's forestry accounts for nearly half of Canada's wood and paper products. The development of iron ore mines in the NE has encouraged development of a steel industry. Construction began in 1979 on the La Grande Complex, on the La Grande R., scheduled to be the world's second-largest hydroelectric project.

History. The first permanent settlement in Quebec dates from 1608 when CHAMPLAIN built a trading post at the site of Quebec City. From then until defeat by the British in the FRENCH AND INDIAN WAR (1754–63), the French controlled the province. Since the advent of British rule in 1763, Quebec's history has been dominated by its effort to preserve its French identity, in which the QUEBEC ACT of 1774 played a significant part. In 1837 a revolt under PAPINEAU flared up. In 1867 Quebec became a founding province of the Dominion of Canada, with considerable autonomy. In the 1960s a French separatist movement emerged, and the Canadian government has since made several concessions in the field of education. In the early 1980s the topic of constitutional reform gained prominence, with Quebec as the focus of the debate on national unity. (See also CANADA.)

QUEBEC, Battle of, the most important battle of the FRENCH AND INDIAN WAR, whose outcome transferred control of Canada from France to Britain. French troops under MONTCALM were defending Quebec City. On the night of Sept. 12, 1759, British troops under WOLFE silently scaled the cliffs W of the city to the Plains of Abraham. After a short, bloody battle the French fled. Both Wolfe and Montcalm were mortally wounded.

QUEBEC, the capital of QUEBEC province, situated on the St. Lawrence R. Founded in 1608 by CHAMPLAIN, it is Canada's oldest city. Quebec has remained essentially French, and more than 90% of its citizens claim French ancestry. Today it is a leading manufacturing center and transatlantic port. Industries include shipbuilding, paper milling, food processing, machinery and textiles. The city is a major tourist attraction. Pop 177,080.

QUEBEC ACT, passed by the British Parliament in 1774, one of the INTOLERABLE ACTS. It guaranteed the use of the French civil code and established religious freedom for the Roman Catholic Church in Quebec, and extended Quebec's boundary to the Ohio and Mississippi rivers.

QUEBEC CONFERENCE, a conference in the city of Quebec, Oct. 1864, that laid the foundations of the Canadian Confederation. Representatives from the British provinces in N America produced a series of 72 resolutions outlining a centralized federal union. This became the basis of the BRITISH NORTH AMERICA ACT (1867) which created the Dominion of Canada.

QUEBEC CONFERENCES, two important conferences held in the city of Quebec during WWII. In Aug. 1943 ROOSEVELT and CHURCHILL met with the Canadian prime minister and the Chinese foreign minister to make arrangements for operations in the Far East and for the Allied invasion of Europe. In Sept. 1944 Roosevelt and Churchill met again to discuss broad military strategy.

QUECHUA, S American Indians, once part of the INCA empire and now living mostly as peasants in the Andean highlands from Colombia to N Chile. Quechua is also the name of the family to which the official language of the Incas belonged, and some 28 languages of the family are still spoken.

QUEEN, Ellery, pen-name and fictional hero of detective writers, Frederic Dannay (1905–   ) and Manfred B. Lee (1905–1972). Their successful *The Roman Hat Mystery* (1929), was followed by over 100 other novels characterized by complexity of plot. *Ellery Queen's Mystery Magazine* was founded in 1941.

QUEEN ANNE'S WAR (1702–13) reflected the War of the SPANISH SUCCESSION. French raids on British territory in the N were beaten off and Acadia Nova Scotia) taken. In the S French and Spanish forces unsuccessfully attacked Charleston, S.C. In the Peace of UTRECHT much territory was theoretically ceded to Britain.

QUEENS, largest borough, in area, of New York City, located at the W end of Long Island. It includes the industrial and commercial centers of Long Island City and Astoria, and residential neighborhoods such as Forest Hills. The site of John F. Kennedy Airport, it was the scene of the 1939–40 and 1964–65 World Fairs. Pop 1,891,325.

QUEENSBERRY RULES, the basic rules of modern BOXING, drawn up in 1865 under the auspices of the 8th Marquess of Queensberry, supplanting the old London prize-ring rules. Innovations included the use of padded gloves instead of bare fists, a 10-second count to determine a knockout, and the division of the bout into rounds with intermissions.

QUEENSLAND, state in NE Australia, 667,000sq mi in area. Tropical and eucalyptus forests in the rugged E contrast with pasture and desert on the vast W plain. It produces sheep, nearly half of Australia's cattle, and such crops as sugarcane, wheat, cotton and fruit. There are valuable oil and mineral deposits. Almost half the population, mainly of British descent, lives in BRISBANE, the state capital. Pop 2,224,100.

QUEMOY, small island in the Formosa Strait, close to mainland China. Ruled by Nationalist Chinese, the island was subjected to shelling from the Communist mainland in the 1950s and 1960s.

QUENEAU, Raymond (1903–1976), French novelist and man of letters. His most widely known books are *Exercises de style* (1947), in which one incident is presented in 99 different literary-styles, and the comic *Zazie* (1959).

QUETZALCOATL, the plumed serpent, ancient Mexican god identified with the morning and evening star. He is said to have ruled the pre-Aztec TOLTEC empire and to have invented books and the calendar. Whether he was an historical chieftain or merely mythological is not certain. MONTEZUMA II welcomed CORTEZ, believing him to be descended from the god.

QUEZON, Manuel Luis (1878–1944), Filipino statesman who played a leading role in the Philippine independence movement before becoming the first president of the Philippine Commonwealth (1935). His presidency, continued (after Japanese invasion) from 1942 in the US, was marked by efforts to improve conditions for the poor.

QUEZON CITY, city of the Philippines since 1948, on Luzon Island, 10mi NE of the capital MANILA. A trading and transportation center, it was named for Manuel QUEZON. Quezon City was the

national capital 1948-76. Pop 956,900.

QUIDS, early US political faction, led by John RANDOLPH, of extreme protagonists of states' rights.

QUIETISM, mystical religious movement originated in 17th-century Spain by Miguel de Molinos (1640–c1697), which later spread to France as the less extreme Semiquietism. Molinos advocated a wholly passive mysticism. After papal condemnations, Quietism (1687) and Semiquietism (1699) collapsed.

QUIMBY, Phineas Parkhurst (1802–1866), US pioneer of mental healing, an early user of SUGGESTION as a therapy. A strong influence on Mary Baker EDDY, he is regarded as a father of the New Thought movement.

QUINCY, city in E Mass., situated on Boston Harbor, 8mi S of Boston, birthplace of Presidents John ADAMS and John Quincy ADAMS. It is an industrial center. The Fore River shipyards are among the most important in the US. Pop 84,743.

QUINCY, Josiah (1772–1864), US politician, educator and author. Elected to Congress in 1804, he resigned in 1813 after opposing the WAR OF 1812. He later distinguished himself as a reforming mayor of Boston (1823–28) and as president of HARVARD UNIVERSITY (1829–45).

QUINE, Willard Van Orman (1908–   ), US philosopher and logician, best known for his rejection of such longstanding philosophical claims as analytic ("self-evident") statements are fundamentally distinguishable from synthetic (observational) statements, and that the concept of synonymy (sameness of meaning) can be exemplified.

QUININE, substance derived from CINCHONA bark from South America, long used in treating a variety of ailments. It was preeminent in early treatment of MALARIA until the 1930s when ATABRINE was introduced; after this more suitable quinine derivatives such as CHLOROQUINE were synthesized. Quinine is also a mild ANALGESIC and may prevent CRAMPS and suppress HEART rhythm disorders. Now rarely used, its side effects include VOMITING, DEAFNESS, VERTIGO and VISION disturbance.

QUINN, Anthony (1915–   ), Mexican-born US actor who won two Academy Awards in supporting roles before becoming an internationally renowned star in such films as *La Strada* (1954) and *Zorba the Greek* (1964).

QUINSY, acute complication of TONSILLITIS in which ABSCESS formation causes spasm of the adjacent jaw muscles, FEVER and severe pain. Incision and drainage of the PUS produce rapid relief, though ANTIBIOTICS are helpful and the TONSILS should be excised later.

QUINTERO, José (1924–   ), Panama-born US stage director recognized as the primary contemporary interpreter of Eugene O'NEILL's work. His productions include *The Iceman Cometh* (1956), *Long Day's Journey into Night* (1956) and *A Moon for the Misbegotten* (1973), for which he won a Tony Award.

QUINTILIAN (Marcus Fabius Quintilian-us: c35 AD–c96 AD), Roman rhetoric teacher, whose famous 12-book *Institutio Oratoria*, covering rhetorical techniques, educational theory, literary criticism and morality, deeply influenced Renaissance culture.

QUIRINO, Elpídio (1890–1956), Filipino statesman. Political aide to Manuel QUEZON for many years prior to WWII, he became an underground leader during the Japanese occupation. He was president of the Philippine republic 1948–54.

QUISLING, Vidkun Abraham Lauritz (1887–1945), Norwegian fascist leader who assisted the German invasion of Norway (1940) and was afterward appointed by HITLER premier of Norway's puppet government (1942–45). He was executed for treason. His name has come to mean "traitor."

QUITO, capital and second largest city of Ecuador and oldest capital in S America, is located just S of the equator at the foot of the Pichincha volcano, at an altitude of 9,350ft. Seized from the INCAS by a Spanish conquistador in 1534, it is famous for its Spanish colonial architecture. It has minor industries. Pop 635,713.

QUITRENTS, system whereby an "incomplete sale" of land was concluded between tenant and landlord, the latter collecting annual rent in perpetuity and retaining the option to repurchase the land at 75% of the sale price. Prevalent in the US in the 17th and 18th centuries, the system largely disappeared in the mid-19th century.

QUOITS, traditional English country game. Each player of each team throws in turn two quoits (iron or rubber rings) in an attempt to ring them over pins (hobs) set into the ground 54–72ft apart.

QUOTAS, limits imposed by governments on the number of immigrants or the quantity (sometimes the value) of goods that may be exported or imported. Tariff quotas allow a certain number of goods to be imported duty-free, quantities above the quota being subject to duty. (See also AFFIRMATIVE ACTION.)

18th letter of the alphabet, corresponding to Greek *rho* and Semitic *rēsh* ("head"). Its present capital form comes from classical Latin; the small letter derives from Carolingian script.

RA, or **Re**, sun god of ancient Egypt, one of the most important gods of the pantheon. From the 6th dynasty all pharaohs claimed descent from Ra. He was commonly represented as a falcon or falcon-headed figure with the solar disk on his head.

RABBI (Hebrew: my master, or my teacher), the leader of a Jewish religious congregation with the role of spiritual leader, scholar, teacher and interpreter of Jewish law. The term originated in Palestine, meaning merely religious teacher, after the return from exile and destruction of the hereditary priesthood, the more official role of a rabbi developing from the Middle Ages.

RABBITS, herbivorous members of the LAGOMORPHA, usually with long ears and a white scut for a tail. Best known is the European rabbit *Oryctolagus cuniculus*. These live in discrete social groups in colonial burrows. Territory is defended by all members of the group and within the group there is distinct dominance ranking.

RABELAIS, François (1494?–1553), French monk, doctor and humanist author of *Gargantua and Pantagruel* (four books 1532–52, arguably a fifth 1564). This exuberant mixture of popular anecdote, bawdry and huge erudition with vastly inventive language and broad satire of tyrants and bigots, recounts two giants' quest for the secret of life.

RABI, Isidor Isaac (1898–   ), Austrian-born US physicist whose discovery of new ways of measuring the magnetic properties of ATOMS and MOLECULES both paved the way for the development of the MASER and the ATOMIC CLOCK and earned him the 1944 Nobel Prize for Physics.

RABIES, or **Hydrophobia**, fatal VIRUS

disease resulting from the bite of an infected animal, usualy a dog. HEADACHE, FEVER, and an overwhelming fear, especially of water, are early symptoms following an INCUBATION period of 3–6 weeks; PARALYSIS, spasm of muscles of swallowing, respiratory paralysis, DELIRIUM, CONVULSIONS and COMA due to an ENCEPHALITIS follow. Wound cleansing, antirabies vaccine and hyperimmune serum must be instituted early in confirmed cases to prevent the onset of these symptoms. Fluid replacement and respiratory support may help, but survival is rare if symptoms appear. Infected animals must be destroyed.

RACCOONS, probably the best known of the American mammals, stout, bear-like animals, 600mm to 1m (2.0–3.3ft) long with a distinctive black mask and five to eight black bands on the bushy tail. They live in trees, alone or in small family groups, descending at night to forage for crayfish, frogs and fish in shallow pools. Family: Procyonidae.

RACE, within a SPECIES, a subgroup most of whose members have sufficiently different physical characteristics from those exhibited by most members of another subgroup for it to be considered as a distinct entity. In particular the term is used with respect to the human species, *Homo sapiens*, the three most commonly distinguished races being CAUCASOID, MONGOLOID and NEGROID (see also AUSTRALOID). However, in practice it is impossible to make unambiguous distinctions between races: a classification by color would yield a quite different result to one by blood-group (see ANTHROPOMETRY). According to DARWIN's theories of EVOLUTION, races arise when different groups encounter different environmental situations. Over generations, their physical characteristics evolve until each group as a whole is physically quite different from its parent stock. Should the isolation of the group continue long enough, and the environment be different enough, the divergent race will eventually become a distinct species, unable to mate with the species from which it originally sprang. This has obviously not happened in the case of man, whose races may interbreed successfully and, in many cases, advantageously. It is not known when man became racially differentiated, but certainly it was at a very early stage in his evolution (see PREHISTORIC MAN).

RACHMANINOV, Sergei Vasilyevich (1873–1943), Russian composer and virtuoso pianist. After a successful career in Russia he left in 1917, settling in Switzerland (until 1935) and then the US. His extensive output of piano music,

symphonies, songs and choral music includes such popular works as the Second Piano Concerto (1901).

RACINE, Jean Baptiste (1639–1699), greatest of French tragic dramatists. After a JANSENIST education at PORT ROYAL schools, he surpassed his rival CORNEILLE with seven tragedies, from *Andromaque* (1667) and *Britannicus* (1669) to *Phèdre* (1677), possibly his masterpiece. His greatness lies in the beauty of his verse, expressing both powerful and subtle emotions, and the creation of tragic suspense in a classically restrained form.

RACING. See AUTOMOBILE RACING; HORSE RACING.

RACISM, the theory that some races are inherently superior to others. The concept of racism in the early 19th century was really an offshoot of NATIONALISM, and emphasis was placed on the development of individual cultures. But at the same time a systematic study of human types was revealing the existence of races distinguished by physical characteristics. Despite the theories of LINNAEUS and BLUMENBACH that environment rather than heredity molded intellectual development, many theorists associated culture with race, and assumed white superiority. Guided by such thinkers as GOBINEAU, a concept of "tribal nationalism" began to appear. It was used to justify IMPERIALISM, the imposition of colonial status on backward peoples, and finally the concept of the "master-race" fostered by the NAZIS. The mass exterminations before and during WWII, together with advances in ANTHROPOLOGY, discredited racism as a tenable intellectual doctrine. (See also RACE.)

RACKHAM, Arthur (1867–1939), English artist best known for his fanciful, delicately-colored illustrations for children's books such as *Grimm's Fairy Tales* (1900), *Peter Pan* (1906) and *A Wonder Book* (1922).

RACQUETS, a game for two or four players, normally played in an enclosed court 60ft long and 30ft wide, with a front wall 30ft high and a back wall 15ft high. Rules are similar to those of SQUASH, but the ball is much harder.

RADAR (*radio detection and ranging*), system that detects long-range objects and determines their positions by measuring the time taken for RADIO WAVES to travel to the objects, be reflected and return. Radar is used for NAVIGATION, air control, fire control, storm detection, in radar astronomy and for catching speeding drivers. It developed out of experiments in the 1920s measuring the distance to the IONOSPHERE by radio pulses. R. A. WATSON-WATT showed that the technique could be applied to detecting aircraft, and from 1935 Britain installed a series of radar stations which were a major factor in winning the Battle of Britain in WWII. From 1940 the UK and the US collaborated to develop radar. There are two main types of radar: **continuous-wave radar**, which transmits continuously, the frequency being varied sinusoidally, and detects the signals received by their instantaneously different frequency; and the more common **pulsed radar**. This latter has a highly directional antenna which scans the area systematically or tracks an object. A cavity magnetron or klystron emits pulses, typically 400 per second, $1\mu s$ across and at a frequency of 3GHz. A duplexer switches the antenna automatically from transmitter to receiver and back as appropriate. The receiver converts the echo pulses to an intermediate frequency of about 30MHz, and they are then amplified, converted to a video signal, and displayed on a CATHODE-RAY TUBE. A synchronizer measures the time-lag between transmission and reception, and this is represented by the position of the pulse on the screen. Electronic processing can reduce noise by adding together successive pulses so that the noise tends to cancel out. Over-the-horizon radar is possible when atmospheric conditions form a "duct" through which the waves travel. Various display modes are used: commonest is the plan-position indicator (PPI), showing horizontal position in polar coordinates. (See also LORAN.)

RADCLIFFE, Ann (born Ann Ward; 1764–1823), English novelist remembered for her GOTHIC NOVELS, notably *The Mysteries of Udolpho* (1794) and *The Italian* (1797).

RADIATION SICKNESS, malaise, nausea, loss of appetite and VOMITING occurring several hours after exposure to ionizing RADIATION in large doses. This occurs as an industrial or war hazard, or more commonly following RADIATION THERAPY for CANCER, LYMPHOMA or LEUKEMIA. Large doses of radiation may cause BONE MARROW depression with ANEMIA, AGRANULOCYTOSIS and bleeding, or gastrointestinal disturbance with distension and bloody DIARRHEA. Skin ERYTHEMA and ulceration, LUNG fibrosis, NEPHRITIS and premature ARTERIOSCLEROSIS may follow radiation and there is a risk of malignancy developing.

RADIATION THERAPY, use of ionizing RADIATION, as rays from an outside source or from radium or other radioactive metal implants, in treatment of malignant DISEASE—CANCER, LYMPHOMA and LEUKEMIA. The principle is that rapidly dividing TUMOR cells are more sensitive to the destructive effects of radiation on NUCLEIC ACIDS and are therefore damaged by doses that are relatively harmless to normal tissues. Certain types of malignancy indeed respond to radiation therapy but RADIATION SICKNESS may also occur.

RADICAL FEMINISM, the most extreme wing of the women's movement, composed of those who reject conventional male-female relationships, especially as represented in the institutions of marriage and the patriarchal family, in favor of a new social and economic order based on feminist (or humanistic) values. A product of the radical 1960s, radical feminists rejected both the reformist, civil rights orientation of the NATIONAL ORGANIZATION FOR WOMEN and the male chauvinism and violence of the radical left. Theoretically, the movement found underpinnings in the radical social criticism by such 19th-century advocates of WOMEN'S RIGHTS as Elizabeth Cady STANTON. Ti-Grace Atkinson was a prominent leader.

RADICAL REPUBLICANS, a militant group of the Republican Party active after the US Civil War, putting pressure on LINCOLN and later Andrew JOHNSON to ensure full civil rights for the Southern blacks. Their most important achievement was the RECONSTRUCTION Act (1867).

RADIO, the communication of information between distant points using radio waves, ELECTROMAGNETIC RADIATION of wavelength between 1mm and 100km. Radio waves are also described in terms of their FREQUENCY—measured in HERTZ (Hz) and found by dividing the velocity of the waves (about 300Mm/s) by their wavelength. Radio communications systems link transmitting stations with receiving stations. In a transmitting station a piezoelectric OSCILLATOR is used to generate a steady radio-frequency (RF) "carrier" wave. This is amplified and "modulated" with a signal carrying the information (see INFORMATION THEORY) to be communicated. The simplest method of modulation is to pulse (switch on and off) the carrier with a signal in, say, MORSE CODE, but speech and music, entering the modulator as an audiofrequency (AF) signal from tape or a MICROPHONE, is made to interact with the carrier so that the shape of the audio wave determines either the amplitude of the carrier wave (amplitude modulation—AM) or its frequency within a small band on either side of the original carrier frequency (frequency modulation—FM). The modulated RF signal is then amplified (see AMPLIFIER) to a high power and radiated from an ANTENNA. At the receiving station, another antenna picks up a minute fraction of the energy radiated from the transmitter together with some background NOISE. This RF signal is amplified and the original audio signal is recovered (demodulation or detection). Detection and amplification often involve many stages including FEEDBACK and intermediate frequency (IF) circuits. A radio receiver must of course be able to discriminate between all the different signals acting at any one time on its antenna. This is accomplished with a tuning circuit which allows only the desired frequency to pass to the detector (see also ELECTRONICS). In point-to-point radio communications most stations can both transmit and receive messages but in radio broadcasting a central transmitter broadcasts program sequences to a multitude of individual receivers. Programs are often produced centrally and distributed to a "network" of local broadcasting stations by wire or MICROWAVE link. Because there are potentially so many users of radio communications—aircraft, ships, police and amateur "hams" as well as broadcasting services—the use of the RF portion of the electromagnetic SPECTRUM is strictly controlled to prevent unwanted INTERFERENCE between signals having adjacent carrier frequencies. The INTERNATIONAL TELECOMMUNICATION UNION (ITU) and national agencies such as the US FEDERAL COMMUNICATIONS COMMISSION (FCC) divide the RF spectrum into bands which it allocates to the various users. Public broadcasting in the US uses MF frequencies between 535kHz and 1605kHz (AM) and VHF bands between 88MHz and 108MHz (FM). VHF reception, though limited to line-of-sight transmissions, offers much higher fidelity of transmission (see HIGH-FIDELITY) and much greater freedom from interference. International broadcasting and local transmissions in other countries frequently use other frequencies in the LF, MF and HF (short wave) bands. (See the electromagnetic spectrum table at ELECTROMAGNETIC RADIATION.)

The Development of Radio. The existence of radio waves was first predicted by James Clerk MAXWELL in the 1860s but it was not until 1887 that Heinrich HERTZ succeeded in producing them experimentally. "Wireless" telegraphy was first demonstrated by Sir Oliver LODGE in 1894 and MARCONI made the first trans-Atlantic transmission in 1901. Voice transmission was first achieved in 1900 but transmitter and amplifier powers were restricted before the advent of Lee DE FOREST's triode ELECTRON TUBE in 1906. Only the development of the TRANSISTOR after 1948 has had as great an impact on radio technology. Commercial broadcasting began in the US in 1920.

RADIO, Amateur, a hobby practiced throughout the world by thousands of enthusiasts, or "hams," who communicate with one another on short-wave radio, by "phone" (voice) or by using International MORSE CODE. Permitted amateur bands include 160, 80, 40, 20, 15 and 10 meters. In the US, the various grades of license may be obtained by passing tests of progressively greater difficulty. CB radio (from "Citizens' Band"), is a less structured, more informal kind of "ham" radio which became popular in the US in the late 1970s and resulted in the establishment of a vast network of amateur radio operators.

RADIOACTIVITY, the spontaneous disintegration of certain unstable nuclei, accompanied by the emission of ALPHA PARTICLES (weakly penetrating HELIUM nuclei), BETA RAYS (more penetrating streams of ELECTRONS) or GAMMA RAYS (ELECTROMAGNETIC RADIATION capable of penetrating up to 100mm of LEAD). In 1896, BECQUEREL noticed the spontaneous emission of ENERGY from URANIUM compounds (particularly PITCHBLENDE). The intensity of the effect depended on the amount of uranium present, suggesting that it involved individual atoms. The CURIES discovered further radioactive substances such as THORIUM and RADIUM, and about 40 natural radioactive substances are now known. Their rates of decay are unaffected by chemical changes, pressure, temperature or electromagnetic fields, and each nuclide (nucleus of a particular ISOTOPE) has a characteristic decay constant or HALF-LIFE. RUTHERFORD and SODDY suggested in 1902 that a radioactive nuclide decays to a further radioactive nuclide, a series of transformations taking place which ends with the formation of a stable "daughter" nucleus. It is now known that for radioactive elements of high ATOMIC WEIGHT, three decay series (the thorium, actinium and uranium series) exist. As well as the natural radioactive elements, a large number of induced radioactive nuclides have been formed by nuclear reactions taking place in ACCELERATORS or NUCLEAR REACTORS (see also IRRADIATION; RADIOISOTOPES). Some of these are members of the three natural radioactive series. Various types of radioactivity are known, but beta emission is the most common, normally caused by the decay of a NEUTRON, giving a PROTON, an electron and an antineutrino (see SUBATOMIC PARTICLES). This results in a unit change of atomic number (see ATOM) and no change in MASS NUMBER. Heavier nuclides often decay to a daughter nucleus with atomic number two less and mass number four less, emitting an alpha particle. If an excited daughter nucleus is formed, gamma-ray emission may accompany both alpha and beta decay. Because the ionizing radiations emitted by radioactive materials are physiologically harmful, special precautions must be taken in handling them.

RADIO ASTRONOMY, the study of the ELECTROMAGNETIC RADIATION emitted or reflected by celestial objects in the approximate wavelength range 1mm–30m, usually by use of a RADIO TELESCOPE. The science was initiated accidentally in 1932 by Karl Jansky who found an interference in a telephone system he was testing: the source proved to be the MILKY WAY. In 1937 an American, Grote Reber, built a 9.5m radio telescope in his back yard and scanned the sky at a wavelength around 2m. After WWII the science began in earnest. Investigation of the sky revealed that clouds of hydrogen gas in the Milky Way were radio sources, and mapping of these confirmed our galaxy's spiral form (see GALAXY).

The sky is very different for the radio astronomer than for the astronomer. Bright stars are not radio objects (our sun is one solely because it is so close), while many radio objects are optically undetectable. Radio objects include QUASARS, PULSARS, supernova remnants (e.g., the CRAB NEBULA) and other galaxies. The work of Martin RYLE in the 1960s and 1970s has enabled radio galaxies that are possibly at the farthest extremities of the universe to be mapped. The universe also has an inherent radio "background noise" (see COSMOLOGY).

RADIOCARBON DATING. See RADIOISOTOPE DATING.

RADIOCHEMISTRY, the use of RADIOISOTOPES in chemistry, especially in studies involving chemical ANALYSIS, where radioisotopes provide a powerful and sensitive tool. Tracer techniques, in which a particular atom in a molecule is "labeled" by replacement with a radioisotope, are used to study reaction rates and mechanisms (see KINETICS, CHEMICAL).

RADIOISOTOPE, radioactive ISOTOPE of an element. A few elements, such as RADIUM or URANIUM, have naturally occurring radioisotopes, but because of their usefulness in science and industry, a large number of radioisotopes are produced artificially. This is done by IRRADIATION of stable isotopes with PHOTONS, or with particles such as NEUTRONS in an ACCELERATOR or NUCLEAR REACTOR. Radioisotopes with a wide range of HALF-LIVES and activities are available by these means. Because radioisotopes behave chemically and biologically in a very similar way to stable isotopes, and their radiation can easily be monitored even in very small amounts, they are used to "label" particular atoms or groups in studying chemical reaction mechanisms and to "trace" the course of particular components in various physiological processes. The radiation emitted by radioisotopes may also be utilized directly for treating diseased areas of the body (see RADIATION THERAPY), sterilizing foodstuffs or controlling insect pests.

RADIOLARIANS, single-celled animals possessing an internal skeleton, usually siliceous but sometimes of strontium sulfate. Members of the Sarcodine class of PROTOZOA, all are marine and are abundant in PLANKTON. The skeletons sink after death and build up into thick sediments.

RADIOISOTOPE DATING, means of dating materials from the geological past in terms of the radioisotopes they contain. All radioisotopes are members of various radioactive decay series (see RADIOACTIVITY), whose half-lives (see HALF-LIFE) are known, so that the proportion of the original isotope in the series compared to the percentage of later entrants in the series in a given sample indicates the age of that sample. Several such series are available for investigation by scientists, perhaps the best known of which is the CARBON-14 series used in archaeology and for other relatively recent geological time spans. Because carbon-14 decays fairly rapidly, the method is usually limited to dating the past 50,000 years. Other decay series used for much more ancient times include the POTASSIUM-ARGON method, the RUBIDIUM-STRONTIUM method, the IONIUM-THORIUM method, and various methods involving series that end in the element LEAD.

RADIOLOGY, the use of RADIOACTIVITY, GAMMA RAYS and X-RAYS in MEDICINE, particularly in diagnosis but also in treatment. (See also RADIATION THERAPY.)

RADIO TELESCOPE, the basic instrument of RADIO ASTRONOMY. The receiving part of the equipment consists of a large parabola, the big dish, which operates on the same principle as the parabolic mirror of a reflecting TELESCOPE. The signals that it receives are then amplified and examined. In practice, it is possible to build radio telescopes effectively far larger than any possible dish by using several connected dishes; this is known as an array.

RADIUM (Ra), radioactive ALKALINE-EARTH METAL similar to BARIUM, isolated from PITCHBLENDE by Marie CURIE in 1898. It has white salts which turn black as the radium decays, and which emit a blue glow due to ionization of the air by radiation. It has four natural ISOTOPES, the commonest being Ra^{226} with HALF-LIFE 1,622 years. Radium is used in industrial and medical radiography. AW 226.0, mp 700°C, bp 1140°C, sg 5.

RAEDER, Erich (1876–1960), German admiral, commander in chief of the German Navy 1928–43. For his aggressive naval strategy, as in the invasions of Denmark and Norway, he was convicted as a war criminal in 1946 (released 1955).

RAFFLES, Sir Thomas Stamford (1781–1826), British colonial administrator who founded Singapore (1819). He persuaded the British government to seize Java, which he governed from 1811 to 1815. His career was marked by his liberalism, especially in his opposition to slavery.

RAGLAN, Fitzroy James Henry Somerset, 1st Baron (1788–1855), commander of British forces in the CRIMEAN WAR. He was widely criticized for the failure of the siege of Sevastopol (1854–55) and for the Earl of CARDIGAN's disastrous Charge of the Light Brigade (1854).

RAGTIME, a style of piano playing in which the left hand provides harmony and a firm beat, while the right hand plays the melody, usually syncopated. Famous exponents of the style, which was the immediate predecessor of JAZZ, are Scott JOPLIN and "Jelly-Roll" MORTON.

RAHMAN, Mujibur (called Sheikh Mujib; 1920–1975), first premier (1972–74) and then president (1974–75) of BANGLADESH. He was secretary and president of the Awami League, whose object was autonomy for E Pakistan. He rebuilt Bangladesh following the war of independence (1971), but was assassinated after assuming dictatorial powers.

RAHMAN, Tunku Abdul (1903–1973), first prime minister of the Federation of Malaya (1957–63) and then of the Federation of Malaysia (1963–70). He helped found the United Malay National Organization in 1945 and was its president 1952–55.

RAHV, Philip (1908–1973), Russian-born US literary critic and editor. As co-editor of the *Partisan Review* (1934–69), he fostered modernism and promoted the careers of such writers as Saul BELLOW, Robert LOWELL and Karl SHAPIRO. As a critic, Rahv believed that literature must be rooted in history and ideas. His works include *Image and Idea* (1949), *The Myth and the Powerhouse* (1965) and *Essays on Literature and Politics: 1932–1972* (1978).

RAILROAD, land transportation system in which cars with flanged steel wheels run on tracks of two parallel steel rails. From their beginning railroads provided reliable, economical transport for freight and passengers; they promoted the Industrial Revolution and have been vital to continued economic growth ever since, especially in developing countries. Railroads are intrinsically economical in their use of energy because the rolling friction of wheel on rail is very low. However, fixed costs of maintenance are high, so high traffic volume is needed. This, together with rising competition and overmanning, has led to the closure of many minor lines in the US and Europe, though elsewhere many new lines are still being built. Maintenance, signalling and many other functions are now highly automated.

Railroads developed out of the small mining tracks or tramways built in the UK and Europe from the mid-16th century. They used gravity or horse power, and the cars generally ran on flanged rails or plateways. These were hard to switch, however, and the system of flanged wheels on plain rails eventually predominated. The first public freight railroad was the Surrey Iron Railway (1801). The modern era of mechanized traction began with TREVITHICK's steam locomotive "New Castle" (1804) (see also STEAM ENGINE). Early locomotives ran on toothed racks to prevent slipping, but in 1813 this was found to be unnecessary. The first public railroad to use locomotives and to carry passengers was the Stockton and Darlington Railway (1825). The boom began when the Liverpool and Manchester Railway opened in 1830 using George STEPHENSON's "Rocket," a much superior and more reliable locomotive. Railroads spread rapidly in Britain, Europe and the US. The first US railroad was the Baltimore and Ohio (1830). The rails were laid on wooden (later also concrete) crossties or sleepers, and were joined by fishplates to allow for thermal expansion. Continuous welded rails are now generally used. Track gauges were at first varied, but the "standard gauge" of 4ft 8½in (1.435m) soon predominated. Railroads must be built with shallow curves and gentle gradients, using bridges, embankments, cuttings and tunnels as necessary.

The sharp increases in oil prices, beginning in the early 1970s, appeared to give railroads a new lease on life. However, the popularity of railroads continued to be limited mostly to commuter lines, and the potential for hauling freight was not fully realized. In the US the national AMTRAK system survived with the aid of federal subsidies. (See also SUBWAY.)

RAIMU (Jules Muraire; 1883–1946), French actor and comedian who starred in music hall revues, stage comedies and film. One of France's most beloved actors, he appeared in more than 30 movies, including the Marcel Pagnol trilogy *Marius* (1931), *Fanny* (1932) and *César* (1934), and *The Well-digger's Daughter* (1940).

RAINIER, Mount, extinct volcano in the Cascade Range and highest peak in Wash., 14,410ft high, lying 40mi SE of Tacoma in Mt Rainier National Park. The fine scenery and skiing slopes in the area attract many tourists.

RAINIER III, Louis Henri Maxence Bertrand (1923–), prince of MONACO since 1949. He married the US actress Grace KELLY in 1956.

RAINS, Claude (1889–1967), English actor noted especially for suavely villainous screen performances. His films include *The Invisible Man* (1933), *Casablanca* (1942), *Caesar and Cleopatra* (1945) and *Notorious* (1946).

RAJPUTS (Sanskrit: kings' sons), military and landowning caste mostly of the Rajasthan (now Rajputana) region, India. Their origins date back nearly 1,500 years, when successive waves of invaders were absorbed into Indian society. Their influence in N and central India has waxed and waned, being at times considerable, and since INDIA's independence (1947) has steadily declined.

RALEIGH, state capital of N.C. and seat of Wake Co., named for Sir Walter RALEIGH; a center for the surrounding agricultural areas and for culture, education and science. Its light industries include chemicals, electronics and textiles. Pop 149,771.

RALEIGH, or **Ralegh, Sir Walter** (1554?–1618), English adventurer and poet, a favorite of Queen Elizabeth I. His efforts to organize colonization of the New World resulted in the tragedy of the LOST COLONY. In 1589 he left court and consolidated his friendship with SPENSER, whose *Faerie Queene* was written partly under Raleigh's patronage. Returning he distinguished himself in raids at Cadiz (1596) and the Azores (1597). James I imprisoned him in the Tower of London 1603–16, where he wrote poetry and his uncompleted *History of the World*. After two years' freedom he was executed.

RAM (the constellation). See ARIES.

RAMADAN, ninth month of the Muslim calendar, during which the revelation of the KORAN to MOHAMMED is commemorated by abstention from food, drink and other bodily pleasures between sunrise and sunset.

RAMAKRISHNA PARAMAHANSA (1836–1886), Indian saint whose teachings, now carried all over the world by the Ramakrishna Mission (founded in Calcutta in 1897), emphasize the unity of all religions and place equal value on social service, worship and meditation. His followers consider him to have been an incarnation of God.

RAMAN, Sir Chandrasekhara Venkata (1888–1970), Indian physicist awarded the 1930 Nobel Prize for Physics for his discovery of the **Raman Effect**: when molecules are exposed to a beam of INFRARED RADIATION, light scattered by the molecules contains frequencies that differ from that of the beam by amounts characteristic of the molecules. This is the basis for Raman SPECTROSCOPY.

RAMAYANA, major Hindu epic poem, composed in Sanskrit in about the 3rd century BC, concerning the war waged by RAMA against Ravān, the demon-king of Lanka, who was terrorizing the earth. Helped by Hanuman, king of the monkeys, Rama eventually rescues his wife, Sita, whom Ravān had abducted, and slays the demon, enabling the righteous once more to live in peace.

RAMBERT, Dame Marie (1888–), ballet producer, director and teacher who founded the **Ballet Rambert** (1935). Polish by birth, she became a British citizen in 1918, and exercised a major influence on British ballet. Among her pupils was Frederick ASHTON.

RAMEAU, Jean Philippe (1683–1764), French composer and one of the founders of modern harmonic theory. He achieved recognition with his *Treatise on Harmony* (1722), and in Paris became a celebrated teacher and composer of some 30 operas, *Hippolyte et Aricie* (1733) being the first.

RAMPAL, Jean-Pierre (1922–), French flutist. A virtuoso known for his pure luxuriant tone, he revived interest in the flute as a solo instrument.

RAMSES II (reigned c1304–1237 BC), "Ramses the Great," Egyptian pharaoh who built hundreds of temples and monuments, probably including ABU SIMBEL and the columned hall at KARNAK. He campaigned against the HITTITES, and celebrated a battle at Kadesh (1300 BC) on many of his monuments, but was eventually obliged to make peace (c1283 BC). His long reign marked a high point in Egyptian prosperity.

RAND, Ayn (1905–), Russian-born US writer. Her "objectivist" philosophy, individualistic, egoistic and capitalist in inspiration, is at the core of such successful novels as *The Fountainhead* (1943) and *Atlas Shrugged* (1957).

RAND, Sally (1904–1979), US dancer and actress who created a sensation—and a new form of entertainment—when she performed a fan dance at the 1933 Chicago World's Fair. She subsequently performed in nightclubs throughout the US.

RAND, The. See WITWATERSRAND.

RANDOLPH, Asa Philip (1889–1979), US Negro labor leader. He became an outspoken socialist during WWI and organized the Brotherhood of Sleeping Car Porters in 1925. His campaigning was instrumental in the setting up of the FAIR EMPLOYMENT PRACTICES COMMITTEE in 1941. In 1963 he directed the March on Washington for Jobs and Freedom.

RANGER MISSIONS, series of nine unmanned US probes of the moon. The first to hit the moon, Ranger 4, impacted Apr. 26, 1962; the first to return photographs, Ranger 7, sent back 4,308 pictures before crashing onto the lunar surface July 31, 1964. The Rangers prepared the way for the Lunar Orbiter and Surveyor missions. The Soviets conducted comparable unmanned missions, starting with Luna 1, launched Jan. 2, 1959, which bypassed the moon at a distance of 4,660 miles, and ending with Luna 15, which soft-landed July 21, 1969, a day after the US landed the first men on the moon.

RANGOON, capital, largest city and chief port of Burma, on the Rangoon R. It is a commercial and manufacturing center with textile, sawmilling, food-processing and petroleum industries. Its gold-domed Shwe Dagon pagoda is the country's principal Buddhist shrine. Rangoon was founded in 1753 as the Burmese capital. It was occupied by the British 1824–26 and retaken by them in 1852, after which it developed as a modern city. During World War II Rangoon was occupied by the Japanese and suffered heavy damage. Pop 2,056,118.

RANK, Otto (1884–1939), Austrian-born US psychoanalyst best known for his suggestion that the psychological TRAUMA of birth is the basis of later anxiety NEUROSIS; and for applying PSYCHOANALYSIS to artistic creativity.

RANKIN, Jeanette (1880–1973), pacifist, feminist, social reformer and first woman elected to the US Congress. She became Republican Congresswoman at large for Montana 1917–19, and returned to the House in 1941, when she cast the only vote against entering WWII. In the 1960s she reemerged as a leader of the campaign against the war in Vietnam.

RANSOM, John Crowe (1888–1974), US poet and proponent of the New Criticism, which emphasized textual, rather than social or moral, analysis. Professor of Poetry at Kenyon College, Ohio, 1937–58, he founded and edited the *Kenyon Review* (1939–59). His poetry includes *Chills and Fever* (1924).

RAPALLO, Treaty of, name of two separate treaties. One, between Italy and Yugoslavia, signed Nov. 12, 1920, temporarily established Fiume (RIJEKA) as a free state. The other, between Germany and the USSR, was signed April 16, 1922. The two countries reestablished diplomatic relations, renounced war debts and claims on one another and agreed on economic cooperation.

RAPE, most commonly, sexual penetration against the subject's will. The legal definition of rape has been in a state of flux in recent years, and statutes are not in agreement. For example, penetration of any bodily orifice may constitute rape in some jurisdictions, and by some definitions a person of either sex may be perpetrator or victim; in fact, however, almost all instances of prosecuted rape involve an assault by a man on a woman. Forceful resistance may not be required to demonstrate the lack of consent by the victim. *Statutory* rape is defined as sexual intercourse with a person below a certain age, which varies from 12 to 18 years. In some countries and in several states of the US, a husband may be charged with rape by his wife.

The women's movement has taken the lead in seeking changes in the rape laws, charging that often the victim, rather than the person accused of rape, appears to be on trial. Further, they contend that many women fail to report rapes because of their dread of appearing at a public trial or of being humiliated by the police. In recent years, however, more women officers are dealing sympathetically with rape victims and medical examiners are demonstrating more sensitivity to the particular emotional problems of the victims. (See also CRIME RATES.)

RAPHAEL (Raffaello Santi or Sanzio;

1483-1520), Italian High RENAISSANCE painter and architect. Born in URBINO, he was early influenced by PERUGINO, as in *Marriage of the Virgin* (1504). In Florence, 1504-08, he studied the work of MICHELANGELO and LEONARDO DA VINCI, being influenced especially by the latter, and painted his famous Madonnas. From 1508 he decorated the Vatican rooms for JULIUS II: the library frescoes, masterly portrayals of symbolic themes, use Raphael's new knowledge of classical art. His SISTINE CHAPEL tapestries (1515-16) and his sympathetic portraits were much imitated. From 1514 he worked rebuilding SAINT PETER'S BASILICA.

RAPP, George (1757-1847), German-born ascetic who founded the Rappites, a PIETIST sect which emigrated to the US and formed several communes. The sect became known as the HARMONY SOCIETY.

RARE EARTHS, the elements SCANDIUM, YTTRIUM and the LANTHANUM SERIES, in Group IIIB of the PERIODIC TABLE, occurring widespread in nature as MONAZITE and other ores. They are separated by CHROMATOG-RAPHY and ION-EXCHANGE resins. Rare earths are used in ALLOYS, including MISCH METAL; and their compounds (mixed or separately) are used as ABRASIVES, for making glasses and ceramics, as "getters," as catalysts (see CATALYSIS) in the petroleum industry, and to make PHOSPHORS, LASERS and MICROWAVE devices.

RARE GASES, former name for the NOBLE GASES.

RASHI (acronym from Rabbi Shlomo Yitzhaqi, 1040-1105), medieval French commentator on the Bible and TALMUD. His classic commentaries on the Old Testament and especially the Talmud have exercised an enduring influence on Jewish scholarship.

RASMUSSEN, Knud Johan Victor (1879-1933), Danish Arctic explorer and ethnologist. From Thule, Greenland, he undertook many expeditions to study Eskimo culture, including the longest dog-sledge journey known, from Greenland to Alaska (1923-24), described in his *Across Arctic America* (1927).

RASPE, Rudolph Erich (1737-1794), German scholar and thief best known for *The Adventures of Baron Münchhausen* (1785), a collection of tall stories.

RASPUTIN, Grigori Yefimovich (1872?-1916), Russian mystic, known as the "mad monk," who gained influence over the Tsarina ALEXANDRA FYODOROVNA after supposedly curing her son's hemophilia in 1905. The scandal of his debaucheries, as well as his interference in political affairs,

contributed to the undermining of the imperial government in WWI. He was assassinated by a group of ultra-conservatives.

RASTRELLI, Bartolomeo Francesco (1700-1771), Italian architect who worked in St. Petersburg (Leningrad). Chief architect to the imperial court from 1736, he did much, through his several baroque and rococo palaces such as the Winter Palace (1754-62), to Europeanize Russian architecture.

RATHBONE, Basil (1892-1967), English film actor often cast as a villain but best remembered for his numerous appearances as Sherlock Holmes. His films include *David Copperfield* (1934), *The Adventures of Robin Hood* (1938) and *The Hound of the Baskervilles* (1939).

RATIONALISM, a philosophical approach based on the view that reality has a logical structure accessible to deductive reasoning and proof, and holding, as against EMPIRICISM, that reason unsupported by sense experience is a source of knowledge not merely of concepts (as in mathematics and logic), but of the real world. Major rationalists in modern philosophy include DESCARTES, SPINOZA, HEGEL and LEIBNIZ.

RATS, a vast number of species of RODENTS belonging to many different families, largely Muridae and Cricetidae. The name is given to any large mouse-like rodent. The best known rats are perhaps the Brown and Black rats, *Rattus norvegicus* and *R. rattus*, familiar farmyard and warehouse pests. A strong exploratory urge, with an ability to feed on almost anything, makes them persistent pests; in addition, they transmit a number of serious diseases such as TYPHUS and PLAGUE. These rats originated in Asia but are now widespread in Europe and America. The New World has its own, Cricetid, rats: the Wood rats or PACK RATS, *Neotoma*; the Cotton rats, *Sigmodon*, and the Rice rats, *Oryzomys*.

RATTIGAN, Sir Terence Mervyn (1911-1977), popular British playwright. He turned from light comedies such as *French Without Tears* (1936) to the more serious, in *The Winslow Boy* (1946), *Ross* (1960) and *In Praise of Love* (1974).

RATTLESNAKES, two genera, *Crotalus* and *Sistrurus*, of PIT VIPERS of the Americas, named for a rattle on the tip of the tail. This rattle is composed of successive pieces of dead skin sloughed off the tail and is vibrated at great speed. Rattlers have moveable fangs which fold up into the roof of the mouth when not in use and are shed and replaced every three weeks. They are extremely venomous snakes, some quite ready to attack humans.

RAUSCHENBERG, Robert (1925–   ), US artist, an initiator of the POP ART of the 1960s. His "combines" (collages) use brushwork with objects from everyday life such as pop bottles and news photos.

RAVEL, Maurice Joseph (1875–1937), influential French composer, known for his adventurous harmonic style and the combination of delicacy and power in such orchestral works as *Rhapsodie Espagnole* (1908) and *Bolero* (1928), and the ballets *Daphnis and Chloé* (1912) and *La Valse* (1920). *Gaspard de la Nuit* (1908) is among his many masterpieces for the piano, his favorite instrument.

RAVENNA, city in NE Italy famous for its superb MOSAICS, notably in the 5th-century mausoleum of Galla Placidia and 6th-century churches (notably San Vitale and Sant'Apollinare Nuovo). Emperor HONOR-IUS made Ravenna his capital; it was seized by ODOACER in 476 and was later seat of the Byzantine EXARCH. Modern Ravenna, an agricultural and manufacturing center, has a port and petrochemical plants. Pop 139,200.

RAVENS, large dark CROWS of the genus *Corvus*. They do not form a natural group but are given the name arbitrarily because of their size. There are three species in Africa, one restricted to Australia, one to the Americas. The most cosmopolitan is the Common raven *C. corax* of North America and Eurasia.

RAY, Man (1890–1976), US abstract artist and photographer, a founder of the New York DADA movement. He recreated several "lost" photographic techniques and produced surrealist films.

RAY, Satyajit (1922–   ), foremost Indian film director. *Pather Panchali* (1954) was his acclaimed debut. His many other films include *Aparajito* (1956), *The Music Room* (1958) and *The World of Apu* (1959).

RAYBURN, Samuel (Sam) Taliaferro (1882–1961), longest-serving US House of Representatives speaker (17 years from 1940) and congressman (1913–61). A dedicated Democrat, he helped build NEW DEAL policy and was uniquely esteemed for his political skills and experience.

RAYMOND, Henry Jarvis (1820–1869), founder-editor of the *New York Times* (1851) who took an active part in forming the REPUBLICAN PARTY. He was in the House of Representatives 1865–67, losing renomination because of his moderate stand on RECONSTRUCTION.

RAYS, a group of cartilaginous fishes whose pectoral fins are generally greatly expanded and wing-like. Rays swim by undulation of these "wings." The highly flattened body and large pectoral fins adapt them for a bottom-living existence. Rays are divided into six groups: SKATES; Rays; MANTA RAYS (which have abandoned bottom-living for a pelagic existence); Electric rays (in which blocks of muscle are adapted as electric batteries); SAWFISHES, and Guitarfishes.

READ, Sir Herbert (1893–1968), British poet and critic, champion of art education, free verse and the English 19th-century Romantic writers. His best-known works are *The Philosophy of Modern Art* (1952) and *The Tenth Muse* (1959). He edited the *Burlington Magazine* 1933–39.

READING, the process of assimilating language in the written form. Initial language development in children is largely as speech (see SPEECH AND SPEECH DISORDERS) and has a primarily auditory or phonetic component; the recognition of letters, words and sentences when written represents a transition from the auditory to the visual mode. The dependence of reading on previous linguistic development with spoken speech is seen in the impaired reading ability of deaf children. Normal reading depends on normal VISION and the ability to recognize the patterns of letter and word order and grammatical variations. In reading, vision is linked with the system controlling EYE movement, so that the page is scanned in an orderly fashion. Reading is represented in essentially the same areas of the brain as are concerned with speech, and disorders of the two often occur together (e.g., DYSPHASIA). In DYSLEXIA, pattern recognition is impaired and a specific defect of reading and language development results. The ability to read and write, and thus to record events, ideas, etc., represented one of the most substantial advances in human civilization after the acquisition of speech itself.

REAGAN, Ronald (1911–   ), 40th US president. Born in Tampico, Ill., he became a film actor in 1937 and in 1947 was elected president of the Screen Actors Guild. He campaigned for GOLDWATER as a conservative Republican in 1964, and was governor of Cal. 1967–75. Defeated for the Republican presidential nomination in 1976, he won it and the presidency in 1980. He supported a strong defense budget, but cut federal domestic programs, as he had cut welfare and similar expenditures as governor.

REALISM, in art and literature, the faithful imitation of real life; more specifically, the artistic movement which started in France c1850 in reaction to the idealized representations of ROMANTICISM and NEOCLASSICISM, with a social dimension derived from scientific progress and the REVOLUTIONS OF 1848. In France the leading painters were COROT, COURBET, DAUMIER and MILLET, and its main literary expression was in the novels of BALZAC, FLAUBERT and ZOLA (see NATURALISM). In the US, EAKINS, Winslow HOMER and the ASHCAN SCHOOL were Realistic painters, and in literature Stephen CRANE, Theodore DREISER, William HOWELLS, Henry JAMES and Frank NORRIS led the movement.

REALISM, in philosophy, is a term with two main technical uses. Philosophers who believe, as PLATO did, that UNIVERSALS exist in their own right, and so independently of perceived objects, are traditionally labeled "realists." Realism in this sense is opposed to NOMINALISM. On the other hand, realism also describes the view that material objects exist independently of our perceptions of them. In this sense it is opposed to certain forms of IDEALISM.

REBEC, three-stringed bowed instrument, the precursor of the VIQLS, of Moorish origin. Popular in medieval Europe, it is now found in the folk music of the Balkans.

REBER, Grote (1911–), US astronomer who built the first RADIO TELESCOPE (1937) and made radio maps of the sky (1940, 1942) which indicated areas of strong radio emissions unrelated to any visible celestial body.

RECALL. See INITIATIVE, REFERENDUM AND RECALL.

RECESSION, that part of the BUSINESS CYCLE where the economy slows and begins to turn downward. It is characterized by decreases in capital investment and incomes, more frequent business failures, and declines in industrial output and employment. In the past, recessions have either ended quickly or, less frequently, been replaced by periods of DEPRESSION, with high unemployment and sharply reduced production. To cut short post-WWII recessions, the US government stepped up spending to create jobs and increased the money supply. In the 1970s, however, INFLATION continued to rise throughout recessionary periods (see STAGFLATION); many economists believe that federal anti-recession efforts contribute to high rates of inflation.

RECITATIVE, lightly accompanied narration or dialogue linking musical numbers in OPERA and ORATORIO. Originally more spoken than sung, it has become increasingly integrated into the musical framework.

RECLAMATION, US Bureau of, agency of the Department of the Interior, created to administer the Reclamation Act of 1902 for reclaiming arid land by irrigation in the 16 W states. Its responsibilities were later progressively expanded.

RECOMBINANT DNA, DNA from two different organisms. Recombinant DNA, created by splicing a gene from one type of cell into the DNA of a cell of another organism, is the key to the new science of GENETIC ENGINEERING.

RECONSTRUCTION, period (1865–77) when Americans tried to rebuild a stable Union after the Civil War. The deadlock inherited by Andrew JOHNSON on Lincoln's death, over who should control Reconstruction, hardened with increasing congressional hostility toward restoring the South to its old position (see WADE-DAVIS BILL). Republicans wanted to press home the Union victory by following the 13th Amendment abolishing slavery (1865) with full civil rights for the Negro, including the vote. Instead, while Congress was not in session, Johnson implemented Lincoln's policy of lenience by giving amnesty in return for a loyalty oath. He also condoned BLACK CODES, which practically reintroduced slavery in another guise. Reconvening (1866) with a landslide victory, however, the radical Republicans took control. Their first Reconstruction Act of 1867 divided ten Southern states into five military areas with a major general for each. Under army scrutiny, black and white voters were registered, and constitutions and governments instituted. In 1868, six Southern states were readmitted to the Union, followed in 1870 by the other four. By ratifying the 14th Amendment (1868) on Negro civil rights, Tenn. escaped the military phase. There were no mass arrests, no indictments for treason and the few Confederate officials jailed were (except for Jefferson DAVIS) soon released. Apart from slaves, the property of the Confederate leaders was untouched, although no help was given to rescue the ruined economy. On readmission, the Southern governments were Republican, supported by enfranchised Negroes, SCALAWAGS (white Republicans) and CARPETBAGGERS (Northern profiteers). Constructive legislation was passed in every state for public schools, welfare taxation and government reform, although the governments were accused of corruption and incompetence. The FREEDMEN'S BUREAU only lasted four years, but it did help to found Atlanta, Howard and Fisk universities for Negroes. Southern conservatives, hostile to the radical Republican policies, turned to the Democrats; societies like the Ku Klux Klan emerged to crusade against Negroes and radicals. Full citizenship for Negroes, though legally assured by the 14th and 15th (1870) amendments, was denied by intimidation, literacy tests and POLL TAX. The Republican Party, secure again in the North, abandoned the Negro. In 1877, when federal troops withdrew (see HAYES, RUTHERFORD), the last GOP governments collapsed and Reconstruction was over.

RECORDER, wind instrument related to the FLUTE but held vertically, with a mouthpiece which channels the airstream, and no keys. Relatively easy to play, soft and sweet in tone, it was most popular about 1600–1700 and is again popular today (see DOLMETSCH, ARNOLD). There are soprano, alto, and (with some keys) tenor and bass recorders.

RECYCLING, the recovery and reuse of any waste material. Of obvious economic importance where reusable materials are available more cheaply than fresh supplies of the same materials, the recycling principle is finding ever wider application in the conservation of the world's natural resources and in solving the problems of environmental POLLUTION. The recycling of the wastes of a manufacturing process in the same process—e.g., the resmelting and recasting of metallic turnings and offcuts—is commonplace in industry. So also is the immediate use of wastes or by-products of one industrial process in another—e.g., the manufacture of cattle food from the grain-mash residues found in breweries and distilleries. These are often termed forms of "internal recycling," as opposed to "external recycling": the recovery and reprocessing for reuse of "discarded" materials, such as waste paper, scrap metal and used glass bottles. The burning of garbage to produce electricity and the extraction of pure water from sewage are other common examples of recycling.

RED BRIGADES, an Italian terrorist organization set up in 1970 with the proclaimed aim of being the vanguard of a coming revolution. While its hard-core membership never numbered more than a few hundred, it was organized in small, highly disciplined cells. They attempted to disrupt Italian society by kidnapings, robberies, so-called "people's trials" and murders. Their most celebrated action was the kidnaping and murder of political leader Aldo Moro in 1978.

RED CLOUD (1822–1909), chief of the Oglala Sioux and leader of the Indian struggle against the opening of the Bozeman Trail. The trail was closed in 1868 following the FETTERMAN MASSACRE.

RED CORPUSCLES, or erythrocytes. See BLOOD.

RED CROSS, international agency for the relief of victims of war or disaster. Its two aims are to alleviate suffering and to maintain a rigid neutrality so that it may cross national borders to reach those otherwise unaidable. An international committee founded by J. H. DUNANT and four others from Geneva secured 12 nations' signatures to the first of the GENEVA CONVENTIONS (1864) for the care of the wounded. Aid was given to both sides in the Danish-Prussian War the same year. During WWI and WWII, the Red Cross helped prisoners of war, inspecting camps and sending food and clothing parcels; it investigated about 5 million missing persons and distributed $200 million in relief supplies to civilians. The International Red Cross won the Nobel Peace Prize in 1917 and 1944. It works through the International Committee (1880), made up of 25 Swiss citizens. Over 100 national Red Cross societies (Red Crescent in Muslim countries) carry out peacetime relief and public health work. The US Red Cross (1882) has some 3,100 chapters.

REDEMPTORISTS (Congregation of the Most Holy Redeemer), a religious order founded 1732 in Naples by St. ALPHONSUS LIGUORI to preach the Gospel to the poor and the abandoned. Now established in five continents, it entered the US in 1832.

REDFIELD, Robert (1897–1958), US cultural anthropologist best known for his comparative studies of primitive and highly civilized cultures, and for his active support of racial integration.

REDFORD, Robert (1936–   ), US film actor, among the most popular of the 1960s and 1970s, who later became a producer and director. He played in *Butch Cassidy and the Sundance Kid* (1969), *The Sting* (1973), and *All the President's Men* (1975) and directed *Ordinary People* (1980), which won an Academy Award.

REDI, Francesco (1627–1697 or 1698),

Italian biological scientist who demonstrated that maggots develop in decaying meat not through SPONTANEOUS GENERATION but from eggs laid there by flies.

RED JACKET (Sagoyewatha; c1758-1830), Seneca Indian chief named for the red coat he wore when an English ally in the Revolution. Later an ally of the US in the War of 1812, he strongly opposed white customs and Christianity for his people in N.Y.

REDON, Odilon (1840-1916), French painter and engraver associated with the Symbolists. His oils, usually of flowers and full of color and light, contrasted with bizarre lithographs such as *The Cyclops*, c1898.

RED POWER, rallying cry of the American Indian Movement (AIM), formed by militant young Indians in the late 1960s. Their objectives were better housing, jobs, and schooling for the many Indians who lived in cities, as well as greater local control of Indian affairs for those who remained on reservations. The movement's history has been punctuated by forceful actions, including the occupation of Alcatraz Island in San Francisco Bay in 1969-71, the takeover of the Washington, D.C., headquarters of the Bureau of Indian Affairs for four days in Nov. 1972, and the 70-day occupation of part of the Oglala Sioux Reservation at historic Wounded Knee, S.D., in 1973.

RED SEA, sea separating the Arabian Peninsula from NE Africa. It extends some 1,300mi from the Bab al-Mandab strait by the Gulf of Aden in the S to the gulfs of Suez (with the Suez Canal) and Aqaba in the N. It is up to 250mi wide and up to 7,800ft deep.

RED SHIFT, an increase in wavelength of the light from an object, usually caused by its rapid recession (see DOPPLER EFFECT). The spectra of distant GALAXIES show marked red shifts and this is usually, though far from always, interpreted as implying that they are rapidly receding from us. (See also COSMOLOGY.)

RED SNAPPER, a perch-like fish of the genus *Lutjanus*, with large mouth and jaws. Valuable commercial fishes of the Indo-Pacific, they are active predators, feeding on other fishes and crustaceans.

REED, Sir Carol (1906-1976), British film director, best known for his classic movies *Odd Man Out* (1947), *The Fallen Idol* (1948) and *The Third Man* (1949). Later films included *The Agony and the Ecstasy* (1965) and the musical *Oliver!* (1968).

REED, John (1887-1920), US journalist and radical, author of the famous eye-witness *Ten Days That Shook The World* (1919) which recounts the Russian October Revolution.

REED, Thomas Brackett (1839-1902), US Republican speaker of the House of Representatives 1889-91 and 1895-99, called "Tsar Reed" for his strong control. His "Reed Rules" (1890) are still the basis for procedure in Congress. He supported high tariffs and opposed the Spanish-US war and the annexation of Hawaii.

REED, Walter (1851-1902), US Army pathologist and bacteriologist who, in 1900, demonstrated the role of the mosquito *Aëdes aegypti* as a carrier of YELLOW FEVER, so enabling the disease to be controlled.

REED INSTRUMENTS. See WIND INSTRUMENTS.

REED ORGAN. See HARMONIUM.

REED, Stanley Forman (1884-1980), US jurist, associate justice (1938-57) of the US Supreme Court, where his moderate's vote was often decisive. As solicitor general (1935-38) under F. D. Roosevelt he argued important cases arising from NEW DEAL legislation.

REEL, lively rustic dance in 4/4 time originating in Scotland about the 16th century. After 1770, the foursome reel dominated, the dancers alternating traveling steps with more elaborate ones in one place.

REFERENDUM. See INITIATIVE, REFERENDUM AND RECALL.

REFLEX, MUSCLE contraction or secretion resulting from nerve stimulation by a pathway from a stimulus via the NERVOUS SYSTEM to the effector organ without the interference of volition. Basic primitive reflexes are stylized responses to stress of protective value to an infant. Stretch or tendon reflexes (e.g., knee-jerk) are muscle contractions in response to sudden stretching of their TENDONS. Conditioned reflexes are more complex responses described by PAVLOV that follow any stimulus which has been repeatedly linked with a stimulus of normal functional significance.

REFORMATION, religious and political upheaval in W Europe in the 16th century. Primarily an attempt to reform the doctrines of the Roman Catholic Church, it led to the establishment of PROTESTANTISM. ANTICLERICALISM spread after the movements led by John WYCLIFFE and the LOLLARDS in 14th-century England and by John HUS in Bohemia in the 15th century. At the same time the PAPACY had lost prestige through its 70-year exile, the BABYLONIAN CAPTIVITY at AVIGNON and the 50-year GREAT SCHISM. RENAISSANCE thought, particularly

HUMANISM, stimulated liberal views, spread by the invention of printing. There were many critics, like Martin LUTHER, of the low moral standards of Rome, and of the sale of INDULGENCES, distributed in Germany by TETZEL. Luther also challenged papal authority and the accepted Roman Catholic doctrines, such as TRANSUBSTANTIATION and CELIBACY, and argued strongly for JUSTIFICATION BY FAITH. Luther's ideas spread in Germany after the Diet of WORMS, 1521, and after the PEASANTS' WAR, when Luther won the support of many German princes and of Denmark and Sweden. The protest made by the Lutheran princes at the Diet of SPEYER (1529) provided the term "Protestant."

The Swiss divine Huldreich ZWINGLI won a large following in Switzerland and SW Germany. He carried out radical religious reforms in Zürich, abolishing the mass. After his death (1531), John CALVIN led the Swiss reform movement and set up a reformed church in Geneva. Calvin's *Institutes of the Christian Religion* (1536) had great influence, notably in Scotland where CALVINISM was led by John KNOX. In France Calvin's religious followers, the HUGUENOTS, were involved in the complex political struggles leading to the Wars of RELIGION, 1562–98. The Protestant movement in the Low Countries was linked with the national revolt which freed the Dutch from Roman Catholic Spain. The English Reformation was initiated by HENRY VIII, who denied papal authority, dissolved and seized the wealth of the monasteries, and made the CHURCH OF ENGLAND autonomous to increase the royal government's power. Henry VIII remained in doctrine a Catholic but the influence of Reformers such as RIDLEY and LATIMER established Protestantism under EDWARD VI, when Thomas CRANMER issued a new prayer book (1549). There was a Roman Catholic reaction under MARY I but in 1558 ELIZABETH I established moderate Protestantism as the basis of the English Church. The religious position of Europe as a whole, however, was not settled for another century.

REFORM BILLS, three acts of Parliament passed in Britain during the 19th century to extend the franchise. The first (1832) abolished rotten boroughs (boroughs which returned two members to Parliament long after their populations disappeared), and enfranchised industrial cities like Birmingham and Manchester, and the propertied middle class. The second bill (1867) gave the vote to urban dwellers and the third (1884) extended it to agricultural workers.

REFORMED CHURCHES, the Protestant churches arising from the REFORMATION that adhere to CALVINISM doctrinally and to PRESBYTERIANISM in church polity, and thus distinct from the LUTHERAN CHURCHES and the CHURCH OF ENGLAND. They grew up especially in Switzerland, Germany, France (see HUGUENOTS), Holland (see DUTCH REFORMED CHURCH), Scotland (see CHURCH OF SCOTLAND), Hungary and what is now Czechoslovakia. Each had its own simple formal LITURGY, and all acknowledged the Reformed Confessions. There are several Reformed Churches in the US, the largest being the CHRISTIAN REFORMED CHURCH.

REFRACTION, the change in direction of energy waves on passing from one medium to another in which they have a different velocity. In the case of LIGHT radiation, refraction is associated with a change in the optical density of the medium. On passing into a denser medium the wave path is bent toward the normal (the line perpendicular to the surface at the point of incidence), the whole wave path and the normal lying in the same plane. The ratio of the sine of the angle of incidence (that between the incident wave path and the normal) to that of the angle of refraction (that between the normal and the refracted wave path) is a constant for a given interface (Snell's law). When measured for light passing from a vacuum into a denser medium, this ratio is known as the refractive index of the medium. Refractive index varies with wavelength (see DISPERSION). On passing into a less dense medium, light radiation is bent away from the normal but if the angle of incidence is so great that its sine equals or exceeds the index for refraction from the denser to the less dense medium, there is no refraction and total (internal) REFLECTION (applied in the reflecting PRISM) results. Refraction finds its principal application in the design of LENSES.

REFRIGERATION, removal of HEAT from an enclosure in order to lower its TEMPERATURE. It is used for freezing water or food, for FOOD PRESERVATION, for AIR CONDITIONING and for low-temperature chemical processes and CRYOGENICS studies and applications. The ancient Egyptians and Indians used the evaporation of water from porous vessels; and the Chinese, Greeks and Romans used natural ice, a method which became a major industry in the 19th-century US. Modern refrigerators are insulated cabinets containing the cooling elements of a HEAT PUMP. The pump may use mechanical compression of refrigerants such as AMMONIA or FREON, or may accomplish compression by absorbing the refrigerant in a secondary fluid such as water and pumping the solution through a heat exchanger to a generator where it is heated to drive off the refrigerant at high pressure. Other cycles, similar in principle, using steam or air, are also used. Refrigeration based on the PELTIER EFFECT is being developed but is not yet economically competitive.

REFUGEE, person fleeing from his native country to avoid a threat or restriction. In the 15th century MOORS and JEWS were expelled from Spain, and religious refugees fled to the New World in the 17th century. In the 20th century refugees have created a world problem. POGROMS forced Jews to leave Russia; in WWI Greeks and Armenians fled from Turkey and about 1.5 million Russians settled in Europe after the RUSSIAN REVOLUTION. In the 1930s Spaniards and Chinese left their respective homelands. The WWII legacy of about eight million refugees led to the UN Relief and Rehabilitation Administration, replaced in 1946 by the International Refugee Organization, which in turn was succeeded by the Office of the UNITED NATIONS HIGH COMMISSIONER FOR REFUGEES. They resettled millions of homeless from, for example, the KOREAN WAR. Many thousand Arabs displaced when Israel was created in 1948 still live in Middle Eastern refugee camps and are a serious political problem. The 1971 war between India and Pakistan over BANGLADESH produced nine million refugees, most of whom subsequently settled in Bangladesh. During the 1970s thousands of refugees from SE Asia—the "boat people"—fled to neighboring countries, many later emigrating to the US. The refugee population of the US was further increased in the 1980s by boat loads of Cubans and Haitians seeking asylum or economic opportunity.

REGAN, Donald (1918–   ), US secretary of the treasury (1981–   ). As chairman of the Wall Street brokerage firm of Merrill Lynch he expanded its services in real estate and money-market funds. One of the architects of the Reagan economic program, he had the task of selling it to his skeptical former colleagues on Wall Street.

REGER, Max (1873–1916), German composer and pianist best known for his organ music and orchestral works. His music is characterized by elaborately structured polyphonic forms.

REGGAE, a popular Jamaican musical style that combines American rock and soul music with CALYPSO and other Latin-American rhythms. The 1973 film *The Harder They Come* introduced reggae to the US, where reggae greats like Bob Marley (1945–1981) were to win huge audiences.

REGIOMONTANUS (1436–1476), born Johann Müller, Prussian mathematician and astronomer whose *Five Books on all Types of Triangles* (1533) laid the foundations for modern TRIGONOMETRY.

REGIONAL THEATER, general term applying to major theater activity in US locations outside New York City. The regional theater movement began in earnest in the late 1940s, the Tyrone Guthrie Company in Minneapolis being perhaps the most distinguished founded at that time. Such companies often stress the classics and the nurturing of indigenous US talent, normally drawing financial support from local sponsors. Important regional theater companies include the Arena Stage in Washington, D.C., The Yale Repertory in New Haven, Conn., The Trinity Players in Providence, R.I., and The American Conservatory Theater in San Francisco.

REHABILITATION, means of enabling the handicapped to lead lives which are as normal as possible considering their disability. The term can cover social disability (treatment of prisoners) as well as physical or mental difficulty. Physical rehabilitation starts once immediate threat to life is absent and its success calls for the active participation of the patient. When the damage has been assessed, a program is designed to stop degeneration of the unaffected parts, to strengthen the injured area and to encourage the patient to accept his handicap realistically. Also efforts are made to remove external sources of anxiety. With the body so strengthened, the patient is prepared for reentry into daily life, through aids and equipment where appropriate, for example, wheelchairs, artificial limbs. Skills are taught, such as braille, and finally help given by social workers in job-finding. In mental disturbances, treatment tries to break down isolation and prevent self-withdrawal through interaction with others. In hospitals, rehabilitation aims to involve patients in social activities and then gradually to detach them from dependence on the center by trips outside until outpatients' visits only are necessary. The federal agency, the Vocational Rehabilitation Administration, makes grants to states to finance programs and encourage their expansion. It carries out research and advises the state agencies who must direct the actual program. Voluntary bodies, charitable foundations and industrial concerns supplement government provisions. (See also OCCUPATIONAL THERAPY.)

REHNQUIST, William Hubbs (1924–), US jurist. After serving as assistant attorney general, he was appointed (1971) by President NIXON to the US Supreme Court as an associate justice, where he became a voice of conservatism.

REICH, Wilhelm (1897–1957), radical Austrian-born US psychoanalyst who broke with FREUD over the function of sexual repression, which Reich saw as the root of individual and collective neurosis. He became known for his controversial theory that there exists a primal life-giving force, *orgone* energy, in living beings and in the atmosphere. His design and sale of orgone boxes for personal therapeutic use led to his imprisonment for violating the Food and Drug Act.

REICHENBACH, Hans (1891–1953), German philosopher of science who was a founder of the Berlin Society for Empirical Philosophy and editor of the *Journal of Unified Science*. He contributed to the theories of probability, relativity and quantum mechanics. He left Germany (1933) and taught at UCLA (1938–53).

REICHSTAG, imperial parliament (see DIET) of the Holy Roman Empire, and from 1871–1945 Germany's lower legislative house, the upper being called the Reichsrat. The ruling body of the WEIMAR REPUBLIC, it was a mere cipher under the NAZI regime. The Reichstag building, burnt down in Jan. 1933, probably as a Nazi propaganda trick, has been restored.

REICHSWEHR, German army rebuilt after WWI, chiefly by Hans von SEECKT, who planned to make it the core of the national army and a mobile shock force.

REID, Thomas (1710–1796), Scottish philosopher who, through his investigations of and rejection of HUME's skepticism, is regarded as a founder of the COMMON SENSE SCHOOL of philosophy.

REID, Whitelaw (1837–1912), US journalist, ambassador to Britain 1905–12. Editor of the New York *Tribune* 1872–1912, he was Republican vice-presidential candidate in 1892.

REIGN OF TERROR, 1793–94, period in the FRENCH REVOLUTION when fanatical Jacobin reformers including ROBESPIERRE, DANTON and Hébert, seized control from the GIRONDINS. They guillotined over 2,600 "counterrevolutionaries" (including Danton and Hébert, eventually) in Paris and sanctioned "Terrors" elsewhere, notably in Nantes. The Terror ended with the guillotining of Robespierre himself in July 1794.

REIMS, city in N France, about 100mi E of Paris on the Besle R. Dating from Roman times, it is famed for its Gothic cathedral built 1211–1430. All but two French kings 1179–1825 were crowned in Reims. Center of champagne and woolen production, it also makes chemicals, machinery and paper. Pop 183,600.

REINCARNATION. See TRANSMIGRATION OF SOULS.

REINDEER, *Rangifer tarandus*, a large ungainly-looking DEER widely distributed in Europe, Asia and North America, where they are referred to as CARIBOU.

REINER, Fritz (1888–1963), Hungarian-born US conductor, director of the orchestras of Cincinnati (1922–28), Pittsburgh (1938–48), Chicago (1953– 62), and the Metropolitan Opera (1948–53).

REINHARDT, Adolf (1913–1967), US painter whose symmetrical, geometric abstractions eventually developed into his famous monochrome paintings. His "black" series features only minor contrasts in violet and olive.

REINHARDT, Django (Jean Baptiste Reinhardt; 1910–1953), Belgian gypsy guitarist who, despite losing the use of two fingers, excelled in the Quintet of the Hot Club of France (1934–39). He was the first foreign musician to influence US JAZZ.

REINHARDT, Max (1873–1943), Austrian theatrical director famous for his vast and spectacular productions—especially of *Oedipus Rex* and *Faust*—and for his elaborate and atmospheric use of stage machinery and management of crowds.

RELATIVITY, a frequently referred to but less often understood theory of the nature of space, time and matter. EINSTEIN's "special theory" of relativity (1905) is based on the premise that different observers moving at a constant speed with respect to each other find the laws of physics to be identical, and, in particular, find the speed of LIGHT waves to be the same (the "principle of relativity"). Among its consequences are: that events occurring simultaneously according to one observer may happen at different times according to an observer moving relative to the first (although the order of two causally related events is never reversed); that a moving object is shortened in the direction of its motion; that time runs more slowly for a moving object; that the velocity of a projectile emitted from a moving body is less than the sum of the relative ejection velocity and the velocity of the body; that a body has a greater MASS when moving than when at rest, and that no massive body can travel as fast as, or faster than, the speed of light (2.998×10^8 m/s—at this speed, a body would have zero length and infinite mass, while time would stand still on it).

These effects are too small to be noticed at normal velocities; they have nevertheless found ample experimental verification, and are commonplace considerations in many physical calculations. The relationship between the position and time of a given event according to different observers is known (for H. A. LORENTZ) as the Lorentz transformation. In this, time mixes on a similar footing with the three spatial dimensions, and it is in this sense that time has been called the "fourth dimension." The greater mass of a moving body implies a relationship between kinetic ENERGY and mass; Einstein made the bold additional hypothesis that *all* energy was equivalent to mass, according to the famous equation $E = mc^2$. The conversion of mass to energy is now the basis of NUCLEAR REACTORS, and is indeed the source of the energy of the sun itself.

Einstein's "general theory" (1916) is of importance chiefly to cosmologists. It asserts the equivalence of the effects of ACCELERATION and gravitational fields (see GRAVITATION), and that gravitational fields cause space to become "curved," so that light no longer travels in straight lines, while the wavelength of light falls as the light falls through a gravitational field. The direct verification of these last two predictions, among others, has helped deeply to entrench the theory of relativity in the language of physics.

RELIGION, a system of belief to which a social group is committed, in which there is a supernatural object of awe, worship and service. It generally provides a system of ETHICS and a worldview that supply a stable context within which each person can relate himself to others and to the world, and can understand his own significance. Religions are found in all societies, and are generally dominant (modern secularism being an exception). Some form of religion seems to fulfill a basic human need. Some features are common to most religions: the recognition of a sacred realm from which supernatural forces operate; a mediating priesthood; the use of ritual to establish a right relationship with the holy (though ritual used to manipulate the supernatural becomes MAGIC); and a sense of group community. It is uncertain by what stages religion evolved; a linear progression from ANIMISM through POLYTHEISM to MONOTHEISM is not now firmly accepted. (See also DUALISM; MYTHOLOGY; PANTHEISM; DEISM; THEISM.) Some religions have no deity as such, but are natural philosophies:

see BUDDHISM; CONFUCIANISM; TAOISM. (See also ANCESTOR WORSHIP; MYTHOLOGY; LITURGY; SACRIFICE; TABOO; THEOLOGY.)

RELIGION, Wars of, French civil wars, 1562–98. They were caused partly by the REFORMATION conflict between the Roman Catholics and the Protestant HUGUENOTS, and partly by the rivalry between the French kings and such great nobles as the dukes of GUISE. The worst event was the SAINT BARTHOLOMEW'S DAY MASSACRE (1572). The Edict of NANTES (1598), established religious freedom and concluded the wars.

REMARQUE, Erich Maria (1898–1970). German novelist famous for his powerful anti-war *All Quiet on the Western Front* (1929), describing the horror of the trenches in WWI. In 1932 Remarque emigrated to Switzerland, later becoming a US citizen. Other works include *The Night in Lisbon* (1962).

REMBRANDT (Rembrandt Harmenszoon van Rijn; 1606–1669), greatest of Dutch painters. Born and trained in Leiden, he moved to Amsterdam in 1631 and achieved recognition with a group portrait, *The Anatomy Lesson* (1632). Adapting the styles of CARAVAGGIO, HALS and RUBENS, his painting became, during 1632–42, BAROQUE in style, as in *Saskia as Flora* (1634), *Blinding of Samson* (1636) and *Night Watch* (1642). The years 1643–56 were notable for his magnificent drawings and etchings, predominantly of New Testament themes, such as *The Three Crosses* (1653–61). From mid-1650s his painting was more solemn and spiritual in mood and richer in color as shown in portraits (*Jan Six*, 1654, *The Syndics of the Amsterdam Cloth Hall*, 1662), a series of moving self portraits, and religious paintings like *David and Saul* (c1658).

REMINGTON, Eliphalet (1793–1861), US FIREARMS developer and manufacturer. Under his eldest son, **Philo Remington** (1816–1889), the Remington companies for a time manufactured the Remington SEWING MACHINE (1870–82) and the Remington TYPEWRITER (1873–86).

REMINGTON, Frederic (1861–1909), US painter, sculptor and writer chiefly known for his portrayals of the Old West, where he traveled extensively. His paintings, usually of Indians, cowboys and horses, skillfully convey violent action and are notable for authenticity of detail.

REMUS. See ROMULUS AND REMUS.

REMUS, Uncle. See HARRIS, JOEL CHANDLER.

RENAISSANCE (French: rebirth or revival), the transitional period between the MIDDLE AGES and modern times, covering the years c1350–c1650. The term was first applied by the historian BURCKHARDT in 1860. The Renaissance was a period of deeply significant achievement and change. It saw the REFORMATION challenge the unity and supremacy of the Roman Catholic Church, along with the rise of HUMANISM, the growth of large nation-states with powerful kings, far-ranging voyages of exploration and a new emphasis on the importance of the individual. It was a period of extraordinary accomplishment in the arts, in scholarship and the sciences, typified in the universal genius of LEONARDO DA VINCI. The origins of the Renaissance are disputed, but its first flowering occurred in Italy. In the world of learning a new interest in secular Latin literature can be detected in the early 14th century, and by the middle of the century PETRARCH and BOCCACCIO were avidly searching for old texts and self-consciously cultivating a prose style modeled on CICERO. They inaugurated an age of research and discovery in which the humanists ransacked the monastic libraries of Europe for old manuscripts, and such scholars as FICINO, BESSARION, POLITIAN, VALLA and ERASMUS set new standards in learning and critical scholarship. Greek was also studied, particularly after the fall of Constantinople in 1453 drove many Greek scholars to the West. The invention of printing (c1440) and the discovery of the New World (1492) by COLUMBUS gave further impetus to the search for knowledge.

The Renaissance marked the end of FEUDALISM and the rise of national governments, in Spain under FERDINAND II of Aragon, in France under FRANCIS I, in England under HENRY VIII and ELIZABETH I, and in Holland. In Italy, however, independent city states— Ferrara, Florence, Mantua, Milan, Venice, papal Rome—engaged in fierce rivalry, providing MACHIAVELLI with his famous "ideal" of a Renaissance prince. Prosperous trading provided money for the arts, and princes like Cosimo de' MEDICI eagerly patronized artists, musicians and scholars. Renaissance PAINTING and SCULPTURE flourished in Florence and Rome with the works of BOTTICELLI, MICHELANGELO and RAPHAEL. Literary revivals occurred in England, France and Spain; SHAKESPEARE and SPENSER were prominent in Renaissance ENGLISH LITERATURE and some of the finest French writing came from RABELAIS and RONSARD. *Musica Reservata*, composed by JOSQUIN DES PRES and LASSUS, was among the styles of Renaissance music. In science the findings of the astronomers COPERNICUS and GALILEO were the basis of modern astronomy and marked a turning point in scientific and philosophical thought.

RENAULT, Mary (pseudonym of Mary Challans, 1905–   ), a British novelist. Her popular fictional accounts of the lives of ancient Greeks include *The Bull From The Sea* (1962), *The Mask of Apollo* (1966), and *The Persian Boy* (1973).

RENI, Guido (1575–1642), Italian BAROQUE painter. After studying at the CARRACCI academy he developed an elegant classical style, using light tones, for religious and mythological themes, such as *Aurora* (1613–14) and *Baptism of Christ* (1623).

RENNER, Karl (1870–1950), Austrian socialist statesman. He was the Austrian Republic's first chancellor (1919–20), president of parliament (1931–33) and, after heading the provisional government, president of Austria, 1945–50.

RENOIR, Jean (1894–1979), French film director, son of Pierre Auguste RENOIR. His motion pictures are characterized by a sensitive feeling for atmosphere and a strong pictorial sense. *La grande illusion* (1937) and *The Rules of the Game* (1939) are his masterpieces.

RENOIR, Pierre Auguste (1841–1919), French Impressionist painter. He started painting—with MONET, PISSARRO and SISLEY—scenes of Parisian life, such as *La Grenouillère* (1869) and *The Swing* (1876), using vibrant luminous colors. After IMPRESSIONISM he became mostly interested in figure painting, and his later works are usually large female nudes set in rich landscapes.

RENWICK, James (1818–1895), US architect who designed Grace Church (1843–46) and St. Patrick's Cathedral (dedicated 1879), New York, and other notable buildings, including the SMITHSONIAN INSTITUTION (1846) and Vassar College (1860).

REPARATIONS, term applied since WWI to monetary compensation demanded by victorious nations for material losses suffered in war. In 1919 Germany was committed to pay enormous reparations to the Allies (although the US subsequently waived all claim). Again, in 1945, reparations were exacted from Germany, and Japan was also assessed.

REPIN, Ilya Yefimovich (1844–1930), Russian painter. A leading proponent of the realistic style, his paintings often expressed criticism of the Russian social order during the late 19th century. Many of his paintings are on display in the museums of Moscow and Leningrad.

REPRODUCTION, the process by which an organism produces offspring, an ability that is a unique characteristic of ANIMALS and PLANTS. There are two kinds of reproduction: asexual and sexual. In **asexual reproduction,** parts of an organism split off to form new individuals, a process found in some animals but which is more common in plants: e.g., the FISSION of single-celled plants; the budding of YEASTS; the fragmentation of filamentous ALGAE; SPORE production in BACTERIA, algae and FUNGI, and the production of vegetative organs in flowering plants (bulbs, rhizomes and tubers). In **sexual reproduction,** special (haploid) CELLS containing half the normal number of CHROMOSOMES, called gametes, are produced: in animals, sperm by males in the TESTES and ova by females in the OVARY; in plants, pollen by males in the stamens and ovules by females in the ovary. The joining of gametes (FERTILIZATION) produces a (diploid) cell with the normal number of chromosomes, the zygote, which grows to produce an individual with GENES inherited from both parents (see also HEREDITY). Fertilization may take place inside the female (internal fertilization) or outside (external fertilization). Internal fertilization demands that sperm be introduced into the female— insemination by copulation— and is advantageous because the young spend the most vulnerable early stages of their life-histories protected inside the mother.

At the molecular level, the most important aspect of reproduction is the ability of the chromosome to duplicate itself (see NUCLEIC ACIDS). The production of haploid cells is made possible by a process called MEIOSIS and is necessary to prevent doubling of the chromosome number with each generation in sexually reproducing individuals. The advantage of sexual reproduction is that the bringing together of genes derived from two individuals produces variation in each generation enabling populations to change and thus adapt themselves to changing environmental conditions (see also EVOLUTION; NATURAL SELECTION).

REPTILES, once one of the most numerous and diverse groups of animals, today reduced to four groups: the CROCODILES; the LIZARDS and SNAKES; the TORTOISES and TURTLES; and the TUATARA. Modern reptiles are characterized by a scaly skin, simple teeth in the jaw, and an undivided heart. They are coldblooded, and sexual reproduction results in the laying of large yolky eggs. However, when fossil groups are considered, the class is not so clearly defined, for the later reptiles merge with their avian and mammalian descendants. Many were fur-covered and warm-blooded and had developed other features of present-day birds and mammals. Some may even have been viviparous.

REPTON, Humphry (1752–1818), English landscape designer. Influenced by the Picturesque movement, his gardens aimed at a gradual transition between the house and its surroundings. (See LANDSCAPE ARCHITECTURE.)

REPUBLIC, (from Latin *res publica*: the state), form of government in which the head of state is not a monarch, and today is usually a president. Popularly, the idea of a republic includes the notion of elected representation and democratic control by the people, but many modern republics do not fulfill this condition. *The Republic* is also the name of the famous dialogue in which PLATO outlined his ideal state.

REPUBLICAN PARTY, one of the two major political parties of the US. It was founded in 1854 by dissidents of the WHIG, DEMOCRATIC and FREE SOIL parties to unify the growing anti-slavery forces. Its first national nominating convention was held in 1856; J. C. FRÉMONT was adopted as presidential candidate. Campaigning for the abolition of slavery and of polygamy in the territories, he captured 11 states. LINCOLN became the first Republican president, and in spite of the unpopularity of the subsequent RECONSTRUCTION policies and the secession of the LIBERAL REPUBLICAN PARTY in 1872, the Republicans remained dominant in US politics, winning 14 out of 18 presidential elections between 1860 and 1932. In an era of scandal, the Republicans consolidated a "pro-business" and "conservative" reputation with the nomination and election of William MCKINLEY in 1896. His successor Theodore ROOSEVELT adopted a progressive stance; he defected to the Bull Moose party (see PROGRESSIVE PARTY) in 1912. In 1932 the Democrats swept to power, not to be dislodged until the election of the Republican president EISENHOWER in 1952. His successors KENNEDY and JOHNSON were Democrats. Barry GOLDWATER failed as presidential candidate in 1960, but Richard NIXON's landslide victory in 1972 marked a zenith of party strength. WATERGATE shattered this, contributing to the defeat of Gerald FORD in the 1976 elections. The Republicans rallied again in 1980 to elect Ronald REAGAN president and to capture control of the Senate.

RESERVE OFFICER TRAINING CORPS (ROTC), US Army recruiting project that holds courses in military leadership in schools and colleges. It grew out of the Land Grant Act of 1862, and began operating full scale under the National Defense Act of 1916. It comprises two to four years of course work and drill plus several weeks of field training. The US Navy and Air Force have similar programs.

RESHEVSKY, Samuel (1911–), Polish-born US chess player. Formerly a child prodigy, he was US champion five times between 1936 and 1946, and one of the great modern masters of the game.

RESIN, a high-molecular-weight substance characterized by its gummy or tacky consistency at certain temperatures. Naturally occurring resins include congo copal and BITUMEN (found as fossils), SHELLAC (from insects) and rosin (from pine trees). Synthetic resins include the wide variety of plastic materials available today and any distinction between PLASTICS and resins is at best arbitrary. The first partially synthetic resins were produced in 1862 using NITROCELLULOSE, vegetable OILS and CAMPHOR, and included Xylonite and later, in 1869, CELLULOID. The first totally synthetic resin was BAKELITE, which was produced by L. H. BAEKELAND in 1910 from PHENOL and FORMALDEHYDE. The work in the 1920s of H. STAUDINGER on the polymeric nature of natural RUBBER and STYRENE resin, which laid the theoretical basis for POLYMER science, was a major factor in stimulating the extremely rapid development of a wide range of synthetic plastics and resins.

RESNAIS, Alain (1922–), French film director associated with the NEW WAVE. His enigmatic, somewhat surreal films, such as *Hiroshima, Mon Amour* (1959) and *Last Year at Marienbad* (1961), were followed by lighter works, including *My American Uncle* (1980).

RESPIGHI, Ottorino (1879–1936), Italian composer, director (1924–26) of the Accademia di Santa Cecilia in Rome. He is best-known for such tone poems as *The Fountains of Rome* (1917) and *The Pines of Rome* (1924).

RESPIRATION, term applied to several activities and processes occurring in all ANIMALS and PLANTS: e.g., the breathing movements associated with the LUNGS, the uptake of OXYGEN and the release of CARBON dioxide, and the biochemical pathways by which the ENERGY locked in food materials is transferred to energy-rich organic molecules for utilization in the multitude of energy-requiring processes which occur in an organism. Breathing movements, if any, and the exchange of oxygen and carbon dioxide, may be called "external respiration," while the energy-releasing processes which utilize the oxygen and produce carbon dioxide are termed "internal respiration" or "tissue respiration." In man, external respiration is the process whereby air is breathed from the environment into the lungs to provide oxygen for internal respiration. Air, which contains about 20% oxygen, is drawn into the lungs via the NOSE or MOUTH, the PHARYNX, TRACHEA and BRONCHI. This is achieved by muscular contraction of the intercostal muscles in the CHEST wall and of the DIAPHRAGM; their coordinated movement, controlled by a respiratory center in the BRAIN stem, causes expansion of the chest, and thus of the lung tissue, so that air is drawn in (inspiration). Expiration is usually a passive process of relaxation of the chest wall and diaphragm, allowing the release of the air, which is by now depleted of oxygen and enriched with carbon dioxide. Exchange of gases with the BLOOD circulating in the pulmonary capillaries occurs across the lung alveoli and follows simple diffusion gradients. Disorders of respiration include lung disease (e.g., EMPHYSEMA, PNEUMONIA and PNEUMOCONIOSIS); muscle and nerve disease (e.g., brain-stem STROKE, POLIOMYELITIS, MYASTHENIA GRAVIS and MUSCULAR DYSTROPHY); skeletal deformity; ASPHYXIA, and disorders secondary to metabolic and HEART disease. In man, tissue respiration involves the combination of oxygen with GLUCOSE or other nutrients to form high-energy compounds. This reaction also produces carbon dioxide and water.

RESTON, James Barrett (1909–), Scottish-born US journalist who won Pulitzer Prizes in 1944 and 1957. He has been associated with the *New York Times* since 1939, being its vice-president 1969–74.

RESTORATION, name given to the return of CHARLES II as king of England in 1660, after the fall of the PROTECTORATE. Coinciding with a national mood of reaction against the PURITANS, the Restoration was widely popular. The Restoration period (1660 to the fall of JAMES II in 1688) was one of irreverent wit, licentiousness and scientific and literary achievement (see RESTORATION COMEDY). Politically, it was a period of uneasy relations between king and parliament, culminating in the GLORIOUS REVOLUTION.

RESTORATION COMEDY, name given to the witty, bawdy and often satirical comedies written after the reopening of the theaters at the RESTORATION (1660). Masters of the genre include CONGREVE, VANBRUGH and WYCHERLEY.

RESURRECTION, the raising of a dead person to life. The resurrection of JESUS CHRIST on the third day after his death and burial is a basic Christian doctrine attested by earliest New Testament tradition. In recognizable but glorified bodily form he appeared to several groups of disciples; though skeptical, they became convinced that he had overcome death. Christians' eternal life is viewed as participation in Christ's resurrection, culminating in the general bodily resurrection of the dead at the SECOND COMING (see also ESCHATOLOGY; IMMORTALITY).

RETINA, part of the EYE responsible for conversion of LIGHT into nerve impulses; it contains nerve cells including the rod and cone receptors for light/dark and color VISION respectively.

REUNION, volcanic island (970sq mi) in the W Indian Ocean, a French possession since 1642 and an overseas department of France since 1946. The islanders, mostly of mixed descent, are nearly all Roman Catholic and speak a Creole patois. Its products include sugar, rum and vanilla. The capital is St. Denis. Pop 484,924.

REUTER, Ernst (1889–1953), German political leader. He became a communist in 1916 as a prisoner of war in Russia, but in 1922 rejoined the German Social Democratic Party. In exile 1935–46, he returned to become mayor of West Berlin from 1948.

REUTERS, an international news agency, based in Britain, which distributes information to local agencies, newspapers, television and radio around the world. Founded by P. J. von Reuter (1816–1899) in Germany in 1849, it moved to London 1851, and is today a trust owned mainly by the British press.

REUTHER, Walter Philip (1907–1970), US labor leader, president of the UNITED AUTOMOBILE WORKERS from 1946 until his death in a plane crash. He was president of the Congress of Industrial Organizations 1952–56, and one of the architects of its merger with the AMERICAN FEDERATION OF LABOR, becoming vice president of the combined organization.

REVELATION, Book of, or **Apocalypse,** the last book of the NEW TESTAMENT, traditionally ascribed to St. JOHN the Apostle but probably written by another John, and dated probably c96. After seven letters to the Asia Minor churches, it consists of a series of apocalyptic visions in Old Testament imagery, giving a Christian philosophy of world history.

REVELS, Hiram Rhoades (1822–1901), pastor and educator, and first black US senator. Elected by the Republicans in Miss. for 1870–71, he was subsequently involved in state politics and became president of Alcorn College, Lorman, Miss.

REVERE, Paul (1735–1818), American revolutionary hero, immortalized by LONGFELLOW for his ride from Boston to Lexington (April 18, 1775) to warn the Massachussetts minutemen that "the British are coming." A silversmith and engraver, he joined in the BOSTON TEA PARTY in 1773. During the REVOLUTIONARY WAR, he served the new government, designing and producing the first Continental money, casting official seals and supervising gunpowder and cannon manufacture. After the war he became a prosperous merchant, known for his copper and silver work and his bronze bells.

REVOLUTIONARY WAR, American, in which Britain's 13 colonies gained their independence. It was a minor war with immense consequences—the founding of the US, and the forging of a new, dynamic democratic ideology in an age of absolutism. Despite elements of civil war and of revolution, the conflict was above all a political, constitutional struggle, and as such began many years before the actual fighting. While the expanding colonies were growing wealthy and independent, Britain adhered to the theory that they were supposed to exist solely for its own profit, and were to be tightly ruled by King and Parliament (see MERCANTILISM; NAVIGATION ACTS). Up to 1763, however, control was lax; but after France had been defeated in the New World (see FRENCH AND INDIAN WARS) Britain decided to restore control and tax the colonies to help pay for it. The Navigation Acts were strictly enforced (see SUGAR ACT), settlement beyond the Appalachian Mountains was forbidden, a standing army was to be sent to America and quartered at colonial expense, and in 1765 a stamp tax (see STAMP ACT) was imposed. The outraged colonists, near rebellion, drew upon liberal ideas from England and the continent (see ENLIGHTENMENT) to assert the principle of no taxation without representation in the English Parliament. After duties levied by the TOWNSHEND ACTS (1767) resistance centered in Boston, leading to the BOSTON MASSACRE (1770) and the BOSTON TEA PARTY (1773). But after the INTOLERABLE ACTS (1774), aimed at Boston, patriot local assemblies took control in all colonies, and non-importation associations and COMMITTEES OF CORRESPONDENCE flourished, culminating in the First CONTINENTAL CONGRESS (1774). In April-June 1775 fighting flared around disaffected Boston (see battles of LEXINGTON; CONCORD; BUNKER HILL), and in July George WASHINGTON took command of the Continental Army. In March 1776 the British were forced to evacuate Boston, but an American attempt to conquer Canada (1775-76) failed. Meantime the Second CONTINENTAL CONGRESS, emboldened by Thomas PAINE's pamphlet *Common Sense*, declared for independence in July 1776. (See Special Article on DECLARATION OF INDEPENDENCE.)

Washington, with never more than 10-20,000 regulars, plus state militia (see MINUTEMEN), fought a defensive war; the British, with regulars, Tories and mercenaries (see HESSIANS), suffered from confused strategy and extended supply lines across the ocean, and were hindered by the small US Navy and some 2,000 privateers (see JONES, JOHN PAUL). After a brief strike at the South, the British took New York City in September 1776, forcing Washington to retreat into New Jersey. The small victories of TRENTON and PRINCETON heartened the patriots, but Philadelphia fell in September 1777. Meantime General BURGOYNE, sweeping down into New York from Canada, was forced to surrender his troops at SARATOGA in October, an American triumph that brought France in as an ally of the US. But Washington, wintering at VALLEY FORGE, was barely able to keep his troops together.

Turning to the South, the British took Savannah (1778) and Charleston (1780), defeating GATES at Camden, S.C., in August, 1870. But after the defeat of KINGS MOUNTAIN in October, the British gradually withdrew N into Va. In 1781 CORNWALLIS, bottled up in Yorktown, Va. by a French fleet and a Franco-American army under Washington, surrendered on October 19, virtually ending the war, though the Treaty of PARIS was not signed until Sept. 4, 1783. The ideological struggle, which had found its best expression in the Declaration of Independence, came to a conclusion with the framing of the Constitution in 1787.

REVOLUTIONS OF 1848, series of unsuccessful revolutionary uprisings in France, Italy, the Austrian Empire and Germany in 1848. They were relatively spontaneous and self-contained, but had a number of common causes: the successful example of the FRENCH REVOLUTION of 1789, economic unrest due to bad harvests and unemployment, and a growing frustration, fired by nationalist fervor, about the repressive policies of conservative statesmen like METTERNICH and GUIZOT. In 1848, a major uprising in Paris overthrew King LOUIS PHILIPPE and Guizot, but it was suppressed and the Second Republic proclaimed. In Italy, during the RISORGIMENTO, short-lived republics were proclaimed, and there was agitation to secure independence from Austria, which was itself shaken by revolutions in Vienna, Prague and Hungary. The demand for a representative government led to an all-German Diet in Frankfurt, which failed in its efforts to unite Germany. In England there was working-class agitation (see CHARTISM), and other European countries were also affected.

REVOLVER, a small hand firearm, or PISTOL, incorporating an automatic loading mechanism in the form of a revolving cylinder. The cylinder usually contains five or six chambers into which cartridges are inserted. Activation of the trigger mechanism, in addition to firing a bullet, automatically aligns a fresh chamber with the breech of the barrel. The first practical revolver design was patented in 1836 by Samuel COLT.

REXROTH, Kenneth (1905–   ), US poet, translator, painter and journalist. He belonged to the BEAT GENERATION of the 1950s, and his works include *The Dragon and the Unicorn* (1952) and *In Defense of the Earth* (1956).

REYNARD THE FOX, leading character in a popular medieval series of FABLES. Appearing first in the area between Flanders and Germany in the 10th century, the tales, with their cunning but sympathetic hero and biting satire, became popular in France, Germany and the Low Countries.

REYNAUD, Paul (1878–1966), conservative French statesman. After holding a number of cabinet posts (from 1930), he became premier in 1940. An opponent of the Nazis, he resigned and spent WWII in prison. Afterwards he returned to politics, held several posts and helped draft the constitution of the Fifth Republic (1958).

REYNOLDS, Burt (1936–   ), US actor and director. After serving an apprenticeship in television, he became a popular leading man in films of the 1970s, appearing in *Deliverance* (1972) and *Smokey and the Bandit* (1977).

REYNOLDS, Quentin (1902–1965), US

journalist best known for his human-interest reporting during WWII. In 1954 he won a celebrated libel case against conservative columnist Westbrook PEGLER.

REYNOLDS, Sir Joshua (1723–1792), perhaps the most famous English portrait painter. Ambitious and popular, he became first president of the ROYAL ACADEMY OF ARTS in 1768. He held that great art is based on the styles of earlier masters, and espoused the "Grand Style." He painted nearly all his notable contemporaries, including his friend Samuel JOHNSON (1772), and published influential *Discourses* (1769–90).

REZA SHAH PAHLEVI (1877–1944), Shah of Iran, 1925–41. An army officer, he led a coup in 1921, becoming prime minister and later (1925) founder of the Pahlevi dynasty. He made important military, administrative and economic reforms, but the Allies forced him to resign in WWII for attempting to keep Iran neutral.

RHAETO-ROMANIC, a group of minor ROMANCE LANGUAGES. They include *Romansh* (spoken in SE Switzerland), *Ladin* (the Italian Tyrol) and *Friulian* (NE Italy), all probably derived from Latin. (See also INDO-EUROPEAN LANGUAGES.)

RHAPSODY, a free musical composition, not written in a set form or style, and often a free or romantic treatment of one or more themes. Well-known examples are LISZT'S *Hungarian Rhapsodies* and GERSHWIN'S *Rhapsody in Blue*.

RHEE, Syngman (1875–1965), president of South Korea. A leader in the movement to win Korean independence from Japan, he was in exile 1910–45, serving as president of the Korean Provisional Government for 20 years. He returned to Korea after WWII, and became the first president of the Republic of Korea (South Korea) in 1948. He led the nation through the Korean War but was forced from office in 1960 because of corruption and mismanagement by some of his appointees.

RHEIMS. See REIMS.

RHESUS MONKEY, *Macaca mulatta*, an omnivorous MACAQUE found in many parts of Asia.

RHETORIC, the art of speaking and writing with the purpose of persuading or influencing others. It was taught by the Greek SOPHISTS in the 5th century BC. The first systematic treatise on it is ARISTOTLE'S *Rhetoric*. CICERO and QUINTILIAN wrote on it, and it was a major course at medieval universities as one of the SEVEN LIBERAL ARTS.

RHEUMATIC FEVER, feverish illness, following infection with STREPTOCOCCUS and caused by abnormal IMMUNITY to the bacteria, leading to systemic disease. SKIN RASH, subcutaneous nodules and a migrating ARTHRITIS are commonly seen. Involvement of the HEART may lead to palpitations, chest pain, cardiac failure, MYOCARDITIS and INFLAMMATION of the PERICARDIUM; murmurs may be heard and the ELECTROCARDIOGRAPH may show conduction abnormality. Sydenham's CHOREA may also be seen, with awkwardness, clumsiness and involuntary movements. Late effects include chronic valve disease of the heart leading to stenosis or incompetence, particularly of the mitral or aortic valves. Such valve disease may occur in the young and middle aged and may require surgical correction. Treatment of acute rheumatic fever includes bed rest, ASPIRIN and STEROIDS. PENICILLIN treatment of streptococcal disease may prevent recurrence. Patients with valve damage require ANTIBIOTICS during operations, especially dental and urinary tract SURGERY, to prevent bacterial endocarditis.

RHEUMATISM, imprecise term describing various disorders of the JOINTS, including RHEUMATIC FEVER and rheumatoid ARTHRITIS.

Rh FACTOR, or RHESUS FACTOR. See BLOOD.

RHINE, Joseph Banks (1895–1980), US parapsychologist whose pioneering laboratory studies of ESP demonstrated the possibility of telepathy (see PARAPSYCHOLOGY).

RHINE RIVER, (German: *Rhein*) longest river in Western Europe, rising in Switzerland and flowing 820mi through Germany and the Netherlands into the North Sea near Rotterdam. It is of great historical and commercial significance, being navigable by seagoing ships up to Cologne, and by large barges as far as Basel. Canals link it to the Rhône, Marne, Ems, Weser, Elbe, Oder and Danube rivers. Some of its finest scenery is along the gorge between Bingen and Bonn, with terraced vineyards, ruined castles and famous landmarks like the LORELEI rock.

RHINITIS, INFLAMMATION of the mucous membranes of the NOSE causing runny nasal discharge, and seen in the COMMON COLD, INFLUENZA and HAY FEVER. Irritation in the nose and sneezing are common.

RHINOCEROSES, a family, Rhinocerotidae, of five species of heavy land animals characterized by a long nasal "horn" or "horns." They are bulky animals with thick, hairless skin, often falling in heavy loose folds. They live in transitional habitat between open grassland and high forest, grazing or browsing on the bushes or shrubs. All five species—the Square-lipped, or White, rhino; the Black rhino; the Great Indian; Sumatran, and Javan rhinos—are on the verge of extinction. The horn is not true horn but is formed of a mass of compacted hairs.

Name of state: Rhode Island (Officially: Rhode Island and Providence Plantations)
Capital: Providence
Statehood: May 29, 1790 (13th state)
Familiar Name: Little Rhody
Area: 1,214sq mi
Population: 947,154
Elevation: Highest—812ft, Jerimoth Hill
Lowest—sea level, Atlantic Ocean
Motto: Hope
State Flower: Violet
State Bird: Rhode Island Red
State Tree: Red maple
State Song: "Rhode Island"

RHODE ISLAND, a New England state in the NE US, the smallest state of the Union. It is bordered on the N and E by Mass., W by Conn., and S by the Atlantic Ocean.
Land. Most of Rhode Island lies W of Narrangansett Bay, which extends 28mi inland. There are two major regions: the Seaboard or Coastal Lowlands, including the islands in Narrangansett Bay and the land E of the bay; and the New England Upland to the W. About two-thirds of the state is forested. The climate ranges from about 28°F in winter to about 70°F in summer.
People. The population is heavily urban (87%), and the largest cities are Providence, Warwick, Pawtucket and Cranston. About 97% of the population is white, and over half is Roman Catholic.
Economy. Manufacturing is still of prime importance, with tourism second and agriculture third. The chief farm products are milk, eggs, potatoes and hay. Apples are the principal fruit crop, and fish and shellfish also contribute to the economy. Principal manufactures include jewelry, electrical machinery, primary and fabricated metals, and plastic and rubber goods.
History. Da VERRAZANO probably reached Rhode Island in 1524, and in 1636 Roger WILLIAMS established the first settlement at Providence on land purchased from the NARRAGANSETT INDIANS. Charles II of England granted a charter in 1663. Religious and political freedom from the start formed part of the colony's traditions. In the 18th century Rhode Islanders resented British interference in their flourishing trade and Rhode Island was the first colony to declare independence from Britain in 1776 but also the last of the original 13 colonies to ratify the US Constitution. A new liberal state constitution followed after DORR'S rebellion in 1842. The fast-expanding textile industry attracted thousands of immigrants while the state became known as the summer home of wealthy industrialists.

Since WWII, varied industries have begun to replace the declining textile industry, but unemployment, at 7.3% in 1980, has been a continuing problem. Lack of jobs has led many people to leave the state. Its population declined 0.3% during the 1970s, making it the only state besides New York to have fewer people at the end of the decade than at its start.

RHODES, Greek Island (540sq mi) and its capital city off the SW coast of Turkey. Its exports include wine, fruit and olive oil. The city of Rhodes was a prosperous city-state in the 3rd century BC. At its harbor stood the COLOSSUS OF RHODES.

RHODES, Cecil John (1853–1902), British statesman and business magnate, who first opened up RHODESIA to European settlement. He founded the De Beers Mining Company in 1880 at Kimberly in South Africa, and in 1889 formed a company to develop the area that is now Rhodesia. Premier of the Cape Colony from 1890, he was forced to resign through his complicity in the JAMESON raid (1896). Much of his £6 million fortune went to found the RHODES SCHOLARSHIPS.

RHODESIA. See ZIMBABWE.

RHODES SCHOLARSHIPS, instituted at OXFORD UNIVERSITY by the bequest of Cecil RHODES for students from the British Commonwealth, the US and Germany. Elections are based on general grounds as well as on academic ability.

RHÔNE RIVER, an important European river, 507mi long, rising in Switzerland and flowing through Lake Geneva and then SW and S through France into the Mediterranean Sea. With its tributaries, particularly the Isère and the Saône, it has a large flow of water, which has been harnessed in major hydroelectric schemes. Navigable in part, it is linked by canal to the CAMARGUE.

RHYME, in poetry, the placing of words with identical or similar sounds in a regular pattern, usually at the ends of lines. Rhymes can be strong (*harp, sharp*), weak (*cotton, rotten*—accent -not on last syllable) or imperfect in other ways. Rhyme has characterized much European poetry since the Middle Ages, and certain forms, for example the BALLAD or SONNET, have set rhyme-patterns.

RHYS, Jean (1894–1979), English novelist, born in Dominica, West Indies. The publication of *Wide Sargasso Sea* (1966)—about the early years of Mrs. Rochester, a character in Charlotte Brontë's *Jane Eyre*—led to the "rediscovery" of Rhys's earlier works, which also focused on alienated women in a male-dominated society. These include *Quartet* (1929), *After Leaving Mr. Mackenzie* (1930), *Voyage in the Dark* (1934) and *Good Morning, Midnight* (1939).

RHYTHM, a regular pattern of stressed beats, especially characteristic of MUSIC and POETRY. In Western music the commonest rhythms are 2/4, 3/4, 4/4 and 6/8 (two, three, four and six beats in a bar). A typical 3/4 rhythm is the waltz. Broken rhythms are called SYNCOPATION. In poetry the term describes the pattern of stressed and unstressed words in a line of verse or a poem.

RHYTHMS, Biological. See BIOLOGICAL CLOCKS.

RIBBENTROP, Joachim von (1893–1946), German Nazi leader, ambassador to the UK 1936–38 and foreign minister 1938–45. He helped to negotiate the Rome–Berlin Axis in 1936 and the Russo–German non-aggression pact of 1939 and to plan the invasion of Poland, but wielded little influence in WWII. He was hanged for war crimes.

RIBERA, Jusepe de (1591–1652), Spanish painter who lived after 1616 in Naples. His work, influenced by CARAVAGGIO, is noted for its combination of naturalism and mysticism, as in the *Martyrdom of St. Sebastian* (1630) and *The Penitent Magdalen* (c1640).

RIBOFLAVIN, or vitamin B₂. See VITAMINS.

RIBONUCLEIC ACID (RNA). See NUCLEIC ACIDS.

RIBOSOMES, tiny granules, of diameter about 10nm, found in CELL cytoplasm. They are composed of PROTEIN and a special form of ribonucleic acid (see NUCLEIC ACIDS) known as ribosomal RNA. The ribosome is the site of PROTEIN SYNTHESIS.

RICARDO, David (1772–1823), English economist, founder with Adam SMITH of the "classical school." He made a fortune as a stockbroker and then devoted his time to economics and politics, becoming a member of Parliament 1819–23. His main work is *Principles of Political Economy and Taxation* (1817), which pioneered the use of theoretical models in analyzing the distribution of wealth. (See also ECONOMICS; RENT; VALUE.)

RICCI, Matteo (1552–1610), Italian Jesuit missionary to China. After teaching in Goa, he entered China in 1583, learned Chinese and eventually won acceptance, reaching Peking in 1601. He introduced Western mathematics, astronomy and geography to the Chinese, and in turn sent the first modern detailed reports of China back to the West.

RICE, *Oryza sativa,* a grain-yielding annual plant of the GRASS family, Graminae. It is grown chiefly in S and E Asia where it is the staple food of hundreds of millions of people. Rice needs hot moist conditions to grow, which historically made it highly dependent on MONSOON rainfall. But improved irrigation, fertilizers, pesticides and the development of the improved varieties have enormously increased the yield. Machinery for planting and harvesting rice is used in the US and parts of South America, but in the Orient rice-farming methods are still primitive, using hand labor. Rice has a reasonable nutrient value, but when "polished" much of its VITAMIN B₁ content is lost, resulting in a high incidence of the deficiency disease, BERIBERI, wherever polished rice is staple.

RICE, Elmer (1892–1967), US dramatist. His plays on social themes include *The Adding Machine* (1923), an expressionist fantasy on mechanization, *Street Scene* (1929), a Pulitzer prize-winning portrait of life in a New York tenement, and the romantic comedy, *Dream Girl* (1945).

RICE, Grantland (1880–1954), US sports journalist noted for his stories and syndicated column, "The Sportlight." He wrote *Only the Brave* (1941).

RICHARD, name of three kings of England. **Richard I** (1157–1199), called *Coeur de Lion* (the Lion Heart), was the third son of Henry II, whom he succeeded in 1189. He spent all but six months of his reign out of England, mainly on the Third CRUSADE. After taking Cyprus and Acre in 1191 and recapturing Jaffa in 1192, he was captured returning to England and handed over to the Emperor HENRY VI who held him for ransom till 1194. After a brief spell in England he spent the rest of his life fighting against PHILIP II in France. **Richard II**

(1367–1400), son of Edward the Black Prince, succeeded his grandfather EDWARD III in 1377. In his minority the country was governed by a group of nobles dominated by his uncle JOHN OF GAUNT. Richard quarreled with them but only began to assert himself after 1397; he executed his uncle the Duke of Gloucester and banished Henry Bolingbroke, Gaunt's son, and confiscated his estates. Bolingbroke returned in 1399 to depose Richard and imprison him in Pontefract castle, where he died. Bolingbroke succeeded as Henry IV. **Richard III** (1452–1485), third son of Richard Plantagenet, Duke of York, and the younger brother of EDWARD IV, usurped the throne in 1483. The traditional picture of him as a hunchbacked and cruel ruler who murdered his nephews in the Tower has little historical backing. He instituted many reforms and encouraged trade, but had little hope of defeating his many enemies gathering in France under Henry Tudor (later HENRY VII). They defeated and killed Richard at BOSWORTH.

RICHARD, Maurice "The Rocket" (1921–   ), Canadian ice hockey player. A wingman, he was the first National Hockey League player to score 50 goals in one season (1944–45). He scored 626 goals during his career with the Montreal Canadiens (1942–61).

RICHARDS, Ivor Armstrong (1893–1979), influential English literary critic and semanticist. He developed with C. K. OGDEN the concept of **Basic English**, a primary vocabulary of 850 words. His books include *The Meaning of Meaning* (with Ogden, 1923) and *Principles of Literary Criticism* (1924).

RICHARDSON, Henry Hobson (1838–1886), influential US architect who pioneered an American Romanesque style. Among his important buildings are the Trinity Church, Boston, and the Marshall Field Wholesale Store in Chicago.

RICHARDSON, Samuel (1689–1761), important English novelist, best known for his novels in epistolary form, especially *Pamela* (1740–41), the story of a servant girl's moral triumph over her lecherous master. *Clarissa* (1747–48), his tragic masterpiece, is also on the theme of seduction. *Sir Charles Grandison* (1753–54) portrays a virtuous hero, in contrast to the amoral hero of FIELDING'S *Tom Jones*.

RICHARDSON, Sir Ralph (1902–   ), English actor. A distinguished interpreter of Shakespeare and the classics, he was knighted in 1947. A star on stage, he generally played supporting roles in motion pictures. His films include *Richard III* (1956) and *Long Day's Journey Into Night* (1962).

RICHARDSON, Tony (1928–   ), British theatrical and film director who won acclaim for John Osborne's *Look Back in Anger* (1956; film 1959), the best-known work of the ANGRY YOUNG MEN. Other productions include *The Entertainer* (1957; film 1960), *A Taste of Honey* (1960; film 1961) and *Loneliness of the Long Distance Runner* (film 1962). He also directed the Academy Award-winning film *Tom Jones* (1963).

RICHELIEU, Armand Jean du Plessis, Duc de (1585–1642), French cardinal, statesman and chief minister to LOUIS XIII for 18 years. By a mixture of diplomacy and ruthlessness he helped make France the leading power in Europe with a monarchy secure against internal revolt. He destroyed HUGUENOT power by 1628, foiled an attempt by Maria de MÉDICIS to oust him in 1630, and suppressed the plots of the Duc de Montmorency in 1632 and of Cinq-Mars in 1642, at the same time reducing the power of the nobles. In foreign policy he opposed the Hapsburgs, intervening against them in the THIRTY YEARS WAR. Richelieu strengthened the navy, encouraged colonial development and patronized the arts.

RICHLER, Mordecai (1931–   ), Canadian novelist and essayist. He lived in Paris and London 1951–72 to escape what he saw as Canada's stifling creative atmosphere. His novels, especially *The Apprenticeship of Duddy Kravitz* (1959) and *Cocksure* (1968), are noted for their wry wit and biting satire.

RICHMOND, state capital of Va. and from 1861 to 1865 capital of the Confederacy. Located at the navigation head of the James R, it is a port and a financial and distribution center, as well as being an important industrial city, with tobacco and food processing, chemicals, metals and wood products. It has many historic buildings and places of higher education. Pop 219,214.

RICHTER, Hans (1843–1916), Hungarian conductor who presented the first performance of WAGNER'S *Ring* cycle at BAYREUTH in 1876. A BRAHMS specialist also, he conducted in England for many years.

RICHTER, Johann Paul Friedrich (1763–1825), German humorous and sentimental novelist, who wrote as Jean Paul. His early works were satirical; but he achieved popularity with such works as *The Invisible Lodge* (1793), *The Life of Quintus Fixlein* (1796) and the four-volume *Titan* (1800–03).

RICHTER, Sviatoslav (1915–   ), Russian pianist, particularly renowned for his sensitive treatment of Beethoven, Schubert, Schumann, Debussy and Prokofiev.

RICHTER SCALE, scale devised by C. F. Richter (1900–   ), used to measure the magnitudes of EARTHQUAKES in terms of the amplitude and frequency of the surface waves. The largest recorded earthquakes are about 8.5 and a great earthquake of magnitude 8 occurs only once every 5–10 years. Because the scale is logarithmic, an increase of one unit corresponds to a ten-fold increase in the size of an earthquake.

RICHTHOFEN, Manfred, Baron von (1892–1918), German WWI airman, nicknamed the "Red Baron." Known for the daring and chivalry with which he led his squadron, he shot down around 80 opponents and was himself killed in action.

RICKENBACKER, Edward Vernon (1890–1973), US air ace of WWI; he shot down 26 aircraft. After the war he became an automotive and airline executive.

RICKETS, VITAMIN D deficiency disease in children causing disordered BONE growth at the EPIPHYSES, with growth retardation, defective mineralization of bone, epiphyseal irregularity on X-RAY, and pliability and tendency to FRACTURE of bones. It is common among the malnourished, especially in cool climates where vitamin D formation in the SKIN is minimal. Treatment is by vitamin D replacement.

RICKETTSIA, organisms partway between BACTERIA and VIRUSES that are obligatory intracellular organisms but have a more complex structure than viruses. They are responsible for a number of diseases (often borne by TICKS or LICE) including TYPHUS, SCRUB TYPHUS and ROCKY MOUNTAIN SPOTTED FEVER; related organisms cause Q FEVER and PSITTACOSIS. They are sensitive to TETRACYCLINES and cause characteristic serological reactions cross-specific to Proteus bacteria.

RICKEY, Branch Wesley (1881–1965), US baseball executive, nicknamed "The Mahatma." As general manager of the St. Louis Cardinals, he pioneered the minor league "farm system," and as a Brooklyn Dodgers executive in 1947, he signed Jackie ROBINSON, thus breaking baseball's color barrier.

RICKOVER, Hyman George (1900–   ), Russian-born US admiral who brought nuclear power to the US Navy. Head of the Navy's electrical division in WWII, he moved to the Atomic Energy Commission in 1947, and developed the first nuclear-powered submarine, the *Nautilus* (1954).

Serving well beyond the usual retirement age, he attained the rank of full admiral at the age of 73.

RIDGWAY, Matthew Bunker (1895–   ), US military leader. During WWII he led the first full-scale US air attack in the invasion of Sicily (1943) and took part in the invasion of France (1944). He became commander of the United Nations forces in Korea (1951), supreme commander of NATO Allied Forces in Europe (1952–53) and US army chief of staff 1953–55.

RIEFENSTAHL, Leni (1902–   ), German film actress and director whose movie *The Blue Light* (1932) brought her to the attention of Adolf Hitler. She subsequently made two documentaries for the Nazis, *Triumph of the Will* (1935) and *Olympiad* (1938), considered among the most brilliant propaganda films ever produced.

RIEGGER, Wallingford (1885–1961), US composer. In many of his works he used TWELVE-TONE techniques. He wrote ballet scores, symphonies and chamber works.

RIEL, Louis (1844–1885), Canadian *métis* (person of mixed Indian and French descent) and rebel leader. In 1869 he organized the *métis* of Red River, now in Manitoba, to oppose Canada's annexation of these territories. He fled to the US after government troops had moved in (1870). On his return to Canada (1873) he was elected to the House of Commons, but was expelled in 1874 and banished in 1875. In 1884 he led another Indian uprising in Saskatchewan, but was captured in May, 1885. His execution for treason became a cause of friction between English and French Canadians.

RIEMANN, Georg Friedrich Bernhard (1826–1866), German mathematician, whose best known contribution to diverse fields of mathematics is the initiation of studies of NONEUCLIDEAN GEOMETRY. Elliptic geometry is often named RIEMANNIAN GEOMETRY for him.

RIEMENSCHNEIDER, Tilman (c1460–1531), German Gothic sculptor in wood and stone. He worked in Würzburg, where many of his works survive, and carved the marble tomb of Emperor Henry II and his wife in Bamberg Cathedral (1499–1513).

RIESMAN, David (1909–   ), US sociologist whose best-known work, *The Lonely Crowd* (1950), explores the changing nature of the US social character in a highly industrialized urban society.

RIFLE, strictly any FIREARM with a "rifled" bore — i.e., with shallow helical grooves cut inside the barrel. These grooves, by causing the bullet to spin, steady it and increase its accuracy, velocity and range. The term "rifle" is more narrowly applied to the long-barreled hand weapon fired from the shoulder. Rifles are generally classified by caliber (see AMMUNITION) or decimal fractions or by mode of action. "Single-shot" rifles are manually reloaded after each discharge; "repeaters" are reloaded from a magazine by means of a hand-operated mechanism that ejects the spent cartridge case and drives a fresh cartridge into the breech. In semiautomatic rifles, chambering and ejection operations are powered by gas produced as the weapon is fired. Today, many rifles have an optional fully automatic action, a single squeeze of the trigger emptying the magazine in seconds.

RIFT VALLEY, or graben, a valley formed by the relative downthrow of land between two roughly parallel FAULTS. The best known are the Great Rift Valley of E Africa, and the Rhine Rift Valley between Basel and Bingen.

RIGAUD, Hyacinthe (1659–1743), or **Hyacinthe Rigaud y Ros,** French portrait painter in the style of VAN DYCK. His subjects included Louis XIV (1701), Louis XV (1715) and BOSSUET (1702).

RIGHTS OF MAN, Declaration of the. See DECLARATION OF THE RIGHTS OF MAN.

RIGHT-TO-DIE LAWS, legislation permitting physicians to withdraw life-sustaining treatment for terminally ill patients under prescribed circumstances. The laws grew out of advances in medicine that permitted doctors to sustain life indefinitely for persons who had no hope for recovery or any ability to function normally. Aside from the expense involved, some patients and their families believed that the right to die with dignity was being denied. In 1976 the N.J. Supreme Court ruled that a hospital respirator being used to sustain the life of Karen Anne Quinlan, 22, long in a comatose state, could be disconnected so that she might "die with grace and dignity"; this was done but she continued to live. That same year Cal. adopted a right-to-die law, and within two years seven more states did the same. The laws required the consent of the patient, if conscious.

RIGHT-TO-WORK LAWS, laws enforced in 19 US states requiring companies to maintain an "open shop." This means that a person may not be prevented from working because he does not belong to a union, nor may he be forced to take up, or maintain, membership in a union.

RIG VEDA. See VEDA.

RIIS, Jacob August (1849–1914), Danish-born US journalist and social reformer whose book, *How the Other Half Lives*

(1890), drew attention to slum conditions in New York City. He worked as a police reporter on the *New York Tribune* (1877–88) and the *New York Evening Sun* (1888–99).

RILEY, James Whitcomb (1849–1916), US poet, known as the "Hoosier poet." *The Old Swimmin' Hole and 'Leven More Poems* (1883), was the first of many popular collections of humorous and sentimental dialect poems.

RILKE, Rainer Maria (1875–1926), German lyric poet. His complex and symbolic poems are preoccupied with spiritual questioning about God and death, as in the *Book of Hours* (1905) and *New Poems* (1907–08). His later *Duino Elegies* (1912–20; published 1923) and the *Sonnets to Orpheus* (1923) are richly mystical. Rilke is one of the great founding figures in modern literature.

RIMBAUD, Arthur (1854–1891), French poet. A precocious youth, he associated with VERLAINE, published *A Season in Hell* in 1873, and thereafter denounced his poetry, becoming an adventurer. His vivid imagery and his "disordering of consciousness," reflected in the fragmented technique of such poems as "The Drunken Boat," have had an enormous influence on modern poetry.

RIMSKY-KORSAKOV, Nikolai Andreyevich (1844–1908), Russian composer and a member of THE FIVE. While still a naval officer he started teaching composition at the St. Petersburg Conservatory (1871). He wrote scores for the operas *The Snow Maiden* (1882) and *The Golden Cockerel* (1907) and a colorful symphonic suite, *Scheherazade* (1888).

RINDERPEST, acute VIRUS disease, particularly of cattle, common in N Africa and S Asia. Although there have been outbreaks in other parts of the world, North America has hitherto remained unaffected by this usually fatal disease.

RINEHART, Mary Roberts (1876–1958), American writer of perennially popular detective stories, including *The Circular Staircase* (1908). She also wrote an autobiography, *My Story* (1931).

RINGLING BROTHERS, five US brothers who created the world's largest CIRCUS. Led by John Ringling (1866–1936), they started with a one-wagon show and became BARNUM and BAILEY'S chief rivals, buying them out in 1907. The combined Ringling Bros., Barnum & Bailey Circus was the world's largest by 1930, and remained in the family's hands until 1967.

RINGWORM, common FUNGUS disease of the SKIN of man and animals which may also affect the HAIR or nails. Ringshaped raised lesions occur, often with central scarring; temporary BALDNESS is seen on hairy skin, together with the disintegration of the nails. ATHLETE'S FOOT is ringworm of the toes, while *tinea cruris* is a variety affecting the groin. Various fungi may be responsible, including *Trichophyton* and *Microspora*. Treatments include topical ointments (e.g., benzyl benzoate) or systemic antifungal ANTIBIOTICS such as Griseofulvin.

RIO DE JANEIRO, second largest city of Brazil, on the Atlantic coast about 200mi W of São Paulo. Located in a picturesque setting, the city is a famous tourist resort. It is also a leading commercial center and port, and also an industrial center, manufacturing clothing, furniture, glassware and foodstuffs. The area was settled by the French (1555–67) and then by the Portuguese. It was the Brazilian capital from 1822 to 1960, when it was supplanted by Brasília. Pop 5,394,900.

RIO DE LA PLATA (English: Plate R), an estuary formed by the Paraná R and Uruguay R, separating Argentina to the S and Uruguay to the N. It flows 171mi SE into the Atlantic.

RIO GRANDE, one of the longest rivers in North America, known in Mexico as the Río Bravo del Norte. It rises in the San Juan Mts in SW Col. and flows 1,885mi SE and S to the Gulf of Mexico at Brownsville, Tex., and Matamoros, Mexico. From El Paso, Tex., to its mouth, it forms the US–Mexico border.

RIO TREATY, Inter-American Treaty of Reciprocal Assistance signed in 1947 by all states of the W hemisphere except Canada, Ecuador and Nicaragua. It binds the signatories not to use force on the American continent without the unanimous consent of the others, and regards an attack against one as an attack against all.

RIPARIAN RIGHTS, or water rights, belonging to owners of land on the edge of streams, rivers and lakes. They allow a landowner to use the water for domestic, agricultural or commercial purposes, usually with the provision that such use should not infringe the rights of other riparian owners.

RIPLEY, George (1802–1880), US social reformer and literary critic. Beginning as a Unitarian pastor, he became a TRANSCENDENTALIST, founded and ran the BROOK FARM community, 1841–47. Later he became an influential literary critic with the *New York Tribune.*

RISORGIMENTO (Italian: resurgence), Italian 19th-century period of literary and political nationalism leading to a unified

Italy in 1870. After 1815, various states, stirred by revolutionaries like MAZZINI, rose against their Austrian or papal rulers. Unification under VICTOR EMMANUEL II was achieved by CAVOUR, who involved the French in wars against Austria, and by the victories of GARIBALDI.

RITES OF PASSAGE, ceremonies within a community to mark the achievement by an individual of a new stage in his life cycle (e.g., birth, puberty, marriage) and his consequent change of role in the community.

RITTENHOUSE, David (1732–1796), American astronomer and mathematician, who invented the DIFFRACTION grating, built two famous ORRERIES, discovered the atmosphere of VENUS (1768) independently of LOMONOSOV (1761), and built what was probably the first American TELESCOPE.

RITTER, Tex (1906–1974), US country singer and film actor who was called "America's Most Beloved Cowboy" in the 1940s. A singing star of the Grand Ole Opry, radio and cowboy movies, he was best known for his recordings of "You Are My Sunshine" and the theme from the film *High Noon.*

RIVERA, Diego (1886–1957), Mexican mural painter. He studied in Europe, returning to Mexico in 1921. He painted large murals of social life and political themes throughout Mexico and also in the US, where his Marxist views aroused controversy.

RIVERA, José Eustasio (1889–1928), Colombian novelist. He is famous for his novel *The Vortex* (1924) which tells of the exploitation of rubber gatherers in the dense, hostile rain forest.

RIVER BRETHREN, Christian revivalist sect originating in 1770 among German settlers in Pennsylvania. They were probably called River Brethren because of their ritual of river baptism. Members reject war and worldly pleasures such as alcohol and tobacco, and wear plain dress.

RIVERS, Larry (1923–   ), US painter. He adapted the style of ABSTRACT EXPRESSIONISM to the popular imagery of well-known pictures or commercial advertisements, as in *Dutch Masters Series* (1963).

RIVERS, William Halse Rivers (1864–1922), British anthropologist and psychologist who initiated the study of experimental PSYCHOLOGY at the University of Cambridge (c1893).

RIVERS AND LAKES, bodies of inland water. Rivers flow in natural channels to the sea, lakes or, as tributaries, into other rivers. They are a fundamental component of the

HYDROLOGIC CYCLE (see DRAINAGE). Lakes are land-locked stretches of water fed by rivers; though the term may be applied also to temporary widenings of a river's course or to almost-enclosed bays and LAGOONS and to man-made reservoirs. Most lakes have an outflowing stream: where there is great water loss through EVAPORATION there is no such stream and the lake water is extremely saline (see also EVAPORITES), as in the Dead Sea. Lakes are comparatively temporary features on the landscape as they are constantly being infilled by silt. In many parts of the world rivers and lakes may exist only during certain seasons, drying up partially or entirely during DROUGHT. The main sources of rivers are SPRINGS, lakes and GLACIERS. Near the source a river flows swiftly, the rocks and other abrasive particles that it carries eroding a steep-sided V-shaped VALLEY (see EROSION). Variations in the hardness of the rocks over which it runs may result in WATERFALLS. In the middle part of its course the gradients become less steep, and lateral (sideways) erosion becomes more important than downcutting. The valley is broader, the flow less swift, and meandering more common. Toward the rivermouth, the flow becomes more sluggish and meandering prominent: the river may form OXBOW LAKES. Sediment may be deposited at the mouth to form a DELTA (see also ESTUARY; CANYON; HYDROELECTRIC POWER.)

RIVIERA, coastal region of the Mediterranean Sea in SE France and NW Italy. It is a major tourist center, noted for its scenery and pleasant climate. The Riviera's fashionable resorts include Cannes, Nice and St. Tropez in France; Monte Carlo in Monaco; and Bordighera, Portofino, Rapallo and San Remo in Italy.

RIYADH, Saudi Arabia city and seat of the Saudi royal family, about 240mi E of the Persian Gulf. It is an important commercial center and has rapidly expanded because of the oil trade. Pop 666,840.

RIZAL, José (1861–1896), Philippine writer and patriot. His novels, *The Lost Eden* (1886) and *The Subversive* (1891), denounced Spanish rule in the Philippines. His execution by the Spanish on false charges of instigating insurrection led to a full-scale rebellion.

RNA, ribonucleic acid. See NUCLEIC ACIDS.

ROAD. See HIGHWAY.

ROBARDS, Jason Jr. (1920–   ), US stage and film actor, especially celebrated for his interpretation of O'NEILL characters, such as Hickey in the Off Broadway production of *The Iceman Cometh* (1956). His films include *A Thousand Clowns*

(1966) and *All the President's Men* (1976), for which he received an Academy Award.

ROBBE-GRILLET, Alain (1922–   ), French novelist, originator of the NEW NOVEL. In works such as *The Voyeur* (1955), *Jealousy* (1957) and the screenplay for *Last Year at Marienbad* (1960), structure, objects and events displace character and story.

ROBBIA, della, Italian Florentine family of sculptors who developed the art of glazed TERRACOTTA relief sculptures. **Luca** (c1399–1482) sculpted the famous marble "Singing Gallery" for Florence cathedral (1431–1438) before turning to glazed relief work. The lunette *Madonna and Angels* (c1450) exemplifies the best of his style. His nephew and pupil **Andrea** (1435–1525) made roundels of *Infants in Swaddling Clothes* (1463) for the Hospital of the Innocents in Florence. Andrea's son, **Giovanni** (1469–1529), produced beautiful reliefs for the Church of St. Maria Novella, Florence; another son, **Girolamo** (1488–1566), worked for the French court.

ROBBINS, Harold (1916–   ), US author. His best-selling novels of adventure, greed and passion among the rich—often inspired by headlines events and personalities—include *The Carpetbaggers* (1967), *The Betsy* (1971), *Lonely Lady* (1976), and *Goodbye Janette* (1981).

ROBBINS, Jerome (1918–   ), US choreographer and director. He danced major roles with the American Ballet Theatre, 1940–44, where he created his first ballet, *Fancy Free* (1944). With the New York City Ballet he was associate artistic director, 1950–59 and a ballet master after 1968. For motion pictures, television and Broadway he has choreographed and directed such productions as *West Side Story* (1957) and *Fiddler on the Roof* (1964).

ROBERTS, Kenneth Lewis (1885–1957), US writer and *Saturday Evening Post* correspondent. He wrote a series of popular historical novels, including *Arundel* (1930), *Rabble in Arms* (1933) and *Northwest Passage* (1937), receiving a special Pulitzer Prize citation for them in 1957. He also wrote travel books.

ROBERTS, Oral (1918–   ), US Protestant evangelist and faith healer who has preached to millions over TV and founded Oral Roberts University in Tulsa, Okla.

ROBERTS, Owen Josephus (1875–1955), US associate justice of the Supreme Court, 1930–45. He was a prosecuting attorney in the TEAPOT DOME scandal 1924 and was involved in economic legislation in the Depression. He led the inquiry into the

PEARL HARBOR disaster, 1941.

ROBERTS, Sir Charles George Douglas (1860–1943), Canadian poet and writer. His simple descriptive poems of the Maritime provinces were an important contribution to the emerging Canadian consciousness. Among his best-known works are animal stories such as *Red Fox* (1905).

ROBERTSON, James (1742–1814), American frontier leader who brought settlers from North Carolina to Tennessee in 1771. He explored the Cumberland R area, founded Nashville (1780) and helped draft the Tennessee Constitution (1796).

ROBERTSON, Oscar, called **"Big O"** (1938–   ), US basketball player. A guard, he played with the Cincinnati Royals, 1960–70, and the Milwaukee Bucks, 1970–78. One of the all-time scorers, he also made over 9,000 assists.

ROBESON, Paul (1898–1976), black US singer and stage and film actor. A bass, he made his concert debut in 1925 and became known for his renditions of spiritual songs. His most famous song was "Ol' Man River" from the musical *Show Boat* (1928). Robeson starred in the play and film of *Emperor Jones* (1925; 1933) and in Shakespeare's *Othello*. Ostracized in the US for his communist beliefs, he lived and sang in Europe 1958–63.

ROBESPIERRE, Maximilien François Marie Isidore de (1758–94), fanatical idealist leader of the FRENCH REVOLUTION. An Arras lawyer, he was elected as a representative of the third estate to the STATES GENERAL in 1789 and rose to become leader of the radical JACOBINS in the National Convention (1793). He liquidated the rival moderate GIRONDINS and as leader of the Committee of Public Safety he initiated the REIGN OF TERROR. He hoped to establish a "Reign of Virtue" by ridding France of all its internal enemies. However, the National Convention rose against him, alienated by his increasing power, by the mass executions and the threat of further purges, and by the new religious cult of the "Supreme Being." He was arrested, summarily tried and executed.

ROBIN, vernacular name for various unrelated species of small birds with red breasts, referring to different species in different countries. They include the European robin, *Erithacus rubecula*, American robin, *Turdus migratorius*, Pekin robin, *Leiothrix lutea*, and Indian robin, *Saxicoloides fulicata*. Most familiar are the European robin (Robin redbreast), an insectivorous thrush of woods and gardens, noted for its beautiful song, and the American robin, a common garden and woodland bird of the US.

ROBIN HOOD, legendary medieval English hero. He is usually depicted as an outlaw, living with his band of "merry men" including Little John, Friar Tuck and Maid Marian in Sherwood Forest in Nottinghamshire and robbing the Norman overlords to give to the poor.

ROBINSON, Bill "Bojangles" (1878–1949), US tapdancer considered the finest practitioner of that art. He starred in vaudeville and musical revues and appeared in several films with Shirley Temple, including *The Little Colonel* (1935), and in the black musical film *Stormy Weather* (1943).

ROBINSON, Edward G. (born Emmanuel Goldberg; 1893–1973), US actor, famous for portrayals of ruthless gangster characters in such films as *Little Caesar* (1931), and *Kid Galahad* (1937), and for his role in *Double Indemnity* (1948).

ROBINSON, Edwin Arlington (1869–1935), US poet, known for his series of terse, sometimes bitter verse characterizations of the inhabitants of the fictitious "Tilbury town." His *Collected Poems* (1921), *The Man Who Died Twice* (1924) and *Tristram* (1927), won Pulitzer prizes.

ROBINSON, Jack Roosevelt, "Jackie" (1919–1972), the first black baseball player to be admitted to the major US leagues. He joined the Brooklyn Dodgers in 1947 and maintained a batting average of .311 through 10 seasons.

ROBINSON, "Sugar" Ray (born Walter Smith; 1921–   ), US boxer who won the world welterweight title in 1946 and the middleweight title in 1951. He retired in 1952, but returned in 1955 to regain it, becoming in 1958 the first boxer to win a divisional world championship five times.

ROBINSON CRUSOE. See DEFOE, DANIEL; SELKIRK, ALEXANDER.

ROBOT (from Czech *robota*, work), or automaton, an automatic machine that does work, simulating and replacing human activity; known as an android if humanoid in form (which most are not). Robots have evolved out of simpler automatic devices, and many are now capable of decision-making, self-programming, and carrying out complex operations. Some have sensory devices. They are increasingly being used in industry and scientific research for tasks such as handling hot or radioactive materials. Science fiction from Capek to Asimov and beyond has featured robots. (See also MECHANIZATION AND AUTOMATION; REMOTE CONTROL.)

ROB ROY (1671–1734), nickname of

Scottish outlaw Robert MacGregor, romanticized in Sir Walter SCOTT's *Rob Roy*. He was evicted and outlawed for cattle theft in 1712 by the Duke of Montrose, whose tenants he then plundered. Hunted for many years he surrendered in 1722, but was pardoned in 1727.

ROCHAMBEAU, Jean Baptiste Donatien de Vimeur, Comte de (1725–1807), French general who commanded French troops sent to help WASHINGTON in the American revolution. Involved in the French Revolution, he narrowly escaped execution in the Reign of Terror, and was later pensioned by NAPOLEON.

ROCKEFELLER, family of US financiers. **John Davison Rockefeller** (1839–1937), entered the infant oil industry at Cleveland, Ohio, at the age of 24, and ruthlessly unified the oil industry into the Standard Oil Trust. He devoted a large part of his later life to philanthropy, creating the ROCKEFELLER FOUNDATION. **John Davison Rockefeller, Jr.** (1874–1960), only son of John D. Rockefeller, followed his father's business and charitable interests. He donated the land for the UN headquarters and helped found the Rockefeller Center in New York. **Nelson Aldrich Rockefeller** (1908–1979), second son of John, Jr., governor of N.Y. 1959–73, was appointed US vice-president in 1974. He sought presidential nomination in 1960, 1964 and 1968. He expanded transportation, welfare, housing and other social services in N.Y. **Winthrop Rockefeller** (1912–1973), son of John, Jr., was Republican governor of Ark. (1967–1970). **David Rockefeller**, (1915–), youngest son of John Jr., was president of the Chase Manhattan Bank and chairman of Rockefeller U. **Jay Rockefeller** (1937–), grandson of John D. Rockefeller, Jr., became Democratic governor of W. Va. in 1976.

ROCKEFELLER FOUNDATION, second largest US philanthropic foundation, with assets totaling about $1 billion. Founded in 1913 by John D. ROCKEFELLER, it supports research in three main areas: medical and natural sciences, agricultural sciences, and the humanities and social sciences.

ROCKET, form of JET-PROPULSION engine in which the substances (fuel and oxidizer) needed to produce the propellant gas jet are carried internally. Working by reaction, and being independent of atmospheric oxygen, rockets are used to power interplanetary space vehicles (SEE SPACE EXPLORATION). In addition to their chief use to power MISSILES, rockets are also used for supersonic and assisted-takeoff airplane propulsion, and sounding rockets are used for scientific investigation of the upper atmosphere. The first rockets—of the firework type, cardboard tubes containing GUNPOWDER—were made in 13th-century China, and the idea quickly spread to the West. Their military use was limited, guns being superior, until they were developed by William CONGREVE. Later Congreve rockets mounted the guide stick along the central axis; and William Hale eliminated it altogether, placing curved vanes in the exhaust stream, thus stabilizing the rocket's motion by causing it to rotate on its axis. The 20th century saw the introduction of new fuels and oxidants, e.g., a mixture of NITROCELLULOSE and NITROGLYCERIN for solid-fuel rockets, or ETHANOL and liquid oxygen for the more efficient liquid-fuel rockets. The first liquid-fuel rocket was made by R. H. GODDARD, who also invented the multistage rocket. In WWII Germany, and afterward in the US, Wernher von BRAUN made vast improvements in rocket design. Other propulsion methods, including the use of nuclear furnaces, electrically-accelerated PLASMAS and ION PROPULSION, are being developed.

ROCKINGHAM, Charles Watson-Wentworth, 2nd Marquess of (1730–1782), British statesman, prime minister 1765–66. He repealed the Stamp Act, 1765 and tried to conciliate the American colonies. During his second term as premier (1782) he urged peace with the US.

ROCK MUSIC, the dominant pop-music style since the late 1950s. Rock music first emerged in the mid-1950s as "rock'n'roll," a white rendition of the black musical mode called *rhythm-and-blues*—a sophisticated blues style that often used amplified instruments to produce a heavy beat. The first national r'n'r hit, and the one that gave the genre its name, was "Rock Around the Clock," by Bill Haley and his Comets (1955). Rock's first superstar, Elvis PRESLEY, hit on a riveting combination of hard-driving rhythm-and-blues with COUNTRY AND WESTERN MUSIC; his lyrics were simple and earthy, and directly addressed the emotional concerns of the young.

The impetus for the transformation of r'n'r into rock music came from England, where the BEATLES in 1960, and in 1964 the ROLLING STONES, remixed the original ingredients, adding wit, sensuality and new musical textures, forms and rhythms.

The 1960s also saw the emergence of *soul music*, a product of rhythm-and-blues and black gospel styles, which would add its sound to rock; *folk-rock*, as in the later work of Bob DYLAN; *acid rock*, an attempt to reproduce musically the hallucinogenic drug experience, using advanced electronic sound technologies to produce its effects; and *glitter rock*, featuring outrageous costuming and incredible makeup (the pop-rock group Kiss is a later example). In the 1970s acid rock was followed by *hard rock* or *heavy metal*, louder and more repetitive; and by eclectic mixtures of the amplified rock sound with country, jazz, calypso and other styles. Other 1970s innovations were: *punk rock*, an attempt to outrage through carefully orchestrated ugliness; and *Disco*, the dance music that uses a rock beat broken into more complex rhythms and with a vocal style directly descended from gospel.

ROCKNE, Knute Kenneth (1888–1931), Norwegian-born US football coach. He played football and was head coach at U of Notre Dame through most of his adult life. He made the small school a national football power, achieving the extraordinary record of 105 victories, five ties and only 12 defeats. He was especially brilliant in devising innovative offensive tackles.

ROCKS, the solid materials making up the earth's LITHOSPHERE. They may be consolidated (e.g., sandstone) or unconsolidated (e.g., sand). The study of rocks is petrology. Strictly, the term applies only to those aggregates of one or more minerals, or of organic material, of widespread occurrence at the EARTH'S surface. Unlike MINERALS, rocks are not necessarily homogeneous and have no definite chemical composition. Together, SILICA and SILICATES make up about 95% of the crustal rocks. There are three main classes of rocks, igneous, sedimentary and metamorphic. Most IGNEOUS ROCKS form from the MAGMA, a molten, subsurface complex of silicates or from LAVA, a term applied to magma that has reached the earth's surface. They are the primary source of all the earth's rocks. SEDIMENTARY ROCKS are consolidated layered accumulations of inorganic and organic material. They are of three types: detrital (clastic), formed of weathered (see EROSION) particles of other rocks (e.g., SANDSTONE); organic deposits (e.g., COAL, some LIMESTONES); and chemical precipitates (e.g., the EVAPORITES). (See also FOSSILS; STRATIGRAPHY.) METAMORPHIC ROCKS have undergone change within the earth under heat, pressure or chemical action. Sedimentary, igneous and even previously metamorphosed rocks may change in structure or composition in this way. (See also GEOLOGY.)

ROCKWELL, Norman (1894–1978), US illustrator, known for his realistic and humorous scenes of US small town life. His work includes magazine covers for *The Saturday Evening Post* and a series of paintings of the FOUR FREEDOMS.

ROCKY MOUNTAINS, principal range of W North America. Extending from N Alaska for over 3,000mi to N.M., they form the continental divide; streams rising on the E slopes flow to the Arctic or Atlantic and on the W toward the Pacific. Rivers rising in the Rockies include the Missouri, Rio Grande, Colorado, Columbia and Arkansas. A relatively new system, the Rockies were formed by massive uplifting forces that began about 70 million years ago. The system can be divided into: the Southern Rocky Mts of S Wyo., Col., and N N.M.; the Central Rocky Mts between Mont. and N Ut.; the Northern Rocky Mts of Wash., Mont. and Ida.; the Canadian Rockies of British Columbia, Alberta and Yukon; and continue as the Brooks Range of Alaska. The highest peak is Mt Elbert (14,433ft). National Parks in the Rockies include JASPER NATIONAL PARK, GLACIER NATIONAL PARK, YELLOWSTONE and GRAND TETON. The Rockies are one of the richest mineral deposits in North America, and a major tourist center.

ROCKY MOUNTAIN SPOTTED FEVER, tick-borne rickettsial disease (see RICKETTSIA) seen in much of the US, especially the Rocky mountain region. It causes FEVER, HEADACHE and a characteristic rash starting on the palms and soles, later spreading elsewhere. TETRACYCLINES are effective, though untreated cases may be fatal.

ROCOCO, 18th century European artistic and architectural style. The term derives from *rocaille* (French: grottowork), whose arabesque and ingenious forms are found in many Rococo works. The style, characterized by lightness and delicacy, emerged c1700 in France, finding expression in the works of BOUCHER, FRAGONARD and others. Some of the greatest achievements of Rococo sculpture and decoration are found in the palaces and pilgrimage churches of Austria and S Germany.

RODCHENKO, Alexander (1891–1956), Russian artist and sculptor, among the most radical of the postrevolutionary avant-garde. He called for an entirely new, wholly abstract art led by artist-engineers, and championed CONSTRUCTIVISM.

RODENTS, the largest order of MAMMALS including some 1,500 species of MICE, RATS, PORCUPINES and SQUIRRELS. Rodents are easily identified by the structure and arrangement of the TEETH. There is a single pair of incisors in the upper and lower jaws which continue to grow throughout life. The wearing surface develops a chisel-like edge. Behind the incisors is a gap, or diastema, to allow recirculation of food in chewing. Furthermore, the cheek skin can be drawn across the diastema in front of the molars and premolars, leaving the incisors free for gnawing. Rodents are predominantly eaters of seeds, grain and other vegetation. Their adaptability in feeding on a variety of vegetable matter allows them to exploit a variety of NICHES.

RODEO, in the US and Canada, contest and entertainment based on ranching techniques; it derives from late 19th-century COWBOY meets when contests were held to celebrate the end of a cattle drive. It usually comprises five main events: *calf-roping*, in which a mounted cowboy must rope a calf, dismount, throw the calf and tie three of its legs together; *steer-wrestling*, in which the cowboy jumps from a galloping horse and wrestles a steer to the ground by its horns; *bareback riding*, on an unbroken horse for 8–10 secs; *saddle-bronc riding*, and *bull-riding*.

RODGERS, Jimmie (1897–1933), US country singer known as "America's Blues Yodeler." He was the first country music star and was widely imitated by younger singers. At the height of his career, he died of tuberculosis.

RODGERS, Richard Charles (1902–1981), US songwriter and composer. He collaborated with librettist Lorenz HART on *A Connecticut Yankee* (1927), *Pal Joey* (1940) and many other Broadway musicals containing countless popular songs. Later he teamed with Oscar HAMMERSTEIN II on the Pulitzer prize-winning *Oklahoma!* (1943), *South Pacific* (1949) and *The King and I* (1951).

RODIN, Auguste (1840–1917), major French sculptor. He rose to fame c1877, and in 1880 began the never-completed *Gate of Hell*, source of such well known pieces as *The Thinker* (1880) and *The Kiss* (1886). His works, in stone or bronze, were characterized by energy and emotional intensity, as in *The Burghers of Calais* (1884–94).

RODNEY, Caesar (1728–1784), American patriot and statesman who helped to bring Delaware into the Revolutionary War. He was Delaware's delegate to the Continental Congress, 1775–76, signed the Declaration of Independence and was president of Delaware, 1778–81.

RODNEY, George Brydges Rodney, 1st Baron (1719–1792), English admiral. His achievements include capturing Martinique (1762) in the SEVEN YEARS WAR, relieving Gibraltar from the Spanish in 1780, and defeating the French West Indies fleet in 1782.

ROEBLING, John Augustus (1806–1869), German-born US bridge engineer who pioneered modern suspension bridge design. His most famous works are the Brooklyn Bridge in New York City, and the Niagara Falls Bridge (1855), using wire rope instead of chains. He died before the completion of the Brooklyn Bridge, finished by his son **Washington Augustus Roebling** (1837–1926).

ROENTGEN (or Röntgen), Wilhelm Conrad (1845–1923), German physicist, recipient in 1901 of the first Nobel Prize for Physics for his discovery of X-RAYS. This discovery was made in 1895 when by chance he (or perhaps his assistant) noticed that a PHOSPHOR screen nearby a vacuum tube through which he was passing an electric current fluoresced brightly, even when shielded by opaque cardboard. (See also ROENTGEN unit).

ROETHKE, Theodore (1908–1963), US poet, influenced by T. S. ELIOT and YEATS, who won a Pulitzer Prize for *The Waking* (1953) and a National Book Award for *Words for the Wind* (1958). Much of his imagery is drawn from nature.

ROE VS. WADE. In a 7-2 decision in this 1973 case, the US Supreme Court ruled that states may not prohibit a woman from having a medically initiated abortion in the first trimester of a pregnancy.

ROGERS, Carl Ransom (1902–   ), US psychotherapist who instituted the idea of the patient determining the extent and nature of his course of therapy, the therapist following the patient's lead.

ROGERS, John (1829–1904), US sculptor known for realistic figural groups such as *The Slave Auction*. His extremely popular works were often massproduced.

ROGERS, Robert (1731–1795), American frontiersman who led the famous British–American *Rogers' Rangers*, commandos who adopted Indian tactics, in the FRENCH AND INDIAN WARS. An associate of Jonathan CARVER, he was involved in various dubious enterprises and was a Loyalist during the Revolution.

ROGERS, William Penn Adair, "Will" (1879–1935), US humorist known for his homespun philosophy and mockery of politics and other subjects previously considered "untouchable." Part Irish and part Cherokee, he became famous in the Ziegfeld Follies of 1916. He also contributed a syndicated column to 350 newspapers.

ROGERS, William Pierce (1913–   ), US lawyer and public official, President NIXON's first secretary of state, 1969–73. He was US attorney general (1957–61) and set up the civil rights division of the Justice Department.

ROGET, Peter Mark (1779–1869), English scholar and physician, remembered for his definitive *Thesaurus of English Words and Phrases* (1852). He described it as a "dictionary in reverse"; if one has the general idea, the book will provide the precise word to convey it.

RÓHEIM, Géza (1891–1953), Hungarian-born US anthropologist best known for his application of the ideas of PSYCHOANALYSIS to ETHNOLOGY studies. He wrote *Psychoanalysis and Anthropology* (1950).

ROHMER, Eric (1920–   ), French film director. He was co-founder and editor (1956–63) of *Cahiers du Cinéma*, which attacked conventional methods of filmmaking. His own films, *My Night at Maud's* (1968), *Claire's Knee* (1970) and *Chloe in the Afternoon* (1972), deal subtly with relationships between sophisticated men and women.

ROKOSSOVSKY, Konstantin Konstantinovich (1896–1968), Russian army commander who defended Moscow in 1941 and defeated the Germans at Stalingrad in 1943. He was deputy premier of Poland, 1952–56, and Russian deputy defense minister, 1956–58.

ROLAND, one of CHARLEMAGNE's commanders, hero of the CHANSON DE ROLAND. Ambushed by Basques at RONCESVALLES in 778, he and his men were massacred because he was too proud to summon help.

ROLAND DE LA PLATIÈRE, Jean Marie (1734–1793), French revolutionary, leader of the GIRONDINS in 1791 and minister of the interior 1792–93. He fled Paris in 1793, after trying to save LOUIS XVI. He committed suicide on hearing of the execution of his wife, Jeanne, whose salon had been an important Girondin intellectual gathering place.

ROLFE, Frederick William (1860–1913), English novelist, also known as Baron Corvo. His works include *Hadrian the Seventh* (1904) and *The Desire and Pursuit of the Whole* (1934).

ROLFE, John (1585–1622), early English settler in Virginia who married the Indian princess POCAHONTAS in 1614. His methods of curing tobacco made it the basis of the colony's later prosperity. He was probably killed in an Indian massacre.

ROLLAND, Romain (1866–1944), French novelist and musicologist who won the 1915 Nobel Prize for Literature. He is best known for his biographies, including *Beethoven* (1909), his WWI pacifist articles *Above the Battle* (1915), and the 10-volume novel-cycle *Jean Christophe* (1904–1912), about the life of a musical genius.

ROLLER SKATING, popular sport and recreation, formerly a pastime of nearly every US child, but now increasingly enjoyed by adults in indoor rinks as well as outdoors. Invented by an unknown Dutchman, the skates consist of four wheels with ball bearings, attached to a shoe or steel platform. The popularity of plastic wheels turned roller skating into a craze in the late 1970s.

ROLLING STONES, British rock music band which, along with the BEATLES, revitalized ROCK MUSIC in the early 1960s and which first introduced conspicuous sexuality, and its own brand of menace, to the rock scene. The Stones' lead singer Mick Jagger (b.1944) and guitarist Keith Richard (b.1943) have composed most of the group's music.

ROLLO, or Hrolf (c860–c932), Viking chieftain, first duke of Normandy. Invading NW France, he was granted Normandy in 911 by the French crown when he adopted Christianity.

RØLVAAG, Ole Edvaart (1876–1931), Norwegian-born novelist, who came to the US in 1869 and wrote in Norwegian. His trilogy *Giants in the Earth* (1927–31) is the story of Norwegian settlers in the US Northwest.

ROMAINS, Jules, pen name of Louis Farigoule (1885–1972), distinguished French author and exponent of unanimism, or the collective personality. He is known for his plays and his 27-volume cycle *Men of Good Will* (1932–46).

ROMAN CATHOLIC CHURCH, major branch of the Christian Church, arising out of the WESTERN CHURCH, consisting of those Christians who are in communion with the pope (see PAPACY). It comprises especially the ecclesiastical organization that remained under papal obedience at the REFORMATION, consisting of a hierarchy of bishops and priests (see MINISTRY), with other officers such as CARDINALS. Roman Catholicism stresses the authority of tradition and of the Church (as capitulated in ECUMENICAL COUNCILS and the papacy) to formulate doctrine and regulate the life of the Church. Members participate in GRACE, mediated through the priesthood, by means of the seven SACRAMENTS: the MASS is central to Roman Catholic life and worship. In the Middle Ages the Church influenced all aspects of life in W Europe, and the prelates controlled vast estates. There was a constant struggle with kings and the emperor over the Church's political claims. The challenge of the Reformation was met by the Council of TRENT and by the COUNTER-REFORMATION, many abuses being remedied and large-scale MISSIONS begun. Doctrinally, Roman Catholic theologians since the Reformation have stressed and elaborated the role of the Virgin MARY and the authority and infallibility of the pope. Other distinctive doctrines include clerical celibacy, LIMBO and PURGATORY. Those held in common with the ORTHODOX CHURCHES (but rejected by Protestants) include the invocation of SAINTS, veneration of images, acceptance of the APOCRYPHA, the entire sacramental system, and MONASTICISM. Especially from the 18th century, ANTICLERICALISM weakened the Church's influence, and the loss of the PAPAL STATES was perhaps its political nadir. Since the Second VATICAN COUNCIL there has been a vigorous movement toward accommodation with the modern world, cautious dealings with the ECUMENICAL MOVEMENT and encouragement of lay participation and vernacular LITURGY. There are now c600 million Roman Catholics, and the Church's economic and political influence remains moderately strong, especially in S Europe, South America and the Philippines. (See also CATHOLIC; CHRISTIANITY; CURIA; MODERNISM; OLD CATHOLICS; UNIATE CHURCHES.)

ROMANCE, work of fiction concerning romantic or chivalric adventures. It derived from the French medieval *roman*, sung or recited by TROUBADORS, and developed into the popular CHANSONS DE GESTE.

ROMANCE LANGUAGES, one of the main groups of the INDO-EUROPEAN LANGUAGES. It comprises those languages derived from the vernacular Latin which was spread by Roman soldiers and colonists, and superseded local tongues. The languages include Italian, the Rhaeto-Romanic dialects of Alpine regions, Provençal French, the Walloon dialect of S Belgium, Spanish, the Catalan dialect around Barcelona, Portuguese and Romanian. Although differentiated by dialects the languages share a similar vocabulary and grammatical development.

ROMAN DE LA ROSE, Le, medieval French poem, an elaborate allegory of love in 22,000 lines, of which 4,058 were written by Guillaume de Lorris c1240. The rest, a meandering dissertation on Christian love, was composed by Jean de Meun, c1280.

ROMANESQUE ART AND ARCHITEC- TURE, artistic style prevalent in Western Christian Europe from c950 to c1200. Romanesque preceded GOTHIC ART AND ARCHITECTURE and is so called because its forms are derived from ROMAN ART AND ARCHITECTURE. The architecture, based on the round Roman arch and improvised systems of vaulting, produced a massive, simple and robust style with great vitality, particularly in the case of NORMAN ARCHITECTURE. Churches had immense towers; interiors were decorated by FRESCOES of biblical scenes. The sculptural style was very varied, vigorous and expressive, and there were carved, sculptured scenes on column capitals, and larger reliefs and figures on exterior portals and tympanums. The production of metalwork flourished, and many of the pilgrimage churches had elaborate reliquaries and valuable treasuries. There are many fine illuminated manuscripts. The Romanesque style was spread by traveling artists and craftsmen throughout Europe.

Official name: Romanian Socialist Republic
Capital: Bucharest
Area: 91,699sq mi
Population: 22,270,000
Languages: Romanian
Religions: Romanian Orthodox, Roman Catholic
Monetary unit(s): 1 Leu = 100 bani

ROMANIA, or Rumania, republic in SE Europe on the Black Sea, lying between the USSR and Hungary to the N and Bulgaria and Yugoslavia to the S.
Land. In the N is the SE end of the Carpathian Mts, separating Moldavia in the E from Transylvania in the W. The Carpathians join the Transylvanian Alps running from E to W. The principal rivers are the Danube in the S and W and the Prut in the NE. The climate is continental, but with severe winters.
People. Over 60% of the population is rural. About 85% are Romanians, with Hungarian and German minorities. Largest cities are Bucharest, the capital, Brasov, Iasi, Timisoara, Constanta, Cluj and Galati.

Economy. Over 60% of the land area is agricultural, but industry provides two thirds of the national income. More than 90% of farmland is collectivized, grain being the most important crop. About 25% of Romania is forested, particularly by conifers. With large oil fields in the Prahova R valley, Romania is the second largest producer of petroleum and natural gas in Europe. Copper, lead, coal and iron ore are mined; principal industries are iron and steel, machinery, textiles and chemicals, and main exports oil-field equipment, furniture, agricultural machinery and textiles.

History. Most of modern Romania was part of ancient DACIA, thoroughly imbued with Roman language and culture, which survived barbarian conquests. After the 13th century the two principalities of Moldavia and Walachia emerged, Turkish dependencies until 1829 and then Russian protectorates. United in 1861, Romania became independent in 1878. After WWI the Romanian-speaking province of Transylvania was acquired from Austria-Hungary. In the 1930s Fascists, especially the IRON GUARD, were dominant, and in 1941 dictator Ion ANTONESCU sided with the Axis powers. Overrun by the USSR in 1944, it became a satellite state, and a republic after King Michael's abdication in 1947. In the 1960s and 1970s Romania achieved greater independence under Nicolae CEAUCESCU, establishing relations with the West.

ROMAN NUMERALS, letters of the Roman ALPHABET used to represent numbers, the letters I, V, X, L, C, D and M standing for 1, 5, 10, 50, 100, 500 and 1000, respectively. All other numbers are represented by combinations of these letters according to certain rules of addition and subtraction; thus, for example, VIII is 8, XL is 40, MCD is 1400 and MCDXLVIII is 1448.

ROMANOV, ruling dynasty of Russia 1613–1917. The name was adopted by a Russian noble family in the 16th century; the first Romanov tsar was MICHAEL. The last of the direct Romanov line was PETER, but succeeding tsars retained the name of Romanov, down to NICHOLAS II (reigned 1894–1917).

ROMANS, Epistle to the, NEW TESTAMENT book written by St. PAUL to the Christians of Rome c58 AD. It presents his major statement of JUSTIFICATION BY FAITH, and the Christian's consequent freedom from condemnation, sin and the law. It stresses God's sovereignty and grace.

ROMANTICISM, 19th-century European artistic movement. Its values of emotion, intuition, imagination and individualism were in opposition to the ideals of restraint, reason and harmony of CLASSICISM. The word "Romantic" was first applied to art by Friedrich von SCHLEGEL in 1798, and later to works emphasizing the subjective, spiritual or fantastic, concerned with wild, uncultivated nature, or which seemed fundamentally modern rather than classical. The Middle Ages were thought to express Romantic values. The evocative qualities of nature inspired poets such as WORDSWORTH, COLERIDGE and LAMARTINE, and painters such as TURNER, PALMER and FRIEDRICH. BLAKE and GOETHE sought to develop new spiritual values; individualism concerned artists as disparate as Walt WHITMAN and GOYA. The lives of BYRON and CHOPIN seemed to act out the Romantic myth. Among the greatest Romantic composers were WEBER, BERLIOZ, MENDELSSOHN, LISZT and WAGNER.

ROMANY, a Dardic Indo-Iranian language, the tongue of GYPSIES, related to SANSKRIT. Gypsies migrated from central to NW India and then to Europe; the three main Romany dialects, Asiatic, Armenian and European, reflect the principal gypsy settlement areas. Romany has acquired much of its vocabulary from the peoples among whom gypsies have traveled.

ROMBERG, Sigmund (1887–1951), Hungarian-born US composer. He settled in the US in 1909, and wrote over 70 operettas and musicals, including *The Student Prince* (1924) and *The Desert Song* (1926). He went on to write many film scores.

ROME, or **Roma,** capital and largest city of Italy, a center of Western civilization for over 2,000 years. "The Eternal City" was capital of the Roman Empire (see ROME, ANCIENT), and is of unique religious significance, with the headquarters of the Roman Catholic Church in the VATICAN CITY. Administration (of the Italian government as well as of Roma province and of the region of LATIUM), religion and tourism are the most important activities of modern Rome, which is also a center for commerce, publishing, movies and fashion. The city is a great transportation hub, but has relatively little industry.

Rome is located on the rolling plain of the Roman Campagna in central Italy, 15mi from the Tyrrhenian Sea, the site of the ancient city being the SEVEN HILLS OF ROME. The Tiber R flows through the city from NE to SW. There are many important relics of classical Rome, such as the FORUM, the COLOSSEUM, the baths of CARACALLA and the PANTHEON. Rome is famous for its squares, Renaissance palaces, churches, basilicas (see SAINT PETER'S BASILICA), CATACOMBS and fountains, of which the best known is the Trevi fountain. There are also many fine museums, art collections and libraries, the Rome opera house, and the Santa Cecilia music academy, the world's oldest (1584). The university, Italy's largest, was founded in 1303. Pop 2,912,000.

ROME, Ancient, initially a tiny city-state in central Italy that, over some six centuries, grew into an empire which at its greatest extent (c117 AD) comprised almost all of the Western world known at the time, including most of Europe, the Middle East, Egypt and N Africa.

According to legend, Rome was founded in 753 BC by ROMULUS AND REMUS, descendants of the Trojan prince AENEAS. Until c500 BC, when the Romans set up an independent republic, the area around the SEVEN HILLS OF ROME was controlled by the Etruscans. (See also ETRUSCAN CIVILIZATION; SABINES.) The Romans were a disciplined, thrifty and industrious people whose genius in organization, administration, building and warfare enabled them not only to create their vast empire, but also to make it one of the most enduring ever.

Throughout the period of the republic (c500–31 BC) warfare was almost continuous. Under government by CONSULS and SENATE, Rome became master of central and S Italy and defeated CARTHAGE (see PUNIC WARS). Expansion continued: Greece, Asia Minor, Syria, Palestine and Egypt were conquered between 250 and 30 BC; Gaul (58–51 BC) and England (after 43 AD) followed. From about 100 BC, Rome began to move steadily toward dictatorship. Civil wars arose from conflicts between senatorial factions, and between rich and poor, PATRICIAN and PLEBEIAN forces. (See GRACCHUS; MARIUS; SULLA; SPARTACUS.) The army leaders POMPEY and Julius CAESAR emerged to form the first TRIUMVIRATE with CRASSUS. After Caesar's assassination and the avenging of his death by Mark ANTONY, his nephew Octavian defeated Mark Antony and CLEOPATRA and became the first emperor, AUGUSTUS.

For more than 200 years (27 BC–180 AD) the Roman empire embodied peace and law (the *Pax Romana*) and provided an excellent road and communication system which facilitated the spread of trade and new ideas, particularly Christianity. Its culture sprang from late Hellenism, but Romans surpassed the Greeks in practical achievements such as law (laying the basis for modern CIVIL LAW), civil engineering, a standard coinage and a system of weights and measures (see also ROMAN ART AND ARCHITECTURE). In literature, poets such as CATULLUS, VERGIL and HORACE, and dramatists such as PLAUTUS and TERENCE followed Greek models. LIVY and TACITUS were important Roman historians, and CICERO Rome's greatest orator. After Augustus, major emperors were TIBERIUS, CLAUDIUS, NERO, VESPASIAN, DOMITIAN, TRAJAN, HADRIAN and MARCUS AURELIUS. The empire was at its largest under TRAJAN (emperor 98–117). But from about 200 a decline set in, with internal strife and barbarian raids, particularly by the GOTHS. DIOCLETIAN (joint emperor 284–305) restored order and revived trade. Under his successor CONSTANTINE I (emperor 306–337) the capital was moved to BYZANTIUM (renamed Constantinople after him) and Christianity officially recognized. THEODOSIUS (emperor 379–95) was the last ruler of the united empire; it was then divided into Eastern and Western. From 376, the VISIGOTHS attacked, sacking Rome in 410. The VANDALS followed. The last puppet Western emperor abdicated in 476, but the BYZANTINE EMPIRE lasted until 1453 (see also JUSTINIAN; BELISARIUS). The HOLY ROMAN EMPIRE was not established until 800.

ROME, Harold (1908–   ), US composer and lyricist. He wrote words and music for many Broadway productions, including *Wish You Were Here*, *Fanny*, *Destry Rides Again* and *I Can Get It for You Wholesale*.

ROMMEL, Erwin (1891–1944), German field marshal, named the "Desert Fox" for his tactical genius as commander of the *Afrika Korps* 1941–43. His E advance ended with the battle of EL ALAMEIN. He commanded Army Group B in N France when the Allies landed in Normandy (he had led an armored division into France, 1940). After being wounded, he was implicated in the July 1944 plot to assassinate Hitler. Given the choice of suicide or trial, he took poison.

ROMNEY, George (1734–1802), English portrait painter, rival of REYNOLDS in late 18th-century London. Influenced by classical sculpture (he spent two years in Italy), he tended to flatter his sitters, among whom was Lady HAMILTON.

RÓMULO, Carlos Pena (1901–   ), Filipino journalist and statesman. His broadcasts during the Japanese occupation of the Philippines were known as "the Voice of Freedom." He won a 1941 Pulitzer Prize, and was ambassador to the US, president of the UN general assembly 1949–50, Filipino education secretary 1966–69, and foreign secretary from 1969.

ROMULUS AND REMUS, mythical founders of Rome (by tradition in 753 BC), twin sons of Rhea Silvia, descendant of AENEAS, by MARS. Abandoned as infants, they were suckled by a she-wolf until adopted by a herdsman. After long rivalry, Remus was killed by Romulus, who became the first king of Rome and was later worshiped as the god QUIRINUS.

RONDO, musical composition, derived from the medieval verse *rondeau*, in which repeats of a refrain or theme alternate with other contrasting sections. It became the finale of 18th-century sonatas and symphonies.

RONSARD, Pierre de (1524–1585), 16th-century French "Prince of Poets," leader of the influential PLÉIADE. Best known as a lyric poet, as in *Sonnets for Hélène* (1578), he also wrote lofty *Hymnes* (1556) on more public subjects and an epic, *La Franciade* (1572).

ROONEY, Mickey (1920–   ), US actor, a gifted entertainer who was a child and teenage star of the 1930s in such films as *A Midsummer Night's Dream* (1935), in which he played Puck, *Boy's Town* (1938), *Babes in Arms* (1939) and the Andy Hardy series. He later played character roles in films and starred in the Broadway musical *Sugar Babies* (1980–81).

ROOSEVELT, (Anna) Eleanor (1884–1962), US humanitarian, wife of Franklin Delano Roosevelt and niece of Theodore Roosevelt. Active in politics and social issues (notably for women and minority groups), she was a UN delegate (1945–53, 1961) and coauthored the Universal Declaration of Human Rights. Her many books included *This is My Story* (1937) and *On My Own* (1958).

Born: Jan. 30, 1882
Died: April 12, 1945
Term of office: March 4, 1933—April 12, 1945
Political party: Democratic

ROOSEVELT, Franklin Delano (1882–1945), 32nd and longest-serving US president (1933–45). His twelve years of office included the Great Depression and a global war. Born of Dutch descent in Hyde Park, N.Y., on Jan. 30, 1882, and brought up in "aristocratic" surroundings, he graduated from Harvard and married his distant cousin, Eleanor Roosevelt, in 1905; they had six children. In 1910, after a spell at Columbia U. law school, he worked in a N.Y. law firm until elected as a Democrat to the N.Y. Senate. He established himself as a leading Democrat and opponent of TAMMANY HALL. In 1913 he became assistant secretary of the navy, and ran unsuccessfully in 1920 as Democratic vice-presidential candidate. He suffered a severe attack of polio in Aug. 1921, and became partially paralyzed. He returned to politics in 1924 and was elected governor of N.Y. in 1928 (reelected 1930) and finally US president in 1933, when he stood against Herbert HOOVER. The GREAT DEPRESSION had begun in 1929, and Roosevelt attempted to combat it with the NEW DEAL, beginning with the "Hundred Days" during which nearly all the preliminary New Deal legislation was passed. Everybody appeared to benefit, farmer, industrialist and worker. (See AGRICULTURAL ADJUSTMENT ADMINISTRATION; CIVILIAN CONSERVATION CORPS; NATIONAL RECOVERY ADMINISTRATION; TENNESSEE VALLEY AUTHORITY.) In 1933 Roosevelt launched the GOOD NEIGHBOR POLICY in Latin America and recognized the Soviet government. After increasing criticism from both sides Roosevelt turned his administration in the second phase of the New Deal sharply to the left, introducing the WAGNER ACT of 1935, the massive relief program of the WORKS PROJECTS ADMINISTRATION, a tax reform bill, a social security act and a youth administration. He was reelected in 1936, but labor violence and his efforts to reform the Supreme Court and purge conservative Congressmen damaged his prestige. Reelected again after WWII had broken out, he tried to keep the US out of war, although aiding Britain (see ATLANTIC CHARTER; FOUR FREEDOMS; LEND-LEASE). But four days after the PEARL HARBOR attack, he declared war against Japan, Germany and Italy. He easily won reelection for a fourth term in 1944 on the slogan "don't change horses in midstream!" However, his health was failing, and he died suddenly on April 12, 1945, of a cerebral hemorrhage.

ROOSEVELT, Theodore (1858–1919), 26th US president (1901–09), affectionately known as "Teddy" or "T.R.," one of the most popular presidents as well as the youngest, at 42. He was at different times both a progressive and a conservative. His great energy took him outside politics on many hunting and exploring expeditions; he published over 2,000 works on history, politics and his travels. Born in New York City into an established middle-class family, he graduated from Harvard and in 1880 married Alice Hathaway Lee, who died four years later leaving a daughter. He became a rancher in Dakota Territory. In 1886 he returned to New York City and married Edith Kermit Carow, by whom he had five children. He ran unsuccessfully as Republican candidate for mayor, but established a reputation as an efficient administrator and reformer while a commissioner for the Civil Service and the New York City police. As assistant secretary of the navy (1897–98), he advocated the buildup of a strong fleet and when war broke out with Spain, he joined it in Cuba with his famous volunteer cavalry troop, the ROUGH RIDERS. He returned a national hero, and for two years served as governor of N.Y. He was persuaded to run with McKinley for vice-president in 1908 and took over the presidency when McKinley was assassinated on Sept. 6, 1901. He tried to regulate the evergrowing industrial and financial monopolies, using the 1890 SHERMAN ANTITRUST ACT. Despite his "trust-busting," he tried to give both labor and business a "square deal." Reelected in 1904, he secured passage of the Hepburn Act (1906) to prevent abuses in railroad shipping rates, and the Pure Food and Drug Act. He was proudest of his conservation program, which added over 250 million acres to the national forests. His foreign policy was intent on expansion (see PANAMA CANAL); but he won the 1906 Nobel Peace Prize for mediating in the RUSSO-JAPANESE WAR (see GENTLEMAN'S AGREEMENT). He also proclaimed the so-called "Roosevelt Corollary" of the MONROE DOCTRINE, reserving the role of international policeman for the US. He withdrew from election in 1904, chosing W. H. TAFT as his successor; he contested the

Born: Oct. 27, 1858
Died: Jan. 6, 1919
Term of office: Sept. 14, 1901–March 3, 1909
Political party: Republican

1912 election for the PROGRESSIVE PARTY. When Woodrow WILSON was elected, he retired from politics to lead an expedition into South America. He died of a blood clot in 1919.

ROOT, in ALGEBRA, one of the equal factors of a given number: if $x^n = c$, then x is the nth root of c, written $x^n \sqrt{c}$ (see EXPONENT; POWER.) The 2nd and 3rd roots of a number are specially named the square and cube roots respectively. Of particular interest is i, the imaginary square root of 1 (see COMPLEX NUMBERS).

ROOT, Elihu (1845–1937), US statesman. A successful corporation lawyer, he reorganized the command structure of the army as war secretary under President McKinley, and as Roosevelt's secretary of state developed a pattern of administration for the new possessions won from Spain. A champion of the League of Nations and the World Court, he won the 1912 Nobel Peace Prize for work as an international negotiator. He was also a N.Y. Republican senator 1909–15.

ROOTS, that part of a PLANT which absorbs water and nutrients from the soil and anchors the plant to the ground. Water and nutrients enter a root through minute root hairs sited at the tip of each root. Roots need oxygen to function and plants growing in swamps have special adaptations to supply it, like the "knees" of BALD CYPRESS trees and the aerial roots of MANGROVE. There are two main types of root systems: the taproot system, where there is a strong main root from which smaller secondary and tertiary roots branch out; and the fibrous root system where a mass of equal-sized roots are produced. In plants such as the SUGAR BEET, the taproot may become swollen with stored food material. Adventitious roots anchor the stems of climbing plants, such as IVY. Epiphytic plants such as ORCHIDS have roots that absorb moisture from the air (see EPIPHYTE). The roots of parasitic plants such as MISTLETOE and DODDER absorb food from other plants.

ROREM, Ned (1923–   ), US composer of melodic art-songs whose texts were drawn from the works of 20th-century American poets. His *Air Music* won the 1976 Pulitzer Prize. He published five volumes of diaries (1966–78).

RORSCHACH, Hermann (1884–1922), Swiss psychoanalyst who devised the **Rorschach Test** (c1920), in which the subject looks at a series of ten symmetrical inkblots, and describes what he sees there. It is intended that, from his description, details of his personality can be deduced.

ROSE, Billy (William Rosenberg;

1899–1966), US showman. He wrote songs during the 1920s ("Me and My Shadow," "That Old Gang of Mine") before producing hit Broadway shows including *Jumbo* (1935) and *Carmen Jones* (1943). He founded several NYC nightclubs and produced the *Aquacade* at the New York World's Fair (1939).

ROSE, Pete (1942–   ), US baseball player. In August 1981 he became the National League player with the greatest number of career hits. He also established records for the most 200-hit seasons (10) and the longest modern NL hitting streak (44 games).

ROSEBERY, Archibald Philip Primrose, 5th Earl of (1847–1929), British Liberal statesman, foreign secretary (1886, 1892–94) and successor as prime minister to GLADSTONE (1894–95). An opponent of Irish HOME RULE, he resigned because his imperialist views were rejected by his party.

ROSENBERG CASE. In 1950, Julius Rosenberg, an electrical engineer, and his wife, Ethel, were indicted for treason, accused of being members of a major Soviet spy ring and of having passed atomic secrets to the Russians. The chief witness against them was Mrs. Rosenberg's brother, David Greenglass, an army sergeant at Los Alamos, who said that the Rosenbergs had recruited him as an enemy agent. They denied the charge, but were convicted and sentenced to death. The case was an international *cause célèbre*; many people believed that the Rosenbergs were innocent (or at least that she was) and/or that the information they had allegedly passed was not of great significance. Nevertheless, in 1953, they were electrocuted at Sing Sing prison, the first US citizens to be executed for treason.

ROSENQUIST, James (1933–   ), US painter who turned his early billboard-painting career into a style of art. His gigantic images of movie stars, such as Kirk Douglas, and objects of cultural impact, such as *F-111*, put him in the vanguard of POP ART.

ROSENWALD, Julius (1862–1932), US businessman and philanthropist. He worked with Sears Roebuck and Co. for 35 years to make it the largest mail-order firm in the world, and gave some $63 million to charities, including the Julius Rosenwald Fund (1917–48) to provide educational facilities for Blacks.

ROSE OF LIMA, Saint (1586–1617), born in Lima, Peru, first canonized saint in the New World and patron saint of South America. She was canonized by Pope Clement X in 1671.

ROSES, Wars of the, intermittent struggle for the English throne between the noble houses of Lancaster (emblem, a red rose) and York (badge, a white rose). Dissatisfied by the weak government of the Lancastrian HENRY VI and the defeats of the English at the end of the HUNDRED YEARS' WAR, the Earl of WARWICK (the "king-maker"), using as figurehead Richard, Duke of York, captured Henry in 1455 and took control of government. MARGARET OF ANJOU, Henry's queen, fought to regain power (1459–64) and killed York but, as Warwick proclaimed York's son EDWARD IV, the attempt failed. A second Lancastrian attempt (1471), this time aided by LOUIS XI of France and the disaffected Warwick, also failed. With Warwick and Henry dead and Margaret captured, Edward reigned in peace until his death in 1483. His young son, EDWARD V, was supplanted by his uncle, RICHARD III. The final Lancastrian claim was made by Henry Tudor, who killed Richard at Bosworth (1485) and was crowned HENRY VII in 1485. He linked York and Lancaster by marrying Elizabeth, the daughter of Edward IV.

ROSETTA STONE, an inscribed basalt slab, discovered in 1799, which provided the key to the decipherment of Egyptian HIEROGLYPHICS. About 1.2m long and 0.75m wide, it is inscribed with identical texts in Greek, Egyptian demotic and Egyptian hieroglyphs. Decipherment was begun by Thomas YOUNG (c1818) and completed by Jean-François CHAMPOLLION (c1821–22). Found near Rosetta, Egypt, the stone is now in the British Museum.

ROSH HASHANAH (Hebrew: head of the year), the Jewish New Year, observed on the first day of the seventh Jewish month, Tishri (usually in Sept.). It is revered as the Day of Judgment when each person's fate is inscribed in the Book of Life. The *shofar* (ram's horn) calls Jews to ten days of penitence which end on YOM KIPPUR.

ROSICRUCIANS, worldwide group of secret brotherhoods claiming esoteric wisdom, tinged with MYSTICISM, sometimes with MASONRY and the CABALA. The movement's stimulus was *Fama Fraternitatis* (1614), relating the purported travels of, and secrets learned by, Christian Rosenkreuz.

ROSS, Betsy (1752–1836), American seamstress who is said to have made, to George Washington's design, the first US flag (1776).

ROSS, Diana (1944–   ), US singer who with Florence Ballard and Mary Wilson comprised the popular singing group, The Supremes. Their hits included "Baby Love" and "I Hear A Symphony." Diana Ross went on to a solo singing and a film career that includes a portrayal of Billie HOLIDAY in *Lady Sings The Blues*.

ROSS, Edward Alsworth (1866–1951), US sociologist and author of *Social Control* (1901), *Social Psychology* (1908) and *The Principles of Sociology* (1920). A political progressive, he taught at the University of Wisconsin (1906–37) and served as chairman of the American Civil Liberties Union (1940–50).

ROSS, Harold Wallace (1892–1951), founder (1925) and lifetime editor of the *New Yorker* magazine. Originally conceived as basically by and for New Yorkers, the magazine won national prestige and has had an enduring effect on American journalism and literature.

ROSS, Nellie (1876–1977), US public official. Elected to succeed her husband, who had died, she was the first woman governor of a state (Wyoming 1935–37). She was director of the US Mint 1933–35.

ROSSELINO, two Italian Renaissance sculptor-architects. **Bernardo** (1409–1464) made the tomb of Leonardo Bruni in Santa Croce, Florence. He taught his brother **Antonio** (1427–1479), whose works in Florence and elsewhere include tombs, fine stone reliefs and incisive portraits.

ROSSELLINI, Roberto (1906–   ), Italian film director. His *Open City* (1946), partly made up of footage of the Italian resistance during WWII, established him as a leader of the neorealist movement. He returned to this style in *Generale della Rovere* (1959), but later turned to educational films.

ROSSETTI, name of two leading English Victorian artists. The poems of **Christina Georgina Rossetti** (1830–1894), a devout Anglican, ranged from fantasy (*Goblin Market*, 1862) to religious poetry. Her brother, **Dante Gabriel Rossetti** (1828–1882), was a founder of the PRE-RAPHAELITES. His paintings, of languid, mystical beauty, have subjects from Dante and medieval romance. As a poet he excelled, notably in his exquisite love sonnets.

ROSSINI, Gioacchino Antonio (1792–1868), Italian composer best known for his comic operas, especially *The Barber of Seville* (1816). The dramatic grand opera *William Tell* (1829), with its famous overture, was his last opera; always lazy by nature, he then retired. He was admired by WAGNER and BEETHOVEN, among others.

ROSSO II (Giovan Battista di Iacopo di Gasparre; 1495–1540), Italian painter. *The Deposition* (1521) exemplifies the elongat-

ed figures, hectic color and emotionalism of his paintings. He decorated the François I gallery at FONTAINEBLEAU and brought MANNERISM to France.

ROSS SEA, Antarctic inlet of the S Pacific Ocean, between Victoria Land and Edward VII Peninsula. Its S limit is the 400mi Ross Ice Shelf, and it contains Ross Island, with the 12,450ft Mt Erebus, the most southerly active volcano known.

ROSTAND, Edmond (1868–1918), French dramatist, famous for his play *Cyrano de Bergerac* (1897), which led a Romantic revival.

ROSTOW, Walt Whitman (1916–   ), US economist; he developed a controversial theory that linked social and political development to economic growth in his books *The Process of Economic Growth* (1952) and *Stages of Economic Growth* (1960). A close adviser to Presidents John F. Kennedy and Lyndon B. Johnson, he played a key role in planning US intervention in Vietnam during the 1960s.

ROSTROPOVICH, Mstislav Leopoldovich (1927–   ), Russian cellist. A celebrated musician, he had works composed for him by PROKOFIEV, SHOSTAKOVICH, and some non-Soviet composers, such as BRITTEN. He made his US debut in 1956, and since the mid-1970s he and his wife, the soprano Galina Vishnevskaya, have lived outside the USSR. He became conductor of the National Symphony Orchestra, Washington, D.C., in 1977.

ROSZAK, Theodore (1907–1981), Polish-born US sculptor. Best known for his sinister, birdlike figures in steel and bronze, he also designed the 45ft spire of the Massachusetts Institute of Technology chapel.

ROTARY INTERNATIONAL, governing body of over 14,000 Rotary Clubs in 148 countries. Members, mostly professional and businessmen, aim to promote high standards of service in both work and welfare spheres. The first was started in 1905 by a Chicago lawyer, Paul Harris; meetings were held in members' offices in rotation.

ROTH, Philip (1933–   ), leading US novelist and short story writer. His protagonists agonize between a traditional Jewish upbringing and modern urban society. His first novel was *Goodbye Columbus* (1959), and his best-known work is *Portnoy's Complaint* (1969), a hilarious, bitter account of sexual frustration. He also wrote *Our Gang* (1971) and *The Ghost Writer* (1979).

ROTHKO, Mark (1903–1970), Russian-born US painter, a leader of New York

ABSTRACT EXPRESSIONISM. On large canvases he used rich and somber colors to create designs of simple, lightly painted rectangular shapes.

ROTHSCHILD, family of European Jewish bankers who wielded considerable political influence for nearly two centuries. The founder of the house was **Mayer Anselm Rothschild** (1743–1812), who established banks at Frankfurt, Vienna, London, Naples and Paris, with his sons as managers. The financial genius who raised the business to dominance in Europe was his son **Nathan Mayer Rothschild** (1777–1836), who handled Allied loans for the campaign against Napoleon. His son **Baron Lionel de Rothschild,** was the first Jewish MP in England.

ROTTERDAM, commercial and industrial seaport in South Holland province, second largest city in the Netherlands. Site of the Rotterdam-Europoort industrial and harbor complex, it lies at the center of an extensive canal system connecting with other parts of the Netherlands and the German Rhine ports and RUHR. Major industries include shipyards and oil refineries. Pop 579,200.

ROUAULT, Georges (1871–1958), French painter and graphic artist known especially for his intense religious paintings such as *The Three Judges* (1913). Influenced by medieval stained glass work, he developed a distinctive style with the use of thick black outlines.

ROULETTE, popular game of chance. The roulette wheel is divided into a series of small compartments, alternatively black and red, numbered 1 to 36 with an additional zero (the US game sometimes has two zeros). A croupier spins the wheel and releases into it a small ivory ball. Players bet on where (usually which number or which color) the ball will settle.

ROUND (in music). See CANON.

ROUNDERS, British game played with a stick and ball by two teams of nine. The game is very similar to, and may be an ancestor of, BASEBALL.

ROUNDHEADS, an originally derogatory name for Puritans in the Parliamentary forces in the English CIVIL WAR. Many wore their hair closely cropped, in sharp contrast to their royalist opponents.

ROUNDWORMS, the **Nematodes,** among the commonest and most widely distributed of invertebrates. Although best known as parasites of man and his domestic animals, the majority are free-living and there are terrestrial, freshwater and marine forms. All roundworms are long and thin, tapering at each end. The outside of the body is covered with a complex cuticle. The sexes are usually separate. The internal organs are suspended within a fluid-filled body cavity or pseudocoel. The free-living and plant-parasitic forms are usually microscopic, but animal-parasitic species may reach a considerable length— the Guinea worm, up to 1m (3.3ft). Nematodes are divided into the Adenophorea, containing the majority of free-living forms, and the Sercenentea, which contains the parasitic orders.

ROUSSEAU, Henri (1844–1910), known as *Le Douanier,* self-taught French "primitive" painter much admired by GAUGUIN, PICASSO and others. He is known mainly for his portraits, landscapes and jungle paintings, such as *Sleeping Gypsy* (1897) and *Virgin Forest at Sunset* (1907).

ROUSSEAU, Jean Jacques (1712–1778), Swiss-born French writer, philosopher and political theorist. He wrote for DIDEROT'S *Encyclopédie* in Paris from 1745. Made famous by his essay on how arts and sciences corrupt human behavior (1749) he argued in an essay on the *Origin of the Inequality of Man* (1755) that man's golden age was that of primitive communal living. *The Social Contract* (1762), influential in the FRENCH REVOLUTION, claimed that when men form a social contract to live in society they delegate sovereignty to a government; but that sovereignty resides ultimately with the people, who can withdraw it when necessary. His didactic novel *Emile* (1762) suggested that education should build on a child's natural interests and sympathies, gradually developing its potential. *Confessions* (1782) describe Rousseau's romantic feelings of affinity with nature.

ROUSSEAU, (Pierre Etienne) Théodore (1812–1867), French landscape painter, a leader of the BARBIZON SCHOOL. His scenes of wooded landscapes at sunset include *Coming out of the Fontainebleau woods* (c1850).

ROUSSEL, Albert Charles Paul Marie (1869–1937), French composer. Although influenced by DEBUSSY, D'INDY and visits to the East, his music was based on contrapuntal rather than tonal construction, varying in style from *The Feast of the Spider* (1913) to *Padmavati* (1914–18).

ROWING, propelling a boat by means of oars. In sport there are two types: *sculling,* in which each oarsman uses two oars, and *sweep rowing,* in which each has one. In the US, competitive team rowing is known as *crew.* For speed, the craft (shells) are long, narrow and light. The first recorded race was held on the Thames R, London (1716).

The annual Oxford-Cambridge race began in 1829, and the Yale-Harvard race in 1852. The most famous international rowing event is England's annual Henley Royal Regatta (from 1839).

ROWLANDSON, Thomas (1756–1827), English caricaturist, etcher and painter. His work is a valuable though satirical record of contemporary English life. His work includes *The English Dance of Death* (1815–16) and illustrations for *The Tour of Dr Syntax in Search of the Picturesque* (3 vols.; 1812–21).

ROXAS Y ACUÑA, Manuel (1894–1948), first president of the Philippine republic, 1946–48; earlier he had been a member of the Japanese-sponsored Philippine puppet government in WWII. His administration was marked by corruption.

ROY, Gabrielle (1909–   ), French-Canadian novelist noted for her portrayals of poor urban workers in *The Tin Flute* (1947) and *The Cashier* (1955). Some of her novels, such as *Street of Riches* (1957), are set in the isolated rural landscape of her native Manitoba.

ROYAL ACADEMY OF ARTS, British institution founded 1768 by George III, first president being Joshua REYNOLDS. It has a president, 40 academicians (RA) and 30–35 associates. It maintains an art school and holds an open summer exhibition.

ROYAL CANADIAN MOUNTED POLICE, Canadian federal police force. It was formed 1873, as the North West Mounted Police, to bring law and order to the new Canadian territories. In 1874, the NWMP numbered 300 men and their persistence and determination became legendary: "the Mounties always get their man." In 1904 the force numbered 6,000 and was given the prefix "Royal." In 1920 it absorbed the Dominion Police and received its present name and duties. Its 19,000 members, including 250 women, serve as a provincial police force in the nation's provinces (excluding Ontario and Quebec).

ROYAL SOCIETY OF LONDON FOR THE IMPROVEMENT OF NATURAL KNOWLEDGE, the premier English scientific society. Probably the most famous scientific society in the world, it also has a claim to be the oldest surviving. It had its origins in weekly meetings of scientists in London in the 1640s and was granted a royal charter by Charles II in 1660. Past presidents include Samuel PEPYS, Sir Isaac NEWTON and Lord RUTHERFORD.

ROYCE, Josiah (1855–1916), US philosopher, a major proponent of IDEALISM. Influenced by HEGEL, and SCHOPENHAUER, he conceived the absolute in terms of will

and purpose in *The World and the Individual* (1901–02). Among his other major works was *The Problem of Christianity* (1913), in which he developed his metaphysic of interpretation and community.

RUBBER, an elastic substance; that is, one which quickly restores itself to its original size after it has been stretched or compressed. Natural rubber is obtained from many plants, and commercially from *Hevea brasiliensis*, a tree native to South America and cultivated also in SE Asia and W Africa. A slanting cut is made in the bark, and the milky fluid latex, occurring in the inner bark, is tapped off. The latex—an aqueous COLLOID of rubber and other particles—is coagulated with dilute acid, and the rubber creped or sheeted and smoked. Natural rubber is a chain POLYMER of ISOPRENE, known as caoutchouc when pure; its elasticity is due to the chains being randomly coiled, but tending to straighten when the rubber is stretched. Known to have been used by the Aztecs since the 6th century AD, and first known in Europe in the 16th century, it was a mere curiosity until the pioneer work of Thomas Hancock (1786–1865) and Charles MACINTOSH. Synthetic rubbers have been produced since WWI, and the industry has developed greatly during and since WWII. They are long-chain polymers, elastomers; the main types are: copolymers of butadiene/styrene, butadiene/nitriles and ethylene/propylene; polymers of chloroprene (neoprene rubber), butadiene, isobutylene and SILICONES; and polyurethanes, polysulfide rubbers and chlorosulfonated polyethylenes. Some latex (natural or synthetic) is used as an adhesive and for making rubber coatings, rubber thread and foam rubber. Most, however, is coagulated, and the rubber is treated by VULCANIZATION and the addition of reinforcing and inert fillers and antioxidants, before being used in tires, shoes, rainwear, belts, hoses, insulation and many other applications.

RUBBER PLANT, or India rubber fig, *Ficus elastica*, a popular house plant, native to India and the E Indies. It was once grown for its gum, which was made into india-rubber erasers. Family: Moraceae.

RUBELLA. See GERMAN MEASLES.

RUBENS, Peter Paul (1577–1640), Flemish artist, one of the greatest BAROQUE painters. Influenced by TINTORETTO, TITIAN and VERONESE, he developed an exuberant style depending on a rich handling of color and sensuous effects. His works include portraits and mythological, allegorical and religious subjects such as *Raising of the*

Cross (1610), *Descent from the Cross* (1612), *History of Marie de Médicis* (1622–25), *Judgment of Paris* (c1638) and portraits of his wife. His works influenced many artists, including VAN DYCK and RENOIR.

RUBICON, river in N central Italy which formed the boundary between Italy and Cisalpine Gaul during the Roman Republic. In 49 BC, Julius CAESAR led his army across the river into Italy, so committing himself to civil war against POMPEY. To "cross the Rubicon" means to take an irrevocable decision.

RUBIK'S CUBE, or Magic Cube, a puzzle of immense popularity in the early 1980s, invented in 1975 by Ernö Rubik, a Hungarian teacher of architecture and design (and, independently, a year later by Terutoshi Ishigi, owner of a Japanese ironworks). The cube is composed of smaller 6-color cubes, 9 to a side, aligned in such a way that, in the starting position, each side of the composite cube shows only one color. Each face can be rotated around its central cube, thus quickly scrambling the solid colors on each side. The small cubes can be arranged in some 43 trillion combinations. It may take even very clever people anywhere from 5 hours to a year of work to return a Rubik's cube to its original alignment, although "champions" can often solve the cube in less than 30 seconds.

RUBINSTEIN, Anton Grigoryevich (1829–1894), Russian piano virtuoso and composer. In 1862 he founded the St. Petersburg Conservatory, where he was director 1862–67 and 1887–91.

RUBINSTEIN, Arthur (1889–), Polish-born US pianist who has remained at the top of his profession for over 70 years. He is especially famous for his interpretations of CHOPIN.

RUBINSTEIN, Helena (1872–1965), Polish-born US cosmetics magnate with an empire of salons in London, Paris, New York and other cities. She introduced tinted face powder and foundation for women, and originated cosmetics for men.

RUBY, deep-red GEM stone, a variety of CORUNDUM colored by a minute proportion of chromium ions. It is found significantly only in upper Burma, Thailand and Sri Lanka, and is more precious by far than diamond. The name has been used for other red stones, chiefly varieties of garnet and spinel. Rubies have been synthesized by the Verneuil flame-fusion process (1902). They are used to make ruby LASERS.

RUBY, Jack (1911–1967), nightclub owner who fatally shot Lee Harvey OSWALD, presumed assassin of President KENNEDY, on Nov. 24, 1963, before a "live" TV audience.

RUDE, François (1784–1855), French sculptor. His neoclassical works include the *Neapolitan Fisherboy* (1833), but most of his works, such as *Departure of the Volunteers of 1792* (1835–36), are dramatically realistic.

RUDOLF (1858–1889), archduke and crown prince of the Austro–Hungarian Empire. He and 17-year-old Baroness Mary Vetsera were found shot in the royal hunting lodge at Mayerling, apparent victims of a suicide pact. The exact circumstances of the deaths, which caused endless speculation, have never been clarified.

RUDOLPH, Paul Marvin (1918–), US architect connected with Yale U. (1958–65), where his campus buildings include a controversial art and architecture building. He turned away from the International style to experiment with externally visible ducts, a futuristic parking facility and stacking mobile home frames.

RUDOLPH, Wilma (1940–), US Olympic sprinter who held world records in the 100- and 200-meter dashes. At the 1960 Olympics she became the first American woman to win three gold medals and the first to win both at 100 and 200 meters.

RUGBY, ball game possibly originated at Rugby school, England during a SOCCER match (1823). Play is on a field 75yd wide by 110yd between goal lines. There are two 40min "halves." In Rugby Union there are 15 players per side, in Rugby League, 13. Each side attempts to ground the oval leather-covered ball beyond the opponents' goal: this, a try, is worth 4 points; place-kicking a goal after a try is 2 further points; and a goal from a free, or penalty kick, or from a drop-kick during play, 3. The game is similar to American FOOTBALL, but little protective equipment is worn and play is almost continuous.

RUGGLES, Carl (1876–1971), controversial US composer. His often dissonant style may be heard in the symphonic poems *Men and Mountains* (1924) and *Sun-Treader* (1927–32). He also achieved recognition as a painter.

RUGS AND CARPETS. Reed mats date from at least 5000 BC, but carpet-weaving with sheep's wool was first highly developed in the Near East. Persian carpets were internationally famous by 600 AD. Their vivid, long-lasting dyes came from natural materials such as bark and roots. Persian designs influenced the 16th- and 17th-century carpets of India's Mogul courts, and the beautiful Chinese carpets produced from the 14th to 17th centuries.

Carpet-weaving spread in the West, particularly in the 17th century, via France, Belgium and England.

Oriental carpets were woven on looms, still the basic technique of carpet-making. Foundation threads (the *warp*) are stretched on the loom; crosswise foundation threads are called the *weft*. The surface material (*pile*) is made by tying small tufts of fiber, usually wool, to the warp. Today, major types of the more expensive loom-made carpets and rugs are: *Axminster, chenille, velvet* and *Wilton. Tufted* carpets are made by machines which do the tufting with hundreds of needles onto a prewoven backing, attached to a latex rubber base. Knitted carpets use a combination of loom and tufting processes. (See also TAPESTRY; WEAVING.)

RUHR, great coal-mining and iron-and-steel industrial region in West Germany. It lies mainly E of the Rhine R, between the valleys of the Ruhr and Lippe rivers, and has more than 30 large cities and towns merged into one industrial megalopolis. Chief cities include Düsseldorf, Essen and Dortmund. Materials are transported by the Rhine R, Dortmund-Ems Canal, Rhine-Herne Canal, and road and rail networks.

RUISDAEL, Jacob van (c1629–1682), greatest Dutch landscape painter of the 17th century. He favored a new heroic-romantic style in which small figures are dwarfed by forests, stormy seas and magnificent cloudscapes.

RUIZ CORTINES, Adolfo (1890–1973), Mexican president, 1952–58. During his presidency, corruption was curbed, the "march to the sea" to aid the maritime industry was initiated, agriculture was assisted through widespread irrigation, and women were given the vote.

RUM, alcoholic liquor, usually produced by distilling fermented MOLASSES. It acquires a brown color from the wooden casks in which it is stored and from added CARAMEL or burnt sugar. It is made mainly in the W Indies. (See also ALCOHOLIC BEVERAGES.)

RUMANIA. See ROMANIA.

RUMANIAN, official language of ROMANIA. Descended from the Latin of DACIA province, it is a ROMANCE LANGUAGE with Greek, Hungarian, Slavic and Turkish influences. In the 18th century, the script changed from Cyrillic to the Latin alphabet.

RUMFORD, Sir Benjamin Thompson, Count (1753–1814), American-born adventurer and scientist best known for his recognition of the relation between WORK and HEAT (inspired by observation of heat generated by FRICTION during the boring of cannon), which laid the foundations for JOULE's later work. He played a primary role in the founding of the ROYAL INSTITUTION (1799), to which he also introduced Humphry DAVY.

RUMI, or Jalal-ad-din Rumi (1207–1273), great Sufi poet and mystic of Persia. His major work was the *Mathnawi*, a poetic exposition of Sufi wisdom in some 27,000 couplets.

RUMINANTS, animals that regurgitate and rechew their food once having swallowed it. They feed by filling one compartment of a three-or four-chambered stomach with unmasticated food, bringing it back up to the mouth again to be fully chewed and finally swallowed. It is an adaptation in many herbivores to increase the time available for the digestion of relatively indigestible vegetable matter.

RUML, Beardsley (1894–1960), US economist, banker and businessman who promoted social science research as president of the Laura Spelman Rockefeller Memorial Fund 1922–29 and dean of the University of Chicago 1931–33. He devised the "pay-as-you-go" income tax plan (1943), was chairman of New York's Federal Reserve Bank 1941–47 and helped to set up the International Monetary Fund and the World Bank.

RUMMY, any of a group of card games derived from Spanish *con quien* (with whom). In basic rummy, devised about 1895, the object is to lay down as many sets (*melds*) of cards as possible. Melds consist of three or four cards of the same value in different suits or sequences of three or four cards in the same suit. Melding an entire hand in one turn is a *rummy*. Gin rummy is a popular two-handed form of the game. Another variation of rummy is CANASTA.

RUMP PARLIAMENT, 60 remaining members of the British LONG PARLIAMENT after Col. Thomas Pride in "Pride's Purge" had ejected all opposition to Oliver CROMWELL's army (1648). They created a high court which tried CHARLES I and had him executed (1649), abolished the House of Lords and monarchy, and established a ruling Council of State. The attempt to pass a bill prolonging its life indefinitely led to the Rump's forcible dissolution by Cromwell (1653–59). Purged members returned in 1660, prior to the RESTORATION. (See CIVIL WAR, ENGLISH.)

RUNDSTEDT, Karl Rudolf Gerd von (1875–1953), German field marshal. In WWII he led army groups in Poland, France and Russia, was military ruler of France, and commander, W Europe, on

D-DAY and during the Battle of the BULGE.

RUNES, characters of a pre-Christian writing system used by the Teutonic tribes of N Europe from as early as the 3rd century BC to as late as the 10th century AD, and sometimes after. The three distinct types are Early, Anglo-Saxon and Scandinavian. The Runic alphabet is sometimes known as **futhork** for its first six characters. (See also WRITING, HISTORY OF.)

RUNNING, a sport since ancient times. There are three basic classes: sprints, middle-distance and long-distance. Varieties include relay racing, STEEPLECHASING and cross-country. Non-competitive running as a form of exercise is often called jogging.

RUNNYMEDE, meadow in Surrey, S England, on the bank of the Thames R. Here King John conceded the barons' demands embodied in the MAGNA CARTA (1215). There is a memorial to President John F. Kennedy (unveiled 1965).

RUNYON, Alfred Damon (1884–1946), US journalist and writer. His entertaining stories of tough-talking gangsters, Broadway actors and the sporting underworld were written in the colorful vernacular of New York City. *Guys and Dolls* (1932), the first of several collections, was the basis of a successful musical (1950).

RUPERT, Prince (1619–1682), count palatine of the Rhine and duke of Bavaria, brilliant royalist cavalry commander in the English CIVIL WAR. Dismissed by his uncle Charles I after surrendering Bristol to parliamentarians (1645), he commanded a fleet which harried Commonwealth shipping (1648–50). After the RESTORATION, he was first lord of the admiralty. He introduced MEZZOTINT to Britain and was a founder of the HUDSON'S BAY COMPANY.

RUPERT'S LAND, or **Prince Rupert's Land,** vast, mineral-rich region of NW Canada granted to the HUDSON'S BAY COMPANY in 1670 by Charles II. Named for PRINCE RUPERT, it comprised the basin of Hudson Bay. In 1818, the US acquired the portion S of the 49th parallel. In 1869, the remainder became part of the NORTHWEST TERRITORIES.

RUPTURE, common name for HERNIA.

RURAL ELECTRIFICATION ADMINISTRATION (REA), agency of the US Department of Agriculture (since 1939), formed 1935 to finance distribution of electricity by giving loans to cooperatives, private utilities, public power districts etc.

RUSH, Benjamin (1746–1813), US physician, abolitionist and reformer. His greatest contribution to medical science was his conviction that insanity is a disease (see MENTAL ILLNESS): his *Medical Enquiries and Observations upon the Diseases of the Mind* (1812) was the first US book on PSYCHIATRY.

RUSHMORE, Mount, or **Mount Rushmore National Memorial,** rises to 5,600ft in the Black Hills, W S.D. In the granite of the NE face, 60ft portraits of presidents Washington, Jefferson, Lincoln and (Theodore) Roosevelt were carved 1925–41 by Gutzon BORGLUM.

RUSK, (David) Dean (1909–   ), US secretary of state, 1961–69, in the Kennedy and Johnson administrations. Previously a university professor and WWII army colonel, he worked in the Department of State (1946–52) and was president of the Rockefeller Foundation (1952–60). He became President Johnson's main spokesman on Vietnam. He later taught international law at the University of Georgia.

RUSKIN, John (1819–1900), English art critic, writer and reformer. The first volume of his *Modern Painters* (1843) championed J. M. W. TURNER. A major influence on the arts, he was behind the Victorian GOTHIC REVIVAL. *Unto This Last* (1862), first of his "letters" to workmen, attacked "laissez-faire" philosophy. An autobiography, *Praeterita* (1885–89), was unfinished.

RUSSELL, prominent family in British politics. The first member to gain national fame was **John Russell** (c1486–1555), created 1st earl of Bedford for helping Edward VI to quell a 1549 rebellion. The family fortune, including Woburn Abbey, Bedfordshire, was acquired during this period. **William, 5th earl** (1613–1700), was a parliamentary general in the Civil War. He was created 1st duke of Bedford in 1694, partly because of the fame, as a patriotic martyr, of his son Lord William RUSSELL (1639–1683), first notable WHIG in the family. The title of Lord John RUSSELL, 1st earl of Kingston Russell (1792–1878; third son of the 6th duke), was inherited by his grandson Bertrand RUSSELL.

RUSSELL, Bertrand Arthur William, 3rd Earl Russell (1872–1970), British philosopher, mathematician and man of letters. Initially subscribing to IDEALISM, he broke away in 1898 eventually to become an empiricist (see EMPIRICISM). His most important work was to relate LOGIC and MATHEMATICS. After having written to FREGE pointing out a paradox in Frege's attempt to reduce all mathematics to logical principles, Russell endeavored to perform this task himself. His results appeared in *The Principles of Mathematics* (1903) and, in collaboration with A. N. WHITEHEAD,

Principia Mathematica (3 vols., 1910–13). Russell was a vehement pacifist for much of his life, his views twice earning him prison sentences (1918, 1961): during the former he wrote his *Introduction to Mathematical Philosophy* (1919). His other works include *Marriage and Morals* (1929), *Education and the Social Order* (1932), *An Inquiry into Meaning and Truth* (1940), *History of Western Philosophy* (1945) and popularizations such as *The ABC of Relativity* (1925), as well as his *Autobiography* (3 vols., 1967–69). He received the 1950 Nobel Prize for Literature and founded the Bertrand Russell Peace Foundation in 1963.

RUSSELL, Bill (William Felton Russell; 1934–   ), US basketball player, in 1966 the first black coach of a major professional sports team. In his 13 years with the Boston Celtics (1956–69) the team won 11 NBA championships. He was one of the best defensive centers in the game's history.

RUSSELL, Charles Marion (1864–1926), US cowboy painter, sculptor and author. His many canvases of frontier life, Indians, horses and cattle camps, usually set in Mont., were enormously popular.

RUSSELL, George William (1867–1935), Irish poet, nationalist, mystic and painter, known under the pseudonym "A.E." A theosophist, he was with W. B. YEATS a leader of the CELTIC RENAISSANCE and a cofounder of Dublin's ABBEY THEATRE.

RUSSELL, Henry Norris (1877–1957), US astronomer who, independently of HERTZESPRUNG, showed the relation between a STAR's brightness and color: the resulting **Hertzsprung-Russell diagram** is important throughout astronomy and cosmology.

RUSSELL, Lillian (1861–1922), US singer, actress, flamboyant beauty of the "Gay Nineties." Born Helen Louise Leonard, she became a star in the show *The Great Mogul* (1881). She married four times, but her affair with "Diamond Jim" BRADY spanned 40 years.

RUSSELL, Lord John, 1st Earl Russell (1792–1878), British Whig statesman and liberal reformer. A leading supporter of the CATHOLIC EMANCIPATION ACT (1830), he also fought for the 1832 REFORM BILL. Twice prime minister (1846–52, 1865–66), he was influential in maintaining British neutrality in the US Civil War.

RUSSELL SAGE FOUNDATION. See SAGE, RUSSELL.

RUSSIAN, native language of 130 million Russians, chief official language of the USSR. Most important of the E Slavic INDO-EUROPEAN LANGUAGES (Byelorussian and Ukrainian diverged from c1300), Russian is written in the 33-character Cyrillic alphabet introduced in the 800s by Christian missionaries. A difficult language for English speakers, it has very different word-roots and is heavily inflected in nouns and verbs. By combining colloquialism with the formal Church Slavonic, the poet PUSHKIN did much to shape modern literary Russian, which is based on the Moscow dialect.

RUSSIAN REVOLUTION, momentous political upheaval which changed the course of world history. It destroyed the autocratic tsarist regime and culminated in the establishment of the world's first communist state, the Soviet Union (1922). Its roots lay in the political and economic backwardness of Russia and the chronic poverty of most of the people, expressed in rising discontent in the middle and lower classes since the late 1800s.

The Revolution of 1905 began on "Bloody Sunday," Jan. 22 (Jan. 9, old Russian calendar), when troops fired on a workers' demonstration in St. Petersburg. Widespread disorders followed, including mutiny on the battleship Potemkin and a national general strike organized by the St. Petersburg *soviet* (workers' council). These events, coupled with the disastrous RUSSO-JAPANESE WAR, forced Tsar Nicholas II to grant civil rights and set up an elected *duma* (parliament) in his "October Manifesto." Under premier B. A. STOLYPIN repression continued until late WWI, in which Russia suffered severe reverses.

The February Revolution (1917). Food shortages and strikes provoked riots and mutiny (March 8–10). A provisional government under the progressive Prince Georgi LVOV was set up (later headed by Alexander KERENSKY) and Nicholas II abdicated (March 15). **The October Revolution (1917).** On Nov. 6 (Oct. 24), the Bolsheviks, led by V. E. LENIN, staged an armed coup. Moscow was seized and the remnants of the provisional government arrested; the constitutional assembly was dispersed by Bolshevik troops and the CHEKA set up. Next day a Council of People's Commissars was set up, headed by Lenin and including Leon TROTSKY and Joseph STALIN. In the civil war (1918–20), the anticommunist "Whites," commanded by A. I. DENIKIN, A. V. KOLCHAK and P. N. WRANGEL were defeated. Russian involvement in WWI ended with the Treaty of BREST-LITOVSK. The tsar and his family were murdered at Ekaterinburg (July, 1918), and the new Soviet constitution made Lenin and the Communist (formerly Bolshevik) Party all-powerful.

RUSSIAN SOVIET FEDERATED SOCIALIST REPUBLIC (RSFSR), largest of the USSR's constituent republics, one of the original four united in the Soviet Union (1922). It holds over 50% of the population, and over 76% of the land area, of the Soviet Union. Its W section is a great plain broken only by the N-S Ural Mts. E of the Yenisey R lie eroded plateaus and ridges, with high, folded mountains in the S. About 83% of the population are Russians and there are some 38 other ethnic groups. The capital and largest city is Moscow, the chief port Leningrad. With 90% of Russia's forests, rich mineral resources and abundant hydroelectric power, the RSFSR provides about 70% of Russia's total industrial and agricultural output. (See USSR.)

RUSSIAN WOLFHOUND. See BORZOI.

RUSSO-FINNISH WARS, two conflicts during WWII. The first, the "Winter War" (1939–40), arose from rejection of Russian demands for military bases in Finland, territorial concessions and the dismantling of the MANNERHEIM line, Finland's defense system across the Karelian isthmus. When the Russians attacked (Nov. 30), the Finns unexpectedly threw them back. But in Feb., 1940 the Mannerheim line was broken and Finland signed the Peace of Moscow (March 12) surrendering about 10% of her territory, including much of KARELIA, Petsamo (now Pechenga) and Viipuri (Vyborg). In the "Continuation War" (1941–44), Finland fought alongside Nazi Germany, and was forced to pay $300 million reparations to the USSR and to lease it the PORKKALA area (returned in 1956).

RUSSO-GERMAN PACT, nonaggression pact signed by MOLOTOV and RIBBENTROP on Aug. 23, 1939. It cleared the way for Hitler's invasion of Poland (Sept 1.) which precipitated WWII, and for the division of Poland between Nazi Germany and Russia (which invaded Sept. 17 from the E).

RUSSO-JAPANESE WAR, 1904–05, culmination of rivalry in the Far East, where both powers sought expansion at the expense of the decaying Chinese empire. Russia occupied Manchuria during the BOXER REBELLION and coveted Korea. On Feb. 8, 1904 the Japanese attacked the Russian naval base of PORT ARTHUR (now Lü-shun) which they captured in Jan., 1905. The Russians were also defeated at MUKDEN in Manchuria and their Baltic fleet, sent to retrieve the situation, was destroyed in the battle of TSUSHIMA (May 27, 1905). Mediation by US president Theodore Roosevelt ended the war in the Treaty of PORTSMOUTH (1905). Russia ceded the Liaotung peninsula and S Sakhalin to Japan, recognized Japan's dominance in Korea and returned Manchuria to China. Russia's disastrous defeat was an immediate cause of the 1905 RUSSIAN REVOLUTION and won Japan great power status.

RUSSO-POLISH WAR, 1919–20, started when newly-constituted Poland, under Józef PILSUDSKI, joined with Ukrainian nationalist Simon PETLYURA to invade the Ukraine. Driven back by Soviet forces almost to Warsaw, the Poles with French aid forced Russian retreat. By the treaty of Riga (March 18, 1921) the Poles regained parts of BYELORUSSIA and the UKRAINE.

RUSSO-TURKISH WARS, fought intermittently over three centuries, were caused by Russia's determination to absorb the Black Sea coast and Caucasus, dominate the Balkans and control the Bosporus and Dardanelles straits. The first major Russian success was the capture of Azov by Peter I (the Great) in 1696. In two wars against the Turks (1768–74, 1787–91), Catherine the Great, allied with Austria, gained the rest of the Ukraine, the Crimea, and an outlet to the Black Sea and the straits. Russia adopted the role of protecting Christians in the declining OTTOMAN EMPIRE. Russia won Bessarabia in the war of 1806–12 and made further gains in the war of 1828–29. When Russia next pressured the Turks, France and Britain intervened, defeating Russia in the CRIMEAN WAR (1853–56). Russia regained territory in the last war of 1877–78, though the terms of the treaty of SAN STEFANO were modified by the congress of BERLIN (1878). Russia and Turkey were again opponents in WWI, and concluded a separate peace treaty (1921).

RUST, a large number of FUNGI which cause many PLANT DISEASES. They form red or orange spots, their spore-bearing organs, on the leaves of infected plants. Spores are carried by the wind to infect new plants. Some rusts are heteroecious: they alternate between two different host plants. The most important rust fungus is probably *Puccinia graminis* which causes black stem rust of wheat. (See also SMUT.)

RUSTIN, Bayard (1910–   ), US civil rights activist and pacifist. One of the original Freedom Riders (1947) for integration in the South, he helped found the SOUTHERN CHRISTIAN LEADERSHIP CONFERENCE and was chief organizer of the 1963 civil rights march on Washington. He became president of the A. Philip Randolph Institute in 1966.

RUTH, Moabite heroine of the Old Testament book bearing her name.

Widowed during a famine in the time of the JUDGES, Ruth followed her Judahite mother-in-law, Naomi, to Bethlehem. She survived by gleaning barley from the fields of her husband's next-of-kin, Boaz, who eventually married her. Their great-grandson was DAVID.

RUTH, Babe (George Herman Ruth; 1895–1948), famous US baseball player. An outstanding pitcher and hitter for the Boston Red Sox, he was sold to the New York Yankees in 1920 for the phenomenal sum of $125,000 and was largely responsible for building the team's prestige. In his 22 major league seasons, he hit 714 homeruns and his lifetime batting average was .342. A flamboyant figure, he was elected to the Baseball Hall of Fame in 1936. He established a season record of 60 homeruns in 1927.

RUTHERFORD, Sir Ernest, 1st Baron Rutherford of Nelson (1871–1937), New Zealand born British physicist. His early work was with J. J. THOMSON on MAGNETISM and thus on RADIO waves. Following ROENTGEN'S discovery of X-RAYS (1895), they studied the CONDUCTIVITY of air bombarded by these rays and the rate at which the IONS produced recombined. This led him to similar studies of the "rays" emitted by URANIUM (see RADIOACTIVITY). He found these were of two types, which he named alpha and beta (see ALPHA PARTICLES; BETA RAYS). As a result of their work on RADIUM, ACTINIUM and particularly THORIUM, he and Frederic Soddy were able in 1903 to put forward their theory of radioactivity. This suggested that the atoms of certain substances spontaneously emit alpha and beta rays, being thereby transformed into atoms of different, but still radioactive, ELEMENTS of lesser ATOMIC WEIGHT. He later showed alpha rays to be positively charged particles, in fact, HELIUM atoms stripped of their two ELECTRONS. He was awarded the 1908 Nobel Prize for Chemistry. In 1911 he proposed his nuclear theory of the ATOM, on which BOHR based his celebrated theory two years later. In 1919 he announced the first artificial disintegration of an atom, NITROGEN being converted into OXYGEN and HYDROGEN by collision with an alpha particle. He was President of the ROYAL SOCIETY from 1925 to 1930. His work was commemorated (1969) by the naming of RUTHERFORDIUM.

RUTLEDGE, John (1739–1800), US lawyer and statesman, champion of American independence. He was twice delegate to the CONTINENTAL CONGRESS. As a delegate to the 1787 Constitutional Convention, he was largely responsible for concessions to slaveholders. He helped frame S.C.'s constitution (1776) and was governor 1779–82. Washington's nomination of him for Chief Justice (1795) was not confirmed by the Senate. His brother **Edward Rutledge** (1749–1800) was delegate to the Continental Congress 1774–76, a signer of the Declaration of Independence, and S.C. governor, 1798–1800.

RUYSDAEL, Jacob van. See RUISDAEL, JACOB VAN.

RUYTER, Michiel Adriaanszoon de (1607–1676), Dutch admiral who fought the English in the DUTCH WARS. After the first (1652), he became vice-admiral of Holland. In the first, he defeated the English off Dunkirk (1666) and destroyed much of the English fleet in the Medway R (1667). In the 3rd, he prevented an Anglo-French invasion of Holland (1673).

Official name: Republic of Rwanda
Capital: Kigali
Area: 10,166sq mi
Population: 5,172,000
Languages: Kinyarwanda, French; Swahili
Religions: Roman Catholic, Animist, Muslim
Monetary unit(s): 1 Rwanda franc=100 centimes

RWANDA, formerly Ruanda, small, landlocked independent republic of E central Africa.

Land. Bordered by Uganda, Tanzania, Burundi and Zaire, Rwanda is largely rugged and mountainous. In the NW, highlands of the GREAT RIFT VALLEY slope in ridges from Mt. Karisimbi (14,784ft); in the E there is a series of plateaus. Average annual temperatures range from 63°F in mountainous areas to 73°F in Rift Valley areas. Average annual rainfall ranges from 30in to 58in.

People. Some 90% of the people are Hutu (Bahutu) Bantu farmers, 9% Tutsi (Watutsi or Watusi) cattle-raisers and 1% pygmy Twa hunters. The population is 98% rural and the rate of illiteracy is about 90%.

Economy. Rwanda is among the world's poorest and most overpopulated countries.

Soil erosion—due to LEACHING caused by heavy rains, poor farming techniques and cattle feeding—imperils cultivation, on which the economy depends. Coffee is the principal cash crop. There are deposits of tin and tungsten.

History. In the 1500s, the majority Hutu group were mastered by the taller Tutsi. From 1897, Rwanda was part of German East Africa and, after WWI, part of the Belgian trust territory, Ruanda-Urundi (administered with Belgian Congo 1925–60). In 1959 a bloody Hutu rising destroyed the Tutsi kingdom and ousted the *Mwami* (king), Kigeri V. About 120,000 Tutsi fled to Burundi. The Hutu party (Parmehutu) set up a republican regime. In 1962 Belgium granted full independence. In 1973 a coup established a military government, which was reconfirmed by referendum in 1978.

RYAN, Nolan (1947–   ), US baseball pitcher. In 1981 he set a major league record by hurling his fifth no-hitter. He has also set records with 19 strikeouts in one game, and 383 in one season. His fastball was once clocked at a record 100.8 mph.

RYDER, Albert Pinkham (1847–1917), major US painter, noted for his darkly poetic landscapes, seascapes and allegorical scenes such as *Toilers of the Sea* (1884), *The Flying Dutchman* (c.1890) and *The Race Track* (1895).

RYDER CUP, golf trophy awarded to winners of a biennial Anglo-US professional team match. The US has won all but four of the matches since 1927, when Samuel Ryder of St. Albans, England, presented the cup.

RYE, *Secale cereale,* hardiest of all CEREAL CROPS. It can grow in poor, sandy soils in cool and temperate climates. Most rye is used for human consumption, but rye grain and middlings (a byproduct of milling) are also fed to livestock. Rye malt is used to make rye whiskey. Rye is also used for cattle pasture. The leading producer of rye is the USSR. The ERGOT fungus disease of rye produces contaminated grains, which yield a drug that helps control bleeding and relieves MIGRAINE.

RYE HOUSE PLOT, radical Whig plot in 1683 to kill Charles II and the Duke of York (later JAMES II) at Rye House, Hertfordshire, and crown the Protestant Duke of MONMOUTH king. Among Whigs arrested on insubstantial evidence, the Earl of Essex apparently committed suicide, and Lord William RUSSELL and Algernon SIDNEY were executed.

RYLE, Gilbert (1900–1976), English philosopher, a major figure at Oxford in the tradition of "ordinary language" philosophy, which views philosophical problems as conceptual confusions resulting from an unwary use of language. In his best-known work, *The Concept of Mind* (1949), he seeks to expose the legacy of such confusions bequeathed by the DUALISM of DESCARTES.

RYSWICK, Treaty of, in 1697, ended the war in which the Great Alliance of the League of Augsburg, England and the Netherlands sought to block expansion of Louis XIV's France (see AUGSBURG, WAR OF THE LEAGUE OF). France gave up most territories won since 1678, but kept all but one of the Hudson's Bay Company forts seized in KING WILLIAM'S WAR. France also recognized William of Orange's right to the English throne, taken in the GLORIOUS REVOLUTION. The Dutch gained trade concessions and the right to garrison forts in the Spanish Netherlands.

RYUKYU ISLANDS, or **Riukiu Islands,** a chain forming a 650mi arc between Japan and Taiwan. Dividing the East China and Philippine seas, the 100-plus islands include the Osumi and Tokara (NE), the Amami and OKINAWA (center) and the Miyako and Yaeyama (SW). Many have coral reefs and some have active volcanoes. There are about 1 million islanders, mostly farmers and fishermen. Disputed with China, the Ryukyus became part of Japan in 1879. After WWII the US gave up the N islands in 1953, and the remainder in 1972. The islands are fully integrated into Japan.

RYUN, Jim (1947–   ), US runner. He was the first high school athlete to run the mile in less than four minutes. At 19, he set a world record of 3:51.3 for the distance, bettering the previous mark by 2.3 seconds. His 1967 record of 3:51.1 stood for eight years.

19th letter of the English alphabet. It derived from the Semitic language and progressed through Phoenician, Greek and Roman to its present form. It is an abbreviation for *south,* and in some languages (e.g. Italian) for *saint.*

SAAR, or Saarland, a West German state

ordering France in the S and W. It is a major coal-mining and iron-and-steel region whose control has historically alternated between France and Germany. After WWI, it was administered by France under the League of Nations. It was reunited with Germany after a plebiscite (1935), occupied by France after WWII and became a German state in 1957.

SAARINEN, name of two modern architects, father and son. **Eliel Saarinen** (1873–1950), the leading Finnish architect of his day, designed the influential Helsinki railroad station (1905–14). In 1923, he emigrated to the US, where he designed numerous buildings in the Midwest. **Eero Saarinen** (1910–1961) collaborated with his father 1938–50. His spectacular work includes the General Motors Technical Center (1948–56), the TWA terminal at Kennedy Airport (1962) and Dulles Airport (1962).

SABBATH, seventh day of the Hebrew week. The Jews observe it as the day of rest laid down in the fourth commandment to commemorate the Creation. It starts at sunset on Friday and ends at sunset on Saturday. Christians adopted Sunday as the Sabbath (Hebrew: rest) to commemorate the Resurrection. (See also BLUE LAW.)

SABER-TOOTHED TIGERS, two genera of extinct CATS of the CENOZOIC: *Smilodon* of North America and *Machairodus* of Europe and Asia. Slightly smaller than lions, but similar in build, saber-toothed tigers had enormous upper canines, up to 230mm (9in) long. They probably preyed on large, thick-skinned animals, using the canines as daggers to pierce the skin.

SABIN, Albert Bruce (1906–), US virologist best known for developing an oral POLIOMYELITIS vaccine, made from live viruses (1955). (See also SALK, J. E.)

SABLE, *Martes zibellina,* a carnivorous fur-bearing mammal related to the MARTENS. The name is also used for the rich pelt. Sable are ground-living mustelids of coniferous forests, now restricted to parts of N Asia. About 500mm (20in) long, they prey on small rodents.

SACAJAWEA (c1784–1884?), Shoshone Indian guide with the LEWIS AND CLARK EXPEDITION. She was the wife of the interpreter, Toussaint Charbonneau, and joined the expedition in 1805. Although not the expert guide that legend portrays, she was invaluable in the expedition's dealings with Indians.

SACCHARIN, or *o*-sulfobenzoic imide, a SWEETENING AGENT, 550 times sweeter than sucrose, normally used as its soluble sodium salt. Not absorbed by the body, it is used by diabetics and in low-calorie DIETETIC FOODS.

SACCO-VANZETTI CASE, famous legal battle which polarized opinion between US liberal-radicals and conservatives in the 1920s. In 1921, Nicola Sacco and Bartolomeo Vanzetti were found guilty of murdering a paymaster and factory guard in Braintree, Mass. Opponents of the verdict claimed that there had been insufficient evidence, and that the trial had been unduly influenced by the fact that Sacco and Vanzetti were aliens and and anarchists and had also been draft-evaders. The Supreme Court of Mass. declined to intervene. Eventually, Governor Fuller and an advisory board ruled the trial fair. The two were executed in 1927.

SACHS, Hans (1494–1576), the most popular German poet and dramatist of his time, one of the MEISTERSINGERS, and by trade a shoemaker. His prolific output included *The Nightingale of Wittenberg* (1523), a work in honor of Luther and the Reformation. He was the model for Wagner's *Die Meistersinger*.

SACHS, Julius von (1832–1897), German botanist regarded as the father of experimental plant physiology. Among his many contributions are his discovery of what are now called CHLOROPLASTS, the elucidation of the details of the GERMINATION process and his studies of plant TROPISMS.

SACKVILLE-WEST, Victoria Mary (1892–1962), English poet, novelist and biographer, associated (like her husband Harold Nicolson) with the BLOOMSBURY GROUP. Her works include the poem *The Land* (1926) and her novels *The Edwardians* (1930) and *All Passion Spent* (1931).

SACRAMENT, in Christian theology, a visible sign and pledge of invisible GRACE, ordained by Christ. The traditional seven sacraments (first listed by Peter LOMBARD) are BAPTISM, Holy COMMUNION, CONFIRMATION, PENANCE, ORDINATION, MARRIAGE and EXTREME UNCTION, of which only the first two are accepted as sacraments by Protestants. In Roman Catholic theology the sacraments, if validly administered, convey grace objectively to the believing recipients; Protestants stress the joining of Word and sacrament, and the necessity of faith.

SACRAMENTO, capital city of Cal. and of Sacramento Co. It lies at the confluence of the Sacramento and American rivers, and is the industrial, transportation, market and commercial center for the important truck- and fruit-farming region of Central Valley. First settled 1839, it became state capital

1854. Pop 275,741.

SACRAMENTO RIVER, largest river in Cal. It rises in Siskiyou Co., NE Cal., and flows about 380mi into Suisun Bay, joining the San Joaquin S of Sacramento, to form the rich agricultural region of Central Valley.

SACRIFICE, a cultic act found in almost all religions, in which an object is consecrated and offered by a PRIEST in worship to a deity. It often involves the killing of an animal or human being and thus the offering up of its life; sometimes a communion meal follows. Sacrifice may also be seen as the expiation of sin, the sealing of a covenant or a gift to the god which invites blessing in return. Ancient Israel had an elaborate system of sacrifices (chief being that of PASSOVER) which ceased when the Temple was destroyed (70 AD). In Christianity Christ's death is viewed as the one perfect and eternal sacrifice for sin (see ATONEMENT); the MASS is a dependent sacrifice. (See also ALTAR.)

SADAT, Anwar el- (1918–81), president of Egypt from 1970. An army officer, he was active in the coup that overthrew King Faruk in 1952. As vice president, he became president on Nasser's death. He expelled Soviet military advisers. His war with Israel and support of an Arab oil boycott against the West (both 1973) were followed by a policy reversal. Establishing close ties with the US, he took initiatives leading to an Egyptian-Israeli peace treaty (1979). He shared the Nobel Peace Prize for 1978. In 1981, while reviewing a parade, Sadat was assassinated by a fanatical group of army officers.

SADDUCEES, aristocratic Jewish religious group in Roman Judea, opposed to the PHARISEES. They rejected the Pharisaic Oral Law and based their faith on the TORAH. Their great political influence ended with the destruction of the Temple at Jerusalem (70 AD).

SADE, Donatien Alphonse François, Comte de (1740–1814), usually known as the Marquis de Sade, French soldier and writer who gave his name to SADISM. He argued that since sexual deviation and criminal acts exist, they are natural. He spent much of his life in prisons and his last 11 years in Charenton lunatic asylum.

SADISM, term deriving from the Marquis de SADE meaning obtaining erotic pleasure from inflicting PAIN on others; possibly a retention of INFANTILE SEXUALITY. (See also MASOCHISM.)

SADOMASOCHISM. See SADISM; MASOCHISM.

SAFETY GLASS, reinforced GLASS used chiefly in automobile windscreens, aircraft, and where bullet resistance is needed. Some safety glass is glass toughened by being heated almost to softening and then cooled; some has wire mesh embedded to guard against shattering; most is a LAMINATE with a thin layer of PLASTIC (polyvinyl butyral) between two glass layers, so that, if broken, the glass fragments adhere to the plastic.

SAGA, epic narrative, usually in prose, of 11th–14th century Scandinavian and Icelandic literature. Sagas often have historical settings, but their content is mainly fictional; their style is spare and understated, often bleak and grim. Probably the greatest saga author was SNORRI STURLUSON, whose *Heimskringla* (c1230) traced the history of the kings of Norway. Subjects of sagas range from odd incidents to histories of individuals, whole families or, as in *Njal's Saga*, of feuds.

SAGAN, Carl Edward (1934– .), US astronomer who specializes in studying planetary atmospheres and surfaces. He is best known for his popular book *The Dragon of Eden* (Pulitzer Prize, 1978) and his television series and book *Cosmos* (1980).

SAGAN, Françoise (1935–), pen name of the French novelist Françoise Quoirez, best known for the precocious and highly successful *Bonjour Tristesse* (1954), written when she was 18, and *A Certain Smile* (1956), both of which deal with the disillusionments of *jeunesse d'orée*.

SAGE, Russell (1816–1906), US financier who amassed a fortune from the wholesale grocery, railroad and other businesses. He left $70 million, part of which his widow used to establish the Russell Sage Foundation (1907), which aims to better US social conditions.

SAGEBRUSH REBELLION, a US political movement of the 1970s and 1980s. Many Westerners became impatient with policies of the US government, which owns a high percentage of Western land—more than half in some states. They sought transfer of substantial portions of this land to the states so that it could be developed economically. Environmentalists opposed this as a "land grab." The Reagan administration was more pro-development than its predecessors, and its policies tended to mollify the "rebels."

SAGITTARIUS (the Archer), a constellation on the ECLIPTIC lying in the direction of the galactic center (see MILKY WAY). Sagittarius is the ninth sign of the ZODIAC.

SAHARA DESERT, the world's largest DESERT, covering about 3,500,000sq mi. It stretches across N Africa from the Atlantic to the Red Sea. The terrain includes sand hills, rocky wastes, tracts of gravel and fertile oases. The central plateau, about 1000ft above sea level, has mountain groups rising well above 6,000ft. Rainfall ranges from under 5in to 15in annually and temperatures may soar above 120°F and plunge to under 50°F at night. Since WWII the Sahara has gained economic importance with the discovery of extensive oil, gas and iron-ore deposits.

SAIGON, See HO CHI MINH CITY.

SAINT AUGUSTINE, Fla., oldest city (founded 1565) in the US, seat of St. John's Co., on the Atlantic coast 35mi SE of Jacksonville: it did not become part of the US until 1821. It is a tourist center with a fishing industry. Pop 11,985.

SAINT BARTHOLOMEW'S DAY, Massacre of, the killing of French HUGUENOTS which began in Paris on Aug. 24, 1572. Jealous of the influence of the Huguenot COLIGNY on her son King CHARLES IX, Catherine de MÉDICIS plotted to assassinate him. When this failed Catherine, fearing Huguenot reaction, persuaded Charles to order the deaths of all leading Huguenots. On the morning of St. Bartholomew's Day thousands were slaughtered. Despite government orders to stop, the murders continued in the provinces until Oct.

SAINT BERNARD, a large mastiff dog with droopy ears and lips and a heavy coat, named for St. Bernard de Menthon, the monks of whose hospice in the Swiss Alps used them as guides and rescue dogs.

SAINT BERNARD PASSES, two passes over the Alps. The Great St. Bernard (8,100ft) links Martigny in Switzerland with Aosta in Italy. The Little St. Bernard (7,177ft) connects the Isère Valley in France with Aosta.

SAINT CROIX, largest island of the US VIRGIN ISLANDS. A tourist center, it markets sugarcane and rum.

SAINTE-BEUVE, Charles Augustin (1804–1869), French writer and critic whose biographical approach revolutionized French literary criticism. His works include the collection of critical essays, *Causeries du Lundi* (1851–62).

SAINT-EXUPÉRY, Antoine de (1900–1944), French writer and aviator who pioneered air routes over South America and NW Africa. In 1939 he became a military reconnaisance pilot, and was killed in action. His books include *Night Flight* (1932) and the children's classic tale, *The Little Prince* (1943).

SAINT-GAUDENS, Augustus (1848–1907), US sculptor famed for his large public monuments. His works include the Adams Memorial (1891) in Rock Creek Cemetery, Washington D.C., and the Robert G. Shaw monument in Boston (1897).

SAINT GOTTHARD PASS, in Switzerland, road and rail route through the Alps from central Europe to Italy. The rail tunnel beneath the pass is over 9mi long and a vehicular tunnel completed in 1980 is the longest in Europe.

SAINT HELENA, British island in the S Atlantic Ocean. Its capital is Jamestown, where NAPOLEON I died in exile in 1821. The climate is temperate, and the island has a growing tourist industry. Pop 6,000.

SAINT JOHN'S, capital city of Newfoundland, Canada, on the SE Atlantic coast. It is a natural deep water harbor and fishing port, and the commercial and transportation center of the province. Pop 86,575.

SAINT-JUST, Louis de (1767–1794), French revolutionary leader. He entered the National Convention 1792 and became president two years later. He supported ROBESPIERRE, helped engineer the downfall of DANTON, and was guillotined when Robespierre fell.

SAINT KITTS-NEVIS, in the E Caribbean with a capital at Basseterre, St. Kitts (officially St Christopher). Scheduled for independence in the 1980s, the islands of St Kitts (65sq mi) and Nevis (36sq mi) were part of St Kitts-Nevis-Anguilla prior to 1980. Exports include sugar, molasses and cotton. Area 101sq mi, pop approx 44,400.

ST. LAURENT, Louis Stephen (1882–1973), Canadian Liberal Prime Minister 1948–57. He became federal minister of justice and attorney general in 1942, and in 1945 played an important role in the setting up of the UNITED NATIONS. As prime minister he strengthened Canada's position in the COMMONWEALTH and was instrumental in founding the NORTH ATLANTIC TREATY ORGANIZATION. Domestically, his greatest achievement was the incorporation of Newfoundland as a Canadian province in 1949.

SAINT-LAURENT, Yves (1936–   ), French fashion designer whose boutique Saint-Laurent Rive Gauche (1966) started a trend for designers to move away from exclusiveness. His nostalgia for the 1930s and his peasant look created major fashion trends of the 1960s and 1970s.

SAINT LAWRENCE RIVER, largest river in Canada, flowing 760mi NE from Lake Ontario to the Gulf of St. Lawrence. It forms 120mi of the US/Canadian border, has been canalized to form the SAINT LAWRENCE SEAWAY.

SAINT LAWRENCE SEAWAY AND

GREAT LAKES WATERWAY, the US/Canadian inland waterway for ocean-going vessels connecting the GREAT LAKES with the Atlantic Ocean, and comprising a 2,342mi-long system of natural waterways, canals, locks, dams and dredged channels (including the WELLAND SHIP CANAL). It was completed in 1959. The waterway, once restricted to small river vessels, has opened the industries and agriculture of the Great Lakes to international trade.

SAINT LOUIS, on the Mississippi R, largest city of Mo. Founded as a fur-trading post by the French in 1763, it was ceded to Spain in 1770, and after reverting briefly to the French became part of the US under the LOUISIANA PURCHASE in 1803. The city expanded rapidly, and became a major inland port, transportation center and market for agricultural center. Pop 453,085.

Official name: State of St. Lucia
Capital: Castries
Area: 238sq mi
Population: 117,465
Languages: English (official), French patois
Religions: Christian
Monetary unit(s): 1 East Caribbean dollar = 10 cents

ST. LUCIA, independent island nation of the Windward Island group in the Caribbean, 250mi from the mainland of South America.
Land. St. Lucia, 27mi long and 14mi wide. is of volcanic origin with one active volcano. The terrain is hilly, with Morne Gimie reaching 3,145ft. The interior is covered with tropical rain forests. The average annual temperature is 79°F.
People. Most of the inhabitants are of African heritage, descendants of slaves, although a few Carib Indians survive. Roman Catholicism is followed by almost 90% of the population.
Economy. Small-scale agriculture is the principal economic activity, with most farms smaller than 5acres. Bananas, and to a lesser extent cacao, coconuts and citrus fruits are grown for export. Industry,

including food processing, electrical components and garments, is being diversified to include an ambitious oil complex. Although tourism is growing, imports exceed exports by 300% and the country is heavily dependent upon foreign aid.
History. The Carib Indians were able to prevent several settlement attempts by the British and French from the early 17th century until 1814 when the island was ceded to Britain. St. Lucia was part of the West Indies Federation from 1958 until it was dissolved in 1962. Full independence from Britain was granted in 1979. A severe 1980 hurricane virtually destroyed the entire banana crop, increasing economic difficulties.

SAINT MARK'S CATHEDRAL (San Marco), Venetian 11th-century church, outstanding example of BYZANTINE ARCHITECTURE, built in the form of a Greek cross surmounted by five large domes. The richly constructed and sculptured West Façade has Gothic additions. Its famous four bronze horses were brought from Constantinople in 1204.

SAINT PAUL, city in E Minn. on the Mississippi R, state capital and seat of Ramsey Co. An enormous port and trans-portation center, its important industries are machinery, electronics equipment, motor vehicles, metal and petroleum products and abrasives. Printing and livestock sales are major activities. Pop 270,230.

SAINT PETER'S BASILICA, Rome, the world's largest church, built on the supposed tomb of St. PETER between 1506 and 1667 by architects including BRAMANTE, RAPHAEL, SANGALLO, MICHELANGELO, Carlo MADERNO and BERNINI. It forms a huge Latin cross capped by a great dome. Gilt, mosaic, bronze and marble embellish the interior and an enormous canopy by Bernini encloses the main altar.

SAINT PETERSBURG. See LENINGRAD.

SAINT PIERRE AND MIQUELON, French islands in the Atlantic Ocean, S of Newfoundland. The capital is Saint Pierre. Chief occupations are codfishing, fox-and mink-farming and tourism. First visited in the 17th century by Breton and Basque fishermen, the islands were long disputed between France and Britain finally becoming French in 1804, a French Overseas Territory in 1946 and French overseas departments in 1976.

SAINT-SAENS, Charles Camille (1835–1921), French composer. He com-posed many large-scale symphonies, piano concertos, symphonic poems and operas like

Samson and Delilah (1877), but today it is his lighter music which is best known, especially *Danse Macabre* (1874) and *Carnival of the Animals* (1886).

SAINT-SIMON, Claude Henri de Rouvroy, Comte de (1760–1825), French proto-socialist philosopher who advocated a state organized by scientists and industrialists. Especially concerned by workingclass conditions, his teachings launched the **Saint Simonism** movement, c1830, calling for meritocracy, female emancipation, nation-alization and abolition of inherited wealth.

SAINT-SIMON, Louis de Rouvroy, duc de (1675–1755), French statesman and writer of *Mémoires* (1739–51), where he brilliantly criticized the court of King LOUIS XIV.

SAINT-SOPHIA. See HAGIA SOPHIA.

SAINT THOMAS, island (32sq mi) of the US VIRGIN ISLANDS. Charlotte Amalie, its capital, is a fine harbor. The economy rests on tourism.

SAINT VITUS' DANCE, or Sydenham's chorea. See CHOREA.

SAKE, or saki, an alcoholic drink made from fermented RICE. It is the national beverage of Japan and contains 14% to 15% by volume of ETHANOL.

SAKHALIN, long, narrow island in USSR (about 30,000sq mi) off the E Siberian coast. It is mountainous, covered largely with tundra and forest: its resources include oil, coal, timber and fish. Its ownership has been much disputed by Japan.

SAKHAROV, Andrei Dimitrievich (1921 –), Soviet physicist who played a prominent part in the development of the first Soviet HYDROGEN BOMB. He sub-sequently advocated worldwide nuclear disarmament (being awarded the 1975 Nobel Peace Prize) and became a leading Soviet dissident.

SAKI. See MUNRO, HECTOR HUGH.

SALADIN (Salah-ad-Din Yusuf ibn-Ayyub; 1138–1193), Muslim leader who crushed the crusaders in Palestine. Becoming Sultan of Egypt in 1174, he established there his own dynasty. He reclaimed Syria and most of Palestine including Jerusalem (1187) from the crusaders, and forced a stalemate on England's RICHARD I (1192) during the third CRUSADE, leaving the Muslims masters of Palestine. He was famed for his chivalry.

SALAM, Abdus (1926–), Pakistani physicist whose research demonstrated that ELECTROMAGNETISM and nuclear "weak interaction," two of the basic forces of nature, were aspects of the same natural phenomenon. For his work, which may be a step toward a "unified field theory"

incorporating all physical laws, he shared the 1979 Nobel Prize in Physics with S. WEINBERG and S. GLASHOW.

SALAMANDER, general term for all tailed AMPHIBIA, comprising eight families. They are long-bodied and retain the tail throughout their life. Their limbs are usually small and are not used for locomotion to any great extent; most movement is achieved by wriggling, with the belly close to, or touching, the ground—effectively "swimming" on land. Salamanders occupy a variety of aquatic, semiterrestrial and terrestrial habitats throughout the world. Most feed on insects and other invertebrates.

SALAMIS, mountainous and fertile Greek island (35sq mi), about 10mi W of Athens. Salamis, chief town and port, is at the W end. The famous naval battle (480 BC), when THEMISTOCLES destroyed the stronger Persian fleet, was fought in the straits to the E of the island.

SALAZAR, António de Oliveira (1889–1970), dictator of PORTUGAL (1932–68). Although he reor-ganized public finances and achieved certain modernizations, education and living standards remained almost static and political freedom was restricted.

SALEM, manufacturing city in NE Mass., a seat of Essex Co., NE of Boston. It was founded in 1626, and a number of 17th-century buildings are still standing. It is famous as the site of witchcraft trials (1692) in which 19 were hanged (see SEWALL, SAMUEL), and as the birthplace of Nathaniel HAWTHORNE. Pop 38,220.

SALEM, state capital of OREGON, seat of Marion Co., founded in 1840 by Methodist missionaries. An agricultural center, it has food-processing plants. Pop 89,233.

SALIERI, Antonio (1750–1825), Italian composer who was for nearly 60 years, court musician in Vienna. His rivalry with Mozart is celebrated. He taught SCHUBERT, BEETHOVEN and LISZT.

SALINGER, Jerome David (1919–), US author whose first novel *The Catcher in the Rye* (1951) became one of the most popular postwar books, its adolescent "hero" Holden Caulfield being presented as a spokesman of his generation. Salinger's short stories, many concerning the Glass family, include *For Esmé—With Love and Squalor* (1950).

SALISBURY, Robert Arthur Talbot Gascoyne Cecil, 3rd Marquess of (1830–1903), British statesman, entered parliament 1853. As Conservative prime minister (1885–86, 1886–92, 1895–1902), he opposed parliamentary reform and Irish

HOME RULE, and acted as his own foreign minister. He maintained good relations in Europe, and successfully expanded the British Empire in Africa and Asia.

SALISBURY, Robert Cecil, 1st Earl of (1563–1612), English secretary of state under ELIZABETH I from 1596, chief minister from 1598. Before Elizabeth's death he negotiated with JAMES VI that monarch's accession to the English throne, and remained chief minister thereafter.

SALISBURY, capital and largest city of Zimbabwe, in a gold-mining and corn-and tobacco-growing area. It is the commercial and transportation hub of the country. It was founded in 1890 by RHODES' Pioneer Column. Pop 627,000.

SALIVA, the watery secretion of the salivary GLANDS which lubricates the MOUTH and food boluses. It contains MUCUS, some gamma globulins and PTYALIN and is secreted in response to food in the mouth or by conditioned REFLEXES such as the smell or sight of food. Secretion is partly under the control of the parasympathetic autonomic NERVOUS SYSTEM. The various salivary glands—parotid, submandibular and sublingual—secrete slightly different types of saliva, varying in mucus and ENZYME content.

SALK, Jonas Edward (1914–   ), US virologist best known for developing the first POLIOMYELITIS vaccine, made from killed viruses (1952–54).

SALLUST (Caius Sallustius Crispus; 86–c34 BC), Roman senator, and first Roman historian to interpret the events which he recorded and to describe limited historical periods, though his accounts are flawed by bias and inaccuracy. His major work is *Bellum Catilinarium*, on the CATILINE conspiracy.

SALMON, large, highly palatable fishes of two genera. The Atlantic salmon, *Salmo salar*, lives in the N Atlantic, while in the N Pacific, there are five species in the genus *Onchorhynchus*. All salmon return to freshwater to breed. While the Pacific salmon die on completion of their first spawning, Atlantic salmon return to the sea, and may come back to spawn a second time. Adult salmon return to their natal streams to breed; they spawn in "redds" in the sand or gravel of the stream bed. The young remain in freshwater until they are about 18 months old, then migrate down to the sea. Adults remain in the sea, feeding, for one to two years before returning to breed. (See also OUANANICHE.)

SALMONELLA, bacteria, some species of which cause FOOD POISONING or ENTERITIS; specific types cause TYPHOID and PARA-TYPHOID FEVER.

SALOMON, Erich (1886–1944), German photographer known for his candid photographs of European statesmen between the world wars. He crashed conferences and banquets and used a new high-speed miniature camera to take the pictures that were collected in *Celebrated Contemporaries in Unguarded Moments* (1931). He died at Auschwitz concentration camp.

SALSA, in popular music, a style that combines Latin and Afro-Cuban rhythms with jazz, soul and rock music. Most popular in the 1950s and 1960s, salsa rhythms are still detectable in many disco compositions.

SALT, common name for **Sodium Chloride** (NaCl), found in seawater and also as the common mineral, rock salt or halite. Pure salt forms white cubic CRYSTALS. Some salt is obtained by solar evaporation from salt pans, shallow depressions periodically flooded with seawater; but most is obtained from underground mines. The most familiar use of salt is to flavor food. (Magnesium carbonate is added to table salt to keep it dry.) It is, however, used in much larger quantities to preserve hides in leather-making, in soap manufacture, as a food preservative and in keeping highways ice-free in winter. Rock salt is the main industrial source of chlorine and caustic soda. mp 801°C, bp 1413°C.

SALT, Chemical, an electrovalent compound (see BOND, CHEMICAL) formed by neutralization of an ACID and a BASE. The vast majority of MINERALS are salts, the best known being common SALT, sodium chloride. Salts are generally ionic solids which are good electrolytes (see ELECTROLYSIS); those of weak acids or bases undergo partial HYDROLYSIS in water. Salts may be classified as normal (fully neutralized), acid (containing some acidic hydrogen, e.g., BICARBONATES), or basic (containing hydroxide ions). They may alternatively be classified as simple salts, double salts (two simple salts combined by regular substitution in the crystal lattice) including ALUMS, and complex salts.

SALT LAKE CITY, 15mi from the Great Salt Lake, capital and largest city in Utah and seat of Salt Lake Co. Founded in 1847 by Brigham YOUNG leading a band of Mormons from persecution, it is the world center of the Church of Jesus Christ of Latter-Day Saints: 65% of its residents are members. It is a commercial and industrial center for minerals, farming, oil refining and chemicals. Pop 163,033.

SALTYKOV, Mikhail Evgrafovich (1826

1889), known as Saltykov-Shchedrin, one of the finest Russian satirists. His *History of a Town* (1869–70), attacked Russian bureaucrats. His only novel is *The Golovlyov Family* (1876), a story of declining gentry.

SALVAGE, in maritime law, a term given either to the rescue of life and property (a ship and its cargo) from danger on water, or to the reward given by a court to those who effect a rescue (called salvors). Under the LAW OF THE SEA, it is the duty of a ship's master to go to the aid of an imperiled vessel. If life or property are saved, the owner of the rescue ship, the master and the crew share in the salvage award. These awards are generous in order to encourage seamen and shipowners to risk their lives and property in rescue operations.

SALVATION, a key religious concept: man's deliverance from the evils of life and of death. It is presupposed that man is in bondage to suffering, SIN, disease, death, decay etc., from which he may be rescued and restored to primordial blessedness. In DUALISM salvation is release of the soul from the corrupting prison of the body; in HINDUISM release from the cycle of rebirth (see TRANSMIGRATION OF SOULS). In Judaism, Christianity and Islam it is liberation from evil into communion with God, and hence deliverance from HELL, the RESURRECTION of the body and (in Christian eschatology) the regeneration of the entire universe. Judaism stresses ethnic salvation, as typified by the Exodus. In these W religions salvation is provided by the "mighty acts" of God, who is the savior (see also ATONEMENT; SACRIFICE); elsewhere salvation may be self-attained by ritual, acquisition of knowledge, asceticism, good deeds or martyrdom. Christianity sees all history as a divine plan of salvation, consequent on Adam's fall (see ORIGINAL SIN), achieved in the INCARNATION, death and resurrection of JESUS CHRIST, and consummated at the LAST JUDGMENT.

SALVATION ARMY, Christian organization founded by William BOOTH (1865). In 1878 the mission became the Army, with Booth as General. Under strict quasimilitary discipline, the members seek to strengthen Christianity and help (also save) the poor and destitute. The Army now operates 8,000 centers in the US alone. Its official journal is *War Cry*.

SALWEEN RIVER, great river of SE Asia. Rising in Tibet it flows 1,750mi SE through China and E Burma into the Gulf of Martaban.

SALZBURG, historic city in central Austria, world famous for its annual music festival (begun 1917). The birthplace of MOZART, it lies on the Salzbach R. Pop 128,800.

SAMARKAND, city in Uzbekistan, USSR, in the Zeravshan R valley. One of the world's oldest cities, it was built on the site of Afrosiab (3000 BC or earlier) and was the great conqueror TAMERLANE'S capital. Pop 476,000.

SAMOA, chain of 10 islands and several islets in the South Pacific, midway between Honolulu and Sydney. Volcanic and mountainous, their total area is about 1,200sq mi. The people are mostly Polynesians. The soil is fertile, producing cacao, coconuts and bananas, and the climate tropical. Savai'i (the largest), Upolu and the other W islands constitute independent WESTERN SAMOA. **American Samoa** consists of the E islands: Tutuila, the Manua group and the Rose and Swains Islands. Discovered by the Dutch in 1722, Samoa was claimed by Germany, Great Britain and the US in the mid-19th century, but in 1899 the US acquired sole rights to what is now American Samoa.

SAMUEL, two Old Testament books (known to Catholics as 1 and 2 KINGS) which tell of the statesman, general and prophet, Samuel (c11th century BC). He united the tribes under SAUL, and chose DAVID as Saul's successor.

SAMUELSON, Paul Anthony (1915–), US economist, advisor to Presidents KENNEDY and JOHNSON and winner of the 1970 Nobel economics prize. His widely used college textbook, *Economics* (1948; 11th ed. 1980), was translated into 21 languages.

SAMURAI, hereditary military class of Japan. From c1000 AD the Samurai dominated Japan, though after c1600 their activities were less military than cultural. Comprising 5% of Japanese, they exerted influence through BUSHIDO, a code which demanded feudal loyalty and placed honor above life. The class lost its power in the reforms of 1868.

SAN ANDREAS FAULT, break in the earth's crust, running 600mi from Cape Mendocino, NW Cal., to the Colorado desert. It was the sudden movement of land along this FAULT that caused the San Francisco EARTHQUAKE, 1906. The fracture, and the motion responsible for this and other quakes, is a result of the abutment of the eastern Pacific and North American plates (see PLATE TECTONICS).

SAN ANTONIO, city in S Tex., seat of Bexar Co., on the San Antonio R 150mi N of the Gulf of Mexico. Founded in 1718, it was the site of the ALAMO (1836). It is one of the largest military centers in the US. Pop 785,410.

SANCTIONS, in international politics, methods such as BOYCOTTS, ECONOMIC SANCTIONS, EMBARGOES or military threat to enforce the decisions of one (or more) states concerning (usually) the social structure of another (or others). Provided for by the League of Nations and UN charters, they have been applied against Italy, Rhodesia and South Africa.

SAND, George (1804–1876), pseudonym of the French novelist Amandine Aurore Lucie Dupin, baronne Dudevant. Her novels, at first romantic, later socially oriented, include *Indiana* (1832) and *The Haunted Pool* (1846). Her life-style—coupled with its partial source, her ardent feminism—caused much controversy, her lovers including CHOPIN and notably de MUSSET. Her memoirs, *Histoire de Ma Vie* (1854–55), provide a graceful justification of her views.

SANDBURG, Carl (1878–1967), American poet and biographer who won Pulitzer prizes for *Abraham Lincoln: the War Years* in 1940 and *Complete Poems* in 1951. He left school at 13, and at 20 fought in the Spanish-American war. While a journalist in Chicago, he wrote vigorous, earthy, free verse, as in *Chicago Poems* (1916) and *Smoke and Steel* (1920). He was also a notable folksong anthologist.

SAN DIEGO, on the Pacific Coast close to the Mexican border, second-largest city of Cal. and seat of San Diego Co. Its natural harbor houses a great Navy base, a large fishing fleet, and lumber and shipbuilding yards. Its heavy industries include aircraft, missiles and electronics factories. Pop 875,504.

SANDINISTAS, the Nicaraguan revolutionary movement that overthrew the Somoza family dictatorship in 1979. Named after the Nicaraguan patriot and guerrilla leader of the 1920s César Sandino, it assembled a broad coalition in the country to defeat Anastasio Somoza and his hated Civil Guard. After the revolution the FSLN (Sandinista National Liberation Front) ruled through a five-man junta attempting to rebuild the war-torn country. Some of its opponents accused it of trying to establish a new dictatorship.

SANDPIPERS, small to medium-sized wading birds forming part of the family Scolopacidae. Most are slim birds, with long straight bills and inconspicuous cryptic plumage. The group includes the stints, knots and "shanks" as well as the true sandpipers, dividing into two major groups, the Calidritine and Tringine pipers.

SANDSTONE, a SEDIMENTARY ROC consisting of consolidated sand, cemente postdepositionally by such minerals a quartz, calcite, or hematite, or set in matrix of clay minerals. The sand grains ar chiefly QUARTZ. The chief varieties ar quartz-arenite, rich in silica; arkose feldspar-rich; graywacke, composed o angular grains of quarts and feldspa and/or rock fragments and over 15% matrix; and subgraywacke, with less matri than graywacke. Sandstone beds may bea NATURAL GAS or PETROLEUM, and ar commonly AQUIFERS. Sandstone is quarrie for building, and crushed for use a AGGLOMERATE.

SAN FRANCISCO, famous city an seaport on the Pacific coast, noted for it cosmopolitan charm. Its economy is base on shipping and shipbuilding, with export of cotton, grain, lumber and petroleum products. It is also the financial, cultura and communications center for the NW Coast. Its many tourist attractions includ Chinatown, the Latin Quarter and Golde Gate Park. There are several museums an art galleries and the famous opera house Founded by the Spanish (as Yerba Buena in 1776, the city passed into US hands i 1846 and was named San Francisco (1847) The GOLD RUSH soon attracted thousands o settlers to the area. Parts of the city wer rebuilt after the earthquake of 1906 (se SAN ANDREAS FAULT). (See also ALCATRAZ GOLDEN GATE.) Pop 678,974.

SAN FRANCISCO BAY, the world' largest natural harbor, 50mi long and up t 12mi wide, spanned by the GOLDEN GATE an San Francisco–Oakland Bay bridges.

SANGALLO, Antonio da (Antonio Cor diani; 1483–1546), Italian architect an military engineer, succeeded RAPHAEL a architect of SAINT PETER'S BASILICA.

SANGER, Frederick (1918–   ), Britis biochemist awarded the 1958 Nobel Priz for Chemistry for his work on the PROTEINS particularly for first determining th complete structure of a protein, that o bovine INSULIN (1955). He shared the 198 Nobel Prize for Chemistry for his researc on NUCLEIC ACIDS, the carriers of genetic traits.

SANGER, Margaret (1883–1966), US pioneer of BIRTH CONTROL and feminism who set up the first birth-control clinic in the US (1916), founded the National Birth Contro League (1917), and helped organize th first international birth-control conference (1927).

SAN JUAN, capital and port of PUERTO RICC on the NE coast of the island. Founded in 1508 by PONCE DE LEON, it is now a trade center producing sugar, rum, metal products, textiles and furniture. Tourism is also important. Pop 522,700.

Official name: Republic of San Marino
Capital: San Marino
Area: 24.1sq mi
Population: 21,000
Language: Italian
Religion: Roman Catholic
Monetary unit(s): 1 lira=100 centesimi

SAN MARINO, world's smallest republic and possibly the oldest state in Europe, located in NE Italy. Built on the three peaks of Mt Titano, its townships include San Marino (the capital) and Serravalle. Tradition reports that San Marino was founded as a refuge for persecuted Christians in the 4th century AD. Many historic buildings remain, and the modern state lives mainly by tourism and the sale of postage stamps. The republic is governed by two "captains-regent" assisted by a 60-member council of state.

SAN MARTÍN, José de (1778–1850), Argentinian general who, with BOLÍVAR, liberated Chile and much of Peru from Spanish rule. Educated in Spain, he served in the Spanish army before returning to South America in 1812. In 1817 he led the Argentinian army over the Andes to Chile and victory against the Spanish: his friend Bernardo O'HIGGINS became ruler of an independent Chile. In 1821, after a series of military victories, he proclaimed Peru independent and became its protector. In 1822 he retired to France.

SAN SALVADOR, capital and largest city of EL SALVADOR. In a volcanic region, it has suffered many earthquakes. Founded in 1525, it is now a trade center, producing textiles, tobacco and soap. Pop 408,811.

SANSKRIT, classical language of the Hindu peoples of India and the oldest literary language of the Indo-European Family. Some early texts date from c1500 BC, including the Vedic texts (see VEDA). Vedic Sanskrit was prevalent roughly 1500–150 BC, Classical Sanskrit roughly 500 BC–900 AD. Sanskrit gave rise to most modern Indian languages as HINDI and

URDU, and is distantly related to the CELTIC LANGUAGES, ROMANCE LANGUAGES and SLAVONIC LANGUAGES.

SANSOVINO, Jacopo (Jacopo Tatti; 1486–1570), Italian sculptor and architect, highly influential in Venice where he designed in a classical style the Library of St. Mark's (1536–38) and sculptured *Mars and Neptune* (1554–56).

SANS SOUCI, ROCOCO palace near Potsdam built for FREDERICK II of Prussia in 1745–47, who lived there for 40 years, making it a magnificent cultural center for such notable guests as VOLTAIRE.

SANTA ANNA, Antonio Lopez de (1794–1876), Mexican general and military dictator who tried to suppress the Texan revolution and fought US troops in the MEXICAN WAR. He helped establish Mexican independence in 1821–29 and became president in 1833. When the Texan settlers revolted against his tyranny (1836), he defeated them at the ALAMO but lost the battle of SAN JACINTO, being himself captured, and had to resign: he was to gain and lose the presidency three further times (1841–44, 1846–47, 1853–55). He spent most of his later years in exile.

SANTA CLAUS, Christmastide bearer of gifts to children. The jolly fat man transported by flying reindeer and dropping presents down chimneys is a comparatively recent (19th-century) legend derived from St. NICHOLAS (introduced as Sinter Klaas to the New World by Dutch settlers), whose feast day (Dec. 6) was a children's holiday. A drawing by cartoonist Thomas NAST is believed to have helped fix the image of a rotund, white-bearded Santa Claus in the popular imagination after such a figure was described in Clement Moore's 1822 poem, "Twas The Night Before Christmas."

SANTA FE, capital of NEW MEXICO on the Santa Fe R, a minor tributary of the nearby Rio Grande. Founded by the Spanish c1610, it is the oldest state capital, ceded to the US after the MEXICAN WAR. Its many Spanish colonial buildings attract large numbers of tourists. Pop 48,899.

SANTA FE TRAIL, overland trade route between W Mo. and Santa Fe, N.M., in use from its opening-up in 1821 until the coming of the Santa Fe railroad in 1880. Manufactured goods passed W, furs and bullion E.

SANTAYANA, George (1863–1952), Spanish-born US philosopher, writer and critic. He was an influential writer on aesthetics in books such as *The Sense of Beauty* (1896). His philosophy was expressed in *The Life of Reason* (1905–06), where he emphasized the importance of reason in understanding the world but was skeptical of what one can really know. *Skepticism and Animal Faith* (1923) suggests a relationship between faith and knowledge.

SANTIAGO, capital and principal industrial, commercial and cultural city of Chile, on the Mapocho R. Industries include textiles, foodstuffs and iron and steel foundries. It was founded 1541 by VALDIVIA. Numerous earthquakes destroyed most of the colonial buildings and Santiago is now a modern city with parks and wide avenues. Pop 3,853,275.

SANTO DOMINGO, capital and chief port of the Dominican Republic, at the mouth of the Ozama R. Its official name was Ciudad Trujillo during 1930–61. Founded by COLUMBUS' brother Bartholomew in 1496, it is the oldest continuously inhabited European settlement in the W Hemisphere with a university dating from 1538. Pop 1,241,131.

SANTOS-DUMONT, Alberto (1873–1932), Brazilian-born pioneer aviator who experimented with balloons and powered dirigibles before flying his successful box-kite airplane (1906) and "Grasshopper" monoplane with undercarriage (1909).

SÃO FRANCISCO RIVER, great river of E Brazil. Partly navigable, it runs 1,800mi N and E from S Minas Gerais state to the Atlantic S of Maceió.

SAÔNE RIVER, important waterway in E France, rises in the S Vosges Mts and flows about 300mi SW to meet the Rhône at Lyons. Barges work the Saône to Corre, 233mi upstream.

SÃO PAULO, largest city and industrial center of Brazil. Capital of São Paulo state, it lies 225mi SW of Rio de Janeiro. Founded in 1554, it grew rapidly with the development of the coffee industry in the 1880s, and still sends coffee to SANTOS. Its other industries are diverse. It is the site of four universities and numerous cultural institutions. Pop 8,407,500.

Official name: Democratic Republic of São Tomé e Príncipe
Capital: São Tomé
Area: 372sq mi
Population: 85,000
Languages: Portuguese, Criolo
Religions: Roman Catholic, Animist
Monetary unit(s): 1 dobra = 100 centavos

SÃO TOMÉ E PRÍNCIPE, a republic in the Gulf of Guinea, off the W coast of Africa, comprising two main islands and several islets.
Land. São Tomé lies 190mi W of Libreville, Gabon. São Tomé Island (330sq mi) is

much larger than Príncipe Island, accounting for almost 90% of the country's area and holding about 90% of its population. The land rises to a 6,640ft peak of volcanic rock, sloping downward to fertile volcanic soil on the E coast. Forests grow near the W shore. Príncipe is similar in land pattern. The islands have a tropical climate.
People and Economy. The country depends heavily on cocoa for its income. Copra, coconuts, palm kernels, bananas and coffee are also important exports. There is a lack of mineral resources and industry is undeveloped. Most of the inhabitants are of mixed African and Portuguese ancestry. African migrant workers and a small group of Europeans are also present.
History. Discovered in the 1400s by the Portuguese, the islands achieved independence in 1975. The withdrawal of skilled Europeans after independence seriously disrupted the former plantation economy.

SAPIR, Edward (1884–1939), US anthropologist, poet and linguist whose most important work was on the relation between language and the culture of which it is a product. He suggested that one's perception of the world is dominated by the language with which one articulates.

SAPPHIRE, all GEM varieties of CORUNDUM except those which, being red, are called RUBY; blue sapphires are best-known, but most other colors are found. The best sapphires come from Kashmir, Burma, Thailand, Sri Lanka and Australia. Synthetic stones, made by flame-fusion, are used for jewel bearings, phonograph styluses, etc.

SAPPHO (6th century BC), Greek poet born in LESBOS. Surviving fragments of her work, mainly addressed to young girls, are among the finest classical love lyrics, combining passion with perfect control of many meters. The terms sapphism and lesbianism, meaning female HOMOSEXUALITY, derive from Sappho and Lesbos.

SARACENS, the name given by medieval Christians to the Arab and Turkish Muslims who conquered former Christian territory in SW Asia, N Africa, Spain and Sicily.

SARAJEVO, capital of the republic of Bosnia and Herzegovina in Yugoslavia, on the Bosna R. Here, Austrian Archduke Francis Ferdinand and his wife were assassinated on June 28, 1914, the event which sparked WWI. Pop 359,500.

SARATOGA, Battles of, a key series of engagements in the American Revolution. On Sept. 17, 1777, a British force led by General John BURGOYNE attacked an American encampment around Bemis

Heights, N.Y., defended by General Horatio GATES. Burgoyne's force, outnumbered, with heavy losses and without reinforcements was forced to retreat, and after further fighting eventually surrendered at Saratoga on Oct. 17. After this important victory, the French recognized American independence and allied themselves with the rebels. (See also REVOLUTIONARY WAR, AMERICAN.)

SARAWAK, a state of the Malaysia federation. A former British colony, Sarawak comprises 48,000sq mi of mostly mountainous country on the NW coast of Borneo. Oil, bauxite, rice, pepper, rubber and sago are its principal products. The state capital is Kuching. Pop 975,918.

SARAZEN, Gene (Eugene Saraceni; 1901–), US golfer who won the PGA championship three times (1922–23, 1933) and the US Open championship twice (1922 and 1932).

SARCOMA, a form of TUMOR derived from connective TISSUE, usually of mesodermal origin in EMBRYOLOGY. It is often distinguished from CANCER as its behavior and natural history may differ, although it is still a malignant tumor. It commonly arises from BONE (osteosarcoma), fibrous tissue (fibrosarcoma) or CARTILAGE (chondrosarcoma). Excision is required, though RADIATION THERAPY may be helpful.

SARDINE, a small, herring-like fish, properly the young of the PILCHARD.

SARDINIA, Italian island in the Mediterranean 120mi to the W of mainland Italy and just S of CORSICA. It is a mountainous area of 9,301sq mi, with some agriculture on the coastal plains and upland valleys. Wheat, olives and vines are grown and sheep and goats raised; fish and cork are also exported. Many different ores are extracted from the ancient mines and tourism is growing in importance. The island is an autonomous region of Italy, with its capital at Caligari.

SARDINIA, Kingdom of, the European state that formed the nucleus of modern, united Italy. In 1720, Sardinia was ceded to Savoy and the duke of Savoy became first ruler of the new kingdom of Sardinia, made up of Savoy, Sardinia and Piedmont, in N Italy. In the 19th century Sardinia championed political reform, national unification and independence from Austria. Through the diplomacy of CAVOUR, prime minister of Victor Emmanuel II, and the conquests of GARIBALDI, almost all of Italy was united under the house of Savoy in the period 1859–61, when Victor Emmanuel was proclaimed king of Italy. (See also RISORGIMENTO.)

SARGASSO SEA, oval area of the N Atlantic, of special interest as the spawning ground of American EELS, many of whose offspring drift across the Atlantic to form the European eel population. Bounded E by the Canaries Current, S by the N Equatorial Current, W and N by the GULF STREAM, it contains large masses of *Sargassum* weed.

SARGENT, John Singer (1856–1925), US painter famous for his many portraits of high society figures in the US and UK. His most famous picture, *Madame X* (1884), showing the alluring Parisian Madame Gautreau, created a furor that obscured the painting's brilliance.

SARNOFF, David (1891–1971), Russian-born US radio and television pioneer. Starting his career as a telegraph messenger boy, he became president of RCA, and later founded NBC, the first commercial TV network (1926).

SAROYAN, William (1908–1981), US author. After short stories like *The Daring Young Man on the Flying Trapeze* (1934) came sketches reflecting his Armenian background (*My Name is Aram*, 1940) and colorful, optimistic accounts of Depression and war years, as in the play *The Time of Your Life* (1939) and the novel *The Human Comedy* (1943), both filmed.

SARRAUTE, Nathalie (1902–), Russian-born French writer, creator of the "antinovel." Her technique, in such accounts of bourgeois life and psychology as *Tropisms* (1939) and *Portrait of a Man Unknown* (1947), rejects that of Realist novelists.

SARTRE, Jean Paul (1905–1980), French philosopher, novelist and playwright, famous exponent of EXISTENTIALISM. His works reflect his vision of man as master of his own fate, with his life defined by his actions: "existence precedes essence." Among his novels are *Nausea* (1938) and the trilogy *The Roads to Freedom* (1945–49). His drama includes *The Flies* (1943) and *No Exit* (1944). Sartre founded his review *Les temps modernes* in 1945. A close associate of Simone de BEAUVOIR and a communist who spoke eloquently for the left, his influence was international. In 1964 he refused the Nobel Prize for Literature.

SASKATCHEWAN, inland prairie province of W Canada. Fifth largest of Canadian provinces, it is North America's most important wheat-growing region.

Land. Falls into two main divisions: the N third of the province is made up of the CANADIAN SHIELD, the S two-thirds of plains and lowlands. The N contains many forests, lakes, swamps and streams and is rich in mineral deposits including copper, zinc and uranium. The S has the best farming soil, and the majority of the population live there. The climate is continental with cold winters (average 15°F in the S and −20°F in the N) and summer temperatures averaging 57°–67°F.

People. This is the only province that has a variety of ethnic inheritances, without a majority of either British or French. Over 25% of the population lives in the two largest cities, Saskatoon and the capital, Regina.

Economy. The economy is heavily dependent on farming, with 60% of Canada's wheat grown in the area. Other crops are barley, rye and flax. Agriculture is declining in relative importance with the discovery of oil and the growth of service-supply industries. The service sector now accounts for 50% of the total gross domestic product. Food processing and distribution and the manufacture of farm machinery are increasing. Oil refining and steel manufacturing are located in Regina and other northern communities. Heavy-oil pools have been discovered in the Lloydminster area, and the province is second in Canada in crude-oil production. Lignite coal, mined since the 1880s, has been strip-mined since 1956.

History. The paleo-Indians, believed to be the first people there, crossed from Asia 20–30,000 years ago. White traders from the HUDSON'S BAY COMPANY first entered the area in 1690. The area was not properly explored until LA VÉRENDRYE visited it 40 years later. Farming settlements spread after the purchase in 1870 of the North West Territories by the new Dominion of Canada. Rapid growth followed after Saskatchewan became a province in 1905. The Depression and war years brought hardship and discontent and led to the rise to power in 1944 of the Cooperative Commonwealth Federation, which remained in office till 1964. Petroleum and petroleum-based industries brought new wealth to the province in the 1970s and 1980s.

Name of province: Saskatchewan
Joined Confederation: Sept. 1, 1905
Capital: Regina
Area: 251,700sq mi
Population: 969,000

SASSOON, Siegfried (1886–1967), English poet and novelist. Decorated for bravery in WWI, he wrote bitterly satirical poetry such as *The Old Hunstman* (1917) and *Counterattack* (1918), which shocked the public with their graphic portrayal of trench warfare, their attacks on hypocritical patriotism and their pacifist conclusions. His novels include *Memoirs of a Fox-Hunting Man* (1928).

SASTRE, Alfonso (1926–   ), Spanish playwright, performances of whose work were once banned in Spain because of their pacifism and commitment to social change. Influenced by CAMUS, SARTRE and Arthur MILLER, Sastre's work includes *Death Thrust* (1959) and *Anna Kleiber* (1960).

SATELLITE, in astronomy, a celestial object which revolves with or around a larger celestial object. In our SOLAR SYSTEM this includes PLANETS; COMETS; ASTEROIDS and meteoroids (see METEOR), as well as the moons of the planets; although the term is usually restricted to this last sense. Of the 32 known moons, the largest is Callisto (JUPITER IV), the smallest PHOBOS. The MOON is the largest known satellite relative to its parent planet; indeed, the earth-moon system is often considered a double planet.

SATELLITES, Artificial, man-made objects placed in orbit as SATELLITES. First seriously proposed in the 1920s, they were impracticable until large enough ROCKETS were developed. The first artificial satellite, Sputnik 1, was launched by the USSR in Oct. 1957, and was soon followed by a host of others, mainly from the USSR and the US, but also from the UK, France, Canada, West Germany, Italy, Japan and China. They have many scientific, technological and military uses. Astronomical observations (notably X-RAY ASTRONOMY) can be made unobscured by the atmosphere. Studies can be made of the RADIATION and electromagnetic and gravitational fields in which the EARTH is bathed, and of the upper ATMOSPHERE. Experiments have been made on the functioning of animals and plants in space (with zero gravity and increased radiation). Artificial satellites are also used for reconnaissance, surveying, meteorological observation, as navigation aids (position references and signal relays), and in communications for relaying television and radio signals. Manned satellites, especially the historic Soyuz and Mercury series, have paved the way for space stations, which have provided opportunities for diverse research and for developing docking techniques; the USSR Salyut and US Skylab projects are notable. The basic requirements for satellite launching are determined by celestial mechanics. Launching at various velocities between that required for zero altitude and the escape velocity produces an elliptical orbit lying on a conic surface determined by the latitude and time of launch. To reach any other orbit requires considerable extra energy expenditure. Artificial satellites require: a power supply—SOLAR CELLS, BATTERIES, FUEL CELLS or nuclear devices; scientific INSTRUMENTS; a communications system to return encoded data to earth; and instruments and auxiliary rockets to monitor and correct the satellite's position. Most have COMPUTERS for control and data processing, thus reducing remote control to the minimum.

SATIE, Erik (1866–1925), French composer whose witty and highly original music was deliberately opposed to that of classic German composers. The word "surrealism" was first used in Apollinaire's notes to Satie's ballet music *Parade* (1917), scored for such instruments as typewriters and sirens. An influential figure in modern music, he encouraged younger French composers, such as Francis POULENC and Georges AURIC and the US composers Aaron COPLAND and Virgil THOMSON.

SATIRE, in literature or cartoons, on stage or screen, the use of broad humor, parody and irony to ridicule a subject. More serious than BURLESQUE, it contains moral or political criticism. In literature, classical satirists ARTISTOPHANES, HORACE and JUVENAL were followed by such writers as RABELAIS, DEFOE, SWIFT and VOLTAIRE.

SATO, Eisaku (1901–1975), prime minister of Japan 1964–72. A Liberal-Democrat, he presided over the reemergence of Japan as a major economic power and was active in foreign affairs. He won the 1974 Nobel Peace Prize.

SATURATION, term applied in many different fields to a state in which further increase in a variable above a critical value produces no increase in a resultant effect. A saturated SOLUTION is one which will dissolve no more solute, an EQUILIBRIUM having been reached; raising the temperature usually allows more to dissolve: cooling a saturated solution may produce **supersaturation**, a metastable state, in which sudden crystallization depositing the excess solute occurs if a seed crystal is added. In organic chemistry, a saturated molecule has no double or triple bonds and so does not undergo addition reactions.

SATURN, the second largest planet in the SOLAR SYSTEM and the sixth from the sun. Until the discovery of URANUS (1781), Saturn was the outermost planet known. It orbits the sun in 29.46 years at a mean distance of 9.54AU. Saturn does not rotate uniformly: its period of rotation at the equator is 10.23h, rather longer toward the poles. This rapid rotation causes a noticeable equatorial bulge: the equatorial diameter is 120.9Mm, the polar diameter 108.1Mm. Saturn has the lowest density of

any planet in the Solar System, less than that of water, and may contain over 60% hydrogen by mass. Its total mass is about 95 times that of the earth. Saturn has 17 known satellites; the largest, Titan, about the same size as MERCURY, has a cold nitrogen atmosphere with traces of methane and other gases. The most striking feature of Saturn is its ring system: composed of countless tiny particles of ice and rock. Three or four major ring divisions are visible from earth, but Voyager space probes revealed the rings to consist of hundreds of narrow ringlets. The rings are about 16km thick and the outermost has an external diameter of about 280Gm.

SATURNALIA, ancient Roman festival in honor of SATURN, god of the harvests. Schools and law courts were closed Dec. 17–23, work and commerce ceased, and both slaves and masters indulged in lavish feasting and the exchanging of gifts.

Official name: The Saudi Arabian Kingdom
Capital: Riyadh
Area: 927,000sq mi
Population: 8,465,000
Language: Arabic
Religion: Muslim
Monetary unit(s): 1 Saudi riyal=20 qursh=100 halalah

SAUDI ARABIA, kingdom covering most of the Arabian peninsula in SW Asia.
Land and Climate. Along the Red Sea in the W, the Hejaz and Asir mountains rise steeply from the coastal Tahimah plain. In the center is the vast barren plateau of NEJD. The Rub al Khali or Empty Quarter (250,000sq mi) in the SE and the An Nafud (25,000sq mi) in the N are sand deserts. In the E are the oil-rich Hasa lowlands. Coastal areas are very humid. In the interior daytime temperatures sometimes reach 120°F; yearly rainfall is generally less than 5in.
People. The population is almost entirely Arab. Riyadh, the capital, the Red Sea port of Jiddah and the holy cities of MECCA and Medina are the main centers. Despite the impact of oil, and the increase in

educational and health facilities, many of the people live a traditional life in villages or as nomads. The strictly fundamentalist Wahabi sect of Sunnite Islam is the state religion.

Economy. Saudi Arabia is the third-largest oil-producer, and the oil and natural gas industry dominates the economy. Profits from exports are being used for industrial development (especially oil refining) and ambitious irrigation projects, and have transformed the country into a world financial power. Other minerals produced include limestone, gypsum, and salt. Chief crops are sorghum, dates, wheat, barley, coffee, citrus fruits and millet. Livestock, raised mainly by nomadic Bedouin, includes camels, cattle, horses, donkeys, sheep and goats.

History. From the 7th century Islam served to unify the Semitic nomad tribes of Saudi Arabia, but rival sheikdoms were later established. In the 1500s Arabia came under control of the OTTOMAN EMPIRE. The WAHABI sect, led by the Saudi rulers of Dariya, conquered most of the Arabian peninsula 1750–1800. Modern Saudi Arabia was founded by IBN SAUD (d. 1953), who conquered Nejd and the Hejaz, joining them with Hasa and Asir, and establishing a hereditary monarchy. Succeeding rulers have been SAUD IV (deposed 1964), FAISAL (assassinated 1975) and Khaled. Saudi Arabia has supported Arab countries in conflict with Israel, but as an ally of the US has become an important moderate voice in Middle Eastern affairs. It plays a major role in the ORGANIZATION OF PETROLEUM EXPORTING COUNTRIES, consistently opposing rapid oil price increases.

SAUD IV (1902–1969), king of Saudi Arabia 1953–64, son and successor of Ibn Saud. His reign saw the new oil revenues flow in but Saud was incompetent to manage state finance. He was forced to abdicate in favor of Faisal, his brother.

SAUL, first king of Israel, c1000 BC. The son of Kish of the tribe of Benjamin, he was annointed by SAMUEL after the tribes decided to unite under a king. His reign was generally successful, but he killed himself after a defeat by the Philistines. His rival DAVID succeeded him.

SAULT SAINTE MARIE CANALS, three short canals on the St. Marys R, forming part of the GREAT LAKES–SAINT LAWRENCE WATERWAY between Lake Superior and Lake Huron. Two of the canals (each 1.6mi) are in the US, and one (1.4mi) is in Canada. They are among the busiest in the world.

SAUSSURE, Ferdinand de (1857–1913), Swiss linguist whose contributions to structural linguistics (e.g., the idea that the structure of a language may be studied both as it changes with time and as it is in the present) have had a formative influence on 20th-century studies of GRAMMAR.

SAVANNAH, first steamship to cross the Atlantic. A sailing packet on the New York-Le Havre route, she was fitted with engines which were used for 85hrs of the May–June 1819 voyage from Savannah, Ga., to Liverpool. The name Savannah was also given to the world's first (and so far only) nuclear-powered merchant ship, which was launched in 1959 and was in service from 1962 to 1970.

SAVINGS, in economics, that part of current INCOME not spent on consumption and retained after taxes. Today, INTEREST-bearing accounts, and purchase of INSURANCE or a MORTGAGE have replaced the traditional mattress as a way of protecting savings. Savings may be channeled direct into INVESTMENT by buying STOCKS or MUTUAL FUNDS. In MACROECONOMICS, if the total amount invested in a country equals the amount saved, the economy will be in equilibrium. If savings exceed investment, production, income and employment will tend to fall. (See also ALL SAVERS CERTIFICATE.)

SAVONAROLA, Girolamo (1452–1498), Italian reformer. A Dominican friar, he campaigned boldly against the MEDICI in Florence. By 1494 the Medici had left and he had created a democratic republic in Florence. He was excommunicated by his opponent, Pope ALEXANDER VI (1495), but continued to preach until his enemies and the rival Franciscans had him hanged and burnt as a heretic.

SAVOY, former duchy in the W Alps, now comprising the departments of Haute-Savoie and Savoie, SE France. The ruling house, founded in 1026 by Count Humbert, played a leading role in uniting Italy (1859–70) and provided the kings of Italy from 1861 to 1946. The historical capital is Chambéry.

SAXONS, a Germanic people who with the ANGLES and the JUTES founded settlements in Britain from c450 AD, supplanting the CELTS (see also ANGLOSAXONS). From modern Schleswig (N Germany) they also spread along the coast to N France before incorporation in CHARLEMAGNE's empire.

SAXONY (German *Sachsen*, French *Saxe*), region and former duchy, electorate, kingdom and state in E Germany, now part of the German Democratic Republic (districts of Leipzig, Dresden, and KarlMarx-Stadt, formerly Chemnitz).

Rich in minerals, the region has many industries and is noted for its textiles and Dresden china.

SAXOPHONE, a brass instrument, classed as woodwind since its sound is produced by blowing through a reed. Patented by the Belgian Adolphe Sax in 1846, the saxophone exists in soprano, alto, tenor, and baritone forms; the bass is rare. Sometimes used in the symphony orchestra, the saxophone is better known for its important role in JAZZ, where it is a leading solo and ensemble instrument. (See also WIND INSTRUMENTS.)

SAYERS, Dorothy Leigh (1893–1957), English writer of detective stories and creator of the popular, impeccably aristocratic and erudite detective Lord Peter Wimsey. He is the hero of some 16 books, beginning with *Whose Body* (1923). Sayers also wrote religious drama.

SCABIES, infectious SKIN disease caused by a mite which burrows under the skin, often of hands or feet; it causes an intensely itchy skin condition which is partly due to ALLERGY to the mite. Rate of infection has a cyclical pattern. Treatment is with special ointments and should include contacts.

SCALE, in music, a term used for various sequences or progressions of notes, ascending or descending. The best-known scales are those of the 24 major and minor keys of conventional western harmony, but there are other types (see KEY). The *chromatic scale* progresses through all the notes of a piano keyboard, going up or down by half-tones. The six-note *whole-tone* scale goes up or down by a whole tone, starting from any note. The *pentatonic scale* has five notes, being the black notes on a piano keyboard or any equivalent sequence. The Greek and medieval MODES are another type of scale, and a new type is used in serial or TWELVE-TONE MUSIC.

SCALLOPS, some 300 species of bivalve MOLLUSKS, family Pectinidae, distinguished by a characteristic shell: the valves being rounded, with a series of ribs radiating across the surface in relief. They have especially well developed eyes on the mantle rim. Unique among bivalves, scallops swim extremely well, propelled by jets of water expelled in snapping shut the shell.

SCAMOZZI, Vincenzo (1552–1616), Italian architect of the late RENAISSANCE. His work includes, in Venice, several palaces and the Procuratie Nuove and the Villa Pisani at Lonigo. His theoretical *Idea of Universal Architecture* (1615) became a classic.

SCANDINAVIA, region of NW Europe. Geographically it consists of the Scandinavian peninsula (about 300,000sq mi) occupied by Norway, Sweden and NW Finland, but the term normally includes Denmark. Because of close historical development, Iceland and the Faroe Islands are also covered by the term in matters of language, culture, peoples and politics. Modern "Norden" is synonymous with this usage.

SCANDINAVIAN LANGUAGES, a Germanic group of Indo-European languages, comprising Danish, Faroese, Icelandic, Norwegian and Swedish. Icelandic preserves many features of OLD NORSE, the common tongue of Viking Scandinavia. The Scandinavian colonists who took their language W to N France, Ireland and England, S to Sicily and E to Kiev and Byzantium were later assimilated or died out.

SCAPA FLOW, a large sea basin in the S Orkney Islands off the N coast of Scotland, the principal anchorage of the British navy in WWI and WWII. In 1919 the crews of the interned German fleet scuttled their ships here.

SCAR, area of fibrous tissue which forms a bridge between areas of normal tissue as the end result of wound healing. The fibrous tissue lacks the normal properties of the healed tissue (e.g., it does not tan). The size of a scar depends on the closeness of the wound edges during healing; excess stretching forces and infection widen scars.

SCARABS, a family of BEETLES which includes the DUNG BEETLES, CHAFERS and Dor beetles. Most of the 20,000 species are scavengers of decaying organic matter, especially dung, or feed on the foliage and roots of growing plants, as do the chafers, many of which may become agricultural pests.

SCARLATTI, Alessandro (1660–1725), Italian composer. A leading musical scholar and teacher, he composed hundreds of church masses, cantatas and oratorios, and over 100 operas. Few are now performed, but he is important for innovations in harmony, thematic development, and the use of instruments. His son **Domenico Scarlatti** (1685– 1757) also composed operas and church music, but is known for his many brilliant sonatas for harpsichord, which influenced Haydn and Mozart and are still widely played.

SCARLET FEVER, or scarletina, INFECTIOUS DISEASE caused by certain strains of *Streptococcus*. It is common in children and causes sore throat with TONSILLITIS, a characteristic SKIN rash and mild systemic symptoms. PENICILLIN and symptomatic treatment is required. Scarlet fever occurs in EPIDEMICS; a few are followed by RHEUMATIC FEVER or NEPHRITIS.

SCARNE, John (1903–   ), US card and gambling expert whose books include *Scarne on Cards* (1950), *Scarne on Magic Tricks* (1952), and *Scarne's Complete Guide to Gambling* (1962). He became widely known for his lectures exposing the tricks used by dishonest professional gamblers.

SCHACHT, Hjalmar Horace Greeley (1877–1970), German financier and banker. He helped halt post-WWI inflation and was finance minister (1934–37) and Reichsbank president (1923–30; 1933–39), but conflict with Goering and Hitler later led to imprisonment. He was acquitted at the NUREMBURG TRIALS.

SCHALLY, Andrew Victor (1926–   ), Polish-born US medical researcher who shared the 1977 Nobel Prize for Physiology or Medicine for his discovery and synthesis of hormones produced by the HYPOTHALMUS. The analysis of these hormones, which control body chemistry, had a revolutionary effect on the study of the functioning of the BRAIN.

SCHAPIRO, Meyer (1904–   ), Lithuanian-born US art historian and critic. One of the most highly regarded and influential art scholars in the US, he taught for many years at Columbia U. Among his books are *Romanesque Art* (1977) and *Modern Art: 19th and 20th Centuries* (1978).

SCHARNHORST, Gerhard Johann David von (1755–1813), Prussian general. After Napoleon's victory (1806) over an army in which he was serving, he reorganized the Prussian army. He laid the foundation of its general staff system and its reliance upon conscripted as opposed to professional men.

SCHEELE, Karl (or Carl) Wilhelm (1742–1786), Swedish chemist who discovered OXYGEN (c1773), perhaps a year before Joseph PRIESTLEY's similar discovery. He also discovered CHLORINE (1774).

SCHELDE RIVER, or Scheldt, important navigable waterway of NW Europe. Rising in Aisne department, NW France, it flows 270mi N and NE to Antwerp, Belgium, then NW, as the East and West Schelde rivers, through Holland to the North Sea. The Delta Plan has sealed off the East outlet (see NETHERLANDS). There are canal links to the Rhine and Meuse rivers.

SCHELER, Max (1874–1928), German philosopher whose important work in phenomenology helped spread its influence throughout the world. His best-known works are *Formalism in Ethics and Non-Formal Ethics of Value* (2 vols.,

1913–16) and *The Nature of Sympathy* (1928).

SCHELLING, Friedrich Wilhelm Joseph von (1775–1854), German idealist philosopher of the Romantic period, a pioneer of speculative thought after KANT. A student contemporary of HEGEL, Schelling later turned to religious philosophy and mythology. Both EXISTENTIALISM and modern Protestant theology have been influenced by him.

SCHERZO (Italian: joke), in music, a quick movement developed by Haydn and Beethoven from the MINUET and trio. It may occur in a symphony, sonata or concerto, or as a separate piece.

SCHIAPARELLI, Elsa (1890–1973), Italian-born French fashion designer who was the first couturière to open her own boutique (1935), which was decorated by Salvador DALI. She was known for her daring fashions, her fabrics designed by Dali, Cocteau and others, and the color "shocking pink." She pioneered in experimenting with synthetics.

SCHIAPARELLI, Giovanni Virginio (1835–1910), Italian astronomer who discovered the ASTEROID Hesperia (1861) and showed that METEOR showers represent the remnants of COMETS. He is best known for terming the surface markings of MARS *canali* (channels). This was wrongly translated as "canals," implying Martian builders: the resulting controversy lasted for nearly a century.

SCHIELE, Egon (1890–1918), Austrian expressionist painter. His work, influenced by the linear style of Gustav KLIMT, has great intensity, sometimes expressed in harsh color and brushwork. It includes nudes, portraits and landscapes.

SCHIFF, Dorothy (1903–   ), US publisher. Born into a wealthy New York investment-banking family, Mrs. Schiff bought the New York *Post* in 1939 and ran it as a politically liberal evening tabloid until 1977, when she sold it to Australian publisher Rupert Murdoch (1977).

SCHIFF, Jacob Henry (1847–1920), German-born US banker and philanthropist who headed the investment banking house of Kuhn, Loeb and Co. from 1885. He financed railroads with E. H. HARRIMAN and was one of the most influential bankers in the US.

SCHILLER, Johann Christoph Friedrich von (1759–1805), playwright, poet and essayist, a leading figure of German literature second only to his friend GOETHE. Human dignity and spiritual freedom are central to his work, which ranges from the poem "Ode to Joy" to the STURM UND DRANG drama *The Robbers* (1781) and the popular play *Wilhelm Tell* (1804). As professor of history at Jena he wrote on the THIRTY YEARS' WAR, later the setting of his great dramatic trilogy *Wallenstein* (1799).

SCHISM, Great. See GREAT SCHISM; PAPACY.

SCHIST, common group of METAMORPHIC ROCKS which have acquired a high degree of schistosity, i.e., the parallel arrangement of sheety or prismatic minerals resulting from regional metamorphism. Schistosity is similar in nature and origin to slaty cleavage (see SLATES) but is coarser. The major constituents of most schists are either MICA, TALC, AMPHIBOLES or CHLORITE.

SCHISTOSOMIASIS, or **bilharzia,** a PARASITIC DISEASE caused by *Schistosoma* species of FLUKES. Infection is usually acquired by bathing in infected water, the different species of parasite causing different manifestations. Infection of the BLADDER causes constriction, calcification and secondary infection, and can predispose to bladder CANCER. Another form leads to GASTROINTESTINAL TRACT disease with LIVER involvement. ANTIMONY compounds are often effective in treatment.

SCHIZOPHRENIA, formerly called **dementia praecox,** a type of PSYCHOSIS characterized by confusion of IDENTITY, HALLUCINATIONS, AUTISM, delusion and illogical thought. The three main types of schizophrenia are CATATONIA; **paranoid schizophrenia,** which is similar to PARANOIA except that the intellect deteriorates; and **hebephrenia,** which is characterized by withdrawal from reality, bizarre or foolish behavior, delusions, hallucinations and self-neglect.

SCHLAFLY, Phyllis (1924–   ), US conservative writer and leader. Author of *A Choice Not an Echo* (1964), which supported Republican candidate Barry Goldwater for president, she became the foremost woman conservative in the US. In books and commentary she has expressed her opposition to abortion and to the EQUAL RIGHTS AMENDMENT.

SCHLEGEL, Friedrich von (1772–1829), German philosopher. His stress on the subjective and spiritual in art and his studies of world history and literature greatly influenced ROMANTICISM in Germany.

SCHLEIERMACHER, Friedrich Ernst Daniel (1768–1834), German Protestant theologian and philosopher. He became famous with *Speeches on Religion* (1799), arguing that religion exists independently of morality or science. His great *The Christian Faith* (1821–22) discussed the essence of religion and Christianity, and the role of doctrine and theology.

SCHLESINGER, name of two famous 20th-century US historians. **Arthur Meier Schlesinger** (1888–1965), best known for his *The Rise of the City, 1878–1898* (1933) in the series he edited, *A History of American Life.* He stressed the cultural, social and economic context of history. **Arthur Meier Schlesinger, Jr.** (1917–   ), his son, won Pulitzer prizes for both *The Age of Jackson* (1945) and *A Thousand Days* (1966), the latter written after a period as special assistant to President Kennedy.

SCHLESINGER, James Rodney (1929–   ), US public official. A teacher of economics noted for his serious intellectual approach to issues, he served under both Republican and Democratic presidents as assistant director of the budget, chairman of the Atomic Energy Commission, director of the Central Intelligence Agency (1973), secretary of defense (1973–75) and secretary of energy (1977–79).

SCHLESINGER, John (1920–   ), British film director who made *Billy Liar* (1963), *Darling* (1965) and *Sunday, Bloody Sunday* (1971) in England and *Midnight Cowboy* (1969), for which he won the Academy Award, and *Marathon Man* (1976) in the US.

SCHLICK, Moritz (1882–1936), German philosopher regarded as the founder of the Vienna Circle, an influential school of LOGICAL POSITIVISM.

SCHLIEFFEN, Alfred von (1833–1913), German general, later field marshal. He drew up the "Schlieffen Plan" (1905) to combat France and her new ally Russia. The bulk of the German army would rapidly advance through Belgium and Holland to crush the French, before returning E to face the Russians. MOLTKE's modification of this plan failed in WWI.

SCHLIEMANN, Heinrich (1822–1890), German archaeologist, best known for his discoveries of Troy (1871–90) and Mycenae (1876–78). (See AEGEAN CIVILIZATION.)

SCHMIDT, Helmut (1918–   ), chancellor of West Germany. A Social Democrat, he was party floor leader in the Bundestag 1962–69, defense minister 1969–72 and finance minister 1972–74. He succeeded Willy Brandt as chancellor (1974) when the latter resigned amid a spy scandal. In a continent plagued with economic difficulties, Germany under Schmidt remained stable and prosperous. However, violent radical groups were a problem.

SCHNABEL, Artur (1882–1951), Austrian-US pianist. Best known for his reflective recordings of Beethoven's sonatas (which he edited), he was also a notable interpreter of Mozart and Schubert.

SCHNITZLER, Arthur (1862–1931), Austrian playwright; he wrote about love, lust and the personality basis of racism, particularly anti-Semitism, in the Vienna of Sigmund Freud. His work included *Anatol* (1893), *Playing with Love* (1896) and *Merry-Go-Round* (1897).

SCHOENBERG, Arnold (1874–1951), German composer, theorist and teacher who revolutionized music by introducing TWELVE-TONE MUSIC. His string sextet *Transfigured Night* (1899) with harmonic clashes was followed by the declaimed songs of *Pierrot Lunaire* (1912) and experiments in whole-tone and finally serial or 12-tone music culminating in his unfinished opera *Moses and Aaron* (1930–51). Schoenberg emigrated to the US in 1933. (See also ATONALITY; SCALE.)

SCHOLASTICISM, the method of medieval Church teachers, or scholastics, who applied philosophic (primarily Aristotelian) ideas to Christian doctrine. They held that though reason was always subordinate to faith, it served to increase the believer's understanding of what he believed. Typical scholastic works are the *commentary* on an authoritative text and the *quaestio*. The latter is a stereotyped form in which the writer sets out opposing authorities and then reconciles them in answering a question. AQUINAS' *Summa Theologica* consists of a systematically constructed series of *quaestiones*. (See also ABELARD; ALBERTUS MAGNUS; BONAVENTURA; DUNS SCOTUS; WILLIAM OF OCKHAM.)

SCHOLLANDER, Don (1946–   ), US swimmer. In 1964, at 18, he became the first swimmer to win four Olympic gold medals. He set nine world records from 1963–68.

SCHONGAUER, Martin (c1430–1491), German engraver and painter, born in Colmar, Alsace. His copper engravings of religious subjects had a profound influence on DÜRER and many others.

SCHOOL PRAYER ISSUE. The gathering political strength of the MORAL MAJORITY and the NEW RIGHT has inspired many attempts to circumvent the US Supreme Court's 8–1 decision of June 17, 1963, which declared that state and local laws requiring recitation of the Lord's Prayer or Biblical verses in public schools were unconstitutional because they violated the first amendment's guarantee of separation of church and state. In 1980, for instance, the school prayer issue arose in such diverse states as Ky., La., Mass., N.Y., S.D. and Tenn. Higher courts, if not lower ones, invariably followed the Supreme Court's lead, extending the constitutional ban on prayer to include such practices as posting of the ten commandments in public school classrooms and the holding of voluntary prayer meetings, which tend to subject nonparticipants to suspicion and social pressure for standing apart. Faced with these court defeats, the New Right's political leader, Sen. Jesse HELMS (R., N.C.), sponsored a bill in 1980 to abolish jurisdiction of the federal courts over state laws permitting "voluntary prayers in public schools," and the House adopted a proposal at the end of the year to prohibit use of federal funds to prevent schools from implementing programs of voluntary meditation and prayer.

SCHOPENHAUER, Arthur (1788–1860), German philosopher, noted for his doctrine of the will and systematic pessimism. In *The World as Will and Idea* (1819), his main work, he argued that will is the ultimate reality, but advocated the negation of will to avoid suffering, and the seeking of relief in philosophy and the arts. Schopenhauer's ideas influenced NIETZSCHE and modern EXISTENTIALISM.

SCHRÖDINGER, Erwin (1887–1961), Austrian-born Irish physicist and philosopher of science who shared with DIRAC the 1933 Nobel Prize for Physics for his discovery of the **Schrödinger wave equation**, which is of fundamental importance in studies of QUANTUM MECHANICS (1926). It was later shown that his WAVE MECHANICS was equivalent to the matrix mechanics of HEISENBERG.

SCHUBERT, Franz Peter (1797–1828), Viennese composer. He wrote nine symphonies, of which the Fifth (1816), Eighth (1822) and Ninth (1828) are among the world's greatest. He is also famous for his piano pieces and chamber music (especially his string quartets), but above all for his over 600 *lieder*, a form he raised to unprecedented heights of expressiveness and virtuosity. As well as individual lieder such as *The Erl King* and *The Trout*, he wrote song cycles, among them *The Maid of the Mill* and *Winter's Journey*.

SCHULBERG, Budd (1914–   ), US novelist. He made his reputation with *What Makes Sammy Run?* (1941), a realistic novel about a self-made movie mogul. His best-known screenplay, *On the Waterfront* (1954) won many awards.

SCHULLER, Gunther (1925–   ), US performer, conductor and composer. A horn player with the Metropolitan Opera

(1945–59), he became president of the New England Conservatory in 1966. Combining JAZZ and TWELVE-TONE techniques in what he called "third-stream music," he wrote chamber and orchestral works and operas.

SCHULTZE, Charles Louis (1924–   ), US economist and budgetary expert who served as President Lyndon Johnson's director of the Bureau of the Budget (1965–67) and headed President Jimmy Carter's Council of Economic Advisers (1977–80).

SCHUMAN, Robert (1886–1963), French statesman. Prime minister 1947–48 and foreign minister 1948–52, he launched the "Schuman Plan" which resulted in the EUROPEAN COAL AND STEEL COMMUNITY, precursor of the COMMON MARKET.

SCHUMAN, William (1910–   ), US composer. His symphonies, chamber music, ballets and opera are known for their rhythmic vivacity and their debt to jazz. His 1942 cantata, *A Free Song*, won the first Pulitzer Prize for music. He was president of the Juilliard School of Music (1945–62) and of Lincoln Center for the Performing Arts (1962–69).

SCHUMANN, Robert Alexander (1810–1856), major German composer whose compositions and music journal greatly influenced the music of his time. He did much to make known the early music of CHOPIN and BRAHMS. Though he wrote orchestral and chamber music, he best expressed his ardent Romanticism in his piano works and *lieder* (songs), most of the latter composed in 1840, when he married Clara Wieck, a leading pianist.

SCHUMPETER, Joseph Alois (1883–1950), Austrian-born Harvard economist. After studying economic development and business cycles, he concluded that monopoly companies and government intervention would stifle the entrepreneur, the moving force of capitalism, and that socialism would result.

SCHURMAN, Jacob Gould (1854–1942), US educator and diplomat. A philosophy professor at Cornell U. (1886–92) and co-founder and editor of the *Philosophical Review* (1892), Schurman served as president of Cornell (1892–1920) and helped build it into a major university. He was subsequently US ambassador to China (1921–25) and Germany (1925–30).

SCHURZ, Carl (1829–1906), German-US statesman. Exiled after the German REVOLUTION OF 1848, he supported Lincoln, who named him minister to Spain (1861). After Civil War service as a brigadier-general he was Republican senator for Mo., and an influential journalist, opposing President Grant's policies. He helped form the LIBERAL REPUBLICAN PARTY and was Hayes' secretary of the interior (1877–81).

SCHUSCHNIGG, Kurt von (1897–1977), Austrian political leader. After Nazis murdered DOLLFUSS in 1934, he succeeded as chancellor, continued the authoritarian Christian Socialist government and tried in vain to preserve independence from Nazi Germany, which occupied Austria and imprisoned him 1938–45. He later taught for 20 years in St. Louis before returning to Austria.

SCHUSTER, Max Lincoln (1897–1970), Austrian-born US publisher who, with partner Richard Leo Simon, founded the publishing house of Simon and Schuster (1924). The firm, which became known for paperback and "how to" books, became one of the giants of the trade book industry.

SCHÜTZ, Heinrich (1585–1672), German composer. Apart from madrigals and *Dafne*, Germany's first opera, his works are vocal settings of sacred texts, in German, with or without instruments; his famous Passions influenced Bach.

SCHWAB, Charles Michael (1862–1939), US industrialist. After helping to build and becoming president of the Carnegie Steel Co. (later J. Pierpoint Morgan's US Steel Corp.), he headed and expanded the rival Bethlehem Steel Corp. from 1903.

SCHWARTZ, Delmore (1913–1966), US poet admired for his rhapsodic yet philosophic style. His works include *In Dreams Begin Responsibilities* (1938), *Summer Knowledge* (1959) and *Last and Lost Poems of Delmore Schwartz* (1979).

SCHWARZENEGGER, Arnold (1947–   ), Austrian bodybuilding champion. The only person to win three major titles in one year (Mr. Universe, Mr. World and Mr. Olympia), he has gained additional renown as a tireless promoter of his sport.

SCHWARZKOPF, Elisabeth (1915–   ), German soprano, famous for operatic performances of Mozart, Strauss and Wagner in Vienna and London and later for her expressive singing of German *lieder*.

SCHWARZWALD. See BLACK FOREST.

SCHWEITZER, Albert (1875–1965), German musician, philosopher, theologian, physician and missionary. An authority on Bach, and a noted performer of Bach's organ music, he abandoned an academic career in theology to study medicine and became (1913) a missionary doctor in French Equatorial Africa (now Gabon). He devoted his life to the hospital he founded there. His many writings include *The Quest of the Historical Jesus* (1906). Schweitzer won the 1952 Nobel Peace Prize for his inspiring humanitarian work.

SCHWINGER, Julian Seymour (1918–   ), US physicist who shared with FEYNMANN and TOMONAGA the 1965 Nobel Prize for Physics for his independent work in formulating the theory of quantum electrodynamics.

SCHWITTERS, Kurt (1887–1948), German artist and writer associated with DADAISM. He made collages and "*Merzbau*," constructions of discarded objects, and poems of disparate print cuttings. He edited a Dadaist magazine, *Merz*, 1923–32.

SCIATICA, a characteristic pain in the distribution of the sciatic nerve in the LEG caused by compression or irritation of the nerve. The pain may resemble an electric shock and be associated with numbness and tingling in the skin area served by the nerve. One of the commonest causes is a SLIPPED DISK in the lower lumbar spine.

SCIENCE FICTION, literary genre which may loosely be defined as fantasy based upon speculation about scientific or social development. Probably the first true science fiction, or sci-fi, work was *Frankenstein* (1818) by Mary SHELLEY; it developed a still popular theme, man's inability to control what his research reveals. Only with the works of Jules VERNE and H. G. WELLS, however, did sci-fi break away from supernatural fantasy. In the US in the 1920s "pulp" magazines popularized the form, but all too often debased it. John W. Campbell's magazine *Astounding* (founded 1937, now called *Analog*) revitalized the genre through its consistently high literary standards; it nurtured writers who today lead the field, among them Isaac ASIMOV, Robert HEINLEIN, Poul Anderson, Hal Clement, Eric Frank Russell and many others. Many sci-fi writers, such as Asimov, Arthur C. CLARKE, Ray BRADBURY, Kurt VONNEGUT and John Wyndham have become household names; others, such as Fritz Leiber, Brian Aldiss, Robert Silverberg, Alfred Bester and Theodore Sturgeon, are less well known outside the field. The critical acclaim they and newer writers such as Larry Niven, Harlan Ellison, Samuel Delany, Stanislav Lem and Ursula K. Le Guin receive indicates that the best science fiction may rank with the best contemporary general fiction.

SCIENTIFIC METHOD. Science (from Latin *scientia*, knowledge) is too diverse an undertaking to be constrained to follow any single method. Yet from the time of Lord BACON, well into the 20th century, the myth has persisted that true science follows a particular method—Bacon's celebrated "inductive method." This allegedly involved collecting a vast number of individual facts about a phenomenon, and then working out what general statements fitted those facts. After the 17th century nobody attempted to follow that program. In the 19th century, philosophers of science came to recognize the possible existence of the "hypothetico-deductive method." According to this model, the scientist studied the phenomena, dreamed up a hypothetical explanation, deduced some additional consequences of his explanation, and then devised experiments to see if these consequences were reflected in nature. If they were, he considered his theory (hypothesis) confirmed. But K. POPPER pointed to the logical fallacy in this last step—the theory had not been confirmed, but merely not falsified; it could, however, be worked with provisionally, so long as new tests did not discredit it. Philosophers of science now recognize that they cannot justly generalize about the psychology of scientific discovery; their role must be confined to the criticism of theories once they have been devised. Historians of science, meanwhile, have pointed to the importance in scientific discovery of "external factors" such as the contemporary intellectual context and the structures of the institutions of science. Once distinct terms— "theory," "model," "hypothesis," "explanation," "description," and "law"— are all now seen to represent different ways of looking at the same thing—the units in what constitutes scientific knowledge at any given time. Indeed there is still no general understanding of how scientists become dissatisfied with a once deeply-entrenched theory and come to replace it with what, for the moment, seems a better version.

SCIENTOLOGY, religio-scientific movement stressing self-redemption which originated in the US in the 1950s and was incorporated as a church in 1965. Based on L. Ron Hubbard's theory of dianetics, a "modern science of mental health," scientology holds that all aspects of individual human behavior are linked and must be harmonized; it also posits a life energy in the universe at large which affects human behavior.

SCILLY ISLANDS, group of rocky islets, 30mi W of the S tip of Cornwall, SW England. The population of the five inhabited islands (6sq mi) engage in tourism and flower growing.

SCIPIO, name of a patrician family of ancient Rome which became famous during the PUNIC WARS. **Publius Cornelius Scipio** (236–184 BC), called Africanus Major, conquered HANNIBAL in the second Punic

War. He drove the Carthaginians from Spain, invaded Africa, and forced Hannibal to return from Italy to meet him. The resulting battle of Zama (202 BC) destroyed Carthaginian power. **Publius Cornelius Scipio Aemilianus** (185–129 BC), his adopted grandson, called Africanus Minor, commanded against Carthage in the third Punic War, capturing and destroying the city in 146 BC. He was an admirer of Greek culture, and his friends included TERENCE and POLYBIUS.

SCONE, Stone of, coronation seat of Scottish kings, removed to Westminster Abbey by Edward I in 1296. Scottish nationalists reclaimed it briefly 1950–51. Traditionally, Scone village, E Scotland, was the PICTS' capital.

SCOPES TRIAL, famous 1925 prosecution of a biology teacher for breaking a new Tenn. law forbidding the teaching of EVOLUTION in state-supported schools. Interwar religious fundamentalism secured such laws in several S states. For the defense Clarence DARROW unsuccessfully pitted himself against the orthodoxy of William BRYAN; the Tenn: supreme court reversed the conviction on a technicality, but the law was repealed only in 1967.

SCORPIO (the Scorpion), a medium-sized constellation on the ECLIPTIC; the eighth sign of the ZODIAC. Scorpio contains the bright star ANTARES.

SCORPIONS, a homogeneous group of terrestrial arachnids (see ARACHNIDA) having two formidable palps (claws) held in front of the head and a stinging tail curled forward over the back. All scorpions have a poisonous sting but few are dangerous to man. The sting is usually used in defense, or with the palps in catching prey. Scorpions are restricted to dry, warm regions of the world and feed on grasshoppers, crickets, spiders and other arthropods.

SCORSESE, Martin (1942–   ), US film director who built his reputation on gritty portrayals of the Italian-American milieu. His films include *Mean Streets* (1973), *Alice Doesn't Live Here Anymore* (1974), *Taxi Driver* (1976) and *Raging Bull* (1981).

SCOTCH. See WHISKEY.

SCOTCH-IRISH, the people of Scottish descent who emigrated to North America from Northern Ireland after 1713. They were largely descendants of the Scots who had colonized Northern Ireland.

SCOTLAND, former kingdom, now part of the UK (see GREAT BRITAIN). Covering N Britain and the HEBRIDES, ORKNEY and SHETLAND islands, it is 30,414sq mi in area. Over 50% of the population is urban; major cities include Edinburgh, the capital and cultural center, Glasgow, the industrial center, Aberdeen and Dundee. English is spoken everywhere, but some 77,000 Scots in the NW also speak GAELIC. Scotland was one of the first industrialized countries; its economy rests on iron and steel, aluminum, shipbuilding, chemicals, North Sea oil and the immensely lucrative whisky industry. Agriculture, mainly grain, sheep and cattle, and fishing are also important. Educational standards are among the world's highest, and cultural life flourishes. Scotland's original inhabitants were the PICTS, displaced by the Scots, Britons and Angles. United under KENNETH I MACALPIN, the country maintained an embattled independence from England, ensured by ROBERT THE BRUCE. A brief Renaissance flowering under JAMES IV ended in disaster at FLODDEN FIELD, and in the turmoil of the REFORMATION. James VI (JAMES I of England) united the crowns of Scotland and England, but union of government came only in 1707. It was widely resented, and England fueled this by attacking Scottish autonomy and prosperity; this helped incite the two JACOBITE rebellions (1715 and 1745). A great cultural rebirth followed, but also the hardships of the INDUSTRIAL REVOLUTION and Highland depopulation for sheep farming. Devolution (i.e., greater autonomy) was defeated by referendum vote in 1979

SCOTLAND, Church of. See CHURCH OF SCOTLAND.

SCOTLAND YARD, headquarters of the Criminal Investigation Department (C.I.D.) of the London Metropolitan Police. Its jurisdiction covers 786sq mi containing more than eight million people. It also coordinates police work throughout Britain and provides national and international criminal records.

SCOTS, English-based dialect of the Scottish Lowlands (not GAELIC, a different language). Its literary form flourished from the 13th to the mid-16th century, in the poetry of William DUNBAR and Gavin Douglas, and was revived by Allan RAMSAY and Robert BURNS in the 18th century.

SCOTT, George C. (1927–   ), US actor. A forceful, gravelly voiced stage and film star, he excelled in such motion pictures as *Anatomy of a Murder* (1959) and *The Hustler* (1962) and won an Academy Award for his performance as *Patton* (1970) and an Emmy Award for his role in the TV version of *The Price* (1971).

SCOTT, Robert Falcon (1868–1912), British explorer remembered for his fatal attempt to be the first to reach the South Pole. In 1911 he led four men with sleds

950mi from the Ross Ice Shelf to the South Pole. They arrived on Jan. 18, 1912, only to discover that AMUNDSEN had reached the Pole a month before. Scurvy, frostbite, starvation and bitter weather hampered the grueling two-month return journey, and the last three survivors died in a blizzard, only 11mi from the next supply point.

SCOTT, Sir Walter (1771–1832), Scottish poet and the foremost Romantic novelist in the English language. Scott was the inventor of the historical novel, and his vivid recreations of Scotland's past were widely read throughout Europe. He started by writing popular narrative poems, including *The Lay of the Last Minstrel* (1805). After these successes he turned to fiction, and completed 28 novels and many nonfiction works. His novels included *Waverley* (1814), *The Heart of Midlothian* (1818) and *Ivanhoe* (1819).

SCOTT, Winfield (1786–1866), US political and military leader, known as "Old Fuss and Feathers" for his obsession with procedure and detail and for his elaborate uniforms. Scott became a hero for his part in the WAR OF 1812. He was active in the Indian wars and in 1846 was appointed a commander in the MEXICAN WAR, and captured Mexico City. In 1852 he was the unsuccessful Whig presidential candidate. He commanded the Union Army until 1861.

SCOTTISH TERRIER, old Scottish breed of terrier now bred as a pet. It is 10in at the shoulder, has a large head, short legs, a deep broad chest and powerful shoulder muscles. It also has a very hard coat of wiry hair.

SCOTTO, Renata (1936?), Italian soprano. After her 1957 appearance at the Edinburgh Festival in Bellini's *La Sonnambula* she became internationally known. She made her Metropolitan Opera debut (1965) in *Lucia di Lammermoor*.

SCOTTSBORO CASES, celebrated US legal cases involving nine uneducated black youths who were accused in 1931 of raping two white women on a freight train in Ala. Indicted and tried in Scottsboro, all the youths were found guilty, and eight were sentenced to death. They had no defense counsel until two lawyers volunteered to aid them on the day of the trial. The first Scottsboro Case, *Powell v. Alabama*, reached the US Supreme Court in 1932. The court reversed the convictions on the ground that failure to provide adequate counsel for the boys violated the "due process" clause of the 14th Amendment. Three years later the second case, *Norris v. Alabama*, reached the US Supreme Court; it reversed the convictions because blacks

had been excluded from the grand jury that indicted the youths. Ultimately, all of the youths but one (who escaped) were released from prison.

SCRABBLE, a trade-marked word game for two to four players. A sophisticated extension of ANAGRAM games, it is played with number-valued letter tiles, the object being to form interlocking words of the greatest possible point value on a marked playing board. Developed in the US in the late 1940s, it has now been adapted for play in many languages and is marketed extensively abroad.

SCRIABIN, Alexander Nikolayevich (1872 – 1915), Russian composer and brilliant pianist, whose work was based on chords of fourths. He wanted performances of his *Prometheus* (1909–10) to be accompanied by a play of colored lights corresponding to the musical tones.

SCRIBE, Augustin Eugène (1791–1861), French playwright and librettist. Besides his libretto for VERDI's *The Sicilian Vespers* he also wrote librettos for AUBER, BELLINI and MEYERBEER.

SCRIPPS, Edward Wyllis (1854–1926), US newspaper publisher, founder of the first newspaper chain and of the wire service that eventually became United Press International. Beginning in the Midwest and West his chain spread into 15 states, by 1922, when Roy Howard, manager of UPI, became a partner. The Scripps-Howard organization subsequently acquired newspapers in nearly every state in the Union.

SCROFULA, TUBERCULOSIS of the LYMPH nodes of the neck, usually acquired by drinking MILK infected with bovine or atypical mycobacteria, and involving enlargement of the nodes with formation of a cold ABSCESS. The eradication of tuberculosis in cattle has substantially reduced the incidence. Treatment includes antituberculous CHEMOTHERAPY. It used to be called the **King's Evil** as the royal touch was believed to be curative.

SCUBA DIVING. See DIVING; SKIN DIVING.

SCULLING. See ROWING.

SCULPTURE, the artistic creation of three-dimensional forms in materials such as stone, metal, wood, or even canvas or foam rubber. (This article deals mainly with Western sculpture. For other periods of sculpture see: AEGEAN CIVILIZATION; BYZANTINE ART AND ARCHITECTURE; CHINESE ART; EGYPTIAN ART AND ARCHITECTURE; JAPANESE ART AND ARCHITECTURE; PRE-COLUMBIAN ART; PREHISTORIC AND PRIMITIVE ART.)

High cost and durability tended to make ancient sculpture an official and conservative art form. This is evident in the monumental sculpture of Egypt, which changed little in 2,000 years. Greek sculptors, who set enduring standards of taste and technique, aimed to portray beauty of soul as well as body, and idealized the human form. In the Archaic period (about 630–480 BC) Egyptian influence is evident in the frontal, stylized figures, showing little movement or emotion. Greater realism led to the classical perfection of PHIDIAS, and in the 4th century to PRAXITELES, with his more sensuous forms and wider range of expression. The HELLENISTIC AGE favored an exaggerated style, of which the LAOCOÖN sculpture and the WINGED VICTORY OF SAMOTHRACE are fine examples. Roman sculpture was deeply indebted to Greek art, but was also under ETRUSCAN influence, and excelled at realistic portraiture.

The Western tradition revived c1000 AD with the elongated, stylized figures of ROMANESQUE, leading to the more graceful and expressive sculptures of GOTHIC ART. RENAISSANCE sculpture, starting about 1350, was dominated by the Italians. GHIBERTI and DONATELLO treated classical models in a new spirit, and MICHELANGELO gave to works such as his *David* an inner tension quite foreign to classicism. The elegant MANNERISM of Benvenuto CELLINI and the elaborate BAROQUE of BERNINI gave way about 1800 to the neoclassical reaction of HOUDON, CANOVA, FLAXMAN and THORVALDSEN. The greatest 19th-century sculptor, RODIN, created a style of partially unworked figures, such as his *Balzac*, influencing EPSTEIN. This century has seen the abstract art of BRANCUSI and ARP, while Henry MOORE and GIACOMETTI showed interest in the human form. Outstanding American sculptors are David SMITH and CALDER, who invented MOBILES.

SCURVY, or VITAMIN C deficiency, involving disease of the SKIN and mucous membranes, poor healing and ANEMIA; in infancy BONE growth is also impaired. It may develop over a few months of low dietary vitamin C, beginning with malaise and weakness. Skin bleeding around HAIR follicles is characteristic, as are swollen, bleeding gums. Treatment and prevention consist of adequate dietary vitamin C.

SCYTHIANS, ancient nomadic people from Central Asia or possibly W Siberia, one of the earliest peoples to learn horsemanship. After the 9th century BC they spread into E Europe and S Russia making raids into the settled Near East. Their power was curbed by the MEDES about 600 BC. The kingdom of the Royal Scyths, 9th–2nd century BC, was defeated by the SARMATIANS. The wealth of the Scythians was shown by their gold and silver objects and jewelry.

SEA-BED MINING, the extraction of resources from the ocean floor. Although there are massive mineral deposits in the rocks of the deep-ocean floors, no technology exists at present for extracting them. Current interest is focused mainly on the small (one- to three-inch) round manganese nodules that litter the floors of deep oceans. The nodules contain iron, cobalt, nickel and copper as well as manganese, and represent a potentially rich minerals source awaiting the development of efficient deep-sea mining methods.

SEABORG, Glenn Theodore (1912–   ), US physicist who shared the 1951 Nobel Prize for Physics with E. W. MCMILLAN for his work in discovering several ACTINIDES (see TRANSURANIUM ELEMENTS): in 1944 AMERICUM and CURIUM, and in 1949 BERKELIUM and CALIFORNIUM. Later discoveries were EINSTEINIUM (1952), FERMIUM (1953), MENDELEVIUM (1955) and NOBELIUM (1957).

SEA COWS, an order, Sirenia, of aquatic mammals. Probably evolved from a marsh-dwelling ancestor related to the elephants, all the Sirenia are completely aquatic and seal-like, with the forelimbs modified into flippers and the hindlimbs fused into the horizontal flukes of a whale-like tail.

SEAGA, Edward (1930–   ), prime minister of Jamaica (1980–   ). Elected as a moderate, he tried to revitalize private industry in Jamaica and developed close ties with the US.

SEA HORSES, small, highly-specialized fishes closely related to PIPEFISHES. Unique among fishes in that the head is set at right angles to the body, they swim with the body held vertically. The body is encased in bony rings or plates. There is no tailfin and the hind part of the body is prehensile and may anchor the fish in seaweed. Males brood the eggs in special pouches on the belly.

SEALE, Bobby (1936–   ), American political activist and writer, co-founder of the Black Panther Party.

SEA LIONS, family Otariidae, eared seals, differing from true SEALS in having external ears and an almost hairless body. These are the animals most commonly seen in circuses and zoos. They are large creatures— males may measure between 2–3m (6.6–9.8ft) —and are active marine carnivores, feeding on fishes, squids and other mollusks.

SEALS, members of the mammal order Pinnipedia, which includes both the SEA

LIONS, and the True seals of the family Phocidae. True seals have no external ears and have a thick coat of strong guard hairs. Seals are animals of the colder seas of both hemispheres. Northern species (subfamily Phocinae) include the Bearded seal, the Gray seal and the Common or Harbor seal. Southern species (subfamily Monachinae) include the Monk seals, ELEPHANT SEALS, Crabeater and Weddell seals. Most seals are gregarious; all are pelagic and many come ashore only to breed. A single, light-colored pup is born and further mating takes place immediately afterward. Males form harems of females on the breeding grounds. Many species are now uncommon, having been formerly extensively hunted for their skins and meat.

SEARLE, Ronald (William Fordham, 1920–), British illustrator and cartoonist. His work ranges from lighthearted, satirical cartoons for *Punch* or *The New Yorker*, to drawings grimly depicting his WWII experiences as a Japanese prisoner.

SEARS TOWER, tallest inhabited building in the world (1,454ft), built in the mid-1970s, Chicago office building of Sears Roebuck. Prefabricated welded steel frames form a vertical core for the 110 floors.

SEASICKNESS. See MOTION SICKNESS.

SEA SNAKES, a family, Hydrophidae, of poisonous SNAKES that live permanently in the sea and are fully adapted to an aquatic existence, swimming with a sculling action of the paddle-shaped tail. They are fully air-breathing but can submerge for long periods. They feed on small fishes, immobilizing them first with a potent, fast-acting venom.

SEATTLE, largest city in Wash., the financial and commercial center and major port of the Pacific Northwest, seat of King Co. Seattle lies on Elliott Bay (Puget Sound), and its chief industries are aerospace production, steel, shipbuilding, food-processing and chemicals. Settled in 1852, Seattle rapidly expanded after the 1897 Alaska gold rush, and again following the boom created by WWII. Pop 493,846.

SEA URCHINS, spiny marine ECHINO-DERMS with spherical to somewhat flattened form, occurring worldwide. The basic structure is a sphere of 20 columns of calcareous plates. Within this "test," the internal structures, gut, gonads and water-vascular system, are looped around the inside wall. The center of the sphere is empty. The test bears tubercles and short spines, and also the pedicellaria: motile, pincer-like organs which clear the surface of detritus. Tube feet protrude through pores

in the test, arranged in double rows down the sides.

SEAWEED, popular name for the ALGAE found around coasts from the shore to fairly deep water. Commonest are the brown algae or wracks. Some, such as bladder-wrack, clothe the rocks between tides; others live up to 12m (39.4ft) deep. The large brown algae (KELPS) sometimes form thick beds of long, tangled fronds, with tough, well-anchored stems. GULFWEED is another widespread species. Delicate green and red seaweeds live mainly in rock pools. Seaweeds provide food and shelter to sea animals; many are used by man for food, fertilizer, iodine and gelatin.

SEBASTIAN, Saint (d. c288), early Christian martyr. Legend relates that he was a captain under the Roman Emperor DIOCLETIAN, and was sentenced, as a Christian, to die by archery (a scene recorded in many Italian paintings). He survived but was finally clubbed to death in the Amphitheater.

SEBASTIANO DEL PIOMBO (c1485–1547), Venetian painter. The warm colors of his early portraits and religious works show GIORGIONE's influence. He moved to Rome in his 20s and was associated with MICHELANGELO. His portrait of Christopher Columbus hangs in the Metropolitan Museum.

SEBORRHEA. See DANDRUFF.

SECESSION, in US history, the withdrawal of the Southern states from the Federal Union, 1860–61. A right of secession, arising from a STATES' RIGHTS interpretation of the Constitution, was claimed in the early 1800s by the defeated Federalist Party in New England. The concept died in the US when the CIVIL WAR ended in the Southern states' defeat.

SECOND COMING, or Parousia (Greek: arrival), in Christian ESCHATOLOGY, the return of JESUS CHRIST in glory to end the present order, to raise the dead (see RESURRECTION) and to summon all to the LAST JUDGMENT. The Second Coming was prophesied by Christ himself and by St. Paul; the early Church, and many ADVENTIST groups since, regarded it as imminent; some cults such as the JEHOVAH'S WITNESSES have repeatedly forecast its date.

SECRET POLICE, an organization, usually beyond democratic control, which aims its largely covert work at silencing political opposition or "threats to national security." Methods may range from surveillance to torture and murder. Notorious systems have been FOUCHÉ's in revolutionary France, the tsarist *Okhrana* and later the CHEKA, KGB and MVD in

Russia, the German GESTAPO and the Italian Fascist *Ovra*.

SECRET SERVICE, US, a branch of the US TREASURY Department. Established 1865 to suppress the counterfeiting of currency, it became responsible for protecting the president after the assassination of President William McKINLEY (1901). It now also guards the vice-president, the president-elect and his family, and presidential candidates.

SECRET SOCIETIES, interest-groups with secret membership, initiation rituals and recognition signs. Most have specific aims: religious (ROSICRUCIANS; the MYSTERIES of ancient Greece); political (CAMORRA; CARBONARI; KU KLUX KLAN); social or benevolent (as in MASONRY and college fraternities); or criminal (MAFIA; MOLLY MAGUIRES).

SECURITIES AND EXCHANGE COMMISSION (SEC), an independent agency of the US government set up in 1934 to protect investors in securities (stocks and bonds). It requires disclosures of the structure of all public companies and registration of all securities exchanged. SEC hears complaints, initiates investigations, issues brokerage licenses, and has broad powers to penalize fraud. (See STOCKS AND STOCK MARKET.)

SEDATIVES, DRUGS that reduce ANXIETY and induce relaxation without causing SLEEP; many are also hypnotics, drugs that in adequate doses may induce sleep. BARBITURATES were among the earlier drugs used in sedation, but they have fallen into disfavor because of addiction, side-effects, dangers of overdosage and the availability of safer alternatives. Benzodiazepines (e.g., Valium, Librium) are now the most often used.

SEDIMENTARY ROCKS, one of the three main ROCK classes of the earth's crust. They consist either of weathered (see EROSION) detrital fragments of igneous, metamorphic or even sedimentary rock transported, usually by water, and deposited in distinct strata. They may also be of organic origin, as in COAL, some organic limestone, or they may be formed by chemical processes, as in the EVAPORITES. Most common are SHALE, SANDSTONE and LIMESTONE. Sedimentary rocks frequently contain FOSSILS, as well as most of the earth's MINERAL resources.

SEDIMENTATION, in its narrowest sense the process of sediment deposition. In GEOLOGY, the term is often used as a synonym of sedimentology, which refers to the origin, transportation, and deposition of sedimentary materials and may include the postdepositional processes involved in the formation of SEDIMENTARY ROCK. In an even broader sense, sedimentation may also include sedimentary PETROLOGY and sedimentary petrography which encompass the description, classification, and interpretation of sedimentary rocks. STRATIGRAPHY is a closely related field.

SEDITION, advocating the violent overthrow of the government. During WWI, Congress passed sedition and espionage acts that banned communications attacking the US government. In appealing convictions under these acts to the US Supreme Court, defendants claimed a violation of their freedom of speech and press. In deciding such cases over the years, the court paid some attention to Justice HOLMES's "clear and present danger" test, but gave more weight to the "evil intent" of the defendants and, without exception, upheld their convictions.

SEED, the mature reproductive body of ANGIOSPERMS and GYMNOSPERMS. It also represents a resting stage which enables the PLANTS to survive through unfavorable conditions. The GERMINATION period varies widely from plant to plant. Seeds develop from the fertilized ovule. Each seed is covered with a tough coat called a testa and it contains a young plant or embryo. In most seeds three main regions of embryo can be recognized: a radicle, which gives rise to the root; a plumule which forms the shoot; and one or two seed leaves or COTYLEDONS which may or may not be taken above ground during germination. Plants that produce one seed leaf are called MONOCOTYLEDONS and those that produce two, DICOTYLEDONS. The seed also contains enough stored food (often in the cotyledons) to support embryo growth during and after germination. It is this stored food which is of value to man. Flowering plants produce their seeds inside a FRUIT, but the seeds of conifers lie naked on the scales of the cone. Distribution of seeds is usually by wind, animals or water and the form of seeds is often adapted to a specific means of dispersal. (See also POLLINATION; REPRODUCTION.)

SEEGER, Alan (1888–1916), US poet. He joined the French Foreign Legion at the outbreak of WWI and was killed in France. Among his *Collected Poems* (1916) is the famous "I Have a Rendezvous with Death."

SEEGER, Pete (1919–), US folk singer. A master of the 5-string banjo and 12-string guitar, he led the 1950s revival of folk with his group the Weavers. Many of his own freedom and pacifist songs have become classics of folk music.

SEEING-EYE DOGS, dogs trained to guide the blind. The majority of US guide dogs are GERMAN SHEPHERDS, and are schooled by The Seeing Eye Inc., founded in 1929 by Dorothy Harrison Eustis.

SEFERIS, George (1900–1971), Greek poet and diplomat. His lyrical, symbolic verse sets tragic modern events against the background of Greece's past. It includes *Turning Point* (1931) and *Poems* (1940). Seferis won the 1963 Nobel Prize for literature.

SEGAL, George (1924–   ), US sculptor. Born in New York City, he is best known for his life-size white figures, resembling plaster casts of his subjects, placed in natural settings, such as a doorway or behind a steering wheel.

SEGHERS, Hercules (c1589–c1638), Dutch etcher and painter famous for his fantastic, forbidding landscapes. To convey light effects he used CHIAROSCURO and, in his masterly etchings, AQUATINT (the first to do so) and colored paper.

SEGOVIA, Andrés (1893–   ), Spanish guitarist, most celebrated of modern players. He has done much to revive serious interest in the guitar, transcribing many pieces for it. FALLA, VILLA-LOBOS and others have composed works for him.

SEINE RIVER, France's principal waterway. Rising on the Langres Plateau NW of Dijon, it winds 475mi NW to PARIS, where over 30 bridges span it, through Rouen and Normandy, to the English Channel. It is the main artery of a far-reaching river system converging on Paris. Canals link it to the Loire, Rhône, Rhine and Schelde rivers.

SEISMOGRAPH, instrument used to detect and record seismic waves caused by EARTHQUAKES, nuclear explosions, etc.: the record it produces is a **seismogram**. The simplest seismograph has a horizontal bar, pivoted at one end and with a recording pen at the other. The bar, supported by a spring, bears a heavy weight. As the ground moves, the bar remains roughly stationary owing to the INERTIA of the weight, while the rest of the equipment moves. The pen traces the vibrations on a moving belt of paper. Seismographs are used in seismic PROSPECTING.

SEISMOLOGY, a branch of geophysics concerned with the study of EARTHQUAKES, seismic waves and their propagation through the EARTH's interior.

SELIGMAN, Charles Gabriel (1873–1940), British anthropologist who did pioneering field research among aboriginal peoples in Africa, New Guinea, Borneo and Ceylon.

SELKIRK, Alexander (1676–1721), Scottish sailor whose life as a castaway inspired Daniel DEFOE's novel *Robinson Crusoe*. In Sept. 1704, after a quarrel with his privateer captain, Selkirk chose to be put ashore on one of the uninhabited Juan Fernández islands. He was rescued in 1709.

SELLERS, Peter (1925–1980), English comic actor who created a staggering array of offbeat characters on British radio's "Goon Show" and in motion pictures. His films include *The Mouse That Roared* (1959), *The Pink Panther* (1963), in which he created the bumbling Inspector Clouseau, *Dr. Strangelove* (1963) and *Being There* (1980).

SELMA-MONTGOMERY MARCH, protest march from Selma, Ala., to the state capital, Montgomery, led by Reverend Martin Luther King, Jr. The march was provoked by the outrageous and violent means used by authorities and others in Selma to keep blacks from registering to vote. It began on Mar. 21, 1965, and ended five days later in Montgomery with 25,000 demonstrators present. The success of this march and the ugliness of the opposition contributed to the passage of the Voting Rights Act of 1965.

SELZNICK, David O. (1902–1965), US motion picture producer. His many commercial and artistic successes included *A Star is Born* (1937), *Gone with the Wind* (1939), *Duel in the Sun* (1946) and *The Third Man* (1949).

SEMANTICS, semasiology or **semology,** the study of meaning, concerned both with the relationship of words and symbols to the ideas or objects that they represent, and with tracing the histories of meanings and changes that have taken place in them. Semantics is thus a branch both of LINGUISTICS and of LOGIC. **General semantics,** propounded primarily by Alfred KORZYBSKI, holds that habits of thought have lagged behind the language and logic of science: it attacks such Aristotelian logical proposals as that nothing can be both not-x and x, maintaining that these are simplifications no longer valid.

SEMAPHORE, system of visual signalling using movable arms, flags or lights to represent letters and numbers. The first such system was introduced by Claude Chappe (1763–1805): it used towers 8 to 16km apart. Semaphore is still used for signalling between ships and on some railroads.

SEMICONDUCTOR, a material whose electrical CONDUCTIVITY is intermediate between that of an insulator and conductor at room TEMPERATURE and increases with rising temperature and impurity concentration. Typical **intrinsic semiconductors** are single crystals of GERMANIUM or SILICON. At low temperatures their valence electron ENERGY LEVELS are filled and no ELECTRONS are free to conduct ELECTRICITY, but with increasing temperature, some electrons gain enough ENERGY to jump into the empty conduction band, leaving a **hole** behind in the valence band. Thus there are equal numbers of moving electrons and holes available for carrying electric current. Practical **extrinsic semiconductors** are made by adding a chosen concentration of a particular type of impurity atom to an intrinsic semiconductor (a process known as doping). If the impurity atom has more valence electrons than the semiconductor atom, it is known as a donor and provides spare conduction electrons, creating an **n-type semiconductor**. If the impurity atom has fewer valence electrons, it captures them from the other atoms and is known as an acceptor, leaving behind holes which act as moving positive charge carriers and enhance the conductivity of the **p-type semiconductor** that is formed. An n- and p-type semiconductor junction acts as a RECTIFIER; when it is forward biased, holes cross the junction to the negative end and electrons to the positive end, and current flows through it. If the voltage connections are reversed, the carriers will not cross the junction and no current flows. Semiconductor devices, such as the TRANSISTOR, based on the p-n junction have revolutionized ELECTRONICS since the late 1940s.

SEMIMETAL. See METALLOID.

SEMINOLE, the last Indian tribe to make peace with the US government. They formed in Fla. out of an alliance including refugee CREEK INDIANS (from Ga.), native APALACHEE INDIANS and runaway Negro slaves. They fought Andrew JACKSON's troops in 1817–18 while Fla. was still a Spanish territory. The major Seminole War began in 1835 when the US government ordered removal to W of the Mississippi. A fierce guerrilla war against overwhelming odds ended in 1842, after which most Seminole were moved to Okla. However, a small band held out in the Everglades until 1934, when they agreed to a settlement.

SEMIOLOGY, or **semiotics,** the study of signs (including LANGUAGE), their uses, and the way in which they are used. Its branches are pragmatics (dealing with the relation between the signs and those using them), syntactics (the relation between different words and symbols) and SEMANTICS.

SEMITIC LANGUAGES, important group, found in the Near East and N Africa, of the Hamito-Semitic language family (see HAMITIC LANGUAGES). Most of the group are now extinct, extant members including Hebrew, Arabic and Maltese. A few were written in CUNEIFORM, but most used alphabets. The N Semitic alphabet, the first fully formed alphabetical WRITING system, is of particular importance as it is from this that most of the letters of the Latin ALPHABET have descended.

SEMMELWEISS, Ignaz Philipp (1818–1865), Hungarian obstetrician who, through his discovery that PUERPERAL FEVER was transmitted by failure of obstetricians to thoroughly clean their hands between performing autopsies of mothers who had died of the disease and making examinations of living mothers, first practised ASEPSIS.

SENATE, Roman (Latin *senes*: elders), originally an advisory council to the kings of ancient Rome, in the later Roman republic the chief governing body as PLEBEIANS challenged the PATRICIAN nobility's monopoly of the 300 life appointments to the senate. Revolts led by the TRIBUNES and by military leaders (see GRACCHI; CINNA; MARIUS) preceded severe curtailment of the powers of the increasingly corrupt Senate, which was thereafter dominated by the emperors.

SENDAK, Maurice Bernard (1928–   ), US illustrator and author of children's books whose inventive renderings of monsters both delight and terrify. His works include the Caldecott Medal winners *Where the Wild Things Are* (1963) and *In the Night Kitchen* (1970). His lively art became known to an even wider public in the 1980s through his stage sets for operas, including *Cosi fan tutte.*

SENECA, Lucius Annaeus (c4 BC–65 AD), Roman statesman, philosopher and writer. The most important feature of his political life is the role he played in restraining the worst excesses of NERO. Writing in highly rhetorical, epigrammatic style, Seneca advocated STOICISM in his *Moral Letters,* essays, one masterly satire and nine bloody, intense tragedies. After implication in a conspiracy he was commanded to suicide.

SENECA FALLS CONVENTION, first women's rights convention in the US, organized by Lucretia MOTT and Elizabeth STANTON and held at Seneca Falls, W central N.Y., 1848. The convention's chief assertion was that women should be entitled to vote.

SENEGAL, a republic located on the bulge of W Africa.

Land. Apart from high borderlands in the E and SE, Senegal is a low-lying country of rolling grassland plains. Four rivers—the

Senegal and the Gambia among them—cross the country. Tropical rain forests cover the SW. Senegal's climate is varied: cool on the coast and hot inland.

People. Among the major ethnic groups, the most numerous are the Wolof, Foulah, Serere, Toucouleur and Diola. Most of the population is illiterate and about 80% are Muslim. The majority live in rural areas, primarily along the Senegal R, and engage in agriculture. Dakar, the capital, is a modern port city and site of the national university.

Economy. Senegal is one of the more prosperous and stable countries in Africa, but a recent period of drought sharply reduced national output of peanuts, on which the economy largely depends. Fish and livestock are also important. Industry, mainly in Dakar, centers around food processing. Calcium and phosphates are important mineral exports.

History. Parts of Senegal were within the medieval empires of Ghana, Mali and Songhai. Under French control from 1895, Senegal was part of the Federation of Mali 1959–60, but declared itself independent in 1960. SENGHOR, president for two decades following independence, was succeeded by Abdou Diouf, formerly prime minister.

Official name: Republic of Senegal
Capital: Dakar
Area: 75,750sq mi
Population: 5,675,000
Languages: French; Wolof, Fulani. Mende spoken
Religions: Muslim, Christian
Monetary unit(s): 1 CFA franc=100 centimes

SENGHOR, Léopold-Sédar (1906–   ), Senegalese statesman and poet, Senegal's first president (1960–1980). He became known for his philosophy of *négritude*, a concept of socialism incorporating black African values.

SENNETT, Mack (1884–1960), Canadian-born US silent movie director-producer, a pioneer of "slapstick humor" on the screen. After working with D. W. GRIFFITH he formed his own Keystone Co.

and made over 1,000 "shorts" with his Keystone Kops, Bathing Beauties and stars like CHAPLIN. W. C. FIELDS and Gloria SWANSON.

SENSATIONALISM, philosophical theory which in its most extreme forms (see CYRENAICS; CONDILLAC) holds that knowledge is composed wholly of sensations, the mind being regarded as a passive *tabula rasa* (clean slate).

SEOUL, capital, largest city and industrial and cultural center of South Korea, on the Han R, 25mi E of Inchon, its seaport. It was founded in 1392 as capital of the Yi dynasty, which it remained until 1910. Seoul changed hands several times in the KOREAN WAR and suffered great damage. Largely rebuilt, it has grown rapidly. Pop 6,879,464.

SEPARATION OF POWERS, political theory developed by MONTESQUIEU from his studies of the British constitution, arguing that the arbitrary exercise of government power should be avoided by dividing it between distinct departments, the EXECUTIVE, LEGISLATURE and JUDICIARY. This was a basic principle of the Founding Fathers in producing the US Constitution; legislative powers were vested in Congress, judicial powers in the Supreme and subsidiary courts and executive powers in the president and his governmental machinery. Each branch was to have its functions, duties and authority, and in theory no branch could encroach upon another. In practice there has always been a degree of necessary overlap. The legislature can oppose and impeach members of the executive, the president can veto legislation and the Supreme Court can adjudicate the actions of the other branches; its members, in turn, are presidential appointees subject to congressional approval. In US history one branch has always tended to dominate others for long periods, but this "checks and balances" effect has at least ensured that power can and does shift between them.

SEPARATISTS, those English religious congregations who sought independence from the state and established church, beginning in 1580 with the Norwich Brownists (see BROWNE, ROBERT). John ROBINSON led refugee Separatists in Leyden, Holland, who were later prominent among the PILGRIM FATHERS. (See also CONGREGATIONAL CHURCHES.)

SEPHARDIM, Spanish Jews who fled the INQUISITION (1480) for Portugal, N Africa, Italy, Holland (notably Amsterdam), the Balkans (Salonika), Near East and America. Sephardim had their own language, literature and ritual.

SEPOY REBELLION, or Indian Mutiny, or the First War of Independence, a mutiny of Sepoys (Hindi: troops) in the Bengal Army of the EAST INDIA COMPANY. It began at Meerut, near Delhi, in May 1857 and spread over N India. The immediate cause was the issuing of cartridges greased with the fat of cows (sacred to Hindus) and pigs (unclean to Muslims), but years of increasing British domination led to a general revolt which was not suppressed until March 1858. As a result the British government took over the rule of India.

SEPTEMBER, ninth month of the year, derived from Latin *septem*, seven, an indication of its old position in the pre-Julian Roman CALENDAR.

SEPTICEMIA, circulation of infective BACTERIA and the white BLOOD cells responding to them in the blood. Bacteria may transiently enter the blood normally but these are removed by the RETICULOENDOTHELIAL SYSTEM. If this system fails and bacteria continue to circulate, their products and those of the white cells initiate a series of reactions that lead to SHOCK, with warm extremities, FEVER or hypothermia. Septic EMBOLISM may occur causing widespread ABSCESSES. GRAM'S STAIN-negative bacteria (usually from urinary or GASTROINTESTINAL TRACT) and STAPHYLOCOCCUS cause severe septicemia. Treatment includes ANTIBIOTICS and resuscitative measures for shock.

SEPTUAGINT, oldest Greek translation of the Hebrew OLD TESTAMENT, probably from an older source than any now extant. The PENTATEUCH was translated in Alexandria at the behest of PTOLEMY II (c250 BC), according to legend by 70 or 72 scholars (hence the name); completed, including the APOCRYPHA, c130 BC.

SEQUOIA NATIONAL PARK, 600sq mi park, S central Cal. (administered with the adjacent KINGS CANYON NATIONAL PARK), established 1890 to preserve the groves of giant SEQUOIA. Lying in the S Sierra Nevada, it includes Mt WHITNEY, highest US peak outside Alaska.

SEQUOYA (c1770–1843), Cherokee Indian silversmith who devised an alphabet whose 85 characters represented every sound in Cherokee language, enabling thousands of Cherokees to read and write. The SEQUOIA tree is named for him.

SERBIA, historic Balkan state, since WWII the easternmost of the six constituent republics of YUGOSLAVIA. The Serbs were SLAVS who settled the Balkans from the 600s onward. Stephen Nemanja (ruled 1168–96) created the first united kingdom, which became a great empire under Stephen Dushan (1331–1355), but after the battle of Kosovo (1389) Serbia remained under Turkish rule until independence was restored in 1878. After WWI occupation by Austria, it became the core of the kingdom of Yugoslavia. Serbia (34,000sq mi) is mountainous and mainly agricultural. Its capital is BELGRADE.

SERBO-CROATIAN, the principal language of Yugoslavia. One of the SLAVONIC LANGUAGES, it is written in Cyrillic (by the majority Serbs) or Latin (by the Croats) characters.

SERIAL MUSIC. See TWELVE-TONE MUSIC.

SERKIN, Rudolf (1903–), Bohemian-born US pianist. He studied with SCHOENBERG in Vienna, made his US debut in 1933 and joined the Curtis Institute of Music, Philadelphia, in 1939. A noted Beethoven interpreter, he has played in concerts all over the world. His son Peter Serkin (1947–) is also a prominent pianist.

SERLING, Rod (1924–1975), US author and TV producer. He wrote the outstanding television plays *Patterns* (1955) and *Requiem for a Heavyweight* (1959) and produced and hosted the TV series *Twilight Zone* (1949–64).

SERMON ON THE MOUNT, Christ's most important discourse, described in Matthew 5–7. Encapsulating most of the principles of Christian ethics, stressing the power of love and God's role as a loving father, it contains also the BEATITUDES and the LORD'S PRAYER.

SERRA, Junípero (1713–1784), Mallorcan Franciscan missionary. A famous preacher and professor, he went to Mexico in 1749 and worked among the Indians of the Sierra Gorda. Franciscans under his leadership established, from 1769 onward, nine missions in present-day Cal., including San Carlos at Monterey.

SERUM, the clear yellowish fluid that separates from BLOOD, LYMPH and other body fluids when they clot. It contains water, PROTEINS, fat, minerals, HORMONES and UREA. Serum therapy involves injecting (horse or human) serum containing ANTIBODIES (GLOBULINS), which can destroy particular pathogens. Occasionally injected serum gives rise to an allergic reaction known as serum sickness; a second injection of the same serum may induce ANAPHYLAXIS.

SERVAN-SCHREIBER, Jean-Jacques (1924–), French journalist who founded the liberal weekly news magazine *L'Express*. His books include the best-selling *American Challenge* (1967).

SERVETUS, Michael (1511–1553), or

Miguel Serveto, Spanish biologist and theologian. In *Christianity Restored* (1553) he mentioned in passing his discovery of the pulmonary circulation (see BLOOD CIRCULATION). For heretical views expressed in this book he was denounced by the Calvinists to the Catholic Inquisition: escaping, he foolishly visited Geneva where he was seized by the Protestants, tried for heresy and burned alive.

SERVICE, Robert William (1874–1958), British-born Canadian writer. His enormously popular, often humorous ballads, starting with *Songs of a Sourdough* (1907), told of the rugged life and characters of the Yukon and of the KLONDIKE gold rush.

SERVOMECHANISM, an automatic control device (see MECHANIZATION AND AUTOMATION) which controls the position, velocity or acceleration of a high-power output device by means of a command signal from a low-power reference device. By FEEDBACK, the error between the actual output state and the state commanded is measured, amplified and made to drive a servomotor which corrects the output. The drive may be electrical, hydraulic or pneumatic.

SESAME STREET, innovative children's television program which aims at imparting basic educational concepts through an entertaining mix of music, talk, puppets and animated comics. Inaugurated 1969 on the Public Broadcasting System (PBS) as an original production of the Children's Television Workshop, the program successfully utilizes media techniques to teach.

SESSIONS, Roger Huntington (1896–), US composer. He studied with Ernest BLOCH and has taught at leading US academic institutions. His orchestral, chamber and choral works are characterized by complexity, POLYPHONY, and rhythmic vitality.

SETON, Elizabeth Ann or Mother Seton (née Bayley: 1774–1821), first native-born US saint. A devout Episcopalian, she was widowed at 28 with five children. In 1805, she converted to Catholicism. She opened an elementary school, now regarded as the basis of the US parochial school system, and in 1813 founded the first US religious society, the Sisters of Charity. She was canonized in 1975.

SEURAT, Georges (1859–1891), French painter, one of a small group representing Neoimpressionism or POSTIMPRESSIONISM. Interested in color from scientific and artistic points of view, he invented POINTILLISM. Best known of his paintings is probably *A Sunday Afternoon on the Island of La Grande Jatte* (1884–86).

SEUSS, Dr. (1904–), pen name of Theodor Seuss Geisal, US author-illustrator of many children's books. His imaginative verse tales (*Horton Hears a Who*, 1954; *How the Grinch Stole Christmas*, 1957) and humorous pictorial fantasies are tremendously popular with the very young.

SEVAREID, Eric (1912–), US broadcast journalist with CBS (1939–77). He covered WWII and was subsequently a Washington correspondent and TV political commentator. An urbane and authoritative presence on the home screen, he was a trenchant critic of McCarthyism, the Vietnam War and the administration of President Richard Nixon.

SEVASTOPOL, Black Sea port of the CRIMEA peninsula, Ukrainian SSR, USSR. Now a major Soviet naval base, industrial city and railroad terminal, the city suffered long sieges in the CRIMEAN WAR (1854–55) and WWII (1941–42).

SEVENTH-DAY ADVENTISTS. See ADVENTISTS.

SEVEN WONDERS OF THE WORLD, the seven greatest structures of the ancient world, as listed by Greek scholars. The oldest wonder (and only survivor) are the PYRAMIDS of Egypt: the others were the HANGING GARDENS OF BABYLON; the 30ft statue of Zeus at OLYMPIA; the great temple of ARTEMIS at EPHESUS; the MAUSOLEUM at Halicarnassus; the COLOSSUS OF RHODES; and the PHAROS of Alexandria.

SEVEN YEARS' WAR (1756–1763), a war between Austria, France, Russia, Saxony, Sweden (from 1757) and (after 1762) Spain on the one side and Britain, Prussia and Hanover on the other. In America the struggle centered on colonial rivalry between Britain and France and formed part of the FRENCH AND INDIAN WARS. In Europe the main dispute was between Austria and Prussia for supremacy in Germany. Austria's MARIA THERESA aimed to recover recently-lost Silesia (see AUSTRIAN SUCCESSION, WAR OF THE). This provoked Prussia to attack Saxony and Bohemia. Although severely pressed, the Prussians avoided complete defeat. By the treaties of Hubertusberg and Paris (1763), Britain emerged as the leading colonial power and Prussia as a major European force.

SEVERSKY, Alexander Procofieff de. See DE SEVERSKY, ALEXANDER PROCOFIEFF.

SEVIER, John (1745–1815), US pioneer and first governor of Tenn. He was prominent in the Carolina Campaign of the

Revolutionary War and became head of the state of Franklin in 1783 (see FRANKLIN. STATE OF). Sevier was made governor of Tenn. in 1796, serving until 1801, and again 1803–09. He was also a congressman (1789–91 and 1811–15).

SEWAGE, the liquid and semisolid wastes from dwellings and offices, industrial wastes, and surface and storm waters. Sewage systems collect the sewage, transport and treat it, then discharge it into rivers, lakes or the sea. Vaulted sewers were developed by the Romans but from the Middle Ages and until the mid-19th century sewage flowed through the open gutters of cities, constituting a major health hazard. Then sewage was discharged into storm-water drains which were developed into sewers. But the dumping of large amounts of untreated sewage into rivers led to serious water POLLUTION, and modern treatment methods arose, at least for major cities. An early solution (still sometimes practiced) was sewage farming, raw sewage being used as FERTILIZER. Chemically-aided precipitation was also tried, but neither proved adequate. Noting that natural watercourses can purify a moderate amount of sewage, sanitary engineers imitated natural conditions by allowing atmospheric oxidation of the organic matter, first by passing it intermittently through a shallow tank filled with large stones (the "trickling filter"), and later much more successfully by the **activated-sludge process**, in which compressed air is passed through a sewage tank, the sludge being decomposed by the many microorganisms that it contains. A by-product is sludge gas, chiefly methane, burned as fuel to help power the treatment plant. Sedimentation is carried out before and after decomposition; the filtered solids are buried, incinerated or dried for fertilizer. The sewer system is designed for fast flow (about 1m/s) to carry the solids; the sewers are provided with manholes, drainage inlets, regulators and, finally, outfalls. Dwellings not connected to the sewers have their own SEPTIC TANK.

SEWARD, William Henry (1801–1872), US politician famous for his purchase of ALASKA from Russia in 1867. Seward served under Thurlow WEED in N.Y. and as a prominent antislavery senator was appointed secretary of state by President Lincoln in 1861. He did much to keep Britain out of the Civil War (see TRENT AFFAIR). Seward survived an assassination attempt by an accomplice of BOOTH and served as President Johnson's secretary of state.

SEWING MACHINE, machine for sewing cloth, leather or books: a major industrial and domestic labor-saving device. There are two main types: chainstitch machines, using a needle and only one thread, with a hook that pulls each looped stitch through the next; and lock-stitch machines, using two threads, one through the needle eye and the other, which interlocks with the first in the material, from a bobbin/shuttle system (to-and-fro or rotary). Chain-stitch machines—the first to be invented, by Barthélemy Thimmonier (1793–1859)—are now used chiefly for sacks or bags. The lock-stitch machines now in general use are based on that invented by Elias HOWE (1846). Zigzag machines differ from ordinary straight-stitch machines in having variously-shaped cams that move the needle from side to side. Almost all US machines are electrically powered, but foot-treadle machines are common elsewhere.

SEX, the totality of the differences between the male and female partners engaged in sexual REPRODUCTION. Examples of sex are found among all levels of life save the VIRUSES. In the higher orders, fertilization is brought about by the fusion of two GAMETES, the male SPERM conveying genetic information to the female EGG, or ovum (see HEREDITY). Many INVERTEBRATES, most PLANTS and some FISHES are HERMAPHRODITE; that is, individuals may possess functioning male *and* female organs. This is not the case with BIRDS and MAMMALS, though these on occasion display **intersexuality**, where an individual may possess a confusion of male and female characteristics. **Sexual behavior** is an important facet of animal behavior (see BREEDING BEHAVIOR; RITUALS): it may also be at the root of AGGRESSION and TERRITORIALITY. To the psychologist, "sex" and "sexual behavior" are used in connection with human drives linked to reproduction, and similarly fantasies, sensations, etc. To the psychoanalyst, sexual behavior has its roots in INFANTILE SEXUALITY as well as INSTINCT; and the term also covers a wide range of behavior derived from or analogous to sexuality and sexual drives. (See also HOMOSEXUALITY.)

SEX EDUCATION, instruction in schools and other social institutions on the subjects of human sexuality and sexual behavior. The instruction seeks to help the student understand the maturing process as related to sex, eliminate anxieties relative to sexual development, learn moral values and guard against damage to mental and physical health. Under the leadership of Dr. Mary Calderone, the Sex Information and Education Council of the US (founded 1963) has encouraged the development of carefully planned programs of study to be given by full-time faculty members to public school pupils at appropriate age levels. Opponents contend that sex education in the schools stimulates an inordinate and premature interest in the subject and that teachers may impose their own values on students.

SEX HORMONES. See ANDROGENS; ESTROGENS; GLANDS; HORMONES.

SEXTANT, instrument for NAVIGATION, invented in 1730 and superseding the ASTROLABE. A fixed telescope is pointed at the HORIZON, and a radial arm is moved against an arc graduated in degrees until a mirror which it bears reflects an image of a known star or the sun down the telescope to coincide with the image of the horizon. The angular elevation of the star, with the exact time (see CHRONOMETER), gives the LATITUDE. The air sextant is a similar instrument, usually periscopic, designed for use in aircraft, and has an artificial horizon, generally a bubble level.

Official name: Republic of Seychelles
Capital: Victoria, on Mahé
Area: 107sq mi
Population: 62,200
Languages: English; French; Creole patois spoken
Religion: Roman Catholic
Monetary unit(s): 1 Seychelle rupee = 100 cents

SEYCHELLES, independent republic of some 85 islands (largest Mahé) in the Indian Ocean NE of the island of Madagascar. The climate is hot and often humid. About 90% of the population lives on Mahé. Most of the population is of mixed French and African descent. Chief products are coconuts and spices, and fishing and tourism are important. First settled by the French in the mid-1700s the islands were taken by the British in 1794 and made a dependency of Mauritius in 1810. They became a separate colony in 1903 and were granted independence in June 1976.

SEYSS-INQUART, Arthur (1892–1946), Austrian NAZI leader, governor of Austria (1938–39) and deputy governor of Poland (1939–40). As high commissioner for Holland (1940–45), his cruelty was notorious. He was executed for WAR CRIMES.

SHACKLETON, Sir Ernest Henry (1874–1922), British Antarctic explorer. He was a member of SCOTT's 1901–04 expedition, and led his own parties in 1908–09 (when he located the S magnetic pole) and 1914–16. He died during a fourth expedition.

SHAFFER, Peter (Levin) (1926–   ), English playwright whose well-crafted, realistic plays are often concerned with a protagonist's struggle against an incomprehensible God. In *Equus* (1973) a psychiatrist envies the passion that a troubled boy experiences while placating a personal horse-god. Similarly in *Amadeus* (1980) the virtuous and successful but mediocre composer SALIERI blames God for bestowing genius on a conceited, sniggering Mozart. Among Shaffer's other works are *Five Finger Exercise* (1958) and *The Royal Hunt of the Sun* (1964).

SHAFTESBURY, name of three important English earls. **Anthony Ashley Cooper** (1621–1683), 1st Earl, was a founder of the WHIG party and a staunch Protestant. After supporting both CROMWELL and the RESTORATION, he became Lord Chancellor in 1672, but was dismissed in 1673 for supporting the TEST ACT. He then built up the Whig opposition to CHARLES II, supporting MONMOUTH and opposing JAMES II's succession. He was acquitted of treason in 1681, but fled to Holland in 1682. **Anthony Ashley Cooper** (1671–1713), 3rd Earl, was a moral philosopher and pupil of John LOCKE. He aimed to found an ethical system based on an innate moral sense. **Anthony Ashley Cooper** (1801–1885), 7th Earl, was a statesman and leading evangelical Christian who promoted legislation to improve conditions in mines and factories and supported many movements for social improvement.

SHAH JAHAN (1592–1666), Mogul emperor of India (1628–58), famous for building the TAJ MAHAL. His reign saw the restoration of Islam as state religion, the conquest of S India and the golden age of Mogul art.

SHAHN, Ben (1898–1969), Lithuanian-born US artist. He used a realistic style to draw attention to social and political events. One of his best-known works is a series of paintings on the SACCO-VANZETTI CASE (1931–32).

SHAKERS, originally an abusive term for the United Society of Believers in Christ's Second Appearing, a millenniastic sect who shook with ecstatic emotion in their worship. Originating among the QUAKERS of England, they were brought by "Mother" Ann Lee to the US in 1774, where they formed celibate communes which flourished until the mid-19th century.

SHAKESPEARE, William (1564–1616), English poet, playwright and actor-manager, one of the giants of world literature. Little is known with certainty of his early life. Son of a prosperous glover, he was born and educated at Stratford-upon-Avon in Warwickshire. In 1582 he married Ann Hathaway, and they had three children. He moved to London c1589, probably as an actor at The Theatre, and by 1592 had made a name as a playwright. From 1594 he wrote and acted for the Lord Chamberlain's Men, and became a shareholding director of their new Globe Theatre in 1598. The theaters closed during the plague of 1592–94; during this time he wrote the two narrative poems *Venus and Adonis* and *The Rape of Lucrece*, and also the sonnets. The company survived the closure, rivalry and Puritan hostility to become the King's Men on the accession of James I in 1603, and in that year were able to buy the Blackfriars Theatre also. Shakespeare invested his money wisely, and so was able to retire to Stratford c1610, although he probably continued to write until 1613. Immensely successful in his time, Shakespeare stood out even against KYD, MARLOWE and Ben JONSON. He was recognized not only as the most richly endowed dramatist but as a poet of extraordinary sensibility and linguistic gifts.

Because his plays were generally not prepared for publication except to eclipse "pirated" versions, they have come down to us with many corruptions and variant readings. The chronology of the works is uncertain, and even the canon itself is disputed. For example, the *Henry VI* cycle is attributed to him alone, but may well have been a collaboration, as also *Henry VIII*. The first collected edition, known as the First Folio, was published in 1623. He probably revised many plays by others (*Pericles* may be one) and probably had a hand in other works, as in the anonymous plays known as the "Shakespeare Apocrypha." It seems certain, however, that it was Shakespeare and no other who wrote the 37 plays that bear his name, among the most popular of which are *Hamlet, Julius Caesar, Richard III, Macbeth, Othello, Henry IV* (parts I and II), and *A Midsummer Night's Dream.*

SHALE, fine-grained detrital SEDIMENTARY ROCK formed by compaction and dessication

of mud (clay and silt). Shales are sometimes rich in FOSSILS; and are laminated (they split readily into layers, or laminae). Their metamorphism (see METAMORPHIC ROCKS) produces SLATE. (See also OIL SHALE.)

SHAMANISM, a primitive religious system centered around a shaman, or medicine man, who in trance state is believed to be possessed by spirits that speak and act through him. The shaman (from the language of the Tungus of Siberia) is expected to cure the sick, protect the tribe, foretell the future, etc. (See also MAGIC, PRIMITIVE.)

SHANGHAI, China's largest city, in SE Kiangsu province. It is a major seaport and a leading commercial and industrial center, producing textiles, iron and steel, ships, petroleum products and a wide range of manufactured goods. In 1842 it was one of the first Chinese ports opened by treaty to foreign trade. Britain (1843), France (1849) and the US (1862) gained concessions to develop the city, and most of it remained under foreign control until after WWII. The British and US concessions were renounced in 1945. Shanghai is now China's film capital and the home of 190 research institutes, colleges and universities. Pop 13,000,000.

SHANKAR, Ravi (1920–   ), Indian sitar player. A virtuoso performer, he stimulated interest in Indian classical music throughout the world with his frequent concert appearances and numerous recordings.

SHANKER, Albert (1928–   ), US labor leader. A New York City public school teacher 1952–59, he was active in the teachers' drive for unionization and led strikes over pay and noneconomic issues as president of the United Federation of Teachers 1964–74. He has headed the American Federation of Teachers since 1974.

SHANNON, Claude Elwood (1916–   ), US mathematician who created modern INFORMATION THEORY. He also applied BOOLEAN ALGEBRA to the theory of electrical switching circuits.

SHAPIRO, Karl (1913–   ), US poet and literary critic. His early poetry, such as *V-Letter and Other Poems* (1944; Pulitzer Prize, 1945), shows the influence of AUDEN and was admired for its verbal conceits. Later work, such as *The Bourgeois Poet* (1964), became more Whitmanesque. His *Collected Poems: 1948–1978* appeared in 1978.

SHAPLEY, Harlow (1885–1972), US astronomer who suggested that CEPHEID VARIABLES are not eclipsing binaries (see

DOUBLE STAR) but pulsating stars. He was also the first to deduce the structure and approximate size of the MILKY WAY galaxy, and the position of the sun within it.

SHARAKU TOSHUSAI (18th century), Japanese color-print artist. Himself a professional NOH dancer, in 1794–95 he produced over 136 striking prints of KABUKI theater performers.

SHARKS, an order, Pleurotremata, of about 250 species of CARTILAGINOUS FISHES of marine and fresh waters. Sharks, with the related RAYS and CHIMAERAS, have a skeleton formed entirely of CARTILAGE. Other distinguishing features are that the GILLS open externally through a series of gill-slits, rather than through a single operculum, and reproduction is by internal fertilization, unlike that of bony fishes. The body is fusiform and the upper lobe of the tail is usually better developed than the lower lobe. Sharks swim by sinuous movements of the whole body; there is no swimbladder (see AIRBLADDER) and they must swim constantly to avoid sinking. All are extremely fast swimmers and active predators. Despite a universal reputation for unprovoked attack, only 27 out of the 250 known species have been definitely implicated in attacks on man.

SHATT-AL-ARAB, river formed by the confluence of the Tigris R and Euphrates R in SE Iraq. It flows 120mi SE into the Persian Gulf, and forms part of the Iran–Iraq border.

SHAVUOT, Jewish festival celebrated on the sixth and seventh days of the month Sivan (usually May). Originally an agricultural festival, it commemorates the receiving of the TORAH on Mt Sinai.

SHAW, "Artie" (Arthur Arshewsky Shaw, 1910–   ), US jazz musician and bandleader. He was a brilliant clarinetist and, in the 1930s and 1940s, led several successful orchestras. His *Begin the Beguine* (1939) is considered one of the finest big band recordings of the "swing" era.

SHAW, George Bernard (1856–1950), British dramatist, critic and political propagandist whose witty plays contained serious philosophical and social ideas. Born in Dublin, he went to London (1876) and became a music and theater critic and a leader of the FABIAN SOCIETY. He began writing his brilliantly witty, ironical and polemical comedies in the 1890s. Success came with such plays as *Major Barbara* (1905), *Caesar and Cleopatra* (1906; written 1899), *Androcles and the Lion* (1912) and *Pygmalion* (1913; later adapted as a musical, *My Fair Lady*). He lost popularity for his opposition to WWI, but regained it with *Back to Methuselah* (1921); *St. Joan* (1923), his greatest success, was followed by the 1925 Nobel Prize in Literature. He continued to write up to his death.

SHAW, Irwin (1913–   ), US novelist, short story writer and playwright who has lived in Europe since 1951. Concerned with large-scale social and political issues, many of Shaw's works pit "gentle people" against the forces of a morally sick American society. Among his best known novels are *The Young Lions* (1948), *Rich Man, Poor Man* (1970) and *Beggarman, Thief* (1977).

SHAWN, Ted (Edwin Meyers Shawn, 1891–1972), US dancer, choreographer and teacher. With his wife, Ruth ST. DENIS, he founded the Denishawn school and company. He led an all-male company of dancers, 1933–40, and in 1941 established an international dance center at Jacob's Pillow in Mass.

SHAYS' REBELLION, Aug. 1786–Feb. 1787, an armed uprising in Mass., led by Daniel Shays (c1747–1825) to protest high taxes and the severity of legal action against debtors during the postwar depression. The insurgents forced courts to drop actions against debtors, but were defeated attacking a federal arsenal. The uprising led to some reforms.

SHECKLEY, Robert (1928–   ), US writer of science fiction. His works includes the novels *Journey Beyond Tomorrow* (1962), *The 10th Victim* (1965), *Futuropolis* (1978) and the short story collections *Untouched by Human Hands* (1953, 1979) and *The Wonderful World of Robert Sheckley* (1979).

SHEEN, Fulton John (1895–1979), US Roman Catholic archbishop, widely known in the US for his popular inspirational radio and television talks, and for his strong conservative stance on many issues.

SHEEP, a diverse genus of mammals best known in the various races of the domestic sheep *Ovis aries* bred for both MEAT and WOOL. Wild sheep are a diverse group of mountain-dwelling forms with some 37 races alive today. They divide into two large groups: the Asiatic sheep, which include the MOUFLONS, urials and ARGALIS, and the American sheep, the Thinhorns and BIGHORNS. Asiatic sheep are long-legged, lightly-built animals which prefer a gentle rolling terrain. American-type sheep by comparison are heavy-set and barrel-chested, and characteristic of steep slopes and rocky areas, in part filling the role played in Europe and Asia by the IBEX. Sheep are social animals; males usually form bands following a dominant ram and females form separate parties following a mature ewe. The rams use their horns and the specially-thickened bone of their foreheads for combat, not only in the rut but also in dominance struggles.

SHEFFIELD PLATE, articles made from SILVER plated on copper by a method of FUSION involving heat and pressure, discovered about 1743 by a Sheffield cutler, Thomas Boulsover. This method was widely used before the advent of ELECTROPLATING.

SHELBY, Isaac (1750–1826), US frontier leader who defeated the British at KING'S MOUNTAIN (1780) and planned the action at COWPENS (1781). He was the first governor of Kentucky, 1792–96. In the WAR OF 1812 he led volunteers who helped defeat the British at the Battle of the THAMES.

SHELDON, Sidney (1917–   ), US dramatist and novelist who also produced scripts for musical films, such as *Easter Parade* (1948). He wrote the Tony Award-winning play *Redhead* (1959) and the best-selling adventure novels *The Other Side of Midnight* (1975) and *Rage of Angels* (1980).

SHELLEY, Mary Wollstonecraft (1797–1851), English writer, daughter of William GODWIN and Mary WOLLSTONECRAFT and wife of Percy Bysshe SHELLEY. Her best-known work is the Gothic horror-story *Frankenstein* (1818). She wrote several other novels and edited Shelley's poems.

SHELLEY, Percy Bysshe (1792–1822), English Romantic poet whose work reflects his revolutionary political idealism and his strong faith in the spiritual power of the imagination. It includes long narrative poems such as *Queen Mab* (1813), *The Revolt of Islam* (1818) and *Epipsychidion* (1821), the verse drama *Prometheus Unbound* (1820) and such famous lyrics as the "Ode to the West Wind." He was drowned in a boating accident in Italy, where he had settled with his second wife, Mary.

SHENANDOAH VALLEY, between the Allegheny and Blue Ridge Mts in NW Va.

About 150mi long and up to 25mi wide, it is a rich farming area famed for its natural beauty. It was the scene of the CIVIL WAR Shenandoah Valley Campaigns (1862–64).

SHENYANG, formerly Mukden, capital of Liaoning province, NE China, on the Hun R. An early capital of the MANCHUS, it was developed by the Russians and Japanese and is now an industrial, agricultural and shipping center for the NE (formerly Manchuria). Pop 4,000,000.

SHEPARD, Sam (1943–   ), US avant-garde playwright noted for his almost cinematic inventiveness in such plays as *Operation Sidewinder* (1970). His books include *The Unseen Hand, and Other Plays* (1971) and *Mad Dog Blues, and Other Plays* (1972). He won the Pulitzer Prize for *Buried Child* (1979).

SHEPPARD, Samuel (1923–1970), US osteopath who was convicted of the brutal slaying of his wife 1954. In 1966 the US Supreme Court overturned his conviction on the ground of prejudicial pretrial publicity, and a second trial acquitted him. Unable to reestablish his medical practice, he spent the last years of his life as a professional wrestler.

SHERATON, Thomas (1751–1806), English furniture designer. His elegant style of furniture was popular around 1800, and his *Cabinet-Maker and Upholsterer's Drawing Book* (1791–94) was very influential.

SHERIDAN, "Little Phil" (Philip Henry Sheridan, 1831–1888), US general and Union CIVIL WAR hero. After successes in the Chattanooga and WILDERNESS campaigns, he commanded the army which defeated General EARLY and devastated the SHENANDOAH VALLEY (1864). In 1865 he won the Battle of FIVE FORKS and helped end the war by cutting off Robert E. LEE's line of retreat from APPOMATTOX. He became commander of the US army 1884.

SHERIDAN, Richard Brinsley (1751–1816), Irish-born English dramatist and politician famous for his witty comedies of manners, including *The Rivals* (1775), *The School for Scandal* (1777) and *The Critic* (1779). A Whig member of Parliament (1780–1812), he played a leading part in the impeachment of Warren HASTINGS.

SHERLOCK HOLMES. See DOYLE, SIR ARTHUR CONAN.

SHERMAN, Roger (1721–1793), American patriot who helped draft, and signed, the Declaration of Independence. He was a member of the 1787 Constitutional Convention and, with Oliver ELLSWORTH, introduced the "Connecticut Compromise." (See UNITED STATES CONSTITUTION.) He was US representative (1789–91) and senator

(1791–93) for Conn.

SHERMAN, two brothers important in the CIVIL WAR era. **William Tecumseh Sherman** (1820–1891), was a Union commander, second in importance only to General Ulysses S. GRANT. He fought in the Battles of BULL RUN (1861), SHILOH (1862) and in the Vicksburg campaign (1862–63). He was given command of the Army of Tennessee and, with Grant, took part in the Chattanooga Campaign (1863). As supreme commander in the West (1864) he invaded Ga., capturing Atlanta and marching on Savannah. He then turned N, pushing General Joseph Johnson's army before him, and accepting its surrender at Durham, N.C., in April, 1865. The destruction he wrought in his attempt to destroy Confederate supplies and communications and break civilian morale made him a hero in the N and a villain in the S. He was US army commander 1869–84. **John Sherman** (1823–1900) was a founding member of the REPUBLICAN PARTY. A senator 1861–77 and 1881–97, and secretary of the treasury 1877–81, he introduced the SHERMAN ANTITRUST ACT and the SHERMAN SILVER PURCHASE ACT.

SHERMAN ANTITRUST ACT (1890), first major federal action to curb the power of the giant business MONOPOLIES which grew up after the Civil War. Its failure to define key terms, such as *trust, combination* and *restraint of trade*, led to loopholes, and it was strengthened by the CLAYTON ANTITRUST ACT (1914).

SHERPA, Buddhist people of NE Nepal, famous as Himalayan guides. Of Tibetan origins and speaking a Tibetan language, they number some 85,000 and raise cattle, grow crops and spin wool in the high valleys of the Himalayas.

SHERRINGTON, Sir Charles Scott (1857–1952), British neurophysiologist who shared with E. D. ADRIAN the 1932 Nobel Prize for Physiology or Medicine for studies of the NERVOUS SYSTEM which form the basis of our modern understanding of its action.

SHERWOOD, Robert Emmet (1896–1955), US playwright who won four Pulitzer prizes: for *Idiot's Delight* (1936), *Abe Lincoln in Illinois* (1938), *There Shall Be No Night* (1940) and his biography *Roosevelt and Hopkins: An Intimate History* (1948).

SHETLAND ISLANDS, or Zetland, archipelago of some 100 islands off N Scotland, constituting its northernmost county. Less than a quarter are inhabited; Lerwick is the chief town and port. The main occupations are fishing and cattle and sheep raising. The Shetlands are famous for their knitted woolen goods and the SHETLAND PONY.

SHETLAND PONY, tiny and shaggy-haired, the smallest of the PONIES, probably a relict of prehistoric British and Scandinavian HORSES. Once restricted to the Shetland Islands, it has now been widely bred as a riding pony for children.

SHIELDS, Brooke (1965–   ), US model and actress. Her modeling career began with her selection as the Ivory Snow baby in 1966. In her early teens, her beauty and mature appearance made her TV advertising's most sought-after model. An instant film star, she appeared in *Pretty Baby* (1978) and *Endless Love* (1981).

SHI'ITES, members of an Islamic sect opposed to the orthodox SUNNITES. The Shi'ites reject the first three caliphs and recognize Ali (Mohammed's son-in-law) and his descendants as rightful successors to Mohammed. They number some 40,000,000, concentrated principally in Iran and Iraq.

SHILOH, Battle of, major conflict of the US CIVIL WAR, fought at Pittsburgh Landing, Tenn. (April 6–7, 1872). The Union army under General Ulysses S. GRANT was forced back by a surprise onslaught of the 40,000-strong Confederate army under General A. S. JOHNSTON. The reinforced Union army routed the Confederates in a counterattack the next day. Casualties were over 10,000 on each side.

SHINGLES, or **herpes zoster,** a VIRUS disorder characterized by development of pain, a vesicular rash and later scarring, often with persistent pain, over the SKIN of part of the face or trunk. The virus seems to settle in or near nerve cells following CHICKENPOX, which is caused by the same virus, and then becomes activated, perhaps years later and sometimes by disease. It then leads to the acute skin eruption which follows the path of the nerve involved.

SHINN, Everett (1876–1953), US painter, member of the EIGHT or ASHCAN SCHOOL. He is best known for his pictures of the theater and music hall world, such as *Revue* (1908).

SHINTO (way of the gods), indigenous religion of Japan originally based on the belief that the royal family was descended from the sun-goddess Amaterasu Omikami. It later absorbed much Buddhist thought and practice. At its core is the idea that *kami* (divine power) is manifest at every moment in every thing; hence attention paid to each moment, however trivial, will lead to the realization of truth. Shinto shrines are plain wooden buildings in which priest and people perform simple rites; the imperial shrine is at Ise. Worship of the emperor and the ZEN influence on martial arts resulted in a close connection between Shinto and Japanese militarism. State Shinto ended after WWII.

SHIPS AND SHIPPING, large seagoing vessels and their uses for transport and warfare. The first ships were probably developed from river craft by the Mesopotamians and Egyptians as early as the 4th millennium BC, and the Mediterranean became the home of the first sea-based civilizations (see MINOAN CIVILIZATION; MYCENAE; PHOENICIA). Early ships had a single sail on a fixed yard-arm, a stern oar for a rudder, and one or more banks of oars, a classic example being the Greek trireme. There is evidence that the Phoenicians ventured in such ships as far as Britain and around Africa before 600 BC. Under the Roman Empire the whole Mediterranean was controlled by a navy, and grain-carrying GALLEYS up to 180ft long were built.

In medieval Europe the VIKING longships developed into square-rigged GALLEONS, with fixed stern rudders. These were capable of long sea voyages, and the 15th and 16th centuries saw the great world explorations of Christopher COLUMBUS, Vasco da GAMA and Ferdinand MAGELLAN. In the age of colonial expansion, world trade and naval rivalry which followed, large navies and shipping fleets developed rapidly, and the great "men o' war" and the grain CLIPPERS represented the culmination of the age of sail.

A steamship first crossed the Atlantic in 1819, and the screw-driven GREAT EASTERN (1858) was the first large iron ship. By the early 20th century steel construction and steam turbines dominated, and passenger liners, warships and cargo ships increased spectacularly in size and power. Modern developments include SUBMARINES, AIRCRAFT CARRIERS, nuclear-powered vessels and supertankers of up to 500,000 tons. (See also BATTLESHIP; BOATS AND BOATING; JUNK; MERCHANT SHIPPING; NAVIGATION; NAVY; TRANSPORTATION; YACHTS AND YACHTING.)

SHIRER, William (1904–), US journalist and author who achieved fame with his CBS news broadcasts from Europe (1937–40) and his subsequent reporting of WWII. His best-selling books include *Berlin Diary* (1941), *The Rise and Fall of the Third Reich* (1960) and *The Collapse of the Third Republic* (1969).

SHOCK specifically refers to the develop-

ment of low blood pressure, inadequate to sustain BLOOD CIRCULATION, usually causing cold, clammy, gray SKIN and extremities, faintness and mental confusion and decreased urine production. It is caused by acute blood loss; burns with PLASMA loss; acute HEART failure; massive pulmonary EMBOLISM, and SEPTICEMIA. If untreated, death ensues. Early replacement of plasma or BLOOD and administration of DRUGS to improve blood circulation are necessary to prevent permanent BRAIN damage and acute KIDNEY failure.

SHOCKLEY, William Bradford (1910–), US physicist who shared with BARDEEN and BRATTAIN the 1956 Nobel Prize for Physics for their joint development of the TRANSISTOR. He is also known for promoting the belief that black people are intellectually inferior to whites.

SHOCK THERAPY, or electroconvulsive therapy (ECT), is a form of treatment used in MENTAL ILLNESS, particularly DEPRESSION, in which carefully regulated electric shocks are given to the BRAINS of anesthetized patients. (Muscle relaxants are used to prevent injury through forceful MUSCLE contractions.) The mode of action is unknown but– rapid resolution of severe depression may be achieved.

SHOEMAKER, "Willie" (William Lee Shoemaker, 1931–), US jockey who rode his 6,033rd winner in 1970, breaking all previous records. By 1972, long before his retirement, he had won a record $50 million in prize money.

SHOGUN, title of the hereditary military commanders of Japan who usurped the power of the Emperor in the 12th century and ruled the country for about 700 years. In 1867 the last TOKUGAWA Shogun was forced to resign and restore sovereignty to the Emperor.

SHOLEM ALEICHEM (1859–1916), pseudonym of Solomon Rabinovitch, Russian-born YIDDISH humorous writer. He was an immensely prolific and popular author, and his novels, short stories and plays tell of the serious and absurd aspects of Jewish life in E Europe. His works include *The Old Country* and *Tevye's Daughters*.

SHOLES, Christopher Latham (1819–1890), US inventor (with some help from others) of the TYPEWRITER (patented 1868). He sold his patent rights to the REMINGTON Arms Company in 1873.

SHOLOKHOV, Mikhail Alexandrovich (1905–), Russian novelist awarded the Nobel Prize in Literature (1965). He is best known for his stories about the Don Cossacks of S Russia. His greatest work is

And Quiet Flows the Don (1928–40).

SHORTHAND, or stenography, any writing system permitting the rapid transcription of speech. The three most used today are Isaac Pitman Shorthand, the first to be commercially developed (c1837), and Gregg Shorthand, developed c1888 by John Robert Gregg, both of which are phonetic, using symbols to represent recurring sounds; and Speedwriting, which uses abbreviations. Shorthand is much used by secretaries, journalists, court reporters, etc. (See also STENOTYPE.)

SHORT PARLIAMENT, convened by the English king CHARLES I in April 1640 to finance the Scottish war. The House of Commons wanted first to settle major grievances, so the king dissolved Parliament in May. (See English CIVIL WAR.)

SHORTSIGHTEDNESS. See MYOPIA.

SHORT TAKEOFF AND LANDING AIRPLANE (STOL), an aircraft that is capable of taking off and landing on a runway with a minimum length of 1,000ft. Since takeoff and landing speeds must be reduced to compensate for the short runway, STOL planes use various wing devices such as flaps, slots and blowers to augment lift and help the craft achieve height quickly. Some STOL aircraft also have VERTICAL TAKEOFF AND LANDING (VTOL) capability.

SHOSHONE INDIANS, group of North American Indians originally inhabiting the territory between SE Cal. and W Wyo. The Shoshone of E Utah and Wyo. were typical buffalo-hunting tribesmen of the plains. In the 18th century the COMANCHE INDIANS split off and moved S to modern Tex. There are about 8,000 Shoshone on reservation lands today.

SHOSTAKOVICH, Dmitri (1906–1975), Russian composer. Some of his music is notably patriotic. His works include the opera *Lady Macbeth of Mzensk* (1934) and 15 symphonies of which the most famous are the Fifth (1937), the Seventh, "the Leningrad," written during the siege of Leningrad (1941), and the Tenth (1953). His important works of chamber music include the *Piano Quintet* (1940).

SHOTGUN, smooth-bore FIREARM fired from the shoulder, designed to discharge a quantity of small lead pellets (shot) in a diverging pattern, which increases the chances of hitting small fast-moving targets such as game-birds. Although repeating shotguns have been available since 1860, the doublebarreled model has retained its popularity. One of the barrels usually has its bore "choked"—i.e., slightly tapered toward the muzzle to limit the pellet spread and increase the lethal range, which is usually about 50 yards.

SHOT PUT. See TRACK AND FIELD.

SHREWS, small mouse-like insectivorous mammals with short legs and long pointed noses. They have narrow skulls and sharp, rather unspecialized teeth for feeding on insects, earthworms and small mammal carrion. They are highly active creatures. The somewhat indigestible nature of their food, combined with the high energy consumption of their constant activity, means that they may eat two to three times their own weight of food in a day. Having a pulse rate sometimes approaching 1,000 beats a minute, few shrews live longer than one year. Family: Soricidae.

SHRIKES, aggressive and predatory passerine birds of the family Laniidae, which kill insects, birds or small mammals (according to size) with their hooked bill. Because they store their victims impaled on thorns like the carcasses hung in a butcher's shop, they are often called butcherbirds. They have a worldwide distribution, living on the edges of woods and forests.

SHRIMP, decapod CRUSTACEANS (suborder Natantia) which use their abdominal limbs to swim instead of crawling like LOBSTERS or CRABS. The body, more or less cylindrical and translucent, bears five pairs of walking legs and two pairs of very long antennae. The eyes are stalked. Shrimp are mostly scavengers or predators and may be found in the open ocean, inshore, in estuaries and even in freshwater. They are fished for food worldwide.

SHRIVER, Robert Sargent (1915–   ), first director of the PEACE CORPS under presidents Kennedy and Johnson (1961–66) and director of the OFFICE OF ECONOMIC OPPORTUNITY under Johnson (1964–68). He was ambassador to France (1968–70) and ran for vice-president on the Democratic ticket with George McGovern in 1972. Thereafter he practiced law and briefly sought the 1976 Democratic presidential nomination.

SHROVE TUESDAY, the last day before Lent begins (see ASH WEDNESDAY). It is a traditional day for MARDI GRAS carnivals such as those in New Orleans and Rio de Janeiro.

SHUBUN (flourished early 15th century), Japanese ink painter. His masterly works, many of them landscapes, led to the development of the distinctively Japanese style.

SHUFFLEBOARD, game in which two or four players use cues to slide disks along a court (52ft by 6ft) which has a triangular scoring area at each end. The object is to knock the opponent's disks into the penalty section while leaving one's own disks in one of the scoring positions on the triangle.

SHUTE, Nevil (1899–1960), English novelist and aeronautical engineer, best known for *On the Beach* (1957), about the world's last survivors of a nuclear war. Many of his works were based on his experiences as an engineer, including *The Mysterious Aviator* (1928) and *No Highway* (1948). *Slide Rule* (1954) is his autobiography.

SIAM. See THAILAND.

SIAMESE CAT, short-haired breed of eastern origin, although not proven to have originated in Thailand. Of svelte "foreign" type with a long, slim body, long tapering tail, wedge-shaped head, and large ears, it has a distinctive coat pattern of darker areas on face (mask), ears, tail and paws which are known as points. Its almond-shaped, slanting eyes are a deep blue. Color varieties are Seal Point (cream body color with seal brown points), Blue (white with blue-gray), Chocolate (ivory with milk chocolate) and Frost (or Lilac, magnolia with lilac). Many associations also recognize Red, Tortoiseshell, Tabby (Lynx) and Cream Points. All white or all lilac cats of Siamese type with blue eyes are known as Foreign White and Foreign Lavender.

Siamese cats become closely involved with their owners and can frequently be taught to walk on a leash. They have rather loud voices and may be very talkative.

SIAN (also Xian), city in NE central China, ancient capital of China for 11 dynasties. Today it is a major transportation and industrial center. The scene of CHIANG KAI-SHEK's kidnapping in 1936, it is famous for fabulous archeological finds of life-size terra-cotta warriors and horses at the tomb of Emperor Qin Shi Huang. There are large steel, chemical and textile industries. Pop 3,000,000.

SIBELIUS, Jean (1865–1957), Finnish composer. His most famous work is *Finlandia* (1900), which expressed his country's growing nationalist feeling. He composed a number of tone poems such as *En Saga* (1892), which evokes the physical beauty and ancient legends of Finland. His works include many pieces for violin and for piano and seven symphonies.

SIBERIA, vast indefinite area of land (about 4,000,000sq mi) in N Asian USSR between the Ural Mts in the W and the Pacific Ocean in the E, forming most of the Russian SFSR. The landscape varies from the Arctic tundra to the great forest zone in the S and the steppes of the W. Summers are mild in most parts, winters extremely severe (as low as −90°F in some parts). Most of the people are Russian; Yakuts, Buryats and Tuvans form autonomous republics. The largest cities are Novosibirsk, Omsk, Krasnoyarsk, Irkutsk and Vladivostok. Siberia has rich natural resources—farmland, forests, fisheries and such minerals as coal, iron ore, tungsten, gold and natural gas. Industrial centers have developed in the regions of Krasnoyarsk and Lake Baikal (the world's deepest lake) and one of the world's largest hydroelectric plants is near Bratsk. Siberia was inhabited in prehistoric times. Russians conquered much of Siberia by 1598. Political prisoners were first sent to Siberia in 1710 and forced-labor camps still exist. The TRANS-SIBERIAN RAILROAD (1905) led to large-scale colonization and economic development.

SIBERIAN HUSKY, dog first bred in Siberia as a sled, guard and companion dog; taken to Alaska c1910 and used for dogsled races. The dog is colored black and white, tan, or gray, weighs 30–60lbs and is 20–25in high.

SICHUAN. See SZECHWAN.

SICILY, largest Mediterranean island (9,925sq mi); part of Italy, but with its own parliament at the capital, Palermo. Its most notable feature is the active volcano, Mt Etna (height varies around 10,900ft). Much of the island is mountainous, but there are lowlands along the coasts. About half the population live in the coastal towns Palermo, Catania, Messina and Syracuse. Agriculture is the mainstay of the economy, though hampered by the low rainfall and feudal land-tenure system. Wheat is the staple crop; grapes, citrus fruits and olives are also grown. Main exports, from Ragusa, are petroleum products. Sicily was the site of Greek, Phoenician and Roman colonies before conquest by the Arabs, who in turn were ousted by ROBERT GUISCARD. The SICILIAN VESPERS (1282) led to Spanish rule, ended by GARIBALDI (1860). In WWII, Sicily was conquered by the Allies (1943) and used as a base for attack on Italy.

SICKERT, Walter Richard (1860–1942), British painter. Trained by WHISTLER and DEGAS, he was from 1905 the main link between English and French art. His scenes of music halls and low-class life are in a rich and direct style.

SIDDHARTHA GAUTAMA. See BUDDHA.

SIDDONS, Sarah (*née* Kemble; 1755–1831), English actress who first appeared in London (without success) at the request of GARRICK (1775). She returned at the request of SHERIDAN (1782), and became the leading tragic actress of her day.

SIDEREAL TIME, time referred to the rotation of the earth with respect to the fixed stars. The sidereal DAY is about four minutes shorter than the solar day since the earth moves each day about 1/365 of its orbit about the sun. Sidereal time is used in astronomy when determining the locations of celestial bodies.

SIDEWINDERS, several species of snake, especially of the RATTLESNAKES, which exhibit a peculiar sideways looping motion when moving rapidly. The name is particularly applied to the Horned rattlesnake, *Crotalus cerastis*, of the southwestern US.

SIDNEY, Sir Philip (1554–1586), Elizabethan poet and courtier, a favorite with the queen and a model of RENAISSANCE chivalry. He had great influence on English poetry, both through his poems, of which the best known are *Arcadia* (c1580) and the love sonnets *Astrophel and Stella* (1591), and through his critical work, *The Defence of Poesie* (1595).

SIEGBAHN, Karl Manne Georg (1886–1978), Swedish physicist who was awarded the 1924 Nobel physics prize for his pioneer work in X-ray SPECTROSCOPY. He devised a way of measuring X-RAY wavelengths with great accuracy and developed an account of X-rays consistent with the BOHR theory of the ATOM. His son, **Kai Siegbahn** (1918–   ), a professor at Uppsala University (from 1954), shared the 1981 Nobel Prize for Physics for his work in developing high-resolution electron spectroscopy.

SIEGFRIED, legendary figure of outstanding strength and courage. He appears in both the Icelandic EDDA and the 13th-century German NIBELUNGENLIED epic, and is the hero of WAGNER'S operas *Siegfried* and *Die Götterdämmerung*.

SIEGMEISTER, Elie (1909–   ), US composer. His teachers included Wallingford Riegger and Nadia Boulanger. An authority on American folk music, he wrote for chamber groups and orchestra such works as *Ozark Set* (1943) and a concerto for clarinet (1956) and composed the score for the Broadway production *Sing Out, Sweet Land* (1944).

SIEMENS, German family of technologists and industrialists. **Ernst Werner von Siemens** (1816–1892) invented, among other things, an ELECTROPLATING process (patented 1842), a differential GOVERNOR (c1844), and a regenerative STEAM ENGINE, the principle of which was developed by his brothers **Friedrich** (1826–1904) and then **Karl Wilhelm** (1823–1883), later **Sir**

(Charles) William Siemens, to form the basis of the OPEN-HEARTH PROCESS. Ernst and Sir William both made many important contributions to TELEGRAPH science, culminating in the laying from the *Faraday*, a ship designed by William, of the ATLANTIC CABLE of 1874 by the company he owned.

SIENA, city in Tuscany, Italy, famous for its GOTHIC ARCHITECTURE and the RENAISSANCE art of DONATELLO, LORENZETTI and PISANO. Its main square is the scene of the historic and colorful *Palio* horse races every summer. Pop 65,700.

SIENKIEWICZ, Henryk (1846–1916), Polish novelist awarded the 1905 Nobel Prize in Literature. His greatest works are a trilogy about 17th-century Poland—*With Fire and Sword* (1884), *The Deluge* (1886) and *Pan Michael* (1888)—and the internationally famous *Quo Vadis?* (1896).

Official name: Republic of Sierra Leone
Capital: Freetown
Area: 27,699sq mi
Population: 3,072,000
Languages: English; Krio, Mende, Temne
Religions: Animist, Muslim, Christian
Monetary unit(s): 1 Leone = 100 cents

SIERRA LEONE, republic in W Africa on the Atlantic Ocean, sharing a common border with Guinea on the NW, N and NE, and with Liberia on the SE.

Land. It consists of a swampy coastal area, wooded inland plains crossed by several rivers and rising grassland in the N. The climate is tropical, with an average temperature of 79° F and annual rainfall of 90–150in.

People. The indigenous population includes over 18 tribes, the Mende of the S and the Temne of the N predominating. The Limba and the Kono are also important ethnic groups. The Creoles, descendants of freed slaves, mainly from the Americas, live around Freetown, the capital and chief port. Bo, Kenema and Port Loko are other urban centers.

Economy. The economy is heavily dependent on diamond mining and production of cocoa and coffee. Rice is the chief food crop. Cattle are raised in the N, pigs and poultry in the W.

History. Named by the Portuguese in 1460, the coastal area became the haunt of slavers: in 1787 Granville SHARP settled freed slaves there. In 1808 it became a British colony. Independent from 1961, Sierra Leone was declared a republic in 1971 under the presidency of Dr. Siaka Stevens.

SIERRA MADRE, great mountain system of Mexico. The E range (*Sierra Madre Oriental*) stretches 1,000mi S from the Rio Grande, forming the E edge of the central plateau and reaching 18,700ft in Orizaba (Citlaltépetl). The *Sierra Madre Occidental*, running SW from Ariz. and N.M., borders the plateau on the W, rising to over 10,000ft. The *Sierra Madre de Sur* parallels the SW coast.

SIERRA NEVADA, mountain range, 420mi long, in E Cal., including Mt Whitney (14,494ft), the highest mountain in the US outside Alaska. The spectacular scenery of the three national parks, Yosemite, King's Canyon and Sequoia, makes the Sierra Nevada a popular vacation area.

SIEYES, Emmanuel Joseph (1748–1836), theorist of the FRENCH REVOLUTION and author of *Qu'est-ce que le Tiers État?* (1789). He advocated national sovereignty and organized the National Assembly. Joining the DIRECTORY in 1799 he took part in the coup of 18 BRUMAIRE that brought NAPOLEON I to power.

SIGNAC, Paul (1863–1935), French painter, leading theorist of neo-impressionism. A friend of Georges SEURAT, he developed POINTILLISM, painting many views of ports, like *Port of St.-Tropez* (1894).

SIHANOUK, Norodom (1922–   ), chief of state of CAMBODIA 1960–70 and 1975–76. King from 1941, he abdicated in 1955 to become premier. Deposed by a coup in 1970, he returned from exile in 1975 as figurehead of the communist victors. He resigned six months later.

SIKHS (from Hindi *sikh*, disciple), religious community of about nine million mostly in the PUNJAB, N India. Their religion, based on the sacred book Ādi Granth, combines elements of HINDUISM and BUDDHISM and was founded by the mystic Nānak, their first GURU, in the 16th century. There is no professional priesthood and officially no CASTE SYSTEM. In the 19th century, under RANJIT SINGH, the Sikhs developed a powerful military state before the British assumed control of India.

SIKKIM, Indian state (since 1975) in the E Himalayas, formerly a constitutional monarchy and protectorate of India. It lies between Tibet, Nepal, Bhutan and India, and covers 2,851sq mi, ranging from Kanchenjunga (28,146ft) to lush tropical forests barely 700ft above sea level. The economy rests on agriculture (rice, corn, millet, and fruits); and cardamom is the chief cash crop. Hydroelectricity and new roads are being developed.

SIKORSKI, Wladyslaw (1881–1943), Polish prime minister (1922–23), war minister (1923–25) and general. After the German invasion in 1939, he became leader of the Polish forces and government in exile.

SIKORSKY, Igor Ivanovich (1889–1972), Russian-born US aircraft designer best known for his invention of the first successful HELICOPTER (flown in 1939). He also designed several AIRPLANES, including the first to have more than one engine (1913).

SILENT FILMS. See MOTION PICTURES.

SILESIA, region of E central Europe, extending from the Sudeten Mts and W Carpathians in the S up the Oder River valley. Mostly in Poland, it covers about 20,000sq mi and has fertile farmlands and forests and great mineral wealth. Upper Silesia is Poland's most important industrial region.

SILICON (Si), nonmetal in Group IVA of the PERIODIC TABLE; the second most abundant element (after oxygen), occurring as SILICA and SILICATES. It is made by reducing silica with coke at high temperatures. Silicon forms an amorphous brown powder, or gray semiconducting crystals, metallic in appearance. It oxidizes on heating, and reacts with the halogens, hydrogen fluoride, and alkalis. It is used in alloys, and to make TRANSISTORS and SEMICONDUCTORS. AW 28.1, mp 1410°C, bp 2355°C, sg 2.42 (20°C). Silicon is tetravalent in almost all its compounds, which resemble those of CARBON, except that it does not form multiple bonds, and that chains of silicon atoms are relatively unstable. **Silanes** are series of volatile silicon hydrides, analogous to PARAFFINS, spontaneously flammable in air and hydrolyzed by water. **Silicon tetrachloride** is a colorless fuming liquid, made by reacting chlorine with a mixture of silica and carbon, the starting material for preparing organosilicon compounds, including SILICONES. mp 70°C, bp 58°C. (For silicon carbide, see CARBORUNDUM; SILICON DIOXIDE, SILICA).

SILICOSIS, a form of PNEUMOCONIOSIS, or fibrotic LUNG disease, in which long-standing inhalation of fine SILICA dusts in mining causes a progressive reduction in the functional capacity of the lungs. The normally thin-walled alveoli and small bronchioles become thickened with fibrous tissue and the lungs lose their elasticity. Characteristic x-ray appearances and changes in lung function occur.

SILK, natural FIBER produced by certain insects and spiders to make cocoons and webs, a glandular secretion extruded from the spinneret and hardened into a filament on exposure to air. Commercial textile silk comes from the various SILKWORMS. The cocooned pupae are killed by steam or hot air, and the cocoons are placed in hot water to soften the gum (sericin) that binds the silk. The filaments from several cocoons are then unwound together to form a single strand of "raw silk," which is reeled. Several strands are twisted together, or "thrown," to form yarn. At this stage, or after weaving, the sericin is washed away. The thickness of the yarn is measured in DENIER. About 70% of all raw silk is now produced in Japan.

SILK-SCREEN PRINTING, method of PRINTING derived from the stencil process (see also DUPLICATING MACHINE). A stencil is attached to a silk screen or fine wire mesh, or formed on it by a photographic process or by drawing the design in tusche (a greasy ink), sealing the screen with glue and washing out the tusche and its covering glue with an organic solvent. The framed screen is placed on the surface to be printed, and viscous ink is pressed through by a rubber squeegee. Each color requires a different screen. The process, which may be mechanized, is used for printing labels, posters, fabrics, and on bottles and other curved surfaces. Since 1938 it has been used by painters, who call it serigraphy.

SILKWORM, the caterpillar of a moth, *Bombyx mori,* which, like many other caterpillars, spins itself a cocoon of silk in which it pupates. The cocoon of *B. mori* is, however, especially thick and may be composed of a single thread commonly 900m (2,950ft) long. This is unraveled to provide commercial SILK. Originally a native of China, *B. mori* has been introduced to many countries. The caterpillar, which takes about a month to develop, feeds on the leaves of the MULBERRY tree.

SILLITOE, Alan (1928–   ), English novelist, short-story writer and poet. Many of his works, such as *Saturday Night and Sunday Morning* (1958) and *The Loneliness of the Long-Distance Runner* (1959), focus on working-class heroes rebelling against an oppressive society.

SILLS, Beverly (1929–   ), US coloratura soprano, born Belle Silverman. She

made her debut at the NY City Opera in 1955 and later became internationally known, acclaimed both as an actress and as a singer. After retiring she became general director of the NY City Opera in 1979.

SILONE, Ignazio (1900–1978), pseudonym of Secondo Tranquilli, Italian writer and social reformer. Opposed to fascism, he spent 1931–44 in exile in Switzerland. His novels include *Bread and Wine* (1937).

SILURIAN, the third period of the PALEOZOIC, which lasted between about 440 and 400 million years ago. (See also GEOLOGY.)

SILVER (Ag), soft, white NOBLE METAL in Group IB of the PERIODIC TABLE, a TRANSITION ELEMENT. Silver has been known and valued from earliest times and used for jewelry, ornaments and coinage since the 4th millennium BC. It occurs as the metal, notably in Norway; in COPPER, LEAD and ZINC sulfide ores; and in ARGENTITE and other silver ores. It is concentrated by various processes including cupellation and extraction with CYANIDE (see also GOLD), and is refined by electrolysis. Silver has the highest thermal and electrical conductivity of all metals, and is used for printed circuits and electrical contacts. Other modern uses include dental ALLOYS and AMALGAM, high-output storage batteries, and for monetary reserves. Although the most reactive of the noble metals, silver is not oxidized in air, nor dissolved by alkalis or nonoxidizing acids; it dissolves in nitric and concentrated sulfuric acid. Silver tarnishes by reaction with sulfur or hydrogen sulfide to form a dark silver-sulfide layer. Silver salts are normally monovalent. Ag^+ is readily reduced by mild reducing agents, depositing a silver MIRROR from solution. AW 107.9, mp 960.8°C, bp 2212°C, sg 10.5 (20°C). **Silver Halides** (AgX) are crystalline salts used in PHOTOGRAPHY. The chloride is white, the bromide pale yellow and the iodide yellow. On exposure to light, a crystal of silver halide becomes activated, and is preferentially reduced to silver by a mild reducing agent (the developer). **Silver Nitrate** ($AgNO_3$) is a transparent crystalline solid, used as an ANTISEPTIC and ASTRINGENT, especially for removing WARTS.

SIMENON, Georges Joseph Christian (1903–   ), Belgian-born French author of over 200 novels and thousands of short stories. He is best known for his detective novels about Inspector Maigret, outstanding works of tightly plotted suspense and psychological insight.

SIMEON STYLITES, Saint (c390–c459) (from Greek *stylos,* pillar), Syrian ascetic and mystic who spent his last 40 years or so on top of a high column.

SIMON, Saint, one of the DISCIPLES OF CHRIST. His names of "the Canaanite" or "Zelotes" may suggest association with the ZEALOTS. His feast-day is Oct. 28.

SIMON, Sir John (1873–1954), British political leader. First elected to Parliament in 1906, he was home secretary, foreign secretary (1931–35), chancellor of the exchequer (1937–40) and lord chancellor (1940–45). In the late 1930s he favored a rapprochement with Nazi Germany and was identified with the appeasement-minded "Cliveden set." He was created a viscount in 1942.

SIMON, Neil (1927–), US writer of comedies for stage and screen. Among his many popular works are *Barefoot in the Park* (1964), *The Odd Couple* (1966), *Plaza Suite* (1969), *The Last of the Red Hot Lovers* (1970), *The Sunshine Boys* (1973) and *Chapter Two* (1978).

SIMON AND GARFUNKEL, singer-guitarists who made their first hit album, *Sounds of Silence*, in 1966. Paul Simon (b.1942), who composed most of their songs, and Art Garfunkel (b.1942) separated in 1970. Their 1981 reunion concert in NYC's Central Park drew over half a million people.

SIMONIDES OF CEOS (c556–469 BC), Greek lyric poet, famous for his epitaphs on the Greeks who fell at MARATHON and THERMOPYLAE. He was also well known for his elegies, odes and epigrams. Very little of his verse has survived.

SIMONS, Menno (c1496–1561), Frisian religious reformer and leader of the peaceful ANABAPTISTS in Holland and Germany. He was a Roman Catholic priest who converted to Anabaptism in 1536. The MENNONITES are named for him.

SIMONSON, Lee (1888–1967), US theatrical designer who co-founded and directed (1919–40) the Theatre Guild, and designed such Guild productions as *Heartbreak House* (1920). He also designed the Metropolitan Opera Company's *Ring* cycle (1947).

SIMONY, the buying and selling of sacred privileges. It is named for Simon Magus, a Samarian magician who tried to buy from St. Peter the power of transmitting the Holy Spirit.

SIMPLON PASS, 29mi long and 6,590ft high, between Brig in Switzerland and Isella in Italy. NAPOLEON I built a road along it in 1800–06. In 1906 the Simplon Tunnel, 12.5mi long, Europe's longest and the world's second-longest railroad tunnel, was opened to traffic.

SIMPSON, O. J. (1947–), US football player. A running back, he is the only professional player to have rushed for more than 2,000 yards in a season, reaching the 2,003 mark in 1973 with the Buffalo Bills. He set another NFL record in 1975 by scoring 23 touchdowns.

SIN, or transgression, an unethical act (see ETHICS) considered as disobedience to the revealed will of God. Sin may be viewed legally as crime—breaking God's commandments—and so deserving punishment (see HELL; PURGATORY), or as an offense that grieves God the loving Father, breaking communion with Him. According to the Bible, sin entered the world in Adam's fall and all mankind became innately sinful (see ORIGINAL SIN). Both for this and for actual sins committed, man becomes guilty and in need of SALVATION. Since sin is rooted in character and will, each sinner bears personal responsibility; hence the need for repentance, CONFESSION and ABSOLUTION (see also PENANCE). Views as to what constitutes sin vary, being partly determined by church authority, social standards and one's own conscience. The traditional "seven deadly sins" are pride, covetousness, lust, envy, gluttony, anger and sloth. The Roman Catholic Church defines a mortal sin as a serious sin committed willingly and with clear knowledge of its wrongness; a venial sin is less grave, does not wholly deprive the perpetrator of grace, and need not be individually confessed. (See also ATONEMENT; IMMACULATE CONCEPTION.)

SINAI PENINSULA, mountainous peninsula between the Gulf of Suez and the Gulf of Aqaba, the N arms of the Red Sea. It is thought that Mt Sinai, where MOSES received the TEN COMMANDMENTS, is one of the S peaks (Jebel Serbal or Jebel Musa).

SINATRA, Frank "the Voice" (Francis Albert Sinatra: 1917–), US singer and film star. He achieved fame as a band singer with Tommy Dorsey before becoming a teenagers' idol as a solo performer during WWII. After making several musical films, he became a dramatic actor of note in *From Here to Eternity* (1953). Known as a master of timing, he has remained one of the world's most popular singer-entertainers.

SINCLAIR, Upton Beall (1878–1968), novelist and social reformer. He is best known for *The Jungle* (1906), a novel exposing the horrors of the Chicago meat-packing industries, and for the 11 *World's End* novels centered on Lanny Budd, one of which, *Dragon's Teeth* (1942), brought him the 1943 Pulitzer Prize.

Official name: Republic of Singapore
Capital: Singapore
Area: 238.5sq mi
Population: 2,362,700
Languages: Malay, Chinese (Mandarin), English, Tamil
Religions: Confucianist, Buddhist, Taoist, Muslim
Monetary unit(s): 1 Singapore dollar = 100 cents

SINGAPORE, republic in SE Asia, at the S end of the Malay Peninsula, consisting of Singapore Island and 60 adjacent islets. It is one of the smallest states in the world. Singapore Island is largely low-lying and fringed by mango swamps, its climate tropical: rainfall averages about 95in yearly. The population is predominantly Chinese, with large Malay and Indian minorities. The capital, Singapore city, has a fine natural harbor and is SE Asia's foremost commercial and shipping center, conducting a flourishing international trade as a free port. It trades in textiles, rubber, petroleum, timber and tin, and produces electrical goods, and petroleum products, and textiles. Shipbuilding and repair is an important new industry. Singapore was founded as a trading post by Sir Thomas RAFFLES in 1819 and became part of the Straits Settlements in 1826. Self-governing from 1959, it joined MALAYSIA as a constituent state in 1963 but withdrew from the federation in 1965.

SINGER, Isaac Bashevis (1904–   ). Polish-born US YIDDISH novelist and short story writer, known for his portrayal of European Jewish life. His work includes *The Family Moskat* (1950), *The Magician of Lublin* (1960) and *The Estate* (1969). He was awarded the 1978 Nobel Prize.

SINGER, Isaac Merrit (1811–1875), US inventor of the first viable domestic SEWING MACHINE (patented 1851). Despite a legal battle with the earlier inventor Elias HOWE, the Singer sewing machine soon became the most popular in the world.

SINGLE-ISSUE POLITICS, the uncompromising pursuit of one political goal to the exclusion of others by a formally organized group. In the US single-issue groups have drawn funds and support away from political parties, which are made up of disparate factions who agree on some issues but disagree on others. School prayers, abortion, the environment and busing are concerns of major single-issue groups.

SINGLE TAX, proposed reform that tax on land value should be a government's sole revenue, stated by Henry GEORGE in *Progress and Poverty* (1879). He argued that economic rent of land results from the growth of an economy, not from an individual's effort; therefore, governments are justified in appropriating all economic rents, thus eliminating the need for other taxes. The proposal was never enacted in the US.

SINHALESE, an INDO-ARYAN LANGUAGE, derived from SANSKRIT, spoken by two-thirds of the people of SRI LANKA. Most other Sinhalese speak TAMIL.

SINKIANG, or Xinjiang, Uyger Autonomous Region, region in NW China between Mongolia and USSR. A predominantly agricultural and pastoral area covering 16% of China's land area, it has very rich mineral resources and vast oil fields. Because of scant rainfall, Sinkiang has extensive irrigation systems. It is a strategic region for the defense of China and the home of 13 minority ethnic groups, most of whom practice Islam. Pop 11,000,000.

SINN FEIN (Erse: we, ourselves), Irish nationalist movement which achieved independence for the Irish Free State in 1922. Formed by Arthur GRIFFITH in 1905, it was first widely supported in 1916 when most of the leaders of the EASTER RISING were martyred. Led by DE VALERA, it set up an Irish Parliament, the DAIL EIREANN, by 1919. (See also IRELAND; IRISH REPUBLICAN ARMY).

SINO-JAPANESE WARS, two bitter conflicts between China and Japan. The first (1894–95) was precipitated by the rivalry of the two nations over Korea. China's navy was totally destroyed and its army routed by the Japanese. The Treaty of SHIMONOSEKI led to Japan becoming a great power. The second (1937–45) was the result of renewed Japanese expansionism in the Far East. Japan conquered Manchuria in 1931 and gradually penetrated into China. In 1937 Japan seized nearly all the coastal cities and industrial areas. The Chinese Nationalists and the communists united to fight the Japanese. After PEARL HARBOR the fighting became part of WWII.

SINUS, large air space connected with the NOSE which may become infected and obstructed after upper respiratory infection and cause facial pain and fever (sinusitis). There are four major nasal sinuses: the maxillary, frontal, ethmoid and sphenoid. *Also*, a blind-ended channel which may discharge PUS or other material onto the skin or other surface. These may be EMBRYOLOGICAL remnants or arise from a foreign body or deep chronic infection (e.g., OSTEOMYELITIS). *Also*, a large venous channel, as in the LIVER and in the large vessels draining BLOOD from the BRAIN.

SINYAVSKY, Andrei (1925–   ), Russian novelist, critic and journalist, who, in his early work, used the pen name Abram Tertz. In the 1950s, his *Lyubimov* (*The Makepeace Experiment*) and short stories in the fantastic mode circulated in the USSR in underground editions. In 1966 Sinyavsky and Yuli DANIEL were convicted of writing works "slanderous" of the USSR. After serving his sentence, Sinyavsky emigrated to France, 1973.

SIOUX INDIANS, the largest North American tribe of the Siouan language group. Also known as the *Dakota* ("allies"), they were originally a federation of seven tribes, the most numerous being the Teton. After repeated revolts against white misrule and treachery, they were finally defeated at WOUNDED KNEE (1890). Today about 35,000 live on reservations.

SIQUEIROS, David Alfaro (1896–1974), Mexican mural painter, best known for his murals in Mexico City on social subjects.

SIRICA, John Joseph (1904–   ), US federal judge who presided over the Watergate burglary trial (1973), which resulted in the sentencing of several of President Richard Nixon's top aides for conspiracy to obstruct justice.

SIRIUS, Alpha Canis Majoris, the Dog Star, the brightest STAR in the night sky. 2.7pc distant, it is 20 times more luminous than the sun and has absolute magnitude +1.4 A DOUBLE STAR, its major component is twice the size of the sun; its minor component (the Pup), the first white dwarf star to be discovered, has a diameter only 50% greater than that of the earth, but is extremely dense, its mass being just less than that of the sun.

SIROCCO, also Sciroeco, in S Europe, warm, humid WIND from the S or SE, originating as a dry wind over the Sahara Desert and gaining humidity from passage over the Mediterranean.

SISLEY, Alfred (1839–1899), Anglo-French painter, a founder of IMPRESSIONISM. His fine landscapes and snow scenes, painted in the 1870s, often show Paris, London and their neighbor-

hoods. His work achieved wide recognition only after his death.

SISTINE CHAPEL, the papal chapel in the Vatican palace, Rome, renowned for its magnificent frescoes by MICHELANGELO and other Renaissance artists like PERUGINO, BOTTICELLI and PINTURICCHIO. It is named for Pope Sixtus IV, who began its construction in 1473, and is used by the College of Cardinals when it meets to elect a new pope.

SISYPHUS, in Greek myth, deceitful king of Corinth who cheated death and so was doomed to everlasting punishment in the Underworld. He had to push a boulder up a steep slope, watch it roll down, and then begin all over again.

SITAR, Indian stringed instrument with a long neck and smallish rounded soundbox. There are usually seven strings—five melody and two drone: these are plucked by a player seated on cushions or the floor. In 1957 the Indian sitar virtuoso Ravi SHANKAR made the first of several concert tours of the US, spreading the popularity of the instrument, which has since been used by ROCK MUSIC groups.

SITTER, Willem de (1872–1934), Dutch astronomer who helped to get EINSTEIN'S theory of RELATIVITY widely known and who proposed a modification to it allowing for a gradual expansion of the universe.

SITTING BULL (c1831–1890), chief of the Teton SIOUX INDIANS who led the last major Indian resistance in the US. Born in S.D., he became head of the Sioux nation and inspired the 1876 campaign that resulted in the massacre at LITTLE BIGHORN. After the Sioux surrender (1881) he retired to Standing Rock reservation, N.D. During the GHOST DANCE Indian police killed him while attempting his arrest.

SITUATION ETHICS, ethical theory denying the binding force of objective moral laws. It holds that the morality of an act is determined by the conditions of a given situation and the intentions of the actor rather than by the objective nature of the behavior. *Situation Ethics: The New Morality* (1966), by Episcopalian theologian Joseph Fletcher, outlines the theory.

SITWELL, name of three distinguished English writers, children of Sir George Keresley Sitwell. **Dame Edith Sitwell** (1887–1964), leading poet and critic, helped launch *Wheels* (1916), a magazine of experimental poetry, wrote the satirical *Facade* (1922; music by William WALTON), and was a master technician of sound, rhythm and symbol. **Sir Osbert Sitwell** (1892–1969), satirist, novelist and short-story writer, is best known for his fantastic novel *The Man who Lost Himself* (1929) and his five-volume autobiography. Sir **Sacheverell Sitwell** (1897–   ), is a poet, art critic and traveler whose work includes *Southern Baroque Art* (1924), *All Summer in a Day* (1926) and *Mozart* (1932).

SI UNITS, the internationally adopted abbreviation for the *Système International d'Unités* (International System of Units), a modification of the system known as rationalized MKSA UNITS adopted by the 11th General Conference of Weights and Measures (CGPM) in 1960 and subsequently amended. It is the modern version of the METRIC SYSTEM. SI Units are the legal standard in many countries and find almost universal use among scientists.

SIX, Les, term coined in 1920 to group six French composers (Darius MILHAUD, Francis POULENC, Arthur HONEGGER, Georges AURIC, Louis Durey and Germaine Tailleferre) inspired by the work of Erik SATIE and Jean COCTEAU.

SIX NATIONS, the enlarged IROQUOIS League formed by the joining of the Tuscarora (1722).

SKAGERRAK, arm of the North Sea some 140mi long and 80mi wide dividing Norway from Denmark and linking the North Sea with the Baltic Sea through the Kattegat.

SKALDIC POETRY, in Old Norse literature, the poetry of the SAGA, recited by Scandinavian court poets (*skalds*) from about 800 onwards. It is noted for its syllabic metrical structure and elaborate metaphors (*kennings*).

SKELETON, in VERTEBRATES, the framework of BONES that supports and protects the soft TISSUES and ORGANS of the body. (See also ENDOSKELETON; EXOSKELETON.) It acts as an attachment for the MUSCLES, especially those producing movement, and protects vital organs such as the BRAIN, HEART and LUNGS. It is also a store of calcium, magnesium, sodium, phosphorus and PROTEINS, while its bone marrow is the site of red BLOOD-corpuscle formation. In the adult human body, there are about 206 bones, to which more than 600 muscles are attached. The skeleton consists of two parts: the axial skeleton (the skull, backbone and rib-cage), and the appendicular skeleton (the limbs). The function of the *axial skeleton* is mainly protective. The SKULL consists of 29 bones, 8 being fused together to form the cranium, protecting the brain. The *vertebral column*, or backbone, consists of 33 small bones (or VERTEBRAE): the upper 25 are joined by LIGAMENTS and thick cartilaginous disks and the lower 9 are fused together. It supports the upper body

and protects the SPINAL CORD which runs through it. The *rib-cage* consists of 12 pairs of ribs forming a protective cage around the heart and lungs and assists in breathing (see RESPIRATION). The **appendicular skeleton** is primarily concerned with LOCOMOTION and consists of the ARMS and pectoral girdle, and the LEGS and pelvic girdle. The limbs articulate with their girdles in ball and socket JOINTS which permit the shoulder and hip great freedom of movement but are prone to dislocation. In contrast the elbows and knees are hinge joints permitting movement in one plane only, but which are very strong.

SKELTON, John (c1460–1529), English court poet and satirist; influential tutor to Henry VIII. His works include burlesques (*Philip Sparrow*, 1508), a morality play, *Magnificence* (1515), and satires directed against Cardinal WOLSEY such as *Colin Clout* (1522).

SKEPTICISM, philosophical attitude of doubting all claims to knowledge, chiefly on the ground that the adequacy of any proposed criterion is itself questionable. Examples of thoroughgoing skeptics, wary of dogmatism in whatever guise, were PYRRHO OF ELIS ("Pyrrhonism" and "skepticism" are virtual synonyms) and HUME. Other thinkers, among them AUGUSTINE, ERASMUS, MONTAIGNE, PASCAL, BAYLE and KIERKEGAARD, sought to defend faith and religion by directing skeptical arguments against the EPISTEMOLOGICAL claims of RATIONALISM and EMPIRICISM. PRAGMATISM and KANT's critical philosophy represent two influential attempts to resolve skeptical dilemmas. (See also AGNOSTICISM.)

SKIDMORE, Louis (1897–1962), US architect and cofounder of the firm of Skidmore, Owings and Merrill (1936), which designed government and corporate projects such as Oak Ridge, Tenn. (1943–45), the US Air Force Academy in Colorado Springs (1954–62), and the Sears Tower in Chicago (1971–73).

SKIING, the sport of gliding over snow on long, thin runners called skis. It began some 5,000 years ago in N Europe as a form of transport and became a sport in the 1800s. In 1924, the Fédération Internationale de Ski was formed and the first Winter Olympics held. Today, skiing is ever-increasing in popularity, as either Alpine downhill slalom or giant slalom obstacle courses, Nordic crosscountry skiing, or ski-jumping. Skis are generally made of laminated wood, fiberglass, plastic, metal or a combination of these. They have safety bindings attaching the boot firmly to the ski; ski poles are used for balance.

SKIN, the TISSUE which forms a sensitive, elastic, protective and waterproof covering of the HUMAN BODY, together with its specializations (e.g., NAILS, HAIR). In the adult human, it weighs 2.75kg, covers an area of $1.7m^2$ and varies in thickness from 1mm (in the eyelids) to 3mm (in the palms and soles). It consists of two layers: the outer, epidermis, and the inner, dermis, or true skin. The outermost part of the **epidermis,** the *stratum corneum,* contains a tough protein called KERATIN. Consequently it provides protection against mechanical trauma, a barrier against microorganisms, and waterproofing. The epidermis also contains cells which produce the MELANIN responsible for skin pigmentation and which provides protection against the sun's ultraviolet rays. The unique pattern of skin folding on the soles and palms provides a gripping surface, and is the basis of identification by FINGERPRINTS. The **dermis** is usually thicker than the epidermis and contains BLOOD vessels, nerves and sensory receptors, sweat glands, SEBACEOUS GLANDS, hair follicles, fat cells and fibers. Temperature regulation of the body is aided by the evaporative cooling of sweat (see PERSPIRATION); regulation of the skin blood flow, and the erection of hairs which trap an insulating layer of air next to the skin (see GOOSEFLESH). The rich nerve supply of the dermis is responsible for the reception of touch, pressure, pain and temperature stimuli. Leading into the hair follicles are sebaceous glands which produce the antibacterial sebum, a fluid which keeps the hairs oiled and the skin moist. The action of sunlight on the skin initiates the formation of VITAMIN D which helps prevent RICKETS.

SKINDIVING, underwater SWIMMING AND DIVING with or without self-contained underwater breathing apparatus (SCUBA). The simplest apparatus is the SNORKEL, generally used with goggles, or mask, and flippers. An AQUALUNG consists of compressed air cylinders with an automatic demand regulator, which supplies air at the correct pressure according to the diver's depth. "Closed-circuit" SCUBA contains a chemical which absorbs carbon dioxide from exhaled air.

SKINNER, Burrhus Frederic (1904–), US psychologist and author whose staunch advocacy of BEHAVIORISM has done much to gain it acceptance in 20th-century PSYCHOLOGY. His best known books are *Science and Human Behavior* (1953); *Walden Two* (1961), a Utopian novel based on behaviorism; and *Beyond Freedom and Dignity* (1971).

SKINNER, Cornelia Otis (1901–1979), US actress and author who wrote the autobiographical *Our Hearts Were Young and Gay* (1942; with E. Kimbrough). She is remembered for solo monologues often written by herself.

SKUNKS, carnivorous mammals of the WEASEL family, Mustelidae, renowned for the foul stink they produce when threatened. There are ten species distributed throughout the Americas. All are boldly-patterned in black and white. Most are nocturnal and feed on insects, mice and eggs. In defense a skunk can expel fine jets of foul-smelling liquid from scent glands under the tail. This can be shot out to a distance of 3m (10ft) with a remarkably accurate aim.

SKYDIVING, the sport of parachute jumping, developed since WWII. In competitions, points are awarded for acrobatic style in the maneuvers made during the free fall (the period before the parachute opens), and for accuracy in landing on target (the center of a 1,000ft circle). Parachutists generally drop from heights up to 13,000ft and open their parachutes at about 2,000ft.

SKYJACKING, the seizing of an aircraft and its passengers for ransom or for the purpose of forcing the airline or a government to accede to certain political demands made by the hijacker, who is often a terrorist. Since 1961 some 200 such incidents have occurred in the US. A rash of these crimes caused security to be tightened in 1972: passengers were required to pass through metal detectors and their baggage was X-rayed. Armed sky marshals—2,500 at one point—were briefly employed by airlines, but fears of gun battles in crowded planes ended that experiment. Israeli commandos freed 105 hostages when they successfully completed a daring raid on a hijacked Air France plane at Entebbe, Uganda, in 1976; German troops freed 86 from a seized Lufthansa airliner at Mogadishu, Somalia, in 1977. In recent years the number of skyjackings has declined.

SKYLAB, US manned space station, launched May 25, 1973. First of its kind, it was converted from a Saturn IVB booster to serve as an orbital laboratory and earth resources monitor. The first of its three crews had to repair serious damage, but all set new endurance records in space.

SKYSCRAPER, a very tall building. From the mid-19th century the price of land in big cities made it worthwhile to build upward rather than outward, and this became practicable with the development of safe electric ELEVATORS. The first skyscraper was the 40m (130ft)-high Equitable Life Assurance Society Building, New York (1870). A major design breakthrough was the use of a load-bearing skeletal iron frame, first used in the 10-story Home Insurance Company Building, Chicago (1885).

SLAPSTICK, style of comedy which is primarily physical. The term derives from a split wooden stick, used by Harlequins in COMMEDIA DELL'ARTE pantomimes, which made a loud noise when used as a weapon. Perhaps the most famous use of slapstick humor, however, was in films of the silent era (1920s), including Mack Sennett's Keystone Kops movies and those of CHAPLIN and KEATON, in which chase sequences and a vast repertoire of sight gags became standard elements. LAUREL AND HARDY carried the tradition into sound films as did former vaudevillians ABBOTT AND COSTELLO.

SLATE, a fine-grained low grade metamorphic rock formed by the regional metamorphism of shale. The parallel orientation of platy minerals in the rock causes the rock to split evenly (slaty cleavage) in a plane that is perpendicular to the direction of the compressive metamorphic stress. (See also METAMORPHIC ROCKS.)

SLATER, Samuel (1768–1835), British-born founder of the US cotton textile industry. As an apprentice in England he memorized the principles of ARKWRIGHT'S machinery. He set up his spinning mill (now a museum) in Pawtucket, R.I., in 1793.

SLAVERY, a practice found at different times in most parts of the world, now condemned in the Universal Declaration of Human Rights.

Slavery generally means enforced servitude, along with society's recognition that the master has ownership rights over the slave and his labor. Some elements of slavery can be found in serfdom, as practiced during the Middle Ages and in Russia up to 1861; in debt bondage and PEONAGE, both forms of enforced labor for the payment of debts; and in forced labor itself, exacted for punishment or for political or military reasons, (examples being the "slave" labor used by the Nazis in WWII, and the Soviet labor camps). In some places a form of slavery or bondage is still practiced today under the guise of exacting a bride price, or the "adoption" of poor children by wealthier families for labor purposes. While peonage is still rampant in South America, actual slavery is reputed to exist in Africa, the Arabian Peninsula, Tibet and elsewhere. Slavery in Saudi Arabia was officially abolished only in 1962.

Warfare was the main source of slaves in ancient times, along with enslavement for debt or as punishment, and the selling of children. But there was not necessarily a distinction in race or color between master and slave. Manumission (the granting of freedom) was commonplace, and in Greece and Rome many slaves or freedmen rose to influential posts: a slave dynasty, the Mamelukes, ruled Egypt from 1250 to 1517. In the West the Germans enslaved many Slavic people (hence "slave") in the Dark Ages. By the 13th century feudal serfdom was widespread in Europe (see SERF). Slavery increased again when the Portuguese, exploring the coast of Africa, began to import black slaves in 1433 to fill a manpower shortage at home. With the discovery of America and the development of plantations, the need for cheap, abundant labor encouraged the slave trade. The British abolished the slave trade in 1807 and slavery in 1833. By constitutional provision, the US slave trade ended in 1808 and the Emancipation Proclamation (1863), issued by President Lincoln, took full effect with the end of the Civil War (1865). See NEGROES, AMERICAN; ABOLITIONISM; MISSOURI COMPROMISE; COMPROMISE OF 1850; KANSAS-NEBRASKA ACT; DRED SCOTT CASE; EMANCIPATION PROCLAMATION; CIVIL WAR, AMERICAN; REPUBLICAN PARTY; RECONSTRUCTION; CIVIL RIGHTS AND LIBERTIES.

SLAVONIC LANGUAGES, a group of INDO-EUROPEAN LANGUAGES spoken by some 225 million people in central and E Europe and Siberia. There are three groups: W Slavonic (Polish, Czech and Slovak), S Slavonic (Slovene, Serbo-Croatian, Macedonian and Bulgarian), and E Slavonic (Russian, Ukrainian and Belorussian). Byzantine missionaries in the 9th century first developed written Slavonic, using a modified Greek alphabet known as Cyrillic. Today, SLAVS converted by the Orthodox Church use Cyrillic characters and Slavs converted by the Roman Church use the Latin alphabet.

SLAVS, largest European ethnic and language group, living today in central and E Europe and Siberia: all speak SLAVONIC LANGUAGES. About 4,000 years ago they migrated to land N of the Black Sea and later split into three groups: the E Slavs, (Russians, Belorussians and Ukrainians), the W Slavs (Czechs, Slovaks and Poles) and the S Slavs (Serbs, Croats, Slovenes, Macedonians, Montenegrins and Bulgarians). Slavonic nations were formed from the 9th century but almost all were overwhelmed by Turkish or Mongol invaders. In the 15th century Russia gained national independence but it was not until WWI that the other Slav nations regained their national identities.

SLEEP, a state of relative unconsciousness and inactivity. The need for sleep recurs periodically in all animals. If deprived of sleep humans initially experience HALLUCINATIONS, acute ANXIETY, and become highly suggestible and eventually, COMA and sometimes DEATH result. During sleep, the body is relaxed and most bodily activity is reduced. Cortical, or higher, brain activity, as measured by the ELECTROENCEPHALOGRAPH; blood pressure; body TEMPERATURE; rate of heartbeat and breathing are decreased. However, certain activities, such as gastric and alimentary activity, are increased. Sleep tends to occur in daily cycles which exhibit up to 5 or 6 periods of orthodox sleep—characterized by its deepness—alternating with periods of paradoxical, or rapid-eye-movement (REM) sleep—characterized by its restlessness and jerky movements of the eyes. Paradoxical sleep occurs only when we are dreaming and occupies about 20% of total sleeping time. Sleepwalking (SOMNAMBULISM) occurs only during orthodox sleep when we are not dreaming. Sleeptalking occurs mostly in orthodox sleep. Many theories have been proposed to explain sleep but none is completely satisfactory. Separate sleeping and waking centers in the HYPOTHALAMUS cooperate with other parts of the BRAIN in controlling sleep. Sleep as a whole, and particularly paradoxical sleep when dreaming occurs, is essential to health and life. Consequently, the key to why animals sleep may reside in a need to DREAM. Sleep learning experiments have so far proved ineffective. A rested brain and concentration are probably the most effective basis for LEARNING.

SLEEPING SICKNESS, INFECTIOUS DISEASE caused by TRYPANOSOMES occurring in Africa and carried by TSETSE FLIES. It initially causes FEVER, headache, often a sense of oppression and a rash; later the characteristic somnolence follows and the disease enters a chronic, often fatal stage. Treatment is most effective if started before the late stage of BRAIN involvement and uses arsenical compounds.

SLEEPWALKING. See SOMNAMBULISM.

SLIDE RULE, an instrument based on LOGARITHMS and used for rapid, though approximate, calculation. Two scales are calibrated identically so that, on each, the distance from the "1" point to any point on the scale is proportional to the logarithm of the number represented by that point. Since

log $(a.b)$ = log a + log b, the multiplication $a:b$ can be performed by setting the "1" point on scale (1) against a on scale (2), then reading off the number of scale (2) opposite b on scale (1). Division is performed by reversing the procedure. In practice, slide rules have several different scales for different kinds of calculation, and a runner (cursor) to permit more accurate readings.

SLIPPED DISK, a common condition in which the intervertebral disks of the spinal column degenerate with extrusion of the central soft portion through the outer fibrous ring. The protruding material may cause back pain, or may press upon the spinal cord or on nerves as they leave the SPINAL CORD (causing SCIATICA). Prolonged bed rest is an effective treatment in many cases, but traction, manipulation or surgery may also be required particularly if there is PARALYSIS or nerve involvement.

SLOAN, Alfred Pritchard (1875–1966), US industrialist, president of General Motors from 1923 and chairman of the board 1937–56. His Sloan Foundation (1934) finances social and medical research, particularly into cancer through the Sloan-Kettering Institute in NYC.

SLOAN, John (1871–1951), US painter, a member of the ASHCAN SCHOOL and influential in the development of US modern art. He is famous for his paintings of nudes and of urban scenes, such as *McSorley's Bar* (1912) and *Wake of the Ferry* (1907).

SLOTHS, slow, tree-dwelling EDENTATE mammals. There are two genera of modern Tree sloths, the two-toed sloths (*Choloepus*) and three-toed sloths or ai (*Bradypus*), descending from the Giant GROUND SLOTHS, *Megatherium* of the PLEISTOCENE. The arms and legs are long, the digits are bound together by tissue and terminate in long, strong claws. With these the sloth can suspend the body from branches. All sloths are South American in origin and vegetarian, feeding on fruits, shoots and leaves.

SLOVAK, the official language of Slovakia. A W SLAVONIC LANGUAGE, it resembles Czech in dialect and is written in the Roman alphabet.

SLOVAKIA, E part of Czechoslovakia, 18,922sq mi in area. It is mostly mountainous, but the mountains slope down to plains and the Danube R in the S and SW. Slovakia has rich farmlands and mineral deposits; shipbuilding and metal processing are also leading industries. The old capital, Bratislava, is an important port on the Danube. Slovakia was mainly under

Hungarian rule from the early 900s to 1918. It was then part of Czechoslovakia until it became a German protectorate in 1939. After WWII it was reincorporated into Czechoslovakia.

SLOVENE, the language of Slovenia. It is a S SLAVONIC LANGUAGE, closely related to Serbo-Croatian, and has 46 individual dialects.

SLOVENIA, NW part of YUGOSLAVIA. It became independent of Austria in 1918 and a constituent republic of Yugoslavia in 1945. Its economy is based chiefly on agriculture and on iron, steel, and aluminum industries. The capital is Ljubljana.

SMALL BUSINESS ADMINISTRATION, independent agency of the US government which furnishes small businesses with practical advice and low-cost loans. The agency also helps small businesses obtain government contracts and aids minority-owned firms.

SMALLPOX, INFECTIOUS DISEASE, now restricted to a few areas, causing FEVER, headache and general malaise, followed by a rash. The rash characteristically affects face and limbs more than trunk and lesions start simultaneously. From a maculopapular appearance, the rash passes into a pustular or vesicular stage and ends with scab formation; the lesions are deep and cause scarring. Major and minor forms of smallpox exist, with high fatality rate in major, often with extensive skin HEMORRHAGE. Transmission is from infected cases by secretions and the SKIN lesions; these are infectious for the duration of the rash. Immunization against smallpox was the earliest form practiced, initially through inoculation with the minor form. Later JENNER introduced VACCINATION with the related cowpox VIRUS (vaccinia is now used). QUARANTINE regulations and contact tracing are important in control of isolated outbreaks. It is important to confirm that apparent cases of CHICKENPOX are not indeed of smallpox.

SMELL, SENSE for detecting and recognizing substances at a distance and for assessing the quality of food. One of the earliest senses to develop in EVOLUTION, it may have been based on the chemotaxis of lower forms. Recognition of environmental odors is of vital importance in recognizing edible substances, detecting other animals or objects of danger, and in sexual behavior and attraction. In recent years, particular odors called pheromones that have specific physiological functions in insect and mammal behavior have been recognized. Smell reception in insects is localized to the antennae and detection is by specialist (pheromone) receptors and generalist (other odor) receptors. In man and mammals, the NOSE is the organ of smell. Respiratory air is drawn into the nostrils and passes across a specialized receptor surface—the olfactory epithelium. Receptor cells detect the tiny concentrations of odors in the air stream and stimulate nerve impulses that pass to olfactory centers in the BRAIN for coding and perception. It is not possible to classify odors in the same way as the primary colors in VISION and it is probable that pattern recognition is more important. Certain animals depend mainly on the sense of smell, while man is predominantly a visual animal. But with training, he can achieve sensitive detection and discrimination of odors.

SMELT, small estuarine fishes related to SALMON. Elongate fishes resembling small trout, they live in large shoals in estuaries and coastal waters of temperate regions of the N hemisphere. Like true salmon, smelt migrate up into fresher water to spawn. Smelt rarely grow to more than about 200mm (8in) but are considered a great delicacy.

SMELTING, in METALLURGY, process of extracting a metal from its ORE by heating the ore in a BLAST FURNACE or reverberatory furnace (one in which a shallow hearth is heated by radiation from a low roof heated by flames from the burning fuel). A reducing agent (see OXIDATION AND REDUCTION), usually COKE, is used, and a FLUX is added to remove impurities. Sulfide ores are generally roasted to convert them to oxides before smelting.

SMETANA, Bedřich (1824–1884), Czech composer. Many of his compositions reflect Smetana's ardent Bohemian nationalism; most famous are the comic opera *The Bartered Bride* (1866) and the symphonic poem *Ma Vlast* ("My Country"; 1874–79).

SMITH, Adam (1723–1790), Scottish economist and philosopher. The free-market system he advocated in *The Wealth of Nations* (1776) came to be regarded as the classic system of economics. Smith drew on the ideas of TURGOT, Quesnay, MONTESQUIEU and his friend David HUME and argued that if market forces were allowed to operate without state intervention "an invisible hand" would guide self-interest for the well-being of all. His concept of the division of labor and the belief that value derives from productive labor were major insights. An earlier work, *Theory of Moral Sentiments* (1759) contrasts with *The Wealth of Nations* in its emphasis upon sympathy rather than self-interest as a basic force in human nature.

SMITH, Alfred Emanuel (1873–1944), US politician elected Governor of New York four times (1918, 1922, 1924, 1926), a TAMMANY HALL politician and a leading figure among the Democrats. Supported by F. D. ROOSEVELT in his bids for the presidency, he failed to gain nomination in 1924 and was beaten by HOOVER in 1928: when Roosevelt became president, Smith opposed the NEW DEAL.

SMITH, Bessie (c1898–1937), US jazz singer, perhaps the greatest BLUES singer. "The Empress of the Blues" came from a poor Tenn. home and first recorded in 1923; later she performed with many leading musicians, including Louis ARMSTRONG and Benny GOODMAN.

SMITH, David (1906–1965), influential US sculptor, famous for his constructions of wrought iron and cut steel. His late works, like *Cubi XVIII* (1964), comprised burnished or painted cubic forms dramatically welded together.

SMITH, Frederick Edwin, 1st Earl of Birkenhead (1872–1930), British Conservative politician and jurist. He was against Irish HOME RULE and prosecuted CASEMENT. Lord Chancellor 1919–22, he served in BALFOUR'S cabinet 1924–28 as secretary of state for India.

SMITH, Ian Douglas (1919–   ), Rhodesian prime minister 1965–80. As leader of a white minority government he declared unilateral independence from Britain in 1965, and made RHODESIA a republic in 1970. A decade of civil strife ended (1980) with the formation of a black regime in Rhodesia, renamed Zimbabwe.

SMITH, John (c1580–1631), English explorer, soldier and writer who established the first permanent English colony in North America. He sailed to Virginia in 1607 and founded a settlement at JAMESTOWN. Smith claimed to have been captured by Chief POWHATAN in 1607 and saved from death by the chief's daughter POCAHONTAS. Smith charted the coast of New England in 1614, publishing his findings in *A Description of New England* (1616).

SMITH, Joseph (1805–1844), founder of the Church of Jesus Christ of the Latter-Day Saints, based on the Bible and the Book of Mormon, which Smith claimed to have found (in the form of hieroglyphs on gold plates) and translated with the help of the angel Moroni. In 1844 he was accused of conspiracy and, while in prison, was murdered by a mob. (See MORMONS; NAUVOO.)

SMITH, Kate (1909–   ), popular radio singer whose 1930s show featured her famous signature song, "When The Moon Comes Over The Mountain." Smith introduced the song "God Bless America" in 1938, made films and recordings, and appeared on her own TV show (1950–54).

SMITH, Robyn (1944–   ), US jockey. In 1973 she became the first woman ever to capture a stakes race, and the first to ride three winners in one afternoon.

SMITH, Walter Bedell (1895–1961), WWII US army chief of staff in Europe. He negotiated the surrenders of Italy (1943) and Germany (1945), was ambassador to the USSR 1946–49, CIA director 1950–53 and undersecretary of state 1953–54.

SMITH, William "Strata" (1769–1839), the "father of stratigraphy." He established that similar sedimentary rock strata in different places may be dated by identifying the fossils each level contains, and made the first geological map of England and Wales (1815).

SMITH ACT, or Alien Registration Act (1940), a federal US law making it a criminal offense to advocate the violent overthrow of the government or to belong to any group advocating this. Used to convict Communist Party leaders, the act also required registration and fingerprinting of aliens.

SMITH AND DALE (Joe Smith, 1884–1981, and Charles Dale, 1882–1971), US vaudeville comedy team, known for sketches filled with zany and incongruous dialogue, such as the classic "Dr. Kronkheit." The pair inspired Neil SIMON'S 1972 play, *The Sunshine Boys*.

SMITHSONIAN INSTITUTION, US institution of scientific and artistic culture, located in Washington, D.C., and sponsored by the US Government. Founded with money left by James SMITHSON, it was established by Congress in 1846. It is governed by a board of regents comprising the US Vice-President and Chief Justice, three Senators, three Representatives and six private citizens appointed by Congress. Although it undertakes considerable scientific research, it is best known as the largest US collection of museums, the "nation's attic:" these include the United States National Museum, the National Air and Space Museum, the National Gallery of Art, the Freer Gallery of Art, the National Portrait Gallery and the National Collection of Fine Arts.

SMOKING, the habit of inhaling or taking into the mouth the smoke of dried tobacco or other leaves from a pipe or wrapped cylinder; it has been practiced for many years in various communities, often using leaves of plants with hallucinogenic or other euphoriant properties. The modern habit of tobacco smoking derived from America and spread to Europe in the 16th century. Mass production of cigarettes began in the 19th century. Since the rise in cigarette consumption, epidemiology has demonstrated an unequivocal association with LUNG CANCER, chronic BRONCHITIS and EMPHYSEMA and with ARTERIOSCLEROSIS, leading to CORONARY THROMBOSIS and STROKE. Smoking appears to play a part in other forms of cancer and in other diseases such as peptic ULCER. It is not yet clear what part of smoke is responsible for disease. It is now known that nonsmokers may be affected by environmental smoke. A minor degree of physical and a large degree of psychological addiction occur.

SMOKY MOUNTAINS. See GREAT SMOKY MOUNTAINS.

SMOLLETT, Tobias George (1721–1771), British writer who developed the PICARESQUE NOVEL in his satires of 18th-century English society. They include *Roderick Random* (1748), *Peregrine Pickle* (1751) and his masterpiece, *Humphry Clinker* (1771), which is written in letter form.

SMUTS, Jan Christiaan (1870–1950), South African lawyer, soldier and statesman. In the BOER WAR he led Boer guerrilla forces in Cape Colony. He worked with BOTHA to create the Union of South Africa (1910) and was in the WWI British war cabinet. He was South African prime minister 1919–24, and minister of justice 1933–39 in the coalition government led by HERTZOG, whom he succeeded as prime minister (1939–48) to bring South Africa into WWII on the British side.

SMYRNA, Turkey. See IZMIR.

SNAILS, herbivorous GASTROPOD mollusks with, typically, a spirally coiled shell, found on land, in freshwater or in the sea. The shell is secreted by the underlying "mantle" and houses the internal organs. The internal structure is similar in all groups, though many land snails (Pulmonates) have their gills replaced with an air-breathing lung. Nonpulmonate snails are mostly unisexual while pulmonates are typically hermaphrodite.

SNAKE BITE. A very small proportion of the world's snakes produce poisonous venom, and most of these live in the tropics. The venom may lead to HEMORRHAGE, PARALYSIS and central NERVOUS SYSTEM disorders as well as local symptoms of pain, EDEMA and ulceration. Treatment aims to minimize venom absorption, neutralize venom with antiserum, counteract the specific effects and support life until venom is eliminated. Antiserum should be used only for definite bites by identified snakes.

SNAKES, an order, Squamata, of elongate legless reptiles. Snakes have a deeply forked tongue covered with sense organs which is flicked in and out of the mouth to test the surroundings. All snakes are carnivorous, feeding on insects, eggs, rodents and other larger mammals depending on size. While those that feed on insects usually feed fairly regularly, snakes taking larger prey may feed only infrequently. To facilitate swallowing of large prey, upper and lower jaws may be dislocated and moved independently. All snakes swallow their prey whole without mastication. While many species have no accessories to assist them in the capture of prey, others are venomous, or subdue their prey by constriction before swallowing. Snakes may be aquatic, terrestrial or arboreal.

SNCC. See STUDENT NATIONAL COORDINATING COMMITTEE.

SNEAD, Sam (1912–   ), US professional golfer. He captured over 150 championships, including the Masters (1949, 1952, 1954) and the USPGA (1942, 1949, 1951).

SNORRI STURLUSON (1179–1241), Icelandic poet and historian. The major figure in medieval Scandinavian literature, he wrote the still popular *Heimskringla* (*Orb of the World*), a vivid and eventful history of Norway's kings. He compiled the prose EDDA, a handbook of Norse mythology, poetic diction and meter.

SNOW, C(harles) P(ercy) (1905–1980), English author, physicist and government official, many of whose works deal with the widening gap between art and technology. He is best known for his *Strangers and Brothers* series: 11 novels (1940–70) about the English professional classes.

SNOW, Edgar (1905–1972), US journalist and author. The first Westerner to visit the Chinese Communists in their remote headquarters in Yenan (1936), he wrote a sympathetic account of their programs and idealism in *Red Star Over China* (1937). A personal friend of MAO TSE-TUNG and CHOU EN-LAI, he was one of the few Americans to visit China regularly after the 1949 revolution about which he wrote *The Other Side of the River* (1962) and *The Long Revolution* (1972).

SNOW, Hank (1914–   ), Canadian-born US country singer who sang with the Grand Ole Opry. His mellow ballads, flat-picking guitar work and personal reserve greatly influenced younger singers such as Johnny Cash.

SNOW BLINDNESS, temporary loss of VISION with severe pain, tears and EDEMA due to excessive ultraviolet light reflected from snow. Permanent damage is rare but protective POLAROID glasses should be used.

SNOWDEN, Antony Armstrong-Jones, 1st Earl of (1930–), husband of Princess Margaret of Great Britain (married 1960, marriage dissolved 1978) and a professional photographer and filmmaker.

SNOWDEN, Philip (1864–1937), British political leader. An early leader of the Labour Party, he served in Commons 1906–18 and 1922–31. He was chancellor of the exchequer 1924 and 1929–31.

SNOW LEOPARD. See OUNCE.

SNOWMOBILE, or motor sled, motorized vehicle with two skis in front and propelled by an endless track, used for traveling over deep snow. First developed in the 1920s to replace dogsleds, they have become popular for recreation and racing since lightweight models were introduced (1959).

SOANE, Sir John (1753–1837), English architect. The severe linear style of his neoclassical Bank of England gave way to more picturesque eccentricity in Dulwich College gallery and his own London home in Lincoln's Inn Fields (now the Soane Museum).

SOAPS AND DETERGENTS, substances which, when dissolved in water, are cleansing agents. Soap has been known since 600 BC; it was used as a medicine until its use for washing was discovered in the 2nd century AD. Until about 1500 it was made by boiling animal fat with wood ashes (which contain the alkali potassium carbonate). Then caustic soda (see SODIUM), a more effective ALKALI, was used; vegetable FATS and oils were also introduced. **Saponification,** the chemical reaction in soap-making, is an alkaline HYDROLYSIS of the fat (an ESTER) to yield GLYCEROL and the sodium salt of a long-chain carboxylic acid. The potassium salt is used for soft soap. In the modern process, the hydrolysis is effected by superheated water with a zinc catalyst, and the free acid produced is then neutralized. Synthetic detergents, introduced in WWI, generally consist of the sodium salts of various long-chain SULFONIC ACIDS, derived from oils and PETROLEUM products. The principle of soaps and detergents is the same: the hydrophobic long-chain hydrocarbon part of the molecule attaches itself to the grease and dirt particles, and the hydrophilic acid group makes the particles soluble in water, so that by agitation they are loosed from the fabric and dispersed. Detergents do not (unlike soaps) form scum in HARD WATER.

Their persistence in rivers, however, causes pollution problems, and biodegradable detergents have been developed. Household detergents may contain several additives: bleaches, brighteners, and ENZYMES to digest protein stains (egg, blood, etc.).

SOAPSTONE, or steatite, METAMORPHIC ROCK consisting largely of compacted TALC with some SERPENTINE and carbonates, formed by alteration of PERIDOTITE. Soft and soapy to the touch, soapstone has been used from prehistoric times for carvings and vessels. When fired, it becomes hard and is used for insulators.

SOCCER, most popular sport in the world, national sport of most European and Latin American countries and fast increasing in popularity in the US and among women. The field measures 115yd by 75yd, the netted goal is 8yd wide and 8ft high and the inflated leather ball 27–28in round. There are two 45min halves, one referee and two linesmen. The aim of each 11-man team is to score by kicking or heading the ball into the opponents' goal. To advance the ball, a player may *dribble* it (repeatedly kick it as he runs with it) or kick it to a teammate. The ball may not be touched with the hand or arm, except by the goalkeeper in the penalty area in front of his goal. Modern professional soccer began in the UK in 1885, in the US in 1967.

SOCIAL CONTRACT, in political philosophy a concept of the formation of society, in which men agree to surrender part of their "natural" freedom to enjoy the security of the organized state. The idea, though of ancient origin, was first fully formulated in the 17th and 18th centuries by Thomas HOBBES (in *Leviathan*, 1651), LOCKE and ROUSSEAU, and was then controversial because it suggested that heads of state ruled only by their subjects' consent.

SOCIAL CREDIT PARTY, Canadian party formed (1935) by William ABERHART. It aimed to implement Clifford Douglas' policy of avoiding economic depression by distributing surplus money as a "social dividend" to increase purchasing power. It failed in this but governed Alberta 1935–71 and British Columbia 1952–72. The party failed to win seats in the 1980 federal parliamentary elections.

SOCIAL DARWINISM, late 19th-century school of thought which held that society evolved on DARWIN'S biological model. Social inequalities were explained (and made to seem natural and inevitable) by the law of "SURVIVAL OF THE FITTEST." Its chief theorist was Herbert SPENCER.

SOCIAL DEMOCRATIC PARTIES,

political parties found in many countries that seek socialism through constitutional reform, not revolution. They usually favor government intervention in the economy and nationalization of powerful industries. The Social Democratic Party of the US joined with the Socialist Labor Party in 1901 to form the SOCIALIST PARTY. In Britain, moderate leaders of the Labour Party broke away to form the Social Democratic Party in 1981.

SOCIAL GOSPEL, a liberal Protestant social-reform movement in the US c1870–1920. It promoted Christian ideas of love and justice in education and social and political service. Among its leaders were Horace BUSHNELL, Washington GLADDEN and Walter RAUSCHENBUSCH.

SOCIALISM, an economic philosophy and political movement which aims to achieve a just, classless society through public ownership and operation of the means of production and distribution of goods. Within this framework it has many forms, the principal two of which are, in common usage, social democratic ("reformist") and revolutionary.

Modern socialism arose in reaction to the hardships of the INDUSTRIAL REVOLUTION, its prevailing ideology of LAISSEZ-FAIRE liberalism and its economic system of CAPITALISM. The FRENCH REVOLUTION promoted hopes of a radically changed social order in the early 1800s. Early experimental cooperative communities in the US included BROOK FARM, NAUVOO and the ONEIDA COMMUNITY. In Europe, insurrectionary socialism in the tradition of the Frenchmen BABEUF and BLANQUI played an important role in the REVOLUTIONS OF 1848 and the PARIS COMMUNE (1871). The work of MARX and ENGELS helped build socialism into a potent force. Their COMMUNIST MANIFESTO (1848) is the best-known socialist document. MARXISM, and its principle of inevitable class conflict leading to the overthrow of capitalism, formed the theoretical basis of the RUSSIAN REVOLUTION of 1917. The offshoots of ANARCHISM and SYNDICALISM developed in the years leading up to WWI; more important was the split between reformist social democrats like the FABIAN SOCIETY seeking gradual reform, and revolutionaries seeking working-class power through extra-legal means. (See LENIN; BOLSHEVISM).

Despite the efforts of such socialists as Eugene V. DEBS and Norman THOMAS, no strong socialist movement has emerged in the US. In West Europe, the SOCIAL DEMOCRATIC PARTIES have formed numerous governments, most recently in France and Greece. In Third World countries, socialism has often been linked with independence movements.

SOCIALIST PARTY, US, formed in 1901 by Eugene V. DEBS and V. L. BERGER out of the Social Democratic Party and a split from the revolutionary Socialist Labor Party, and led for many years by Norman THOMAS. It reached its peak in 1912 when, with a membership of 118,000, it got 56 socialist mayors and one congressman (Berger) elected while winning 897,000 votes for its presidential candidate (Debs). It opposed US involvement in WWI. In 1919 many radicals left to join the COMMUNIST PARTY. In 1936 right-wing members separated from the Thomas faction to form the Social Democratic Federation, but in 1958 they rejoined and the party was readmitted to the Socialist International. In 1973 a group led by Michael HARRINGTON split off from the Socialist Party to form the Democratic Socialist Organizing Committee, with the aim of working within the Democratic Party. The Socialist Party candidate for president, David McReynolds, won only 6,720 votes in 1980.

SOCIALIST REALISM, USSR Communist Party artistic doctrine since the early 1930s, and the dominant philosophy and style in most communist countries. The doctrine holds that, in order to serve the people and the revolution, artistic and literary works should be realistic (representational), yet portray, with "positive" heroes, the workers' progress towards socialism.

SOCIALIST WORKERS PARTY, US political party founded in 1938 in support of Leon TROTSKY's call for a Fourth International. This Marxist, anti-Soviet party favors nationalizing most industry and eliminating the military budget. It has had little success in US electoral politics; in 1980 its two presidential candidates, running in different states, received 46,416 votes.

SOCIALIZATION, in psychology and sociology, the process by which individuals are indoctrinated, by parents, teachers and peers, into accepting and following the written and unwritten rules of conduct of a particular society.

SOCIAL PSYCHOLOGY, a branch of psychology concerned with group processes and interactions among individuals. Subjects studied by social psychologists include conformity, altruism, interpersonal attraction and the development of values.

SOCIAL SCIENCES, group of studies concerned with man in relation to his cultural, social and physical environment; one of the three main divisions of human knowledge, the other two being the natural sciences and the HUMANITIES. Although social scientists usually attempt to model their disciplines on the natural sciences, aspiring to achieve a similar level of consensus, their efforts in this direction continue to be frustrated by the crudeness of their conceptual tools in relation to the complexity of their subject matter and the limited scope afforded for controlled experiments. The social sciences are usually considered to include: ANTHROPOLOGY; ARCHAEOLOGY; CRIMINOLOGY; DEMOGRAPHY; ECONOMICS; EDUCATION; POLITICAL SCIENCE; PSYCHOLOGY; and SOCIOLOGY.

SOCIAL SECURITY, government programs for protecting people from hardship due to loss of income through old age, disability, unemployment, injury, sickness, etc. State social-security systems developed in Europe after 1883, when Germany started a compulsory health insurance scheme. In 1911 Britain adopted an unemployment insurance program. In the US, in the GREAT DEPRESSION, the Social Security Act (1935) established a federal program of old-age insurance and a federal-state program of UNEMPLOYMENT INSURANCE. It also provided federal grants for public assistance, public health and child welfare services. The federal plan has become compulsory, except for railway and government workers, who have their own schemes, and special types of workers who are not regularly employed. The plan is financed by equal employer and employee contributions. Old-age and survivor benefits are paid to retired workers and their dependents or to survivors of workers who have died. The amount people receive is related to their average monthly earnings over a number of years. The aging of the US population has recently threatened the solvency of this system. The social-security tax has become a heavy burden for workers as the ratio of retirees to taxpayers has increased in favor of the former. In the early 1980s, the Reagan administration began to consider alternatives for reforming the system: reducing benefits, raising the retirement age or funding the social-security program from general revenues.

Disability benefits are paid to workers and dependents in the event of disability lasting over a year. Health Insurance for the Aged (see MEDICARE) was added in 1965. Those over 65 are automatically helped with payment for hospital and post-hospital care; a supplementary medical-insurance scheme, at an extra voluntary premium, covers 80% of doctors' and some other bills. (See also WELFARE.) A claimant of unemployment insurance is usually eligible for about half his earnings. Public assistance, which in some states predates 1935, differs in being financed through federal grants (largely) and state revenues, rather than individual contributions. It goes to the care of the elderly, disabled, the blind and their dependents. WORKMEN'S COMPENSATION, dating from the early 1900s, and varying widely between states, aids those workers injured at work or with industrial disease. A few states administer sickness insurance plans. Government social-insurance schemes are more comprehensive in most W European and communist countries. In the US private insurance companies play a more prominent role.

SOCIAL SETTLEMENTS, also known as settlement houses, centers of SOCIAL WORK in deprived areas of cities. The first, Toynbee Hall in London, was set up in 1884. In the US, in the late 19th century, many settlements, such as HULL HOUSE, were formed, often to help new immigrants. Their activities today include counselling, adult education, nurseries, sport and recreation.

SOCIAL WORK, the activity of trained social workers which has as its aim the alleviation of social problems. Casework, group work and community organization are employed. Casework involves close cooperation with individuals or families who are under mental, physical or social handicaps. Group work developed from work in early SOCIAL SETTLEMENTS, and involves group education and recreational activities. Community organization involves the identification of community problems and the coordination of local welfare services, both public and private, in solving them. A social worker's training may include psychology, sociology, law, medicine and criminology. She or he might specialize in family service, child welfare or medical, psychiatric or correctional social work. (See also WELFARE.)

SOCIETY ISLANDS, a S Pacific group, in W FRENCH POLYNESIA, including the Windward and Leeward archipelagoes. Named for Britain's Royal Society, the 14 islands have been French since 1843. Most of the population lives on the largest, TAHITI. Copra, sugar and tourism are important.

SOCIETY OF FRIENDS. See QUAKERS.

SOCIETY OF JESUS. See JESUITS.

SOCINIANISM, a 16th-century humanistic religious doctrine developed in Poland by the Italians Laelius Socinus and his nephew

Faustus. A forerunner of and profound influence on modern UNITARIANISM, it rejected the Trinity and the divinity of Jesus.

SOCIOBIOLOGY, a controversial theory that attempts to prove the influence of natural selection on human and animal behavior. The theory postulates that genes can influence behavior as well as physiology, and that behavior may therefore be as subject to the laws of evolution as is the physical development of the species.

SOCIOLINGUISTICS. See LINGUISTICS.

SOCIOLOGY, systematic study that seeks to describe and explain collective human behavior—as manifested in cultures, societies, communities and subgroups—by exploring the institutional relationships that hold between individuals and so sustain this behavior. Sociology shares its subject matter with ANTHROPOLOGY, which traditionally focuses on small, relatively isolated societies, and social PSYCHOLOGY, where the emphasis is on the study of subgroup behavior. The main emphasis in contemporary sociology is on the study of social structures and institutions and on the causes and effects of social change. Some current areas of inquiry are the family, religion, work, politics, urban life and science. Sociologists attempt to model their investigations on those of the physical sciences. Mainly because of the complexity of its subject matter and the political implications of social change, questions as to its proper aims and methods remain far from settled. There can be little doubt, however, that sociological concepts such as "internalization"—the processes by which the values and norms of a particular society are learned by its members (see SOCIALIZATION)—and "institutionalization"—the processes by which norms are incorporated in a culture as binding rules of behavior—do often illuminate important social problems. The two great pioneers of modern sociology were Emile DURKHEIM and Max WEBER. Leading US sociologists include the pioneers William SUMNER and George MEAD, and C. Wright MILLS, Talcott PARSONS and Daniel BELL.

SOCIOMETRY, usually refers to techniques of measurement employed mainly by psychologists and sociologists in attempting to determine the relative strengths of interpersonal preferences and the relative status of individuals within groups. The term is sometimes applied to any attempt to quantify interpersonal relationships.

SOCRATES (c469–399 BC), Greek philosopher and mentor of PLATO. He wrote nothing, but much of his life and thought is vividly recorded in the dialogues of PLATO. The exact extent of Plato's indebtedness to Socrates is uncertain—e.g., it is still disputed whether the doctrine of the Forms is Socratic or Platonic; but Socrates made at least two fundamental contributions to Western philosophy: by shifting the focus of Greek philosophy from COSMOLOGY to ETHICS; and by developing the "Socratic method" of inquiry. He argued that the good life is the life illuminated by reason and strove to clarify the ideas of his interlocutors by leading them to detect the inconsistencies in their beliefs. His passion for self-consistency was evident even in his death: ultimately condemned for "impiety," he decided to accept the lawful sentence— and so remain true to his principles—rather than make good an easy escape.

SODIUM (Na), a soft, reactive, silvery white ALKALI METAL. It is the sixth most common element, occurring naturally in common salt and many other important minerals such as cryolite and Chile saltpeter. It is very electropositive, and is produced by ELECTROLYSIS of fused sodium chloride (Downs process). Sodium rapidly oxidizes in air and reacts vigorously with water to give off hydrogen, so it is usually stored under kerosine. Most sodium compounds are highly ionic and soluble in water, their properties being mainly those of the anion. Sodium forms some organic compounds such as alkyls. It is used in making sodium cyanide, sodium hydride and the ANTIKNOCK ADDITIVE tetraethyl lead. Its high heat capacity and conductivity make molten sodium a useful coolant in some nuclear reactors. AW 23.0, mp 98°C, bp 883°C, sg 0.971 (20°C). **Sodium Bicarbonate** ($NaHCO_3$) is a white crystalline solid, made from sodium carbonate and carbon dioxide. It gives off carbon dioxide when heated to 270°C or when reacted with acids, and is used in BAKING POWDER, fire extinguishers and as an ANTACID. **Sodium Borates** are sodium salts of BORIC ACID, differing in their degree of condensation and hydration; BORAX is the most important. They are white crystalline solids, becoming glassy when heated, and used in the manufacture of detergents, water softeners, fluxes, glass and ceramic glazes. **Sodium Carbonate** (Na_2CO_3), or (Washing) Soda, is a white crystalline solid made by the SOLVAY PROCESS. It is used in making glass, other sodium compounds, soap and paper. The alkaline solution is used in disinfectants and water softeners. mp 851°C. **Sodium Hydroxide** (NaOH), or **Caustic Soda**, is a white deliquescent solid.

usually obtained as pellets. It is a strong ALKALI, and absorbs carbon dioxide from the air. It is made by ELECTROLYSIS of sodium chloride solution or by adding calcium hydroxide to sodium carbonate solution. Caustic soda is used in the production of cellulose, plastics, soap, dyestuffs, paper and in oil refining. mp 318°C, bp 1390°C. **Sodium Nitrate** (NaNO₃), or **Soda Niter**, is a colorless crystalline solid, occurring naturally in Chile saltpeter. Its properties are similar to those of potassium nitrate (see POTASSIUM), but as it is hygroscopic it is unsuitable for gunpowder. mp 307°C. **Sodium Thiosulfate** (Na₂S₂O₃), or **Hypo**, is a colorless crystalline solid. It is a mild reducing agent, used to estimate iodine, and as a photographic fixer, dissolving the silver halides which have remained unaffected by light. (For sodium chloride, see SALT.)

SODIUM PENTOTHAL. See PENTOTHAL SODIUM.

SOFIA, capital and largest city of Bulgaria, its commercial and cultural center, between the Balkan Mts of the N and the Vitosha Mts in the S. Its industry, built up since WWII, includes machinery, textiles and electrical equipment. Pop 1,032,000.

SOFTBALL, type of BASEBALL played with a softer, larger ball (12in in circumference) and a thinner bat. The bases are 60ft apart and the pitcher stands 46ft from home plate. The ball is pitched underhand and a game lasts only seven innings. Softball was developed in Chicago in 1888 by G. W. Hancock as an indoor form of baseball. Many countries, particularly in the Americas, now compete in the annual amateur world championships.

SOIL, the uppermost surface layer of the earth, in which plants grow and on which, directly or indirectly, all life on earth depends. Soil consists, in the upper layers, of organic material mixed with inorganic matter resultant from weathering (see EROSION; HUMUS). Soil depth, where soil exists, may reach to many meters. Between the soil and the bedrock is a layer called the subsoil. Mature (or zonal) soil may be described in terms of four **soil horizons**: A, the uppermost layer, containing organic matter, though most of the soluble chemicals have been leached (washed out); B, strongly leached and with little or no organic matter (A and B together are often called the topsoil); C, the subsoil, a layer of weathered and shattered rock; and D, the bedrock. Three main types of soil are commonly distinguished: **pedalfers**, associated with temperate, humid climates, have a leached A-horizon but contain IRON

and ALUMINUM salts with clay in the B-horizon; **pedocals**, associated with low-rainfall regions, contain CALCIUM carbonate and other salts, and **laterites** or latosols, tropical red or yellow soils, heavily leached and rich in iron and aluminum. Soils may also be classified in terms of texture (see CLAY; SILT; SAND). LOAMS, with roughly equal proportions of sand, silt and clay, together with humus, are among the richest agricultural soils. (See also PERMAFROST; PODZOL.)

SOIL EROSION, the wearing away of soil, a primary cause of concern in agriculture. There are two types: **Geological erosion** denotes those naturally occurring EROSION processes that constantly affect the earth's surface features; it is usually a fairly slow process and naturally compensated for. **Accelerated erosion** describes erosion hastened by the intervention of man. **Sheet erosion** occurs usually on plowed fields. A fine sheet of rich topsoil (see SOIL) is removed by the action of RAIN water. Repetition over the years may render the soil unfit for cultivation. In **rill erosion**, heavy rains may run off the land in streamlets: sufficient water moving swiftly enough cuts shallow trenches that may be plowed over and forgotten until, after years, the soil is found poor. In **gully erosion**, deep trenches are cut by repeated or heavy flow of water. WIND erosion is of importance in exposed, arid areas. (See also CONSERVATION; LAND RECLAMATION.)

SOLAR CELL, device for converting the ENERGY of the sun's radiation into electrical energy. The commonest form is a large array of SEMICONDUCTOR p-n junction devices in series and parallel. By the PHOTOELECTRIC EFFECT each junction produces a small voltage when illuminated. Solar cells are chiefly used to power artificial SATELLITES. Their low efficiency (about 12%) has so far made them uncompetitive on earth except for mobile or isolated devices.

SOLAR ENERGY, the ENERGY given off by the SUN as ELECTROMAGNETIC RADIATION. In one year the sun emits about 5.4×10^{33}J of energy, of which half of one-billionth $(2.7 \times 10^{24}$J) reaches the earth. Of this, most is reflected away, only 35% being absorbed. The power reaching the ground is at most 1.2kW/m^2, and on average 0.8kW/m^2. Solar energy is naturally converted into WIND power and into the energy of the HYDROLOGIC CYCLE, increasingly exploited as HYDROELECTRIC POWER. Plants convert solar energy to chemical energy by PHOTOSYNTHESIS, normally at only 0.1% efficiency; the cultivation of ALGAE in ponds can be up to 0.6% efficient, and is being developed to provide food and fuel. Solar heat energy may be used directly in several ways. Solar evaporation is used to convert brine to SALT and distilled water. Flat-plate collectors—matt-black absorbing plates with attached tubes through which a fluid flows to collect the heat—are beginning to be used for domestic water heating, space heating, and to run air-conditioning systems. Focusing collectors, using a parabolic mirror, are used in solar furnaces, which can give high power absorption at high temperatures. They are used for cooking, for high-temperature research, to power heat engines for generating electricity, and to produce electricity more directly by the SEEBECK effect. Solar energy may be directly converted to electrical energy by SOLAR CELLS.

SOLAR SYSTEM, the sun and all the celestial objects that move in ORBITS around it, including the nine known planets (MERCURY; VENUS; EARTH; MARS; JUPITER; SATURN; URANUS; NEPTUNE; PLUTO), their 32 known moons, the ASTEROIDS, COMETS, meteoroids (see METEOR) and a large quantity of gas and dust. The planets all move in their orbits in the same direction, and, with the exceptions of Venus and Uranus, also rotate on their axes in this direction: this is known as direct motion. Most of the moons of the planets have direct orbits, with the exception of four of Jupiter's minor moons, the outermost moon of Saturn and the inner moon of Neptune, whose orbits are retrograde (see RETROGRADE MOTION). Most of the planets move in elliptical, near circular orbits, and roughly in the same plane. The origins of the solar system are not known, though various theories have been proposed (see NEBULAR HYPOTHESIS; PLANETESIMAL HYPOTHESIS). It would not appear to be unique among the stars (see PLANET).

SOLAR WIND, the electrically charged material thrown out by the sun at an average speed of 400km/s. The "quiet" component is a continuous stream to which is added an "active" component produced by bursts of activity on the sun's surface. The solar wind affects the magnetic fields of the earth and Jupiter, and causes the tails of COMETS.

SOLDERING, joining metal objects using a low-melting-point ALLOY, **solder,** as the ADHESIVE. Soft solder, commonly used in electronics to join wires and other components, is an alloy of mainly lead and tin. The parts to be joined are cleaned, and heated by applying a hot soldering iron (usually having a copper bit). A FLUX is used to dissolve oxides, protect the surfaces, and enable the solder to flow freely. The solder melts when applied, solidifying again to form a strong joint when the iron is withdrawn. Solder is often supplied as wire with a core of noncorrosive rosin flux. Soldering at higher temperatures is termed BRAZING.

SOLÉR, Antonio (1729–1783), Spanish composer noted for his instrumental church music. Organist at the ESCORIAL monastery from 1752, he was taught by Domenico SCARLATTI.

SOLERI, Paolo (1919–   ), Italian-born US architect. A visionary planner, he published in *Sketchbooks* (1971) his designs for Mesa City, a solar-powered desert metropolis. He began work on Arcosanti, a scaled-down version, in 1970. His buildings include Domed Desert House (1951) near Cave Creek, Ariz., and the Solimene Ceramics factory in Vietri sul Mare, Italy.

SOLID, one of the three physical states of matter, characterized by the property of cohesion: solids retain their shape unless deformed by external forces. True solids have a definite melting point and are crystalline, their molecules being held together in a regular pattern by stronger intermolecular forces than exist in liquids or gases. Amorphous solids are not crystalline, melt over a wide temperature range and are effectively supercooled liquids.

SOLIDARITY, independent Polish labor union spontaneously formed by workers in 1980 and eventually recognized by the Communist government following nation-wide strikes which began in the shipyards of Gdansk to protest a rise in meat prices. The strike's leader and popular hero, Lech WALESA, was elected head of the 10 million-strong Solidarity Union which together with Rural Solidarity (a union of 2.5 million farmers) rivals the power of the official government. The democratizing process set in motion by Solidarity inaugurated an ongoing period of tension with the USSR.

SOLID STATE PHYSICS, branch of physics concerned with the nature and properties of solid materials, many of which arise from the association and regular arrangement of atoms or molecules in crystalline solids. The term is applied particularly to studies of SEMICONDUCTORS and solid-state electronic devices.

SOLOMON, second son of DAVID and BATHSHEBA who ruled ancient Israel about 970–933 BC at the height of its prosperity and gained a reputation for great wisdom.

His success in establishing lucrative foreign trade and his introduction at home of taxation and forced labor enabled him to finance a massive building program which included a temple and royal palaces on an unprecedented scale of opulence. His story is told in 1 Kings 1–11 and 2 Chronicles 1–9 of the OLD TESTAMENT. Biblical writings later attributed to him include PROVERBS, ECCLESIASTES and the SONG OF SOLOMON.

Official name: Solomon Islands
Capital: Honiara
Area: 11,500sq mi
Population: 217,000
Languages: English (official), pidgin lingua franca
Religions: Christian
Monetary unit(s): 1 Solomon Island dollar = 100 cents

SOLOMON ISLANDS, an independent country, extending across an area of over 232,000sq mi in the SW Pacific.

Land. The mountainous Solomon Island archipelago, composed of 21 large islands and many smaller islets, is of volcanic origin; four volcanoes are intermittently active. The highest peak, Mt Makarakombou (8,028ft), is on Guadalcanal, the largest island where Honiara, the capital, is located. The Solomons are well watered and covered with dense tropical rain forests, with grasslands on the N plains of Guadalcanal. The climate is equatorial, and temperatures vary little during the year; yearly rainfall, averaging 120in, is concentrated from Nov. to Apr.

People and Economy. The population is almost 95% Melanesian with Polynesian, Micronesian, European and Chinese minorities. Most follow the traditional life-style, living in small villages, fishing and growing coconuts, taro, yams and cassava. Exports, formerly exclusively copra, now also include fish and timber. Tourism is increasingly important.

History. The Solomons were largely ignored by Europeans until the 19th century, when islanders were forcibly recruited to labor overseas. By 1900 Britain had assumed control. Invaded by the Japanese in 1942, the islands were only recaptured by US forces after heavy fighting in 1943. Since independence in 1978 the Solomons have been plagued by regional disputes.

SOLON (c639–559 BC), Athenian lawgiver and poet, one of the SEVEN SAGES. Elected *archon* (government leader) of Athens in 594 BC, he repealed the repressive laws of DRACO and freed those enslaved for debt. Dividing citizens into four income classes, he reformed the Greek oligarchy by allowing members of all four classes to sit in the assembly and the law courts. Later he resisted the tyrant PISISTRATUS.

SOLSTICES, the two times each year when the sun is on the points of the ECLIPTIC farthest from the equator (see CELESTIAL SPHERE). At the summer solstice in late June the sun is directly overhead at noon on the TROPIC of Cancer; at winter solstice, in late December, it is overhead at noon on the Tropic of Capricorn.

SOLTI, Sir Georg (1912–), Hungarian-born British conductor. He is best known for his great recordings of Wagner and Richard Strauss and was musical director of Covent Garden (1961–71), beginning in the 1970s of the Paris Opera and most recently of the Chicago Symphony.

SOLUTION, a homogeneous molecular mixture of two or more substances, commonly of a solid and a liquid, though solid/solid solutions also exist. The liquid component is usually termed the SOLVENT, the other component, which is dissolved in it, the *solute*. The **solubility** of a solute in a given solvent at a particular temperature is usually stated as the mass which will dissolve in 100g of the solvent to give a saturated solution (see SATURATION). Solubility generally increases with temperature. For slightly soluble ionic compounds, the **solubility product**—the product of the individual ionic solubilities—is a constant at a given temperature. Most substances are solvated when dissolved: that is, their molecules become surrounded by solvent molecules acting as LIGANDS. Ionic crystals dissolve to give individual solvated ions, and some good solvents of high dielectric constant (such as water) cause certain covalent compounds to ionize, wholly or partly (see also ACID). Analogous to an ideal gas, the hypothetical **ideal solution** is one which is formed from its components without change in total volume or internal energy: it obeys RAOULT'S law and its corollaries, so that the addition of solute produces a lowering of the freezing point, elevation of the boiling point and increase is in osmotic pressure (see OSMOSIS), all proportional to the number of MOLES added. (See also DISSOCIATION; ELECTROLYSIS; EQUIVALENT WEIGHT.)

SOLZHENITSYN, Alexander Isayevich (1918–   ), Russian novelist. His own experience of Stalin's labor camps was described in *One Day in the Life of Ivan Denisovich* (1962), acclaimed in the USSR and abroad. But *The First Circle* and *Cancer Ward* (both 1968) were officially condemned. He accepted the 1970 Nobel Prize for literature by letter. His expulsion in 1974 and his warnings on the moral and political fate of the West drew worldwide publicity. Solzhenitsyn's works include *August 1914* (1971) and *The Gulag Archipelago* (1974).

SOMALI-ETHIOPIAN WAR, border conflict in western Africa. The British gave the largely Somali-populated region of the Ogaden to Ethiopia in 1948 and ever since it has been disputed between Somalia and Ethiopia. In 1974 local Somalis with the support of the Somalian government began to push the Ethiopians out of the region. By 1978 they were in almost total control. However, the Marxist government of Ethiopia with the support of Soviet arms and Cuban troops recaptured most of the province in 1978–79. This border war resulted largely in huge numbers of fleeing refugees living in camps in Somalia.

Official name: Somali Democratic Republic
Capital: Mogadishu
Area: 246,149sq mi
Population: 3,649,000
Languages: Somali; Arabic, English, Italian spoken
Religions: Muslim
Monetary unit(s): 1 Somali shilling = 100 centesimi

SOMALI REPUBLIC, or Somalia, occupying the E "horn" of Africa, comprises two former colonies, British Somaliland and Italian Somaliland, which gained independence and united on July 1, 1960.
Land. Although its E coast lies along the Indian Ocean, Somalia is mainly desert. A narrow, barren N coastal plain, hemmed in by high mountains, gives way to high plateaus, dry savanna plains and to the country's most fertile area, between the Shibeli and Juba rivers in the S. The climate is hot; yearly rainfall varies from about 3in in the N to 20in in the S. Wildlife includes big game and many species of antelope.
People. The population consists mainly of Somalis belonging to northern nomadic or southern farming clans. Somali, the national language, lacks a written form. Arabic (widely spoken), Italian and English are the written languages. The literacy rate is about 15%. Most Somalis move from place to place with their herds and portable woodframe huts; others live in small villages or trade centers built around a well.
Economy. Somalia ranks as one of the world's poorest countries, its development hampered by various factors, among them a lack of natural resources, undeveloped infrastructure, periodic drought and shortages of skilled labor and expertise. Agriculture accounts for the major share of revenues and employment.
History. Europeans colonized Somalia in the late 1800s. Independent Somalia continued its heavy dependence on US and Italian aid. In 1969 President Shermarke was assassinated and a revolutionary council headed by Maj. Gen. Mohammed Siyad took control. The Somali Democratic Republic was declared a socialist state. An armed conflict with Ethiopia erupted in 1963–64 and again in 1977–78 over the disputed territory of the OGADEN. Despite a tacit truce clashes recurred, and hundreds of thousands of refugees streamed into Somalia. Despite assistance by international agencies, Somalia's already meager resources were further strained.
SOMATOTYPES, in ANTHROPOMETRY, descriptions of physique, sometimes supposedly also descriptive of temperament. The individual is classified by three digits representing the extent of his endomorphy (plumpness), mesomorphy (muscularity) and ectomorphy (slenderness), respectively.
SOMME RIVER, in N France, rises near Saint-Quentin and flows W and NW some 150mi through Amiens to its English Channel estuary at Saint-Valéry. Scene of the greatest WWI battle of attrition (July–Nov. 1916), it saw over a million casualties of all nations. On July 1 alone there were 57,000 British casualties (19,000 killed).
SOMNAMBULISM, or sleepwalking, state in which the body is able to walk and perform other automatic tasks while consciousness is diminished. Often seen in

anxious children, it is said to be unwise to awaken them as intense fear may be felt.

SOMOZA, the name of a Nicaraguan family, three members of which controlled Nicaragua from 1936 to 1979. In 1936 **Anastasio Somoza Garcia** (1896–1956) deposed his uncle, President Sacasa, becoming president himself in 1937. Assassinated after 20 years of nepotistic dictatorship, he was succeeded by his son **Luis Somoza Debayle** (1922–1967), who held formal office until 1963. In 1967 Anastasio's second son **Anastasio Somoza Debayle** (1925–1980) was elected president. Replaced by a puppet triumvirate in 1972, he retained control of the army and was reelected president in 1974. His corrupt rule led to a revolt in 1977 by leftist Sandinist guerrillas, who gradually gained broad support and forced him to flee the country for exile in Paraguay in 1979. A year later Somoza was assassinated in Asuncíon.

SONAR, *sound navigation and ranging,* technique used at sea for detecting and determining the position of underwater objects (e.g. submarines; shoals of fish) and for finding the depth of water under a ship's keel (see ECHO SOUNDER). Sonar works on the principle of echolocation: high-frequency SOUND pulses are beamed from the ship and the direction of and time taken for any returning ECHOES are measured to give the direction and range of the reflecting objects.

SONATA, in music, term used in the 17th and early 18th centuries to describe works for various small groups of instruments, as opposed to the CANTATA. Since the late 18th century, it has been restricted to works for piano or other solo instrument (the latter usually with keyboard accompaniment), generally in three movements.

SONG, a musical setting of words, usually a short poem, often with instrumental accompaniment. There are two basic kinds: songs in which each verse repeats the same tune, and songs with a continuous thematic development. The origins of the song are lost in the history of FOLK MUSIC and POETRY (poetry was originally sung); it became a mature art in Western cultures in OPERA arias, the German *lied*—those of SCHUBERT are supreme examples—and the French *chanson.* The song-forms that have most influenced 20th-century popular music are probably the BALLAD and the BLUES. (See also HYMN.)

SONG OF ROLAND. See CHANSON DE ROLAND.

SONG OF SOLOMON, or **Song of Songs,** or **Canticles,** OLD TESTAMENT book tradition- ally ascribed to Solomon. A series of exquisite love poems, it has been interpreted by both Jews and Christians as an allegorical description of God's love for his people.

SONIC BOOM, loud noise generated in the form of a shockwave cone when an airplane traveling faster than the speed of sound overtakes the pressure waves it produces. Because of sonic boom damage, supersonic planes are confined to closely defined flight paths.

SONNET, a LYRIC poem of fourteen lines with traditional rules of structure and rhyme scheme. Devised in 13th-century Italy and perfected by PETRARCH, it entered English literature in the 16th century, and was adopted by such poets as SHAKESPEARE, MILTON, KEATS and WORDSWORTH as a vehicle for concentrated thought and feeling, very often of love.

SON OF SAM, pseudonym of David Richard Berkowitz, also called the .44 caliber killer, who terrorized New York City in 1976–77 with nighttime attacks on young women and their companions, killing six people and wounding seven. The seemingly random attacks, mostly in quiet, residential neighborhoods, caused police to set up a 300-man task force to pursue every clue. Traced to his home by a parking ticket on his car, the 24-year-old Berkowitz was arrested Aug. 10, 1977; he was sentenced to maximum prison terms for each of the murders on June 13, 1978.

SONTAG, Susan (1933–), US novelist, short-story writer, filmmaker and essayist. Her best-known books include *Against Interpretation* (1966), *On Photography* (1977), *Illness as Metaphor* (1978) and *Under the Sign of Saturn* (1980).

SOONERS, name given to the many Okla. homesteaders who entered the INDIAN TERRITORY in advance of the date of the first official "run"—April 22, 1889. Okla. is familiarly known to this day as the Sooner State.

SOPHISTS, "wise men," name given to certain teachers in Greece in the 5th and 4th centuries BC, the most famous of whom were GORGIAS and PROTAGORAS. They taught RHETORIC and the qualities needed for success in political life. PLATO attacked them for taking fees, teaching skepticism about law, morality and knowledge, and concentrating on how to win arguments regardless of truth—attacks still reflected in the modern word "sophistry."

SOPHOCLES (c495–406 BC), great Athenian dramatist, together with AESCHYLUS and EURIPIDES one of the founders of Greek tragedy. Only seven plays survive, the best-known being *Oedipus Rex, Oedipus at Colonus, Antigone* and *Electra*. They dwell on the tragic ironies of human existence, particularly on the role of fate. Heroic figures, tricked by fate into acts necessitating moral retribution, suffer in the event more harshly than they seem to deserve. The plays are highly dramatic (Sophocles regularly won first prize in the dramatic competitions), and contain much noble poetry.

SORBONNE, a college founded in Paris in 1253 by Robert de Sorbon. It was a famous medieval theological center, rebuilt in the 17th century by RICHELIEU and re-established in 1808 after being closed in the French Revolution. Its name is often used to refer to the University of Paris, into which it was incorporated in the 19th century.

SOREL, Georges (1847–1922), French sociologist, philosopher of revolutionary SYNDICALISM and author of *Reflections on Violence* (1908). Despising democracy and the bourgeoisie, he believed in the moral regeneration of society through violence. He influenced both FASCISM and the far left.

SORGE, Richard (1895–1944), German-born Soviet spy; as a German newspaper correspondent in Japan during WWII, he was able to warn Soviet officials of Germany's plan to invade Russia and of Japan's decision not to mount a similar attack. Arrested by the Japanese, he was executed for espionage.

SORGHUM, widely cultivated CEREAL CROP (*Sorghum vulgare*), the most important grown in Africa. It grows best in warm conditions and is most important as a drought-resistant crop. For human food, the grain is first ground into a meal and then made up into porridge, bread or cakes. The grain is also used as a cattle feed and the whole plants as forage. There are many types in cultivation including *durra* and KAFFIR. Family: Graminae.

SOROKIN, Pitirim Alexandrovich (1889–1968), Russian-US sociologist. He distinguished between "sensate" (empirical, scientific) and "ideational" (mystical, authoritarian) societies, and wrote *Social and Cultural Dynamics* (1937–41).

SOUL MUSIC, a flamboyant, highly emotional vocal and instrumental music created by blacks out of the rhythms and style of GOSPEL MUSIC. Soul first became known to the US public at large in the late 1950s through such big-name singers as James BROWN and Ray CHARLES, and reached the height of popularity in the 1960s with the recordings of Aretha FRANKLIN and Otis Redding.

SOUND, mechanical disturbance, such as a change of pressure, particle displacement or stress, propagated in an elastic medium (e.g. air or water), that can be detected by an instrument or by an observer who hears the auditory sensation it produces. Sound is a measurable physical phenomenon and an important stimulus to man. It forms a major means of communication in the form of spoken language, and both natural and manmade sounds (of traffic or machinery) contribute largely to our environment. The EAR is very sensitive and will tolerate a large range of sound energies, but enigmas remain as to exactly how it produces the sensation of hearing. The Greeks appreciated that sound was connected with air motion and that the PITCH of a musical sound produced by a vibrating source depended on the vibration FREQUENCY. Attempts to measure the velocity of sound in air date from the 17th century. Sound is carried as a longitudinal compressional wave in an elastic medium: part of the medium next to a sound source is compressed, but its elasticity makes it expand again, compressing the region next to it and so on. The velocity of such waves depends on the medium and the temperature, but is always much less than that of light. Sound waves are characterized by their wavelength and frequency. Humans cannot hear sounds of frequencies below 16Hz and above 20kHz, such sounds being known as infrasonic and ULTRASONIC respectively. The sound produced by a TUNING FORK has a definite frequency, but most sounds are a combination of frequencies. The amount of motion in a sound wave determines its loudness or softness and the intensity falls off with the square of distance from the source. Sound waves may be reflected from surfaces (as in an ECHO), refracted or diffracted, the last property enabling us to hear around corners. The intensity of a sound is commonly expressed in DECIBELS above an arbitrary reference level; its loudness is measured in PHONS.

SOUND RECORDING, the conversion of SOUND waves into a form in which they can be stored, the original sound being reproducible by use of playback equipment. The first sound recording was made by Thomas EDISON in 1877 (see PHONOGRAPH). In modern electronic recording of all kinds, the sound is first converted by one or more MICROPHONES into electrical signals. In the case of **mechanical recordings** (discs, or records), these signals—temporarily recorded on magnetic tape—are made to vibrate a stylus that cuts a spiral groove in a rotating disc covered with lacquer. The master disc is copied by ELECTROFORMING to produce stamper dies used to press the plastic copies. (See also HIGH-FIDELITY.) In **magnetic recording**, the microphone signals activate an ELECTROMAGNET which imposes a pattern of magnetization on moving magnetic wire, discs or tape with a ferromagnetic coating (see also MAGNETISM; TAPE RECORDER). **Optical recording**, used for many motion-picture sound tracks, converts the microphone signals into a photographic exposure on film using a light beam and a variable shutter. The sound is played back by shining a light beam through the track onto a PHOTOELECTRIC CELL. As with the playback equipment for the other recording methods, this reproduces electrical signals which are amplified and fed to a LOUDSPEAKER.

SOUSA, John Philip (1854–1932), US band master and composer. He wrote many light operas, but is best remembered today for his military marches, including "The Stars and Stripes Forever" and "The Washington Post." Sousa was leader of the Marine Band in Washington before forming a world-touring band of his own.

SOUSAPHONE, a coiled TUBA, or helicon, named for the US bandleader John Philip Sousa, who had suggested the idea for such an instrument. It is equipped with a flexible end, or "bell," that can be moved about to send sound in any direction.

Official name: Republic of South Africa
Capital: Pretoria
Area: 472,359sq mi
Population: 28,410,000
Languages: Afrikaans, English
Religions: Christian, Bantu
Monetary unit(s): 1 Rand = 100 cents
SOUTH AFRICA, independent republic occupying the southern tip of Africa. It is bounded N by Namibia (South West Africa), which it rules, Botswana, Rhodesia, Mozambique and Swaziland, and it surrounds the republic of LESOTHO. It comprises four provinces: the Cape, Natal, Transvaal and the Orange Free State.
Land. A vast system of grassland plateaus is separated from narrow coastal plains by the

ranges of the Great Escarpment, which reaches 11,000ft in the Drakensberg Mts in the E. The westward-flowing Orange R drains most of the interior plateau. The climate is mainly warm temperate. Much of the land in the W is arid or semiarid. Rainfall is greatest in the S and E.
People. The population is about 70% black African (mainly ZULU and XHOSA), 17.5% white, 9.5% of mixed descent and 3% Asiatic. About two-thirds of the whites are Afrikaners. Government is entirely white-controlled, which has been assured by the exclusion of blacks from the general franchise. About half the people are urban, the largest cities being Johannesburg, Durban, Cape Town, Pretoria and Port Elizabeth. The black Africans speak a variety of BANTU languages; many speak AFRIKAANS or English as well. Most of the population is Christian, belonging to a wide variety of churches.
Economy. South Africa produces most of the world's gem diamonds and gold, has large coal reserves and is also rich in uranium, iron ore, asbestos, copper, manganese, nickel, chrome, titanium and phosphates. Mining contributes the major share of export earnings, but accounts for only 12–13% of the gross domestic product. The largest contributor is manufacturing, which includes food processing, iron, steel and oil-from-coal production, engineering and textiles. Industry and mining are concentrated in the S and E. South Africa is self-sufficient in food production and is a major exporter of food to neighboring countries. The leading crops are corn, sugarcane and a variety of fruits. Wool is a major export. Dairying also flourishes.
History. South Africa was already inhabited by BUSHMEN, HOTTENTOTS, and Bantu peoples from the N when white settlement began in 1652, with the Dutch establishing a colony at Cape Town. The main period of British rule (1806–1910) saw the GREAT TREK (1835–43), the founding of BOER (Dutch farmer) republics inland, and the BOER WAR (1899–1902). In 1910 the Union of South Africa was formed out of the various colonies (now the four provinces), and during WWI South West Africa was wrested from the Germans. Since 1948 South Africa has been ruled by the Afrikaner-led National Party, which has set up an efficient and repressive state apparatus to implement the policies of APARTHEID. In recent years several tribal and racial "homelands" have been designated (see BANTUSTANS). Three—the Transkei, Bophuthatswana and Venda—have already been granted "independence"

but are not recognized by any country other than South Africa. The Ciskei was scheduled for independence in late 1981. Other homelands are: Gazankulu, KwaZulu, Lebowa, Qwaqwa, Ndebele and KaNgwane. The homelands encompass only 13% of South Africa's land area. In 1961 the country became a republic and left the Commonwealth largely because of differences over its apartheid policies.

SOUTH AMERICA, the southern half of the two Western Hemisphere continents, linked with the northern by the narrow land bridge of CENTRAL AMERICA. It comprises twelve independent republics: Argentina, Bolivia, Brazil, Chile, Colombia, Ecuador, Guyana, Paraguay, Peru, Suriname, Uruguay and Venezuela, and one European possession, French Guiana.

Land and resources. Roughly triangular in shape, South America is surrounded by the Caribbean Sea on the N, the Atlantic Ocean on the E and the Pacific Ocean on the W. It has a coastline of about 15,000mi. The most prominent feature is the Andean mountain system, with more than 50 peaks exceeding 20,000ft. Mt Aconcagua (22,834ft) in Argentina is the highest mountain in the Western Hemisphere. Other features include three major river basins: the Amazon (the world's most voluminous river), Paraná, and Orinoco; the Brazilian and Guiana highlands in the E and NE; and the pampas grassland and Patagonian plateau of Argentina. The world's largest tropical rain forest is in the Amazon river basin. The climate varies from extreme cold in the high Andes to tropical humid heat in the lowlands near the equator. Native plants include beans, pumpkins, squashes, tomatoes, peanuts, pineapples, red peppers, tapioca, rubber, tobacco, and cocoa. Produce of the tropical forests, which cover about half the area, includes hardwoods, brazil and cashew nuts, quinine and quebracho bark. Sugarcane, coffee and oil palms are important imported crops. Among the native animal species are hummingbids, parrots, and the condor; jaguar, llama and alpaca; anteaters, sloths, tapirs and armadillos; and piranhas, anacondas and boa constrictors. South America is rich in mineral resources, many far from fully developed. The most abundant resources are oil in the N (mainly in Venezuela) and iron ore (in Brazil, Venezuela, and Colombia); other minerals include copper, tin, lead, zinc, manganese, gold, nitrate and bauxite. There is very little coal but considerable hydroelectric potential.

People. There are four main groups: the native Indians; white Europeans, mainly of Spanish or Portuguese descent; Negros, who originally came as slaves; and people of mixed Indian, Negro, and European ancestry (mestizo usually means of Indian-European and mulatto of Negro-European origin). The total population is almost 250 million. The chief official languages are Spanish and Portuguese (the latter is spoken in Brazil). In Guyana, Suriname and French Guiana, the official languages are English, Dutch and English, and French, respectively. The most widely spoken Indian languages are Guaraní (in Paraguay), Quechua (in Peru, Bolivia and Ecuador) and Aymará (in Bolivia). Two countries, Argentina and Uruguay, have a predominantly European population; three countries, Peru, Bolivia, and Ecuador, have large Indian populations; and the rest are inhabited by people of mixed descent. About 90% of South Americans are nominally Catholic.

Name of state: South Carolina
Capital: Columbia
Statehood: May 23, 1788 (8th state)
Familiar name: Palmetto State
Area: 31,055sq mi
Population: 3,119,208
Elevation: Highest—3,560ft., Sassafras Mountain; Lowest—sea level, Atlantic Ocean
Motto: Animis opibusque parati (Prepared in mind and resources); Dum spiro spero (While I breathe, I hope)
State flower: Yellow jessamine
State bird: Carolina wren
State tree: Palmetto
State song: "Carolina"

SOUTH CAROLINA, state of the SE US bordered to the N by N.C., S and E by the Atlantic Ocean, and S and SW by Georgia. It is one of the original 13 colonies.

Land. The three main regions are the Atlantic coastal plain, occupying the SE two-thirds of the state, the Piedmont plateau in the NW, and the Blue Ridge Mts in the extreme NW. Rivers include the Pee Dee, Santee, Edisto and Savannah. Summers are hot (average daily temperature over 70°F) and winters mild. Rainfall averages 47in per year.

People. The population is about 55% rural, and mainly Protestant. Columbia, Charleston and Greenville are the major cities. Blacks make up about 31% of the population.

Economy. Once overwhelmingly agricultural, the economy is now based principally on manufacturing. Textiles and clothing, employing 40% of the manufacturing workforce, are most important, followed by chemicals, and the manufacture of machinery. Agricultural produce includes tobacco, soybeans, cotton and peaches. Livestock farming is increasing, and the state's forests, covering two-thirds of its area, support growing lumber and paper industries.

History. South Carolina was first settled as a PROPRIETARY COLONY in 1670, but dissatisfaction with the proprietors led the colonists to revolt in 1719, and the province became a royal colony in 1729. During the REVOLUTIONARY WAR, victories at KING'S MOUNTAIN and COWPENS offset the fall of Charleston to the British in 1780. In 1786 the capital was moved to Columbia to help unify the two sections of the state, the rich planters of the lowlands and the poorer farmers of the Piedmont. In the NULLIFICATION and STATES' RIGHTS controversies preceding the CIVIL WAR, slave-owning South Carolina took the radical lead, and became the first state to secede from the Union. The first shots of the Civil War were fired at FORT SUMTER, and South Carolina experienced bitter fighting and an equally bitter Reconstruction period, followed by continuing agricultural depression and chronic political corruption. The black majority was effectively disenfranchised, and even in the 1960s, there was resistance to INTEGRATION. Since WWII an industrial and agricultural revival has brought new prosperity; and South Carolina has been growing rapidly, its population rising 20.4% during the 1970s, with unemployment also high at 8.4% in 1980. South Carolina has the unenviable reputation of being a place where large amounts of nuclear wastes have been stored, often with insufficient care—a problem that was finally addressed in 1980 by major legislation covering the disposal of toxic and nuclear wastes.

SOUTH CHINA SEA, part of the Pacific Ocean, bounded by mainland Asia and Malaysia to the N and W, Borneo to the S, and the Philippines to the E. It is tropical, and subject to frequent typhoons.

SOUTH DAKOTA, state of the north-central US, bounded on the N by N.D., E by Ia. and Minn., S by Neb., and W by Mont. and Wyo.

Land. South Dakota can be divided into the rugged Great Plains in the W and center, the more fertile Central Lowlands to the E, and the semi-arid BADLANDS and Black Hills to the SW. The state is bisected by the Missouri R. Climate is continental, with low humidity and great seasonal temperature changes. Rainfall ranges from about 13in per year in the NW to 25in in the SE.

People. South Dakota has the lowest population density of all the states E of the Rockies. It is also one of the least urbanized, with only about 45% of the population living in urban areas. Sioux Falls and Rapid City are the biggest cities. There are large Indian reservations bordering Lake Oahe (on the Missouri R.). The largest religious denomination is the Lutheran Church.

Economy. Agriculture, particularly livestock and livestock produce, provides 80% of the total value of all goods produced in the state. Leading crops include wheat, corn and oats. Manufacturing is dominated by food processing. Gold is mined in the Black Hills where the Homestake Mine at Lead is the largest in the western hemisphere. The Black Hills, Badlands National Park, and other areas are popular with tourists.

History. Home of the ARIKARA, CHEYENNE and SIOUX Indians, South Dakota became part of the US with the LOUISIANA PURCHASE (1803) and was explored by LEWIS AND CLARK (1804–06). Settlement was first

Name of State: South Dakota
Capital: Pierre
Statehood: Nov. 2, 1889 (40th state)
Familiar name: Sunshine State, Coyote State
Area: 77,047sq mi
Population: 690,178
Elevation: Highest—7,242ft., Harney Peak; Lowest—962ft., Big Stone Lake
Motto: Under God the People Rule
State flower: American pasqueflower
State bird: Ring-necked pheasant
State tree: Black Hills spruce
State song: "Hail, South Dakota"

stimulated by the fur trade, but by the 1850s farmers had begun to move in. In 1861 South Dakota was included in the Dakota territory with its capital at Yankton. Increasing conflict with Indian tribes was settled by the Laramie Treaty (1868) which created the Great Sioux Reservation. General CUSTER violated the treaty in a search for gold in the Black Hills (1874), and soon the area was flooded with miners and prospectors; Indian resistance came to an end at WOUNDED KNEE (1890). New railroads brought more farmers, and the population tripled between 1880 and 1890.

The boundary with North Dakota was drawn and both states entered the Union in 1889, but the boom was already almost over and the state suffered from successive droughts and depressions from which it did not recover until after WWII. Since then hydroelectric projects, control of the Missouri R, farm mechanization, industrial expansion and expanded tourism have marked a new prosperity. Population has been increasing slowly, rising 3.6% during the 1970s, and unemployment has been relatively low, at 4.6% in 1980.

SOUTHEAST ASIA TREATY ORGANIZATION (SEATO), a defense treaty signed by Australia, France, Great Britain, New Zealand, Pakistan, the Philippines, Thailand and the US after the French had withdrawn from Indochina in 1954. Its aim was to prevent communist expansion. There was a headquarters at Bangkok, Thailand, but no standing forces. The treaty was invoked by the US in the VIETNAM WAR. Pakistan withdrew in 1972. SEATO terminated itself in 1977.

SOUTHERN CHRISTIAN LEADERSHIP CONFERENCE (SCLC), a nonviolent CIVIL RIGHTS organization founded by Martin Luther KING, Jr, and others in 1957. It played a major part in the 1963 civil rights march on Washington and other antidiscrimination campaigns. After the assassination of King in 1968, leadership was taken by the Rev. Ralph ABERNATHY.

SOUTHERN CROSS, Crux, a small, bright constellation near the S celestial pole. The four bright stars forming the cross are Acrux (Alpha), Mimosa (Beta), Gacrux (Gamma) and Delta Crucis.

SOUTHERN RHODESIA. See ZIMBABWE.

SOUTHEY, Robert (1774–1843), English Poet Laureate from 1813, a friend of WORDSWORTH and COLERIDGE. His large output includes long narrative poems, journalism, histories, biographies and verse collections. Famous in his day as a poet, he is now more admired as a prose writer,

notably for his *Life of Nelson* (1813).

SOUTH POLE, the point in Antarctica through which passes the earth's axis of rotation. It does not coincide with the earth's S Magnetic Pole (see EARTH). It was first reached by Roald Amundsen (Dec. 14, 1911). (See also CELESTIAL SPHERE; MAGNETISM; NORTH POLE.)

SOUTH SEA BUBBLE, popular name for speculation in the South Sea Company, created in England in 1711 to trade with Spanish America. In 1720 the company's proposal to take over the NATIONAL DEBT, aided by fraudulent promotions, pushed shares to fantastic prices. In the subsequent collapse many were ruined.

SOUTHWEST AFRICA. See NAMIBIA.

SOUTINE, Chaim (1894–1943), Russian-born French expressionist painter. His style uses vivid primary colors and twisting, rhythmic forms, as in *Pastry Cook* (1922).

SOVEREIGNTY, supreme political power in a state. In political theory debates on sovereignty center on the role of the sovereign and on the nature of supreme power—by what rights, and by whom, it should be wielded. A *sovereign state* is one that is independent of control by other states (but see INTERNATIONAL LAW; UNITED NATIONS).

SOVIET, the basic political unit of socialist Russia (from *sovet*, a council). The soviets, ranging in importance from rural councils to the Supreme Soviet, the major legislative body of the Soviet Union, are elected policy-making and administrative units. The first soviets were the strike committees set up during the 1905 revolution.

SOVIET UNION. See UNION OF SOVIET SOCIALIST REPUBLICS.

SOYBEAN, *Glycine max* or *G. soja,* a LEGUMINOUS PLANT native to E Asia providing food, animal feed and industrial raw material. It has been grown as a staple food in China for over 5,000 years. Richer in PROTEIN than most MEAT, it also contains calcium, VITAMINS, minerals, acids and lecithin. Soy flour is used to make artificial meats and is also an important food in times of famine. Soybean oil is used in the manufacture of margarine, paints, soap, linoleum, textiles, paper and agricultural sprays. Over half of the world's soybean crop is now grown in the US.

SOYER, Raphael (1899–), Russian-born US artist. Called the "dean of American realism," Soyer is best known for his street scenes and portraits of lonely inhabitants of New York's Lower East Side. His brothers, **Moses** (1899–1974) and **Isaac** (1907–1981), were also realist painters.

SPAAK, Paul Henri (1899–1972), Belgium's first Socialist premier (1938–39, 1947–49), and deputy premier (1961–65). He was foreign secretary several times between 1936 and 1966, and was president of the UNITED NATIONS General Assembly in 1946. He was influential in setting up the European COMMON MARKET and was secretary-general of the NORTH ATLANTIC TREATY ORGANIZATION 1957–61.

SPAATZ, Carl Andrew (1891–1974), US Air Force officer who fought in both world wars, taking a number of high command positions during WWII, and in 1945 directing the strategic bombing of Japan. He was Air Force Chief of Staff 1947–48.

SPACE, in MATHEMATICS, a bounded or unbounded extent. In GEOMETRY this extent may be in one, two or three DIMENSIONS, its nature being viewed differently in different geometries. According to EUCLIDEAN GEOMETRY space is uniform and infinite, so that we may talk of a LINE of infinite extent or a POLYGON of infinite AREA. In RIEMANNIAN GEOMETRY, however, all lines are of less than a certain, finite extent; and in LOBACHEVSKIAN GEOMETRY, there is a similar maximum of area. The term is also often used for sets that have some kind of structure imposed on them, as in "topological space" and "VECTOR space." (See SET THEORY; TOPOLOGY; ALGEBRA, ABSTRACT.)

SPACE EXPLORATION. At 10:56pm EDT on July 20, 1969, Neil ARMSTRONG became the first man to set foot on the MOON. This was the climax of an intensive US space program sparked off by the successful launch of the Russian artificial SATELLITE Sputnik 1 in 1957, and accelerated by Yuri GAGARIN's flight in Vostok 1, the first manned spacecraft, in 1961. Later that year Alan SHEPARD piloted the first American manned spacecraft, and President Kennedy set the goal of landing a man on the moon and returning him safely within the decade. On Feb. 20, 1962 John GLENN orbited the earth three times in the first MERCURY craft to be boosted by an Atlas rocket, but it was Valery Bykovsky who set the one-man endurance record with a 5-day mission in June 1963. The next Russian mission involved two craft, Vostoks 5 and 6, and made Valentina TERESHKOVA the first woman cosmonaut. Alexei Leonov completed the first space-walk in Oct. 1964: but then it was the turn of the GEMINI MISSIONS to break all records. Both countries lost men, on the ground and in space: among them V. I. GRISSOM, E. H. WHITE and R. B. Chaffee—in a fire on board Apollo during ground tests—and the crew of Soyuz 11, killed during reentry in 1971, though earlier

Soyuz had docked successfully with the first space station and set new records. Unmanned probes such as Orbiter, Ranger and Surveyor were meanwhile searching out Apollo landing sites, while Russian Luna and Lunokhod craft were also studying the moon. In 1968 Apollo 7 carried out an 11-day earth-orbit flight, and at Christmas Apollo 8 made 10 lunar orbits. The lunar landing craft was tested on the Apollo 9 and Apollo 10 missions, leaving the way clear for the triumphant success of Apollo 11. Apollo 12 was equally successful, landing only 600 yards from the lunar probe Surveyor 3, but the Apollo 13 mission was a near disaster: an explosion damaged the craft on its way to the moon, and re-entry was achieved only with great difficulty. Apollo 14 had no such problems in visiting Fra Mauro, and the collection of a very wide range of samples. Apollo 16 brought back over 200lbs of moon rock, and in Dec. 1972 Apollo 17 made the last lunar landing. In 1973 the SKYLAB missions returned attention to the study of world resources from space, and movements toward cooperation in this field were demonstrated by the joint Apollo/Soyuz mission in 1975. Exploration of the planets has been carried out by unmanned probes. the MARINER series to Mars, Venus and Mercury; the PIONEER missions to the outer planets, and a number of Russian contributions, such as the Venera soft-landing missions to Venus, the Zond bypass probe and the Mars soft-landing craft. Results from the two American VIKING probes that soft-landed on Mars in 1976 did not conclusively show existence of life there. VOYAGER 1 and 2 revealed a wealth of new information about JUPITER and SATURN.

SPACE SHUTTLE, nickname for Space Transportation System (STS) spacecraft, the first craft designed to orbit the earth and return intact. It is intended mainly to place payloads in orbit more cheaply than can be done by conventional rockets and retrieve them if necessary, and also to fly astronauts to and from large space stations. It carries an enormous disposable fuel tank for its rocket engine and two solid-fuel boosters that are dropped by parachute and recovered. When the shuttle returns, it lands like a glider. In Feb. 1981, astronauts John Young and Robert Crippen took the $9.9 billion *Columbia* shuttle on its first flight, a 54 1/2 hour mission, which concluded with a perfect landing in the Mojave Desert in Cal.

SPACE-TIME, a way of describing the geometry of the physical universe arising from EINSTEIN'S special theory of

RELATIVITY. Space and time are considered as a single 4-dimensional continuum rather than as a 3-dimensional space with a separate infinite 1-dimensional time. Time thus becomes the "fourth dimension." Events in space-time are analogous to points in space and invariant space-time intervals to distances in space.

SPAHN, Warren Edward (1921–), US baseball player who won 363 games, more than any other lefthanded pitcher. He pitched a lifetime total of 57 scoreless games. Spahn began his major league career with the Boston Braves in 1942, and retired in 1965.

Official name: Spanish State
Capital: Madrid
Area: 194,883sq mi
Population: 37,430,000
Languages: Spanish; Catalan, Galician, Basque
Religions: Roman Catholic
Monetary unit(s): 1 peseta = 100 céntimos

SPAIN, a country occupying about four-fifths of the Iberian Peninsula S of the Pyrenees Mts in SW Europe. It includes the BALEARIC ISLANDS and the CANARY ISLANDS. The largely arid plateau of the Meseta forms most of the interior. The Andalusian or Baetic Mts near the Mediterranean coast include the SIERRA NEVADA, rising to Mulacen (11,421ft), the highest peak in mainland Spain. The Guadalquivir R drains the fertile Andalusian plains, and narrow coastal plains lie along the E and SE coasts. The climate is mainly dry with cold winters and hot summers, more extreme on the Meseta. In N Spain the climate is equable, and the S and E coasts enjoy a Mediterranean climate.

People. About 40% of the population is urban. Regional differences are marked and the BASQUE provinces, GALICIA and CATALONIA have preserved their own languages.

Economy. Tourism makes the most important contribution to Spain's income, followed by industry and agriculture. Mineral wealth includes mercury, iron ore, coal, pyrites, potash and salt. Oil was found near Burgos in 1964. Manufacturing industries center on the N provinces, especially Catalonia, and include textiles, chemicals, iron and steel, paper, explosives and armaments. Agriculture is equally divided between crops and livestock. Oranges, olive oil and wine are exported. Fishing is important.

History. Spain was settled successively by Celts, Phoenicians, Greeks and Carthaginians (3rd century BC). A more enduring influence was that of the Romans, who conquered Spain during the second of the PUNIC WARS and remained dominant until the VANDALS and VISIGOTHS appeared in the 5th century AD. The last invaders were the MOORS (711 AD). The Christian kingdoms in the N achieved a gradual reconquest completed in the reign (1474–1504) of Ferdinand V (FERDINAND II of Aragon) and his wife ISABELLA of Castile. They introduced the INQUISITION and financed the voyages of COLUMBUS. Soon Spain had won a vast empire in the New World and N Africa, joined with the HAPSBURG lands by the election of Charles I as CHARLES V, Holy Roman Emperor. Under his son PHILIP II a period of outstanding cultural achievement unfolded with such figures as CERVANTES, Lope de VEGA, VELÁSQUEZ and El GRECO. At the same time Spain's political power declined. The Netherlands revolted in 1568, and the ARMADA was defeated in 1588. The War of the SPANISH SUCCESSION resulted in heavy losses. The French, invading in 1808, were driven out in the PENINSULAR WAR; but after the revolt of the Latin American colonies and the SPANISH-AMERICAN WAR the Empire was all but dead. After the SPANISH CIVIL WAR General FRANCO became dictator. On his death (1975) JUAN CARLOS succeeded, thus restoring the monarchy.

SPALDING, Albert (1888–1953), US violinist. An exquisite and restrained stylist, he was the first internationally recognized US-born violin virtuoso. He played with major orchestras in Europe and the US and composed several compositions for the violin.

SPALLANZANI, Lazzaro (1729–1799), Italian biologist who attacked the contemporary belief in the SPONTANEOUS GENERATION of life by demonstrating that organisms which usually appeared in vegetable infusions failed to do so if the infusions were boiled and kept from contact with the air.

SPANISH, a Romance language spoken by over 145,000,000 people in Spain and Latin America. Modern Spanish arose from the Castilian dialect centered on the town of Burgos in N central Spain.

SPANISH-AMERICAN WAR (1898), war fought between the US and Spain, initially over the conduct of Spanish colonial authorities in CUBA. Strong anti-Spanish feeling was fomented in the US by stories of the cruel treatment meted out to Cuban rebels, and the hardships suffered by American business interests. Though President Cleveland took no action, his successor, William McKINLEY, had promised to recognize Cuban independence. He succeeded in obtaining limited self-government for the Cubans, but an explosion aboard the US battleship *Maine* (1898), from which 260 died was blamed on the Spanish, and McKinley sent an ultimatum, some of whose terms were actually being implemented when Congress declared war on April 25. On May 1 George DEWEY destroyed the Spanish fleet in Manila harbor. What remained was trapped in Santiago harbor by Admiral W. T. SAMPSON, and destroyed on July 3 by American forces which had already shattered Spanish land forces. Santiago surrendered on July 17. General Nelson A. Miles occupied Puerto Rico, and on Aug. 13 troops occupied Manila. The Treaty of PARIS (Dec. 10, 1898) ended Spanish rule in Cuba. The US gained the islands of GUAM, PUERTO RICO and the PHILIPPINES, thus acquiring an overseas empire with accompanying world military power and responsibilities.

SPANISH CIVIL WAR (1936–39), major conflict between liberal and conservative forces in Spain. After the bloodless overthrow of the monarchy in 1931, the democratic republican government proposed far-reaching reforms which alienated conservatives. On the election (1936) of the POPULAR FRONT, a left-wing coalition, the rightists under General FRANCO resorted to force. Supported by Hitler and Mussolini, Franco was on the verge of shattering the republicans when the Soviet Union began to send them aid. The West remained aloof. Madrid fell to Franco in 1938, Barcelona in 1939. Over 600,000, many of them foreign volunteers, died in the war, and the country suffered massive damage. The Luftwaffe's systematic destruction of GUERNICA, a preview of Hitler's *blitzkrieg*, shocked the world.

SPANISH MAIN, former name of the N coast of the South American mainland, now part of Colombia and Venezuela. It was the hunting ground of the English pirates and buccaneers who attacked the Spanish treasure fleets.

SPANISH MOSS, or Florida moss, *Tillandsia usneoides*, an EPIPHYTE that can be found festooning trees such as oaks and cypresses and even telephone poles and wires in the southeastern US. It absorbs water through scaly hairs on the leaves and stem. It is used as a substitute for horsehair stuffing and for insulation.

SPANISH SUCCESSION, War of the (1701–1714), conflict between France on the one hand and a Grand Alliance of England, Holland, Austria and the smaller states of the Holy Roman Empire on the other. The childless Charles II of Spain willed his kingdom and its empire to France on his deathbed. The Grand Alliance sought to prevent France from becoming the dominant European power. Though the decisive battles were fought in Europe, there were also engagements overseas, including North America (see FRENCH AND INDIAN WARS). The Duke of Marlborough and Prince Eugene of Savoy won such remarkable victories as BLENHEIM (1704), Ramillies (1706) and Malplaquet (1709), but LOUIS XIV fought on. The accession of CHARLES VI as the new emperor removed obstacles to the recognition of Philip of Anjou as PHILIP V of Spain. England made a separate peace in 1712 and a general settlement of differences in the Peace of UTRECHT followed in 1713.

SPARK, Muriel Sarah (1918–), Scottish writer best known for her witty, often satirical novels, including *Memento Mori* (1959), *The Prime of Miss Jean Brodie* (1961; later made into a play and a film) and *The Mandelbaum Gate* (1965).

SPARROWS, small gregarious seed-eating birds forming the subfamily Passerinae of the weaver-bird family Ploceidae. There are eight genera, five confined to Africa, the other three, the True sparrows, Rock sparrows and Snow finches, also found in the Palearctic. Of the true sparrows, one species, the House sparrow, *Passer domesticus*, has been successfully introduced to the Americas. Closely associated with human habitation, it is the only bird not known to occur at all in a "natural" habitat, but always with man.

SPARTA, or Lacedaemon, city of ancient Greece, the capital of Laconia in the Peloponnesus, on the Eurotas R. Its society was divided into three classes: the HELOTS, the free perioeci, and the Spartiates, whose rigorous military training became a byword. There were two hereditary kings, though real power resided with the five annually elected EPHORS. Founded in the 13th century BC, Sparta dominated the Peloponnesus by 550 BC. Despite alliance with Athens in the PERSIAN WARS, Sparta fought and won the PELOPONNESIAN WAR against Athens (431–404 BC) but a series of revolts and defeats destroyed Spartan power, and in 146 BC the city became subject to Roman rule.

SPARTACUS (d. 71 BC), leader of the Gladiators' War, a slave revolt against ancient Rome (73–71 BC). With an army of runaway slaves Spartacus heavily defeated forces sent against him and gained control of S Italy, but after his death in battle the revolt was quickly crushed, and 6,000 slaves were crucified along the Appian Way.

SPARTACUS LEAGUE, German revolutionary socialist group active after WWI and named for the slave leader SPARTACUS by its leaders, Karl LIEBKNECHT and Rosa LUXEMBURG. The league became the nucleus of the German Communist Party, but its attempt to seize power in Jan. 1919 was crushed by the government of Friedrich EBERT, and Liebknecht and Luxemburg were murdered while under arrest.

SPASSKY, Boris Vasiliyevich (1937–), Russian journalist and chess master. He won the Soviet chess championship in 1962 and was world champion 1969–72. He lost the world title to the young American player, Bobby FISCHER, in 1972 in what was probably the most widely publicized series of chess matches in history.

SPASTIC PARALYSIS, form of PARALYSIS due to DISEASE of BRAIN (e.g., STROKE) or SPINAL CORD (e.g., MULTIPLE SCLEROSIS), in which the involved MUSCLES are in a state of constantly increased tone (or resting contraction). Spasticity is a segmental motor phenomenon where muscle contraction occurs without voluntary control.

SPEAKER, Tristram E. (1888–1958), outstanding American League outfielder elected to the Baseball Hall of Fame in 1937. He compiled a lifetime batting average of .344 and set a major league record for doubles (793).

SPECIAL EFFECTS, in cinema, techniques developed to enhance visual illusion, especially important in "disaster movies" and ambitious science fiction films, such as *Star Wars*. Most effects are produced in special studios, and are added to the film after it is shot. A great many techniques are employed, including animation, the use of miniature models, and slow-speed or fast-speed ("slow motion") photography. An important and increasingly sophisticated technique is creation of a composite picture—using several different images superimposed within a single film frame—often with the aid of electronic memories and timers to match perspectives, light, and camera angles.

SPECIAL FORCES, commonly known as the Green Berets, branch of the US Army trained for action behind enemy lines, including intelligence work and the instructing of native units in guerrilla tactics and counterinsurgency. Created after the Korean War, the Special Forces troops were highly active in the VIETNAM WAR.

SPECIES. See TAXONOMY.

SPECTROSCOPY, the production, measurement and analysis of spectra (see SPECTRUM), an essential tool of astronomers, chemists and physicists. All spectra arise from transitions between discrete energy states of matter, as a result of which PHOTONS of corresponding energy (and hence characteristic FREQUENCY or wavelength) are absorbed or emitted. From the energy levels thus determined, atomic and molecular structure may be studied. Moreover, by using the observed spectra as "fingerprints," spectroscopy may be a sensitive method of chemical ANALYSIS. Most of the different kinds of spectroscopy, corresponding to the various regions of ELECTROMAGNETIC RADIATION, relate to particular kinds of energy-level transitions. **Gamma-ray spectra** arise from nuclear energy-level transitions; **X-ray spectra** from inner-electron transitions in atoms; **ultraviolet and visible spectra** from outer (bonding) electron transitions in molecules (or atoms); **infrared spectra** from molecular vibrations; and **microwave spectra** from molecular rotations. There are several more specialized kinds of spectroscopy. **Raman spectroscopy,** based on the effect discovered by C. V. RAMAN, scans the scattered light from an intense monochromatic beam. Some of the scattered light is at lower (and higher) frequencies than the incident light, corresponding to vibration/rotation transitions. The technique thus supplements infra-red spectroscopy. **Mössbauer spectroscopy,** based on the MÖSSBAUER EFFECT, gives information on the electronic or chemical environments of nuclei; as does **nuclear magnetic resonance spectroscopy** (nmr), based on transitions between nuclear SPIN states in a strong magnetic field. **Electron spin resonance spectroscopy** (esr) is similarly based on electron spin transitions when there is an unpaired electron in an ORBITAL, and so is used to study FREE RADICALS. The intrument used is a **spectroscope,** called a *spectrograph* if the spectrum is recorded photographically all at once, or a *spectrometer* if it is scanned by wavelength and calibrated from the instrument.

SPECTRUM, the array of colors produced

on passing LIGHT through a PRISM; also, by extension, the range of a phenomenon displayed in terms of one of its properties. ELECTROMAGNETIC RADIATION arranged according to wavelength thus forms the electromagnetic spectrum, of which that of visible light is only a minute part. Similarly the mass spectrum of a particular collection of ions displays their relative numbers as a function of their masses. (See SPECTROSCOPY; MASS SPECTROSCOPY.)

SPEECH AND SPEECH DISORDERS. Speech may be subdivided into conception, or formulation, and production, or phonation and articulation, of speech (see VOICE). Speech development in children starts with associating sounds with persons and objects, comprehension usually predating vocalization by some months. Nouns are developed first, often with one or two syllables only; later acquisition of verbs, adjectives, etc., allows the construction of phrases and sentences. A phase of babbling speech, where the child toys with sounds resembling speech, is probably essential for development. READING is closely related to speech development, involving the association of auditory and visual symbols. Speech involves coordination of many aspects of BRAIN function (HEARING, VISION, etc.) but three areas particularly concerned with aspects of speech are located in the dominant hemisphere of right-handed persons and in either hemisphere of left-handed people (see HANDEDNESS). DISEASE of these parts of the brain leads to characteristic forms of dysphasia or APHASIA, ALEXIA, etc. Developmental DYSLEXIA is a childhood defect of visual pattern recognition. Stammering or stuttering, with repetition and hesitation over certain syllables, is a common disorder, in some cases representing frustrated left-handedness. Dysarthria is disordered voice production and is due to disease of the neuromuscular control of voice. In speech therapy, attempts are made to overcome or circumvent speech difficulties, this being particularly important in children (see also DEAFNESS).

SPEEDOMETER, instrument for indicating the speed of a motor vehicle. The common type works by magnetic INDUCTION. A circular permanent magnet is rotated by a flexible cable geared to the transmission. The rotating magnetic field induces a magnetic field in an aluminum cup, so tending to turn it in the same direction as the magnet. This TORQUE, proportional to the speed of rotation, is opposed by a spiral spring. The angle through which the cup turns against the spring measures the speed. The speedometer is usually coupled with an **odometer**, a counting device geared to the magnet, which registers the distance traveled.

SPEER, Albert (1905–1981), German Nazi leader who was Hitler's architect. For his organization of slave labor for Germany during WWII, the international tribunal at Nuremberg sentenced him to 20 years imprisonment in SPANDAU. After his release he wrote revealingly of the inner workings of the Nazi regime.

SPELEOLOGY, the scientific study of CAVES. The world's first speleological society was founded in France in 1895, and interest soon became worldwide. The US National Speleological Society was founded in 1939. Less academic cave exploration is called spelunking.

SPENCER, Herbert (1820–1903), English philosopher, social theorist and early evolutionist. In his multivolume *System of Synthetic Philosophy* (1862–96), he expounded a world view based on a close study of physical, biological and social phenomena, arguing that species evolve by a process of differentiation from the simple to the complex. His political individualism deeply influenced the growth of SOCIAL DARWINISM, US social thinking.

SPENDER, Stephen Harold (1909–   ), English poet and critic, coeditor of the literary magazine *Encounter* 1953–65. His poetry collections include *Poems* (1933), *Ruins and Visions* (1942) and *The Generous Days* (1971).

SPENGLER, Oswald (1880–1936), German philosopher whose cyclic view of history is expressed in *The Decline of the West* (1918–22), a study of the rise and fall of civilizations. He believed that Western civilization was entering a period of decline, a view much favored between the wars.

SPENSER, Edmund (c1522–1599), English poet, best known for the six books of his unfinished epic poem *The Faerie Queene* (1590–96), an allegorical work celebrating the moral values of Christian chivalry. Steeped in English folklore, the poem displays the monumental scope of a Homer or Vergil. His other works include *The Shepheardes Calender* (1579) and *Epithalamion* (1595).

SPERM WHALES, or Cachalots, a family of Toothed Whales, with two species: the cachalot, *Physeter catodon*, and Pigmy Sperm whale, *Kogia breviceps*. They are among the best known of all WHALES because of the enormous, squared head. The front of the head contains a huge reservoir of **spermaceti** oil, perhaps used as a lens to focus the sounds produced by the whales in echolocation. Spermaceti solidifies in cool air to form a wax once used for candles and cosmetics. Sperm whales are also the source of AMBERGRIS, a secretion in the gut produced in response to irritation by the beaks of SQUIDS, an important prey item. Sperm whales are found in all oceans, migrating from the poles into warmer waters during the breeding season. It is a deep water whale, capable of diving to 500m (1,640ft) or more. Females and young form large schools of up to several hundred animals. Males tend to travel alone or in small groups.

SPHINX, mythical monster of the ancient Middle East, in Egypt portrayed as a lion with a human head and used as a symbol of the pharaoh. In Greek mythology the sphinx propounded a riddle to travelers on the road to Thebes: when OEDIPUS answered correctly the sphinx threw herself from her rocky perch.

SPIDERS, an order, Araneida, of the Arachnida, with the body divided into two parts, and with four pairs of walking legs. Unlike INSECTS, spiders have no antennae, have simple, not compound, EYES, and no larval or pupal stages. They are an incredibly diverse group of some 26,000 species. The evolution of spiders is closely linked with that of the insects on which they prey: as insects developed abilities of jumping, gliding and later flying, and evolved stings and other defenses, so the spiders developed so as still to be able to capture their changing prey. Thus from primitive running spiders have evolved such groups as the JUMPING SPIDERS; WOLF SPIDERS; Trapdoor spiders, and, of course, the Web-spinners.

SPIELBERG, Steven (1946–   ), US film director noted for his suspense-filled thrillers, including *Duel* (1971), *Jaws* (1975) and *Raiders of the Lost Ark* (1981).

SPILLANE, Mickey (Frank Morrison, 1918–   ), American detective story writer. His books, describing the violent adventures of private detective Mike Hammer, include *I, The Jury* (1947).

SPINAL CORD, the part of the central NERVOUS SYSTEM outside the SKULL. It joins the BRAIN at the base of the skull, forming the *medulla oblongata*, and extends downward in a bony canal enclosed in the VERTEBRAE. Between the bone and cord are three sheaths of connective TISSUE called the *meninges*. A section of the cord shows a central core of *gray matter* (containing the cell bodies of nerve fibers running either to the muscles or within the cord itself), completely surrounded by *white matter*

(composed solely of nerve fibers). There is a central canal containing CEREBROSPINAL FLUID, which opens into the cavities of the brain.

SPINAL TAP, or lumbar puncture, procedure to remove CEREBROSPINAL FLUID (CSF) from the lumbar spinal canal using a fine needle. It is used in diagnosis of MENINGITIS, ENCEPHALITIS, MULTIPLE SCLEROSIS and TUMORS. In NEUROLOGY, it may be used in treatment, by reducing CSF pressure or allowing insertion of DRUGS.

SPINELLO DI LUCA SPINELLI (c1346–1410), Italian painter of the late Gothic period, also known as Spinello Aretino, whose most important works are two series of frescoes at the Campo Santo, Pisa and the Palazzo Pubblico, Siena.

SPINET, type of small HARPSICHORD which probably originated in 16th-century Italy. Inside the wing-shaped cabinet a single set of strings is set at an oblique angle to the keyboard. The name is also used for a small upright piano.

SPINNING, the ancient craft of twisting together FIBERS from a mass to form strong, continuous thread suitable for weaving. The earliest method was merely to roll the fibers between hand and thigh. Later two sticks were used: the distaff to hold the bundle of fibers, and a spindle to twist and wind the yarn. Mechanization began with the spinning wheel, invented in India and spreading to Europe by the 14th century. The wheel turned the spindle by means of a belt drive. In the 15th century the flyer was invented: a device on the spindle shaft that winds the yarn automatically on a spool. Improved WEAVING methods in the Industrial Revolution caused increased demand which provoked several inventions. The spinning jenny, invented by James HARGREAVES (c1767), spun as many as 16 threads at once, the spindles all being driven by the same wheel. Richard ARKWRIGHT's "water frame" (1769), so called from being water-powered, had rollers and produced strong thread. Then Samuel CROMPTON produced a hybrid of the two—his "mule"—which had a movable carriage, and was the forerunner of the modern machine. The other modern spinning machine is the ring-spinning frame (1828) in which the strands, drawn out by rollers, are twisted by a "traveler" that revolves on a ring around the bobbin on which they are wound.

SPÍNOLA, António Sebastião Ribeiro de (1910–   ), Portuguese army officer and political leader. Chief of staff in Portuguese Guinea 1968–72, in Mar. 1974 he was dismissed from the army for asserting in a book that Portuguese military victory in Africa was impossible. In April he led a military coup, and became provisional president until Sept. (See PORTUGAL.)

SPINOZA, Baruch or **Benedict de** (1632–1677), Dutch philosopher and rationalist (see RATIONALISM) who held that God is nature, or all that is, an interpretation which brought him expulsion from the Amsterdam Jewish community. Though influenced by DESCARTES, he rejected Descartes' dual substance theory and claimed that matter and mind are attributes of the one substance: God. His most famous work is *Ethics* (1677). Organized "in the geometric style" like EUCLID's *Elements*, it contains the development of his PANTHEISM, which is both rationalist and mystical.

SPIRITUAL, a form of religious folk song developed by the Negro slaves and their descendants in the southern US states. It usually consists of a number of verses for solo voice, with a rhythmic choral refrain.

SPIRITUALISM, religious movement based on belief in the survival of the human personality after death and its ability to communicate with those left behind, usually through a medium. Spiritualist beliefs have had powerful effects, both for good and for bad, on the advance of psychic research (see PARAPSYCHOLOGY).

SPIROCHETE, spiral BACTERIA, species of which are responsible for RELAPSING FEVER. YAWS and syphilis (see VENEREAL DISEASES).

SPITTELER, Carl Friedrich Georg (1845–1924), Swiss poet, winner of the 1919 Nobel Prize for Literature. His heroic epics *Prometheus and Epimetheus* (1881) and *Olympic Spring* (1900–05; 1910) stressed spiritual nobility.

SPITZ, a general term for a group of stocky northern dogs including the chow chow, Samoyed and Pomeranian. They have a long, dense coat, tail curved over the back, and pointed, erect ears. The 25lb American spitz has a white coat.

SPITZ, Mark (1950–   ), US swimmer who captured a record seven gold medals during the 1972 Olympics. An intense competitor, he set 27 individual world records in the freestyle and butterfly between 1967 and 1972. He also won two gold medals in the 1968 Olympics.

SPLEEN, spongy vascular lymphoid organ (see LYMPH) between the STOMACH and DIAPHRAGM on the left side of the ABDOMEN. A center for the RETICULOENDOTHELIAL SYSTEM, it also eliminates worn-out red BLOOD cells, recycling their iron. Most of its functions are duplicated by other organs. The spleen was classically the source of

black bile, or melancholy (see HUMORS).

SPOCK, Benjamin McLane (1903–   ), known worldwide as "Dr. Spock," US pediatrician and pacifist best known for his (*Common Sense Book of*) *Baby and Child Care* (1946), which advocated a more liberal attitude on the part of parents, and *Bringing up Children in a Difficult Time* (1974).

SPODE, British family of pottery makers. **Josiah Spode** (1733–1797), founded the Spode works at Stoke-on-Trent and introduced transfer decoration and oriental motifs. **Josiah Spode** (1754–1827), developed stone china, porcelain and BONE CHINA. He popularized the willow pattern and gained royal patronage. (See also POTTERY AND PORCELAIN.)

SPOHR, Ludwig (Louis) (1784–1859), violinist, composer and one of the first orchestral conductors. As a performer he did much to make Beethoven's early string quartets well known. Among his extensive works are 9 symphonies and 11 operas, including *Faust* (1816) and *Jessonda* (1823).

SPOILS SYSTEM, the use of appointments to public offices to reward supporters of a victorious political party. With the growth of a two-party system in the US, political patronage increased. It was President Jackson's friend Senator William L. Marcy who said in 1832 that "to the victor belong the spoils," and the system soon operated on every political level. The PENDLETON ACT of 1883, introducing competitive entrance examinations for public employees, marked the gradual introduction of a merit system.

SPONGES, primitive animals of both marine and fresh water, phylum Parazoa (Porifera). Sponges are true ANIMALS, although they have only a simple body wall and no specialized organ or tissue systems. They may be solitary or colonial. They are filter-feeders, straining tiny food particles out of water drawn in through pores all over the body surface, and expelled through one or more exhalant vents. The body wall is strengthened by spicules of CALCITE or SILICA, or by a meshwork of PROTEIN fibers: spongin. Sponges with spongin skeletons are fished for bath sponges. Sponges can exhibit REGENERATION to a remarkable degree. A sponge strained through silk to break it up into its component cells can reorganize itself into a functional sponge.

SPONTANEOUS COMBUSTION, COMBUSTION occurring without external ignition, caused by slow OXIDATION or FERMENTATION which (if heat cannot readily escape) raises the temperature to burning point. It may occur when hay or small coal is stored.

SPONTANEOUS GENERATION, or **abiogenesis,** theory, dating from the writings of ARISTOTLE, that living creatures can arise from nonliving matter. The idea remained current even after it had become clear that higher orders of life could not be created in this way; and it was only with the work of REDI, showing that maggots did not appear in decaying meat to which flies had been denied access, and PASTEUR, who proved that the equivalent was true of microorganisms (i.e., BACTERIA), that the theory was finally discarded.

SPORE, minute single or multicelled body produced during the process of reproduction of many plants, particularly BACTERIA, ALGAE and FUNGI and in some PROTOZOA. The structure of spores varies greatly and depends upon the means of dissemination from the parent. Some, e.g., the zoospores of algae, are motile.

SPRAIN. See LIGAMENT.

SPRING, a naturally occurring flow of water from the ground. This may be, for example, an outflow from an underground stream; but most often a spring occurs where an AQUIFER saturated with GROUNDWATER intersects with the earth's surface. Such an aquifer, if confined above and below by aquicludes, may travel for hundreds of kilometers underground before emerging to the surface, there, perhaps, in desert areas giving rise to OASES. Spring water is generally fairly clean, since it has been filtered through the permeable rocks; but all spring water contains some dissolved MINERALS. (See also GEYSER; HOT SPRINGS; WELL.)

SPUTNIK. See SATELLITES, ARTIFICIAL.

SPYRI, Johanna (née Heusser; 1829–1901), Swiss writer of children's books. *Heidi* (1880–81), set in the Swiss Alps, has become a worldwide classic.

SQUARE DANCE, popular, lively American folk dance in which four couples formed in a square carry out steps and formations under the direction of a caller. It dates back to the quadrille dances of 15th-century Europe. (See also FOLK DANCING.)

SQUARE DEAL, policy of Theodore ROOSEVELT, when presidential candidate (1912), seeking to reconcile the demands of both workers and industrialists.

SQUASH, game similar to racquetball but played with a softer, less bouncy ball. Singles squash is played on an indoor court 18½ft wide by 32ft long. Doubles squash requires a larger court. The ball may be hit against any of the four walls as long as it bounces on the front wall before striking the ground. The opponent must strike the ball before it bounces twice.

SQUATTER SOVEREIGNTY, or "popular sovereignty," a doctrine intended to end congressional controversy over the expansion of slavery just before the US Civil War. The inhabitants of a territory were to be allowed to decide for themselves whether or not to permit slavery. It was applied to Ut. and N.M. through the COMPROMISE OF 1850, and a popular sovereignty clause was included in the KANSAS-NEBRASKA ACT (1854) which repealed the MISSOURI COMPROMISE.

SQUIDS, shell-less CEPHALOPOD mollusks, order Teuthoidea. Although a few species live in coastal waters the majority are open ocean forms. Squids are streamlined animals with ten arms around the head, facing forward. The mantle at the rear of the body houses the gills and the openings of the excretory, sex and digestive organs. Sudden contraction of the whole mantle cavity sends out a blast of water that can be directed forward or backward by a movable funnel, providing the main means of propulsion. All squids can swim very rapidly and are active predators of fish, shooting out the long arms, provided with suckers and hooks, to grab their prey.

SQUINT. See STRABISMUS.

SQUIRRELS, one of the largest families, Sciuridae, of rodents. Commonly, the name refers only to Tree squirrels (see also GROUND SQUIRRELS). Tree squirrels are found in most forested parts of the world. Typically they have long bushy tails and short muzzles. They are diurnal, feeding on seeds, nuts and leaf buds, with some insect or other animal food. A number of temperate species, while not true hibernants, store food for the winter and enter deep torpor.

SRI LANKA, formerly Ceylon, independent island republic within the British Commonwealth, separated from SE India by the Gulf of Mannar, Palk Strait and Adam's Bridge, a 30mi chain of shoals.

Land. Sri Lanka is about 270mi N–S and 140mi E–W. The mountainous central S area rises to Pidurutalagala (8,281ft) and ADAM'S PEAK (7,360ft); the major rivers, including the Mahaweli Ganga, rise here. Around the mountains stretches a coastal plain, up to 100mi wide in the N. Climate is tropical, but the island situation gives more equable temperatures than mainland India (around 81°F at Colombo). Rainfall ranges from 40in in the N to 200in in the SW mountains. In many areas the original dense tropical forest has been cleared for agriculture.

People. The few cities include the capital,

COLOMBO on the W coast, Jaffna in the N, Kandy in the S central mountains, Trincomalee on the E coast and Galle in the SW. Buddhist Sinhalese form 75% of the fast-growing population, and SINHALESE is the official language. Others include the Hindu Tamils (people of S Indian origin, who live mainly in the N and E), the forest Veddas (probably the aboriginal inhabitants), the Burghers (Christian descendants of Dutch-Sinhalese ancestors), the Moors and Malay Muslims.

Economy. Sri Lanka produces about one third of the world's tea and over 150,000 tons of rubber a year. Coconuts are commercially grown for their oil, but rice, the main food crop, has to be supplemented in many years by imports. Several irrigation schemes have, however, improved annual rice yields. The country is the world's chief producer of high-grade graphite. Power is mainly hydroelectric. There is a good road and rail system.

History. The island was settled around 550 BC by Sinhalese, a people from the Indian subcontinent who built ANURADHAPURA and made the island a center of Buddhist thought after the religion was introduced here in the 3rd century BC. From the 12th to the 16th century the Tamils held the N part. Europeans arrived in the 1500s, lured by the spice trade; they called the island Ceylon. Held by the Portuguese (landed 1505), the Dutch (after 1658) and finally the British (from 1796), the island attained independence in 1948 and became a republic in 1956. In 1972 Ceylon adopted a new constitution and the Sinhalese name Sri Lanka. In the late 1970 and early 1980s, sporadic violence flared up between the

Official name: Democratic Socialist Republic of Sri Lanka
Capital: Colombo
Area: 25,332sq mi
Population: 14,500,000
Languages: Sinhalese, English, Tamil
Religions: Buddhist, Hindu, Christian, Muslim
Monetary unit(s): 1 Sri Lanka rupee=100 cents

Sinhalese and the Tamil minority.

SS (abbreviation of *Schutzstaffel*: defense echelons) or Blackshirts, dreaded elite corps of Nazi Germany, commanded by HIMMLER. It comprised the secret police (see GESTAPO), Hitler's personal bodyguard, the guards of the concentration and extermination camps, and some divisions of picked combat troops. (See NAZISM.)

SST (SUPERSONIC TRANSPORT), general term for passenger airplanes that fly faster than sound, including the Anglo-French CONCORDE and the Soviet Tu-144, and specifically a controversial plane that was to have been built in the US. A subject of bitter dispute during the late 1960s, the proposed plane was attacked by environmentalists, who feared it would cause huge sonic booms and pollute the upper atmosphere, while the government, wanting to help the domestic aerospace industry, pressed ahead despite adverse recommendations on economic, technical and environmental grounds by its own scientists. It took a major battle in the Senate at the end of 1970 to kill the project.

STAEL, Anne Louise Germaine, Madame de (1766–1817), French-Swiss novelist and critic, celebrated personality and liberal opponent of Napoleon's regime, daughter of Jacques NECKER. A noted interpreter of German ROMANTICISM, she maintained brilliant salons in Paris and in exile near Geneva. She had liaisons with TALLEYRAND and CONSTANT.

STAFFORD, Jean (1915–1979), US author noted for her sensitive, well-crafted novels and stories. Her *Collected Stories* (1969) won a Pulitzer Prize in 1970.

STAGE DESIGN. See THEATER.

STAGG, Amos Alonzo (1862–1965), US football coach. His career spanned 71 seasons, including 41 (1892–1932) with the University of Chicago. He was in the first All-American team (1889), developed many football formations and also promoted basketball.

STAINED GLASS, pieces of colored glass held in place by a framework, usually of grooved lead strips (cames), to form patterns or pictures in a window. The earliest such windows date from the 11th century, but the art reached its highest development in the great period of GOTHIC ARCHITECTURE, c1150–1500: the series of windows made 1200–1240 for CHARTRES cathedral is perhaps the most famous example. Interest revived with the work of Edward BURNE-JONES and, in the US, the designs of Louis TIFFANY and John LA FARGE. Among recent masters of stained glass are the painters MATISSE, Fernand LÉGER,

ROUAULT and CHAGALL. The glass is colored during manufacture, by mixing it with various metallic oxides; then cut according to the artist's full-scale cartoons. Details may be painted on to the glass with colored enamels, which fuse to the glass surface when it is heated.

STAINLESS STEEL, corrosion-resistant STEEL containing more than 10% chromium, little carbon, and often nickel and other metals. Made in the ELECTRIC FURNACE, there are four main types: ferritic, martensitic, austenitic and precipitation-hardening. Stainless steel is used for cutlery and many industrial components.

STALACTITES AND STALAGMITES, rocky structures found growing downward from the roof (stalactites) and upward from the floor (stalagmites) of CAVES formed in LIMESTONE. Rainwater percolates through the rocks above the cave and, as it contains atmospheric CARBON dioxide, can dissolve calcium carbonate en route. On reaching the cave, the water drips from the roof to the floor; as a drop hangs, some water evaporates, leaving a little calcium carbonate as CALCITE on the roof. Repetition forms a stalactite; and evaporation of the fallen water on the floor forms a stalagmite. On occasion, the rising stalagmite and descending stalactite fuse to form a pillar.

STALIN, Joseph (1879–1953), dictatorial ruler of the Soviet Union from 1929 until his death. Born Josif Vissarionovich Dzhugashvili, a Georgian village shoemaker's son intended for the priesthood, he joined the Georgian Social Democratic Party in 1901, becoming its Tiflis organizer in 1905. In 1912 LENIN coopted him onto the Bolshevik central committee, to which he was elected in 1917. After the RUSSIAN REVOLUTION he advanced rapidly. In 1922 he was elected general secretary of the Russian Communist Party. In the struggle for the leadership after Lenin's death (1924) he ousted from the Politburo first Trotsky (1925) then Kamenev and Zinoviev (1926). In 1928 he launched a vast development and industrialization program that involved the forced collectivization of agriculture and massive social redeployment. He also sought to "Russianize" the Soviet Union, attempting to eradicate by force the separate identities of minorities. Dissent was met with a powerful secret police, informers, mass deportations, executions and show trials. In 1935 Stalin initiated the first of the great "purges" which spared neither his family nor former political associates. Equally ruthless in foreign affairs, he partitioned Poland with Germany, and invaded Finland (1939) and imposed communist rule on the Baltic states (1940). The reversal of German fortunes on the WWII Eastern Front strengthened his hand. In 1945 at YALTA he sealed the postwar fate of East Europe to his satisfaction. Thereafter, he pursued COLD WAR policies abroad and supported rapid industrial recovery at home until his death, from a brain hemorrhage. Almost immediately a process of "destalinization" began, culminating in KHRUSHCHEV'S 1956 attack on the Stalinist terror and personality cult.

STALINGRAD, Battle of, decisive engagement in WWII, fought in the vicinity of Stalingrad (now Volgograd) from Aug. 1942 to Feb. 1943. The 500,000-strong German 6th army under von Paulus surrounded the city on Sept. 14, 1942, but was itself encircled early in 1943 by a Russian army under ZHUKOV and forced to surrender. Not only was the German invasion halted, but the psychological initiative was wrested from the Nazis for the remainder of the war.

STAMITZ, Johann Wenzel Anton (1717–1757), Czech-born German composer and musician. As concertmaster of the court orchestra at Mannheim from 1745 and founder of the Mannheim school of symphonists, he had a profound influence on the work of Mozart.

STAMMER. See SPEECH AND SPEECH DISORDERS.

STAMP ACT (1765), the first direct tax imposed by the English Parliament on the 13 American colonies. All legal and commercial documents, pamphlets, playing cards and newspapers were to carry revenue stamps, which would help finance the British army quartered in America. The colonists balked at the idea of "taxation without representation," and delegates from nine colonies met in the Stamp Act Congress held in New York to protest against the law. A boycott of British goods finally led Parliament to repeal the Stamp Act in March 1766.

STAMP COLLECTING, or philately. The first postage stamps, the famous "Penny Blacks" and "Twopenny Blues," were issued in England on May 1, 1840: the first in the US appeared in 1847, and by 1860 most countries had adopted the prepaid postage stamp system. Today stamp catalogs list over 200,000 items. Serious collectors, who generally specialize in particular countries, periods or themes, make a close study of each stamp's paper, ink, printing method, perforations, cancellation (if used), design, information content and historical occasion. Stamps can also be a good investment: sums of up to $380,000 have been paid for rare specimens.

STANDARD OF LIVING, statistical measure which attempts to rate the quality of life in a nation or a group in terms of its level of consumption of food, clothing, and other basic goods and services including transportation, education and medical care. The standard is generally expressed in monetary terms according to latest costs.

STANDISH, Miles (c1584–1656), Lancashire-born military adviser to the PILGRIMS and an important member of the PLYMOUTH COLONY, serving as its assistant governor and treasurer. About 1631 he helped found Duxbury, Mass. Longfellow's poem about him has no factual basis.

STANFORD, Leland (1824–1893), US railroad pioneer and politician. Governor of Cal. (1861–63) and a Cal. Republican senator (1885–93), he also helped found and became president of the Central Pacific and Southern Pacific railroads and he established Stanford University (1885).

STANFORD-BINET TEST, an adaptation of the Binet-Simon test for INTELLIGENCE, introduced by TERMAN (1916, revised 1937), and used primarily to determine the IQs of children. (See also BINET.)

STANISLAVSKI, Konstantin (1863–1938), Russian actor, director and producer. Born Konstantin Sergeyevich Alekseyev, he originated an influential approach, known as "the method," which involves subordination of personal style to an attempt to analyze, assimilate and live out the emotional content of the enacted role. In 1898 he founded the MOSCOW ART THEATER.

STANLEY, Sir Henry Morton (1841–1904), British explorer, soldier and journalist. Born John Rowlands, he took the name of a US merchant who adopted him. He fought in the US Civil War and in 1869 was sent to Africa by the *New York Herald* to find the missionary and explorer David LIVINGSTONE. Their famous meeting by Lake Tanganyika occurred in 1871. Stanley continued Livingstone's exploration (1874–77), crossing the continent E–W.

STANLEY, Wendell Meredith

(1904–1971), US biochemist who shared with J. NORTHROP and J. SUMNER the 1946 Nobel Prize for Chemistry for his first crystallization of a VIRUS.

STANLEY CUP, presented annually to the winner of the National Hockey League post-season playoffs. Lord Stanley, Governor General of Canada, first presented the award to the Canadian champion in 1893. Since 1926 it has been identified solely with the NHL. (See ICE HOCKEY.)

STANTON, Edwin McMasters (1814–1869), US politician, an able Civil War secretary of war (1862–68) and important ally of the Radical Republicans during RECONSTRUCTION. As US attorney general in the last months of President BUCHANAN's cabinet, he stood against Southern secession. He resigned following President JOHNSON's narrow escape from impeachment (1868).

STANTON, Elizabeth Cady (1815–1902), US abolitionist and campaigner for women's rights In 1848, with Mrs. Lucretia MOTT, she organized the first women's rights convention in the US, at Seneca Falls, N.Y., and in 1869 founded the Woman Suffrage Association with Susan B. ANTHONY.

STAPHYLOCOCCUS, BACTERIUM responsible for numerous SKIN, soft tissue and BONE infections, less often causing SEPTICEMIA, a cavitating PNEUMONIA, bacterial endocarditis and enterocolitis. BOILS, CARBUNCLES, IMPETIGO and OSTEOMYELITIS are commonly due to staphylococci. Treatment usually requires drainage of PUS from ABSCESSES and ANTIBIOTICS.

STAR, a large incandescent ball of gases held together by its own gravity. The SUN is a fairly normal star in its composition, parameters and color. The lifespan of a star depends upon its mass and luminosity: a very luminous star may have a life of only one million years, the sun a life of ten billion years, the faintest main sequence stars a life of ten thousand billion years. Stars are divided into two categories, Populations I and II. The stars in Population I are slower moving, generally to be found in the spiral arms of GALAXIES, and believed to be younger. Population II stars are generally brighter, faster moving and mainly to be found in the spheroidal halo of stars around a galaxy and in the GLOBULAR CLUSTERS. Many stars are DOUBLE STARS. It is believed that stars originate as condensations out of INTERSTELLAR MATTER. In certain circumstances a protostar will form, slowly contracting under its own gravity, part of the energy from this contraction being radiated, the remainder heating up the core: this stage may last several million years. At last the core becomes hot enough for thermonuclear reactions (see FUSION, NUCLEAR) to be sustained, and stops contracting. Eventually the star as a whole ceases contracting and radiates entirely by the thermonuclear conversion of hydrogen into helium: it is then said to be on the main sequence. When all the hydrogen in the core has been converted into helium, the now purely helium core begins to contract while the outer layers continue to "burn" hydrogen: this contraction heats up the core and forces the outer layers outward, so that the star as a whole expands for some 100–200 million years until it becomes a red giant star. Although the outer layers are comparatively cool, the core has become far hotter than before, and thermonuclear conversions of helium into carbon begin. The star contracts once more (though some expand still further to become supergiants) and ends its life as a white dwarf star. It is thought that more massive stars become neutron stars, whose matter is so dense that its PROTONS and ELECTRONS are packed together to form NEUTRONS; were the sun to become a neutron star, it would have a radius of less than 20km. Finally, when the star can no longer radiate through thermonuclear or gravitational means, it ceases to shine. Some stars may at this stage undergo ultimate gravitational collapse to form BLACK HOLES. (See also CARBON CYCLE; CEPHEID VARIABLES; CONSTELLATION; COSMOLOGY; GALACTIC CLUSTER; MAGELLANIC CLOUDS; MILKY WAY; NEBULA; NOVA; PULSAR; QUASAR; SOLAR SYSTEM; STAR CLUSTER; SUPERNOVA; UNIVERSE; VARIABLE STAR.)

STARCH, a CARBOHYDRATE consisting of chains of GLUCOSE arranged in one of two forms to give the polysaccharides amylose and amylopectin. Amylose consists of an unbranched chain of 200–500 glucose units, whereas amylopectin consists of chains of 20 glucose units joined by cross links to give a highly branched structure. Most natural starches are mixtures of amylose and amylopectin; e.g., potato and cereal starches are 20%–30% amylose and 70%–80% amylopectin. Starch is found in plants, occurring in grains scattered throughout the CYTOPLASM. The grains from any particular plant have a characteristic microscopic appearance and an expert can tell the source of a starch by its appearance under the microscope. Starches in the form of rice, potatoes and wheat or other cereal products supply about 70% of the world's food.

STAR CHAMBER, English law court, formally set up in 1487, abolished (1641) by the LONG PARLIAMENT. Operating outside COMMON LAW, with no jury, it was speedy and efficient, but also arbitrary and cruel, particularly under CHARLES I.

STARFISHES, a class, Asteroidea, of star-shaped marine ECHINODERMS, with five-fold symmetry. A starfish consists of a central disk surrounded by five or more radiating arms. There is a dermal skeleton of CALCITE plates and a water-vascular system gives rise to rows of tube feet on the lower surface by which the animal moves about. The mouth is on the lower surface. Most species are carnivorous or omnivorous scavengers. Starfishes can regenerate (see REGENERATION) lost or damaged parts.

STARLINGS, a family, Sturnidae, of over 100 species of song birds. They have slender bills, an upright stance and smooth glossy plumage. Originally an Old World group, they are now found elsewhere. They feed on insects, other invertebrates and seeds, probing with the bill into turf or among leaves. They flock for feeding and roosting, with communal roosts of up to 500,000 birds.

STARR, Belle (c1848–1889), US outlaw. Her exploits with Jesse JAMES and Cole YOUNGER were made famous in *Belle Starr, the Bandit Queen; or the Female Jesse James* (1889) by Richard K. Fox. Her Okla. home became famous as an outlaw refuge.

STAR-SPANGLED BANNER, The, US national anthem, officially adopted by act of Congress in 1931. Francis Scott KEY wrote the words in 1814, during the War of 1812, and they were later set to the tune of an old English drinking song, "To Anacreon in Heaven."

STATE, COUNTY AND MUNICIPAL EMPLOYEES, American Federation of (AFSCME), largest US union of public employees (c650,000), chartered in 1936. It represents men and women working for the federal government, nonprofit agencies and universities, as well as state, county and municipal government employees. The AFSCME has had only two presidents, Arnold S. Zander (1935–64) and Jerry Wurf (1964–). Headquarters are in Washington, D.C.

STATE, US Department of, oldest executive department of the US government. Originally in charge of domestic as well as foreign affairs, it now conducts US foreign policy. It collects and analyzes information from abroad, gives policy advice to the US president and negotiates treaties and agreements. The US Foreign Service maintains some 280 diplomatic and consular offices. The secretary of state, senior member of the president's cabinet, is assisted by undersecretaries, and assistant secretaries who run regional bureaus.

STATES GENERAL, or **estates-general,** assemblies in European countries in the late Middle Ages which, in Germany, Poland, France and the Netherlands, evolved into modern parliaments. The "estates" were social classes, usually the clergy, the nobility and privileged commoners such as the new bourgeoisie of the towns. Though peasants were not represented, the estates spoke for the whole country, usually when summoned by the ruler to discuss a specific item. Their role was consultative rather than legislative.

STATES' RIGHTS, the rights of individual states in relation to the US federal government. The states' power, enshrined in the ARTICLES OF CONFEDERATION, was curtailed by the Constitution in the interests of federalism. Controversy soon arose over the relation between states' and federal rights: Thomas JEFFERSON opposed the federalists' advocacy of strong central government and declared with James MADISON, in the KENTUCKY AND VIRGINIA RESOLUTIONS (1798–99), that individual states could decide whether to enforce federal legislation or not. In the HARTFORD CONVENTION (1814–15), federalist New England expressed defiance of the Madison administration in the War of 1812, and in the 1850s several Northern states refused to implement the FUGITIVE SLAVE LAWS. The most extreme states' rights position was taken by John CALHOUN and set forth in N.C.'s NULLIFICATION ordinance (1832). Calhoun held that the Constitution in no way diminished state sovereignty; this view led logically to the doctrine of SECESSION. The Northern victory in the Civil War demolished the extreme states' rights position of nullification and secession, but states' rights has remained an important rallying cry, notably in the area of federal civil rights law. By 1980, the states' rights philosophy had found some favor in the West, where many in the "Sagebrush Rebellion" wanted their states to take control of large tracts of federal land. Some states sought exemption from the national 55mph auto speed limit.

STATIC, an accumulation of electric charge (see ELECTRICITY) responsible, e.g., for the attractive and repulsive properties produced in many plastics and fabrics by rubbing. It leaks away gradually through warm damp air, but otherwise may cause small sparks (and consequent RADIO interference) or violent discharges such as LIGHTNING.

STATICS, branch of MECHANICS dealing with systems in EQUILIBRIUM, i.e., in which all FORCES are balanced and there is no motion.

STATISTICAL MECHANICS, branch of physics that explains the thermodynamic properties of a material system (see THERMODYNAMICS) in terms of the properties of the molecules or other particles of which it is composed. Statistical mechanics can be regarded as a generalization of KINETIC THEORY. Its foundations were laid by L. BOLTZMANN, who postulated that the ENTROPY of a system in a given state is proportional to the LOGARITHM of the PROBABILITY of the system's being in that state. The other thermodynamic quantities, such as TEMPERATURE and PRESSURE, can then be derived.

STATISTICS, the area of mathematics concerned with the manipulation of numerical information. The science has two branches: descriptive statistics, dealing with the classification and presentation of data, and inferential or analytical statistics, which studies ways of collecting data, its analysis and interpretation. Sampling is fundamental to statistics. Since it is usually impractical to treat every element in a population (the group under consideration), a representative (often random) sample is instead examined, its properties being ascribed to the whole group. The data is analyzed in series of PARAMETERS such as the STANDARD DEVIATION and the MEAN of the data distribution. The distribution may be presented as a HISTOGRAM, a frequency polygon, or a frequency curve. Ideally, a statistician aims to devise a mathematical model of the distribution, especially if it approximates to normality (see NORMAL DISTRIBUTION); there are many tests which he can use to determine whether or not his model "fits" (see CHI-SQUARED TEST; STUDENT'S t-DISTRIBUTION). Statistics is used throughout science, wherever there is an element of PROBABILITY involved, and also in industry, politics, market analysis and traffic control. (See also STOCHASTIC PROCESS; VARIANCE.)

STATUE OF LIBERTY. See LIBERTY, STATUE OF.

STAUBACH, Roger (1942–   ), US football player. He won the Heisman Trophy as the Naval Academy's quarterback in 1963, spent four years in the Navy and joined the Dallas Cowboys at age 27. He was noted for passing accuracy, with an 11-year 83.5% efficiency rating, 1969–79.

STEADY STATE THEORY. See COSMOLOGY.

STEALTH, proposed penetrating manned strategic bomber almost invisible to enemy radar. A multibillion dollar aircraft, Stealth would replace the B-52. Stealth's top-secret technology has not yet been developed but will incorporate a radar-absorbent coating and ultrastreamlined shape. Aircraft could be ready in the 1990s. Stealth technology would leapfrog current technology, thus slowing the development of countermeasures.

STEAM ENGINE, the first important heat ENGINE, supplying the power that made the Industrial Revolution possible, and the principal power source for industry and transport (notably railroad locomotives and steamships) until largely superseded in the 20th century by steam TURBINES and the various INTERNAL-COMBUSTION ENGINES. The steam engine is an external-combustion engine, the steam being raised in a BOILER heated by a furnace; it is also a RECIPROCATING ENGINE. There are two main types: condensing, in which the pressure drop is caused by cooling the steam and so condensing it back to water; and noncondensing, in which the steam is exhausted to the atmosphere. The first major precursor of the steam engine was Thomas SAVERY's steam pump (1698), worked by the partial vacuum created by condensing steam in closed chambers. It had no moving parts, however, and the first working reciprocating engine was that of Thomas NEWCOMEN (1712): steam was admitted to the cylinder as the piston moved up, and was condensed by a water spray inside the cylinder, whereupon the air pressure outside forced the piston down again. James WATT radically improved Newcomen's engine (1769) by condensing the steam outside the cylinder (thus no longer having to reheat the cylinder at each stroke) and by using the steam pressure to force the piston up. He later found that, if steam were admitted for only part of the stroke, its expansion would do a good deal of extra work. (The principles involved were later studied by CARNOT and became the basis of THERMODYNAMICS.) Watt also invented the double-action principle—both strokes being powered, by applying the steam alternately to each end of the piston—the flyball GOVERNOR, and the crank and "sun-and-planet" devices for converting the piston's linear motion to rotary motion. The compound engine (1781) makes more efficient use of the steam by using the exhaust steam from one cylinder to drive the piston of a second cylinder. Later developments included the use of high-pressure steam by Richard TREVITHICK and Oliver Evans.

STEEL, an ALLOY of IRON and up to 1.7%

carbon, with small amounts of manganese, phosphorus, sulfur and silicon. These are termed carbon steels; those with other metals are termed alloy steels; low-alloy steels if they have less than 5% of the alloying metal, high-alloy steels if more than 5%. Carbon steels are far stronger than iron, and their properties can be tailored to their uses by adjusting composition and treatment. Alloy steels—including STAINLESS STEEL— are used for their special properties. Steel was first mass-produced in the mid-19th century, and steel production is now one of the chief world industries, being basic to all industrial economies. The US, the USSR and Japan are the major producers. Steel's innumerable uses include automobile manufacture, shipbuilding, skyscraper frames, reinforced concrete and machinery of all kinds. All steelmaking processes remove the impurities in the raw materials—PIG IRON, scrap steel and reduced iron ore—by oxidizing them with an air or oxygen blast. Thus most of the carbon, silicon, manganese, phosphorus and sulfur are converted to their oxides and, together with added FLUX and other waste matter present, form the SLAG. The main processes are the BESSEMER PROCESS, the Linz-Donawitz or basic oxygen process and the similar electric-arc process used for highest-quality steel, and the OPEN-HEARTH PROCESS. Most modern processes use a basic slag and a basic refractory furnace lining: acidic processes are incapable of removing phosphorus. When the impurities have been removed, desired elements are added in calculated proportions. The molten steel is cast as ingots which are shaped while still red-hot in ROLLING MILLS, or it may be cast as a continuous bar ("strand casting"). The properties of medium-carbon (0.25% to 0.45% C) and high-carbon (up to 1.7% C) steels may be greatly improved by heat treatment: ANNEALING, CASEHARDENING and TEMPERING. Steel metallurgy is somewhat complex: unhardened steel may contain combinations of three phases—austenite, ferrite and cementite—differing in structure and carbon content; hardened steel contains martensite, which may be thought of as ferrite supersaturated with carbon.

STEELE, Sir Richard (1672–1729), English author and politician, best remembered for his wide-ranging essays in two periodicals founded with ADDISON, the *Tatler* (1709) and *Spectator* (1711). He was an active Whig member of Parliament, a journalist and a successful playwright, though his sentimental comedies are not now performed.

STEEN, Jan (1626–1679), Dutch genre

painter, a master of color and facial expression. His 700 surviving works include jovial scenes of eating, drinking and revelry, portraits, landscapes and classical and biblical scenes.

STEEPLECHASING, horse-racing over a course with such obstacles as fences, hedges and water. It originated in England as a race from one church steeple to another. The world's most famous steeplechase is the English Grand National, first run in 1839. US steeplechases are normally held at racing tracks or hunts. Steeplechases on foot are now an Olympic sport.

STEFANSSON, Vilhjalmur (1879–1962), Canadian arctic explorer and author. He became an authority on Eskimo life and arctic survival. Stefansson also charted several islands in the W Canadian Arctic. He was a northern studies consultant at Dartmouth College, N.H., from 1947.

STEFFENS, Lincoln (1866–1936), US journalist. One of the MUCKRAKERS, he wrote for *McClure's Magazine* and the *American Magazine* and was famous for his exposés of corruption in politics and business. A selection of his articles was published in *The Shame of the Cities* (1904) and his autobiography (1931) is a classic of the muckraking era.

STEICHEN, Edward (1879–1973), pioneer US photographer. After studying in Paris he worked in fashion, advertising and theater. At New York City's Museum of Modern Art he mounted the 1955 *Family of Man* exhibition.

STEIN, Gertrude (1874–1946), US author and celebrated personality who lived in Paris from 1903. Her first important work was *Three Lives* (1909). Stein is best known for her experimental syntax and her friendships with such figures as PICASSO, HEMINGWAY, MATISSE and GIDE. They are described in *The Autobiography of Alice B. Toklas* (1933).

STEINBECK, John (1902–1968), US author who came to the fore in the 1930s with his novels about poverty and social injustice. He won a Pulitzer Prize for *The Grapes of Wrath* (1939), about migrant farm workers in Cal., and the 1962 Nobel Prize for Literature. His other works include *Tortilla Flat* (1935), *Of Mice and Men* (1937), *Cannery Row* (1945), *East of Eden* (1952) and *The Winter of Our Discontent* (1961).

STEINEM, Gloria (1934–), US feminist and writer, notably of a lively column in *New York* magazine; a skillful publicist for the women's movement. A co-founder (1971) of the National Women's Political Caucus, she also founded

(1972) and edited *Ms.* magazine, whose pages have consistently criticized women's traditional place in society.

STEINER, Maximilian (1888–1971), Austrian-born film composer who initiated the use of symphonic-style music for movies. His orchestrations for such classics as *King Kong* (1933) and *Gone With the Wind* (1939) incorporated special effects and were composed for maximum psychological impact and drama.

STEINER, Rudolf (1861–1925), Austrian founder of ANTHROPOSOPHY, an attempt to recapture spiritual realities ignored by modern man. He founded the Waldorf School movement, and stressed music and drama as aids to self-discovery. Works include *The Philosophy of Spiritual Activity* (1922).

STEINKRAUS, William (1925–), US equestrian. He was a member of six Olympic teams, 1952–72, and won four medals, including a gold in individual jumping (1968). He was named Rider of the Decade in 1970.

STEINMAN, David Barnard (1886–1960), US engineer whose pioneering aerodynamic studies led to the construction of extremely long yet stable bridges. He designed more than 400 bridges including the Triborough (NYC; 1936) and Mackinac Straits (Michigan; 1957).

STEINMETZ, Charles Proteus (1865–1923), formerly **Karl August Rudolf Steinmetz**, German-born US electrical engineer who is best remembered for working out the theory of alternating current (1893 onward), thereby making it possible for AC to be used rather than DC in most applications.

STEINWAY, German-American family of piano manufacturers. **Henry Engelhard** (1797–1871), who changed his name from Steinweg after migrating in 1851 from Germany to the US, founded the family business in 1853. In 1855 he began building pianos with cast-iron frames. The business was carried on by his sons **Christian Friedrich Theodore** (1825–1889) and **William** (1835–1896).

STELLA, Joseph (1877–1946), Italian-born US artist, best known of America's futurist painters. He was fascinated by the world of steel and electricity and filled his canvases with images of bridges, skyscrapers and subways.

STENCIL. See SILK-SCREEN PRINTING.

STENDHAL (1783–1842), pen name of Marie-Henri Beyle, French pioneer of the psychological novel. *The Red and the Black* (1830) and *The Charterhouse of Parma* (1839) explore the search for happiness through love and political power, with minute analysis of the hero's feelings. His treatment of the figure of the "outsider," his social criticism and brilliant ironic prose style make him one of the greatest and most "modern" of French novelists.

STENGEL, Casey (1890–1975), US baseball manager. A popular and garrulous figure, he led the New York Yankees to seven world championships 1949–58, and managed the New York Mets 1962–65. He was elected to the Baseball Hall of Fame in 1966.

STEN GUN, simple type of submachine gun, used extensively in WWII by British airborne troops and supplied to partisans in occupied Europe, since it could use 9mm pistol ammunition.

STENNIS, John Cornelius (1901–   ), US legislator. A Democrat, he was a Mississippi circuit judge until elected US senator in 1947. As Armed Services Committee chairman he backed Vietnam involvement but called for limits to presidential powers to commit troops. He recovered from being shot in a robbery attempt in 1973.

STENO, Nicolaus (1638–1686), or **Niels Stensen,** Danish geologist, anatomist and bishop. In 1669 he published the results of his geological studies: he recognized that many rocks are sedimentary (see SEDIMENTARY ROCKS); that FOSSILS are the remains of once-living creatures and that they can be used for DATING purposes, and established many of the tenets of modern crystallography.

STENOGRAPHY. See SHORTHAND.

STENOTYPE, system of machine SHORTHAND that uses a keyboard machine like a typewriter except that several keys may be depressed at once. Letter groups phonetically represent words. The machine, silent in operation, is capable of 250 words/min.

STEPHEN, Saint (d. c36 AD), first Christian martyr. Accused of blasphemy, he was stoned to death (Acts 6–8). His feast day is Dec. 26.

STEPHEN, Sir Leslie (1832–1904), English man of letters. He edited (1882–91) *The Dictionary of National Biography.* A freethinker, he wrote major studies of 18th-century English literature and philosophy. Virginia WOOLF was his daughter.

STEPHEN (c1097–1154), king of England 1135–54. A nephew of Henry I, he was briefly supplanted (1141) by Matilda, Henry's daughter. Though a just and generous ruler, he was not strong enough to govern the warring factions of his realm.

STEPHEN I, Saint (977–1038), first king

of Hungary, often regarded as founder of the state. His formal coronation in 1000 marked Hungary's entry into Christian Europe. He established a strong church, and modeled his administration on German lines.

STEPHENS, Alexander Hamilton (1812–1883), vice-president of the Confederate States of America 1861–65. A congressman from Ga. (1843–59), he opposed secession, but stayed loyal to his state in the Civil War. He led the delegation to the Hampton Roads peace conference (1865). Imprisoned for six months after the war, he returned to serve again in Congress (1873–82) and as governor of Ga. (1882–83).

STEPHENSON, British family of inventors and railroad engineers. **George Stephenson** (1781–1848) first worked on stationary STEAM ENGINES, reconstructing and modifying one by NEWCOMEN (c1812). His first LOCOMOTIVE, the *Blucher,* took to the rails in 1814: it traveled at 4mph (about 6.5km/h) hauling coal for the Killingworth colliery, and incorporated an important development, flanged wheels. About this time, independently of DAVY, he invented a SAFETY LAMP: this earned him £1,000 (then about $5,000), which helped finance further locomotive experiments. In 1821 he was appointed to survey and engineer a line from Darlington to Stockton: in 1825 his *Locomotion* carried 450 people along the line at a rate of 15mph (about 25km/h), and the modern RAILROAD was born. This was followed in 1829 by the success of the *Rocket,* which ran the 40mi (65km) of his new Manchester–Liverpool line at speeds up to 30mph (about 48km/h), the first mainline passenger rail journey. His only son **Robert Stephenson** (1803–1859) helped his father on both of these lines, and with the *Rocket,* but is best known as a BRIDGE builder, notably for the tubular bridges over the Menai Straits, North Wales (1850), and the St. Lawrence at Montreal (1859).

STEPINAC, Aloysius (1898–1960), Yugoslav Roman Catholic cardinal. Archbishop of Zagreb (1937), he denounced TITO's communism, was accused of Nazi collaboration, and imprisoned 1946–51. On his elevation to cardinal (1952) Yugoslavia broke off relations with the Vatican.

STEREOCHEMISTRY, the study of the arrangement in space of atoms in molecules, and of the properties which depend on such arrangements. The two chief branches are the study of STEREOISOMERS and stereospecific reactions (which involve only one isomer); and CONFORMATIONAL ANALYSIS, including the study of steric effects on reaction rates and mechanisms.

STEREOPHONIC SOUND. See HIGH FIDELITY.

STEREOSCOPE, optical instrument that simulates BINOCULAR VISION by presenting slightly different pictures to the two eyes so that an apparently three-dimensional image is produced. The simplest stereoscope, invented in the 1830s, used a system of mirrors and prisms (later, converging lenses) to view the pictures. In the color separation method the left image is printed or projected in red and seen through a red filter, and likewise for the right image in blue. A similar method uses images projected by POLARIZED LIGHT and viewed through polarizing filters, the polarization axes being at right angles. The pictures are produced by a stereoscopic camera with two lenses a small distance apart. The stereoscope is useful in making relief maps by aerial photographic survey.

STERILIZATION, surgical procedure in which the FALLOPIAN TUBES are cut and tied to prevent eggs reaching the WOMB, thus providing permanent CONTRACEPTION. The procedure is essentially irreversible and should only be performed when a woman has completed her family. It may be done by a small abdominal operation, at CESARIAN SECTION or through an instrument, the laparoscope. (See also VASECTOMY.) *Also*, the treatment of medical equipment to ensure that it is not contaminated by BACTERIA and other microorganisms. Metal and linen objects are often sterilized by heat (in AUTOCLAVES). Chemical disinfection is also used and plastic equipment is exposed to GAMMA RAYS.

STERN, Isaac (1920–   ), US violinist. Born in Kremenets, USSR, he studied and made his debut in 1931 in San Francisco.

STERN, Lina Solomonovna (1878–1968), Russian physiologist who did pioneering research in the chemical foundation of physiological processes. The most prominent woman scientist in the USSR, she directed the Moscow Institute of Physiology (1925–49) and was the first woman elected to the Soviet Academy of Sciences (1939).

STERNBERG, Joseph von (1891–1969), Viennese-born US film director. He is most famous for the films he made with Marlene DIETRICH. These include *The Blue Angel* (1930), *Morocco* (1930) and *Shanghai Express* (1932).

STERNE, Laurence (1713–1768), English novelist and clergyman, author of *The Life and Opinions of Tristram Shandy, Gentleman* (1760–67). One of the most widely read novels of its day, this whimsical work proceeds by association of ideas and

conversation rather than by plot structure. *A Sentimental Journey* (1768) recounts travels in France and Italy.

STEROIDS, HORMONES produced in the body from CHOLESTEROL, mainly by the ADRENAL GLANDS, and related to ESTROGENS and ANDROGENS. All have chemical structures based on that of the STEROLS. Cortisol is the main glucocorticoid (steroids that regulate GLUCOSE metabolism) and aldosterone the main mineralocorticoid (regulating SALT, POTASSIUM and WATER balance). Increased amounts of cortisol are secreted during times of stress, e.g., SHOCK, SURGERY and severe infection. Steroids, mainly of the glucocorticoid type, are also given in doses above normal hormone levels to obtain other effects, e.g., the suppression of INFLAMMATION, ALLERGY and IMMUNITY. Diseases that respond to this include ASTHMA, MULTIPLE SCLEROSIS, some forms of NEPHRITIS, inflammatory GASTROINTESTINAL TRACT disease and cerebral EDEMA; SKIN and EYE conditions may be treated with local steroids. High-dose systemic steroids may have adverse effects if used for long periods; they may cause ACNE, osteoporosis, hypertension, fluid retention, altered facial appearance and growth retardation in children.

STETHOSCOPE, instrument devised by René H. Laënnec (1781–1826) for listening to sounds within the body, especially those from the HEART, LUNGS, ABDOMEN and blood vessels.

STEUBEN, Friedrich Wilhelm Augustin, Baron von (1730–1794), Prussian soldier who trained the CONTINENTAL ARMY. Arriving in America in 1777 with an introduction from Benjamin Franklin, he was appointed inspector general of the army by Congress in 1778. He organized Washington's troops in Valley Forge into an effective fighting force, seen at the battle of MONMOUTH (1778) and siege of YORKTOWN (1780).

STEVENS, US family of inventors and engineers. **John Stevens** (1749–1838) made many contributions to steamboat development, including the first with a screw PROPELLER (1802) and the first seagoing steamboat (*Phoenix*, 1809). He also built (1825) the first US steam locomotive. His son **Robert Livingston Stevens** (1787–1856) assisted his father, and invented the inverted-T rail still used in modern RAILROADS (1830) as well as the technique of fastening them to wooden sleepers. **Edwin Augustus Stevens** (1795–1868), another son, also made contributions to railroad technology.

STEVENS, George (1905–1975), US

director of such classic films as *Swing Time* (1936), *Gunga Din* (1939), *Talk of the Town* (1942) and *Shane* (1952). He won Academy Awards for *A Place in the Sun* (1951) and *Giant* (1956).

STEVENS, John Paul (1920–   ), US jurist, served on the US Court of Appeals and then, by appointment of President Ford (1975), on the US Supreme Court as an associate justice.

STEVENS, Thaddeus (1792–1868), controversial US politician. A staunch opponent of slavery, he wielded great power as a Vt. congressman and chairman of the US Senate Ways and Means Committee during the Civil War. He afterward dominated the joint committee on RECONSTRUCTION, leading the Radical Republicans with Senator SUMNER. He held that the defeated Southern states were "conquered provinces," subject to the will of Congress. He proposed the 14th Amendment, fought for Negro suffrage, and led in the impeachment of President Andrew Johnson.

STEVENS, Wallace (1879–1955), US poet. He worked for a Connecticut insurance company and achieved wide literary recognition only with the 1955 Pulitzer Prize for his *Collected Poems*. Rich in imagery and vocabulary, his often difficult verse explores the use of imagination to ease tragic reality and give meaning to its confusion.

STEVENSON, Adlai Ewing, name of two US politicians. Adlai Ewing Stevenson (1835–1914), a lawyer and Democratic representative for Ill. (1875–76, 1879–80), was elected US vice-president in Cleveland's second term (1893–97). Adlai Ewing Stevenson (1900–1965), his grandson, also a lawyer, was special assistant to the secretary of the navy (1941–44) and a delegate to the UN (1946–47). In 1948 he was elected governor of Ill., where he backed reform. He was chosen as Democratic presidential candidate in 1952 and 1956 but lost to Eisenhower. His policies of halting the arms race and promoting the economies of Africa and Asia were unpopular at home. He lost the 1960 nomination to Kennedy. From 1961 to his death he was US ambassador to the UN.

STEVENSON, Robert Louis (1850–1894), Scottish author best known for such adventure stories as *Treasure Island* (1883) and *Kidnapped* (1886). He also wrote *Dr. Jekyll and Mr. Hyde* (1886), a horrific tale of inherent good and evil, and the sensitive verse of *A Child's Garden of Verses* (1885), as well as short stories, essays and travel books. A sufferer from tuberculosis, he sailed with his US wife to the South Pacific (1888) and settled in Samoa, where he continued to write and tell stories.

STEVINUS, Simon (1548–1620), or **Simon Stevin**, Dutch mathematician and engineer who made many contributions to HYDRO-STATICS; disproved, before GALILEO, ARISTOTLE's theory that heavy bodies fall more swiftly than light ones; introduced the DECIMAL SYSTEM into popular use; and first used the parallelogram of forces in MECHANICS.

STEWARD, Julian Haynes (1902–1972), US anthropologist. A major exponent of cultural evolution, he was among the first anthropologists to emphasize ecology as a determinant of culture. He edited the *Handbook of South American Indians* (7 vol., 1946–59) and wrote *Theory of Culture Change* (1955).

STEWART, Dugald (1753–1828), Scottish philosopher, a major member of the COMMON SENSE SCHOOL and a principal disciple of Thomas REID.

STEWART, James (1908–   ), US film actor known for his slow drawl and a screen image that exuded shyness and honesty. He appeared in many film classics including *Mr. Smith Goes to Washington* (1939), *It's a Wonderful Life* (1946) and *Rear Window* (1954). He won an Academy Award for *The Philadelphia Story* (1940).

STEWART, Potter (1915–   ), associate justice of the US Supreme Court 1958–1981. Appointed by President Eisenhower, he held a moderate point of view and often cast a "swing" vote.

STIEGEL, Henry William (1729–1785), German-born US iron and glass manufacturer. He emigrated to Philadelphia in 1750, made a fortune manufacturing iron stoves, and in 1760 founded Manheim, Pa., where he established a famous glass-factory. Extravagance led to bankruptcy in 1774.

STIEGLITZ, Alfred (1864–1946), US photographer who helped make photography a recognized art form; and who founded the gallery "291" in New York, where he put on pioneering exhibitions. A founding member of the Photo-Secession, he is known for his city and cloudscapes and many portraits of his artist wife, Georgia O'KEEFFE.

STIFTER, Adalbert (1805–1868), Austrian writer noted for his fine descriptions of nature and his gentle praise of humble virtues. His works include *Colored Stones* (1853: a collection of short stories) and the novel *Indian Summer* (1857).

STILL, William Grant (1895–1978), US composer whose three ballets, two symphonies and three operas are largely devoted to black themes. Langston HUGHES wrote the libretto for his opera *Troubled Island* (1938).

STIMSON, Henry Lewis (1867–1950), US lawyer and statesman, author of the "Stimson Doctrine." As secretary of state (1929–33), he declared at the time of Japan's invasion of Manchuria that the US would not recognize any territorial changes or treaties which impaired US treaty rights or were brought about by force. Recalled from retirement to become secretary of war (1940–45), he strongly advocated development and use of the atomic bomb.

STINNES, Hugo (1870–1924), German industrialist. Before, during and after WWI he built up a vast industrial empire. A founder of the right-wing National People's party, he served in the Reichstag (parliament) 1920–24.

STIRLING ENGINE, a type of EXTERNAL-COMBUSTION ENGINE invented in Scotland by the Rev. Robert Stirling in 1816. Long in disuse, the Stirling engine has recently become a subject of investigation as a possible substitute for the gasoline engine, but so far has not proved practical. Different versions of the Stirling engine exist, but all involve a gas (usually air) circulating in a closed system of cylinders and pistons and deriving energy from an external source of heat.

STOCHASTIC PROCESS, any process governed by the laws of PROBABILITY: for example, the BROWNIAN MOTION of the submicroscopic particles in a colloidal solution (see COLLOID). The term is usually confined to processes that develop through time, each step taking place according to probabilities that depend on the results of the previous steps.

STOCKHAUSEN, Karlheinz (1928–), German composer and theorist. An experimenter with a variety of avant-garde musical techniques, including electronic, twelve-tone and aleatory music, he studied with Frank Martin, Messiaen and Milhaud and was much influenced by Anton Webern. He has produced work like *Gruppen* (1959), in which three orchestras play "groups" or blocks of sounds against each other, and the electronic *Kontakte* (1959–60).

STOCKHOLM, capital of Sweden, an architecturally fine city on a network of islands on the E coast. It is Sweden's major commercial, industrial, cultural and financial center, and an important port. Chief industries are machinery, paper and print, shipbuilding, chemicals and foodstuffs. Founded in the 13th century, it was long

dominated by the HANSEATIC LEAGUE. Liberated in a national uprising in 1523, it became the capital in 1634. Pop 653,900.

STOCKMAN, David (1946–), US public official. An active member of the anti-Vietnam War movement in the 1960s, he gradually moved to a more conservative outlook. In 1976 he was elected to Congress as a Republican from Michigan, serving two terms. He established a reputation as a critic of government spending and was chosen in 1981 by President Reagan as director of the Office of Management and Budget. He played a leading role in Reagan's effort to cut domestic federal spending.

STOCKS AND STOCK MARKET. Stocks represent shares of ownership in a corporation or public body. Issuing stocks provides a means for companies to raise CAPITAL (see INVESTMENT). Individuals buy stocks because they can easily be converted into cash and may gain in value. The initial par value of a stock is determined by the assets of the company, such as its plant, machinery, property. But par value has no bearing on the market value of a stock, which is the price people are willing to pay. If a company is seen to be doing well, the market value can soar above its original par value. This is one way an investor can make capital gains by owning stocks. A stockholder also expects to receive an annual dividend based on the profits of the company. Stocks can be divided into two categories, preferred and common. The preferred stockholder is entitled to a fixed percentage claim on profits prior to the common stockholder, who then gets the rest. Depending on profits, the common stockholder may either get no dividend, or get a much higher return than the preferred stockholder; common stocks are more speculative.

The stock market, or exchange, is the place where people who want to sell and buy stocks can get together. Most transactions are carried out by stockbrokers, who are paid a commission on each transaction. In the US, a customer may also buy stocks on credit, but he must pay an amount, or margin, specified by the Federal Reserve System, toward the transaction, with the balance advanced by the broker. All stock exchanges in the US are registered and regulated by the SECURITIES AND EXCHANGE COMMISSION. (See AMERICAN STOCK EXCHANGE; NEW YORK STOCK EXCHANGE.)

STOICISM, ancient Greek school of philosophy founded by ZENO OF CITIUM, who taught in a STOA in Athens c300 BC. Much influenced by the CYNICS, the Stoics believed that man should live rationally and in harmony with nature, and that virtue is the only good. In performing his duty the virtuous man should be indifferent to pleasure, as well as to pain and misfortune, thus rising above the effects of chance and achieving spiritual freedom and conformity with the divine reason controlling all nature. Stoicism was influential for many centuries; among the most famous of the later Stoics were SENECA, EPICTETUS and MARCUS AURELIUS.

STOKER, Bram (Abraham Stoker; 1847–1912), British writer and theatrical manager best known for his classic novel of horror, *Dracula* (1897). In addition, he was manager to Henry IRVING 1878–1905.

STOKOWSKI, Leopold (1882–   ), brilliant, flamboyant British-born US conductor. He gained his early reputation as musical director of the Philadelphia Orchestra (1912–36), and it was under his baton that they played the music for Disney's *Fantasia* (1940). He was noted especially for his modern repertoire and innovative orchestration.

STOLYPIN, Pyotr Arkadevich (1862–1911), prime minister of imperial Russia 1906–11. Ruthless in suppressing unrest and opposition, he yet instituted land reforms aimed at creating a conservative landowning peasantry, thereby making right-wing enemies. He was assassinated by a revolutionary who was also a police agent.

STOMACH, the large distensible hopper of the DIGESTIVE SYSTEM. It receives food boluses from the ESOPHAGUS and mixes them with hydrochloric acid and the stomach ENZYMES; fats are partially emulsified. After some time, the pyloric SPHINCTER relaxes and food enters the DUODENUM and the rest of the GASTROINTESTINAL TRACT. Diseases of the stomach include ULCER, CANCER and pyloric stenosis, causing pain, anorexia or VOMITING; these often require SURGERY.

STONE, Edward Durell (1902–1978), US architect whose works include the US pavilion for the 1958 Brussels World's Fair, the US embassy in Delhi (1958) and the J. F. Kennedy Center in Washington, D.C. (1971).

STONE, Harlan Fiske (1872–1946), appointed attorney general in 1924 to restore confidence in the scandal-ridden Justice Department, became associate justice (1925–41) and chief justice (1941–46) of the US Supreme Court. He was noted for his dissenting opinions, many upholding NEW DEAL legislation.

STONE, Irving (1903–   ), US author noted for carefully researched biographical novels such as *Lust for Life* (1934) about Van Gogh, *The Agony and the Ecstasy* (1961) about Michelangelo, and *The Passions of the Mind* (1971) about Freud.

STONE, I(sidor) F(einstein), (1907–   ), US journalist who founded and wrote *I. F. Stone's Weekly* (1953–71). The prestigious journal maintained a constant stream of criticism and comment on US politics, in particular attacking McCarthyism and the Vietnam War.

STONE, Lucy (1818–1893), US reformer and campaigner for women's rights. A fervent abolitionist, she helped to found the American Woman Suffrage Association (1869) and edited its magazine *Woman's Journal* (1870–93).

STONE AGE, the stage in man's cultural development preceding the BRONZE AGE and the IRON AGE (see also PRIMITIVE MAN). It is characterized by man's use of exclusively stone tools and weapons, though some made of bone, wood, etc., have been used. It is split up into three periods: the **Paleolithic,** or Old Stone Age, began with the emergence of man-like creatures, the earliest stone tools being some 2.5 million years old and associated with the australopithecines (see PREHISTORIC MAN). Paleolithic tools, if worked at all, are made of chipped stone. The **Mesolithic,** or Middle Stone Age, was confined exclusively to NW Europe. Here, between c10,000 and c3000 BC, various peoples enjoyed a culture showing similarities with both Paleolithic and Neolithic. The **Neolithic,** or New Stone Age, began in SW Asia about 8000 BC and spread throughout Europe between 6000 and 2000 BC; it was signaled by the development of agriculture, with consequent increase in stability of the population and hence elaboration of social structure. The tools of this period are of polished stone. Apart from farming, men also worked mines. The Neolithic merged slowly into the Early Bronze Age.

STONEHENGE, the ruins of a MEGALITHIC MONUMENT, dating from the STONE AGE and early BRONZE AGE, on Salisbury Plain, S England. Its most noticeable features are concentric rings of stones surrounding a horseshoe of upright stones, and a solitary vertical stone, the Heel Stone, some 100m to the NE. Stonehenge was built between c1900 BC and c1400 BC in three distinct phases. It appears to have been both a religious center and an observatory from which predictions of astronomical events could be made.

STONEWARE. See POTTERY AND PORCELAIN.

STOPES, Marie Charlotte Carmichael

(1880–1958), British pioneer of sex education and family planning. A professional paleobotanist, she wrote *Wise Parenthood* (1918) and set up (1921) the first birth-control clinic.

STOPPARD, Tom (1937–   ), English playwright best known for *Rosencrantz and Guildenstern Are Dead* (1966), an existentialist drama centering on two minor characters from Shakespeare's *Hamlet*. The scintillating dialogue that critics admired in this play are also evident in *Travesties* (1974).

STOREY, David (Malcolm) (1933–   ), English playwright and novelist whose two best-known works, the novel *This Sporting Life* (1960) and the play *The Changing Room* (1971), are based on his years as a professional rugby player.

STORKS, large, heavily-built birds, family Ciconiidae, with long legs and necks, long, stout bills and commonly black and white plumage. The long legs and slightly webbed feet are adaptations for wading in shallow water, where they feed on freshwater animals and large insects. They tend to be gregarious and characteristic greeting ceremonies may be observed at nests and roosts. The family is largely of tropical distribution, the two temperate-breeding species undertaking long migrations to their breeding grounds.

STORM AND STRESS. See STURM UND DRANG.

STORM TROOPER (Sturmabteilungen, or SA), the strongarm gangs set up in Germany in 1921 by Ernst ROEHM to destroy resistance to the Nazis. They grew into a private army 2,000,000 strong, but were virtually disbanded after Hitler had Roehm killed in 1934.

STORY, Joseph (1779–1845), associate justice of the US Supreme Court from 1811, author of nine great legal commentaries and professor of law at Harvard from 1829. He participated in many historic decisions shaping federal law under Chief Justice MARSHALL, and exercised a great influence on US jurisprudence and legal education.

STOUT, Rex Todhunter (1886–1975), American writer of detective novels featuring the sedentary, beer drinking, orchid-growing gourmet and sleuth, Nero Wolfe. Wolfe was introduced in *Fer-de-Lance* (1929).

STOWE, Harriet Elizabeth Beecher (1811–1896), US author famous for the antislavery novel *Uncle Tom's Cabin* (1852). Born into the BEECHER family, she moved to Cincinnati, Ohio, in 1832, and there learned about slavery in nearby Ky.

Her other books include the documentary *The Key to Uncle Tom's Cabin* (1853), and the novels *Dred: A Tale of the Great Dismal Swamp* (1856) and *The Minister's Wooing* (1859).

STRABISMUS, cross-eye, or **squint,** a disorder of the EYES in which the alignment of the two ocular axes is not parallel, impairing binocular VISION; the eyes may diverge or converge. It is often congenital and may require SURGERY if orthoptics fail. Acquired squints are usually due to nerve or muscle disease and cause double vision.

STRABO (c63 BC–c23 AD), Greek geographer and historian. His *Historical Sketches* in 47 books are almost entirely lost, but the 17 books of his *Geography* have survived and are a principal source for our knowledge of ancient geography.

STRACHEY, Giles Lytton (1880–1932), English biographer and critic prominent in the BLOOMSBURY GROUP. His irreverent studies of the famous in *Eminent Victorians* (1918), and *Queen Victoria* (1921) caused a stir but suited the iconoclastic mood which followed WWI. They are still admired for their wit, irony and style. His last major work was *Elizabeth and Essex* (1928).

STRADIVARI, or **Stradivarius, Antonio** (c1644–1737), Italian violin maker, most famous of a group of fine craftsmen who worked in Cremona (see also AMATI; GUANERI). Stradivarius violins, violas and cellos are today highly prized.

STRAND, Paul (1890–1976), US photographer, a protégé of STIEGLITZ, who began his career with pictures of New York City's streets, moved on to still-life photos of the wilderness and film documentaries, and, after his move to France in 1950, became a photo essayist. His subjects included Italian peasants (1954), Hebrides fishermen (1968), and Egyptian fellahin (1969).

STRASBERG, Lee (1901–   ), Austrian-born US acting teacher and stage director, advocate of STANISLAVSKI'S "method" acting. A founder and director of the Group Theatre (1930–37), he became director of the Actor's Studio in New York in 1948, instructing BRANDO and others. Subsequently, he himself appeared as an actor in *The Godfather* (1972) and other films.

STRASSMANN, Fritz (1902–   ); German physicist who worked on uranium FISSION with Otto HAHN after Lise MEITNER had fled Germany (1938). All three shared the 1966 Fermi Award.

STRATEGIC AIR COMMAND (SAC), main US nuclear striking force, containing all US land-based ballistic missiles and long-range bombers. SAC is linked to US warning systems and is a specified command under the Defense Department. Its mission is global.

STRATEGIC ARMS LIMITATION TALKS (SALT), negotiations between the US and the USSR aimed at preventing the expansion of strategic weapons in both countries. SALT I, which began in 1969 and terminated in 1972, achieved the ABM Treaty and the Interim Agreement on some offensive weapons. SALT II was initiated in 1972. A treaty was signed in 1979 but is as yet unratified.

STRATEGY, the general design behind a war or military campaign. In a wider sense it involves "grand strategy": delineation of broad political objectives. Strategy cannot be reduced to a set of general rules, but it always involves long-term planning; defining military objectives; analyzing one's own and the enemy's strength; understanding the geography of the land and planning moves accordingly; assessing options and preparing contingency plans; organizing transport, supplies and communications; anticipating enemy actions and determining when and where to fight. Strategy and strategic theories are continually modified by technological, social and political changes. Since WWII, nuclear weapons at one extreme and GUERRILLA WARFARE at the other have made obsolete conventional strategy and it has become impossible to separate purely military strategy from wider political and economic objectives.

STRATFORD-UPON-AVON, market town in W central England, home of SHAKESPEARE. A tourist meeca, it contains his birthplace (now a museum), his tomb in Holy Trinity church, and the riverside theater where the Royal Shakespeare Company performs. Anne Hathaway's cottage is nearby. The town also supports some light industry. Pop 19,449.

STRATHCONA AND MOUNT ROYAL, Donald Alexander Smith, 1st Baron (1820–1914), Canadian fur trader, financier, statesman and builder of the Canadian Pacific railroad (1885). Emigrating from Scotland in 1838, he joined the Hudson's Bay Company, eventually becoming governor in 1889. A member of the Canadian Parliament 1871–80, 1887–96, he was High Commissioner in London 1896–1914.

STRATIGRAPHY, the branch of GEOLOGY concerned with the description, sequence, classification and correlation of bodies of stratified rock, their depositional environments and their vertical and lateral relationships. (See also PALEONTOLOGY; ROCKS; SEDIMENTARY ROCKS.)

STRAUS, Nathan (1848–1931), German-born US merchant and philanthropist who purchased R. H. Macy and Co. in New York City and developed it into the world's largest department store. He was a leader in the field of child health and established milk distribution centers throughout the US.

STRAUS, Oscar (1870–1954), Austrian composer, famous for *The Chocolate Soldier* (1908) and about 50 other operettas. He left Europe to escape the Nazis but later returned to Austria.

STRAUSS, Franz Joseph (1915–   ), West German political leader, head of the conservative Bavarian Christian Social Union. As minister of defense (1956–62), he advocated German rearmament. Criticized for the arrest of the editors of the magazine *Der Spiegel*, he lost his post, but returned as finance minister 1966–69.

STRAUSS, Johann, name of two famous Viennese composers of WALTZES. **Johann, the Elder** (1804–1849) achieved immense popularity and established the distinctive light style of the Viennese waltz. **Johann, the Younger** (1825–1899), wrote many favorites, including *The Blue Danube* (1866), *Tales from the Vienna Woods* (1868) and the opera *Die Fledermaus* (*The Bat*, 1873).

STRAUSS, Lewis Lichtenstein (1896–1974), US banker, member (1946–50) and chairman (1953–58) of the US Atomic Energy Commission, where he clashed with OPPENHEIMER over the development of the hydrogen bomb, which he supported. He became Secretary of Commerce 1958–59.

STRAUSS, Richard (1864–1949), German composer and conductor, the last of the great Romantic composers. He leapt to fame with the tone poem *Don Juan* (1888). Other symphonic poems include *Till Eulenspiegel* (1895), *Thus Spake Zarathustra* (1896), *Don Quixote* (1898) and *A Hero's Life* (1898). After 1900 he concentrated on vocal music, and with von HOFMANNSTHAL as librettist produced brilliantly scored and popular operas, including *Salome* (1905), *Elektra* (1909), *Der Rosenkavalier* (1911) and *Die Frau ohne Schatten* (1919).

STRAVINSKY, Igor Fyodorovich (1882–1971), one of the greatest modern composers, born in Russia. Taught by RIMSKY-KORSAKOV, he caused a sensation with his scores for DIAGHILEV's ballets: *The Firebird* (1910), *Petrouchka* (1911) and *The Rite of Spring* (1913). From 1920 he lived in France, adopting an austere neoclassical style, as in *Symphonies of Wind Instruments* (1920), the opera *Oedipus Rex* (1927) and *Symphony of Psalms* (1930). Emigrating to the US in 1939, he became a US citizen in 1945. Later works include *Symphony in Three Movements* (1942–45) and the opera *The Rake's Progress* (1951). He finally adopted TWELVE-TONE composition in works like *Agon* (1953–57) and *Threni* (1958).

STREAMLINING, the design of the shape of a body so as to minimize drag as it travels through a fluid; essential to the efficiency of aircraft, ships and submarines. At subsonic speeds turbulent flow is minimized by using a shape rounded in front, tapering to a point behind (see AERODYNAMICS; AIRFOIL; FLUID MECHANICS). At SUPERSONIC speeds a different shape is needed, thin and pointed at both ends, to minimize the shock waves.

STREAM OF CONSCIOUSNESS, a literary technique in which a character's thoughts are presented in the jumbled, inconsequential manner of real life, apparently without the author imposing any framework on them. Its best-known exponents are Marcel PROUST, James JOYCE and Virginia WOOLF.

STREEP, Meryl (1949–), US actress noted for her offbeat beauty and incisive performances. Her films include *Kramer vs. Kramer* (1978) and *The French Lieutenant's Woman* (1981).

STREICHER, Julius (1885–1946), German Nazi journalist. In 1923 he founded *Der Stürmer*, a fanatical anti-Semitic periodical which he edited until 1945. He was tried at NUREMBERG and hanged.

STREISAND, Barbra (1942–), US singer and actress whose off-beat beauty, irrepressible personality and unique singing style won her a huge following during the 1960s and 1970s. She achieved fame in the Broadway musical *I Can Get It For You Wholesale* (1962) and starred in such film musicals as *Funny Girl* (1968), for which she won an Academy Award, and *Hello Dolly* (1969) and in several dramatic films, including *The Way We Were* (1973).

STREPTOCOCCUS, BACTERIUM responsible for many common infections including sore throat, TONSILLITIS, SCARLET FEVER, IMPETIGO, cellulitis, ERYSIPELAS and PUERPERAL FEVER; a related organism is a common cause of PNEUMONIA and one type may cause endocarditis on damaged HEART valves. PENICILLIN is the ANTIBIOTIC of choice. RHEUMATIC FEVER and BRIGHT'S DISEASE are late immune responses to streptococcus.

STRESEMAN, Gustav (1878–1929), German statesman awarded the 1926 Nobel Peace Prize. He founded (1918) and led the conservative German People's Party, was chancellor of the Republic in 1923 and foreign minister 1923–29. He followed a program of moderation and reconciliation with Germany's former enemies, and as an author of the LOCARNO TREATIES (1925) took Germany into the League of Nations as an equal of the other powers.

STRIKES AND LOCKOUTS. See UNIONS.

STRINDBERG, Johan August (1849–1912), Swedish playwright and novelist. His biting, pessimistic plays, *Mäster Olof* (1873), *The Father* (1887) and *Miss Julie* (1888) made a deep mark on modern drama; his novel *The Red Room* (1879) about injustice and hypocrisy won acclaim. Later plays such as *The Ghost Sonata* (1907) combine dream sequences with Swedenborgian religious mysticism.

STRINGED INSTRUMENTS, musical instruments whose sound is produced by vibrating strings or wires, the pitch being controlled by their length and tension. In the BALALAIKA, BANJO, GUITAR, HARP, LUTE, MANDOLIN, SITAR, UKULELE and ZITHER, the vibration is produced by plucking with the fingers or a plectrum. In the KEYBOARD INSTRUMENTS (CLAVICHORD, HARPSICHORD, PIANO, SPINET, VIRGINAL) the strings are either plucked or struck by hammers operated by depressing the keys. The VIOLA and VIOLIN families are played with a horsehair bow, which is drawn across the string.

STROBOSCOPE, instrument that produces regular brief flashes of intense light, used to study periodic motion, to test machinery and in high-speed photography. When the flash frequency exactly equals that of the rotation or vibration, the object is illuminated in the same position during each cycle, and appears stationary. A gas discharge lamp is used, with flash duration about 1 μs and frequency from 2 to 3,000Hz.

STROESSNER, Alfredo, General (1912–), president of Paraguay since 1954. Army commander in 1951, he ousted his predecessor in a coup, and created an efficient and stable totalitarian regime.

STROHEIM, Erich von (1885–1957), German-born US film director. Beginning under D. W. GRIFFITH, he became known for his realism, careful construction and attention to detail, as in *Greed* (1924) and *The Wedding March* (1928). He was also a distinguished screen actor, appearing in *La Grande Illusion* (1937) and *Sunset Boulevard* (1950).

STROKE, or cerebrovascular accident, the sudden loss of some aspect of BRAIN function due to lack of BLOOD supply to a given area; control of limbs on one side of the body, APHASIA or dysphasia, loss of part of the visual field or disorders of higher function are common. Stroke may result from

EMBOLISM, ARTERIOSCLEROSIS and THROMBOSIS, or HEMORRHAGE (then termed apoplexy). Areas with permanent loss of blood supply do not recover but other areas may take over their function.

STRONTIUM (Sr), reactive, silvery-white ALKALINE-EARTH METAL, occurring as strontianite ($SrCO_3$) and celestite ($SrSO_4$), found mainly in Scotland, Ark. and Ariz. Strontium is made by ELECTROLYSIS of the chloride or reduction of the oxide with aluminum. It resembles calcium physically and chemically. The radioactive isotope Sr^{90} is produced in nuclear FALLOUT, and is used in nuclear electric-power generators. Strontium compounds are used in fireworks (imparting a crimson color), and to refine sugar. AW 87.6, mp 769°C, bp 1384°C, sg 2.54.

STRUVE, Otto (1897–1963), Russian-born US astronomer known for work on stellar evolution (see STAR) and primarily for his contributions to astronomical SPECTROSCOPY, especially his discovery thereby of INTERSTELLAR MATTER (1938).

STRYCHNINE, poisonous ALKALOID from NUX VOMICA seeds causing excessive SPINAL CORD stimulation. Death results from spinal CONVULSIONS and ASPHYXIA.

STUART, Gilbert (1755–1828), US portrait painter, creator of the famous portrait head of George Washington (1796). Praised for his color, technique and psychological insight, he painted nearly 1,000 portraits and created a distinctive US portrait style.

STUART, James Ewell Brown (1833–1864), Confederate cavalry officer. Resigning from the US Army, he won command of a Confederacy brigade after the first Battle of BULL RUN (1861), and began his famous cavalry raids in 1862. Promoted to command all the cavalry in the N Va. Army, he was killed in the WILDERNESS campaign.

STUART, Steuart or Stewart, House of, ruled Scotland 1371–1714 and Scotland and England 1603–1714. The first Stuart king, **Robert II** (reigned 1371–90) was a hereditary steward of Scotland whose father had married a daughter of Robert the BRUCE. A descendant, **James IV**, married Margaret, daughter of HENRY VII of England. Their grandson, **James VI**, became JAMES I of England in 1603. Between 1603 and 1714, six Stuarts ruled: James I, his son CHARLES I (1625–49), CHARLES II (1660–85), JAMES II (deposed 1688), MARY II (wife of WILLIAM III) and ANNE (1702–14). (For the Stuart pretenders descended from James II, see JACOBITES.)

STUBBS, George (1724–1806), English animal painter famous for his pictures of horses, such as *Mares and Foals* (c1760–70), and *Lion Devouring a Horse* (1769). The etchings of his *Anatomy of the Horse* (1766) came from years of anatomical study.

STUDENT NONVIOLENT COORDINATING COMMITTEE (SNCC), a leading nonviolent CIVIL RIGHTS organization of the 1960s, notably in the Southern integration and voter registration campaigns. Later, under the leadership of H. Rap Brown and Stokely CARMICHAEL, it promoted the idea of BLACK POWER.

STUDENTS FOR A DEMOCRATIC SOCIETY (SDS), US leftwing student organization founded in 1960. It spread through US universities and spearheaded opposition to the VIETNAM WAR. By 1970 it had split into many irreconcilable factions including the WEATHERMEN.

STURGEON, Theodore (1918–   ), US science-fiction writer noted for his romantic, antibourgeois inclinations. His works include "It" (1940), "Microcosmic God" (1941), and *More Than Human* (1953).

STURGEONS, primitive, often large, fishes from temperate waters of the N Hemisphere. Slow-moving and bottom-living, they feed on invertebrates, using the fleshy BARBELS around the mouth to detect prey. Many species migrate into fresh water to breed. They are important fishes commercially, prized for the eggs removed from the migrating females for CAVIAR. The flesh is also extremely good. (See also BELUGA.)

STURM UND DRANG (German: storm and stress), name given to a period of literary ferment in Germany c1770–84. Influenced by ROUSSEAU, its leading figures, HERDER, GOETHE and SCHILLER, espoused an antirationalist and rebellious individualism in opposition to the prevailing classicism.

STUTTER. See SPEECH AND SPEECH DISORDERS.

STUYVESANT, Peter (c1610–1672), Dutch governor (1647) of NEW NETHERLAND. Autocratic and unpopular, he lost Dutch territory to Connecticut in 1650, conquered and annexed NEW SWEDEN in 1655, and finally surrendered New Netherland to England in 1664 after his citizens failed to support him against a surprise English attack. He retired to his farm "the Bouwerie," now New York's Bowery.

ST. VINCENT, independent island nation, part of the Windward Island group in the Caribbean Sea.

Land. The principal island, St. Vincent (133sq mi), is of volcanic origin, and a mountainous spine runs down the center of the island reaching 4,000ft at Soufrière, an active volcanic peak that erupted in 1979, causing extensive crop damage. The 5 small main islands of the Grenadines extend to the SW. The climate is tropical, with annual rainfall averaging 60–150in.

People. About 65% of the inhabitants are descendants of slaves brought from Africa; minorities include persons of Portuguese, East Indian and indigenous Carib Indian (2%) descent. Most of the population belongs to the Anglican church.

Economy. Agriculture employs about 65% of the labor force and provides all exports, principally arrowroot (90% of the world's supply) and bananas, followed by spices and cacao. Staple crops include yams, plantains, maize and peas. The small industrial sector mostly processes food crops.

History. St. Vincent was discovered by Christopher Columbus in 1498. Although both Britain and France subsequently contested control of the island, it was left largely to the Carib Indians until 1797 when following a war with both the French and Caribs, the British were victorious, deporting most of the Indians. Since full independence was achieved in 1979 the country has faced tensions from an independence movement in the Grenadines.

Official name: St. Vincent and the Grenadines
Capital: Kingstown
Area: 150sq mi
Population: 118,000
Languages: English
Religions: Christian
Monetary unit(s): 1 East Caribbean dollar = 10 cents

STY. See BOIL.

STYRON, William (1925–), US novelist and winner of the 1968 Pulitzer Prize for *The Confessions of Nat Turner* (1967), a controversial first-person account of an 1831 slave rebellion. Other novels are *Lie Down in Darkness* (1951) and *Sophie's Choice* (1979).

SÜ-CHOW, or **Hsü-Chou,** city in E central China. It is a commercial and rail center in a coalmining area, and manufactures steel, textiles and machinery. Pop 800,000.

SUBATOMIC PARTICLES, or **Elementary Particles,** small packets of matter-energy which are constituent of ATOMS or are produced in nuclear reactions or in interactions between other subatomic particles. The first such particle to be discovered was the (negative) ELECTRON (e^-), the constituent of CATHODE RAYS. Next, the **nucleons** were discovered; first the (positive) PROTON (p^+); then, in 1932, the (neutral) NEUTRON (n°). The same year saw the discovery of the first antiparticle, the positron (or antielectron, $\bar{e}^+$—see ANTIMATTER), and from that time the number of known subatomic particles, found in COSMIC RAYS or detected using particle ACCELERATORS, grew rapidly, until by the early 1980s more than 100 were known or suspected. As yet no attempt to find theoretical order in this multitude of particles, many of which are highly unstable and have very short HALF-LIVES, has proved entirely successful. A first division of the particles classifies them according to whether their *SPIN*, *S*, is a whole number (bosons), or a whole number plus $\frac{1}{2}$ (fermions). Another division groups them into classons, leptons and hadrons. The **classons** are massless bosons which are associated with the fields known to classical physics: the familiar PHOTON associated with ELECTROMAGNETIC RADIATION and the as yet hypothetical graviton, the particle associated with GRAVITATION. The **leptons** are the electrons, the *neutrinos* and the *muons*. These fermions interact with the classical fields and the "weak force" involved in beta-decay. The neutrinos, of rest MASS zero, are products in various decay processes. The **hadrons**, including the mesons, nucleons and hyperons, interact additionally with the "strong force"—the intense force that holds the atomic nucleus together in spite of the mutual electric repulsion of its constituent protons. Boson hadrons are known as *mesons*; these were originally postulated as mediating the "strong force" in a similar way to that in which photons mediate the classical electromagnetic field. The mesons include the *pions* (pi mesons) and the heavier *kaons* (*K*-mesons). Fermion hadrons are known as *baryons*. These include the nucleons (protons and neutrons), and the heavier *hyperons*. The omega-minus particle (Ω^-) is a quasi-stable hyperon with a half-life of about 0.1ns. A recent attempt to explain the multiplicity of subatomic particles has involved postulating the existence of an order of yet smaller particles, called quarks, supposed to be constituent of all the conventional particles.

SUBLIMATION, in psychoanalysis, the process whereby energies derived from instinctive DRIVES, particularly the sexual and aggressive (see SEX; AGGRESSION), are channelled into noninstinctive behavior, such as creative cultural pursuits, through INHIBITION or other methods.

SUBMARINE, a ship capable of underwater operation. The idea is an old one, but the first working craft was not built until 1620, by Cornelis Drebbel; it was a wooden frame covered with greased leather. The first submarine used in warfare was invented by David BUSHNELL (1776). Called the Turtle, it was a one-man, hand-powered, screw-driven vessel designed to attach mines to enemy ships. In the Civil War the Confederate States produced several submarines. Propulsion, the major problem, was partly solved by the Rev. G. W. Garrett, who built a steam-powered submarine (1880). In the 1890s John P. HOLLAND and his rival Simon Lake designed vessels powered by gasoline engines on the surface and by electric motors when submerged, the forerunners of modern submarines. They were armed with TORPEDOES and guns. Great advances were made during WWI and WWII, which demonstrated the submarine's military effectiveness. The German U-boats were notably efficient, and introduced SNORKELS to hinder detection while recharging batteries. But none of these vessels could remain submerged for very long, and a true (long-term) submarine awaited the advent of nuclear power, independent of the oxygen of the air for propulsion. The first nuclear-powered submarine was the U.S.S. *Nautilus* (1955), which in 1958 made the first voyage under the polar ice-cap. The US, USSR, UK and France have nuclear submarine fleets fitted with ballistic missiles. The US has three classes of SSBNs (ballistic missile submarine, nuclear-powered) in deployment: the Polaris, which is being phased out; the Poseidon; and the ultramodern Trident. The USS *Ohio*, the first of the Trident submarines, began sea trials in June 1981. Submarines when on station at sea are the most survivable of the nuclear strategic systems. A number of nuclear-powered attack submarines in the *Los Angeles* class have recently been added to the US arsenal.

Modern submarines are streamlined vessels, generally with a double hull, the inner being a pressure hull with fuel and ballast tanks between it and the outer hull. The submarine submerges by flooding its ballast tanks to reach neutral buoyancy, i.e., displacing its own weight of water (see ARCHIMEDES), and dives using its hydrofoil diving planes. Submarines are equipped with PERISCOPES and INERTIAL GUIDANCE systems. As well as their military uses, submarines are used for oceanographic research and exploration, salvage and rescue.

SUBWAY, an underground railroad system designed for efficient urban and suburban passenger transport. The TUNNELS usually follow the lines of streets, for ease of construction by the cut-and-cover method in which an arched tunnel is built in an open trench, covered with earth and the street restored. Outlying parts of the system usually emerge to the surface. The first subway was built in London (1860–63) by the cut-and-cover method; it used steam trains and was a success despite fumes. A three-mile section of London subway was built (1886–90) using a shield developed by J. H. Greathead: this is a large cylindrical steel tube forced forward through the clay by hydraulic jacks; the clay is removed and the tunnel walls built. Deep tunnels are thus possible, and there is no surface disturbance. This London "tube" was the first to use electrically-powered trains, which soon replaced steam trains everywhere. Elevators were provided for the deep stations, later mostly replaced by escalators. Many cities throughout the world followed London's lead, notably Paris (the Métro, begun 1898) and New York (begun 1900). The New York subway, using the multiple-unit trains developed by Frank SPRAGUE, is now the largest in the world. The Moscow subway (begun 1931) is noted for its palatial marble stations. With increasing road traffic congestion in the 1960s, the value of subways was apparent, and many cities extended, improved and automated their systems; some introduced quieter rubber-tired trains running on concrete guideways.

SUCCOTH. See SUKKOTH.

SUCCULENTS, plants that have swollen leaves or stems and are thus adapted to living in arid regions. CACTI are the most familiar but representatives occur in other families, notably the Crassulaceae (STONECROPS and houseleeks) and Aizoaceae (LIVING STONES, mesembryanthemum). Many succulents have attractive foliage and colorful, though often short-lived, flowers.

SUCRE, legal capital of BOLIVIA, some 8,500ft high in the Andes, about 250mi SE of La Paz, the administrative capital.

Founded in 1538, it is now a commercial and agricultural center. Pop 63,625.

SUCRE, Antonio José de (1795–1830), South American revolutionary leader, BOLÍVAR's chief aide and first president of Bolivia (1826–28). He liberated Colombia, Ecuador and Peru from Spanish rule, with a final victory at AYACUCHO (1824). He retired to Ecuador 1828, but returned to repel a Peruvian attack 1829. He was assassinated after presiding over a congress aimed at keeping Ecuador, Colombia and Venezuela united.

SUCROSE ($C_{12}H_{22}O_{11}$), or cane sugar, disaccharide CARBOHYDRATE, commercially obtained from SUGAR BEET, SUGARCANE and Sweet SORGHUM. As table sugar, sucrose is the most important of the SUGARS. It comprises a GLUCOSE unit joined to a FRUCTOSE unit. Sucrose, glucose and fructose all exhibit OPTICAL ACTIVITY and when sucrose is hydrolyzed the rotation changes from right to left. This is called inversion and an equimolar mixture of glucose and fructose is called invert sugar. The ENZYME which hydrolyzes SUCROSE to glucose and fructose is called invertase.

Official name: Democratic Republic of the Sudan
Capital: Khartoum
Area: 967,500sq mi
Population: 18,766,000
Languages: Arabic; English
Religions: Muslim, Animist, Christian
Monetary unit(s): 1 Sudanese pound = 100 piastres

SUDAN, the largest country in Africa, lies S of Egypt and W of Ethiopia; its NE coastline is along the Red Sea.

Land. Sudan has swamp and tropical rain forest in the S, savanna grassland in the central region, desert and semidesert in the N and W. There are mountains in the NE, S, center and W. The country is bisected by the N-flowing Nile and its tributaries, along which the bulk of the population and almost all the towns are found. The climate is hot and rainfall ranges from almost nil in the N to almost 60in per year in the S.

People. There are two main groups: the Arab-speaking Muslims of the N, who make up over 75% of the population, and the black African and Nilotic peoples of the S, mainly animist in belief. There have been continuing disputes between N and S, the latter resisting Muslim domination. About 90% of the people are rural, and the rate of illiteracy is high. There are, however, several universities.

Economy. The Sudan is basically agricultural, and most people live by subsistence farming. The chief cash crops are cotton, gum arabic and peanuts. Domestic crops include millet, sorghum, wheat and sugarcane. Livestock are raised in large numbers. Manufacturing is limited. The only port is Port Sudan on the Red Sea.

History. Called NUBIA in ancient times, N Sudan was colonized by Egypt c2000 BC. By 800 BC it had come under the CUSH kingdom, which by 600 AD had given way to independent Coptic Christian states. In the 13th–15th centuries these collapsed under Muslim expansion, and the Muslim Funj state was established, lasting until Egypt invaded the Sudan in 1821. The nationalist MAHDI led a revolt in 1881, after which a series of campaigns resulted in joint Anglo-Egyptian rule in 1899. Since independence in 1956 the country has had alternating military and civilian governments, the regime led by President Ja'Far Muhammad Numayri having been installed in 1969. In recent years nearly a half million refugees from neighboring countries have streamed into Sudan, further unsettling an already fragile economy.

SUDETENLAND, region of W Czechoslovakia. Originally it designated the area of the Sudetes Mts on the Bohemia-Silesia border, but came to apply to all the German-speaking Bohemian and Moravian borderlands incorporated into Czechoslovakia in 1919. The Sudetenland was ceded to Nazi Germany by the MUNICH AGREEMENT in 1938, and restored to Czechoslovakia in 1945.

SUE, Eugène (1804–1857), French novelist, best known for his sensational serialized tales of low-life Paris such as *The Mysteries of Paris* (1842–43) and *The Wandering Jew* (1844–45); they embraced his ideal of social reform.

SUEZ CANAL, ship canal in Egypt linking the Red Sea with the E Mediterranean; 101mi long, it cut over 4,000mi off the route from Britain to India and has been a major commercial waterway since its opening in 1869. Without locks, the canal runs N–S, passing through Lake Timsah and the Bitter Lakes. It has a minimum width of 179ft and a dredged depth of almost 40ft.

Work began in 1859 under de LESSEPS, after the Ottoman khedive of Egypt had conceded a 99-year lease to the Suez Canal Company. The controlling interest was French, and in 1875 the khedive sold his 44% shareholding to the British government, which had initially been hostile. An international convention guaranteeing the canal's neutrality was signed in 1888. Egyptian interest increased after 1936 and culminated in 1956 when NASSER nationalized the canal, prompting an invasion by Britain and France. After UN intervention the canal reopened in 1957 under Egyptian control. It was closed again by the ARAB-ISRAELI WAR of 1967, but in 1974 agreement was reached, and after the canal had been cleared of wreckage it was reopened in 1975. The canal was deepened 1976–80 to permit the passage of oil tankers up to 500,000 tons and 53ft draft.

SUFFOCATION. See ASPHYXIA.

SUFISM, Muslim mystical philosophical and literary movement dating from the 10th and 11th centuries. Stressing personal communion with God, it has spread throughout Islam in a variety of forms.

SUGAR BEET, *Beta vulgaris,* a plant whose swollen root provides almost half the world's sugar. It was first extensively grown in Europe to replace cane sugar from the W Indies, supplies of which were cut off during the Napoleonic Wars. Careful breeding has improved the sugar yield. Sugar beet is grown in all temperate areas where cool summers ensure good sugar formation. Family: Chenopodiaceae.

SUGARCANE, grass of the genus *Saccharum,* from which the world obtains over half its sugar. Originally native to E Asia, it has been grown extensively in the Indies and America since the 18th century and now is cultivated in most warm humid areas. The fibrous material (bagasse) left after juice extraction is made into board. Family: Gramineae. (See also MOLASSES.)

SUGARS, sweet, soluble CARBOHYDRATES (of general formula $C_x(H_2O)_y$), comprising the monosaccharides and the disaccharides. **Monosaccharides** cannot be further degraded by HYDROLYSIS and contain a single chain of CARBON atoms. They normally have the suffix -ose and a prefix indicating the length of the carbon chain; thus trioses, tetroses, pentoses, hexoses and heptoses contain 3, 4, 5, 6 and 7 carbon atoms respectively. The most abundant natural monosaccharides are the hexoses, $C_6H_{12}O_6$, (including GLUCOSE), and the pentoses, $C_5H_{10}O_5$ (including xylose). Many different isomers of these sugars are possible and often have names reflecting their source, or a property,

e.g., FRUCTOSE is found in fruit, arabinose in gum arabic and the pentose, xylose, in wool. **Disaccharides** contain two monosaccharide units joined by an oxygen bridge. Their chemical and physical properties are similar to those of monosaccharides. The most important disaccharides are SUCROSE (cane sugar), LACTOSE and MALTOSE. (Table sugar consists of sucrose). The most characteristic property of sugars is their sweetness. If we accord sucrose an arbitrary sweetness of 100, then glucose scores 74, fructose 173, lactose 16, maltose 33, xylose 40 (compare SACCHARIN 55,000). The sweetness of sugars is correlated with their solubility.

SUHARTO (1921–   ), president of Indonesia from 1968. A veteran general, he opposed the corrupt SUKARNO regime and crushed the communist coup it sponsored in 1965; he has held effective power since, and has restored the country's prosperity.

SUICIDE, the act of voluntarily taking one's own life. In some societies (notably Japan: see HARA-KIRI) suicide is accepted or even expected in the face of disgrace. Judaism, Islam and Christianity, however, consider it a sin. Until 1961 the UK sought to discourage it by making it a crime, and it still is in some US states. Motivation varies enormously where there is no social sanction; a suicide attempt is often thought to be an implicit "plea" for help, and may result from extreme DEPRESSION. Several notable literary figures have died in this manner, among them Ernest Hemingway, Anne Sexton and Sylvia Plath. Suicide is the cause of 1.4% of all deaths in the US each year; the suicide rate is 12.7 per 100,000 population. The comparative rate for Britain is 7.8, and for Switzerland 23.8. Émile DURKHEIM's *Suicide* (1897) is the classic study of the subject.

SUITE, musical form developed in Germany and France in the 17th and 18th centuries, consisting of a set of dance movements in the same or related keys. The regular combination was allemande, courante, sarabande, gigue; additional movements such as the minuet, gavotte or bourée could be added.

SUKARNO (1901–1970), first president of Indonesia 1945–67. A leader of the independence movement from 1927, he collaborated with the Japanese in WWII, and was instrumental in creating the republic in 1945. His flamboyant and corrupt rule became a dictatorship in 1959; he veered toward the communist bloc, while his policies ruined the economy. Implicated in an attempted communist coup (1965), he was gradually ousted by SUHARTO.

SUKKOTH, or Feast of Tabernacles, an

autumn Jewish festival. It recalls the *sukkot* (huts) used in the wanderings in the wilderness and originally celebrated the end of the harvest. Symbolic *sukkot* are still made from branches.

SULEIMAN I (1494–1566), sultan of the Ottoman Empire 1520–66. He extended its borders W to Budapest and E to Persia and maintained a powerful Mediterranean fleet. Called the Magnificent by Europeans and *Kanuni* (lawgiver) by his subjects, he brought Turkish culture and statecraft to its zenith.

SULFA DRUGS, or **sulfonamides,** synthetic compounds (containing the —SO$_2$NH$_2$ group) that inhibit the multiplication of invading BACTERIA, thus allowing the body's cellular defense mechanisms to suppress infection. The first sulfa drug, sulfanilamide (Prontosil), was synthesized in 1908 and used widely as a dye, before, in 1935, DOMAGK reported its effectiveness against STREPTOCOCCI. Since then it has proved effective against several other bacteria including those causing SCARLET FEVER, certain VENEREAL DISEASES and MENINGITIS. This and the many other sulfa drugs are now generally used in conjunction with ANTIBIOTICS.

SULFUR (S), nonmetal in Group VIA of the PERIODIC TABLE. There are large deposits in Tex. and La., and in Japan, Sicily and Mexico; the American sulfur is extracted by the FRASCH PROCESS. It is also recovered from natural gas and petroleum. Combined sulfur occurs as SULFATES and SULFIDES. There are two main allotropes of sulfur (see ALLOTROPY): the yellow, brittle rhombic form is stable up to 95.6°C, above which monoclinic sulfur (almost colorless) is stable. Both forms are soluble in carbon disulfide; they consist of eight-membered rings S$_8$. Plastic sulphur is an amorphous form made by suddenly cooling boiling sulfur. Sulfur is reactive, combining with most other elements. It is used in gunpowder, matches, as a fungicide and insecticide, and to vulcanize rubber. AW 32.1, mp 113°C (rh), 119°C (mono), bp 445°C, sg 2.07 (rh, 20°C). **Sulfur dioxide** (SO$_2$) is a colorless, acrid gas, formed by combustion of sulfur. It is an oxidizing and reducing agent and is important as an intermediate in the manufacture of sulfur trioxide and SULFURIC ACID. It is also used in petroleum refining and as a refrigerant, disinfectant, preservative and bleach. It reacts with water to give sulfurous acid (H$_2$SO$_3$), which is corrosive. Thus sulfur dioxide in flue gases is a harmful cause of POLLUTION. mp −73°C, bp −10°C. **Sulfites** are salts containing the ion SO$_3{}^{2-}$,

formed from sulfur dioxide and BASES; readily oxidized to SULFATES. Bisulfites are acid sulfites, containing the ion HSO$_3{}^-$. **Sulfur Trioxide** (SO$_3$) is a volatile liquid or solid formed by oxidation of sulfur dioxide (see CONTACT PROCESS). It reacts violently with water to give SULFURIC ACID. mp 17°C (α), bp 45°C (α). **Thiosulfates** are salts containing the ion S$_2$O$_3{}^{2-}$, usually prepared by dissolving sulfur in an aqueous sulfite solution. They are mild reducing agents, and form LIGAND complexes; in acid solution they decompose to give sulfur and sulfur dioxide. (For sodium thiosulfate, see SODIUM.)

SULLA, Lucius Cornelius (138–78 BC), Roman general and dictator. Turning against his former commander MARIUS, he became the first Roman to lead an army against Rome (88 BC). He fought MITHRADATES in Asia Minor, 87–83 BC, and returned to defeat the Marians in a civil war. As dictator, 82–79 BC he massacred opponents for their property and restored the SENATE's power.

SULLIVAN, Anne (née Macy; 1866–1936), US teacher of Helen KELLER. Partially blind herself, in 1887 she taught Helen to read and communicate through the touch alphabet, and became her lifelong companion.

SULLIVAN, Sir Arthur Seymour (1842–1900), British composer best known for his partnership with W. S. GILBERT on their famous operettas. He also composed oratorios, grand operas and hymn tunes whose popularity has not endured to the same extent.

SULLIVAN, Ed (1902–1974), US newspaper columnist and television personality who hosted one of TV's most successful and longest-running programs, *The Ed Sullivan Show* (1948–71). Nervous and uneffusive, he presided over an entertaining mix of animal acts, chorus-line routines ' and appearances by some of the brightest performing talents of his era.

SULLIVAN, Harry Stack (1892–1949), US psychiatrist who made important contributions to SCHIZOPHRENIA studies and originated the idea that PSYCHIATRY depends on study of interpersonal relations (including that between therapist and patient).

SULLIVAN, John L(awrence) (1858–1918), US boxer, last world heavyweight champion 1882–89 under London Prize Ring (bareknuckle) rules. He lost his first defense of it under QUEENSBURY RULES in 1892 to "Gentleman" Jim Corbett after 21 rounds. The colorful "Boston Strong Boy" was the first nationally famous boxing champion.

SULLIVAN, Louis Henry (1856–1924), US architect famous for his office buildings that pioneered modern design. He was a partner of Dankmar ADLER in Chicago (1881–95). His works include the Auditorium (1889) and the Carson Pirie Scott building (1899–1904) in Chicago, and the Guaranty Building in Buffalo (1894–95). His functionalism was expressed in his famous maxim "form follows function." Frank Lloyd WRIGHT was his pupil.

SULLY, Thomas (1783–1872), English-born US portrait painter. He studied briefly under Gilbert STUART, and became popular and prolific. Queen Victoria (1839) and several US presidents sat for him.

SULLY-PRUDHOMME, René François Armand (1839–1907), French PARNASSIAN poet, winner of Nobel Prize for Literature, 1901. He began writing melancholy and subjective poetry, but *La Justice* (1878) and *Le Bonheur* (*Happiness*; 1888) are philosophical.

SULZBERGER, Arthur Hays (1891–1968), US newspaperman. As publisher of the *New York Times* 1935–61 he upheld the high journalistic standards of his predecessor Adolph Ochs. He joined the *Times* in 1918 and was chairman of the board 1957–68.

SUMATRA, second-largest island of Indonesia. On the Equator, with a hot, wet climate, it is heavily forested and rich in oil, bauxite and coal, producing 70% of Indonesia's wealth. Export crops include rubber, coffee, pepper and tobacco. Medan and Palembang are the chief cities.

SUMERIANS, inhabitants of S MESOPOTAMIA from earliest times, with a great civilization dating from c3300 BC. They established agriculture-based city-states such as ERECH, KISH, NIPPUR and UR, built irrigation canals, and achieved remarkable technical and artistic prowess, developing CUNEIFORM writing. Sumer fell to the AKKAD kingdom c2400 BC, and after a brief revival c2000 BC was absorbed into BABYLONIA.

SUMNER, Charles (1811–1874), US antislavery politician, senator from Mass. 1851–74. A law graduate (1833), he became an aggressive abolitionist and worked for world peace and prison and educational reform. Chairman of the Senate Foreign Relations Committee (1861–71), he was a prominent radical Republican during RECONSTRUCTION, and active in impeaching President Andrew JOHNSON.

SUMNER, William Graham (1840–1910), US sociologist who expounded social Darwinism. This belief, based on DARWIN's theory of evolution, stated that social progress depends upon unrestrained competition, economic LAISSEZ-FAIRE and acceptance of inherent inequalities. He wrote *Folkways* (1907), examining the role of custom in society.

SUMO, type of Japanese wrestling in which great importance is put on size and weight, poundages up to 300 being not uncommon. The contests are usually brief.

SUN, the star about which the earth and the other planets of the SOLAR SYSTEM revolve. The sun is an incandescent ball of gases, by mass 69.5% hydrogen; 28% helium; 2.5% carbon, nitrogen, oxygen, sulfur, silicon, iron and magnesium altogether, and traces of other elements. It has a diameter of about 1,393Mm, and rotates more rapidly at the equator (24.65 days) than at the poles (about 34 days). Although the sun is entirely gaseous, its distance creates the optical illusion that it has a surface: this visible edge is called the PHOTOSPHERE. It is at a temperature of about 6000K, cool compared to the center of the sun (13,000,000K) or the corona (average 2,000,000K); the photospheres of other stars may be at temperatures of less than 2000K or more than 500,000K. Above the photosphere lies the **chromosphere**, an irregular layer of gases between 1.5Mm and 15Mm in depth. It is in the chromosphere that SUNSPOTS, FLARES and **prominences** occur: these last are great plumes of gas that surge out into the corona and occasionally off into space. The **corona** is the sparse outer atmosphere of the sun. During solar ECLIPSES it may be seen to extend several thousand megameters and to be as bright as the full moon, though in fact it extends the orbit of JUPITER. The earth lies within the particles and radiation flowing outward from the sun, termed the SOLAR WIND. The sun is a normal STAR, common in characteristics although slightly smaller than average. It lies in one of the spiral arms of the MILKY WAY.

SUNBURN, burning effect on the SKIN following prolonged exposure to ULTRAVIOLET RADIATION from the sun, common in travelers from temperate zones to hot climates. First-degree BURNS may occur but usually only a delayed ERYTHEMA is seen with extreme skin sensitivity. Systemic disturbance occurs in severe cases. Fair-skinned persons are most susceptible.

SUN DANCE, religious ceremony observed by a number of Plains tribes of American Indians during the 19th century, involving fasting, self-torture and the seeking of visions.

SUNDAY, Billy (1862–1935), US revivalist preacher noted for his flamboyance and his vivid version of fundamentalist theology. He claimed to have saved over a million souls and is thought to have collected over $1 million in doing so. He was a professional baseball player before his conversion.

SUNFLOWER, tall plants of the genus *Helianthus,* with large disk-shaped yellow and brown flowers which twist around to face the sun. Most of the 60 species are native to the US. The Common sunflower (*Helianthus annuus*) is cultivated in many parts of the world. The seeds yield an oil and the remainder becomes cattle feed. Family: Compositae.

SUNNITES, the orthodox majority of the followers of ISLAM, distinct from the SHI'ITES. The term refers to the traditional Way (*sunna*) of the Prophet MOHAMMED.

SUNSPOTS, apparently dark spots visible on the face of the SUN. Vortices of gas associated with strong electromagnetic activity, their dark appearance is merely one of contrast with the surrounding photosphere. Single spots are known, but mostly they form in groups or pairs. They are never seen at the sun's poles or equator. Their cause is not certainly known. Their prevalence reaches a maximum about every 11 years.

SUNSTROKE, or heatstroke, rise in body TEMPERATURE and failure of sweating in hot climates, often following exertion. DELIRIUM, COMA and CONVULSIONS may develop suddenly and rapid cooling should be effected.

SUN YAT-SEN (1866–1925), Chinese revolutionary, revered as the ideological father of modern China. Influenced by MARX and Henry GEORGE, he founded (1894) a movement against the MANCHUS. Exiled in 1895, he formulated the principles of *democracy, nationalism* and *socialism* underlying the KUOMINTANG, the party he founded and led. In 1911 the Manchus were overthrown and Sun returned to China. First president of the new republic, he soon resigned (1912) to YÜAN SHIH-KAI, whose rule became increasingly dictatorial. After a second exile (1913–17), in 1921 Sun led a rival "national" government at Canton. In the ensuing struggle against the rulers in Peking, he cooperated with the communists and organized a military academy under CHIANG KAI-SHEK who succeeded him on his death. (See also CHINA.)

SUPERCONDUCTIVITY, a condition occurring in many metals, alloys, etc., at low temperatures, involving zero electrical RESISTANCE and perfect DIAMAGNETISM. In such a material an electric current will persist indefinitely without any driving voltage and applied MAGNETIC FIELDS are exactly cancelled out by the magnetization they produce. In **type I superconductors**, both these properties disappear abruptly when the temperature or applied magnetic field exceed critical values (typically 5K and 10^4A/m), but in **type II superconductors** the diamagnetism decay is spread over a range of field values. Large ELECTROMAGNETS sometimes use superconducting coils which will carry large currents without overheating, and the exclusion of fields by superconducting materials can be exploited to screen or direct magnetic fields. Superconductivity was discovered by H. KAMERLINGH-ONNES in 1911, and is due to an indirect interaction of pairs of ELECTRONS via local elastic deformations of the metal CRYSTAL.

SUPEREGO, according to FREUD'S METAPSYCHOLOGY, the third and last part of the psychic apparatus to develop, a part of the EGO containing self-criticism, INHIBITIONS, etc., and also the individual's ego ideal or ideal self.

SUPERIOR, Lake, largest of the North American GREAT LAKES, the world's largest freshwater lake. It is about 350mi long and 160mi wide, covering approximately 31,800sq mi and having a maximum depth of over 1,330ft. It is bounded E and N by Ontario, W by Minn., and S by Wis. and Mich. Some 200 rivers drain into it, the largest being the St. Louis. It is part of the GREAT LAKES-ST. LAWRENCE WATERWAY, its principal port, Duluth-Superior, marking the W end of that system.

SUPERNOVA, a NOVA which initially behaves like other novae but, after a few days at maximum brightness, increases to a far higher level of luminosity (a supernova in the ANDROMEDA galaxy, 1885, was one tenth as bright as the entire galaxy). It is thought that supernovae may be caused by the gravitational collapse of a star, or cloud of gas and dust, into a neutron STAR.

SUPPÉ, Franz von (1819–1895), Austrian composer of light music, especially light opera in the style of OFFENBACH. His works include *Poet and Peasant* (1846).

SUPPLY AND DEMAND, in economics, central concepts which seek to explain changes in prices, production and consumption of goods and services. Demand for a product depends largely on its price; usually, the higher the price, the less the quantity demanded. This relationship may be plotted as a demand curve. A supply curve may similarly be obtained showing that supply of a product is related to its price. The intersection of the two curves shows the equilibrium between the amount demanded and the amount supplied at a given price. Demand may also be explained by UTILITY, while supply can be explained by the producer's profit motive. The economic theory of SUPPLY-SIDE ECONOMICS emphasizes the supply of goods, whereas KEYNESIAN ECONOMICS places more attention on demand.

SUPPLY-SIDE ECONOMICS, theory of economic management that focuses on stimulating production rather than manipulating demand. In the traditional dichotomy between supply and demand, supply-side economists emphasize the former as opposed to the emphasis of KEYNESIAN ECONOMICS on the latter. The chief measure advocated by supply-siders for the US today is drastic tax reduction, which is intended to inspire increased investment in business, leading to higher employment. The theory also calls for a cutback in government spending to achieve a balanced and much smaller budget, thus eliminating deficit spending which causes inflation and drains funds from the private sector. The leading supply-side theorist is Arthur B. LAFFER of the University of California; important advocates include Rep. Jack KEMP of N.Y. and David STOCKMAN, director of the Office of MANAGEMENT AND BUDGET under President Ronald Reagan. Supply-side thinking has dominated Reagan's economic policies, but it is still a minority view among economists.

SUPREMATISM, art movement c1913–19 originated by the Russian-Polish painter Kasimir MALEVICH, establishing a system of non-representational composition in terms of pure geometric shapes and patterns. The movement's influence on graphic design and typography has been significant.

SUPREME COURT, highest court of the US, with the authority to adjudicate all cases arising under US law, including constitutional matters. The number of member justices is set by statute and so varies; presently the Court has a Chief Justice and eight other Associate Justices. The president appoints the justices as vacancies arise, but nominees must be confirmed by majority vote of the senate. Most nominees are easily confirmed, but the process is not perfunctory; Richard Nixon had two successive nominees rejected by the senate in 1970. Great care is taken in confirmation since justices serve "during good behavior" for life or until retirement. They can, however, be impeached and convicted for high crimes and misdemeanors. Although theoretically above politics,

the Court is vitally important to them, since it alone can determine the constitutionality of both state and federal laws. This power of "judicial review" is not explicitly stated in the Constitution, but is rather an operational precedent established by Chief Justice John MARSHALL in the cases of MARBURY V. MADISON (1803) and MARTIN V. HUNTERS LESSEE (1816). It may also overrule its own previous decisions, a provision that has kept it a living, vital body able to change with the times. A good example of this is the decision in BROWN V. BOARD OF EDUCATION (1954), forbidding racial segregation in education, which overruled PLESSY V. FERGUSON (1896). In 1981, Sandra Day O'CONNOR became the first woman to sit on the High Court.

SUPREME SOVIET, in the USSR, the supreme state and legislative body. Its two chambers—the 767-member Soviet of the Union and the 750-member Soviet of Nationalities—have equal legislative rights, are elected to four-year terms and meet twice a year. Committees continue work between sessions. The Supreme Soviet elects its PRESIDIUM in joint session, appoints the Supreme Court and approves the Council of Ministers, the top executive and administrative body whose chairman heads the government.

SURFACE TENSION, FORCE existing in any boundary surface of a liquid such that the surface tends to assume the minimum possible area. It is defined as the force perpendicular to a line of unit length drawn on the surface. Surface tension arises from the cohesive forces between liquid molecules and makes a liquid surface behave as if it had an elastic membrane stretched over it. Thus, the weight of a needle floated on water makes a depression in the surface. Surface tension governs the wetting properties of liquids, CAPILLARITY and detergent action.

SURFING, the art of riding a wooden or foam plastic surfboard on the fast-moving incline of a wave. It requires exceptional balance, timing and coordination. Surfing originated in Hawaii and has become an international sport, with particular popularity along the coasts of California, Australia, Brazil, Peru and South Africa.

SURGERY, the branch of MEDICINE chiefly concerned with manual operations to remove or repair diseased, damaged or deformed body tissues. With time, surgery has become more complex and has split up into a number of specialities. In 1970 ten surgical speciality boards existed in the US and Canada: general surgery; OPHTHALMOLOGY; otolaryngology; OBSTET-

RICS and GYNECOLOGY; ORTHOPEDICS; colon and rectal surgery; urology; PLASTIC SURGERY; neurosurgery, and thoracic (chest) surgery. **Otolaryngology** deals with the EAR, LARYNX (voicebox) and upper respiratory tract: tonsillectomy is one of its most common operations. **Colon and rectal surgery** deals with the large intestine. **Urological surgery** deals with the urinary system (KIDNEYS, ureters, BLADDER, urethra) and male reproductive system. **Neurosurgery** deals with the NERVOUS SYSTEM (BRAIN, SPINAL CORD, nerves); common operations include the removal of TUMORS, the repair of damage caused by severe injury, and the cutting of dorsal roots (rhizotomy) and certain parts of the spinal cord (cordotomy) to relieve unmanageable pain. **Thoracic surgery** deals with structures within the chest cavity. There are also a number of subspecialities; thus **cardiovascular surgery**, a subspeciality of thoracic surgery, deals with the heart and major blood vessels.

Official name: Republic of Suriname
Capital: Paramaribo
Area: 63,037sq mi
Population: 394,500
Languages: Dutch, Sranang Tongo, Hindi, Javanese
Religions: Christian, Hindu, Muslim
Monetary unit(s): 1 Suriname Guilder = 100 cents

SURINAME, republic on the NE coast of South America, bounded W by Guyana, S by Brazil and E by French Guiana.
Land. The country, about the size of Georgia, consists of unexplored forested highlands and flat Atlantic coast. The climate is tropical, with heavy rains.
People and economy. The population consists of about 38% East Indians, 31% Creoles, 15% Javanese, 10% Bush Negroes and 6% Europeans, Chinese and Amerindians. The official language is Dutch, but most people speak the Creole Sranang Tongo. Hindi, Javanese, Chinese, English,

French and Spanish are also spoken. The basis of the economy is bauxite, which provides about 85% of foreign exchange. The main crops are rice, sugar, fruits, coffee and bananas.
History. England gave Suriname to the Dutch (1667) in exchange for New Amsterdam (now New York City), and the country was subsequently known as Dutch Guiana. It became a self-governing part of the Netherlands in 1954 and gained full independence in 1975. The first years of independence were marked by an exodus of some 40,000 Surinamese to the Netherlands and by border disputes with French Guiana and Guyana. A bloodless military coup took place in 1980.

SURREALISM, movement in literature and art which flourished between WW I and WW II, centered in Paris. Writers such as André BRETON and COCTEAU, and painters such as DALI, MIRO, MAGRITTE, TANGUY and ERNST were surrealists. They owed much to FREUD, emphasizing the world of dream and fantasy and believing that the unconscious mind reveals a truer reality than the natural world. In paintings, everyday objects were often placed in a dream-like setting and apparently unrelated objects were juxtaposed.

SURREY, Henry Howard, Earl of (c1517–1547), English poet who with his friend Thomas WYATT introduced the SONNET from Italy into England. In his translations from Vergil, Surrey was the first to employ BLANK VERSE in English.

SURVEYING, the accurate measurement of distances and features on the earth's surface. For making MAPS and charts, the LATITUDE and longitude of certain primary points are determined from astronomical observations. Geodetic surveying, for large areas, takes the earth's curvature into account (see GEODESY). After a base line of known length is established, the positions of other points are found by triangulation (measuring the angles of the point from each end of the base line) or by trilateration (measuring all the sides of the triangle formed by point and base line). Trigonometry, in particular the SINE RULE, yields the distances or angles not directly measured. A series of adjacent triangles is thus formed, each having one side in common with the next. Distances are measured by tape or electronically, sending a frequency-modulated light or microwave beam to the farther point and back, and measuring the phase shift. Angles are measured with the THEODOLITE or (vertically) the alidade. Vertical elevations are determined by LEVELS. Much modern surveying is done by PHOTOGRAMMETRY, using the STEREOSCOPE to determine contours.

SURVEYOR MISSIONS, a series of seven unmanned US probes in 1966–68 of the moon, five which made successful soft landings, returning a total of more than 85,000 pictures to the earth, along with data on the strength and composition of the lunar surface. The Surveyors were the final unmanned probes prior to the manned Apollo moon missions. They were not the first to send back pictures from the moon's surface: The Russian Luna 9 began transmitting close-up photos after landing Feb. 3, 1966, four months before Surveyor 1's soft landing on June 2.

SURVIVAL OF THE FITTEST, term first used by Herbert SPENCER in his *Principles of Biology* (1864) and adopted by Charles Darwin to describe his theory of EVOLUTION by NATURAL SELECTION.

SUSLOV, Mikhail Andreyevich (1902–), Soviet party leader. An orthodox Stalinist while Stalin was alive, Suslov rose steadily through the Communist party ranks, saw important service during WWII and helped form the Cominform in 1947. He was editor of Pravda 1949–50. A member of the ruling Politburo from 1955, he became its most rigid ideologue. With an instinct for survival he at first supported Khrushchev and then helped overthrow him in 1964. He opposed any suggestion of relaxing party rule in the USSR.

SUTHERLAND, Donald (1935–), Canadian actor who alternates between comedy and brooding realism. His films include *M*A*S*H* (1970), *Klute* (1971) and *Ordinary People* (1980).

SUTHERLAND, Graham (1903–1980), English painter. His work includes landscapes and portraits, but he is best known for his post-WWII *Thorns* series, symbolic of Christ's Passion.

SUTHERLAND, Joan (1926–), Australian soprano, internationally known as one of the foremost exponents of the art of BEL CANTO. She made her debut in Sydney (1950), her US debut in Dallas (1960), and her Metropolitan debut (1961) in *Lucia di Lammermoor*. Her husband, **Richard Bonynge,** often conducts for her, has been her coach and writes fioritura interpolated into the music she sings.

SUTTER, John Augustus (1803–1880), Swiss-born pioneer of the US who founded a colony on the site of present-day Sacramento, Cal., and established a rich personal empire based on agriculture. His land was overrun and his property destroyed in the GOLD RUSH of 1848. He died bankrupt.

SUTTON, William (1901–1980), US bank robber; known as "Willy the Actor," he bluffed his way into bank vaults disguised as a fireman, Western Union messenger, and even as a policeman. During his colorful career, he robbed banks of an estimated $2 million. Although a tireless jailbreaker, he spent the greater part of his life in jail.

SUVERO, Mark Di (1933–), US sculptor. His work is distinguished by its monumental size and moveable parts. Usually made from steel, old tires, aged timbers and similar materials, his "constructivist" sculptures sometimes make political statements.

SUZUKI, Shinichi (1898–), Japanese music teacher who devised successful techniques for teaching children (as young as three years old) how to play the violin. Utilizing the basic principles of exposure, imitation and reinforcement, his "talent education movement" spread throughout the world.

SVEVO, Italo (1861–1928), Italian fiction writer, born Ettore Schmitz. His masterpiece is the witty and perceptive psychological novel *Confessions of Zeno* (1923). He first became widely known through his friend and admirer James JOYCE.

SWAHILI, a Bantu language (influenced by Arabic) which is the LINGUA FRANCA of much of E Africa, especially near the coast. It also refers to some of the inhabitants of this area.

SWALLOWS, family, Hirundinidae, of some 78 species of birds. All have long sickle-shaped wings and long forked tails. The plumage is generally dark, often with a metallic sheen. Many species have lighter underparts. The legs and feet are small and weak: they can perch on wires or tree branches, but are adapted to spend most of their time on the wing, feeding on insects caught in flight. Many species are migratory. (See also MARTINS.)

SWANS, a small group of large long-necked aquatic birds of the family Anatidae. There are eight species, seven within the genus *Cygnus*. Five of these are found in the N Hemisphere; all are white in adult plumage, but have different colored bills. These are the Trumpeter swan, Bewick's swan, Whooper, Whistling and Mute swans. The two remaining cygnids are the Black swan of Australia and the Black-necked swan of South America. Most feed on vegetation.

SWANSON, Gloria (1897–), US film actress, one of the most glamorous personalities of the silent era. She made one of several comebacks in the Hollywood classic *Sunset Boulevard* (1950), playing the role of an aging movie queen.

SWASTIKA (Sanskrit: good fortune), ancient symbol of well-being and prosperity employed by such diverse peoples as Greeks, Celts, Amerindians and the Hindus of India, based on the form 卐. In the 20th century it gained notoriety as the hated symbol of NAZISM.

Official name: Swaziland
Capital: Mbabane
Area: 6,705sq mi
Population: 552,000
Languages: English, Siswati, Zulu and Afrikaans
Religions: Christian, Traditional beliefs
Monetary unit(s): 1 Lilangeni = 100 cents
SWAZILAND, a kingdom in SE Africa, bordered by Mozambique to the E, and the Republic of South Africa on three sides.

Land. It has three main regions: the mountainous High Veld in the W, the lower Middle Veld and the Low Veld rising in the E to the narrow Lebombo range. The four major rivers, running W–E, are being developed for irrigation and could provide abundant hydroelectricity. Temperatures average from 60°F in the W to 72°F in the E.

People and economy. Swazis and a smaller number of Zulus constitute 97% of the population. Coloureds (of mixed ancestry) and Europeans make up the rest. Agriculture, including forestry, is the largest single sector in the economy. Sugar, wood pulp, asbestos, fruits, iron ore and canned meats are the main exports. Swaziland has close communication, economic and trade links with South Africa, its principal trade partner.

History. Settled by the Swazis, a BANTU people, and unified as a kingdom in the 1800s, Swaziland was administered by both Britain and then South Africa. The country became self-governing in 1963 and fully independent in 1968, under King Sobhuza II.

SWEATSHOP, place of work with long hours, poor pay and bad conditions. Such places usually exploited those who found difficulty in obtaining employment, such as women, unskilled laborers, newly arrived immigrants and children. Sweatshops were curbed by the growth of organized labor (see UNIONS).

Official name: Kingdom of Sweden
Capital: Stockholm
Area: 173,686sq mi
Population: 8,310,000
Languages: Swedish
Religions: Swedish Lutheran
Monetary unit(s): 1 Krona = 100 öre
SWEDEN, Scandinavian kingdom of N Europe, bounded W by Norway, NE by Finland, E by the Gulf of Bothnia, SE by the Baltic Sea and SW by the North Sea.

Land. There are two main regions. Norrland ("the northland") occupies most of the country and slopes down from the Köle Mts on the Norwegian border to the Gulf of Bothnia. Its northernmost parts lie within the Arctic Circle and include part of LAPLAND. Sparsely populated, Norrland contains most of the country's vast wealth of timber and its principal iron mines. To the south are the intensively cultivated lowlands where the major cities, including STOCKHOLM and GÖTEBORG, and the manufacturing industries are concentrated. In Feb., the coldest month, temperatures are below 32°F throughout Sweden but average 5°F and lower in the N. Summer temperatures average 60°F in the N and slightly higher in the S.

People. The population is almost entirely Swedish except for a minority of a few thousand Lapps in the N. More than 75% of the people are urban. Sweden enjoys one of the highest living standards in the world and an outstanding range of social services.

Economy. Sweden's forests cover about 55% of the country; it has rich deposits of iron ore, abundant hydroelectricity and enough good farmland to be almost self-sufficient in food. Metals and metal products dominate industry. Main exports are machinery, iron, steel, paper, wood pulp, timber and motor vehicles.

History. The Swedes were first recorded by the historian Tacitus in the 1st century AD.

During the period of the VIKINGS they were known as Varangians in Russia where they pioneered a trade route as far as the Black Sea. Throughout the Middle Ages their history was tied to that of NORWAY and DENMARK. The Danes, dominant from the KALMAR UNION (1397), were driven out in 1523. In the 17th century GUSTAVUS II (Gustavus Adolphus) made Sweden a leading European power. In 1809 the monarchy became constitutional; a new constitution took effect in 1975. Sweden took no part in WWI and WWII. The Social Democrats have been the predominant political party through much of Sweden's 20th century history.

SWEDENBORG, Emanuel (1688–1772), Swedish scientist, theologian and religious mystic. He had won recognition as a natural scientist when in 1745 he became the recipient of spiritual revelations. In his subsequent teachings he denied the Trinity, saying that Christ alone was God. He later claimed that Christ's second coming occurred in 1757. The Church of the New Jerusalem, founded (1788) after his death, embodies the theology set forth in his numerous works.

SWEDISH, one of the Germanic SCANDINAVIAN LANGUAGES, spoken by about 9 million people in Sweden, Finland, Estonia, the US and Canada. Old Swedish developed from Old Norse c800 AD and gave place to modern Swedish c1500 with the onset of standardization.

SWEETBREADS, the pancreatic tissue (see PANCREAS) or THYMUS GLANDS of various animals sold as MEAT.

SWIFT, Gustavus Franklin (1839–1903), US butcher and businessman. First (1875) to slaughter cattle in Chicago for shipment E, he introduced refrigerated railroad cars, founded the giant Swift & Co., and pioneered the manufacture of meat byproducts.

SWIFT, Jonathan (1667–1745), Anglo-Irish writer, a journalist, poet and outstanding prose satirist. He was born in Ireland, and ordained in 1694. Two of his satires were published in 1704: *The Battle of the Books* and *The Tale of a Tub*. He became a Tory in 1710, taking over *The Examiner*, the Tory journal. From 1714, he lived in Ireland, as Dean of St. Patrick's, Dublin. He deplored the plight of the Irish poor in the *Drapier's Letters* (1724). His masterpiece is *Gulliver's Travels* (1726), a children's fantasy as well as a political and social satire.

SWIFTS, small, fast-flying insectivorous birds, very like SWALLOWS but placed with the HUMMINGBIRDS in the order Apodiformes. Both swifts and hummingbirds have very small feet and extremely short arm bones, the major flight feathers being attached to the extended hand bones. Entirely aerial, most species feed and even sleep on the wing.

SWIMMING AND DIVING, most popular of water sports. Common swimming styles include the *side stroke*, a simple sidewise propulsion for distance swimming and lifesaving; *breaststroke*, a froglike arm-and-leg thrust which is probably the oldest stroke; *backstroke*, overarm or, for distance endurance, an inverted breaststroke; and *crawl*, the most common freestyle form, using an overarm pull and a flutter kick rather than the thrusting propulsion characteristic of most other strokes. The *butterfly*, a modified breaststroke which thrusts the head and arms up from the water and incorporates a dolphin kick, has become a popular competitive style. Synchronized swimming, or water ballet, is popular among US women. Distance swimming has produced many well-publicized attempts to cross the English Channel and other large bodies of water. Fancy diving dates back to 17th-century Sweden and Germany. Competitions include forward, backward, reverse, inward, twisting and armstand dives in layout (extended), tuck (rolled in a ball, pike (bent at waist, legs straight) and free positions, from a platform . or springboard. Several kinds of swimming and diving events have been part of OLYMPIC GAMES competitions. (See also DROWNING; LIFESAVING; ARTIFICIAL RESPIRATION.)

SWINBURNE, Algernon Charles (1837–1909), English lyric poet and critic. A friend of the PRERAPHAELITES, he led a dissolute life, ending in 30 years' seclusion. He won success with *Atalanta in Calydon* (1865), a poetic drama. *Poems and Ballads* (1866, 1878, 1889) dealt with the psychology of sexual passion. They shocked contemporaries but are now widely appreciated for their resonant language and powerful rhythms.

SWING. See JAZZ.

SWISS GUARDS, Swiss mercenary soldiers who served in various European armies, most notably as bodyguards to the French monarchs 1497–1792 and 1814–30. The colorfully uniformed Papal Swiss Guard at the Vatican Palace in Rome dates back to the late 1400s.

SWITHIN, or Swithun, Saint (c800–862), Anglo-Saxon bishop of Winchester and chaplain to EGBERT. Tradition says that St. Swithin's Day (July 15) determines the weather for the next 40 days.

SWITZERLAND, a landlocked central

European confederation.

Land. The country borders Germany, Austria, Liechtenstein, Italy and France. In the far NW the JURA MOUNTAINS extend into France. The hills and plains of the Swiss Plateau, a SW–NE band in the NW, contain rich farming land, many lakes (lakes GENEVA and LUCERNE the largest) and 66% of the people (including Geneva, Lausanne, Bern and Zürich). The Swiss ALPS in the S and SE are little populated but attract many tourists. Climate varies greatly: temperature decreases and precipitation increases the higher the altitude. Sheltered S valleys have hot summers and mild winters, but elsewhere winters are cold, with heavy snowfalls.

People. The four official language groups are German (70%), French (19%), Italian (10%) and ROMANSH (1%). The population is divided almost equally between Protestant and Roman Catholic. There are some 650,000 foreign, mainly S European, workers. The 22 cantons (states) retain much autonomy and choose a 44-member Council of States, which with the directly elected 200-member National Council elects a 7-member executive Federal Council every 4 years. A president and vice-president are similarly elected each year. Women obtained the vote in 1971.

Economy. Highly industrialized, and with plentiful hydroelectric power, Switzerland exports watches, jewelry, precision tools and instruments, textiles and chemicals. Dairy cattle are raised. Cheese and chocolate are important exports, and tourism and international banking major industries.

History. Rome conquered the HELVETII in 58 BC. The area came under the ALEMANNI, the BURGUNDIANS, the FRANKS, and the HOLY ROMAN EMPIRE (962). HAPSBURG oppression led to the Perpetual Covenant between Uri, Schwyz and Unterwald (1291), the traditional beginning of the Swiss Confederation. Wars against Austria resulted in virtual independence in 1499. Religious civil wars divided the country in the REFORMATION (see CALVIN, JOHN; ZWINGLI, HULDREICH) but it stayed neutral in the Thirty Years' War and independence was formally recognized by the 1648 Peace of WESTPHALIA. French revolutionary armies imposed a centralized Helvetic Republic 1798–1803. The 1815 Congress of VIENNA restored the Confederation. After a three-week civil war a federal democracy was set up in 1848. Switzerland remained neutral in both world wars and is still outside the UN.

SWORD, ancient principal form of hand weapon, its metal blade longer than a dagger. Leaf-shaped Bronze Age swords gave way to short flat blades in Rome, and longer laminated iron (in Damascus) and tempered steel (notably in Toledo) weapons. Asian curved cutting blades (the Turkish *scimitar*) inspired the cavalry *saber*. Japanese SAMURAI used a longer two-handed version. The thrust-and-parry *rapier* became the weapon of the DUEL and FENCING.

SWORDFISHES, a family of perch-like fishes, Xephiidae, with the snout prolonged into a powerful, flattened sword. Swordfishes are found worldwide, mainly in tropical oceans. The sword is reputed to be used to thrash among shoals of fish, the swordfish feeding at leisure on the injured fish. They are solitary animals which may weigh up to 680kg (1,500lb).

SYDNEY, oldest and largest city in Australia, capital of New South Wales. Famous for its natural harbor, Harbor Bridge and opera house, Sydney was founded as a penal colony in 1788. Sydney ships wool, wheat and meat and is a major commercial, industrial, shipping, cultural and recreational center. Met pop 3,193,300.

SYLLOGISM, the logical form of an argument consisting of three statements: two premises and a conclusion. The conclusion of a valid syllogism follows logically from the premises and is true if the premises are true. (See also LOGIC.)

SYMBIONESE LIBERATION ARMY, a US criminal group that professed to champion the poor. In 1974, in Berkeley, Cal., this "army" kidnapped Patricia Hearst, daughter of newspaper executive Randolph Hearst, who distributed millions

Official name: Swiss Confederation
Capital: Bern
Area: 15,941sq mi
Population: 16,370,000
Languages: German, French, Italian; Romansh
Religions: Roman Catholic, Protestant
Monetary unit(s): 1 Swiss franc = 100 rappen (German) or centimes (French)

of dollars in food to the poor as ransom. In a bizarre twist, Miss Hearst joined her captors and participated in a bank robbery. Six "army" members died in a shoot-out with police in Los Angeles, and the arrest in 1975 of Miss Hearst and three others ended this organization. She was convicted on the bank-robbery charge and imprisoned briefly.

SYMBIOSIS, the relationship between two organisms of different species in which mutual benefit is derived by both participants. The main types of symbiotic relationship are commensalism and mutualism. Commensalism implies eating at the same table, e.g., the Sea anemone that lives on the shell occupied by the Hermit crab: the anemone hides the crab but feeds on food scattered by the crab. Mutualism is more intimate, there being close physiological dependence between participants. An example is seen in bacteria that live in the gut of herbivorous mammals. Here the bacteria aid digestion of plant material.

SYMBOLISM, a literary movement begun by a group of French poets in the late 19th century including Laforgue. MALLARMÉ, VALÉRY and VERLAINE. Influenced by BAUDELAIRE, SWEDENBORG and WAGNER, the symbolists aimed to create poetic images, or symbols, which would be apprehended by the senses and reach the preconscious world of the spirit. Though shortlived as a movement, symbolism influenced such great writers as JOYCE, PROUST, RILKE and YEATS.

SYMINGTON, Stuart (1901–   ), US political leader. He was secretary of the air force (1947–50) before serving as a Democratic US senator from Missouri (1953–77).

SYMMETRY, regularity of form describable by the geometrical or other operations that leave the form unchanged. The human body has a rough left-right symmetry; its form is left unchanged by *reflection* (interchange of equidistant points on opposite sides) in a vertical plane through its center. The form of an infinitely long picket fence is left unchanged by *translation* (motion without rotation) by certain amounts to the left or right. A circle is unchanged by any *rotation* about its center. There may be more than one kind of symmetry operation: a circle is also unchanged by reflection in any diameter. Two symmetry operations performed in succession give another symmetry operation. All the symmetry operations that can be applied to a given form constitute a mathematical group.

Symmetry plays an important role in PHYSICS. The possible classes of CRYSTALS are defined by their symmetry groups. All physical laws, so far as is known, are left unchanged by simultaneous reflections of space, time and electric charge (interchange of positive and negative), as well as by rotations of space and translations of space and time. The special theory of RELATIVITY is defined by the LORENTZ group. SUBATOMIC PARTICLES show abstract symmetries in which their interactions with other particles are unchanged when different kinds of particles are substituted for one another in certain ways.

SYMPHONIC POEM, or tone poem, a form of orchestral music in one movement, popular about 1850–1900, which describes a story or a scene. LISZT originated the form, but Richard STRAUSS is the most noted composer in the field.

SYMPHONY, the major form of music for ORCHESTRA. Developed from the OVERTURE, by 1800 it had four movements: a fairly quick movement in SONATA FORM; a slow movement; a MINUET and trio; and a quick RONDO. HAYDN and MOZART played a central role in developing the classical symphony. BEETHOVEN introduced the SCHERZO and a new range of emotion. Major symphonic composers include in the 1800s SCHUBERT, BERLIOZ, MENDELSSOHN, BRAHMS, BRUCKNER, DVORAK and MAHLER, and in the 1900s STRAVINSKY, PROKOFIEV, SHOSTAKOVITCH, VAUGHAN WILLIAMS, ELGAR, SIBELIUS and NIELSEN.

SYNAGOGUE (Greek: house of assembly), Jewish place of worship. The synagogue became the center of communal and religious life after destruction of the Temple in Jerusalem (70 AD) and dispersal of the Jews. Most synagogues have an ark containing the TORAH, an "eternal light," two candelabra, pews and a platform (*bimah*) for readings and conduct of services. Some strict Orthodox synagogues still segregate women. (See JUDAISM.)

SYNANON, communal organization founded in 1958 in Cal. by Charles E. Dederich for the treatment of drug addicts and alcoholics. Under the tyrannical and increasingly erratic leadership of Dederich, Synanon's reputation for effecting cures was gradually undermined by reports of abuses and violence within the community. Threats and attacks occurred against anyone who left or who criticized the organization and the accumulation of a large fortune by Dederich. In 1980, Dederich, Lance Kenton (son of band leader Stan Kenton) and Joseph Musico pleaded guilty to charges of attempted murder of Los Angeles lawyer Paul Morantz, who had been bitten (in 1978) by a rattlesnake placed in his mailbox. Dederich was then forced to resign as head of Synanon.

SYNAPSE, the point of connection between two nerves or between nerve and muscle. An electrical nerve impulse releases a chemical transmitter (often ACETYLCHOLINE) which crosses a small gap and initiates electrical excitation (or inhibition) of the succeeding nerve or muscle. (See NERVOUS SYSTEM.)

SYNCOPATION, in music, the conscious contradiction of regular rhythm by stressing a normally unstressed beat, or eliminating the expected beat by a rest or tied note. It is a feature of JAZZ and the music of many modern composers.

SYNCOPE. See FAINTING.

SYNDICALISM (French *syndicat*: labor union), a revolutionary labor movement aiming at seizing control of industry through strikes, sabotage, even violence, and, as its ultimate weapon, the general strike. It originated in late 19th-century France, from the theories of PROUDHON and G. SOREL. Syndicalists agree with Marxist class analysis (see MARXISM) but like anarchists reject any state organization (see ANARCHISM). Syndicalism was strong in France and Italy in the early 1900s and found US expression in the industrial unionism of the INDUSTRIAL WORKERS OF THE WORLD. WWI and the advance of communism overtook the syndicalists; their influence lasted longest in Spain, but was finally destroyed in the civil war 1936–39.

SYNERGISM, the working together of two or more agencies (e.g., synergistic MUSCLES, or a chemical with a mechanical phenomenon, or even a chemist with a physicist) to greater effect than both would have working independently.

SYNFUELS, synthetic fuels, especially oil and gas derived from coal and shale. Interest in the development of synfuels was stimulated by President Jimmy Carter, who in 1980 signed the bill creating the US Synthetic Fuels Corporation, intended to promote the development of a domestic synfuel industry. President Ronald Reagan has supported 2 synfuel projects, and research is also being done in this area by some large oil companies.

SYNGE, John Millington (1871–1909), Irish dramatist. Influenced by the CELTIC RENAISSANCE, he studied Irish peasant life and dramatized his view of Irish myth and character in his plays *In the Shadow of the Glen* (1903), *Riders to the Sea* (1904), *The Tinker's Wedding* (1908), and his most famous work, *The Playboy of the Western World* (1907). He was encouraged by W. B. YEATS and with him helped organize the Abbey Theatre in Dublin.

SYNOPTIC GOSPELS, the three GOSPELS (Matthew, Mark and Luke) which—unlike the Gospel of JOHN—have a large degree of subject-matter and phraseology in common. Modern scholars commonly regard Mark as prior and suppose that Matthew and Luke also used Q, a lost source containing the non-Marcan material common to each, and other sources peculiar to each.

SYNTAX. See GRAMMAR.

SYNTHETIC FIBER, man-made textile FIBER derived from artificial POLYMERS, as opposed to regenerated fibers (such as rayon) made from natural substances, or to natural fibers. Almost all types of long-chain polymer may be used: NYLON, the first to be discovered, is a polyamide; Dacron is a polyester, useful for nonstretch clothing. Other widely-used synthetic fibers include ORLON, POLYETHYLENE and FIBERGLASS. Polyurethane fibers are ELASTOMERS, used in stretch fabrics. To make the fibers, the polymer is usually converted to a liquid by melting or dissolving it; this is extruded through a spinneret with minute holes, and forms a filament as the solvent evaporates (dry spinning) or as it passes into a suitable chemical bath (wet spinning). The filaments are drawn (stretched) to increase strength by aligning the polymer molecules. They may then be used as such, or cut into short lengths which are twisted together, forming yarn.

SYPHILIS. See VENEREAL DISEASES.

SYRACUSE, or Siracusa, city in SE Sicily. Founded by Corinthians c734 BC, it became a brilliant center of Greek culture, notably under HIERO I and DIONYSIUS THE ELDER. Syracuse was defeated in the PUNIC WARS by Rome (211 BC). Later conquerors were the Arabs (878) and Normans (1085). The modern provincial capital, a port and tourist center, has many ancient monuments. Pop 124,111.

SYRIA, republic in SW Asia bordered by Turkey (N), Iraq (E), Jordan (S), and Israel, Lebanon and the Mediterranean (W).

Land. The Euphrates R flows SE through Syria. To the N lie rolling plains, to the S the Syrian Desert, ending in the SW with the Jebel Druz plateau and fertile Hauran plains. Further W lie the Anti-Lebanon Mts with Mt Hermon (9,232ft) in the S, and the Ansariya range with the cultivated coastal plain beyond it in the N. The warm Mediterranean climate gives way inland to a more extreme temperature range. Annual rainfall (Nov.–March) is heaviest (about 50in) on the W Ansariya slopes, while the desert has less than 5in.

People. After Damascus the largest cities are Aleppo, Homs and Hama (all in fertile zones E of the mountains) and the seaport of Latakia. Over 80% of the people are Arab-speaking Muslims, mostly SUNNITE, but there are nomadic BEDOUIN, and Kurdish, Turkish and Armenian minorities. Christian Orthodox churches claim some 500,000 members. There are about 120,000 DRUZES. Government programs have reduced illiteracy to some 50%. There are universities at Damascus, Aleppo, and Latakia.

Economy. About half the people work in agriculture. Many large estates were expropriated beginning in 1958 and redistributed, and attempts are being made to increase yields through modern methods and irrigation. Industry includes textiles, iron and steel, and assembly of transportation and electrical equipment. Exports include cotton, fruits and vegetables, and phosphates. Most oil revenues are derived from pipe lines crossing the country, but income from oil drilled in the NE is increasing. The large Euphrates Dam power station opened in 1978.

History. Part of the ancient HITTITE empire, Syria was conquered by Assyrians, Babylonians, Persians and Greeks. Under the SELEUCIDS after the death of ALEXANDER THE GREAT, it was later incorporated into the Roman empire by POMPEY. The Arabs conquered Syria in the 600s (see MAMELUKES; OMAYYADS; SALADIN; SELJUKS). Part of the OTTOMAN EMPIRE from 1516, Syria was mandated to the French after WWI and became fully independent in

Official name: The Syrian Arab Republic
Capital: Damascus
Area: 71,772sq mi
Population: 8,347,000
Languages: Arabic; Armenian, Kurdish, Turkish
Religions: Muslim, Christian, Druze
Monetary unit(s): 1 Syrian pound=100 piastres

1946. It joined with Egypt in the UNITED ARAB REPUBLIC 1958–61. From the late 1950s, emphasis in trade shifted toward the USSR and E European countries. The ruling BAATHIST Party, which assumed control of the government in 1963, favors socialism and pan-Arab nationalism, but in the early 1980s faced growing unrest especially from the fundamentalist Muslim Brotherhood. Since 1967 Israel has occupied the Golan Heights in the SW. In 1976 Syrian troops intervened in the Lebanese civil war in support of the Palestinians and have continued their presence.

SYRIAC, an ARAMAIC language of the NW Semitic group. It was used in early Christian writings but was largely superseded by Arabic after the spread of Islam. Closely related to Hebrew, Syriac is still spoken by small groups in the Middle East.

SZASZ, Thomas Stephen (1920–   ) Hungarian-born US psychiatrist and prominent critic of traditional psychiatry. He believes that "mental illness" is a mythical concept used by the state to control and limit the freedom of deviants in US society. Among his books are *The Myth of Mental Illness* (1961) and *The Manufacture of Madness* (1971).

SZELL, Georg (1897–1970), Hungarian-born US conductor. He established his reputation in Germany but emigrated to the US when the Nazis rose to power. Szell's many recordings with the Cleveland Orchestra have gained international acclaim.

SZENT-GYÖRGI VON NAGYRAPOLT, Albert (1893–   ), Hungarian-born US biochemist awarded the 1937 Nobel Prize for Physiology or Medicine for work on biological COMBUSTION processes, especially in relation to VITAMIN C.

SZIGETI, Joseph (1892–1973), US violinist. Born in Hungary, he emigrated to the US in the 1920s. Szigeti is particularly famous for his performances of virtuoso contemporary works.

SZILARD, Leo (1898–1964), Hungarian-born US physicist largely responsible for the US embarking on the development of the atom bomb (see MANHATTAN PROJECT). In 1945 he was a leader of the movement against using it. Later he made contributions in the field of molecular biology.

SZOLD, Henrietta (1860–1945), founder in 1912 of the Women's Zionist Organization of America (Hadassah). Baltimore born, she moved to Palestine in 1920, and directed medical and rehabilitation work, particularly for children.

20th letter of our alphabet. Last letter of the ancient North Semitic alphabet, it became the 19th letter of the Greek (as *tau*) and Roman alphabets. The small t developed in 6th-century Roman script.

TABLE TENNIS, or **Ping Pong**, indoor game similar to a small-scale version of TENNIS. It is played by two or four players on a table divided by a 6 in-high net into two 5ft × 4½ft courts. The players use wooden rackets to strike a hollow celluloid ball over the net into the opposite court. The game is administered by the International Table Tennis Federation, and biennial world tournaments are held.

TACHÉ, Sir Étienne Paschal (1795–1865), Canadian politician, premier 1856–57 and 1864 65 of the province of Canada. He presided over the historic Quebec Convention (1865) leading to federation of British North American colonies.

TACHYCARDIA. See HEART.

TACITUS, Cornelius (c55–c120 AD), Roman historian. His most famous works are critical studies of the 1st-century empire, the *Histories* and *Annals*. A son-in-law of AGRICOLA, of whom he wrote a biography, he rose to consul (97), and proconsul of Asia (112). His *Germania* is the earliest study of the Germanic tribes.

TAFT, Lorado (1860–1936), US sculptor, author of a pioneering *History of American Sculpture* (1903). Typical of his allegorical monuments (often fountains) is *The Fountain of the Great Lakes* in Chicago. He taught at Chicago Art Institute from 1886.

TAFT, Robert Alphonso (1889–1953), US senator from Ohio, 1938–53. Eldest son of W. H. TAFT, he studied law, served in the Ohio legislature, and became a leading conservative Republican. Taft was a fiscal conservative, an opponent of the NEW DEAL and an isolationist. His most famous congressional achievement was the TAFT-HARTLEY ACT.

TAFT, William Howard (1857–1930), 27th president of the US. An enormous, self-effacing man, he had the misfortune to succeed Theodore ROOSEVELT and suffered in comparison. He never wanted to be president and was politically inept; yet the achievements of his administration were substantial.

After a promising legal career, in which he served as state judge, US solicitor general and federal judge, Taft became first civil governor of the Philippines (1901). In 1904 he became Roosevelt's secretary of war and his concerns included the reorganization of the PANAMA CANAL project and the settlement of the RUSSO-JAPANESE WAR. In 1908 Roosevelt named him- his successor, and Taft easily defeated William Jennings Bryan.

The new president's policies were based largely on those of Roosevelt. He increased prosecutions under the SHERMAN ANTITRUST ACT and introduced controls on government expenditure. His domestic reforms included a bill requiring disclosure of campaign funds in federal elections. In foreign affairs his efforts at international peace-keeping failed through poor management, and his "dollar diplomacy" poisoned relations with Latin America. Taft's inability to reduce tariffs effectively, his failure to curb the powers of Speaker CANNON, and his dismissal of chief forester Gifford PINCHOT alienated progressive Republicans. With progressive support Roosevelt began to attack Taft and ran against him in the 1912 election on a BULL MOOSE ticket. The split allowed the Democrat Woodrow WILSON to sweep into power.

Taft's defeat allowed him to return to his legal career and in 1921 he achieved a lifelong ambition when he was appointed chief justice of the Supreme Court, thus becoming the only man to serve as both chief justice and president.

TAFT-HARTLEY ACT, the Labor-Management Relations Act of 1947, sponsored by Sen. Robert A. TAFT and Rep. Fred Hartley. It was passed over the veto of President TRUMAN and amended the WAGNER ACT. The act defined "unfair labor practices," and banned boycotts, sympathy strikes and strikes in interunion disputes. A federal arbitration service was set up and states were empowered to prohibit union shop agreements. A further controversial provision was presidential power to seek an 80-day injunction against a strike in cases of "national emergency." (See also LANDRUM-GRIFFIN ACT.)

TAGALOG, a people who comprise over 20% of the population of the Philippines. Their majority in Manila gives them preeminence in business, administration and the arts. Since 1937 Tagalog (or Pilipino) has been the national language.

TAGORE, Sir Rabindranath (1861–1941), Bengali Indian poet, painter, musician and mystic who founded what is now Visva-Bharati U. to blend the best in Indian and Western culture. His literary work includes many songs, poems, plays, novels, short stories and essays. He received the 1913 Nobel Prize for Literature.

TAGUS RIVER, or Tajo, longest river in the Iberian peninsula. It flows W 556mi from the Montes Universales in central Spain to the Atlantic coast of Portugal at LISBON.

TAHITI, largest of the Society Islands in the S Pacific, the center of FRENCH POLYNESIA. Its 400sq mi are mountainous and rich in tropical vegetation. The 95,600 people are Polynesians, with some French and Chinese. PAPEETE is the capital. Tahiti, claimed for France by BOUGAINVILLE in 1768, was visited by James COOK and William BLIGH. Its beauty inspired GAUGUIN.

TAINE, Hippolyte Adolphe (1828–1893), French critic and historian who devised a "scientific" method of criticism based on study of an author's environment and historical situation. The implications of his determinism greatly influenced the growth of literary NATURALISM. His most famous work is *History of English Literature* (1864).

TAIPEI, or T'ai-pei, capital and largest city of TAIWAN, lying to the N on the Tanshui R. A major industrial city, with steel plants, oil refineries and glass factories, Taipei is also the cultural and educational center of Taiwan. Founded in the early 1700s, it became capital of the Nationalist Chinese government in 1949. Pop 2,196,200.

TAIPING REBELLION (1851–64), great Chinese peasant uprising. Agrarian discontent was channeled into a mass movement by the mystic leader Hung Hsiu-ch'üan, who claimed to be the brother of Christ. His regime in Kwangsi province survived 10 years but was finally crushed with the help of Charles GORDON and his 3,000 mercenaries. The rebellion seriously weakened the Manchu dynasty.

TAIWAN. See CHINA, REPUBLIC OF.

TAJ MAHAL, a MAUSOLEUM built by the Mogul emperor Shah Jahan for his wife Mumtaz-i-Mahal at Agra in N India. Faced in white marble, the central domed tomb stands on a square plinth with a minaret at each corner, surrounded by water gardens, gateways and walks. It took some 20,000 workmen over 20 years to complete (1632–54).

TALBOT, William Henry Fox (1800–1877), English scientist and inventor of the Calotype (Talbotype) method of PHOTOGRAPHY. In Calotype a latent image in silver iodide is developed in gallic acid and fixed in sodium thiosulfate giving a paper "negative." Thus, for the first time, any number of positive prints could be made from a single exposure by contact printing.

TALLAHASSEE, state capital of Fla., seat of Leon Co. Famous for its gardens, the city is the commercial center of NW Fla. and has light industry and two state universities. Pop 81,548.

TALLCHIEF, Maria (1925–   ), US ballerina. From 1948 to 1965 she was prima ballerina of the New York City Ballet, where BALANCHINE created many roles for her.

TALLEYRAND (Charles-Maurice de Talleyrand-Perigord; 1754–1838), French statesman. He was a member of the National Assembly during the FRENCH REVOLUTION, helped Napoleon found the First Empire (1804), assisted the restoration of the Bourbon kings (1814), then helped oust them in favor of a constitutional monarchy (1830). Talleyrand is best remembered for his brilliant diplomacy at the Congress of Vienna (see VIENNA, CONGRESS OF) and in the negotiations (1830–31) between France and Britain which set up the state of Belgium.

TALLIS, Thomas (c1505–1585), English composer and organist. He was a close associate of William BYRD, with whom he shared a state monopoly in the printing of music. Tallis is famous for his solemn, elaborately constructed choral church music and for his development of COUNTERPOINT.

TALMADGE, name of two Georgia political leaders. **Eugene Talmadge** (1884–1946) was governor three times between 1933 and 1943. He supported segregation and opposed Roosevelt's New Deal programs and federal social security legislation. His son, **Herman Eugene Talmadge** (1913–   ), was governor 1948–55 and US senator 1956–1981. He is remembered as an incisive questioner of witnesses during Watergate.

TALMUD, (Hebrew: teaching), ancient compilation of Jewish oral law and rabbinical teaching, begun 5th century AD. There are two versions: Babylonian and Palestinian. It has two parts: the MISHNAH and the GEMARA. These contain a wealth of traditional wisdom, legends and stories, comment on the Old Testament and record early legal decisions. The Talmud is second only to the Bible in prestige, and its study has been the core of Jewish education for over 1,000 years.

TAMAYO, Rufino (1899–   ), Mexican

painter. He combines the strength and color of native and pre-Columbian art with Expressionist and Surrealist styles. He has painted several frescoes but is best known for his small paintings of Indian figures.

TAMBOURINE, a PERCUSSION INSTRUMENT comprising a skin stretched across a hoop fitted with bells or "jingles" which rattle as it is tapped or shaken. Originating in the Middle East, it is used in folk music and in some orchestral scores.

TAMERLANE (c1336–1405), or Timur the Lame, Mongol conqueror. Claiming descent from GENGHIS KHAN, by 1370 he controlled from his capital SAMARKAND what is now Soviet Turkmenistan. He conquered Persia (1387), the Caucasus (1392), Syria (1400) and the Ottoman Turks (1402) in the W, and invaded India and sacked Delhi (1398). He died planning to invade China. The empire rapidly disintegrated.

TAMIL, a DRAVIDIAN language spoken by some 40 million, principally in SE India and NE Ceylon. It is the main language of Tamil Nadu (formerly Madras) state. Tamil has its own script, and a rich ancient literature.

TAMMANY HALL, nickname from the 1800s for the corrupt New York Democratic Party machine, also the name of its Madison Avenue offices. The patriotic society of Tammany (a wise Delaware Indian chief) was founded in 1789, with a ritual based on Indian custom. It became a Democratic machine, dominating the city after c1830, with corruption common under "bosses" like William TWEED. Its influence spread beyond New York, but the reforms of LA GUARDIA (mayor, 1933–45) led to its decline.

TANAKA, Kakuei (1918–   ), Japanese prime minister 1972–74. He built up a construction business, headed the Liberal Democratic Party from 1965 and held cabinet posts from 1968. Acquitted in 1949 on bribery charges, he was charged in the 1976 Lockheed bribery scandal. The subsequent trial continued for years, and Tanaka remained active in politics.

TANEY, Roger Brooke (1777–1864), chief justice of the US (1836–64) whose DRED SCOTT CASE decision helped bring on the Civil War. As President Jackson's secretary of the treasury (1833–35), he crushed the Second BANK OF THE UNITED STATES. As chief justice, he steered a middle course on STATES' RIGHTS, and continued John MARSHALL'S liberal interpretation of the Constitution. (See also SUPREME COURT OF THE UNITED STATES.)

TANGANYIKA. See TANZANIA.

TANGANYIKA, Lake, in W Tanzania and E Zaire, in the Great Rift Valley. Africa's second-largest lake, it is 420mi N–S, 30–45mi E–W and up to 4,710ft deep. It has important fisheries.

TANGE, Kenzo (1913–   ), Japanese architect and city planner who combines modern techniques and materials with traditional Japanese design. His design for the Hiroshima Peace Hall (1955–56) was influenced by LE CORBUSIER. He also designed the dramatic National Gymnasium for the 1964 Tokyo Olympic Games.

TANGO, Latin American dance, originating in Argentina, with long, gliding steps, deep bendings of the knees and syncopated music. It was a popular ballroom dance after WWI.

TANGUY, Yves (1900–1955), French Surrealist painter, who lived in the US from 1939. Influenced by CHIRICO, he painted a dream-like world of strange inhuman shapes inhabiting a lunar landscape. (See SURREALISM.)

TANIZAKI, Junichiro (1886–1965), Japanese novelist and short-story writer. A leading neoromantic influenced by POE, BAUDELAIRE and WILDE, he infused his work with sensuality, cruelty and mysterious demonic forces. Among his works is *The Makioka Sisters* (1948; tr. 1957).

TANK, armored combat vehicle, armed with guns or missiles, and self-propelled on caterpillar treads; the chief modern conventional ground assault weapon. Tanks were first built in 1915 by Britain and used from 1916 against Germany in WWI. These early tanks were very slow, and development between the wars greatly improved speed and firepower. The Spanish civil war and WWII showed the effectiveness of concentrated tank attacks. Amphibious and airborne tanks were developed. Heavy tanks proved cumbersome, and were generally abandoned in favor of the more maneuverable (though more vulnerable) light and medium tanks. Improved models are now used where heavy guns are needed. Light tanks (less than 25 tons) are used mainly for infantry support.

Newer tanks like the US Army's M-1 or Abrams are carefully armored against the growing proliferation of highly accurate antitank missiles and the armor-penetrating projectiles of larger caliber high-velocity guns. The M-1 features a variety of the British Chobham armor, especially designed to dissipate kinetic energy. Like most new main battle tanks it has a lightly armored skirt and more streamlined profile to decrease vulnerability.

Tanks may be forced to return to a visual communication system (pennants, flags, flares etc.) due to the sophisticated jamming techniques developed for use in an electronic warfare scenario.

Development of a new breed of tank is being accompanied by a new series of armored personnel carriers. Heavily armed and ARMORED, and fast enough to follow tanks into battle, they will provide the manpower which is increasingly being seen as an essential support of tank operations.

TANKER, ship designed to carry liquid cargo in bulk, notably crude oil, gasoline or natural gas. The first tanker (1886), a 300ft vessel, carried 3,000 tons of oil. Some tankers today hold 100 times as much: a 483,939-ton vessel (the *Globtik London*, 1975) has been built in Japan. Ships this size greatly reduce per-ton transport costs, but cannot enter many ports; some large tankers transfer their cargo to smaller tankers offshore. In gross tonnage tankers account for over a third of all MERCHANT SHIPPING.

TANNENBERG (Polish: Stebark), village in N Poland, 15mi SE of Ostróda, site of two important battles. In 1410, the TEUTONIC KNIGHTS were defeated by the Lithuanians and Poles, and in WWI (August, 1914), the Germans severely defeated the Russians. Up to 1945 Tannenberg was in Germany.

TANNING, the conversion of animal hide into LEATHER. After cleaning and soaking, a tanning agent is applied that converts the GELATIN of the hide into an insoluble material which cements the PROTEIN fibers together and makes them incorruptible. Until the end of the 19th century vegetable extracts containing TANNINS were used; then the process was greatly shortened by using CHROMIUM salts, and also FORMALDEHYDE and FORMIC ACID.

TANTRAS, the texts of Tantrism, a system of esoteric Hindu and Buddhist practices. Tantras are often dialogues between the male and female aspects (in Hinduism SHIVA and SHAKTI) of a supreme deity. They instruct in meditation and YOGA (including ritual sex) as a means of reaching ultimate truth through mind and body. They date from c500 AD.

TANZANIA, republic in E Africa, on the Indian Ocean. It was formed (1964) by the union of Tanganyika with the island of ZANZIBAR.

Land. Tanzania is a beautiful country, with plateaus, mountain ranges, Africa's highest peak (Mt. Kilimanjaro), Rift Valley lakes and the S part of Lake Victoria. Inland the climate is hot and dry with some rain Dec.–May. Coral reefs and mangrove swamps line the coast. Grasslands and open woods dominate the extensive plains,

famous for their wildlife.

People. The vast majority (94%) are rural. There are over 100 BANTU tribes, each with distinctive languages and customs. There are Indian, Arab and European minorities. The illiteracy rate is high, but there is a modern university in **Dar es Salaam.**

Economy. Since 1967 Tanzania, guided by President NYERERE, has attempted to institute socialism through communal farming villages. Due to various factors, including some resistance to these programs, food production dropped sharply, creating deep problems in the agriculture-based economy. Coffee and cotton are primary exports. Other important exports are cloves (from Zanzibar), pyrethrum, sisal, tobacco and tea. Manufacturing centers around the processing of primary commodities. Tanzania's involvement 1978–79 in unseating Idi AMIN of Uganda also created economic dislocations.

History. OLDUVAI GORGE in N Tanzania has the world's earliest known human and pre-human remains. In historical times, the coast and Zanzibar came under Arab control from the 700s AD. Germany established a mainland protectorate (1891), but after WWI the region passed to Britain by League of Nations mandate. Tanganyika gained independence in 1961, Zanzibar in 1964. The capital was transferred from Dar es Salaam to Dodoma beginning in 1975.

Official name: United Republic of Tanzania
Capital: Dodoma
Area: 362,821sq mi
Population: 17,884,000
Languages: Swahili, English; Bantu dialects
Religions: Animist, Muslim, Christian
Monetary unit(s): 1 Tanzanian shilling = 10 cents

TAOISM, ancient Chinese philosophy, in influence second only to CONFUCIANISM, derived chiefly from the book *Tao-te Ching* (3rd century BC) attributed to LAO-TSE. It advocated a contemplative life in accord with nature, unspoiled by intellectual evaluations. Tao ("The Way") was considered impossible to describe save in cryptic imagery. Taoism later became a polytheistic religion.

TAP DANCE, an exhibition dance in which the toes and heels are tapped rapidly against a hard surface. Metal-tipped shoes clarify the complicated rhythms. Tap dancing developed in black communities in the US and on vaudeville stages, reaching a high point in the dancing of Bill ROBINSON and being carried to more sophisticated level by Fred ASTAIRE.

TAPE RECORDER, instrument for SOUND RECORDING on magnetic tape, and subsequent playback. The tape, consisting of small magnetic particles of iron oxides on a thin plastic film base, is wound from the supply reel to the take-up reel by a rotating capstan which controls the speed. The tape passes in turn: the erase head, which by applying an alternating field reduces the overall magnetization to zero; the recording head; and the playback head. Standard tape speeds are $1\frac{7}{8}$, $3\frac{3}{4}$, $7\frac{1}{2}$, 15 or 30 in/s, the higher speeds being used for HIGH-FIDELITY reproduction. **Cassettes** contain thin tape handily packaged, running at $1\frac{7}{8}$ in/s. The somewhat larger **cartridges** contain an endless loop of tape on a single reel. Most recorders use two, four or even more tracks side by side on the tape.

TAPESTRY, a fabric woven with colored threads to form a design and used to cover walls and furniture. Warp threads are stretched on a loom, and colored threads, or wefts, are woven over and under them and then compacted (see also WEAVING). Tapestries were known in ancient Egypt, Syria, Persia and China. N Europe's great era of tapestry-making began in the 1300s, notably at ARRAS in Flanders. It reached a peak in the GOBELIN tapestries of the 1600s. Great painters who have made tapestry designs include Raphael and Rubens. The BAYEUX TAPESTRY is in fact embroidery.

TAPEWORMS, intestinal parasites, so named because they are long and flat, forming the class Cestoda of the FLATWORM phylum Platyhelminthes. A scolex, or head, only 1.5–2mm (about 0.06in) in diameter is attached to the gut and behind this the body consists of a ribbon of identical flat segments, or proglottids, each containing reproductive organs. These proglottids are budded off from behind the scolex. Mature proglottids containing eggs pass out with the feces where larval stages can infect intermediate hosts.

TAPIRS, a family, Tapiridae, of large brown or black and white UNGULATES related to RHINOCEROSES. They are plump, thick-skinned vegetarian animals characterized by a short mobile nasal "trunk" and with four toes on the front feet and three on the hind feet. Of four living species, the largest, *Tapirus indicus* occurs in Malaya, the others being South American.

TARANTELLA, lively Italian dance with six beats to the bar. It is linked with tarantism, hysterical dancing once common near Taranto. The dance supposedly cured the bite of a tarantula spider.

TARANTULA, popular name, originally of the large WOLF SPIDER *Lycosa tarantula*, but now used for various unrelated giant SPIDERS throughout the world. All are long and hairy and eat large insects or small vertebrates. Their venom seldom has serious effects on humans.

TARBELL, Ida Minerva (1857–1944), US journalist, a leader of the MUCKRAKERS. Her exposure of malpractice in *The History of the Standard Oil Company* (1904) led to successful prosecution of the company in 1911.

TARGET SHOOTING, competitive shooting with a firearm at a target, usually a cardboard square with a central black bullseye surrounded by concentric circles. The closer a hit to the bullseye, the more it scores. The sport became popular in the 19th century; it has been an event of the Olympic Games since 1896.

TARIFFS, customs duties on exports or, more commonly, imports. The aim is generally to protect home industries from foreign competition, though it may be merely to provide revenue. During the 17th and 18th centuries the European powers created tariff systems that gave their colonies preferential treatment, but Britain's tariffs, by limiting North America's trade, helped provoke the Revolutionary War. In the early 1800s the FREE TRADE movement, bolstered by the economic philosophy of LAISSEZ-FAIRE, helped limit the spread of tariffs. However, US federal tariffs imposed to aid Northern industry damaged the South and contributed to the Civil War. US and European tariffs were moderate in the early 1900s but, after the Great Depression, both the US and UK adopted high tariffs, with a consequent decline in INTERNATIONAL TRADE. In 1947 the US and 22 other nations signed the GENERAL AGREEMENT ON TARIFFS AND TRADE (GATT) aimed at reducing trade discrimination. GATT has only partly achieved this, notably in the "Kennedy Round" (1964–67), involving over 50 nations and a broad range of commodities. By the 1980s, high EUROPEAN ECONOMIC COMMUNITY tariffs against food imports and a general trade recession roused fears of revived PROTECTIONISM. (See also ECONOMICS; EUROPEAN FREE TRADE ASSOCIATION.)

TARKINGTON, Newton Booth (1869–1946), US writer famous for his novels reflecting Midwestern life and character, as in his *Penrod* (1914). He worked for *The Saturday Evening Post*, was an Ind. representative (1902–03), and won two Pulitzer prizes (1919, 1922) for *The Magnificent Ambersons* (1918) and *Alice Adams* (1921).

TAROT, pack of 78 PLAYING CARDS used for fortune telling or for the card game *tarok* (tarot or tarocchi). There are four suits each of 14 cards (cups, pentacles, swords and wands) and a major arcana of 22 cards (also called tarots) which in the card game operate as permanent trumps.

TARPONS, powerful, silvery fishes renowned for their fighting powers when hooked as game fishes. There are two species, primarily marine, the Indo-Pacific tarpon, *Megalops cyprinoides*, and the Atlantic tarpon *Tarpon atlanticus*, which may grow to 2.5m (8ft) and weigh 130kg (287lb).

TARSKI, Alfred (1902–   ), Polish-born US mathematician and logician who was one of the most influential figures in 20th-century philosophy. A professor at the U. of Cal. at Berkeley (1942–68), he made fundamental contributions to the fields of metamathematics, semantics and symbolic logic.

TASHKENT, capital of the Uzbek SSR and fourth largest city in USSR, located in Chirchik Valley W of Chatkal Mts. One of the oldest cities in Asia, it was an important trading center for Arab, Muslim and Mongol empires. Major products are textiles and agricultural machinery. Rebuilt after a devastating earthquake in 1966, it is an important cultural center. Pop 1,821,000.

TASMAN, Abel Janszoon (c1603–1659), Dutch sailor and S Pacific explorer. Sailing from Java in Dutch East India Company service (1642–43, 1644), he discovered Tasmania and New Zealand (1642), which he thought were parts of Australia, then Tonga and Fiji (1643).

TASMANIA, smallest Australian state (26,383sq mi, pop 414,000). The 150mi Bass Strait separates Tasmania from the SE mainland. It includes King, Flinders and Macquarie islands, as well as the main island (christened by TASMAN Van Diemen's Land). Tasmania's forests contain the unique TASMANIAN DEVIL and THYLACINE. Chief cities are HOBART (the capital), Launceston, Burnie and Devonport. Impor-

tant industries are livestock (dairying, wool), horticulture, lumber and newsprint, mining and mineral processing (zinc, copper, lead). (See also TASMANIANS.)

TASS (Telegraph Agency of the Soviet Union), the state monopoly news agency of the USSR. Founded in 1925, it is managed by the Propaganda Department of the Communist Party's Central Committee.

TASSO, Torquato (1544–1595), Italy's major late Renaissance poet, a master of lyrical, sensuous, often mournful verse. His works include the pastoral drama *Aminta* (1573) and his masterpiece *Jerusalem Delivered* (completed 1575), an epic based on the First Crusade.

TASTE, special SENSE concerned with the differentiation of basic modalities of food or other substances in the mouth; receptors are distributed over the surface of the TONGUE and are able to distinguish salt, sweet, sour, bitter and possibly water as primary tastes. Much of what is colloquially termed taste is actually SMELL, perception of odors reaching the olfactory EPITHELIUM via the naso-PHARYNX. Receptors for sweet are concentrated at the tip of the tongue, for salt and sour along the sides, with bitter mainly at the back. Taste nerve impulses pass via the BRAIN stem to the cortex.

TATARS, or **Tartars**, Turkic-speaking people of the USSR, where some 4,500,000 live in the Tatar Autonomous SSR, along the Volga R, in the Ural Mts. and the Uzbek and Kazakh SSRs. Most are Sunnite Muslims. Tatar also describes the E Mongolian tribes, part of the GOLDEN HORDE, which seized much of Russia in the 1200s (see MONGOL EMPIRE).

TATE, John Orley Allen (1899–1979), distinguished US writer, critic and teacher. Born in Ky., he helped found the FUGITIVES and advocated the "new criticism," with its stress on a work's intrinsic qualities. His own work includes several collections of his poetry and essays, biographies and a novel.

TATI, Jacques (1908–   ), French pantomimist and actor who wrote, directed and starred in the comic film masterpieces *Monsieur Hulot's Holiday* (1952) and *Mon Oncle* (1958).

TATLIN, Vladimir (1885–1956), Russian painter and sculptor, leader of CONSTRUCTIVISM. Influenced by PICASSO's cubist reliefs, he made in 1913 abstract reliefs of tin, wood, glass and plaster and *Corner-reliefs* (1915) suspended on wire. In 1920 he planned a symbolic monument to the Third INTERNATIONAL.

TATTING, craft using thread and a shuttle to produce a lace-like fabric. Long popular in Italy, France and the East, it was widely practiced in the courts of 18th-century Europe.

TATTOOING, decorating the body by injecting colored pigment beneath the surface of the skin, a method of personal adornment used throughout history, but especially elaborated among the Maori.

TATUM, Arthur "Art" (1910–1956), brilliant self-taught US jazz pianist. His command of jazz styles was comprehensive and influenced jazz and non-jazz musicians alike.

TATUM, Edward Lawrie (1909–1975), US biochemist awarded the 1958 Nobel Prize for Physiology or Medicine with G. W. BEADLE and J. LEDERBERG for work with Beadle showing that individual GENES control production of particular ENZYMES (1937–40).

TAURUS (the Bull), a large constellation on the ECLIPTIC; the second sign of the ZODIAC. It contains the CRAB NEBULA, the GALACTIC CLUSTERS the Hyades and PLEIADES, and the bright star Aldebaran.

TAURUS MOUNTAINS, a range in S Turkey, parallel with the Mediterranean coast and extending NE as the Anti-Taurus. It has many peaks of 10,000ft to 12,000ft. The range is well wooded and has various mineral deposits.

TAUSSIG, Helen Brooke (1898–   ), US pediatrician and cardiologist who developed the "blue baby operation" (1945; with surgeon Alfred Blalock) which increased blood circulation to the lungs and stimulated research on the surgical correction of congenital heart defects.

TAVERNER, John (c1495–1545), English composer whose ornate masses and motets are among the finest early Tudor music. After 1530 he turned from music to suppressing monasteries as an agent of Thomas Cromwell.

TAWNEY, Richard Henry (1880–1962), British historian and social theorist. His best known book *Religion and the Rise of Capitalism* (1926), connects the hard work and individualism of the Protestants of N Europe in the 16th and 17th centuries with the growth of capitalism there.

TAXATION, the raising of revenue to pay for government expenditure. Broadly speaking, a tax can be described as direct or indirect: income tax is paid directly to the government, but sales taxes are collected indirectly through government charges on goods or services. A tax is also progressive or regressive: income tax is usually progressive (its rate rises as the taxable sum increases); sales taxes tend to be regressive (their burden decreases as the taxpayer's income increases).

Modern taxation serves three purposes. It meets government expenditure on public services, administration and defense. In some countries social justice is promoted by the redistribution of income: the rich are taxed at higher rates than the poor, who may receive grants from revenue. Control of the economy is achieved by adjusting direct or indirect taxes to curb consumption or encourage investment. It is often difficult to achieve all three objectives equally effectively.

In the US the Constitution at first required that taxes be levied in proportion to the population, and that indirect taxes must be uniform throughout all states. An INCOME TAX, which does not meet these requirements, was permitted by the 16th Amendment in 1913, and came to replace TARIFFS and EXCISES as a principal source of revenue. During and after WWI, the federal government developed its individual and corporation income taxes, expanded excises, and introduced an estate INHERITANCE TAX and a social security payroll levy. By WWII federal taxes had reached new peaks and become important in regulating the economy, being used to curb inflation and prevent profiteering. The major form of state and local taxation is now the *property tax*; states also tax gasoline, retail sales and automobiles, and many states and cities tax income. A taxpayers' revolt against high property taxes began in Cal. in 1978, when voters approved a state constitutional amendment restricting taxes on real property, and the revolt soon spread to other states (see PROPOSITION 13). It also took the form of organized opposition to high federal INCOME TAX, which culminated in the newly elected Reagan administration's reduction of personal income tax rates by 25% over three years, beginning Oct. 1, 1981.

TAX COURT, US federal tribunal established in 1924 to rule on disputes between taxpayers and the INTERNAL REVENUE SERVICE. Most decisions may be appealed to the US Court of Appeals.

TAXIDERMY, stuffing animal skins to make lifelike replicas. Taxidermy is now practiced mainly in large museums, though it originated in the production of hunting trophies; nowadays, rather than stuffing, the animal's form is duplicated and the skin stretched over.

TAXONOMY, the science of classifying PLANTS and ANIMALS. The theory of EVOLUTION states that organisms come into being as a result of gradual change and that closely related organisms are descended from a relatively recent common ancestor.

One of the main aims of taxonomy is to reflect such changes in a classification of groups, or taxa, which are arranged in a hierarchy such that small taxa contain organisms that are closely related and larger taxa contain organisms that are more distantly related. Taxa commonly employed are (in their conventional typography and starting with the largest): Kingdom, Phylum, Class, Order, Family, *Genus* and *Species*.

TAX SHELTER, an investment made less for the sake of profit than for purposes of reducing taxes, typically by deducting special depreciation allowances from current income. Traditional tax shelters include oil, gas, real estate and cattle. The reduction on Jan. 1, 1982, of the maximum tax rate for individuals from 70% to 50% has diminished, but did not end, the attractiveness of tax shelters.

TAYLOR, Alan John Percivale (1906–   ), British historian known for his iconoclastic interpretations of the origins of European wars of the 19th and 20th centuries. His books include *The Struggle for Mastery in Europe, 1848–1918* (1954), *The Origins of the Second World War* (1961) and *Revolutions and Revolutionaries* (1980).

TAYLOR, (Joseph) Deems (1885–1966), US composer. During his long career in music he worked as critic, radio commentator, network consultant and president of the American Society of Composers, Authors and Publishers (AS-CAP). His works include the operas *The King's Henchman* (1926) and *Peter Ibbetson* (1931).

TAYLOR, Elizabeth (1932–   ), film actress, one the classic screen beauties. After *Lassie Come Home* (1943) and *National Velvet* (1944), her adult successes included *Cat on a Hot Tin Roof* (1958) and *Butterfield 8* (1960), for which she won an Academy Award. With Richard BURTON, with whom she had a highly publicized romance and marriage, she starred in *Cleopatra* (1963) and *Who's Afraid of Virginia Woolf?* (1966).

TAYLOR, Frederick Winslow (1856–1915), US mechanical engineer who pioneered the principles of scientific management. He introduced TIME-AND-MOTION STUDY and held that careful analysis of every factory operation by man and machine alike was necessary for operational efficiency. These theories came to be known as **Taylorism.**

TAYLOR, Laurette (1884–1946), US stage actress who starred in a series of sentimental comedies, notably *Peg O' My Heart* (1912) and was popular through the 1920s. After a long period of inactivity due to alcoholism, she made a spectacular comeback in *The Glass Menagerie* (1945), giving one of the more memorable performances in Broadway history.

TAYLOR, Maxwell Davenport (1901–   ), US Army general who largely organized the US army's first airborne units in WWII. He commanded the Eighth Army in Korea 1953–55, headed the US and UN Far East commands 1954–55, was US army chief of staff 1955–59 and ambassador to Vietnam 1964–65.

TAYLOR, Telford (1908–   ), US legal scholar and attorney, who was chief US prosecutor at the Nuremberg war crimes trials. A law professor at Columbia University (1958–76), he wrote several books including *Nuremberg and Vietnam* (1970), *Courts of Terror* (1976) and *Munich: The Price of Peace* (1979).

TAYLOR, Zachary (1784–1850), 12th US president. Known as "Old Rough and Ready" to his soldiers, Taylor was a bold and resourceful general in the Mexican War and one of the most popular presidents of his period. Nevertheless, his brief term in the White House—he died after only 16 months in office—has been all but forgotten, though he did take a bold stand against the extension of slavery, the one burning issue of his term. Three things shaped his life: he was 40 years a soldier (doing much to open the West to settlement); his parents belonged to the wealthy planting aristocracy of old Va.; and he himself was brought up in Ky., on the frontiers of an expanding nation. He fought in the WAR OF 1812 and the BLACKHAWK WAR (1832), and subdued the SEMINOLE Indians in Fla.; his defeat of General SANTA ANNA'S forces in the MEXICAN WAR made him a national hero.

Standing as a Whig, he became president in 1849; his term was marked by the CLAYTON-BUTLER TREATY. More important, the acquisition of vast new territories threatened to upset the precarious balance between slave states and free (15 of each) established by the MISSOURI COMPROMISE of 1820. Determined to prevent expansion of slavery even though it might preserve the Union, and undoubtedly influenced by such advisors as William H. SEWARD, Taylor refused to compromise, even if it meant war. His sudden death in 1850 postponed the issue.

TAY-SACHS DISEASE, an inherited fatal disorder found primarily among Jews of or from eastern Europe. Among this group, as many as one out of 30 may be carriers. The disease is caused by a deficiency or defect in the enzyme hexosaminidase A, or sometimes in both hexosaminidase A and B, which allows fatty substances (sphyngolipids) to accumulate in the brain. The condition usually appears at 3 to 6 months of age and is characterized by mental retardation, blindness, muscular weakness, and a cherry-red spot on the retina of each eye. Death commonly occurs between the ages of 3 and 5 years. Individuals capable of transmitting this disease to their children can be detected by medical screening procedures.

TBILISI, or **Tiflis,** capital of the Georgian SSR, SW USSR, on the Kura R. It is a major manufacturing, cultural and educational center and transportation hub. The city was founded c450 AD as the capital of the ancient Georgian Kingdom. Pop 1,080,000.

TCHAIKOVSKY, Peter Ilich (1840–1893), Russian composer. He studied with Anton RUBINSTEIN, became professor at Moscow Conservatory and gave concerts of his own music in Europe and the US. His gift for melody and brilliant orchestration, plus the drama, excitement and emotional intensity of his music, makes him the most popular of all composers. Works such as the 1st Piano Concerto (1875), the Violin Concerto (1878) and *Pathetique* Symphony (No. 6; 1893) are known and loved by millions, and ballet owes much of its popularity to his *Swan Lake* (1876), *Sleeping Beauty* (1889) and *Nutcracker* (1892). His operas include *Eugene Onegin* (1879), *The Queen of Spades* (1890) and *The Maid of Orleans.*

TCHELITCHEW, Pavel (1898–1957), Russian-born US painter. He designed ballets, notably for DIAGHILEV, but is best known for such studies of perspective and metamorphosis as *Hide-and-Seek* (1941).

TEA, the cured and dried young leaves and tips of the tea plant (*Thea sinensis*) which are made into a drink popular throughout the world. Tea has been drunk in China since early times, but it was not until the early 1600s that the Dutch introduced it into Europe. Although expensive, it soon became fashionable. In the UK and the British colonies, the East India Company enjoyed a monopoly of the China tea trade until 1833; it was the attempt of the British government to levy a tax on tea imports into the American colonies that led to the BOSTON TEA PARTY of 1773. Today, the chief producers are India and Sri Lanka (Ceylon). Tea contains the stimulant CAFFEINE. The term tea is also used to describe many other local drinks produced

from the leaves of a vast array of plants. Family: Theaceae.

TEAGARDEN, Weldon John, "Jack" (1905–1964), US trombonist and jazz singer, one of the first (artistically) successful white jazzmen. He played with Paul WHITEMAN and after WWII with Louis ARMSTRONG. He led his own bands 1939–47 and 1951–57.

TEAK, a deciduous tree (*Tectona grandis*) whose wood is one of the most valuable in the world. Teaks grow in tropical climates from E India to Malaysia. The hard, oily wood is used for house construction, furniture, railroad sleepers etc. Several other trees produce a similar hardwood also called teak. Family: Verbenaceae.

TEAMSTERS (International Brotherhood of Teamsters, Chauffeurs, Warehousemen and Helpers of America), largest US labor union. Formed by an amalgamation in 1903, it has nearly 2,000,000 members, largely in trucking and warehousing. Its outstanding presidents were Daniel Tobin (1907–52), Dave Beck (1952–57) and Jimmy HOFFA (1957–71), although the latter two were jailed for corruption. In 1957 the Teamsters were expelled from the AFL-CIO.

TEAPOT DOME, scandal over government malpractice under President HARDING. The naval oil reserve at Teapot Dome, Wyo., was leased in 1922 by agreement of secretary of the interior Albert FALL to the Mammoth Oil Co. with no competitive bidding. A Senate investigation followed and the lease was canceled. Fall was later convicted of receiving another bribe in a similar transaction.

TEAR GAS, volatile substance that incapacitates for a time by powerfully irritating the eyes, provoking tears. Various halogenated organic compounds are used, including α–chloracetophenome (**Mace gas** or CN), and the even more potent CS gas. They are packed in grenades and used for riot control. (See also CHEMICAL AND BIOLOGICAL WARFARE.)

TEARS, watery secretions of the lacrymal GLANDS situated over the EYES which provide continuous lubrication and protection of cornea and sclera. A constant flow runs across the surface of the eye to the nasolacrymal duct at the inner corner, where tears drain into the NOSE. Excess tears produced in states of high emotion and conjunctival or corneal irritation overflow over the lower eyelid.

TEBALDI, Renata (1922–   ), Italian soprano. She was chosen by TOSCANINI to participate in La Scala's post-WWII reopening in 1946. In 1950 she made her

American debut in San Francisco as Aïda, and in 1955 she bowed at the Metropolitan as Desdemona in *Otello*.

TECTONICS, an area of study in geology dealing with the development of the broader structural features of the EARTH and their deformational origins. (See also PLATE TECTONICS; DIASTROPHISM.)

TECUMSEH (c1768–1813), great SHAWNEE INDIAN chief, warrior and orator who sought after the Revolution to unite Midwestern tribes against encroachment of their homelands. Despite British and widespread Indian support the effort failed with defeat of his brother TENSKWATAWA at the battle of TIPPECANOE (1811). Tecumseh died fighting for the British at the battle of the THAMES.

TEDDER, Arthur William (1890–1967), British air chief marshal. He was commander of the Royal Air Force in the Middle East 1940–43, then headed the Mediterranean Air Command and was deputy Supreme Allied Commander under Eisenhower, helping to plan and carry out the invasion of Europe.

TEETH, the specialized hard structures used for biting and chewing food. Their numbers vary in different species and at different ages, but in most cases an immature set of teeth (milk teeth) is replaced during growth by a permanent set. In man the latter consists of 32 teeth comprising 8 incisors, 4 canines, 8 premolars and 12 molars, of which the rearmost are the late-erupting wisdom teeth. ("Dentition" refers to the numbers and arrangement of the teeth in a species.) Each tooth consists of a crown, or part above the gum line, and a root, or insertion into the BONE of the jaw. The outer surface of the crowns is covered by a thin layer of enamel, the hardest animal tissue. This overlies the dentine, a substance similar to bone, and in the center of each tooth is the pulp which contains blood vessels and nerves. The **incisors** are developed for biting off food with a scissor action, while the **canines** are particularly developed in some species for maintaining a hold on an object. The **molars** and **premolars** are adapted for chewing and macerating food, which partly involves side-to-side movement of one jaw over the other. Maldevelopment and CARIES of teeth are the commonest problems encountered in DENTISTRY.

TEHERAN, or Tehran, capital and largest city of Iran, lies S of the Elburz Mts at about 3,800ft. Dating from the 1100s and Mogul destruction of nearby Ray (1220), it became capital in 1788. Modern Teheran is a manufacturing, transportation, and cultural center. The city was the center of the Iranian revolution of the later 1970s and early 1980s. Pop 4,496,159.

TEHERAN CONFERENCE, inter-allied conference of WWII, held in Teheran Nov.–Dec. 1943 and attended by Stalin, Roosevelt and Churchill. Important items were coordination of landings in France with a Soviet offensive against Germany from the E, future Russian entry into the war against Japan, and agreement on Iran's future independence.

TEILHARD DE CHARDIN, Pierre (1881–1955), French Jesuit, philosopher and paleontologist. He was in China 1923–46, where he studied Peking Man (see PREHISTORIC MAN). *The Phenomenon of Man* (1938–40) attempted to reconcile Christianity and science with a theory of man's evolution toward final spiritual unity. His superiors held his views to be unorthodox and warned against them; fame came to him and his ideas only post-humously.

TEKTITES, controversial, nonvolcanic glassy objects, usually of less than 100mm diameter, found only in certain parts of the world. Most are rich in SILICA: they resemble OBSIDIAN, though have less water. Despite suggestions that they are of extraterrestrial, particularly lunar, origin, it seems most likely that they have resulted from meteoritic impacts on terrestrial rock in the remote past.

TEL AVIV-JAFFA or -Yafo, second-largest city in Israel, on the Mediterranean coast NW of Jerusalem. It is a modern city-port and Israel's chief manufacturing center as well as a tourist resort. Tel Aviv was Israel's first capital, from 1948 to 1950 (when JAFFA was incorporated). Pop 339,800.

TELEGRAPH, electrical apparatus for sending coded messages. The term was first applied to Claude Chappe's SEMAPHORE. Experiments began on electric telegraphs after the discovery (1819) that a magnetic needle was deflected by a current in a nearby wire. In 1837 W. F. Cooke and Charles WHEATSTONE patented a system using six wires and five pointers which moved in pairs to indicate letters on a diamond-shaped array. It was used on English railroads. In the same year Samuel MORSE, in partnership with Alfred Vail, and helped by Joseph HENRY, patented a telegraph system using MORSE CODE in the US. The first intercity line was inaugurated in 1844. At first the receiver embossed or printed the code symbols but this was soon replaced by a sounding device. In 1858 Wheatstone invented a high-speed automatic Morse telegraph, using punched paper tape in transmission. The TELEX system, using teletypewriters, is now most popular. In 1872 Jean-Maurice-Émile Baudot invented a multiplexing system for sharing the time on each transmission line between several operators. Telegraph signals are now transmitted not only by wires and land lines but also by submarine cables and radio.

TELEMANN, Georg Philipp (1681–1767), versatile and prolific German composer, a master of all the musical forms of his day. His oratorios and other sacred music, over 40 operas and many instrumental works, are noted for their liveliness of rhythm and tunefulness.

TELEOLOGY (from Greek *telos*, end), the study of an action, event or thing with reference to its purpose or end. PLATO and ARISTOTLE argued that the purpose, perfection and good of a thing, which Aristotle called its "final cause," was the ultimate explanation of the thing. The teleological view of nature has declined since the rise of science. The teleological argument, or argument "from design," argues from the order and perfection of nature to the existence of a divine Creator.

TELEPATHY. See ESP.

TELEPHONE, apparatus for transmission and reproduction of sound by means of frequency electric waves. Precursors in telecommunication included the megaphone, the speaking tube and the string telephone—all of which transmitted sound as such— and the TELEGRAPH, working by electrical impulses. Although the principles on which it is based had been known 40 years earlier, the telephone was not invented until 1876, when Alexander Graham BELL obtained his patent. Bell's transmitter worked by the voltage induced in a coil by a piece of iron attached to a vibrating diaphragm. The same apparatus, working in reverse, was used as a receiver. Modern receivers use the same principle, but it was soon found that a more sensitive transmitter was needed, and by 1878 the carbon MICROPHONE (invented by Thomas EDISON) was used. A battery-powered DC circuit connected microphone and receiver. In 1878 the first commercial exchange was opened in New Haven, Conn., and local telephone networks spread rapidly in the US and elsewhere. Technical improvements made for longer-distance transmission included the use of hard-drawn copper wire, underground dry-core CABLE, and two-wire circuits to avoid the cross-talk that occurred when the circuit was completed via ground. Distortion in long circuits was overcome by introducing loading coils at intervals to increase the INDUCTANCE. The introduction also of repeaters, or AMPLIFIERS, made long-distance telephone calls possible. Today, MICROWAVE RADIO links, and COMMUNICATIONS SATELLITES and OPTICAL FIBERS are used. Telephone subscribers are connected to a local exchange, these in turn being linked by trunk lines connecting a hierarchy of switching centers so that alternative routes may be used. When a call is dialed, each digit is coded as pulses or pairs of tones which work electromechanical or electronic switches.

TELEPHOTO. See FACSIMILE.

TELESCOPE, Optical, instrument used to detect or examine distant objects. It consists of a series of lenses and mirrors capable of producing a magnified IMAGE and of collecting more light than the unaided eye. The refracting telescope essentially consists of a tube with a LENS system at each end. Light from a distant object first strikes the objective lens which produces an inverted image at its focal point. In the terrestrial telescope the second lens system, the eyepiece, produces a magnified, erect image of the focal image, but in instruments for astronomical use, where the image is usually recorded photographically, the image is not reinverted, thus reducing light losses. The reflecting telescope uses a concave MIRROR to gather and focus the incoming light, the focal image being viewed using many different combinations of lenses and mirrors in the various types of instrument, each seeking to reduce different optical ABERRATIONS. The size of a telescope is measured in terms of the diameter of its objective. Up to about 30cm diameter the resolving power (the ability to distinguish finely separated points) increases with size but for larger objectives the only gain is in light gathering. A 500cm telescope can thus detect much fainter sources but resolve no better than a 30cm instrument. Because mirrors can be supported more easily than large lenses, the largest astronomical telescopes are all reflectors. (See also ASTRONOMY; GALILEO; OBSERVATORY; RADIO TELESCOPE.)

TELEVISION, the communication of moving pictures between distant points using wire or radio transmissions. In television broadcasting, centrally prepared programs are transmitted to a multitude of individual receivers, though closed-circuit industrial and education applications are of increasing importance. Often, a sound signal is transmitted together with the picture information. In outline, a television CAMERA is used to form an optical IMAGE of the scene to be transmitted and convert it into electrical signals. These are amplified and transmitted, either directly by cable (closed-circuit) or as radio waves, to a receiver where the scene is reconstituted as an optical image on the screen of a CATHODE-RAY TUBE. Today most television cameras are of the image orthicon or vidicon types, these having largely replaced the earlier iconoscope and orthicon designs. Since it is impossible to transmit a whole image at once, the image formed by the optical LENS system of the camera is scanned as a sequence of 525 horizontal lines, the varying light value along each being converted into a fluctuating electrical signal and the whole scan being repeated 30 times a second to allow an impression of motion to be conveyed without noticeable flicker. The viewer sees the image as a whole because of the persistence of VISION effect. In color television, the light entering the camera is analyzed into red, green and blue components—corresponding to the three primary COLORS of light—and electrical information concerning the saturation of each is superimposed on the ordinary luminance (brightness) monochrome signal. In the color receiver this information is recovered and used to control the three electron beams which, projected through a shadow mask (a screen containing some 200,000 minute, precisely positioned holes), excite the mosaic of red, green and blue PHOSPHOR dots which reproduce the color image. All three color television systems in use around the world allow monochrome receivers to work normally from the color transmissions.

Development of television. Early hopes of practical television date back to the early days of the electric TELEGRAPH, but their realization had to await several key developments. First was the discovery of the photoconductive properties of selenium, followed by the development of the cathode-ray tube (1897) and the ELECTRON TUBE (1904). The first practical television system, demonstrated in London in 1926 by J. L. BAIRD, used a mechanical scanning method devised by Paul Nipkow in 1884. Electronic scanning dates from 1923 when ZWORYKIN filed a patent for his iconoscope camera tube. Television broadcasting began in London in 1936 using a 405-line standard. In the US public broadcasting began in 1941, with regular color broadcasting in 1954. US television broadcasts are made in the VHF (Channels 2–13) and the UHF (Channels 14–83) regions of the RF spectrum (see RADIO). (See also ELECTRONICS; VIDEOTAPE.)

TELL, William, legendary 14th-century Swiss hero. Ordered by the Austrian bailiff Gessler to bow to a hat on a pole as a symbol of Austrian supremacy, he refused and was forced to shoot an apple from his son's head with a crossbow; in this almost impossible task he succeeded. Later he killed Gessler.

TELLER, Edward (1908–   ), Hungarian-born US nuclear physicist who worked with FERMI on nuclear FISSION at the start of the MANHATTAN PROJECT, but who is best known for his fundamental work on, and advocacy of, the HYDROGEN BOMB.

TELSTAR, US artificial SATELLITE, launched July 10, 1962, the first to relay TELEVISION signals across the Atlantic. It weighed 170lb. Broadcasts ended (Feb. 1963) after Van Allen belt radiation damaged some of the 1,000 transistors.

TELUGU, a DRAVIDIAN language of S India. There are some 40 million Andhras (Telugu speakers), mainly in ANDHRA PRADESH. The extensive literature is written in a script derived from SANSKRIT.

TEMPERA, painting technique in which dry pigments are "tempered" or bound with egg yolks and water. Applied to a panel coated with GESSO, in thin, drying layers, it produces a luminous mat surface. Especially popular 1200–1500 in Italy, it has been revived by modern artists.

TEMPERATURE, the degree of hotness or coldness of a body, as measured quantitatively by THERMOMETERS. The various practical scales used are arbitrary: the FAHRENHEIT scale was originally based on the values 0°F for an equal ice-salt mixture, 32°F for the freezing point of water and 96°F for normal human body temperature. Thermometer readings are arbitrary also because they depend on the particular physical properties of the thermometric fluid etc. There are now certain primary calibration points corresponding to the triple points, boiling points or freezing points of particular substances, whose values are fixed by convention. The thermodynamic, or ABSOLUTE, temperature scale, is not arbitrary; starting at ABSOLUTE ZERO and graduated in KELVINS, it is defined with respect to an ideal reversible heat engine working on a CARNOT cycle between two temperature T_1 and T_2. If Q_1 is the heat received at the higher temperature T_1, and Q_2 the heat lost at the lower temperature T_2, then T_1/T_2 is defined equal to Q_1/Q_2. Such absolute temperature is independent of the properties of particular substances, and is a basic THERMODYNAMIC function. It is an intensive property, unlike HEAT, which is an extensive property—that is, the temperature of a body is independent of its mass or nature; it is thus only indirectly related to the heat content (internal energy) of the body. Heat flows always from a higher temperature to a lower. On the molecular scale, temperature may be defined in terms of the statistical distribution of the kinetic energy of the molecules.

TEMPERATURE, Body. Animals fall into two classes: COLD-BLOODED ANIMALS, which have the same temperature as their surroundings, and WARM-BLOODED ANIMALS, which have an approximately constant temperature maintained by a "thermostat" in the brain. The normal temperature for most such animals lies between 95°F (35°C) and 104°F (40°C); it is greatly reduced during HIBERNATION. For man, the normal mouth temperature usually lies between 97°F (36°C) and 99°F (37.2°C), the average being about 98.6°F (37.0°C). It fluctuates daily, and in women monthly. The temperature setting is higher than normal in FEVER. When the body is too hot, the blood vessels near the skin expand to carry more blood and to lose heat by radiation and convection, and the sweat glands produce PERSPIRATION which cools by evaporation. When the body is too cold, the blood vessels near the skin contract, the metabolic rate increases and SHIVERING occurs to produce more heat. Fat under the skin, and body hair (FUR in other animals), help to keep heat in. If these defenses against cold prove inadequate, **hypothermia** results: body temperature falls, functions become sluggish, and death may result. Controlled cooling may be used in surgery to reduce the need for oxygen.

TEMPERATURE HUMIDITY INDEX (THI), formerly **discomfort index,** an empirical measure of the discomfort experienced in various warm weather conditions, and used to predict how much power will be needed to run air-conditioning systems. It is given by

$$THI = 0.4(T_1 + T_2) + 15$$

where T_1 is the dry-bulb temperature and T_2 the wet-bulb temperature in degrees Fahrenheit (see HYGROMETER). When the index is 70 almost everyone feels comfortable; at 80 or more, no one.

TEMPERING, heat-treatment process in METALLURGY, used to toughen an ALLOY, notably STEEL. The metal is heated slowly to the desired temperature, held there while stresses are relieved and excess solution precipitates out from the supersaturated solid solution, and then cooled, usually by rapid quenching. The temperature determines the properties produced, and may be chosen to retain hardness.

TEMPLE, Shirley Jane (1928–   ), US child film star and later a politician. She made her movie debut at three and became pheonomenally popular in such films of the 1930s as *Little Miss Marker* and *The Little Colonel*. She retired from films in 1949. After working on television in the 1950s Shirley Temple Black (her married name) took up Republican politics. She became a US delegate to the UN in 1969, ambassador to Ghana in 1975, and US Chief of Protocol 1976.

TEMPLE, a (usually large) building for religious worship. The Jewish temple, a successor to the TABERNACLE, was envisaged by King DAVID and built by SOLOMON at Jerusalem, becoming the central shrine where alone SACRIFICE could legally be offered. This First Temple was destroyed by the Babylonian invasion in 586 BC. The Second Temple was built in 520 BC and was used until HEROD the Great built the most splendid and last temple, destroyed by the Romans in 70 AD.

TENANT, a person who has temporary occupation or use of another person's real property (house or apartment) usually under terms spelled out in a lease. A lease may run for a year or more; to avoid mistakes or misunderstandings it should describe the premises being rented. If the premises are in an apartment building having a garage, laundry room and storage areas, the tenant's right to use these facilities should be specified, along with any extra charges for their use. A tenant cannot sublease a house or apartment to another person (a subtenant) unless the owner (landlord) gives written permission, and the tenant remains responsible for the subtenant's obligations to the landlord. A lease may specify certain other restrictions and responsibilities, i.e. regarding pets or noise.

TEN COMMANDMENTS, or the Decalogue, the moral laws delivered by God to Moses on Mt. Sinai, as recorded in the Bible (Exodus 20:2–17; Deuteronomy 5:6–21). They provide the foundation for Jewish and Christian teaching.

TENDON, fibrous structure formed at the ends of most MUSCLES, which transmits the force of contraction to the point of action (usually a BONE). They facilitate mechanical advantage and allow bulky power muscles to be situated away from small bones concerned with fine movements, as in the HANDS.

TENG HSIAO-PING (1904?–   ), Chinese political leader. A life-long revolutionary who joined the Chinese Communist Party in the 1920s, Teng (also spelled Deng Xiaoping) became the party's secretary general in the 1950s. During the Cultural Revolution of the 1960s he was dismissed from his post, but he again emerged as a top aide to Premier Chou En-lai in the 1970s. After the death of Mao Tse-tung in 1976 Teng became China's most prominent leader but modestly kept the title of deputy chairman.

TENIERS, David, the younger (1610–1690), Flemish painter. A master colorist, he studied under his father, David Teniers the elder (1587–1649), and became one of the most famous, sought-after and prolific painters of his time. His over 2,000 surviving works mainly comprise genre scenes of peasant life, still lifes and landscapes.

Name of state: Tennessee
Capital: Nashville
Statehood: June 1, 1796 (16th state)
Familiar name: Volunteer State, Big Bend State
Area: 42,244sq mi
Population: 4,590,750
Elevation: Highest—6,642ft., Clingmans Dome. Lowest—182ft., Mississippi River
Motto: Agriculture and Commerce
State flower: Iris
State bird: Mockingbird
State tree: Tulip poplar
State song: "Tennessee Waltz"

TENNESSEE, state of the south central US, bordered on the N by Ky. and Va., E by N.C., S by Ga., Ala., and Miss., and W by Ark. and Mo. across the Mississippi R. It is considered one of the border states between North and South.

Land. It forms a narrow parallelogram extending from the Mississippi R in the W to the Blue Ridge region (with the GREAT SMOKY MOUNTAINS and Clingmans Dome, 6,642ft). Other regions include the Appalachian ridge-and-valley farming region, the coal-rich Cumberland Plateau and the fertile central Nashville Basin bounded by a broad Highland Rim. Farther W the N Gulf Coastal Plain slopes down to the alluvial Mississippi Bottoms. Dams on the Tennessee and Cumberland rivers have formed many lakes (including Kentucky

Lake, 247sq mi). The climate is humid (average 50in annual precipitation) and temperate.

People. Over 60% of the population now lives in the metropolitan areas of MEMPHIS, NASHVILLE, CHATTANOOGA and KNOXVILLE. Most Tennesseans are native-born. Blacks constitute about 16% of the population.

Economy. Tennessee is now a predominantly industrial state. Its industries produce chemicals, foodstuffs, electrical machinery and metal, stone, clay and glass products. Research centers include OAK RIDGE (atomic energy). Much of the state's electricity is derived from the TENNESSEE VALLEY AUTHORITY, which speeded changeover from a primary-products to a manufacturing economy. Mining (stone, zinc, phosphate, coal), livestock (notably cattle and thoroughbred horses), and tobacco, cotton and corn contribute significantly to the economic base.

History. Among Indians encountered by DE SOTO and later white explorers were the CHEROKEE, CHICKASAW and SHAWNEE. The region was ceded to England by the Treaty of PARIS (1763). Settlers drew up North America's first written constitution, the WATAUGA ASSOCIATION, in 1772 and formed the independent state of FRANKLIN (784–88). Bitterly divided over slavery, Tenn., the last Southern state to join the Confederates and the first to rejoin the Union, was the site of major Civil War battles. It has provided three US presidents: Andrew JACKSON, James K. POLK and Andrew JOHNSON. During the 1940s and '50s, Tennessee was transformed from an agricultural state to a basically urbanized, manufacturing state; and with its expanding economy, and generally more liberal attitudes than neighboring states, it emerged as a leader of the revitalized "New South." Its population rose 16.9% during the 1970s, but at the end of the decade it was plagued by a series of government scandals and hurt by the national recession, which decreased its tax revenues and forced cutbacks in state programs.

TENNESSEE RIVER, principal tributary of the Ohio R. Formed by the junction of Holston and French Broad rivers near Knoxville, Tenn., it flows SW into Ala., then NW and N back across Tenn. and into Ky. It drains some 40,000sq mi. On its 652mi length are many dams and power facilities under the control of the TENNESSEE VALLEY AUTHORITY.

TENNESSEE-TOMBIGBEE WATERWAY, known as the Tenn-Tom Waterway, 232mi. water project near Florence, Ala. Begun in 1971 and expected to be completed by 1988, the Tenn-Tom Waterway will link the Tennessee River with the Black Warrior-Tombigbee Waterway, thus offering access from the Tennessee R. to the Gulf of Mexico. At a projected cost of $1.96 billion, it will be the largest water project in US history, and has been strongly opposed by environmentalists and other groups.

TENNESSEE VALLEY AUTHORITY (TVA), US federal agency responsible for developing the water and other resources of the Tennessee R Valley, established (1933) as one of the early measures of Roosevelt's NEW DEAL. The Authority has 26 major dams on the Tennessee R and its tributaries. The dams and reservoirs have made it possible to eliminate major flooding. Locks make the Tennessee navigable throughout, and TVA hydroelectric and steam plants provide most of the region's electricity. TVA projects have involved also conservation, agriculture and forestry.

TENNIEL, Sir John (1820–1914), English artist noted for his illustrations for Lewis CARROLL's *Alice's Adventures in Wonderland* and *Through the Looking-Glass*, and for hundreds of political cartoons for the English satirical magazine, *Punch* (1850–1901).

TENNIS, racket game played on a rectangular court by two or four players. The court, divided by painted lines into sections, is bisected by a net 3½ft high; the object is to hit the hollow ball (of cloth-covered rubber, about 2½in in diameter and 2oz in weight) over the net into the opposite court such that the opposing player is unable to return it. The racket has a metal or laminated wood frame with gut or nylon strings forming an oval "head," is about 27in long and weighs 12oz–1lb. Tennis originated in 15th-century France as indoor *court* tennis, and took its present form, *lawn* tennis, in 1870. It was first played in the US 1874. In 1877 England held the first Wimbledon Championship. Dwight DAVIS donated the Davis Cup in 1900. The International Lawn Tennis Federation regulates rules and play in over 80 countries.

TENNYSON, Alfred, 1st Baron Tennyson (1809–1892), English poet. His *Poems* (1842) established him as a great poet. His well-known philosophic elegy *In Memoriam* (1850) became the favorite of Queen Victoria, who appointed him POET LAUREATE. "Official" work included *The Charge of the Light Brigade* (1855). *Idylls of the King* (1842–1885) are based on the legends of King Arthur. His mastery of sound and rhythm, both vigorous and delicate, is

perhaps best seen in such haunting lyrics as "The Lotus Eaters" and "The Lady of Shalott."

TENSKWATAWA (c1768–1834), or "Shawnee Prophet," Shawnee Indian who aimed with his twin TECUMSEH for a Northwest Indian confederacy. Famous for his "messages from God" and prediction of an eclipse, he urged rejection of the white man. He rashly engaged in the disastrous battle of TIPPECANOE (1811).

TEQUILA, a type of Mexican brandy or mescal that is produced by the fermentation of the stems and leaf bases of a number of AGAVE species, particularly *Agave tecqualana*.

TER BORCH, Gerard (1617–1681), Dutch painter. Much traveled (Italy, France, England, Westphalia, Spain), he painted small, delicate portraits and dignified interior genre scenes. His group portrait *The Peace of Münster* (1648) is of historical note.

TERENCE (Publius Terentius Afer; c185–159 BC), Roman playwright. All his comedies (most based on MENANDER) survive: *The Woman from Andros, The Mother-in-Law, The Self-Tormentor, The Eunuch, Phormio* and *The Brothers*. Their refined realism, humor and language later influenced development of the COMEDY OF MANNERS.

TERESA OF ÁVILA, Saint (1515–1582), Spanish nun and mystic who reformed the CARMELITES; a patron saint of Spain. Canonized in 1622, she was proclaimed a "Doctor of the Roman Catholic Church" in 1970. Her *Interior Castle* (1588), *Life* (1611) and other writings are classics of spiritual literature.

TERMAN, Lewis Madison (1877–1956), US psychologist best known for developing the STANFORD-BINET TEST.

TERMITES, or white ants, primitive insects closely related to COCKROACHES, found in all warm regions. They have a complicated social system and live in well-regulated communities with different castes taking distinct roles. They build large nests of soil mixed with saliva, in which the colony of king, queen, workers, soldiers and juveniles live. Soldiers and workers are sterile individuals whose development has been arrested at an early stage. Termites feed on wood and vegetation, digesting the food with the aid of symbiotic PROTOZOA or BACTERIA in the gut.

TERNS, a subfamily, Sterninae, of the GULL family. All have long, pointed wings and deeply-forked tails while most are white with gray back and black head cap in the breeding season. Terns plunge into the sea to catch fish. The Arctic tern, *Sterna paradisaea*, yearly migrates from the Arctic to the Antarctic and back again.

TERRA COTTA (Italian: baked earth), any fired earthenware product, especially one made from coarse, porous CLAY, red-brown in color and unglazed. Being cheap, hard and durable, it has been used from ancient times for building and roofing, and for molded architectural ornament and statuettes. Its use for sculpture and plaques was revived in the Renaissance and in the 18th century. (See also POTTERY AND PORCELAIN.)

TERRAPINS, the name given to seven geographical races of *Malaclemys terrapin*. They are moderate-sized TURTLES, up to 250mm (10in) long, living in coastal waters of eastern North America.

TERRITORIALITY, a behavioral drive causing animals to set up distinct territories defended against other members of the same species (conspecifics) for the purposes of establishing a breeding site, home range or feeding area. It is an important factor in the spacing out of animal populations. Territoriality is shown by animals of all kinds: birds, mammals, fishes and insects, and may involve displays or the scent-marking of boundaries. A territory may be held by individuals, pairs or even family groups.

TERRITORIAL WATERS, in international law, the belt of sea adjacent to a country and under its territorial jurisdiction. Important for control of shipping, seabeds and fisheries, such limits used to extend 3mi, and more recently 12mi, from low-water mark. A 200mi limit has been accepted by some countries.

TERRITORY, in politics, an area under a government's control. Named territories have lower status than the mother country. All but 19 US states were once territories; Alaska and Hawaii were the last incorporated territories (with full Constitutional rights) to gain statehood. US territories include the Virgin Islands and Guam. Federated States of Micronesia, formerly a UN Trust Territory administered by the US, became a self-governing territory in association with the US in 1981.

TERRORISM, the use of actual or threatened violence for political ends. The level of terrorism increased markedly in the 1970s as antigovernment groups throughout the world turned to violent acts such as bombing, hijacking, kidnapping, and murder. Much of the increase was due to Palestinians and their allies who gave up hope of defeating Israel by conventional military tactics after the rout of the Arab

nations in the 1967 war. The more active terrorist groups of the period included the Japanese Red Army (3 of whose members killed 28 people and wounded 76 at Tel Aviv's Lod airport in 1972), the Palestinian BLACK SEPTEMBER group (responsible for the deaths of 11 Israeli athletes at the 1972 Munich Olympics), the BAADER-MEINHOF GANG in Germany, the Italian RED BRIGADES (who kidnapped and killed the former Italian premier, Aldo MORO, in 1978), the TUPAMAROS in Uruguay, and the WEATHERMEN in the US. While receiving much publicity (one of their aims), terrorists actually account for relatively few deaths (less than 2,000 in the 1970s) compared with other causes (nearly 10 times as many people are murdered every year by ordinary criminals in the US alone). Terrorists are very hard to catch, however, because their groups are small, tightly organized, and highly mobile.

TERRY, Dame (Alice) Ellen (1847–1928), English actress. In her partnership with Henry IRVING at the London Lyceum (1878–1902) she became famous in roles from Shakespeare, but also acted in modern plays.

TERTIARY, the period of the CENOZOIC before the advent of man, lasting from about 65 to about 2–3 million years ago. (See also GEOLOGY.)

TERTULLIAN (Quintus Septimius Florens Tertullianus; c160–c225), early Christian Latin writer, born Carthage. Converted on return to Carthage from Rome, he wrote apologetics, polemics and ascetic works in which, aided by his law training, he denounced paganism, heresies and licentiousness.

TERTZ, Abram. See SINYAVSKY, ANDREI.

TESLA, Nikola (1856–1943), Croatian-born US electrical engineer whose discovery of the rotating magnetic field permitted his construction of the first AC INDUCTION MOTOR (c1888). Since it is easier to transmit AC than DC over long distances, this invention was of great importance.

TESTES, pair of male GONADS, which in humans lie in the scrotum suspended from the perineum below the PENIS. This position allows a lower temperature than in the ABDOMEN, thus favoring SPERM production, the principal function of the testes. ANDROGEN hormones (mainly TESTOSTERONE) are also secreted by the testes under the control of HYPOTHALAMUS and PITUITARY GLAND. The testes develop at the back of the abdomen and descend in the FETUS and infant. Failure to descend in childhood may require surgical correction.

TESTOSTERONE, ANDROGEN STEROID produced by the interstitial cells of the TESTES, and to a lesser extent by the ADRENAL GLAND ortex, under the control of LUTEINIZING HORMONE. It is responsible for most male sexual characteristics—VOICE change, HAIR distribution and sex-organ development.

TETANUS, or **lockjaw**, BACTERIAL DISEASE in which a TOXIN produced by anaerobic tetanus bacilli growing in contaminated wounds causes MUSCLE spasm due to nerve toxicity. Minor cuts may be infected with the bacteria which are common in soil. The first symptom may often be painful contraction of jaw and neck muscles; trunk muscles including those of RESPIRATION and muscles close to the site of injury are also frequently involved. Untreated, many cases are fatal, but ARTIFICIAL RESPIRATION, anti-serum and PENICILLIN have improved the outlook. Regular VACCINATION and adequate wound cleansing are important in prevention.

TET OFFENSIVE, in the Vietnam War, a coordinated cluster of attacks against cities and bases in South Vietnam by Vietcong and North Vietnamese forces, beginning on Jan. 30, 1968, the first day of the Tet (New Year) holiday. The offensive, which included a brief occupation of part of the US embassy in Saigon, was costly to the enemy; nevertheless, it converted many Americans to the view that the war could not be won.

TETRACYCLINES, broad-spectrum ANTI-BIOTICS (including Aureomycin and Terramycin) which may be given by mouth. While useful in BRONCHITIS and other minor infections, they are especially valuable in diseases due to RICKETTSIA and related organisms; they can also be used in ACNE. Staining of TEETH in children and deterioration in KIDNEY failure cases are important side effects.

TEUTONIC KNIGHTS, religious military order established (1198) in Palestine. It successfully invaded, Germanized and Christianized Prussia in the 1200s. It declined after defeat by a Polish-Lithuanian army at TANNENBERG (1410). Its last branch, in central and S Germany, was dissolved by Napoleon (1805).

TEUTONS, originally a German tribe, defeated by the Romans in Gaul (102 BC). "Teutons" became synonymous with JUTES, ANGLES and SAXONS, then with "North Germans" in general; "teutonic" came to describe the languages of Scandinavia, Germany, Belgium and Holland.

TEXAS, second-largest US state, bordered by Mexico, N.M., Okla., Ark., La., and the Gulf of Mexico. It is the only state to have been an independent republic before attaining statehood.

Land. The West Gulf Coastal Plain extends inland 150–300mi to the Balcones escarpment and contains the state's richest soils. Less fertile are the Texas Great Plains (W half of the Panhandle and along the Pecos R), which reach W to N.M. In the extreme W the Basin and Range (Trans-Pecos) region is crossed by the Rocky Mts. Sam Rayburn Lake, on the Angelina R, is the largest of many man-made lakes. Mean annual temperature ranges from 55°F in the Panhandle to 74°F along the lower Rio Grande in the S. Annual rainfall is 55in in the E but diminishes to only 10in in the W.

People. As of 1980, Texas is the third most populous state, up from fourth place in 1970. More than 80% of the population is urban, the largest urban areas being HOUSTON, Dallas-Fort Worth, San Antonio, and El Paso. More than 20% are of Spanish origin and were born or have parents who were born in neighboring Mexico. Population densities are highest in the West Gulf Plain and lowest in the drier W.

Economy. Texas leads the states in production of oil and natural gas and is also rich in sulfur and low-grade coal deposits. It is a leading agricultural state and a major producer of cotton, beef cattle, sheep, citrus, rice, wheat, pecans and peanuts. Large petrochemical industries are concentrated along the Gulf. Food-processing and manufacture of transportation equipment, machinery, metals and textiles are important. NASA's Manned Spacecraft

Name of state: Texas
Capital: Austin
Statehood: Dec. 29, 1845 (28th state)
Familiar name: Lone Star State
Area: 267,339sq mi
Population: 14,228,383
Elevation: Highest—8,751ft., Guadalupe Peak. Lowest—sea level, Gulf of Mexico
Motto: Friendship
State flower: Bluebonnet
State bird: Mockingbird
State tree: Pecan
State song: "Texas, Our Texas"

Center was established near Houston in 1964 and has since stimulated the manufacture of scientific and electronic equipment.

History. The subject of French, Spanish and US (1803) claims, Texas became part of independent Mexico 1821. After defeat at the ALAMO, victory for US settlers at SAN JACINTO preceded the independent republic (1836–45) and entrance into the US. The MEXICAN WAR ended Mexican claims (1848). Despite the views of governor Sam HOUSTON, Texas joined the Confederates (1861); it was readmitted to the Union in 1870. Railroads (later 1800s), discovery of oil (1901) and WWII helped economic development.

During the 1970s, Texas began to diversify its economic base and oil and gas production declined despite extensive drilling. So exuberant was its growth in this period that it became a magnet drawing new residents from all over the US— Houston attracting people at a rate of 1000 per month in 1980. The population of the state as a whole jumped 27.1% during the decade of the 1970s, including a net immigration of more than 1 million people. Its problems include the need for more water for industry and irrigation. Tensions also continue between white and Mexican-Americans and, despite its great wealth, Texas has one of the poorest records of any state in spending for social services.

Texas is governed under its 5th (1876) constitution; its 31 senators serve four-year terms, its 150 representatives two years.

TEXAS RANGERS, a law enforcement body, part of the Texas department of public safety. The first were ten men employed (1823) by S. F. AUSTIN to protect settlers from Indian and Mexican raiders. In 1935 the Rangers were merged with the state highway patrol.

TEY, Josephine (1896–1952), pen name of Elizabeth Mackintosh, Scottish novelist and playwright who also used the name Gordon Daviot. She wrote several highly successful detective stories, beginning with *The Man in the Queue* (1929).

THACKERAY, William Makepeace (1811–1863), English novelist, essayist and illustrator. He did much to shape *Punch*, and was first editor of *The Cornhill Magazine* (1860). His best known (and best) novel is *Vanity Fair* (1848), a gentle satire of the early 19th-century middle classes; its central character is the sly but good-natured Becky Sharp. His other novels include *Barry Lyndon* (1844), *Pendennis* (1850) and *Henry Esmond* (1852).

Official name: Kingdom of Thailand
Capital: Bangkok
Area: 209,411
Population: 46,455,000
Languages: Thai; English, Chinese, Malay, tribal languages
Religions: Buddhist; Muslim, Christian, Animist
Monetary unit(s): 1 baht = 100 satangs

THAILAND, (formerly Siam), monarchy in SE Asia. The N part borders Kampuchea (Cambodia), Laos and Burma; the S extends between the Gulf of Thailand and Bay of Bengal down the Malay Peninsula to Malaysia.

Land. In the N are densely wooded N–S hill ranges rich in teak. The populous central region comprises the rice-producing alluvial plain of the Chao Phraya R. The drier NE Khorat Plateau drains E to the Mekong R. The narrow S region is mostly mountainous and forested, with some rice plains and many islands off the W coast. Rainfall ranges from an average 80in in the S and W to 40in in the E.

People. The Thais are of Mongol descent; most are Theravada Buddhists. Thai language is of the Sino-Tibetan family and written in script of Sanskrit origin. Chinese form an important urban minority; there are hill peoples in the N and Malays, most of whom are Muslims, in the S. Bangkok, the capital, and adjacent Thon Buri are by far the largest cities.

Economy. Rice is the chief crop in an agricultural economy, with sugarcane, cotton, corn, coconuts, rubber and tobacco also grown. Draft water buffalos are the principal livestock, though there are timber elephants. Fishing and forestry (teak, oils, resins, bamboo) are important. Textiles (including famous Thai silks) produced in Bangkok and Thon Buri are among the few manufactures. Thailand is one of the world's largest exporters of rice. Other exports include corn, rubber and teak. Trade is mainly with the West.

History. The Thais migrated from S China about 1000 AD. Their center moved S under the Sukhothai (c1220–1350), Ayuth-

ia (1350–1778) and Chakri (1782–)
dynasties. Siam lost territorial influence in
the 1800s to the British (in Burma and
Malaya) and French (in Laos and
Cambodia) but kept its independence.
Thailand was invaded by Japan in WWII.
In the early 1950s it sent troops to Korea,
joined the SOUTHEAST ASIA TREATY
ORGANIZATION (headquartered in Bangkok)
and later supported the US in Vietnam. The
overthrow of Marshal Thanom Kittika-
chorn (1973) coincided with increased
militancy among workers, peasants and
students. Communist guerrilla activity
continued in the NE, N and S and
withdrawal of US troops began in 1975 (see
MAYAGÜEZ INCIDENT).After a bloody confrontation with leftists, a military government was re-established (1977). A new
constitution was promulgated in 1978,
however, and general elections were held in
1979.

THALBERG, Irving (1899–1936), US film
producer. The "boy genius" of Hollywood,
Thalberg became head of production at
MGM at 24 and for the next 12 years
produced such classic films as *Grand Hotel*
(1932), *Mutiny on the Bounty* (1935),
Camille (1936), *The Good Earth* (1937)
and the Marx Brothers' *A Night at the
Opera* (1935).

THALES (early 6th century BC), ancient
Greek PRESOCRATIC philosopher, one of the
SEVEN SAGES. He is reputed to have invented
geometry and to have attempted the first
rational account of the universe, claiming
that it originated from water.

THALIDOMIDE, mild SEDATIVE
introduced in the late 1950s and withdrawn
a few years later on finding that it was
responsible for congenital deformities in
children born to mothers who took the DRUG.
This was due to an effect on the EMBRYO in
early PREGNANCY, in particular causing
defective limb bud formation.

THAMES RIVER, England's chief waterway, winds E 210mi from the Cotswolds to
its North Sea estuary. On its banks lie
OXFORD, READING, ETON, WINDSOR CASTLE,
RUNNYMEDE, HAMPTON COURT PALACE and
GREENWICH. Canals link it to the West and
Midlands. Above LONDON it displays fine,
gentle scenery; below London it is of
considerable importance for shipping. It is
tidal up to Teddington (10mi W of
London).

THANKSGIVING DAY, since 1863, an
annual US national holiday to give thanks
for blessings received during the year. It is
celebrated on the fourth Thursday in
November with feasting and prayers. The
tradition was begun by the colonists of

Plymouth, Mass., in 1621, and can be
traced back to the English harvest festivals.
In Canada, it is celebrated on the second
Monday in October.

THANT, U (1909–1974), Burmese diplomat, UNITED NATIONS secretary-general
1961–71. A cautious and unassertive
negotiator, he was involved in the Cuban
Missile Crisis (1962), and in peace
negotiations in Indonesia (1962), Congo
(1963), Cyprus (1964) and the India-
Pakistan war (1965).

THARP, Twyla (1942–), US dancer
and choreographer, a student of Merce
CUNNINGHAM and Alwin Nikolais. She made
her debut with the Paul Taylor Dance
Company in 1965, then formed her own
company. In her many innovative dances,
she has blended ballroom, jazz and tap
dance with traditional ballet forms.

THATCHER, Margaret (1925–),
British prime minister. She entered
Parliament in 1959 and served 1970–74 as
secretary of state for education and science.
In 1975 she was elected Conservative Party
leader, and in 1979, when the Conservatives
won a parliamentary majority, Mrs.
Thatcher became Britain's first woman
prime minister. To fight inflation she
introduced austerity measures, but this kept
unemployment high and contributed to
domestic unrest. She took a firm line
against the hunger strikes and terrorist
tactics of the Irish Republican Army.

THEATER, term used to refer to drama as
an art form as well as to the building in
which it is performed.

According to Aristotle, the drama of
ancient Greece, the ancestor of modern
European drama, grew out of the
DITHYRAMB. The invention of TRAGEDY is
credited to THESPIS and the form was refined
successively by AESCHYLUS, SOPHOCLES and
EURIPIDES. COMEDY was a separate and later
development of Greek theater. The plays of
ARISTOPHANES are the only remains of Greek
Old Comedy (5th century BC), a form that
was extremely licentious and still close to its
ritual origins. Middle and New Comedy
(4th and 3rd centuries BC respectively)
became increasingly sentimental; only the
New Comedy plays of MENANDER, with their
complex, often romantic plots, remain from
these periods. Greek drama was performed
at religious festivals in outdoor
AMPHITHEATERS built into hillsides; that at
EPIDAURUS is still used each summer. The
Roman plays of PLAUTUS, TERENCE and
SENECA show their Greek antecedents, but
MIME and PANTOMIME were the popular
theatrical forms in the Roman Empire and,
through the COMMEDIA DELL'ARTE, provide

the only direct link between ancient and medieval European drama.

Medieval drama evolved in the Church from musical elaborations of the service. Eventually these developed into MYSTERY PLAYS and were moved out of doors onto play wagons. Miracle Plays, based on the lives of the saints and on scripture, also developed; whole cycles of plays were performed at religious festivals. MORALITY PLAYS (such as EVERYMAN) and INTERLUDES appeared in the 15th century. During the RENAISSANCE the rediscovery of Greek and Roman dramatic texts led directly to the growth of secular drama. Buildings for the performance of plays were erected in Elizabethan times, one of the most famous being the Globe Theatre, associated with SHAKESPEARE. By the end of his career a roofed building inside which the audience ranged around an open stage came into use. The modern form of the stage, with painted scenery and a *proscenium arch* across which a curtain falls between acts, was established by the 17th century.

In England the drama went through distinct phases associated with the Renaissance, the RESTORATION and NEOCLASSICISM before settling into a long period of MELODRAMA and sentimentality. On the Continent, classical and neoclassical drama, represented supremely by CORNEILLE and RACINE in France, gave way to a period of ROMANTICISM during which SCHILLER and GOETHE in Germany, and later HUGO in France and PUSHKIN in Russia, made lasting contributions.

Drama of the modern era began with efforts by IBSEN, STRINDBERG, CHEKOV, ZOLA and George Bernard SHAW to reintroduce realism, honest character portrayal and serious social and political debate into the theater. Many experiments with dramatic form (EXPRESSIONISM, SURREALISM, NATURALISM) and language characterize this phase in the theater. This century has produced dramatists of considerable merit such as O'NEILL, BRECHT, LORCA, BECKETT, IONESCO, Tennessee WILLLIAMS, Arthur MILLER, Edward ALBEE, and Harold PINTER. In recent times Western audiences have also become interested in Oriental theater, especially Japanese NOH and KABUKI drama. The term theater comprehends also such forms as MUSICAL COMEDY, VAUDEVILLE and OPERA as well as plays. See also COSTUME DESIGN and STAGE DESIGN.

THEATER OF THE ABSURD, term used to describe plays in which traditional values are shown as unable to fulfill man's emotional and spiritual needs. Human experience is seen as chaotic and without purpose, and man is often depicted as a victim of technology and bourgeois values. BECKETT, IONESCO, GENET, ALBEE and PINTER have been identified with this genre.

THEBES, ancient Egyptian city, 419mi S of Cairo, famous for its temples to AMON and its tombs of the pharaohs, capital of Egypt from c2100 BC, reaching its peak under the 17th and 18th dynasties (c1600 BC–1306 BC; see AMENHOTEP; KARNAK; LUXOR; TUTANKHAMEN). Already in decline by 1100 BC, it was sacked by the Assyrians in 661 BC and finally destroyed by the Romans in 29 BC.

THEISM, a philosophical system, as distinguished from DEISM and PANTHEISM, that professes the existence of a personal, transcendent God who created, preserves and governs the world. Orthodox Christian philosophy is a developed form of theism. (See also MONOTHEISM; PROVIDENCE.)

THEMISTOCLES (c525 BC–c460 BC), Athenian statesman and naval strategist. During the PERSIAN WARS, he foresaw that the Persians would return, and persuaded the Athenians to build the fleet with which he won the battle of SALAMIS (480 BC). As ARCHON from 493 BC, he built up the fortifications of Athens. ARISTIDES and other rivals were exiled by OSTRACISM, and in 471 BC he was ostracized himself by his aristocratic enemies, eventually retiring to Persia.

THEOCRACY, probably the oldest form of government in which power and authority are seen as derived directly from God, and rulers are considered either incarnations or representatives of divine power. In ancient times theocracy was widespread, ranging from the Egyptians to the Inca empires, Persia to China and Japan. During the Middle Ages in Europe the Roman Catholic Pope claimed ultimate authority in governing based on his religious authority, and later kings used the "divine right of kings" to justify their absolutist rule. Early Puritan colonies in New England like Massachusetts Bay and New Haven had leaders who claimed to derive their authority from God. While today secular and religious authority are for the most part separated in the Western democracies, their fusion in such political units as the Iranian Islamic Republic is still strong.

THEOCRITUS (c300–c250 BC), Alexandrian Greek poet of the HELLENISTIC AGE, whose polished, artificial *Idylls* created the genre of the PASTORAL. He was imitated by VERGIL and many later poets.

THEODOLITE, surveying instrument comprising a sighting TELESCOPE whose orientation with respect to two graduated angular scales, one horizontal, the other vertical, can be determined. It represents a development of the *transit*, which traditionally included only the horizontal scale.

THEOLOGY, the science of religious knowledge; the formal analysis of what is believed by adherents of a religion, making its doctrine coherent, elucidating it logically and relating it to secular disciplines. Its themes, therefore, are universal: GOD, man, the world, the Scriptures, SALVATION, ETHICS, the cultus, and ESCHATOLOGY. However, most religions have no well-developed theology. The concept arose in Greek thought, but its elaboration took place only in Christianity. The early Church Fathers and Doctors formulated doctrine in contemporary philosophical terms, and major advances were made by resolving controversies. In the Middle Ages SCHOLASTICISM developed, partly in reaction to the influence of NEOPLATONISM, and divided theology into NATURAL THEOLOGY and revealed theology (see REVELATION). From the Reformation each branch of PROTESTANTISM began to develop its own distinctive theology. From the Enlightenment rationalist theology became dominant, leading to MODERNISM and the modern critical view of the Bible. Partly in reaction arose NEO-ORTHODOXY, and the existentialist theology of NIEBUHR and TILLICH. The chief divisions of theology are: Biblical studies (including linguistic and other auxiliary disciplines), leading to the interpretation of Scripture; Biblical theology (the development of ideas in the Biblical writings); historical theology; systematic theology; and apologetics.

THEOPHRASTUS (c370–c285 BC), Greek philosopher, pupil of ARISTOTLE and his successor as head of the PERIPATETIC SCHOOL, generally considered the father of modern BOTANY.

THEOSOPHY (literally, divine wisdom), a mystical system of religious philosophy claiming direct insight into the divine nature. The speculations of such philosophers as PLOTINUS, Jakob BÖHME and SWEDENBORG are often called theosophical, as are many Eastern philosophies. The Theosophical Society was founded 1875 by Madame BLAVATSKY.

THÉRÈSE OF LISIEUX, Saint (1873–1897), the "Little Flower of Jesus," a French Carmelite nun who practiced the "little way"—achieving sanctity in performing the humblest tasks. Her spiritual autobiography was published posthumously.

THERMAL POLLUTION, the release of excessive waste heat into the environment, notably by pumping warm water from power plant cooling towers into rivers and lakes. This may kill off some living species, decrease the oxygen supply, and adversely affect reproduction.

THERMIDOR, 11th month of the new calendar adopted in the FRENCH REVOLUTION, in force 1793–1805. It covered the period July–August (the name signifies heat). The coup marking the downfall of ROBESPIERRE (July 27, 1794) is called the coup of 9 Thermidor.

THERMOCOUPLE, an electric circuit involving two junctions between different METALS or SEMICONDUCTORS; if these are at different temperatures, a small ELECTROMOTIVE FORCE is generated in the circuit (Seebeck effect). Measurement of this emf provides a sensitive, if approximate THERMOMETER, typically for the range 70K–1000K, one junction being held at a fixed temperature and the other providing a compact and robust probe. Semiconductor thermocouples in particular can be run in reverse as small refrigerators. A number of thermocouples connected in series with one set of junctions blackened form a thermopile, measuring incident radiation through its heating effect on the blackened surface. Thermoelectricity embraces the Seebeck and other effects relating heat transfer, thermal gradients, ELECTRIC FIELDS and currents.

THERMODYNAMICS, division of PHYSICS concerned with the interconversion of HEAT, WORK and other forms of ENERGY, and with the states of physical systems. Being concerned only with bulk matter and energy, classical thermodynamics is independent of theories of their microscopic nature; its axioms are sturdily empirical, and then from them theorems are derived with mathematical rigor. It is basic to ENGINEERING, parts of GEOLOGY, METALLURGY and PHYSICAL CHEMISTRY. Building on earlier studies of the thermodynamic functions TEMPERATURE and heat, Sadi CARNOT pioneered the science by his investigations of the cyclic heat ENGINE (1924), and in 1850 CLAUSIUS stated the first two laws. Thermodynamics was further developed by J. W. GIBBS, H. L. F. von HELMHOLTZ, Lord KELVIN and J. C. MAXWELL.

In thermodynamics, a *system* is any defined collection of matter: a *closed system* is one that cannot exchange matter with its surroundings; an *isolated system* can exchange neither matter nor energy. The *state* of a system is specified by determining all its properties such as pressure, volume, etc. A system in stable

EQUILIBRIUM is said to be in an equilibrium state, and has an equation of state (e.g., the general GAS law) relating its properties. A *process* is a change from one state A to another B, the path being specified by all the intermediate states. A *state function* is a property or FUNCTION of properties which depends only on the state and not on the path by which the state was reached; a differential dX of a function X (not necessarily a state function) is termed a *perfect differential* if it can be integrated between two states to give a value $X_{AB} = \int_{A}^{B} dX$ which is independent of the path from A to B. If this holds for all A and B, X must be a state function.

There are four basic laws of thermodynamics, all having many different formulations that can be shown to be equivalent. The **zeroth law** states that, if two systems are each in thermal equilibrium with a third system, then they are in thermal equilibrium with each other. This underlies the concept of temperature. The **first law** states that for any process the difference of the heat Q supplied to the system and the work W done by the system equals the change in the internal energy U: $\Delta U = Q - W$. U is a state function, though neither Q nor W separately is. Corollaries of the first law include the law of conservation of ENERGY, Hess' law (see THERMOCHEMISTRY), and the impossibility of PERPETUAL MOTION machines of the first kind. The **second law** (in Clausius' formulation) states that heat cannot be transferred from a colder to a hotter body without some other effect, i.e., without work being done. Corollaries include the impossibility of converting heat entirely into work without some other effect, and the impossibility of PERPETUAL MOTION machines of the second kind. It can be shown that there is a state function ENTROPY, S, defined by

$$\Delta S = \int dQ/T,$$ where T is the absolute temperature.

The entropy change ΔS in an isolated system is zero for a reversible process and positive for all irreversible processes. Thus entropy tends to a maximum (see HEAT DEATH). It also follows that a heat ENGINE is most efficient when it works on a reversible CARNOT cycle between two temperatures T_1 (the heat source) and T_2 (the heat sink), the EFFICIENCY being $(T_1 - T_2)/T_2$. The **third law** states that the entropy of any finite system in an equilibrium state tends to a finite value (defined to be zero) as the temperature of the system tends to absolute

zero. The equivalent NERNST heat theorem states that the entropy change for any reversible isothermal process tends to zero as the temperature tends to zero. Hence absolute entropies can be calculated from specific heat data. Other thermodynamic functions, useful for calculating equilibrium conditions under various contraints, are: **enthalpy** (or heat content) $H = U + pV$; the **Helmholtz free energy** $A = U - TS$; and the **Gibbs free energy** $G = H - TS$. The free energy represents the capacity of the system to perform useful work. **Quantum statistical thermodynamics**, based on QUANTUM MECHANICS, has arisen in the 20th century. It treats a system as an assembly of particles in quantum states. The entropy is given by $S = \ln P$ where k is the BOLTZMANN constant and P the statistical probability of the state of the system. Thus entropy is a measure of the disorder of the system.

THERMOPYLAE, Battle of (480 BC), famous battle in which a small Greek force under LEONIDAS held up the invading Persian army for three days (see PERSIAN WARS). Thermopylae, a narrow pass in E central Greece, was on the principal route from the N. The battle has become celebrated as an example of heroic resistance.

THERMOSTAT, device for maintaining a material or enclosure at a constant temperature by automatically regulating its HEAT supply. This is cut off if the TEMPERATURE rises and reconnected if it falls below that required. A thermostat comprises a sensor whose dimensions or physical properties change with temperature and a relay device which controls a switch or valve accordingly. **Bimetallic strips** are widely used in thermostats; they consist of two metals with widely different linear thermal coefficients fused together. As the temperature rises, the strip bends away from the side with the larger coefficient. This motion may be sufficient to control a heater directly.

THESSALONIANS, Epistles to the, two NEW TESTAMENT books written c51 AD by St. PAUL to the Christians in Salonika, Macedonia. They contain an early expression of Paul's theological ideas, particularly about Christ's second coming.

THIAMINE, or aneurin, alternative name for VITAMIN B_1.

THIBAUD, Jacques (1880–1953), French violinist who was recognized as the leading master of the French school of classical violin playing. He appeared frequently as part of a trio with cellist Pablo CASALS and pianist Alfred Cortot.

THIERS, Louis Adolphe (1797–1877),

French statesman, first president (1871–73) of the Third Republic. An influential journalist and popular historian of the French Revolution, he supported LOUIS PHILIPPE (1830) and held ministerial posts under him; opposed NAPOLEON III (1851) and was briefly exiled; negotiated the FRANCO-PRUSSIAN WAR's peace treaty and crushed the PARIS COMMUNE (1871).

THIEU, Nguyen van (1923–   ), president of South Vietnam, 1967–75. An army officer, he helped overthrow DIEM (1963), becoming premier in 1965 and president after KY's fall. He was reelected (1971) in elections widely thought to be rigged, but after US troops had withdrawn his dictatorial regime gradually collapsed, and he resigned in April, 1975. (See VIETNAM.)

THIRD WORLD, term often applied to the unaligned nations of Africa, Latin America and Asia as opposed to "Western" or communist countries.

THIRST AND HUNGER, complex specific sensations or desires for water and food respectively, which have a role in regulating their intake. Thirst is the end result of a mixture of physical and psychological effects including dry mouth, altered BLOOD mineral content, and the sight and sound of water; hunger, those of STOMACH contractions, low blood sugar levels, HABIT, and the SMELL and sight of food. Repleteness with either inhibits the sensation. Food and water intake are regulated by the HYPOTHALAMUS, and are closely related to the control of HORMONE secretion and other vegetative functions, being part of the system preserving the HOMEOSTASIS (constancy) of the body's internal environment. DRUGS, SMOKING, systemic disease and local BRAIN damage are among the many factors influencing thirst and hunger. Excessive thirst may be a symptom of DIABETES or KIDNEY failure (UREMIA), but organic excessive hunger is rare.

THIRTY-NINE ARTICLES, set of doctrinal statements, issued in 1571, outlining the position of the CHURCH OF ENGLAND on theological and civil matters. Formal assent to the articles was required of all Anglican clergy until 1865, when a less rigorous requirement of general approval was substituted.

THIRTY YEARS' WAR, a series of European wars, 1618–1648. Partly a Catholic-Protestant religious conflict, they were also a political and territorial struggle by different European powers, particularly France, against its greatest rivals the HAPSBURGS, rulers of the HOLY ROMAN EMPIRE. War began when BOHEMIAN Protestants revolted. They were defeated by TILLY (1620), who went on to subjugate the PALATINATE (1623). In 1625 Denmark, fearing Hapsburg power, invaded N Germany, but was defeated in 1629, when the emperor FERDINAND II issued the Edict of Restitution, restoring lands to the Roman Catholic Church. In 1630 the Swedish king GUSTAVUS ADOLPHUS led the Protestant German princes against Ferdinand. He was killed at LÜTZEN (1632), and by 1635 the Swedes had lost support in Germany, and the German states concluded the Peace of Prague. But now France, under RICHELIEU, intervened. Further wars ensued, with France, Sweden and the German Protestant states fighting in the Low Countries, Scandinavia, France, Germany, Spain and Italy against the Holy Roman Empire, Spain (another Hapsburg power) and Denmark. Peace negotiations, begun in 1640, were completed with the Peace of WESTPHALIA (1648).

THO, Le Duc (1911–   ), member of the North Vietnamese Politburo who, with Henry KISSINGER, was awarded the Nobel Peace Prize in 1975 for negotiating the ceasefire (1973) ending the VIETNAM WAR. He refused the prize on the ground that peace in Vietnam had not in fact been achieved.

THOMAS, Dylan Marlais (1914–1953), Welsh poet who first achieved recognition with *Eighteen Poems* (1934). His prose includes the quasiautobiographical *Portrait of the Artist as a Young Dog* (1940) and *Adventures in the Skin Trade* (1955); his poetry *Deaths and Entrances* (1946) and *Collected Poems* (1952). Perhaps his most famous work is *Under Milk Wood* (1954), originally a radio play.

THOMAS, Kurt (1955–   ), the first gymnast to be named outstanding amateur athlete in the US (1979). He won the world championship that year with two gold and three silver medals. He invented the "Thomas Flair," a pommel horse routine.

THOMAS, Lowell (1892–1981), US news broadcaster, world traveler and travelogue producer. A foreign correspondent during WWI, he was an eyewitness to the desert campaigns of Colonel T. E. LAWRENCE, about whom he wrote the best-selling, *With Lawrence in Arabia* (1924). A pioneer daily network-news broadcaster, he was on the air longer than anyone in radio history (1930–76).

THOMAS, Norman Mattoon (1884–1968), US socialist leader who ran six times for the presidency as a Socialist Party candidate. He helped found the American Civil Liberties Union (1920) and the League for Industrial Democracy (1922). An ardent pacifist, he tried to keep the US out of WWII. Many of his radical proposals eventually became law.

THOMAS, Saint, or Didymus (Greek: twin), one of the 12 APOSTLES, known as "Doubting Thomas" because he would not believe Christ's resurrection until he put his fingers in Christ's wounds. His subsequent career, and martyrdom at Madras, are recounted in the apocryphal *Acts of Thomas*.

THOMAS, Seth (1785–1859), US pioneer of mass production of clocks. He built his first factory (1812) at Plymouth, Conn., in a district later named Thomaston.

THOMAS A KEMPIS (Thomas Hemerken von Kempen; c1380–1471), German religious writer and Augustinian friar at Zwolle in the Netherlands. He is famous as the probable author of *On the Imitation of Christ* which, for its gentle humanity, has had an influence among Roman Catholics second only to the Bible.

THOMAS AQUINAS, Saint. See AQUINAS, SAINT THOMAS.

THOMISM, philosophical system of Thomas AQUINAS and his commentators, a synthesis of the thinking of ARISTOTLE and such early Church Fathers as AUGUSTINE. Long the official philosophical doctrine of the Roman Catholic Church, it has had a revival since the 1800s (as neo-Thomism). A central theme is the distinction between areas in which faith and reason should operate.

THOMPSON, Dorothy (1894–1961), US journalist. A foreign correspondent during the 1920s, she became a syndicated columnist for the New York *Herald Tribune* (1936) and was one of the most influential women in the US. An aggressive anti-fascist during the 1930s, she became a prominent anti-communist during the Cold War era. She was married to Sinclair LEWIS.

THOMSON, James (1700–1748), British poet who wrote *Rule Britannia* (1740). He is otherwise best known for his blank-verse *The Seasons* (1726–30), a celebration of Nature, which foreshadowed the Romantic period.

THOMSON, Sir Joseph John (1856–1940), British physicist generally regarded as the discoverer of the ELECTRON. It had already been shown that CATHODE RAYS could be deflected by a MAGNETIC FIELD; in 1897 Thomson showed that they could also be deflected by an ELECTRIC FIELD, and could thus be regarded as a stream of negatively charged particles. He showed their mass to be much smaller than that of the HYDROGEN atom—this was the first discovery of a SUBATOMIC PARTICLE. His model of the ATOM, though imperfect, provided a good basis for RUTHERFORD'S more satisfactory later attempt. Thomson was awarded the 1906 Nobel Prize for Physics.

THOMSON, Tom (1877–1917), Canadian artist who painted Canadian northland scenes in vivid tones. *A Northern Lake*, perhaps his best-known canvas, was purchased by the Canadian government and placed in the Ottawa National Gallery.

THOMSON, Virgil (1896–   ), US composer and music critic. Influenced by the SIX in Paris, he became a leading "Americanist." His works include the operas *Four Saints in Three Acts* (1928) and *The Mother of Us All* (1947) in collaboration with Gertrude Stein, symphonies and instrumental, chamber and film music. He won a 1949 Pulitzer Prize for his *Louisiana Story* score.

THOMSON OF FLEET, Roy, Baron (1894–1976), Canadian-born British newspaper publisher whose Thomson Organization, Ltd., was believed to control more newspapers than any other company in the world. His empire included numerous Canadian papers and radio stations as well as *The Scotsman* and *The Times* of London (acquired 1967).

THOR, Norse god, great god of thunder and provider of rain, subsidiary only to ODIN. The EDDAS recount his feats with Mjolnir, his magic hammer. The name Thursday comes from "Thor's Day."

THOREAU, Henry David (1817–1862), US writer, philosopher and naturalist. He was taught TRANSCENDENTALISM by Ralph Waldo EMERSON. *Walden* (1854) records his life in harmony with nature at WALDEN POND, near Concord, Mass. A fierce opponent of slavery, Thoreau withheld his poll tax in 1845 in protest, and defended the HARPERS FERRY raid in *A Plea for John Brown* (1859). His essay *Civil Disobedience* (1849) has influenced GANDHI, TOLSTOY and modern civil rights leaders with its defense of CIVIL DISOBEDIENCE against an unjust state.

THOREZ, Maurice (1900–1964), French communist leader. Rising rapidly in the party he became secretary general in 1930 and was elected to the chamber of Deputies in 1932, where he adhered to the Soviet line. He headed the party until his death.

THORFINN KARLSEFNI (11th century), Icelandic explorer who colonized North America. He sailed to Greenland, then (c1004) followed the route of Leif ERICSON to VINLAND, where he and 160 others attempted for two to three years to set up colonies.

THORNDIKE, Edward Lee (1874–1949), US psychologist whose system of psychology, connectionism, had a profound influence on US school education techniques, especially his discovery that the learning of one skill only slightly assists in the learning of another, even if related.

THORNTON, William (1759–1828), US architect and inventor. Though without formal training, he won (1793) the competition to design the Capitol, Washington, D.C. His revised designs (1795) were used for the exteriors of the N and S wings.

THORPE, James Francis "Jim" (1888–1953), US athlete, first man to win both decathlon and pentathlon at the Olympic Games (1912). He was half American Indian and starred with the Carlisle (Pa.) Indian school football team. After being barred from amateur athletics for having played semi-pro baseball, he became a legendary professional football star. He was named the greatest US athlete since 1900 in a 1950 Associated Press poll.

THORVALDSEN, Bertel (1770–1844), Danish sculptor, an apostle of NEOCLASSICISM, and one of the most successful sculptors of the 19th century. The Thorvaldsen Museum, Copenhagen, houses many of his works.

THOUSAND ISLANDS, group of over 1,500 islands, some Canadian, some US, in St. Lawrence R at the outlet of Lake Ontario. ST. LAWRENCE ISLANDS NATIONAL PARK includes 13 of them. Thousand Islands International Bridge (actually five bridges) is 8½mi long and carries traffic across the river.

THRACE, ancient region in the E Balkan Peninsula, SE Europe, bordering the Black and Aegean seas. It included modern NE Greece, S Bulgaria and European Turkey. The modern Thrace, an administrative region of Greece, comprises the SW parts of the old; while E Thrace constitutes European Turkey.

THREE MILE ISLAND, site in the Susquehanna River, near Middletown, Penn., of a nuclear reactor that on Mar. 28, 1979, began to emit "puffs" of radiation as a result of malfunction of the cooling system, aggravated by problems with the computer monitors and some human error. Initial reports downplayed the crisis, but it developed that a core meltdown was a possibility and that a large, potentially explosive hydrogen bubble had formed in the reactor; also, it was learned that no workable plans existed for evacuating the area. Luckily, catastrophe was averted without fatalities or known injury within 12 days. The accident at Three Mile Island was succeeded by numerous other serious if less dramatic setbacks to the nuclear power industry.

THREE-PENNY OPERA, The, song play by Kurt WEILL and Berthold BRECHT, first performed in Berlin, Germany, in 1928. Weill's music, ranging from operatic choruses and arias to jazz, captures the harsh satirical mood of Brecht's modernization of an 18th-century work, *The Beggar's Opera* by John Gay.

THROMBOSIS, the formation of clot (thrombus) in the HEART or BLOOD vessels. It commonly occurs in the legs and is associated with VARICOSE VEINS but is more serious if it occurs in the heart or in the brain arteries. Detachments from a thrombus in the legs may be carried to the lungs as an embolus (see EMBOLISM); this may have a fatal outcome if large vessels are occluded. The treatment includes ANTICOAGULANTS.

THRUSHES, slender-billed song-birds of the subfamily Turdinae. The plumage is often gray or red-brown and many species have speckled or striated breasts. The tail is usually rounded or square and is held erect in some species. Birds of worldwide distribution, they feed largely on insects, worms and snails, but many species also take fruit and berries.

THUCYDIDES (c460–c400 BC), greatest Greek historian and first to probe the relationship between historical cause and effect. An Athenian naval commander exiled for his incompetence over the siege of Amphipolis (424 BC), he spent the rest of his life traveling, interviewing soldiers and writing his *History of the Peloponnesian War*, in which he stressed accuracy, objectivity and analysis of individual motivation.

THUGS, secret society of ritual murderers in India, dating back to the 1600s. Devotees of Kali, Hindu goddess of destruction, they traveled in gangs, strangling and robbing their victims. The last known Thug was hanged by the British in 1882.

THULE, in classical times, the northernmost land, perhaps Iceland. It is now the name of a settlement on Baffin Bay, NW Greenland, with a USAF base; and of a pre-European Eskimo culture.

THURBER, James Grover (1894–1961), US humorist and cartoonist. The sophisticated humor of his writing contrasts with the simplicity of his line drawings. Several stories, such as *The Secret Life of Walter Mitty* (1942), were filmed. He contributed to the *New Yorker* from 1927. His collections include *My Life and Hard*

Times (1933) and *The Thurber Carnival* (1945).

THURMOND (James) Strom (1902–   ), US political leader, senator from South Carolina (1954–   ). A hardline supporter of states' rights, he opposed federal civil rights legislation and federal welfare. He was governor 1947–51 and the 1948 States' Rights Democratic presidential candidate, carrying four states. During his Senate career he shifted to the Republican party, and in 1981 he became president pro tempore of the Senate.

THURSTONE, Louis Leon (1887–1955), US psychologist whose application of the techniques of STATISTICS to the results of PSYCHOLOGICAL TESTS permitted their more accurate interpretation and demonstrated that a plurality of factors contributed to an individual's score.

THYMUS, a ductless two-lobed gland lying just behind the breast bone and mainly composed of lymphoid cells (see LYMPH). It plays a part in setting up the body's IMMUNITY system. Autoimmunity is thought to result from its pathological activity. After PUBERTY it declines in size.

THYROID GLAND, a ductless two-lobed gland lying in front of the trachea in the neck. The principal HORMONES secreted by the thyroid are thyroxine and triiodothyroxine; these play a crucial role in regulating the rate at which cells oxidize fuels to release ENERGY, and strongly influence growth. The release of thyroid hormones is controlled by thyroid stimulating hormone (TSH) released by the PITUITARY GLAND when blood thyroid-hormone levels are low. Deficiency of thyroid hormones (hypothyroidism) in adults leads to **myxedema**, with mental dullness and cool, dry and puffy skin. Oversecretion of thyroid hormones (hyperthyroidism or thyrotoxicosis) produces nervousness, weight loss and increased heart rate. GOITER, an enlargement of the gland, may result when the diet is deficient in iodine. (See also CRETINISM.)

THYSSEN, Fritz (1873–1951), German industrialist who in 1926 inherited an iron and steel empire that controlled most of Germany's ore reserves. One of Adolf Hitler's major financial supporters, he organized an alliance of Nazis and industrialists that helped the Nazis take power in 1933. Disenchanted with the regime, he fled to France, but was captured and spent WWII in a concentration camp.

TIBER, river in central Italy, flowing 252mi from the Appenines S through Umbria and Latium and SW through Rome to the Tyrrhenian Sea near Ostia. Ancient ROME was built on its E bank.

TIBERIUS (42 BC–37 AD), or Tiberius Claudius Nero, second Roman emperor (from 14 AD). A general, he was adopted heir by AUGUSTUS. His reign, although generally peaceful, was often tyrannical, resulting in unrest in Rome.

TIBET (also Xizang), autonomous region of China in central Asia, bordering Burma, India, Nepal, Bhutan and Sikkim. The 471,660sq mi of Tibet ("The Roof of the World") averages 12,000ft in altitude. The Kunlun Mts. in the N are almost as high as the Himalayas, across the great Ch'iang T'ang plateau to the S. The Brahmaputra, Indus, Mekong and Yangtze rivers rise in Tibet.

Tibetans follow Buddhist LAMAISM, headed by the Dalai Lama and the Panchen Lama. Until 1965 there were many monasteries and 20% of the male population were monks. After 1965, the Chinese expropriated large estates and have greatly decreased emphasis on religion. The pastoral, livestock-based economy has been affected by roadbuilding and new cement, chemical, paper, textile and other industries. Tibet has deposits of coal and iron (exploited in the NE) and other minerals.

By the mid-1950s Chinese rule in eastern Tibet caused open dissent and, in 1959, a revolt which was suppressed. The Dalai Lama fled from the capital LHASA to India. Tibet became an autonomous region in 1965. There are thought to be some 300,000 Chinese in the country in addition to some 1,500,000 Tibetans. There are an additional 1,500,000 Tibetans living outside of Tibet.

TIC, a stereotyped movement, habit spasm or vocalization which occurs irregularly, but often more under stress, and which is outside voluntary control. Its cause is unknown. **Tic douloureux** is a condition in which part of the FACE is abnormally sensitive, any TOUCH provoking intense PAIN.

TICKS, a group of parasitic arthropods, with the MITES members of the order Acarina. Unlike most other arthropods, there is no head and the THORAX and ABDOMEN are fused. All ticks are blood-sucking external parasites of vertebrates. They are divided into two main families: the soft ticks, Argasidae, and hard ticks, Ixodidae. Ticks transmit more diseases to man and domestic animals than any other arthropod group except the mosquitoes.

TICONDEROGA, by Lake George, NE N.Y., village and site of Fort Ticonderoga, which commanded the route between Canada and the Hudson R valley. Taken (1759) by the British in the FRENCH AND

NDIAN WAR, it fell (1775) in the Revolutionary War to the GREEN MOUNTAIN BOYS led by Ethan ALLEN and Benedict ARNOLD. It was recaptured (1777) by General BURGOYNE. The fort is now a museum.

TIDAL POWER, form of HYDROELECTRICITY produced by harnessing the ebb and flow of the TIDES. Barriers containing reversible TURBINES are built across an estuary or gulf where the tidal range is great. The Rance power plant in the Gulf of St. Malo, Brittany, the first to be built (1961–67), produces 240MW power, mostly at ebb tide.

TIDES, the periodic rise and fall of land and water on the earth. Tidal motions are primarily exhibited by water: the motion of the land is barely detectable. As the earth-moon system rotates about its center of gravity, which is within the earth, the earth bulges in the direction of the moon and in the exactly opposite direction, owing to the resultant of the moon's gravitational attraction and the centrifugal forces resulting from the system's revolution. Toward the moon, the lunar attraction is added to a comparatively small centrifugal force; in the opposite direction it is subtracted from a much larger centrifugal force. As the moon orbits the earth in the same direction as the earth rotates, the bulge "travels" round the earth each lunar day (24.83h); hence most points on the earth have a high tide every 12.42h. The sun produces a similar though smaller tidal effect. Exceptionally high high tides occur at full and new moon (spring tides), particularly if the moon is at perigee (see ORBIT); exceptionally low high tides (neap tides) at first and third quarter. The friction of the tides causes the DAY to lengthen 0.001s per century.

TIEGS, Cheryl (1948–   ), US model and cover girl. One of the most photographed women of all time, her wholesome blonde California beauty made her "the all-American model" of the fashion world in the late 1970s.

TIEN SHAN, great mountain system of Soviet central Asia and W China. It curves E from the NE PAMIRS for 1,500mi and covers some 70,000sq mi. Pobeda Peak (24,406ft) is the range's highest.

TIENTSIN, (also Tianjin), capital of Hopei province, N China, on the Hai R 80mi SE of Peking. It is a great industrial center and sea, river and canal port with major steel, chemical and textile industries. It is the seaport for Peking and is near major coal-producing areas. The city suffered badly during the 1976 earthquake centered in Tangshan, a few miles away. Pop 7,000,000.

TIEPOLO, Giovanni Battista (1696–1770), great Venetian painter. Influenced initially by VERONESE, he developed his own colorful, airy but exuberant style in frescoes and ceilings in N Italy, Würzburg palace (Germany) and the royal palace in Madrid.

TIERRA DEL FUEGO, island group off S South America. Discovered (1520) by MAGELLAN and now divided between Chile and Argentina, its sparsely populated 28,470sq mi comprise one large and many small islands. Sheep and oil are the economic mainstays.

TIFFANY, Charles Lewis (1812–1902), US jeweler and retailer. The stock in his first store, opened in 1839, was limited mainly to ordinary glassware and stationery, but it soon included Bohemian glass, jewelry, silverware and rare porcelain. Tiffany began manufacturing his own jewelry in 1848, and, by 1870, had extended his operations to Paris and London. The firm name, Tiffany & Co., was adopted in 1853.

TIFFANY, Louis Comfort (1848–1933), US artist and designer, a leader of ART NOUVEAU. Son of jeweler Charles Tiffany, he created decorative objects of iridescent "favrile" or Tiffany glass.

TIFLIS. See TBILISI.

TIGER, *Panthera tigris,* the major CAT of Asia, with distinct races in different parts of that continent. Closely related to LIONS, they are the largest of all the cats, with a tawny coat broken with dark, vertical stripes providing excellent camouflage against natural patterns of light and shade. Tigers do not chase after food but prefer to stalk and spring. For the most part they are solitary animals, hunting in the cool of the day and otherwise lying up in the shade to rest.

TIGRIS RIVER, easternmost of the two great rivers of ancient Mesopotamia. The Tigris-Euphrates valley was the cradle of Middle-East civilizations (see BABYLONIA; NINEVEH; SUMER). Baghdad, city of the ABBASIDS, now capital of Iraq, stands on its banks. It rises in the Taurus Mts. in Turkey and flows 1,180mi SE through Iraq to the Euphrates at Al Qurnah.

TIKHONOV, Nikolai (1896–   ), Russian poet, prose writer and Soviet literary official. Tikhonov's early poetry describes his experiences with the Red Army during the Civil War. In the late 1920s he wrote short stories depicting romantic adventures in the Soviet East. For many years he served as president of the Union of Soviet Writers and as a member of the Supreme Soviet.

TILDEN, Samuel Jones (1814–1886), US

lawyer and politician. An early leader of the BARNBURNERS and FREE SOIL movements, he proved corruption among New York City politicians led by William TWEED. Governor of N.Y. 1875–76, he lost the hotly contested 1876 presidential election to Republican Rutherford B. HAYES by one electoral vote.

TILDEN, William (Bill) Tatem, II (1893–1953), US tennis champion. From 1920 to 1930 he was the top-ranked US player, winning US, Wimbledon singles (first American to do so) and Davis Cup titles. He turned professional in 1931.

TILLICH, Paul Johannes (1886–1965), German-born theologian and teacher. He attempted to synthesize Christianity and classical and modern existentialist philosophy in such works as *Systematic Theology* (1951–63) and the shorter, more popular *The Shaking of the Foundations* (1948) and *The Courage to Be* (1952). Dismissed from Frankfurt U. by the Nazis, he taught at New York, Harvard and Chicago universities.

TIMBUKTU, or Tombouctou, trading town and ancient city in central Mali, W Africa, near the Niger R. It was a wealthy trading and Muslim cultural center in the MALI EMPIRE (1300s) and under the SONGHAI (1400–1500s). Pop 10,445.

TIME, a concept dealing with the order and duration of events. If two events occur nonsimultaneously at a point, they occur in a definite order with a time lapse between them. Two intervals of time are equal if a body in equilibrium moves over equal distances in each of them; such a body constitutes a clock. The sun provided man's earliest clock, the natural time interval being that between successive passages of the sun over the local meridian—the solar DAY. For many centuries the rotation of the earth provided a standard for time measurements, but in 1967 the SI UNIT of time, the SECOND, was redefined in terms of the frequency associated with a cesium energy-level transition. In everyday life, we can still think of time in the way Newton did, ascribing a single universal time-order to events. We can neglect the very short time needed for light signals to reach us, and believe that all events have a unique chronological order. But when velocities close to that of light are involved, relativistic principles become important; simultaneity is no longer universal and the time scale in a moving framework is "dilated" with respect to one at rest— moving clocks appear to run slow (see RELATIVITY).

TIME-AND-MOTION STUDY, analysis of how a worker performs a given task, by study of his movements, methods and equipment. Changes can be made by laying out the job differently or adding labor-saving tools. F. W. TAYLOR was a pioneer in time-and-motion study. (See HUMAN ENGINEERING; LINEAR PROGRAMMING.)

TIMOR, largest and easternmost of the Lesser SUNDA ISLANDS, 400mi NW of Australia. Since Dec. 1975, when the former Portuguese (eastern) Timor was occupied by Indonesian troops, the whole island has been under Indonesian control.

TIMOTHY, Saint, one of St. PAUL's companions, said to have been bishop of Ephesus after Paul. He was recipient of two of Paul's epistles (1 and 2 Timothy), which emphasize moral discipline and obedience to civil and religious authority.

TIMPANI, kettledrums, first used in orchestral music in the 1600s, having a calfskin head over a hollow brass or copper hemisphere. A set of timpani usually consists of three drums. Pitch is governed by the tension of the head, which can be adjusted. Tone may be varied by the type of stick and by the region of the head struck.

TINBERGEN, Jan (1903–   ), Dutch economist who shared the first (1969) Nobel Prize for Economic Science with Ragnar FRISCH for work in developing dynamic models (see ECONOMETRICS).

TINBERGEN, Nikolas (1907–   ), Dutch ethologist awarded with K. LORENZ and K. von FRISCH the 1973 Nobel Prize for Physiology or Medicine for their individual, major contributions to the science of ANIMAL BEHAVIOR.

TINGUELY, Jean (1925–   ), Swiss sculptor best known for his *metamécaniques*, machine-like forms of KINETIC ART. Some themselves produce paintings.

TIN PAN ALLEY, popular name of an area in NYC, centering on 7th Avenue between 48th and 52nd Streets, which served as the headquarters of the popular-music publishing business, c.1900–35.

TIN (Sn), silvery-white metal in Group IVA of the PERIODIC TABLE, occurring as CASSITERITE in SE Asia, Bolivia, Zaire and Nigeria. The ore is reduced by smelting with coal. Tin exhibits ALLOTROPY: white(β) tin, the normal form, changes below 13.2°C to gray (α) tin, a powdery metalloid form resembling GERMANIUM, and known as "tin pest." Tin is unreactive, but dissolves in concentrated acids and alkalis, and is attacked by HALOGENS. It is used as a protective coating for steel, and in alloys including solder (see SOLDERING), BRONZE, PEWTER, BABBITT METAL and type metal. AW 118.7, mp 232°C, bp 2270°compounds, used as biocides, and also inorganic compounds; in (II) and tin (IV) salts. Tin (IV) Oxide (SnO_2), white powder prepared by calcining CASSITERITE or burning finely divided tin; used in glazes and as an abrasive. subl 1800°C. Tin (II) Chloride ($SnCl_2$), white crystalline solid, prepared by dissolving tin in hydrochloric acid, used as a reducing agent, in tinplating, and as a mordant for dyes. mp 246°C, bp 652°C.

TINTORETTO (Jacopo Robusti; 1518–1594), Venetian MANNERIST painter. His paintings and FRESCOES are characterized by free brushwork, dramatic viewpoint, movement, monumental figures and rich colors. He sought to express drama through color and light, as in the Scuola di S. Rocco *Life of Christ* (1564–87).

TIOMKIN, Dmitri (1899–1979), Russian-born US film composer who wrote in a soaring romantic style. His 160 scores included four Academy Award winners: those for *High Noon*, *The Alamo*, *The High and the Mighty*, and *The Old Man and The Sea*.

TIPPECANOE, Battle of (Nov. 7, 1811), between TECUMSEH's Shawnees, led by TENSKWATAWA, and US troops led by William HARRISON, near the Tippecanoe R, Ind. There were heavy casualties on both sides, but the "great victory" helped Harrison to the presidency in 1840. (See INDIAN WARS.)

TIRE, ring-shaped cushion fitted onto a wheel rim as a shock absorber and to provide traction. The pneumatic tire (filled with compressed air) was patented in 1845 by R. W. Thomson, an English engineer, who used a leather tread and a rubber inner tube. Solid rubber tires were more popular, however, until the pneumatic tire was reinvented by John Boyd DUNLOP (1888), whose outer tube was of canvas covered by vulcanized rubber. The modern tubeless tire (without inner tube) dates from the 1950s. The basic structure of a tire comprises layers (plies) of rubberized fabric (usually polyester cord). The plies are combined with "beads"—inner circular wire reinforcements—and the outer tread and sidewalls on a tire-building drum. The tire is then shaped and vulcanized (see VULCANIZATION) in a heated mold under pressure, acquiring its tread design. Three types of tire are made: the bias-ply tire has the plies with cords running diagonally, alternately in opposite directions; the bias-belted tire is similar, with fiberglass belts between plies and tread; the radial-ply tire has the cords running parallel to the axle, and steel-mesh belts.

TIROL, a state in W Austria. Over half its original area was ceded to Italy in 1919 (see ALTO-ADIGE). Austria's highest peak, Grossglockner (12,461ft) is there. Farming, lumber and tourism are its main activities. The capital is Innsbruck. Pop 540,771.

TIROS, acronym for *T*elevision and *I*nfra-*R*ed *O*bservation *S*atellite, the initial US weather satellites. The first of 10 Tiros satellites was orbited Apr. 1, 1960; together, they made more than 500,000 cloud-cover photographs. The Tiros satellites were followed by larger and more versatile craft, including Nimbus (1964), ESSA (for Earth Science Services Administration, 1966), NOAA (for National Oceanic and Atmospheric Administration, 1970), SMS (for Synchronous Meteorological Satellite, later changed to GOES, for Geostationary Operational Environmental Satellite, 1974), and Tiros-N (1978). The Soviets have similar Meteora weather satellites (first launched 1969) and the two nations have exchanged meteorological data from satellites since 1966.

TIRPITZ, Alfred von (1849–1930), German admiral. As navy secretary (1897–1916) he built up the battle fleet to rival the British navy, precipitating an Anglo-German arms race. In WWI his fleet proved to be relatively useless.

TIRSO DE MOLINA (Gabriel Téllez; c1584–1648), Spanish dramatist and friar. His historical, cloak-and-dagger and religious works are notable for insight into character. His *Rake of Seville* (1630) introduced DON JUAN to the stage.

TISSUES, similar CELLS grouped together in certain areas of the body of multicellular ANIMALS and PLANTS. These cells are usually specialized for a single function; thus MUSCLE cells contract but do not secrete; nerve cells conduct impulses but have little or no powers of contraction. The cells are held together by intercellular material such as COLLAGEN. Having become specialized for a single or at most a very narrow range of functions, they are dependent upon other parts of the organism for items such as food or oxygen. Groups of tissues, each with its own functions, make up ORGANS. Connective tissue refers to the material in which all the specialized body organs are embedded and supported. It includes ADIPOSE TISSUE and the material of LIGAMENTS and TENDONS. (See also HISTOLOGY.)

TITANIC, 46,328-ton British liner which sank in 1912 after hitting an iceberg on her maiden voyage to New York. At least 1,500 of the 2,200 aboard drowned. After the disaster (caused mainly by excessive speed), lifeboat, radio watch and ice patrol provisions were improved.

TITANIUM (Ti), silvery gray metal in

Group IVB of the PERIODIC TABLE; a TRANSITION ELEMENT. Titanium occurs in RUTILE and in ILMENITE, from which it is extracted by conversion to titanium (IV) chloride and reduction by magnesium. The metal and its alloys are strong, light, and corrosion- and temperature-resistant, and, although expensive, are used for construction in the aerospace industry. Titanium is moderately reactive, forming tctravalent compounds, including titanates (TiO_3^{2-}), and less stable di- and trivalent compounds. **Titanium (IV) oxide** (TiO_2) is used as a white pigment in paints, ceramics, etc. **Titanium (IV) chloride** ($TiCl_4$) finds use as a catalyst. AW 47.9, mp 1660°C, bp 3287°C, sg. 4.54.

TITANS, in Greek myth, the children of URANUS (Heaven) and GAEA (Earth), including CRONUS, Coeus, HYPERION, OCEANUS and IAPETUS, all of great strength and height. Cronus overthrew Uranus and swallowed his own children—one, ZEUS, escaped. He and the other Olympians rebelled and defeated the Titans.

TITCHENER, Edward Bradford (1867–1927), British-born US psychologist, a disciple of WUNDT, who played a large part in establishing experimental PSYCHOLOGY in the US, especially through his *Experimental Psychology* (4 vols., 1901–05).

TITIAN (c1480/90–1576), Venetian painter, leading Renaissance artist. Born Tiziano Vecellio, he worked for BELLINI and GIORGIONE, who influenced his early work. He became Venice's official painter 1516. His perceptive portraits, monumental altarpieces, historical and mythological scenes are famous for their energetic composition, use of rich color and original technique.

TITICACA, Lake, on the Peru-Bolivia border in the Andes Mts. About 120mi long, it is the largest lake in South America (3,200sq mi) and the world's highest navigable lake (12,500ft). It was the center of the TIAHUANACO civilization.

TITO, (Josip Broz) (1892–1980), communist president of YUGOSLAVIA (1953–1980), founder of the post-WWII republic. He became a communist while a WWI prisoner of war in Russia and later spent several years in Yugoslav jails. General secretary of the Communist Party from 1937, Tito organized partisan resistance to the Nazis in WWII, eclipsing the CHETNIKS, and after the war established a socialist republic. He served as prime minister (1945–53) before becoming president. Tito broke with STALIN in 1948. He suppressed home opposition, while working for workers' self-management and reconciliation of nation. minorities. Later years saw a substanti. liberalization of his policies. On th international scene, Tito became a organizer and leading spokesman for "thir world," or neutralist countries.

TITUS (Flavius Sabinus Vespasianus (39–81 AD), Roman emperor, successo (79) to his father VESPASIANUS. A successf soldier, he captured (70) Jerusalem in th Jewish revolt (66–70). Berenice, sister HEROD Agrippa II, became his mistress. H was popular for lavish entertaining, and ai to victims of VESUVIUS (79) and of the fire Rome (80).

TLINGIT INDIANS, largest group North American INDIANS of the NW coas now living in SE Alaska and numberin about 7,000. They belong to the Koluscha linguistic family and resemble HAID Indians in their complex social organiza tion. Many still live by fishing, woodcarv ing, basketry and weaving. (See als ALASKA.)

TM. See TRANSCENDENTAL MEDITATION.

TNT, or **trinitrotoluene,** pale yellow crystalline solid made by nitration TOLUENE. It is the most extensively used hig EXPLOSIVE, being relatively insensitive t shock, especially when melted by stear heating and cast. MW 227.1, mp 82°C.

TOADS, name strictly referring only t members of the family Bufonidae, but a the terms "frog" and "toad" are the onl common names available for all the 2,00 species of tailless amphibians, "frog" is use for those which have smooth skins and liv in or near water, and "toad" for all thos with warty skins and living in drier areas Toads are independent of water except fo breeding, the larvae—TADPOLES—bein purely aquatic. Most toads feed nocturnall on small animals.

TOBACCO, dried and cured leaves o varieties of the tobacco plant (*Nicotianc tabacum*), used for smoking, chewing and as SNUFF. Native to America, tobacco wa introduced to Europe by the Spanish in the 16th century and from there spread to Asi and Africa. Today the US remains the world's largest producer, followed by China, India and the USSR. Consumptior is increasing despite the health hazards o SMOKING. Tobacco is grown in alluvial o sandy soils and may be harvested in abou four months. Cultivation is dependent on hand labor. Family: Solanaceae.

TOBEY, Mark (1890–1976), US painter strongly influenced by Chinese calligraphy and Zen Buddhism. He developed his "white writing" style in the 1930s in small abstracts representing street scenes. His ater, delicately colored abstracts have more intricate linear rhythms.

TOBIN, Daniel Joseph (1875–1955), Irish-born US labor leader. As president of the TEAMSTERS UNION (1907–52), he built it into one of the most powerful unions in the US. He was also a vice-president of the AFL (1933–52).

TOBIN, James (1918–   ), US economist; Yale professor who won the 1981 Nobel Memorial Prize in Economic Science for his research in relating the effects of financial markets to consumption, prices, production and investment, as well as his studies of government monetary policies and budgets. He had served as one of President Kennedy's economic advisers.

TOBIT (Tobias), Book of, in the APOCRYPHA, recounts how Tobias, son of the devout but blinded Jew Tobit (or Tobias), successfully undertakes a dangerous journey, helped by the Angel RAPHAEL, to exorcise a demon from, and marry, Sara. He then helps Tobit regain his sight.

TOBOGGANING, winter sport of riding flat runnerless sleds (toboggans) with curved endpieces down slopes at up to 60mph. Toboggans are of American Indian origin. Today they are 4–9ft long by 18in wide, made of wood or metal. (See also BOBSLED.)

TOCQUEVILLE, Alexis (Charles Henri Clérel) de (1805–1859), French historian famous for his analysis of the strengths and drawbacks of democracy. He discussed his observations in the US in *Democracy in America* (1835–40). He was impressed but foresaw a threat to individual liberty in the "tyranny of the majority," a theme developed in *The Old Regime and the French Revolution* (1856). A moderate liberal politician, he was French foreign minister in 1849.

TODD, Mike (1907–1958), US impresario who produced burlesque revues on Broadway starring Gypsy Rose LEE and Mae WEST during the 1930s and helped develop Cinerama and a 70-mm film process, Todd-AO, during the 1950s. He also produced the lavish Academy Award-winning film *Around the World in 80 Days* (1956).

TOGLIATTI, Palmiro (1893–1964), Italian Communist Party leader (1926–64). He cofounded the party, now West Europe's largest, in 1921, became COMINTERN secretary (1935) and returned from exile (1944) to serve in several governments.

TOGO, West African republic, a 70mi-wide strip extending 340mi N from the Gulf of Guinea between Ghana and Dahomey. From the central Togo Mts. a grassy

plateau slopes E to the Mono R and S to the sandy coastal plain. The N is savanna country. The climate is hot and humid, averaging 81°F, with yearly rainfall of 40–70in. The economy is agricultural: chief exports are cacao and coffee, but cassava, corn and cotton are also important. Large phosphate deposits are worked NE of the seaport capital LOMÉ. Over 90% of the people live in rural areas, mostly in the S. The population is made up almost entirely of African Negroes from the Ewe, Ouatchi, Mina, Kabre and other ethnic groups. French is the official language, Ewe the most widely used.

Formerly the E part of the German protectorate of Togoland, the area was administered by France after WWI and became independent in 1960. Since a military coup in 1967 it has been ruled by Étienne Eyadèma, who suspended the constitution and dissolved the legislative body.

Official name: Republic of Togo
Capital: Lomé
Area: 21,853sq mi
Population: 2,022,000
Languages: French; tribal languages
Religions: Animist; Christian; Muslim
Monetary unit(s): 1 CFA franc=100 centimes

TOJO, Hideki (1884–1948), Japanese general and militarist statesman, prime minister and virtual dictator (1941–44) who ordered the attack on Pearl Harbor. A professional soldier, he was chief of staff of the army in China (1937), and minister of war from 1940. He was forced to resign when the US took Saipan (1944). Convicted of war crimes, he was hanged.

TOKYO, capital of Japan. It lies at the head of Tokyo Bay on the SE coast of Honshu Island, and contains over 10% of Japan's population. Founded in the 12th century as Edo, it became capital of the TOKUGAWA shoguns in 1603; it was renamed and made imperial capital in 1868. Reconstruction after earthquake and fire (1923) and the air raids of WWII transformed much of Tokyo. It is today a center of government, industry, finance and education: the National Diet (parliament) meets here; most of Japan's great corporations have their head office in Maurunochi district; Tokyo University (founded 1877) is one of hundreds of educational institutions. Tokyo has many parks, museums and temples, the Imperial Palace and the Kabukiza theater (see KABUKI). Industries (with large complexes to the W) include printing, shipbuilding, metal manufactures, automobiles, chemicals and textiles. The harbor and airport are Japan's busiest. Pop (city) 8,448,400; (metropolis) 11,596,000.

TOKYO ROSE (Iva D'Aquino 1916–   ), US traitor. An American born to Japanese parents, she broadcast to US troops from Japan during WWII, seeking to undermine their morale and urging them to return home. After the war she was convicted of treason and imprisoned.

TOLEDO, city in central Spain 40mi SW of Madrid, seat of Toledo province, former Roman and Visigoth capital, famous for sword blades since prosperous Moorish rule (712–1085). Landmarks are the Alcázar (citadel), Gothic cathedral (the archbishop is Spain's primate) and EL GRECO's house. Pop 354,635.

TOLKIEN, John Ronald Reuel (1892–1973), British author and scholar, celebrated for his tales *The Hobbit* (1937) and the trilogy *The Lord of the Rings* (1954–55), which present a mythical world of elves and dwarfs, partly based on Anglo-Saxon and Norse folklore. Tolkien was professor of Anglo-Saxon, then of English language and literature, at Oxford University.

TOLSTOY, Aleksei Nikolaevich, (1883–1945), Russian novelist and playwright, best known for his trilogy *The Road to Calvary* (1921–40), the novella *Nikita's Childhood* (1920) and the novel *Peter the First* (1929–34). A nobleman distantly related to Leo Tolstoy, he left Russia in 1917 but returned in 1922 and became a supporter of Stalin's regime.

TOLSTOY, Leo Nikoleyevich, Count (1828–1910), Russian novelist. Educated at Kazan University, he served in the army, married in 1862 and spent the next 15 years on his estate at Yasnaya Polyana near Moscow. In this happy period he produced his masterpieces: *War and Peace* (1865–69), an epic of vast imaginative scope and variety of character, tells the story of five families against the background of the Napoleonic invasion of Russia. *Anna Karenina* (1875–77), the tragic story of an adulterous affair, is remarkable more for its psychological

portrayal. In later years Tolstoy experienced a spiritual crisis, recounted in his *Confession* (1882), and embraced a ascetic philosophy of Christian anarchism His other works include *Childhood* (1852) *The Cossacks* (1863) and *Resurrection* (1899).

TOLTEC, Indian civilization dominant i the central Mexican highlands between th 900s and 1100s. The Toltec god wa QUETZALCOATL. The Toltecs, sophisticate builders and craftsmen, erected thei capital at Tollán (ruins near modern Tula 60mi N of Mexico City). The dominan group were Nahuatl speakers. AZTECS an others overran the area and adopted variou aspects of Toltec culture.

TOMAHAWK, light hatchet or war club o certain North American Indians. Originall a chip or stone fixed to a stick, it gained ar iron ax head through trade with Europeans Often incorporating a pipe bowl and stem, i had ceremonial value and was usually buried at the end of hostilities.

TOMATO, *Lycopersicon esculentum*, herbaceous plant, native to South America, bu introduced to Europe in the 16th century and now cultivated worldwide. Most of the crop is canned or processed to make prepared foods, a relatively small proportion being grown for salad use. In northerr latitudes, tomatoes are grown under glass but the bulk is grown as a field crop. Italy Spain, Brazil and Japan are among the leading producers. Family: Solanaceae.

TOMONAGA, Shinichiro (1906–   ) Japanese physicist who shared with FEYNMAN and SCHWINGER the 1965 Nobel Prize for Physics for their independent work on quantum electrodynamics.

TOM THUMB, General (1838–1883) pseudonym for the US midget Charles Sherwood Stratton, who toured Europe and the US with the entertainer P. T. BARNUM His adult height was only 40in.

TONALITY, the quality of music based on the tonic, or principal note of a particular KEY, as in most classical music; such music is tonal. Tonality compares with polytonality the simultaneous use of many keys, and ATONALITY, the use of none.

TONE POEM. See SYMPHONIC POEM.

TONGA, or Friendly Islands, constitutiona monarchy in the S Pacific.
Land. The kingdom comprises over 15C islands of which the chief groups are Tongatapu, Háapai, and Vaváu. The climate is tropical. The capital is Nukúalofa on Tongatapu. The present kingdom wa founded in 1845 by George Tupu I and became a British protectorate in 1900. I achieved independence in 1970.

People and Economy. The population is mainly Polynesian with about 300 Europeans. The economy is agricultural, with copra, bananas, and vanilla the chief exports. Promising petroleum deposits were located near Tongatapu in 1977.

History. The islands were discovered in 1616 by the Dutch explorer Jakob Lemaire and later visited by Abel Tasman (1643) and James Cook (1773).

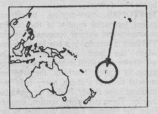

Official name: Kingdom of Tonga
Capital: Nukúalofa
Area: 270sq mi
Population: 97,800
Languages: Tongan, English
Religions: Christian
Monetary unit(s): 1 Páanga=100 seniti

TÖNNIES, Ferdinand Julius (1855–1936), German sociologist noted for his distinction between rural communities governed by traditions rooted in the family and urban groupings based on rational self-interest and economic and legal interdependence. His theories are expressed in *Community and Society* (1887).

TONSILLITIS, INFLAMMATION of the TONSILS due to VIRUS or BACTERIAL infection. It may follow sore throat or other pharyngeal disease or it may be a primary tonsil disease. Sore throat and red swollen tonsils, which may exude PUS or cause swallowing difficulty, are common; LYMPH nodes at the angle of the jaw are usually tender and swollen. QUINSY is a rare complication. ANTIBIOTIC treatment for the bacterial cause usually leads to a resolution but removal of the tonsils is needed in a few cases.

TONSILS, areas of LYMPH tissue aggregated at the sides of the PHARYNX. They provide a basic site of body defense against infection via the mouth or NOSE and are thus particularly susceptible to primary infection (TONSILLITIS). As with the ADENOIDS, they are particularly important in children first encountering infectious microorganisms in the environment.

TONY AWARDS, annual awards for achievement in the US theater, inaugurated in 1947 and named for Antoinette Perry

(1888–1946), an actress, manager, and theatrical producer. Awards are accorded by the League of New York Theaters, various theater arts unions and other organizations in such categories as best play, best musical, direction, choreography, featured actor and set, costume and lighting design.

TOOMEY, Bill (1939–   ), US decathlon star. He won the gold medal in the event at the 1968 Olympics, and, in 1969, set a world record with 8,417 points.

TOPAZ, aluminum SILICATE mineral of composition $Al_2S:O_4(F, OH)_2$, forming prismatic crystals (orthorhombic) which are variable and unstable in color, and valued as GEM stones. The best topazes come from Brazil, Siberia and the US.

TOPEKA, capital of Kan., seat of Shawnee Co., on the Kansas R 55mi W of Kansas City. It is a railroad center, processes grain and meat, and makes iron and steel products and automobile tires. The MENNINGER Foundation is here. Pop 115,266.

TOPOLOGY, branch of mathematics that studies properties of geometrical figures or abstract spaces that are independent of shape or distance. **Point-set topology** deals with ways of defining "nearness" of elements, or points, of a set (see SET THEORY) without necessarily assigning numerical distances to pairs of points. Such a definition is called "a topology on the set" and the set is called a **topological space**. The topology makes it possible to define continuous FUNCTIONS on the space. **Algebraic topology,** or combinatorial topology, uses abstract algebra (see ALGEBRA, ABSTRACT) to treat the ways in which geometrical figures fit together to form figures of higher dimension, disregarding shape. For example a sphere is topologically the same as a cube, but it is distinct from a torus (doughnut) because if the surfaces of the figures are divided into triangles the algebraic relationships between the triangles will be different in the two cases.

TORAH (Hebrew: law, teaching), the PENTATEUCH (first five books of the Bible) kept in the Ark of every SYNAGOGUE. In a wider sense it is the whole body of oral and written teaching central to JUDAISM, and includes the rest of the Hebrew Bible, Rabbinic Codes, the TALMUD and MIDRASH.

TORNADO, the most violent kind of STORM; an intense WHIRLWIND of small diameter, extending downward from a convective cloud in a severe THUNDERSTORM, and generally funnel-shaped. Air rises rapidly in the outer region of the funnel, but descends in its core, which is at very low pressure. The funnel is visible owing to the formation of cloud droplets by expansional cooling in this low-pressure region. Very high winds spiral in toward the core. There is almost total devastation and often loss of life in the path of a tornado—which itself may move at up to 200m/s. Though generally rare, tornadoes occur worldwide, especially in the US and Australia in spring and early summer. (See also WATERSPOUT.)

TORONTO, capital of Ontario province and York Co., second-largest city in Canada (after Montreal), on the NW shore of Lake Ontario. It is a major port as well as a commercial, manufacturing and educational center and the cultural focus of English-speaking Canada. Its products include chemicals, machinery, electrical goods and clothing. The French Fort Rouillé (c1750) was replaced by the English York (1793), which was sacked in the War of 1812, renamed in 1834 and was Canada's capital 1849–51 and 1855–59. Pop 633,315.

TORPEDO, self-propelled streamlined missile that travels underwater, its explosive warhead detonating when it nears or strikes its target. The torpedo was invented by Robert Whitehead, a British engineer, in 1866. Modern torpedoes are launched by dropping from airplanes or by firing from ships or submarines. They are electrically driven by propellers and guided by rudders controlled by a GYROPILOT. Many can be set to home in acoustically on their target. Rocket-propelled torpedoes are fired as guided missiles, and convert into torpedoes when they enter the water near their target. Torpedoes are now chiefly antisubmarine weapons.

TORQUEMADA, Tomás de (1420–1498), Spanish Dominican prior, fanatical general of Spain appointed by Ferdinand and Isabella in 1483. Using the INQUISITION to enforce religious and political unity, he was responsible for expelling 200,000 Jews from Spain and burning over 2,000 heretics.

TORRICELLI, Evangelista (1608–1647), Italian physicist and mathematician, a one-time assistant of GALILEO, who improved the telescope and microscope and invented the mercury BAROMETER (1643).

TORSION, strain produced by a twisting motion about an axis (a TORQUE), such as a couple applied perpendicular to a cylinder axis. The resistance of a bar of given material to torsion is a measure of its rigidity and elasticity.

TORT (French: wrong), in law, a wrongful act against a person or his property for which that person can claim damages as compensation. It is distinguished from a crime, which the state will prosecute; it is up to the injured party to sue for redress of a tort. The same wrongful act, an ASSAULT for example, may be both actionable as a tort and prosecuted as a crime. Torts range from personal injury to SLANDER or LIBEL; they include TRESPASS and damage or injury arising through NEGLIGENCE. Wrongful breach of an agreement, however, is covered by the law of CONTRACT.

TORTOISES, slow-moving, heavily-armored terrestrial reptiles of the tropics, subtropics and warmer temperate regions. The body is enclosed in a box-like shell into which the head and limbs can be withdrawn. The shell is covered with horny plates or scutes. Toothless, the jaws are covered to form a sharp, horny beak. All tortoises move slowly, feeding on vegetable matter. There are many species, ranging from the familiar garden tortoises to the 1.4m (4.6ft) giant tortoises of the Galapagos and Seychelles.

TORTURE, deliberate infliction of extreme pain. It has been used for centuries as punishment or to extract information or confessions from prisoners, for religious (as in the INQUISITION) and, more often, purely political reasons. Banned by England's 1689 Bill of Rights, by the US Constitution's 8th Amendment and by the GENEVA CONVENTIONS, it was widely practiced by Axis countries in WWII, and still survives, even with refinements like electric shocks. Some consider BRAINWASHING to be mental torture.

TORY, popular name of the Conservative and Unionist Party, one of Britain's two chief parties. The term (originally describing Irish highwaymen) was applied in 1679 to supporters of the future JAMES II of England. In the main, Tories became staunch church and king men, and "Tory" was applied to loyalist colonists in the American Revolution.

TOSCANINI, Arturo (1867–1957), Italian conductor, perhaps the greatest of his time, famous for dedication to each composer's intentions. He became musical director of LA SCALA in Milan (1898) and went on to conduct the New York Metropolitan (1908–14) and Philharmonic orchestras (1926–36). The NBC Symphony Orchestra was created for him in 1937.

TOTALITARIANISM, a system of government in which the state exercises wide-ranging control over individuals within its jurisdiction. Usually, a totalitarian state has but one political party, led by a dictator, and an official ideology that is disseminated through the mass media and educational system, with suppression of dissent. Nazi Germany and the Soviet Union are exemplary totalitarian states.

TOTEM, an object, animal or plant toward which a TRIBE. CLAN or other group feels a special affinity, often considering it a mythical ancestor. Killing of the totemic animal or animals by members of the group is TABOO, except, with some peoples, ritually during religious ceremonies. Totem poles, on which are carved human and animal shapes representing the particular warrior's heritage, were at one time common among the AMERINDS.

TOULOUSE-LAUTREC, Henri de (1864–1901), French painter and lithographer who portrayed Parisian nightlife. Of an old aristocratic family, he was crippled at 15, studied art in Paris and settled in MONTMARTRE to paint the entertainers who lived there, such as Jane Avril and Aristide Bruant. Influenced by DEGAS and by Japanese prints, his work did much to popularize the lithographic poster.

TOURÉ, Sékou (1922–   ), president of the Republic of Guinea since he led it to independence in 1958. A labor leader in French colonial times, a Marxist and a political writer, Touré was the winner of the 1960 Lenin Peace Prize.

TOURNAMENT, a series of games, originally a combat between armored knights, usually on horseback. Popular in Europe in the Middle Ages, it provided both entertainment and training for war. In the 13th century the dangerous *Melée* was replaced by the *joust* contest between only two knights who tried to unhorse each other with lance, mace and sword.

TOURNEUR, Cyril (c1575–1626), English dramatist, supposed author of *The Revenger's Tragedy* (1607) and *The Atheist's Tragedy* (1611). These two revenge tragedies are powerful, violent and pessimistic.

TOUSSAINT L'OUVERTURE, Pierre François Dominique (c1743–1803), Haitian black patriot and general. A freed slave of French St.-Domingue, W Hispaniola (Haiti), he headed the 1791 slave revolt and through military success and diplomacy took all Haiti amid French, Spanish, British and mulatto resistance. Despite his capture (1802) and death in France, Haiti became independent in 1804.

TOWER OF LONDON, ancient fortress on the Thames R in E London. Built 1078–1300, mainly by WILLIAM I the Conqueror and HENRY III, its massive stone buildings are enclosed by high walls and a moat. It has been palace, prison, arsenal and mint. Today it houses the crown jewels and an armor museum. Here Thomas MORE, Anne BOLEYN and Roger CASEMENT were executed. Rudolf HESS was its last prisoner.

TOWNES, Charles Hard (1915–   ), US physicist awarded the 1964 Nobel Prize for Physics with N. BASOV and A. PROKHOROV for independently working out the theory of the MASER and, later, the LASER. He built the first maser in 1951.

TOWN MEETING, a directly democratic form of local government, mainly in New England (Mass., N.H. and Vt.). In colonial days, all enfranchised citizens met to choose officials, decide taxes and discuss affairs. In the 1800s meetings became an annual event called by warrant. Today, many town meetings are attended only by officials and elected representatives, but others are fully attended by the public when significant local issues are discussed.

TOWNSEND, Francis Everett (1867–1960), US reformer, author of the Townsend Plan (1933), a SHARE THE WEALTH program by which citizens over 60 were to receive $200 a month, the money to be raised by a federal tax. Claimed supporters of the plan numbered 5,000,000, but Congress rejected it.

TOWNSHEND ACTS (1767), four British parliament acts, initiated by Charles TOWNSHEND, which suspended the Massachusetts Assembly and imposed duties on lead, glass, paint, paper and tea imports to America. They proved hugely unpopular. The BOSTON MASSACRE and repeal of all but the tea tax took place on the same day in 1770. (See also BOSTON TEA PARTY.)

TOXIC SHOCK SYNDROME (TSS), a rare and sometimes fatal disease associated with the use of tampons. TSS is characterized by high fever, vomiting and diarrhea, followed by a sharp drop in blood pressure that may bring on fatal shock. At greatest risk are women under 30 during their menstrual periods. The incidence is low, with a frequency of about 3 cases per 100,000 women annually in the US, and the mortality rate is about 10%.

TOXIN, a poisonous substance produced by a living organism. Many microorganisms, animals and plants produce chemical substances which are poisonous to some other organism; the toxin may be released continuously into the immediate environment or released only when danger is imminent. Examples include FUNGI which secrete substances which destroy BACTERIA (as ANTIBIOTICS these are of great value to man) and poisonous spiders and snakes which deliver their toxin via fangs. In some organisms, the function of toxins is obscure, but in many others they play an important role in defense and in killing prey. The symptoms of many INFECTIOUS DISEASES in man (e.g., CHOLERA; DIPHTHERIA; TETANUS) are due to the release of toxins by the bacteria concerned. (See also ANTITOXINS.)

TOYNBEE, Arnold Joseph (1889–1975), English historian whose principal work, *A Study of History* (12 vols., 1934–61) divides the history of the world into 26 civilizations and analyzes their rise and fall according to a cycle of "challenge and response."

TOYS, play-objects, principally for children. Some toys, such as balls, marbles, tops, rattles, whistles, pull-along toys, DOLLS, PUPPETS and miniature animals, have been universally popular throughout the ages. Mechanical toys, construction kits and working models of machinery are more recent innovations, as is the famous "Teddy Bear," named for Theodore ("Teddy") Roosevelt, who once refused to shoot a bear cub while out hunting. Educationalists such as FROEBEL and MONTESSORI have stressed the creative role of play in children's development, and toys and "play materials" are now an essential part of the modern educational curriculum.

TRACHOMA, INFECTIOUS DISEASE due to an organism (bedsonia) intermediate in size between BACTERIA and VIRUSES, the commonest cause of BLINDNESS in the world. It causes acute or chronic CONJUNCTIVITIS and corneal INFLAMMATION with secondary blood-vessel extension over the cornea resulting in loss of translucency. Eyelid deformity with secondary corneal damage is also common. It is transmitted by direct contact; early treatment with SULFA DRUGS or TETRACYCLINE may prevent permanent corneal damage.

TRACK AND FIELD, athletic sports including running, walking, hurdling, jumping for distance or height and throwing various objects. In modern times organized athletic contests developed rapidly from the 1860s onwards. The revival of the OLYMPIC GAMES in 1896 gave international and national competition an enormous boost, and in 1913 the International Amateur Athletics Federation was set up. Track and field events now constitute a popular sport throughout the world, and the training of champions is a serious business, backed up by government-sponsored programs, particularly in communist countries. The Olympic Games have developed into a quadrennial world championship, conducted in an atmosphere of intense rivalry, and politics has overtaken professionalism as the major problem confronting the organizers. **Track events.** Distances raced vary from the 60-yd dash sprint to the marathon (26mi 385yds). Hurdlers and steeplechasers have to clear a set number of obstacles. In relay races a baton is passed from one runner to the next. **Field events.** In high jump and pole vault the contestant who clears the greatest height with the least number of attempts wins. A long jump running or triple jump (hop, step and jump) competitor is permitted six jumps. Throwing events also permit six throws. The javelin is a spear thrown by running up to a line and releasing. The shot, a solid iron ball, is "put" from the shoulder. The discus is a circular plate, released with a sweeping sidearm action. The hammer throw consists of throwing an iron ball attached to a handle by a wire. All-around events include the 10-event decathlon and the 5-event pentathlon.

TRACY, Spencer (1900–1967), US film actor who played a wide variety of roles in a distinguished 37-year Hollywood career. He won Academy Awards for his roles in *Captains Courageous* (1937) and *Boys' Town* (1938) and costarred with longtime friend Katharine HEPBURN, in such hits as *Woman of the Year* (1942) and *Pat and Mike* (1952).

TRADE UNIONS. See UNIONS.

TRAFALGAR, Battle of, decisive naval engagement of the NAPOLEONIC WARS fought on Oct. 21, 1805. The British fleet of 27 warships under NELSON met a combined French and Spanish fleet of 33 ships off Cape Trafalgar (SW Spain). By attacking in an unorthodox formation Nelson surprised the enemy, sinking or capturing 20 vessels without loss, but was himself killed.

TRAGEDY, form of serious drama originating in ancient Greece, in which exceptional characters are led, by fate and by the very qualities that make them great, to suffer calamity and often death. ARISTOTLE, in his famous definition, spoke of purification (*catharsis*) through the rousing of the emotions of pity and fear. The great classical tragedians were AESCHYLUS, SOPHOCLES and EURIPIDES. Supreme in modern times is SHAKESPEARE. Great tragedians include Lope de VEGA, CALDERÓN DE LA BARCA, CORNEILLE, RACINE, GOETHE and SCHILLER. In the 19th and 20th centuries, whose drama usually shuns the heroic dimension of tragedy, the greatest exponents are probably IBSEN and O'NEILL. (See also THEATER.)

TRAJAN (Marius Ulpius Trajanus; c53–117 AD), famous Roman emperor responsible for great extensions of the empire and vast building programs. He conquered Dacia (Romania) and much of PARTHIA, and rebuilt the Roman FORUM. Adopted heir by NERVA in 97 AD, he became emperor in 98. He was known as a capable administrator and a humane and tolerant ruler.

TRAKL, Georg (1887–1914) Austrian EXPRESSIONIST poet. His intense lyrics, with their haunting imagery, reveal a preoccupation with death and decay. An addict, he died of an overdose of cocaine while serving in the army.

TRANQUILIZERS, agents which induce a state of quietude in anxious or disturbed patients. Minor tranquilizers are SEDATIVES (e.g., benzodiazepines) valuable in the anxious. In psychosis (see MENTAL ILLNESS), especially schizophrenia and (hypo) mania, major tranquilizers are required to suppress abnormal mental activity as well as to sedate; phenothiazines (e.g., chlorpromazine) are often used.

TRANS-CANADA HIGHWAY, all-weather, high-standard 4,860mi-long highway crossing Canada from Victoria, British Columbia, to St. John's (Newfoundland). The world's longest national highway, it was originally planned in 1948, and completed in 1965.

TRANSCENDENTALISM, an idealistic philosophical and literary movement which flourished in New England c1835–60. Regarding rationalist UNITARIANISM and utilitarian philosophy as morally bankrupt and shallow, the Transcendentalists took their inspiration from the German idealists, notably KANT, from COLERIDGE and from Eastern mystical philosophies. They believed in the divinity and unity of man and nature and the supremacy of intuition over sense-perception and reason as a source of knowledge. The major figures were Ralph Waldo EMERSON and Margaret FULLER, who edited *The Dial* (1840–44), Henry David THOREAU and Amos Bronson ALCOTT. The movement had considerable influence on US literature (HAWTHORNE; MELVILLE; WHITMAN) and politics (ABOLITIONISM; WOMEN'S RIGHTS; BROOK FARM).

TRANSCENDENTAL MEDITATION (TM), a form of meditation taught by the Maharishi Mahesh Yogi (an Indian guru now living in Switzerland) and by his disciples. It calls for 20-minute periods of quiet twice a day during which one repeats a phrase (mantra), thus clearing the mind of conscious thinking; this can produce profound relaxation and a sense of transcending daily cares. Similar types of meditation are taught by other organizations and individuals, including some physicians, for those who reject the quasi-mystical jargon associated with TM.

TRANSFERENCE, the coloration of an individual's perception of a person (or object) by his ASSOCIATION of that person with another, probably a parental figure. In PSYCHOANALYSIS, the term means specifically the effects of this process on a patient's attitudes toward his analyst.

TRANSFORMATIONAL-GENERATIVE GRAMMAR, a system of linguistic analysis developed originally by Zellig S. Harris and greatly elaborated by his student Noam CHOMSKY in the 1950s and '60s. A generative grammar is one whose rules enable the generation of the infinite number of well-formed sentences possible in any language; transformation rules govern correct linguistic transformations (as from the active to passive voice). In Chomsky's later work, his grammar included phonology, syntax and SEMANTICS, and thus was intended systematically to relate sound to meaning.

TRANSFORMER, a device for altering the voltage of an AC supply (see ELECTRICITY), used chiefly for converting the high voltage at which power is transmitted over distribution systems to the normal domestic supply voltage, and for obtaining from the latter voltages suitable for electronic equipment. It is based on INDUCTION: the "primary" voltage applied to a coil wound on a closed loop of a ferromagnetic core creates a strong oscillating MAGNETIC FIELD which in turn induces in a "secondary" coil wound on the same core an AC voltage proportional to the number of turns in the secondary coil. The core is laminated to prevent the flow of "eddy" currents which would otherwise also be induced by the magnetic field and would waste some ENERGY as HEAT.

TRANSFUSION, Blood, a means of BLOOD replacement in ANEMIA, SHOCK or HEMORRHAGE by intravenous infusion of blood from donors. It is the simplest and most important form of transplant, though, while of enormous value, it carries certain risks. Blood group compatibility based on ANTIBODY AND ANTIGEN reactions is of critical importance as incompatible transfusion may lead to life-threatening shock and KIDNEY failure. Infection (e.g., HEPATITIS) may be transmitted by blood, and FEVER or ALLERGY are common.

TRANSISTOR, electronic device made of semiconducting materials used in a circuit as an AMPLIFIER, RECTIFIER, detector or switch. Its functions are similar to those of an ELECTRON TUBE, but it has the advantage of being smaller, more durable and consuming less power. The early and somewhat unsuccessful point-contact transistor has been superseded by the junction transistor, invented in 1948 by BARDEEN, BRATTAIN and SHOCKLEY. The junction transistor is a layered device consisting of two p-n junctions (see SEMICONDUCTOR) joined back to back to give either a p-n-p or n-p-n transistor. The three layers are formed by controlled addition of impurities to a semiconductor crystal, usually SILICON or GERMANIUM. The thin central region (p-type in an n-p-n transistor and n-type in a p-n-p one) is known as the *base*, and the two outer regions (n-type semiconductor in an n-p-n transistor) are the *emitter* and *collector*, depending on the way an external voltage is connected. To act as an amplifier in a circuit, an n-p-n transistor needs a negative voltage to the collector and base. If the base is sufficiently thin, it attracts ELECTRONS from the emitter which then pass through it to the positively charged collector. By altering the bias applied to the base (which need only be a few volts), large changes in the current from the collector can be obtained and the device amplified. A collector current up to a hundred times the base current can be obtained. This type of transistor is analogous to a triode ELECTRON TUBE, the emitter and collector being equivalent to the CATHODE and ANODE respectively and the base to the control grid. The functioning of a p-n-p transistor is similar to the n-p-n type described, but the collector current is mainly holes rather than electrons. Transistors revolutionized the construction of electronic circuits, but are being replaced by INTEGRATED CIRCUITS in which they and other components are produced in a single silicon wafer.

TRANSITION ELEMENTS, the elements occupying the short groups in the PERIODIC TABLE— i.e., Groups IIIB to VIII, IB and IIB—in which the *d*-ORBITALS are being filled. The transition elements are all metals, and include most of the technologically important ones. In general they are dense, hard and of high melting point. Their electronic structures, with many loosely-bound unpaired *d*-electrons, account for their properties: they exhibit many different VALENCE states, and are generally good catalysts. They form many stable ORGANOMETALLIC COMPOUNDS and carbonyls (compounds in which carbon monoxide, CO, acts as a ligand) with specially stable "push-pull" bonding. The second and third row transition elements are less reactive than the first row, and stable in higher valence states.

TRANSMIGRATION OF SOULS, the belief that on death the souls of men and animals pass into new bodies of the same or different species as punishment or reward for previous actions. Central to Buddhist and Hindu thought (see also KARMA; NIRVANA), the doctrine is part of much mystical philosophy, and is often found in mystery cults and theosophical speculations (see MYSTERIES; THEOSOPHY).

TRANSMISSION, in engineering, a device for transmitting and adapting power from its source to its point of application. Most act by changing the angular velocity of the power shaft, either by step-variable means—GEARS, as in automobiles, or CHAINS, as in bicycles—with fixed ratios and no slip, or by stepless means—belt-and-pulley systems or traction drives employing adjustable rolling contact—with continuously variable ratios but liable to slip. In an AUTOMOBILE with manual transmission, the flywheel on the engine crankshaft is connected to the gearbox via the clutch, two plates that are normally held tightly together by springs so that through friction they rotate together. When the clutch pedal is depressed, the plates are forced apart so that the engine is disengaged from the rest of the transmission. This is necessary when changing gear: sliding different sets of gears into engagement by means of a manual lever. Modern gearboxes have synchromesh in all forward gears: a coned clutch device that synchronizes the rotation of the gears before meshing. The gearbox is coupled to the final drive by a drive shaft with universal joints. A crown wheel and pinion, connected to the half-shafts of each drive wheel via a DIFFERENTIAL, complete the system. In automatic transmission there is no clutch pedal or gear lever; a fluid clutch (see FLUID COUPLING), combined with sets of epicyclic gears selected by a GOVERNOR according to the program set by the driver, provides a continuously variable torque ratio for maximum efficiency at all speeds.

TRANSPIRATION, the loss of water by EVAPORATION from the aerial parts of PLANTS. Considerable quantities of water are lost in this way, far more than is needed for the upward movement of solutes and for the internal metabolism of the plant alone. Transpiration is a necessary corollary of PHOTOSYNTHESIS, in that in order to obtain sufficient CARBON dioxide from the air, considerable areas of wet surface, from which high loss of water by evaporation is inevitable, have to be exposed. Plants have many means for reducing water loss, STOMATA playing an important part. XEROPHYTES in particular are adapted for minimizing transpiration. (See also WILTING.)

TRANSPLANTS, organs that are removed from one person and surgically implanted in another to replace lost or diseased organs. Autotransplantation is the moving of an organ from one place to another within a person where the original site has been affected by local disease (e.g., skin grafting—see PLASTIC SURGERY). Blood TRANSFUSION was the first practical form of transplant. Here BLOOD cells and other components are transferred from one person to another. The nature of BLOOD allows free transfusion between those with compatible blood groups. The next, most important, and now most successful of organ transplants, was that of the KIDNEY. Here a single kidney is transplanted from a live donor who is a close relative or from a person who has recently suffered sudden DEATH (e.g., by traffic accident or irreversible BRAIN damage), into a person who suffers from chronic renal failure. The kidney is placed beneath the skin of the abdominal wall and plumbed into the major ARTERIES and VEINS in the PELVIS and into the BLADDER. High doses of STEROIDS and IMMUNITY suppressants are used to minimize the body's tendency to reject the foreign tissue of the graft. These doses are gradually reduced to lower maintenance levels, but may need to be increased again if rejection threatens. Here, tissue typing methods are used additionally to blood grouping to minimize rejection. HEART transplantation has been much publicized, but is limited to a few centers, many problems remaining. LIVER and LUNG transplants have also been attempted although here too the difficulties are legion. Corneal grafting is a more widespread technique in which the cornea of the EYE of a recently dead person replaces that of a person with irreversible corneal damage leading to BLINDNESS. The lack of blood vessels in the cornea reduces the problem of rejection. Grafts from nonhuman animals are occasionally used (e.g., pig SKIN as temporary cover in extensive BURNS). Both animal and human heart valves are used in cardiac surgery.

TRANSPORTATION, US Department of, responsible for the development and coordination of national transport policies and agencies. Set up in 1966, it reports to Congress on the optimum use of federal transportation funds. It supervises the federal Aviation, Highway, Railroad and Urban Mass Transportation administrations, the US COAST GUARD, the SAINT LAWRENCE SEAWAY Development Corpora-

tion and the National Transportation Safety Board.

TRANS-SIBERIAN RAILROAD, in the USSR, longest railroad in the world, stretching 5,787mi from Moscow to Vladivostock on the Sea of Japan, a journey which takes eight days. Its construction (1891–1916) had a dramatic effect on the development of Siberia.

TRANSUBSTANTIATION, Roman Catholic doctrine that in Holy COMMUNION the substance of the bread and wine is changed into that of the body and blood of Christ. It affirms belief in the REAL PRESENCE. (See also CONSUBSTANTIATION.)

TRANSURANIUM ELEMENTS, the elements with atomic numbers greater than that of URANIUM (92—see PERIODIC TABLE; ATOM). None occurs naturally: they are prepared by bombardment (usually with NEUTRONS or ALPHA PARTICLES) of suitably-chosen lighter ISOTOPES. All are radioactive (see RADIOACTIVITY), and those of higher atomic number tend to be less stable. Those so far discovered are the ACTINIDES from neptunium through lawrencium, RUTHERFORDIUM and HAHNIUM. Only neptunium and plutonium have been synthesized in large quantity; most of the others have been produced in weighable amounts, but some with very short HALF-LIVES can be studied only by special tracer methods.

TRANSVAAL, second-largest province in the Republic of South Africa, between the Vaal and Limpopo rivers in the NE. It is mainly high VELD 3,000–6,000ft above sea level. The capital is PRETORIA and the largest city is JOHANNESBURG. Mineral wealth includes gold, silver, diamonds, coal, iron ore, platinum, asbestos and chrome. Its farmlands are noted for their cattle, corn and tobacco. (See also BOER WAR; SOUTH AFRICA.)

TRAPPISTS, popular name for Cistercians of the Reformed, or Strict, Observance, a Roman Catholic monastic order founded by de RANCÉ, abbot of La Trappe in Normandy, France 1664–1700, who instituted a rigorous discipline of silence, prayer and work. There are 12 US abbeys. The abbot general lives in Rome.

TRAPSHOOTING, sport of shooting with a shotgun at clay discs or "pigeons" sprung into the air from a "trap." It developed in England in the 19th century originally as a means of target practice for sportsmen. In the US today there are more than 100,000 trapshooting enthusiasts.

TREASON, behavior by a subject or citizen which could harm his sovereign or state. In many countries, including England before the 19th century, treason has been loosely defined and used as a political weapon. The US Constitution, however, states that treason consists only in levying war against the US or in adhering to its enemies, "giving them Aid and Comfort," and evidence of two witnesses or a confession in open court is necessary to secure a conviction.

TREASURY, US Department of, executive department of the US government, established in 1789 and responsible for federal taxes, customs and expenditure. It also plays a major role in national and international financial and monetary policies. Its head, the secretary of the treasury, the second-ranking member of the President's cabinet, is an *ex officio* governor of the INTERNATIONAL MONETARY FUND. The department's other responsibilities include the US SECRET SERVICE, and the bureaus of Customs, MINT, Engraving and Printing, Internal Revenue and Narcotics.

TREATY, an agreement in writing between two or more states. Treaties are bilateral (between two states) or multilateral (between several states), and cover matters such as trade, tariffs, taxation, economic and technical cooperation, diplomatic relations, international boundaries, extradition of criminals, defense and control of arms and aggression—anything on which international agreement is needed. Historically the most famous treaties have been those ending wars, such as the treaties of PARIS, VERSAILLES, WESTPHALIA. Some treaties, for example the NORTH ATLANTIC TREATY ORGANIZATION, are military; others set up international organizations: examples are the UNITED NATIONS; the COMMON MARKET (set up by the Treaty of Rome); the FOOD AND AGRICULTURE ORGANIZATION; the INTERNATIONAL TELECOMMUNICATIONS UNION. These have become an important part of modern INTERNATIONAL RELATIONS. (See also INTERNATIONAL LAW.)

TREATY PORTS, ports, notably in China and Japan, opened by treaty to foreign trade and whose foreign residents enjoyed EXTRATERRITORIALITY. In China 69 ports were opened—the first five to the British in 1842 after the OPIUM WAR. The system in Japan lasted 1854–99 but in China continued until WWII.

TREE, woody perennial PLANT with a well defined main stem, or trunk, which either dominates the form throughout the life cycle (giving a pyramidal shape) or is dominant only in the early stages, later forking to form a number of equally important branches (giving a rounded or flattened form to the tree). It is often difficult to distinguish between a small tree and a SHRUB, but the former has a single trunk rising some distance from the ground before it branches while the latter produces several stems at, or close to, ground level. The trunk of a tree consists almost wholly of thick-walled water-conducting cells (xylem) which are renewed every year (see WOOD), giving rise to the familiar ANNUAL RINGS. The older wood in the center of the tree (the heartwood) is much denser and harder than the younger, outer sapwood. The outer skin, or the BARK, insulates and protects the trunk and often shows characteristic cracks, or falls off leaving a smooth skin. Trees belong to the two most advanced groups of plants, the GYMNOSPERMS and the ANGIOSPERMS (the flowering plants). The former include the cone-bearing trees such as the PINE, SPRUCE and CEDAR; they are nearly all evergreens and mostly live in the cooler regions of the world. The angiosperms have broader leaves and much harder wood; in tropical climates they are mostly EVERGREEN, but in temperate regions they are DECIDUOUS. (See also FORESTRY; FORESTS.)

TRENT, Council of (1545–1563), the 19th ECUMENICAL COUNCIL of the Roman Catholic Church, at Trent, N Italy. In response to the REFORMATION, the council, first summoned by Pope PAUL III, formally redefined the Church's doctrines and banned many abuses. The council's reforms and doctrinal canons were the basis of the COUNTERREFORMATION and became definitive statements of Catholic belief.

TRENT AFFAIR, naval incident in the US CIVIL WAR that nearly brought Britain to military support of the South. In Nov. 1861, Charles WILKES, commanding *San Jacinto*, stopped the British ship *Trent* and seized the two Southern agents, MASON AND SLIDELL. Britain demanded an apology for this violation of the freedom of the sea and ordered 8,000 troops to Canada. The men were freed in December.

TRENTON, Battle of, American victory in the REVOLUTIONARY WAR, fought on Dec. 26, 1776. To forestall a British attack on Philadelphia, George WASHINGTON crossed the Delaware R at night and surprised a British force of 1,500 HESSIANS at Trenton, N.J. The battle was won in 45 minutes, rallying Washington's army and the American cause.

TRENTON, city in N.J., state capital and seat of Mercer Co., on the Delaware R. Settled by Quakers in 1679, it is now a major industrial center, producing steel cable, pottery, plastics, metal goods and textiles. Pop 92,124.

TREVELYAN, George Macauley (1876–1962), British historian who rejected the "scientific" approach to history in favor of a more humanistic and literary approach. He taught at Cambridge (1927–51) and was best known for a colorful study of Garibaldi (3 vols., 1907–11), a one-volume *History of England* (1926), *England Under Queen Anne* (3 vols., 1903–34), and *English Social History* (1942).

TREVINO, Lee (1939–   ), US golfer. In 1973 he became the fourth golfer ever to earn $1 million. In 11 weeks in 1971, he won the US, Canadian and British Opens and two other tournaments.

TREVITHICK, Richard (1771–1833), British mining engineer and inventor primarily remembered for his work improving the STEAM ENGINE and for building the first railroad LOCOMOTIVE (c1804).

TREVOR-ROPER, Hugh Redwald (1914–   ), British historian. A professor at Oxford (1957–80), he wrote many works ranging from studies of the Elizabethan era to those of contemporary history. His best known books include *The Last Days of Hitler* (1947) and *The European Witch-Craze of the 16th and 17th Centuries* (1969).

TRIAL, judicial examination and determination of criminal prosecutions and law suits. In the US the right of an accused person to a speedy and public trial by a jury of his peers is guaranteed in the Constitution. Trials in COMMON LAW countries such as the UK and US are "adversary" proceedings, in which the court impartially decides between the evidence of two parties; under CIVIL LAW systems trials tend to be more "inquisitorial," allowing more scope for pretrial investigation and the court itself a greater role in the gathering of evidence. Under both systems the judge ensures that procedure is followed and that rules of evidence are observed, and determines the guilty offender's sentence; in common law systems he decides questions of law. Questions of fact are left to a JURY, if there is one; jury trial is more expensive and time-consuming, and so is reserved for more serious offenses. Although the US trial system today is designed to be as fair as possible, complexity, delay and expense create many serious flaws.

TRIANGLE, one of the musical PERCUSSION INSTRUMENTS. It consists of a steel or iron rod, bent into a triangle with one corner open. It is suspended by a string from the player's hand and struck with a metal rod.

TRIASSIC, the first period of the MESOZOIC era, which lasted from about 225 to 190 million years ago. (See also GEOLOGY.)

TRICHINOSIS, infestation with the larva of a worm (*Trichinella*), contracted from eating uncooked pork etc., causing a feverish illness. EDEMA around the eyes, MUSCLE pains and DIARRHEA occur early; later the LUNGS, HEART and BRAIN may be involved. It is avoided by the adequate cooking of pork. CHEMOTHERAPY may be helpful in severe cases.

TRIDENT, ballistic missile submarine, nuclear-powered (SSBN). The USS Ohio, the first in this new class, began sea trials in June 1981. The 18,750 ton, 560-ft submarine carries 24 missiles that can be launched from tubes placed at midship. Missiles are capable of striking targets to a distance of 4,000 nautical miles. Their MIRV payloads allow each to hit several targets. Trident submarines swim more quietly, faster and deeper than earlier SSBNs and can remain at sea one-fourth longer.

TRIESTE, city-seaport in NE Italy at the head of the Adriatic Sea, with steel, oil and shipbuilding industries. A busy port in Roman times, it was part of Austria, 1382–1919, and then of Italy. Claimed by Yugoslavia in 1945, it was made a Free Territory 1947–54, then restored to Italy. Pop 260,000.

TRIGONOMETRY, the branch of GEOMETRY that deals with the ratios of the sides of right-angled TRIANGLES, and the applications of these ratios. The principal ratios, when considering ANGLE A of triangle ABC whose sides opposite the angles A, B and C respectively are a, b and c, where b is the HYPOTENUSE, are:

name	abbreviation	ratio
tangent	tan A	$\dfrac{a}{c}$
sine	sin A	$\dfrac{a}{b}$
cosine	cos A	$\dfrac{c}{b}$
cotangent	cot A	$\dfrac{c}{a}$
cosecant	cosec A	$\dfrac{b}{a}$
secant	sec A	$\dfrac{b}{c}$

As can be seen, the cotangent is the reciprocal of the tangent, the cosecant that of the sine, and the secant that of the cosine. The basis of trigonometric calculations is the PYTHAGOREAN THEOREM, which in trigonometric forms reads $\sin^2 A + \cos^2 A = a$; this is true for any angle A.

From these ratios are derived the **trigonometric functions**, setting y equal to tan x, sin x, etc. These FUNCTIONS are termed transcendental (nonalgebraic). Of particular importance is the sine wave, in terms of which many naturally-occurring

WAVE MOTIONS, such as SOUND and LIGHT, are studied.

TRILLING, Lionel (1905–1975), US literary critic and author. *The Liberal Imagination* (1950), and studies of Matthew Arnold (1939), E. M. Forster (1943) and Freud (1962) are informed by psychological, philosophical and sociological insights and methods.

Official name: Republic of Trinidad and Tobago
Capital: Port-of-Spain
Area: 1,980sq mi
Population: 1,133,000
Language: English
Religions: Roman Catholic, Hindu, Muslim
Monetary unit(s): Trinidad and Tobago dollar=100 cents

TRINIDAD AND TOBAGO, independent state in the West Indies consisting of the islands Trinidad (1,864sq mi) and Tobago (116sq mi) off the coast of Venezuela.
Land. Trinidad is very fertile and mainly flat, rising to about 3,000ft in the N, and Tobago has a mountain ridge 1,800ft high and is densely forested. The climate is tropical, with a rainfall range of 50-100in.
People. The population is mostly Negro (43%) and East Indian (36%), and there are also whites and Chinese. The literary rate is 92%.
Economy. The country, one of the most prosperous in the Caribbean, is rich in oil, natural gas and asphalt—Trinidad is famous for the large pitch lake near La Brea—and produces sugarcane, cocoa and fruit, but has to import many foodstuffs.-Tourism is a growing industry.
History. Trinidad was discovered by COLUMBUS in 1498 and settled by the Spaniards, but British rule was establishd in 1802. Trinidad and Tobago joined the West Indies Federation in 1958 but left in 1962 to become independent. Eric Williams was premier from 1962 until his death in 1981. In 1976 Trinidad and Tobago became a republic.

TRINITY, the central doctrine of Christian theology, that there is one GOD who exists in three Persons and one Substance. The definition of the doctrine, implicit in the New Testament, by the early ECUMENICAL COUNCILS (notably NICAEA and Constantinople) was the product of violent controversy with such heresies as ARIANISM, MONOPHYSITISM, NESTORIANISM and Monarchianism. It is classically summed up in the ATHANASIAN CREED. The three Persons—the Father, the Son (see INCARNATION; JESUS CHRIST) and the HOLY SPIRIT—are each fully God: coequal, coeternal and consubstantial, yet are distinct. The Son is "eternally begotten" by the Father; the Holy Spirit "proceeds" from the Father and (in Western theology) from the Son. The doctrine is a mystery, being known by REVELATION and being above reason (though not unreasonable). Hence it has been challenged by rationalists (see DEISM; SOCINIANISM; UNITARIANISM) and by such sects as the JEHOVAH'S WITNESSES and MORMONS.

TRIPLE ALLIANCE, name of several European alliances: between England, Sweden and the Netherlands against France (1668); between England, France and the Netherlands (1717; see also QUADRUPLE ALLIANCE); between Germany, Austria-Hungary and Italy (1882).

TRIPLE ENTENTE, informal diplomatic understanding between Britain, France and Russia which acted as a counterweight to the TRIPLE ALLIANCE of 1882. It lasted 1907–17. After the outbreak of WWI, it became a military alliance. (See also ENTENTE CORDIALE.)

TRIPOLI, seaport and capital of Libya, North Africa, founded by the PHOENICIANS c7th century BC. It is an important industrial, commercial and tourist center. Pop 481,295.

TRIPPE, Juan Terry (1899–1981), US businessman who founded Pan American World Airways (1927) and built it into one of the largest international airlines. As its president, 1927–68, he initiated international airmail service (1927) and transatlantic passenger service (1939).

TRIUMVIRATE, in ancient Rome, a group of three leaders sharing office or supreme power. The First Triumvirate (60–53 BC) was formed by Julius CAESAR, POMPEY and CRASSUS. The Second Triumvirate (43–36 BC) consisted of Octavian (later the Emperor AUGUSTUS), Marcus LEPIDUS and Mark ANTONY.

TROBRIAND ISLANDS, small group of coral islands in the Solomon Sea, SW Pacific Ocean, part of Papua-New Guinea. Losuia is the principal settlement and stands on the largest island, Kiriwina. The islands are famous through the work of the anthropologist Bronislaw MALINOWSKI.

TROJAN WAR, conflict between Greece and Troy, made famous by HOMER's *Iliad*. PARIS, son of PRIAM of Troy, carried off HELEN, wife of Menelaus of Sparta, and took her to Troy. The Greeks, led by AGAMEMNON, MENELAUS, ODYSSEUS, ACHILLES and other heroes, swore to take revenge. They besieged Troy for 10 years, then pretended to sail away, leaving a huge wooden horse outside the city, with Greek soldiers concealed in its belly. The Trojans dragged it into the city, and that night the soldiers opened the city gates to the Greek army. Most of the Trojans were killed and the city was burnt. The legend is thought to have been based on an actual conflict of c1250 BC.

TROLLOPE, Anthony (1815–1882), English novelist, famous for his six *Barsetshire* novels about middle-class life in an imaginary cathedral town, including *The Warden* (1855) and *Barchester Towers* (1857). He was a sharp but sympathetic observer of social and political behavior, as revealed in his political *Palliser* novels, such as *Phineas Finn* (1869) and *The Prime Minister* (1876).

TROMBONE, musical instrument, one of the brass WIND INSTRUMENTS. It has a slide mechanism to alter the length of the playing tube and increase the note range. Developed from the sackbut, it was first used in a symphony by BEETHOVEN in 1808.

TROPICS, the lines of latitude lying 23½°N (**Tropic of Cancer**) and S (**Tropic of Capricorn**) of the equator. They represent the farthest southerly latitudes where the sun is, at one time of the year, directly overhead at noon. This occurs at the time of the summer SOLSTICE in each hemisphere. The term is used also of the area between the two tropics.

TROPISMS, movements of PLANTS in response to external directional stimuli. If a plant is laid on its side, the stem will soon start to bend upward again. This movement (geotropism) is a response to the force of gravity. The stem is said to be negatively geotropic. Roots are generally positively geotropic and grow downward. Phototropisms are bending movements in response to the direction of illumination. Stems are generally positively phototropic (bend toward the light). Most roots are negatively phototropic, although some appear unaffected by light. Some roots exhibit positive hydrotropism: they bend toward moisture. This response is more powerful than the response to gravity; roots can be deflected from their downward course if the plants are watered only on one

side. Tropisms are controlled by differences in concentration of growth HORMONES. (See also AUXINS.)

TROTSKY, Leon (Lev Davidovich Bronstein; 1879–1940), Russian revolutionary communist, a founder of the USSR. President of the Petrograd (Leningrad) soviet in the 1905 revolution, he escaped from prison to France, Spain and New York. In 1917 he returned, went over to BOLSHEVISM and led the Bolshevik seizure of power in the October RUSSIAN REVOLUTION. As commissar of foreign affairs (1917–18) he resigned over the treaty of BREST-LITOVSK and became commissar of war (1918–25), organizing the Red Army into an effective force. After LENIN's death (1924) he lost power to STALIN and was deported (1929). Bitterly opposed to Stalin's "socialism in one country," he continued to advocate international revolution, founded the Fourth INTERNATIONAL and attacked Stalinism in *The Revolution Betrayed* (1937). He was murdered in Mexico City by a Stalinist agent.

TROUBADOURS, courtly poet-musicians of Provence, S France, c1100–c1300. Their poems, written in PROVENÇAL, mostly on the theme of love, were sung. Troubadours developed the conventions of courtly love, and influenced poetry and music in Germany (see MINNESINGER), Italy, Spain and England.

TROUT, members of the SALMON family found in fresh waters of the N hemisphere, best known as the Brown trout, *Salmo trutta*, of Europe and the Rainbow trout, *S. gairdneri*, of the US. They are solid, powerful, active, usually spotted fishes that favor highly-oxygenated and cool waters. Most species have a variety of forms, some of which spend part of their time in the sea, migrating into fresh water to breed (e.g., the Sea trout, a race of *S. trutta*).

TROY, city of ancient NW Asia Minor, near the Dardanelles, described in HOMER's *Iliad* and rediscovered by SCHLIEMANN in 1870. The earliest site (Troy I) dates from c3000 BC. Troy II contained an imposing fortress and had wide trade contacts. Its famous treasure of gold, copper and bronze indicates a wealthy community. Troy VI, c2000–1300 BC, had a citadel surrounded by huge limestone walls, and large houses built on terraces. It was destroyed by earthquake. The rebuilt Troy VIIa was probably Homer's Troy. It was looted and destroyed by fire c1250 BC. Troy VIII was a small Greek village. Troy IX was the Greek and Roman city of Ilium.

TRUCK, automotive vehicle used for transporting freight by road. The typical long-distance truck is an articulated vehicle comprising a two- or three-axled "truck tractor" coupled to a two-axled "semi-trailer." A two- or three-axled "full trailer" may in addition be coupled to the semitrailer. Most trucks are powered by a DIESEL ENGINE, have a manual TRANSMISSION with perhaps as many as 16 forward gears, and have AIR BRAKES. In the US, trucks carry about 40% of all intercity freight (compared with the railroads' 30%); the industry is organized under a trade association, American Trucking Associations Inc., while the American Association of State Highway Officials regulates truck sizes and weights. Overall supervision of trucking is undertaken by the INTERSTATE COMMERCE COMMISSION.

TRUDEAU, Garry (1948–   ), US cartoonist who created the strip *Doonesbury* (1970), which brilliantly satirized contemporary US political and social life and appeared in more than 400 newspapers. He won the 1974 Pulitzer Prize.

TRUDEAU, Pierre Elliott (1919–   ), Canadian prime minister. A law professor, he entered parliament in 1965, became minister of justice in 1967 and succeeded Lester PEARSON as prime minister and Liberal Party leader (1968). He has sought to promote a dialogue between the provincial and federal governments and to contain the Quebec separatist movement, giving the French language equal status with English. In 1970 he recognized the People's Republic of China. Briefly out of office (1979–80), he returned to cope anew with the constitutional issue that threatened to break Canada apart.

TRUFFAUT, François (1932–   ), French film director and critic. A leading New Wave director, he attracted attention for his series of semi-autobiographical films, including *The 400 Blows* (1959), *Stolen Kisses* (1968) and *Day for Night* (1973). His other films include *Jules and Jim* (1961), *Small Change* (1976) and *The Last Metro* (1980).

TRUFFLE, underground fungi of the genus *Tuber* that have long been regarded as a delicacy. Pigs and dogs are trained to find them by scent. Some grow up to 1kg (2.2lb) and resemble potatoes; most are much smaller.

TRUJILLO MOLINA, Rafael Leonidas (1891–1961), Dominican dictator 1930–61, and president 1930–38, 1942–52. He introduced much material progress, but savagely suppressed political opposition and feuded with neighboring countries. He was assassinated.

TRUMAN, Harry S (1884–1972), 33rd president of the US. Inexperienced and virtually unknown, he became president after F. D. ROOSEVELT's sudden death, and in the difficult post-WWII years attempted to contain communist expansion and to continue the NEW DEAL programs. Truman entered politics in 1919 with help from the Kansas City boss T. J. PENDERGAST who in 1934 backed his election as a Mo. senator. In 1940 he gained prominence as head of a committee investigating corruption in the defense industries, and in 1944 was chosen by Roosevelt as his vice-presidential candidate to replace Henry Wallace. On becoming president Truman accepted the German surrender, was involved in the establishment of the UNITED NATIONS, attended the POTSDAM CONFERENCE and made the controversial decision to use the atom bomb against Japan, thus ending the war. He took a tough line over Russia's attempted annexation of Poland. At home, amid economic difficulties and labor unrest, a hostile Congress blocked most of his FAIR DEAL program, and passed the TAFT-HARTLEY ACT over Truman's veto. As the COLD WAR hardened, he regarded communist expansion as the major threat, and responded with the TRUMAN DOCTRINE and the MARSHALL PLAN, followed by the POINT FOUR PROGRAM and the setting-up of the NORTH ATLANTIC TREATY ORGANIZATION. (See also BERLIN AIRLIFT.) Truman's unpopularity at home made his decision to run again in 1948 seem hopeless, but despite all predictions he won by a narrow margin. During his second term Truman again had his Fair Deal measures blocked by Congress, except for a Housing Act (1949), was embroiled in the anti-communist hysteria generated by MCCARTHY, and had his seizure of the steel industry during a strike declared unconstitutional. He sent troops to fight the KOREAN WAR, and amidst controversy over US Far East policy, removed General MACARTHUR for insubordination.

TRUMAN DOCTRINE, US declaration (1947), aimed to combat communist expansion, particularly in Greece and Turkey, stating the US would "support free peoples who are resisting attempted subjugation by armed minorities or by outside pressures."

TRUMBULL, John (1750–1831), US poet and judge. A leader of the HARTFORD WITS, he is best known for *The Progress of Dulness* (1772–73) and *M'Fingal* (1775–82), a mock-epic based on Samuel BUTLER's *Hudibras*, satirizing the British Tories.

TRUMBULL, John (1756–1843), US painter. He studied with Benjamin WEST in London where he started *The Battle of Bunker's Hill* (1786). He made 36 life portrait studies for his best-known work, *The Signing of the Declaration of Independence* (1786–94), one of his four monumental pictures on revolutionary themes for the US Capitol rotunda (1817–24). He is also well known for his portraits of George Washington.

TRUMPET, musical instrument, one of the brass WIND INSTRUMENTS. The modern trumpet comprises a cylindrical tube in a curved oblong form which flares out into a bell. Three piston valves, first introduced c1815, regulate pitch. The standard orchestral trumpet is generally in B Flat. The trumpet is a popular dance and jazz-band instrument.

TRUST, in law, a legal relationship in which property is administered by a trustee, who has some of the powers of an owner, for the benefit of a beneficiary; the trustee is obliged to act only in the beneficiary's best interest, and can derive no advantage except an agreed fee. His powers are limited to those specified or implied in the document establishing the trust. The trustee may be an individual, perhaps looking after the property of a child until it comes of age, or a corporate body; banks and trust corporations often act as trustees of larger properties. Trusts are a major feature of EQUITY law. Certain categories of trust, generally those with some charitable or other aim beneficial to the public, may be given tax relief. Under a specialized form, the corporate trust, a group of trustees held the stock and thus controlled the operations of companies that would normally have been competitors; this enabled Standard Oil Co. and others to control whole industries and to fix prices to suit themselves. These monopolistic business communications continued to be called trusts even after they were replaced by the "holding company." The Sherman Antitrust Act (1890) attacked the trusts, but enforcement was vitiated by US Supreme Court decisions. Enforcement of antitrust legislation in recent years has been complicated by the growth of huge conglomerates, which control many companies in different industries.

TRUST TERRITORY, formerly a dependent territory administered under UNITED NATIONS supervision. A trustee nation was responsible for developing the trust territory and assisting it to independence. The Trusteeship Council helped the General Assembly and Security Council supervise trust territories. Of the 11 Trust Territories (mostly former MANDATES of the LEAGUE OF NATIONS)—British Cameroons, French Cameroons, Ruanda-Urundi, Italian Somaliland, Tanganyika, British Togoland, French Togoland, Nauru, Pacific Islands, New Guinea and Western Samoa — the US-administered Pacific Islands were the last to be terminated (1981).

TRUTH, Sojourner (c1797–1883), US abolitionist. A slave until 1827, originally called Isabella, she traveled the North from 1843 preaching Negro emancipation and women's rights. In the mid-1860s in Washington D.C. she worked to resettle ex-slaves.

TRUTH-IN-LENDING ACT, a 1968 law requiring the clear disclosure of credit terms, especially the interest rate figures on an annual basis. The law applies to banks, credit-card companies, car dealers, department stores, and others who extend consumer credit. Its formal name is the Consumer Credit Protection Act.

TRUTH SERUM. See PENTOTHAL, SODIUM.

TSETSE FLIES, 20 species of muscoid flies of the genus *Glossina*. They are true winged flies very like HOUSEFLIES except that the mouthparts are adapted for piercing the skin of mammals and sucking blood. Widespread in tropical Africa, their significance lies in that some species act as vectors of the TRYPANOSOMES which cause SLEEPING SICKNESS in humans.

TSHOMBE, Moïse Kapenda (1919–1969), president 1960–63 of the Congolese breakaway state of Katanga. Backed by Belgian interests, he opposed LUMUMBA and the UN. He returned from exile to be premier (1964–65) of the Congo (ZAIRE). Dismissed, he was sentenced to death, and died in prison in Algeria.

TSIOLKOVSKY, Konstantin Eduardovich (1857–1935), Russian physicist who pioneered ROCKET science, but who is perhaps most important for his role in educating the Soviet government and people into acceptance of the future potential of SPACE EXPLORATION. He also built one of the first WIND TUNNELS (c1892). A large crater on the far side of the MOON is named for him; and the timing of Sputnik I's launch marked the 100th anniversary of his birth.

TSUNAMI, formerly called tidal wave, fast-moving ocean wave caused by submarine EARTHQUAKES, volcanic eruptions, etc., found mainly in the Pacific, and often taking a high toll of lives in affected coastal areas. In midocean, the wave height is usually under 1m, the distance between succeeding crests of the order of 200km, and the velocity about 750km/h. Near the coast, FRICTION with the sea bottom slows the wave, so that the distance between crests decreases, the wave height increasing to about 25m or more.

TUAREGS, a BERBER tribe in the Sahara, about 300,000 in number. Its people are fair-skinned; the social system comprises noble families; a large number of vassal tribes, and Negro slaves. Adult men, but not women, wear a blue veil. Tuareg script is like that of the ancient Libyans.

TUBA, low-pitched brass musical WIND INSTRUMENT with three to five valves. It is held vertically. There are tenor, baritone, euphonium, bass and contrabass tubas—the CC contrabass being popular in orchestras, the BB contrabass in bands.

TUBB, Ernest (1914–), US country singer who began his long career by imitating his idol, Jimmie Rodgers. A star with the Grand Ole Opry (from 1942), he worked with such vocalists as the ANDREWS SISTERS, Minnie Pearl and Loretta LYNN.

TUBER, swollen underground stems and roots which are organs of perennation and vegetative propagation and contain stored food material. The potato is a stem tuber. It swells at the tip of a slender underground stem (or stolon) and gives rise to a new plant the following year. Dahlia tubers are swollen roots.

TUBERCULIN, PROTEIN derivative of the mycobacteria responsible for TUBERCULOSIS. This may be used in tests of cell-mediated IMMUNITY to tuberculosis, providing evidence of previous disease (often subclinical) or immunization (BCG). The substance was originally isolated by KOCH.

TUBERCULOSIS (TB), a group of INFECTIOUS DISEASES caused by the BACILLUS *Mycobacterium tuberculosis,* which kills some 3 million people every year throughout the world. TB may invade any organ but most commonly affects the respiratory system where it has been called consumption or phthisis (see also LUPUS VULGARIS and SCROFULA). In 1906 it killed 1 in every 500 persons in the US, but today it leads to only 1 in 30,000 deaths, because of effective drugs and better living conditions. The disease is spread in three ways: inoculation via cuts, etc.; inhalation of infected sputum; and ingestion of infected food. In pulmonary TB there are two stages of infection. In primary infection there are usually no significant symptoms: dormant small hard masses called tubercles are formed by the body's defenses. In postprimary infection the dormant BACTERIA are reactivated due to weakening of the body's defenses and clinical

symptoms become evident. Symptoms include fatigue, weight loss, persistent cough with green or yellow sputum and possibly blood. Treatment nowadays is mainly by triple drug therapy with streptomycin, para-aminosalicylic acid (PAS) and isoniazid, together with rest. Recovery takes about 2 years.

The TUBERCULIN skin test can show whether a person has some IMMUNITY to the disease, though the detection of the disease in its early stages, when it is readily curable, is difficult. Control of the disease is accomplished by preventive measures such as X-RAY screening, BCG vaccination, isolation of infectious people and food sterilization.

TUBMAN, Harriet Ross (c1820–1913), US fugitive slave and abolitionist. She was active in the UNDERGROUND RAILROAD after 1850. Nicknamed "Moses," she helped over 300 slaves to freedom. In the Civil War she was a Union spy and scout.

TUBMAN, William Vacanarat Shadrach (1895–1971), president of Liberia (1944–71). He made extensive economic, social and educational reforms and extended the rights of tribespeople and women.

TUCKER, Sophie (1884–1966), Russian-born US vaudeville singer and entertainer known as the "Last of the Red Hot Mamas," and famous for her rendition of the song "Some of These Days."

TUDOR, Antony (1909–), English choreographer who introduced dramatic, emotional themes into US ballet. He was a founder (1939) of the American Ballet Theatre, where his *Dark Elegies* (1937) and *Pillar of Fire* (1942) became part of the repertory.

TUDOR, House of, reigning dynasty of England, 1485–1603. Of Welsh descent, Henry Tudor, Earl of Richmond and heir to the HOUSE of LANCASTER, ended the WARS of THE ROSES by defeating Richard III in 1485 and became HENRY VII, first Tudor king. After him came HENRY VIII (reigned 1509–47), EDWARD VI (1547–53), MARY I (1553–58) and ELIZABETH I (1558–1603). Under the Tudors England became a major power and enjoyed a flowering of the arts.

TULAREMIA, or Rabbit Fever, INFECTIOUS DISEASE due to BACTERIA, causing FEVER, ulceration, LYMPH node enlargement and sometimes PNEUMONIA. It is carried by wild animals, particularly rabbits, and insects. ANTIBIOTICS are fully effective in treatment.

TUMOR, strictly, any swelling on or in the body, but more usually used to refer only to an abnormal overgrowth of tissue (or neoplasm). These may be benign proliferations such as fibroids of the WOMB, or they may be forms of CANCER, LYMPHOMA or SARCOMA, which are generally malignant. The rate of growth, the tendency to spread locally and to distant sites via the BLOOD vessels and LYMPH system, and systemic effects determine the degree of malignancy of a given tumor. Tumors may present themselves as a lump, by local compression effects (especially with BRAIN tumors), by bleeding (GASTROINTESTINAL TRACT tumors) or by systemic effects including ANEMIA, weight loss, false HORMONE actions, NEURITIS etc. Treatments include surgery, RADIATION THERAPY and CHEMOTHERAPY.

TUNA, or tunny, large oceanic members of the MACKEREL family. They are powerful, torpedo-shaped fishes, the dorsal and pectoral fins folding away into grooves to reduce drag in rapid swimming. Active carnivores, feeding especially on squid, all are important sport and food fishes.

TUNDRA, the treeless plains of the Arctic Circle. For most of the year the temperature is less than 0°C, and even during the short summer it never rises above 10°C. The soil is a thin coating over PERMAFROST. Tundra vegetation includes lichens, mosses and stunted shrubs. Similar regions on high mountains (but generally without permafrost) are **alpine tundra**.

TUNGSTEN (W), or **wolfram**, hard, silvery-gray metal in Group VIB of the PERIODIC TABLE; a TRANSITION ELEMENT. Its chief ores are SCHEELITE and WOLFRAMITE. The metal is produced by reduction of heated tungsten dioxide with hydrogen. Its main uses are in tungsten steel ALLOYS for high-temperature applications, and for the filaments of incandescent lamps. It is relatively inert, and resembles MOLYBDENUM. Cemented **tungsten carbide** (WC) is used in cutting tools. AW 183.9, mp 3410°C, bp 5660°C, sg 19.3 (20°C).

TUNIS, commercial and industrial city and capital of Tunisia, in NE Tunisia. It produces carpets, textiles and olive oil. Nearby are the ruins of ancient CARTHAGE. Pop 550,404.

TUNISIA, North African republic on the Mediterranean Sea, with Algeria to the W and Libya to the SE.

Land. The 639mi coastline has several good harbors. In the NW the Atlas mountains form a high wooded plateau and rise to 5,000ft in the W. The Medjerda R is the only permanent river; it irrigates a major wheat-producing area. In the S beyond Chott Djerid and other salt lakes lies the Sahara Desert. The summers are hot and dry, the winters mild and wet. Annual rainfall varies from 30in in the N to 4in in the S.

People. Tunisia is the most densely populated of North African countries. Most people live in the fertile N. The population is predominantly BERBER and Arab. There are small French, Italian and Maltese minorities. Tunis, the capital and primary port, Sfax, Sousse, Bizerta and Kairouan are the largest cities; 40% of the population live in towns.

Economy. Crude petroleum is the country's principal export, followed by clothing, olive oil and phosphates. The main crops are wheat, barley and other grains; olives, citrus, dates and wine grapes; and vegetables. Industry has traditionally centered around food processing but is expanding. Tunisia's rich oil deposits, its political stability and educated work force have enhanced development, but inflation and unemployment have kindled unrest in recent years.

History. Formerly a Phoenician colony, Tunisia was conquered in 146 BC by the Romans, in 439 AD by the VANDALS, in 533 by the Byzantines, in 670 by the Arabs, in 1574 by Turkish pirates and in 1881 by the French who made it a protectorate. Habib BOURGUIBA founded the nationalist Neo-Destour Party in 1934 and after Tunisia's independence (1956) became president of the Tunisian republic in 1957. Still in power, he has largely created modern Tunisia.

Official name: Republic of Tunisia
Capital: Tunis
Area: 63,362sq mi
Population: 6,476,000
Languages: Arabic; French
Religions: Muslim
Monetary unit(s): 1 dinar = 1,000 millimes

TUNNEL, underground passageway, usually designed to carry a highway or railroad, to serve as a conduit for water or sewage, or to provide access to an underground working face (see MINING). Although tunnels have been built since prehistoric times, tunneling methods remained primitive and hazardous until the 19th century. Modern softground tunneling was pioneered by Marc BRUNEL, who in 1824 invented the "tunneling shield"—a device subsequently improved (1869–86) by James Greathead. The Greathead shield is basically a large steel cylinder with a sharp cutting edge driven forward by hydraulic rams. Used in conjunction with a compressed-air atmosphere, it protects excavating workmen against cave-ins and water seepage. Tunneling through hard rock is facilitated by an array of pneumatic drills mounted on a "jumbo" carriage running on rails. Explosives are inserted in a pattern of holes drilled in the rock face and then detonated. Increasingly used today, however, are automatic tunneling machines called "moles," with cutting heads consisting of a rotating or oscillating wheel that digs, grinds or chisels away the working face. Another common tunnel-building method—used in constructing the New York SUBWAY—is "cut-and-cover," which involves excavating a trench, building the tunnel-lining and then covering it. The world's longest vehicular or railroad tunnel is the 19.8km (12.3mi) Simplon II in the Alps, completed in 1922.

TUNNEY, Gene (James Joseph; 1898–   ), US world heavyweight boxing champion, 1926–28. In 1926 he beat Jack DEMPSEY in the controversial fight of the "long count." He retired undefeated in 1928, having lost only one of his professional bouts.

TUPAMAROS, Uruguayan urban guerilla movement. Named for Tupac Amaru, an 18th-century Inca who rebelled against the Spaniards, the Tupamaros sought to exploit growing economic difficulties and social unrest in Uruguay in the 1970s. Their objective was creation of a leftist regime.

TUPOLEV, Andrei Nikolayevich (1888–1972), Russian aircraft designer. He was responsible for more than 100 designs, including the Tu-20 Bear turboprop bomber (1955) and the world's first supersonic passenger airliner, the Tu-144 (1969).

TURBINE, machine for directly converting the kinetic and/or thermal ENERGY of a flowing FLUID into useful rotational energy. The working fluid may be air, hot gas, steam or water. This either pushes against a set of blades mounted on the drive shaft (impulse turbines) or turns the shaft by reaction when the fluid is expelled from nozzles (or nozzle-shaped vanes) around its circumference (reaction turbines). Water turbines were the first to be developed. They now include the vast inward-flow reaction turbines used in the generation of HYDROELECTRICITY and the smaller-scale tangential-flow "Pelton wheel" impulse

types used when exploiting a very great "head" of water. In the 1880s, Charles Algernon Parsons (1854–1931), a British engineer, designed the first successful steam turbines, having realized that the efficient use of high-pressure steam demanded that its energy be extracted in a multitude of small stages. Steam turbines thus consist of a series of vanes mounted on a rotating drum with stator vanes redirecting the steam in between the moving ones. They are commonly used as marine engines and in thermal and nuclear power plants. GAS TURBINES are not as yet widely used except in airplanes (see JET PROPULSION) and for peak-load electricity generation.

TURBOJET. See JET PROPULSION.

TURBOT, *Scophthalmus maximus*, a large FLATFISH from shallow waters of the N Atlantic and European coasts. They are fine food fishes, growing to over 18kg (40lb). The body is not scaled, but is covered on the eyed left side with warty tubercles.

TURENNE, Henri de la Tour d'Auvergne, Vicomte de (1611–1675), French military commander. During the THIRTY YEARS' WAR, his brilliant campaigns of 1644–47 helped secure the Peace of WESTPHALIA (1648). He supported first CONDÉ then LOUIS XIV in the FRONDE civil war (1648–50), fought against the Spanish (1654–59) and was killed in action in the third DUTCH WAR of 1672–78.

TURGENEV, Ivan Sergeyevich (1818–1883), great Russian writer. A liberal and pro-Western opponent of serfdom, he wrote of peasant and country life, at the same time embracing social and political themes. After criticism of his greatest novel, *Fathers and Sons* (1862), he lived mostly abroad. His plays include *A Month in the Country* (1850). Short stories such as *Torrents of Spring* (1872) are among his finest works.

TURGOT, Jacques (1727–1781), French economist and reformer. One of the PHYSIOCRATS, he favored free trade and a land tax and anticipated the Law of DIMINISHING RETURNS. He lost his post (1776) as comptroller general of finances when he pressed for an end to compulsory labor.

TURING, Alan Mathison (1912–1954), British mathematician who was a pioneer in computer theory. He helped design and construct computers at the National Physical Laboratory at Teddington (1945–48) and the University of Manchester (after 1949) and developed early programming techniques.

TURKESTAN, or Turkistan, historic region in central Asia, extending from the Caspian Sea to the Mongolian desert. It

An Atlas of the Earth and Universe

In the beginning, there may have been a supernova—a star that exploded, almost completely destroying itself and shining, for a few days, as brightly as a small galaxy. Current cosmological theory suggests that our solar system condensed out of the material ejected from supernovas over a period of several billion years. Further, the event may have been triggered by the concussion of another supernova, comparatively close at hand—perhaps less than 60 light years away. This theory is suggested by analysis of the atomic composition of meteorites, whose isotope ratios differ slightly from those of normal rocks. The earth has three main zones: the atmosphere, the hydrosphere (the world's waters), and the lithosphere (the solid body of the world). The atmosphere not only provides us with oxygen, but shields us from much of the harmful radiation of the sun and protects us from excesses of heat and cold. The hydro-

The Crab Nebula in the constellation Taurus is the remnant of a supernova, or exploding star, recorded by Chinese astronomers in 1054 AD. At the nebula's center is a small, very dense pulsar, rotating about 30 times a second.

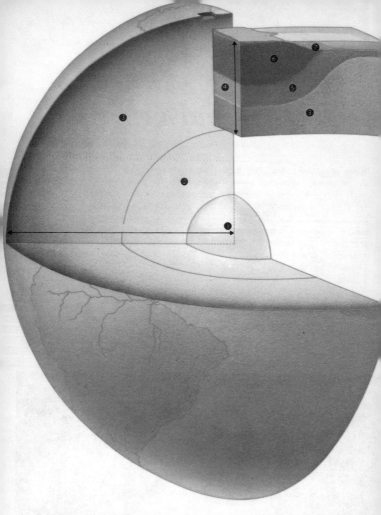

(A) The earth probably comprises a solid core (1), an outer liquid core (2), and a solid mantle (3) of iron and magnesium silicates. (B) An enlarged section of the outermost layers of the earth (4). The upper part of the mantle (3) is fairly plastic. Above it is the earth's crust: Basaltic material up to 5 mi thick forms the oceanic crust (5) while granitic material underlies continental land masses (6). Recent sediments (7) result from erosion.

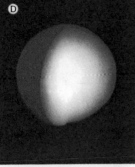

Early in the earth's formation (C), the materials compressed near its center melted to produce a molten core. As the earth cooled (D), the crust formed. With more cooling (E), the layers separated out into core, mantle, and crust.

sphere, meanwhile, is extensive, with some 70% of the earth's surface being covered by water in liquid and solid (ice) form.

The earth's solid body, in turn, can also be divided into three zones: the core, the mantle, and the crust. The core with a diameter of about 7000 km and a temperature of about 3000K, is at least partly liquid, though the central region (the inner core) probably is solid. The core's density ranges from about 9.5 to perhaps more than 15 tonnes/m^3 and it probably is composed mainly of nickel and iron. The mantle, with an outer diameter of about 12686 km, ranges in density from about 5.7 tonnes/m^3 toward the core to 3.3 tonnes/m^3 toward the crust. The earth's crust, the planet's outermost layer and the one to which all human activity is confined, is some 35km thick (though much less beneath the oceans).

The crust of the earth is composed of three types of rocks: igneous, sedimentary, and metamorphic. From fossils in sedimentary rocks, it appears that life on this planet began about 570 million years ago, with human beings emerging about 4 million years ago.

The earth's crust, once thought to be relatively fixed, is now known to be composed of a mosaic of plates that shift over long periods of time, changing the configurations of the continents and the ocean basins. This is the theory of ''plate tectonics'' — the modern version of the continental-

The continents as they were some 190 million years ago, before they began drifting to their present positions. Red areas indicate overlaps in the continental shelves. The single supercontinent has been named Pangaea.

drift theory proposed by Alfred Wegener in 1912. The mechanism that powers the moving plates is still not perfectly understood, but it probably involves convection currents in the earth's mantle. In this scheme, the light continental rocks ride on top of basalt plates somewhat like packages on a conveyor belt. When plates move apart, new crust is created along the global

Deep sea trench and accompanying volcanic islands. Dense oceanic plate (1) is being subducted beneath lighter continental plate (2), causing deep earthquake activity, the production of lava, and turbidites (3) on the trench floor.

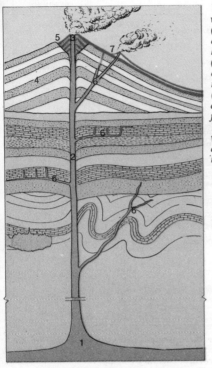

Left: *cross section of a volcano. (1) magma, (2) main conduit, (3) main outlet, (4) layers of ash and lava from prior eruptions, (5) large explosion crater, or caldera, partly filled with new volcanic matter, (6) branches of main conduit, (7) parasitic cone formed by one of these. Below: world's major volcanoes are distributed in a "ring of fire" along plate margins.*

midocean ridge. At the same time, when one plate pushes beneath another, old crust is melted as the heavier plate descends into the mantle. The movement of the plates against one another builds mountains, creates faults, causes earthquakes, and explains why the world's volcanoes are located where they are.

aeon	era	period	epoch	time since commencement (million years)
Phanerozoic	Cenozoic	Quaternary	Holocene (Recent)	0.01
			Pleistocene	4
		Tertiary	Pliocene	10
			Miocene	25
			Oligocene	40
			Eocene	55
			Paleocene	65
	Mesozoic	Cretaceous		135
		Jurassic		190
		Triassic		225
	Paleozoic	Permian		280
		Pennsylvanian	Carboniferous	315
		Mississippian		345
		Devonian		400
		Silurian		440
		Ordovician		500
		Cambrian		570
Cryptozoic	Proterozoic	Precambrian		
	Archeozoic (Archean)			
	Azoic			4550

Geological time scale showing the aeons, eras, periods, and epochs since the formation of the world nearly 4.6 billion years ago. The scale is derived from analysis of the sequences of rock strata and the fossils they contain.

The theory of plate tectonics is the most significant recent development in the earth sciences but it builds, of course, on the work of geologists of the past few hundred years. Most early geological knowledge came from the practical experience of mining engineers, with some of the first geological treatises coming from the pen of Georgius Agricola in the 16th century. Geology was not really established as a science until the opening of the 19th century, however, when field observations began to become truly detailed. William Smith (1769–1839), the "father of stratigraphy," showed how the succession of fossils could be used to index the stratigraphic column, and he and others produced impressive geological maps. Charles Lyell's classic *Principles of Geology* (1830–33) restated (in much clearer form) James Hutton's principle of uniformitarianism, which holds that the same agencies are at work in nature today, operating at the same intensities, as they always have throughout geological time. Lyell's work provided the foundation for much of the later development of the science of geology. Significant contributions also were made by his contemporary, Louis Agassiz, who first proposed (1840) that large areas of the northern continents had been covered by sheets of ice in the geologically recent past.

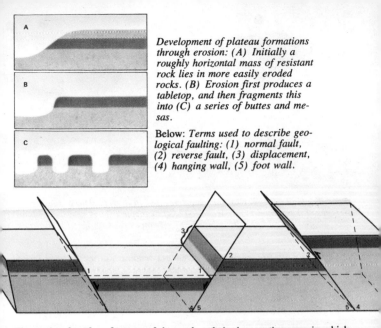

Development of plateau formations through erosion: (A) Initially a roughly horizontal mass of resistant rock lies in more easily eroded rocks. (B) Erosion first produces a tabletop, and then fragments this into (C) a series of buttes and mesas.

Below: Terms used to describe geological faulting: (1) normal fault, (2) reverse fault, (3) displacement, (4) hanging wall, (5) foot wall.

The study of surface features of the earth—their shapes, the ways in which they are formed, and the processes that are continually influencing the evolution of the landscape—is called geomorphology. One of the classic studies of geomorphology is karst topography: the landforms that develop through solution of limestone by rainwater (see illustration below). The gradual infiltration

Karst formation in which water creates complex underground channels in limestone: (1) phreatic zone, (2) sinkhole, (3) polje, (4) vadose region, (5) swallow holes, (6) vauclusian spring, (7) limestone pavement, (8) kamenitza.

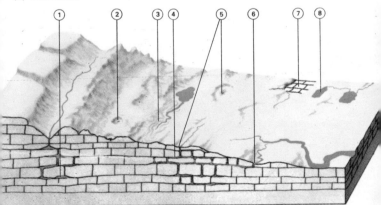

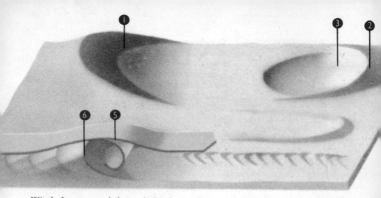

Wind shapes sand dunes behind coastlines and in deserts. Dunes can be crescentic or barchan (1), parabolic (2), or hairpin (3). A crescentic dune over which the wind regularly blows (5) advances as its ridge (6) migrates forward.

of water, usually following zones of natural weakness in the rock, produces extremely complex systems of underground channels, sinkholes, and caverns.

The earth's landscape also is continually sculpted by wind, rivers, and—perhaps most dramatically—glaciers. There are three recognized types of glacier: ice sheets and caps, mountain or valley glaciers, and piedmont glaciers.

Glaciers and glaciated landforms: (1) head of glacier, (2) firn or névé, (3) region of ground morain deposition, (4) terminal morain, (5) drumlin, (6) braided stream, (7) kettle, (8) medial moraine, (9) lateral morain, (10) U-shaped valley, (11) arête, (12) hanging valley, (13) cirque, (14) tarn, (15) ice fall.

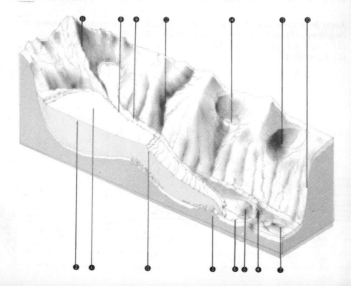

River valley development: A young valley (left) has a deep V-shape, produced by fast-flowing water near the river source. A mature valley (above) has been eroded into wider flatter, form by slower flow near river outlet.

Glaciers form wherever conditions are such that annual precipitation of snow, sleet, and hail exceeds the amount that can be lost through evaporation or melting. The occurrence of glaciers depends much on latitude as well as on local topography; there are several glaciers at high altitudes on the equator. In the great ice ages of the past (the most recent of which reached its maximum about 18,000 years ago), glaciers determined much of the world's climate, drastically affected sea levels (the more of the world's water budget that is locked up in ice, the lower the sea level), and very possibly created delugelike floods when they melted (glaciologists now think that ice sheets decay about five times as quickly as they grow). Even today, glaciers account for 75% of the world supply of fresh water, with the Antarctic ice sheet alone representing 85% of this.

Changing rivers: Arrows show the different patterns in the movement and deposition of eroded materials in (1) a straight river with a symmetrical bed, and (2) a winding river with an asymmetrical bed.

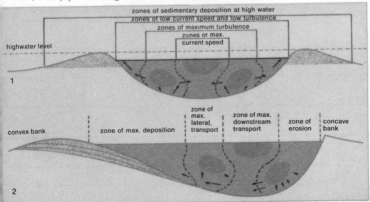

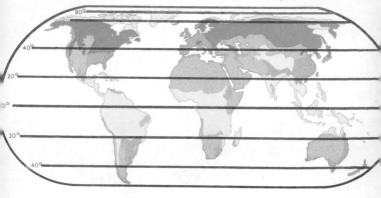

Map showing the distribution and extent of the Arctic tundra lands (darker area); similar regions on high *mountains are called alpine tundra. Vegetation includes lichens, mosses, and stunted shrubs.*

Closely related to geology is geography. Where geologists seek to explain the earth's surface by probing beneath it, geographers tend to concentrate on the surface itself. There is much overlap between the disciplines, however, and physical geography, which deals with the physical structures of the earth, and so includes climatology and oceanography, is akin to physical geology. Other key branches of geography include economic geography, political and regional

The climates of the world according to the classification of Vladimir Köppen. This takes into account temper- *ature patterns, rainfall and vegetation. The categories correspond roughly to zoning by latitude.*

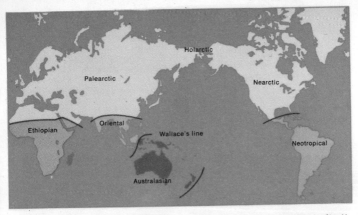

Alfred R. Wallace's 1876 zoographic divisions, reflecting the distribution of animal species and populations, is still valid today. ("Wallace's line" divides Asian from Australasian fauna.)

geography, historical geography, and applied geography. The field of biogeography is concerned with the distribution of plant and animal life about the globe and is thus intimately related to biology and ecology. Finally, mathematical geography deals with the size, shape, and motions of the earth and is thus linked to astronomy.

Forests are vital to the preservation of an environment hospitable to man as well as to a great range of other animals and plants. Destruction of forest lands is considered a critical contemporary ecological problem.

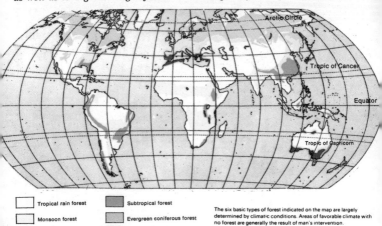

	Tropical rain forest
	Monsoon forest
	Temperate forest
	Subtropical forest
	Evergreen coniferous forest
	Hardwood forest

The six basic types of forest indicated on the map are largely determined by climatic conditions. Areas of favorable climate with no forest are generally the result of man's intervention.

The International Date Line (shown left in red) follows an irregular course approximating to the 180th meridian. This is in order to avoid the confusion it would cause if it crossed land areas. To the west of the line it is one day later than it is to the east.

The rotation and revolution of the bodies of the solar system provide not only cyclic variety but also clues used by humans to analyze the nature of the system itself. Eclipses can be terrifying phenomena, but they reveal basic elements in the structure of the solar system.

Below: *world's time zones with longitude at top; the second row of numbers indicates the hours that a given time zone is ahead of or behind Greenwich Mean Time. In the USSR local time is 1 hour later than sun* *time; in dotted areas (a), local times differ by a half hour from sun time; (b) is the International Date Line. Bottom: variations in length of the natural day.*

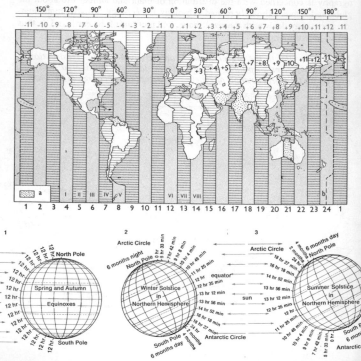

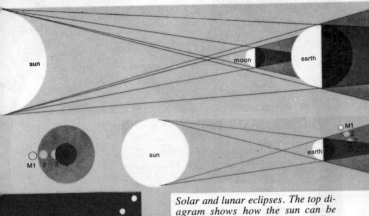

Solar and lunar eclipses. The top diagram shows how the sun can be eclipsed by the moon. Lower diagrams show eclipse of the moon by the earth; at M1 the moon is outside Earth's shadow; at M3 a real eclipse starts; at M4 it is total. Left: series of short exposures at 15 minute intervals of solar eclipse at Chicago in 1954.

Eclipses of the sun and moon have since ancient times given scientists insight into the relative motions of the Earth, moon, and sun; eclipses involving the satellites of Jupiter are also visible from Earth. Beginning in the 19th century, scientists have made major studies of the sun during eclipses, especially spectroscopic studies. In the 20th century, scientists have also depended upon eclipses for major tests of relativity theory.

Below: *orbit of a satellite of Jupiter, invisible from Earth at points 2–5.*

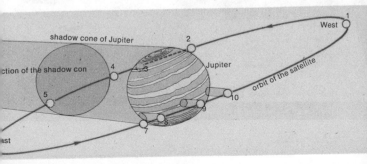

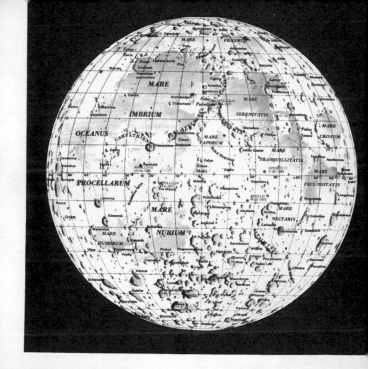

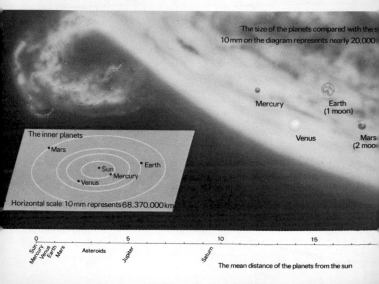

The size of the planets compared with the s
10 mm on the diagram represents nearly 20,000

Mercury

Earth
(1 moon)

Venus

Mars
(2 moo

The inner planets

Mars

Sun

Earth

Venus

Mercury

Horizontal scale: 10 mm represents 68,370,000 km

0				5		10		15	

Sun
Mercury
Venus
Earth
Mars

Asteroids

Jupiter

Saturn

The mean distance of the planets from the sun

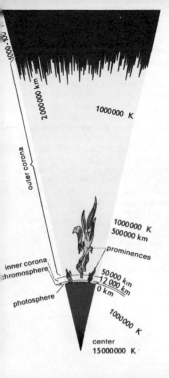

The solar system has become our new frontier. The moon (far left) has been reached by man (note the dates of the Apollo landings, in red). Voyager I and II have sent us superb photos of Jupiter and Saturn, and Voyager II is going to Uranus and Neptune (scheduled for approaches in 1986 and 1989). All depends, of course, on the sun (shown in sectional diagram to left). The sun, an incandescent ball of gases, is a normal, smallish star, lying in one of the spiral arms of the Milky Way. The temperature at the center of the sun is more than 15,000,000 K (see diagram); in the sun's chromosphere occur sunspots, flares and prominences, the last being great plumes of gas that surge out into the corona and occasionally off space. The

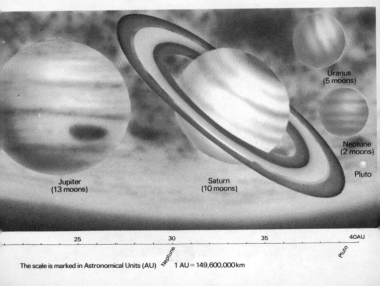

The scale is marked in Astronomical Units (AU)   1 AU = 149,600,000km

earth lies within the sun's corona, called (at this distance) solar wind. Binary stars (left) revolve around a common center of gravity; a star and a black hole can do the same. Below see the effect of a black hole, Cygnus X-1, on the accretion disk of gases from such a star: (a) the disk, a few million km in diameter, orbiting the black hole; (b) the disk near the hole, its shape distorted by X-rays; (c) even nearer the hole, gravity triumphs; (d) even closer, with the disk now a few kms across, gravity is sucking the gases directly into the black hole.

There appear to exist in the universe black holes; a black hole is formed when a supernova from a sufficiently massive star collapses in upon itself, creating an ever–more–intense gravitational field, until finally nothing, not even light, can escape it. It is possible that the universe may end as a vast black hole. And it is also possible that the explosion of such a black hole would re-create the universe anew.

consists today of the S Kazakh, Kirgiz, Tadzhik, Turkmen and Uzbek SSRs in the USSR, Chinese Turkestan and part of NE Afghanistan. It has been the home of TURKIC-speaking peoples since c500 AD and was important for its great trade routes linking Europe with the Far East. The chief city is SAMARKAND.

Official name: Republic of Turkey
Capital: Ankara
Area: 309,947sq mi
Population: 45,356,000
Languages: Turkish; Kurdish
Religions Muslim
Monetary unit(s): Turkish Lira (or pound)=100 kurus (or piastres)

TURKEY, a republic in extreme SE Europe and Asia Minor, bounded by the Black Sea, USSR, Iran, Iraq, Syria, the Mediterranean, Greece and Bulgaria.
Land. Turkey is mountainous, with an extensive semiarid plateau in Asia Minor; the highest peak is Mt. ARARAT (16,945ft). The Euphrates and the Tigris rivers rise in the E; other rivers include the Kizil Irmak, Sakarya and Büyük Menderes. The strategic BOSPORUS and DARDANELLES separate European from Asian Turkey. Earthquakes occur frequently. The climate is Mediterranean around the coastal lowlands, but more extreme and drier inland, with harsh winters toward the NE.
People. The TURKISH-speaking population descends largely from the TATARS, who entered Asia Minor in the 1000s AD. There are small Kurdish and Arab minorities. Some 60% live in rural areas. Illiteracy is about 40%.
Economy. Agriculture is the basis of the economy. The chief crops are grains, cotton, fruits and tobacco. Cattle are raised on the Anatolian plateau. Turkish industry has been developed greatly since WWII and includes steel, iron and textile manufacture. There are large deposits of coal, iron and other metals, and some oil.
History. Formerly part of the HITTITE, PERSIAN, ROMAN, BYZANTINE, SELJUK and OTTOMAN empires, Turkey became a republic in 1923 under ATATURK, who initiated a vast program of reform and modernization aiming at establishing Turkey as a modern democratic state on European lines. Neutral for most of WWII, Turkey afterwards aligned herself with the West, joining the NORTH ATLANTIC TREATY ORGANIZATION and accepting substantial US aid. Democratic rule was shaken by an army coup in 1960, since when military intervention in government has continued, amid increasing economic difficulties, civil unrest and political instability. Tension with Greece has almost led to war on several occasions. In 1974 Turkey invaded and occupied most of Cyprus.

TURKEYS, two species of large New World game birds in their own family, Meleagrididae. The Common turkey, *Meleagris gallopavo*, occurs in open woodland and scrub of North America and is the ancestor of the domestic turkey. The head and neck of both species are naked and with wattles; a fleshy caruncle overhangs the bill. The naked skin in the Common turkey is red; in the Ocellated turkey, blue.

TURKIC LANGUAGES, a group of ALTAIC LANGUAGES spoken by the TURKS in Turkey, E Europe and central and N Asia. They include Turkish, Azerbaijani, Turkoman, Uzbek, Kirghiz, Tatar, Kazakh and Chuvash. Vowel harmony and wide use of suffixes are characteristic. Latin or Cyrillic have replaced Arabic script since the 1920s–30s.

TURKISH, a TURKIC language, official language of Turkey, also spoken by minorities in E Europe and SW Asia. Evolved during the OTTOMAN EMPIRE, it was written in Arabic script until ATATURK introduced a modified Latin alphabet in 1928.

TURKS, a family of TURKIC speaking, chiefly Muslim peoples extending from Sinkiang (W China) and Siberia to Turkey, Iran and E European USSR. They include the Tatars, Kazakhs, Uzbeks, Kirghiz, Turkmens, Vighurs, Azerbaijanis and many others. The Turks spread through Asia from the 6th century onwards, were converted to Islam in the 10th century. In the W they controlled vast lands under the SELJUKS (1000s–1200s) and OTTOMAN EMPIRE (1300s–1923).

TURKS AND CAICOS ISLANDS, a British colony comprising two island groups SE of the Bahamas, West Indies. There are six inhabited and over 30 smaller islands. The chief industries are sponge and shellfish collection and salt production. Pop 7,200.

TURNER, Frederick **Jackson** (1861–1932), US historian. A Harvard professor (1910–24), he propounded an influential thesis about the American frontier and its role in shaping US individualism and democracy. *The Frontier in American History* (1920) reprinted earlier papers. He won a Pulitzer Prize for his study of sectionalism in the US (1932).

TURNER, Joseph Mallord William (1775–1851), outstanding Romantic landscape painter, perhaps the greatest British painter. His work is famous for its rich treatment of light and atmosphere, in oil, watercolor or engraving. His paintings include *The Fighting Téméraire* (1839) and *Rain, Steam and Speed* (1844). He left some 20,000 works to the nation. (See also ROMANTICISM.)

TURNER, Ted (1938–), American business executive and sportsman. The Atlanta entrepreneur built his family's billboard business into a multimillion dollar communications conglomerate. He is a pioneer in the cable television industry. He is also a champion yachtsman, winner of the 1977 and 1980 America's Cup and the owner of the Atlanta Braves baseball club.

TURPENTINE, exudate obtained from injured PINE trees. This is distilled to give the RESIN, rosin, and the ESSENTIAL OIL, oil of turpentine (also known as turpentine). The chief constituent of oil of turpentine, used as a solvent and thinner for PAINTS and VARNISHES, is pinene.

TURTLES, aquatic relatives of TORTOISES, divisible into freshwater and marine groups. Like the tortoises, the body is encased in a horny shell. There are no teeth in the gums and the mouth has become adapted to form a sharp horny bill. Turtles are largely vegetarians. In freshwater forms the limbs normally retain free fingers and toes; in marine turtles they are modified into flat flippers, increasing their swimming ability. The amount of time spent in the water by the various species varies enormously: many of the freshwater species go for more or less extensive walks on land; others, like the marine turtles, leave the water only to lay their eggs. These are laid in scrapes in sand or soil on beaches and are left to incubate themselves. The young turtles make straight for the water on hatching.

TUSCANY, region in W central Italy, extending from the Apennine Mts. to the W coast. It is mostly mountainous, with fertile river valleys and coastal strip. Agricultural products include cereals, olive oil and Chianti wine. Iron and other minerals are mined; the chief manufactures are textiles, chemicals and machinery. Center of the ancient ETRUSCAN civilization, Tuscany has many famous cities such as Florence, Lucca, Pisa and Siena.

TUSKEGEE INSTITUTE, private college in Tuskegee, Ala. Founded by Booker T. WASHINGTON in 1881, it was one of the first colleges to educate freed slaves. The institute trained black school teachers and supported the work of George W. CARVER. Today it offers a wide range of subjects and has a fine library of American black history.

TUSSAUD, Marie Grosholtz (1760–1850), Swiss wax modeler. Forced to make death masks of guillotined aristocrats in the French Revolution, she left Paris to found (1802) her famous London WAX MUSEUM. Today the waxworks contain tableaus and hundreds of models of well-known people.

TUTANKHAMEN (reigned c1350 BC), Egyptian pharoah. He died at 18 but is famous for his tomb, discovered in THEBES by Howard CARTER in 1922 with its treasures intact. His solid gold coffin, gold portrait mask and other treasures are in the Cairo museum.

Official name: Tuvalu
Capital: Funafuti
Area: 10sq mi
Population: 7,349 on Tuvalu, about 2,000 abroad
Languages: English, Tuvaluan
Religions: Christian
Monetary unit(s): 1 Australian dollar = 100 cents

TUVALU (formerly Ellice Islands), an independent island nation composed of nine small atolls, spread over more than 500,000sq mi in the W Pacific.

Land. The largest island, Vaitupu, covers only 2sq mi. No spot on these coral atolls rises more than 16ft above sea level. The soil is poor and there are no rivers and little vegetation besides coconut palms. The average annual temperature is 86°F; most of the rainfall occurs between Nov. and Feb.

People and Economy. The inhabitants are Polynesian, with almost 30% living on the island of Funafuti. Although traditional subsistence farming and fishing are important, about 2,000 Tuvaluans have gone abroad for employment, many to

Nauru. Copra is the only export although he sale of postage stamps abroad also produces income.

History. The islands were largely ignored by Europeans until the 19th century, when whaling took place in the area. The population was reduced from 22,000 to 8,000 between 1850 and 1875 because of disease and forcible recruitment for labor abroad. A British protectorate over both the Ellice and Gilbert (now KIRIBATI) islands was established in 1892. In 1974 Ellice Islanders voted for separate status, achieving independence in 1978.

TWAIN, Mark (1835–1910), pen name of Samuel Langhorne Clemens, US author and popular humorist and lecturer. After being a printer's apprentice (1848–53), he led a wandering life, becoming a Mississippi river pilot (1857–61) and then a journalist, establishing a reputation with his humorous sketches. In 1869 he produced his first bestseller, *The Innocents Abroad*, followed by *The Adventures of Tom Sawyer* (1876), *The Prince and the Pauper* (1882), his masterpiece *Huckleberry Finn* (1884) and the satirical *A Connecticut Yankee in King Arthur's Court* (1889). *Huckleberry Finn*, the story of a raft trip down the Mississippi, exemplifies Twain's gift of blending humor with realism. In later life, Twain lost most of his money through speculation and suffered the loss of his wife and daughters. His works became increasingly pessimistic and bitingly satirical, as in *The Tragedy of Pudd'nhead Wilson* (1894) and *The Man who Corrupted Hadleyburg* (1899).

TWEED, William Marcy (1823–1878), New York City politician. He became boss of TAMMANY HALL in 1868 and with the help of his cronies, known as the Tweed Ring, exercised corrupt control over the Democratic Party machine running New York. Tweed defrauded the city of over 30 million dollars, but was eventually convicted and died in jail.

TWELVE-TONE MUSIC, or serial music, a type of music, developed in the 1920s, which rejects TONALITY as the basis for composition. Its most famous exponent, SCHOENBERG, laid down a method of composition which attempted to free music from the 8-note OCTAVE and its associated conventions. Twelve-tone compositions are constructed around a specific series of the twelve notes of the CHROMATIC SCALE. Later 20th-century composers have used the principles of twelve-tone composition with greater freedom. (See ATONALITY.) Later composers of twelve-tone music include STRAVINSKY, SESSIONS, PISTON, KRENEK, HENZE, DALLAPICCOLA, SHOSTAKOVICH and Schoenberg's pupils WEBERN and BERG.

TWELVE TRIBES OF ISRAEL, the twelve family groups into which the ancient Hebrews were divided. According to the Bible they were descended from and named for ten sons of JACOB and two sons of JOSEPH. Those descended from Jacob's sons were ASHER, BENJAMIN, DAN, GAD, Issachar, JUDAH, NAPHTALI, REUBEN, SIMEON, ZEBULUN; the two from Joseph's sons were EPHRAIM and MANASSEH. When the Jews finally reached the Promised Land they divided the country between these twelve family groups. A thirteenth tribe, LEVI, had no portion of land set aside for it. (See also JEWS.)

TWINS. See MULTIPLE BIRTHS; SIAMESE TWINS.

TWIST, dance of the early 1960s, introduced by pop singer Chubby CHECKER. The twist is danced without touching one's partner and consists in rotating the hips and upper body in opposite directions. The dance was almost universally popular for several years.

TWO SICILIES, Kingdom of the, a kingdom uniting SICILY and S Italy (see NAPLES). Originally founded by Normans in the 1000s, it was reunited by ALFONSO V of Aragon in 1442. A branch of the BOURBON family succeeded to the kingdom in 1759 and held it until the proclamation of a united Italy in 1861.

TYLER, John (1790–1862), tenth US president (1841–45). A Va. aristocrat, he studied law and was elected to the Va. legislature (1811–16, 1823–25, 1839), and served in Congress (1817–21). He became governor of Va. (1825–27), and then a US senator (1827–36). A conservative, he believed in STATES' RIGHTS and the restriction of federal power, opposing the MISSOURI COMPROMISE and the bill authorizing President JACKSON to use force against S.C. during the NULLIFICATION crisis. He broke with the Democrats and was chosen by the WHIGS to run for vice-president with William Henry HARRISON, who became president in 1841 but died within a month of his inauguration.

TYLER, Wat (d. 1381), leader of the English Peasants' Revolt (1381), England's first popular rebellion, protesting high taxation after the BLACK DEATH. Tyler and his Kentish followers captured Canterbury, then took the TOWER OF LONDON. RICHARD II promised abolition of serfdom and feudal service. At a second meeting with the king, Tyler was stabbed and the revolt was brutally crushed.

TYLOR, Sir Edward Burnett (1832–1917), British anthropologist whose work, culminating in *Primitive Culture* (1871), established him as a father of cultural ANTHROPOLOGY. In 1896 he was appointed the first Professor of Anthropology in the University of Oxford.

TYNAN, Kenneth (1927–1980), influential English drama critic whose controversial opinions were expressed in witty, elegant, often stinging reviews. An admirer of Brecht, he believed that theater was a "kind of sociology" encompassing ethics, politics and economics. His works include *Tynan Right and Left* (1967), *A View of the English Stage* (1975), *Show People* (1980) and the bawdy stage review *Oh, Calcutta!*

TYNDALE, William (c1494–1536), English bible translator, theologian and Protestant martyr. His NEW TESTAMENT, printed in Germany (1526), was suppressed in England. He lived abroad in hiding, translating the PENTATEUCH (1529–30) and Book of Jonah (1531). In 1535 he was captured in Antwerp, tried and burned for heresy. (See also BIBLE.)

TYNDALL, John (1820–1893), British physicist who, through his studies of the scattering of light by colloidal particles or large molecules in SUSPENSION (the **Tyndall effect**), showed that the daytime sky is blue because of the Rayleigh SCATTERING of impingent sunlight by dust and other colloidal particles in the air (see COLLOID).

TYPESETTING. See LINOTYPE; MONOTYPE; PRINTING.

TYPEWRITER, writing machine activated manually or electrically by means of a keyboard. Normally, when a key is depressed, a pivoted bar bearing a type character strikes an inked ribbon against a sheet of paper carried on a cylindrical rubber "platen," and the platen carriage automatically moves a space to the left. In some electric models all the type is carried on a single rotatable sphere that moves from left to right and strikes a fixed platen. The first efficient typewriter was developed in 1868 by C. L. SHOLES.

TYPHOID FEVER, INFECTIOUS DISEASE due to a SALMONELLA species causing FEVER, a characteristic rash, LYMPH node and SPLEEN enlargement, GASTRO-INTESTINAL TRACT disturbance with bleeding and ulceration, and usually marked malaise or prostration. It is contracted from other cases or from disease carriers, the latter often harboring asymptomatic infection in the GALL-BLADDER or urine, with contaminated food and water as major vectors. Carriers must be treated with ANTIBIOTICS (and have their gall-bladder removed if this site is the source); they must also stop handling food until they are free of the bacteria. VACCINATION may help protect high risk

persons; antibiotics—chloramphenicol or cotrimoxazole—form the treatment of choice.

TYPHUS, INFECTIOUS DISEASE caused by RICKETTSIA and carried by LICE, leading to a feverish illness with a rash. Severe HEADACHE typically precedes the rash which may be erythematous or may progress to skin HEMORRHAGE; mild respiratory symptoms of cough and breathlessness are common. Death ensues in a high proportion of untreated adults, usually with profound SHOCK and KIDNEY failure. Recurrences may occur in untreated patients who recover from their first attack, often after many years (Brill-Zinsser disease). A similar disease due to a different but related organism is carried by fleas (Murine typhus). Chloramphenicol or TETRACYCLINES provide suitable ANTIBIOTIC therapy.

TYPOGRAPHY, the design and layout of printed type. The object of typography is to enhance the legibility of a printed page, or as in advertising and display, to attract the reader's attention. Early typefaces were derived from medieval Gothic and Renaissance humanistic scripts. A typeface usually consists of a set or *font* of capital and lower-case letters in three styles: roman, *italic* and **bold**, each cut in a range of sizes (measured in *points*). Famous typefaces include those produced by BASKERVILLE, BODONI, GARAMOND and Eric GILL. Good typography calls for intelligent positioning of word patterns set in types of appropriate face and size (see PRINTING).

TYRANNOSAURUS, the largest of the carnivorous DINOSAURS—bipedal and measuring up to 5.8m (19ft) in walking pose, with powerful hindlimbs and feet, enormous head and massive jaws but tiny forelimbs. They lived during the late CRETACEOUS.

TYRANT, a dictator in ancient Greece. With the growth of democracy in 5th-century BC Athens the word took on its present pejorative sense though in fact many tyrants were able and popular rulers. Some of the most famous were DIONYSIUS I and II, HIERO I and II and PISISTRATUS.

TYRE, town, and ancient PHOENICIAN city-port on the coast of Lebanon. After 1400 BC it began to dominate Mediterranean trade, and established colonies in Spain and CARTHAGE. Frequently mentioned in the Bible and famed for its silks and dyes, it was sacked by ALEXANDER THE GREAT (322) but recovered under the ROMAN EMPIRE. It was finally destroyed by the MAMELUKES in 1291. Today the small town of Sur occupies the site.

TYROL. See TIROL.

TYRRHENIAN SEA, part of the Mediterranean Sea bounded by the W coast of Italy, and by Corsica, Sardinia and Sicily. The strait of Messina in the S connects with the Ionian Sea. Its ports include Naples and Palermo.

TZARA, Tristan (1896–1963), Romanianborn French poet, founder of the DADA movement. In Paris he published the *Seven Dada Manifestos* (1924), working with André BRETON to destroy conventional values and language. He moved toward SURREALISM, and his mature lyrical poetry is more humanistic.

TZ'U-HSI (1835–1908), Chinese Dowager Empress. She was regent for her son and later her nephew, and finally ruled directly, dominating Chinese affairs for nearly 50 years. Her corrupt rule through a clique of conservative officials contributed to China's defeat in the SINO-JAPANESE WAR (1895) and to the BOXER REBELLION. Three years after her death the CH'ING dynasty was overthrown.

U

21st letter of the English alphabet, derived from the Semitic *waw* via the Greek *upsilon*. In the Roman alphabet, *V* (lower case *u*) was both vowel and consonant, and the modern *u* and *v* date from the 16th century.

UCCELLO, Paolo (1397–1475), Florentine early RENAISSANCE painter, noted for his use of perspective. His best-known works are the *Creation* and *Noah* scenes (c1431–50) in Santa Maria Novella, Florence, and the three richly decorative panels of *The Battle of San Romano* (c1455–60).

UDALL, Nicholas (c1505–1556), English schoolmaster, scholar and playwright. Headmaster of ETON (1534–41) and Westminster (1554–56), he wrote the first known English comedy, *Ralph Roister Doister* (c1553).

UFFIZI, 16th-century palace in Florence, Italy, built to designs by VASARI for Cosimo I de' MEDICI. It houses one of the world's finest art collections, rich in classical, Dutch, Flemish and, notably, Italian Renaissance paintings and sculptures.

Official name: Republic of Uganda
Capital: Kampala
Area: 91,134sq mi
Population: 13,674,000
Languages: English; Bantu languages, Swahili
Religions: Christian, Muslim; tribal religions
Monetary unit(s): 1 Uganda shilling=100 cents

UGANDA, landlocked republic in E central Africa, bordering Kenya, Sudan, Zaire, Rwanda and Tanzania.

Land. Uganda lies on the equator and has an average elevation of 4,000ft. The fertile plateau is bounded by the GREAT RIFT VALLEY and Ruwenzori Mts to the W and high mountains to the E. The White Nile, whose source is Lake Victoria in the SE, is harnessed for electricity at Owens Falls dam. Except in the arid N and parts of the S, annual rainfall is about 40in, and temperatures rarely exceed 85°F or fall below 60°F.

People. Uganda has over a dozen major tribes, of which Bantu-speaking groups form a majority. The Baganda in the S are the most numerous. The bulk of the population depends on agriculture, but Nilotic-speaking peoples in the N tend to be herdsmen. Illiteracy is high. Kampala's Makerere University was once regarded as one of Africa's most important seats of learning, but declined during the period that Uganda was ruled by Maj. Gen. Idi AMIN DADA, 1971–79.

Economy. The economy is agricultural and most farms are small, growing subsistence crops and raising livestock. Despite severe economic dislocation under Amin's rule, Uganda remained one of the world's major producers of coffee, which accounts for almost all its export earnings. Other export crops include tea, peanuts, and tobacco. Copper is the principal mineral.

History. The BUGANDA kingdom, which succeeded the Bunyoro kingdom, became a British protectorate in 1894. The protectorate was extended to other kingdoms and by 1914 the present boundaries of Uganda became fixed. Uganda became independent in 1962. In 1971 Maj. Gen. Idi Amin Dada deposed President Milton Obote in a military coup. In 1972 he expelled Uganda's Asian population, attracting world attention. Through the Amin years internal strife prevailed. In 1979 Tanzania invaded Uganda and Amin fled. By 1981, after two presidents, Uganda again chose Obote to rule the nation.

UGRO-FINNIC LANGUAGES, the more important of the branches of the Uralic language family (see URAL-ALTAIC LANGUAGES). The Finnic division includes Finnish and Estonian; the Ugric, Hungarian.

UKRAINE, constituent Soviet Socialist Republic in the W USSR, third largest in area and second only to the RSFSR in population and economic importance. Mostly steppes, the Ukraine extends from the Carpathian Mts E to the Donets Ridge and Sea of Azov, and from the Black Sea N to Belorussia. The Dnieper R flows N, dividing the Ukraine. In the NW lie the Polesye (Pripyat, Pripet) marshes; in the S, a fertile CHERNOZEM region.

The "breadbasket of the Soviet Union" is the second most productive agricultural area of the USSR (wheat and other grains, root crops and flax) and accounts for 25% of the heavy industrial output. It is rich in oil, gas, coal, hydroelectricity, and iron. Major centers are KIEV (the capital), DNEPROPETROVSK, DONETSK (and the DONETS BASIN), KHARKOV and ODESSA. Culturally distinct UKRAINIAN speakers comprise over 75% of the people. The COSSACKS ("outlaws") arose in opposition to Polish and, later, Russian rule. The Ukraine was briefly independent, 1918–20, and nationalism remains. (See USSR.)

UKRAINIAN, or Ruthenian, East Slavic SLAVONIC LANGUAGE. Distinguished from RUSSIAN since c1200 and written in a modified CYRILLIC alphabet, it emerged as a literary language in the 18th century. It is the official language of the Ukraine, with some 41,000,000 speakers.

ULANOVA, Galina (1910–   ), Russian prima ballerina of the BOLSHOI THEATER, Moscow, from 1944–62. She excelled as a dramatic and lyric dancer, notably in *Swan Lake* and Prokofiev's *Romeo and Juliet.*

ULBRICHT, Walter (1893–1973), leader of post-WWII East Germany. A founder member (1918) of the German Communist Party, he became first deputy premier (1949) and head of state (1960–73) of the German Democratic Republic. An uncompromising Stalinist, he headed the Socialist Unity Party from 1950 until replaced (1971) by Erich HONECKER. He built the BERLIN WALL (1961), and in 1968 sent troops to Czechoslovakia.

ULCER, pathological defect in SKIN or other EPITHELIUM, caused by INFLAMMATION secondary to infection, loss of BLOOD supply, failure of venous return or CANCER. Various skin lesions can cause ulcers, including infection, arterial disease, VARICOSE VEINS and skin cancer. Aphthous ulcers in the MOUTH are painful epithelial ulcers of unknown origin. Peptic ulcers include gastric and duodenal ulcers, although the two have different causes; they may cause characteristic pain, acute HEMORRHAGE, or lead to perforation and PERITONITIS. Severe scarring or EDEMA around the pylorus may cause stenosis with VOMITING and STOMACH distension. ANTACIDS, rest, stopping SMOKING, and licorice derivatives may help peptic ulcer but surgery may also be needed.

ULLMAN, Liv (1939–   ), Norwegian actress whose work with Ingmar BERGMAN made her an international star. Her films include *Persona* (1966), *Cries and Whispers* (1972) and *Scenes from a Marriage* (1974).

ULSTER, historic province split since 1920 into the three-county Ulster province of IRELAND and six-county Northern Ireland (see IRELAND, NORTHERN).

ULTRAMONTANISM, in Roman Catholicism, the movement to strengthen the authority of the pope and CURIA. It arose in reaction to Gallicanism (the 16th-to 18th-century movement for autonomy of the French church), JANSENISM and liberal tendencies, and finally triumphed at the First VATICAN COUNCIL (1870), which defined papal infallibility and universal jurisdiction. Some of its opponents seceded as OLD CATHOLICS.

ULTRASONICS, science of SOUND waves with frequencies above those that humans can hear (>720kHz). With modern piezoelectric techniques, ultrasonic waves having frequencies above 24kHz can readily be generated with high efficiency and intensity in solids and liquids, and exhibit the normal wave properties of REFLECTION, REFRACTION and DIFFRACTION. They can thus be used as investigative tools or for concentrating large amounts of mechanical energy. Low-power waves are used in thickness gauging and HOLOGRAPHY, high-power waves in surgery and for industrial homogenization, cleaning and machining.

ULTRAVIOLET   RADIATION, ELECTROMAGNETIC RADIATION of wavelength between 0.1nm and 380nm, produced using gas discharge tubes. Although it constitutes 5% of the energy radiated by the sun, most falling on the earth is filtered out by atmospheric OXYGEN and OZONE, thus protecting life on the surface from destruction by the solar ultraviolet light. This also means that air must be excluded from optical apparatus designed for ultraviolet light, similar strong absorption by glass necessitating that lenses and prisms be made of QUARTZ or FLUORITE. Detection is photographic or by using fluorescent screens. The principal use is in fluorescent tubes (see LIGHTING) but important medical applications include germicidal lamps, the treatment of RICKETS and some skin diseases and the VITAMIN-D enrichment of milk and eggs.

ULYSSES, Latin name for ODYSSEUS.

UMBILICAL CORD, long structure linking the developing EMBRYO or FETUS to the PLACENTA through most of PREGNANCY. It consists of BLOOD vessels taking blood to and from the placenta, and a gelatinous matrix. At BIRTH the cord is clamped to prevent blood loss and is used to assist delivery of the placenta. It undergoes ATROPHY and becomes the navel.

UMBRIA, ancient region in the Apennine Mts., central Italy. It is chiefly agricultural, with expanding industry based on hydroelectricity, notably at Terni. The capital is Perugia, center of the medieval Umbrian painters.

UN-AMERICAN ACTIVITIES COMMITTEE, renamed Committee on Internal Security in 1969, US House of Representatives body formed in 1938 to investigate subversive activities in the US. HUAC won notoriety after WWII for its investigation of alleged communist influence in government, unions, education and the film industry. Richard M. NIXON played a key role in its investigations leading to conviction of Alger HISS (1950). Its activities were paralleled in the 1950s by Joseph McCARTHY'S anti-communist witch-hunts.

UNAMUNO, Miguel de (1864–1936), leading Spanish philosopher and writer, rector of Salamanca University from 1900. Influenced by KIERKEGAARD, he explored the faith-reason conflict and man's desire for immortality in *The Tragic Sense of Life* (1913), and in essays and novels such as *Mist* (1914). "The Christ of Velázquez" (1920) is his finest poem. Politically outspoken, he was exiled 1924–30.

UNCERTAINTY PRINCIPLE, or **indeterminacy principle,** a restriction, first enunciated by W. K. HEISENBERG in 1927, on the accuracy with which the position and MOMENTUM of an object can be established simultaneously: the product of the accuracies attainable in each cannot be less than the PLANCK CONSTANT. Relevant only near the atomic level, the principle arises from the wave nature of matter: the wave function (see WAVE MECHANICS) of a particle consists of a superposition of waves with slightly different momenta producing a localized disturbance of which neither the position nor the momentum is precisely defined.

UNCLE REMUS. See HARRIS, JOEL CHANDLER.

UNCLE SAM, popular figure officially adopted as a US national symbol in 1961. He is portrayed as a white-haired and bearded, angular gentleman dressed in the Stars and Stripes. The image was developed by 19th-century cartoonists. The name possibly derives from "Uncle Sam" Wilson, a War of 1812 beef supplier to the US army, from Troy, N.Y.

UNCONSCIOUS, that part of the mind in which events take place of which the individual is unaware; i.e., the part of the mind that is not the CONSCIOUS. Unconscious processes can, however, alter the behavior of the individual (see also DREAMS; INSTINCT). FREUD termed the unconscious the ID. (See also COLLECTIVE UNCONSCIOUS.)

UNDERGROUND RAILROAD, secret network which helped slaves to escape from the US South to the Northern States and Canada before the Civil War. Neither underground nor a railroad, it was named for its necessary secrecy and for the railroad terms used to refer to its operation. Most of the "conductors" were themselves slaves, Harriet TUBMAN being the best known. Abolitionists, notably Quakers such as Levi COFFIN, ran "stations" providing food and shelter along the way. Some 40,000–100,000 slaves escaped this way. (See also ABOLITIONISM.)

UNDSET, Sigrid (1882–1949), Norwegian novelist. For her epic trilogy set in medieval Norway, *Kristin Lavransdatter* (1920–22), she won the 1928 Nobel literature prize. Her contemporary novels dealt with modern woman and Roman Catholicism.

UNDULANT FEVER. See BRUCELLOSIS.

UNEMPLOYMENT, a situation where people who are normally members of the labor force, and are willing and able to work, cannot find employment. Large-scale unemployment can itself pose or exacerbate serious social problems. It can be caused by numerous factors, often beyond the control of the individual worker. Seasonal layoffs occur because certain jobs, for example in agriculture, are not available all year round.

Cyclical unemployment occurs during an economic DEPRESSION or recession, when production declines along with reduced demand. Increased mechanization and automation in industries could in the long run create jobs for a small number of skilled workers, but in the short term usually create unemployment by displacing large numbers of manual or semiskilled workers. Structural unemployment is caused by shifts in a nation's demand pattern. Some declining industries, such as coalmining, may have to lay off workers; without proper retraining, it will be difficult for them to find other jobs, although unemployment compensation is paid to such workers for specific periods of time. Keynesian economists seek to solve the unemployment problem by government intervention, maintaining that increased government spending and expansion of credit can stimulate the economy and thus reduce unemployment (see KEYNESIAN ECONOMICS). But other economists argue that full employment is incompatible with low INFLATION and a stable BALANCE OF PAYMENTS.

UNEMPLOYMENT INSURANCE, a type of SOCIAL SECURITY providing income to people involuntarily unemployed. Most modern industrial nations have programs of this kind, financed by the government, employers, employees, or a combination of these.

In the 1800s some labor unions initiated unemployment benefits for out-of-work members. France introduced a voluntary national scheme in 1905, and Britain the first compulsory insurance program in 1911. In the US the first unemployment insurance law was passed in Wis. in 1932; three years later the Social Security Act established a federal–state program, now administered by the Department of LABOR.

UNGARETTI, Giuseppe (1888–1970), Italian poet. Influenced by the poets of French SYMBOLISM, his evocative verse, in a condensed, purified language, marked a new direction in Italian poetry.

UNIATE CHURCHES, those Eastern churches which accept the pope's authority and Roman Catholic doctrines, but retain their own languages, rites and canon laws, the administration of both bread and wine in COMMUNION, baptism by immersion and marriage of the clergy. An example is the MARONITE church.

UNICORN, mythical creature with the body of a white horse and one straight horn on its forehead. It has appeared in the art and legends of India, China, Islam, and medieval Europe, where it was associated with virginity, and with Christ.

UNIDENTIFIED FLYING OBJECT (UFO). See FLYING SAUCER.

UNIFICATION CHURCH, religious organization of Korean origin that became highly visible in the US in the late 1960s. Based on the ideas of the Reverend Sun Myung Moon, who represents himself as an elect leader and seer, the organization recruits and regiments young people, who dedicate their lives to it in highly disciplined fashion. Accused of "programming" its adherents by brain-washing techniques, the Unification Church was investigated by Congress in 1977 and has been attacked by both parents and business competitors. See MOONIES.

UNIFIED FIELD THEORY, theory which tries to incorporate electromagnetic together with the strong and weak nuclear forces into the general theory of RELATIVITY. If successful, one set of equations would describe these fundamental force fields, including gravity, in terms of the geometry of space-time. Einstein made the first attempt to produce such a theory; he wanted to represent physical reality entirely in terms of fields, yet, in his general theory of relativity, particles still exist as SINGULARITIES— regions where field equations break down.

UNIFORM CODE OF MILITARY JUSTICE, the law governing all members of the US armed forces. It sets out procedures for COURT-MARTIAL and military justice. Enacted in 1950, it unified the codes and laws of the Army, Navy, Air Force and Coast Guard.

UNIFORMITARIANISM, the principle originally opposed to CATASTROPHISM and attributed to J. HUTTON and C. LYELL that the same geologic processes are at work in nature today as have always existed and operated throughout geologic time. Recently, geologists have suggested discarding this concept in favor of *actualism*, the more general concept that the laws of nature have remained invariant through time.

UNION OF SOVIET SOCIALIST REPUBLICS (USSR) or Soviet Union. The largest country in the world, it encompasses

649,412sq mi of the Eurasian land mass.
s maximum W-E extent, E Europe to the
acific, exceeds 6,500mi. It extends
800mi–3,000mi N-S from the Arctic to its
ontiers with Turkey, Iran, Afghanistan,
hina and Mongolia.

This vast country, most of which lies in
he high latitudes N of the 50th parallel, has
population of over 260,000,000, exceeded
nly by China and India. There are more
han 170 ethnic groups, the three chief Slav
roups—Russians, Ukrainians and
elorussians—making up more than 70% of
he population. The Soviet Union comprises
5 federated republics, each of which is
nhabited mainly, but not exclusively, by a
najor ethnic group. The Russian Soviet
ederated Socialist Republic (RSFSR) is
he largest and its capital, Moscow, is also
he capital and largest city of the USSR.
everal republics have subdivisions—
utonomous republics, autonomous oblasts
regions) and national okrugs (districts)—
eflecting minority ethnic groups.

he Land. W of the Yenisey R (about
0°E) are the vast W Siberian and E
European plains, divided by the N-S Ural
Mts (which also divide Asia from Europe).
The W Siberian plain, never above 600ft
nd with large marshy areas, is drained to
he N by the Ob and Irtysh rivers and to the
5 is separated by the Kazakh hills from the
argely arid Aral-Caspian lowlands drained
by the Amu and Syr rivers. The E European
plain is drained N by the Dvina and Pechora
ivers, and S by the Dnieper, Don and Volga
ivers. E of the Yenisey are the Central
Siberian plateau between the Yenisey and
Lena rivers, and the Taimyr region along
he Arctic, including the N Siberian
owland. Mountain regions include the
Caucasus, NE Siberia and the Kamchatka
peninsula (with its active volcanoes) and the
Altai-Sayan region NW of Mongolia.
Russia's highest peaks are in the Pamir
ranges of central Asia near the Afghan-
Tibetan border. More modest mountain
areas are Baikalia, between Lake Baikal
and the Amur R in the SE, and the Amur
maritime region between that river and the
Pacific Ocean.

Climate and Vegetation. Most of the USSR
has a continental climate marked by severe
winters. The Arctic coast is icebound for
most of the year and more than 50% of the
country is snow-covered for about six
months. But summers are usually warm; the
Crimean coast enjoys mild winters and
warm summers. The vegetation zones, N-S,
comprise tundra, *taiga* (forest zone), the
treeless grassland steppes, the semi-desert
and desert zone and the subtropical

vegetation zone bordering the Black Sea.

People. The population is unevenly
distributed: over two-thirds live in the
European plain, with heavy concentrations
around Moscow, Leningrad and Kiev, the
only three cities with more than 2 million
inhabitants. Although there has been some
intermingling, the 170 or more ethnic
groups are mainly territorially distinct. Slav
groups (including Russians, who comprise
55% of USSR population) predominate in
the European USSR, Siberia and the far E
and non-Slav groups in the Caucasus and
Soviet Central Asia. More than 100
languages are spoken along with Russian,
the official and universal language.

Economy. The USSR has a planned
socialist economy in which all resources and
means of production belong to the state. An
industrial superpower second only to the
US, the USSR is self-sufficient in most
minerals and energy resources including
coal (Donets and Kuznetsk basins,
Karaganda and Pechora), oil and natural
gas (Volga-Ural oil field, N Caucasus,
Baku, W Siberia) and iron ore (Krivoi Rog,
Urals, NW Kazakhstan and E Siberia).
Industry is concentrated notably in the
Urals and E Ukraine (iron, steel, heavy
engineering) and manufacturing in cities
like Moscow, Leningrad, Kiev, Kharkov,
Minsk, Riga and Voronezh. Only about
10% of the land can be used for farming.
About 60% of Soviet agricultural output
comes from the 20,800 state farms and
26,500 collective farms. In recent years
disastrously small grain harvests have
necessitated substantial grain imports from
the West (US, Canada, Australia).

History. The SLAVS probably first entered
Russia from the W in the 400s AD. In the
800s Scandinavian conquerors known as
"Russes," led by RURIK, settled in Novgorod
and Kiev, whose ruler, VLADIMIR, was
converted to Christianity c989. After the
12th-century Tatar invasions (see MOGUL
EMPIRE), Moscow rose to preeminence. Its
Grand Prince IVAN IV (the Terrible) was the
first to be crowned tsar (1547). The election
of MICHAEL as tsar (1613) established the
ROMANOV dynasty which ruled until the
Russian Revolution. PETER the Great
founded St. Petersburg (now Leningrad)
and made it imperial capital (1721). His
program of westernization and Russian
expansion continued under CATHERINE the
Great. Russia survived invasion by
Napoleon (1812) but was in decline during
the 19th century (nevertheless the greatest
period of Russian literature). Reforms,
including liberation of the serfs (1861),
failed to check internal unrest which

culminated in the Russian Revolution. The throne was toppled and power seized from the moderates under KERENSKY by the BOLSHEVIKS led by LENIN. After civil war (1918–20) the USSR was proclaimed (1922). The power struggle following Lenin's death (1924) was won by Joseph STALIN, who led Russia to victory in WWII. After his death (1953), leadership eventually passed to Nikita KHRUSHCHEV, who denounced Stalin's tyrannies and inaugurated "peaceful co-existence" with the West. China then broke with the USSR; in the 1960s and 1970s the rift increased. Khrushchev was deposed in 1964 and succeeded by Aleksei KOSYGIN as premier and Leonid BREZHNEV as party leader. Since Kosygin's retirement in 1980, Brezhnev has assumed sole leadership. In June, 1972 the USSR and the US signed the Strategic Arms Limitation Treaty (SALT II). Ratification by the US has been delayed as a protest over the USSR's presence in Afghanistan.

Government and Politics. The Soviet Union is a federation of 15 constituent republics. Each republic elects delegates to the Supreme Soviet, which, according to the Soviet constitution, is "the highest organ of state power in the USSR." It is the main legislative body and appoints the Supreme Court and the Council of Ministers and elects the Presidium. It consists of two chambers, the Soviet of the Union (with one deputy for every 300,000 of population) and the Soviet of Nationalities, which has representatives from all constituent and autonomous republics, autonomous regions and national areas. The Supreme Soviet has only two sessions a year so that between sessions the highest state authority is its Presidium, consisting of 37 members elected from both houses. Its chairman is the president of the USSR, the nominal head of state, but executive power rests in the Council of Ministers. Its chairman is premier of the USSR and its members, including the 15 premiers of the constituent republics are chosen by him with the approval of the Supreme Soviet. Similarly, each republic has its own council of ministers and supreme soviet. The Communist Party of the Soviet Union (CPSU) is the only legal political party and provides all candidates for office whom the voter can only approve or reject. The Soviet constitution guarantees freedom of speech, of the press, of assembly and the right to demonstrate freely, but in practice these rights are reserved for the CPSU. The party comprises a relatively small percentage of the total population, with about 15 million members, and remains an elite organization. An All-Union Party Congress should meet once every four years but often meets less frequently. In theory, the party elects a Central Committee of about 350 members who in turn elect the Politburo and the Party Secretariat, whose first secretary (currently Leonid Brezhnev) is the most powerful man in both the party and the USSR. In practice, power flows downwards from the Party Secretary.

UNIONS, workers' organizations formed to improve pay, working conditions and benefits. There were medieval craft GUILDS in Europe, but modern labor unions arose out of the new concentrations of workers in the INDUSTRIAL REVOLUTION. A craft (horizontal) union organizes workers with a particular skill; an industrial (vertical) union includes all workers in an industry. Employer-controlled company unions are unaffiliated to labor groupings.

Unions negotiate contracts with employers by COLLECTIVE BARGAINING. A CLOSED SHOP or UNION SHOP increases bargaining strength but may be barred by RIGHT-TO-WORK LAWS. A dispute may be referred to ARBITRATION, or members may resort to strikes, slowdowns or featherbedding, PICKETING, BOYCOTT, and, rarely, sit-downs or work-ins.

In the US, local craft unions existed from the late 1700s. The influence of the socialistic KNIGHTS OF LABOR (1869–1917) gave way to that of the craft unions of the American Federation of Labor (founded 1886). In the early 1900s a revolutionary upsurge was expressed through the INDUSTRIAL WORKERS OF THE WORLD, but the Protocol of Peace ending the 1910 strike by the International Ladies' Garment Workers' Union set a pattern for union-management cooperation that accelerated in WWI. The industrial union-based Congress of Industrial Organizations was formed in the 1930s, a time of NEW DEAL legislation to improve industrial relations (see WAGNER ACT). The TAFT-HARTLEY ACT (1947) placed restrictions on unions and the LANDRUM-GRIFFEN ACT (1959) curbed union corruption. In recent years, union organizing has lagged as the US economy has become more service-oriented; the percentage of US workers belonging to unions has declined from nearly 30% in 1964 to less than 25% as of 1980.

The AMERICAN FEDERATION OF LABOR AND CONGRESS OF INDUSTRIAL ORGANIZATIONS merger occurred in 1955. Britain has one Trades Union Congress, but many countries have rival Christian and socialist bodies. Internationally, the Christian World

Confederation of Labor claims 12 million members, the communist-led World Federation of Trade Unions 160 million, and the International Confederation of Free Trade Unions (the 1949 AFL-CIO-backed breakaway from the WFTU) 56 million.

UNION SHOP, industrial situation where all new employees at a workplace must join a particular union. (See also CLOSED SHOP.)

UNITARIANISM, unorthodox Protestant faith that rejects the TRINITY and Christ's deity and asserts the unipersonality of God. It developed out of SOCINIANISM; and many 18th-century English Presbyterians became Unitarian. Joseph PRIESTLEY gave it a great impetus in the US, where liberal, rationalist Unitarianism preaching toleration and universal salvation was developing in CONGREGATIONAL CHURCHES. The American Unitarian Association, led by William CHANNING, was founded in 1825. Theodore PARKER and Ralph Waldo EMERSON were notable Unitarians.

UNITARIAN UNIVERSALIST ASSOCIATION, US Protestant church formed (1961) by merger of the Universalist Church of America and the American Unitarian Association. The Association brings together over 240,000 members from two churches with similar histories and views (see UNITARIANISM; UNIVERSALISM).

UNITAS, John (1933–), US football player, one of the game's great quarterbacks. He joined the Baltimore Colts in 1956 and led them to three championships (1958, 1959 and 1968). He set a record for completed passes and yards gained passing.

Official name: United Arab Emirates
Capital: Abu Dhabi
Area: 32,000sq mi
Population: 1,063,830
Languages: Arabic; English
Religions: Muslim
Monetary unit(s): 1 UAF dirham = 100 fils

UNITED ARAB EMIRATES, formerly Trucial States, oil-rich federation of emirates in the E Arabian Peninsula, on the Persian Gulf and Gulf of Oman. It comprises Abu Dhabi, Ajman, Dubai, Fujairah, Ras al-Khaimah, Sharjah and Umm al-Qaiwain. From 1820 truces linked the sheikhs with Britain. The independent federation was formed in 1971, neighboring BAHRAIN and QATAR opting for separate statehood.

Land and People. The country has a 400mi coastline and is mostly desert, with oases. In the E mountains rise to over 8,000ft, giving way to a fertile littoral strip where dates, grains and tobacco are cultivated. Herding, fishing and pearling are traditional occupations and Dubai has long been a center of Middle East trade. Most of the people are Sunnite Muslim Arabs and are farmers or nomads. The population has recently increased rapidly; there are Iranian, Black, Indian, Pakistani and European minorities, who now outnumber the indigenous population.

In 1958 oil was discovered in Abu Dhabi, the largest state. Its per capita income is now one of the world's highest, and its output is among the highest of members of the ORGANIZATION OF PETROLEUM EXPORTING COUNTRIES. Duhai and Sharjah are the other significant oil exporters.

UNITED ARAB REPUBLIC, union of Egypt and Syria proclaimed in 1958, as a step toward pan-Arab union. Cairo was capital, and NASSER president. The UAR formed with Yemen the nominal United Arab States (1958–61). Resenting Egyptian dominance, Syria seceded in 1961. A 1963 attempt to unite Egypt, Syria and Iraq failed. Egypt was named the UAR until 1971, when a loose Federation of Arab Republics (Egypt, Syria and Libya) was formed.

UNITED AUTOMOBILE WORKERS (United Automobile, Aerospace and Agricultural Implement Workers of America), the second largest US industrial labor union, with local unions in Canada. Founded in 1935, it won recognition at General Motors, Chrysler and Ford (1937–41). Its 1,500,000 members are in automobile, space, aviation and metal industries. The UAW cofounded the CIO, but left the AFL-CIO in 1968. Walter REUTHER was president 1946–70, and Leonard WOODCOCK served 1970–77. UAW headquarters are in Detroit.

UNITED CHURCH OF CANADA, Canadian Protestant church formed 1925 by union of the Methodist and most Presbyterian and Congregationalist churches. Ecumenical, national and missionary, it has a PRESBYTERIAN form of organization, stresses the rights of congregations, and has men and women ministers. It was joined in 1968 by Canada's Evangelical United Brethren Church and has over a million adult communicants.

UNITED CHURCH OF CHRIST, a US Protestant body set up by the 1957 union (with its 1961 constitution) of the Congregational Christian Churches and the Evangelical and Reformed Church. It gives strong local autonomy combined with national services and organization, and has over 2,000,000 members.

UNITED EMPIRE LOYALISTS, people of the original 13 colonies who remained loyal to Britain during the American Revolution and emigrated to Canada. The largest group, some 50,000, left New York City in 1783, and established New Brunswick (1784) and Upper Canada (now Ontario; 1791).

Official name: United Kingdom of Great Britain and Northern Ireland
Capital: London
Area: 94,217sq mi
Population: 55,950,000
Languages: English; Welsh, Gaelic
Religions: Church of England, Roman Catholic, Church of Scotland
Monetary unit(s): 1 Pound = 100 pence

UNITED KINGDOM, or the United Kingdom of Great Britain and Northern Ireland, a constitutional monarchy of NW Europe occupying the whole of the British Isles except the Republic of Ireland. The United Kingdom (UK) thus comprises the island of Great Britain (England, Scotland, and Wales) and Northern Ireland. The Isle of Man and the Channel Islands are both Crown dependencies and are not strictly part of the UK.

Land. England, largest country in the UK, has a hilly backbone—the Pennines—running N from Derbyshire to the Scottish border. This extends from the Solway Firth to Berwick-upon-Tweed. W of the N Pennines (Cross Fell, 2,930ft), is the scenic Lake District, set amid the Cumbrian Mts, and containing England's highest point (Scafell Pike, 3,210ft) and largest lake (Windermere, 5.69sq mi). Lowlands, sometimes with low hills, stretch across the rest of England. Among them are the fertile Fens bordering on the Wash and, SE of the

Chiltern Hills, the London basin with the Thames R.

Scotland has rolling southern uplands, and fertile central lowlands deeply penetrated by the firths (estuaries) of the Clyde R (leading to Glasgow) and the Forth R (leading past Edinburgh, the capital city). The Tay (118mi) is Scotland's longest river. N of the Ochil hills are the rugged Scottish Highlands. Ben Nevis (4,406ft), in the Grampian Mts, is the highest peak in the British Isles. SE of Glen More (the Great Glen) and its chain of lochs, are the Cairngorm Mts (Ben Macdhui, 4,296ft). Scotland's many islands include the Inner and Outer Hebrides to the NW and the Orkney and Shetland groups to the N.

Wales centers on the Cambrian Mts (Snowdon 3,560ft). The many rivers flowing from the Welsh massif include the Severn (220mi), the UK's longest river.

Northern Ireland is often called Ulster because it occupies most of that ancient province. Lough Neagh (153sq mi) is the largest lake in the British Isles. To the SE are the granite Mourne Mts (Slieve Donard, 2,796ft). The Erne R drains the SW.

Climate. Britain enjoys a mainly mild climate with changeable weather. The warm N Atlantic Drift and prevailing westerly winds are major influences. Rainfall, heaviest in the W and mountains, averages 40in yearly. Winter temperatures average 40°F, summer averages ranging from 54°F in the far N, to 61°F in the usually warmer S.

People. With an estimated population of about 56 million, the UK is one of the world's most densely populated countries. More than five sixths of the people live in England. Most British are urban-dwelling, with London, the nation's capital, the largest of some eight major conurbations.

As a result of immigration the UK now has a multiracial society. Immigrants from India, Pakistan, the West Indies and other Commonwealth countries number at least 1,500,000.

Government. MAGNA CARTA and the English CIVIL WAR checked the power of the monarch. Cabinet government and parliamentary democracy developed during the 18th and 19th centuries. Today the supreme legislative body is Parliament, comprising the House of Commons, whose 635 members are elected for a five-year term by all citizens over 18, and the House of Lords with about 1,170 members. The government is conducted by a prime minister and cabinet, normally provided by the majority party in the Commons from among its members of Parliament.

Culture and Beliefs. Education is free and compulsory from 5 to 16. English is the universal language, but Welsh is widely spoken in Wales, and Gaelic survives in parts of Scotland. There are two established churches, the CHURCH OF ENGLAND and CHURCH OF SCOTLAND. The many other religious groups include Roman Catholics, Methodists, Baptists, Unitarians, Congregationalists, Quakers, Jews and Muslims.

Economy. Scene of the world's first industrial revolution in the 18th century, the UK based its economic development on its coal and iron deposits. Recently North Sea oil and natural gas have been exploited. Industrial raw materials and food, however, often have to be imported. (British farms, though efficient, provide only half of the nation's food.) To pay for imports the UK exports manufactured goods and provides services like banking, insurance and shipping. Major industries include iron and steel, engineering, textiles, chemicals and shipbuilding. Most industries are privately owned, but some of the most important, like coalmining, iron and steel, electric power, railroads and the chief airlines, are wholly or partly owned by the state. Since WWII the UK has failed to keep pace in economic growth with other W European countries. Membership in the EEC (1973) did not solve her chronic balance of payments difficulties and in 1976 the problem of inflation was exacerbated by a severe drought.

History. After the Roman occupation (c100–400 AD) England was invaded by Angles, Saxons, Jutes and Danes. The Norman conquest (1066) introduced the feudal system and the first centralization of power. Wales, conquered in 1282, was legally joined to England in 1536. Scotland was united with England under the monarchy of James VI and I (1603) and then by Act of Union (1707). Northern Ireland remained part of the UK after the S became independent (1922).

Maritime expansion began under Elizabeth I (1558–1603) and reached its height in the 1700s and 1800s, building up the 19th-century British Empire. British power was greatly weakened by both world wars, and with successive grants of independence from 1945, the empire was transformed into the Commonwealth of Nations. Remaining colonies include the Falkland Islands (claimed by Argentina), Gibraltar (claimed by Spain) and Hong Kong.

UNITED MINEWORKERS OF AMER- ICA (UMW), US industrial union formed in 1890. Under John L. LEWIS (president 1920–60), it took militant stands on pay, safety, and political questions. A cofounder of the CIO in 1935 (now unaffiliated), it had 308,000 members in 1979. Ex-president Tony Boyle was convicted (1974) of murdering his left-wing rival Joseph Yablonski.

UNITED NATIONS, international organization of the world's states which aims to promote peace and international cooperation. Successor to the LEAGUE OF NATIONS, it was founded at the 1945 SAN FRANCISCO CONFERENCE prepared by the "Big Three" Allied Powers of WWII; 51 states signed the charter. Membership had grown to 117 in 1955, and to 155 by 1981. The headquarters are in New York.

The UN has six major organs. The *General Assembly,* composed of delegates from all member states, meets once a year and provides a general forum, but has little power of action. The *Security Council* has five permanent members each with a veto (China, France, Great Britain, the US and the USSR) and ten elected members. Intended to be a permanent peacekeeping body with emergency executive powers, it has often been hamstrung by the Soviet veto. The *Economic and Social Council,* with 27 elected members, deals with "nonpolitical" matters, coordinating the work of the specialist agencies and operating important commissions of its own, such as those on children, refugees and human rights. The *Trusteeship Council* is responsible for UN TRUST TERRITORIES. The INTERNATIONAL COURT OF JUSTICE is the UN's principal organ for INTERNATIONAL LAW. The *Secretariat* is the administrative body headed by the Secretary General, who is an important figure with considerable executive power and political influence (SEE LIE, TRYGVE; HAMMARSKJÖLD, DAG; THANT, U; WALDHEIM, KURT).

Other organs are the UNITED NATIONS CONFERENCE ON TRADE AND DEVELOPMENT, the Office of the UNITED NATIONS HIGH COMMISSIONER FOR REFUGEES, and the UNITED NATIONS CHILDREN'S FUND.

Major specialized agencies affiliated with the UN include the FOOD AND AGRICULTURE ORGANIZATION, GENERAL AGREEMENT ON TARIFFS AND TRADE, INTERNATIONAL ATOMIC ENERGY AGENCY (UN-sponsored), INTERNATIONAL CIVIL AVIATION ORGANIZATION, INTERNATIONAL LABOR ORGANIZATION, INTERNATIONAL MONETARY FUND, INTERNATIONAL TELECOMMUNICATION UNION, UNITED NATIONS EDUCATIONAL, SCIENTIFIC AND

CULTURAL ORGANIZATION, UNIVERSAL POSTAL UNION, WORLD BANK, WORLD HEALTH ORGANIZATION, and WORLD METEOROLOGICAL ORGANIZATION.

UNITED NATIONS CHILDREN'S FUND (UNICEF), UN organization formed 1946 as the UN International Children's Emergency Fund to help in countries devastated in WWII. It became a permanent body in 1953, retaining the UNICEF acronym and specializing in child welfare, family planning and nutrition programs in disaster areas and in many poorer countries. It is financed voluntarily. In 1965 UNICEF was awarded the Nobel Peace Prize.

UNITED NATIONS EDUCATIONAL, SCIENTIFIC AND CULTURAL ORGANIZATION (UNESCO), a UN agency established 1946 to promote international collaboration through science, education and cultural activities, thus advancing the human rights and freedoms laid down in the UN charter. Its policy-making general conference meets biennially at the Paris headquarters. UNESCO has helped develop education in poorer countries and arranges scientific and cultural exchanges.

UNITED NATIONS HIGH COMMISSIONER FOR REFUGEES, Office of the, UN agency, the 1951 successor to the International Refugee Organization. It has cared for refugees from many countries, and supports their right to be free from arbitrary expulsion, to work and be educated in their new homes. It received in 1954 the Nobel Peace Prize, and again in 1981 it won the award for its humane work in helping displaced people. The separate UN Relief and Works Agency for Palestine Refugees (established 1949) is based in Beirut.

UNITED NATIONS RELIEF AND REHABILITATION ADMINISTRATION (UNRRA), body set up (1943) by WWII Allied Powers to help newly liberated regions. It provided emergency supplies and refugee camps and repatriated 7,000,000 refugees, mainly in China and E and S Europe. Its successors were the International Refugee Organization (1946–52) and the Office of the UNITED NATIONS HIGH COMMISSIONER FOR REFUGEES.

UNITED PRESBYTERIAN CHURCH IN THE USA, created in 1958 through merger of the Presbyterian Church in the USA and the United Presbyterian Church of North America. It is the largest Presbyterian body in the US, representing over 9,000 churches with more than 3,000,000 members. It has many overseas missionaries and is concerned with Christian social action. (See PRESBYTERIANISM; REFORMED CHURCHES.)

UNITED PRESS INTERNATIONAL (UPI), world's largest independent news agency, created by the 1958 merger of United Press (formed by Edward W. SCRIPPS) and William R. HEARST'S International News Service. At its height in the 1950s, it had some 200 bureaus (half in the US) sending news and pictures to over 5,000 clients.

UNITED SERVICE ORGANIZATIONS (USO), independent, nonprofit grouping of organizations formed 1941 to provide recreational, entertainment, religious and social facilities for the US armed forces. It is recognized by the US Department of Defense. Affiliates include the YMCA, YWCA and Salvation Army.

UNITED STATES CONSTITUTION, the supreme law of the nation. Written in Philadelphia in the summer of 1787, the Constitution was approved by the 55 delegates representing the 13 original states and went into effect on March 4, 1789, after ratification by the required nine states. The document was the sum of the young nation's experience to that point. The actions of the virtually autonomous states and the failure of the country's first constitution, the ARTICLES OF CONFEDERATION, convinced the Founding Fathers that a strong executive and a powerful federal government were needed if the US were to survive as a cohesive entity. Many compromises were necessary before final agreement was reached. The conflicting desires of large and small states resulted in a bicameral legislature, one house based on population size, the other house with an equal number of seats for each state (see CONGRESS). North and South compromised on including slaves in population totals. Most important, though, was the eventual, if begrudging, recognition by all states that a strong central government would be needed if the US was to be more than just a loose confederation. The states allayed their fears by constructing a SEPARATION OF POWERS to limit governmental power (see STATES' RIGHTS; EXECUTIVE; JUDICIARY; LEGISLATURE). A BILL OF RIGHTS to guarantee personal freedoms was also added as the first ten amendments to the Constitution. The document has proven adaptable and flexible; its timelessness is indicated by the addition of only 16 amendments since 1791. (See also PRESIDENCY, US; ELECTORAL COLLEGE; CONSTITUTIONAL LAW.)

UNITED STATES OF AMERICA (USA or US), world's fourth-largest country after the USSR, Canada and China. The 48 conterminous states span North America from coast to coast. With Alaska, separated from them by Canada, they form the continental US. The 50th state is Hawaii. The federal capital is Washington, D.C. (District of Columbia). Overseas territories include Puerto Rico, the American Virgin Islands, Guam, American Samoa and BELAU, MARSHALL ISLANDS, Federated States of MICRONESIA, and NORTHERN MARIANAS, formerly in the Trust Territory of the Pacific Islands. Other dependencies include Johnson, Midway, Wake and other Pacific islands.

Land. The conterminous US can be divided into six natural regions: the *Atlantic and Gulf Coastal Lowlands* stretching S from Long Island to Florida and then W to Mexico, averaging 200mi wide, with many lagoons and sandbars and, on the Gulf Coast, the Mississippi R delta; the *Appalachians*, running NE-SW from Nova Scotia (Canada), a low mountain system that includes the White Mts of N.H. (Mt Washington, 6,288ft), the Great Smoky Mts (Clingmans Dome, 6,643ft), the Black Mts of N.C. (Mt Mitchell, 6,684ft) and, to the W, the ridge and valley belt and the Allegheny Plateau; the *Central* or *Interior Plains*, stretching W to the Rocky Mts, a region drained chiefly by the Mississippi-Missouri river system and its branches and containing various uplands such as the Black Hills of Dakota, and the Ozarks; the *Rocky Mts*, with peaks exceeding 14,000ft, glacial features and many national parks; the *Western Plateau and Basin* or *Intermontane Region*, separated from the Pacific coastlands by the Cascade and Sierra Nevada ranges and containing such features as the Grand Canyon and the Great Salt Lake; and the *Pacific Coastlands*, extending S from Puget Sound

Official name: United States of America
Capital: Washington, D.C.
Area: 3,536,855sq mi
Population: 226,504,825
Languages: English
Religions: Protestant, Roman Catholic, Jewish
Monetary unit(s): 1 US Dollar = 100 cents

to the long Central Valley of California.

Climate is greatly influenced by the geographic position of the conterminous US between large oceans on the E and W, with a warm and shallow sea to the S and the Canadian landmass to the N. The W winds from the Pacific bring heavy rainfall to the NW coast in winter and the fall, but rainfall decreases rapidly immediately E of the western mountains before increasing again along the Atlantic and Gulf coasts. Winter temperatures vary greatly, being relatively high along the sheltered Pacific coast, but often extremely low in the interior and the E. Snowfall can be heavy in the N. Summer temperatures are mainly high, averaging over 75°F in most areas. The SE becomes subtropical and humid. Tornadoes can occur in spring, especially in the Mississippi valley, and summer thunderstorms and hurricanes are frequent along the S Gulf and Atlantic coasts.

Vegetation. The natural vegetation ranges from the mixed forests of the Appalachians to the grasslands of the Great Plains, and from the conifers of the Rocky Mts and NW states to the splendid redwoods of California, the cacti and mesquite of the SW deserts, and the tropical palms and mangroves of the Gulf.

People. The US is the world's fourth-largest nation by population after China, India and the USSR. Until 1840 immigrants came mostly from England and Scotland, but thereafter increasingly from other, mainly European, lands including Ireland, Germany, Scandinavia and, from the 1860s, Italy and the Slavic countries. Since 1820 more than 46 million immigrants are estimated to have been admitted, but since 1921, a quota system has been in force, annual admissions since 1968 being limited to 120,000 from the W Hemisphere and 170,000 from the E. Under the Refugee Act of 1980 an average of 50,000 political refugees can be received each year. The first Negroes came as slaves (from 1619). Today there are some 26 million black Americans, of whom the majority still live in the South and in large cities like Washington, D.C., New York and Chicago. Indians, the original inhabitants, are found in all states, with major concentrations in the Great Plains and the West. Other significant national groups include Spanish-Americans (Mexicans and Puerto Ricans), Chinese and Japanese. About 75% of Americans are urban-dwelling and about 16% of the total population live in the highly urbanized Boston to Washington, D.C. stretch of the Atlantic coastal belt which contains the most densely populated states, New Jersey and Rhode Island. During the 1960s California overtook New York to become the most populous state in the Union. The US has many religious groups, the strongest being the Protestants (73,700,000, chiefly Baptists, Methodists, Lutherans and Presbyterians) and Roman Catholics (49,800,000). There is a nationwide system of public education and only 2% of the population is illiterate.

Economy. In 1980 the Gross National Product of the US was $2,629 billion, almost four times that of the USSR, its nearest rival as the world's leading economic nation. The American economy is predominantly free-enterprise. The US can grow nearly all temperate and subtropical crops and is self-sufficient in essential foods. About half the land surface is occupied by farms, with dairying important in the N and NE, livestock and feed grains in the Midwest (the Corn Belt), wheat on the plains, livestock on the High Plains and the intermontane areas of the W, and also in the S (along with dairying and various crops). Texas, the rest of the S, and California lead in cotton and there are various specialty crops like fruit, rice, citrus fruits and sugarcane in the S. There are valuable forests and fisheries. The rich mineral resources include coal (Appalachians, Indiana-Illinois, Alabama), iron ore (near Lake Superior), petroleum and natural gas (Texas, Louisiana, the Great Plains and Alaska) and other vital minerals. But reserves of some minerals are declining and the US has increasingly become an importer of ores and oil. Major products include steel (Pittsburgh, Chicago-Gary and elsewhere), automobiles (Detroit), aircraft and aerospace products (the West and on the Great Plains), electric and electronic equipment (New England and increasingly the Sun Belt states), textiles (North and South Carolina, Georgia) and most kinds of consumer goods. Some consumer goods industries, like tobacco and meat-packing, are located near their raw materials; others are widely scattered to meet their markets.

History. For an account of the original inhabitants of America and their dispossession, see INDIANS; INDIAN WARS. The first permanent European settlement was Spanish (St. Augustine, Florida, 1565). Early English settlements were in Virginia (Jamestown, 1607), Massachusetts (Plymouth, 1620), Maryland (1634), Connecticut (1636) and Pennsylvania (1681). From these and from French, Dutch and Swedish settlements came the original 13 colonies. Later opposition to

Britain's colonial policy led to the REVOLUTIONARY WAR (1775–83) and independence as a federal republic with George WASHINGTON as first President (1789). Expansion westward followed. The area of the US was doubled by the LOUISIANA PURCHASE (1803) and later Florida was purchased from Spain (1819). The WAR OF 1812 with Britain ended US prospects of conquering Canada. Texas was annexed in 1845 and other territories gained by the Treaty of Guadalupe Hidalgo ending the MEXICAN WAR (1848). The GADSDEN PURCHASE (1853) brought southern New Mexico and southern Arizona into the Union, and Alaska was purchased from Russia in 1867. Rivalry between North and South culminated in the CIVIL WAR (1861–65). There followed a period of RECONSTRUCTION (1865–77) and rapid development during which the first transcontinental railroad was completed (1869). Hawaii was annexed in 1898, and other overseas territories came under US rule as a result of the SPANISH-AMERICAN WAR. The US entered WORLD WAR I in 1917, but the prosperity which followed the war was ended by the GREAT DEPRESSION of the 1930s. Franklin D. ROOSEVELT'S NEW DEAL was an innovative program to halt this economic decline. The Japanese attack on PEARL HARBOR (1941) brought the US into WORLD WAR II. The nation emerged from that war as leader of the West and a "superpower" engaged in worldwide rivalry with the communist bloc (see COLD WAR), which led to its participation in the KOREAN WAR (1950–53) and the VIETNAM WAR (1961–73). At the start of the 1980s the US was beset with nagging "stagflation" (recession combined with high rates of unemployment and inflation), government deficits, cutbacks in government services, rising crime rates and ethnic and class bitterness. A Republican sweep in the 1980 elections represented a taxpayers' revolt against the social programs undertaken in the 1960s. Nevertheless, the US remains economically immensely powerful and a major force in world affairs.

UNITED STEELWORKERS OF AMERICA, third largest US union with 1,286,000 members. Superseding the Amalgamated Association of Iron, Steel and Tin Workers, the CIO's Steel Workers' Organizing Committee, recognized by the US Steel Corporation in 1937, took its present name in 1942.

UNITED WAY OF AMERICA (UWA), US organization which raises funds for health, recreation and welfare agencies, founded 1918. Over 200 major national organizations have been helped by the United Way's funds. It has 2,322 local chapters.

UNIVERSAL, philosophical term referring to any possible attribute of more than one particular. Redness, for example, is the universal common to all red things. The question arises whether the general term naming a universal refers to an entity that exists independently of thought or is merely a principle of classification. (See also IDEALISM; REALISM; CONCEPTUALISM; NOMINALISM.)

UNIVERSALISM, heretical Christian doctrine that everyone will ultimately be saved (see SALVATION). HELL is denied. The Universalist Church in the US was formed by Hosea BALLOU and other New England nonconformists. Liberal and syncretist, in 1961 it joined the Unitarians to form the UNITARIAN UNIVERSALIST ASSOCIATION.

UNIVERSAL POSTAL UNION (UPU), a UN agency (since 1947) that determines procedures for the reciprocal flow of foreign mail. Its operations are based on the first (1875) Universal Postal Convention. The Universal Postal Congress meets every five years. Headquarters are in Bern, Switzerland. (See also POSTAL SERVICES.)

UNKNOWN SOLDIER, in the US and some European countries after WWI, the unidentified body of a soldier killed in action, whose tomb is a national symbol honoring those killed in the war. The first US Unknown Soldier was buried in ARLINGTON NATIONAL CEMETRY, Va., on Nov. 11, 1921.

UNSER, Bobby (1934–   ) and **Al** (1939–   ), US race car drivers. Racing from the mid-1960s, the brothers had each won the Indianapolis 500 three times by 1981 and had also each been national champions.

UNTERMEYER, Louis (1885–1977), US poet and anthologist known particularly for his parodies and for popular anthologies such as *Modern American Poetry* (1919, frequently revised).

UPANISHADS, ancient Hindu scriptures (c1000 BC–600 BC) attached to the latter half of each VEDA and containing secret or mystical doctrine. They are of lesser authority than the *Aranyakas* and *Brahmanas* (expository texts), being intended more for the philosophical inquirer.

UPDIKE, John Hoyer (1932–   ), US novelist, short-story writer, poet and critic. With precise craftsmanship, he dissects contemporary life in such novels as *Rabbit, Run* (1960), *The Centaur* (1963), *Couples* (1968), *Bech: A Book* (1970), *Rabbit Redux* (1971), *The Coup* (1978) and *Rabbit Is Rich* (1981) and short-story collections like *The Music School* (1966).

UPJOHN, Richard (1802–1878), British-born US architect, famous for his Gothic Revival churches, such as Trinity Church, New York City (1846). He was president of the American Institute of Architects 1857–76.

Official name: Republic of Upper Volta
Capital: Ouagadougou
Area: 105,838sq mi
Population: 6,814,000
Languages: French; Mossi spoken
Religions: Animist; Muslim; Christian
Monetary unit(s): 1 CFA franc=100 centimes

UPPER VOLTA, a landlocked West African republic, N of Ghana and S of Mali.

Land. The country is a dry plateau drained by the upper streams of the Volta R. Rainfall averages 10–45in yearly, but is not retained by the thin soil, which supports little more than poor savanna; the N and NE is semidesert (see SAHEL). Temperatures range between 68°F and 95°F. The wet season lasts from June to October.

People. The largest ethnic group is the Voltaic Mossi (48%); other Voltaic groups are the Bobo, Lobi and Gurunsi. There are also Mande and Senufo groups, and Fulani and Tuareg nomads. The population is 95% rural and concentrated in the S and E. The illiteracy rate is about 90%.

Economy. Upper Volta is among the poorest countries in the world, possessing few natural resources. Subsistence agriculture supports about 95% of the population. Principal exports are cotton, karite nuts and oil, live animals and peanuts. Landlocked, it relies on rail connections to the port of Abidjan in the Ivory Coast for imports and exports. As many as 1.5 million workers are employed outside the country, primarily in the Ivory Coast and Ghana. Their remittances home provide important revenues.

History. Part of the powerful Mossi empire since c1000 AD, the region of Upper Volta was annexed by the French in 1896 and became a full French colony in 1919. It became independent in 1960. The military seized power in 1966 and gave way to a democratic civilian government in 1978.

URAL-ALTAIC LANGUAGES, collective term for the Uralic language family and the ALTAIC LANGUAGES. The 20 or so languages of the Uralic family (best known being Finnish and Hungarian) are in two branches, the UGRO-FINNIC LANGUAGES and the relatively unimportant Samoyedic languages.

URAL MOUNTAINS, 1,250mi-long mountain system in W USSR. Running N–S from the Kara Sea into Kazakhstan N of the Aral Sea, they are the traditional boundary between Europe and Asia. Mt Narodnaya (6,214ft), in the N section, is the highest peak. The Urals are heavily forested and rich in minerals.

URANIUM (U), soft, silvery-white radioactive metal in the ACTINIDE series; the heaviest natural element. Uranium occurs widely as PITCHBLENDE (uranite), CARNOTITE and other ores, which are concentrated and converted to uranium (IV) fluoride, from which uranium is isolated by electrolysis or reduction with calcium or magnesium. The metal is reactive and electropositive, reacting with hot water and dissolving in acids. Its chief oxidation states are $+4$ and $+6$ and the uranyl (UO_2^{2+}) compounds are common. Uranium has three naturally-occurring ISOTOPES: U^{238} (HALF-LIFE 4.5×10^9yr) U^{235} (half-life 7.1×10^8yr) and U^{234} (half-life 2.5×10^5yr). More than 99% of natural uranium is U^{238}. The isotopes may be separated by fractional DIFFUSION of the volatile uranium (VI) fluoride. Neutron capture by U^{235} leads to nuclear FISSION, and a chain reaction can occur which is the basis of NUCLEAR REACTORS and of the ATOMIC BOMB. U^{238} also absorbs neutrons and is converted to an isotope of PLUTONIUM (Pu^{239}) which (like U^{235}) can be used as a nuclear fuel. Uranium is the starting material for the synthesis of the TRANSURANIUM ELEMENTS. Some of its compounds are used to color ceramics. AW 238.0, mp 1132°C, bp 3818°C, sg 19.05 (α).

URANUS, the third largest planet in the SOLAR system and the seventh from the sun. Physically very similar to NEPTUNE, but rather larger (53 mm ± 5% equatorial radius), it orbits the sun every 84.02 years at a mean distance of 19.2AU, rotating in 10.75h. The plane of its equator is tilted 98° to the plane of its orbit, such that the rotation of the planet and the revolution of its five known moons, which orbit closely parallel to the equator, are retrograde (see RETROGRADE MOTION). In 1977 the planet was discovered to have five rings, like those of SATURN but much fainter.

URBAN LEAGUE, National, philanthropic US interracial agency founded in 1910 to end segregation and promote the economic and social welfare of disadvantaged groups. It has been particularly effective in the area of equal job opportunities, and pursues programs in such fields as housing, education, health and welfare.

URBAN RENEWAL, name applied to city programs designed to eliminate slums and replace them with improved housing and amenities. See CITY PLANNING; HOUSING AND URBAN DEVELOPMENT, US DEPARTMENT OF; MODEL CITIES.

URDU, Indic language of the Indo-European family, a form of HINDUSTANI (see also HINDI). It has borrowed heavily from Arabic and Persian. Spoken by some 20 million people, it is an official language of India and Pakistan.

UREMIA, the syndrome of symptoms and biochemical disorders seen in KIDNEY failure, associated with a rise in blood UREA and other nitrogenous waste products of PROTEIN metabolism. Nausea, VOMITING, malaise, itching, pigmentation, ANEMIA and acute disorders of fluid and mineral balance are common presentations, but the manifestations depend on the type of disease, rate of waste buildup, etc. DIETARY FOODS may reduce uremic symptoms in chronic renal failure but dialysis or TRANSPLANTATION may be needed.

UREY, Harold Clayton (1893–1981), US chemist awarded the 1935 Nobel Prize for Chemistry for his discovery of DEUTERIUM, an isotope of HYDROGEN having one proton and one neutron in its nucleus, and who played a major role in the MANHATTAN PROJECT. He was also important as a cosmologist: his researches into geological dating using OXYGEN ISOTOPES enabled him to produce a model of the atmosphere of the primordial planet earth; and hence to formulate a theory of the planets having originated as a gaseous disk about the sun (see SOLAR SYSTEM). He was a leading theorist about the origin of the MOON.

URINE, waste product comprising a dilute solution of excess salts and unwanted nitrogenous material, such as UREA and deaminated PROTEIN, excreted by many animals. The wastes are filtered from the BLOOD in the KIDNEYS or equivalent structures and stored in the BLADDER till excreted. The passage of urine serves not only to eliminate wastes, but also provides a mechanism for maintaining the water and salt concentrations and pH of the blood. While all MAMMALS excrete their nitrogenous wastes in urine, other groups—birds, insects and fishes—excrete them as AMMONIA or in solid crystals as URIC ACID.

URIS, Leon (1924–   ), US popular novelist best known for *Exodus* (1957), about the history of modern Israel. His other bestselling novels include *QB VII* (1970) and *Trinity* (1976).

Official name: Oriental Republic of Uruguay
Capital: Montevideo
Area: 63,037sq mi
Population: 2,788,400
Languages: Spanish
Religions: Roman Catholic
Monetary unit(s): 1 new Uruguayan peso=10 centesimos

URUGUAY, the smallest republic in South America, bordered by Argentina (W), Brazil (N and E), the Atlantic and the Río de la Plata in the S.

Land. A narrow coastal strip rises to low ridges (highest point 1,644ft), grassland plains and wooded valleys. The climate is temperate and rainfall (average 35in) is spread throughout the year. The Uruguay and Negro are the chief rivers.

People. The people are mostly of Spanish and Italian descent, and over 80% urban. About two-fifths of the population live in Montevideo. There are some 300,000 MESTIZOS, mainly in the N.

Economy. The economy is based on cattle and sheep; meat, wool and hides provide 80% of the country's exports. Wheat, oats, flax, oilseeds, grapes, fruit and sugarbeet are grown. Meat-packing and tanning are the chief industries, and textiles, chemicals, plastics, electrical and other goods are manufactured. There are important fisheries, but few mineral resources.

History. The region was visited (1516) and settled (1624) by the Spanish, who resisted Portuguese incursions and founded Montevideo in 1726. José ARTIGAS led the independence movement 1810–20, and

Uruguay became independent in 1828. In the early 20th century, the government under Jose Batlley Ordóñez introduced economic and social reforms and Uruguay subsequently became one of the most developed Latin American countries. Labor unrest and leftist Tupamaro guerrilla activities in the late 1960s led to a military takeover in 1973. Repression in the following years was widespread but abated somewhat in 1979. The military promised a return to civilian rule in the 1980s.

USO. See UNITED SERVICE ORGANIZATIONS.

USTINOV, Peter Alexander (1921–   ), English actor and playwright, also a famous raconteur and mimic. He has appeared in many movies and has often acted in his own plays, *Romanoff and Juliet* (1956) being probably the best-known.

USURY, charging an exorbitant rate of INTEREST, usually to persons in financial distress; more strictly, the charging of interest at a higher rate than legally allowed. Before the Middle Ages, the charging of *any* interest was called usury and condemned by the Church, so that rich non-Christians, especially Jews, were forced by the nobility to become moneylenders.

Name of state: Utah
Capital: Salt Lake City
Statehood: Jan. 4, 1896 (45th state)
Familiar name: Beehive State
Area: 84,916sq mi
Population: 1,461,037
Elevation: Highest—13,498ft., Kings Peak
Lowest—2,000ft, Beaverdam Creek
Motto: Industry
State flower: Sego lily
State bird: Seagull
State tree: Blue spruce
State song: "Utah, We Love Thee"

UTAH, a state in the W US, bordered on the N by Ida. and Wyo., on the E by Col., S by Ariz., and W by Nev.
Land. Utah falls into three regions: the ROCKY MOUNTAINS in the NE, the COLORADO PLATEAU in the S and E and the GREAT BASIN in the W. The NW is dominated by the GREAT SALT LAKE and desert. The Colorado

R and its tributary the Green R drain much of the E half. Average temperatures vary from 84°F in July in the SW to 20°F in January in the NE. Much of Utah is semiarid; annual rainfall varies from less than 5in to 50in (in the Wasatch Mts).

People. Over two-thirds of the population are MORMONS, whose headquarters are at Salt Lake City. Roman Catholics constitute the second-largest denomination. The population is 98% white; Indians number about 19,256. Salt Lake City, the state capital, is by far the largest city, followed by Ogden and Provo.

Economy. Since WWII manufacturing and mining have overtaken farming as the mainstays of the state economy. Large industries produce primary metals, transportation equipment, missiles and aerospace components, and foodstuffs including beet sugar, dairy products, flour and meat. Utah possesses large deposits of copper, oil, bituminous coal, uranium, iron and other metals. Extensive irrigation projects have opened up new farm land. The principal crops are hay, wheat, barley and sugar beet. Livestock-raising (cattle, sheep and poultry) is also important. Tourism is a fast-expanding industry.

History. Visited by Spanish missionaries in 1776 and later exploited by traders, Utah was first settled by the persecuted Mormons in 1847. It became part of the US in 1848, but did not become a state until 1896, after decades of strife with the federal government and warfare with the UTE INDIANS (for whom the state is named). The original 1895 constitution has remained in force. Since WWII, Utah has enjoyed a long period of prosperity. Significant reserves of oil, natural gas, and uranium were discovered, starting in 1948, and irrigation for agriculture was improved by the large Central Utah Project, undertaken in 1967. The state's population increased 38% during the 1970s, but it remains remarkably homogeneous and virtually all white, with the result that Utah lacks the ethnic tensions common in other states. Much attention has been given in recent years to controlling development of Utah's natural resources, and environmentalists— as well as leaders of the Mormon church, who had come out against the proposal on theological grounds—were greatly relieved when the Reagan administration scrapped plans in 1981 for building 4,600 shelters for mobile MX missiles in Utah and neighboring Nevada.

UTAMARO, Kitagawa (1753–1806), Japanese artist famous for his elegant color prints of women. Highly popular in Japan,

they were also admired by the French Impressionists.

UTERUS. See WOMB.

UTILITARIANISM, a theory of ETHICS that the rightness or wrongness of an action is determined by the amount of happiness its consequences produce for the greatest number of people. Although the good action is that which brings about the greatest amount of happiness, it is not dependent on motive: an agent's bad motive may lead to others' happiness. The theory dates from the 18th-century thinker Jeremy BENTHAM who believed that actions were motivated by pleasure and pain and that happiness can be assessed by the quantity of pleasure; but J. S. MILL's *Utilitarianism* (1863) argued that some pleasures should be sought for their intrinsic quality.

UTILITY, in classical economics, defines the psychological satisfaction of consuming a given quantity of a particular good or service. It is an important concept in explaining demand. Goods with higher utility may be in greater demand and command a higher PRICE (see SUPPLY AND DEMAND). The concept underlies the law of MARGINAL UTILITY.

UTOPIA, term now used to denote any imaginary ideal state. Based on Greek words meaning "no place," it was coined by Sir Thomas MORE as the title of his *Utopia* (1516), in which he described a just society free of internal strife. Blueprints for such societies have been offered by many other authors, ranging from PLATO to MARX. Utopian thinking in 19th-century America was largely influenced by the theories of FOURIER; utopian experiments included Brook Farm (1841–47); a popular utopian romance was Edward BELLAMY's *Looking Backward* (1888). Aldous HUXLEY's *Brave New World* (1932) and George ORWELL's *1984*, by contrast, are dystopias, or satirical attacks on totalitarian utopian schemes.

UTRECHT, Peace of (1713–14), a series of treaties between England, France, the Netherlands, Portugal, Prussia, Spain and the Holy Roman Empire which concluded the War of the SPANISH SUCCESSION (see also FRENCH AND INDIAN WARS). It marked the end of a period of French expansion and the beginnings of the British Empire. Britain gained Newfoundland, Acadia (Nova Scotia) and the Hudson Bay territory from France, which retained New France (Quebec), recognized the Protestant succession in England and renounced PHILIP v of Spain's claim to the French throne. From Spain Britain gained Gibraltar and Minorca and a monopoly over the slave trade. Austria gained Milan, Naples,

Sardinia and the Catholic Netherlands.

UTRILLO, Maurice (1883–1955), French painter best known for his Paris street scenes. His finest works, painted between about 1908 and 1914, capture the atmosphere of old Montmartre.

UZBEKISTAN, or Uzbek Soviet Socialist Republic, a republic of the USSR, bordering on Afghanistan. Much of it is desert but irrigated agriculture flourishes in the SE. Uzbeks, a Turkic people, comprise 65% of the population. The major cities are TASHKENT and SAMARKAND. It is Russia's chief cotton-producer and is also noted for its fruits, silk, rice, wheat, corn, grapes and sheep. There are rich deposits of coal, oil, natural gas and copper, and many industries. (See USSR.)

V 22nd letter of the English alphabet. Its origins are the same as those of the letter U, out of which it developed. In English the use of "v" for the consonantal sound was firmly established by the 17th century. "V" stands for five in Roman numerals.

V-1, or "flying-bomb," small pilotless airplane, with a ramjet engine, used by Germany during WWII against Britain and Belgium. It flew at about 360mph, carried a 2,000lb bomb and had a range of about 150mi.

V-2, German WWII ballistic MISSILE which was the basis of modern US and Russian long-range missiles and space-exploration vehicles. It flew at about 3,500mph and used ETHANOL and liquid oxygen fuel. Its range was about 220mi.

VACCINATION, method of inducing IMMUNITY to INFECTIOUS DISEASE due to BACTERIA or VIRUSES. Based on the knowledge that second attacks of diseases such as SMALLPOX were uncommon, early methods of protection consisted of inducing immunity by deliberate inoculation of material from a mild case. Starting from the observation that farm workers who had accidentally acquired cowpox by milking infected cows were resistant to smallpox, JENNER in the 1790s inoculated cowpox material into nonimmune persons who then showed resistance to smallpox. PASTEUR extended this work to experimental chicken CHOLERA, human ANTHRAX and RABIES. The term vaccination became general for all methods of inducing immunity by inoculation of products of the infectious organism. ANTITOXINS were soon developed in which specific immunity to disease TOXINS was induced. Vaccination leads to the formation of antibodies and the ability to produce large quantities rapidly at a later date (see ANTIBODIES AND ANTIGENS); this gives protection equivalent to that induced by an attack of the disease. It is occasionally followed by a reaction resembling a mild form of the disease, but rarely by the serious manifestations. Patients on STEROIDS, with immunity disorders or ECZEMA may suffer severe reactions and should not generally receive vaccinations.

VACUUM, any region of space devoid of ATOMS and MOLECULES. Such a region will neither conduct HEAT nor transmit SOUND waves. Because all materials which surround a space have a definite VAPOR PRESSURE, a perfect vacuum is an impossibility and the term is usually used to denote merely a space containing air or other gas at very low PRESSURE. Pressures less than $0.1\mu Pa$ occur naturally about 800km above the earth's surface, though pressures as low as 0.01nPa can be attained in the laboratory. The low pressures required for many physics experiments are obtained using various designs of vacuum PUMP.

VACUUM TUBE, an evacuated ELECTRON TUBE.

VAGRANCY, act of roaming about or loitering by a person who has no job and refuses to seek employment. The police in many cities have used vagrancy statutes as authority to arrest individuals they suspect are "up to no good." In 1972, however, the US Supreme Court, in a decision broad enough to invalidate the vagrancy statutes of many states and cities, unanimously held a Jacksonville, Fla., vagrancy ordinance unconstitutional as a violation of a person's right to "due process of law."

VAIHINGER, Hans (1852–1933), German philosopher and KANT scholar whose major work, *The Philosophy of "As If"* (1911), argued that human beings invent fictions to satisfy their needs and then treat reality "as if" it conformed to their inventions.

VALENTINE, Saint, a Christian priest in Rome who was martyred c270 AD. His traditional association with love probably reflects the near-coincidence of his feast-day (Feb. 14) with the ancient Roman fertility festival of LUPERCALIA (held Feb. 15). The practice of sending Valentine cards dates from the 19th century.

VALENTINO, Rudolph (1895–1926), Italian-born American cinema actor, known as "the great lover." The greatest romantic male star of the silent film era, Valentino's credits included *The Four Horsemen of the Apocalypse* (1921), *The Sheik* (1921) and *Blood and Sand* (1922).

VALENZUELA, Fernando (1961–   ), US baseball pitcher. A pudgy, crowd-pleasing rookie lefthander for the Los Angeles Dodgers, he displayed a baffling screwball and a veteran's poise in 1981 to win 13 games and lead the National League in strikeouts (180), complete games (11) and record shutouts (8) for a freshman. He defeated Houston and Montreal in the NL playoffs, then beat the New York Yankees, 5–4, in the third World Series game, helping L.A. to become world champions.

VALERY, Paul (1871–1945), French poet, essayist and critic. His early verse, *Album de vers anciens* (1920), was influenced by MALLARMÉ. His best-known works are *La Jeune Parque* (1917) and *Le Cimetière marin* (1920). He wrote on poetry in *Monsieur Teste* (1896), and on philosophical and critical themes.

VALHALLA, in Norse mythology, the vast splendid "hall of the slain," in ASGARD where warriors killed in battle were entertained by ODIN. On RAGNAROK, the day of doom, they were to march out with Odin to battle with the giants.

VALKYRIES (choosers of the slain), ODIN'S battle maidens in Norse myth, who transported the souls of the warriors they had chosen in battle to VALHALLA. See also BRUNHILD.

VALLANDIGHAM, Clement Laird (1820–1871), US Representative from Ohio (1858–63), leader of the pro-South COPPERHEADS during the Civil War, and a KNIGHTS OF THE GOLDEN CIRCLE commander. Court-martialed for "treasonable" sympathies (1863) he was "exiled" to the Confederacy. He returned to Ohio in 1864, but his political influence waned after the Civil War.

VALLEE, Rudy (1901–   ), US singer and actor. A popular singing bandleader and recording star in the 1920s, he hosted radio's first network variety show (1929–39). Later, as a comedic actor, he appeared in several Hollywood films and on the New York stage.

VALLEY FORGE, Revolutionary War encampment of Washington's CONTINENTAL ARMY on the Schuylkill R, 22mi NW of Philadelphia, Pa., Dec. 1777–June 1778. The army of 11,000 men was nearly destroyed by a harsh winter and lack of supplies. Hundreds of soldiers died, many deserted, and mutiny was feared. But morale was restored, and the Prussian Baron von STEUBEN introduced efficient drilling.

VALMY, Battle of, victory of the French Revolutionary army, under Charles DUMOURIEZ, over the invading Austro-Prussian forces at Valmy, NE France, in Sept. 1792. It saved Paris and the FRENCH REVOLUTION.

VALOIS, House of, French royal dynasty, 1328–1589. Starting with PHILIP VI (1328–50) the direct line ended with Charles VIII, who was followed by LOUIS XII (1498–1515) of the ORLÉANS branch. The Angoulême branch succeeded, ending in HENRY III (1574–89).

VALUE, in classical economics, the quality of a good or service that yields UTILITY when consumed. If a good with use-value can be exchanged for other goods or money, it has exchange-value as well. This is the more common sense of the term. Value theory therefore often coincides with PRICE theory. For SMITH, RICARDO and MARX, the basic measure of value was labor (see LABOR THEORY OF VALUE).

VALUE-ADDED TAX (VAT), a tax on the value added to goods or services at each stage in their production and distribution. It originated in France in 1954 and was later extended throughout the Common Market; it has been considered at various times in the US. In effect, VAT is a sales tax computed on the difference between what a producer pays for a raw material or semi-finished product and what he sells it for. The cost of the tax is borne ultimately by consumers. It is a regressive tax because it bears most heavily on low-income people who spend more and save less than those with high incomes. For government, VAT has the advantage of being broader than most sales taxes and thus produces large revenues even at low rates. The tax is virtually self-enforcing; producers who make tax payments submit claims for credit for the taxes included in their suppliers' prices, and this tends to discourage non-payment along the line.

VAMPIRE, in folklore, a spirit of the dead, which left its grave at night to suck the blood of living persons. Victims who died would be decapitated or buried with a stake through their hearts, to prevent them from also becoming vampires. (See DRACULA; STOKER, BRAM.)

VAMPIRE BATS, BATS which feed on the blood of larger mammals and birds; the only parasitic mammals. A slit is cut with the teeth and blood lapped from the wound, anticoagulants in the saliva ensuring a constant flow. They occur in South and Middle America and contribute to the debilitation of agricultural workers. They can transmit RABIES.

VAN ALLEN RADIATION BELTS, the belts of high-energy charged particles, mainly PROTONS and ELECTRONS, surrounding the earth, named for Van Allen, who discovered them in 1958. They extend from a few hundred to about 50,000km above the earth's surface, and radiate intensely enough that astronauts must be specially protected from them. The mechanisms responsible for their existence are similar to those involved in the production of the AURORA.

VANBRUGH, Sir John (1664–1726), English dramatist and BAROQUE architect. His comedies include *The Relapse* (1696) and *The Provoked Wife* (1697). With HAWKSMOOR he built several grand houses, such as Blenheim Palace and Castle Howard, noted for the interplay of architectural masses.

VAN BUREN, Martin (1782–1862), eighth US president (1837–41), political heir to JACKSON. A consummate politician, he was called "the little magician" for his political maneuvering, use of patronage and power over the press.

Of Dutch descent and born in Kinderhook, N.Y., the son of a farmer and tavern keeper, he studied law locally and was admitted to the bar (1803). He entered politics, was elected to the N.Y. senate (1813–20), became prominent among the Democrats and rivaled De Witt CLINTON for control of N.Y. Elected to the US senate for 1821–28 he maintained his power through TAMMANY HALL and his creation of the ALBANY REGENCY. As a Jeffersonian Van Buren stood for STATES' RIGHTS and opposed internal improvements. After unsuccessfully promoting W. H. CRAWFORD in 1824, he supported General Jackson for president in 1828. Briefly N.Y. governor for 1828–29, he became Jackson's secretary of state. One of the most powerful men in Washington, he developed the SPOILS SYSTEM. His resignation in 1831 assisted Jackson in removing the followers of vice-president CALHOUN from the government. Van Buren was Jackson's vice-president 1832–36, and in 1836 won the presidency for the Democrats. Shortly after his inauguration a financial panic broke out, bringing Van Buren great unpopularity. One crisis remedy was the INDEPENDENT TREASURY SYSTEM, passed by Congress in 1840. Van Buren also settled the CAROLINE AFFAIR and the AROOSTOOK WAR. Presidential candidate again in 1840

he was defeated by William HARRISON's "log cabin and hard cider" campaign in which Harrison's frontier background was contrasted with Van Buren's alleged luxurious tastes. In 1844 Van Buren failed to receive the Democratic nomination because he opposed the annexation of Texas. He ran in 1848 for the anti-slavery FREE SOIL PARTY, splitting the Democrats and contributing to Zachary TAYLOR's victory. At the outbreak of the Civil War he supported Lincoln.

VANCE, Cyrus (1917–   ), US public official. A Wall Street lawyer, he was secretary of the army (1962–63) and deputy secretary of defense (1964–67). An experienced diplomatic troubleshooter, he served as President Jimmy Carter's secretary of state (1977–80) before resigning in protest over the abortive attempt to rescue US diplomatic hostages in Iran.

VANCOUVER, largest city in British Columbia, on the Burrard Inlet, Strait of Georgia, and third-largest in Canada. It is an important Pacific port and a major manufacturing center for wood, paper, iron, steel and chemical products. Other industries are shipbuilding, oil refining and fish processing. After becoming the terminus of the trans-Canada railroad (1886) it rapidly expanded. Pop 410,190.

VANDALS, ancient Germanic people. They gradually migrated from S of the Baltic to Pannonia and Dacia. In the 5th century they invaded the Roman Empire, ravaging Gaul and Spain. Under GENSERIC they established a strong Vandal kingdom in North Africa (429) which extended to Sicily, and in 455 they sacked Rome. The Vandals were finally defeated by the Byzantine BELISARIUS, after which they disappeared as a unified people.

VAN DE GRAAF GENERATOR. See ELECTROSTATIC GENERATOR.

VANDENBERG, Arthur Hendrick (1884–1951), US Republican senator from Mich. (1928–51). A leading isolationist until PEARL HARBOR, he was an important architect of the post-WWII bipartisan foreign policy, supporting the UN, NATO and the MARSHALL PLAN (1949).

VANDERBILT, wealthy American family whose fortune was built on steamship and railroad empires. **Cornelius Vanderbilt** (1794–1877), known as "Commodore," began with a ferry service which grew into an international steamship business. In the 1860s, he purchased a number of small E railroads. His group dominated the NE by the 1870s and controlled the New York-Chicago route. He established Vanderbilt University at Nashville, Tenn. His son, **William Henry Vanderbilt** (1821–1885), was president of the New York Central Railroad and his eldest son, **Cornelius Vanderbilt II** (1843–1899), next controlled the rail empire and amassed another fortune. Another son, **George Washington Vanderbilt** (1862–1914), established the 100,000 acre Biltmore estate near Asheville, N.C. **Harold Sterling Vanderbilt** (1884–1970) won the AMERICA'S CUP three times and invented contract BRIDGE.

VANDERBILT, Gloria (1924–   ), US heiress and designer. She became famous as a child when she was caught up in a bizarre custody battle between her mother, Gloria Morgan Vanderbilt, and her aunt, Gertrude Vanderbilt Whitney. She became a talented painter and, as a fashion designer in the late 1970s, became associated with a line of designer jeans. She married, among others, Leopold STOKOWSKI and Sidney LUMET.

VAN DER GOES, Hugo (c1440–1482), Flemish painter. The sophisticated symbolism, naturalist details and oil paint technique of his major work, the Portinari altarpiece *Adoration of the Shepherds* (c1475), greatly influenced Italian RENAISSANCE art.

VAN DER WEYDEN, Rogier. See WEYDEN, ROGIER VAN DER.

VAN DINE, S. S. (1888–1939), pen name of Willard Huntington Wright, US mystery story writer and creator of the erudite, snobbish Philo Vance, detective-hero of numerous novels of the 1920s and 1930s.

VAN DOREN, name of two US men of letters. **Carl Clinton Van Doren** (1885–1950), critic and biographer, was famous for his work on the history of American literature. His biography *Benjamin Franklin* won a 1939 Pulitzer Prize. His brother **Mark Albert Van Doren** (1894–1972) wrote poetry, novels, short stories and criticism of English and American literature. His *Collected Poems 1922–1938* won a 1940 Pulitzer Prize.

VAN DRUTEN, John William (1901–1957), English dramatist whose plays include *Bell, Book and Candle* (1950), and *I Am A Camera* (1951) based on Christopher ISHERWOOD'S *Goodbye to Berlin* (1939).

VAN DUSEN, Henry Pitney (1897–1975), US Protestant theologian. A prominent liberal, he was an advocate of the SOCIAL GOSPEL and a leader of the ECUMENICAL MOVEMENT. He was president of Union Theological Seminary in New York (1945–63) and a founder of the WORLD COUNCIL OF CHURCHES (1948).

VAN DYCK, Sir Anthony (1599–1641), Flemish BAROQUE portrait and religious painter. He was a pupil of RUBENS and his portrait style, influenced by his study of Venetian art, was one of elegantly posed figures and rich but refined color and handling, particularly of materials. He painted Italian and English nobility and was court painter from 1632 to CHARLES I of England, who knighted him. He had great influence on the development of English art.

VAN EYCK, Jan (c1390–1441), Flemish painter, the leading early Netherlandish artist who collaborated with his older brother Hubert (c1370–1426) on his most famous painting, the Ghent altarpiece. Completed in 1432, it comprises more than 250 figures in 20 panels. Van Eyck's other important works include a number of portraits, among which *Giovanni Arnolfini and His Bride* (1434) is especially familiar. All are remarkable for realistic, closely observed details. He was the first painter to develop effects of richness, brilliance and intensity in oil paint.

VAN GOGH, Vincent (1853–1890), Dutch POSTIMPRESSIONIST painter. His early, dark-toned work, done in Holland, focuses on peasant life. Later (1886–88), in Paris, he met GAUGUIN and SEURAT. In 1888 he moved to Arles, in southern France, where—among many other paintings—he produced *Sunflowers* in a direct style and the symbolic *The Night Café* using color suggestively. After a fit of insanity, in which he cut off his left ear (1889), he painted at the asylums of St. Rémy and Auvers. In *Portrait of Dr. Gachet* (1890) he attempted to express ideas and emotion in and through paint. He committed suicide.

VANUATU (formerly New Hebrides), independent republic composed of about 80 small islands, extending for about 500mi in the W Pacific Ocean.

Land. The largest island, Espiritu Santo (1,524sq mi), is followed in size by Efate, site of Vila, the capital. The islands are of volcanic origin, and there are six active volcanoes. The rugged, mountainous interiors, densely covered with tropical rain forests, give way to narrow coastal strips where most of the inhabitants live. SE trade winds prevail; rainfall averages 90in per year.

People and Economy. The inhabitants, 90% Melanesian, speak a variety of different dialects, giving rise to a mutually intelligible pidgin. There are small Chinese, British and French minorities. About 70% of the people live in rural villages, practicing traditional subsistence agriculture, raising coconuts, other fruits, yams, taro and pigs for both food and ceremonial purposes. Industries produce copra, fish and beef for export. Manganese has been mined since 1961, and more than 30,000 tourists visited Vanuatu in 1979. Special tax laws have made Vanuatu a banking center.

History. Settlements existed at least as early as 1300 BC, but it was not until the 18th century that the British and French explored the islands. During the 19th century strife broke out between native inhabitants and British and French settlers. In 1906 a joint British-French condominium was established to rule the islands. In 1980 on the eve of independence, fighting broke out on Espiritu Santo, where guerrillas demanded separate status. Fighting ended after British peace-keeping forces arrived, and independence was granted.

VAN VECHTEN, Carl (1880–1964), US music critic, novelist and photographer. He wrote *The Music of Spain* (1918), novels such as *Peter Whiffle* (1922) and *Nigger Heaven* (1926), and an autobiography, *Sacred and Profane Memories* (1932). Subsequently he took up photography and promoted Negro culture at Yale U.

VAN VLECK, John Hasbrouck (1899–1980), US mathematical physicist who used QUANTUM MECHANICS in advancing the theory of MAGNETISM and was awarded the 1977 Nobel Prize in Physics.

VARANASI, or Benares, commercial city in N central India, on the Ganges R. It is very ancient and is the most holy Hindu city (known in this context as Kasi). It has more than 1500 temples. *Ghats* (steps) lead down to the river where pilgrims bathe in the waters. Pop 583,856.

VARÈSE, Edgard (born Edgar; 1883–1965), French-born US composer. Trained under ROUSSEL and D'INDY, he went to the US in 1915 and became a citizen in 1926. In 1921 he helped organize the International Composers Guild to promote such avant-gardists as Berg, Schoenberg and Webern. He explored new rhythms, harmonies and the effects of dissonance. From the 1950s his compositions used electronic equipment.

VARGAS, Getúlio Dornelles (1883–1954), Brazilian statesman, president of Brazil 1930–45 and 1951–54. He set up a "New State" (1937), and a strongly centralized government-promoted industrial, economic and social development. Opposition during his second term led him to commit suicide.

VARIABLE STARS, stars that vary in brightness. There are two main categories. **Extrinsic variables** are those whose variation in apparent brightness is caused by an external condition, as in the case of eclipsing binaries (see DOUBLE STAR). **Intrinsic variables** vary in absolute brightness owing to physical changes within them. They may vary either regularly or irregularly: NOVAE and SUPERNOVAE are irregular intrinsic variables, though some novae erupt in an approximate cycle. Pulsating variables, which vary in size, are the most common type of variable star: they include the RR Lyrae stars, with periods from 1.5h to little over a day, W Virginis stars and RV Tauri stars (all three types appearing principally in GLOBULAR CLUSTERS); long period and semiregular variables, which are red giants; and, possibly erroneously, the CEPHEID VARIABLES. Types of variable stars whose periods are known to have a relationship to their absolute brightness are especially important in that they can be used to determine large astronomical distances.

VARICOSE VEINS, enlarged or tortuous VEINS in the legs resulting from incompetent or damaged valves in the veins, with the pressure of the venous BLOOD causing venous distension and subsequent changes in the vein wall. Although unpleasant in appearance, they are more important for causing venous stagnation, with skin ECZEMA and ULCERS on the inside of the ankle, HEMORRHAGE and EDEMA. Treatment is by stripping or sclerosing injections.

VARRO, Marcus Terentius (116–27 BC), greatest scholar of Ancient Rome, a prolific writer on a great variety of subjects. Of his many books only *On Farming* and *On the Latin Language* have substantially survived.

VASARI, Giorgio (1511–1574), Italian MANNERIST painter, architect and writer. His *Lives of the Most Eminent Italian Architects, Painters & Sculptors* (1550), a major source of knowledge of the Italian RENAISSANCE, is about the progress of art in Italy in the 13th—16th centuries.

VASCULAR SYSTEM, the BLOOD CIRCULATION system, comprising BLOOD, ARTERIES, CAPILLARIES, VEINS and the HEART; the LYMPH vessels form a further subdivision. Its function is to deliver nutrients (including OXYGEN) to, and remove wastes from, all organs, and to transport HORMONES and the agents of body defense.

Official name: Vatican City State
Area: 0.15sq mi
Population: 1,000
Languages: Italian; Latin (administrative and legislative)
Religions: Roman Catholic
Monetary unit(s): 1 Lira = 100 centesimi

VATICAN CITY, the world's smallest independent state, in Rome, Italy, ruled by the Pope, and the spiritual and administrative center of the ROMAN CATHOLIC CHURCH. The city is dominated by SAINT PETER'S BASILICA and by the Vatican Palace, the largest residential palace in the world. The city has many art treasures in the SISTINE CHAPEL, the Vatican Museum, and the Vatican Archive and Library which contain many priceless manuscripts. The Vatican has its own currency, postage stamps, broadcasting station, bank, railroad station, newspaper (*L'Osservatore Romano*) and army of SWISS GUARDS. The city does not have income tax and there is no restriction on the import or export of funds. It maintains diplomatic relations with many countries through ambassadors called *nuncios* and sends apostolic delegates to other countries, including the US and Canada, for religious matters. The official independence of the Vatican City from Italy was established in 1929 in the LATERAN TREATY between the PAPACY and the Italian government.

VATICAN COUNCILS, the two most recent Roman Catholic ECUMENICAL COUNCILS, held at the Vatican. The First Vatican Council (1869–70), summoned by Pius IX, saw ULTRAMONTANISM'S triumph. It restated traditional dogma against materialism, rationalism and liberalism. On the papal primacy, it defined the pope's jurisdiction as universal and immediate; it also declared the pope to be infallible when, speaking *ex cathedra*, he defines a doctrine of faith or morals. Some dissenters seceded as OLD CATHOLICS. The Second Vatican Council (1962–65), summoned by John XXIII, aimed at renewal of the Church, the updating of its organization and attitude to the modern world, and the ultimate reunion of all Christian churches (see ECUMENICAL MOVEMENT). Protestant and Orthodox observers attended. Along with calling for a reform of the MINISTRY and LITURGY, including increased lay participation and use of vernacular languages, the Council decreed that the bishops with the pope form a body ("collegiality") and that the Virgin MARY is "Mother of the Church."

VATTEL, Emerich de (1714–1767), Swiss jurist. His treatise, *The Law of Nations*, based on Christian von Wolff's *Jus Gentium* (1749), claimed that international law should be based on natural laws. His theory of liberty had great influence in the American colonies.

VAUBAN, Sébastien Le Prestre, Marquis de (1633–1707), French military engineer, known for his siege tactics and defense fortifications. In 1673 he dug parallel and concentric trenches around Maastricht and in 1688 introduced ricochet gunfire and socket bayonets.

VAUDEVILLE, term for variety shows, deriving from *Vau de Vire*, a French valley and source of 15th-century songs, or from *Voix de Ville*, French street songs. It was applied from the 1880s to US shows with musical, comic, dramatic, acrobatic and juggling acts. Noted artists included Eddie CANTOR, Will ROGERS and W. C. FIELDS. Vaudeville declined in the 1930s.

VAUGHAN, Henry (1622–1695), Welsh poet. Some of his best religious and mystical verse, such as "The Retreate," "The Sap" or "I walkt the other day," influenced by the METAPHYSICAL POET George HERBERT, appeared in his *Silex Scintillans* (1651–55).

VAUGHAN WILLIAMS, Ralph (1872–1959), English composer. He was influenced by secular and religious Tudor music and thus acquired methods of expression which differed from traditional classical music. His works, many drawing on English folk music, include *Norfolk Rhapsodies* (1906–07), *Fantasia on a Theme of Tallis* (1909), nine symphonies and five operas.

VAUGHN, Sarah (1924–   ), US jazz singer and stylist famous for her renditions of songs in the Bop mode ("Shulie a Bop," 1964), for her marvelously precise scat singing and for the richness and flexibility of her delivery in such ballads as *Lover Man* (first recorded in 1944).

VEBLEN, Oswald (1880–1960), US

mathematician best known for his contributions to projective and differential GEOMETRY and especially for his pioneering role in the development of TOPOLOGY, set out in *Analysis Situs* (1922).

VEBLEN, Thorstein Bunde (1857–1929), influential US economist and social theorist. In *Theory of the Leisure Class* (1899) he used the satirical concept of "conspicuous consumption" (that people acquire goods for their status, rather than for their utility or value). *The Theory of Business Enterprise* (1904) attacked the capitalist system, and *The Engineers and the Price System* (1921) foreshadowed TECHNOCRACY.

VEDA (Sanskrit: knowledge), most ancient of Indian scriptures, believed to have been inspired by God, and basic to HINDUISM. There are four *Samhitas* or collections of MANTRAS—the Rig, Yajur, Sama and Atharva-Veda. The oldest may date from 1500 BC. Vedic literature consists of the Veda itself, the *Brahmanas* and *Aranyakas* (later expository supplements), and the UPANISHADS.

VEDANTA (Sanskrit: end of knowledge), system of Hindu philosophy, based at first on the UPANISHADS (the final part of the VEDA), and later on the *Brahma Sutras*, commentaries on the Upanishads, which date from the 1st century AD. The Vedanta concern the relation of the individual (*atman*) to the Absolute (*Brahman*).

VEGA, Lope de (1562–1635), poet and Spain's first great dramatist. He created the *comedia*, a drama with comic, tragic, learned and popular elements. Vitality, wit and intricate plot typify *Peribañez*, *Fuenteovejuna* and *The Knight of Olmedo*. Lope's 500 surviving works also include lyrical verse, the autobiographical *La Dorotea* (1632), religious and light "cloak-and-sword" plays.

VEINS, thin-walled collapsible vessels which return BLOOD to the HEART from the tissue CAPILLARIES and provide a variable-sized pool of blood. They contain valves which prevent back-flow—especially in the legs. Blood drains from the major veins into the inferior or superior VENA CAVA. Blood in veins is at low pressure and depends for its return to the heart on intermittent muscle compression, combined with valve action.

VELÁZQUEZ, Diego Rodríguez de Silva y (1599–1660), great Spanish painter. In 1623, he became court painter to King Philip IV of Spain. His style was influenced strongly by his Flemish contemporary RUBENS and also by Italian artists of the High RENAISSANCE. His masterpieces include *The Drunkards, Christ on the Cross* and *Maids of Honor*.

VELD, or **veldt,** open GRASSLAND of South Africa, divided into three types: High Veld, around 1500m above sea level, which is similar to the PRAIRIES; Cape Middle Veld, somewhat lower, covered with scrub and occasional low ridges of hills; and Low Veld, under about 750m above sea level.

VELDE, Henri Clemens van de (1863–1957), Belgian ART NOUVEAU architect and designer, interested in the idea of pure form in architecture. He founded (1906) and taught at the Weimar School of Applied Art which became the BAUHAUS in 1919.

VELIKOVSKY, Immanuel (1895–1979), Russian-born US astronomical theorist, author of *Worlds in Collision* (1950) and other popular and controversial books. He asserted that the planet Venus was formed by an explosion of Jupiter, and that its near-collision with Earth before it settled into a planetary orbit caused cataclysmic upheavals described in ancient histories and myths.

VELOCITY, the rate at which the position of a body changes, expressed with respect to a given direction. Velocity is thus a VECTOR quantity, of which the corresponding scalar is **speed**: the rate of change in the position of a body without respect to direction. Translational velocity, usually expressed in calculus as

$$V = \frac{ds}{dt}$$

refers to movement through space; angular or rotational velocity,

$$\omega = \frac{d\theta}{dt}$$

to rotation about a given axis. (See also ACCELERATION.)

VENDÉE, maritime department of W France, in Poitou, on the Atlantic. It was the scene of the peasants' counterrevolutionary **War of the Vendée** (1793–96), which threatened the new republican state. Savagely crushed at the outset, the peasants continued to resist and eventually achieved their aims of freedom of worship and freedom from conscription.

VENEREAL DISEASES, those INFECTIOUS DISEASES transmitted mainly or exclusively by sexual contact, usually because the organism responsible is unable to survive outside the body and the close contact of genitalia provides the only means for transmitting viable organisms. **Gonorrhea** is an acute BACTERIAL DISEASE which is frequently asymptomatic in females who therefore act as carriers, although they may suffer mild cervicitis or urethritis. In males it causes a painful urethritis with urethral discharge of PUS. ARTHRITIS, SEPTICEMIA and other systemic manifestations may also occur, and urethral stricture follow. Infection of an infant's eyes by mothers carrying the gonococcus causes neonatal OPHTHALMIA, previously a common cause of childhood BLINDNESS. Gonorrhea is best treated with PENICILLIN. **Syphilis**, due to *Treponema pallidum*, a SPIROCHETE, is a disease with three stages. A painless genital ULCER or chancre—a highly infective lesion—develops in the weeks after contact; this is usually associated with LYMPH node enlargement. Secondary syphilis, starting weeks or months after infection, involves systemic disease with FEVER, malaise and a characteristic rash, mucous membrane lesions and occasionally MENINGITIS, HEPATITIS or other organ disease. If the disease is treated with a full course of penicillin in the early stages, its progression is prevented. Tertiary syphilis takes several forms; e.g., gummas—chronic granulomas affecting SKIN, EPITHELIUM, BONE or internal organs—may develop. Largely a disease of blood vessels, tertiary syphilis causes disease of the AORTA with aneurysm and aortic valve disease of the HEART, with incompetence. Syphilis of the NERVOUS SYSTEM may cause TABES DORSALIS, primary EYE disease, chronic meningitis, multifocal vascular disease resembling STROKE or general PARESIS with mental disturbance, personality change, failure of judgment and muscular weakness. Penicillin may only partially reverse late syphilis. Congenital syphilis is a disease transmitted to the FETUS during PREGNANCY and leads to deformity and visceral disease. Other venereal diseases include Reiter's disease with arthritis, CONJUNCTIVITIS and urethritis (in males only); genital trichomonas; THRUSH; *Herpes simplex* virus, and "nonspecific urethritis." Tropical venereal diseases include chancroid; lymphogranuloma venereum, and granuloma inguinale.

VENEZUELA, republic of N South America, bounded N by the Caribbean Sea, E by Guyana, S by Brazil and W by Colombia.

Land. The country's four main regions are the Venezuelan Highlands (W and N), an extension of the Andes; the oil-producing Maracaibo Lowlands, almost completely enclosed by mountains; the great central grassland plain of the Orinoco (the LLANOS); and the mineral-rich Guiana Highlands, S of the Orinoco R, very sparsely populated but covering about half the country.

People. The population is mainly MESTIZO. Of the rest, about 20% are of European

Official name: Republic of Venezuela
Capital: Caracas
Area: 352,143sq mi
Population: 13,122,000
Languages: Spanish
Religions: Roman Catholic
Monetary unit(s): 1 Bolívar=100 céntimos

stock (mainly Spanish), 7% Negroes and 6% Indians. The population is over 70% urban and the literacy rate is over 80%.

Economy. Venezuela now produces about 14% of the world's output of oil (its share declined in the 1970s). It also produces natural gas and iron ore. Chief agricultural products are coffee, rice and cocoa. Oil revenues finance industrial diversification, public works and welfare programs.

History. Venezuela was discovered by COLUMBUS, but may have been named by VESPUCCI. When the first Spanish settlement was founded (at Cumaná, 1521) the country was inhabited by ARAWAKS and CARIBS. Their fierce resistance did not prevent Spanish penetration. Venezuelan independence, unsuccessfully attempted by Francisco de MIRANDA (1806), was proclaimed by a national congress in 1811. Miranda became dictator in 1812, but was imprisoned by the Spanish. Simón BOLÍVAR led the independence struggle and triumphed in 1821. The country became part of Greater Colombia, but broke free as an independent republic in 1830. Dictatorships and revolts followed. General Juan Vicente Gómez (president 1908–35) granted oil concessions to foreign companies until 1983. In 1958, the corrupt Marcos Pérez Jiménez dictatorship was overthrown by Rómulo BÉTANCOURT, and democracy was restored. The nationalization of the petroleum industry (with compensation) in 1976 was smooth and peaceable.

VENICE, city in NE Italy, seaport capital of the Veneto region and Venezia province. It comprises 118 islands in the Lagoon of Venice at the head of the Adriatic Sea. Transport is mainly along the famous canals by motorboat and gondola. Venice is built on piles sunk deep into the mud and is linked by a causeway to the mainland. The first DOGE (duke or ruler) was elected in 697. Venice rose to control trade between Europe and the East. At its height (15th century), Venice ruled many areas along the coast of the E Mediterranean, the Aegean and parts of the Black Sea. Its power weakened during the long struggle with the Ottoman Empire (c1453–c1718). Venice is now a major tourist resort, boasting unique beauty and a magnificent cultural heritage. Pop 358,300.

VENIZELOS, Eleutherios (1864–1936), Greek statesman, premier of Greece (1910–15; 1916–20; 1928–32; 1933). He promoted the alliance which defeated Turkey in the first of the BALKAN WARS (1912–13) and, after CONSTANTINE I's abdication (1917), brought Greece into WWI on the Allied side.

VENTRILOQUISM, way of speaking to make the voice seem to come from a source other than the speaker's mouth. An ancient art, ventriloquism is still practiced, the ventriloquist usually having a dummy with whom he appears to converse. Edgar BERGEN, who created the dummies Charlie McCarthy and Mortimer Snerd, was a popular US phenomenon of the 1930s and 1940s.

VENTRIS, Michael George Francis (1922–1956), English linguist who deciphered one of the MINOAN LINEAR SCRIPTS (Linear B).

VENTURI, Robert (1925–), US architect. A controversial critic of the purely functional and spare designs of orthodox modern architecture, he set forth his "counterrevolutionary" views in *Complexity and Contradiction in Architecture* (1966) and *Learning from Las Vegas* (1972).

VENUS, the planet second from the sun in the SOLAR SYSTEM. Its diameter is 12.1Mm, slightly smaller than that of the earth. Its face is completely obscured by dense clouds containing sulfuric acid, though the USSR's Venera-9 and Venera-10 (Oct. 1975) landing have provided photographs of the planet's rocky surface. Venus revolves about the sun at a mean distance of 0.72AU in 225 days, rotating on its axis in a retrograde direction (see RETROGRADE MOTION) in 243 days. Its atmosphere is 97% carbon dioxide and its surface temperature is about 750K. Venus has no known moons, and could not support life.

VENUS DE MILO, famous armless statue of the Greek goddess APHRODITE. It was carved in marble c150 BC and was discovered 1820 on the island of Melos. It is now in the Louvre in Paris.

VENUS' FLYTRAP, *Dionaea muscipula,* INSECTIVOROUS PLANT native to the sandy country of the Carolinas. The outer part of each leaf forms a pad, hinged in the middle and edged with stiff teeth. Sensitive hairs protrude from the pad's center. When an insect brushes the hairs, the pad rapidly folds, catching the insect behind the teeth. Special secretions digest the soft parts of the insect's body. Family: Droseraceae.

VERDI, Giuseppe (1813–1901), Italian opera composer. He rose to fame during the struggle for Italian unification and independence; early operas such as *Nabucco* (1842) express these political ideals. By the time of *Rigoletto* (1851), *Il Trovatore* (1853) and *La Traviata* (1853) he had developed his powerful individual style well beyond the conventions inherited from ROSSINI, DONIZETTI and BELLINI. *Don Carlos* (1867), *Aida* (1871) and the *Requiem* honoring MANZONI (1874) are works of his maturity. The two great Shakespearian operas of Verdi's old age, *Otello* (1887) and *Falstaff* (1893), were written to libretti by BOITO.

VERDUN, Battle of (Feb.–Dec. 1916), major WORLD WAR I engagement. The Germans launched a concentrated offensive against the fortified salient of VERDUN. The French dared not abandon this position and the Germans hoped to compel them to exhaust their forces in its defense. Total casualties were well over 700,000. No significant advantage was gained by either side.

VERDUN, Treaty of (843 AD), treaty concluding the civil war between the heirs of LOUIS I, by which CHARLEMAGNE'S empire was divided between his three grandchildren (Louis' sons). LOTHAIR I kept the title emperor and received Italy and a narrow strip of land from Provence to Friesland. Louis the German received the lands between the Rhine and Elbe. Charles the Bald held the area W of the Rhine.

VERGA, Giovanni (1840–1922), Italian novelist and short-story writer whose work had a strong influence on modern Italian neo-realist fiction. His story *Cavalleria Rusticana* (1880) was the basis for his own play and Pietro Mascagni's opera.

VERGENNES, Charles Gravier, Comte de (1717–1787), French statesman. As foreign minister 1774–87, he supported the American colonies in the Revolutionary War and joined them in a military alliance (1778). He negotiated the Treaty of PARIS (1783).

VERGIL, or **Virgil** (Publius Vergilius Maro; 70–19 BC), Roman poet, one of the greatest writers of EPIC. Born at Mantua, he studied at Cremona, Milan and finally Rome, where MAECENAS became his patron and Octavian (later the emperor AUGUSTUS) his friend. He won recognition with his *Eclogues* or *Bucolics*, PASTORAL poems reflecting the events of his own day. The *Georgics*, a didactic poem on farming, uses the world of the farmer as a model for the world at large. His last ten years were spent on his epic masterpiece, the *Aeneid*, about the wanderings of AENEAS and his struggle to found ROME.

VERISSIMO, Erico (1905–), Brazilian historian and novelist, author of *Crossroads* (1935), *Consider the Lilies of the Field* (1938), and the trilogy *Time and the Wind*.

VERLAINE, Paul Marie (1844–1896), French poet, an early and influential exponent of SYMBOLISM. While imprisoned 1873–75 for shooting and wounding his friend and lover Arthur RIMBAUD, he wrote *Romances sans Paroles* (1874), one of his finest volumes. After a period of religious piety he returned to his life of Bohemian dissipation and died in poverty.

VERMEER, Jan (1632–1675), Dutch painter who spent his entire life in Delft. His interior scenes are noted for superb control of light, precise tonality, cool harmonious coloring and classical composition. Of the fewer than 40 works attributed to him his masterpieces include *The Letter* and *Head of a Girl* (both c1665).

Name of state: Vermont
Capital: Montpelier
Statehood: March 4, 1791 (14th state)
Familiar name: Green Mountain State
Area: 9,609sq mi
Population: 511,456
Elevation: Highest—4,393ft, Mount Mansfield; Lowest—95ft, Lake Champlain
Motto: Freedom and Unity
State flower: Red clover
State bird: Hermit thrush
State tree: Sugar maple
State song: "Hail, Vermont!"

VERMONT, state of the NE US, in New England, bounded N by Quebec, W by N.Y., S by Mass. and E by N.H. It is among the ten smallest and least populated states and the only New England state without a coastline.

Land. The Green Mts form the major geographical region, comprising several virtually continuous ranges running N–S through Vt.'s center. Most fertile are the broad Connecticut R Valley in the E and the Champlain Valley in the NW. The climate is cool, with long, cold winters.

People. Vermont remains a predominantly rural state with fewer than one third of the population living in urban areas. Burlington is the largest city. Most of the population is white, with French-speaking Canadian immigrants a significant minority.

Economy. The chief source of income is manufacturing, much of it based on the state's marble and granite quarries and talc and asbestos production. Dairy farming is the chief agricultural activity, and Vermont is also justly famed for its maple sugar products. Tourism is important, skiing in the Green Mts being a major attraction.

History. Vt. was one of three states (with Hawaii and Texas) recognized by the US government as independent republics before they joined the Union. When the French explorer de CHAMPLAIN arrived in 1609, the region was inhabited by Iroquois Indians from N.Y., who had driven out the original Algonquins. Champlain aided the Algonquins in their defeat of the Iroquois and claimed the region for France. In 1763, England gained Vt. as a result of the treaty ending the FRENCH AND INDIAN WARS. In 1770, Ethan ALLEN organized the GREEN MOUNTAIN BOYS to resist N.Y. claims to Vt. lands and to drive out N.Y. settlers. When the Revolutionary War broke out, the Green Mountain Boys joined other patriots to fight the British. The state's 1777 constitution prohibited slavery and was the first to provide for universal male suffrage. Vt. remained an independent republic until 1791, when it became the 14th state.

Vermont has maintained its independent, almost insular spirit into the 20th century; and after more than a hundred years of very slow population growth, is now beginning to increase more quickly, rising 14.8% during the 1970s. Its unemployment rate is low, at 5.6% in 1980, but so is its per capita income of $7329 in 1979; only 5 states had lower income figures that year.

VERNE, Jules (1828–1905), popular French novelist and a father of the modern genre of SCIENCE FICTION. He often incorporated genuine scientific principles in his imaginative adventure fantasies, and anticipated the airplane, submarine, television, space travel, etc. His most famous novels include *Journey to the Center of the Earth* (1864), *Twenty*

Thousand Leagues Under the Sea (1870) and *Around the World in Eighty Days* (1873).

VERONESE, Paolo (Paolo Caliari; 1528–1588), Venetian painter of rich, brilliantly colored religious, historical and mythological pictures. Works such as *Triumph of Venice* (post-1577) include crowds of people in splendid costumes and settings. The Inquisition admonished him for details in *Feast in the House of Levi* (1573).

VERRAZANO, Giovanni da (c1485–c1528), Italian navigator who discovered New York and Narragansett bays while exploring the North American coast in 1524. Some time after 1526, he set out for Central America and never returned.

VERRAZANO-NARROWS BRIDGE, suspension bridge across the narrows at the entrance to New York Harbor, completed 1964. It has a main span of 4,260ft, the world's longest.

VERROCCHIO, Andrea del (c1435–1488), Italian RENAISSANCE sculptor and painter. In pictures such as *Madonna and Child* (1468–70) he treated figures and landscape sculpturally. His greatest work, finished by Leopardi, the bronze equestrian *Monument to Bartolommeo Colleoni* (1483–96), in Venice, shows his mastery of composition, technique and rich detailing.

VERSAILLES, French city, 12mi SW of Paris. It is world-famous for its magnificent Palace of Versailles, built for King LOUIS XIV in the mid-1600s. The seat of the French court for over 100 years, it was made a national museum in 1837, and the palace and its formal gardens are one of France's greatest tourist attractions. The modern city is principally a residential suburb of Paris.

VERSAILLES, Treaty of, agreement ending WORLD WAR I, imposed on Germany by the Allies on June 28, 1919. It also set up the LEAGUE OF NATIONS. Under the treaty, Germany lost all her colonies, Lorraine was given to France, Eupen-Malmédy to Belgium, Posen and West Prussia to Poland, and Memel (Klaipeda) to the Allies. GDANSK became a free city, the Saar (with its coalfields) was to be under international administration for 15 years, the Rhineland was to be demilitarized and occupied by the Allies for 15 years at German cost. Heavy REPARATIONS were imposed, and Germany's armed forces drastically reduced. German resentment of the treaty's harshness was a factor in the rise of NAZISM and the eventual outbreak of WWII.

VERSE, language with a regular rhythm often characteristic of POETRY. Verse may be used as a general term for all such language (as opposed to prose), or to describe a single line of poetry or a QUATRAIN or stanza of a ballad or hymn. Verse generally has RHYME. The pattern of stressed beats in a line of verse is called the *meter*, and the study of the various types of meter and rhyme in poetry is called *prosody*, which employs a technical language to analyze the rhythmic units (called *feet*) making up the different styles of verse. (See also BLANK VERSE; FREE VERSE.)

VERTEBRATES, subphylum of the CHORDATES, containing all those classes of animals which possess a backbone—a spinal column made up of bony or cartilaginous VERTEBRAE.

VERTICAL TAKEOFF AND LANDING AIRPLANE (VTOL), AIRPLANE that can lift-off and land vertically, such as a HELICOPTER; now chiefly associated with "jump-jet" systems in which the exhaust gases of horizontally mounted jet engines can be deflected downward. The British Hawker "Harrier" military strike airplane, capable of supersonic speeds in level flight, is the best-known example. See also SHORT TAKEOFF AND LANDING AIRPLANE (STOL).

VERWOERD, Hendrik Frensch (1901–1966), Dutch-born South African politician, premier 1958–66. A professor of psychology from 1927, he became editor of the Afrikaans nationalist newspaper *Die Transvaler* (1937). A senator from 1948, he was appointed minister of native affairs (1950), and enforced APARTHEID rigorously, stressing "separate development" and creating the BANTUSTANS. He was assassinated.

VESALIUS, Andreas (1514–1564), Flemish biologist regarded as a father of modern ANATOMY. Initially a Galenist he became, after considerable experience of dissection, one of the leading figures in the revolt against GALEN. In his most important work, *On the Structure of the Human Body* (1543), he described several organs for the first time.

VESPUCCI, Amerigo (1454–1512), Italian navigator for whom America was named. In two voyages (1499–1500, 1501–02) he explored the coast of South America, and deduced that the "New World" must be a continent and not part of Asia. The name "America" first appeared on a map published in 1507.

VESTA, Roman virgin goddess of the domestic hearth, identified with the Greek goddess Hestia. In her sanctuary in Rome, a perpetual flame was tended by six VESTAL

VIRGINS.

VESTAL VIRGINS, in ancient Rome, priestesses chosen very young, who had to serve the shrine of VESTA for 30 years. Punishment for breaking their vow of chastity was burial alive. Their chief responsibility was to tend the sacred flame in Vesta's temple.

VESUVIUS, Mount, the only volcano on mainland Europe, in S Italy near Naples. Its height, c4,000ft, varies with each eruption. Capped by a plume of smoke, it is a famous landmark. Its lower slopes are extremely fertile. In 79 AD it destroyed the cities of POMPEII and HERCULANEUM. Recent eruptions occurred in 1906, 1929 and 1944.

VETERANS ADMINISTRATION, US federal agency established in 1930, responsible for administering all laws authorizing benefits for ex-servicemen and their dependents or beneficiaries. Its comprehensive program of medical care, pensions, housing, educational and other assistance was set up by the Serviceman's Readjustment Act of 1944, popularly known as the G.I. BILL OF RIGHTS.

VETERANS DAY, a US holiday, celebrated on 11 November, to honor American servicemen, past and present. Originally known as Armistice Day, it was first designated by Woodrow WILSON to commemorate the end of WWI.

VETERANS OF FOREIGN WARS, organization for all veterans of all US wars since the Civil War. Known as the VFW, it was founded in 1899 by veterans of the Spanish–American War. It helps rehabilitate ex-servicemen and aims to promote patriotism and a community spirit.

VETERINARY MEDICINE, the medical care of sick animals, sometimes including the delivery of their young. It is practiced separately from human MEDICINE since animal diseases differ largely from those affecting humans. Veterinarians treat domestic, farm, sport and zoo animals. Sometimes diseases can be controlled only through the slaughter of known or suspected carriers.

VETO, in politics, the power of the executive to reject legislation. It is a Latin word meaning "I forbid," pronounced by the Roman TRIBUNES when they exercised their right to block laws passed by the SENATE. Under the US Constitution (Article I, Section 7), the President can veto any bill passed by Congress, but this can be overridden by a two-thirds majority in both houses. In the Security Council of the UNITED NATIONS, the five permanent members (China, France, Great Britain, the US and USSR) each possess a veto over proceedings.

VIBRAPHONE, musical instrument of the PERCUSSION group. A modern version of the XYLOPHONE, it has tuned metal bars struck by a hammer. Beneath each bar is an electrically operated resonator to give the distinctive vibrating sound.

VICENTE, Gil (c1470–c1536), major Portuguese poet and dramatist. Between 1502 and 1536 he produced some 44 plays for the Portuguese court. Full of verve and satire, and with many exquisite songs, they include comedies, farces, morality plays and tragi-comedies.

VICE-PRESIDENT, the second-highest elected official of the US. Constitutionally and politically this office does not carry great power, and its holder must rely on the confidence and discretion of the President for any power he wields. The Vice-President was originally intended to perform two roles: that of a neutral presiding officer in the Senate, and that of a constitutional successor on the death or resignation of a President. Eight Vice-Presidents have succeeded on the death of their predecessor. In the past Vice-Presidential nominees were often nonentities chosen for party political reasons rather than for ability (though several have become excellent presidents), but the increase in presidential duties with WWII has been partly responsible for giving the Vice-President a greater share in political and legislative matters, in particular as a member of the National Security Council.

The 25th Amendment (1967) permits the President to fill a vacancy in the office of Vice-President, subject to the approval of Congress. The amendment permits the Vice-President to act as President when the President is disabled, and even to declare the President disabled if the latter is unable or unwilling to do so.

VICHY, health resort in S central France, famous for its mineral springs. Its chief industry is bottling Vichy water. In WWII it was the seat of the "Vichy government" of Marshal Henri PÉTAIN, which was set up in unoccupied France in 1940 and under LAVAL continued to collaborate with the Nazis after the whole of France was occupied in 1942.

VICKERS, Jon (1927–　), Canadian tenor. He made many concert appearances before going on to the opera stage at Covent Garden, London, in 1957 in Verdi's *A Masked Ball*. At first specializing in Italian repertory, he later became a heldentenor (heroic tenor) in Wagnerian opera.

VICTORIA, state in SE Australia, the next smallest and most densely populated in the country. It is divided E–W by an extension of the Australian Alps, with lowlands, hills and valleys in the S and low plains N and W. The climate is temperate. Agriculture is important: wheat, oats, barley and grapes are grown, and cattle and sheep raised. Automobiles, textiles and processed foods are produced and coal and some gold are mined. Melbourne is the capital and largest city.

VICTORIA, Lake, or Victoria Nyanza, lies in the Great RIFT VALLEY of East Africa, bordered by Tanzania, Uganda and Kenya. It is the second-largest freshwater lake in the world and the largest lake in Africa, c200mi long and c150mi wide.

VICTORIA, Tomás Luis de (c1548–1611), Spanish composer. A priest in Rome, he was influenced by PALESTRINA, and composed some of the finest religious choral music of the Renaissance. Returning to Spain in 1594, he wrote his great *Requiem* in 1605.

VICTORIA, or Hong Kong, seaport and capital of HONG KONG colony, in the NW of Hong Kong Island. A center of world trade and site of Hong Kong U., it also has many light industries. Pop 501,680.

VICTORIA (1819–1901), Queen of Great Britain and Ireland from 1837 and Empress of India from 1876. As a young queen she depended heavily on the counsel of Lord MELBOURNE. Her life was transformed by marriage in 1840 to Prince ALBERT, who became the greatest influence of her life. A devoted wife and mother (she bore nine children), she mourned for the rest of her life after his death in 1861. She had strong opinions and believed in playing an active role in government, and her relations with a succession of ministers colored the political life of her reign. Her dislike of PALMERSTON and GLADSTONE and fondness for DISRAELI, for example, were notorious. In old age she became immensely popular and a symbol of Britain's imperial greatness.

VICTORIA FALLS, one of Africa's most spectacular sights, on the Zambesi R in S-central Africa between Zimbabwe and Zambia, where the mile-wide river plunges c400ft into a narrow fissure. They were named for Britain's Queen Victoria by LIVINGSTONE in 1855.

VICUÑA, *Lama vicugna,* a member of the CAMEL family living in the western High Andes at up to 5,000m (16,400ft). They are believed to be the original of the domesticated ALPACAS. Vicuñas are graceful animals living in family groups of a stallion and up to 20 mares, occupying a fixed territory.

VIDAL, Gore (1925–   ), US novelist and playwright. Novels such as *Washington*

D.C. (1967), *Myra Breckenridge* (1968), *Burr* (1973) and *1876* (1976) provide an urbane, satirical view of a corrupt society. His historical novel, *Julian* (1964), is also of note. Plays include *Visit to a Small Planet* (1956) and *The Best Man* (1960).

VIENNA (Wien), capital of Austria, on the Danube R, one of the world's great cities. Associated with HAYDN, MOZART, BEETHOVEN and the STRAUSS family, it is a celebrated musical, theatrical and cultural center, and has many famous buildings and museums, including the Hofburg, Schönbrunn and Belvedera palaces, the Cathedral of St. Stephen, the State Opera, the Art History Museum and the City Hall. A Roman town, it became the residence of the HAPSBURGS in 1282. It was besieged by the Turks in 1529 and 1683. A great period of prosperity and building began in the 18th century, and Vienna was capital of the Austro–Hungarian empire until 1918, when the modern republic of Austria was formed. In WWII it was occupied by the Nazis and bombed by the Allies. The modern city is also a commercial and industrial center, producing machinery, metals, textiles, chemicals, furniture, handicrafts and food products. Pop 1,592,800.

VIENNA, Congress of, assembly held in Vienna, 1814–15, to reorganize Europe after the NAPOLEONIC WARS. Effective decision-making was carried out by METTERNICH of Austria, Tsar ALEXANDER I of Russia, CASTLEREAGH and WELLINGTON of Britain, von HUMBOLDT of Prussia and TALLEYRAND of France. Among other territorial adjustments, the Congress established the German Confederation and the kingdoms of the Netherlands and Poland (under Russian rule), and restored the PAPAL STATES and the kingdoms of SARDINIA and NAPLES. Austria gained parts of Italy, Prussia gained parts of Austria, and Britain gained overseas territories. The major powers thus distributed territories to achieve a new balance of power, ignoring the nationalist aspirations of the people concerned. (See also PARIS, TREATY OF; TRIPLE ALLIANCE; QUADRUPLE ALLIANCE.)

VIENTIANE, capital and largest city of Laos. On the Mekong R near the Thailand border, it is a commercial center with small-scale industries. Pop 176,600.

VIETNAM, republic in SE Asia, united in 1976 after nearly 35 years of war.

Land. Narrow and S-shaped, Vietnam is a 1000mi-long strip bordered by Kampuchea (Cambodia), Laos and China W and N and the Gulf of Tonkin, the South China Sea and the Gulf of Thailand E and S. A heavily forested mountainous backbone and a narrow coastal strip link the Red R delta in the N and the Mekong R delta in the S. Vietnam has a tropical monsoon climate, with high humidity and rainfall.

People. Nearly 90% of the people are Vietnamese, concentrated in the two great deltas. There are urban Chinese minorities, and several highland tribal peoples, such as the MEO, (Hmong), who preserve their own cultures. Hanoi (the capital), Ho Chi Minh City (formerly Saigon), Hue, Da Nang and Haiphong are the chief cities.

Economy. Vietnam has an agricultural economy based principally on rice-growing in the Mekong and Red R deltas. Other crops include corn, cotton, hemp, sugarcane, rubber, coffee and tea. Fishing and forestry are locally important. Minerals, including coal, iron, tin, zinc, lead and phosphates, are found mainly in the N, where most of the country's industry, chiefly the manufacture of iron and steel, chemicals and textiles, is concentrated. There is also some manufacturing industry around Ho Chi Minh City. Offshore oil deposits have been found.

History. Established as a distinct people by the 2nd century BC, the Vietnamese occupy the historic regions of TONKIN (N), ANNAM (center) and COCHIN CHINA (S). Tonkin and Annam were conquered by China in 111 BC. In the 2nd century AD the CHAMPA kingdom emerged in central Vietnam. The Chinese were driven out in 939, and the Annam empire grew, defeating the Champas (1471) and expanding S into Cochin China. European traders and missionaries began to arrive in the 1500s. The French captured Saigon in 1859 and in 1862 annexed Cochin China, which was later merged into French INDOCHINA. After

Official name: Socialist Republic of Vietnam
Capital: Hanoi
Area: 127,246
Population: 52,742,000
Language: Vietnamese
Religions: Buddhist, Taoist
Monetary unit(s): 1 Dông = 100 xu

Japanese occupation in WWII, a republic was proclaimed under HO CHI MINH (1945). The French attempt to reassert their authority (1946–54) ended in defeat at DIEN BIEN PHU. At the GENEVA CONFERENCE (1954) the country was divided, pending nationwide free elections, into communist North Vietnam, under Ho Chi Minh, and noncommunist South Vietnam. The French withdrew from Vietnam and, with US backing, the regime of Ngo Dinh DIEM delcared an independent republic in the South (1955) and refused to hold free elections (1956). The VIETNAM WAR ensued, with South Vietnam being aided by increasing numbers of US troops. A cease-fire agreement was finally signed in 1973 and US troops were withdrawn. Communist forces, however, launched a major offensive and by 1975 had control of all of South Vietnam. The unified Socialist Republic of Vietnam was proclaimed in 1976.

VIETNAM WAR, conflict in South Vietnam between South Vietnamese government forces backed by the US, and communist guerrilla insurgents, the Vietcong, backed by North Vietnam. The conflict originated in 1941 when a Vietminh guerrilla force was formed under HO CHI MINH to fight the Japanese. After 1946 it fought the French colonial government, defeating them at DIEN BIEN PHU. The GENEVA CONFERENCE then temporarily divided Vietnam at the 17th parallel between the Communists (North) and the Nationalists (South). Ngo Dinh DIEM, the South Vietnamese premier, cancelled national elections and declared the South independent in 1956. The Viet Nam Cong San (Vietnamese Communists), or Vietcong, was then formed to oppose his increasingly corrupt regime. The Vietcong were equipped and trained by North Vietnam, with Chinese backing, and included North Vietnamese troops especially in the later stages of the war. The Vietcong fought a ferocious guerilla campaign that led Diem to call in US support forces under the US-South Vietnamese military and economic aid treaty of 1961. In 1963 he was overthrown by his officers; after a period of turmoil Nguyen van THIEU became president in 1967. In 1965 the US had begun bombing the North in retaliation for the use of Northern troops in the South; increasing numbers of US combat troops began to arrive in 1965 and totaled nearly 550,000 by 1968. The large-scale US campaign proved unable to do more than hold back the well-entrenched Vietcong; Vietnamese civilians suffered terribly at the hands of both sides. The use of napalm and defoliants by the US Air Force, in a vain attempt to reduce the jungle that gave the Vietcong a great advantage in cover and mobility, provoked international controversy, as did the great publicity given to alleged atrocities committed by a few US troops. This feeling, and the mounting toll roused world opinion to the war, as well as large antiwar demonstrations in the US. Fruitless peace talks began in Paris (1968) and in 1969 President NIXON announced the "vietnamization" of the war by building up South Vietnamese forces and withdrawing US combat troops. The war had spread to Cambodia and Laos before a ceasefire signed in Jan. 1973 preceded the total withdrawal of US troops a few months later. The South was then overrun by Vietcong and North Vietnamese forces; the war effectively ended with the fall of Saigon in May 1975.

VIGNOLA, Giacomo da (1507–1573), Italian architect, painter and sculptor. He designed the Villa Giulia in Rome (1550–55) and the Villa Farnese at Caprarola (1559–73). His designs for the Jesuit church Il Gesù and his *Rules of the Five Orders of Architecture* (1562) helped create the BAROQUE style.

VIGNY, Alfred Victor, comte de (1797–1863), French Romantic poet, novelist and playwright. His pessimistic works deal with solitude, alienation and spiritual conflict. The posthumous collection *Les Destinées* (1864) contains his most famous poems.

VIGO, Jean (1905–1934), French film director whose films *A Propos de Nice* (1930), *Zéro de Conduit* (1933) and *L'Atalante* (1934) combined elements of stark realism with surrealistic sequences and influenced generations of filmmakers.

VIKING PROGRAM, series of US unmanned space probes designed to land on and study Mars. Viking 1 landed on July 20, 1976, sending back TV pictures; its soil-analysis experiments yielded results which suggest the presence of life, but may represent only unusual chemical reactions. Viking 2 landed Sept. 3, 1976.

VIKINGS, or "Norsemen," the Norwegian, Swedish and Danish seafarers who harassed Europe from the 9th to the 11th centuries. Expert shipbuilders and navigators, they were capable of long sea voyages, and their ferocity made them the terror of Europe. The Norwegians raided Scotland, Ireland and France, and colonized the Hebrides, Orkneys, the Faroes, Iceland and Greenland. They may also have discovered America (see VINLAND). The Danes raided England, France, the Netherlands, Spain and Italy. The Swedes went down the E shores of the Baltic, through what is now W Russia, and reached the Bosporus and Byzantium. In addition to being raiders the Vikings also traded and created permanent settlements. They united the Hebrides and the Isle of Man into a kingdom. The Shetlands, the Orkneys and Caithness became an earldom. Kingdoms were also set up in Ireland and Russia (see VARANGIANS). In 878 the Danish founded the DANELAW in NE England. In N France the Viking ROLLO was granted a dukedom in 911, which was the origin of the NORMAN kingdom. Remarkable for their restless energy, the Vikings exerted a considerable influence on European history.

VILLA, Francisco, known as **Pancho Villa** (1877–1923), Mexican bandit, revolutionary leader and popular hero. He helped MADERO to power in 1911. He then supported CARRANZA (1913–14), but fell out with him. Villa and ZAPATA captured Mexico City but were defeated in 1915 by Gen. Álvaro Obregón. In 1916 he raided US territory and evaded capture by a US punitive force for 11 months. An outlaw until 1920, when the Mexican government retired him with full pay as a general, he was assassinated on his ranch.

VILLA-LOBOS, Heitor (1887–1959), Brazilian composer. Director of national musical education from 1932, he created a synthesis of classical and Brazilian folk music in numerous works, including *Chôros* (1920–29) and *Bachianas Brasileiras* (1930–44).

VILLARD, Henry (1835–1900), German-born US journalist and financier. Correspondent for the *New York Herald* and *New York Tribune* in the Civil War, he later (1881) acquired the New York *Evening Post* and *The Nation*. Entering the railroad business in 1873, he created the Oregon Railway and Navigation Co. (1879), and became president of the Northern Pacific (1881–84, 1888–93). In 1890 he formed the Edison General Electric Co.

VILLELLA, Edward (1936–   ), US dancer. With the New York City Ballet from 1957, he became noted for his dramatic intensity and athleticism. He was famous in the title role of BALANCHINE's *Prodigal Son.*

VILLON, François (1431– after 1463), French poet who led a wandering, criminal life. In his coarse and cynical *Lais* ("Legacy") and *Testament*, which contain some celebrated lyrics, he both relishes and regrets his misspent life and expresses his horror of death.

VINCENT DE PAUL, Saint (c1580–

1660), Roman Catholic priest who pioneered charities in France. In 1625 he founded the Congregation of the Mission (Lazarists), an order of secular priests devoted to rural missionary work. Later (1633) he founded the Daughters of Charity to help the poor in towns.

VINLAND, a region of E North America discovered c1000 AD by VIKING explorers, probably led by Leif ERICSON, and briefly settled c1004 by THORFINN KARLSEFNI. Some scholars believe it was in New England, others favor Newfoundland (where Viking remains have been found). The Norse sagas describe the discovery of a fertile region where grapes grew, hence "Vin(e)land." (See also KENSINGTON RUNE STONE.)

VINSON, Frederick Moore (1890–1953), Chief Justice of the US 1946–53. A Ky. Democrat, he was a member of the House of Representatives 1923–29, 1931–37 and Secretary of the Treasury 1945–46. While he was chief justice, the Supreme Court made important civil-liberty rulings.

VIOL, the 15th–17th century forerunner of the VIOLIN. Viols have sloping shoulders, frets, a low bridge and a soft, mellow tone. The six strings are tuned in fourths. The treble, alto, tenor and bass (*viola da gamba*) viols are all held upright, as was the double-bass *violone,* which became today's DOUBLE-BASS. Interest in the viol has revived in the 20th century.

VIOLA DA GAMBA. See VIOL.

VIOLIN, smallest, most versatile and leading member of the bowed, four-stringed violin family (violin, VIOLA, CELLO, DOUBLE-BASS). Violins succeeded the VIOL in the 1600s, differing in their flexibility, range of tone and pitch, arched bridge, squarer shoulders, narrower body and lack of frets. The violin proper, derived from the 16th-century arm viol, is tuned in fifths and ranges over 4½ octaves above G below middle C. Perfected by the craftsmen of CREMONA, it became a major solo instrument. The principal violinist leads the ORCHESTRA, violins forming most of the string section. Classical string quartets have two violins.

VIOLONCELLO. See CELLO.

VIPERS, a family of SNAKES with highly-developed venom apparatus, found in Europe, Africa and Asia. Vipers are short, stoutly-built and typically terrestrial. They lie in wait for their prey—lizards or small mammals—strike, injecting venom from modified salivary glands through the hollow poison fangs, and then wait for a while before tracking down their victim. One of the best known species is the ADDER.

VIRCHOW, Rudolf (1821–1902), Pomer-anian-born German pathologist whose most important work was to apply knowledge concerning the CELL to PATHOLOGY, in course of which he was the first to document LEUKEMIA and EMBOLISM. He was also distinguished as an anthropologist and archaeologist.

VIRGIL. See VERGIL.

VIRGINAL, type of small HARPSICHORD, its strings parallel to the single keyboard. There is one wire per note. Encased in a small rectangular box, the virginal was popular c1550–1650.

VIRGIN BIRTH, Christian doctrine that JESUS CHRIST was conceived by the Virgin MARY through the Holy Spirit's power, without a human father. Though stated in the GOSPELS of Matthew and Luke and embodied in the CREEDS, it has been criticized in the past 100 years as a legendary tradition endangering Jesus' full humanity. (See also INCARNATION.)

Name of state: Virginia
Capital: Richmond
Statehood: June 25, 1788 (10th state)
Familiar names: Old Dominion; Mother of Presidents
Area: 40,817sq mi
Population: 5,346,279
Elevation: Highest—5,729ft, Mount Rogers; Lowest—sea level, Atlantic Ocean
Motto: Sic Semper Tyrannis (Thus Always to Tyrants)
State flower: Dogwood
State bird: Cardinal
State tree: Dogwood
State song: "Carry Me Back to Old Virginny"

VIRGINIA, state of the E US, the largest and oldest of the original 13 colonies. It is bounded N by Md., S by N.C. and Tenn., W by Ky., and NW by W. Va.

Land. The major regions are: the TIDEWATER coastal plain, extending about 100mi inland; the Piedmont, a rolling plateau rising to 2,000ft where it meets the Blue Ridge Mts., and the broad Appalachian Ridge and Valley Region in the W. There are many rivers, most of which run SE to Chesapeake Bay. The Potomac R forms most of the Va.–Md. boundary. Nearly two-thirds of Va. is forest. The climate is mild.

People. Since 1950 Virginia has been transformed from a predominantly rural to a predominantly urban state. Population is concentrated in the E where Norfolk, Portsmouth, and Richmond are the largest cities; Roanoke is the largest city in the W. Blacks total 1,008,311.

Economy. Va.'s strong economy is based on manufacturing (notably chemicals, tobacco, textiles, shipbuilding and foodstuffs) and agriculture (primarily tobacco and livestock). Tourism is a major addition to the economy. There are large coal deposits in the SW.

History. After Sir Walter RALEIGH'S expedition to North America in the late 16th century, the name "Virginia" (for Elizabeth I, the "Virgin Queen") was applied to all of North America not claimed by Spain or France. In May 1607, colonists sent out by one of the VIRGINIA COMPANIES established the first permanent English settlement in the New World at JAMESTOWN.

In 1612 John ROLFE began to raise tobacco, which was to be for long the basis of Va.'s economy. In 1619 the first Negroes came to Va., as indentured servants, and by 1715 constituted about 25% of the population. Intermittent conflicts with the POWHATAN INDIANS reached a peak in 1622 when the Indians killed some 350 colonists in a single attack, reducing the colony by a third. In 1619 the first house of burgesses met at Jamestown, and the settlers' participation in their own governmental affairs continued after Va. became a royal colony in 1624. The British government of the RESTORATION attempted strict enforcement of the NAVIGATION ACTS limiting colonial trade to England. This was a contributing cause of BACON'S REBELLION in 1676.

Va. took a leading role in the REVOLUTIONARY WAR and events leading to it. Her distinguished patriots included Patrick HENRY, Thomas JEFFERSON, and George WASHINGTON. In May 1776, the fifth Virginia Convention declared the colony an independent commonwealth and the following month it became the first American colony to adopt a constitution and a declaration of rights. Va.'s Robert E. LEE led the South during the CIVIL WAR. In 1863 the W counties of Va. which had refused to secede formed the new state of WEST VIRGINIA. Most historic of states, Va. was the scene of the British surrender at YORKTOWN (1781) and the Confederate surrender at APPOMATTOX, and has provided eight US presidents. In the 20th century, Virginia has become increasingly urbanized and industrialized with numerous military facilities contributing to the state's economic sturdiness. It was dominated for many years (1926–66) by Harry F. Byrd Sr., under whose leadership the state vigorously resisted desegregation and civil rights for black voters.

VIRGINIA COMPANIES, two companies of merchant-adventurers granted patents by the English crown in 1606 for colonizing America. The LONDON COMPANY, authorized to settle anywhere from present-day S.C. to N.Y., founded JAMESTOWN in 1607 (see also VIRGINIA). The PLYMOUTH COMPANY, granted rights from present-day Va. to Me., fared badly. It was reorganized (1620) into the COUNCIL FOR NEW ENGLAND, which made the original grant to the PILGRIM FATHERS and PURITAN settlers.

VIRGIN ISLANDS, westernmost group of the Lesser Antilles in the WEST INDIES, E of Puerto Rico. The W islands belong to the US and the E group to Britain. Discovered and claimed for Spain by Christopher COLUMBUS (1493), the Virgin Islands were settled chiefly by English and Danes in the 1600s. England secured the British Virgin Islands in 1666. The Danish West Indies were acquired by the US for strategic reasons in 1917 and became the US Virgin Islands. The economy of both groups now depends on tourism but farming (food crops, livestock) and fishing are important. The Virgin Islands of the US, a US territory covering 133sq mi, comprise St. Thomas, St. John, St. Croix and some 65 islets. Charlotte Amalie, the capital and only city, stands on St. Thomas. Pop 95,200. The British Virgin Islands are separated from the American islands by a strait called The Narrows. Covering 59sq mi, the group consists of about 30 mainly uninhabited islands. The largest is Tortola, which has the capital and chief port, Road Town. Pop 13,000.

VIRGO (the Virgin), a large constellation on the ECLIPTIC; the sixth sign of the ZODIAC. It contains the bright spectroscopic binary (see DOUBLE STAR) Spica and a cluster of galaxies.

VIRUS, submicroscopic parasitic microorganism comprising a PROTEIN or protein/lipid sheath containing nucleic acid (DNA or RNA). Viruses are inert outside living cells, but within appropriate cells they can replicate (using raw material parasitized from the cell) and give rise to the manifestations of the associated VIRAL DISEASE in the host organism. Various viruses infect animals, plants and BACTERIA (in which case they are BACTERIOPHAGES). Few drugs act specifically against viruses, although IMMUNITY can be induced in susceptible cells against particular viruses. Various pathogenic organisms formerly regarded as large viruses are now distinguished as *bedsonia.*

VISCONTI, Luchino (1906–1976), Italian director in film and theater (notably operas for Maria CALLAS). His films include the neorealist *Ossessione* (1942), *Rocco and his Brothers* (1960), studies of decadence in times past (*The Leopard*, 1964; *Death in Venice*, 1971) and *Conversation Piece* (1975).

VISHINSKY, Andrei Yanuarievich (1883–1954), Russian statesman and jurist. Chief state prosecutor in the purge trials of 1936–38, he was deputy commissar (1940–49) and commissar (1949–53) for foreign affairs, and the USSR's chief UN delegate.

VISIGOTHS (West Goths), Germanic people who in the 200s AD invaded Roman DACIA, under FRITIGERN defeated the Romans at Adrianople (378) and, led by ALARIC I, invaded Thrace and N Italy and sacked Rome (410). They founded (419) a kingdom in S Gaul and Spain, but ALARIC II lost (507) the N lands to CLOVIS, king of the Franks. Roderick, last Gothic king of Spain, lost his throne to the Moors 711. (See also GOTHS; OSTROGOTHS.)

VISION, the special sense concerned with reception and interpretation of LIGHT stimuli reaching the EYE; the principal sense in man. Light reaches the CORNEA and then passes through this, the AQUEOUS HUMOR, the lens and the VITREOUS HUMOR before impinging on the RETINA. Here there are two basic types of receptor: **rods** concerned with light and dark distinction, and **cones**, with three subtypes corresponding to three primary visual COLORS: red, green and blue. Much of vision and most of the cones are located in the central area, the macula, of which the FOVEA is the central portion; gaze directed at objects brings their images into this area. When receptor cells are stimulated, impulses pass through two nerve cell relays in the retina before passing back toward the BRAIN in the optic nerve. Behind the eyes, information derived from left and right visual fields of either eye is collected together and passes back to the opposite cerebral hemisphere, which it reaches after one further relay. In the cortex are several areas concerned with visual perception and related phenomena. The basic receptor information is coded by nerve interconnections at the various relays in

such a way that information about spatial interrelationships is derived with increasing specificity as higher levels are reached. Interference with any of the levels of the visual pathway may lead to visual symptoms and potentially to BLINDNESS.

VITALISM, the theory, dating from ARISTOTLE, that there is a distinguishing vital principle ("life force") in living organisms that is absent from nonliving objects. (See BERGSON.)

VITAMINS, specific nutrient compounds which are essential for body growth or METABOLISM and which should be supplied by normal DIETARY FOODS. They are denoted by letters and are often divided into fat-soluble (A, D, E and K) and water-soluble (B and C) groups. Vitamin A, or retinol, is essential for the integrity of EPITHELIUM and its deficiency causes SKIN, EYE and mucous membrane lesions; it is also the precursor for RHODOPSIN, the retinal pigment. Vitamin-A excess causes an acute encephalopathy or chronic multisystem disease. Important members of the **vitamin B** group include thiamine (B_1), riboflavin (B_2), Niacin, Pyridoxine (B_6), Folic acid and cyanocobalamin (B_{12}). **Thiamine** acts as a coenzyme in CARBOHYDRATE metabolism and its deficiency, seen in rice-eating populations and alcoholics, causes BERIBERI and a characteristic encephalopathy. **Riboflavin** is also a coenzyme, active in oxidation reactions; its deficiency causes epithelial lesions. **Niacin** is a general term for nicotinic acid and nicotinamide, which are coenzymes in carbohydrate metabolism; their deficiency occurs in millet- or maize-dependent populations and leads to PELLAGRA. **Pyridoxine** provides an enzyme important in energy storage and its deficiency may cause nonspecific disease or ANEMIA. **Folic acid** is an essential cofactor in NUCLEIC ACID metabolism and its deficiency, which is not uncommon in PREGNANCY and with certain DRUGS, causes a characteristic anemia. **Cyanocobalamin** is essential for all cells, but the development of BLOOD cells and GASTROINTESTINAL-TRACT epithelium and NERVOUS SYSTEM function are particularly affected by its deficiency, which occurs in pernicious ANEMIA and in extreme vegetarians. Pantothenic acid, Biotin, Choline, Inositol and Para-aminobenzoic acid are other members of the B group. **Vitamin C**, or **ascorbic acid**, is involved in many metabolic pathways and has an important role in healing, blood cell formation and bone and tissue growth; SCURVY is its deficiency disease. **Vitamin D**, or **calciferol**, is a crucial factor in CALCIUM metabolism, including the growth and structural maintenance of BONE; lack causes RICKETS, while overdosage also causes disease. **Vitamin E**, or **tocopherol**, appears to play a role in blood cell and nervous system tissues, but its deficiency is uncommon and its beneficial properties have probably been overstated. **Vitamin K** provides essential cofactors for production of certain CLOTTING factors in the LIVER; it is used to treat some clotting disorders, including that seen in premature infants. Vitamin A is derived from both animal and vegetable tissue and most B vitamins are found in green vegetables, though B_{12} is found only in animal food (e.g., liver). Citrus fruit are rich in vitamin C. Vitamin D is found in animal tissues, COD LIVER OIL providing a rich source. Vitamins E and K are found in most biological material.

VITRUVIUS POLLIO, Marcus (1st century BC), Roman architect, military engineer and author of *Architectura*, dedicated to AUGUSTUS. This sole surviving Roman work on the subject had an enormous influence on RENAISSANCE architects.

VIVALDI, Antonio (c1680–1741), Venetian composer, notably for the violin. He wrote vocal music, sonatas, some 450 concertos for violin and other instruments (helping establish the three-movement form: see CONCERTO), and *concerti grossi* including the famous *Four Seasons*. His work has a sparkling clarity, strong rhythms, and a wealth of melody.

VIVISECTION, strictly, the dissection of living animals, usually in the course of physiological or pathological research; however, the use of the term is often extended to cover all animal experimentation. Although the practice remains the subject of considerable popular controversy, it is doubtful whether research, particularly medical, can be effectively carried on without a measure of vivisection.

VLADIMIR, Saint, or **Vladimir I** (c956–1015), Russian grand duke of KIEV (c980–1015) who, after successful wars against Bulgars, Byzantines and Lithuanians, became a Christian c988, married Anna, sister of Byzantine Emperor BASIL II, and began the mass conversion of his people to Eastern Orthodox Christianity.

VLAMINCK, Maurice de (1876–1958), French painter. An admirer of VAN GOGH and a leader of FAUVISM, he evolved an expressionist style in thickly painted, often somber, but brilliantly lit landscapes.

VOICE, the sound emitted in speech (see SPEECH AND SPEECH DISORDERS), the method of communication exclusive to *Homo*

sapiens. It is dependent for its generation upon the passage of air from the LUNGS through the TRACHEA, LARYNX, PHARYNX and MOUTH and its quality in each individual is largely determined by the shape and size of these structures and the resonance of the NOSE and nasal SINUSES. Phonation is the sounding of the elements of speech by the action of several small muscles on the vocal cords of the larynx; these regulate the air passing through and vibrate when tensed against this air stream. Articulation consists in the modulation of these sounds by the use of the TONGUE, TEETH and lips in different combinations. Vowels are produced mainly by phonation while consonants derive their characteristics principally from articulation.

VOICE OF AMERICA, the radio division of the United States Information Agency, established 1942 to explain the US role in WWII. Its network now broadcasts, in English and other languages, a favorable view of life in the US to many (chiefly communist) countries.

VOLCANISM, or **vulcanicity**, the processes whereby MAGMA, a complex of molten silicates containing water and other volatiles in solution, rises toward the earth's surface, there forming IGNEOUS ROCKS. These may be extruded on the earth's surface (see LAVA; VOLCANO) or intruded into subsurface rock layers as, for example, DIKES, SILLS and LACCOLITHS. (See also FUMAROLE; GEYSER; HOT SPRINGS.)

VOLCANO, fissure or vent in the earth's crust through which MAGMA and associated material may be extruded onto the surface. This may occur with explosive force. The extruded magma, or LAVA, solidifies in various forms soon after exposure to the atmosphere. In particular it does so around the vent, building up the characteristic volcanic cone, at the top of which is a crater containing the main vent. There may be subsidiary vents forming "parasitic cones" in the slopes of the main cone. If the volcano is dormant or extinct the vents may be blocked with a *plug* (or *neck*) of solidified lava. On occasion these are left standing after the original cone has been eroded away. Volcanoes may be classified according to the violence of their eruptions. In order of increasing violence the main types are: Hawaiian, Strombolian, Vulcanian, Vesuvian, Peléan. Volcanoes are generally restricted to belts of seismic activity, particularly active plate margins (see PLATE TECTONICS), but some intraplate volcanic activity is also known as in the case of Hawaii (see HOT SPOTS). At mid-ocean ridges magma rises from deep in the mantle and is added to the receding edges of the plates (see SEA-FLOOR SPREADING). In MOUNTAIN regions, where plates are in collision, volatile matter ascends from the subducted edge of a plate, perhaps many km below the surface, bursting through the overlying plate in a series of volcanoes. (See also EARTHQUAKES.)

VOLCKER, Paul (1927–   ), US economist and chairman of the Federal Reserve Board. He served as under secretary for monetary affairs in the Treasury department 1969–74 and president of the New York Reserve Bank 1975–79 before being appointed 1979 to head the Federal Reserve by President Carter. He was architect of the Board's tight-money policy that kept interest rates on borrowing high in order to contract the money supply and dampen inflation.

VOLGA RIVER, chief river of Russia and the longest in Europe. It rises in the Valdai Hills NW of Moscow and flows 2,293mi through Gorki, Kazan, Kuibyshev, Saratov, Volgograd and Astrakhan to its Caspian Sea delta. Draining an area of some 530,000sq mi, it is the main artery of the world's greatest network of commercial waterways linking the White, Baltic, Caspian, Azov and Black seas.

VOLGOGRAD, or (1925–51) Stalingrad or (to 1925) Tsaritsyn, important industrial city on the Volga R, S Russian SFSR, USSR. It was the site of heroic resistance to the Germans in WWII (see STALINGRAD, BATTLE OF). It has iron-and-steel, machine manufacturing, chemical, textile and hydroelectric plants. Pop 939,000.

VOLLEYBALL, a popular game for two teams of six, who volley (using any part of the body above the waist) a large inflated ball across a high net, conceding points by failing to return the ball or by hitting it out of court. Invented at the Holyoke (Mass.) YMCA in 1895 by W. G. Morgan, it became an Olympic event at Tokyo (1964).

VOLSTEAD ACT, the United States National Prohibition Act, introduced by Minn. Representative Andrew J. Volstead. Passed in 1919, over the veto of President Wilson, it provided for enforcement of the 18th Amendment prohibiting the sale, manufacture or transportation in the US of intoxicating liquors. It proved unenforceable, and was modified, then repealed, in 1933. (See PROHIBITION.)

VOLSUNGA SAGA, late-13th-century Icelandic prose heroic saga, based partly on heroic lays in the Poetic EDDA. Like the Germanic NIBELUNGENLIED, it recounts the exploits of Sigurd (SIEGFRIED) and the Völsungs. This legendary material inspired WAGNER.

VOLTA, Alessandro Giuseppe Antonio Anastasio (1745–1827), French physicist who invented the voltaic pile (the first BATTERY) and thus provided science with its earliest continuous electric-current source. Volta's invention (c1800) demonstrated that "animal electricity" could be produced using solely inanimate materials, thus ending a long dispute with the supporters of GALVANI's view that it was a special property of animal matter.

VOLTAIRE (1694–1778), pen name of François-Marie Arouet, French satirist, polemicist, poet, dramatist, novelist, historian and letter-writer, one of the PHILOSOPHES and a genius of the ENLIGHTENMENT. An enemy of tyrants everywhere, he spent much of his life in exile, including 23 years at his property on the Swiss border. His *Letters Concerning the English Nation* (1733) extolled religious and political toleration and the ideas of NEWTON and LOCKE. The famous tale *Candide* (1759), a rational skeptic's attack on the optimism of LEIBNIZ, shows Voltaire's astringent style at its best. A friend of FREDERICK II of Prussia, Voltaire contributed to DIDEROT's *Encyclopedia* and wrote his own *Philosophical Dictionary* (1764).

VOLUNTEERS OF AMERICA, a voluntary philanthropic society founded in New York City (1896) by Ballington and Maud BOOTH after a split with the Salvation Army. It aims to win converts to Christianity and provides many social services. Though it retains military forms and titles, it is run democratically.

VON BRAUN, Wernher. See BRAUN, WERNHER VON.

VONDEL, Joost van den (1587–1679), Dutch national poet. His sonorous verse celebrated the successes of the United Provinces. He translated French, Latin and Greek authors. His dramas, on political, national and religious themes, include *Palamedes* (1625), *Gijsbrecht van Aemstel* (1637) and *Lucifer* (1654).

VONNEGUT, Kurt, Jr. (1922–   ), US novelist noted for his satire and "black humor," with science, religion and war among his targets. His novels, some of which carry overtones rooted in science fiction, include *Player Piano* (1951), *Cat's Cradle* (1963), *God Bless You, Mr. Rosewater* (1965), *Slaughterhouse Five* (1969) and *Jailbird* (1976).

VON NEUMANN, John (1903–1957), Hungarian-born US mathematician who put QUANTUM MECHANICS on a rigorous mathematical foundation. He created GAME THEORY, and made important contributions to the theory of COMPUTERS as well as many branches of abstract mathematics.

VOODOO, a folk religion, chiefly of Haiti, with West African and added Roman Catholic and native West Indian elements. It involves worship of the spirits of saints and ancestors who may "possess" participants. Prayers, drumming, dancing and feasts are part of the ritual. A cult group's priest or priestess is believed to act as a medium, work charms, lay curses and recall zombies (the "living dead").

VOROSHILOV, Kliment Yefremovich (1881–1969), Ukrainian Russian army and political leader. An early Bolshevik and associate of STALIN (whom he succeeded as head of state, 1953–60), he played an important role in organizing Soviet military forces as commissar of defense (1925–1940). He held important military commands during WWII.

VORSTER Balthazar Johannes (John) (1915–), prime minister of South Africa 1966–78. On the right of the Nationalist Party, he was in charge of education (1958–61), and as minister of justice (1961–66) responsible for some of the most repressive APARTHEID laws. He sought later to improve relations with Black Africa. Elected president in 1978, he resigned in 1979 after being accused of false testimony on expenditure of government funds.

VOTING, formal collective expression of approval or rejection of a candidate for office or of a course of action. The ELECTION of officers is a basic feature of DEMOCRACY, but universal adult suffrage is recent: US women obtained the vote only in 1920. Sometimes voting is compulsory, as in Australia and in communist states.

In the US, voting originally followed English parliamentary practice, with the addition of the New England TOWN MEETING. Ballot papers first appeared in Mass. in 1634. Most US states now use voting machines to ensure secrecy, speed and accuracy. Voting through INITIATIVE, REFERENDUM AND RECALL is allowed for in many states. (See also POLL; PUBLIC OPINION; PLEBISCITE.)

VOTING RIGHTS ACT OF 1965, US law aimed at eliminating local laws and practices that served to prevent blacks and other minorities from voting. It was strongly backed by President Lyndon B. Johnson, who signed it into law.

VOYAGER PROGRAM, two unmanned US probes of the outer solar system. Voyager 1 made close approaches to JUPITER in March 1979 and SATURN in Nov. 1980. Voyager 2 by-passed Jupiter in July 1979,

swung aroung Saturn in Aug. 1981, and is scheduled to continue to URANUS in 1986 and NEPTUNE in 1989. The probes provided remarkable close-up views of the two giant planets and their satellites, revealing, among other things, the existence of a ring around Jupiter, active volcanoes on Jupiter's moon Io and a completely unexpected complexity in Saturn's ring system.

VOZNESENSKY, Andrei, (1933–) Russian poet who became popular in the early 1960s. One of the most outspoken and experimental contemporary Soviet poets, he was criticized by the Soviet literary establishment in the 1970s, but continued to write and publish prolifically.

VTOL. See VERTICAL TAKEOFF AND LANDING AIRPLANE.

VUILLARD, Jean Édouard (1868–1940), French painter known particularly for his intimate and richly decorative interior domestic scenes. He was influenced by Japanese art.

VULGATE, the Latin version of the BIBLE, so-called because it became the most widespread (Latin, *vulgata*) in use. Largely the work of St. JEROME, who revised earlier Old Latin translations, it was collected together in the 6th century and universally established by 800. In 1546 the Council of TRENT confirmed the Vulgate as the sole official version of the Roman Catholic Church.

VULTURES, two groups of large, soaring, diurnal BIRDS OF PREY. The New World vultures are a primitive family, Cathartidae; the Old World vultures are a branch of the Accipitridae, being most closely related to certain EAGLES. All vultures are adapted to feed on animal carrion. Their heads and necks are wholly or partially naked; several have specialized tongues to feed rapidly on liquid flesh or bone marrow.

23rd letter of the English alphabet, originally (as the name indicates) a "double U." The form "uu," appearing in the earliest Old English texts, was replaced by the letter *wen* (ρ) in the 700s, but reinstated by French-speaking scribes after the

NORMAN CONQUEST (1066).

WAGE AND PRICE CONTROL, in economics, policy of countering INFLATION by government controls on the separate but interdependent movements of PRICES and wages. The policy may contain percentage or flat-rate limits on increases, and is sometimes preceded by a "freeze" or standstill period. The policy may be legally binding, or voluntary with back-up powers of government intervention. It usually entails a system of notification of price or wage increases. Its use has increased in Western countries since the 1960s, although President Nixon's 90-day wage-price freeze in 1971 only temporarily interrupted the steadily increasing US inflation of the 1970s.

WAGNER, Honus (John Peter Wagner; 1874–1955), US baseball player, one of the greatest shortstops. He played for the Pittsburgh Pirates for 21 years and was their coach for another 19. He was one of the first five men elected to the Baseball Hall of Fame in 1936.

WAGNER, Richard (1813–1883), major German opera composer. His adventurous and influential works mark the high point of Romanticism in music. A conductor in provincial opera houses, he achieved his first success with *Rienzi* (1840). *Der Fliegende Holländer (1841)*, *Tannhäuser* (1844) and *Lohengrin* (1848) pioneered his new ideas in music and drama (see OPERA); these were fulfilled in the myth-cycle *Der Ring des Nibelungen: Das Rheingold* (1853–54), *Die Walküre* (1854–56), *Siegfried* (1856–69) and *Die Götterdämmerung* (1874). Involved in the 1848 Dresden revolution, Wagner fled to Switzerland, where he wrote *Tristan und Isolde* (1859) and the comic opera *Die Meistersinger von Nürnberg* (1868). Ludwig II of Bavaria helped him found the BAYREUTH Festival. *Parsifal* (1882) was his last opera. In private life Wagner was often self-centered and bigoted.

WAGNER, Robert Ferdinand (1877–1953), German-born US reforming politician. After serving as a N.Y. senator (1910–18)

and justice (1919–26), he became a Democratic US senator (1927–49), and helped create the NEW DEAL program, particularly in labor, social security and housing (see WAGNER ACT).

WAGNER, Robert Ferdinand, Jr. (1910–   ), US politician and administrator. Son of R. F. WAGNER, he held posts in New York (1938–41, 1946–53), and served three terms as mayor (1954–65), introducing controversial reforms in housing, education and civil rights. He was US ambassador to Spain 1968–69.

WAGNER ACT, popular name for the National Labor Relations Act, a key part of the NEW DEAL legislation, enacted in July, 1935. Sponsored by R. F. WAGNER, it guaranteed workers the right to organize and bargain collectively, and defined some unfair labor practices. It also set up the NATIONAL LABOR RELATIONS BOARD.

WAHABI, a Muslim reform movement begun in 18th-century Arabia. It aimed to restore ISLAM to its primitive simplicity, and its influence spread as far as Africa and Sumatra. In Arabia the movement followed the fortunes of the royal family, becoming firmly established under IBN SAUD.

WAILING WALL, part of the western wall of the ancient Temple in Jerusalem, destroyed by the Romans in 70 AD. It is held sacred by the Jews, who gather there to pray and bewail their sufferings. Until the 1967 Arab-Israeli War, it was in Jordanian territory.

WAIN, John (1925–   ), English novelist, poet, critic and short-story writer best known for *Hurry On Down* (1953), a satirical novel about post-WWII Britain. Other works include the poetry collections *A Word Carved on a Sill* (1956) and *Weep Before God* (1961), a biography, *Samuel Johnson* (1974), and the novel *The Pardoner's Table* (1978).

WAINWRIGHT, Jonathan Mayhew (1883–1953), US general, veteran of WWI and hero of BATAAN and CORREGIDOR in the defense of the Philippines during WWII. Despite great courage in a hopeless situation, he had to surrender to the Japanese in 1942. A prisoner of war until 1945, he was awarded the Congressional Medal of Honor on his return.

WAITE, Morrison Remick (1816–1888), US lawyer, chief justice of the US Supreme Court 1874–88. He first gained prominence in the ALABAMA CLAIMS dispute (1871–72). His most influential opinions concerned STATES' RIGHTS and the interpretation of the Fourteenth Amendment.

WAJDA, Andrzej (1926–   ), Polish director noted for his avant-garde stage work and the political daring of his films, which include *Kanal* (1955), *Ashes and Diamonds* (1958) and *Man of Marble* (1976).

WAKSMAN, Selman Abraham (1888–1973), Russian-born US biochemist, microbiologist and soil scientist. His isolation of STREPTOMYCIN, the first specific antibiotic (a term he coined) against TUBERCULOSIS, won him the 1952 Nobel Prize for Physiology or Medicine.

WALCOTT, Jersey Joe (1914–   ), US boxer who was the oldest fighter in modern times to win the world heavyweight championship when he knocked out Ezzard Charles in 1951. He lost the title in 1952 to Rocky MARCIANO.

WALD, George (1906–   ), US chemist and prominent pacifist whose work on the chemistry of VISION brought him a share, with H. K. Hartline and R. A. Granit, of the 1967 Nobel Price for Physiology or Medicine.

WALDENSES, a reforming Christian sect founded in Lyons, France, in the 12th century. They preached poverty, rejected the PAPACY and took the Bible as their sole authority, for which they were excommunicated (1184) and persecuted. The survivors united with the Protestants in the REFORMATION. The Waldensian Church still exists, with several offshoots in the US.

WALDHEIM, Kurt (1918–   ), Austrian diplomat and minister of foreign affairs (1968–70), from 1972 secretary general of the UNITED NATIONS. He worked especially to strengthen the UN's peacekeeping role and increase aid to poor countries.

WALES, historic principality of GREAT BRITAIN, politically united with England since 1536. It is a large roughly rectangular peninsula projecting into the Irish Sea W of England. Covering 8,016sq mi, it is dominated by the Cambrian Mts (Snowdon, 3,560ft). Rivers include the Severn, Wye, Usk, Taff and Teifi. The climate is mild and wet. The population (2,774,700) live mainly in the S near the rich coalfields. About 20% speak both WELSH and English. The largest cities are Cardiff, the capital, and Swansea. Major industries, including coalmining, steel, oil-refining, man-made fibers and electronics, are concentrated in the S. Agriculture, mostly cattle and sheep raising, predominates elsewhere. Devolution (i.e. greater local autonomy), long sought by the Welsh nationalist movement (Plaid Cymru) was defeated by referendum vote in 1979.

WALESA, Lech (1943–   ), Polish labor leader. An electrician, he had been active in union organizing for several years before becoming head of SOLIDARITY (1980), a national union that wrung many concessions from the government, unprecedented in the Soviet bloc.

WALKER, James John (1881–1946), New York politician. A member (1915–20) and minority leader (1921–25) of the state Senate, he became Democratic mayor of New York (1926–32), instituting popular reforms. He resigned in a corruption scandal.

WALKER, Mary Edwards (1832–1919), US surgeon and feminist, the first woman to be commissioned a surgeon in the Union army (1864). Later she practiced in Washington D.C. and campaigned for women's rights.

WALKER, Ralph Thomas (1889–1973), US architect whose works include the New York Telephone Company and the Irving Trust buildings in Manhattan. He also specialized in the design of research laboratories, and created one of the basic photographic techniques of cinerama.

WALKER, William (1824–1860), US adventurer. He tried to create a republic out of Lower Cal. and Sonora, Mexico (1853–54), then joined a revolution in Nicaragua, becoming president 1856–57. Ousted partly by VANDERBILT interests, but regarded by many as a hero, he was captured by the British and shot in attempting to regain Nicaragua.

WALKER CUP, a golf competition held every other year between men's amateur teams from the US and Great Britain. This match play competition, consisting of both foursome and singles matches, is named for former US Golf Association president George H. Walker.

WALLABIES, a large and diverse assemblage of kangaroo-like MARSUPIALS, generally smaller than true KANGAROOS, but like them in having large strong hindfeet and limbs and a long tail. They are herbivorous animals of Australia, Tasmania and New Guinea. All wallabies produce a single young, suckling it in the marsupium or pouch.

WALLACE, Alfred Russel (1823–1913), British socialist naturalist regarded as the father of ZOOGEOGRAPHY. His most striking work was his formulation, independently of C. DARWIN, of the theory of NATURAL SELECTION as a mechanism for the origin of species (see EVOLUTION). He and Darwin presented their results in a joint paper in 1858 before the Linnean Society.

WALLACE, Edgar (1875–1932), prolific English writer and playwright. He was especially successful with his detective stories and thrillers, notably *The Red Circle*

(1913).

WALLACE, George Corley (1919–   ), US political leader, governor of Ala. 1963–67, 1971–75. He served in the state legislature 1946–58, and achieved notoriety in 1963 with his unsuccessful attempt to prevent racial integration at the University of Alabama. He ran for president as an independent in 1968, receiving 13% of the vote. He was paralyzed in an attempted assassination while campaigning for the Democratic nomination in 1972. His 1976 campaign for the nomination came to little owing to Jimmy CARTER'S successes in the South.

WALLACE, Henry Agard (1888–1965), 33rd Vice-President of the US (1941–45). A distinguished agricultural economist and plant geneticist, he was appointed secretary of agriculture in 1933. His success with NEW DEAL farm programs led to the vice-presidency. He became secretary of commerce (1945), but was dismissed in 1946 for criticizing TRUMAN. He stood in 1948 as candidate for the PROGRESSIVE PARTY.

WALLACE, Irving (1916–   ), US popular novelist. More than 135 million copies of his books have been sold worldwide, including *The Chapman Report* (1960), *The Prize* (1962), *The Seven Minutes* (1969) and *The Second Lady* (1980). With his family he has compiled the nonfiction bestsellers *The People's Almanac* (1975) and *The Book of Lists* (1977).

WALLACE, Lew (1827–1905), US author, soldier and diplomat, known for his best-selling novel *Ben Hur* (1880). He served in the Mexican and Civil Wars, became Governor of N.M. (1878–81) and minister to Turkey (1881–85).

WALLENBERG, Raoul (1912–1947?), Swedish diplomat. While representing Sweden in Budapest during WWII, he issued passports to 5,000 Jews to keep them out of Nazi hands. Soviet authorities arrested him as a spy in 1945 and claimed he died in prison in 1947. In 1981 an international association said evidence indicated he might be alive and urged the Soviet Union to investigate.

WALLENDA, Karl (1905–1978), German-born circus performer. He created the first high-wire pyramid with his troupe (1925) and led the "Flying Wallendas," the most successful daredevil act in history, to triumphs throughout the world. He fell to his death while trying to walk a wire between two ten-story buildings in San Juan, Puerto Rico.

WALLER, Thomas "Fats" (1904–1943), US jazz pianist and composer. Original and influential, he made hundreds of popular recordings and wrote such songs as *Ain't Misbehavin'* and *Honeysuckle Rose*. He was also a brilliant performer on the organ.

WALLIS, John (1616–1703), British mathematician and cryptographer whose *Arithmetica infinitorum* (Arithmetic of Infinities, 1655) laid the foundations for much of modern algebra, introducing the concept of the LIMIT and the symbol ∞ for INFINITY. From this work were later developed CALCULUS and the BINOMIAL THEOREM.

WALLOONS, the French-speakers of the S half of BELGIUM. There has long been friction between them and the Flemish-speaking majority, who have resented French political and cultural domination. Separate regional administrations were set up in 1974.

WALL STREET, the financial center of the US, in Lower Manhattan, New York, the home of the New York Stock Exchange, many other commodity exchanges and head offices of banks, insurance and brokerage firms. The term also refers to the nation's aggregate financial interests.

WALPOLE, Horace, 4th Earl of Orford (1717–1797), son of Sir Robert, English novelist, letter-writer and connoisseur. His *Castle of Otranto* (1765) was the first GOTHIC NOVEL; and his famous villa, Strawberry Hill, helped stimulate the GOTHIC REVIVAL. Over 3,000 of his letters survive.

WALPOLE, Sir Robert (1676–1745), English statesman often described as Britain's first prime minister. A WHIG, he held ministerial posts 1708–17. Recalled after the SOUTH SEA BUBBLE to be first lord of the Treasury and chancellor of the Exchequer (1721), he dominated Parliament, creating political and financial stability. Facing opposition and unpopularity as Britain became involved in European wars from 1739, he resigned in 1742, becoming 1st Earl of Orford.

WALPURGIS NIGHT, the night of Apr. 30/May 1 when, according to central European legend, witches assembled on mountaintops to consort with the devil. Of ancient pagan origin, it has been mistakenly associated with 8th-century German St. Walburga.

WALRUSES, two subspecies of seal-like marine mammals, *Odobenus rosmarus*, distinguished by having the upper canines extended into long tusks which in a mature adult may reach 1m (3.3ft). Walruses are found in shallow water around Arctic coasts, often hauling out onto rocks or ice floes to bask. They feed almost exclusively n mollusks.

WALTER, Bruno (Bruno Walter Schlesinger; 1876–1962), German-born US conductor. He was a protégé of Gustav MAHLER'S, but his career in Europe was cut short by the Nazis, and he lived in the US from 1939. He was renowned for his interpretations of Mahler, Wagner, Beethoven and Brahms.

WALTHER VON DER VOGELWEIDE (c1170–c1230), most famous of the German MINNESINGERS. He wandered from court to court, until granted a fief by Emperor FREDERICK II. Apart from love poems, he composed political and religious poetry.

WALTON, Izaak (1593–1683), English writer remembered for *The Compleat Angler* (1653), a series of dialogues on the art of fishing which also praise the peaceful and simple life. He wrote biographies of friends he admired, like John DONNE.

WALTON, Sir William Turner (1902–   ), English composer. He had a brilliant early success with his music for Edith SITWELL'S *Façade* (1923). Other works include the oratorio *Belshazzar's Feast* (1931), film scores, notably for Shakespeare films, and the opera *Troilus and Cressida* (1954).

WALTZ, dance with three beats to the bar, originating from the LÄNDLER. Its popularity in the 19th century was due largely to the music of the STRAUSS family.

WAMBAUGH, Joseph (1937–   ), US writer whose intense novels about policemen are drawn from his experience as a detective sergeant with the Los Angeles Police Department (1960–74). His best known novels are *The New Centurions* (1971) and *The Onion Field* (1973).

WAMPUM, strings of shell beads prized by North American Indians, who used them as money in trading. The early white settlers also accepted them as currency, but the production of counterfeit glass beads undermined their value in the early 18th century.

WANAMAKER, John (1838–1922), US businessman whose department stores pioneered advertising techniques and personnel welfare and training. He was postmaster general 1889–93.

WANDERING JEW, according to a legend first recorded in the 13th century, a Jew who taunted Jesus on the way to Calvary and who was doomed to wander the world until Jesus returned.

WANG WEI (699–759), Chinese painter and poet. He is traditionally the originator of the monochrome ink-wash technique and founder of the renowned "Southern" School

of landscape painting. His poetry and painting are imbued with a personal feeling for the beauty of nature.

WANK, Roland Anthony (1898–1970), Hungarian-born US architect known for his low-rent housing designs (1930) in New York City. He was named head architect of the Rural Electrification Administration and Tennessee Valley Authority (1933–44).

WANKEL ENGINE, INTERNAL COMBUSTION ENGINE that produces rotary motion directly. Invented by the German engineer Felix Wankel (1902–   ), who completed his first design in 1954, it is now used in automobiles and airplanes. A triangular rotor with spring-loaded sealing plates at its apexes rotates eccentrically inside a cylinder, while the three combustion chambers formed between the sides of the rotor and the walls of the cylinder successively draw in, compress and ignite a fuel-and-air mixture. The Wankel engine is simpler in principle, more efficient and more powerful weight for weight, but more difficult to cool, than a conventional reciprocating engine.

WAPITI, the North American subspecies of the RED DEER, *Cervus elephas*. It differs from the typical European red deer in being larger and in that the terminal points to the antlers are in the same plane as the beam and do not form a "crown." Wapiti, once the most abundant deer in North America, are now severely reduced in numbers and range.

WAR, organized armed conflict between groups of people or states. War is not found elsewhere in the animal kingdom. Since recorded history began, man has been involved in hostility, for different aims: power, territory, wealth, ideological domination, security, independence. Until modern times, most wars were fought with limited means for limited aims, but modern weapons of mass destruction and total warfare can eliminate whole populations and endanger the survival of the human race. (See GENEVA CONVENTIONS; GUERRILLA WARFARE; NUCLEAR WARFARE; STRATEGY; WAR CRIMES.)

WARBLERS, small perching birds related to THRUSHES and FLYCATCHERS. Almost all have thin, pointed bills and they are mainly insectivorous. While some, tropical, species are brightly-colored, most are olive or brown. The common name refers to the melodious songs produced by many of the species.

WARBURG, Otto Heinrich (1883–1970), German biochemist awarded the 1931 Nobel Prize for Physiology or Medicine for his work elucidating the chemistry of cell RESPIRATION.

WAR CRIMES, in INTERNATIONAL LAW, the violation of the laws and rules of WAR. The first systematic attempt to frame laws for warfare was by GROTIUS (1625). Since 1864 various agreements have laid down principles for the treatment of combatants and civilians, and attempted to outlaw certain weapons (see GENEVA CONVENTIONS; HAGUE PEACE CONFERENCES; KELLOGG-BRIAND PACT).

Few have been convicted of war crimes. A Confederate officer, Henry WIRZ, was executed in 1865. An attempt was made to try the Kaiser after WWI, and some German officers were tried (mostly acquitted) by a German court. The only major war-crimes trial has been the NUREMBERG TRIALS. Here three categories of war crime were defined: crimes against peace (planning and waging aggressive war); "conventional" war crimes (murder of civilians or prisoners of war, plunder etc.); and crimes against humanity (murder, enslavement or deportation of whole populations). The principle of individual responsibility was also established. (See also MY LAI.)

WARD, Aaron Montgomery (1843–1913), US businessman. In 1872, with a capital of $2,400, he started up the mail-order firm which became the vast house of Montgomery Ward & Co.

WARD, Artemas (1727–1800), American leader in the REVOLUTIONARY WAR. As governor of Massachusetts (1774–75), he besieged Boston until WASHINGTON arrived, and was second in command of the Continental Army 1775–76. He served in Congress 1791–95.

WARD, Artemus (1834–1867), pen-name of Charles Farrar Browne, US journalist and humorist. The character of Artemus Ward, an irreverent traveling showman, became a household name for his pungent and comically ungrammatical comments. Browne also became a popular lecturer.

WARD, Barbara (1914–1981), British economist and commentator on the relations between the Western powers and developing nations. She stressed the importance of economic aid and international cooperation in such books as *The Rich Nations and the Poor Nations* (1962), *Spaceship Earth* (1968) and *Progress for a Small Planet* (1979).

WARD, Lester Frank (1831–1913), US sociologist and paleontologist. A fervent evolutionist, he pioneered US sociology with such works as *Dynamic Sociology* (1883), *The Psychic Factors of Civilization* (1893)

and *Glimpses of the Cosmos* (6 vols. 1913–1918).

WARD, Robert (1917–   ), US composer who studied at both the Eastman and Juilliard schools of music. The influence of jazz and American folk melodies is heard in his works, which include the Pulitzer Prize-winning opera *The Crucible* (1961).

WAR DEPARTMENT, former executive department of the US government, reconstituted in 1947 as the Department of the Army, a branch of the US Department of DEFENSE. It was first set up in 1789 to supervise the nation's military establishment, and also ran the Navy until 1798. It was headed by a civilian secretary who was automatically a member of the president's cabinet. After 1947, the secretary of war lost his cabinet post and became secretary of the army, responsible to the new secretary of defense.

WAR HAWKS, group of expansionist US Congressmen who in 1810–12 helped precipitate the WAR OF 1812. Mostly Southerners and Westerners, they hoped to remove British hindrance to expansion in the Northwest and gain Florida from Spain, Britain's ally.

WARHOL, Andy (1930?–   ), US artist and filmmaker, famous for his POP ART paintings. His highly innovative, often erotic and often lengthy films include *Chelsea Girls* (1966) and *Lonesome Cowboys* (1969).

WARM-BLOODED ANIMALS, or Homoiotherms, animals whose body TEMPERATURE is not dependent on external temperature but is maintained at a constant level by internally-generated metabolic heat. This constant temperature enables the chemical processes of the body, many of them temperature-dependent, to be more efficient. Modern animals which have developed this homoiothermy are the MAMMALS and BIRDS, and it is now believed that PTERODACTYLS, THERAPSIDS, and many other extinct REPTILES may also have been warm-blooded.

WARNER, Glenn S. "Pop" (1871–1954), US football coach. He coached all-American JIM THORPE at Carlisle Indian School 1899–1915, produced three undefeated U. of Pittsburgh teams 1915–24 and led three Stanford elevens to the Rose Bowl 1924–33. During his 46 years as a coach, Warner pioneered both the single and double wing formations.

WARNER, Jack L. (1892–1978), US film producer who, with his three brothers, founded Warner Brothers, one of the largest and most successful Hollywood film studios. Warner Brothers produced the first full-length sound film, *The Jazz Singer* (1927), and was the first studio to produce for television.

WARNER, Seth (1743–1784), a hero of the American REVOLUTIONARY WAR and a leader of the GREEN MOUNTAIN BOYS. He helped capture Fort TICONDEROGA, took CROWN POINT (1775) and was largely responsible for the American victory at BENNINGTON (1777).

WAR OF 1812, conflict between the US and Great Britain, 1812–15. It originated in the maritime policies of Britain and France in the NAPOLEONIC WARS. In 1806 Napoleon tried to prevent neutrals from trading with Britain (see CONTINENTAL SYSTEM; BERLIN DECREE; MILAN DECREE). Britain retaliated with ORDERS IN COUNCIL to prevent neutrals from trading with France. US trade slumped, and after the CHESAPEAKE incident she responded with the EMBARGO ACT (1807) and the NONINTERFERENCE ACT (1809), banning trade with the belligerents. However, the chief sufferer from the ban was the US. MACON'S BILL No. 2 (1810) lifted the ban, with certain provisions, but after agreement with Napoleon the US reimposed sanctions against Britain. Anti-British feeling, fed by WAR HAWKS and by the conviction that British support of the Indians (see TIPPECANOE, BATTLE OF) was hindering US expansion, led to war being declared on June 18, 1812.

The US was unprepared and in internal conflict over the war, and her attempted invasion of Canada (1812) was a failure. (See Sir Isaac BROCK.) Early naval successes led to a retaliatory British blockade. US successes came in 1813 with the Battles of Lake ERIE and the THAMES. In 1814 US troops held their own at Chippaewa and LUNDY'S LANE, and by a victory at PLATTSBURGH halted a British advance on the Hudson Valley. In Chesapeake Bay a British force that had sacked Washington was repelled in its attempt to take Baltimore. There was military stalemate, and peace negotiations started in June, 1814. The Peace of GHENT, signed on Dec. 22, 1814, was essentially a return to the status quo before the war. A fortnight later, Andrew JACKSON, unaware of the peace, defeated the British at the Battle of NEW ORLEANS. The war had several far-reaching effects on the US: the military victories promoted national confidence and encouraged expansionism, while the trade embargo encouraged home manufactures.

WAR OF THE PACIFIC (1879–1884), war fought by Chile against Bolivia and Peru over control of the nitrate-rich Atacama Desert in Bolivia (now N Chile's Antofagasta Province), bordering the Pacific. Chile conquered and annexed the desert and parts of Peru. (See also TACNA-ARICA DISPUTE.)

WAR ON POVERTY, the totality of the administrative programs of President Lyndon B. Johnson that were aimed at eliminating poverty in the US and alleviating its effects. Johnson's declaration of "a war on poverty" occurred in his State of the Union speech of 1964; this crusade was essential to his vision of the Great Society.

WARREN, Earl (1891–1974), US Chief Justice 1953–69. Attorney general (1939–43) and governor (1943–53) of Cal., he was Republican vice-presidential candidate in 1948. Appointed to the Supreme Court by Eisenhower, he led it to a number of liberal judgements, notably the one in Brown v. Board of Education of Topeka, Kan. (1954) declaring racial segregation in schools unconstitutional. See also WARREN REPORT.

WARREN, Robert Penn (1905–   ), US novelist, poet, critic, and university teacher. He was a member of the FUGITIVES. Most of his poetry and popular novels have a Southern setting and political and moral themes. His three Pulitzer prizes include one for *All the King's Men* (1946).

WARREN REPORT, report of the commission set up by Lyndon JOHNSON to investigate the assassination of President John KENNEDY. It comprised Earl WARREN, US representatives Hale Boggs and Gerald FORD, US senators Richard RUSSELL and John S. Cooper, Allen DULLES and John J. McCloy, attorney and ex-president, World Bank. The report, released in Sept. 1964, concluded that neither putative assassin Lee OSWALD nor his killer Jack RUBY was part of a conspiracy. It criticized the FBI and Secret Service and recommended reforms in presidential security.

WARSAW (Warszawa), largest city and capital of Poland and of Warsaw province, on the Vistula R. It is a commercial, industrial, cultural and educational center and transportation hub. Chief products are machinery, precision instruments, motor vehicles, electrical equipment, textiles and chemicals. Warsaw replaced Kraków as capital in 1596 and has frequently fallen into Swedish, Russian, Prussian or German hands. Much of the city was razed in WWII but it has been carefully reconstructed. Pop 1,572,000.

WARSAW PACT, or Warsaw Treaty Organization, mutual defense pact signed 1955 in Warsaw by the USSR and its communist neighbors Albania, Bulgaria,

Czechoslovakia, East Germany, Hungary, Poland and Romania, after formation of the NORTH ATLANTIC TREATY ORGANIZATION (NATO). Its unified command has headquarters in Moscow. In 1968 (when Albania formally withdrew), Pact forces invaded Czechoslovakia to overthrow an independent-minded regime. In 1980–81 the USSR used pact maneuvers and threats of intervention by pact members to discourage labor unrest in Poland.

WART, scaly excrescence on the SKIN caused by a VIRUS which may arise without warning and disappear equally suddenly. Numerous remedies have been suggested but local freezing or CAUTERIZATION are often effective. Verrucas are warts pushed into the soles of the feet by the weight of the body.

WARWICK, Richard Neville, Earl of (1428–1471), "The Kingmaker," most powerful English noble of his time. A Yorkist (see ROSES, WARS OF THE), he drove out HENRY VI and installed Edward of York as EDWARD IV (1461). He virtually ruled England, but lost royal favor, rose against Edward and reinstated Henry (1471). Warwick was defeated by Edward and killed at the battle of Barnet. He featured in Lytton's *The Last of the Barons* (1843).

Name of state: Washington
Capital: Olympia
Statehood: Nov. 11, 1889 (42nd state)
Familiar name: Evergreen State; Chinook State
Area: 68,192sq mi
Population: 4,130,163
Elevation: Highest—14,410ft, Mount Rainier; Lowest—sea level, Pacific Ocean
Motto: Alki (By and By)
State flower: Coast rhododendron
State bird: Willow goldfinch
State tree: Western hemlock
State song: "Washington, My Home"
WASHINGTON, a NW Pacific state of the US bordering Ida., Ore., and British Columbia, Canada.
Land. The state is divided by the N–S CASCADE RANGE, which reaches 14,410ft (Mt RAINIER). The W half of the state is largely fertile lowland, deeply penetrated by Puget Sound. The E is mostly semiarid plateau intersected by deep canyons, the largest of which is dammed by the GRAND COULEE DAM on the COLUMBIA RIVER. The Columbia and its tributary Pend Oreille and the Snake and Yakima rivers provide irrigation just E of the Cascades, and a large amount of hydroelectricity. The climate is mild and damp (up to 150in rain per year) in the W, drier and more extreme to the E.

People. The population is predominantly urban and concentrated in the NW on the shores of Puget Sound, where Seattle and Tacoma are the largest cities. The E is more sparsely populated, with Spokane the principal city. Blacks constitute less than 3% of the population, and there are over 60,000 Indians and more than 20 reservations.

Land. The economy depends primarily on manufactures, notably aircraft, food-processing, timber products, aluminum and chemicals. Agriculture (apples, cherries, wheat, livestock, and dairying), fishing, mining, lumber (half of Wash. is forest) and tourism are also important. The state is an important producer of hydroelectric power.

History. The first recorded landing on the Wash. coast was made by Spaniards in 1775, and James COOK and George VANCOUVER soon followed. The LEWIS AND CLARK EXPEDITION descended the Columbia R in 1805, and fur traders gradually moved in. In 1846 the 49th-parallel boundary with Canada was fixed. The area was included in the Oregon Territory (1848); Washington Territory, set up in 1853, lost part of W Ida. in 1863, and achieved statehood in 1889. The opening of the railroad in 1883 and the Alaska and Klondike gold rush in the 1890s boosted population, while labor conflicts gave Wash. a radical name. Though WWI brought a stimulus to the economy (especially shipbuilding), a collapse followed, and the situation worsened in the Great Depression. However, industries set up in WWII, postwar hydroelectric schemes, the expanding aerospace industry and diversification have brought increasing prosperity. On May 18, 1980, a devastating volcanic explosion at MOUNT SAINT HELENS tore off the peak and collapsed one side of the mountain; the immediate destruction affected some 44,000 acres (from which most people had been evacuated), and a cover of volcanic ash fell in 3 states.

WASHINGTON, Booker Taliaferro (1856–1915), black US educator. Born of a Va. slave family, he was chosen 1881 to head a new school for blacks; the TUSKEGEE INSTITUTE, Ala. This he built up from two unequipped buildings to a complex with over 100 buildings and 1,500 students. Washington urged industrial education as the way to economic independence, favoring racial cooperation rather than political action. His extensive writings included an autobiography, *Up From Slavery* (1901).

WASHINGTON, D.C., capital of the US, coextensive with the federal District of Columbia. It covers 69.2sq mi on the E bank of the Potomac R, but the metropolitan area now includes parts of Md. and Va. The focal point is the domed CAPITOL, home of the CONGRESS OF THE US. To the NW lies the WHITE HOUSE. Other important buildings are the headquarters of numerous government departments and agencies, the SUPREME COURT, PENTAGON (in Va.), FEDERAL BUREAU OF INVESTIGATION and LIBRARY OF CONGRESS. Also a cultural and educational center, Washington is the site of the SMITHSONIAN INSTITUTION, the NATIONAL GALLERY OF ART and the John F. Kennedy Center for the Performing Arts. There are many parks and famous memorials: the WASHINGTON MONUMENT, the LINCOLN MEMORIAL, and the JEFFERSON MEMORIAL. There is little industry, but many large corporations and other organizations have their offices there, including the FEDERAL RESERVE SYSTEM.

History. In 1783, the CONTINENTAL CONGRESS voted for a federal city. President Washington chose the present site in 1790 as a compromise between North and South, and the capitol was built at its center. In 1800 Congress moved from Philadelphia. During the WAR OF 1812, the government buildings were burned down (1814) by British troops, and new and more splendid plans were made. Since then the population has risen steadily. Washington, long a gateway for blacks emigrating N, is a focus for demonstrations as well as government. There is an elected mayor but Congress retains the right to review the city's budget and legislation. A subway opened in 1976. Pop 637,651.

WASHINGTON, George (1732–1799), first president of the US (1789–97). Born into a wealthy Va. family, he showed an early aptitude for surveying, in 1749 becoming surveyor of Culpeper Co. He first attracted notice with a report (1753) on the French threat in the Ohio Valley, and became commander in chief of the Va. militia (1755–58) after distinguishing himself in the mission of Edward BRADDOCK (see FRENCH AND INDIAN WARS). Returning to MOUNT VERNON, the estate he inherited in 1760, he married (1759) and became a member of the Va. house of burgesses (1759–74) and a justice of the peace (1760–74). His anti-British feelings were exacerbated by British taxes (see STAMP ACT, TOWNSHEND ACTS). He became a delegate to the CONTINENTAL CONGRESS (1774–75) and was appointed commander in chief of the Continental Army in 1775 (see REVOLUTIONARY WAR). From ill-trained and ill-equipped troops, he created a disciplined army, secured the fall of Boston (1776) but narrowly extricated himself after defeat at LONG ISLAND.

After successes at Trenton and Princeton, 1777 marked a low point in the war. Washington survived an attempt to displace him and wintered 1777–78 in VALLEY FORGE. Alliances with France (1778) and Spain (1779) changed the course of the war. Victory was secured by the capture of YORKTOWN (1781), and after peace had been reached (1783) Washington resigned and returned to Mount Vernon.

Dissatisfied with the 1781 ARTICLES OF CONFEDERATION, Washington played a major role in securing the adoption of the UNITED STATES CONSTITUTION, and was unanimously elected president in 1789. Believing in a strong central government, he created a federal judiciary (1789) and a national bank (1791), and put through other far-reaching financial measures. These led to party conflict centering on Thomas JEFFERSON and Alexander HAMILTON. His second term of office was marked by controversy over foreign affairs, as with the JAY TREATY and his efforts to keep the US neutral in Britain's war with France (1793). There were also Indian insurrections (see FALLEN TIMBERS, BATTLE OF) and internal dissension (see WHISKEY REBELLION). He refused a third term of office. His integrity, patience and high sense of duty and justice made him a great leader and won him the title of "Father of His Country."

WASHINGTON CONFERENCE, post-WWI meetings convened by US President HARDING and held in Washington, D.C., 1921–22. The US, Britain, Japan, France and Italy agreed to limit their capital ships in the ratio 5:5:3:1⅔:1⅔ respectively, to restrictions on submarine warfare and a ban on use of poison gas. France, Japan, Britain and the US agreed to respect each other's Pacific territories. A nine-power treaty with the additional signatures of Belgium, China, the Netherlands and Portugal guaranteed China's territorial integrity.

WASHINGTON MONUMENT, stone obelisk in Washington, D.C., honoring George WASHINGTON. Begun 1848, it was completed in 1884. Faced with white marble, it is 555ft high. Visitors may go to the top by elevator, or by climbing 898 steps.

WASHINGTON'S BIRTHDAY, a legal holiday in most states, celebrated on the third Monday in February in honor of George Washington. He was born Feb. 11, 1732, but the 1752 calendar reform made it Feb. 22. The Monday holiday also honors Abraham Lincoln, who was born on Feb. 12.

WASPS, stinging insects, banded black and yellow, related to BEES and ANTS in the order Hymenoptera. There are a number of families; most are solitary, but members of the Vespoidea are social, forming true colonies with workers, drones and queen(s). Most of the solitary species are hunting wasps. These make nest cells in soil or decaying wood, in which they place one or more paralyzed insects before the egg is laid, to act as a living larder for the larva when it hatches. Social wasps congregate to form a permanent colony with both adults and young. The nest is usually constructed of "wasp paper," a thick pulp of wood fibers and saliva. The adults feed the developing larvae on dead insects which have been killed by biting in the neck; the sting, which in solitary wasps is used to paralyze the prey, is reserved for defense. Adult wasps feed on carbohydrate: NECTAR, aphid honeydew or jam.

WASSERMANN TEST, screening test for syphilis (see VENEREAL DISEASES) based on a nonspecific serological reaction which is seen not only in syphilis but also in YAWS and diseases associated with immune disorders. More specific tests are available to discriminate between these.

WASTE DISPOSAL, disposal of such matter as animal excreta and the waste products of agricultural, industrial and domestic processes, where an unacceptable level of environmental POLLUTION would otherwise result. Where an ecological balance exists (see ECOLOGY), wastes are recycled naturally or by technological means (see RECYCLING) before accumulations affect the quality of life or disrupt the ecosystem. The most satisfactory waste-disposal methods are therefore probably those that involve recycling, as in manuring fields with dung, reclaiming metals from scrap or pulping waste paper for remanufacture. Recycling, however, may be inconvenient, uneconomic or not yet technologically feasible. Many popular waste-disposal methods consequently represent either an exchange of one form of environmental pollution for another less troublesome, at least in the short term—e.g., the dumping or burying of non-degradable garbage or toxic wastes— or a reducing of the rate at which pollutants accumulate—e.g., by compacting or incinerating bulk wastes before dumping. Urban wastes are generally disposed of by means of dumping, sanitary landfill, incineration and SEWAGE processing. Agricultural, mining and mineral-processing operations generate most solid wastes—and some of the most intractable waste-disposal problems: e.g., the "factory" farmer's problem of disposing of surplus organic wastes economically without resorting to incineration or dumping in rivers; the problems created by large mine dumps and open-cast excavations; and the culm-dumps that result from the processing of anthracite COAL. Another increasingly pressing waste-disposal problem is presented by radioactive wastes. Those with a "low level" of RADIOACTIVITY can be safely packaged and buried; but "high-level" wastes, produced in the course of reprocessing the fuel elements of NUCLEAR REACTORS, constitute a permanent hazard. Even the practice of encasing these wastes in thick concrete and dumping them on the ocean bottom is considered by many environmentalists to be an inadequate long-term solution (see also NUCLEAR ENERGY).

WATER (H_2O), pale-blue odorless liquid which, including that trapped as ICE in icecaps and glaciers, covers about 74% of the earth's surface. Water is essential to LIFE, which began in the watery OCEANS; because of its unique chemical properties, it provides the medium for the reactions of the living CELL. Water is also man's most precious natural resource, which he must conserve and protect from POLLUTION (see also WATER SUPPLY). Chemically, water can be viewed variously as a covalent HYDRIDE, an OXIDE, or a HYDROXIDE. It is a good solvent for many substances, especially ionic and polar compounds; it is ionizing and itself ionizes to give a low concentration of hydroxide and hydrogen ions (see pH). It is thus both a weak ACID and a weak BASE, and conducts electricity. It is a good, though labile, LIGAND, forming HYDRATES. Water is a polar molecule, and shows anomalies due to HYDROGEN BONDING, including contraction when heated from 0°C to 4°C. Formed when hydrogen or volatile hydrides are burned in oxygen, water oxidizes reactive metals to their ions, and reduces fluorine and chlorine. It converts basic oxides to hydroxides, and acidic oxides to OXY-ACIDS. (See also DEHYDRATION; HARD WATER; HEAVY WATER; HYDROLYSIS; POLYWATER; STEAM.) mp 0°C, bp 100°C, triple point 0.01°C, sg 1.0.

WATERCOLOR, painting technique in which the pigment is mixed with water before application, more particularly the aquarelle technique of thin washes, mastered by such English artists as COTMAN and J. M. W. TURNER around 1800. Infelicities cannot be painted over, but watercolor permits powerful effects of transparency, brilliance and delicacy. Famous US watercolorists include Winslow HOMER and John MARIN. (See also FRESCO; GOUACHE; TEMPERA.)

WATERGATE, series of scandals which brought down President NIXON's administration. On June 17, 1972, five men were arrested carrying electronic eavesdropping equipment in the Watergate office building headquarters of the Democratic Party national committee, Washington, D.C. Investigations opened a trail which led to Nixon's inner councils. Nixon easily won reelection in Nov. 1972; but his public support eroded after a televised US Senate investigation, newspaper revelations (notably by Carl Bernstein and Bob Woodward in the *Washington Post*) and testimony of Republican Party and former governmental officials clearly implicated him and his senior aides in massive abuse of power and obstruction of justice involving campaign contributions, the CIA, the FBI, the Internal Revenue Service, and other agencies. The House of Representatives Judiciary Committee voted to impeach Nixon in July 1974, and his ouster from office became inevitable; he resigned on Aug. 9, 1974. One month later he was granted a full pardon by Gerald FORD. Almost three score individuals, including former US attorney general John MITCHELL and senior White House staff were convicted of Watergate crimes, about half serving jail sentences.

WATERLOO, Battle of (June 18, 1815), the final engagement of the NAPOLEONIC WARS. Having escaped from exile on Elba and reinstated himself with a new army, NAPOLEON I faced a coalition of Austria, Britain, Prussia and Russia. He decided to attack, advancing into Belgium to prevent an Anglo-Dutch army under WELLINGTON from uniting with the Prussians. After separate battles with the British and Prussians on June 16, the French army, led by Marshall NEY, attacked Wellington's strongly defended position at Waterloo, S of Brussels. The intervention of a Prussian force under BLÜCHER allowed Wellington to take the offensive. The French were routed, losing some 25,000 men. Napoleon abdicated four days later.

WATER POLO, ball game for two teams of seven played in a pool 19–30yd long, up to 20yd wide and at least 3ft deep. The goals at each end are 10ft wide, their cross-bars 3ft above water. The 26–27in-round ball may be moved on the surface by one hand, passed or dribbled in front of the body. Devised in England in the 1870s, the game became an Olympic event in 1900.

WATER POWER. See HYDROELECTRICITY; TURBINE.

WATERS, Ethel (1900–1977), US actress and singer. Her stage successes include *Mamba's Daughters* (1939), *The Member of the Wedding* (1950) and the stage and screen musical *Cabin in the Sky* (1940).

WATER SKIING, sport in which a motorboat tows the skier along the surface of the water at the end of a line. Originating in S France and the US in the 1920s, it is now a popular recreation. National and international competitions include slalom races, trick riding and distance jumping. Jumps of 150ft and speeds of over 100mph have been achieved.

WATER SNAKES, nearly 80 species of the genus *Natrix*, which also includes the European Grass snake. They are nonvenomous snakes living on fish and amphibians. The Eurasian water snakes lay eggs, while the two New-World species are viviparous.

WATER SPANIEL, American, sporting dog developed in the US, standing 18in high and weighing 45lb. It is excellent for both flushing and retrieving game, although its curly waterproof coat can be a hindrance in some cover. The coat may be liver or dark chocolate, with white on toes and breast permissible.

WATSON, James Dewey (1928–   ), US biochemist who shared with F. H. C. CRICK and M. H. F. WILKINS the 1962 Nobel Prize for Physiology or Medicine for his work with Crick establishing the "double helix" molecular model of DNA. His personalized account of the research, *The Double Helix* (1968), became a best-seller.

WATSON, John Broadus (1878–1958), US psychologist who founded BEHAVIORISM, a dominant school of US psychology from the

1920s to 1940s, and whose influence is still strong today.

WATSON, Thomas John (1874–1956), US business executive who took over an ailing computing company in 1914, changed its name to International Business Machines Corp., 1924, and built it into one of the world's largest corporations. Under his presidency, 1914–49, and chairmanship, 1949–56, IBM became the leader in electronic data-processing equipment.

WATSON, Tom (1949–   ), US golfer. In the late 1970s he replaced Jack Nicklaus as the premier figure on the professional tour. He won the Masters (1977) and British Open (1977, 1980), and, from 1977–80, led the tour in stroke average and earnings.

WATSON-WATT, Sir Robert Alexander (1892–1973), British physicist largely responsible for the development of RADAR, patenting his first "radiolocator" in 1919. He perfected his equipment and techniques from 1935 through the years of WWII, his radar being largely responsible for the British victory of the BATTLE OF BRITAIN.

WATT, James (1938–   ), US secretary of the Interior (1981–   ). Deputy assistant secretary of the Interior during the Nixon administration, he later became president of the Mountain States Legal Foundation and a leading spokesman for the "sagebrush rebellion" in the West, which advocated giving federal lands to the states and private enterprise. His antienvironmental positions and abrasive manner earned him the condemnation of major conservationist organizations.

WATT, James (1736–1819), Scottish engineer and inventor. His first major invention was a STEAM ENGINE with a separate CONDENSER and thus far greater efficiency. For the manufacture of such engines he entered partnership with John ROEBUCK and later (1775), more successfully, with Matthew BOULTON. Between 1775 and 1800 he invented the sun-and-planet gear wheel, the double-acting engine, a throttle valve, a pressure gauge and the centrifugal governor—as well as taking the first steps toward determining the chemical structure of water. He also coined the term HORSEPOWER and was a founding member of the LUNAR SOCIETY.

WATTEAU, Jean-Antoine (1684–1721), French (of Flemish descent) draftsman and painter, strongly influenced by RUBENS. His gay, sensuous paintings have a melancholy quality. They include theater scenes, *fêtes galantes, The Embarkation for Cythera* (1717) and *Gilles* (c1718).

WATTS, Andre (1946–   ), US pianist.

He made his debut at age 16 with the New York Philharmonic over national television. He is best known for his brilliant interpretations of the music of Franz LISZT.

WATTS RIOT, in April 1965, a five-day riot in Watts, a predominantly black district of Los Angeles; whites and white-owned stores were particular targets. The approximately 10,000 rioters were opposed by some 15,000 National Guardsmen and police; 34 people died in the violence.

WATUSI (English version of Swahili *Watutsi*), the Tutsi people of BURUNDI and RWANDA in Central Africa (formerly Ruanda-Urundi). In the 1400s and 1500s the invading Watusi imposed a feudal system on the native Hutu, who revolted in 1959 and drove out their rulers. The Tutsi king of Burundi was deposed in 1966. The Watusi differ ethnically from other African peoples. Many attain a height of 7ft.

WAUGH, name of three English writers, the sons of journalist and publisher Arthur Waugh (1886–1943). **Alexander Raban (Alec) Waugh** (1898–1981) is the author of over 40 novels and travel books including *Loom of Youth* (1918) and *Island in the Sun* (1956). **Evelyn Arthur St. John Waugh** (1903–1966) wrote mainly satire, both elegant and biting. His conversion to Roman Catholicism in 1930 had a deep effect on his work. His novels include *Decline and Fall* (1928), *Vile Bodies* (1930), *Scoop* (1938), *Put out More Flags* (1942), *Brideshead Revisited* (1945) and his WWII trilogy *The Sword of Honour* (1952–61). Evelyn's son **Auberon Alexander Waugh** (1939–   ) is a novelist and miscellaneous writer. His novels include *Bed of Flowers* (1972).

WAVELL, Archibald Percival Wavell, 1st Earl (1883–1950), British field marshal. He served in WWI, and was WWII British commander-in-chief, Middle East, defeating the Italians in N Africa 1940, and in India (from 1941), and viceroy and governor general of India in the years before independence (1943–47).

WAVE MECHANICS, branch of QUANTUM MECHANICS developed by SCHRÖDINGER which considers MATTER rather in terms of its wavelike properties (see WAVE MOTION) than as systems of particles. Thus an orbital ELECTRON is treated as a 3-dimensional system of standing waves represented by a *wave function.* In accordance with the UNCERTAINTY PRINCIPLE, it is not possible to pinpoint both the instantaneous position and velocity of the electron; however, the square of the wave function yields a measure in space-time. The pattern of such probabilities provides a model for the "shape" of the electron ORBITAL involved. Given wave functions can be obtained from the Schrödinger wave equation. Usually, and not unsurprisingly, this can only be solved for particular values of the ENERGY of the system concerned.

WAVE MOTION, a collective motion of a material or extended object, in which each part of the material oscillates about its undisturbed position, but the oscillations at different places are so timed as to create an illusion of crests and troughs running right through the material. Familiar examples are furnished by surface waves on water, or transverse waves on a stretched rope; SOUND is carried through air by a wave motion in which the air molecules oscillate parallel to the direction of propagation, and LIGHT or RADIO waves involve ELECTROMAGNETIC FIELDS oscillating perpendicular to it. The maximum displacement of the material from the undisturbed position is the *amplitude* of the wave, the separation of successive crests, the *wavelength*, and the number of crests passing a given place each second, the *frequency*. The product of the wavelength and the frequency gives the *velocity of propagation*. According to the direction and form of the local oscillations of the medium, different *polarizations* of the wave are distinguished (see POLARIZED LIGHT). *Standing waves* (apparently stationary waves, where the nodes and antinodes— points of zero and maximum amplitude—appear not to move) arise where identical waves traveling in opposite directions superpose. The characteristic properties of waves include propagation in straight lines; REFLECTION at plane surfaces; REFRACTION—a change in direction of a wave transmitted across a plane interface between two media; DIFFRACTION— diffuse SCATTERING by impenetrable objects of a size comparable with the wavelength; and INTERFERENCE—the cancellation of one wave by another wave half a wavelength out of step (or *phase*) so that the crests of one wave fall on the troughs of the other. If the *wave velocity* is the same for all wavelengths, then quite arbitrary forms of disturbance will travel as waves, and not simply regular successions of crests and troughs. When this is not the case, the wave is said to be *dispersive* and localized disturbances move at a speed (the *group velocity*) quite different from that of the individual crests, which can often be seen moving faster or slower within the disturbance "envelope," which becomes progressively broader as it moves. Waves carry ENERGY and MOMENTUM with them just like solid objects; the identity of the apparently irreconcilable wave and particle concepts of matter is a basic tenet of QUANTUM MECHANICS.

WAVES (Women Accepted for Voluntary Emergency Service), women of the US Navy (excluding nurses); originally meaning those recruited from Aug. 1942 for the WWII US Navy Women's Reserve. In the mid-1970s, women were integrated into the active-duty Navy. Women may not serve on combat vessels but can do duty on training and repair ships, as well as in supply, air and sea communications, and traffic control.

WAX, moldable water-repellent solid. There are several entirely different kinds. Animal waxes were the first known: *wool wax* when purified yields LANOLIN; *beeswax*, from the honeycomb, is used for some candles and as a sculpture medium (by carving or casting); *spermaceti wax*, from the sperm whale, is used in ointments and cosmetics. **Vegetable waxes**, like animal waxes, are mixtures of ESTERS of longchain ALCOHOLS and CARBOXYLIC ACIDS. *Carnauba wax*, from the leaves of a Brazilian palm tree, is hard and lustrous, and is used to make polishes; *candelilla wax*, from a wild Mexican rush, is similar but more resinous; *Japan wax*, the coating of sumac berries, is fatty and soft but tough and kneadable. **Mineral** waxes include *montan wax*, extracted from lignite (see COAL), bituminous and resinous; *ozokerite*, an absorbent hydrocarbon wax obtained from wax shales, and *paraffin wax* or petroleum wax, the most important wax commercially: it is obtained from the residues of PETROLEUM refining by solvent extraction, and is used to make candles, to coat paper products, in the electrical industry, to waterproof leather and textiles, etc. Various **synthetic** waxes are made for special uses.

WAYNE, Anthony (1745–1796), American Revolutionary general whose daring tactics earned him the name "mad Anthony." In 1779 he executed the brilliant victory of Stony Point over the British, and he was with Lafayette at the siege of YORKTOWN (1781). After defeating the Indians at FALLEN TIMBERS in 1794, he negotiated the Treaty of GREENVILLE (1795), in which the Indians ceded most of Ohio.

WAYNE, John (Marion Morrison; 1907–1979), US film actor. The archetypal western hero, he appeared in such popular films as *Stagecoach* (1939), *Fort Apache* (1948), and *She Wore a Yellow Ribbon* (1949), and won an Academy Award for *True Grit* (1969). A supporter of conservative political causes, he directed and starred in *The Green Berets* (1968), a film which supported US involvement in

Vietnam.

WAYS AND MEANS COMMITTEE, US House of Representatives standing committee, responsible for assessing all tax and public finance bills, and the main source of revenue legislation.

WEASEL, *Mustela nivalis*, a small carnivorous mammal very like the STOAT but smaller and lacking the black tail tip. A slender lithe red-brown creature, which often kills prey many times its own size, it measures only up to 280mm (11in) in the male, 200mm (7.9in) in the female. The normal diet is mice, voles and fledgling birds, though rabbits may be taken. The many races of weasel are distributed throughout Europe, Africa and North America.

WEATHERMEN, violent faction within the NEW LEFT, formed in 1969 by radical dissenters from the STUDENTS FOR A DEMOCRATIC SOCIETY. The name comes from a line in a Bob Dylan song, "You don't need a weatherman to know which way the wind blows"; it was subsequently changed to "Weather People" and "Weather Underground." Three members of the group were killed in 1970 when an accident in handling bombs blew up a townhouse in New York City belonging to lawyer John Wilkerson, father of one of the Weathermen. Thereafter the organization operated in secrecy, but by 1980 three who had long been sought by the FBI had turned themselves in: Mark Rudd, Cathlyn Wilkerson, and Bernadine Dohrn. In Oct. 1981, the Weather Underground again made headlines when it was found that they were responsible for an attempted robbery of a Brink's armored car in Nanuet, N.Y., in which two policemen and a guard were killed. Among the suspects arrested was Katherine Boudin, daughter of radical lawyer Leonard Boudin; she had remained underground since escaping death in the 1970 townhouse explosion.

WEAVER, James Baird (1833–1912), US politician. Elected to the House of Representatives (1879–80, 1885–88) on the GREENBACK PARTY ticket, he was the party's presidential candidate in 1880. He organized the People's Party and as their presidential candidate (1892) won over a million popular and 22 electoral votes. His career declined with the demise of POPULISM.

WEAVER, Robert Clifton (1907–   ), US economist and secretary of the Department of HOUSING AND URBAN DEVELOPMENT (1966–69), first black member of the US cabinet. He was the administrator of the N.Y. Rent Commis-

sion (1955–59) and led the federal Housing and Home Finance Agency (1961–66).

WEAVING, making a fabric by interlacing two or more sets of threads. In "plain" weave, one set of threads—the *warp*—extends along the length of the fabric; the other set—the *woof*, or *weft*—is at right angles to the warp and passes alternately over and under it. Other common weaves include "twill," "satin" and "pile." In basic twill, woof threads, stepped one warp thread further on with each line, pass over two warp threads, under one, then over two again, producing diagonal ridges, or wales, as in denim, flannel and gaberdine. In satin weave, a development of twill, long "float" threads passing under four warp threads give the fabric its characteristically smooth appearance. Pile fabrics, such as corduroy and velvet, have extra warp or weft threads woven into a ground weave in a series of loops that are then cut to produce the pile. Weaving is usually accomplished by means of a hand- or power-operated machine called a loom. Warp threads are stretched on a frame and passed through eyelets in vertical wires (heddles) supported on a frame (the harness). A space (the shed) between sets of warp threads is made by moving the heddles up or down, and a shuttle containing the woof thread is passed through the shed. A special comb (the reed) then pushes home the newly woven line. (See also TEXTILES; RUGS AND CARPETS; BASKET WEAVING.)

WEBB, name of two English social reformers and economists. **Beatrice Webb** (née Potter, 1858–1943) studied working life for her *Life and Labour of the People in London* (1891–1903). Her husband, **Sidney James Webb, 1st Baron Passfield** (1859–1947), was a Labour Member of Parliament (1922–29) and held several Cabinet posts. The couple were leading intellectuals of the Labour movement and wrote together a *History of Trade Unionism* (1894). They were FABIANS and helped found the London School of Economics in 1895, and the left-wing journal *The New Statesman* in 1913.

WEBER, Carl Maria Friedrich Ernst von (1786–1826), German composer, pianist and conductor who established Romantic opera and paved the way in Germany for WAGNER, with the operas *Der Freischütz* (*The Marksman*; 1821), *Euryanthe* (1823) and *Oberon* (1826). He wrote a number of orchestral and chamber works, notably for the piano, including the well-known *Invitation to the Dance* (1819).

WEBER, Dick (1929–   ), US bowler.

He won more titles and money, and was named to more All-American teams, than any other bowler. He was the first to roll three 300 games in one tournament.

WEBER, Max (1864–1920), German economist and sociologist. In *The Protestant Ethic and the Spirit of Capitalism* (1904–05) he argued that the Calvinist emphasis on hard work helped develop business enterprise. He believed that many causes such as law, religion and politics combined with economics to determine the course of history. He defined a methodology for sociology.

WEBERN, Anton von (1883–1945), Austrian composer who studied with SCHOENBERG and developed his TWELVE-TONE MUSIC form into a concentrated and individual style. His works include *Five Pieces for Orchestra* (1911–13), two symphonies, three string quartets and a number of songs.

WEBSTER, Daniel (1782–1852), US statesman, lawyer and orator whose advocacy of strong central government earned him the name of "defender of the Constitution." Early in his career, nonetheless, he defended STATES' RIGHTS and championed New England interests as N.H. member of the House of Representatives (1813–17) and Mass. representative (1823–27) and senator (1827–41). As New England interests changed from shipping to industry, Webster became nationalist, and supported protective tariffs despite his earlier castigation of trade restrictions. His battle against NULLIFICATION began in 1830, and continued throughout the crisis of 1832–33; in his efforts to preserve the Union he supported the COMPROMISE OF 1850. (See also WEBSTER-ASHBURTON TREATY.)

WEBSTER, John (c1580–c1625), English Jacobean playwright best remembered for his two powerful revenge tragedies, *The White Devil* (c1610) and *The Duchess of Malfi* (c1615). Both are set in Renaissance Italy. Webster sometimes collaborated with other playwrights, notably John FORD and Thomas DEKKER.

WEBSTER, Margaret (1905–1972), British actress and director, best known as a Shakespearean director, especially for *Othello* (1943), which ran for 295 performances, a record for a production of Shakespeare.

WEBSTER, Noah (1758–1843), US lexicographer whose works such as *The Elementary Spelling Book*, called the "Blue-Backed Speller" (1829; earlier versions 1783–87), helped standardize American spelling. He compiled a grammar (1784) and a reader (1785). Working on dictionaries from 1803 he published *An American Dictionary of the English Language* (1828), with 70,000 entries and 12,000 new definitions. Today his name is often applied to dictionaries that are in no way based on his work.

WEBSTER-ASHBURTON TREATY (1842), agreement between the US and Great Britain settling the line of the NE border of the US between Me. and New Brunswick. Signed by Daniel WEBSTER for the US and Lord Ashburton for Great Britain, the treaty also agreed on joint suppression of the slave trade.

WEDEKIND, Frank (1864–1918), German playwright who attacked the hypocrisy and sexual mores of his times, notably in *Spring Awakening* (1891). His "Lulu plays," *Earth-Spirit* (1895) and *Pandora's Box* (1903), center on Lulu, a personification of natural sensuality, and inspired an opera by BERG. Many of his techniques foreshadowed EXPRESSIONISM.

WEDEMEYER, Albert Coady (1897–), US general, given the Distinguished Service Medal for his work as chief of the strategy section in WWII. He commanded US troops in China (1944–46) and the US 6th Army (1949–51).

WEDGWOOD, Josiah (1730–1795), outstanding English potter, inventor of Wedgwood ware. He patented his cream Queen's Ware in 1765; for the designs on his blue and white Jasper Ware he frequently employed John FLAXMAN. Wedgwood introduced new materials and machinery; his factory at Etruria, Staffordshire, was the first to acquire steam engines.

WEEDKILLERS. See HERBICIDES.

WEEGEE (Arthur Fellig; 1900–1968), Austrian-born US photographer whose use of a police radio to locate scenes of crime and violence in New York enabled him to record more four-alarm fires than any other photographer in history. Among his books were *Naked City* (1945).

WEEVILS, the largest animal family, Curculionidae, 35,000 species of oval or pear-shaped BEETLES having a greatly drawn out head or snout bearing strong chewing mouthparts. They feed on hard vegetable matter, seeds and wood; the larvae, developing within seeds, are legless. Weevils are important economic pests of cotton and grain crops; also of stored peas, beans and flour.

WEGENER, Alfred Lothar (1880–1930), German meteorologist, explorer and geologist. His *The Origin of Continents and Oceans* (1915) set forth "Wegener's hypothesis," the theory of CONTINENTAL

DRIFT, whose developments were in succeeding decades to revolutionize man's view of the planet he lives on (see also PLATE TECTONICS).

WEIDENREICH, Franz (1873–1948), German-born US physical anthropologist and anatomist best known for his work on fossil remains of *Sinanthropus*, *Pithecanthropus* and *Meganthropus* (see PREHISTORIC MAN), and for his chronological arrangement of the various stages in man's evolution.

WEIDMAN, Charles (1901–1975), US dancer and choreographer. After studying with Ted SHAWN he conducted a school and company with Doris HUMPHREY, 1927–45, and then by himself. Pantomine and humor are important elements in many of his works, including *Flickers* (1941) and *Fables for Our Time* (1947).

WEIGHT, the attractive FORCE experienced by an object in the presence of another massive body in accordance with the law of universal GRAVITATION. The weight of a body (measured in newtons) is given by the product of its MASS and the local ACCELERATION due to gravity (g). Weight differs from mass in being a VECTOR quantity.

WEIGHTLIFTING, body building exercise and competitive sport. As a contest it has long been popular in Turkey, Egypt, Japan and Europe and has been a regular event in the Olympic Games since 1920. There are three basic lifts: the snatch (from the floor to over the head in a single motion); the clean and jerk (two movements—first to the chest and then over the head); and the military or two-hand press (similar to the clean and jerk, but retaining a "military" stance).

WEIGHTS AND MEASURES, units of WEIGHT, LENGTH, AREA and VOLUME commonly used in the home, in commerce and in industry. Although like other early peoples the Hebrews used measures such as the foot, the cubit (the length of the human forearm) and the span, which could easily be realized in practice using parts of the body, in commerce they also used standard containers and weights. Later, weights were based on the quantity of precious metal in coins. During and after the Middle Ages, each region evolved its own system of weights and measures. In the 19th century these were standardized on a national basis, these national standards in turn being superseded by those of the METRIC SYSTEM. In the western world, only the British Empire and the US retained their own systems (the Imperial System and the US Customary System) into the mid-20th

century. With the UK's adoption of the International System of Units (SI UNITS), the US has found itself alone in not using metric units, although, as has been the case since 1959, the US customary units are now defined in terms of their metric counterparts and not on the basis of independent standards. In the US the administration of weights and measures is coordinated by the National Bureau of Standards (NBS) who also publish the version of the International System used in this volume. (See also APOTHECARIES' WEIGHTS; TROY WEIGHT.)

WEIL, Simone (1909–1943), French Jew, philosopher, religious mystic and left-wing intellectual. She was active in the Spanish Civil War and the French Resistance in WWII. She converted from Judaism to Christianity c1940. Her books include *Oppression and Liberty* (1955).

WEILL, Kurt (1900–1950), German-born US composer. His most original music is for the two satirical operas on which he collaborated with BRECHT, *The Threepenny Opera* (1928) and *The Rise and Fall of the City of Mahagonny* (1930). He came to the US in 1935, and became a successful Broadway composer.

WEIMAR, city in SW East Germany, on the Ilm R, manufacturing agricultural machinery, electrical equipment and chemicals. It was capital of the Saxe-Weimar duchy from 1547, and its court became the German cultural and intellectual center in the 18th and 19th centuries, attracting BACH, GOETHE, SCHILLER, HERDER, LISZT and NIETZSCHE. It was the first site of the BAUHAUS. BUCHENWALD concentration camp was nearby. In 1919 the constitution of the German republic was adopted at Weimar. Pop 62,800.

WEINBERG, Steven (1933–   ), US physicist who shared the 1979 Nobel Prize in Physics for work demonstrating that two of the basic forces of nature, ELECTROMAGNETISM and the weak interaction (the cause of radioactive decay in certain atomic nuclei) are aspects of a single interaction.

WEINBERGER, Caspar (1917–   ), US secretary of Defense (1981–   ). A California Republican, he was appointed state director of finance by then Governor Reagan in 1968. He served in the Nixon administration as deputy director 1970–72 and director 1972 of the Office of Management and Budget, and as secretary of Health, Education and Welfare 1973–75. Although in the past he earned the nickname of "Cap the Knife" for his budget-cutting zeal, he emerged as a staunch defender of military expenditures under Reagan.

WEINGARTNER, Felix (1863–1942), Austrian conductor and composer who conducted the Berlin Royal Opera, the Vienna State Opera and the Vienna Philharmonic. He conducted throughout the world, composed six symphonies and eight operas, and wrote several books on conducting and musical interpretation.

WEISMANN, August (1834–1914), German biologist regarded as a father of modern GENETICS for his demolition of the theory that ACQUIRED CHARACTERISTICS could be inherited, and proposal that CHROMOSOMES are the basis of HEREDITY. He coupled this proposal with his belief in NATURAL SELECTION as the mechanism for EVOLUTION.

WEISS, Peter (1916–   ), German playwright, artist and filmmaker, now living in Sweden, having fled Nazi Germany in 1934. With the appearance of his innovative *Marat/Sade* (1963), essentially about revolutionary idealism versus aristocratic individualism, Weiss was acclaimed the successor of BRECHT as the foremost German dramatist. He is also well known for *The Investigation* (1965), a five-hour docudrama detailing Nazi atrocities.

WEISSKOPF, Victor (1908–   ), Austrian-born US physicist who helped develop the first atomic bombs while a group leader on the Manhattan Project (1943–46). After WWII he championed nuclear disarmament and helped found the *Bulletin of the Atomic Scientists*. He headed the European Center for Nuclear Research (CERN) in Geneva from 1961 to 1965.

WEIZMANN, Chaim (1874–1952), Polish-born Zionist leader, first president of Israel from 1949. He emigrated to England in 1904 and became an eminent biochemist and director of the British Admiralty laboratories in 1916. He helped secure the BALFOUR DECLARATION (1917), which promised a Jewish state in Palestine. He was head of the World Zionist Organization (1920–29) and of the JEWISH AGENCY (1929–31, 1935–46). (See ZIONISM.)

WELD, Theodore Dwight (1803–1895), US abolitionist, a founder of the American Antislavery Society (1833–34). He organized 70 agents to campaign in the North, edited the *Emancipator*, lobbied Congress and wrote the influential *American Slavery As It Is* (1839), a basis for H. B. STOWE's *Uncle Tom's Cabin*.

WELDING, bringing two pieces of metal together under conditions of heat or pressure or both, until they coalesce at the joint. The oldest method is forge welding, in which the surfaces to be joined are heated to welding temperature and then hammered together on an anvil. The most widely used method today is metal-arc welding: an ELECTRIC ARC is struck between an ELECTRODE and the workpieces to be joined, and molten metal from a "filler rod"—usually the electrode itself—is added. Gas welding, now largely displaced by metal-arc welding, is usually accomplished by means of an oxyacetylene torch, which delivers the necessary heat by burning ACETYLENE in a pure OXYGEN atmosphere. Sources of heat in other forms of welding include the electrical RESISTANCE of the joint (resistance welding), an electric arc at the joint (flash welding), a focused beam of ELECTRONS (electron-beam welding), pressure alone, usually well in excess of 1,400,000kPa (cold welding), and friction (friction welding). Some more recently applied heat sources include hot PLASMAS, LASERS, ULTRASONIC vibrations and explosive impacts.

WELFARE, direct government aid to the needy. In the US various programs, operated by the SOCIAL SECURITY office and by state and local government, provide aid to the handicapped, aged, poor (see POVERTY) and unemployed. Benefits to the aged are more-or-less standardized nationally, but the form of, amount of and qualifications for other benefits differ from state to state. Benefits fall under many programs, such as veterans' aid and WORKMEN'S COMPENSATION. All welfare programs are linked to programs which do not give direct financial assistance, such as housing, FOOD STAMPS, MEDICARE and MEDICAID. This patchwork of programs caused inequalities and hardships, which resulted in part in the reduction of federal revenues for welfare programs during the presidency of Ronald Reagan in the 1980s.

WELK, Lawrence (1903–   ), US bandleader who worked his way up from dancehalls to a network TV show in 1955. He played unsophisticated old-fashioned polkas and waltzes for a huge and faithful following.

WELLAND SHIP CANAL, Canadian waterway running 27.6mi from Port Colborne on Lake Erie to Port Weller on Lake Ontario to form a major link of the SAINT LAWRENCE SEAWAY. The canal was built 1912–32, modernized in 1972 and has a minimum depth of about 30ft. It has eight locks to overcome the 326ft difference in height between lakes Erie and Ontario.

WELLES, (George) Orson (1915–   ), US actor, director and producer. In 1938 his

Mercury Theater's realistic radio production of H. G. WELLS' *War of the Worlds* made thousands of listeners panic. His first motion picture, of which he was director, co-writer, and star, was *Citizen Kane* (1941), loosely modeled on the life of newspaper magnate W. R. HEARST. It was an astonishing tour de force, now considered one of the finest films ever made. Innovative camera work and film editing continued to characterize his work in such films as *The Magnificent Ambersons* (1942), *The Lady from Shanghai* (1947), *Macbeth* (1948) and *Touch of Evil* (1958). He acted in most of his own films and in such other classics as *The Third Man* (1949), *Moby Dick* (1956) and *Treasure Island* (1972).

WELLES, Sumner (1892–1961), US diplomat who was regarded as the leading governmental expert on Latin America and was the chief architect of President Roosevelt's "Good Neighbor Policy." He served as assistant secretary (1933; 1934–37) and later under secretary of state (1937–43) for Latin American affairs.

WELLESLEY, Richard Colley Wellesley, Marquess, 2nd Earl of Mornington (1760–1842), British statesman in India. As governor general of Bengal and governor of Madras (1797–1805) he greatly extended British authority in India. When lord lieutenant of Ireland (1821–28, 1833–34), he favored CATHOLIC EMANCIPATION.

WELLESLEY COLLEGE, Wellesley, Mass., private institution for women founded in 1870. Instruction is in small classes and emphasis is placed on individual development through intensive study of the liberal arts and sciences. Wellesley is known for the beauty of its campus.

WELLINGTON, city, capital of New Zealand since 1865, at the S of North Island. Founded in 1840, it is the nation's second largest city and an important port and transportation center. Pop 349,000.

WELLINGTON, Arthur Wellesley, 1st Duke of (1792–1852), British general and statesman, "the Iron Duke," who defeated NAPOLEON I at the battle of WATERLOO. After distinguished military service in India (1796–1805), he drove the French from Spain and Portugal in the PENINSULAR WARS and entered France in 1813. After being created duke, he led the victorious forces at Waterloo (1815). Serving the Tory government for 1819–27, he became prime minister (1828–30), passed the CATHOLIC EMANCIPATION BILL but opposed Parliamentary reform. In 1842 he became commander-in-chief for life.

WELLS, Henry (1805–1878). US pioneer expressman. Associated with W. FARGO from 1844, he founded Wells, Fargo and Co. (1852) to supply express mail to Cal. and the West. By acquiring the OVERLAND MAIL COMPANY (1866) he owned the greatest US stagecoach network.

WELLS, H. G. (Herbert George; 1866–1946), British writer and social reformer. After being a draper's apprentice he studied science and taught. After such early science-fiction as *The Time Machine* (1895) and *The War of the Worlds* (1898), he wrote novels on the lower middle class, including *Kipps* (1905) and *The History of Mr. Polly* (1910). A founder of the FABIAN SOCIETY, he was a social prophet (*A Modern Utopia*; 1905). After WWI he popularized knowledge in *Outline of History* (1920) and *The Science of Life* (1931).

WELSH, or Cymraeg, one of the Brythonic group of CELTIC LANGUAGES, still widely spoken in Wales. There is a rich literature, particularly of poetry.

WELSH TERRIER, breed of dog developed in Wales to hunt foxes, badgers and otters. It is about 15in high and about 20lb in weight, and has a wiry black-and-tan coat.

WELTY, Eudora (1909–   ), US novelist and short-story writer, known for sensitive tales of Miss. life. She superbly depicted atmosphere and characters in *The Wide Net* (1943), *The Ponder Heart* (1954), *The Optimist's Daughter* (1972; Pulitzer Prize) and others.

WEN, or sebaceous CYST, blocked SEBACEOUS GLAND, often over the scalp or forehead, which forms a cyst containing old sebum under the SKIN. It may become infected. Its excision is a simple procedure.

WENCESLAUS, Saint (c907–929), Duke of Bohemia, famous for his efforts to Christianize his people. The song *Good King Wenceslaus* refers to him.

WERFEL, Franz (1890–1945), Austrian novelist, poet and playwright, whose early plays and poetry such as *Der Spiegelmensch* (1920) were important works of German EXPRESSIONISM. His novels include *Embezzled Heaven* (1939) and *The Song of Bernadette* (1941).

WERTHEIMER, Max (1880–1943), German psychologist who founded (with Kurt Koffka and Wolfgang Köhler) the school of GESTALT PSYCHOLOGY. He taught at Frankfurt and Berlin before emigrating to the US (1933), and wrote *Productive Thinking* (1945).

WERTMULLER, Lina (1928–   ), Italian film director whose movies combined raucous comedy, violence and an antibourgeois political message. Her popular films of the 1970s were *The Seduction of Mimi*, *Love and Anarchy*, *Swept Away* and *Seven Beauties*.

WESKER, Arnold (1932–), English playwright, one of the "angry young men" to emerge in England in 1956. His early plays, such as the trilogy *Chicken Soup with Barley* (1958), *Roots* (1959) and *I'm Talking about Jerusalem* (1960), are committed to the ideals of socialism. The later, more introspective *Chips with Everything* (1962) and *The Friends* (1970) explore themes of "private pain."

WESLEY, name of two evangelistic preachers who with George WHITEFIELD founded METHODISM. **John Wesley** (1703–1791), ordained 1725, and his brother **Charles** (1707–1788), ordained 1735, formed an Oxford "Holy Club" of scholarly Christians, known as "Methodists" for their "rule and methods." In 1738 the brothers were profoundly influenced by the MORAVIAN CHURCH and John particularly by LUTHER'S *Preface to the Epistle to the Romans.* Aiming to promote "vital, practical religion" the Wesleys took up evangelistic work by field or open-air preaching. Rejected by the church, they were enthusiastically received by the people, and they organized conferences of itinerant lay preachers. Charles composed more than 5,500 hymns.

WESSEX, Anglo-Saxon kingdom in S England, roughly comprising modern Somerset, Dorset, Wiltshire and Hampshire. Probably first settled by the SAXON Cedric in 495, it was at its largest under EGBERT (802–39). ALFRED THE GREAT (871–99) checked the Danish invasions and by 927 ETHELSTAN overturned DANELAW and controlled all England. Thomas HARDY revived the name in his novels.

WEST, Benjamin (1738–1820), American-born painter. After studying in Rome he settled in London (1763), becoming official history painter to King George III and a founder of the ROYAL ACADEMY OF ARTS. His best-known works are *The Death of General Wolfe* (1771) and *Penn's Treaty with the Indians* (1776).

WEST, Dame Rebecca (Cicily Isabel Fairfield; 1892–), British novelist, critic and journalist. *Black Lamb and Grey Falcon: A Journey through Yugoslavia* (1941) is perhaps her finest work. Her novels include *Birds Fall Down* (1966).

WEST, Mae (1892–1980), US stage and screen actress who was the sultry mistress of provocative innuendo and a sex symbol of Hollywood films of the 1930s. Frequently at odds with the censors, she immortalized the phrase "come up 'n' see me sometime" and

starred in such movies as *She Done Him Wrong* (1933), *I'm No Angel* (1933) and *My Little Chickadee* (1940).

WEST, Morris (1916–), Australian author best known for his novels *The Devil's Advocate* (1959) and *The Shoes of the Fisherman* (1963), the last about a Ukrainian cardinal who becomes the first modern non-Italian pope.

WEST, Nathanael (1903–1940), pseudonym of Nathan Weinstein, US novelist. His satiric novels, *Miss Lonelyhearts* (1933), the story of an agony columnist, and *The Day of the Locust* (1939) are bitter and disturbing, with sudden flashes of humor.

WEST BANK, uplands to the west of the Dead Sea and Jordan River, formerly part of the kingdom of Jordan but occupied by Israel since its victory in the Six Day War of 1967. Historically known as Judea and Samaria, the West Bank contains such famous cities as Bethlehem, Jericho, Hebron, and the Old City of Jerusalem. The status of the West Bank, along with that of the Gaza Strip in southwestern Israel, has been at the center of most Arab-Israeli disputes. The Camp David Agreement of 1978 between Egypt and Israel specified that the 1.3 million Palestinian Arabs in the two areas would be given "full autonomy and self-government" for a five-year period during which the ultimate sovereignty of the territories would be determined. As of 1981, however, the parties were still arguing over the details of self-government. At the same time Israel, while reducing its military presence on the West Bank, began to increase its settlements there.

WESTERMARCK, Edward Alexander (1862–1939), Finnish anthropologist and philosopher. He was equally famous for *The History of Human Marriage* (1891), which demonstrated the importance of monogamy, and for *The Origin and Development of Moral Ideas* (1906–08), in which he held that morality was based on social approval, not truth.

WESTERN AUSTRALIA, largest Australian state (975,920sq mi), first settled 1826–29, covering the W third of the country. Beyond the narrow coastal strip and fertile SW, it is mostly dry plateau with vast desert wastes. Major products are wool, wheat and lumber; chief minerals are gold, coal and iron. Its capital is Perth.

WESTERN CHURCH, one of the two great branches of the Christian Church (see EASTERN CHURCH). The Latin-speaking church of the western Roman empire, it was increasingly dominated by Roman usage and by the papacy, whose claims of supremacy grew and were enforced. It thus developed into the ROMAN CATHOLIC CHURCH, though the Protestant churches formed at the Reformation share the common western tradition. (See also CHRISTIANITY; GREAT SCHISM.)

WESTERN EUROPEAN UNION (WEU), defensive economic, social and cultural alliance (1955) among Belgium, France, Great Britain, Italy, Luxembourg, the Netherlands and West Germany. It supervised German rearmament. The Council of Europe took over its economic and cultural activities (1960).

WESTERN FEDERATION OF MINERS (WFM), radical US miners' union of the W states formed in 1893. In its earlier days it clashed with federal, state and company forces. In 1905 WFM leader W. D. HAYWOOD, falsely charged, was acquitted of a former governor's murder. The WFM cofounded the INDUSTRIAL WORKERS OF THE WORLD (1905), seceded to rejoin (1911) the AMERICAN FEDERATION OF LABOR and became the International Union of Mine, Mill and Smelter Workers (1916).

WESTERN FICTION, an enduring genre in US literature and the performing arts. Its setting consisted of the plains, mountains and canyons of the West between the end of the Civil War and 1900. Familiar characters are the lanky cowboy, the homesteader's sweet young daughter, the hard-bitten pioneer, the taciturn lawman, the sinister gun-slinger and the American Indian—sometimes noble, sometimes savage. The simple recurring themes involve love, friendship, greed and determination to tame the wild land. In the early dime novels by Ned Buntline, Zane Grey, Luke Short and others, a lone man on horseback prevails over an outlaw, rustler or renegade Indian. Other novelists, including Owen WISTER (*The Virginian*) and A. B. Guthrie (*The Big Sky*) paid more attention to historical detail. Western films have ranged from dusty shoot'em-ups to serious dramas by directors like John FORD. Gary COOPER and John WAYNE were but two of many Western film heroes. Radio and television presented such continuing adventures as *The Lone Ranger*, *Death Valley Days*, *Gunsmoke* and *Bonanza*, and revived the early movies of such cowboy stars as William BOYD (Hopalong Cassidy). Writers such as Louis L'AMOUR continue to churn out Western fiction for a market that never seems to flag.

WESTERN RESERVE, NE region of Ohio on the S shore of Lake Erie. In 1786, Conn. refused to cede this area to the NORTHWEST TERRITORY. In 1792, 500,000 acres were granted to Conn. citizens whose land was destroyed during the Revolution. The remaining land was sold to a land company which built Cleveland. The region joined the Northwest Territory 1800.

WESTERN SAHARA, former Spanish province in NW Africa, comprising 102,680sq mi of, mainly, desert on the Atlantic coast, rich in phosphate deposits. Despite active independence movements among native Arabs and Berbers, it was formally divided between neighboring Morocco and Mauritania in 1975. Mauritania withdrew in 1979 following protracted guerilla warfare with Algerian-backed Polisario rebels.

Official name: The Independent State of Western Samoa
Capital: Apia
Area: 1,093sq mi
Population: 155,821
Languages: Samoan; English
Religion: Christian
Monetary unit(s): 1 Western Samoa tālā = 10 sene

WESTERN SAMOA, independent state in the SW Pacific Ocean, comprising two large islands, Savai'i and UPOLU, and seven smaller islands, only two of which are inhabited.

Land. Most of the islands are mountainous, volcanic, forested and fertile. The climate is rainy and tropical.

People and Economy. The people are Polynesian and the majority live in Upolu, where Apia, the capital and chief port, stands Samoans speak probably the oldest Polynesian language in use. The economy is agricultural, the main exports, being copra, bananas and cacao. Tourism is important. The current development program, backed by foreign aid, aims to expand agriculture and encourage modest industrialization (e.g., soap, lumber).

History. The islands were probably discovered by the Dutch explorer, Jacob Roggeveen (1722). Germany, Great Britain and the US jointly administered the islands 1889–99 and agreed in 1899 that SAMOA should be divided between the US and

Germany. In 1914 New Zealand seized German Samoa, later administering it by League of Nations mandate, and as a UN trust territory. It became independent as Western Samoa in 1962. It joined the UN in 1976.

WESTERN SCHISM. See GREAT SCHISM.

WEST INDIES, chain of islands extending from Fla. to the N coast of South America, separating the Caribbean Sea and the Gulf of Mexico from the Atlantic Ocean. An alternative name (excluding the Bahamas) is the Antilles. The West Indies comprises three main groups: the BAHAMAS to the NE of Cuba and Hispaniola; the Greater Antilles (Cuba—the largest island in the West Indies, Hispaniola [HAITI and DOMINICAN REPUBLIC], Jamaica and Puerto Rico); and the Lesser Antilles (LEEWARD and WINDWARD ISLANDS, Trinidad and Tobago and Barbados); together with the NETHERLANDS ANTILLES and other islands off the Venezuelan coast. Many of the islands are mountainous and volcanic with lagoons and mangrove swamps on their coastlines. The climate is warm but there are frequent hurricanes. The principal crop is sugarcane. Tourism is an important industry. After COLUMBUS reached the West Indies (1492) they were settled by the Spanish followed by the English, French and Dutch who exploited the spices and sugar, using African slaves. The political status of the islands varies widely.

WEST INDIES ASSOCIATED STATES, regional association of former British dependencies in the Caribbean established in 1967. The original five states—Antigua, Dominica, Grenada, St. Kitts-Nevis-Anguilla and St. Lucia—were joined by St. Vincent in 1969. Grenada terminated the association in 1974, Dominica in 1978, St. Lucia and St. Vincent and the Grenadines in 1979 and St. Kitts and Nevis in 1980 when Anguilla reverted to colonial status. Regional legal, financial, transport, and tourist institutions remain.

WESTINGHOUSE, George (1846–1914), US engineer, inventor and businessman who pioneered the use of high-voltage AC electricity. In 1869 he founded the Westinghouse Air Brake Company to develop the air BRAKES he had invented for RAILROAD use. From 1883 he did pioneering work on the safe transmission of NATURAL GAS. In 1886 he founded the Westinghouse Electric Company, employing notably TESLA, to develop AC INDUCTION MOTORS and transmission equipment: this company was largely responsible for the acceptance of AC in preference to DC for most applications—in spite of opposition from the influential EDISON.

WESTMINSTER, Statute of (1931), British parliamentary act abolishing Britain's power to legislate for its dominions. It gave the dominions complete independence in the COMMONWEALTH OF NATIONS although they owed common allegiance to the British crown.

WESTMINSTER ABBEY, great English Gothic church in London, traditional scene of English coronations since that of WILLIAM the Conqueror, and a burial place for English monarchs and famous subjects. The present building, started in 1245, is on the site of a church (1065) built by EDWARD THE CONFESSOR.

WESTMINSTER CONFESSION, Reformation confession of faith (see CREED) forming the subordinate doctrinal standard of most REFORMED CHURCHES. A detailed statement of CALVINISM, it was produced 1643–46 by the Westminster Assembly, a synod called by the LONG PARLIAMENT to reform the Church of England. The assembly also issued the two Westminster Catechisms. (See also PURITANS.)

WESTMORELAND, William Childs (1914–   ), US general, US Army chief of staff 1968–72. He was superintendent of WEST POINT 1960–63 and the US commander in Vietnam 1964–68.

WESTON, Edward (1886–1958), US photographer, one of the most influential of the 20th century. He aimed for clarity of detail (using large-view cameras and small apertures) and composition, and seldom cropped, enlarged or touched up. His best work is of still lifes, nudes and sand dunes.

WESTPHALIA, Peace of, treaties signed by Sweden, France, Spain, the Holy Roman Empire and the Netherlands concluding the THIRTY YEARS' WAR in 1648. The treaties recognized the sovereignty of the German states of the Holy Roman Empire; declared the Netherlands and Switzerland independent republics; and granted religious freedom to Calvinists and Lutherans in Germany. Sweden acquired W Pomerania and Stettin; France Alsace, Metz, Toul and Verdun; and Brandenburg E Pomerania.

WEST POINT, site of, and common name for, the US Military Academy in SE N.Y., an institute of higher education which trains officers for the regular army. Established by Act of Congress in 1802, its training methods and traditions were set down by Colonel Sylvanus THAYER, superintendent of the academy 1817–33. Candidates for entry (since 1976 of either sex) to the academy must be unmarried US citizens aged 17–22 and must meet minimum academic requirements. Cadets are enlisted in the regular army on entrance. Graduates are awarded a BS and a commission as 2nd lieutenant, and are expected to serve in the army for at least four years.

Name of state: West Virginia
Capital: Charleston
Statehood: June 20, 1863 (35th state)
Familiar name: Mountain State; Panhandle State
Area: 24,181sq mi
Population: 1,949,644
Elevation: Highest—4,863ft, Spruce Knob Lowest—240ft, Potomac River
Motto: Montani Semper Liberi (Mountaineers are always free)
State flower: Rhododendron
State bird: Cardinal
State tree: Sugar maple
State songs: "The West Virginia Hills," "This is My West Virginia," "West Virginia, My Home Sweet Home"

WEST VIRGINIA, state in E US in the heart of the Appalachians. It is bordered on the N by Ohio, Penn. and Md., on the E by Va.; S by N.C. and Tenn., and W by Ky.
Land. Most of West Virginia lies in the Appalachian Plateau, whose E edge is formed by the hills of Allegheny Front (over 4,500ft), the state's highest area. In the NE the Blue Ridge Mountains region is an area of fertile slopes and river valleys. The state's rugged terrain has the highest average elevation (over 1,500ft) E of the Mississippi. The chief rivers are the Ohio, on the NW border, the Potomac and the Kanawtha. The climate is mild, the annual temperature range 34–70°F, and the annual rainfall about 45 in. Much of the land is forested.
Population. West Virginia is 60% rural. Most urban dwellers live in the industrial centers along the river valleys. Charleston and Huntington are the largest cities. Over 95% of the people are white.
Economy. The economy is dominated by manufacturing and mining. Its prosperity has long been dependent on its bituminous COAL industry, but today other minerals such as natural gas, petroleum, stone and sand are also exploited. Leading industries

produce chemicals, iron and steel. Lumber is a significant resource. Farming is largely confined to the fertile river valleys.
History. West Virginia's history until 1861 is essentially that of VIRGINIA, although West Virginia was distinguished by its isolation from the state capital, the fact that few West Virginians owned slaves, and its economy—small-scale farming and industries based on mineral resources. In 1861 the West Virginians refused to secede from the Union with Va. They declared their independence, adopted a constitution (1862) and became 35th state of the Union in 1863.

In the early 20th century, the state's rapid expansion in the coal, gas and steel industries was accompanied by severe labor-management conflicts and by riots, notably in the mines, which were resolved only by the NEW DEAL legislation. Nevertheless, the state remained poor, the land and water resources damaged by coal strip mining, and many people left the state. In the 1970s major efforts were made to attract new industry, alleviate poverty, and control strip mining. Although successful to some extent—as reflected in an 11.8% population rise in the decade—unemployment, which reached 10% in 1980, remains a serious problem.

WETBACKS, slang term for illegal Mexican immigrants in the US, which derives from how some immigrants avoid immigration control points—by swimming the Rio Grande. The number of "wetbacks" living in California and other SW states was estimated at 3–6 million in 1980. (See also CHICANO.)

WEYDEN, Rogier Van der (c1400–1464), Flemish painter, the most influential painter of his period. Trained by CAPIN and influenced by VAN EYCK, he is noted for his tragic and emotional depiction of the scenes of the Passion such as *Descent from the Cross* (c1435) and *Calvary Triptych* (c1440–45). His portraits have the same intensity.

WEYL, Hermann (1885–1955), German mathematician and mathematical physicist noted for his contributions to the theories of RELATIVITY and QUANTUM MECHANICS.

WEGAND, Maxime (1867–1965), French general. He defended Warsaw (1920) in the RUSSO-POLISH WAR. As commander in chief in France he recommended the Franco-German armistice (1940). Although serving the VICHY government in North Africa (1941), he was exonerated of German collaboration (1948).

WHALES, an order, Cetacea, of large wholly-aquatic mammals. All are highly-adapted for life in water, with a torpedo-shaped body, front limbs reduced and modified as steering paddles, and hind limbs absent. They have a tail of two transverse flukes and swim by up-and-down movements of this tail. Most species have a fleshy dorsal fin which acts as a stabilizer. The neck is short, the head flowing directly into the trunk. The body is hairless and the smooth skin lies over a thick layer of BLUBBER which has an insulating function but also acts to smooth out the passage of water over the body in rapid swimming. The nose, or blowhole, is at the top of the head, allowing the animal to breathe as soon as it breaks the surface of the water. Modern whales divide into two suborders, the Mysticeti, or Whalebone Whales, and the Odontoceti, or Toothed whales. Whalebone whales feed on PLANKTON straining the enormous quantities they require from the water with special plates of whalebone, or BALEEN, developed from the mucus membrane of the upper jaw. Whalebone whales, the RIGHT WHALES, RORQUALS and Gray whales, are usually large and slow-moving. The group includes the BLUE WHALE, the largest animal of all time. Toothed whales, equipped with conical teeth, feed on fishes and squids. With the SPERM WHALE and NARWHAL, the group also includes the DOLPHINS and PORPOISES.

WHALING, the hunting of WHALES, originally for oil, meat and BALEEN, practiced since the 900s if not earlier. The Basques and Dutch hunted from land and pioneered methods of flensing and boiling whale meat. American whaling started in the 1600s, and whaling ports such as Nantucket and New Bedford grew to great size in the 1700s. Whaling became safer after the invention (1856) of harpoons with explosive heads which caused instantaneous death and avoided the dangerous pursuit of a wounded whale. From the 1800s, whalers moved S in pursuit of the SPERM WHALE. Development of factory ships which processed the catch on board facilitated longer expeditions. In the 1900s whaling has centered on Antarctic waters. Reconaissance aircraft and electronic aids are now used. Whale products include oils, AMBERGRIS, spermaceti, meat and bone meal. Despite the (voluntary) restrictions of the International Whaling Convention, whales are still overfished, and many species face extinction.

WHARTON, Edith (1862–1937), US novelist, poet, and short-story writer, a friend of Henry JAMES. She wrote subtle and acerbic accounts of society in New York, New England and Europe, including The House of Mirth (1905), Ethan Frome (1911) and The Age of Innocence (1920, Pulitzer Prize).

WHEAT, Triticum aestivum, the world's main CEREAL CROP; about 300 million tons are produced every year, mostly used to make flour for bread and pasta. Wheat has been in cultivation since at least 7000BC and grows best in temperate regions of Europe, America, China and Australia. The USSR is the largest producer, followed by the US and Canada. There are many varieties of wheat and different parts of the grain are used to produce the various types of flour. Grains comprise an outer husk called the bran and a central starchy germ (which is embedded in a PROTEIN known as GLUTEN.) Wheat is graded as hard or soft depending on how easily the flour can be separated from the bran. Wheat for bread is hard wheat and contains a lot of gluten. Soft wheat flours containing more STARCH and less protein are used for pastries. There are two main types of wheat; these are sown either in the fall (winter wheat), or in the spring (spring wheat). Harvesting is carried out by COMBINE HARVESTERS which cut and thresh the crop in one operation. Wheat is vulnerable to several diseases including SMUT, RUST, ARMY WORM and HESSIAN FLY. Family: Gramineae.

WHEATLEY, Phillis (c1753–1784), black US poet. Born in Africa, she was sold to John Wheatley of Boston, who educated her. Her Poems on Various Subjects, Religious and Moral was published in London in 1773.

WHEATSTONE, Sir Charles (1802–1875), British physicist and inventor who popularized the "Wheatstone bridge" for measuring voltages; and invented the electric TELEGRAPH (with the help of Joseph HENRY) before MORSE (1837), the STEREOSCOPE (1838) and the concertina (1829).

WHIG, an English and a US political party. In England, the term was applied in 1679 to Protestant opponents of the English Crown led by SHAFTESBURY (see GLORIOUS REVOLUTION). The Whigs enjoyed a period of dominance c1714–60, notably under Robert WALPOLE. Largely out of office under Charles FOX, they were increasingly associated with Nonconformism, mercantile, industrial and reforming interests. After the Whig ministries of 2nd Earl GREY and Lord MELBOURNE, the Whigs helped form the LIBERAL PARTY in the mid 1800s.

The US Whig Party was formed c1836 from diverse opponents, including the NATIONAL REPUBLICANS of Andrew JACKSON and the Democrats. Its leaders were Henry

CLAY and Daniel WEBSTER, and a national economic policy was its principal platform. Whig President W. H. HARRISON died in office and was succeeded 1841 by John TYLER, who was disowned by the Whigs when he vetoed their tariff and banking bills. Clay, the next Whig candidate, lost the 1844 election. During the second Whig presidency (1849–53; Zachary TAYLOR and Millard FILLMORE), the party was already divided by the issues of slavery and national expansion; the COMPROMISE OF 1850 did not last and Winfield SCOTT was heavily defeated in the 1852 election. The party never recovered, and many Whigs joined the new REPUBLICAN PARTY.

WHIPPET, English sporting and racing dog, derived from an 18th-century cross between greyhound and terrier. It is slender and light (10–28lb), stands 18–22in high and can run at up to 35mph. Its smoothhaired coat is usually white, tan, or gray.

WHISKEY, strong spirituous DISTILLED LIQUOR, drunk mixed or neat, made from grain. When from Scotland or Canada, whisky is spelt without an "e". The ingredients and preparation vary. In the US corn and rye are commonly used: 51% corn for *bourbon whiskey* and 51% rye for *rye whiskey*. A grain mash is allowed to ferment, then distilled, diluted and left to age. Bourbon and rye whiskey stand in oak barrels for four years. *Canadian whisky* is made from corn, rye and malted (germinated) barley and aged for 4–12 years. *Irish whiskey* uses barley, wheat, oats and rye, and vessels called potstills for the distilling process. *Scotch whisky* is the finest form: the best types are pure barley malt or grain whiskies, but blended varieties are cheaper. The secret of its flavor is supposed to be the peat-flavored water of certain Scottish streams. Whiskey is one of the most popular of ALCOHOLIC BEVERAGES. In the US an average of 16 bottles per person are drunk every year.

WHISKEY REBELLION, 1794, uprising of W. Pa., mainly Scotch-Irish farmer settlers against the federal excise tax imposed on whiskey by secretary of the treasury HAMILTON in 1791. Federal officers were attacked, some were tarred and feathered and one had his house burnt down. Resistance increased when official measures were taken to obtain the tax. At Hamilton's insistence, President Washington sent in 13,000 militiamen to suppress the insurgents. They met no resistance, and Washington pardoned two ringleaders convicted of treason. Federalists claimed a victory—the federal government had demonstrated the power to enforce its law.

WHIST, four-player card game. A 52-card pack is evenly dealt and the last card exposed to show trumps. Partners (facing players) aim to win tricks. Played in 17th-century England, it became popular and fashionable in the 1800s and 1900s. Solo whist and BRIDGE were 19th-century developments.

WHISTLER, James Abbott McNeill (1834–1903), US painter, etcher, and wit who lived in Paris and London. He advocated "art for art's sake," and stressed simplicity of color and design, as in the famous portrait of his mother, *Arrangement in Gray and Black* (1872), and *Falling Rocket: Nocturne in Black and Gold* (1874). His etchings were among the finest of his day, and his decorated interiors foreshadowed ART NOUVEAU.

WHITBY, Synod of, held 663 or 664 in the kingdom of Northumbria, England, to decide between Celtic and Roman church usage. King OSWY chose Roman practice, thus affecting not only the reckoning of Easter but linking the English church more closely with that of the rest of Europe.

WHITE, Andrew Dickson (1832–1918), US educator and diplomat, first president (1867–85) of Cornell U., founded as a nonsectarian university based on his liberal principles. He was a N.Y. senator 1864–67, US ambassador to Germany 1897–1903 and led the US delegation to the 1899 Hague peace conference.

WHITE, Byron Raymond (*"Whizzer"*) (1917–   ), US jurist. Once famous as a professional football player, he was appointed by President Kennedy as US deputy attorney general (1961) and associate justice of the Supreme Court (1962–   ).

WHITE, Edward Douglass (1845–1921), US jurist. A judge of the La. supreme court 1879–80, US senator 1890–94 and associate justice of the US Supreme Court from 1894, he was appointed chief justice by Taft in 1910. Generally a conservative, he wrote the "rule of reason" into antitrust law.

WHITE, E(lwyn) B(rooks) (1899–   ), US writer noted for his witty, well-crafted essays in the *New Yorker* (from 1926) and *Harper's* (1938–43). His work includes poems, the satire *Is Sex Necessary?* (1929, with THURBER), and such children's books as *Charlotte's Web* (1952).

WHITE, George (1890–1968), US theatrical producer who presented 13 editions of his spectacular Broadway *Scandals* (1921–39), a series of enormously popular musical revues.

WHITE, Joshua Daniel (1908–1969), US folksinger whose religious convictions and travels with black minstrels deeply influenced his style. His renditions of such standards as "Sometimes I Feel Like a Motherless Child" and "Frankie and Johnny" reflected the tone of the ballads and prison songs he heard in his youth, as well as the teaching of his mentor, Blind Lemon Jefferson.

WHITE, Leslie Alvin (1900–   ), US anthropologist whose theories of cultural evolution were heavily influenced by the work of Karl Marx. His major works are *The Science of Culture* (1949) and *The Evolution of Culture* (1959).

WHITE, Minor (1908–1976), US photographer associated with Ansel ADAMS, Alfred STIEGLITZ and Edward WESTON. Known as a mystical and abstract artist, he co-founded (1952) and edited the journal *Aperture* and taught at several schools, including MIT (1965–74).

WHITE, Patrick (1912–   ), Australian novelist, winner of the 1973 Nobel Prize for Literature. His long novels, set mostly in Australia, include *The Tree of Man* (1955), *Voss* (1957), *Riders in the Chariot* (1961), *The Vivisector* (1970), and *The Eye of the Storm* (1974).

WHITE, Pearl (1889–1939), popular US actress in early silent movies, heroine of such serials as *The Perils of Pauline*, noted for the cliff-hanging ending to each short episode.

WHITE, Stanford (1853–1906), US architect, noted for interior and decorative work. He cofounded (1879) the famous firm MCKIM, Mead, and White. Their work developed from domestic Shingle Style to "Beaux Arts" classical-Renaissance, as in the 1890 Madison Square Garden and the Century Club, New York. He was shot dead by the husband of his mistress Evelyn Nesbit Thaw.

WHITE, T(erence) H(anbury) (1906–1964), English novelist, noted for *The Once and Future King* (four books, 1938–58), a retelling of the legends of King Arthur (adapted for the musical *Camelot*) and *The Goshawk* (1951).

WHITE, Walter Francis (1893-1955), US Negro leader, from 1931 secretary of the National Association for the Advancement of Colored People. His works include his autobiography, *A Man Called White* (1948).

WHITE, William Allen (1868–1944), US journalist and author. A small-town liberal Republican, White became famous for his editorials in his own Emporia (Kan.) *Gazette* (1923 Pulitzer Prize). His

posthumous autobiography won a 1946 Pulitzer Prize.

WHITEFIELD, George (1714–1770), English evangelist, founder of Calvinist Methodism. He joined the Methodists, led by WESLEY, whom he followed (1738) to Ga., the first of seven missions to America (see GREAT AWAKENING). Adopting Calvinist views on predestination, he led the Calvinist Methodists from 1741.

WHITEHEAD, Alfred North (1861–1947), English mathematician and philosopher. He was co-author with Bertrand RUSSELL of *Principia Mathematica* (1910–13), a major landmark in the philosophy of mathematics; and while teaching at Harvard University (from 1924) he developed a monumental system of metaphysics, most comprehensively expounded in his *Process and Reality* (1929).

WHITE HOUSE, official home of the President of the US, in Washington, D.C. It was designed in the manner of an 18th-century English gentleman's country house by James HOBAN (1792). It was severely damaged by the British in 1814, but rebuilt and extended (and painted white) by 1818. In 1824 Hoban added the semicircular south portico. The grounds were landscaped in 1850 by Andrew DOWNING. Major renovations, including the addition of the executive office building, were carried out in the early 20th century by the architectural firm of MCKIM, Mead and White. From 1948 onward the building was extensively rebuilt.

WHITEMAN, Paul (1891–1967), US bandleader of the 1920s and 1930s. He is remembered for his collaboration with GERSHWIN and for his elaborate arrangements of jazz and dance music.

WHITE MOUNTAINS, a section of the APPALACHIAN MOUNTAINS covering c1,200sq mi in W Me. and N.H. It includes the Presidential, Sandwich, Carter-Moriah and Franconia ranges. The highest peak, Mt. Washington (6,288ft), is in the Presidential Range. Deep canyons, called "notches," have been carved out by glaciers. The area is noted for scenic beauty.

WHITE RUSSIANS, an alternative name for the Belorussians, an East SLAV people who live mostly in the BELORUSSIAN SOVIET SOCIALIST REPUBLIC in W USSR. The name "White Russian" has also been used for the anti-communist groups who fought the BOLSHEVIKS in the RUSSIAN REVOLUTION and Civil War (1917–20).

WHITMAN, Walter "Walt" (1819–1892), major US poet. Born in Long Island, N.Y., he became a printer and journalist. His *Leaves of Grass* (1855; expanded in successive editions) was praised by EMERSON and THOREAU but did not at first achieve popular recognition. Other works include the Civil War poems, *Drum Taps* (1865); *Democratic Vistas* (1871), studies of American democracy; and the autobiographical *Specimen Days* (1882–83). He rejected regular meter and rhyme in favor of flowing FREE VERSE, and celebrated erotic love, rugged individualism, democracy and equality, and expressed an almost mystical identification with America.

WHITNEY, Eli (1765–1825), US inventor of the COTTON GIN (1793), from which he earned little because of patent infringements, and pioneer of MASS PRODUCTION. In 1798 he contracted with the US Government to make 10,000 muskets: he took 8 years to fulfill the 2-year contract, but showed that with unskilled labor muskets could be put together using parts that were precision-made and thus interchangeable, a benefit not only during production but also in later maintenance.

WHITNEY, Gertrude Vanderbilt (1875–1942), US sculptor. She was best known for her monuments commemorating the victims of WWI, and for her fountain sculpture. The Whitney Studio Club, which she established in New York (1918), was a center for American avant-garde art and led to the founding of the Whitney Museum of American Art (1930).

WHITNEY, John Hay (1904–   ), US diplomat and publisher. Born to wealth, he was active in Republican politics and served as ambassador to Great Britain (1957–61). He published the New York *Herald Tribune* (1961–67), served as chairman of the *International Herald Tribune* (from 1967) and published several prominent US magazines.

WHITNEY, Mount, a mountain in the Sierra Nevada range of E central Cal., at 14,494ft the highest in the US outside Alaska. It was named for the geologist Josiah Dwight Whitney (1819–1896), who discovered it in 1864.

WHITTIER, John Greenleaf (1807–1892), US Quaker poet and abolitionist. From 1833 to 1865 he was a campaigning journalist and collected his antislavery poems in *Voices of Freedom* (1846). He later returned to New England themes in his "Yankee pastorals." The autobiographical *Snow-Bound* (1866) and *The Tent on the Beach* (1867) are among his best-known works.

WHITTINGTON, Richard (c1358–1423), English merchant and lord mayor of London, made famous in legend as the poor Dick Whittington with his cat, but in fact the son of a wealthy knight. He was mayor 1397–98, 1407–08 and 1419–20, and bequeathed his considerable fortune to charitable and public purposes.

WHITTLE, Air Commodore Sir Frank (1907–   ), British aeronautical engineer who invented the first aircraft JET PROPULSION unit (patented 1937, first used in flight 1941).

WHO, The, British rock music group whose early hit, "My Generation" (1965), and rock opera *Tommy* (1969) are considered central to the development of rock music.

WHOLESALE PRICE INDEX. See PRODUCER PRICE INDEX.

WHOOPING COUGH, or **pertussis,** BACTERIAL DISEASE of children causing upper respiratory symptoms with a characteristic whoop or inspiratory noise due to INFLAMMATION of the LARYNX. It is usually a relatively mild illness, except in the very young, but VACCINATION is widely practiced to prevent it.

WHOOPING CRANE, *Grus americana,* a tall white wading bird with a red cap on the head. Once widespread through North America, they have for several decades been close to extinction and have been preserved only by determined conservation measures.

WHORF, Benjamin Lee (1897–1941), US linguist best known for proposing the theory that a language's structure determines the thought processes of its speakers. (See also LINGUISTICS.)

WIELAND, Christoph Martin (1733–1813), German poet and novelist. His urbane and satirical works include the verse romance *Oberon* (1780), the psychological novel *Agathon* (1773) and the satire *The Abderites* (1774). He translated much of Shakespeare (1762–66).

WIENER, Norbert (1894–1964), US mathematician who created the discipline CYBERNETICS. His major book is *Cybernetics: Or Control and Communication in the Animal and the Machine* (1948).

WIESENTHAL, Simon (1908–   ), Polish-born hunter of Nazi war criminals. Having lost a large number of relatives in Nazi concentration camps during WWII; he established the Jewish Documentation Center in Vienna, Austria, through which he located more than 1,000 former Nazis accused of war crimes, including Adolf EICHMANN.

WIG, a covering for the head of real or artificial hair, worn as a cosmetic device, as a mark of rank or office, as a disguise or for theatrical portrayals. Known since ancient times, wigs became fashionable in 17th- and 18th-century Europe, when elaborate headpieces for women and full, curled wigs for men came into wide use. The latter are still worn in British law courts. In the 1960s wigs came back into fashion for women, and the toupee to conceal baldness became acceptable for men.

WIGGLESWORTH, Michael (1631–1705), English-born American Puritan poet, pastor at Malden, Mass., from 1656. His *Day of Doom* (1662) was extremely popular. He also wrote *Meat out of the Eater* (1669), on the moral benefits of affliction.

WIGHTMAN CUP, an annual event between women's tennis teams. The trophy, donated by Mrs. Hazel Hotchkiss Wightman (winner of 60 US tennis tournaments), was for competition among women's teams throughout the world. However, since its inception in 1923, only the US and England have participated in the matches.

WIGMAN, Mary (1886–1973), German dancer and choreographer, born Marie Wiegmann. Her free theatrical style marked a departure from classical dance. Through Hanya HOLM and other pupils at her school in Dresden, she influenced the development of modern dance.

WIGNER, Eugene Paul (1902–   ), Hungarian-born US physicist who shared with J. H. D. JENSEN and M. G. MAYER the 1963 Nobel Prize for Physics for his work in the field of nuclear physics. He also worked with FERMI on the MANHATTAN PROJECT, and received the 1960 Atoms for Peace Award.

WILBERFORCE, William (1759–1833), English philanthropist and antislavery campaigner. A member of Parliament (1780–1825), he secured the abolition in the British Empire of the slave trade (1807) and of slavery itself (1833). A leader of the CLAPHAM SECT, he supported missionary work and devoted most of his fortune to evangelical and charitable purposes.

WILBUR, Richard (1921–   ), US poet and critic who won a Pulitzer Prize for *Things of this World* (1956). Using a formal structure and a witty style, he incorporated philosophy and myth into poems about ordinary life.

WILDCATS, various species of small CATS distributed throughout the world. The name often refers specifically to the European wildcat, *Felis sylvestris*, a heavier version of the domestic cat, living in crevices in rock and preying mainly on mice and voles. It is extremely fierce and intractable.

WILDE, Oscar Fingal O'Flahertie Wills (1854–1900), Irish wit and playwright. A dandy and aesthete, believing in "art for art's sake," he achieved celebrity with the novel *The Picture of Dorian Gray* (1891)

and witty society comedies such as *Lady Windermere's Fan* (1892), *An Ideal Husband* (1895) and *The Importance of Being Earnest* (1895), and the biblical *Salome* (written in French; 1893). His career was shattered by his imprisonment for homosexuality (1895–97), which prompted his best known poem, *The Ballad of Reading Gaol* (1898).

WILDEBEEST, or **gnu,** ungainly-looking African ANTELOPES of the genus *Connochaetes.* The White-tailed gnu, a southern species, is now rare outside captivity while the Brindled gnu (Blue wildebeest) still roams the plains of E Africa in vast herds—a major prey of the LION.

WILDER, Billy (1906–   ), Austrian-born US film director, known for his keen satire and realistic observation. After years as a screenwriter, he directed such films as *Sunset Boulevard* (1950), *Some Like it Hot* (1959) and *The Apartment* (1960).

WILDER, Thornton Niven (1897–1975), US novelist and playwright. Novels include *The Bridge of San Luis Rey* (1927; Pulitzer Prize) and *The Ides of March* (1948). Plays such as *Our Town* (1938), *The Skin of Our Teeth* (1942) and *The Matchmaker* (1954) experiment with stylized techniques.

WILDERNESS ROAD, an early American pioneer route. It ran from Va. through the Cumberland Gap into the Ohio Valley. Laid out in 1775 by Daniel BOONE, it was the main route W until c1840.

WILHELMINA (1880–1962), Queen of the Netherlands from 1890 to 1948 (her mother was regent until 1898). She was primarily responsible for Dutch neutrality during WWI. After her Golden Jubilee in 1948, she abdicated in favor of JULIANA, her daughter.

WILKES, Charles (1789–1877), US naval officer and explorer. Head of the US Navy department of charts and instruments (1833), he explored the Pacific, ANTARCTICA and the NW coast of America (1838–42), and was the first to designate Antarctica a separate continent. In 1861 he precipitated the TRENT AFFAIR.

WILKES, John (1727–1797), English politician and champion of liberty. Expelled from Parliament 1764, reelected and expelled again four times 1768–69, he became a popular champion of electors' rights, individual liberty and freedom of the press. Lord mayor of London (1774), he returned to Parliament (1774–90), where he supported parliamentary reform and opposed the war with America.

WILKINS, Maurice Hugh Frederick (1916–   ), British biophysicist who shared with F. H. CRICK and J. D. WATSON the 1962 Nobel Prize for Physiology or Medicine for his X-RAY DIFFRACTION studies of DNA, work that was vital to the determination by Crick and Watson of DNA's molecular structure.

WILKINS, Roy (1901–1981), US CIVIL RIGHTS leader and executive secretary (director) of the NATIONAL ASSOCIATION FOR THE ADVANCEMENT OF COLORED PEOPLE 1955–1970. He was assistant secretary from 1931 and edited the journal, *Crisis* (1934–49). Dedicated to nonviolence, he came under criticism from younger militants in the 1960s and 1970s.

WILL, legal document by which a person (the testator) gives instructions concerning the disposal of his or her PROPERTY after death. Under most jurisdictions a will must be attested in order to be legally valid: independent witnesses, who have nothing to gain under the will, must attest that the signature on the will is in fact that of the testator who has signed in their presence. Wills may be revoked during the life of the testator or altered by codicils. Wills generally appoint executors to administer the estate of the deceased and carry out his or her instructions. When a person dies intestate (without making a will), the property is normally divided among the next of kin.

WILLARD, Emma Hart (1787–1870), US campaigner for women's education. In 1821 she founded Troy Female Seminary, later renamed for her, which pioneered collegiate courses for women. She retired in 1838, but continued her educational work.

WILLARD, Frances Elizabeth Caroline (1839–1898), US temperance leader and reformer, president of the WOMAN'S CHRISTIAN TEMPERANCE UNION from 1879. A brilliant speaker and capable organizer, she also worked for women's suffrage and social reforms.

WILLARD, Frank Henry (1893–1958), US cartoonist who created and drew (with Fred Johnson) the popular comic strip *Moon Mullins*, which was carried by more than 400 newspapers throughout the US.

WILLARD, Jess (1883–1968), US heavyweight boxing champion of the world. He won the title by beating Jack JOHNSON in 1915, and lost it in 1919 to Jack DEMPSEY.

WILLIAM (German Wilhelm), name of two German emperors. **William I** (1797–1888), became king of Prussia in 1861. Conservative, autocratic and militaristic, under BISMARCK'S guidance he organized the unification of Germany, largely through the AUSTRO-PRUSSIAN WAR (1866) and the FRANCO-PRUSSIAN WAR

(1870–71), from which Prussia emerged as the leading German power. He was proclaimed emperor at Versailles in 1871. **William II** (1859–1941), grandson of William I and also of Queen VICTORIA, succeeded in 1888. Impulsive and with a passion for military affairs, he dismissed Bismarck (1890), reinforced the TRIPLE ALLIANCE and promoted the nationalistic imperialism that was a factor leading to WWI. In 1918 he was forced to abdicate, and found asylum in Holland.

WILLIAM, name of four kings of England. **William I, the Conqueror** (1027–1087), duke of Normandy from 1035, became king in 1066 by defeating HAROLD at HASTINGS (see NORMAN CONQUEST), and had suppressed all opposition by 1071. He was a harsh but capable ruler, reorganizing England's military and landholding systems, building many castles and creating a strong feudal government (see FEUDALISM). The DOMESDAY BOOK was compiled by his order. His son, **William II "Rufus"** (the Red; c1056–1100), succeeded in 1087. Autocratic and brutal, he spent much time fighting, in England (against his own barons, 1088), France (1091, 1094, 1097–99), Scotland (1091–92) and Wales (1096–97), and quarreled with St. ANSELM over the independence of the Church. He was killed (probably deliberately) by an arrow while hunting in the New Forest. **William III, Prince of Orange** (1650–1702), was *stadtholder* (ruler) of Holland. His marriage in 1677 to MARY, Protestant daughter of JAMES II, resulted in Parliament inviting him to accept the crown jointly with his wife after the GLORIOUS REVOLUTION (1688). He subdued JACOBITE resistance in Ireland (see BOYNE, BATTLE OF THE) and Scotland, and ruled alone after Mary's death (1694). **William IV** (1765–1837) succeeded his brother GEORGE IV in 1830. He exercised little political influence, and was succeeded by his niece, VICTORIA.

WILLIAM AND MARY COLLEGE, Williamsburg, Va., the second oldest institution of higher learning in the US. Chartered in 1693 by King William and Queen Mary, it pioneered the elective system and the study of history and modern languages. The scholastic honor society PHI BETA KAPPA was founded there in 1776.

WILLIAMS, Bert (1876–1922), Bahamian-born black US entertainer, considered one of the greatest comedians of his day. He was a member of the vaudeville team of Walker and Williams, 1895–1909, and starred in the ZIEGFELD *Follies*, 1910–19.

WILLIAMS, Emlyn (1905–   ), Welsh

actor and playwright, noted for his semi-autobiographical play *The Corn Is Green* (1941) and for one-man shows in which he portrayed Dylan THOMAS and Charles DICKENS.

WILLIAMS, Hank (1923–1953), US country singer and composer, a legendary figure in country music who had a magnetic stage personality. He recorded such hits as "I'm So Lonesome I Could Cry" and "Your Cheatin' Heart."

WILLIAMS, John T. (1932–   ), US composer and conductor. His scores for such films as *Jaws* (1976), *Star Wars* (1977) and *Superman* (1978) brought him international fame. In 1980 he succeeded Arthur FIEDLER as conductor of the Boston Pops Orchestra.

WILLIAMS, Ralph Vaughan. See VAUGHAN WILLIAMS, RALPH.

WILLIAMS, Roger (c1603–1683), British-born clergyman, founder of RHODE ISLAND. A firm believer in religious freedom, he emigrated to Massachusetts Bay Colony in 1631. He became a pastor at Salem, but was banished for criticizing the expropriation of Indian lands and the enforcement of religious principles by civil power. In 1636 he founded PROVIDENCE in Rhode Island and obtained a charter for the colony (1644). Its constitution exemplified his principles of religious freedom, separation of church and state, democracy and local autonomy, all of which were influential in shaping US traditions.

WILLIAMS, Shirley (1930–   ), British political leader. She served as education secretary in a Labour government (1976–79), then broke with the party because of its leftward drift and helped form the Social Democratic Party (1981).

WILLIAMS, Ted (1918–   ), US base-ball player who achieved a major league batting average of .344 and hit 521 home runs. He joined the Boston Red Sox in 1939 and won six American batting champion-ships before retiring in 1960. A left-hand hitting outfielder, he was the last major leaguer to achieve a .400 season batting average (.406 in 1941).

WILLIAMS, Tennesse (1911–   ), US playwright whose emotionally intense plays deal with the warping effects on sensitive characters of failure, loneliness and futile obsessions. His first success, *The Glass Menagerie* (1945), was followed by *A Streetcar Named Desire* (1947) and *Cat on a Hot Tin Roof* (1955), both of which received Pulitzer Prizes. Other plays include *Sweet Bird of Youth* (1959) and *Night of the Iguana* (1961).

WILLIAMS, William Carlos (1883–1963),

US poet. A doctor, he wrote about ordinary life in N.J., especially in the long reflective poem *Paterson* (1946–58). *Pictures from Breughel* (1963) won a Pulitzer Prize. He also wrote plays, fiction and essays, including *In the American Grain* (1925), a study of the American character.

WILLIAMSBURG, restored colonial town in SE Va., on the James R. The city (colonial capital of Virginia until 1780) contains over 500 original or reconstructed 18th-century buildings, including the Governor's Palace and the Capitol in which the Virginia Assembly met. Much of the restoration work was undertaken by John D. Rockefeller, Jr. Pop 9,870.

WILLIAMSON, Nicol (1938–   ), Scottish-born British actor who joined the Royal Shakespeare Co. in 1962. He won a New York Drama Critics Award for his performance as Bill Maitland in *Inadmissible Evidence* (1965) and is noted for his portrayal of Hamlet (1969). He has also appeared in films.

WILLIAM THE SILENT (1533–1584), founder of Dutch independence. Son of the count of Nassau, he became Prince of Orange (1544) and *stadtholder* (ruler) of Holland, Zeeland and Utrecht (1559). Resisting PHILIP II of Spain's oppressive anti-Protestantism, he had his estates confiscated (1567) and fled to Germany. He became a Protestant and led the revolt against Spanish rule, becoming first *stadtholder* of the independent united Northern Provinces in 1579.

WILLKIE, Wendell Lewis (1892–1944), US businessman and political leader. A lawyer and Democrat (1914–33), he became president of a giant utility company and led business opposition to the NEW DEAL. Joining the Republicans, he was presiden-tial candidate in 1940, gaining a large popular vote. *One World* (1943) was a plea for international cooperation.

WILLS, Helen Newington (1906–   ), US tennis star. Between 1923 and 1938 she won seven US singles titles and eight Wimbledon championships.

WILMINGTON TEN, group of civil rights activists convicted of conspiracy and arson in the aftermath of a week of racial violence in Wilmington, N.C., in 1971. Three prosecution witnesses later said their testimony had been coerced, but it was not until Dec. 4, 1980, that a federal appeals court unanimously reversed the original convictions.

WILMOT PROVISO, an attempt by Democratic representative David Wilmot in 1846–47 to outlaw slavery in new US territories. A $5million appropriation for a territorial settlement to the MEXICAN WAR had been proposed in Congress; Wilmot's amendment would have banned slavery in any territory purchased. Twice passed by the House but dropped by the Senate, the Proviso made slavery an explosive issue and led to bitter controversy.

WILSON, Angus (1913–), English novelist and short story writer who satirizes English class attitudes and social life. His novels include *Hemlock and After* (1952), *Anglo-Saxon Attitudes* (1956) and *No Laughing Matter* (1967).

WILSON, Charles Erwin (1890–1961), US industrialist who was president of General Motors 1941–53 and Secretary of Defense 1953–57. He was known for his remark that "what was good for our country was good for General Motors, and vice versa," which the press reported as, "What's good for General Motors is good for the country."

WILSON, Colin (1931–), English writer whose books often explore the dichotomy between reason and vision. His many works include such nonfiction as *The Outsider* (1956), *The Strength to Dream* (1962), *Introduction to the New Existentialism* (1966) and such fiction as *Man without a Shadow* (1963) and *The Space Vampires* (1976).

WILSON, Edmund (1895–1972), US critic and writer who investigated the historical, sociological and psychological background to literature. His prolific imaginative and critical output includes *Axel's Castle* (1931), a study of SYMBOLISM; *To the Finland Station* (1940) on the intellectual sources of the Russian Revolution; *The Wound and the Bow* (1941) on neurosis and literature; the explosive novel *Memoirs of Hecate County* (1949); and *Patriotic Gore* (1962), a study of Civil War literature.

WILSON, James (1742–1798), American jurist and signer of the Declaration of Independence, who played an important role in the 1787 Constitutional Convention. He became associate justice of the US Supreme Court from 1789 and first law professor at the University of Pa. from 1790.

WILSON, (James) Harold (1916–), British statesman. An Oxford economist, he entered Parliament (1945), became president of the Board of Trade (1947–51), leader of the Labour Party (1963) and prime minister 1964–70 and 1974–76. Identified initially with the left wing and known for his tactical skill, he preserved party unity during a period of economic crisis and division over the COMMON MARKET. He was knighted in 1976.

WILSON, Robert (1936–), US

physicist whose discovery of cosmic MICROWAVE radiation emanating from the universe at large provided strong evidence for the "big bang" theory of the origin of the universe. He shared the 1978 Nobel Prize in Physics for his discovery.

WILSON, Woodrow (1856–1924), 28th president of the US, 1913–21. Of Presbyterian stock, Wilson inherited a moral fervor and an impatient idealism which influenced his political life and contributed to the personal tragedy of his last years. After growing up in Ga. and S.C., he studied history and political science at Princeton (BA, 1879) and John Hopkins (PhD, 1886). Teaching followed at Bryn Mawr (1885–88), Wesleyan (1888–90) and Princeton (from 1890), where in 1902 he was elected president. His innovations strengthened the university but his attempt to abolish the aristocratic "eating clubs" aroused bitter controversy. Encouraged by N.J. Democratic political bosses, Wilson in 1910 ran for governor and, on being elected, energetically pushed through ambitious reforms which drew national attention. He captured the 1912 Democratic presidential nomination after 46 ballots and won the ensuing election because of a Republican split. Assuming legislative leadership, and with a Democratic majority in Congress, Wilson achieved much, including the UNDERWOOD TARIFF (1913), which also provided for graduated income tax; the FEDERAL RESERVE SYSTEM (1913); the FEDERAL TRADE COMMISSION and CLAYTON ANTITRUST ACT (1914); the Federal Child Labor law, the Federal Farm Loans Act and an eight-hour day for railroad employees (1916). The constitutional amendments establishing PROHIBITION, women's votes and direct election of senators were also passed. In foreign affairs Wilson was led to intervene in Haiti, Nicaragua, the Dominican Republic and Mexico. In Europe, he struggled to maintain US neutrality in WWI, before finally declaring war on Germany in 1917. He directed US war mobilization and urged a peace of reconciliation based on his famous

FOURTEEN POINTS (1918). Wilson headed the US delegation at VERSAILLES (1919). Compromises were forced on him there, but he salvaged the LEAGUE OF NATIONS. In 1919, the Treaty signed, Wilson sought ratification of the League from a Republican-controlled Congress which demanded "reservations" protecting US sovereignty. He refused compromise and went on a countrywide speaking tour to gain support, but collapsed from the strain and suffered a stroke (Oct. 2, 1919). For the remaining 17 months of his term, the government was run informally by the cabinet, aided by his wife. Ratification failed, and although he was awarded the Nobel Peace Prize in 1920, Wilson retired a sick and disappointed man.

WIMBLEDON CHAMPIONSHIPS. See TENNIS.

WINCHELL, Walter (1897–1972), US newspaper columnist. A powerful figure in the world of journalism, he wrote an influential nationally syndicated gossip column (from 1929) and had his own radio show (1930–50) whose signature was the dots and dashes of transatlantic wireless. He was a brash and controversial figure who was a notorious "red-baiter" during the McCarthy era.

WINCKELMANN, Johann Joachim (1717–1768), German archaeologist and art theorist. His *Thoughts on the Imitation of Greek Works in Painting and Sculpture* (1755) and *History of Ancient Art* (1764) created the Greek Revival in art and building.

WIND, body of air moving relative to the earth's surface. The world's major wind systems are set up to counter the equal heating of the earth's surface and are modified by the rotation of the earth. Surface heating, at its greatest near the equator, creates an equatorial belt of low pressure known as the doldrums and a system of CONVECTION currents transporting heat toward the Poles. The earth's rotation deflects the currents of the N Hemisphere to the right and those of the S Hemisphere to the left of the directions in which they would blow, producing on a nonrotating globe the NE and SE TRADE WINDS, the PREVAILING WESTERLIES and the Polar Easterlies. Other factors influencing general wind patterns are the different rates of heating and cooling of land and sea and the seasonal variations in surface heating (see MONSOON). Mixing of air along the boundary between the Westerlies and the Polar Easterlies—the polar front—causes depressions in which winds follow circular paths, counterclockwise in the N Hemisphere and clockwise in the S Hemisphere

(see CYCLONE). Superimposed on the general wind systems are local winds—winds, such as the CHINOOKS, caused by temperature differentials associated with local topographical features such as mountains and coastal belts, or winds associated with certain CLOUD systems. (See also ATMOSPHERE; HURRICANE; JET STREAM; MONSOON; TORNADO; WEATHER FORECASTING; WHIRLWIND.)

WINDFALL PROFITS TAX, a special tax often imposed on businesses. When a new law has the effect of increasing the profits of an industry, the tax may be imposed to avoid public criticism. In the US, a windfall profits tax was passed in 1980 to recover from oil companies part of the profits realized from the decontrol of oil prices.

WIND INSTRUMENTS, musical instruments whose sound is produced by blowing air into a tube, causing a vibration within it.

In *woodwind* instruments the vibration is made either by blowing across or into a specially shaped mouthpiece, as with the FLUTE, PICCOLO, RECORDER and its relative the flageolet; or by blowing such that a single or double reed vibrates, as in the CLARINET, SAXOPHONE, OBOE, ENGLISH HORN and BASSOON. The pitch is altered by opening and closing holes set into the tube.

In *brass* instruments, the vibration is made by the player's lips on the mouthpiece. The BUGLE and various types of posthorn have a single unbroken tube. The CORNET, FRENCH HORN, TRUMPET and TUBA have valves to vary the effective tube length and increase the range of notes; the TROMBONE has a slide mechanism for the same purpose.

WINDMILL, machine that performs WORK by harnessing wind power. In the traditional windmill, the power applied to a horizontal shaft by four large radiating sails was transmitted to milling or pumping machinery housed in a sizable supporting structure. The windmill's modern cousin is the wind turbine, often seen in remote rural areas. Here a multibladed turbine wheel mounted on a steel derrick or mast and pointed into the wind by a "fantail" drives a pump or electric generator.

WINDSOR, House of, name of the ruling dynasty of the United Kingdom of Great Britain and Northern Ireland, adopted by King GEORGE V in 1917 to replace Saxe-Coburg-Gotha (from Albert, Queen VICTORIA'S husband) when anti-German feeling was high.

WINDSOR CASTLE, principal residence of British sovereigns since the 11th century. Begun by WILLIAM I, it stands about 20mi W.

of London. The Round Tower, built in 1180, is the castle's center, and St. George's Chapel (1528) is a fine example of English Perpendicular architecture.

WIND TUNNEL, tunnel in which a controlled stream of air is produced in order to observe the effect on scale models or full-size components of airplanes, missiles, automobiles or such structures as bridges and skyscrapers. An important research tool in AERODYNAMICS, the wind tunnel enables a design to be accurately tested without the risks attached to full-scale trials. "Hypersonic" wind tunnels, operating on an impulse principle, can simulate the frictional effects of flight at over five times the speed of sound.

WINDWARD ISLANDS, group of islands in the Lesser Antilles, WEST INDIES, stretching toward Venezuela. They include St. Lucia, St. Vincent the Grenadines, Grenada, and Martinique. The area is about 950sq mi and the people mainly Negro, producing bananas, cacao, limes, nutmeg and cotton. The tourist industry is growing.

WINE, an ALCOHOLIC BEVERAGE made from fermented grape juice; wines made from other fruits are always named accordingly. Table wines are red, rosé or "white" in color; red wines are made from dark grapes, the skins being left in the fermenting mixture; white wines may be made from dark or pale grapes, the skins being removed. The grapes— normally varieties of *Vitis vinifera*—are allowed to ripen until they attain suitable sugar content—18% or more—and acidity (in cool years or northern areas sugar may have to be added). After crushing, they undergo FERMENTATION in large tanks, a small amount of sulfur dioxide being added to inhibit growth of wild yeasts and bacteria; the wine yeast used, *Saccharomyces cerevisiae*, is resistant to it. When the alcohol and sugar content is right, the wine is cellared, racked off the lees (from which argol is obtained—see TARTARIC ACID), clarified by FILTRATION or fining (adding absorbent substances such as BENTONITE, GELATIN and ISINGLASS), aged in the wood and bottled. Sweet wines contain residual sugar; dry wines little or none. The alcohol content of table wines varies from 8% to 14% by volume. Sparkling wines—notably champagne—are made by secondary fermentation under pressure, in bottles or in tanks. Fortified wines, or dessert wines— including sherry, port and madeira—have brandy added during or after fermentation, and contain about 20% alcohol. Vermouth is a fortified wine flavored with wormwood

(see ABSINTHE) and other herbs. Major wine-producing areas of the world include France, Germany, Spain and Portugal, Italy, and, in the US, Cal.

WINNIPEG, capital of Manitoba, Canada, 45mi S of Lake Winnipeg, at the confluence of the Assiniboine and Red rivers. A major transportation and commercial center, it is one of the world's largest grain markets. Industries include food-processing, clothing, railroad stock, agricultural equipment and furniture. Met pop 578,220.

WINTHROP, name of three distinguished American colonists. **John Winthrop** (1588–1649), led the English "Great Migration" to Salem in 1630, founded Boston and was 12 times elected governor of the Massachusetts Bay Colony. His journal, *The History of New England*, is an important historical source. His eldest son, **John Winthrop** (1606–1676), went to America in 1631. After founding the colony of Saybrook in 1635, he became governor of Connecticut (1657, 1659–76), receiving in 1662 a charter from Charles II uniting New Haven and Connecticut. His son **John Winthrop** (1638–1707), left Mass. to join CROMWELL's army in England, returning (1663) to fight the Dutch, the French and the Indians. He was Connecticut's agent in London (1693–97) and from 1698 a popular governor.

WIRETAPPING, interception of telephone conversations or telegraph messages without the knowledge of those communicating. Wiretapping and the use of other "bugging" devices by private citizens are prohibited by US federal and state laws, but there has always been argument about whether police and other government officials should be able to use wiretapping to detect crimes and collect evidence. In 1968 Congress passed a new law allowing wiretapping to be used in cases involving national security and certain serious crimes, providing that a court order was first obtained. (See also WATERGATE.)

Name of state: Wisconsin
Capital: Madison
Statehood: May 29, 1848 (30th state)
Familiar name: Badger State

Area: 56,154sq mi
Population: 4,705,335
Elevation: Highest—1,952ft, Timm's Hill
Lowest—581ft, Lake Michigan
Motto: Forward
State flower: Wood violet
State bird: Robin
State tree: Sugar maple
State song: "On, Wisconsin!".

WISCONSIN, state in the north central US bordered by Lake Michigan (E), the Mississippi and St. Croix rivers (W) and Lake Superior (N).

Land. Wisconsin consists mostly of gently rolling pasturelands and heavily wooded, hilly upland. There are over 8,000 lakes, formed by glacial action, and much outstandingly beautiful scenery. Some 45% of the surface is forested, the rest rich agricultural land. The largest river, the Wisconsin, drains into the Mississippi. The climate is continental, with hot humid summers and long cold winters.

People. The population is largely of European origin, chiefly German, Polish and Scandinavian. Two-thirds are urban dwellers, of whom half live around Milwaukee in the more densely populated SE.

Economy. Wisconsin is the leading US producer of milk, cheese and butter, and also produces hay, fruit and vegetables. Food-processing is an important industry, overshadowed, however, by other manufacturing, which produces heavy machinery, transportation equipment, farm and electrical equipment and paper. Tourism is a growing industry. Minerals include sand, gravel, zinc and iron.

History. The area was first visited by the French (1634), who set up fur-trading posts and fought against the FOX Indians (c1690–1740). It became British in 1763 and part of the US in 1783. Intensive settlement began in the 1800s, and resistance by the Fox and SAUK Indians was crushed in the BLACK HAWK WAR (1832). (Other Wis. Indians were the KICKAPOO, MENOMINEE, OJIBWA and WINNEBAGO.) Becoming the 30th state in 1848, Wis. acquired a reputation for progressivism under LA FOLLETTE in the early 1900s. In the 1920s, the state became predominantly urban, and it is now an important manufacturing center, though suffering somewhat in the 1980s from the decline of the automotive industry. The state is also notable for nurturing such diverse political figures as the late Sen. Joseph McCarthy on the far right and former US Senator Gaylord Nelson, known for his efforts to save the environment and early opposition

to the Vietnam War.

WISDOM OF SOLOMON, a book of the Old Testament APOCRYPHA, traditionally ascribed to Solomon but probably written in the 2nd or 1st century BC. An example of Jewish "wisdom" literature, it praises wisdom and outlines God's care for the Jews.

WISE, Isaac Mayer (1819–1900), US rabbi, a founder of American Reform Judaism. He organized the Union of American Hebrew Congregations (1873) and founded the Hebrew Union College, Cincinnati (1875). He wrote novels and historical and religious works.

WISSLER, Clark (1870–1947), US anthropologist. In works such as *The American Indian* (1917) and *Man and Culture* (1923) he developed the concept of culture areas, thus making a fundamental contribution to ETHNOGRAPHY.

WISTER, Owen (1860–1938), US author, best known for his classic western *The Virginian* (1902) and a biography of his friend Theodore Roosevelt (1930).

WITCHCRAFT, the manipulation of supernatural forces toward usually evil ends. It has existed in most cultures throughout history, and still has its devotees in modern technological society. In the Christian West witchcraft developed from surviving pagan beliefs. Witches were held responsible for disease and misfortune, and to acquire their evil power from the devil, whom they worshiped in obscene rituals (satanism, devil-worship, is not synonymous with witchcraft). From the 14th to 17th centuries a witch-hunting epidemic arose in Europe, and many thousands of innocent people were tortured and executed in fanatical and hysterical persecutions. (See also MAGIC, PRIMITIVE; SALEM.).

WITCH DOCTOR, popular name for a tribal priest and doctor, or "medicine man," in many primitive cultures. He combines a knowledge of traditional lore and herbal remedies with an authority derived from his alleged magic power, particularly to combat WITCHCRAFT. (See also MAGIC, PRIMITIVE; SHAMANISM.)

WITTE, Count Sergei Yulyevich (1849–1915), Russian statesman. A capable finance minister (1892–1903), he promoted industry and modernization. Recalled in 1905 to negotiate the Treaty of PORTSMOUTH, he became the first constitutional Russian premier after the 1905 Revolution (1905–06), but conservative pressures forced his dismissal.

WITTGENSTEIN, Ludwig (1889–1951), Austrian philosopher, whose two chief works, *Tractatus Logico-Philosophicus*

(1921) and *Philosophical Investigations* (published posthumously in 1953), have profoundly influenced the course of much recent British and US philosophy. The *Tractatus* dwells on the logical nature and limits of language, understood as "picturing" reality. The *Investigations* rejects the assumption in the *Tractatus* that all representations must share a common logical form and instead relates the meanings of sentences to their uses in particular contexts: philosophical problems are attributed to misuses of language. Wittgenstein was professor of philosophy at Cambridge U., England (1929–47).

WITWATERSRAND, or The Rand, gold-bearing rocky ridge, 62mi long and 23mi wide, in S Transvaal, NE South Africa. It produces one-third of the world's gold output, and is South Africa's major industrial region, with Johannesburg located in its center.

WOBBLIES. See INDUSTRIAL WORKERS OF THE WORLD.

WODEHOUSE, P. G. (Sir Pelham Granville; 1881–1975), English humorous novelist and short-story writer. His comic characters include the popular Bertie Wooster and his imperturbable valet, Jeeves. Works include *The Inimitable Jeeves* (1924) and *Much Obliged, Jeeves* (1971). He became a US citizen in 1955.

WOLCOTT, name of a prominent Connecticut family. **Roger Wolcott** (1679–1767), became chief justice and governor of the colony (1750–54). His *Poetical Meditations* (1725) was the first book of verse published in Conn. His son **Oliver Wolcott** (1726–1793), served in the Continental Congress (1775–78, 1780–84), signed the Declaration of Independence and was governor of Conn. (1746–97). **Oliver Wolcott, Jr.** (1760–1833), was US comptroller (1791–95), secretary of the treasury (1795–1800) and governor of Conn. (1817–27).

WOLF, *Canis lupus*, powerful carnivore ranging throughout the deciduous and coniferous forests and tundra of the N Hemisphere. Broadchested, with small pointed ears and long legs, wolves are pack hunters, preying on the huge northern moose, deer and elk herds. In the summer, with the onset of the breeding season and with small mammal prey more readily available, the packs break up into smaller groups. Wolf packs have distinct territories, and within the pack there is a complex social structure under a top male and female.

WOLF, Hugo (1860–1903), Austrian composer who led an unstable life of poverty

and died insane. He is best known for his lieder, published in groups like *The Spanish Song Book* (1889) and *The Italian Song Book* (1891, 1896). He also wrote the opera *Der Corregidor* (1896), a string quartet and the well-known *Italian Serenade* (1894).

WOLFE, James (1727–1759), British general whose capture of Quebec was the decisive victory in the last of the FRENCH AND INDIAN WARS. He fought in the War of the AUSTRIAN SUCCESSION (1742–45) and at Falkirk and CULLODEN MOOR in the JACOBITE rebellion of 1745–46. Second in command under AMHERST (1758), he distinguished himself in the capture of LOUISBURG, and was chosen to lead the attack on Quebec. By brilliant strategy, aided by good luck, he routed the French; but died of his wounds. (See QUEBEC, BATTLE OF.)

WOLFE, Thomas Clayton (1900–1938), US novelist whose works constitute an autobiographical epic. *Look Homeward, Angel* (1929), *Of Time and The River* (1935) and the posthumous *The Web and The Rock* (1939) and *You Can't Go Home Again* (1940) are rich in detail and characterization, and capture the author's vividly felt sense of place.

WOLFF, Christian (1679–1754), German philosopher and mathematician who developed and popularized the ENLIGHTENMENT in Germany. He championed the ideas of DESCARTES and LEIBNITZ in numerous works published under the general title *Vernünftige Gedanken* ("Rational Ideas").

WOLFRAM VON ESCHENBACH (c1170–1220), medieval German poet and MINNESINGER. His fame rests on a few lyrics and the chivalrous epic *Parzival* (see PARSIFAL), in which the quest for the HOLY GRAIL becomes a spiritual journey.

WOLLSTONECRAFT, Mary (1759–1797), English writer and champion of women's rights. Her *Vindication of the Rights of Women* (1792) is an eloquent plea for equality of the sexes in all spheres of life. She married William GODWIN in 1797, and died giving birth to his daughter (later Mary SHELLEY).

WOLSEY, Thomas (c1475–1530), English cardinal and statesman. He became a royal chaplain in 1507, and under HENRY VIII rose to favor, becoming bishop of Lincoln and then archbishop of York in 1514. Made a cardinal and appointed lord chancellor of England in 1515, he amassed great wealth and wielded almost absolute political power until 1529, when he failed to secure the annulment of Henry's marriage and was dismissed. He died journeying to face treason charges.

WOMAN'S CHRISTIAN TEMPER-ANCE UNION (WCTU), US organization seeking legislation against the consumption of alcohol. Founded 1874, it became a worldwide organization in 1883 through the efforts of Frances WILLARD. It also conducts research into tobacco and narcotics.

WOMBATS, heavy, stockily-built, burrowing marsupials of Australia, closely related to KOALAS. They share many anatomical features with placental burrowing rodents. Nocturnal animals, they emerge from their holes to feed on grasses and roots.

WOMEN IN THE AIR FORCE (WAF), the women's branch of the US Air Force from 1948 until the mid-1970s. Women have been fully integrated in the Air Force since that time although they may not fly in combat missions. Before 1948, women were part of the Army Air Corps and known as Air WACS.

WOMEN'S ARMY CORPS (WAC), the women's branch of the US Army. It replaced the Women's Army Auxiliary Corps (WAAC) in 1943, becoming a part of the army with its own commanding officer. In the mid-1970s, WAC was integrated into the regular rank system of the US Army. Women in the army are presently referred to as EWs (enlisted women).

WOMEN'S CLUBS, General Federation of (GFWC), umbrella organization, founded 1890, which unites women's clubs throughout the world and promotes their common interests in education, industry, philanthropy, literature, art, science and culture. It has 10 million members.

WOMEN'S LIBERATION MOVEMENT, movement advocating a basic change in the social role of women and seeking to give them an equal place in society. "Women's Lib" spread rapidly in the US, Europe, Australia and Japan in the 1960s and 1970s. Women's groups want equal opportunities for all jobs, the same rates of pay, legislation against discrimination in sex and childbearing matters, and equality in male–female relationships. Prominent leaders are Germaine GREER, Kate MILLET, Gloria STEINEM and Betty FRIEDAN. (See also NATIONAL ORGANIZATION FOR WOMEN; RADICAL FEMINISM.)

WOMEN STRIKE FOR PEACE (WSP), founded 1961 to advance the cause of general and complete disarmament under international control. Purposefully unstructured at the national level, WSP operates through autonomous local groups which conduct vigils, forums, letter-writing campaigns, etc. More than 100,000 women have been active at various times in its protests against the nuclear arms race, the draft, and the Vietnam War.

WONDER, Stevie (1950–), highly regarded blind rock music composer, singer and instrumentalist. Since the age of ten, when he made his first recording with MOTOWN Records, he has composed and recorded a huge body of work, including the hit album *Songs in the Key of Life* (1976).

WOOD, the hard, dead tissue obtained from the trunks and branches of TREES and SHRUBS. Woody tissue is also found in some herbaceous PLANTS. Botanically, wood consists of *xylem* tissue which is responsible for the conduction of water around the plant. A living tree trunk is composed of (beginning from the center): the *pith* (remains of the primary growth); wood (xylem); CAMBIUM (a band of living cells that divide to produce new wood and phloem); PHLOEM (conducting nutrients made in the leaves), and the bark. The wood nearest the cambium is termed *sapwood* because it is capable of conducting water. However, the bulk of the wood is *heartwood* in which the xylem is impregnated with LIGNIN which gives the cells extra strength but prevents them from conducting water. In temperate regions, a tree's age can be found by counting its ANNUAL RINGS. Commercially, wood is divided into hardwood (from deciduous ANGIOSPERM trees) and softwood (from GYMNOSPERMS). (See also FORESTS; FORESTRY; LUMBER; PAPER.)

WOOD, Grant (1891–1942), US painter, exponent of the 1930s style "regionalism." Strongly influenced by Gothic and Early Renaissance painting, he realistically depicted the people and places of Iowa, as in *American Gothic* (1930).

WOOD, Leonard (1860–1927), US general and administrator. He led the ROUGH RIDERS' attack (1898). Though an excellent military governor of Cuba (1899–1902), he ruthlessly crushed (1903–08) Philippine opposition to US occupation. He was US chief of staff (1910–14), advocated WWI "preparedness" but had no WWI command. He lost the Republican presidential nomination (1920) and became governor general of the Philippines, reversing the US self-government policy.

WOODCHUCK, or groundhog, *Marmota monax,* a familiar GROUND SQUIRREL of woodlands of North America. A large rodent, up to 600mm (2ft) long, with a short bushy tail, the woodchuck is diurnal, feeding on greenstuff near the entrance of the communal burrow. The only woodland ground squirrel, it can be a notable pest.

WOODCOCK, Leonard Freel (1911–),

US labor leader, president of the UNITED AUTOMOBILE WORKERS from 1970 to 1977, when he was named the first US chief of mission to Communist China; he became ambassador in 1978.

WOODCUT AND WOOD ENGRAVING, two techniques of producing pictures by incising a design on a block of wood, inking the design and then pressing the inked block onto paper. Those parts of the design which are to be white are cut away and not inked, leaving in relief the areas to be printed. Woodcut is the older method, originating in China and Japan, and used in Europe from the 14th century, particularly for book illustration. The greatest artist in the medium was Albrecht DÜRER. In wood engraving the artist uses a tool called a *burin*, producing a design of white lines on a black background. It became popular in 18th- and 19th-century Europe.

WOODEN, John (1910–   ), US basket-ball coach. The head coach at UCLA for over a quarter of a century (1948–75), he led the Bruins to an unprecedented ten NCAA championships in his last 12 years (1964, 1965, 1967–73, 1975).

WOODHULL, Victoria Claflin (1838–1927), US social reformer who, with her sister **Tennessee,** advocated woman suffrage, free love and socialism, and published the first English translation of MARX and ENGELS' *Communist Manifesto* in 1872. She was the first woman presidential candidate, for the Equal Rights Party (1872).

WOODPECKERS, a family, Picidae, of birds specialized for obtaining insect food from the trunks and branches of trees. The 210 species occur worldwide except in Australasia. All have wedge-shaped tails which may be pressed against the trunk of a tree as a prop. The bill is strong and straight and the muscles and structure of head and neck are adapted for driving the bill powerfully forward into tree bark and absorbing the shock of the blow. The tongue is long and slender for picking out insects. One group, the SAPSUCKERS, also feed on tree sap. Woodpeckers also use the bill during courtship "drumming" and to hack out nesting holes in tree trunks.

WOODS, Lake of the, on the Canadian–US border, in SE Manitoba, SW Ontario and N Minn. About 70mi long and 1,485sq mi in area, it is fed by the Rainy R and drains into Lake Winnipeg. It is a popular tourist location.

WOODSTOCK, rock and folk music festival in 1969 in Bethel, N.Y., near the artists' community of Woodstock, where the festival was originally scheduled. The event came immediately to symbolize the benign aspects of the counterculture spirit of the '60s. Attended by some 400,000 (mostly young) people, the festival was distinguished by disorganization; good humor; good music; marijuana; some nudity; crises with regard to traffic, toilets, and food supplies, and universal opposition to the Vietnam War.

WOODWARD, Comer Vann (1908–   ), US historian of the American South. A professor at Johns Hopkins (1946–61) and Yale (1961–77), he wrote several influential works including *Origins of the New South* (1951), *The Strange Career of Jim Crow* (1955), and *The Burden of Southern History* (1960).

WOODWARD, Robert Burns (1917–1979), US chemist who has synthesized QUININE (1944), CHOLESTEROL (1951), CORTISONE (1951), STRYCHNINE (1954), LSD (1954), reserpine (1956; see RAUWOLFIA SERPENTINA), CHLOROPHYLL (1960) and VITAMIN B_{12} (1971). He received the 1965 Nobel Prize for Chemistry for his many organic syntheses.

WOODWINDS. See WIND INSTRUMENTS.

WOOL, animal FIBER that forms the fleece, or protective coat, of sheep. Coarser than most vegetable or synthetic fibers, wool fibers are wavy (up to 10 waves/cm) and vary in color from the usual white to brown or black. They are composed of the protein KERATIN, whose molecules are long, coiled chains, giving wool elasticity and resilience. Reactive side groups result in good affinity for DYES, and enable new, desirable properties to be chemically imparted. Wool lasts if well cared for, but is liable to be damaged by some insect larvae (which eat it), by heat, sunlight, alkalis and hot water. It chars and smolders when burned, but is not inflammable. Wool strongly absorbs moisture from the air. It is weakened when wet, and liable to form felt if mechanically agitated in water. Wool has been used from earliest times to make cloth. Sheep are shorn, usually annually, and the fleeces are cleaned—the wool WAX removed is the source of LANOLIN—and sorted, blended, carded (which disentangles the fibers and removes any foreign bodies) and combed if necessary to remove shorter fibers. A rope of woolen fibers, roving, is thus produced, and is spun (see SPINNING). The woolen yarn is woven into cloth, knitted, or made into carpets or blankets. The main producing countries are Australia, New Zealand, the USSR and India. Because the supply of new (virgin) wool is inadequate, inferior textiles are made of reprocessed wool.

WOOLF, Virginia (1882–1941), English novelist and essayist. The daughter of Sir

Leslie STEPHEN, she married the critic **Leonard Sidney Woolf** (1880–1969) and they established the Hogarth Press (1917). Novels using STREAM OF CONSCIOUSNESS, such as *Mrs. Dalloway* (1925), *To the Lighthouse* (1927) and *The Waves* (1931), concern her characters' thoughts and feelings about common experiences. Some of her brilliant criticism was published in *The Common Reader* (1925). Subject to fits of mental instability, she finally drowned herself.

WOOLLCOTT, Alexander (1887–1943), US journalist, wit, drama critic and popular broadcaster whose books include *While Rome Burns* (1934). His personality inspired the comedy *The Man Who Came to Dinner* in which he once played the leading part.

WORD PROCESSING, the use of electronic equipment to improve the efficiency of office procedures. A **word processor** is basically an electronic typewriter with information-storage devices similar to those of a COMPUTER and a CATHODE-RAY TUBE screen on which text is displayed. This makes it possible to edit or correct the text before it is typed; the processor "remembers" the corrections and prints out the final version. The processor can also make the right-hand margins even and produce documents in any desired format. The automation of offices has gone far beyond this, however, to include word processors, copying machines and computer and data-storage facilities interconnected to provide for input and output wherever needed. In many newspaper offices the word-processing equipment is connected directly to electronic typesetting machines.

WORDSWORTH, William (1770–1850), English poet, one of the greatest poets of ROMANTICISM. He spent much of his life in the Lake District about which he wrote, and his poetry shows his strong affinity with nature. In collaboration with COLERIDGE he composed *Lyrical Ballads* (1798; includes "Tintern Abbey"), written in deliberately ordinary language to suit the simplicity of their themes. In 1805 he wrote *The Prelude* and in 1806 "Ode: Intimations of Immortality," a lament on the loss of the poetic vision of his youth. He was appointed Poet Laureate in 1843.

WORKMEN'S COMPENSATION, the provision by employers of medical, cash and sometimes rehabilitation benefits for workers who are injured in accidents at work. In the US all states have had workmen's compensation laws since 1949, but 20% of all workers are unprotected, notably railroad employees and merchant seamen, who are covered by other legislation. Before the first effective US compensation acts, passed in 1908–11, injured employees were dependent on their employers' financial goodwill or on winning a negligence suit against them. Present laws are based on the principle of "liability without fault"; despite safety precautions, accidents are likely to occur and the cost of prevention should be a legitimate business cost. (See also SOCIAL SECURITY.)

WORLD BANK, officially the International Bank for Reconstruction and Development, a specialized agency of the United Nations, founded 1945. Its headquarters are in Washington, D.C. From capital (limited to $24 billion) it loans money to its 134 member states for investment, foreign trade and repayment of debts. Members own shares of $100,000, and belong to the INTERNATIONAL MONETARY FUND. The bank is self-sustaining and profit-making. In 1960 it set up the INTERNATIONAL DEVELOPMENT ASSOCIATION.

WORLD COUNCIL OF CHURCHES, international association of over 200 Protestant, Anglican, Eastern Orthodox and Old Catholic churches in 90 countries. Founded 1948, with headquarters in Geneva, it promotes Christian unity, religious liberty, missionary cooperation, interfaith doctrinal study and service projects such as refugee relief. It meets every seven years.

WORLD HEALTH ORGANIZATION (WHO), specialized agency of the United Nations founded 1948 and based in Geneva. Its services are available to all nations and territories. WHO advises countries on how to develop health services, combat epidemics and promote health education and standards of nutrition and sanitation. It also coordinates the standardization of drugs and health statistics, and researches into mental health and pollution.

WORLD METEOROLOGICAL ORGANIZATION (WMO), specialized agency of the United Nations, in Geneva, established 1951 to promote international meteorological observation and standardization.

WORLD'S FAIRS. See FAIRS AND EXPOSITIONS.

WORLD TRADE CENTER, the tallest building in the world when built in the early 1970s in New York City (surpassed by the SEARS-TOWER 1973). Built by the N.Y. Port Authority, the twin towers (each 110 stories) rise 1,350ft over the lower West Side of Manhattan.

WORLD WAR I, global conflict waged from 1914 to 1918 primarily between two European power blocs: the "Central Powers," Germany and Austria–Hungary; and the "Allies," Britain, France and Russia. Their respective alliance structures, imperial rivalries and mutual distrust escalated a minor conflict into "The Great War." The spark was struck at SARAJEVO on June 28, 1914, when the Austrian Crown Prince FRANZ FERDINAND was assassinated by a Serbian nationalist. Austria, awaiting a pretext for suppressing Slav nationalism, declared war on Serbia (July 28), with Germany's blessing. Russia immediately mobilized, and France rejected a German demand that she declare herself neutral.

The Two Fronts. Germany declared war on Russia (Aug. 1) and on France (Aug. 3) and invaded Belgium, the shortest route to Paris, hoping to win a quick victory in the W before turning to face Russia. Britain entered the war (Aug. 4) in support of Belgium and France. Although initially successful, the German advance was halted by the French on the MARNE (Sept. 1914) and a stalemate developed. Terrible trench warfare along a 300mi front was to drag on for over three years at a cost of several million lives. Meanwhile, the Germans had defeated a Russian invasion force at TANNENBERG in East Prussia (Aug. 1914) and established an eastern front. In Oct., Turkey joined the Central Powers against Russia, and in a vain attempt to aid the Russians the Allies sent a fleet to the Dardanelles and forces to the GALLIPOLI PENINSULA.

Outside Europe. After the Gallipoli disaster, the Allies attacked Turkey through her empire in the Middle East, leaving her ultimately with little more than Anatolia. Farther afield, British, French and South African troops overran Germany's African possessions, while the Japanese (who had entered the war in Sept. 1914) and Australasian troops captured German possessions in the Far East and the Pacific.

Attrition in the West. Italy was induced to join the Allies in May 1915, and engaged an Austrian army in the Alps. Major features of the stalemate in the W were the German offensive at VERDUN (Feb. 1916) and the

Allied counteroffensive at the SOMME (July 1916). Britain maintained a naval blockade of the Continent, while German submarines mauled Allied mercantile shipping. An attempt by the German fleet to lift the blockade at JUTLAND (May 1916) failed. The sinking of three US merchantmen in March 1917 and the ZIMMERMAN TELEGRAM brought the US into the war on April 6. In March 1917 the tsar had been overthrown and Russia's resolve further weakened. In Nov. 1917 the BOLSHEVIKS seized power, and peace terms were concluded between Russia and Germany at BREST-LITOVSK (March 1918). Despite a massive final German offensive in 1918 which drove the Allies back to the Marne, Allied numbers, boosted by US contingents, eventually began to tell. In September the Hindenburg Line was breached. The Central Powers sued for peace, and an armistice came into effect on Nov. 11, 1918. The Treaty of VERSAILLES (June 28, 1919) imposed on Germany, formalized the Allied victory. The dead on both sides totaled 8.4 million.

WORLD WAR II, second global conflict, which lasted from 1939 until 1945, involving civilian populations on an unprecedented scale. The harsh terms of the Treaty of VERSAILLES after WWI had left Germany embittered and unstable. Deep economic depression, the lot of Germany in the 1920s, from 1929 afflicted Japan, Italy, the rest of Europe, and North America. Germany and Italy became FASCIST dictatorships, Japan aggressively militaristic. The Allies were weary of war, but the LEAGUE OF NATIONS, without US membership, proved ineffectual. With the coming to power of HITLER and NAZISM in Germany (1933), the Versailles arrangements began to crumble. Germany rearmed and, on the pretext of defending German ethnic nationals, laid claim to certain neighboring territories. Hitler annexed Austria in March 1938 (see ANSCHLUSS), and by the MUNICH AGREEMENT (Sept. 1939) was given the SUDETENLAND. In March 1939 he occupied the rest of Czechoslovakia, and on Aug. 23 signed a nonaggression pact with the USSR.

Outbreak of War. The German invasion of Poland (Sept. 1, 1939) elicited ultimatums from Britain and France. On Sept. 3 both nations declared war on Germany. The Germans overran Poland; and the USSR, which had invaded Poland from the east, also invaded Finland and the Baltic states. Swift Nazi invasions of Denmark and Norway (April 1940) and of the Low Countries and France (May–June 1940) followed; and within a few weeks of the evacuation of a British expeditionary force from DUNKERQUE, Hitler and his Italian ally MUSSOLINI were unchallenged on the Continent. A concerted German attempt to neutralize Britain's air cover was thwarted by the Royal Air Force in the autumn (see BATTLE OF BRITAIN). Hitler now concentrated on night-bombing and U-boat attacks on British shipping. In June 1941 Germany suddenly invaded the USSR, initially making rapid gains. Late in 1941 Germany and Italy found a new ally in Japan, a nation bent on the conquest of Eastern Asia and the Western Pacific. On Dec. 7, 1941, she surprised and crippled the US fleet at PEARL HARBOR, Hawaii. The US immediately declared war, but at first fared badly in the Pacific.

Turn of the Tide. The first major US victories were recorded at CORAL SEA and MIDWAY (June 1942). In North Africa, Allied supremacy was established at EL ALAMEIN (Oct.–Nov. 1942). On the Russian front, early in 1943, the Germans lost the initiative at STALINGRAD. Sicily fell to Anglo-American forces (July 1943), and Mussolini was driven from power. In September the invasion of Normandy on D-DAY (June 6, 1944) signaled the last phase of the war in Europe. German forces, already expelled from Russia, had by Sept. 1944 been driven from most of France and Belgium. The BATTLE OF THE BULGE (Dec. 1944) proved to be the final German counteroffensive. As Russian forces at last entered Berlin itself, Hitler committed suicide (Apr. 30, 1945) and eight days later all German resistance ceased. The fate of conquered Europe was subsequently settled at the YALTA CONFERENCE and the POTSDAM CONFERENCE. (See also CONCENTRATION CAMPS; NUREMBERG TRIALS.)

Defeat of Japan. Allied forces had begun eroding the Japanese Asian empire from 1943; and by mid-1945 island-hopping assaults by US forces, culminating in IWO JIMA and OKINAWA, had swept Japan from the Western Pacific. The ATOMIC BOMB was dropped on HIROSHIMA and NAGASAKI (Aug. 6 and 9, 1945), and on Aug. 14 Japan accepted terms of unconditional surrender. (See also COLD WAR; UNITED NATIONS.)

WORM, term used for any elongate, cylindrical invertebrate, such as the EARTHWORMS, ROUNDWORMS, HAIRWORMS, or ACORN WORMS. The word has no taxonomic validity; animals commonly referred to as worms belong to many unrelated groups—Chordates, Annelids and Platyhelminths. However, the term is sometimes restricted to the phylum ANNELIDA.

WORTH, Charles Frederick (1825–1895), fashion designer whose Maison Worth in Paris and London was the arbiter of women's fashions for more than a century. Court dressmaker to European royalty, Worth created the ancestor of the tailor-made suit. The House of Worth in London is still in operation.

WOUK, Herman (1915–   ), US novelist, best known for *The Caine Mutiny* (1951; Pulitzer Prize), about the events on a US WWII mine sweeper, made into a successful film. *Marjorie Morningstar* (1955), *Youngblood Hawke* (1962) and *The Winds of War* (1972) were also popular novels.

WOUNDED KNEE, Battle of, massacre by US soldiers of more than 200 SIOUX Indian men, women and children at Wounded Knee Creek, SW S.D. on Dec. 29, 1890. The Indians, roused by the GHOST DANCE, had fled from their reservation but had been recaptured and disarmed. A slight Indian scuffle prompted the US attack. In 1973, 200 members of the American Indian Movement occupied the Wounded Knee Reservation for 69 days, demanding a Senate investigation into the conditions of Indians.

WRANGEL, Baron Ferdinand Petrovich von (1796–1870), Russian explorer. He led an expedition to the polar regions of NE Siberia 1820–24, was governor of Russian Alaska 1829–35 and director of the RUSSIAN-AMERICAN COMPANY 1840–49. He opposed the sale of Alaska to the US.

WRANGEL, Baron Piotr Nikolayevich (1878–1928), Russian general. Leader 1920–21 of the White Army against the Red Army at the end of the Russian Civil War, he lost the Crimea 1921 but organized an efficient evacuation to Constantinople.

WREN, Sir Christopher (1632–1723), greatest English architect. He had a brilliant early career as a mathematician and professor of astronomy, Oxford (1661–73), and was a founder-member of the ROYAL SOCIETY OF LONDON (president 1681–83). In 1663 he turned to architecture, in which he was largely self-taught. After the Great Fire of London (1666) Wren was appointed principal architect to rebuild London, where he was responsible for 52 churches, all of different design. His greatest building was the new St. Paul's Cathedral, noted for its monumental BAROQUE facade. He also worked at Greenwich (see GREENWICH OBSERVATORY), Oxford and Cambridge.

WRENS, the name of several groups of small birds. The true wrens are the Troglodytidae, a family of 60 species of small perching birds. The name is also used for some 80 species, Malurinae, of warbler of Australia and New Guinea, and the New Zealand wrens, Xenicidae. True wrens are compact little birds with short to long tails cocked upward. They occur in Middle and North America, though one species, *Troglodytes troglodytes*, has spread across Europe. Wrens live in thick cover, feeding on insects picked from foliage with the slender bill.

WRESTLING, in the West, sport in which two persons grapple and try to pin one another's shoulders to the floor by means of various holds. An ancient Greek sport, wrestling became a recognized Olympic Sport in 1904. In the US the preferred form is the freestyle or catch-as-catch-can. The Greco-Roman form, popular in Europe, forbids holds below the waist or leg holds. Bouts are divided into three periods of 3min each. The match is over when a wrestler pins both his opponent's shoulders for the count of 3 (a fall). Matches can also be won on points awarded by the referee for skilled maneuvers. (See also SUMO.)

WRIGHT, Frances "Fanny" (1795–1852), Scottish–US reformer. After her tour of the US (1818–20) she wrote *Views of Society and Manners in America* (1821) and settled there. She was a radical freethinker, campaigning against slavery and for women's rights and birth control.

WRIGHT, Frank Lloyd (1869–1959), greatest 20th-century US architect. He studied engineering, joined the architect L. SULLIVAN and was influenced by the Arts and Crafts movement. His pioneering "prairie" style (Robie House; 1908–09)—strong, horizontal lines, low-pitched, hipped roofs, open plan and change of internal levels—influenced DE STIJL. He articulated massive forms clearly (Larkin Building, 1904) and, though he liked natural materials and locations, was innovative in his use of reinforced concrete, dramatic cantilevering and screen walls (Falling Water House, 1936–37; Johnson's Wax Building, 1936–49; GUGGENHEIM MUSEUM, 1946–59).

WRIGHT, Joseph (1734–1797), English painter, known as "Wright of Derby," remembered for his realistic portraits, his early treatment of industrial subjects and his candlelight scenes.

WRIGHT, Orville (1871–1948) and **Wilbur** (1867–1912), US aeronautical engineers who built the first successful powered heavier-than-air aircraft, flown first at Kitty Hawk, N.C., on Dec. 17, 1903, over distances of 120–852ft (37–260m). Their early experiments were with gliders, influenced by the work of Otto LILIENTHAL:

Wilbur incorporated the AILERON (1899), a major step forward in their first man-carrying glider, flown at Kitty Hawk in 1900. In 1901 they built and experimented with a WIND TUNNEL, and their findings were used for their 1902 glider, by far the most advanced of its time. Following their first successful powered flight in 1903, they made further developments and by 1906 they were able to stay aloft for more than an hour. The American Wright Company for manufacturing airplanes was formed in 1909. (See also FLIGHT, HISTORY OF.)

WRIGHT, Richard (1908–1960), black US novelist and social critic. His works include *Uncle Tom's Children* (1938), stories of Southern racial prejudice; *Native Son* (1940) about a victimized black in Chicago; and *Black Boy* (1945) his autobiography.

WRIGLEY, William, Jr. (1861–1932), US businessman who started a chewing-gum business 1891 and developed it into the world's largest gum producer. He also owned the Chicago Cubs.

WRITING, History of. Human communication has two primary forms: the transient, e.g. speech, SIGN LANGUAGE; and the permanent or semipermanent, of which the most important is writing. Forerunners of writing are the use of carved sticks or knotted cords to convey information; but the earliest form of writing was the PICTOGRAPHY of ancient Sumeria and Egypt. Originally the pictographs depicted objects, but some 5,000 years ago there developed IDEOGRAMS (representing ideas) and logograms (words). Sumerian CUNEIFORM and Egyptian HIEROGLYPHICS had complex word signs, as does Chinese to this day. The Hittites, Egyptians and Mesopotamians devised symbols for specific sounds; that is, phonetic writing. During the 2nd millennium BC the Semitic ALPHABETS emerged, and from these were derived the Greek and later Roman alphabets and so, in time, our own. (See also LANGUAGE.)

WU, Chien-shiung (1912–   ), Chinese-born US physicist. She designed and executed research on beta decay which proved that the PARITY principle does not hold for weak interactions of SUBATOMIC PARTICLES.

WUHAN, city in central China, and capital of Hubei Province, where the Han and Yangtze rivers meet, comprising the former cities of Hankow, (Hankou,) Hanyang and Wuchang. It is the leading industrial, commercial and transportation center of Central China, is a port for large ocean-going vessels, and has China's largest iron–steel complex and largest textile mill.

It has heavy-machinery, food and cement industries. Pop 3,700,000.

WUNDT, Wilhelm (1832–1920), German psychologist regarded as the father of experimental PSYCHOLOGY. By opening the first psychological institute at Leipzig in 1879, he ushered in the modern era of psychology.

WUORINEN, Charles (1938–   ), US composer who helped found the avant-garde Group for Contemporary Music. His symphonies, vocal music, opera, solo instrumental and chamber works, and electronic music include *Time's Encomium* (1970), which won the first Pulitzer Prize for an all-electronic composition.

WYATT, Sir Thomas (c1503–1542), English poet and courtier who, with the Earl of SURREY, introduced the Italian sonnet form to England. His poems— modeled on PETRARCH'S—were published in *Tottel's Miscellany* (1557). His son, **Sir Thomas the Younger** (c1521–1554) was executed for leading an army from Kent to London against the proposed marriage of Queen MARY to Philip II of Spain (1554).

WYCHERLEY, William (c1640–1716), English playwright of RESTORATION COMEDY. He won success and court favor with *Love in a Wood* (1671). *The Country Wife* (1675) and *The Plain Dealer* (1676) sardonically criticize hedonistic and licentious London society.

WYCLIFFE, John (c1330–1384), English religious reformer, a precursor of the REFORMATION. He attacked the institutional Church and papal authority, and claimed the Bible was the external "exemplar" of the Christian religion and the sole criterion of doctrine. His attack on TRANSUBSTANTIATION forced his retirement in 1382 but he was protected by JOHN OF GAUNT. His followers translated the Latin VULGATE Bible into English. He influenced the LOLLARDS and Jan HUS.

WYETH, Andrew Newell (1917–   ), US painter. His work depicts scenes of strange, lonely rural life in a highly detailed style that seems almost photographic. His best known picture is *Christina's World* (1948).

WYLER, William (1902–1981), US motion-picture director. He won Academy awards for *Mrs Miniver* (1942), *The Best Years of Our Lives* (1946) and *Ben Hur* (1958). His other films include *Wuthering Heights* (1939), *Friendly Persuasion* (1956) and *Funny Girl* (1968).

WYLIE, Elinor Hoyt (1885–1928), US poet and novelist. Her verse included *Nets to Catch the Wind* (1921) and *Black Armour* (1923). Her first novel, *Jennifer Lorn* (1923), is about 18th-century India.

WYLIE, Philip Gordon (1902–1971), US essayist and novelist. His *Generation of Vipers* (1943) is a stinging analysis of US society. He also wrote a number of novels, notably *The Disappearance* (1951), and film scripts.

WYNDHAM, John (1903–1969), English science-fiction writer. Among his books are *The Day of the Triffids* (1951, in the US *The Revolt of the Triffids*) and *The Midwich Cuckoos* (1957, in the US *Village of the Damned*).

Name of state: Wyoming
Capital: Cheyenne
Statehood: July 10, 1890 (44th state)
Familiar names: Equality State; Cowboy State
Area: 97,914sq mi
Population: 470,816
Elevation: Highest—13,804ft, Gannett Peak
Lowest—3,100ft, Belle Fourche River
Motto: Equal Rights
State flower: Indian paintbrush
State bird: Meadow lark
State tree: Cottonwood
State song: "Wyoming"

WYOMING, a state in the W US, bordered on the N by Montana, E by S.D. and Neb., S by Col. and Utah, and W by Ida. and Utah.

Land. Wyoming has the second highest average elevation of any state (6,700ft) and comprises four major regions: the Great Plains in the E; the Middle Rocky Mts in the W; S Rocky Mts in the S; and the Wyoming Basin in the SW leading to the historic South Pass through the Rockies, whose highest point in the state is Gannett Peak (13,804ft). The Great Plains are 3,100–6,000ft in height. The major rivers are the Snake, Green and Yellowstone. The climate is cool and dry; annual rainfall is in the range of 5–40in.

People. Next to Alaska, Wyo. has the smallest population of all the states; its people include about 5,000 Indians and 2,500 blacks. Most of the remaining people trace their ancestry to European countries. About 60% live in towns, the largest cities being Cheyenne and Casper.

Economy. Mining, livestock raising and tourism are the basis of the economy. Coal, oil, and natural gas are the chief mineral products. Cattle provide most of the livestock income, but Wyo. ranks second only to Tex. in sheep and wool production. The important tourist industry is based on the magnificent scenery and the Yellowstone and Grand Teton national parks. Wyo. is one of the least industrialized states, the principal manufactures being processed food and wood and clay products.

History. John COLTER made the first records of the region (1807), and expeditions first crossed Wyo. in 1811. Over the next 30 years the fur trade developed and settlers passed through Wyo. on the OREGON TRAIL. Indians resenting encroachment on their lands attacked wagon trains and army forts but peace was restored by 1876. In 1868 Wyoming became a Territory and was the first state or territory to enfranchise women (1869). Cattle and oil industries developed in the 1880s. In 1890 Wyoming became a state. The valuable oil resources led to the TEAPOT DOME scandal (1924). Despite agricultural expansion Wyo. was part of the 1930s DUST BOWL. Since WWII uranium and tourist industries have prospered, and going into the 1980s, the state has displayed the signs and scars of rapid, booming success. The population grew 41% in the 1970s, with mobile homes providing much of the new housing. Strip mining for coal expanded, and many new oil wells came into production in the Overthrust Belt. In 1980, the legislature passed an unusual bill claiming federal lands for exploitation.

WYOMING VALLEY MASSACRE, event in the Revolutionary War. A force of Loyalists, Butler's Rangers and Iroquois Indians led by John BUTLER defeated a band of 300 Connecticut settlers led by Zebulon BUTLER in WYOMING VALLEY in July 1778. A massacre ensued in which the Indians butchered the survivors. The incident horrified both sides; it made the English wary of Indian allies and prompted Washington to attack the Iroquois (1779).

WYSS, Johann David (1743–1818), Swiss author who wrote *The Swiss Family Robinson* (4 vols. 1812–27), edited by his son, **Johann Rudolf** (1781–1830).

WYSZYNSKI, Stefan (1901–1981), Polish Catholic cardinal, archbishop of Warsaw and primate of Poland. Arrested for his attacks on the communist government's persecution of the Church in 1953, he was released after GOMULKA's rise to power (1956). His funeral was a national event attended by Pope JOHN PAUL II.

24th letter of the English alphabet, related to the Greek "chi." "Christ" in Greek begins with chi, so "X" came to be used for Christ, as in Xmas. "X" also stands for ten in Roman numerals.

X AND Y CHROMOSOMES, or sex chromosomes, the CHROMOSOMES which determine the sex of a person (as well as carrying some genetic information not related to sex determination). Sex chromosomes are inherited (see HEREDITY) in the same way as the other 22 human chromosome pairs, normal persons being either XX (female) or XY (male). The Y chromosome carries little genetic information and it is largely the properties of the X chromosome that determine "sex-linked" characteristics in males. Sex-linked characteristics include HEMOPHILIA and COLOR BLINDNESS, which are carried as recessive genes in females.

XENAKIS, Yannis (1922–   ), Greek avant-garde composer who developed "stochastic" music using computer-programmed sequences based on mathematical probability, as in *Métastasis* (1955) and *Achorripsis* (1958).

XENOPHON (431–355 BC), Greek soldier and author. An Athenian and an admirer of SOCRATES, he joined the Greek expedition supporting CYRUS the Younger (401), and after its defeat led the Greeks back in a heroic 1,500mi march recounted in his famous *Anabasis*. He later fought for Sparta, whose conservative militarism he admired. Retiring to the country, he wrote Greek history, memoirs of Socrates, a romanticized account of CYRUS the Great's education, and works on horsemanship and politics.

XEROGRAPHY, an electrostatic copying method. Light reflected from the original is focused onto an electrostatically charged (see ELECTRICITY), selenium-coated drum. Selenium is photoconductive (see PHOTOCONDUCTIVE DETECTOR), so where the light strikes the drum, the charge leaks away, leaving a reversed electrostatic image of the original on the drum. This is dusted with "toner," a dry ink powder which sticks only to the charged image. The toner is then transferred to a sheet of ordinary paper and fixed by applying heat. The paper thus carries a positive copy of the original. Repeated exposure on the rotating drum is needed to produce further copies. Other electrostatic copying processes form a positive print on paper specially coated with zinc oxide.

XERXES, name of two kings of ancient PERSIA. **Xerxes I** (ruled 486–465 BC) continued the war against Greece started by his father DARIUS I. His vast army crossed the Hellespont in 480 BC, and despite a check at THERMOPYLAE, destroyed Athens. However, his fleet was defeated at SALAMIS, and he returned to Persia leaving the army to be defeated at PLATAEA (479). He was murdered in a court intrigue. **Xerxes II,** his grandson, was murdered in 424, after ruling for 45 days.

X-RAY ASTRONOMY, the study of the X-RAYS emitted by celestial objects. Since the earth's atmosphere absorbs most X-radiation before it reaches the surface, observations are usually made from high altitude balloons, satellites and rockets. A number of celestial X-ray sources are known, including the sun and the CRAB NEBULA.

X-RAYS, highly energetic, invisible ELECTROMAGNETIC RADIATION of wavelengths ranging between 0.1pm to 1nm. They are usually produced using an evacuated ELECTRON TUBE in which ELECTRONS are accelerated from a heated CATHODE toward a large tungsten or molybdenum ANODE by applying a POTENTIAL difference of perhaps 1MV. The electrons transfer their energy to the anode which then emits X-ray PHOTONS. X-rays are detected using PHOSPHOR screens (as in medical fluoroscopy), with GEIGER and SCINTILLATION COUNTERS and on photographic plates. X-rays were discovered by ROENTGEN in 1895, but because of their extremely short wavelength their wave nature was not firmly established until 1911, when von LAUE demonstrated that they could be diffracted from crystal LATTICES. X-rays find wide use in medicine both for diagnosis and treatment (see RADIOLOGY) and in engineering where RADIOGRAPHS are used to show up minute defects in structural members. X-ray tubes must always be carefully shielded because the radiation causes serious damage to living tissue.

XYLOPHONE, a PERCUSSION INSTRUMENT consisting of a series of tuned wooden blocks set in a frame and struck with special hammers. Of ancient origin, it was widespread in Asia and Africa before being introduced in Europe. (See also GLOCKENSPIEL; VIBRAPHONE.)

XYZ AFFAIR, diplomatic incident which nearly led to open war between the US and France in 1798. President ADAMS sent J. MARSHALL and E. GERRY with C. PINCKNEY to settle disputes with France following the JAY TREATY. They were met by three unnamed agents, later called X, Y and Z, who demanded US loans and bribes before opening negotiations. When this was announced in Congress, there was uproar, but Adams averted war and reopened negotiations with TALLEYRAND, the French foreign minister.

25th letter of the English alphabet. Like U, V and W it is derived from the Semitic "waw" via the Greek "upsilon," which was transliterated as Y by the Romans. In Old and Middle English Y and I tended to be used interchangeably.

YACHTS AND YACHTING. Now a popular international sport and pastime, yachting developed in the early 19th century as steam began to supplant sail in commercial vessels. It became established on an organized basis with the setting-up of the New York Yacht Club in 1844. In 1851 the first race for the AMERICA'S CUP took place and subsequent races for the cup played a major role in the evolution of yacht design. After WWI the trend moved away from large, expensive yachts, and popular "one-design" classes emerged, with the Bermuda rig predominating. Small-keel yachts and catboats are now raced and sailed for pleasure throughout the world. Ocean racing is also popular and recently single-handed transatlantic and round-the-world races have attracted enormous public attention. (See also BOATS AND BOATING; CATAMARAN; MOTORBOATING.)

YAK, *Bos mutus,* the shaggy ox of the high plateau of Tibet. Yaks are distinguished by the long fringe of hair on shoulders, flanks, thighs and tail, and the long incurved horns. Wild yaks are large animals, up to 2m (6.6ft) at the shoulder, with black coats. Domestic yaks, kept as beasts of burden and for their milk, are smaller and may be any of a variety of colors.

YAKIMA INDIANS, a North American tribe of Plateau Indians belonging to the Sahaptin-Chinook language family. They lived along the Columbia and Yakima rivers in Wash. In 1859 they were settled in a reservation in Wash. after a three-year war against the white settlers (1855–58). They now number some 7,000.

YALE UNIVERSITY, US university chartered in 1701 as a collegiate school, first at Killingworth, Milford and Saybrook, then (1716) at New Haven, Conn., its present site. Renamed Yale College in 1718 in honor of Elihu YALE, it expanded greatly in the 19th century and was renamed Yale University in 1887.

YALOW, Rosalyn Sussman (1921–   ), US medical researcher who shared the 1977 Nobel Prize for Physiology or Medicine for helping to develop the technique, called radioimmunoassay (RIA), for measuring minute amounts of hormones, vitamins or enzymes that could not be detected by other means.

YALTA CONFERENCE, A meeting held near YALTA Feb. 4-11, 1945, between CHURCHILL, ROOSEVELT and STALIN representing the major Allied powers in WWII. Plans were agreed for the treatment, after the war, of Germany (including its division into occupation zones, elimination of its war industries and prosecution of war criminals). The foundation of a new Polish state was decided upon and the setting-up of the UNITED NATIONS was discussed. The USSR was persuaded to join in the war against Japan.

YAMAMOTO, Isoroku (1884–1943), commander of the Japanese fleet in WWII. He planned and commanded the attack on PEARL HARBOR (1941) and MIDWAY ISLAND (1941). He was killed in an air ambush.

YAMASHITA, Tomoyuki (1885–1946), Japanese army commander in WWII. His forces overran Malaya and captured Singapore (1942). He later commanded Japanese forces in the Philippines, surrendering in 1945. He was hanged by the Allies for the atrocities committed by his troops.

YANG, Chen Ning (1922–   ), Chinese-born US physicist who shared with Tsung Dao LEE the 1957 Nobel Prize for Physics for their studies of violations of the conservation of PARITY.

YANGTZE RIVER, China's longest river. It rises in the Kunlun Mts of Tibet and flows 3,434mi into the E China Sea, draining an area (about 750,000sq mi) which includes

China's richest agricultural land along its lower reaches. Its main tributaries are the Min, Wu and Han. It is navigable for oceangoing ships for some 600mi, as far as Wuhan. The $2 billion Gezhouba Dam, China's largest water-control project, is being built on the Yangtze at Yichang.

YANKEE, slang term of uncertain origin, probably Dutch Outside the US, it refers to anyone from the US; inside the US, it normally refers to a New Englander, especially someone descended from colonists. In the South it refers to Northerners, a tradition dating from the CIVIL WAR.

YAWS, a disease, caused by an organism related to that of syphilis (see VENEREAL DISEASES), common in the tropics. It occurs often in children and consists of a local lesion on the limbs; there is also mild systemic disease. Chronic destructive lesions of SKIN, BONE and CARTILAGE may develop later. The WASSERMANN TEST is positive as in syphilis and PENICILLINS are the treatment of choice.

YEAR (yr), name of various units of time, all depending on the revolution of the earth about the sun. The *sidereal year* (365.25636 mean solar DAYS) is the average time the earth takes to complete one revolution measured with respect to a fixed direction in space. The *tropical year* (365.24220 mean solar days), the year measured by the changing SEASONS, is that in which the mean longitude of the sun moves through 360°. The *anomalistic year* (365.25964 mean solar days) is the average interval between successive terrestrial perihelions (see ORBIT). The *civil year* is a period of variable duration, usually 365 or 366 days (leap year), depending on the type of CALENDAR in use.

YEASTS, single-celled plants classified with the FUNGI. Some cause diseases of the skin and mucous membranes (see THRUSH), while others, notably the strains of *Saccharomyces cerevisiae*, baker's yeast, are used in baking (see LEAVEN), brewing and wine-making. Yeasts employ either or both of two metabolic processes: FERMENTATION involves the anaerobic decomposition of hexose SUGARS to yield alcohol (ETHANOL) and CARBON dioxide; "respiration" involves the exothermic decomposition of various sugars in the presence of oxygen to give carbon dioxide and water. Yeasts are also grown as a source of food rich in B-complex VITAMINS.

YEATS, William Butler (1865–1939), Irish poet and dramatist, leader of the CELTIC RENAISSANCE in Ireland and one of the world's greatest lyric poets. Nationalism is a major element in his early poetry, such as

The Wanderings of Oisin (1889), which draws on Irish legend. Yeats cofounded (1899) Dublin's Irish Literary Theatre, later the ABBEY THEATRE. His mature poetic works, often symbolic and mystical, treat universal themes. They include *The Wild Swans at Coole* (1917), *The Tower* (1928) and *Last Poems* (1940). Yeats was awarded the Nobel Prize for Literature in 1923.

YELLOW FEVER, INFECTIOUS DISEASE caused by a VIRUS carried by MOSQUITOS of the genus *Aëdes* and occurring in tropical America and Africa. The disease consists of FEVER, headache, backache, prostration and VOMITING of sudden onset. PROTEIN loss in the URINE, KIDNEY failure, and LIVER disorder with JAUNDICE are also frequent. HEMORRHAGE from mucous membranes, especially in the GASTROINTESTINAL TRACT is also common. A moderate number of cases are fatal but a mild form of the disease is also recognized. VACCINATION to induce IMMUNITY is important and effective as no specific therapy is available; mosquito control provides a similarly important preventive measure.

YELLOW JOURNALISM, vulgar and sensational newspaper reporting whose sole aim is to attract readers. The term originated with the "Yellow Kid" comic strip in the Sunday supplement of Joseph PULITZER'S New York *World* (1896). This began a "yellow journalism" circulation war in the city with Randolph HEARST'S *Journal.*

YELLOW RIVER, or Hwang Ho, river of N China, flowing 2,903mi from the Kunlun Mts. generally E to the YELLOW SEA. It is named for its fertile yellow silt, and often nicknamed "China's Sorrow" because of terrible floods and destructive changes of course. In 1955 a major flood-control and hydroelectric project was begun.

YELLOWSTONE NATIONAL PARK, oldest and largest US national park, created 1872 and covering 3,472sq mi, mostly in NW Wyo. It contains some of the most spectacular geological wonders in the US, including the OLD FAITHFUL geyser, thousands of hot springs and mud pools, petrified forests, black glass cliffs and the Grand Canyon of the Yellowstone R. Wildlife abounds in the forests covering most of the park.

YEMEN, People's Democratic Republic of, also called Southern Yemen, independent state in the S of the Arabian peninsula bordering on the Arabian Sea and commanding the entrance to the Red Sea. It includes also the islands of Kamaran, Perim and Socotra. It is bordered by Oman (E), Saudi Arabia (N) and the YEMEN ARAB REPUBLIC (W).

Land. The land rises from the hot, arid coastal plain with its palm oases to a high plateau broken by a ridge of mountains which reach 8,000ft before falling away N to the Rub'al-Khali desert. The Wadi Hadramaut is a fertile valley running parallel to the coast. Coastal temperatures average 84°F; annual rainfall, 2in on the coast, reaches 20–30in in the highlands inland. Dams across the wadis (seasonal rivers) help conserve water for agriculture.

People. Most of the population are SUNNITE Muslim Arabs of various tribes, living in the few fertile areas like the Wadi Hadhramaut, or nomadically in the extreme N. Aden is the largest city and chief port. Other centers are Madinat ash Sha'b, and Mukalla.

Economy. Yemen is basically agricultural. Long-staple cotton, coffee, tobacco and dates are exported. Subsistence crops include millet, sesame and sorghum. Fishing along the coast is a major source of food and export revenue. Salt is mined but there is little industry, consisting mostly of oil refining. Remittances from Yemenis working abroad are an important source of income. The country is heavily dependent on foreign aid, supplied mostly by the USSR and other Eastern Bloc countries.

History. Under British control from the 1830s Southern Yemen became fully independent (1967) under the rule of the Marxist National Liberation Front, after the collapse of the Federation of SOUTH ARABIA. After a brief war in 1972, unification with the more moderate neighboring Yemen Arab Republic was agreed upon in principle but relations between the two governments have

Official name: People's Democratic Republic of Yemen
Capital: Aden
Area: 130,066sq mi
Population: 1,853,000
Languages: Arabic
Religions: Muslim
Monetary units(s): 1 Yemeni dinar=1,000 fils

remained tense, making unification unlikely.

Official name: Yemen Arab Republic
Capital: San'ā
Area: 75,000sq mi
Population: 5,650,000
Language: Arabic
Religion: Muslim
Monetary unit(s): 1 Yemeni riyal=100 fils

YEMEN ARAB REPUBLIC, independent state on the SW Arabian peninsula bordering on the Red Sea. It is bounded by Saudi Arabia (N and NE) and by the People's Democratic Republic of YEMEN (S).

Land. Beyond the Red Sea coast with its coral reefs and low beaches lies the Tihamah, a dry coastal plain, and farther inland a foothill region crossed by wadis (seasonal rivers). The land then rises E to lofty mountain crests (some over 12,000ft high) and a mosaic of plateaus and upland plains. Fertile valleys leading E eventually give way to the Rub'al-Khali desert beyond the basin of the Wadi Abrad. Though the coastal lowlands are hot, arid and humid (as are the E desert fringes), the highlands have the most favored climate in Arabia, with annual rainfall of 16–32in and sometimes more.

People. The population is mostly of south Arabian stock, but with African elements along the coast and in the S. About half are SUNNITE Muslims, and the other half SHI'ITES, a division which creates social and political problems. Most people live in the highlands. The largest towns are the port of Hodeida, Sanā (the capital) and Ta'izz.

Economy. The land is the most fertile on the Arabian peninsula and agriculture—mostly cotton and coffee—accounts for 80% of export earnings, with livestock, sorghum, millet, qat (a narcotic shrub), citrus fruits, bananas, and dates also raised. Salt is currently the only exploited mineral. The small industrial sector includes textiles, cement, salt processing and traditional crafts. Many Yemenis work abroad and their remittances are a major source of income in a country largely dependent on foreign aid, coming mostly from the USSR before 1975 and from the US, Saudi Arabia and Kuwait since then.

History. Once part of the ancient kingdom of Saba (the Biblical Sheba, see SABAEANS), the country was ruled from the 9th to 20th centuries by competing local imams, although sometimes under nominal control of foreign powers including the Ottomans, until 1962 when an army coup led to the proclamation of a republic. Civil war followed, in which Saudi Arabia backed the royalist tribes and Egypt the new republican regime, but was ended by mediation in 1970, with the republicans controlling the government. War with the neighboring Marxist People's Democratic Republic of Yemen erupted in 1972, and a ceasefire was followed by an agreement for the two countries to unify, although brief renewed fighting in 1979 made prospects for unification doubtful.

YEN CHIA-KAN (1905–   ), nationalist Chinese president. He held numerous government posts in China 1938–49 and in TAIWAN from 1950; he became vice-president of the Republic of China in 1966 and succeeded to the presidency in 1975 on the death of CHIANG KAI-SHEK, serving until 1978.

YENISEI, or Yenisey, major river of central Siberia, USSR. Formed by the confluence of the Bolshoi and the Maly Yenisei rivers near the Mongolian border, it flows 2,566mi N through Siberia into the Arctic Ocean. It has enormous hydroelectric potential.

YERKES, Charles Tyson (1837–1905), US financier. He was highly successful and controlled Chicago's transportation system. His financial and political manipulations caused a public scandal and he was forced to sell out (1899). He then helped build the London underground railway system.

YERKES, Robert Mearns (1876–1956), US pioneer of comparative (animal/human) PSYCHOLOGY and of intelligence testing. He initiated the first mass psychological testing program in WWI, involving nearly 1¼ million US soldiers. During the 1920s and 1930s he was the world's foremost authority on PRIMATES.

YEVTUSHENKO, Yevgeny (1933–   ), Russian poet who became a spokesman for "liberal" forces in Soviet literature in the early 1960s. His best-known poems include "Babi Yar" (1961), dealing with Soviet anti-Semitism, and "The Heirs of Stalin" (1963), warning of the persistence of Stalinism.

YIDDISH, a language spoken and written by Jews in many parts of the world, belonging to the Germanic group of INDO-EUROPEAN LANGUAGES. It evolved in Germany in the Middle Ages and was spread by Jewish migrations. It uses the Hebrew alphabet and was standardized in 1934–36 in conferences of the Yiddish Scientific Institute (YIVO).

YIN AND YANG, two principles in Chinese philosophy, representing the passive and the active forces of the universe. Yin stands for earth, female, passive, dark and receiving; Yang for heaven, male, active, light and generative. All things exist through their interaction. The symbol for Yin-Yang is a circle divided into two curved forms, one dark, the other light.

YIPPIES, members of the radical Youth International Party, founded in 1968 by Abbie HOFFMAN, Jerry RUBIN, and others. The Yippie party still exists, but it was prominent for only two years, during which it was known for its outrageous, theatrical, and sometimes witty protests against the VIETNAM WAR and just about everything else. In 1974, after skipping bail on a cocaine-selling charge, Abbie Hoffman went semi-underground (becoming a prominent environmentalist under an alias); in 1980 he turned himself in and was convicted.

YOGA (Sanskrit, union), forms of spiritual discipline practiced in BUDDHISM and HINDUISM. Through these disciplines the Yogi (one who follows Yoga) strives to free the mind from attachment to the senses and to achieve *Samadhi*, or union with *Brahma*, the deity, and fusion into oneness. There are three varieties of yoga: *karma-yoga*, salvation through action; *jnana-yoga*, salvation through knowledge; and *bhakti-yoga*, salvation through devotion. In each the student passes through eight levels of attainment, supervised by a *guru* or teacher. The practice of *hatha-yoga*, based on physical postures and control, has increasingly become popular in the Western World.

YOKOHAMA, second-largest city in Japan, on the W shore of Tokyo Bay, a leading national seaport and part of Tokyo's industrial belt, S Honshu Island. It is a trading center and supports large shipbuilding, iron, steel, chemical, machinery and oil industries. It also has several universities. Yokohama was a fishing village when visited by Commodore Matthew Perry in 1854. Its growth began in 1859, when it became a foreign-trade port. Pop 2,763,300.

YOM KIPPUR, the Jewish Day of Atonement, the most sacred day in the Jewish religious calendar. It falls on the tenth day after the Jewish New Year and is marked by repentance, prayers and abstention from food, drink, sex and work.

YORK, Alvin Cullum (1887–1964), US soldier, WWI hero. During the Argonne-Meuse offensive in France in 1918 Sergeant York silenced an entire enemy machine-gun unit, killing at least 25 Germans and taking 132 prisoners. He was awarded the Congressional Medal of Honor and the French Croix de Guerre.

YORK, House of, ruling dynasty of England 1461–1485, a branch of the PLANTAGENET family, whose symbol was the white rose. The three Yorkist kings were EDWARD IV (1461–83), his son EDWARD V (April–June 1483) and RICHARD III (1483–85), who was killed at the Battle of Bosworth Field by Henry Tudor (HENRY VII) who established the House of TUDOR as the ruling family.

YORKSHIRE TERRIER, toy terrier, first bred in 19th-century Yorkshire, England. It is about 9in high at the shoulder, 4–7lbs in weight and has a long straight silky coat, tan and dark steel-blue in color.

YORKTOWN, town in SE Va., seat of York Co., on the York R., site of the last campaign of the REVOLUTIONARY WAR. In Oct. 1781, 16,000 American and French troops, led by Washington and Rochambeau, laid siege to 7,247 British troops under Lord CORNWALLIS in Yorktown. With naval reinforcements defeated by Comte de GRASSE and escape impossible, Cornwallis surrendered on Oct. 19th.

YORUBA, African people in SW NIGERIA. A highly urbanized people, they are organized into many kingdoms and their economy is principally agricultural. Yoruba culture exists also in Cuba and Brazil because of large slave importations.

YOSEMITE NATIONAL PARK, park in E Cal., established in 1890, 1,189sq mi of spectacular mountain scenery formed during the last glacial period of the current ice age, on the W slopes of the Sierra Nevada. Its chief attractions are the Yosemite Valley, its granite walls 2,500–3,500ft high; Yosemite Falls, the highest falls in North America; and the Mariposa Grove of "Big Trees"— 200 Giant sequoias.

YOUMANS, Vincent (1898–1946), US composer who wrote some of the most popular musical comedies of the 1920s, among them *No, No, Nanette* and *Hit the Deck*. His songs included "Tea for Two," "Without a Song" and "I Want To Be Happy."

YOUNG, Andrew (1932–   ), US clergyman and civil rights leader. He helped draft the Civil Rights and Voting Rights acts (1964 and 1965) and served in the US House 1971–76. As the first black US ambassador to the UN (1977–79), he stirred up frequent controversy with undiplomatic public statements.

YOUNG, Brigham (1801–1877), US MORMON leader. He joined the Mormons in 1832 and quickly rose to prominence. After three years as a missionary in England he took over the leadership on the death of Joseph SMITH (1844), and led his people to Salt Lake City, Ut., in 1846. Young established a thriving city on a sound commercial basis and became first governor of Utah in 1850. He may have had as many as 27 wives.

YOUNG, Denton True (1867–1955), US baseball player, called "Cy", short for cyclone, for his amazingly fast right-hand pitching. He played in major league baseball for 22 seasons, and in 1937 was elected to baseball's Hall of Fame for pitching the most games (906) and winning the most games (511).

YOUNG, Lester Willis, "Pres" (1909–1959); US jazz tenor saxophonist. His style was a major influence on the development of progressive jazz in the 1940s. Young played with many artists including Count BASIE and Billie HOLIDAY.

YOUNG, Owen D. (1874–1962), US lawyer, industrial executive and statesman. He had a very successful career in industry, but is chiefly remembered as an international statesman. He presided at the 1929 Paris Reparations Conference and produced the Young Plan for German WWI REPARATIONS, considered a triumph of diplomacy.

YOUNG, Thomas (1773–1829), British linguist, physician and physicist. His most significant achievement was, by demonstrating optical INTERFERENCE, to resurrect the wave theory of LIGHT, which had been occulted by NEWTON's particle theory. He also suggested that the eye responded to mixtures of three primary colors (see VISION), and proposed the modulus of ELASTICITY known as *Young's modulus* (E— see MATERIALS, STRENGTH OF).

YOUNG, Whitney Moore, Jr. (1921–1971), US civil rights leader. As director of the National Urban League from 1961 he worked for better job and housing conditions for black Americans and was one of the most influential black leaders of the 1960s.

YOUNG AMERICANS FOR FREEDOM (YAF), organization of conservative young people (up to age 39) that promotes the values of private enterprise and a reduced role for government in national life. Founded 1960 at the Sharon, Conn., home of journalist William F. BUCKLEY, Jr., YAF has some 55,000 members in 650 local groups.

YOUNG MEN'S CHRISTIAN ASSOCIATION (YMCA), worldwide organization that seeks, through programs of sport, religious and current affairs study groups and summer camps, to promote a healthy way of life based on Christian ideals. The first US branch was founded in 1851 and there were 9 million members in 1,842 US associations in 1979. The YMCA operates in more than 80 countries.

YOUNG WOMEN'S CHRISTIAN ASSOCIATION (YWCA), an international organization which promotes a Christian way of life through educational and recreational activities and social work. The movement, started in the US in 1858, now has 2.5 million members.

YOURCENAR, Marguerite (1904–) pen name of Marguerite de Crayencour, French author who became a US citizen in the 1940s. The first woman elected to the Académie Française (1980), she is best known for the historical novel *Hadrian's Memoirs* (1951) and *Coup de Grâce* (1939).

YÜAN SHIH-K'AI (1859–1916), Chinese soldier and president. His efforts to check Japan in Korea led to the Sino-Japanese war of 1894–95. He supported the Dowager Empress Tz'u Hsi and helped suppress the Boxer movement (1900). Supported by his army during the Revolution, he emerged as president 1912–16 but was unable to establish himself emperor.

YUCATÁN, peninsula (55,400sq mi) dividing the Gulf of Mexico from the Caribbean. It contains British Honduras, part of Guatemala and three Mexican states. The climate is hot and humid, and farming and forestry are the main activities. The N is the leading producer of henequen. The people are of MAYA Indian stock and CHICHÉN ITZÁ, a famed Maya site, is on the peninsula.

Official name: Socialist Federal Republic of Yugoslavia
Capital: Belgrade
Area: 98,725sq mi
Population: 22,340,000
Languages: Serbo-Croatian, Slovenian, Macedonian
Religions: Orthodox, Roman Catholic, Muslim
Monetary unit(s): 1 Dinar=100 para

YUGOSLAVIA, socialist federal republic, the largest country in the Balkan Peninsula, bordered by Austria, Hungary and Italy to the N, by Romania and Bulgaria to the E, and by Greece to the S.

Land. It is divided into six republics: Serbia, Croatia, Bosnia and Herzegovina, Macedonia, Slovenia and Montenegro. The country comprises four geographical areas: the Alpine NW, the fertile N plains, the rugged mountain region in the S and the beautiful island-studded Dalmatian coast, developed for tourism. Most of Yugoslavia is drained by the Danube R which flows SE from the Hungarian border across the plains. The climate varies from being continental in the N to being warm and mild in the S.

Population. The people include Serbs, Croats, Slovenes, Macedonians, Montenegrins and many minority groups. Both the Roman and Cyrillic alphabets are used. About 41% of the population are urban-dwellers, the largest cities being the federal capital Belgrade, Zagreb, Skopje, Sarajevo and Ljubljana. Industry is widespread, the most important industrial region being the Sava Valley.

Economy. Mining, industry, agriculture and tourism are the basis of the economy. Yugoslavia has rich mineral resources of lignite, iron, lead, copper, bauxite, gas and oil. The chief industrial products are iron, steel, machinery, textiles, metal goods and chemicals. Manufactured goods are the leading exports, traded mainly to West Germany, Italy and the USSR. Crops grown in the Danube R area include corn, wheat, rye, sugar, beets, potatoes and fruit. There are extensive vineyards. Yugoslavia is associated with the COMMON MARKET. All major industries are nationalized.

History. What is now Yugoslavia belonged to the OTTOMAN EMPIRE. By 1914 AUSTRIA-HUNGARY controlled Croatia, Slovenia, and Bosnia and Herzegovina, while Serbia and Montenegro were independent. In 1918 the "Kingdom of the Serbs, Croats and Slovenes" was created, its name changed to Yugoslavia in 1929. After the German invasion (1941) rival resistance groups were organized by the royalist MIHAJLOVIC and the communist TITO. In 1945 Tito proclaimed Yugoslavia a federal republic of six states and established a communist government. Yugoslavia was expelled from the COMINFORM in 1948, and relations with the USSR have since been uneasy, President Tito pursuing an "independent national communism" for Yugoslavia. Internal tensions have centered on nationalist aspirations of the constituent republics, notably Croatia, and on problems of intellectual freedom. After the death of Tito in 1980, a collective state presidency was established.

YUKAWA, Hideki (1907–1981), Japanese physicist who postulated the meson (see SUBATOMIC PARTICLES) as the agent bonding the atomic nucleus together. In fact, the mu-meson discovered shortly afterwards (in 1936) by C. D. ANDERSON, does not fulfill this role and Yukawa had to wait until C. F. Powell discovered the pi-meson in 1947 for vindication of his theory. He received the 1949 Nobel Prize for Physics.

YUKON RIVER, one of the five longest rivers in North America, flowing from N British Columbia for 1,979mi through Yukon Territory into Alaska, then SW to the Norton Sound on the Bering Sea. It is navigable for about 1,770mi.

Name of territory: Yukon
Joined Confederation: June 13, 1898
Capital: Whitehorse
Area: 207,076sq mi
Population: 22,010

YUKON TERRITORY, a subarctic territory in NW Canada lying between the North-West Territories and Alaska. The territory consists of high mountain peaks and ranges surrounding a heavily forested central plateau drained by the Yukon R. Winters are long and cold. The original population, Canadian Indians, live as hunters and trappers, and the white population is concentrated in the S and central valleys. The capital is Whitehorse, which contains half the total population. Mining is the chief economic activity with lead, zinc, gold, tungsten and platinum the chief minerals. Some natural gas is produced in the Beaver R field, and the search for petroleum continues. The Klondike gold rush brought prosperity to the area, but gold reserves were running low by 1911 and the population dropped sharply— it rose again in WWII when the building of the Alaska Highway and airports on the staging route to Alaska brought new settlers. Since then Yukon's economy has expanded gradually.

26th and last letter of the English alphabet. It was taken by the Romans from the Greek "zeta," which in turn came from the ancient

Semitic "zayin." Its sound is often represented by "s" in English, as in "busy."

ZAGROS MOUNTAINS, system in SW Iran, its parallel ranges running NW–SE along the Iraq border and Persian Gulf.

ZAHARIAS, Mildred "Babe" Didrikson (1914–1956), US athlete. An All-American basketball player (1930), she won (1930–32) national hurdles, javelin, baseball throw, broad- and high-jump titles, set (1932) Olympic 80m hurdles and javelin records, and became top US woman amateur and (after 1947) professional golfer.

ZAHAROFF, Sir Basil (1850–1936), Turkish-born armaments dealer and financier—the "mystery man of Europe"—who sold arms for the Nordenfelt (Swedish) and later Vicker-Armstrong (British) munitions firms. Accused of fomenting world crises and called a "merchant of death," he supplied weapons during the Boer, Russo-Japanese and Balkan wars as well as WWI.

Official name: Republic of Zaire
Capital: Kinshasa
Area: 905,562sq mi
Population: 28,904,000
Languages: French, Swahili, Tshiluba, Kikongo, Lingala
Religions: Roman Catholic, Protestant, Animist
Monetary unit(s): 1 Zaire = 100 makuta = 10,000 sengi

ZAIRE, a nation in W central Africa and the third-largest country in Africa, formerly known as the Belgian Congo and, after independence, as the Democratic Republic of the Congo. In 1971 it was renamed Zaire.

Land. Central Zaire, which straddles the equator, is a large, low plateau covered by rain forest. The plateau rim surrounding the Zaire R basin averages 3,000ft, but highlands in the SE exceed 6,000ft and the Ruwenzori Range (Mts of the Moon) bordering Uganda exceeds 16,000ft. A series of lakes lie on the E border. The CONGO (Zaire) R, one of the largest rivers in Africa, flows W to the Atlantic, where the country narrows to a 25mi-wide coastline. Zaire is a hot, rainy country, with coastal temperatures averaging 79°F. Wild life abounds in the country.

People. The population is divided among numerous groups; about 200 languages are spoken—most of them Bantu. The Kongo people are most numerous. Other important groups are the Mongo, Luba and Zande. Nilotic-speaking peoples live primarily in the N. Pygmies live in the E. About 80% of the population is rural and engaged in agriculture. The rate of literacy is estimated at 35%; there is a national university with three main campuses. The largest cities are KINSHASA, the capital, and Lubumbashi and KISANGANI.

Economy. The mainstay of Zaire's economy is its mineral sector. Cobalt is the principal export; followed by copper. Diamonds are also important. Cash crops include coffee, rubber, palm oil, cocoa and tea. Despite its mineral wealth and a diversified industrial sector, Zaire has been beset by severe economic problems, causing it to look to the international banking community for assistance. Hydroelectricity from newly constructed Inga Dam on the Congo R, is expected to play a large role in the nation's future development.

History. In 1885 Belgium's King Leopold II took control of an area he called the Congo Free State; in 1908 it became the Belgian Congo. It gained independence in 1960, with KASAVUBU president and Lumumba premier. Unrest erupted shortly afterward, and Tshombe later urged the secession of Katanga (SHABA), a mineral-rich area. The UN sent troops to restore order. In 1965, following continuing unrest, Maj. Gen. Joseph MOBUTU took control.

ZAIRE RIVER. See CONGO RIVER.

ZALE, Tony (1913–   ), US middleweight boxing champion. From 1934–48 he won 70 out of 88 fights, 46 by knockouts. He won two of three legendary meetings with Rocky GRAZIANO.

ZAMBEZI RIVER, SE Africa, fourth-largest river in Africa. Rising in NW Zambia, it flows 1,700mi S, then E along the Zambia-Zimbabwe border, through Mozambique to enter the Mozambique Channel of the Indian Ocean through a 2,500sq mi delta. (See also KARIBA DAM; VICTORIA FALLS.)

ZAMBIA, formerly Northern Rhodesia, landlocked republic of S central Africa.

Land. Mostly savanna plateau 3,000-5,000ft above sea level, it rises in the NE to 7,000ft in the Muchinga Mts. Dissecting the plateau are the Kafue and Luangwa rivers, flowing S to join the

ZAMBIA RIVER (here marked by the VICTORIA FALLS). In the N are lakes Bangweulu and Mweru and the S end of Lake Tanganyika. Although in the tropics, Zambia has a relatively mild climate because of altitude; however, temperatures can reach 100°F during the hot season (Sept–Nov). Annual rainfall ranges from 20in to 50in.

People. The Zambian people are predominantly Bantu, with over 70 tribes and many languages. About two-thirds live by subsistence agriculture. There are European and Asian minorities.

Economy. Zambia is one of the world's top producers of copper, which in 1979 accounted for over 80% of export earnings. Cobalt is the second-largest export earner; lead, zinc, manganese and sulfur are also exported. Cash crops include tobacco, sugarcane and wheat. Zambia's economy was severely dislocated because of the country's support of Zimbabwe guerrillas during the Rhodesian war. Damage caused by air raids, the disruption of transit routes to the sea and the loss of Rhodesia as a trade partner brought Zambia near economic collapse. Zimbabwe's independence inspired hope for mutually beneficial economic relations.

History. European traders and missionaries came to Zambia in the 19th century. David LIVINGSTONE came in 1855; in 1888 Cecil Rhodes led the way for British commercial interests. As N Rhodesia the area became a British protectorate in 1924. From 1953 to 1963 it formed part of the Federation of RHODESIA and NYASALAND, with S Rhodesia (now Zimbabwe) and Nyasaland (now Malawi). It became independent in 1964, with Kenneth KAUNDA as president.

Official name: Republic of Zambia
Capital: Lusaka
Area: 290,586sq mi
Population: 4,520,000
Languages: English; Bemba, Nyanja, Tonga
Religions: Christian, Muslim, Hindu
Monetary unit(s): 1 Zambian Kwacha=100 ngwee

ZAMYATIN, Yevgeny Ivanovich (1884–1937), Russian writer. His satires include *The Islanders* (1917), about England, and *We* (1922), a forecast of communist society in the 2500s. An early Bolshevik, he lost favor with Soviet officials (but influenced young writers), and died in Paris.

ZANGWILL, Israel (1864–1926), English writer and Zionist. Born of E European parents, he described Jewish life in *Children of the Ghetto* (1892), *Dreamers of the Ghetto* (1898), and *The Melting Pot* (1903), a play about US Jewish immigrants.

ZANUCK, Darryl F. (1902–1979), US film producer. He co-founded Twentieth Century-Fox (1933), was its production head (1935–52) and its president (1962–71). Although most of his movies provided escapist entertainment, he also made such socially significant films as *The Grapes of Wrath* (1940), *Gentlemen's Agreement* (1948), *The Snake Pit* (1948) and *Pinky* (1949).

ZANZIBAR, island, part of Tanzania, E. Africa. Center from c1700 of an Omani Arab sultanate with extensive mainland territories, British protectorate (1890–93), independent sultanate (1963), and republic (1964), Zanzibar island united 1964 with nearby PEMBA and with Tanganyika to form Tanzania. The chief exports are cloves and copra.

ZAPATA, Emiliano (c1883–1919), Mexican agrarian revolutionary. From 1910 he led his fellow Indian peasants of Morelos state in the S in revolt against DÍAZ and the big landowners. Later he opposed presidents MADERO, HUERTA and CARRANZA for failing to carry out land reforms. He was assassinated by an army officer supporting Carranza.

ZAPOTEC INDIANS, ancient native people of SE Oaxaca, S Mexico, and their descendants. They created a formative pre-Columbian culture about 2,000 years ago. Monte Albán, W of Oaxaca city, contains magnificent ruins of tombs, stelae, temples and plazas.

ZARATHUSTRA, or Zoroaster. See ZOROASTRIANISM.

ZEBRA, three species of striped HORSES of Africa. The characteristic black and white striped coat surprisingly makes the animal inconspicuous at long range. The three species—Plains zebra, Mountain zebra and Grévy's zebra—differ in stripe pattern, habitat and behavior. Plains and Mountain zebra live in permanent nonterritorial stallion groups, but Mountain zebra are adapted to life in more arid regions. Grévy's zebra, with very narrow stripes, are territorial animals.

ZECHARIAH, 11th of the MINOR PROPHETS of the Old Testament. The book, dated c520 BC, foretells the rebirth of Israel. The more apocalyptic visions in chapters 9–12 are of later, possibly Greek, authorship. With HAGGAI, Zechariah urged the rebuilding of the Temple at Jerusalem.

ZEISS, Carl (1816–1888), German optical manufacturer who founded a famous workshop at Jena in 1846. Realizing that optical technology had much to gain from scientific research, in the mid-1860s he formed a fruitful association with the physicist, Ernst ABBE.

ZEN (Chinese: *Ch'an*), form of BUDDHISM which developed in China from c500 AD and spread to Japan c1200, exerting great influence on Japanese culture. The word means "meditation." Zen differs markedly from traditional Buddhism, abhorring images and ritual, scriptures and metaphysics. There are some 9,000,000 adherents in two sects in Japan. Rinzai Zen uses *koan* (paradoxical riddles) to shock into sudden enlightenment; Soto Zen stresses contemplation.

ZEND-AVESTA, or Avesta, the sacred book of ZOROASTRIANISM, written in Avestan, an Iranian language similar to Vedic Sanskrit. The *Gathas* (songs) derive from Zoroaster himself, but the present Avesta was written down in the Sassanian period (3rd–4th centuries AD). It is the major text of PARSEES.

ZENGER, John Peter (1697–1746), German-born American printer, whose acquittal (1735) on a charge of seditious libel was an important victory for freedom of the press. Sponsored by opponents of the unpopular New York colonial governor, William Cosby, Zenger had founded the New York *Weekly Journal* in 1733, and proceeded to publish bitter attacks on him. At the trial he was defended by Andrew HAMILTON.

ZENO OF CITIUM (c335–263 BC), ancient Greek philosopher, founder of STOICISM. Influenced by the CYNICS, he developed a complete philosophy, but is most famous for declaring that only virtue is to be desired; a wise man should be indifferent to all else, including pain, pleasure, possessions and wealth.

ZENO OF ELEA (c450 BC), Greek philosopher, member of the ELEATIC school. He is most important for his paradoxes, best known of which is the "Achilles and tortoise" paradox (in a race, the tortoise is given a start: by the time Achilles reaches the point where the tortoise *was*, the tortoise has advanced—therefore Achilles can never

overtake the tortoise). Zeno defended the Eleatic concept that being is one and changeless by showing the contradictions entailed in claiming the reality of motion and plurality.

ZEOLITE. See ION EXCHANGE.

ZEPHANIAH, Old Testament prophet. In the reign of King Josiah of Judah (640–630 BC) he wrote the ninth book of the MINOR PROPHETS, denouncing evil in Judah and predicting the "Day of the Lord." The end of the last (third) chapter, predicting salvation for the remnant, was probably added later.

ZEPPELIN, Count Ferdinand Adolf August Heinrich von (1838–1917), German aeronautical engineer who designed and built almost a hundred powered BALLOONS (1900 on), called zeppelins for him.

ZEROMSKI, Stefan (1864–1925), Polish novelist, short-story writer and playwright. He was the first to realistically depict the social injustices of Polish life and has been called "the conscience of Polish literature." He is best known for *Ashes* (3 vols., 1904; tr. 1928).

ZERO POPULATION GROWTH, the close approximation in numbers of births and deaths needed to stabilize a nation's population and prevent annual increases. To stabilize the US population at its present level, the replacement ratio for families (excluding illegitimate births) is 2.54 children per fertile married woman. Zero Population Growth is also the name of an organization formed in 1968 by Richard Bowers, Paul Ehrlich and Charles Remington to inform the public and legislators of the disadvantages of continued population growth.

ZEUS, supreme god of Greek mythology. His mother RHEA saved him from his jealous father CRONUS. Later he led the Olympian gods in overthrowing Cronus and the other TITANS. By lot he became god of earth and sky (POSEIDON won the sea, HADES the underworld). He ruled from Mt. OLYMPUS, from which his thunderbolt threatened mortals. By his wife HERA, by Metis (Wisdom), Themis (mother of the Seasons and Fates), Eurynome (mother of the Muses), MNEMOSYNE, and DEMETER he sired many gods. Zeus' mortal loves included LEDA, IO, and EUROPA. His offspring included ATHENA and HERCULES. Romans equated him with Jupiter (Jove).

ZHDANOV, Andrei Aleksandrovich (1896–1948), Soviet leader. Chosen (1934) by STALIN to succeed KIROV as Communist Party secretary of LENINGRAD (in whose WWII defense he was active), he became a full member of the POLITBURO (1939) and

Supreme Soviet chairman (1946), before organizing the COMINFORM.

ZHUKOV, Georgi Konstantinovich (1896–1974), Soviet general, hero of the defeat of the Germans at STALINGRAD (1943) and entry into Berlin (1945). After the death of STALIN (who had blocked his career), he was defense minister 1955–57, and briefly a full member of the Communist Party presidium (1957).

ZIEGFELD, Florenz (1869–1932), US theatrical producer. In 1907 he launched the Ziegfeld Follies, an annual revue famous for its spectacular staging and beautiful girls; it ran for 24 years. Ziegfeld also produced musicals including *Sally* (1920) and *Showboat* (1927).

ZIGGURAT, brick pyramid temple built in many cities of ancient MESOPOTAMIA between about 3,000 and 600 BC. More than 30 are known, with bases up to 320ft square and original heights as much as 150ft. The biblical Tower of Babel may have been a Ziggurat.

Official name: Republic of Zimbabwe
Capital: Salisbury
Area: 150,803sq mi
Population: 7,435,000
Languages: English, Sindebele, Chisona
Religions: Christianity, Animism
Monetary unit(s): 1 Zimbabwe dollar = 100 cents

ZIMBABWE, formerly Rhodesia, is a landlocked republic in the heart of southern Africa, bordering Mozambique, South Africa, Botswana and Zambia.

Land. Zimbabwe lies astride a high plateau between the ZAMBEZI and Limpopo rivers. The High VELD is over 4,000ft and extends SW–NE across the country. The Middle Veld, land between 3,000ft and 4,000ft, is most extensive in the NW. The Low Veld, land below 3,000ft, occupies land near river basins in the N and S. Mt Inyangana in the E highlands rises to 8,503ft. Temperatures are moderated by altitude, ranging between 54°F and 85°F. Rainfall varies from 20in a year in the W to 60in in the E.

People. The African population is primarily Bantu and falls into two broad groups: the Shona and the Ndebele. Other tribes are the Tonga, Sena, Hlengwe, Venda and Sotho. Most live in rural areas, where they depend on subsistence agriculture. Whites (former Rhodesians), Coloureds (of mixed ancestry) and Asians make up about 5% of the population.

Economy. Zimbabwe is a major food exporter in Southern Africa and is rich in mineral resources. Modern European farms are vital to the economy and produce the main cash crop, tobacco. The black population lives mainly by subsistence farming and by raising cattle, but new government policies will make land available to Africans for commercial agriculture. Gold is the chief export; other important minerals are iron ore, asbestos, chrome, copper and nickel. The industrial sector, which was expanded in response to economic sanctions against Rhodesia in 1965, is diversified and active.

History. Bushmen paintings and tools indicate that Zimbabwe had Stone Age inhabitants. Bantu tribes settled the area c400AD, and during the 1400s the Shona civilization established an empire, calling its capital Zimbabwe. In 1889 the British South Africa Co. of Cecil RHODES (after whom Rhodesia was named) obtained a charter from Britain to colonize and administer the area. In 1953 the country became part of the Federation of RHODESIA AND NYASALAND. In 1965, as the wave of independence swept through Africa, Prime Minister Ian SMITH'S government refused to allow black majority rule and illegally declared independence for white-ruled Rhodesia. However, after years of international pressure, local dissension and warfare, and the brief administration of a controversial transitional government, Zimbabwe became legally independent in April 1980 and Robert Mugabe was elected president.

ZIMBALIST, Efrem (1890–   ), Russian-born US virtuoso violinist. He directed the Curtis Institute of Music in Philadelphia, 1941–68, and composed several pieces for violin and orchestra.

ZIMMERMAN TELEGRAM, secret message sent by Arthur Zimmerman, the German foreign secretary, in Jan., 1917, proposing a German-Mexican alliance against the US. Sent via the German ambassador in the US to the German minister in Mexico, it was intercepted by the British and shown to President Woodrow WILSON, who made it public. It influenced the US decision to enter WWI.

ZINC (Zn), bluish-white metal in Group IIB of the PERIODIC TABLE, an anomalous

TRANSITION ELEMENT. It occurs naturally as SPHALERITE, SMITHSONITE, HEMIMORPHITE and WURTZITE, and is extracted by roasting to the oxide and reduction with carbon. It is used for GALVANIZING; as the cathode of dry cells, and in ALLOYS including BRASS. Zinc is a vital trace element, occurring in red BLOOD cells and in INSULIN. Chemically zinc is reactive, readily forming divalent ionic salts (Zn^{2+}), and zincates (ZnO_2^{2-}) in alkaline solution; it forms many stable LIGAND complexes. Zinc oxide and sulfide are used as white pigments. Zinc chloride is used as a FLUX, for fireproofing, in dentistry, and in the manufacture of BATTERIES and FUNGICIDES. AW 65.4, mp 420°C, bp 907°C, sg 7.133 (25°C).

ZINOVIEV, Grigori Evseyevich (1883–1936), Russian communist leader. A close friend of LENIN in exile (1909–17), he became head of the Third INTERNATIONAL (Comintern) 1919–26, and a POLITBURO member 1921–26. After Lenin's death he supported STALIN, who then turned against him; he was finally executed in the 1936 "Great Purge." The "Zinoviev Letter" (1924), containing Zinoviev's purported instructions for a revolution in Britain, was a forgery.

ZINZENDORF, Count Nikolaus Ludwig von (1700–1760), German leader of the MORAVIAN CHURCH. In 1722 he helped some Moravians to form a community called Herrnhut, and became their leader and bishop (1737), founding communities in the Low Countries, England and America. His emphasis on emotion greatly influenced Protestant theology.

ZION, in the Old Testament, the ancient citadel of David, on the SE hill of JERUSALEM. In a wider sense it symbolizes the whole of Jerusalem, and also the Jewish people and their aspirations.

ZITHER, STRINGED INSTRUMENT related to the DULCIMER and PSALTERY. It is placed across the knees and the strings, which stretch across a shallow sound box, are plucked. The zither is a traditional folk instrument of central Europe.

ZOLA, Émile (1840–1902), French novelist and founder of NATURALISM. His works proclaim his "scientific" vision of life determined entirely by heredity and environment. His first success *Thérèse Raquin* (1867) was followed by the *Rougon-Macquart* cycle (20 volumes, 1871–93) depicting, with powerful and often lurid realism, the fortunes of a contemporary family. It includes his celebrated studies of alcoholism (*The Dram-shop*, 1877), prostitution (*Nana*, 1880) and life in a mining community

(*Germinal*, 1885). In 1898 Zola threw himself into the DREYFUS AFFAIR with the pamphlet *J'accuse*, attacking the army.

ZOO, or zoological garden, a collection of wild-animal species preserved for public education, scientific research and the breeding of endangered species. The first modern zoo was that of the Royal Zoological Society at Regent's Park, London, established in 1826.

ZOOGEOGRAPHY, the study of the geographical distribution of animal species and populations. Physical barriers, such as wide oceans and mountain ranges, major climatic extremes, intense heat or cold, may prevent the spread of a species into new areas, or may separate two previously like populations, allowing them to develop into distinct species. The presence of these barriers to movement and interbreeding, both now and in the past, are reflected in the distributions and later adaptive radiations of animal species, resulting in the zoogeographical distributions we find today. The major zoogeographic regions of the world are the Ethiopian (sub-Saharan Africa); the Oriental (India and SE Asia); the Australasian (including Australia, New Guinea and New Zealand); the Neotropical (Central and South America), and the Holarctic (the whole northerly region, often divided into the Nearctic—North America—and the Palearctic—most of Eurasia with N Africa).

ZOOLOGY, the scientific study of animal life. Originally concerned with the classification of animal groups (see ANIMAL KINGDOM), comparative ANATOMY and PHYSIOLOGY, the science now embraces studies of EVOLUTION, GENETICS, EMBRYOLOGY, BIOCHEMISTRY, ANIMAL BEHAVIOR and ECOLOGY.

ZOOM LENS, in motion-picture and TV photography, a device that allows a photographer to take telephoto to close-up shots with a single LENS. It contains several lens elements whose relationship determines the focal length. Using an internal cam system and an external control, the lens elements are moved to provide a continuous series of focal lengths and the rapidly enlarging effect of "zooming in."

ZOOPLANKTON, the animal elements of the PLANKTON, made up of small marine animals, PROTOZOA, and, principally, the larvae of other marine creatures, mainly MOLLUSKS and CRUSTACEA.

ZORACH, William (1887–1966), Lithuanian-born US sculptor. Abandoning his early painting career, he turned to traditional works of carved wood and stone, noted for their simplicity and monumental character. They include *Spirit of the Dance* (1932).

ZOROASTRIANISM, Persian religion based on the teachings of Zoroaster (Greek form of *Zarathustra*), a sage who lived in the 6th century BC. It was founded on the old Aryan folk-religion, but abolished its polytheism, establishing two predominant spirits: Ahura-Mazda (Ormazd), the spirit of light and good; and Ahriman, the spirit of evil and darkness (see DUALISM). Zoroastrianism includes the belief in eternal reward or punishment after death according to man's deeds. Its scriptures are the ZEND-AVESTA. Almost wiped out in the 7th century by the Muslim conquest of Persia, Zoroastrianism survives among the PARSEES.

ZOSHCHENKO, Mikhail (1895 1958), Russian humorist, born in the Ukraine. His popular short stories of the 1920s satirized everyday Soviet life. Although his works became more conventional in the 1930s, he was attacked by the party and expelled from the Union of Soviet Writers in 1946. He was rehabilitated after Stalin's death.

ZUIDER ZEE. See IJSSELMEER.

ZUKERMAN, Pinchas (1948–   ), Israeli-born violinist, violist and conductor who came to New York (1962) as a protégé of Isaac Stern. He performed with orchestras throughout the world and made his conducting debut in 1974.

ZULULAND, the NE region of Natal Province, South Africa. It borders on Mozambique (N), the Indian Ocean (E), Swaziland (W) and the Buffalo and Tugela rivers (S and SW). It produces sugarcane, cotton and maize. Cattle raising is the traditional occupation of the Zulus, a BANTU people who comprise most of the population. Traditionally they live in beehive-shaped huts in fenced compounds called *kraals*. Zululand was annexed by the British in 1887 after prolonged Zulu resistance to white conquest. Many Zulu men now work as MIGRANT LABOR in mines and cities.

ZUNI INDIANS, North American PUEBLO INDIANS of the Zuñian linguistic stock. They were first discovered by the Spanish in 1539. The Zuñi live mainly by agriculture and produce fine jewelry. They have retained their ancient religion, which they celebrate in magnificent festivals noted for their dancing and costumes. About 4,000 live at Zuñi, W N.M.

ZURBARÁN, Francisco de (1598–1664), Spanish BAROQUE painter. He was in-

fluenced by CARAVAGGIO and is known for his realistic and CHIAROSCURO treatment of religious subjects and still-lifes. Among his masterpieces is *The Apotheosis of St. Thomas Aquinas* (1631).

ZÜRICH, city in NW Switzerland, Switzerland's largest city and chief economic, banking and commercial center. It lies on Lake Zürich and the Limmat and Sihl rivers. Zürich manufactures textiles, paper and machine tools. The site was once occupied by Neolithic lake-dwellers, Celtic HELVETII and Romans. Pop 377,000; met pop 707,000.

ZWEIG, Arnold (1887–1968), German novelist. He wrote an eight-vol. epic that includes his best-known novel, *The Case of Sergeant Grischa* (1927) which powerfully indicted militarism in its description of WWI and its effects on German society.

ZWEIG, Stefan (1881–1942), Austrian biographer and novelist. He is best known for his psychological studies of historical figures and writers such as Erasmus, Mary Queen of Scots and Balzac. He wrote of European culture in *The Tide of Fortune* (1928).

ZWICKY, Fritz (1898–1974), Swiss-born US astronomer and astrophysicist best known for his studies of SUPERNOVAS, which he showed to be quite distinct from, and much rarer than, NOVAS. He also did pioneering work on JET PROPULSION.

ZWINGLI, Huldreich (1484–1531), influential Swiss leader of the REFORMATION. In 1523 the city of Zürich accepted his 67 Articles demanding such reforms as the removal of religious images, simplification of the Mass and the introduction of Bible readings. Zwingli was killed in the war between the Catholic and Protestant cantons.

ZWORYKIN, Vladimir Kosma (1889–1981), Russian-born US electronic engineer regarded as the father of modern TELEVISION: his kinescope (patented 1924), little adapted, is our modern picture tube; and his iconoscope, though now obsolete, represents the basis of the first practical television camera. He has also made important contributions to the ELECTRON MICROSCOPE.

ZYGOTE, CELL produced by the fusion of two GAMETES and which contains the DIPLOID chromosome number. The offspring is then produced by mitotic division (see MITOSIS) of the zygote to give $2, 4, 8, 16, 32 \ldots 2^n$ cells.